CENTER FOR BLACK MUSIC RESEARCH

International Dictionary of
Black Composers

CENTER FOR BLACK MUSIC RESEARCH

International Dictionary of
Black Composers

Volume 1
Abrams – Jenkins

Editor
SAMUEL A. FLOYD JR.
CENTER FOR BLACK MUSIC RESEARCH
COLUMBIA COLLEGE CHICAGO

FITZROY DEARBORN PUBLISHERS
CHICAGO • LONDON

FITZROY DEARBORN PUBLISHERS
919 North Michigan Avenue, Suite 760
Chicago, IL 60611
USA

or

FITZROY DEARBORN PUBLISHERS
310 Regent Street
London W1R 5AJ
England

British Library Cataloguing in Publication Data
International Dictionary of Black Composers
1. Composers, Black — Dictionaries
I. Columbia College Center for Black Music Research
780.9'22

ISBN 1-884964-27-3

Library of Congress Cataloging in Publication Data is available

First published in the USA and UK 1999

Typeset by Print Means, Inc., New York, New York
Printed by Braun-Brumfield Inc., Ann Arbor, Michigan
Cover design by Peter Aristedes, Chicago Advertising and Design, Chicago, Illinois

Cover photograph: Edward Kennedy ("Duke") Ellington; courtesy of the Hogan Jazz Archive,
Howard-Tilton Memorial Library, Tulane University

The paper used in this book meets the minimum requirements of
American National Standard for Information Sciences –
Permanence of Paper for Printed Library Materials.
ANSI Z39.48-1984

Editorial Staff

CONTENTS

PREFACE

The *International Dictionary of Black Composers* (*IDBC*) provides information about a cross-section of composers of African heritage who reside in locations around the world, including North and South America, Europe, Africa, and the islands adjacent to and between any of these continents, including, for example, the islands of the Caribbean. The *IDBC* differs from similar reference tools in that it contains not only biographical sketches, works lists, bibliographies, and discographies but also critical essays about the composers and some of their most important works, giving users not only facts but also interpretive perspectives from scholars in the field. The *IDBC* also differs in that it embraces not only composers of music for the concert hall but also composers of popular and vernacular musical forms and styles.

Composers of concert and theater music have been included if they (1) have written compositions that have been commercially published or recorded and (2) have a substantial corpus of work. Composers of vernacular music have been included if they have composed music that has circulated within performing repertories and have had a substantial impact on the elaboration of the traditions of blues, ragtime, jazz, gospel, and a variety of popular genres. Developed after intensive consultation and deliberation with scholars who specialize in various vernacular musics, these criteria were designed to reflect musical practice. Obviously, they are effective only to the degree that the music is available in reproducible form: unfortunately, some composers of vernacular music never recorded or published their music, even though it might have had currency in performing repertories.

Of the 185 entries in this book, 87 are about classical composers. It was our intention to focus on the composers of classical music because composers of vernacular and popular genres have always been part of our common knowledge and because it is rare indeed that black composers of music for the concert hall get significant public notice. Notwithstanding, we have produced a forum for the notice, study, and validation of all genres of music, dedicated as we are to recognizing the contributions of black composers of all forms and styles to the continuing elaboration of music the world over.

In the realm of black music,* where public approbation and visibility are concerned, composers of music for the concert hall are the ones who are marginalized. Although some users of the *IDBC* will view the privileging of these composers as bias against vernacular musics, designed to exclude composers in these genres, the criteria we developed were designed to *include* vernacular composers who have had substantial *compositional* impacts on the elaboration of the traditions they represent, without having them numerically overwhelm the book and contribute to the continuing marginalization of composers of music for the concert hall.

While users committed to the vernacular forms and styles will decry the absence of many composers of vernacular music, those who view vernacular products as "ephemeral" will question whether they belong here at all; and some individuals from both persuasions will criticize the freezing of vernacular musical texts in written forms that may not represent their true or potential essences. All things considered, the *IDBC* staff's approach to the difficult problems surrounding this question has resulted in the best compromise possible, given limitations of space and time.

In addition to trying as much as possible to adhere to the criteria set forth at the outset of the project, the staff has attempted to achieve a mix of figures representing compositional practice

---

*For the purposes of the *IDBC*, *black music* is defined as any music composed by people of African descent. It includes African-American vernacular music (calls, cries, hollers, spirituals, ragtime, blues, jazz, R&B, black gospel, and all forms to which these genres have given birth), African music, and concert-hall music by black composers in any country.

throughout the diaspora and across genres. Although this project has been guided by advice from its editorial advisory board, the final choices were made by the editors, who chose to include a few individuals who do not meet the project's criteria but who, for historical reasons, should be present in the work.

Similarly, several talented, younger contemporary composers of music for the concert hall have not been included because they have not had a chance to establish publication records or because their careers or output will not yet sustain the kind of treatment required for the essays. Perhaps future editions of this work can embrace these young composers.

Nineteenth-century composers of popular music are included in this publication primarily because of their historical and cultural importance; composers from the turn of the century through the 1910s are included because their music has been stylistically influential. That so few composers in this latter category have been included seems to support the notion that the importance of an artist's work is best determined from a chronological distance of several decades; many of the most popular composers from the turn of the century—for example, Ernest Hogan and Ford Dabney—are now seen as having had little or no musical influence in succeeding years. The situation with contemporary composers of popular music is similar. Al Green, for example, was important as a performer partly on the strength of the music he composed for himself to perform, but the music he produced did not influence stylistically that of composers who followed him. It is possible and even likely that, from decades of distance in the future, some of the composers for whom entries are included in the *IDBC* would be excluded from an updated version of the book.

Nevertheless, some historically significant figures remain absent: the Chevalier J.J.O. Meude-Monpas, active in the 1770s, whose extant works number fewer than five and who obviously made no recordings; Joseph Emidee (ca. 1770–mid-1830s), of Falmouth, England, by way of Guinea, West Africa, and Brazil, none of whose music is extant; John Thomas Douglass (1847–1886), the first black composer to write an opera (*Virginia's Ball,* produced in New York in 1868), whose works are now lost; Newport Gardner (1746–1826), who was briefly a student of Andrew Law and whose choral work "Promise Anthem" (written in 1764 and published in 1826) is one among a larger body of works that are now lost; and the 20th-century composer Melville Charleton, whose papers reside in private hands and were not available to this project for consultation.

Acknowledgements

The Center for Black Music Research would like to express its appreciation to the administration of Columbia College Chicago for support of the completion of the *International Dictionary of Black Composers.* In addition to the members of the editorial advisory board, we owe significant thanks to Portia Maultsby and Robert Pruter, who gave extremely valuable advice about the inclusion of composers of contemporary popular music; John Graziano and Thomas Riis, who were consulted about turn-of-the-century composers of popular music; and Johann Buis, who provided editorial assistance on several of the African entries.

We would like to acknowledge the assistance of three people at ASCAP in the preparation of the music lists; they are Frances Richard, Sam Perlman, and Cia Toscanini. Additional help with several of the music lists came from Dan Singer, Anthony Saggese, and Jeff Cohen at BMI. Others who deserve mention are Deborrah Richardson, Assistant Chair, Archives Center, National Museum of American History, Smithsonian Institution, for providing access to the Martin and Morris Music Company Records, ca. 1930–1985 collection; Wayne Shirley, Librarian at the Music Division, Library of Congress, for assistance with the thematic catalog of Joaquim Emérico Lobo de Mesquita; Diana Lachatanere, Manuscripts Curator at the Schomburg Center for Research in Black Culture, New York Public Library, for information about W. C. Handy scores; Amy Beth Hale at SESAC for identifying the names of writers societies (e.g., ASCAP, BMI) to which each of the composers belongs; and Cynthia Schmidt for assistance with solicitation of contributors for the African composers. We appreciate the assistance of Gisele Elie, Hildegard S. Gardère, Yves Gardère, Marie Helene Villard, and Dania Wittenberg for assistance with the music list and brief biography of Justin Elie.

Extensive assistance with the brief biography and music lists of some of the composers was provided by a group of people to whom we extend our heartfelt thanks: Kathy Sebastien for Allen Toussaint; Peter Sims for Dizzy Gillespie; Father Peter O'Brian for Mary Lou Williams; Douglas Yoel and Lynda Bramble for Billy Taylor; John Corbett for George Clinton; and Stephen Charpié for Frank Johnson.

Extensive assistance in locating photographs was provided by Frank Driggs of the Frank Driggs Collection; Marsha Estell and Celeste Williams of Fitzroy Dearborn Publishers; Ann K. Kuebler, Archives Specialist, Archives Center, National Museum of American History, Smithsonian Institution; and Antony M. Toussaint and Mary Yearwood of the Schomburg Center for Research in Black Culture, New York Public Library.

At various times during the life of the project, research assistance was provided by graduate students from the University of Chicago and Northwestern University. We would like to acknowledge, from the University of Chicago, Mark Blackbird, Adrian P. Childs, Catherine Cole, Robert W. Fried, Joan Bentley Hoffman, Bernardo Enzo Illari, Jennifer More, Hillary Poriss, Leon Shernoff, Kate van Orden, and Chien-Chang Yang, and from Northwestern University, Keith Carpenter, Marsha Coffey, Kathy Pisaro, and Mark-Daniel Schmid.

Poetry and Lyrics Permissions

Lyrics from "Come On in the Room" by Alex Bradford © 1952 (Renewed) Roberta Martin Studio of Music, All Rights Administered by Unichappell Music Inc. (BMI), All Rights Reserved, Used by Permission, WARNER BROS. PUBLICATIONS U.S. INC., Miami, FL 33014; Dorothy Love Coates' additional lyrics to "Get Away Jordan" © 1993 Savgos Music, Inc./Dorothy Love Coates Music, reprinted by permission; Arthur H. Cunningham's poem "Let Others Dream" reprinted courtesy of the estate of Arthur H. Cunningham; the introduction to *African-American Celebration* © 1984 by Roger Dickerson, reprinted by special permission from Roger Dickerson; lyrics from "Soulsville" by Isaac Hayes © 1971 (Renewed) Irving Music, Inc. (BMI), All Rights Reserved, Used by Permission, WARNER BROS. PUBLICATIONS U.S. INC., Miami, FL 33014; "Get Up, Stand Up" written by Bob Marley and Peter Tosh, copyright © 1974 Fifty-Six Hope Road Music, Ltd., Odnil Music, Ltd., and Stuck On Music, Used By Permission, All Rights Reserved; introductory poem to Frederick Tillis's *A Festival Journey* reprinted courtesy of Frederick Tillis, poet and composer.

INTRODUCTION

Each entry in the *IDBC* consists of as many as 11 parts, as follows: the name of the composer; a brief biographical paragraph; a photograph or other illustrative representation of the composer; a list of all the composer's compositions that could be located or identified in published sources of information, together with available discographical information about each; a bibliography of scholarly articles, books, dissertations, and theses *about* the composer and a bibliography of books or articles of any kind that were written *by* the composer; a list of the principal archives that hold scores and materials related to the composer; a critical essay about the composer; as many as four critical essays about the composer's compositions; and a list of the important sources used by the author in preparing the essays.

The essays were written by contributing scholars who have expertise or some compelling interest in their subjects. Their names appear at the ends of the essays, and information about them appears in the "Notes on Contributors" section. For the most part, all remaining portions of the book—biographical sketches, works lists, publications lists, and bibliographical and discographical information—were prepared by the dictionary staff of the Center for Black Music Research, whose names are included either on the title page or in the preface.

Work on the parts of the entries that precede the essays was compiled for the most part by researchers contracted by the Center for Black Music Research, who used standard bibliographic tools. In a few cases, where information about a composer was generally not available in the United States, the contributing authors were asked to provide this information. In general, the sources for the information include general reference books, biographies, and standard bibliographic tools such as OCLC (On-line Computer Library Center), RILM (Répertoire internationale de litterature musicale), and others.

A questionnaire requesting complete information was sent to each living composer or, if the composer was recently deceased, a surviving family member. The information that was received, either in the form of the completed questionnaire or a resume, was arranged according to a predetermined format. Because the reordering often produced evidence of a lack of some kinds of information, draft versions of the biographical paragraphs were sent to the composers, asking for assistance in completing and bringing them up to date. All of the composers were cooperative, and many provided extensive assistance. For all of the entries in the book, the biographical paragraphs and the lists were sent to the essay authors, asking that they vet them and fill in any obviously missing information.

Composer's Name

For each entry, the composer's proper name was used as the basis for the form of the name chosen to introduce the entry. Nicknames are included in parentheses at the end of the name. Where known, names that are commonly limited to an initial are completed in parentheses, for example, "Johnson, James P(rice)."

Brief Biographical Paragraph

The brief biographical paragraph in each entry is subdivided into as many as nine sections. The first section gives information about the composer's birth and death dates. In a few cases, the composer's birth name is included in this opening section; an example is Leslie Adams, who was born as Harrison Leslie Adams.

The remaining sections begin with boldface headings and consist of the following types of information: Education, Military Career, Composing and Performing Career, Teaching Career, Commissions, Memberships, Honors/Awards, and Mailing Address. Within each section, the information is presented in the following order: location, event, date. These items appear in chronological order and are separated by semicolons.

The Commissions section contains a list of the names of the commissioning body and the dates the works were completed, those dates having been chosen for listing because of the impossibility of gathering exact commission dates. Commissions for works-in-progress are not included.

Mailing addresses are included for living composers only if they have granted permission.

Music List

The music list for each entry is organized by medium. In order to provide consistency throughout the book, the order in which the categories appear was determined at the outset of the manuscript preparation process. This order is maintained for the majority of cases, exceptions being made only in two cases, as follows: (1) When many of a composer's works are published in one or more collections, for reasons of conserving space, complete publication information about those collections is given at the head of the list. A shortened form is given in the individual entries. (2) In cases where a composer wrote pieces for jazz ensemble and for concert music and his or her jazz works constitute the primary focus of the output, the order was adjusted to place the concert works later in the list, thus reflecting more accurately the nature of the oeuvre.

For a few composers whose output was very extensive—for example, Duke Ellington—a selected list was prepared in conjunction with the authors of the essays. This step was taken to avoid overbalancing the book with the output of a few composers and misrepresenting the relative importance of other composers who may have been less prolific.

Compositions that were set for more than one medium by a composer are listed under the rubrics of their original settings, with indications of other media for which the work was set included in the entry.

Works written under a pseudonym are listed at the end of the music list under a heading that indicates the names under which they were composed. For example, the entry for Avril Coleridge-Taylor carries two such lists: "As Gwendolen Coleridge-Taylor" and "As Peter Riley."

As the research was in progress on the music lists, it became clear that the titles of certain compositions were located in sources—particularly those that are narrative in nature—that did not include documentation of the works' existence; examples included compositions that are mentioned in passing in books or articles, particularly those of the 19th century. As working lists were prepared, such works were marked as unverified, and efforts were made to verify their existence and authorship. A work was subsequently deemed verified if its title was listed on a printed program as having been performed, if the work was found to be included in an archival collection, if a sound recording of the work was found to exist, if the piece was listed in a composer's self-produced works list or the composer him- or herself verified its existence, if the piece was the composer's Ph.D. dissertation or master's thesis, if there exists a film release date (in the case of film soundtracks), or if viable documentation exists that the work is available from the composer. All compositions whose titles were found in the bibliographic record but could not be verified either as actually composed or as composed by the person to whom they are attributed are included in a section at the end of the music list titled "Not Verified."

Exclusions

The purpose of the *IDBC* is to focus on composers (as opposed to performers, bandleaders, arrangers, or myriad other such roles that they may have played in their lives); therefore, the editorial process excluded certain kinds of information in the music lists. Because the music lists are intended to present a list of the original compositions by the subjects of the entries, all decisions about exclusions were grounded in that effort. Thus, excluded are the following categories of information:

Arrangements by others of the composer's works
Arrangements by the composer of someone else's work
Arrangements by the composer of other pieces or melodies composed by others,
    including spirituals
Lead sheets, fake books, piano reductions, and cue sheets
Works that are in progress

Format of Individual Entries

The entries in the music lists are presented in paragraph format; the following listing of the various parts of the entry is provided here in order to help users of the book understand the format and its rationale:

Title of the piece
Performing forces
Composition date
Publication information
Series title and number
Copyright date
List of contents
Miscellaneous information
Year of premiere
Recording date
Discography

In each case, the parts of the entry are listed in the same order as presented here. Where no information for a given part of the entry is available, that part is omitted; for example, available information about works by vernacular composers often includes only the title, recording date, and discographical list; thus, the remaining parts of the format will not be found for those items.

Title of the piece. Included are both the complete title of the work and alternate titles under which it has been published. To the degree possible, titles have been typeset to distinguish large-scale works from those composed in smaller forms: large-scale works are set in italic type, smaller works in quotes. However, common titles of musical works, such as Sonata in E-flat Major, are neither italicized nor quoted, in accordance with common practice, as documented in the *Chicago Manual of Style* (14th edition; University of Chicago Press, 1993).

Performing forces. A list of the instruments for which the work was composed is included in parentheses behind the title of the work. For the category "Dramatic Music," the name of the genre—ballet, opera, oratorio, musical, cantata, and the like—is indicated in the field normally reserved for performing forces.

For choral pieces, where the composer arranged the same piece for more than one voicing, abbreviations for the voicings are listed as performing forces, separated by semicolons, for example, "(SATB; SSA; SATT)."

For solo instrumental or vocal music, it is assumed that the songs are accompanied by piano and, for the most part, are not so indicated in the performing forces. Unaccompanied works are so identified, for example, "(SSA unaccompanied)"; when pieces are accompanied by instruments other than piano, those instruments are identified, for example, "(SATB, organ)."

Composition date. The composition date is identified in the entry by position—that is, in every case, the date following the title and performing forces is the date the work was composed, unless otherwise identified. Every effort has been made to secure the composition dates, although they are much more frequently available or known for concert-music works than for vernacular pieces, which are most often available only on sound recordings.

Publication information. When a composition has been published in a printed edition, the standard bibliographic format of city, name of publisher, and date of publication are given. Because the project's intention was to document as far as possible the first edition of each work, if citations were found for more than one edition, the earliest complete citation is used.

Series title and number. Where a published composition is included in a series, the name of the series and the number of the publication in the series is given.

Copyright date. Copyright dates that are separate from publication information are included only in cases where neither a composition date nor a printed publication is available. An example of such a date may be found in the works of Lucie Campbell, where the date that a song was copyrighted is frequently earlier than the publication date.

List of contents. For multimovement works, a list of the titles of the movements is given, separated by semicolons.

Miscellaneous information. Included here are indications of, for example, the title of a musical show for which the piece was written or in which it was performed, alternate performing forces, commissions, co-composers, gospel-music arrangers, a notation that the work was withdrawn by the composer, and any other important information not covered by the standardized format categories.

For the most part, gospel songs were not notated by their composers but were part of an oral tradition. In preparation for publication, a second person (or sometimes the composer him- or herself) transcribed and provided an accompaniment for the melodies. The published versions were used as the basis for gospel performances by other singers and/or instrumentalists. Because this procedure is the accepted practice for gospel-music publications, information is included about the published versions, and the entries include the names of the arrangers.

Year of premiere. When available, the year of the first performance of the piece is given.

Recording date. This date is the earliest recording date available in the general bibliographic sources. It is included for pieces for which no composition date or copyright date is available in order to provide for the user some sense of when the work was composed. For the most part, this category is pertinent only to vernacular music, where other dates are often not available.

Discography. It is not the purpose of this dictionary to provide a complete discography for each composition listed. But because it is important to provide users with information about how sound recordings of the cited compositions may be consulted, a list of as many as five labels on which the piece can be found has been included. Because this book is designed primarily for the lay reader, it focuses on current or easily available recordings rather than on first recordings. Preference is given to recordings available on CD and, for jazz and popular-music composers, to performances by the composers themselves.

This discographical information is not intended either to be complete or to serve as a chronological source of recordings of a given work; thus, the record label name and numbers are listed alphabetically. Some lists include record numbers for multiple releases of the same recording; where this information was gathered in the course of the research, the various releases are indicated by connecting the record numbers with the word "or," for example, "Okeh 4789 or Okeh 8046."

Indications of the names of the groups who recorded the various versions of a work have been omitted in the discographies.

Only recordings of complete works have been considered for inclusion in the list; on this basis, recordings of single movements are not among those cited.

Vernacular Composers

Because the purpose of this project is to list song writers as *composers* rather than as performers, a series of questions arose, many of which came to the fore in the preparation of the composers' music lists. Unless there existed a monograph or published discography about a composer, the research on the music lists was accomplished primarily through database searches. For vernacular composers, the three primary databases that were consulted are OCLC, the MUSE databases located in record stores, and the All-Music Guide. In every case, information was cross-verified among these sources to allow for the highest level of accuracy available.

The difficulty that we encountered in attempting to view the compositional output of this group of composers was the lack of clarity in and information missing from the existing bibliographic record. For the most part, these sources do not identify the names of the composers to the same extent as they do the performers. Second, for jazz and popular music, sound recordings—the primary source of information about these works—are usually cataloged under the name of the performer, so searching for a person's *compositions* was accordingly made more difficult. In a number of cases, these sources did not yield information about works composed by one person but performed by another.

These difficulties were compensated by having the lists vetted by one or more of the following individuals or research sources: the composers themselves; the databases posted on the Internet Web sites of ASCAP and BMI, supplemented by assistance from the individuals from those companies who are mentioned in the acknowledgments section in the preface; the individuals acknowledged in the preface for work on particular composers; and the contributors of the essays for the individual composers. In addition, many of the lists in this category were sent through the research protocol more than once over the course of the project, using additional sources that were found or that proved to be particularly useful.

Publications List

The publications list for each entry is subdivided into published materials written *about* the composer and those written *by* the composer. The first of these sections is further subdivided into lists of books and monographs, dissertations and theses, and articles. In the second section, the composer's own publications are listed in a single alphabetical list. For a few composers, no publications have been listed because none were found in the context of the search protocol.

Publications about the Composer

This bibliography is not intended as a complete listing of all printed materials about the composer. Rather, its purpose is to give readers—in particular, lay readers—a starting point for additional information about the person to whom it is devoted and to present a picture of the state of the research about him or her to date. Rather stringent guidelines were established to limit the materials to be included.

The books and monographs included in the list are devoted entirely to the composer. Preference is given to the original edition of the books, and reprint editions are not included.

Dissertations and theses are cited if the composer is the principal subject or a principal figure of the work, if the name of the composer is in the title, or if the name of the composer appears in the abstract for the dissertation.

In general, articles about a composer are cited if they appear in scholarly journals. The research on the publications lists for the vernacular composers quickly revealed that this criterion excluded all but a few citations, so the search for this group of composers was expanded to include non-scholarly periodicals such as *Metronome, Down Beat,* and *Billboard*; however, short writings of a newsy nature (one to two pages in length) have been excluded. In a few instances, when publications lists turned out to be extremely short, this criterion was broadened further.

Under the "Articles" rubric are also listed bibliographic entries for chapters about the composers that appear in books that are not entirely devoted to them. However, these have been excluded in cases in which such writings are too numerous reasonably to list; thus, book chapters about Duke Ellington are not included, whereas similar writings about Margaret Bonds, about whom little has been written, are.

Articles published in popular magazines or newspapers are not included. The list does not include transcriptions of taped interviews unless they appear within the context of an edited and published work or appear in scholarly journals. Reviews, whether of concerts or recordings, are also not included.

Moreover, we have not included book or record reviews written by composers about other composers' works or included composers' introductions or prefaces to other people's books. History and subject books, such as Tilford Brooks' *America's Black Music Heritage,* Hildred Roach's *Black American Music: Past and Present,* and Eileen Southern's masterly *The Music of Black Americans: A History,* have not been cited, although on occasion they do offer substantive and useful analysis and information.

Publications by the Composer

Articles *by* a composer are cited regardless of where they were published. Some lists also include typescripts when references to them are given in sources such as OCLC and they are held by an archive. In the case where a composer has been a regular columnist to several newspapers and periodicals over an extended time, a single entry notes the years during which such activity took place.

Principal Archives

Only archives are listed that hold major collections of compositions or vertical file information about composers. The primary libraries and archives in which copies of the composers' works are held were identified and compiled from *Manuscript Collections, National Union Catalog; Pre-1956 Imprints, National Union Catalog; Music, National Union Catalog;* OCLC; RILM; RISM (Répertoire internationale des sources musicale); and *Resources of American Music History,* edited and compiled by D. W. Krummel, et al. (University of Illinois Press, 1981).

Essays

Each entry contains a series of 500- to 1,000-word critical essays: an essay about the composer and between one and four critical essays about the composer's works. The set of essays is concluded by a list of the primary references consulted by the author in the preparation of the essays. The essay set is closed by the name of the contributing author.

The composer essays of most of the pre–20th-century entries tend to be shorter than those of 20th century composers, since information for the former is in most cases scant. Exceptions include the 18th-century Chevalier de Saint-Georges, of whom quite a bit is known.

Of the works essays, in a very few cases in which extant works were not available for consultation, essays were developed from secondary-source commentary (e.g., Gutíerrez). In the case of vernacular composers who generally wrote songs and other shorter compositions that would not easily support an essay of the length required by the project, the works essays are frequently combined into a single essay titled "Selected Works."

In most cases, the entire set of essays was written by a single author; however, there are a few instances in which one author contributed the composer essay and a second author provided the works essays. In these cases, the authors' names immediately follow the essays that they wrote.

Because the book is intended primarily for lay readers, and in view of the space limitations established by the publisher, authors were strongly encouraged to limit their use of figures and musical examples. The examples that have been included in the book are limited to short rhythmic examples, progressions of chord symbols, or notation of four to eight measures, depending on the number of staves in the system. In general, authors were encouraged to discuss the music relying on words rather than notation.

CONTRIBUTORS

T. J. Anderson
Naomi André
Reid Badger
Gabriel Banat
William C. Banfield
Thomas Bauman
Amy C. Beal
James Bennighof
Edward A. Berlin
Egberto Bermudez
Geoffrey Block
Todd Borgerding
Rob Bowman
Horace Clarence Boyer
Idalmis S. Braña Mola
Malcolm J. Breda
Christopher A. Brooks
Rae Linda Brown
Scott E. Brown
Jerry Cadden
Hansonia L. Caldwell
Joyce Carlson-Leavitt
Marva Griffin Carter
William H. Chapman Nyaho
Stephen K. Charpié
Mark Clague
Rebecca T. Cureau
Celia E. Davidson
Reno De Stefano
Scott DeVeaux
Kurt Dietrich
Greg Downey
John E. Druesedow
Caleb Dube
J. Emanuel Dufrasne-González
Ed Duling
Ernest F. Dyson
J. Michele Edwards
Victoria Eli Rodríguez
David Evans
Suzanne Flandreau
Samuel A. Floyd Jr.
Luvenia A. George
Maya C. Gibson

John Graziano
Jeffrey Green
James C. Hall
Deborah Hawkins
Marsha J. Heizer
Andrew Homzy
Elliott S. Hurwitt
Reuben Jackson
John Andrew Johnson
Timothy M. Kalil
Mark Katz
Charles E. Kinzer
Wolfram Knauer
Gerhard Kubik
Michael Largey
Richard C. Littlefield
Luiz Fernando Vallim Lopes
Paul S. Machlin
Jeffrey Magee
Eric Marshall
Olivia Mattis
Michael Meckna
Ingrid Monson
Kimberlyn Montford
Gayle M. Murchison
Maurice Peress
Samuel Perlman
Brian Priestley
Robert Pruter
Gerhard Putschögl
Ronald M. Radano
Guthrie P. Ramsey Jr.
John O. Robison
Timothy Rommen
Brent M. Runnels
Georgia A. Ryder
Michael Saffle
David Sanjek
Mark-Daniel Schmid
Cynthia Schmidt
Denise A. Seachrist
Ann Sears
Gayle Sherwood
Giles Smith

XX INTERNATIONAL DICTIONARY OF BLACK COMPOSERS

Jean E. Snyder
Greg A Steinke
Robert Stevenson
Willie Strong
Lester Sullivan
Kathryn Talalay
Jewel T. Thompson
Robert T. Townsend
Mark Tucker

Thomas Turino
Walter van de Leur
Victoria von Arx
Helen Walker-Hill
Kristin Wendland
Richard Will
Lorraine P. Wilson
Lucius Wyatt

ALPHABETICAL LIST OF ENTRIES

COMPOSER NAMES, PSEUDONYMS, AND VARIANTS

Abrahams, Richard. *See* Abrams, Muhal Richard

Abrams, Muhal Richard

Adams, Alton Augustus

Adams, Harrison Leslie. *See* Adams, Leslie

Adams, Leslie

Akers, Doris Mae

Aldridge, Amanda Christina Elizabeth.
   See Aldridge, Amanda Ira

Aldridge, Amanda Ira (Montague Ring)

Anderson, T(homas) J(efferson)

Arnold, Maurice

Baiocchi, Regina Harris

Baker, David N(athaniel)

Banfield, William Cedric

Bankole, Ayo

Barès, Basile Jean

Barrelhouse Tom. *See* Dorsey, Thomas Andrew

Bartholomew, Dave Louis

Batiste, Alvin

Bayeke, Mwenda wa. *See* Bosco, Mwenda Jean

Berry, Charles Edward Anderson.
   See Berry, Chuck

Berry, Chuck

Bethune, Thomas Greene Wiggins
   ("Blind Tom")

Blake, ("Blind") Arthur

Blake, James Hubert ("Eubie")

Bland, Ed(ward)

Blind Boone. *See* Boone, John William

Blind Tom. *See* Bethune, Thomas Greene
   Wiggins

Bonds, Margaret

Boone, John William ("Blind Boone")

Bosco, Mwenda Jean

Boulogne, Joseph de.
   See Saint-Georges, Chevalier de

Bradford, Alex E.

Braxton, Anthony

Brewster, W(illiam) Herbert, Sr.

Brooks, George. *See* Henderson,
   Fletcher Hamilton, Jr. ("Smack")

Brooks, Shelton Leroy

Brown, James

Brown, Tom. *See* Waller, Thomas
   Wright ("Fats")

Burleigh, Harry [Henry] T(hacker)

Calhoun, Charles. *See* Stone, Jesse A.

Campbell, Lucie

Capers, Valerie Gail

Carter, Roland

Chambers, Stephen Alexander.
   See Hakim, Talib Rasul

Charles, Ray

Cleveland, James Edward

Clinton, George

Coates, Dorothy Love

Cole, Robert Allen ("Bob")

Coleman, Ornette

Coleman, Randolph Denard Ornette.
   See Coleman, Ornette

Coleridge-Taylor, Avril

Coleridge-Taylor, Gwendolen.
   See Coleridge-Taylor, Avril

Coleridge-Taylor, Samuel

Coltrane, John

Cook, William Mercer. *See* Cook, Will Marion

Cook, Will Marion

Cordero, Roque

Crouch, Andraé

Cunningham, Arthur

Da Costa, Noel G.

Daoud, Rageh

Davis, Anthony Curtis

Davis, Gussie Lord

Dawson, William Levi

Dédé, Edmond

Dett, R(obert) Nathaniel

Dickerson, Roger Donald

Dixon, Willie James

Dorsey, Thomas Andrew

Durán, Alejo

Durán Díaz, Gilberto Alejandro.
   See Durán, Alejo

El-Dabh, Halim

Redman, Don(ald) Matthew
Riley, Peter. *See* Coleridge-Taylor, Avril
Ring, Montague. *See* Aldridge, Amanda Ira
Rivers, Gertrude. *See* Robinson, Gertrude Rivers
Robinson, Gertrude Rivers
Robinson, Ray Charles. *See* Charles, Ray
Roldán y Gardes, Amadeo
Rudd, Dorothy. *See* Moore, Dorothy Rudd
Russell, George
Russell, Oswald
Russell, Selbourne Oswald Alfred. *See* Russell, Oswald
Ryder, Noah Francis
Saint-Georges, Chevalier de
Sancho, Ignatius
Schuyler, Philippa Duke
Scott, James
Scruggs, Mary Elfrieda. *See* Williams, Mary Lou
Shorter, Wayne
Silver, Horace Ward Martin Tavares
Singleton, Alvin
Smith, Chris
Smith, Florence Beatrice. *See* Price, Florence Beatrice
Smith, Hale
Smith, Irene Britton
Snaër, François-Michel-Samuel
Sowande, Fela
Still, William Grant
Stone, Jesse A.
Strayhorn, William Thomas ("Billy")

Strothotte, Maurice Arnold. *See* Arnold, Maurice
Swanson, Howard
Taylor, Cecil Percival
Taylor, William Edward, Jr. ("Billy")
Threadgill, Henry Luther
Tillis, Frederick C.
Tindley, Charles Albert
Tizol, Juan Vincente Martinez
Toussaint, Allen
Toussaint, Clarence. *See* Toussaint, Allen
Tyers, William H.
Valera Chamizo, Roberto
Vee Jay. *See* Price, Florence Beatrice
Veloso, Caetano Emanuel Viana Teles
Viana Filho, Alfredo da Rocha. *See* Pixinguinha
Vodery, William Henry Bennett ("Will")
Walker, George Theophilus, Jr.
Wallen, Errollyn
Waller, Thomas Wright ("Fats")
White, Clarence Cameron
Wiggins, Thomas Greene. *See* Bethune, Thomas Greene Wiggins ("Blind Tom")
Williams, Clarence
Williams, Henry F.
Williams, James Kimo
Williams, Mary Lou
Wilson, Olly W(oodrow), Jr.
Wonder, Stevie
Work, John Wesley, III
Work, Julian Cassander

ABRAMS, MUHAL RICHARD

Born Richard Abrahams in Chicago, Ill., September 19, 1930. **Education:** Mainly self-taught from age 17; Chicago Musical College, 1948–52; Chicago, Governors State University, studied electronic music. **Composing and Performing Career:** Composed and arranged for pianist Walter "King" Fleming Jazz Orchestra, 1955; Chicago, performed with visiting soloists, including James Moody, Eddie Harris, and many others; co-founder with Walter Perkins of group MJT+3, 1955; formed the Experimental Band, which included Donald Rafael Garrett, Roscoe Mitchell, and Joseph Jarman, 1961; toured and recorded as soloist and with others, including various Muhal Richard Abrams groups, 1970s; moved to New York, N.Y., 1977; continued composing and performing with various ensembles, including the Muhal Richard Abrams Sextet, 1977–present. **Teaching Career:** Taught jazz composition and improvisational classes at the Banff Center, Banff, Canada, Columbia University, New York, N.Y., California Institute of the Arts, Valencia, Calif., Syracuse University, Syracuse, N.Y., and BMI Composers workshop, New York, N.Y.; taught privately, 1977–present. **Commissions:** City of Chicago for the 1982 New Music America Festival; The Kitchen, 1982; McKim Fund, ca. 1986; Brooklyn Philharmonic, 1988; Center for Black Music Research, Columbia College Chicago, and the Friends of the Chicago Public Library, 1991; Bang on the Can, 1992; String Trio of New York, 1992; Rova Saxophone Quartet, 1994; Newband, 1995. **Memberships:** Association for the Advancement of Creative Musicians (AACM), co-founder and first president, 1965; AACM School of Music, founder, 1969; AACM, New York City chapter, president; National Endowment for the Arts and the New York State Council on the Arts, former music panelist; National Jazz Service Organization and Meet the Composer, member, board of directors. **Honors/Awards:** First recipient, International JazzPar Award, by the Danish Jazz Center, Copenhagen, Denmark, 1990. **Mailing Address:** RPR Management, P.O. Box 612, Times Square Station, New York, NY 10108-0612.

MUSIC LIST

JAZZ ENSEMBLE

[The following list of titles includes only works that were composed by the subject of the entry; it is not a list of recordings that were made by the subject. Although the composer may have made recordings of his own works, the list is not restricted to those recordings but in many cases includes performances by other artists of the composer's work. The list is made up of publication and discographical data, in cases where such information is available. Although no effort has been made to include documentation of the earliest recording of the works listed, the date of the earliest recording that is readily available has been given. —Ed.]

"Afrisong." Recorded, 1975: India Navigation IN-1058; Whynot Records-PA-7121.

"Aleph the Fool." Recorded, 1973: Atlantic 311.

"Ancient and Future Reflections." Recorded, 1981: Black Saint BSR 0061 CD.

"Arhythm Songy." Recorded, 1977: Black Saint BSR 0017.

"B Song." Recorded, 1978: Arista Novus 1978.

"Balladi." Recorded, 1977: Black Saint BSR 0017.

"Ballad for New Souls." Recorded, 1975: Delmark DS-430.

"Ballad for Old Souls." Recorded, 1975: Delmark DS-430.

"Balu." Recorded, 1980: Black Saint BSR 0041.

"Before and After." Recorded, 1994: Black Saint 120-141-2.

"Big T." Recorded, 1989: UMO CD 101.

"The Bird Song." 1967. Recorded, 1967: Delmark DD 413.

"Blessed Be the Heavens at 12." Recorded, 1983: Black Saint BSR 0071.

"Bloodline." Recorded, 1983: Black Saint 120 117-2; Black Saint BSR 0071.

"Blu Blu Blu." Recorded, 1990: Black Saint 120 117-2.

"Blues for M." Recorded, 1975: India Navigation IN-1058; Whynot Records-PA-7121.

"Blues Forever." Recorded, 1981: Black Saint BSR 0061 CD.

"Blues to You." Co-composer, Marty Ehrlich. Recorded, 1997: New World 80512.

"Bud P. (Dedicated to Bud Powell)." Recorded, 1978: Novus Records AN 3000.

"C. C.'s World." Recorded, 1986: RPR Records RPR 1001.

"Chambea." Recorded, 1981: Black Saint BSR 0061 CD.

"Charlie in the Parker." Recorded, 1977: Black Saint BSR 0017; New World/CounterCurrents 80409-2.

"Cluster for Many Worlds." Recorded, 1981: Black Saint BSR 0061 CD.

"Colors in Thirty-third." Recorded, 1986: Black Saint BSR 0091 CD.

"Continuous Variation." New York: Ric Peg, 1988.

"Crossbeams." Recorded, 1994: Black Saint 120-141-2; New World 80512.

"Cycles Five." Recorded, 1990: Black Saint 120 117-2.

"D Song." Recorded, 1978: Novus Records AN-3007.

"Dabadubada." Recorded, 1996: Black Saint 120 161-2.

"Direflex." Recorded, 1986: RPR Records RPR 1001.

"DizBirdMonkBudMax (A Tribute)." Recorded, 1993: Black Saint 120 132-2.

"Down at Peppers." Recorded, 1984: Black Saint BSR 0081.

"Down the Street from the Gene Ammons Public School." Recorded, 1982: Black Saint BSR 0051.

"Drumbutu." Recorded, 1993: Black Saint 120 132-2.

"Drumman Cyrille." Recorded, 1986: Black Saint BSR 0091 CD.

"Du King (Dedicated to Duke Ellington)." Recorded, 1982: Black Saint BSR 0061 CD.

"Duet for One World." Recorded, 1981: Black Saint BSR 0061 CD.

"Duo 1." Recorded, 1978: Novus Records AN 3000.

"Duo 2." Recorded, 1978: Novus Records AN 3000.

"Egypic." Recorded, 1955: Argo Records LP 621.

"Eleven over Four." Recorded, 1995: New World 80469-2.

"Encore." Recorded, 1994: Black Saint 120-141-2.

"End of the Line." Recorded, 1955: Argo Records LP 621.

"Ensemble Song." Recorded, 1995: New World 80469-2.

"Excerpts." New York: Ric Peg, 1992. Recorded, 1977: Original Jazz Classics OJCCD-479-2.

Muhal Richard Abrams; courtesy of Anthony Barboza

"Fafca." Recorded, 1980: Black Saint BSR 0041.

"The Fairness of Life." Recorded, 1982: Black Saint BSR 0051.

"Familytalk." Recorded, 1993: Black Saint 120 132-2.

"Fanfare." Recorded, 1989: UMO CD 101.

"Fortex." Recorded, 1989: UMO CD 101.

"GMBR." Recorded, 1996: Black Saint 120 161-2.

"Half Step." Recorded, 1989: UMO CD 101.

"The Harmonic Veil." Recorded, 1994: Black Saint 120-141-2.

Hearinga Suite. Recorded, 1989: Black Saint 120 103-2. Contents: Hearinga; Conversations with the Three of Me; Seesall; Aura of Thoughts-Things; Oldfotalk; Finditnow; Bermix.

"The Heart Is Love and 'I Am.'" Recorded, 1983: Black Saint BSR 0071.

"How Are You?" Recorded, 1975: Delmark DS-430.

"Hydepth." Recorded, 1995: New World 80469-2.

"Hymn to the East." Recorded, 1975: India Navigation IN-1058; Whynot Records-PA-7121.

"Illuso." Recorded, 1993: Black Saint 120 132-2.

"In Retrospect." Recorded, 1975: Delmark DS-430.

"The Infinite Flow." Recorded, 1975: India Navigation IN-1058; Whynot Records-PA-7121.

"Imagine." Recorded, 1996: Black Saint 120 161-2.

"Inner Lights." Recorded, 1984: Black Saint BSR 0081.

"Inneroutersight." Recorded, 1979: Black Saint BSR 0032.

"Introspection." Recorded, 1986: Black Saint BSR 0091 CD.

"J. G." Recorded, 1975: Black Saint 120 003-2.

"Ja Do Thu (Dedicated to Jarman)." Recorded, 1978: Novus Records AN 3000.

"Journey Home as Seen through the Fairness of Life." Recorded, 1982: Black Saint BSR 0051.

"The Junction." Recorded, 1994: Black Saint 120-141-2.

"Laja." Recorded, 1984: Black Saint BSR 0081.

"Levels and Degrees of Light." Recorded, 1967: Delmark Records DD 413.

"Lifea Blinea." Recorded, 1978: Novus Records AN 3000.

"Linetime." Recorded, 1996: Black Saint 120 161-2.

"Little Brother." New York: Arc Music, 1957.

"Little Girl." New York: EMI Unart, 1967.

"Malic." Recorded, 1980: Black Saint BSR 0041.

"Mama and Daddy." Recorded, 1980: Black Saint BSR 0041.

"March of the Transients." Recorded, 1975: Delmark DS-430.

"Marching with Honor." Recorded, 1996: Black Saint 120 161-2; New World 80512.

"Meditation." Recorded, 1993: Black Saint 120 132-2.

"Metamor." Recorded, 1986: RPR Records RPR 1001.

"MGD." New York: Ric Peg, 1990.

"Miss Amina." Recorded, 1982: Black Saint BSR 0051.

"Miss Richarda." Recorded, 1986: Black Saint BSR 0091 CD.

"Munktmunk." Recorded, 1986: Black Saint BSR 0091 CD.

"My Thoughts Are My Future—Now and Forever." Recorded, 1967: Delmark DD 413.

"The New People." Recorded, 1975: India Navigation IN-1058; Whynot Records-PA-7121.

"Nickie." Co-composer, Anthony Braxton. Recorded, 1976: Arista AL 4101.

"No Lands Man." Recorded, 1955: Argo Records LP 621.

"No Name." Recorded, 1955: Argo Records LP 621.

"Nusped." New York: Ric Peg, 1991.

"Ode to the Imagination." Recorded, 1990: Black Saint 120-133-1.

"One and Four Plus Two and Seven." Recorded, 1975: Delmark DS-430.

"One for Peggy." Co-composer, Amina Claudine Myers. Recorded, 1982: Black Saint BSR 0051.

"One for the Whistler." Recorded, 1990: Black Saint 120 117-2.

"One Line, Two Views." Recorded, 1995: New World 80469-2.

"One Merger." New York: Ric Peg, 1996.

"OQA." Recorded, 1977: Black Saint BSR 0017.

"Over the Same Over." Recorded, 1996: Black Saint 120 161-2.

"Panorama." Recorded, 1975: Black Saint 120 003-2.

"Peace on You." Recorded, 1975: India Navigation IN-1058; Whynot Records-PA-7121.

"Personal Conversations." Recorded, 1984: Black Saint BSR 0081.

"Petsrof." Recorded, 1990: Black Saint 120 117-2.

"Piano-Cello Song." Recorded, 1986: Black Saint BSR 0091 CD.

"Plus Equal Minus Balance." Recorded, 1990: Black Saint 120 117-2.

"Positrain." Recorded, 1984: Black Saint BSR 0081; Black Saint BSRMJ-001.

"The Prism 3." Recorded, 1995: New World 80469-2.

"Quartet to Quartet." Recorded, 1981: Black Saint BSR 0061 CD.

"Rejoicing with the Light." Recorded, 1983: Black Saint BSR 0071.

"Reunion." Co-composer, Roscoe Mitchell. Recorded, 1990: Black Saint 120-133-1.

"Richard's Tune." Recorded, 1978: Atlantic SD 8802.

"Ritob." Recorded, 1977: Black Saint BSR 0017; Black Saint BSRMJ-001; UMO CD 101.

"Roots." Recorded, 1975: India Navigation IN-1058; Whynot Records-PA-7121.

"Roots of Blue." Recorded, 1986: RPR Records RPR 1001.

"Saturation Blue." New York: Ric Peg, 1986.

"Scaledance." Recorded, 1994: Black Saint 120-141-2.

"Scenes and Colors." Recorded, 1990: Black Saint 120-133-1.

"Septone." Recorded, 1990: Black Saint 120 117-2.

"Sightsong." Recorded, 1975: Black Saint 120 003-2.

"Song for All." Recorded, 1996: Black Saint 120 161-2.

"Soprano Song." Recorded, 1986: Black Saint BSR 0091 CD.

"Sound Image of the Past, Present and Future." Recorded, 1993: Black Saint 120 132-2.

"Spihumonesty." Recorded, 1979: Black Saint BSR 0032.

"Spiral to Clarity." Recorded, 1983: Black Saint BSR 0071.

"Steamin' up the Road." Recorded, 1996: Black Saint 120 161-2.

"Stretch Time." Recorded, 1989: Black Saint 120 103-2; Black Saint 120 117-2.

"String Song." Recorded, 1978: Novus Records AN-3007.

"Swang Rag Swang." Recorded, 1982: Black Saint BSR 0051.

"Symtre." Recorded, 1989: UMO CD 101.

"Temporarily out of Order." Recorded, 1955: Argo Records LP 621.

"Textures 95." Recorded, 1995: New World 80469-2.

"Things to Come from Those Now Gone." Recorded, 1975: Delmark DS-430.

"Think All, Focus One." Recorded, 1995: Black Saint 120-141-2.

"Thousand Years." Omaha, Nebr.: Had's Music, 1967.

"Time into Space into Time." Recorded, 1986: RPR Records RPR 1001.

"Transparency of Lobo Lubu." Recorded, 1982: Black Saint BSR 0051.

"Transversion 1." New York: Ric Peg, 1991.

"Tribute to Julius Hemphill and Don Pullen." Recorded, 1995: New World 80469-2.

"Triverse." Recorded, 1979: Black Saint BSR 0032.

"Turbulence." Co-composer, Eddie Harris. Recorded, 1973: Atlantic 311.

"Two over One." Recorded, 1975: Black Saint 120 003-2; Original Jazz Classics OJCCD-479-2.

"Unichange." Recorded, 1979: Black Saint BSR 0032.

"Unity." Recorded, 1975: Black Saint 120 003-2.

"View from Within." Recorded, 1984: Black Saint BSR 0081.

"Voice Song." Recorded, 1978: Novus Records AN-3007.

"W. W." Recorded, 1975: Black Saint 120 003-2.

"Wherever I Go." Chicago: Conrad Music, 1976.

"Wise in Time." Recorded, 1969: Delmark DE-423.

"Young at Heart." Recorded, 1969: Delmark DE-423.

"Zambezi Dance." Recorded, 1972: Atlantic 1611.

INSTRUMENTAL SOLOS
Violin
Duet for Violin and Piano. New York: Ric Peg, 1986. Commissioned by the McKim Fund.

Piano
Improvisation Structures I–II–III–IV–V–VI. Unpublished manuscript. Premiere, 1983.

Trio. Unpublished manuscript. Contents: Trio no. 1; Trio no. 2; Trio no. 3. Premiere, 1984.

Piano, Four Hands
Piano Duet no. 1. Unpublished manuscript. Premiere, 1986.

SMALL INSTRUMENTAL ENSEMBLE
Strings
String Quartet no. 2. Unpublished manuscript. Premiere, 1985.

String Quartet no. 3. Unpublished manuscript. Commissioned by Bang on the Can. Premiere, 1992.

"Strings and Things." ca. 1992. Unpublished manuscript. Commissioned by the String Trio of New York. Recorded: Black Saint 120 131-2.

Woodwinds
Saxophone Quartet no. 1. ca. 1994. Unpublished manuscript. Commissioned by the Rova Saxophone Quartet.

Combinations
"New Horizons." ca. 1995. Unpublished manuscript. Commissioned by Newband.

FULL ORCHESTRA
Folk Tales '88. Unpublished manuscript. Commissioned by the Brooklyn Philharmonic. Premiere, 1988.

Odyssey of King. Unpublished manuscript. Premiere, 1984.

Saturation Blue. Unpublished manuscript. Premiere, 1986.

Transversion I, op. 6. New York: Ric Peg, 1983. Premiere, 1991.

ORCHESTRA (CHAMBER OR FULL) WITH SOLOISTS
NOVI (jazz quartet, symphony orchestra). Unpublished manuscript.

Variations for Solo Saxophone, Flute, and Chamber Orchestra. New York:

Ric Peg, 1983. Commissioned by the City of Chicago for the 1982 New Music America Festival. Premiere, 1982.

What a Man (mezzo-soprano, tenor, bass-baritone, woodwinds, trumpet, trombone, tuba, percussion, piano, string quartet). 1991. Unpublished manuscript. Commissioned by the Center for Black Music Research, Columbia College Chicago and Friends of the Chicago Public Library. Premiere, 1991.

VOICE WITH INSTRUMENTAL ENSEMBLE
Quintet for Voice (Soprano), Piano, Harp, Cello, and Violin. Unpublished manuscript. Commissioned by The Kitchen. Premiere, 1982.

PUBLICATIONS

ABOUT ABRAMS
Articles
Coudert, F. M. "Trophée pour un prophète: Muhal Richard Abrams." *Jazz Magazine* 395 (July–August 1990): 50–51.

DeMuth, Jerry. "Muhal Richard Abrams: Jazz Innovator, Founder of the A.A.C.M." *Contemporary Keyboard* 4, no. 5 (1978): 20+.

Giddins, Gary. "Muhal Richard Abrams: Meet This Composer." *Jazz Forum* 120 (1989): 4–6. Originally published in *The Village Voice*, June 29, 1989.

Jost, Ekkehard. "Katalysator, Ratgeber und Vaterfigur Muhal Richard Abrams." *Jazz Podium* 31 (March 1982): 21–26.

Litweiler, John. "Chicago's Richard Abrams: A Man with an Idea." *Down Beat* 34, no. 20 (1967): 23+.

———. "Interview with Muhal Richard Abrams." *Chicago Reader* (May 9, 1975): 13.

———. "Muhal Richard Abrams." *Down Beat* 59, no. 11 (1992): 60.

Macnie, Jim. "Muhal Richard Abrams' Abstract Blues." *Musician* 145 (November 1990): 30+.

Martin, T. "The Chicago Avant-Garde." *Jazz Monthly* 157 (1968): 12.

McRae, Barry. "Beyond the Mainstream: Avant Courier Muhal Richard Abrams." *Jazz Journal International* 33, no. 4 (1980): 25+.

Silverman, Leigh, and Larry Birnbaum. "The World According to Muhal." *Ear: New Music News* 13, no. 4 (1988): 18+.

Townley, Ray. "Profile: Muhal Richard Abrams." *Down Beat* 41, no. 14 (1974): 34.

———. "Richard Abrams." *Coda* 10, no. 1 (1973): 4, 42.

BY ABRAMS
"The Social Role of Jazz." With David N. Baker and Charles Ellison. In *Reflections on Afro-American Music,* edited by Dominique-René de Lerma, 101–110. Kent, Ohio: Kent State University Press, 1973.

"Special Reports: The Association for the Advancement of Creative Musicians." With John Shenoy Jackson. *Black World* 23, no. 1 (1973): 72–74.

* * * * *

Pianist, composer, clarinetist, administrator, and educator, Muhal Richard Abrams (born Richard Abrahams) has exercised profound influence as a catalytic figure in post-1960 avant-garde black music and partially composed improvisation. He initiated the Chicago free jazz movement and became a respected mentor within the apprenticeship system of his Experimental Band and later the Association for the Advancement of Creative Musicians (AACM). Abrams' pedagogical emphasis on the varied history of black music has had a profound impact on younger generations of musicians and composers, including Roscoe Mitchell, Henry Threadgill, Anthony Braxton, and George Lewis. The stylistically diverse music that he has composed and performed often juxtaposes abstract sonic explorations of unconventional timbres and textures with familiar black music of the past and present.

Though Abrams attended the Chicago Musical College for four years, he was mostly self-taught, beginning with the piano at age 17 and continuing with clarinet and flute. In 1950, during the height of the bebop era, he began writing and arranging for Walter "King" Fleming's band and performing with musicians on tour (including Miles Davis, Max Roach, and Sonny Rollins) and in local venues. His piano playing, for which he developed an original sound during this time, blends the virtuosity and rhythmic approach of Art Tatum, the stride piano style of James P. Johnson, and techniques of ragtime and boogie woogie.

In 1955, Abrams co-founded, with Walter Perkins, the post-bebop quartet MJT+3, for which Abrams wrote compositions and arrangements. When the group disbanded, he studied formal compositional techniques, using the Schillinger system and the music theory texts of the German composer Paul Hindemith. His growing interest in exploring the world of sound through original composition, combined with the desire to liberate musicians from dependence on mainstream performance venues, led Abrams and multi-instrumentalist Donald Garrett to establish Chicago's Experimental Band in 1961. The Experimental Band was essentially a rehearsal band dedicated to the ideals of unlimited musical discovery, collective improvisation, and creative equality among the players.

During the early 1960s, clubs increasingly favored employing disc jockeys as a popular and inexpensive way to feature music, thus threatening the livelihood of many nightclub musicians. Musicians were growing dissatisfied with limitations on repertoire when playing for money in clubs, and as that context allowed increasingly less personal expression and musical growth for creative musicians, it became clear that a self-governing framework was necessary to counter the dominance of the music industry. The larger social context of the Civil Rights struggle, Black Nationalist movement, and grass-roots community organizations in South Side Chicago neighborhoods contributed further to a climate of political, economic, social, and musical self-determination.

In 1965, the Experimental Band evolved permanently into the first musicians' collective of wide-reaching historical significance, a non-profit organization called the Association for the Advancement of Creative Musicians (AACM), with Abrams as its first president (other founders included pianists Phil Cohran and Jodie Christian and drummer Steve McCall). Experimental Band alumni Joseph Jarman, Roscoe Mitchell, Henry Threadgill, Anthony Braxton, Malachi Favors, Lester Bowie, and many others joined as active members. The organization's primary goals were musical: to create employment, performance, and recording opportunities for musicians; to train young musicians within a structured apprenticeship system; to provide AACM composers with a context in which original music could be performed; and to establish a big band that featured original works by its members, while spawning smaller bands that developed their own distinctive voices (such as the Art Ensemble of Chicago, Creative Construction Company, and Air). As a mentor, cultural missionary, and spiritual leader within the AACM, Abrams emphasized an informed awareness of black music history while encouraging individualistic experimentation with new forms of music. In addition, he established a venue for publishing original scores by AACM composers (Richarda Music).

Abrams' own music as composer and bandleader was not recorded until 1967. On the first album of his works, *Levels and Degrees of Light*, his fully developed pianistic style is evident, as is his unconventional clarinet playing. The three pieces recorded on this album, sketched only in outlines, stress melodic and rhythmic elements over harmonic structural frameworks and demonstrate a keen sense of form developed through impressionistic and expressive timbres and textures. Abrams introduces extensive unaccompanied solo playing, sensitive use of silence, and dense, free group improvisation combined with instrumental use of the voice, poetry, and the playful colors of many "little instruments." His 30-minute introspective solo piano narrative, "Young at Heart," recorded on Delmark nearly two years later (*Young at Heart/Wise in Time*), exemplifies his highly ornamented melodic style, while the partner piece "Wise in Time" finds him exploring extended piano techniques, such as playing directly on the strings of the piano, while a quartet (trumpet, alto saxophone, bass, drums) improvises freely.

Following the lead of many of his former Chicago-based AACM colleagues, Abrams moved to New York City in 1977, where he continued composing and recording (almost exclusively on the Italian record label Black Saint), while playing in a number of large and small ensembles that reflected the musical interdependence fostered by the AACM, including the Muhal Richard Abrams Sextet. His growing popularity in the international arena culminated in his winning the first International JazzPar Award in Denmark in 1990. This prestigious award confirmed the technical excellence, experimental sensibility, and original musical voice of Abrams' prolific compositional output, and it publicly recognized his international influence on improvised music of the past 30 years.

Despite the lack of more widespread recognition among mainstream listeners, Abrams' commitment to the progress of heterogeneous creative music thrives as he remains active as a composer, performer, and teacher. Abrams the composer liberally explores diverse instrumental combinations (for example, a recent piece for symphony orchestra and jazz quartet, or writing for Newband's ensemble of original Harry Partch instruments) as well as the possibilities of computer-age instruments, such as the Disklavier. Abrams the performer continues to develop solo piano improvisational structures; and the skills of Abrams the teacher have been sought by the Banff Center in Banff, Canada; Columbia University; the California Institute of the Arts in Valencia; and many other schools. His compositions, such as *Hearinga Suite* (1989) for jazz orchestra, and recent recordings, such as *One Line, Two Views* (1995), demonstrate that Abrams, the multifaceted musician, continues to cultivate his original voice.

AMY C. BEAL

THE BIRD SONG (1967)

"The Bird Song" is the longest piece on Muhal Richard Abrams' earliest recording and release, *Levels and Degrees of Light* (1967; Delmark DD 413), which includes two other compositions by Abrams, "Levels and Degrees of Light" and "My Thoughts Are My Future—Now and Forever." "The Bird Song" lasts an impressive 23 minutes and covers a rich and esoteric musical landscape typical of his early compositions. As recorded on June 7, 1967, "The Bird Song" features the composer on piano and clarinet, poet David Moore's poem and voice, Leroy Jenkins on violin, Charles Clark and Leonard Jones on bass, Thurman Barker on drums, Anthony Braxton on alto saxophone, and (Kalaparusha) Maurice McIntyre on tenor saxophone. Although the recording was barely reviewed at the time of its release, it has in recent years been recognized as a seminal sound document of late-1960s Chicago free jazz.

Record producer Chuck Nessa's historic recordings of Abrams' compositions on the Chicago blues label Delmark Records quickly followed similar documentation of fellow Association for the Advancement of Creative Musicians (AACM) composers Roscoe Mitchell (*Sound,* 1966) and Joseph Jarman (*Song For,* 1967). These recordings all share a progressive exploration of improvisational structures and a common sensitivity to unconventional tone colors; they also exemplify the influence of Abrams' musical vision and his generosity in promoting younger composers. Twenty years later, composer, multi-instrumentalist, and AACM member Anthony Braxton, whose *3 Compositions of New Jazz* (1968) was recorded by Delmark shortly after *Levels and Degrees of Light,* summarized Abrams' profound influence on this group: "The thrust of Abrams' work can be traced back to the time zone of the fifties—from his involvement with hard bop, to the founding of the Experimental Band, to the theatre work he contributed in the sixties, and to the inspiration he provided for all of the musicians in the AACM. Muhal's piano music is like a history of black music—encompassing every area and period of black music, yet offering something that is uniquely different at the same time. . . . I believe Muhal's contribution to creative music represents one of the significant offerings of the post-[Albert] Ayler continuum."

"The Bird Song" demonstrates the many levels and degrees of Abrams' luminous music, guiding the listener through a series of impressionistic, perhaps programmatic soundscapes that lead into the future, far from their place of origin. The piece combines stasis, mystery, and tranquillity with drive, energy, and density. As an early example of Abrams' compositional style, "The Bird Song" exemplifies his sensitive layering of instrumental colors, an ability to blend disparate sonorities with both humor and a nod toward abstraction. Although the piece is dominated by traditional jazz instrumentation (reeds, piano, bass, drums), Abrams embellishes the sound with violin and voice, extended playing techniques, and sound effects such as bird calls and bells.

The piece opens with unmetered, heterophonic high reeds playing a tonal-sounding melody with wide, consonant leaps. This introduction is soon interrupted by Moore's poem, which opens with the words "Birds and prophecy." Unaccompanied, Moore recites a poem that blends cityscapes of modern Chicago ("midwestern maroon brick," "Chicago dust"), cynical American symbolism ("ruins of a cursed land, star-spangled," "wrecked cities"), and issues of slavery ("they come from Cancer's Tropics," "brothers imprisoned in chickenwire," "demons of Nordic snows") with colorful adjectives and nature imagery ("golden doves through the windows of high-rise ruins," "sparrows of yellow," "silver doves," "magenta fowl flying"), while also referring to jazz ("*our* music," "doomed and shrouded in what was jazz"). Following the four-minute recitation, the two basses enter as if from afar, and, like the reeds, in extremely high registers (playing harmonics, or flageolet tones), similarly twittering like strangled birds. They move restlessly, in disjointed, spasmodic lines. As the drums enter with atmospheric cymbal rolls, the texture thickens and becomes more urgent, foreshadowing the burst of energy to come.

The absence of reeds in this section creates a new music far removed from traditional expectations of jazz. The sense of rising tension in the strings is unexpectedly pierced by bird calls that blend with the instrumental melodies while providing countermelodies to the already established texture. Various kinds of "little instruments" (an assortment of noisemakers, percussion, and non-Western instruments, including shakers and bells used frequently by AACM musicians) add new colors to the texture, and the cymbal pulse periodically grows more regular and urgent. New sounds fade in and out of the frame, until Abrams' piano and Braxton's saxophone cause a rupture in the otherwise static scene.

The new section drives forward like high energy music of the recent jazz past, accompanied by urgent free drumming and continued use of the "little instruments." This is collective group improvisation at its most exciting. The swirling piano riff is echoed by bells and the angular, free saxophone solo. Musically, the chaotic natural world of birds is juxtaposed with the chaotic modern world of urban decay, much as it was in Moore's poem. The dynamic level and tempo have been raised considerably from the previous section, and this climax provides no breathing space: the agonized shrieks and virtuosic phrases of Braxton's and McIntyre's extroverted playing demand attention as one multivoiced organism. The high tessitura of the opening continues to dominate the choice of pitches, as energetic drumming punctuates the pulse.

Three minutes before the close of the piece, the energy suddenly drops off (perhaps depicting Moore's apocalyptic vision: "the end of Armageddon," or "century twenty-one, and the clocks of Rome stand mute"). The motion and dynamics soften, and the bird calls, bells, cymbal rolls, and the ornamented violin and bass harmonics are heard again, as if they were there all along, covered by the dense central energy section. In the final minutes of the piece, the high strings and percussion gradually recede into silence. Heard as a large arch form that builds to a central climax before fading back to its original texture, "The Bird Song" reveals compositional planning and structural resolution.

Abrams' "Bird Song" moves breathlessly and fills every possible space of its musical landscape, perhaps symbolizing the constant nervous motion of birds or aurally illustrating Moore's poetic connection between birds and the oppression of black Americans ("singing their colored calls over wrecked cities"). The inclusion of this eloquently declaimed verse demonstrates progressive openness to the incorporation of unconventional elements in a partially composed collective improvisation. This piece also centralizes the composer's preference for nonchordal structures and exploration of unconventional tone color. As a visual representation of his music, his original water-color painting on the cover of the record jacket features a colorful palette full of contrast: organic ancient symbols amid angular geometric shapes complement the unpredictable and asymmetrical curves of the natural world.

AMY C. BEAL

LEVELS AND DEGREES OF LIGHT (1967)

"Levels and Degrees of Light," the title track of the album that also includes "The Bird Song," explores the melodic limits of pentatonic improvisation as well as the textural and timbral possibilities that grow out of a small group of instruments consisting of voice (Penelope Taylor, on the recording), vibraphone, cymbals, and clarinet. The work begins with a section devoted to exploration of the human voice. A pentatonic scale is the basis for the melodic material, and the range is continually expanded upward. This causes a psychological heightening of tension, performed in dramatic fashion. The continual addition and exploration of higher degrees of the scale by the vocalist also suggests similarities with the practice of Hindustani musicians as they introduce and improvise on the successive degrees of a particular raga. The cymbals and vibraphone punctuate the vocalist's phrases, contributing both harmonic and dynamic elements to the work. These instruments enhance the entrance of each new phrase with *crescendo* cymbal rolls and arpeggiated chords. In addition, they freely improvise material underneath the vocal phrases. The constant presence of these instruments creates a sense of drone, albeit very flexibly applied, which is also reminiscent of Hindustani music. This continual interplay between the accompanying instruments and the voice creates a quality not unlike waves crashing onto land; while perhaps not particularly eloquent, this analogy conveys the tension and release as well as the continual variation inherent in each phrase.

The second section of "Levels and Degrees of Light" explores the range and timbral characteristics of the clarinet. Continuing the interplay between solo and accompaniment that was initiated in the vocal section, the clarinet becomes increasingly more adventurous in terms of range and tonal quality with each passing phrase. A new interval, an ascending ninth, is added to the melodic material. In addition, the melodic range is continually expanded toward the upper limits of the instrument. The dynamics of this section are pushed beyond the limits of the instrument, resulting in overblown, violent passages in which the pitch becomes less focused and the instrument fairly screams its material. This section offers a much more emotionally charged solo part and becomes far more climactic than the vocal section. This is most likely due to the fact that the clarinet is pushed to its limits while the vocal part remains contained within traditional techniques.

The structure of the work can be described in relationship to this interplay, the formal implications of which seem to indicate that the piece is built upon a combination of the principles of variation technique and free improvisation. Variation is inherently part of each successive phrase, and the continual return to a "tonic" pitch reinforces this. Yet it is clear that no one theme is being developed; rather, the entire scale seems to be subjected to exploratory improvisation. Here, then, is an example of the partially composed nature of Abrams' music: while the structure is provided by the composer, the material within the sections is based on improvisatory techniques.

The treatment of the melodic material of both sections is interesting when it is viewed in relationship to the title of the work. When applied to the two solo instruments, voice and clarinet, questions of levels and degrees of light can be answered in any number of ways. Most directly, the range and timbral characteristics of each instrument seem to illustrate the meaning of the title.

TIMOTHY ROMMEN

THINK ALL, FOCUS ONE (1995)

"Think All, Focus One" is the title track from the album that was released by Black Saint Records in 1995. Abrams performs this approximately five-and-a-half-minute work on solo and background synthesizers in addition to percussion samples. The general structure of the work is ternary (ABA'). The A section begins in two-part polyphonic texture. The lower part moves rapidly while the upper part moves more slowly and lyrically against the lower line. The harmonic implications of these two lines are decidedly posttonal in nature. No clear key center emerges from this passage, and their vertical combination sounds almost polytonal at times. Yet a sense of direction prevails throughout this opening section. Abrams utilizes a thick analog synthesizer tone and makes free use of modulation effects, such as vibrato. In addition, the range of the lower part is surprisingly wide, reaching down to notes that are so low in pitch that they are difficult to distinguish from one another. Abrams seems to be exploiting the sonic quality of the slower soundwaves rather than the pitch content at these points in the A section.

The goal of the A section coalesces at the point at which various percussion samples are introduced into the texture (about 55 seconds into the piece). These include tubular bells, triangles, toms, and a synthesized drum kit, to name but a few. During this portion of the work, the analog synthesizer sound draws out the moment into a feeling of stasis through the use of a repeating chord that asserts its presence even as the musical focus shifts to the rhythmic and textural elements introduced by the percussion instruments. A return to the two-voice texture, with percussive accompaniment, concludes the A section.

The B section concerns itself primarily with percussive sounds and is just over two minutes long. Abrams explores a new set of sounds in this section, including filtered and primarily attack-oriented tones. The most striking of these sounds are the types of tones that do not convey strong pitch content. While a pitch is discernible in each of the tones, pitch is treated as only one of the many parameters of each tone and is subordinated to parameters such as attack and timbre. Abrams prefers lower registers when exploring these tones, using the slower cycles per second of each soundwave to add to the ambiguity of the tone. When combined, these techniques of sound modeling result in tones that are particularly airy and without definitive pitch content. Abrams integrates these types of tones with more traditional percussive sounds and creates a soundscape that derives interest primarily from rhythmic variation and creativity. He does retain the focused, original analog sound in this section, but it plays a minor role. The B section concludes by elision. The lower voice of the two-part polyphonic texture in the A section asserts itself as the percussive instruments gradually drop out.

The A' section begins with much of the material from the A section. The polyphonic texture is reintroduced and this portion of the A' section moves toward the same goal as did the first A section, arriving at the static, reiterated chord and the introduction of percussion samples. Yet the concluding portion of this section introduces a pad sound to explore the sonic texture, focusing attention on this previously unheard sound rather than on the percussion instruments. The pad sound is at the interval of a minor second in both low and high registers, giving the most extended glimpse of tonal language in the entire piece. "Think All, Focus One" concludes by introducing a solo percussion motive, which then fades into silence.

This work demonstrates Abrams' free experimentation with sound and technology and also illustrates his partially composed structures. The A section is mirrored by the A' section in all but the concluding measures, whereas the various percussion sections seem derived from improvisatory technique. In a sense, then, Abrams has applied the spirit of his Experimental Band to technology.

TIMOTHY ROMMEN

REFERENCES

Davis, Francis. *In the Moment: Jazz in the 1980s.* New York: Da Capo Press, 1986.

Heffley, Mike. *The Music of Anthony Braxton.* Westport, Conn.: Greenwood Press, 1996.

Jost, Ekkehard. *Free Jazz.* New York: Da Capo Press, 1974.

Litweiler, John. "Chicago's Richard Abrams: A Man with an Idea." *Down Beat* 34, no. 20 (1967): 23+.

Radano, Ronald M. "Jazzin' the Classics: The AACM'S Challenge to Mainstream Aesthetics." *Black Music Research Journal* 12, no. 1 (1992): 79–95.

ADAMS, ALTON AUGUSTUS

Born in St. Thomas, Danish West Indies (U.S. Virgin Islands), November 4, 1889; died in St. Thomas, November 23, 1987. **Education:** Mrs. Vialet's School, St. Thomas, beginning at age six; Moravian Town School, St. Thomas; began musical studies at age eight or nine; solfège and flute studies with John Pierre; studied flute with Albert Francis; University of Pennsylvania, correspondence course offered by Dr. Hugh A. Clarke, studied harmony, counterpoint, and composition, 1906–09, diploma and letter of commendation, 1909; School of Musical Theory of Carnegie Hall, New York, N.Y., certificate in harmony, counterpoint, and composition, 1914; University Extension Conservatory of Music, Chicago, Ill., B.Mus.; Royal Academy of Music, London, correspondence studies. **Military Service:** U.S. Navy, Chief Petty Officer and bandmaster, 1917–34; Naval Reserves, 1934–42; recalled to active duty as Chief Musician, 1942–47; 10th Naval District, San Juan, Puerto Rico, Naval Censor, 1943–45. **Composing and Performing Career:** St. Thomas, played flute and piccolo in the Municipal Band under Lionel Roberts, 1906–10; organized and directed the Adams Juvenile Band (later the St. Thomas Juvenile Band), 1909, first concert, 1910; organized three Navy Bands (one in St. Thomas, two in St. Croix), 1917–18; Virgin Islands, organized public school music program, 1918; supervisor of music in public schools, 1918–31; helped establish first public library, 1920; toured eastern United States with U.S. Navy Band of the Virgin Islands, including stops in Washington, D.C., Philadelphia, New York, and Boston, 1924; Central Park, New York, N.Y., conducted the Goldman Band, 1924; St. Thomas, opened private music studio, ca. 1924; tour of British West Indies, 1930; Cuba, directed Navy band, 1931–34; Guantánamo Bay, Cuba, formed first racially integrated U.S. Navy band, 1942; St. Thomas, reorganized Virgin Islands Band, 1943; New York, N.Y., hosted radio show, *Concert Hall,* beginning 1963; conducted the Goldman Band, 1963, 1967; conducted U.S. Field Band, 1979. **Commissions:** Cyril Daniel, ca. 1911. **Memberships:** St. Thomas Power Authority, chairman, 1944–50; Associated Negro Press, executive staff, beginning 1955; Virgin Islands Hotel Association, president, 1952–71; Virgin Islands Press Association, president, 1956–58; Virgin Islands Council on the Arts, 1966–69. **Honors/Awards:** Received a Boehm-system flute for articles in *Jacobs' Band Monthly,* ca. 1916; RCA Letter of Commendation, 1924; Virgin Islands Citation, 1967; American Legion Award for Outstanding Leadership and Cultural Contributions to the Virgin Islands, 1970; cited in U.S. Congressional Record for outstanding military service and discipline, 1975; Virgin Islands Council on the Arts, Distinguished Artist Award, ca. 1975; Alton Adams Day, ca. 1975; Virgin Islands Chamber of Commerce Award for Outstanding Contributions to the Virgin Islands, 1975; Virgin Islands Hotel Association, Alton A. Adams Sr. Scholarship Fund; Fisk University, Nashville, Tenn., honorary doctorate, 1979; College of the Virgin Islands, Trustees Distinguished Achievement Award, 1983; Virgin Islands Medal of Honor from the Sixteenth Legislature of the Virgin Islands, 1986.

MUSIC LIST

INSTRUMENTAL SOLOS
Piano

"Doux rêve d'amour: Valse pour piano." ca. 1911. Columbus, Ohio: Burt M. Cutler, 1912. Commissioned by Cyril Daniel. Also arranged for band.

"Questions." Unpublished manuscript.

"Sincerity: Valse." ca. 1911. Unpublished manuscript.

"Until: Valse." Unpublished manuscript. Also arranged for wind band.

CONCERT BAND

"Caribbean Echoes: Valse Tropical." Unpublished manuscript. Also arranged for piano.

"Childhood Merriment: Valse Caprice." ca. 1924. Unpublished manuscript. Also arranged for piano.

"The Governor's Own." 1921. New York: Carl Fischer, 1921. Originally entitled "Governor Oman." Also arranged for small orchestra, full orchestra, and piano. Premiere, 1921. Recorded: Columbia A-7579 or New World Records NW 226 or New World Records 80266-2.

"H.M.S. Ingolf March." ca. 1911. Unpublished manuscript. Presumed lost. Premiere, 1911.

"The Spirit of the U.S.N." 1924. Boston: Cundy-Bettoney, 1925. Recorded: CBMR001.

"Virgin Islands March" (wind band). 1917; revised 1965. Boston: Walter Jacobs, 1919. Originally published in *Jacobs' Band Monthly* 4, no. 10 (October 1919). Also arranged for piano; trio also arranged for SATB. Official territorial anthem of the Virgin Islands, 1963–present.

CONCERT BAND WITH SOLOIST

"Warbling in the Moonlight" (piccolo, band accompaniment). Unpublished manuscript.

SOLO VOICE

"Sweet Virgin Isles." Unpublished manuscript.

"Welcome to Our President" (medium voice). Unpublished manuscript.

PUBLICATIONS

ABOUT ADAMS
Articles

Floyd, Samuel A., Jr. "Alton Augustus Adams." *Black Perspective in Music* 5, no. 2 (1977): 173–187.

Giglioli, Arturo. "Alton A. Adams." *Jacobs' Band Monthly* 1, no. 6 (1916): 29–30.

Schlesinger, Tanya. "Alton Adams: A Point of View." *All-Ah-Wee* 1, no. 3 (1977): 28–32.

Seltzer, Frank R. "Famous Bandmasters in Brief." *Jacobs' Band Monthly* (1920): 18ff.

BY ADAMS

"About Mr. H. A. VanderCook and his 'Modern Method of Cornet Playing.'" *Musical Messenger* (1924).

Memoirs. ca. 1977–87. Alton Augustus Adams Collection, Center for Black Music Research, Columbia College, Chicago, Ill.

"Music Appreciation: An Appeal for Its Study." *Music Bulletin* (October 1929): 8–17.

"A Treatise on Band Music." n.d. Alton Augustus Adams Collection, Center for Black Music Research, Columbia College, Chicago, Ill.

"Whence Came the Calypso?" *Caribbean* 7 (1953): 218–220, 230, 235. Reprinted in *Virgin Islands Magazine* 8 (1953): 35+.

Regular columns in *Army and Navy Musician* [Elkhart, Ind.], *Dominant* [New York, N.Y.], *Metronome* [New York, N.Y.], *Music Bulletin, Musical Enterprise* [Camden, N.J.], *Pittsburgh Courier, St. Croix Herald, St. Thomas Bulletin,* and the *St. Thomas Times.* Also contributed to the *Amsterdam News, Life,* the *New York Times,* the *San Juan Star, Sports Illustrated,* the *St. Thomas Daily News,* and *Time.*

Regular contributing editor to *Jacobs' Band Monthly,* 1916–19.

Editor, the *St. Thomas Times,* 1920–22, *St. Thomas Bulletin,* 1940-42.

PRINCIPAL ARCHIVES

Alton Augustus Adams Collection, Center for Black Music Research, Columbia College, Chicago, Illinois.

Van Sholten Collection, Enid M. Boa Library, St. Thomas, United States Virgin Islands.

* * * * *

The accomplishments of Alton Adams assure him of an important role in music history: first black bandmaster of the U.S. Navy (1917–34); first bandmaster of a racially integrated unit in the U.S. Navy (Guantánamo Bay, Cuba, 1942–47); composer of one of the top-selling marches for Carl Fischer in 1921, "The Governor's Own"; and distinguished music educator and author. Yet his unique position and numerous writings make his life and work a valuable resource for those interested in many areas of historical endeavor, including U.S. naval history, the history of the Virgin Islands, the sociology of music, and issues of class and ethnicity during the Harlem Renaissance.

The career of Alton Adams cannot be separated from the history of the Virgin Islands, where he was born and lived. Throughout his musical life, he continually rejected opportunities from such institutions as the U.S. Army, Philadelphia's Wanamaker Stores, and the Hampton Institute that would have taken him away from his home on St. Thomas. The symbiosis between Adams and the Virgin Islands seems to be the key to understanding both his music and his muse.

Born into a community of middle-class artisans who had in most cases purchased their freedom from slavery through hard work and determination, Adams wholeheartedly adopted their elite values of individualism, education, cultural sophistication, and community responsibility. His music education was gained through self-study. As St. Thomas lacked an institution for music instruction, he learned by listening, reading, and, most importantly, by doing. He began his studies on the flute. After some early experiments using a hand-made six-hole instrument cut to size

from "the protruding stems of the papaya tree," he received the gift of a flageolet from his grandmother and began learning how to play by transcribing by ear two hymns, "Nearer My God to Thee" and "Safe in the Arms of Jesus." Because it was cheaper than a full-sized flute, his father purchased a wooden piccolo along with an instruction book through a U.S. mail-order house for $2.10. He studied the piccolo and elementary theory with a local amateur, but his six months of lessons were cut short by the teacher's death. Following local custom, he then apprenticed himself to a local shoemaker, who was, not coincidentally, a flutist himself and the leader of a local town band. Adams remained dedicated to the self-study of music, often practicing late into the night. Much of his authority and success as a bandmaster resulted from his own instrumental prowess. As his own teacher, he seems to have developed strong pedagogical skills and was able to pass his hard-earned knowledge along to the members of his Juvenile Band, who were all rank beginners. He gave them each instrument lessons and taught them *solfège,* rhythm, and music history.

Adams' development as a composer is a bit more difficult to trace. After discovering a copy of *Etude Magazine* in the wrappings of a shipment of shoemaking tools, he subscribed. From this magazine and others, including *Metronome, Musical Observer,* and *Musical Courier,* he discovered an inspiring motivation: "In the pages of these journals I became aware of the higher purpose and mission of music as a civilizing agency as well as a precise art form requiring many years of study and practice, struggle and sacrifice," wrote Adams in his memoirs. Responding to an advertisement in *Etude,* he enrolled in a correspondence course in music theory and composition offered by Dr. Hugh A. Clarke, professor of music at the University of Pennsylvania. Correspondence study was both a necessity and a respected tradition in the Virgin Islands; he studied for three years and received strong encouragement and finally a special letter of commendation from Clarke in 1909. Later, he also completed correspondence courses with the School of Musical Theory of Carnegie Hall (1914) and the Royal Academy of Music in London. He received a bachelor's degree from the University Extension Conservatory of Music in Chicago through correspondence coursework.

Adams' compositional style appears to have resulted from a combination of his correspondence work in theory, harmony, and orchestration and his own experience, self-study, and experimentation. As a virtuoso flutist, he developed a gift for melodic balance and invention. His marches frequently eschew the typical melody and accompaniment texture of most band music in favor of a polyphonic interplay of as many as four separate and simultaneous melodies. Many of his melodies make use of chromatic passing tones to create a particularly graceful and lyrical effect.

For his self-study in composition, Adams relied on the traditional pedagogical technique of copying scores: "Assiduously I would put into band and orchestral score the immortal 'Stars and Stripes Forever,' 'El Capitán,' 'Right Forward,' 'Semper Fidelis,' 'Manhattan Beach,' 'King Cotton,' and others . . . so as to clearly analyze and study their content—harmonic progressions, instrumental arrangements, and those original patterns of bass movements so characteristic of their unique style." His conception of melody, rhythm, form, and key structure reflects his analyses of Sousa's marches.

Alton Augustus Adams; courtesy of the Alton A. Adams Jr. Collection, Center for Black Music Research, Columbia College Chicago

The composer's borrowings from Sousa served a social function as well. While coming from a "native" and, furthermore, "black" Virgin Islander, these sounds expressed an undeniable patriotism that served to assure both U.S. officials and potential visitors in the Islands' growing tourist industry of the loyalty, sophistication, and essential Americanness of Virgin Islanders. For Adams, Sousa's music represented "the popular expression and embodiment of the spirit of America itself." To imitate Sousa was to emulate an American spirit that was comfortable, safe, and beyond criticism, thus placing Adams, his band, and Virgin Islanders as a whole into an ideological safe haven.

Although Adams was frequently referred to as the "Sousa of his Race," to call him a mere imitator would be to neglect his own creative efforts. While he certainly attempted to capture the patriotic spirit and rhythmic energy of Sousa, his rhythmic construction is generally more economical. Furthermore, his more frequent use of syncopation may reflect the influence of local Caribbean dance musics that he often arranged for his ensembles. Unfortunately, a comprehensive analysis of Adams' musical style may never be possible; a fire that burned his home on St. Thomas in 1932 destroyed the great majority of his music manuscripts.

Despite his dedication to the mastery of craft, compositional technique for Adams represented simply the means to an end—that of education and community service. He believed that "teaching is the greatest contribution a person could make to society." But teaching meant a myriad of possibilities: teaching discipline and a trade to the youths in his St. Thomas Juvenile Band; teaching the world about the existence of the Virgin Islands; and even teaching people of different races to live and work together in harmony. According to Adams, "The very nature of music prevents it from being the slave of any class or race or nation." In fact, each of his compositions seems to respond to a specific community need and to perform several social functions. Inspired by a particular social problem, he would compose extremely quickly; he composed his most successful march, "The Governor's Own," in a single evening and premiered it the following day after discovering that the U.S. naval governor had been publicly embarrassed by another local musician.

When the United States took over the Danish West Indies for tactical reasons near the climax of World War I, Adams already had trained an impressive ensemble known as the Adams Juvenile Band. When a concert by the Juvenile Band was overheard by the wife of one of the newly arrived naval administrators, the band, said Adams, became "a liaison, a bridge of communication, between the new naval officials and the community, . . . a facilitator of cross-cultural dialogue and understanding, as well as a means of demonstrating the need and value of cooperation, unity and harmony." At the request of the naval governor, James Oliver, President Woodrow Wilson signed the directive that established the Navy Band of the United States Virgin Islands on June 2, 1917, making the Adams Juvenile Band the first black band in the U.S. Navy and making Adams the navy's first black bandmaster.

Adams took maximum advantage of this unprecedented opportunity by expanding the band's role as liaison into that of community leader. It appears that his own professionalism and bearing, as well as the band's polished appearance, legendary discipline, and musical skill helped win the admiration, respect, and largesse of the white naval administration. Based on this respect, he created two additional bands: one on St. Croix and a second on St. Thomas. He created the public school music program with the help of the Red Cross and also helped establish the first public library on the Virgin Islands. He even created the first local newspaper on the island, the *St. Thomas Times,* dedicated to cultural and education news.

The band's repertoire fulfilled in a sonic existence Adams' dreams of a society based upon merit without racial, class, or ethnic barriers. According to Adams, the band's wide-ranging repertoire included "marches, classics, local folk melodies, waltzes, sacred music, popular tunes, songs, overtures, even jazz." For him, the classics meant not only his band arrangement of Schubert's *Unfinished Symphony* but a wide variety of operatic arias and overtures. His Emersonian vision of American society was utopian and idealistic, so much so that he continually minimized and dismissed his own experiences with racial discrimination. On the public surface, race had no position in his social equation. Underneath this veneer however, he was keenly aware of the example set by himself and his band and was motivated by this opportunity to influence racial politics.

In 1924, the band toured in eastern seaboard cities of the U.S. mainland. The tour not only reached hundreds of thousands of people through concerts, newspaper reports, and radio broadcasts, but it was enormously successful on other levels. Adams and the band were hailed as geniuses in the black communities they visited, and they performed special-request concerts for black audiences who had been barred from attending their regular performances. In short, the band became a focal point of black identity, pride, and cultural politics during the formative period of the Harlem Renaissance. Adams came into contact with many black musical leaders of the Harlem Renaissance, including Harry T. Burleigh, William Dawson, W. C. Handy, and Lucien H. White.

After the tour, the band's fortunes declined rapidly. A recording contract, radio performances, and plans for additional American and European tours came to nothing. Adams himself ceased to compose for band; there is no evidence today of any substantial works that can be solidly dated to the period following the 1924 tour. Despite his later accomplishments, Adams' own account of his musical career in his memoirs ends with this tour, which he called, "the apogee of the Navy Band's success." Personal tragedy may have contributed to this cessation of compositional activity; the fire that destroyed his manuscripts in 1932 also took the life of his 12-year-old daughter, Hazel, and he felt this loss very deeply. His march "Childhood Merriment: Valse Caprice" is based upon a melody Hazel had hummed one day while playing.

For Adams, the Virgin Islands were not only a paradise of natural beauty, but a paradise of social opportunity. At the periphery of the United States, Adams benefited from both the legacy of racial tolerance left behind by the Dutch and, as he has reported, the U.S. naval administration's remarkably open embrace of a newly acquired territory. This unique situation minimized racial discrimination and realized for a brief time Adams' American dream of individual liberty, hope, and opportunity. He not only took maximum advantage of this opportunity but discovered his only real source of artistic inspiration and purpose—the community and people of the Virgin Islands.

Adams was recalled to active duty during World War II to take over the direction of his old unit in Cuba. Although it was initially an all-white unit, he received permission to recall several of his original bandsmen, thus creating the navy's first racially integrated ensemble. After his final retirement from the military in 1947, Adams returned to St. Thomas and resumed his dedication to community leadership and established flourishing careers as a journalist and a guest-house proprietor.

VIRGIN ISLANDS MARCH (1917)

The "Virgin Islands March" exemplifies Adams' claim that "there is no other force which can socialize, energize, and guide the emotions of the masses, from childhood to maturity, like good music." This composition functions as a catalyst toward identity and a vehicle for its publicity on at least seven different levels: (1) as a calling card for the composer; (2) as music for Adams' own band; (3) as music for the local island community; (4) as a compliment to its dedicatee, Captain William Russell White of the U.S.S. Vixen; (5) as music for the U.S. naval government; (6) as music raising international awareness of the Virgin Islands; and (7) with lyrics added, as the official anthem of the Virgin Islands and a personal statement of Adams' own hope for universal brotherhood.

The "Virgin Islands March" is about melody, being "more lyrical," according to Adams, than his other works. The clarity of this march results primarily from the prominence, solidity, and infectious energy of its tune. Written at the beginning of his naval career in 1917, its moderate difficulty level likely reveals its function as a teaching piece for the three bands under Adams' care.

The "Virgin Islands March" embraces a variety of conventional instrumental devices from the traditional band repertoire, thereby instructing players in the general role of each instrument: the flute, clarinet, and saxophone parts frequently carry the melody, which emphasizes scalar decorations of a lyrical tune; the alto horns play rhythmic off-beat parts that complement the firm harmonic architecture of the basses; the baritones and trombones play lyrical countermelodies; and the cornets double the melodies of the upper woodwinds and punctuate cadences and transitions. Thus, the band's mastery of this march would equate to the mastery of the basic skills necessary to play any piece in the band's repertory and would be a stepping-stone to Adams' more challenging works, "The Governor's Own" and "The Spirit of the U.S.N." In addition, his choice of rhythms avoids tricky 16th-note figures and first introduces all of the more challenging rhythms in the melody against the metronomic clarity of the basses, repeats them several times, and only then allows them to be imitated by other instruments in brief counterstatements. These countermelodies respond to the melody in a polyphonic conversation that gives the work a coherence that is easy for even an inexperienced player to grasp and replicate. The melody is therefore the rhythmic pedagogue of the work as a whole.

This march gave the bandsmen a sense of pride, purpose, and direction. Writing about the qualities of the bandleader, Adams observed, "The main objective of the teacher or leader is to inspire in his pupils the feeling that the thing being done is a vital one, vital to the life of the community and done with a real love in their heart for the work." While the "Virgin Islands March" does not appear to refer explicitly to any local traditions or tunes, its title alone is capable of producing a strong association. For both its players and audiences, the march served as a catalyst to a local sense of place, purpose, and ownership that resisted the pervasive force of Americanization.

Two years after its composition, Adams dedicated the march to his commanding officer. He described the multiple functions of this gesture in his dedication letter to the captain dated November 10, 1919: "Sir, this is but a feeble effort of mine to express to you the heartfelt gratitude we owe to you . . . especially for your kind interest and teaching in the development of our moral and intellectual status. We trust, with God's help, to carry on the noble work—which you have carefully . . . entrusted to us, that is: that our lives should be as shining examples to our fellow natives." Using a rhetoric of self-effacement, Adams deftly employed his composition not only to express deference and gratitude, but, more importantly, to encourage the future largesse of his superiors. While the dedication gave White credit for the creation of the band, it also gave White the responsibility for its continued success and indeed even responsibility for the moral and intellectual status of *all* the islands' natives. By allowing himself to become the shining example of the naval government's racial policies, Adams became the measure of this policy and thereby gained considerable power.

The "Virgin Islands March" was performed throughout the 1924 U.S. tour of the band, and the composer took every opportunity to introduce the work by describing the islands with particular attention to their tropical beauty. The harmonic coloring and rhythmic vitality of the march could only have made his description more vivid in the minds of his listeners. The association between the colorful and energetic musical soundscape and the island's tropical landscape transforms the march into a potent advertisement repeated again and again not only by Adams' own band but by bands throughout the United States. An article in the *Metronome* from 1924 observes that "if these islands are nearly as good as the music their land discourses, they are indeed worth seeing and helping."

In 1963, the legislature of the Virgin Islands officially accepted Adams' rededication of the "Virgin Islands March" to the people of the Virgin Islands and suggested that it be performed at "all significant state occasions." Immediately following this rededication, Governor Paiewonsky appointed Adams as chairman of a committee of seven government and community leaders brought together to create words for this now official song. Enacting Adams' vision of a tolerant and democratic society, the committee solicited verses from the islands' inhabitants regardless of race, religion, gender, or class. For the first time in more than 20 years, Adams began composing again and wrote an additional four-part choral setting of the trio section that can be inserted into the original composition. Arranged from the contributions of 24 island residents, the final version of the text includes four verses set to the tune of the trio strain. While praising the natural beauty of the island and noting the loyalty of Virgin Islanders to the U.S., the text was primarily "a song in praise of brotherhood." Its patriotic sentiments reflect idealized notions of freedom, democracy, liberty, truth, love, and peace. With this new text and legal mandate, the march critiqued the attitudes of racial intolerance stemming from the U.S. mainland in the 1960s and actively distanced itself from this influence. As an anthem, the march confronted and displaced the "Star Spangled Banner" and thus reminded a new generation of islanders that their heritage of racial tolerance was unique and historically distinct from that of the U.S. mainland.

The second work by Alton Adams to be published, the "Virgin Islands March" made his reputation among bandsmen in the United States during the 1920s. In *Jacobs' Band Monthly*, Frank Seltzer wrote of this march, "It is a delightful concert number, and one of those parade marches that puts life and vim in the tired marchers." *Nicholl's Master Musician Music Review* called it "a tuneful swinging march. . . . The arrangement is exceptionally good; the melodies are splendid." Even Adams' idol, John Philip Sousa, wrote to him to express his admiration of the work: "My dear Sir:—We rehearsed the march and I find it very effective and hope that it will prove a success. Believe me."

THE GOVERNOR'S OWN (1921)

As a boy, and before the advent of radio, Alton Adams would secretly listen in "rhapsodic ecstasy" to "phonograph concerts" outside the residence of an islander with a sizable collection of "beautiful music—orchestral and band selections [and] operatic arias." He was "particularly impressed by the marches of Sousa, so full of the spirit of militant vigor and courage." After these concerts, he would daydream and "imaginatively conduct Sousa's band in one of [his] own compositions." Little did he know then that one day Sousa himself would conduct his compositions or that he would conduct his own music with Goldman's famous band to great applause and an encore.

"The Governor's Own" is a clear response to the works of Sousa. Like the majority of Sousa's marches, it begins with a four-measure introduction leading to the first of three sections or strains. Adams placed the first two sections in the key of A-flat major and the third section, or trio, in D-flat major, thus mimicking the typical key pattern of Sousa's works by adding a single flat to the key signature in the final strain. Each of these sections would then be repeated, but without the *da capo* return to the beginning so typical of earlier marches as well as the march's 17th- and 18th-century ancestor, the minuet and trio form.

While Adams learned his lessons in form via Sousa, their respective styles began to diverge when it came to melodic treatment and counterpoint. Although Adams' syncopated rhythms and polyphony invoke his African heritage, the main reason why he and Sousa sound different is simply that the ensembles for which they wrote were so different. Sousa's concert ensemble was actually a cross between the brass band and the symphony orchestra. He typically wrote for an ensemble of 60 or more musicians, including players of the harp and contrabassoon. In contrast, Adams' 1924 touring ensemble, which gathered musicians from all three of the bands under his command, still numbered a scant 38. It included the conductor; seven B-flat clarinets, one alto clarinet, and one bass clarinet; two alto and two tenor saxophones; five cornets; three trumpets; five trombones; four alto horns; one euphonium; four tubas; snare drum; and a combined bass drum/

cymbals part. Furthermore, while Sousa's band was at its best in the auditorium, Adams' ensemble played almost exclusively outdoors. The combination of reduced instrumentation and unfavorable performance venues limited the instrumental palate and dynamic subtlety of his works in favor of greater clarity and carrying power.

Adams' real gift was for melody, specifically polyphonic counterpoint—the ability to combine several melodies into a simultaneous musical argument. While Sousa found variety in the softer dynamics and differing instrumental colors, Adams created variety by layering different instrumental sections atop one another. These multiple melodies not only grabbed the listener's attention but made sure that the band could be heard by keeping the entire ensemble playing at almost all times.

According to Adams, the principal theme of "The Governor's Own" was inspired by its dedicatee, Admiral James C. Oman, the naval governor of the Virgin Islands, from 1919 to 1921, whom Adams described as "a short, jaunty, snappy sort of fellow." The melody seems to depict the governor himself, but it also echoes Sousa's energetic melodies from "King Cotton" and "Manhattan Beach" in its use of rests to invigorate the otherwise stepwise motion of the melodic line (see Ex. 1). The characteristic use of chromatic neighbor and passing notes is also apparent.

Adams' economy of rhythm comes into play as he subtly transforms the rhythmic motive from each section into its successors. In this way, he provides an organic unity to the whole by balancing variety with repetition. He transfers at least one small rhythmic idea into each subsequent formal section and gives these transplanted ideas new life by shifting them against the metric flow of the pulse. For example, the two 16ths and eighth-note motive of the opening melody is transferred into one of the countermelodies of the trio section. By shifting the motive into an off-beat position against the pulse, the original "military" motive sounds new, more lyrical and flowing, while maintaining a link to earlier music in the composition. Thus, the music achieves an inexhaustible sense of variety and melodic progression while using only a limited set of rhythmic motives.

Although Adams' published marches have nearly disappeared from the contemporary band repertoire, his compositions were extremely popular in the early- to mid-1920s. An advertisement by its publisher, Carl Fischer, proclaimed "The Governor's Own" to be one of the "Four Leading American Compositions" of 1924. The work even became the official commencement march for Howard University and is acknowledged to be among Adams' very best compositions.

Example 1. "The Governor's Own," melodic line, mm. 9-17

THE SPIRIT OF THE U.S.N. (1924)

Adams' last complete work for band, "The Spirit of the U.S.N." [United States Navy], was written in 1924 on Long Island, New York, just prior to the band's U.S. tour. The work was dedicated to "President Calvin Coolidge as an expression of the loyalty and patriotism of the people of the Virgin Islands to the United States." As an affirmation of the Virgin Islanders' firm commitment to their new owners, the work was intended to premiere for the President at a concert in Washington, D.C. The tragic death of the President's son, however, forced the navy's executive officer to decline the invitation to attend the concert.

"The Spirit of the U.S.N." reveals the growing musical skill of Adams' ensemble as well as his mature compositional fluency. The compact four-measure introduction sets the principal devices of the composition into play: a whistling tune in the upper woodwinds floats above a melodic bass line and exclamatory counterstatements. Unlike Sousa, Adams introduces his polyphonic countermelodies from the very beginning of the first strain: the solo baritone rises stepwise from underneath the seafaring melody, providing a smooth lyrical contrast to the quick syncopated tune. Technically and rhythmically, this march is Adams' most difficult to perform. It makes increased use of differences in instrumental coloring and idiomatic writing than his earlier work, and its form is more complex as a break strain is added to the trio section. The work successfully integrates the concept of a melodic bass line, which Adams admired so much in Sousa's compositions.

Published in 1925, "The Spirit of the U.S.N." never achieved the success of Adams' earlier works. Maybe it was the composition's high level of technical difficulty or the aural complexity of its polyphonic counterpoint that limited its success. In any event, the work's poor commercial performance gives further indication of Adams' rapid decline in popularity following the 1924 tour.

WARBLING IN THE MOONLIGHT (N.D.)

While no recordings of Alton Adams playing the flute or piccolo appear to have been made, contemporary accounts, anecdotal evidence, his writings on flute technique, and his one solo work for piccolo and band, "Warbling in the Moonlight," all seem to point to the conclusion that he was a true virtuoso on these instruments. In an article for *Jacobs' Band Monthly,* Boston bandmaster Frank Seltzer called Adams "a virtuoso on the flute and piccolo" and noted that "his solos frequently [are] the one great feature of his many concerts."

At the top of his own list of the qualifications of a bandmaster, Adams wrote: "1. an innate musical ability." Playing a solo work in front of his band at concerts would have established his preeminent position as leader of the ensemble. Furthermore, the solo concerto was an expected element in the band program ritual. Many prominent American bands were directed by virtuoso soloists who had left Sousa's ensemble to form their own, among whom were Herbert L. Clark, cornet, Arthur W. Pryor, trombone, and Simone Mantia, euphonium. Each of these performer/conductors played solos with their bands. In many ways, then, audiences expected the director to be the finest musician in the ensemble, and the solo concerto was a means of demonstrating this leadership. For this purpose, Adams earlier had arranged "The Mocking Bird," by

flutist Fred Lax for piccolo with band accompaniment. Adams' performances of this work in each city of the 1924 tour only fostered his reputation; a Boston paper remarked, "The piccolo solo by Mr. Adams . . . was wildly applauded."

"Warbling in the Moonlight" provided yet another opportunity for the composer to shine as a soloist with his band. Not surprisingly, he provided two solo cadenzas that emphasize the technical virtuosity and interpretive acumen of the performer. One cadenza is so packed with notes in sweeping runs that a single measure takes up more than the entire width of a manuscript page. The accompaniment is a straightforward arpeggiated Alberti bass and is among the simplest music that Adams ever wrote, but it serves its purpose well. This transparent texture allows the solo voice to stand out from the accompaniment in high relief. In the few instances that the band accompaniment does become thick and loud, the piccolo is placed in its uppermost register in order to make the soloist clearly audible. The piccolo's lowest, and therefore quietest, register appears only in the cadenzas, when there is no competing accompaniment.

Neither the flute nor piccolo was a common solo instrument for outdoor band concerts; the louder and more penetrating brass instruments were much more typical. The choice of the brilliant-sounding piccolo over the more mellow flute undoubtedly was made to allow the solo voice more prominence. The lack of flutes and piccolos from the accompanying ensemble further highlights the timbre of the solo voice, allowing its distinctive color to stand out from the accompaniment not simply because of its volume, but because of its unique tone quality and tessitura.

"Warbling in the Moonlight" is essentially a modified march. The first solo cadenza is inserted after the standard four-measure introduction. The first section, marked "Tempo di Polka," capitalizes on the rapid articulation and clarity of the piccolo above a thin, but rhythmic, chordal accompaniment. Next, a 16-measure interlude by the full band adds variety and gives the soloist a rest before the next solo strain. The next strain's eight-measure *tutti* is cut short by another solo cadenza that flows smoothly into the trio section. True to the typical march key structure, the trio adds a flat, placing the piece in the key of D-flat major—a somewhat unusual key for band. For the D-flat piccolo, however, this modulation lands the soloist in the facile key of C major. Thus, a climactic pyrotechnic display is facilitated by idiomatic patterns in a comfortable key. The use of trills and rearticulated pitches maximizes the listener's excitement while minimizing the technical demands of the piece. This is not to say that the work is simplistic, but rather that the composer has custom tailored this work to the needs of a conductor/soloist who must pick up his instrument cold after directing a long concert and still execute a convincing, if not commanding, rendition with a maximum of titillating effect.

It is in the climactic trio that Adams finally indulges his talent for polyphonic countermelodies by inserting two additional melodies into the mixture, one played by the baritones, and another by the cornets and clarinets. The piccolo's highest register and more active rhythms help capture the audience's ear despite the increased volume and complexity of the accompaniment. Following the repeat of the trio and another 16-measure interlude by the full ensemble, the texture thins and the piccolo part becomes increasingly angular and frenetic as the remainder of the work never repeats, but becomes ever more virtuosic as it accelerates. A surprising fermata suspends the accompaniment momentarily before a climactic coda rushes toward a conclusion that caps the soloist's technical display and ushers in the audience's applause. "Warbling in the Moonlight" is a virtuosic showpiece that demonstrates Adams' choreography of musical form to achieve a specific goal—to both entertain his audience and establish his own commanding musical presence.

REFERENCES

Adams, Alton Augustus. "En Route with the Navy Band of the Virgin Islands." Unidentified Virgin Islands newspaper clipping found in Adams' scrapbook, ca. July 1924. Alton Augustus Adams Collection, Center for Black Music Research, Columbia College, Chicago, Ill.

———. "John Philip Sousa: As Man and Musician 1854–1932." Alton Augustus Adams Collection, Center for Black Music Research, Columbia College, Chicago, Ill.

———. Memoirs. ca. 1980s. Alton Augustus Adams Collection, Center for Black Music Research, Columbia College, Chicago, Ill.

———. "A Music Week Contribution." ca. 1935–41. Alton Augustus Adams Collection, Center for Black Music Research, Columbia College, Chicago, Ill.

———. "The Power of Music." Lecture for Community Music Association of the Virgin Islands, n.d. Alton Augustus Adams Collection, Center for Black Music Research, Columbia College, Chicago, Ill.

———. "Testimonials: Printed at the *St. Thomas Times* Office, St. Thomas, V.I." ca. 1921–22. Alton Augustus Adams Collection, Center for Black Music Research, Columbia College, Chicago, Ill.

———. "Virgin Island Band Charms City." *Boston Chronicle.* Undated newspaper clipping found in Adams' scrapbook, ca. August 1924. Alton Augustus Adams Collection, Center for Black Music Research, Columbia College, Chicago, Ill.

———. "Virgin Islands Navy Band Visits United States and Has Successful Tour." Unidentified newspaper clipping found in Adams' scrapbook, 1924. Alton Augustus Adams Collection, Center for Black Music Research, Columbia College, Chicago, Ill.

Floyd, Samuel A., Jr. "Alton Augustus Adams." *Black Perspective in Music* 5, no. 2 (1977): 173–187.

Seltzer, Frank R. "Famous Bandmasters in Brief." *Jacobs' Band Monthly* (1920): 18ff.

MARK CLAGUE

ADAMS, LESLIE

Born Harrison Leslie Adams in Cleveland, Ohio, December 30, 1932. **Education:** Cleveland, Ohio, public schools, early piano training with Dorothy Smith and Mina Eichenbaum; Glenville High School, voice lessons with John Howard Tucker; Oberlin College Conservatory of Music, Oberlin, Ohio, studied composition with Herbert Elwell and Joseph Wood, voice with Robert Fountain, piano with Emil Danenberg, B.M., 1955; studied composition with Robert Starer, 1959; studied composition with Vittorio Giannini, 1960; California State University at Long Beach, studied under Leon Dallin, M.Mus., 1967; Ohio State University, Columbus, Ohio, studied composition with Marshall Barnes, 1968–73, Ph.D., 1973; studied orchestration with Marcel Dick, Edward Mattila, and Eugene O'Brien, 1978–83. **Composing and Performing Career:** New York, N.Y., served as piano accompanist for various ballet and dance companies, received numerous performances of his compositions by a variety of artists, 1957–62; Karamu House, Cleveland, Ohio, associate musical director, 1964–65; Kaleidoscope Players, Raton, N.Mex., musical director, 1967–68; Karamu House, composer-in-residence, 1979–80; Cuyahoga Community College, Cleveland, Ohio, guest composer, 1980; Cleveland Music School Settlement, composer-in-residence, 1981–82; Cleveland, Ohio, Accord Associates, Inc., founder and president, 1980–86, executive vice-president and composer-in-residence, 1986–92; Cleveland, Ohio, Creative Arts, Inc., executive vice-president and composer-in-residence, 1997–present. **Teaching Career:** Soehl Junior High School, Linden, N.J., vocal music instructor, 1962–63; Raton, N.Mex., secondary schools, vocal music supervisor and choir director, 1966–67; Florida A&M University, Tallahassee, assistant professor of music, 1968; University of Kansas, Lawrence, associate professor of music, director of the University choir, director of choral clinics, 1970–78. **Commissions:** Broken Arrow Elementary School, 1975; Kansas Composers Forum of Kansas Music Teachers Association, 1979; Cuyahoga Community College, 1979; Ohio Chamber Orchestra, 1981; University of Kansas, 1983; Paul Kaye Singers, Minneapolis, Minn., 1985; Borg-Warner Foundation, 1989; Cleveland Chamber Symphony, 1990; American Guild of Organists, 1991; Cleveland Orchestra, 1994; Historic First Presbyterian Church of East Cleveland, Ohio, 1997. **Memberships:** Advisory Council, Musical Arts Association (Cleveland Orchestra), 1982; Phi Kappa Phi; Phi Mu Alpha Sinfonia; Phi Delta Kappa; Pi Kappa Lambda; American Choral Directors Association; American Guild of Organists. **Honors/Awards:** National Association of Negro Women, Inc., New York, winner, composition competition, 1963; National Education Defense Act Fellowship, 1969–70; National Award for Original Composition for Choral Ensemble, Christian Arts, Inc., New York, 1974; National Endowment for the Arts award, 1979; Rockefeller Foundation Study and Conference Center, Bellagio, Italy, scholar-in-residence, 1979; Yaddo Artists Colony, Saratoga Springs, N.Y., fellowships, 1980, 1984; Cleveland Foundation Fellow, 1980; Jennings Foundation Fellow, 1981; "Meet the Artist," Cleveland, Ohio, Public Schools, featured composer, 1981–82, 1983–84, 1991. **Mailing Address:** c/o Creative Arts, Inc., 9409 Kempton Avenue, Cleveland OH 44108.

MUSIC LIST

INSTRUMENTAL SOLOS
Violin
Intermezzo for Violin and Piano. 1953. New York: American Composers Alliance, 1984. Premiere, 1954.

Pastorale for Violin and Piano. 1952. New York: American Composers Alliance, 1990. Premiere, 1953.

Sonata for Violin and Piano. 1961. New York: American Composers Alliance, 1982. Premiere, 1961.

Cello
Sonata for Cello and Piano. 1975. New York: American Composers Alliance, 1981. Premiere, 1978.

Horn
Sonata for Horn and Piano: *Empire.* 1961. New York: American Composers Alliance, 1962. Premiere, 1961.

Piano
"Contrasts for Piano." 1961. Unpublished manuscript. Premiere, 1961.

Etude in G Minor. 1977. Readfield, Wisc.: Vivace Press, 1998.

Four Pieces. 1951. Unpublished manuscript. Contents: A Spanish Caprice; By the Brookside; Waltz; Sad Story.

Theme and Variations in A-flat Minor or "Variations on a Serious Theme." 1953. Unpublished manuscript. Premiere, 1953.

Three Preludes for Piano. 1961. New York: American Composers Alliance, 1983. Premiere, 1961.

Organ
"Offering of Love." 1991. New York: American Composers Alliance, 1992. Commissioned by the American Guild of Organists.

Prelude and Fugue for Organ. 1979. Readfield, Wisc.: Vivace Press, 1997. Commissioned by the Kansas Composers Forum of Kansas Music Teachers Association. Premiere, 1980.

SMALL INSTRUMENTAL ENSEMBLE
Brass
Trombone Quartet. 1975. New York: American Composers Alliance, 1990. Premiere, 1977.

Combinations
"Night Song for Flute and Harp." 1983. New York: American Composers Alliance, 1986. Premiere, 1989.

FULL ORCHESTRA
Ode to Life. 1979; revised 1983. New York: American Composers Alliance, 1983. Commissioned by Cuyahoga Community College, Cleveland, Ohio. Premiere, 1979.

Leslie Adams; courtesy of the composer

Romance. 1960. Unpublished manuscript. Note: orchestrated from "Contrasts for Piano."

Symphony no. 1. 1983. New York: American Composers Alliance, 1983. Commissioned by the University of Kansas.

Western Adventure. 1994. New York: American Composers Alliance, 1994. Contents: Cowboy's Race Across the Plains; Past an Indian Village; The Grand Cattle Roundup. Commissioned by the Cleveland Orchestra. Premiere, 1995.

ORCHESTRA (CHAMBER OR FULL) WITH SOLOISTS

Concerto for Piano and Orchestra or *CitiScape.* 1964. New York: American Composers Alliance, 1981. Note: master's thesis, California State University, Long Beach. Premiere, 1976.

Dunbar Songs or *Three Songs on Texts of Paul Laurence Dunbar* (medium voice and orchestra). 1981. New York: American Composers Alliance, 1983. Contents: The Meadow Lark; He/She Gave Me a Rose; The Valse. Commissioned by the Ohio Chamber Orchestra. Also arranged for high voice and piano. Premiere, 1981.

Hymn to Freedom (soprano, tenor, baritone, chamber orchestra). 1989. New York: American Composers Alliance, 1990. Contents: When Storms Arise; Lead Gently, Lord. Commissioned by the Borg-Warner Foundation for the Black Music Repertory Ensemble, Center for Black Music Research, Columbia College Chicago. Premiere, 1989. Recorded: "Lead Gently, Lord," Center for Black Music Research CBMR-0001.

Love Expressions. 1990. Geneva, Ohio: Henry Carl Music, 1990. Contents: Love Waltz; Love Ballad. Commissioned by the Cleveland Chamber Symphony. Premiere, 1990.

ORCHESTRA (CHAMBER OR FULL) WITH CHORUS

Christmas Lullaby (children's chorus, orchestra). 1993. Cleveland, Ohio: Cleveland Orchestra, 1995. Premiere, 1993.

SOLO VOICE

"Amazing Grace" (high voice). 1992. New York: American Composers Alliance, 1992. Premiere, 1992.

"Anniversary Song" (medium voice). 1993. New York: American Composers Alliance, 1993. Premiere, 1995.

"Break, Break, Break" (low voice). 1951. Unpublished manuscript.

"Christmas Lullaby" (medium voice). 1983. New York: American Composers Alliance, 1983. Premiere, 1995.

"The Constant Lover" (medium voice). 1951. Unpublished manuscript.

"Daybirth" (medium voice). 1994. New York: American Composers Alliance, 1994. Premiere, 1994.

Five Songs on Texts by Edna St. Vincent Millay or *Five Millay Songs.* 1960. New York: American Composers Alliance, 1978. Contents: Wild Swans; Branch by Branch; For You There Is No Song; The Return from Town; Gone Again Is Summer the Lovely. Originally titled *Songs of Love and Likelihood.* Also arranged for medium voice and orchestra; "For You There Is No Song," also arranged for chorus. Premiere, 1961. Recorded: "For You There Is No Song," University of Michigan SM-0015.

"Flying" (high or medium-high voice). 1993. New York: American Composers Alliance, 1993. Premiere, 1995.

"From a Hotel Room" (high voice). New York: American Composers Alliance, 1994. Also arranged for low voice.

"Hark, to the Shouting Wind!" (low voice). 1951. Unpublished manuscript.

"I Hear a Voice" (low voice). 1951. Unpublished manuscript.

"Love Memory" (high or medium-high voice). 1990. New York: American Composers Alliance, 1990. Premiere, 1993.

"Love Request" (high or medium-high voice). 1993. New York: American Composers Alliance, 1993. Premiere, 1994.

"Lullaby Eternal" (high or medium-high voice). 1993. New York: American Composers Alliance, 1993. Premiere, 1995.

"Midas, Poor Midas" (high voice). New York: American Composers Alliance, 1994. Premiere, 1995.

"Night" (low voice). 1951. Unpublished manuscript.

"Of Man's First Disobedience (from *Paradise Lost*)" (low voice). 1951. Unpublished manuscript. Premiere, 1953.

"On the Sea" (low voice). 1953. Unpublished manuscript. Premiere, 1953.

Six Songs (on Texts by African-American Poets) or *African-American Songs.* 1961. New York: American Composers Alliance, 1978. Contents: Prayer; Drums of Tragedy; The Heart of a Woman; Night Song; Since You Went Away; Creole Girl. Also arranged for medium voice and orchestra; "Prayer," "The Heart of a Woman," "Since You Went Away," and "Creole Girl" also arranged for chorus. Premiere, 1961.

"Song of Thanks" (low or medium voice). 1993. New York: American Composers Alliance, 1993. Premiere, 1993.

"Song of the Innkeeper's Children" (medium voice). 1992. New York: American Composers Alliance, 1992. Premiere, 1995.

"Song to Baby Jesus" (high or medium-high voice). 1992. New York: American Composers Alliance, 1992. Premiere, 1993.

"Teach Me, O Lord (from Psalm 119)" (low voice). 1951. Unpublished manuscript.

"Turn Away Mine Eyes" (low voice). 1951. Unpublished manuscript.

Two Vachel Lindsay Songs (low voice). 1952–53. Unpublished manuscript. Contents: The Leaden-Eyed; Factory Windows. Premiere, 1953.

"What Love Brings" (high or medium voice). 1991. New York: American Composers Alliance, 1992. Premiere, 1996.

"A White Road" (low voice). 1961. Unpublished manuscript. Premiere, 1964.

The Wider View (high or medium-high voice). 1988. New York: American Composers Alliance, 1990. Contents: To the Road!; Homesick Blues; Li'l' Gal (or My Man); Love Come and Gone; The Wider View; Love Rejoices. Premiere, 1989.

CHORAL MUSIC

"Asperges Me" (SSAATTBB chorus, SATB quartet, organ). 1952. Unpublished manuscript.

"A Christmas Wish" (SSAATTBB). 1991. Unpublished manuscript.

"Hosanna to the Son of David" (SATB). 1969. Fort Lauderdale, Fla.: Walton Music, 1976. Premiere, 1973.

"Hymn to All Nations" (SATB). 1997. New York: American Composers Alliance, 1997. Commissioned by the Historic First Presbyterian Church, East Cleveland, Ohio. Premiere, 1997.

"Love Song" (SATB). 1969. New York: Lawson-Gould Music, 1982. Premiere, 1994.

"Madrigal" (SATB unaccompanied). 1969. Aurora, Colo.: Now Music, 1991. Premiere, 1973.

"Man's Presence—A Song of Ecology" (two-part children's chorus). 1975. New York: American Composers Alliance, 1990. Commissioned by the Broken Arrow Elementary School, Lawrence, Kansas. Premiere, 1975.

"Psalm 23" (SATB unaccompanied, incidental baritone solo). 1970. New York: American Composers Alliance, 1990. Also arranged for SATB and piano.

"Psalm 121" (SATB chorus unaccompanied, solo SATB quartet). 1969. New York: American Composers Alliance, 1983. Note: winner, 1974 National Competition for Choral Composition, Christian Arts, Inc. Premiere, 1972.

Seven Amen Chorale Responses (SATB unaccompanied). 1953. Unpublished manuscript.

"There Was an Old Man" (SATB). 1970. New York: Lawson-Gould Music, 1985. Premiere, 1973.

"Under the Greenwood Tree" (SATB unaccompanied). 1969. New York: American Composers Alliance, 1983. Premiere, 1978.

"Vocalise" (SATB, two bassoons or two cellos, optional SATB quartet). 1973. New York: American Composers Alliance, 1990.

DRAMATIC MUSIC

Blake (opera in four acts). 1986. New York: American Composers Alliance, 1990. Premiere, 1997.

The Congo (theater piece for solo reader, speaking group, percussion). 1955. Unpublished manuscript. Premiere, 1955.

A Kiss in Xanadu (ballet in three scenes). 1954; revised 1973. New York: American Composers Alliance, 1990. Premiere, 1954.

The Righteous Man, A Cantata to the Memory of Dr. Martin Luther King, Jr. or Cantata no. 1 (SSAATTBB, orchestra). 1985. New York: American Composers Alliance, 1986. Commissioned by the Paul Kaye Singers, University of Minnesota. Also arranged for chorus and piano. Premiere, 1986.

INCIDENTAL MUSIC

All the Way Home (orchestra). 1965. Unpublished manuscript. Incidental music to a play by Tad Mosel. Premiere, 1965.

PUBLICATIONS

ABOUT ADAMS
Dissertation

McCorvey, Everett David. "The Art Songs of Black American Composers." D.M.A. thesis, University of Alabama, 1989.

Articles

Dawkins, Darlene. "Leslie Adams, Composer: Man and His Music." *Clubdate* 8, no. 2 (1987): 48–52.

Green-Crocheron, Karen. "Meeting Composer Leslie Adams." *Galore Magazine* (May 1982): 31.

Roach, Hildred. "Composer Leslie Adams." In *Black American Music: Past and Present,* 172–175. 2nd ed. Malabar, Fla.: Robert E. Krieger, 1985.

Turner, Diana. "Leslie Adams." *Artspace* 6, no. 6 (September/October 1983): 14.

Williams, Yvonne. "Leslie Adams and the Making of the Opera *Blake:* An Interview with the Composer." In *New Perspectives on Music: Essays*

in Honor of Eileen Southern, edited by Josephine Wright and Samuel A. Floyd Jr., 173–209. Warren, Mich.: Harmonie Park, 1992.

Wyatt, Lucius R. "Leslie Adams." *Black Music Research Newsletter* 7, no. 1 (1985): 3–4.

BY ADAMS

"The Mahlerian Mystique." *Journal of the Graduate Music Students at the Ohio State University* 1 (1969): 1–4.

"The Problems of Composing Choral Music for High School Use." Ph.D. diss., Ohio State University, 1973.

PRINCIPAL ARCHIVES

Leslie Adams Collection, Center for Black Music Research, Columbia College, Chicago.

Leslie Adams Music Archive, Cleveland Public Library, Cleveland.

* * * * *

Best known for his choral writing and art songs, Leslie Adams has also made significant contributions to the genres of instrumental music and opera. Currently a full-time composer, he has initiated many educational projects involving both public schools and the community at large. Adams' music has earned him national attention, as his numerous commissions, honors, and awards attest.

Born Harrison Leslie Adams in 1932, in Cleveland, Ohio, his early training included piano lessons with Dorothy Smith and Mina Eichenbaum and voice lessons with John Howard Tucker. Adams completed a bachelor of music degree at Oberlin College Conservatory of Music in 1955, where he had studied composition with Herbert Elwell, voice with Robert Fountain, piano with Emil Danenberg, and conducting. Following private compositional study with Robert Starer in 1959 and Vittorio Giannini in 1960, Adams studied composition with Leon Dallin at California State University at Long Beach (now Long Beach State University), receiving a master of music degree in 1967. His Ph.D. in composition was awarded by Ohio State University in 1973, where he studied with Henry L. Cady and Marshall Barnes.

Adams' Ph.D. dissertation, "The Problems of Composing Choral Music for High School Use," addresses both compositional and educational issues, two areas that for him remain connected. In addition to teaching appointments at Florida A&M University (Tallahassee) and University of Kansas (Lawrence), Adams has served as composer-in-residence at Karamu House in Cleveland (1979–80) and the Cleveland Music School Settlement (1981–82).

Adams' compositional development falls into two general periods, including smaller works prior to 1980 and large-scale compositions since that time. His first major works include two dramatic compositions, the ballet *A Kiss in Xanadu* (1954, revised 1973), and *The Congo* (1955) for solo reader, speaking group, and percussion. Later works show an interest in traditional solo and chamber instrumental genres, such as his Sonata for Violin and Piano and Sonata for Horn and Piano: *Empire* (both 1961), the Concerto for Piano and Orchestra (1964), Sonata for Cello and Piano (1975), and the Prelude and Fugue for Organ (1979). Choral settings and solo songs have been a continuing presence in Adams' output. Of particular note are the two collections for solo voice and piano: *Five Songs on Texts by Edna St. Vincent Millay* or *Five Millay Songs* (1960); and *Six Songs (on Texts by African-American Poets), or African-American Songs* (1961). Adams' choral music spans both the secular and sacred worlds, ranging from biblical settings ("Psalm 121" from 1969; "Psalm 23" from 1970) to social commentary (an arrangement of "We Shall Overcome" from 1963; "Man's Presence—A Song of Ecology," from 1975).

In 1977, Adams decided to devote his time exclusively to composition and commenced advanced private study in orchestration with Marcel Dick (1978–83). The results have been several large-scale works that utilize the full orchestra. Works from this period include the *Dunbar Songs* or *Three Songs on Texts of Paul Laurence Dunbar* for voice and orchestra (1981), as well as several unpublished choral arrangements of selections from the *Five Millay Songs* and *Afro-American Songs*. His *Ode to Life* for orchestra was completed in 1979, through a commission from the Cuyahoga Community College of Cleveland, Ohio, and revised in 1983. In 1983, Adams also completed his Symphony no. 1, commissioned by the University of Kansas. His *Western Adventure* for full orchestra (1994), commissioned by the Cleveland Orchestra, was premiered in 1995.

Also during the 1980s, Adams combined his growing activity in orchestral writing with his long-standing interest in dramatic vocal and choral music. The results were several large-scale works, including the opera *Blake* (1986); *The Righteous Man, A Cantata to the Memory of Dr. Martin Luther King, Jr.,* or Cantata no. 1 (1985, commissioned by the Paul Kaye Singers, University of Minnesota); and the *Hymn to Freedom* for soloists and chamber orchestra (1989).

Adams has situated his work in the tradition of William Grant Still's definition of black music: to have "some characteristics of the black experience," including the use of syncopation, and "qualities or characteristics of the [Negro] spiritual." Furthermore, Adams states that black music has "an identifiable quality to it. . . . [T]here is something unique indeed about listening to [music] . . . [with a] black signature. There is definitely something different compared to . . . German art songs or German folk songs, the same way there is a different quality in the German folk song and the French *chanson*. . . . [E]ach one has its own unique qualities and expressions."

Adams' music is basically tonal, with clear emphasis on lyric melodies, even in instrumental compositions. As a result, his works are extremely accessible to contemporary audiences. Yet Adams does not sacrifice technical or thematic complexity. He credits the often emotional effect of his music with the statement, "Music comes from the heart; technique is the servant of emotions." Adams has received considerable national recognition for his compositions, including awards and fellowships from the National Association of Negro Women (1963) and the National Endowment for the Arts (1979). He is currently executive vice-president and composer-in-residence of Creative Arts, Inc., a nonprofit arts organization in Cleveland that promotes the work of minority artists.

FOR YOU THERE IS NO SONG (1960)

This art song from *Five Songs on Texts by Edna St. Vincent Millay* has proven to be one of Adams' most enduring compositions. Millay's lyrics reflect a conservative, romantic style that nonetheless addresses contemporary political and feminist issues. As a highly trained pianist and singer, Millay's sensitivity to poetic melody and sound effects is uniquely suited to Adams' melodic yet dramatic idiom.

Adams' setting of "For You There Is No Song" complements Millay's poetry in its stylistic blend of traditional romantic harmonic language with emphasis on melody and occasional modernist twists. Throughout the song, he uses a diatonic musical language. The song is written in B-flat minor; he uses the natural minor form of the scale, without the raised seventh. Most memorable is the voice's overarching, haunting melody, which is placed against the piano's arpeggiated accompaniment. Coupled with its straightforward text setting, this striking melody gives the work the quality of a spiritual, while syncopations between piano and voice add a subtle level of rhythmic interplay at key textual points. Both elements—spiritual-like melodies and syncopation—characterize what Adams has called the identity of black music.

A close examination of the song reveals precise craftsmanship in the tightly structured interwoven thematic ideas. The main melodic idea of the work is an appoggiatura, introduced in measure 3 by the vocal line in the resolution from *c* to *b*-flat. This appoggiatura figure reappears in the melody as suspended sevenths, ninths, elevenths, and thirteenths against the piano's bass. This extended tonality gives the piece a rich harmonic canvas, culminating in quartal and quintal harmony in the piano (mm. 27–30). Furthermore, the appoggiatura constantly resolves on shorter rhythmic values, adding a sense of rhythmic and melodic direction and thrust.

The recurring appoggiatura figure creates the impression of a simply constructed, "natural" melody based on stepwise motion. Moreover, this hymnic melody lends itself to text illustration in the most dramatic manner. At the end of the first verse, on Millay's invocation of "the sound of a strong voice breaking," the melody introduces a *g*-natural against an F-minor chord (see Ex. 1). When viewed within the context of the previous motives, this pitch appears as an unresolved appoggiatura, illustrating the "strong voice" painfully breaking against the piano accompaniment.

Example 1. "For You There Is No Song," mm. 10-11

Adams' sensitive setting of Millay's work is exceptionally concise while maintaining emotional and musical breadth. Its blend of African-American traditions with the harmonic language of the romantic art song creates a paradoxically personal and universal vocabulary uniquely suited to Millay's touching poetry.

BLAKE (1986)

Blake is Leslie Adams' grand opera. It was begun in 1980 while the composer was in residence at Yaddo, and the full orchestration was completed in 1986. The work is in four acts, utilizing full orchestra, an auxiliary percussion ensemble, soloists, and double chorus.

The opera is based on the novel *Blake: Or, the Huts of America* by Martin R. Delaney. Parts of Delaney's work were originally published in 1959 in installments of the *Anglo-African Magazine*. The complete book was published in 1970. *Blake* has been described by Yvonne Williams as "the most important black novel of the period, and . . . one of the most significant and revealing novels ever written by an Afro-American." Delaney's novel was adapted by librettist Daniel E. Mayers of Brooklyn College, City University of New York.

The story concerns the lives, loves, and trials of African Americans on the eve of the Civil War. John-Henry Blake (tenor) is a slave on the Mississippi plantation of the cruel Major Frank Stevens (bass). When Blake returns from an errand, he finds that Stevens has given away Blake's wife Miranda (soprano) to a visiting couple from Charleston, South Carolina. The remainder of the story traces Blake's and Miranda's struggle to reunite and preserve their dignity against the dehumanizing backdrop of the antebellum South. The opera culminates in a fictional slave uprising in the Great Dismal Swamp on the border of Virginia and North Carolina, concurrent with the attack on Fort Sumter and the beginning of the Civil War.

Adams' setting of *Blake* is harmonically conservative, with an emphasis on lyric melody. Romantic opera conventions are evident in the reuse of themes and motives throughout the opera, particularly Blake's main theme, which recurs at crucial points in the story. The plantation owner Stevens sings a bass aria, "Our Losses Will Be Great," typical of villains in 19th-century grand opera. Miranda's lullaby "Hush Sweet Baby Chile" demonstrates Adams' unique melodic gift once again; this piece has proven especially appealing to audiences. Adams uses a traditional orchestral prelude along with trios, duets, and choral ensembles throughout the work. These more conservative elements from romantic opera are combined with African-American traditions. In addition to using syncopated rhythms and spiritual-like melodies (as in Miranda's lullaby), the final ensemble uses a gospel style.

Perhaps the most intriguing section of *Blake* occurs in act 3, scene 2. Here, an improvisatory section is played by an auxiliary percussion ensemble that Adams describes as Afro-Cubano. This group is separate from the orchestral percussion section and includes seven parts: three conga drums, cowbell, clave, *palitos* (two sticks that play the *palito* rhythm), and *shakere* (gourd rattle). The ensemble performs patterns that Adams describes as "African" rhythms: "There is an improvisatory section . . . which will be performed differently at each performance. This will allow for the musicians to bring their own passions to bear on the score within the framework of so many measures. . . . I felt that [spontaneity] was important, particularly when dealing with such authentic instruments and the style of performance. The original folk approach was certainly not sitting there in front of a musical score, but bringing to bear the performers' own emotions to their instrumental expressions is what I attempted to recreate in *Blake*."

Highlights of *Blake* were introduced to various audiences gradually, through "in-progress" concerts between 1983 and 1985. Adams described these concerts as follows: "[W]e had an idea to take *Blake* and go directly to the people in the community . . . to reveal the opera-in-progress as it was being composed, and, little by little, show the community what's going on and how it was developing [in order to] build interest and build an audience. . . . The idea was to 'test the waters' and the audience's response, and I think there is an advantage to do this for a new work, without giving too much of it away so that there's something left."

These performances included presentations for students and general audiences at Karamu House and Cuyahoga Community College in Cleveland and at Oberlin College Conservatory of Music. Parts of *Blake* were presented at a gala that was televised live, and sections were later partially staged with costumes and sparse set in a formal context. In some cases, the scenes were presented with an introduction by Adams, sometimes with a post-concert discussion. All of these activities reflect his continuing interest in various venues of music education while also addressing composers' challenges to build an audience in the late 20th century. The work was given its formal premiere in 1997.

REFERENCES

Williams, Yvonne. "Leslie Adams and the Making of the Opera *Blake*: An Interview with the Composer." In *New Perspectives on Music: Essays in Honor of Eileen Southern,* edited by Josephine Wright and Samuel A. Floyd Jr., 173–209. Warren, Mich.: Harmonie Park, 1992.

GAYLE SHERWOOD

AKERS, DORIS MAE

Born in Brookfield, Mo., May 21, 1923; died in Minneapolis, Minn., July 26, 1995. **Education:** Began playing piano by ear, at age six. **Composing and Performing Career:** wrote first song, "Keep the Fire Burning in Me," age 10; organized five-piece band, Dot Akers and Her Swingsters, and performed throughout Missouri, 1930s and 1940s; Los Angeles, Calif., formed the Simmons-Akers Singers, 1948; directed, composed, and performed with various white congregations; Sky Pilot Choir, Sky Pilot Church, solo artist and director, 1958–60; songs performed by Stamps Quartet in the documentary film, "Elvis Presley on Tour," 1972; Columbus, Ohio, music director and songleader for evangelist Charlotte Gore, 1960–; Minneapolis, Minn., Grace Temple of Deliverance, Director of Music, 1990–95. **Honors/Awards:** Gospel Music Composer of the Year, 1960; Gospel Music Composer of the Year, 1961; RCA Victor, Most Outstanding Album, 1964; Manna Music, Gold West Plaque, in recognition of one million records sold, "Lord, Don't Move the Mountain," 1973; Grant A.M.E. Church, Magna Recognita Cum Lauda in Music; Hampton University, National Church Music Award for Meritorious Service Achievement to Sacred Music Composition, 1995.

MUSIC LIST

[The following list of titles includes only works that were composed by the subject of the entry; it is not a list of recordings that were made by the subject. Although the composer may have made recordings of her own works, the list is not restricted to those recordings but in many cases includes performances by other artists of the composer's work. The list is made up of publication and discographical data, in cases where such information is available. Although no effort has been made to include documentation of the earliest recording of the works listed, the date of the earliest recording that is readily available has been given. —Ed.]

"All You Need." Hollywood, Calif.: Manna Music, 1961. Recorded: Manna Records MS-2059; Worship Records WLP-803.

"Ask What You Will." Hollywood, Calif.: Manna Music, 1959.

"Bread That's Cast upon the Water." Hollywood, Calif.: Manna Music, 1959.

"Can I Have This Happiness?" Hollywood, Calif.: Manna Music, 1973.

"Deeper in the Lord." Hollywood, Calif.: Manna Music, 1958.

"Don't Stop Using Me." Hollywood, Calif.: Manna Music, 1958.

"Don't You Just Love the Lord?" Hollywood, Calif.: Manna Music, 1975. Recorded: Manna Records MS-2059.

"God Is So Good to Me." Hollywood, Calif.: Manna Music, 1956. Arranger, Thurston G. Frazier. Recorded: Columbia/Legacy CK 66911; RCA Victor LSP-2644; Sing MSP9034.

"God Spoke to Me One Day." Los Angeles: Simmons and Akers Music Studio, 1949. Arranger Charles J. Levy.

"God Will If You Will." Hollywood, Calif.: Manna Music, 1957. Recorded: Manna Records MS-2059.

"Grow Closer." Hollywood, Calif.: Manna Music, 1955. Arranger, Thurston G. Frazier. Recorded: Christian Faith Recording SK6041; Sing MSP9034.

"He Delivered Me." Los Angeles: Simmons and Akers Music Room, 1948. Arranger, Charles J. Levy.

"He Knows and He Cares." Hollywood, Calif.: Manna Music, 1958. Arranger, Thurston G. Frazier.

"He's Alright with Me." Los Angeles: Simmons and Akers Gospel Music Studio, 1950. Arranger, Gwendolyn Cooper. Recorded: RCA Victor LPM 1481.

"He's a Light onto My Pathway and a Lamp unto My Feet." Los Angeles: Simmons-Akers Music House, 1957. Arranger, Gwendolyn Cooper. Recorded: RCA Victor LPM 1481.

"He's Everywhere." Hollywood, Calif.: Manna Music, 1954. Recorded: Savoy SL 14732.

"Highway to Heaven." Recorded: Christian Faith Records SK 6041; Marantha! Music CD 08755; Sing MSP9034.

"Holy Spirit, Thanks for the Rain." Recorded: Manna Records MS-2059.

"Honey in That Rock." Hollywood, Calif.: Manna Music, 1960.

"How Big Is God." Hollywood, Calif.: Manna Music, 1960.

"I Cannot Fail the Lord." Hollywood, Calif.: Manna Music, 1958. Recorded: Christian Faith Recording SK6041; RCA Victor LSP 1945; Sing MSP9034.

"I Felt the Spirit." Los Angeles: Manna Music, 1959.

"I Found Something." Los Angeles: Trio Music. Arranger, Maxine Blackburn. Recorded: RCA Victor LPM 1481.

"I Just Got Religion." Hollywood, Calif.: Manna Music, 1960. Recorded: RCA Victor LSP-2644; Sing MSP9034.

"I Know the Story." Hollywood, Calif.: Manna Music, 1959.

"I Never Knew Joy Before." Los Angeles: Simmons and Akers Music Studio, 1949. Arranger, Charles J. Levy.

"I Stopped Dying and Started Living." Hollywood, Calif.: Manna Music, 1973.

"I Sure Do Love the Lord." Hollywood, Calif.: Manna Music, 1959.

"I Want a Double Portion of God's Love." Chicago: Martin and Morris Music Studio, 1947. Arranger, Kenneth Morris.

"I Want to Go Deeper in the Lord." Hollywood, Calif.: Manna Music, 1955. Arranger, Thurston G. Frazier.

"I Was There When the Spirit Came." Los Angeles: Simmons and Akers Music Studio, 1949. Arranger, Kenneth Morris. Recorded: Christian Faith Recording SK6041; Sing MSP9034.

"I Won't Move Unless He Tells Me." Hollywood, Calif.: Manna Music, 1973.

"I'm Glad to Know There's a Heaven." Hollywood, Calif.: Manna Music, 1967.

"I'm Not Satisfied Yet." Hollywood, Calif.: Manna Music, 1963.

"If I Didn't Know." Hollywood, Calif.: Manna Music, 1973.

"Is There Peace Anywhere?" Hollywood, Calif.: Manna Music, 1964. Recorded: RCA Victor LPM 3335.

"It Is Jesus." Hollywood, Calif.: Manna Music, 1968.

"It Means a Lot to Know Jesus for Yourself." Los Angeles: Simmons and Akers Music Studio, 1951. Arranger, Don Lee White.

"It Rained." Hollywood, Calif.: Manna Music, 1964.

"It's Real, It's Real, It's Real." Recorded: Manna Records MS-2059.

"Jesus Is Born Today." Los Angeles: Simmons and Akers Music Studio Music, 1954.

"Jesus Is the Name." Los Angeles: Simmons and Akers Music Studio, 1948. Arranger, Charles J. Levy. Recorded: RCA Victor LPM 1481.

"Keep the Fire Burning in Me." 1933. Chicago: Martin and Morris, 1947. Arranger, Kenneth Morris.

"Lead Me, Guide Me." Los Angeles: Hill and Range Songs, 1955. Arranger, Maxine Blackburn. Recorded: Specialty SPS 2132.

"Lead On, Lord Jesus." Hollywood, Calif.: Manna Music, 1955.

"Life Eternal." Hollywood, Calif.: Manna Music, 1955. Arranger, Charles J. Levy. Recorded: RCA Victor LPM 1481.

"Look at the Cross Again." 1955. Unpublished manuscript.

"Look to the Hills." Los Angeles: Simmons-Akers, 1952. Arranger, Don Lee White. Recorded: Specialty SPS-2147.

"Lord, Don't Move the Mountain." Los Angeles: Manna Music, 1958. Co-composer, Mahalia Jackson. Recorded: MCA Records MCA-28061; RCA Victor LSP.

"Lord Is My Light." Hollywood, Calif.: Manna Music, 1973.

"Lord, Keep My Mind on Thee." Hollywood, Calif.: Manna Music, 1963.

"Meet Me in Heaven." Hollywood, Calif.: Manna Music, 1958. Recorded: RCA Victor LPM 1481.

"Mine Just for the Asking." Hollywood, Calif.: Manna Music, 1958.

"My Expectation." n.p.: Charles Levy, 1951.

"My Heart Is Filled with Jesus' Love." Hollywood, Calif.: Manna Music, 1968.

"My Song of Assurance." Hollywood, Calif.: Manna Music, 1964. Recorded: RCA Victor LPM 3335.

"No One but the Lord." Hollywood, Calif.: Manna Music, 1959.

"Prayer Is the Answer." Hollywood, Calif.: Manna Music, 1964.

"A Servant for Thee." 1955. Unpublished manuscript.

"The Smile on His Face Never Fades." Hollywood, Calif.: Manna Music, 1958. Recorded: RCA Victor LPM 1481.

"Sweet Jesus." Hollywood, Calif.: Manna Music, 1953. Recorded: Christian Faith Recording SK6041; RCA Victor LSP 2864; Sing MSP9034.

"Sweet Peace." Hollywood, Calif.: Manna Music, 1967.

"Sweet, Sweet Spirit." Los Angeles: Simmons and Akers Music Studio, 1962. Recorded: MC-JC-11; Music City Records LP69; Savoy SL 14704; Word WST-8549.

"That's the Lord, That's His Way." Recorded: Manna Records MS-2059.

"These Times Must Come." Hollywood, Calif.: Manna Music, 1973.

"Trouble." Hollywood, Calif.: Manna Music, 1958.

"Walk in the Sunshine." Hollywood, Calif.: Manna Music, 1963.

"Wanna Go to Heaven?" Hollywood, Calif.: Manna Music, 1968.

"You Can't Beat God Giving." Los Angeles: Simmons and Akers Music Studio, 1957. Recorded: Gospel 1007; Savoy DBL7012.

PUBLICATIONS

ABOUT AKERS
Books and Monographs

Farrer, Carl. *The Songs of Doris Akers.* Culver City, Calif.: Manna Music, 1981.

BY AKERS

Favorite Gospel Songs. Hollywood, Calif.: Manna Music, 1965.

* * * * *

Doris Mae Akers was the youngest in a line of gospel composers who developed African-American gospel music from its earliest manifestations at the turn of the 20th century to its "golden age" of 1945–60. She maintained in her compositions the integrity of this tradition when, in the late 1960s, gospel began to take on many of the sounds of contemporary popular music. Moreover, it was she who bridged the gap between African-American and white gospel music. Akers' compositions are included in all the major mainline and African-American hymnals and have been recorded by such artists as George Beverly Shea, Mahalia Jackson, the Roberta Martin Singers, Brother Joe May, Dr. J. Robert Bradley, Aretha Franklin, the Stamps-Baxter Quartet, and numerous church choirs. Elvis Presley sang one of her songs in the 1972 documentary, "Elvis on Tour." Gospel and blues singer Linda Hopkins featured an Akers song in her Broadway musical, *Besse and Me* (1976). Perhaps Akers' greatest honor came in 1987 when the National Organization of Black Catholics named their official hymnal after her 1955 composition, "Lead Me, Guide Me."

Born one of ten children to Floyd and Pearl Akers in 1923 in the small village of Brookfield, Missouri, she moved with her family to Kirksville, Missouri, at the age of five. She attended elementary school in Kirksville but showed little interest in school. She was interested in music, however, and learned to play the piano by ear at the age of six. At age 10 she composed her first song, "Keep the Fire Burning in Me." By age 12 she had organized her own band, "Dot Akers and Her Swingsters," and played a repertoire of swing jazz and other styles of popular music of the 1930s and 1940s. She left school at the age of 15 and began traveling with female evangelists, serving as their pianist and music director.

Her inspiration for playing and composing gospel music, according to Akers, came not from other gospel musicians but from the sermons preached by the evangelists. It was not until 1945, that, while playing for an evangelist in Los Angeles, she came under the influence of an active gospel community. There she encountered Sallie Martin, J. Earle Hines, the gospel choir of John L. Branham's St. Paul Baptist Church, Earl Amos Pleasant, and Eugene Douglas Smallwood, all of whom were popular local gospel performers.

In 1946 Akers became the pianist and a singer with the Sallie Martin Singers. She left the group in 1948 to form the Simmons-Akers Singers with Vernell Simmons, a Chicago native who had come to Los Angeles with the Sallie Martin Singers, and Louise Byrd, newly arrived from New Orleans. The Simmons-Akers Singers, later Simmons-Akers Trio, gained a national reputation singing not only the songs of Akers but also those of Thomas A. Dorsey, Lucie Campbell, Kenneth Morris, and Eugene Smallwood. Though the Martin and Morris Music Studio had published her songs since her arrival in Los Angeles, in 1955 Akers and Simmons opened their own firm, Simmons and Akers Music House. Akers' tenure with the Sallie Martin Singers, the formation of her own group, and the establishment of a publishing house solidified her renown in the African-American gospel music world.

In 1956, while performing her latest composition, "God Is So Good to Me," with a Los Angeles choir on a star-studded 25-act gospel extravaganza at Wrigley Field in Chicago, Akers captured

Doris Mae Akers; courtesy of Manna Music, Inc.

the interest of two listeners who would make her a gospel star: the celebrated movie actor-singer Roy Rogers and Tim Spencer, president of Manna Music, the premier publishing house of white gospel music. After she demonstrated her songs for Spencer, he became her publisher and invited her and her singers to record for RCA Victor. In addition to marketing her compositions and recordings to the African-American audience, Spencer covered the white gospel market through the white-owned Book and Bible Store chain. Within a few short months, Akers had a huge following among white gospel music lovers.

In 1958, a group of white singers in Los Angeles asked her to organize a group in which they could sing African-American gospel. Akers, in conjunction with the Sky Pilot church, organized the Sky Pilot Singers, a group of 100 singers, mostly white, who sang African-American gospel with an African-American sound. The group became extremely popular in the Los Angeles area, broadcasting over radio, making several recordings, and traveling throughout the West Coast presenting concerts and serving in special religious services. Akers conducted the Sky Pilot Choir until 1968, when requests for solo appearances, workshops, and clinics took up most of her time. After two years of traveling with the Sky Pilot Choir, in 1960 she accepted the position of music director for Baptist minister Dr. Charlotte Gore of Columbus, Ohio, the sister of the celebrated Baptist preacher, Reverend Dr. Herman Gore Sr. In Columbus, Akers directed a 75-voice choir for nightly services and played for funerals, weddings, baptisms, and special concerts. Because of her duties in Columbus, she had little time for composing. In 1990, however, the Reverend Dr. Willa Grant Battle, pastor of the Grace Temple Deliverance Center in Minneapolis, Minnesota, invited Akers to serve as her music director, with the understanding that ample time would be allotted for composing. On October 24, 1990, she assumed the position of music director at Grace Temple Deliverance Center, an independent denomination that combined elements of Baptist, Methodist, Pentecostal, and Spiritualist doctrines and service practices. She remained active in that position until early 1995 when, due to spinal cancer that left her paralyzed from the waist down, her appearances at services became sporadic until her death on July 16, 1995.

While Dorsey celebrated the colorful language of the Southern African-American in bluesy melodies and jazzy syncopation and Lucie Campbell captured the quiet sincerity of the long-suffering Christian in plaintive melodies and simple harmonies, Doris Mae Akers moved closer to the poetic and musical expressions of the educated, middle-class African-American. With sophisticated poetry that celebrated standard English and the witty turn of a phrase, melodies that had the shape of popular songs, and the harmonies of the trained musician, Akers gently moved gospel music in a direction that allowed Edwin Hawkins, for example, with his 1969 recording of "O Happy Day," to propel it from its classic manifestations to one in which the romanticized harmonies and rhythms of contemporary popular music were ascendant.

LEAD ME, GUIDE ME (1955)

"Lead Me, Guide Me" has aspects in common with gospel songs ranging from the works of Charles Albert Tindley, who wrote during the first two decades of the 20th century, to those of James Cleveland, who published into the mid-1970s. The words and music were composed by the same person, the format was a verse-refrain of eight or 16 bars (32 or 64 bars were less common), and the keys in which the songs were published were those in which the composers sang them. All of this is true of "Lead Me, Guide Me."

"Lead Me, Guide Me" is in the key of E-flat major in 3/4 meter (9/8 is the actual meter in performance). The text is based on Psalms 31:3, in which David implores God: "Therefore for Thy name's sake lead me, and guide me." In her setting, Akers cites her frailties—"I am weak, I am lost, I am blind"—as justification for requesting leadership and guidance. The semiformal language of the text, completely devoid of the homespun and picturesque phrases of a Kenneth Morris or a Thomas A. Dorsey and set to hymn-like chords, gives a certain piety to her plea. Employing a form of verse and refrain, Akers has assigned eight bars to the refrain and 16 to the verse (the portion of the song in which a story is told or a situation presented).

The refrain (in this song, always sung before the verse) is composed of four phrases of four bars each and a rhyme scheme of aabb. It opens with a three-tone, stepwise descending motive that comes to rest on the tonic. This motive is immediately repeated, suggesting sincerity of request through repetition. There are no other motivic repetitions in the refrain, though repeated tones are prevalent. Akers withholds the climax of the refrain until the final phrase, when she sets the words "Lead me, oh, Lord" to three stepwise ascending tones and one stepwise downward tone (*f-g-a*-flat-*g*) and completes the song with the words "Lead me" on two additional stepwise descending tones (*f-e*-flat). The *a*-flat, then, is used here as the apex to which the lyrics climb and from which they descend.

The harmony of the refrain contains several chromatically altered chords that were being used by only a few other composers (e.g., Roberta Martin and Alex Bradford); they were, however, common in Akers' harmonic language. The rhythm appears almost ordered or prescribed. Of the 16 bars of the refrain (the published version omits the 16th bar, which continues the sustained tones of bar 15), eight begin with half notes followed by either a quarter note or two eighth notes. Rather than rendering the rhythm static, however, this formula gives eloquence to the lyric.

While the refrain begins with a three-tone stepwise descending motive, the verse begins with its inversion, a three-tone ascending motive. The verse is composed of four phrases of four measures each. The first three phrases of the verse begin with the ascending motive, the top tone of which is repeated, except in the case of the third phrase, which drops to a lower tone before repetition begins. The fourth phrase, beginning on the third scale degree, like the opening of the verse and chorus, repeats that tone twice and then descends to the tonic in its final bar. As in the refrain, there is an order to the rhythm of the 16 bars of the verse: nine employ a rhythm of repeated long-short values (half note followed by a quarter or two eighth notes); the remaining bars have three quarter notes.

Only five tones, the first five tones of the E-flat major scale (*e*-flat-*f-g-a*-flat-*b*-flat) are used in the melody of the verse. Akers has used these tones in such a way that only careful analysis will reveal her economy, since the melody is more complex than a simple scale. The verse's harmony, like that of the refrain, is vintage Akers, including judiciously placed altered chords. The climax of the verse, which occurs in the third phrase, is marked by the highest tone and the loudest point of the song.

Akers recorded "Lead Me, Guide Me" with her own group in the early 1950s, but her recording went almost unnoticed. It was not until 1955 that Brother Joe May recorded the song and moved it into gospel's standard repertoire. The song has remained popular since 1955 and was chosen by the National Office for Black Catholics as the title of their 1987 African-American hymnal.

LORD, DON'T MOVE THE MOUNTAIN (1958)

"Lord, Don't Move the Mountain" was composed by Akers and her long-time friend, gospel singer Mahalia Jackson. The text, written by Akers, promotes an alternative to the passivity suggested by Christ in Matthew 17:20, in which he directed his followers to have faith equal to "a grain of mustard seed" and they would be able to move mountains. Instead, Akers requests the strength to take action:

Lord, don't move the mountain
But give me the strength to climb it.
Please don't move that stumbling block,
But lead me, Lord, around it.

In addition to tampering with the concept of the scriptures, Akers disregards established musical conventions by setting an aggressive text in a minor key (E minor). While no tempo is specified (not unusual in gospel songs, which often leave tempo choices to performers), a moderately slow tempo is usually employed in singing this song. The steady 4/4 meter suggests the motion indicated in the text. The song is divided into two equal parts, refrain and verse, each eight bars in length, with the harmony of each suggesting their further division into two equal four-bar sections. Though the tones *d* and *d*-sharp are used interchangeably, the melody of the refrain is based on the minor pentatonic scale (for example, *a-c-d-e-g*). Composed of four phrases, the melody revolves around one tone, *e*. The first phrase of the refrain begins on this central tone, ascends, and turns back on itself at the final note; the second phrase has the same initial contour but does not turn back at the end. The third phrase stretches over an octave (unlike the other phrases which remain within a relatively small interval) and is the most dramatic in the refrain. Here Akers employs what might be called "suggested" text painting: she has the phrase begin on a high *e* and move down a sixth instead of an octave for the word "block," suggesting an obstacle in the path of the melody. The final phrase is similar to the third in that it begins on a high tone (the fifth) and gradually moves down to the tonic.

Phrases one and two of the verse—like phrase three of the refrain—each begin on a high note and, like a mirror of the first phrase of the refrain, descend toward a cadence. Phrase three begins on the same high tone as phrases one and two but descends down an octave for the close. Phrase four is almost identical to the closing phrase of the refrain.

Five tones are used in the melody, and Akers uses only five chords to support it. The basic harmonies are I, IV, and V, the same chords employed in the blues. The other two chords, based on the sixth scale degree (*c-e-g* and *c-sharp-e-g*), provide harmonic excitement. The text is set syllabically (each syllable sung to only one tone), except in a few instances where one syllable is set to two or three tones.

While Akers employed restraint in musical matters in this song, the selection of the few musical ideas employed resulted in a composition that is regarded as one of the most effective songs in the literature. "Lord, Don't Move the Mountain" was recorded by former Caravans singer Inez Andrews in 1972 and was the biggest gospel hit of that year, lasting three months on the R&B charts. Akers was awarded Manna Music's Gold West Plaque in honor of one million records sold.

SWEET, SWEET SPIRIT (1962)

Doris Akers' most popular composition, "Sweet, Sweet Spirit," is the African-American gospel song most included in mainline and African-American hymnals. The text of "Sweet, Sweet Spirit" recounts the blessings of those who possess the "spirit" and pleads with the Lord to let the "spirit" remain with them. It is set and published in the keys of F, G, and A-flat major, that of G major being the first published. The verse and the refrain each are 16 bars of four-measure phrases. The song features a poetic scheme of abab for the first verse, and aabb for the second and third. Surprisingly, although all seven tones of the diatonic scale are used in the melody of the verse, Akers has been extremely economical: the melody, harmony, and rhythm of the first phrase returns in the third phrase, while the same principle applies to the second and fourth phrases. Thus, only two musical ideas are expressed in the course of 16 bars. In highlighting the text, Akers uses only the basic gospel chords, the same as those of the blues, until she inserts two altered chords at the verse's final cadence.

The refrain has a poetic scheme of aabb, while the melody is organized into a scheme of aba'c. The first phrase is based on a revolving motive beginning on a high *d;* it is divided into two semi-phrases of two bars, with the same motive repeated in each. The second phrase, beginning on *b*, a third lower than the beginning tone of the first phrase, moves downward to an *a* on a dominant chord (the third chord of the blues) to divide the entire refrain into two large harmonic units. The third phrase is a combination of phrases one and two: its first two bars employ the melody of the first two bars of the first phrase, and its second two bars, the first two of the second phrase. The fourth phrase, the "hook" (that part of the text or tune that sets the song apart) in the refrain, introduces a new motive that ascends, only to turn and descend; it is assigned to the phrase "without a doubt we'll know," which is immediately repeated for the words "that we have been redeemed." The melody of the last two bars of the refrain linger around the home key of G in preparation for the final cadence.

"Sweet, Sweet Spirit" is unusual in that its popularity was gained from the singing of church choirs and congregations. Although Akers and Dr. J. Robert Bradley each recorded the song, their recordings somehow met with only moderate success; yet, according to Akers, "Sweet, Sweet Spirit" gave her the most spiritual satisfaction of all her songs. The song has become so popular that it is included in the official hymnals of the United Methodist, National Baptist Convention, and Seventh-Day Adventist denominations.

YOU CAN'T BEAT GOD GIVING (1957)

Akers composed "You Can't Beat God Giving" to celebrate two beloved scriptures: Mark 12:42–44, which tells the story of the widow who, responding to the call for the "offering" during a service conducted by Christ, gave her last two pennies and was therefore immortalized; and John 3:16, where the ultimate gift was given, for God "gave his only begotten Son." The sentiment of total and unconditional giving of one's self to the Lord was replaced, however, by a strong emphasis on generous donations during the collection in the traditional African-American church service. Despite this misinterpretation, the song has become a staple for the offertory.

Like most Akers compositions, "You Can't Beat God Giving" is a song in recognition of the greatness of the Supreme Being expressed through adoration and praise. The textual hook comes in the text "the more you give, the more He gives to you; just keep on giving for it's really true, you can't beat God giving no matter how hard you try." It is lamentable that "You Can't Beat God Giving" is so extremely popular because of a misinterpretation of the lyrics.

Because those lines are so expressive of a major tenet in African-American Christianity and they appear in the refrain, its verses are seldom sung, leaving the refrain the only known part of the song.

"You Can't Beat God Giving" is cast in the conventional form of verse and refrain, is in the key of G major, and is set in 4/4 meter (12/8 is the actual meter in performance). The independent piano part is little more than a doubling of the melody. The significance of the accompaniment, however, is in the rhythmic articulation of the four beats in the bar while the voices hold tones or observe rests.

The text of the refrain bears two extrinsic qualities of a limerick: it has five lines set syllabically and a rhyme scheme of aabba; but the relationship ends there. While a limerick is usually a nonsense poem with specified stresses to each line, "You Can't Beat God Giving" is a serious religious song, and Akers has adjusted the form to give more attention to ideas than to poetic stresses. For example, lines one and five have 13 stresses; while line two, which ordinarily should have corresponding stresses, has 16. Lines three and four each have 10 stresses. Notwithstanding the five lines of text, the melody is set in four phrases of four bars each by setting a little more than a single line of text in each phrase. Employing only five tones (pentatonic) of the conventional diatonic (seven tones) scale, the melodies of the first and fourth phrases begin (bar one) and end (bar four) in the same way, though the interior bars differ enough to give each of them individual character. Of more interest is the fact that the song is actually built on a "concluding" phrase, since the first phrase has the melodic contour, harmony, and lyrics customarily reserved for the last phrase of a song.

The second and third phrases, beginning as did the first and fourth on the same tone (the third scale step), unfold with a predictable harmonic progression in which the middle of the refrain reaches the dominant chord and the third phrase highlights the subdominant chord. This leads directly to a repetition of the first phrase, which is actually a cadential phrase. The melody, set low in the vocal range, always descends, except in the fourth phrase, which begins on the same tone as the others, ascends to an octave above the tonic in a disjunct melodic swirl, then turns on itself and closes with the final tones of the first phrase.

The harmonic basis for the first and fourth phrases is a popular cadential cliché of 1950s gospel music in which the opening chord progresses to a chord of tension that leads directly to a cadence (I–v/vi–vi–IV–V–I). The second and third phrases then lead to the dominant harmony, which divides the refrain into two large sections, and then to the concluding phrase.

The verse of "You Can't Beat God Giving" is less well known but is no less finely crafted. From a compositional point of view, it is more sophisticated than the refrain. Composed of four lines and four phrases, the verse carries the responsibility of giving textual credence to the refrain. With textual phrases such as "should we receive and never give?" and "And what I give would never be compared with what I share," the verse demands a musical individuality that would complement the refrain. With four lines, a poetic scheme of aabb, and a melodic setting that employs six tones of the diatonic scale and includes the repetition of the first idea set a step higher (the second phrase), Akers fashions four phrases from eight bars by employing two-bar instead of four-bar phrases. The harmonies move so rapidly that the first four bars proceed from tonic to dominant ninth, a progression that required eight measures in the refrain. The final two bars move swiftly through the cadential progression to the conclusion of the verse. While there are no new harmonies introduced in the verse, the composer's judicious use of the primary harmonies ensures the familiarity upon which most gospel songs depend.

The one famous recording of "You Can't Beat God Giving" is that made in 1958 by Albertina Walker and the Caravans. From this very popular recording, the song moved into the repertoire of choirs and congregations so thoroughly that, even into the late 1990s, few congregations would donate as liberally during the "offering" without the song as they would with its strains filling the sanctuary.

REFERENCES

Boyer, Horace Clarence. *How Sweet the Sound: The Golden Age of Gospel.* Washington, D.C.: Elliott and Clark, 1995.

DjeDje, Jacqueline Cogdell. "Gospel Music in the Los Angeles Black Community: A Historical Overview." *Black Music Research Journal* 9, no. 1 (1989): 81–79.

Farrer, Carl. *The Songs of Doris Akers.* Culver City, Calif.: Manna Music, 1981.

Jackson, Irene V. *Afro-American Religious Music: A Bibliography and a Catalogue of Gospel Music.* Westport, Conn.: Greenwood Press, 1979.

HORACE CLARENCE BOYER

ALDRIDGE, AMANDA IRA (MONTAGUE RING)

Born Amanda Christina Elizabeth Aldridge in Norwood, London, England, March 10, 1866; died in London, England, March 9, 1956. **Education:** Came from a highly musical family: father, Ira Aldridge, was an actor and singer, mother was a Swedish singer, sister was a dramatic contralto engaged for several seasons at the Royal Opera House, brother was a pianist, conductor, and composer; studied piano as a child; attended a Belgian convent school, 1875–77; Royal College of Music, London, England, studied voice with Jenny Lind and George Henschel, elocution with Madge Kendall, harmony and counterpoint with Sir Frederick Bridge and Frances E. Gladstone, 1883–87. **Composing and Performing Career:** Successful concert career as Amanda Ira Aldridge until attack of laryngitis permanently injured her voice; pursued compositional career as Montague Ring, 1906–34; leading orchestras and military bands in London performed her works and some of her dances were used at principal opera houses. **Teaching Career:** Private voice-production and diction instructor, coached many outstanding students in Hanover studio, including Marian Anderson, Roland Hayes, Paul Robeson, Muriel Smith, and Ida Shepley. **Honors/Awards:** Foundation Scholarship to attend Royal College of Music.

MUSIC LIST

INSTRUMENTAL SOLO
Piano
Bagdad Suite. London: Chappell, 1929. Contents: The Royal Guard; The Garden Beautiful; Hail, O Caliph the Great.
Carnival Suite of Five Dances. 1924. London: Chappell, 1924. Contents: Cavalcade; Pierrette; Harlequin; Columbine; Frolic.
"Clorinda" (two-step with chorus ad lib.). London: J. B. Cramer, 1906.
Four Moorish Pictures: An Eastern Suite. London: Ascherberg, Hopwood and Crew, 1927. Contents: Prayer Before Battle; Dance of the Slave Girls; Twilight Dance; Dance of Triumph.
"Frivolette." London: Chappell, 1917.
"Gloriana: Ragtime." London: Chappell, 1913.
"Have You Forgotten? Waltz." London: Regent Music, 1911.
"Laughing Love: Waltz." London: Chappell.
"Lazy Dance: La Paresseuse." London: Chappell, 1913.
"Mirette: Serenade" (with vocal refrain). London: Walsh, Holmes, 1934.
T'Chaka: African Suite. New York: Bosworth, 1927. Contents: Before the Battle; Monorah; War Dance.
"Teach Me How to Two Step." London: Ascherberg, Hopwood and Crew, 1910.
Three African Dances. London: Chappell, 1913. Contents: The Call to the Feast; Luleta's Dance; Dance of the Warriors.
Three Arabian Dances: Suite. 1919. London: Chappell, 1919. Contents: Carnival; By the Fountain; Bedouin.
Three Pictures from Syria: Suite. London: Metzler, 1924. Contents: The Desert Patrol; Beneath the Crescent Moon; The Pursuit.
"Watch Me. Fox-trot." London: Chappell, 1919.

Concert Band
"On Parade: March." London: Boosey and Hawkes, 1914.

Solo Voice
"Assyrian Love Song." London: Elkin, 1921.
"At Cupid's Ball." London: Chappell, 1923.
"Azalea" (medium voice). London: Ascherberg, Hopwood and Crew, 1907.
"Blue Days of June" (low voice). London: Chappell, 1915.
"The Bride" (high voice). London: Chappell, 1910.
"The Fickle Songster" (medium voice). London: Cary, 1908.
"Little Brown Messenger." London: G. Ricordi, 1912.
"Little Missie Cakewalk." London: Lublin, 1908.
"Little Rose in My Hair" (medium voice). London: Chappell, 1917.
"Love's Golden Day." London: Chappell, 1917.
"Miss Magnolia Brown." London: Francis, Day and Hunter, 1907.
"My Dreamy, Creamy Colored Girl." London: Ascherberg, Hopwood and Crew, 1907.
"My Little Corncrack Coon." London: Lublin, 1908.
"Noontide" (voice and piano). London: Elkin, 1922.
"Simple Wisdom." London: Lublin, 1908.
"Song of Spring." London: Boosey and Hawkes, 1908.
"Summah Is de Lovin' Time." London: Chappell, 1925.
"A Summer Love Song." London: Boosey, 1907.
"Supplication." London: Leonard, 1914.
"Thou Art with Me." London: Cramer, 1910.
Through the Day (medium voice). London: Boosey, 1910. Contents: Morning; Noon; Evening.
"'Tis Morning" (high voice). London: Boosey, 1910.
Two Little Southern Songs (medium voice). London: Chappell, 1912. Contents: Kentucky Love Song; June in Kentucky.
Two Songs of the Desert (high voice). New York: G. Ricordi, 1923. Contents: An Eastern Lullaby; A Warrior's Love Song.
"When the Colored Lady Saunters Down the Street." London: Ascherberg, Hopwood and Crew, 1907.
"Where the Paw Paw Grows." London: Ascherberg, Hopwood and Crew, 1907.

NOT VERIFIED
"Swedish Polka" (ca. 1914).

PUBLICATIONS

ABOUT ALDRIDGE
Articles
"Obituary." *Musical Courier* 153 (June 1956): 22.
Scobie, Edward. "For More Than 100 Years the Aldridge Family Has Ruled London's Music and Theatre Fields." *Chicago Defender* (August 3, 1952).

BY ALDRIDGE
"I Remember Jenny Lind." *Our World* 9 (January 1954): 63–65.

PRINCIPAL ARCHIVES

Amanda Aldridge Papers, Laurence Brown Papers, Music Archives,
　　Schomburg Center for Research in Black Culture, New York Public
　　Library, New York City.
Helen Walker-Hill Collection, American Music Research Center,
　　University of Colorado, Boulder, Colorado.
Ira Aldridge Papers, Special Collections, Deering Music Library,
　　Northwestern University.
Music Collection, British Library.

* * * * *

In an autobiographical sketch, Amanda Aldridge remarked that when she began composing in her thirties, she adopted the name "Montague Ring" to keep her composing apart from her singing and teaching. She also reported, in a letter to a Mrs. Overton, that "fortunately, I have found favor with the public through my efforts in composition." Indeed, her light, fashionable pieces were played by all the leading orchestras and military bands and danced at the principal opera houses. Her music was recorded, broadcast, and used for incidental film music.

The gender-neutral pseudonym may have aided this success. In adopting the name, she may also have felt that the crowd-pleasing style of music she wrote was slightly at odds with her standing as a serious concert artist and with her position as a vocal coach of British bluebloods and of such luminaries as Roland Hayes, Marian Anderson, and Paul Robeson, and that it therefore needed to be "kept apart." Her career as a concert singer, which flourished from 1896 to 1905 and extended on a less frequent basis to 1915, was slowing down after a bout she had with severe laryngitis; so the income from her publishing royalties certainly came at a time when it was needed. Her mother, a cultivated Swedish musician and excellent singer, had, as Aldridge said, "no head for business" and, according to Herbert Marshall, Ira's biographer, lost the considerable fortune that Aldridge's father, the distinguished African-American tragedian Ira Aldridge, had accumulated. Aldridge became the sole support of her aging mother, who died in 1915, and her invalid sister Luranah, who died in 1932.

Amanda Christina Elizabeth Aldridge was born on March 10, 1866, 18 months before her father's death, and grew up in the London suburb of Upper Norwood, within a few minutes' walk of the Crystal Palace, an exhibition and pleasure resort noted for its symphony concerts. She made her singing debut there in 1881. Two years later, at the age of 17, she won a scholarship to the newly formed Royal College of Music, where she studied harmony and counterpoint with Frederick Bridge and Frances Edward Gladstone. She also studied voice with George Henschel and diction with Madge Kendall, and she was one of nine voice students accepted by the great Swedish soprano, Jenny Lind. Lind admired Aldridge's father and urged her to use his name, Ira, as her middle name—advice which Aldridge followed for the rest of her life. Except for a period of three childhood years at a convent school in Ghent, Belgium, Aldridge remained in England until her death one day before her 90th birthday in 1956.

In Aldridge's time, concerts usually included light, popular music alongside the weightier classics to lend variety to programs and maintain audience interest. In keeping with this practice, Montague Ring's songs "June in Kentucky" and "Swedish Polka" were performed on her sister Luranah's vocal concert programs along with Beethoven's "Creation Hymn," Brahms's "Sapphische Ode," and a viola solo, Galliard's "Sarabande and Two Hornpipes," played by Maud Aldis. The concert recital as variety show was still a strong tradition.

Under the name Montague Ring, Aldridge composed and published at least 30 songs, seven suites for pianoforte (also arranged for orchestra and military band), and various other incidental pieces that were well received by the public. The publication of her known works began in 1906 with "Clorinda," a two-step with ad-lib. chorus that was also arranged for solo cornet and military band, and ended in 1934 with "Mirette," a serenade in tango rhythm, also designed for light entertainment and dancing. Her publications in 1907 and 1908 were popular songs drawing on the American minstrel and coon song traditions: "My Dreamy, Creamy Colored Girl," "When the Colored Lady Saunters Down the Street," "Miss Magnolia Brown," and "My Little Corncrack Coon," several of them in Chappell & Company's popular "Sixpenny Edition." These songs also incorporated another popular trend, a song "followed by a dance for pianoforte." While the obviously popular genre continued with pieces like "Teach Me How to Two-Step" (1910), "Frivolette" (1917), and "Lazy Dance: La Paresseuse" (1913), more serious compositions also were published, songs such as "Thou Art with Me" and the cycle *Through the Day.* These display the composer's considerable compositional skills. By 1925, she had turned to American Negro poets in her settings of Paul Laurence Dunbar's "Summah Is de Lovin' Time" and "'Tis Morning."

Her other favorite genre, the suite of pieces for pianoforte, was also intended for arrangement for dance orchestra and military band, although it is not known how much of this arranging she did herself. Although she indicates in the piano scores her wishes for specific instrumentations, the published works list H. M. Higgs as the orchestrator and Dan Godfrey as the band arranger. Six of the seven suites employ African or Arabian themes, as evidenced by their titles: *Bagdad Suite, Four Moorish Pictures, T'Chaka: African Suite, Three African Dances, Three Arabian Dances,* and *Three Pictures from Syria.* Their musical materials are also non-Western: gapped scales, melodies constructed of short repeated motives, extensive repetition, hypnotic rhythmic patterns, exploited color and timbre, all of which are characteristic of the music of specific localities. One of her sets, *Carnival Suite of Five Dances,* is based on the themes of the Italian and French *commedia dell'arte.* The contrast of the typical late romantic European harmonic and melodic styles with the African/Arabian styles in this work demonstrates her skill in the deliberate use of specialized geographical styles and atmospheric color.

Aldridge credits her mother, Pauline von Brandt Aldridge, with encouraging this skill. "She never wearied of trying to induce me to write down the melodies that I sometimes hummed or played. I also feel that my mother influenced the development of the African side of me—by her veneration and pride in the memory of our father Ira Aldridge."

The critical acclaim Amanda Ira Aldridge received for her singing also applies to her success as Montague Ring in composi-

Amanda Ira Aldridge; photo provided by Helen Walker-Hill; courtesy of the Special Collections Department, Northwestern University Library, Evanston, Illinois

tion: "If manners make the man," said a 1905 article in the London *Times* (June 5), "they also go for much in the formation of an artist. Miss Aldridge's style is excellent, and her intelligence far beyond dispute; the combination may well serve to explain the measure of her success."

THROUGH THE DAY (1910)

In *Through the Day*, Ring's cycle of three songs entitled "Morning," "Noon," and "Evening," she creates an overall unity of design, moving from stability in the first two songs, to unpredictability and variety in form, tonality, and melodic and rhythmic movement in the last song. The interpretation of the texts by P. J. O'Reilly is thereby given an unexpected twist: after the "Awake!" of morning and the "drowsy hush" of noon, the "rest and peace" of evening, rather than coming to rest, is transmuted into mystery and change, awaiting the "radiant Dawnlight."

Each of the three poems is constructed in two stanzas, and Ring sets the first two straightforwardly in binary form (AA'). The last song is essentially through-composed, that is, it repeats portions of the second stanza's text but with continuously changing melody. The tonality of the first two songs remains firmly in E-flat major, with few altered chords; whereas the third song changes both mode (to major) and key, with considerable melodic and harmonic chromaticism. The vocal setting of the words for all three songs is primarily syllabic, shifting from smooth, stepwise motion in the first, to repeated notes in narrow compass in the second song, to a variety of contours in the third.

Rhythmically, too, regularity of pattern gives way to a restless irregularity in the third song. Thus the increasing complexity contributes to the overall shape of the cycle. Although each of the songs could be performed by itself, none of them can be fully understood without the others.

In "Morning," the quickening pace of "fresh winds," "joyous lambs," and "life in the dawning day" is established by the fast and vigorous (*Allegro vivace*) 9/8 meter, moving in flowing triplets that frequently alternate with duplets. The rising and falling stepwise vocal line is contained within an octave, with occasional octave leaps underlining "skies above" and "heavens calling." Only the last two lines of the two stanzas vary the melody, so that the song concludes with an emphasis on "Awake!" and a long-held final note (high *e*-flat) on "day!" In the piano part, a simple waltz accompaniment occasionally yields to more elaborate skipping chords on "lambs at play" and double-note trills on "lark in the heavens calling."

In the smooth and tranquil (*tranquillo e molto legato*) "Noon," the stasis of the "hushed and drowsy" landscape is evoked by a stationary undulating piano accompaniment (in double sixths and fifths). The melodic line hovers around the note *g*, rising above it to *e*-flat only when the sun "scatters the drowsy kine" and when the lark ascends "lo! on happy wings." Harmonies change rarely, and then no faster than once per measure.

Since this song is marked *Molto tranquillo* (with much tranquillity), one would expect "Evening" to continue toward even more stillness, but the voice and piano enter together with a steadily moving, on-the-beat, quarter-note harmonic rhythm and widening vocal range, dipping low (to *a*-flat below middle *c*) on

"valleys green." The modality begins in E-flat minor for the first stanza, shifting to A-flat major for the concluding stanza, with chromaticism incorporated into both the vocal melody and the accompanying harmony. On "It is eventide," the vocal line droops in half steps and does the same again at "Rest then, all ye weary, Ye with heavy eyes," underscored by a chromatically falling harmonic progression. The rhythmic declamation repeatedly begins phrases after downbeat rests, accompanied by a syncopated rhythmic ostinato in the piano that creates a purposeful forward movement.

The second stanza text is repeated, but with the line "When life's evening cometh, Ye shall rest likewise" omitted. This omission foreshortens the repetition and, together with the continuously changing melodic and harmonic material, shifts the meaning to emphasize "Till the radiant Dawnlight Calls ye to arise."

The skilled and subtle musical setting of the cycle's three poems shows a deeper side of Ring's musical creativity, in contrast to the popular, lighthearted spirit of her "Sixpenny Edition" songs. Well within the late romantic style, they nevertheless indicate an original and sensitive creative instinct.

THREE AFRICAN DANCES (1913)

This suite of dances was the first of six such suites Ring composed with titles that locate their inspiration in Arabia or Africa, and the publications of arrangements of several of them for orchestra and/or military band testifies to the popularity of this genre of music. A 19th-century European taste for the far-away and exotic (probably related to the growth of colonies abroad), further stimulated by the Paris World Exposition of 1899, had created a vogue for music, literature, and art evoking the Far and Near East, as well as Africa and America. In addition to *Three African Dances,* several others, including *Bagdad Suite for Pianoforte* (1929), *Three Pictures from Syria* (1924), and *Three Arabian Dances* (1919), were all arranged for orchestra by H. M. Higgs, and the last-named composition was also arranged for military band by Dan Godfrey for the London publishing house of Chappell & Co. *Three African Dances* was revived in 1989 for performances and a recording by the Black Music Repertory Ensemble of the Center for Black Music Research in Chicago, orchestrated very effectively for that occasion by composer Hale Smith.

The first mention of a performance of *Three African Dances* appears in a review in *The African Times and Orient Review,* "by an African," of Aldridge's sister Luranah Aldridge's vocal recital at Queen's Hall on June 7, 1913. The reviewer reported that "The able assistance of Miss Ira Aldridge (Montague Ring), her sister, gave the afternoon programme its pleasing variety. What African that heard her rendering of her own pianoforte solo, 'The Call to the Feast,' can forget the drum of the Cabalistic brotherhood of the Nigerian 'Osugbo' within the sacred square of the Para, the rhythmic solemnity of the aristocratic dance of the chiefs, or the terminal scene of the great ceremony when Adimu, Adamu, Ogunran, and the 'Dancing Girls' whirl in the gentle poetry of motion in the lengthening shadows of evening and the 'call home' dies away under the flickering glow of the evening stars, which flash upon the tired resting limbs of a sleeping town! In 'Luleta's Dance' Montague Ring made the woodland ring with laughter and the very trees to wave in sheer merriment. Her audience saw and heard the light tripping, seductive movement of the Togoland 'Keri-Keri,' the minuet grace of the Fanti 'Adenkum,' and the almost tragic, but majestic measures of the Apollonian 'Kuntum.'"

Granting an obviously imaginative reporting style, "the African's" mention of specific African ceremonies, songs, and musical traditions raises the possibility that Aldridge may have drawn upon authentic materials, although it is not known what access she may have had to them. On the other hand, the evocative quality of this music, its hypnotic, steady rhythmic motion and repetition of short melodic motives and themes, its use of exotic chromatic variants of minor and major modes, and its atmospheric coloristic effects could remind an African of the music of his homeland in a generalized way. Ring's affinity for unifying her sets of pieces is apparent here through similar modality—C minor, F minor, and B minor—and through references to melodic motives from the preceding pieces in the last, "Dance of the Warriors."

A note in the piano score at the end of the first section of the opening "Call to the Feast" (instructing the performer to repeat it only when used with orchestral parts), suggests that Aldridge herself might have had a hand in orchestrating the work, although H. M. Higgs is credited with the orchestration in the 1913 edition. At any rate, the voicing and register of both the melody and the accompaniment parts immediately bring to mind the sound of particular instruments, particularly percussion and bell sounds. The four-measure introduction consists of a drum-like pattern, *pianissimo,* establishing the key (C minor) and preparing for the *misterioso* melody, whose winding, circling contours evoke the snake charmer's flute. This 16-measure A section alternates (in an ABACBA form) with other melodic material, each in 16-measure sections with a transitional measure added here and there to interrupt the regularity of phrase lengths.

"Luleta's Dance" is a sinuous slow dance (*Lento, ma non troppo*) marked *plaintivo.* The exoticism of the languid, *rubato* movement and ornamented melody is enhanced by the unusual five-measure phrasing. A tonal shift (from F minor to A-flat major) marks a contrasting, faster (*Più mosso*) section before the return of the key and tempo of the opening.

"Dance of the Warriors," in *Vivace* tempo, heightens the animation with vigorously accented melodic motives and strongly rhythmic percussive accompaniments. Melodic contours suggest themes from the preceding two movements. Themes A and B from the first movement ("Call of the Feast") are stated clearly and simultaneously just before the conclusion. In this penultimate section, marked "broadly," the prevailing homophonic texture—a single melody supported by chords—is finally broken by this striking contrapuntal event to bring the entire work to a climactic and unified close.

CARNIVAL SUITE OF FIVE DANCES (1924)

This set of pieces was published in piano score and was soon followed by arrangements and parts for orchestra by H. M. Higgs and for military band by Dan Godfrey. It is the only one of Montague Ring's suites to be based on non-African/Arabian themes, taking its subject from the French and Italian *commedia dell'arte* with its stock characters, Pierrot, Harlequin, and Columbine. This European program is underscored by musical materials very different from those of her other suites. In place of the minor keys, gapped scales, and melodies composed of repeated short motives, so characteristic of African music, she employs major keys and longer and more continuous melodies with a wider tonal compass. The rhythmic durations within these melodies are more varied. While the accompaniment patterns retain the predominantly homophonic, repeated rhythmic patterns of her other suites, there are also more virtuosic octave and chordal passages. The harmonies are the most distinctively European element: the slow and simple harmonic rhythm (of tonic-dominant support) is frequently broken by passages in which the chords change on every beat, with a variety of function and color. The emphasis is on melodic and harmonic variety that reflects a worldly and restless European mind-set, rather than the more static rhythmic, timbral, and coloristic effects reflecting an African aesthetic.

The first of the five dances, "Cavalcade," is an *Allegro* introductory fanfare and march (in ABACA form). The right hand presents the C-major melody doubled in parallel staccato sixth chords. With a shift to a second melody (in F major), the texture lightens momentarily to prepare a triumphant build-up to close the second A section. The C section (in A-flat major) also starts with a softer more lyrical theme and features more chromatic harmonic progressions. It likewise closes with a powerful *crescendo* in octave fireworks, leading to the return of the A section.

In "Pierrette," Ring chose the more delicate, whimsical feminine form of the luckless Pierrot, portraying her in a graceful medium tempo (*Allegretto con grazia*) with "tempo *rubato.*" The E-flat major melody trips lightly (in staccato sixteenths and triplet sixteenths), with an oom-pah chordal accompaniment pattern in wide leaps. The harmonies are likewise playfully varied and unpredictable. The form is also ABACA.

"Harlequin" begins with a two-measure introductory gesture marked *scherzando,* followed by a broad, eight-measure melodic line (in G major). A middle section marked *cantabile* (in E-flat major) leads back to both introductory gesture and broad melody.

"Columbine" introduces the classic *commedia dell'arte* heroine in waltz meter, in *Tempo lento e rubato* with a gracefully descending chromatic melodic line (in E-flat major) doubled in thirds. She executes a charming *cadenza* before repeating her languidly flowing dance tune.

The set concludes with a fast "Frolic" beginning in F major, lightly ornamented with triplets, but moving to D-flat major and predictably expanding into pyrotechnical octaves, double sixths, and chords in wide leaps, to bring the entire set to a satisfactory climactic close.

THREE PICTURES FROM SYRIA (1924)

This suite for piano consists of "The Desert Patrol," "Beneath the Crescent Moon," and "The Pursuit." Pianistically demanding, it is "Dedicated to Janet, Lady Lacon" and perhaps was fitted to this person's pianistic abilities. The modalities of the piece are prevailingly minor but with relatively frequent modulations, and the melodies are constructed of repeated short motives. The tonal range is wide, and the melodies elaborate. Counterpoint is used, both between the hands and within the right-hand part, and passages in double thirds and octaves are frequent and lengthy.

The first movement, "The Desert Patrol," moderately fast (*Poco allegretto*), carries the indication "Soft drum taps on each beat throughout," which suggests that the composer had orchestration in mind. Theme A (in A minor), while employing repeated motives, is unusually broad, stretching over four measures and evoking the vastness of the desert. It is then repeated with an added ornamental line above it, also in the right hand, which requires some dexterity. A second repetition finds the parts reversed, the melody now in the left hand in octaves. The middle section (D minor) also has a long four-measure theme, B, ranging over two octaves. It, too, repeats, this time with the ornamental line below it, and modulates through several keys in which both themes are combined—theme A in octaves in the left hand, and theme B in the right hand. The piece closes with a final statement of theme A becoming softer and softer until it fades into the distance.

"Beneath the Crescent Moon," marked *Moderato* and "languidly," is in 3/4 time and features staccato double-third passages in the right hand. The melody (F minor) is eight measures long and, like the previous ones, unusually broad. The waltz-like harmonic rhythm (frequency of chord changes) is fast, with frequent modulation. Only the chromatic scale would differentiate this movement from a European waltz.

The last movement, "The Pursuit," to be played "with fire" (*Allegro con fuoco*), requires considerable facility, particularly in the rapid left-hand octaves and the combined melody and coloristic pedal effects in the right hand, including long trills. The form ABACDA contains four distinct themes and moves through four keys in the D section. The key returns to F minor for the climactic, final A section, which features a melodic counterpoint by left-hand octaves.

Both the contrapuntal passages and the technically difficult coloristic effects suggest that the composer was thinking in orchestral terms. Each melodic line might have had its own instrumentation in mind. But as a solo piano piece, this work is effective and presents satisfying challenges.

REFERENCES

Aldridge, Amanda Ira. Autobiographical letter to Mrs. Overton. Held in the Ira Aldridge Collection, Deering Music Library, Northwestern University, Evanston, Illinois.

By an African. "Miss Luranah Aldridge's Vocal Recital." *The African Times and Orient Review* July (1913): 3.

Marshall, Herbert, and Mildred Stock. *Ira Aldridge: The Negro Tragedian.* New York: Macmillan, 1958.

Royal College of Music Register, 1883–87. London, England.

Scobie, Edward. "For More Than 100 Years the Aldridge Family Has Ruled London's Music and Theatre Fields." *Chicago Defender* August 3, 1952.

HELEN WALKER-HILL

ANDERSON, T(HOMAS) J(EFFERSON)

Born in Coatesville, Pa., August 17, 1928. **Education:** Studied piano with his mother, age five; studied violin with Louis von Jones, age ten; Washington, D.C., and Cincinnati, Ohio, public grammar schools; Scott High School, Coatesville, Pa., 1942–46; West Virginia State College, Institute, W.Va., studied orchestration and conducting with Edward C. Lewis, theory with Ted Phillips, and music education with P. Ahmed Williams, 1946–50, B.Mus., 1950; Pennsylvania State University, University Park, Pa., studied composition with George Ceiga, 1950–51, M.Mus. Ed., 1951; Cincinnati Conservatory of Music, studied composition with T. Scott Huston, summer 1954; University of Iowa, Iowa City, studied composition with Phillip Bezanson, theory and composition with Richard Hervig, 1954–55, 1956–58, Ph.D., 1958; Aspen School of Music, Aspen, Colo., studied composition with Darius Milhaud, summer 1964. **Composing and Performing Career:** Junior high school, formed own jazz group, 1941; toured with Tate Wilburn's jazz orchestra of Cincinnati, summer 1943; High Point, N.C., worked with both school groups and a trio with Jackie McLean and Dannie Richmond, 1951–54; *Introduction and Allegro,* published by Composers' Facsimile Edition, ACA, 1959; orchestrated and helped stage Scott Joplin's *Treemonisha* for its premiere, 1972; Boston Pops Orchestra (Tufts Night), guest conductor, 1976, 1977; Oklahoma Arts Institute Orchestra, Quartz Mountain, Okla., conductor, 1984; Chicago, Ill., conductor for premiere performance, Black Music Repertory Ensemble, 1988. **Teaching Career:** High Point, N.C., public schools, instrumental music instructor, 1951–54; Fisk University, 1966; West Virginia State College, Institute, W.Va., instructor, 1955–56; Langston University, Langston, Okla., professor of music and chairman of music department, 1958–63; Tennessee State University, Nashville, professor of music, 1963–69; Atlanta Symphony, Atlanta, Ga., composer-in-residence, 1969–71; Morehouse College, Atlanta, Ga., Danforth Visiting Professor, 1971–72; Tufts University, Medford, Mass., music department, professor and chairman, 1972–80, Austin Fletcher Professor of Music, 1976–90, emeritus, 1990–present; University of Minnesota, Minneapolis, Hill Distinguished Visiting Professor, 1990; California State University, Chico, Calif., Distinguished Visiting Professor, 1991; Northwestern University, Evanston, Ill., composer-in-residence, April 1992, April 1997; University of Michigan, Ann Arbor, Visiting King/Chavez/Parks Professor, March 1993; Ohio State University, Columbus, Ohio, composer-in-residence, May 1994; Duke University, Durham, N.C., adjunct professor of music, spring 1995. **Commissions:** Oklahoma City Junior Symphony Orchestra, 1961; West Virginia State College, 1965; Fisk University, 1966; Thor Johnson, 1968; Robert Shaw, 1970; Berkshire Music Center, Tanglewood, Mass., and Fromm Music Foundation, 1971; Thomas A. Ayres, 1972; Symphony of the New World, 1974; National Endowment for the Arts, 1975; American Wind Symphony of Western Pennsylvania and American Wind Symphony, Norfolk, Va., 1976; Thomas Everett, 1977; Richard Hunt, 1978, 1980, 1986, 1988; Union United Methodist Church, Boston, Mass., 1979; Indiana University and

the National Endowment for the Arts, 1982; Chicago Children's Choir, 1982; ASCAP Foundation and Meet the Composer, 1986; Pennsylvania State New Music Performance, 1987; Music School at Rivers, Weston, Mass., 1988; Cleveland State University, 1988; University of Massachusetts, Amherst, 1988; Boston Athenaeum, 1992; Yo Yo Ma, 1993; Mallarmé Chamber Players with assistance by North Carolina Arts Council, 1994; Bill T. Jones/Arnie Zane Dance Company, 1994; James Dargan, 1996; Eva-Marie Worthington, 1997; David Potuch, 1998. **Memberships:** Festival of Contemporary Music, Atlanta University Center, participant, 1968; American Music Project, Minneapolis Symphony Orchestra, participant, 1968; Advisory Committee, Black Music Center, Indiana University, Bloomington, chairperson, 1969–72; Elma Lewis School of Fine Arts, Boston, Mass., board member, 1975–90; Committee on the Status of Minorities, College Music Society, chairperson, 1976–80; Harvard Musical Association, Boston, Mass., resident member, 1976–90, board member, 1989–90; New York Philharmonic Celebration of Black Composers, participant, 1977; Committee on Tenure and Promotions, Tufts University, Medford, Mass., 1978–81; Massachusetts Council for the Arts and Humanities, 1978–81; St. Botolph Club, Boston, Mass., associate member, 1980–90; Meet the Composer, New York, N.Y., advisory board, 1982; National Endowment for the Arts Artists in Education Panel, Washington, D.C., 1983–85; Institute for the Arts, Boston, Mass., board member, 1983–85; U.U.A. Hymnbook Resources Commission, 1988–91; Still Going On, planning committee, 1994–95; American Association of University Professors; American Composers' Alliance; American Music Center; BMI; Boston Musica Viva, Boston, Mass. past board member; College Music Society, past board member; Music Educators' National Conference (M.E.N.C.); Black Music Caucus, M.E.N.C., founding member, first national chairman; Videmus, past board member; Phi Mu Alpha Sinfonia; Sonneck Society. **Honors/Awards:** MacDowell Colony, Peterborough, N.H., fellowship, summers 1960, 1961, 1963, 1968; Copley Foundation Award, 1964; Fromm Foundation Award, 1964, 1971; Rockefeller Center Foundation Grant, Composer-in-Residence Program, 1969, 1970; Yaddo Foundation, Saratoga Springs, N.Y., fellowship, 1970, 1971, 1974, 1977; Phi Beta Kappa, honorary member, 1977; National Association of Negro Musicians, Distinguished Achievement Award, 1979; National Black Music Caucus, M.E.N.C., Leadership Award, 1980; Pennsylvania State University, Alumni Fellow, 1982; Norlin/MacDowell Fellow, 1983; Tufts University, Class of 1983 Senior Faculty Citation for Outstanding Service, 1983; College of the Holy Cross, Worcester, Mass., honorary doctorate, 1983; Rockefeller Foundation, Study and Conference Center, Scholar-in-Residence, Bellagio, Italy, 1984, 1994; West Virginia State College, honorary doctorate, 1984; Tufts University, Lillian Leibner Award for Distinguished Teaching and Advising, 1985; John Simon Guggenheim Foundation Fellowship, 1988–89; Djerassi Foundation, IBM-Michael Stillman Fellowship in Music, 1988; Escola da Musica, Universidade Federal da Bahia, Salvador, Bahia, Brazil, artistic

T. J. Anderson; courtesy of the composer; photo by Richard Wood

residency, 1988; Virginia Center for the Creative Arts, fellow, 1989; Atlanta's First All-Black Symphony and Chorus, Achievement Award, 1990; College of Arts and Architecture, Pennsylvania State University, Distinguished Alumnus Award, 1990; Sterling Patron, Phi Mu Epsilon, 1990; Mary Hudson Onley Ward, Hall of Black Achievement, Boston, Mass., 1991; Bridgewater State College, Mass., honorary doctorate, 1991; National Humanities Center, Research Triangle Park, N.C., fellow, 1996–97; St. Augustine's College, Raleigh, N.C., honorary doctorate, 1996; National Black Music Caucus, Atlanta, Ga., National Achievement Award, 1997. **Mailing Address:** 111 Cameron Glen Drive, Chapel Hill, NC 27516.

MUSIC LIST

INSTRUMENTAL SOLOS
Violin
"Broke Baroque." 1996. New York: American Composers Alliance, 1996. Commissioned by James Dargan. Premiere, 1997.

Viola
"Variations on a Theme by Alban Berg." 1977. New York: American Composers Alliance, 1977. Premiere, 1978.

Cello
"Spirit Songs." 1993. New York: American Composers Alliance, 1993. Commissioned by Yo Yo Ma.

Clarinet
"Swing Set." 1972. New York: American Composers Alliance, 1972. Commissioned by Thomas A. Ayres. Premiere, 1973.

Harp
"Spring Song" (unaccompanied harp). 1996. Unpublished manuscript. Premiere, 1996.

Trumpet
"Sunstar" (trumpet and cassette recorder). ca. 1984. New York: American Composers Alliance, 1984. Premiere, 1994.

Piano
"Boogie Woogie Fantasy." 1997. New York: American Composers Alliance, 1997. Premiere, 1998.

"Call and Response." 1982. Berlin: Böte und Bock, 1983. Note: may be performed with "Watermelon" and "Street Song" as *Urban Recollections*. Premiere, 1982.

"Passacaglia and Blues." 1989. New York: American Composers Alliance, 1989. Premiere, 1990.

"Play Me Something." 1979. New York: American Composers Alliance, 1979. Premiere, 1979.

"Street Song." 1977. Berlin: Böte und Bock, 1979. Note: may be performed with "Call and Response" and "Watermelon" as *Urban Recollections*. Premiere, 1979.

"Watermelon." 1971. Berlin: Böte und Bock, 1971. Note: may be performed with "Call and Response" and "Street Song" as *Urban Recollections*. Premiere, 1972.

Organ
"In Memoriam: Graham Wootton." ca. 1985. Unpublished manuscript. Premiere, 1985.

Piano, Four Hands
Five Portraitures of Two People. 1965. New York: American Composers Alliance, 1967. Premiere, 1968.

SMALL INSTRUMENTAL ENSEMBLE
Strings
"Connections: A Fantasy for String Quintet." 1966. New York: American Composers Alliance, 1967. Premiere, 1968.

"Grace" (string quartet). 1994. New York: American Composers Alliance, 1994. Commissioned by Bill T. Jones/Arnie Zane Dance Company.

String Quartet no. 1. 1958. Unpublished manuscript. Note: Ph.D. dissertation, University of Iowa, 1958.

"Vocalise" (violin, harp). 1980. New York: American Composers Alliance, 1980. Commissioned by Richard Hunt for Jacques and Gail Israelevitch. Premiere, 1980.

Woodwinds
"Echoes" (oboe, bassoon). 1987. Berlin: Böte und Bock, 1991. Commissioned by Pennsylvania State New Music Performance. Premiere, 1988.

Five Etudes and a Fancy for Woodwind Quintet. 1964. New York: American Composers Alliance, 1967. Premiere, 1964.

Brass
"Fanfare to the School Volunteers for Boston" (brass ensemble). ca. 1986. New York: American Composers Alliance, 1986. Premiere, 1986.

"Inaugural Piece" (three trumpets, three tenor trombones). 1982. New York: American Composers Alliance, 1982. Premiere, 1982.

Combinations
b Bop in 2 (alto saxophone, two cassette recorders). 1998. Unpublished manuscript. Commissioned by David Potuch. Premiere, 1998.

"Bridging and Branching" (flute, double bass). 1986. Berlin: Böte und Bock, 1987. Commissioned by Richard Hunt. Premiere, 1986.

Five Bagatelles for Oboe, Violin, and Harpsichord. 1963. New York: American Composers Alliance, 1963. Premiere, 1963.

Five Easy Pieces (violin, piano, Jew's harp). 1974. New York: American Composers Alliance, 1974. Premiere, 1974.

Huh! (What Did You Say?) (three performing stations: violin; violin, viola, cello; clarinet). 1997. New York: American Composers Alliance, 1997.

"Intermezzi" (clarinet, alto saxophone, piano). 1983. Berlin: Böte und Bock, 1983. Premiere, 1984. Recorded: New World Records 80423-2.

"Ivesiana" (violin, cello, piano). New York: American Composers Alliance, 1988. Commissioned by the Music School at Rivers, Weston, Mass. Premiere, 1988.

"Minstrel Man" (bass trombone, percussion). 1977. Berlin: Böte und Bock, 1978. Commissioned by Thomas Everett. Premiere, 1978.

Shouts (three performing stations: oboe; violin, cello; piano). 1997. New York: American Composers Alliance, 1997. Commissioned by Eva-Maria Worthington. Premiere, 1997.

"Transitions: A Fantasy for Ten Instruments" (flute, clarinet, bassoon, horn, trumpet, trombone, violin, viola, cello, piano). 1971. New York: American Composers Alliance, 1971. Commissioned by Berkshire Music Center, Tanglewood, Mass., and the Fromm Music Foundation. Premiere, 1971.

"Whatever Happened to the Big Bands?" (alto saxophone, trumpet, trombone). 1991. Berlin: Böte und Bock, 1994. Premiere, 1992.

CHAMBER ORCHESTRA

Bahia, Bahia. 1990. New York: American Composers Alliance, 1990. Premiere, 1998.

Chamber Symphony. 1968. New York: American Composers Alliance, 1969. Commissioned by Thor Johnson. Premiere, 1969. Recorded: Composers Recordings CRI SD 258.

Fanfare (trumpet, four mini-bands). 1976. New York: C. F. Peters, 1976. Commissioned by the American Wind Symphony of Western Pennsylvania and the American Wind Symphony, Norfolk, Va. Premiere, 1976.

New Dances. 1960. New York: American Composers Alliance, 1967. Premiere, 1960.

FULL ORCHESTRA

Chamber Concerto (Remembrances). 1988. New York: American Composers Alliance, 1989. Commissioned by Cleveland State University for the Cleveland Chamber Symphony. Premiere, 1988.

Classical Symphony. 1961. New York: American Composers Alliance, 1961. Commissioned by the Oklahoma City Junior Symphony Orchestra. Premiere, 1961.

Intervals. 1970–71. New York: American Composers Alliance, 1972. Commissioned by Robert Shaw.

Introduction and Allegro. 1959. New York: American Composers Alliance, 1959. Premiere, 1959.

Messages: A Creole Fantasy. 1979. New York: Carl Fischer (rental). Premiere, 1980.

Pyknon Overture. 1958. Unpublished manuscript. Note: Ph.D. dissertation, University of Iowa, 1958.

Squares: An Essay for Orchestra. 1965. New York: American Composers Alliance, 1966. Commissioned by West Virginia State College. Premiere, 1966. Recorded: Columbia M33434.

Symphony in Three Movements. 1964. New York: American Composers Alliance, 1966. Premiere, 1964.

Tone Poem of a Steel Mill. 1951. Unpublished manuscript. Note: a student work composed during the composer's graduate studies at Pennsylvania State University, 1950–51.

ORCHESTRA (CHAMBER OR FULL) WITH SOLOISTS OR CHORUS

Concerto for Two Violins and Chamber Orchestra. 1988. New York: American Composers Alliance, 1988. Commissioned by Richard Hunt for Elliot Golub, Nisanne Graff, and Music of the Baroque. Premiere, 1988.

Horizons '76 (soprano, orchestra). 1975. New York: American Composers Alliance, 1975. Commissioned by the National Endowment for the Arts for the Bicentennial of the United States.

In Memoriam Malcolm X (mezzo-soprano, orchestra). 1974. New York: American Composers Alliance, 1974. Commissioned by the Symphony of the New World. Premiere, 1974.

Six Pieces for Clarinet and Chamber Orchestra. 1962. New York: American Composers Alliance, 1966. Premiere, 1962.

Spirituals (orchestra, jazz quartet, chorus, children's choir, tenor, narrator). 1979. New York: American Composers Alliance, 1979. Commissioned by the Union United Methodist Church, Boston, Mass. Premiere, 1982.

What Time Is It? (boys choir, jazz orchestra). 1986. New York: American Composers Alliance, 1986. Commissioned by the ASCAP Foundation and Meet the Composer. Premiere, 1986.

BAND

"In Memoriam Zach Walker." 1968. New York: American Composers Alliance, 1968. Premiere, 1969.

Rotations. 1967. New York: American Composers Alliance, 1967.

"Trio Concertante" (clarinet, trumpet, trombone, band). 1960. New York: American Composers Alliance, 1960. Premiere, 1961.

SOLO VOICE

"Ancestral Voices" (bass, piano). 1988. New York: American Composers Alliance, 1988. Premiere, 1990.

"Block Songs" (soprano, children's toys). 1972. New York: American Composers Alliance, 1972. Premiere, 1976.

"A Musical Kaddish 'In Sea' for John Zimarowski" (soprano, piano). 1995. New York: American Composers Alliance, 1995. Premiere, 1995.

VOICE WITH INSTRUMENTAL ENSEMBLE

Egyptian Diary (soprano, two percussionists). 1991. New York: American Composers Alliance, 1991. Premiere, 1992.

"First Love: A Song for Nadia" (voice, combo). 1997. New York: American Composers Alliance, 1997.

Seven Cabaret Songs (jazz singer, flute, viola, cello, piano). 1994. New York: American Composers Alliance, 1994. Contents: I Dream a World; Ain't Cut Drylongso; Between Man and Himself; In Dahomey; X-Rated; Sassy Cook; Sing the Blues. Commissioned by the Mallarmé Chamber Players with assistance by the North Carolina Arts Council. Premiere, 1995.

VOCAL DUET

Songs of Illumination (soprano, tenor, piano). 1989. New York: American Composers Edition, 1989. Premiere, 1990.

CHORAL MUSIC

"Dear John, Dear Coltrane" (SATB). ca. 1989. New York: American Composers Alliance, 1989. Commissioned by the University of Massachusetts, Amherst. Premiere, 1990.

"Here in the Flesh" (congregation, piano). 1993. In *Singing the Living Tradition* (Boston: Beacon Press, Unitarian Universalist Association, 1993). Premiere, 1993.

"Jonestown" (children's chorus). 1982. New York: American Composers Alliance, 1982. Commissioned by the Chicago Children's Choir. Premiere, 1984.

"This House" (male chorus, four chromatic pitch pipes). 1971. New York: American Composers Alliance, 1978. Premiere, 1972.

Thomas Jefferson's Minstrels (baritone, male glee club, jazz band). 1982. New York: American Composers Alliance, 1982. Premiere, 1983.

DRAMATIC MUSIC

Beyond Silence (cantata for tenor, clarinet, trombone, viola, cello, piano). 1973. New York: American Composers Alliance, 1973. Premiere, 1973.

Personals (cantata for narrator, mixed chorus, brass septet). 1966. New York: American Composers Alliance, 1967. Commissioned by Fisk University. Premiere, 1966.

Re-Creation: A Liturgical Music-Drama (three speakers, dancer, violin, cello, trumpet, alto saxophone, piano, drums). 1978. New York: American Composers Alliance, 1978. Commissioned by Richard Hunt. Premiere, 1978.

The Shell Fairy (operetta for four solo voices, chorus, dancers, piano or chamber orchestra). 1976–77. New York: American Composers Alliance, 1977.

Soldier Boy, Soldier (opera). 1982. New York: American Composers Alliance, 1982. Commissioned by Indiana University and the National Endowment for the Arts. Premiere, 1982.

Thomas Jefferson's Orbiting Minstrels and Contraband: A 21st Century Celebration of 19th Century Form (string quartet, woodwind quintet, jazz sextet, dancer, soprano, glee club, computer, visuals, keyboard synthesizer). 1984. New York: American Composers Alliance, 1984. Premiere, 1986.

Variations on a Theme by M. B. Tolson (cantata for soprano, violin, cello, alto saxophone, trumpet, trombone, piano). 1969. New York: American Composers Alliance, 1969. Premiere, 1970. Recorded: Nonesuch 71303.

Walker (chamber opera). 1992. Boston: Boston Athenaeum. Commissioned by the Boston Athenaeum. Premiere, 1993 (concert version).

PUBLICATIONS

ABOUT ANDERSON
Books and Monographs
A Birthday Offering to T. J. Anderson. Baltimore: Morgan State University, 1978.

Dissertations
Oliver, Christine Evangeline. "Selected Orchestral Works of Thomas J. Anderson, Arthur Cunningham, Talib Rasul and Olly Wilson." Ph.D. diss., Florida State University, 1978.

Thompson, Bruce Alfred. "Musical Style and Compositional Techniques in Selected Works of T. J. Anderson." Ph.D. diss., Indiana University, 1979.

Articles
Baker, David N., Lida M. Belt, and Herman C. Hudson, eds. "Thomas Jefferson Anderson, Jr." In *The Black Composer Speaks,* 1–14. Metuchen, N.J.: Scarecrow Press, 1978.

Hunt, Joseph. "Conversation with Thomas J. Anderson: Blacks and the Classics." *Black Perspective in Music* 1, no. 2 (1973): 156–165.

De Lerma, Dominique-René, ed. "Black Composers and the *Avant Garde:* T. J. Anderson, Jr., Hale Smith, and Olly Wilson." In *Black*

Music in Our Culture: Curricular Ideas on the Subjects, Materials, and Problems, 62–78. Kent, Ohio: Kent State University Press, 1970.

———. "The Composer and His Relationship to Society: T. J. Anderson, David N. Baker, John Carter, John E. Price, and Herndon Spillman." In *Reflections on Afro-American Music,* 76–89. Kent, Ohio: Kent State University Press, 1973.

Thompson, Bruce Alfred. "The Influence and Use of Jazz and Blues in the Music of T. J. Anderson." *Jazz Research* 19 (1987): 157–175.

BY ANDERSON
"Images of Blacks in Instrumental Music and Song," with Lois Anderson. In *Images of Blacks in American Culture,* edited by Jessie Carney Smith. New York: Greenwood Press, 1988.

"Introduction." In *The Continuing Enslavement of Blind Tom, 1865–1887,* by Geneva Handy Southall. Minneapolis, Minn.: Challenge Productions, 1983.

"Introduction to the Conversation." In *Why Sing,* vii-viii. Concord, Mass.: National Humanities Faculty, 1975.

"On *Soldier Boy, Soldier:* The Development of an Opera." *Black Music Research Journal* 10, no. 1 (1990): 160–166.

"Racial and Ethnic Directions in American Music." *College Music Society Report,* no. 3, edited by T. J. Anderson. Boulder, Colo.: College Music Society, 1982.

"So You Want to Write an Opera." [Medford, Mass.] *Tufts Criterion* (1983).

* * * * *

Thomas Jefferson (T. J.) Anderson has characterized his role as a composer as that of a musical anthropologist, that is, as a documentor, interpreter, and re-creator of culture. He developed that role in creating his own unique system of composing music, which is, in his own words, "organized around basic patterns or note groupings which have the potential to exist in varying environments." Anderson's distinctive compositional voice, his wide-ranging output, and the craft that drives them have established him as a composer of significant achievement and stature.

Anderson's formative years were spent in Washington, D.C., and Cincinnati, Ohio, in a home in which both parents were educators. His mother, also a professional musician, provided inspiration and instruction for his development as a musician by teaching him to play the piano. He studied the violin with Louis von Jones of Howard University. In high school, he played the trumpet, began to lead his own jazz band, toured in the summers with a professional jazz orchestra, and played in the school band and orchestra. The young Anderson was interested in all kinds of music, and his favorite composer at that time was Edward MacDowell. Beginning college in 1946, Anderson majored in music education, played in the band and orchestra, and began making musical arrangements. After earning a bachelor's degree in music at West Virginia State College (1950) and a master's degree in education at Pennsylvania State University (1951), Anderson taught instrumental music in the public schools of High Point, North Carolina (1951–54), while also continuing to perform with the groups of his high school years and with friends such as Jackie McLean and Danny Richmond.

After three years of teaching, he entered graduate school in 1954 at the University of Iowa, where he became interested in composition and decided to pursue it as a profession. He took a one-year position as instructor at West Virginia State College (1955–56), then returned for two more years to Iowa, where he was awarded the doctorate in 1958.

Although his first major composition was *Tone Poem of a Steel Mill,* Anderson recognizes *Pyknon Overture,* his doctoral dissertation, as his first significant composition. He subsequently held positions at West Virginia State College, Langston University, and Tennessee State University, and eventually became the Austin Fletcher Professor of Music at Tufts University. He retired in 1990 to compose on a full-time basis.

During his doctoral studies, Anderson worked with Philip Bezanson and Richard Hervig. He had studied with Scott Huston in the summer of 1954 at the Cincinnati Conservatory of Music and, ten years later, with Darius Milhaud at the Aspen School of Music. This varied study and Anderson's own "global" musical orientation resulted in his development of a musical style that synthesizes Eastern, Western European classical, and African-American traditions. His mature style results from a fusion of influences from Purcell, Berg, and Webern to jazz, spirituals, blues, and the avant-garde, presented within the context of an atonal/pantonal musical language. Southern describes it as "distinctive for [its] use of melodic fragments in ever-shifting melodic and rhythmic patterns and [its] intense instrumental coloring." According to Slonimsky, Anderson's style is "audaciously modern" though lyrical, "taut and intense" though "[pan]tonal," and based on resources that are "quaquaversal" within a musical context that is all-embracing. Extra-musical influences have impacted Anderson's style and his compositional process, influences as diverse as the work of visual artists Richard Hunt, Paul Shimon, Charles Young, Hyde Solomon, and Anne Truitt; other influences include personal conversations with conductors Guy Fraser Harrison, Thor Johnson, and Robert Shaw, and the poetry of Robert Hayden, Pauline Harrison, M. B. Tolson, Pearl Lomax, and Milton Kessler.

Since 1959, when well-known groups in socially important venues began to perform Anderson's works, his compositions have received steady exposure to the listening public, and he has become, according to composer Hale Smith, one of the few black composers whose works have been fortunate enough to escape being consigned solely to "black only" concert programs. Anderson believes, however, that, in society, the fact that particular composers are black is only significant because their perspective is black and because they explore the fundamental issues of existence. Be that as it may, he said in a radio interview with Wayne Pond, "As we live together in a diverse nation, this diversity—difficult as it may be at times—influences the overall process of people 'becoming,' which in turn makes us a nation."

VARIATIONS ON A THEME BY M. B. TOLSON (1969)

Variations on a Theme by M. B. Tolson, a 16-minute cantata for soprano, violin, cello, alto saxophone, trumpet, trombone, and piano, is based on a text by the poet M. B. Tolson. Its thin, transparent, Webern-like texture is typical of its time, and its flow is angular though lyrical, jazz-like though classically avant-garde. The words, through which the poet describes aspects of the black experience in America, are enlivened by the texture and expressiveness of the music. Solo moments for the instruments abound throughout, and cadenzas are interspersed among musical declamations with speech and speech-like singing. Declamatory settings alternate with musically "bothered" text, as words are syllabically stretched and melismas cascade. Jazz influences are manifest both rhythmically and through inflection (bent notes, smears, etc.), while cross-rhythms, polyrhythms, implied polymeters, tonal blending and distortion, and moments of "composed improvisation" (where everything is specified exactly but sounds improvised) also contribute significantly to the effectiveness of the work. *Variations* closes with a quiet chorale-like ending for saxophone and the two string instruments.

Variations on a Theme by M. B. Tolson was first performed in 1970 by Bernadine Oliphant and the Atlanta Symphony Chamber Players with the composer conducting. The work was recorded in 1974 on the Nonesuch label.

THOMAS JEFFERSON'S ORBITING MINSTRELS AND CONTRABAND (1984)

This work for string quartet, woodwind quintet, jazz sextet, dancer, soprano, glee club, keyboard synthesizer, computer, and visuals, is meant as a 21st-century celebration of 19th-century form. It has its origins in Anderson's opera *Soldier Boy, Soldier,* through an intervening work entitled *Thomas Jefferson's Minstrels,* which was set as a 19th-century minstrel show with an inverted approach that utilizes a black interlocutor and a white glee club. Then came *Thomas Jefferson's Orbiting Minstrels and Contraband,* which "represents a view of the past, present, and future" and whose goal is to be an articulation of the 21st century. As Anderson imagines, "You, the audience, are [in] a space colony in which we, the performers, have come to present a minstrel show." Embracing influences from his composition "Intermezzi" (1983), from the music of Charles Ives, and from avant-garde jazz to create "deliberate incongruities," simultaneous performances staged at six different stations feature different instrumental and instrumental/vocal combinations in as many different tempos; the tempos are always controlled, relative, and in free time. The completion of the composition requires that the audience substitute for the usual applause conversation with the performers and with each other about what they have experienced. This work involved a large collaborative team, and Anderson indicates in his notes about the piece that they attempted to create a "prophecy" for the next century based on a mutual respect "for differences, scientific exploration and the creative imagination of the world's best minds." So in the theatrical sense, there is no specific plot to the work.

The first performance of *Thomas Jefferson's Orbiting Minstrels and Contraband* took place on February 12, 1986, at Northern Illinois University in DeKalb. It is a full evening's work, running approximately one hour and 30 minutes.

Figure 1. "Whatever Happened to the Big Bands?"

	A	B	Trans.	C	Trans.	D	Cadenza	E
Tpt.	Allegro	Moderato	RT	Presto	RT	Allegretto	Duo	Adagio
Sax.	Moderato	Adagio	RT	Allegretto	RT	Allegro	Solo	Presto
Tbn.	Allegretto	Presto	RT	Moderato	RT	Adagio	Duo	Allegro
Time line		4:00	5:00		8:00		11:00	12:30

WHATEVER HAPPENED TO THE BIG BANDS? (1991)

Written for alto saxophone, trumpet, and trombone, "Whatever Happened to the Big Bands?" was inspired by the music of the big band era, which Anderson views as "one of the major developments in the history of American music." The piece is meant to be a musical resolution of the question of what really happened, since two answers are usually given, one claiming that the bands were "destroyed" by bebop, the other that they are alive and well in schools and universities. According to notes written by Anderson for the published score, the work is "organized around sounds and techniques used during [the big band] era," with the use, for example, of a riff popularized by bandleader Fletcher Henderson that moves into bebop figures and ultimately gives way to what Anderson characterizes as a "more plastic organization of jazz styles," which is, it might be added, uniquely his own.

The work is published as three separate parts, with no score having been written. Each of the three parts has its own internal organization and is not coordinated with the others, yet, they are related to each other in such a way that careful planning will yield a coherent performance. In performance, the players sit as far away as possible from each other and are instructed not to allow each other's dynamics or accents to influence their separate, individual performances. The composition/performance is controlled by an overall timeline ("TL") that contains precise indications of where particular sections (for all three instruments) are to start at the same time. Sections within individual parts are controlled by a relative-time duration ("RT") specified in seconds. The performers are instructed to perform as if they are playing three concurrently presented compositions.

"Whatever Happened to the Big Bands?" should be performed within a time framework of 12 minutes and 30 seconds, with events taking place as outlined in Figure 1. Each of the three instruments generally has the same set of eight movements, but in different order. Although the movement indications are identical for the different parts, the material contained in each part differs musically, though retaining similarities in terms of motivic, rhythmic, and scalar construction. Thus, although each player's performance is exactly specified, subsequent readings of the work will produce slightly different results, even though starts and stops are quite precise. The "concurrent compositions" present a special challenge for the performer to think on several levels that must be interpreted within the individual part as well as within the composition as a whole.

WALKER (1992)

Walker, a one-act chamber opera in five scenes, is, according to program notes by Rodney Armstrong, "based on the last day in the life of David Walker, black abolitionist martyr, who migrated from North Carolina to Boston in 1825 and ran a clothing store on Beacon Hill until his death in 1830. [The] libretto expands on the historic details of Walker's life and plays on the conflicts between the idealism expressed in both violent and nonviolent responses to slavery. It dramatizes Walker's struggle to come to terms with his past, his hopes for the future, and his alienation from friend and fellow abolitionist William Lloyd Garrison before Walker's mysterious death."

The work is scored for chamber orchestra, with prologue and interlude-cadenzas for soprano, contralto, tenor, two baritone voices, and bass. This one-hour-and-15-minute work includes a cast consisting of Walker, his wife Eliza, Garrison, Catherine Healy (an Irish friend), Barbados (an ex-slave), and the figure (who signifies a white southerner). The opera opens with Garrison talking to Walker. As the drama unfolds, the seriousness of Walker's threatened situation in Boston becomes apparent. The libretto is set for the most part in declamatory style, with brief sections of recitative. The overall melodic style is lyrical, yet somewhat angular in a pantonal framework. The texture of the accompaniment is simple and clear throughout, yet not simplistic. Rhythmic figurations are of a simpler variety than one finds in many of Anderson's other compositions. But the approach serves the situation well, since there is always effective contrapuntal interplay between the voices and between the voices and the accompanying orchestral parts.

Between the opera's scenes unique transitions take place—a series of cadenzas scored both for solo instruments and for larger, varying combinations of instruments. It is in the cadenzas and in selected moments of the general accompaniment that Anderson's penchant for structured improvisation emerges and complements the overall approach to the underscoring and setting of the libretto. Here and there traces of jazz emerge, as in scene four between David and Catherine in "The Lesson" and in later moments as the opera spins out to its end. "The Lesson," followed by Walker's aria, "A Time to Murder," is one of the more powerful moments in the score. Other touching moments come toward the end of the opera, in a duet between David and Eliza and in Eliza's final aria, which might be described as a kind of agonized spiritual.

Walker was commissioned by the Boston Athenaeum and first performed in that organization's facility on December 9, 1993, in a concert staging with two pianos, under the direction of Donna Roll of the Longy School of Music. The work showcases the multifaceted talents and technical mastery of the composer and his librettist/collaborator, Nobel Laureate Derek Walcott.

REFERENCES

Anderson, T. J. "On *Soldier Boy, Soldier:* The Development of an Opera." *Black Music Research Journal* 10, no. 1 (1990): 160–166.

————. Program notes, *Thomas Jefferson's Orbiting Minstrels and Contraband.* DeKalb, Ill.: Northern Illinois University, February 12, 1986.

————. Radio interview by Wayne Pond. *Soundings.* Program no. 778. National Humanities Center, spring 1995.

————. Telephone conversation with the author, April 12, 1995.

————. Telephone conversation with the author, June 29, 1995.

Armstrong, Rodney. Program notes, *Walker.* Boston: Boston Athenaeum, December 9, 1993.

DeVoto, Mark. "Honoree." In *100 Years of the Tufts Music Department 1895–1995.* Program booklet. Medford, Mass.: Tufts University, 1995.

Oliver, Christine Evangeline. "Selected Orchestral Works of Thomas J. Anderson, Arthur Cunningham, Talib Rasul and Olly Wilson." Ph.D. diss., Florida State University, 1978.

Schneck, Carolyn. "Composer in Residence: T. J. Anderson Tells His Life through His Music." *Winchester* [Mass.] *Star,* January 27, 1983.

Southern, Eileen. *The Music of Black Americans.* 2nd ed. New York: W. W. Norton, 1983.

Slonimsky, Nicholas. "T(homas) J(efferson) Anderson (, Jr.)." In *Baker's Biographical Dictionary of Musicians.* 8th ed. New York: Schirmer's Books, 1992.

Smith, Hale. "Here I Stand." In *Readings in Black American Music,* edited by Eileen Southern, 323–326. 2nd ed. New York: W. W. Norton, 1983.

Thompson, Bruce Alfred. "Musical Style and Compositional Techniques in Selected Works of T. J. Anderson." Ph.D. diss., Indiana University, 1979.

————. "The Influence and Use of Jazz and Blues in the Music of T. J. Anderson." *Jazz Research* 19 (1987): 157–175.

Wadsworth, Ann. Letter to the author on behalf of the Library of Boston Athenaeum, June 27, 1995.

GREG A STEINKE

ARNOLD, MAURICE

Born Maurice Arnold Strothotte in St. Louis, Mo., January 19, 1865; died in New York, N.Y., October 23, 1937. **Education:** Cincinnati, Ohio, Cincinnati College of Music, 1880–83; Kullak's Academy, Berlin, Germany, studied with Heinrich Urban, ca. 1883; Cologne Conservatory, studied with Woellner, Neitzel, and G. Jensen; Breslau, Germany, studied with Max Bruch, ca. 1885; National Conservatory, New York, N.Y., studied composition with Antonin Dvorák, 1892. **Composing and Performing Career:** Madison Square Garden, New York City, *American Plantation Dances* premiered by National Conservatory Orchestra, 1893; Columbian World Exposition, Chicago, Ill., served as piano accompanist for the musical program of "Colored People's Day," 1893; St. Louis, active as a conductor of light opera, ca. 1887; Princess Theatre, London, conductor, toured Germany, ca. 1897–1905; Brooklyn, N.Y., opera *The Merry Benedicts* produced, 1896; *American Rhapsody* premiered by the New York Orchestra under Modest Altshuler, 1932. **Teaching Career:** St. Louis, taught violin, ca. 1887; New York, N.Y., active as violin teacher, ca. 1892–1937.

MUSIC LIST

INSTRUMENTAL SOLOS
Violin
"Amerikanisches Ständchen" or "Minstrel Serenade," op. 32. ca. 1884. London: Breitkopf and Härtel, 1894.
Tunes from Everywhere: Twenty Five Selected Melodies of All Nations. Cincinnati, Ohio: Willis Music, 1927.
"Violin Sonata: Example of Negro Tune." Unpublished manuscript.

Piano
"Absence from Home." New York: Luckhardt and Belder, n.d.
"Banjoenne." Unpublished manuscript.
"California Rose Waltz." Brooklyn, N.Y.: Ernest Walterstrack, 1903.
"Caprice Espagnol." Unpublished manuscript.
"The Caravan." New York: Theodore Presser, 1927.
"Danse de la Midway Plaisance." Boston: Oliver Ditson, 1893.
Fantasia in C Minor. London: Cary and Co., 1916.
"The Fortune-Teller" or "La Zingara." Cincinnati: J. Church, 1902.
"Frühlingstraum." London: J. H. Larway, 1912. Note: also published by Cary and Co., 1913.
Gavotte in D Minor. London: Cary and Co., 1916.
"The Magic Fountain," op. 37. New York: M. Witmark and Sons, 1897.
"Motion." London: Cary and Co., 1913.
Nocturne in F Minor. London: Cary and Co., 1915.
"The Old Castle (La chateau)." Cincinnati: J. Church, 1902.
"Polish Dance." London: Cary and Co., 1916.
"Souvenir de Seville, serenade pour pianoforte." New York: Luckhardt and Belder, 1895.
Technical Exercises for the Development of Independence of Motion. London: Cary and Co., 1913.
Toccata in A Minor. London: Cary and Co., 1915.
"Trepack, Russian Dances." London: Cary and Co., 1914.

Two Pianos, Eight Hands
"Valse élégante," op. 30. Leipzig: Boosey and Hawkes, 1893.

STRING ORCHESTRA
Tarantelle. Unpublished manuscript.

FULL ORCHESTRA
Amerikanische Tänze or *American Plantation Dances,* op. 33. 1894. New York: P. L. Jung, 1894. Note: also arranged for piano four-hands; concert band; and the second movement, for solo piano. Premiere, 1894.
American Rhapsody. 1932. Unpublished manuscript.
Dramatic Overture. Unpublished manuscript.
Symphony in F Minor. Unpublished manuscript.
Turkish March. Unpublished manuscript.

SOLO VOICE
"La belle mexicaine," or "Mandolinata," op. 35. New York: Widmer-Stigler, 1894.
"Barcarolle." Unpublished manuscript.
"Clover Blossoms." Brooklyn, N.Y.: Ernest Walterstrack, 1903.
"Du meines Herzens Lieb (Lady of My Heart)." Leipzig: Boosey and Hawkes, n.d.
"I Think of Thee in Silver Night." Unpublished manuscript.
"The Lad Who Wears the Blue." New York: N. Weinstein, 1898.
"Ein Marlein." Unpublished manuscript.
"The Roses in My Garden." New York: E. J. Bricker, 1918.
"Say I'm Not Forsaken." New York: Luckhardt and Belder, 1897. Note: from the opera *The Merry Benedicts.*
"Yearning." New York: M. Witmark and Sons, 1902.

DRAMATIC MUSIC
The Merry Benedicts (opera). Unpublished manuscript. Premiere, 1896.
The Wild Chase (cantata). ca. 1885. Unpublished manuscript.

PERFORMING FORCES UNKNOWN
"Bully Jig." Unpublished manuscript.

NOT VERIFIED
Cleopatra (opera).

PUBLICATIONS

BY ARNOLD
Orchestration Simplified with Practical Exercises for the Student. New York: Luckhardt and Belder, 1918.

* * * * *

Maurice Arnold's American debut as a composer was made on January 23, 1893, at a gala concert led by Antonin Dvorák that appears to have been designed especially to feature Dvorák's many African-American students at the National Conservatory of Music of America. "Long before the hour fixed for the opening, the [Madison Square Garden] hall was filled with an immense throng of people. At eight o'clock there was hardly standing room." In attendance were Maestro and Mrs. Anton Seidl. The conductor of the New York Philharmonic had only five weeks earlier led the world premiere of Dvořák's Symphony no. 9 ("From the New World"), which received critical and popular acclaim. Dvořák was at the height of his success in the United States. Imagine, therefore, the honor bestowed upon two of his students—one, possibly both, being African American—when at the concert he turned over his baton and invited them to the podium: Maurice Arnold, whose original surname was Strothotte and who led the orchestra in his brand new composition *American Plantation Dances*; and Edward H. Kinney, organist and choirmaster of St. Philip's Episcopal Church. Kinney directed the orchestra and the 130-voice all-black choir, among them the boy sopranos and altos from St. Philip's, in the "Inflammatus" from Rossini's Stabat Mater, with Mme. Sissieretta Jones, the celebrated "Black Patti," as guest soloist.

Arnold had independently arrived at the idea of incorporating African-American music into his compositions a decade before coming to New York to study with Dvořák. In 1883, he began studying in Europe, leaving his first teacher, Heinrich Urban, in Berlin, because, reported the musical journalist Rupert Hughes, "he discouraged me when I attempted to imbue a suite with a Negro Plantation spirit."

I believe that it is Maurice Arnold and his *American Plantation Dances* that Dvořák refers to in the first of his several *New York Herald* interviews: "'When I first came here last year I was impressed with this idea [to study and build upon plantation melodies] and it has developed into a settled conviction. These beautiful and varied themes are the product of the soil.' And saying so Dvořák sat down at his piano and ran his fingers lightly over the keys. It was his favorite pupil's adaptation of a southern melody." Later in the article, he comes back to Arnold: "Among my pupils at the National Conservatory of Music I have discovered strong talents. There is one young man upon whom I am building strong expectations. His compositions are based upon Negro melodies, and I have encouraged him in this direction." The only possible portion of the *American Plantation Dances* about which Dvořák may have been speaking is a lilting skipping dance in F major featuring the clarinet, which appears to have influenced Dvořák's celebrated "Humoresque No. 7."

Another of Arnold's ardent fans was the composer and symphonic band leader, Edwin Franko Goldman, who in 1893 was a 15-year-old cornet student in Dvořák's orchestra. In his unpublished manuscript, Goldman remembers Antonin Dvořák:

My instructor in harmony at the conservatory was Maurice Arnold, who in those days was known as Maurice A. Strothotte. [Arnold, obviously an advanced student, was also a faculty member.] Dvořák was very fond of him, and considered him his most promising pupil. Arnold wrote much music, including a symphony, a grand opera, chamber music, and many other worthwhile works, but he never achieved the success and recognition he deserved. He was entirely too modest for his own good and never seemed able to bring himself to the fore. The work which Dvořák admired the most was Arnold's *American Plantation Dances*.

The choice of a solo clarinet for the catchy tune that caught Dvořák's fancy is perhaps explained in a later portion of Goldman's memoir: "Dvořák was greatly interested in the negroes, and especially their music. In the students orchestra there were a number of them. I recollect a first violinist named Craig, a clarinetist named Bailey and in particular Harry T. Burleigh. . . . Often when the first clarinet had a solo passage, Dvořák would go over to Bailey and put his arms around him and cry 'Bravo!'"

Arnold's later music did not fulfill the promise of his *American Plantation Dances*. Among the 15 published chamber works listed in the *Catalogue of Printed Music* in the British Library are a few provocative pieces: a "Valse élégante" for two pianos, eight hands (1893), and "Dance de la Midway Plaisance," for piano (1893), a "souvenir of the famous [Persian] Danse du Ventre," obviously inspired by his Chicago World's Fair experience. Both of these date from before or during his time with Dvořák. Perhaps one could have found more interesting music in his larger, unpublished works, but his manuscript scores, like those of many other American composers of the period, including Cook and Europe, have disappeared.

Despite its inspired moments, Arnold's *American Plantation Dances* clings safely to tradition. Arnold was in the unenviable position of trying to paint an American landscape using a European palette, thus canceling out many of the very qualities that attracted Dvořák—and as he astutely observed, most Americans—to "Negro" music in the first place, but it does not realize Dvořák's inspired theory. To do this, a new kind of American orchestra would have to be created with its own unique sound. Within a decade this task was begun in earnest by Will Marion Cook and James Reese Europe, who said in an interview that appeared in the New York *Evening Post*, "[W]e have developed a kind of symphony music that, no matter what else you may think, is different and distinctive, and that lends itself to the playing of the peculiar compositions of our race."

Arnold participated in a landmark event in African-American music history when he served as the piano accompanist for the musical portion of the program presented at the Colored People's Day celebration given at the Chicago Columbian World Exposition on August 25, 1893.

After his success with the *American Plantation Dances*, Arnold settled in New York. He spent a season as conductor at London's Princess Theatre and toured Germany, and, in 1896, his opera *The Merry Benedicts* was produced in Brooklyn. In the years before World War I, Arnold published several "characteristic" piano works and a book of technical exercises for Cary and Company of London.

We know very little about Arnold's activity toward the end of his life. A piano piece published by Theodore Presser, "The Caravan," appeared in the April 1927 issue of *The Etude* and was rated as "An effective number in oriental style. Grade 3." In that same year, Arnold was one of three former Dvořák pupils to publish almost simultaneously a spiritual text setting of the Largo from the Symphony no. 9 ("From the New World"). Arnold's was entitled "Mother Mine."

In a letter to the editor printed in the August 31, 1932, issue of the *New York Times,* Arnold criticizes music educators for condemning jazz and upholding "the high-brow adult 'standpoint' toward children and the 'unmusical'." He reminds the reader that Wagner "lacked the gift of absolute pitch and perhaps it may have been an advantage to him." *Baker's Biographical Dictionary* notes that his *American Rhapsody* was premiered by the New York orchestra under Modest Altshuler in 1932, only a month earlier. Despite these sentiments, after his *American Plantation Dances,* Arnold had clearly turned away from his African-American musical heritage, away from Dvořák's vision, and toward a musical style of bland anachronisms.

There is a passing reference to "the black student Maurice Arnold" in John Clapham's *Dvořák,* the first complete biography of the composer in English. But there can be no doubt that Arnold lived as a white person at the end of his life. His last address, 120 East 89th Street, is in the heart of Yorktown, Manhattan's German district, and the 1920 census for that residence records no "colored" occupants. His *New York Times* obituary of October 24, 1937, explains that Arnold was his professional name, and his death certificate was filed under Strothotte.

AMERICAN PLANTATION DANCES (1893)

American Plantation Dances was published in the form of an autograph condensed score, probably in Arnold's own hand. Arnold carefully noted his instrumentation, including an indication in the third movement for the percussion to use "blocks of sandpaper," something that was used by kit drummers in the dance bands and theater orchestras of the early 1900s. This must be the first use not only of sandpaper but of a pop music effect—the actual sound of a cakewalk drummer—in a classically scored work.

The four-movement work has charming moments. It begins with a strutting bass tune in D minor accompanied by syncopated rhythms and flurries in the strings. This attention-getter introduces an airy barn dance tune in F major, lightly decorated by inner strings. There is no development of this material. The opening movement functions as a brief introduction for the material that follows.

The second movement, a lilting, skipping dance in F major featuring the clarinet, reminds one rather strikingly of Dvořák's celebrated "Humoresque no. 7." The two works share the same or similar plagal cadences, phrase lengths, and gavotte rhythm. Arnold's tune predates the "Humoresque no. 7" by a year and probably was its inspiration. A middle section, really a bridge, is a classic development section in miniature. The tonality changes every two measures until the tune reappears in A-flat major and leads us smoothly back to the home key and Arnold's beautifully placed solo clarinet tune.

The third movement is a bolero (*Allegro brillante*) in A major. Arnold displays his European languages in this most American work, describing the drum, which along with a clarinet and *pizzicato* strings carries the rhythm, as a French *tambour petit,* while later making a special note that "Die kleine Trommel muss etwas schnarrend klingen" (the small drum is supposed to be played with the snare engaged). A solo oboe presents a syncopated banjo tune, reminiscent of a barn dance, in the bolero context. The following development section begins in the relative minor and quickly moves to C major before returning to a recapitulation of the tune for full orchestra. The movement ends with a skillful conclusion of the bolero rhythm and the tune: the orchestra subsides to a whisper and then brings the listener to attention with a sudden final A-major chord.

The last movement begins with a somber double bass theme in D minor, which slowly and most brilliantly builds into a full-blown cakewalk played by the oboe and accompanied by the strings. The cakewalk tune grows in size and excitement while staying in the home key, very much like a dance-band treatment. A closing lick is introduced, which tumbles into a virtuosic passage for the strings leading back to the cakewalk for the last time. The piece ends with 12 measures of closing figures in D.

The *New York Herald* reporter who was at the 1894 premiere of this composition commented about the last movement: "There is such a gay swing about the last [movement] that nearly every boy in the choir marked time with his head. And I am pretty sure that under cover of that friendly gallery front, they were all patting 'juba.'" Following Arnold's indications, a full score of the *American Plantation Dances* was made by the author and performed in 1992.

REFERENCES

Arnold, Maurice. "The Caravan." *Etude* (April 1972).

———. Letter to the editor. *New York Times* (August 31, 1932).

Clapham, John. *Dvořák.* New York: W. W. Norton, 1979.

Europe, James Reese. "The Negro's Place in Music." [New York] *Evening Post* (March 13, 1914): 7.

Goldman, Edwin Franko. "Edwin Franko Goldman Remembers Antonin Dvořák." Unpublished manuscript, 1940.

Hughes, Rupert. *Famous American Composers.* Boston: L. D. Page, 1900.

Obituary, Maurice Arnold. *New York Times* (October 24, 1937).

Slonimsky, Nicolas. *Baker's Biographical Dictionary of Musicians.* 4th ed. New York: G. Schirmer, 1940.

MAURICE PERESS

BAIOCCHI, REGINA HARRIS

Born in Chicago, Ill., July 16, 1956. **Education:** Studied guitar at age nine; Richards Vocational High School, Chicago, studied chorus and recorder with Judith Cammon Rogers, 1971; Paul Laurence Dunbar Vocational High School, Chicago, studied counterpoint and chorus with Nathaniel Green, trumpet, theory, arranging, and composition with Willie A. Naylor, 1971–74; Roosevelt University, studied composition with Robert Lombardo, piano with Ludmilla Lazar, piano and theory with Lucia Santini, 1974–79, B.A. in composition, 1979; Illinois Institute of Technology, Institute of Design, Chicago, 1982–86; New York University, Public Relations Certificate, 1991; DePaul University, Chicago, studied composition with George Flynn, 1994–95, M.M., 1995; studies jazz piano with Alan Swain and composition with Hale Smith, 1995–present. **Composing and Performing Career:** Began composing at age ten; Orchestral Suite performed at the Detroit Symphony Orchestra/Unisys Corporation Symposium, 1992; Mostly Music, Inc., Chicago, composer-in-residence, 1992; Wayne State University, Detroit, Mich., guest composer, 1993, 1994; Northeastern Illinois University, Chicago, guest composer/public relations lecturer, 1993, 1994; Columbia College Chicago, guest composer, 1995; Northwestern University, Evanston, Ill., guest composer, 1996; Chicago, Steppenwolf Theatre, composer/music director, 1997. **Commissions:** Richard Nunley Jr., 1978; American Women Composers Midwest, 1989; Philadelphia, St. Mary's Episcopal Church, 1992; Mostly Music, Inc., 1991–92; Matthew Arau, 1994. **Memberships:** American Women Composers; International League of Women in Music, ASCAP. **Honors and Awards:** City of Chicago Department of Cultural Affairs, CAAP Grant, 1992, 1993, 1994, 1996; AT&T grant, 1994; National Endowment for the Arts/Randolph Street Gallery Regional Artist Program Grant, 1995; Chicago Music Association, recognition award, 1995; ASCAP, Special Awards Grant, 1996, 1997; Art Institute of Chicago and the Lila Wallace/Reader's Digest Fund, 1997; Herb Alpert/Cal Arts, fellowship and recognition award nominee, 1997. **Mailing Address:** P.O. Box 450, Chicago, IL 60690-0450.

MUSIC LIST

INSTRUMENTAL SOLOS
Flute
"Autumn Night" (unaccompanied alto flute). 1991. Unpublished manuscript. Premiere, 1991.

Trumpet
"Miles per Hour" or "Jazz Sonatina" (unaccompanied trumpet). 1990. Unpublished manuscript. Premiere, 1990.

Percussion
Deborah (marimba, vibes, traps, xylophone, piano). 1994. Unpublished manuscript. Note: received a CAAP Grant from the City of Chicago. Contents: Jael; Rwanda's Prayer; Per-cussing up a Storm! Premiere, 1994.

"Skins" (two hand drummers, one multi-percussionist). 1997. Unpublished manuscript.

Piano
Equipoise by Intersection (two piano etudes). 1978. Bryn Mawr, Pa.: Hildegard Press. Etude no. 2 in *Black Women Composers: A Century of Piano Music, 1893–1990* (Bryn Mawr, Pa.: Hildegard Press, 1992). Recorded: Leonarda CD-LE339.
"Liszten, My Husband Is Not a Hat." 1994. Unpublished manuscript. Note: received an AT&T grant. Premiere, 1994.

SMALL INSTRUMENTAL ENSEMBLE
Strings
"Realizations." 1978. Unpublished manuscript. Premiere, 1978.

Brass
QFX (brass quintet). 1993. Unpublished manuscript. Contents: March of the Impotent Ants; Bosnia's Tear; Brass Tacks. Note: received a CAAP Grant from the City of Chicago. Premiere, 1993.

Combinations
"After the Rain" (soprano saxophone, bass, piano, congas, bongos, rain stick, claves, drum set). 1994. Unpublished manuscript. Commissioned by Matthew Arau. Premiere, 1994.
Chasé (flute, alto flute, B-flat clarinet, oboe, bassoon, piano). 1979. Unpublished manuscript. Note: first movement is for B-flat clarinet and piano, second and third movements for *tutti*. First movement commissioned by Richard Nunley Jr.
Sketches for Piano Trio (violin, cello, piano). 1992. Unpublished manuscript. Commissioned by St. Mary's Episcopal Church, Philadelphia. Contents: Sketches for the Ninth; Miriam's Muse; Variations on Two Puerto Rican Folk Songs by Rafael Hernández; Pentasketch. Premiere, 1992.

FULL ORCHESTRA
Muse. 1997. Unpublished manuscript. Premiere, 1997.
Orchestral Suite. 1991–92. Unpublished manuscript. Contents: Against the O.D.S.; Mother to Nique; Thunder. Premiere, 1992.
Teddy Bear Suite. 1992. Unpublished manuscript. Contents: Ode to Her Child; Legacy; Gwen's Cue.
Three Pieces for Greg. 1994. Unpublished manuscript. Contents: Windows; Best Friends; Pentasketch.

ORCHESTRA (CHAMBER OR FULL) WITH SOLOISTS
African Hands (concerto for orchestra and four African hand drums: ashiko, bata, congas, dgembe). Unpublished manuscript. Contents: Muse; Mbira; Oge. Note: received an ASCAP Special Awards Grant. Premiere, 1997.

SOLO VOICE
"Darryl's Rose" (voice, piano, optional rhythm section: bass, drums, piano). 1995. Unpublished manuscript.

"Legacy" (soprano, piano). 1992. Unpublished manuscript. Commissioned by Mostly Music, Inc. Premiere, 1992.

"Mason Room" (baritone, piano). 1993. Unpublished manuscript.

"Message to My Muse." 1997. Unpublished manuscript. Premiere, 1997.

"Rainbows." Unpublished manuscript.

VOICE WITH INSTRUMENTAL ENSEMBLE

"Dream Weaver" (voice, saxophone, piano). 1997. Unpublished manuscript. Premiere, 1997.

"A Few Black Voices" (two voices, tenor saxophone, percussion). 1992. Unpublished manuscript. Commissioned by Mostly Music, Inc. Premiere, 1992.

"Foster Pet" (soprano, oboe, piano, percussion). 1991. Unpublished manuscript. Commissioned by Mostly Music, Inc. Premiere, 1991.

"Friday Night" (voices, trumpet, saxophone, rhythm). 1995. Unpublished manuscript. Premiere, 1995.

Langston Hughes Songs. ca. 1991. Unpublished manuscript. Commissioned by Mostly Music, Inc. Premiere, 1991.

"Shadows" (voice, bassoon, percussion, piano). 1992. Unpublished manuscript. Commissioned by Mostly Music, Inc. Premiere, 1992.

Zora Neale Hurston Songs (mezzo-soprano, piano, cello). 1989; revised 1992. Unpublished manuscript. Contents: How It Feels to Be Colored Me; I Am Not Tragically Colored. Commissioned by American Women Composers Midwest. Premiere, 1990.

VOCAL ENSEMBLE

"Crystal Stair" (two voices, piano). 1991. Unpublished manuscript. Commissioned by Mostly Music, Inc. Premiere, 1992.

"Much in Common" (two sopranos, piano). 1993. Unpublished manuscript. Premiere, 1993.

CHORAL MUSIC

"Father We Thank You" (two-part choir). 1986. Unpublished manuscript.

"I've Got a Mother/Father." Unpublished manuscript.

"Nobody's Child." 1993. Unpublished manuscript.

"Psalm 138." 1990. Unpublished manuscript.

"Send Your Gifts" (SATB, baritone solo). 1984. Unpublished manuscript.

"Who Will Claim the Baby?" (SATB, solo voice). 1984. Unpublished manuscript. Note: received a CAAP Grant from the City of Chicago. Premiere, 1992.

DRAMATIC MUSIC

Bwana's Libation (ballet: voice, guitar, saxophone, percussion). 1992. Unpublished manuscript. Contents: Ancestor's Medley; First Fruits; Legends; Say No! to Guns. Commissioned by Mostly Music, Inc. Premiere, 1992.

Dreamhoppers (one-act music drama). 1997. Unpublished manuscript. Note: received an ASCAP Special Awards Grant. Premiere, 1997.

Gbeldahoven: No One's Child (one-act chamber opera). 1996–97. Unpublished manuscript. Note: received a CAAP Grant from the City of Chicago. Premiere, 1996.

INCIDENTAL MUSIC

Nikki Giovanni. 1997. Unpublished manuscript. Incidental music for the play.

JAZZ ENSEMBLE

"We Real Cool" (solo instrument [trumpet, saxophone, or voice], piano, bass, drums). ca. 1990; revised 1995, 1997. Unpublished manuscript. Also arranged for solo piano.

PUBLICATIONS

BY BAIOCCHI

"Black Curtains Up: A Peek at Opera Written by African-Americans in the Twentieth Century." Part of master's thesis, DePaul University, 1995.

"Capers, Valerie," "Gail Davis-Barnes," "Geraldine de Haas," "Danniebelle Hall," "Hilda Harris," "Margaret Harris," "Patricia Prattis Jennings," "Betty Jackson King," "Marsha Mabrey," "Portia Maultsby," "Nkeiru Okoye," "Kay George Roberts," and "Gertrude Jackson Taylor." In *Black Women in America.* New York: Carlson Publishing, 1996.

"Gbeldahoven: No One's Child." Program notes presented at Harold Washington Library Auditorium, Chicago, Ill., October 6, 1996, and at the Art Institute of Chicago, April 20, 1997.

"Nurturing Jazz in the City that Works: Geraldine de Hass, Founder of Jazz Unities, Chicago." *Black Women in America Encyclopedia,* music volume. New York: Carlson Publications, 1996.

"Sounds from the Motherland: African-Inspired Music by Women Composers." Program annotations from American Women Composers Midwest tribute to Betty Jackson King, 1994.

* * * * *

Regina Harris Baiocchi has established herself as one of the most important composers of the younger generation of African-American women composers in Chicago. Through her use of black gospel music, Negro spirituals, and jazz, along with blues, work songs, African chants, and classical European models, she has forged a voice that continues to gain recognition. Active also as a writer of novels, plays, short stories, and poems, she is a musician whose rich literary background informs her approach to composing.

Baiocchi has received performances of her works by the Detroit Symphony Orchestra (Orchestral Suite, 1992, and *Muse,* 1997), and the Southeast Symphony Orchestra in Los Angeles (Orchestral Suite, 1992). Chicago Symphony Orchestra trumpeter George Vasbergh performed "Miles per Hour" in 1990. Her chamber work *QFX,* written in 1993, was premiered by the Chicago Brass Quintet in October 1993 and performed by the Milwaukee Brass Quintet in June 1994. In 1995, she was awarded a grant from the National Endowment for the Arts Regional Artist Program to write a percussion piece (which became *African Hands,* a concerto for hand drums and orchestra) and decided to devote herself entirely to composing. Even before this decision, Baiocchi was recognized as a dynamic creative voice; in 1992, she was chosen to be a participant in the Detroit Symphony Orchestra/Unisys Corporation Symposium and was a Composer-in-Residence for Mostly Music, Inc. (for which she wrote "A Few Black Voices," "Foster Pet," "Shadows," and "Legacy" in connection with a children's music education program). In 1997, she was composer/music director for the Steppenwolf Theatre in Chicago, where she collaborated with poet Nikki Giovanni,

Regina Harris Baiocchi; courtesy of the composer; photo, Pete Thurin; design, Ginann; makeup, Marilyn Allen; hair, Biko

and she composed and conducted the music for a play (*Nikki Giovanni*) adapted from Giovanni's poetry. Since 1993, Baiocchi has been a guest lecturer at Indiana University (Bloomington, Ind.), Northwestern University (Evanston, Ill.), Northeastern Illinois University (Chicago), Columbia College Chicago, and Wayne State University (Detroit, Mich.).

Baiocchi came from a creative family in which the arts were valued at home and were a part of daily life. Her parents were avid jazz listeners. Her mother was a church choir member, and her father, a visual artist, also played bluegrass fiddle and harmonica. Her paternal grandmother was a church organist at the Church of God in Christ in Chicago where, from an early age, Regina regularly heard spirituals and gospel songs imbued with a strong tradition of improvisation and a rich harmonic background of altered seventh and ninth chords.

It is not surprising that many of Baiocchi's early works are for chorus. In addition to the church choirs to which she was exposed through her family's musical activities and in which she had sung since she was four years old, she sang in the Grand Boulevard Community Girls' Choir, led by Larney J. Webb, the organist and choir director at the Metropolitan African Methodist Episcopal Church in Chicago. This choir, made up of 30 voices, sang spirituals and classical repertory in four to six parts. Baiocchi's early music experiences also included guitar lessons when she was nine years old. As soon as she had mastered the basic chords, she began composing songs for voice and guitar as well as short solo guitar pieces. At St. Elizabeth Catholic Church, the oldest black Catholic church in Chicago, Baiocchi had the opportunity to expand her choral activities and play the guitar publicly at a young age. Throughout elementary school and high school, she played guitar for the guitar masses and sang in the youth gospel choir (which sang primarily contemporary gospel and inspirational music). In college, at Roosevelt University, she was hired at age 20 as the adult choir director of St. Elizabeth's, for which she programmed both spirituals and classical music.

Baiocchi's commitment to music is reflected in her educational pursuits. She attended the Paul Laurence Dunbar Vocational High School, where she learned to play the trumpet, French horn, and flute, which she played (in various combinations) in the concert band, orchestra, and jazz band. Surrounded by a supportive environment with encouraging teachers and other talented student musicians, she had many opportunities to compose and write music for school ensembles. After completing high school, she attended Roosevelt University in Chicago, where she graduated in 1979 with a bachelor of music degree in composition and theory. In 1995, she received a master of music degree in composition from DePaul University. Her studies in music were supplemented by courses in design at the Illinois Institute of Technology's Institute of Design, and she received a public relations certificate from New York University.

Early in her compositional career, Baiocchi was heavily influenced by the music she had heard in her Roman Catholic church. She wrote songs and choral pieces with religious texts in traditional Western harmonies that utilized the plagal cadences that so frequently conclude religious hymns. One compositional approach she used in high school was to find a favorite chord or interval and then write pieces that exploited this sonority; for example, she focused on the dominant seventh chord or the more dissonant tritone interval. During this time, she was also very interested in the musical styles of singers Betty Carter and Cassandra Wilson, pianist Gerri Allen, composer Dorothy Rudd Moore, and the various styles demonstrated by the multi-volume Columbia Records Black Composers Series, compiled by musicologist Dominique-René de Lerma and conducted by Paul Freeman. Among her most influential teachers are Hale Smith, Alan Swain, and Willie A. Naylor; other important teachers were Nathaniel Green, Judith Cammon Rogers, Lucia Santini, Ludmilla Lazar, George Flynn, and Robert Lombardo.

A unique feature about Baiocchi's career as a composer is the extent to which her activities as a literary writer complement her musical compositions. She started writing poetry at the age of six, and her earliest musical compositions were guitar songs in which she set her own poems to music. Throughout her life, she has continued to be an active and accomplished writer; she has written two novels, four plays, nine short stories, and over 200 poems in addition to one opera libretto, a one-act music drama, and the texts to her songs. She has received the *Essence Magazine*/McDonald's Literary Achievement Award for her short story "Mama's Will," and her poetry has appeared in the *Chicago Tribune Magazine, Aim Magazine,* and *World of Poetry.*

Baiocchi has always been interested in how people perceive music and how words can function as a way for explaining music. She has frequently written short poems meant to informally accompany her musical compositions. The relationship between the poem and the music is a sophisticated one: the poem does not provide an analytical narrative for how the notes relate to each other; instead, the poem illuminates a deeper level of what she hopes to accomplish musically, functioning as a type of program note. She views the music and the poem functioning as metaphorical blueprints for each other, expressing similar emotions in different media.

Baiocchi's musical influences are drawn largely from Western classical models (in terms of harmonic language and genre) into which she masterfully integrates stylistic features from jazz, gospel music, and spirituals. She has been able to assert her own voice in various genres, ranging from two early piano etudes that employ a 12-tone row (*Equipoise by Intersection*, 1978), to a bossa nova for soprano saxophone, percussion, and piano ("After the Rain," 1994), to orchestral works, chamber works, solo pieces for piano, flute, and trumpet, vocal works (choral pieces and solo songs), and a four-act ballet (*Bwana's Libation,* 1992).

Many of Baiocchi's works have a strong connection to a literary text, whether they are settings of or inspired by specific texts. Several of Baiocchi's instrumental works have programmatic titles that are connected to political and/or social themes: "Rwanda's Prayer" (second movement from the three-movement percussion work *Deborah,* 1994), "Bosnia's Tear" (second movement from the three-movement brass quintet *QFX,* 1993), "Variations on Two Puerto Rican Songs by Rafael Hernández" (third movement from the four-movement *Sketches for Piano Trio,* 1992), and "Say No! to Guns" (last movement from the four-movement ballet *Bwana's Libation*). Her Orchestral Suite (1991–92) was written in reaction to the military action, Desert Shield.

In the late 1990s, many of Baiocchi's compositional efforts have focused on dramatic music. In 1997, she completed the libretto and music of her one-act chamber opera, *Gbeldahoven: No One's Child,* based on the lives of Zora Neale Hurston and Langston Hughes during the Harlem Renaissance. Baiocchi also wrote the text for her next dramatic composition, *Dreamhoppers* (1997). This one-act music drama explores the lives of four African-American women, each of whom attempted suicide and is receiving treatment in an Illinois state mental institution. In a way that exhibits thoughtfulness and care, Baiocchi treats the issues of self-discovery, creativity, race relations, and survival with insight, sensitivity, and dignity. Complementing her other compositional efforts, both of these dramatic works present themes that illustrate the richness of African-American life in the 20th century.

ZORA NEALE HURSTON SONGS (1989; REVISED 1992)

These two songs, "How It Feels to Be Colored Me" and "I Am Not Tragically Colored," represent Baiocchi's first compositional efforts based on the life and works of the African-American writer, folklorist, and critic Zora Neale Hurston. (Baiocchi revisited the life of Hurston in 1994 as she began work on her opera about the lives of Hurston and Langston Hughes in *Gbeldahoven: No One's Child.*) The two songs can be seen as a set, both written at the same time, based on the same subject, written in the same B-flat minor key, and employing the same ensemble: mezzo-soprano, cello, and piano. The texts for the two songs are adapted from Hurston's essay "How It Feels to Be Colored Me," published in 1928, early in Hurston's career. Both works were commissioned by American Women Composers Midwest (AWCM) and performed in 1990 on the AWCM concert series of music by African-American women in Chicago and Washington, D.C.

"How It Feels to Be Colored Me" is an extended set piece of 83 measures that showcases all three performers without compromising the prominence of the singer. The first half of the song emphasizes the opening line, "How it feels to be colored me." The opening words, "How it feels," are initially presented twice to the same melodic phrase (*b*-flat, *b*-natural, *a*-flat), then repeated for a modified second verse using the same pitches (mm. 19–21). The vocal climax is reached on a high *b*-flat in measures 29 and 33; the return of the opening phrase, transposed up a minor third, reflects the intensity of the climax (mm. 36–38). The second half of the song includes an extended section for the piano that contrasts lyricism with great rhythmic vitality using the extreme high and low registers and an added *pizzicato* texture provided by the cello. This section carries the stage directions "Zora primps, prances. . . ." (m. 41) and "Zora continues to primp, prance . . ." (m. 50). The voice re-enters with a reference to the opening motive, using its original pitches but with a different text and rhythm (mm. 68–69). The final line of the song is introduced with an unaccompanied improvisational measure marked *sotto voce,* which the voice half-sings, half-speaks, "But, on second thought," providing just enough contrast to the preceding texture to make the final line stand out in relief to the rest of the piece: "I'll never know just how it feels to be colored you. And you'll never know how good it feels to be Colored Me."

"I Am Not Tragically Colored" is a shorter work (40 measures) that displays a stronger jazz influence. Though both songs

utilize the same two-octave vocal range for the singer (*b*-flat below middle *c* to high *b*-flat), "I Am Not Tragically Colored" has a lower *tessitura.* After an opening descending chordal figure in the piano, the first vocal line is delivered *a cappella* in a "staccato whisper; loud, breathy whisper." The melody of the vocal line is then repeated (with minor changes in the text), accompanied by an ascending *pizzicato* ostinato figure in the cello. Throughout the song, the cello imitates the jazz double bass and mainly plays *pizzicato.* The voice joins this style, and there are periodic directions in the score for the singer to perform "with jazz feel" (m. 10) and the option to "substitute words with playful hums or scats" (mm. 28–29). Whereas "How It Feels to Be Colored Me" presents an introspective soliloquy of self-discovery, "I Am Not Tragically Colored" shows a slightly mischievous and somewhat defiant side of the central protagonist; both are traits that have been used to describe Hurston's own character.

LISZTEN, MY HUSBAND IS NOT A HAT (1994)

"Liszten, My Husband Is Not a Hat" marks Baiocchi's return to the solo piano genre after a 16-year hiatus; her two piano etudes, *Equipoise by Intersection,* date from 1978. The title of this programmatic work, "Liszten, My Husband Is Not a Hat," reveals two sources of influence that have had a powerful impact on Baiocchi's compositional career: literature and 19th-century romantic pianism. She was drawn to the study of a musician's struggle with reality by the case study "The Man Who Mistook His Wife for a Hat" by British clinical neurologist Oliver Sacks. Though not in direct imitation of a specific Lisztian virtuosic display, Baiocchi's writing for the piano frequently contains a lyricism that invokes the romanticism of the 19th century.

"Liszten My Husband Is Not a Hat" is an 80-measure work made up of diverse sections that present contrasting moods and states of mind. Musically, the piece follows a loose ABA' organization, with measures 1–6 acting as an introduction and measures 7–20 reappearing in an altered form in measures 61–74. This type of ternary form was very common in 19th-century piano pieces that were meant to feature the performer's technical ability and exploit the full range of the piano; in this way, Baiocchi's work refers to Liszt's legacy for the piano. Additionally, by using the piano to imitate other instruments, such as the *quasi arpa* sections (beginning in mm. 7 and 61), Baiocchi invokes the sensibilities of the romantic era. The section from the end of measure 25 to the middle of measure 35 resembles the particular musical style of Liszt as Baiocchi reduces the texture to one line in the low bass and then gradually layers on the other voices in a four-part imitative counterpoint that builds in expanded range, rhythmic complexity, and intensity until the polyphonic texture breaks down into octave triplets in measure 36.

Oliver Sacks's clinical study comes from a collection of case studies that was published in 1987 and became a national bestseller, *The Man Who Mistook His Wife for a Hat and Other Clinical Tales.* Baiocchi was particularly interested in the relationship between sanity and insanity and how the protagonist (a musician) was unable to function comfortably in everyday life unless he was talking about music; music for him became a reference point for reality. In her score, Baiocchi portrays sudden shifts in mental states by sudden shifts in register, dynamics, rhythmic texture, and melodic fragments. The work starts out "Reflectively" and frequently shifts between *ritard, a tempo,* and *accelerando*; the expression marking *loco* is interspersed throughout the score.

GBELDAHOVEN: NO ONE'S CHILD (1996–97)

Gbeldahoven: No One's Child, a chamber opera in one act, represents Baiocchi's first compositional venture into opera. Set in 1930 during the Harlem Renaissance, the opera treats the relationships among writers Zora Neale Hurston, Langston Hughes, and their literary patroness Charlotte van der Veer Quick Mason. Mason, a widowed white philanthropist has commissioned Hurston and Hughes to collaborate on writing a play. To facilitate this process, Mason has hired Louise Thompson as a stenographer to aid the creative writers and relies on her adviser, Alain Locke, to help her decide if the project is worthy of production funds. The fictional plot centers on the complicated situations that arise from the interactions of the characters as they deal with sexism, ageism, and racism, and how misunderstandings of these issues often work to separate people of color from society at large.

Writing her own libretto for this opera, Baiocchi was able to use both her literary and musical talents to great success. The title of the work, *Gbeldahoven,* is a word that Baiocchi invented to represent and embody the spirit of what one can become or positive dreams and aspirations. Baiocchi approached the libretto through a series of literary stages. After finding a subject in which she was interested, she wrote it out as a novel. She then took the story and, going through several drafts, turned it into a play. The play became the basis for the first version of the libretto (over two hours long). The two-hour version of the opera received its premiere reading at the Harold Washington Library Auditorium in Chicago (October 1996). The final version was cut to one hour and was presented in a concert reading at the Art Institute of Chicago on April 20, 1997. Through each revision, Baiocchi was able to fully develop each character as an individual and give careful thought to the importance each word has in projecting the story.

Gbeldahoven: No One's Child consists of 13 arias connected by a recitative-like, musically set dialogue. The opera also features a play within a play and a dance scene. The musical language encompasses a variety of styles and represents Baiocchi's most ambitious project to date. Her music, in general and particularly in an extended work such as *Gbeldahoven,* reflects the idioms of African chant, spirituals, blues, jazz, gospel, art songs, works songs, and rap music.

"Godmother's Lesson" is a wistful aria sung by Charlotte Mason midway through the opera. Preferring to be called "godmother" by Hughes and Hurston, Mason has just discovered in the preceding recitative ("Hell hath no Fury!") that she is referred to as "guardmother" behind her back and learns that her money cannot buy affection and loyalty. The mood of the aria moves from reflection to agitation and finally a defeated resignation when she realizes that things will never be the same for her.

The opening vocal lines of the aria present the musical material in a way that reflects the dramatic situation of Godmother (Mason) slowly coming to terms with her realization. In the first phrase, the melody is restricted to the filled-in interval of the perfect fifth, *d*-flat to *a*-flat (mm. 10–11). The second phrase (mm. 12–13) expands the vocal range up a fourth and contains the filled-in interval of *g*-flat to *d*-flat, an octave above the opening note in measure 10. By measure 15, the beginning of the third phrase, the voice has ascended to high *a*-flat and in the following measures continues to encompass all the notes that came before. Thus, Godmother's gradual understanding of the situation is musically reflected in the expanding range of the vocal line. Baiocchi uses the technique of a gradually expanding vocal range again at the very end of the aria to emphasize the final line, "Things will never be the same. Never!"

"Godmother's Lesson" is a hauntingly beautiful aria that captures the humanity in a character that could easily be seen as villainous in a less sophisticated portrayal. Through her sensitive approach to the relationship between the text and music, Baiocchi has found a compelling way of expressing the dramatic situation that underlies the plot. By using historical characters to explore themes that were rising to the surface in 1930 and that are still very relevant in the 1990s, Baiocchi has brought insight into the interplay of creativity and racial identity in 20th-century America.

REFERENCES

Baiocchi, Regina H. Program notes, *Gbeldahoven: No One's Child.* Harold Washington Library Auditorium, Chicago, Ill., October 6, 1996, and the Art Institute of Chicago, April 20, 1997.

——.Telephone interview with the author, May 14, 1997.

Walker-Hill, Helen. "Black Women Composers in Chicago: Then and Now." *Black Music Research Journal* 12, no. 1 (1992): 1–23.

——. *Music by Black Women Composers: A Bibliography of Available Sources.* CBMR Monographs, no. 5. Chicago: Columbia College, Center for Black Music Research, 1995.

NAOMI ANDRÉ

BAKER, DAVID N(ATHANIEL)

Born in Indianapolis, Ind., December 21, 1931. **Education:** Indianapolis, Ind., public schools; Crispus Attucks High School, studied tuba with LaVerne Newsome and Russell Brown, theory and composition with Norman Merrifield, 1946–49; Jordan Conservatory, studied tuba and trombone, late 1940s; Indiana University–Bloomington, studied theory and composition with Bernard Heiden, Juan Orrego-Salas, and Thomas Beversdorf, 1949–54, B.Mus.Ed., 1953, M.Mus.Ed., 1954; Berklee School of Music, Boston, Mass., mid-1950s; School of Jazz, Lenox, Mass., diploma, 1959; studied composition privately with George Russell, John Lewis, William Russo, Gunther Schuller, and John Eaton, among others; studied cello privately with Leopold Teraspulsky, Russell Brown, Gary Hoffman, Daniel Rothmuller, Helga Winold, Barbara Wirth, Jules Eskin, and Janos Starker; studied trombone privately with J. J. Johnson, John Marcellus, Charles Small, Lewis Van Haney, John Clark, Bobby Brookmeyer, Thomas Beversdorf, and William Adam; studied bass privately with Murray Grodner and Buell Neidlinger. **Composing and Performing Career:** Began playing professionally with local groups, 1948; played in the bands of Maynard Ferguson, 1957, Quincy Jones, 1961, George Russell, 1962, Wes Montgomery, early 1960s, and Lionel Hampton; frequently performed with symphony orchestras and chamber groups, occasionally as soloist, ca. 1962–present; U.S. and abroad, toured widely with university jazz groups and his own sextet, 1950s–present; frequent lectures and workshops and clinics. **Teaching Career:** Lincoln University, Jefferson City, Mo., 1956–57; Indianapolis, public schools, 1958–59; private teaching, 1960–66; Indiana Central College, Indianapolis, 1963–64; Indiana University, Department of Jazz Studies, Distinguished Professor of Music, Chairman of the Jazz Department, 1966–present; has also taught at Indiana State University, Miami (Ohio) University, New England Conservatory of Music, San Diego State College, Chicago State University, and Wichita State University, to name a few. **Commissions:** Jamey Aebersold, 1962; Meredian String Quartet, 1962; Howard Liva, 1963; Montreal Brass Quintet, 1966; Hugh Partridge, 1966, 1973; Christian Theological Seminary, 1966, 1968; Peter Gordon, 1967; National Lutheran Campus Ministry, 1967; David Collins, 1967; United Christian Missionaries, 1968; Natalie Hinderas, 1968; James Nelson, 1968; Janice Albright, 1969; Indianapolis Arts Council, 1969; Josef Gingold, 1969; Faith for a City, 1970; Fisk Jubilee Singers, 1970; Sidney Foster, 1970; American Conservatory Percussion Ensemble, 1971; James Pellerite, 1971; Frina and Ken Boldt Duo, 1971; Harvey Phillips, 1971, 1975; Helena Freire, 1971; Andrew Jacobs Jr., 1972; Gary Karr, 1972; Thomas Beversdorf, 1972; Grand Valley State College, 1972; Rita Sansone, 1972; William Brown, 1973, 1986; Bertram Turetsky, 1973; Paul Freeman, 1973; Marina Svetlova, 1974; Louisville Symphony Orchestra, 1974; J. B. Floyd and Stere-Opticon, 1975; Edith Diggory, 1975; J. C. Penney, 1975; Janos Starker, 1975, 1980; Ruggiero Ricci, 1975, 1976; Webb-Hornibrook Duo, 1976; Beaux Arts Trio, 1976, 1992; Western Arts Trio, 1976; McKim Fund of the Library of Congress, 1979; Michael Limoli, 1986; Bill Evans, 1987; New York Philharmonic,

1987; Carole Wincenc, 1987; Ronen Chamber Ensemble, 1988; Dominic Spera, 1988; Lee Konitz, 1989; Columbus Pro Musica, 1990; Plymouth Music Series, 1990; Frank Bongiorno, 1990; Indiana University School of Law, 1992; Meet the Composer, 1993; Indiana University, 1995. **Memberships:** Afro-American Music Bicentennial, Hall of Fame and Museum, member, advisory board; American Federation of Musicians, Local 161-710 and Local 3, member; American Music Center, member, board of directors; American Recording Orchestra of Duke University, board member; American Symphony Orchestra League, member, board of directors; Arts Midwest, board of directors; Atlantic Center for the Arts (New Smyrna Beach, Fla.), member, advisory board; Broadcast Music Inc., member; Contemporary Music Project, member; Jazz Action Coalition, president; Jazz Advisory Panel, Kennedy Center, Washington, D.C., chairman; Jazz, Folk, and Ethnic Advisory Panel, National Endowment for the Arts, Washington, D.C., chairman; Jazz Masterworks Editions, Smithsonian Institution, member, executive board; Indiana Arts Commission, member; Interlochen Arts Academy, member, advisory board; International Association of Jazz Educators, vice-president; Minnesota Composers Forum, member; Mu Phi Epsilon, honorary Sterling Patron; National Council on the Arts, member; National Jazz Foundation, member; National Jazz Service Organization, president; National Music Council, member, board of directors; Recorded Anthology of American Music, Inc., member; Jazz Masters in Monaco, musical/artistic director; Smithsonian Institution, senior consultant to the Music Programs; State Department Folk Music and Jazz Advisory Panel, member; Young American Symphony Orchestra, member, Artistic Advisory Board; The Pulitzer Prizes, Nominating Jury in Music, 1995–present. **Honors/Awards:** Crispus Attucks High School, Indianapolis, Ind., Hall of Fame; Indiana University Scholastic Achievement Award, 1954; Indiana University Philharmonic Gold Award, 1954; Indiana Music Promoters Merit Award, 1959; *Down Beat* magazine, Hall of Fame Scholarship Award, 1959; Notre Dame Collegiate Jazz Festival, Best Big Band, 1959; Indiana University Cream and Crimson Award; *Down Beat* magazine, New Star Award (trombone), 1962; Notre Dame Collegiate Jazz Festival, Cellist with Best Jazz Group, 1964; National Association of Negro Musicians, Outstanding Musician Award, 1968; *Down Beat* magazine, Award for Best Composition of the 1970 National Collegiate Jazz Festival, 1970; Pulitzer Prize nomination, 1973; Indiana Distinguished Citizen Award, 1976; National Association of Negro Musicians Special Award, 1976; Indianapolis, Ind., Key to the City; Indianapolis Jazz Hall of Fame, member; Grammy Award nomination, 1979; National Endowment for the Arts, grant; National Association of Jazz Educators, Hall of Fame Award, 1981; Dr. Martin Luther King Drum Major Award, 1982; Leadership Development Center, Outstanding Achievement in Business and the Professions Award: Arts/Music/Theatre, 1983; President's Award for Distinguished Teaching, Indiana University-Bloomington, 1986; *Jazz Educators Journal,* Jazz Educators Poll Winner, 1986; *Down Beat* magazine, Lifetime Achievement

Award, 1987; Indianapolis Musicians (Local 3) and the American Federation of Musicians, Artistic Achievement Award, 1988; Indiana General Assembly, Resolutions in honor of David N. Baker Jr., 1989; Arts Midwest, Jazz Masters Award, 1990; Governor's Arts Award, State of Indiana, 1991; New York Brass Conference for Scholarships, honoree, 1991; Indiana University School of Journalism, Sigma Delta Chi Leather Medal Award, 1991; Wabash College, Indiana, honorary doctorate, 1993; *Down Beat* magazine, Jazz Education Hall of Fame, 1994; Eva Janzer Cello Center, Indiana University School of Music, Chevalier du violoncello, 1995; National Federation of Music Clubs, 1995; National Endowment for the Arts, Certificate, Ambassador to the Arts, 1995; Indianapolis chapter, Links, Inc., "Salute to Indiana's African American Jazz Artists," honoree; Indianapolis, "Stars in the Sidewalk," honoree. **Mailing Address:** Indiana University, School of Music M309, Bloomington, IN 47401.

MUSIC LIST

INSTRUMENTAL SOLO
Violin
"Deliver My Soul." 1968. St. Louis, Mo.: MMB Music, 1968. Note: adaptation of "Deliver My Soul" from *Psalm 22*. Premiere, 1968.

"Ethnic Variations on a Theme of Paganini." 1976. St. Louis, Mo.: MMB Music, 1976. Commissioned by Ruggiero Ricci. Note: based on Paganini's 24th caprice.

"Improvisation no. 1 for Unaccompanied Violin." 1975. Unpublished manuscript. Commissioned by Ruggiero Ricci.

"Improvisation no. 2 for Unaccompanied Violin." 1975. Unpublished manuscript. Commissioned by Ruggiero Ricci.

Jazz Suite: For Violin and Piano. 1979. St. Louis, Mo.: MMB Music, 1979. Commissioned by the McKim Fund of the Library of Congress. Contents: Mintons; Harlem; Saturday Night; Perfume/ Perspiration; Jamaican Jam; 52nd Street. Recorded: Grenadilla GSC 1056.

Sonata for Violin and Piano or Sonata in One Movement. 1967. St. Louis, Mo.: MMB Music, n.d. Commissioned by David Collins. Premiere, 1967.

Suite for Unaccompanied Violin. 1975. St. Louis, Mo.: MMB Music, 1975. Commissioned by Ruggiero Ricci.

Viola
Sonata for Viola and Piano. 1966. Unpublished manuscript. Commissioned by Hugh Partridge.

Cello
"The Dude." 1962. Unpublished manuscript. Also arranged for jazz ensemble.

"Electric Stere-Opticon" (cello, electronic instruments). 1975. Unpublished manuscript. Commissioned by J. B. Floyd and Stere-Opticon.

Piece for Violoncello and Piano. 1966. Unpublished manuscript.

Sonata for Solo Cello. St. Louis, Mo.: MMB Music, 1990. Recorded: Liscio Recordings LAS-21793.

Sonata for Violoncello and Piano. 1973. New York: Associated Music, 1975. Recorded: Columbia M-33432, vol. 6; Laurel LR-817-CD.

Clarinet
Sonata for Clarinet and Piano. St. Louis, Mo.: MMB Music, 1990. Contents: Blues; Loneliness; Dance. Recorded: Indiana University School of Music, 1994–95, no. 581.

Flute
"Inspiration." 1987. St. Louis, Mo.: MMB Music, 1987. Also in *National Flute Association 20th Anniversary Anthology of American Flute Music* (New York: Oxford University Press, 1992). Commissioned by Carole Wincenc. Recorded: Indiana University School of Music Program, 1990–91, no. 1.

Six poèmes noir pour flûte et piano. 1974. St. Louis, Mo.: MMB Music, 1974. Contents: Rêve; Papillon, Omniscient; Chanson; Image; Nocturne.

Sonata for Flute and Piano. St. Louis, Mo.: MMB Music, n.d.

Piano
Five Short Pieces for Piano. 1970. St. Louis, Mo.: MMB Music, 1970. Contents: Rêve; To Bird; Passacaglia; Evening Song; Blues Waltz (née Terrible T).

Jazz Dance Suite. 1988. St. Louis, Mo.: MMB Music, 1988.

Sonata for Piano. 1968. St. Louis, Mo.: MMB Music, 1968. Commissioned by Natalie Hinderas. Contents: Black Art; A Song—After Paul Laurence Dunbar; Coltrane.

Two Pianos
Sonata for Two Pianos. 1971. Unpublished manuscript. Commissioned by Frina and Ken Boldt Duo.

INSTRUMENTAL ENSEMBLE
Strings
Impressions for Two Cellos. 1988. St. Louis, Mo.: MMB Music, 1988. Recorded: Indiana University School of Music Program, 1989–1990, no. 121.

"Pastorale" (string quartet). 1959. n.p.: Fema Music Publications, 1959. Recorded: Indiana University School of Music Program, 1990–91, no. 503.

"Reflections on a Summer's Day" (cello choir). 1986. St. Louis, Mo.: MMB Music, 1986.

"Refractions for Cello Quartet." 1993. St. Louis, Mo.: MMB Music, 1993. Recorded: Indiana University School of Music, 1993–94, no. 500.

Sonata for Viola, Guitar, and Contrabass. 1973. Unpublished manuscript. Commissioned by Hugh Partridge.

Sonata for Violin and Cello. 1974. Unpublished manuscript.

String Quartet no. 1. 1962. Unpublished manuscript. Commissioned by the Meredian String Quartet.

"Summer Memories" (string quartet). St. Louis, Mo.: MMB Music, 1988.

Two Cello String Quintet. 1987. St. Louis, Mo.: MMB Music, 1987. Recorded: Indiana University School of Music Program, 1987–88, no. 149.

Woodwinds
Duet for Alto Saxophones. 1990. St. Louis, Mo.: MMB Music, 1990.

"Faces of the Blues: A Fantasy for Alto Saxophone and Saxophone Quartet." 1990. St. Louis, Mo.: MMB Music, 1990. Commissioned by Frank Bongiorno. Premiere, 1988. Recorded: Indiana University School of Music Program, 1989–90, no. 818; Liscio Recordings LCD-09193.

David N. Baker; courtesy of the composer; photo by Steve Sheldon

Fantasy for Woodwind Quintet. 1969. Unpublished manuscript.

Theme and Variations (woodwind quintet). 1970. St. Louis, Mo.: MMB Music, 1970.

Woodwind Quintet no. 1 (flute, oboe, clarinet, bassoon, horn). St. Louis, Mo.: MMB Music, n.d.

Brass

"Passions" (brass quintet). 1966. Unpublished manuscript. Commissioned by the Montreal Brass Quintet.

"Romanza and March" (three trombones). 1961. Unpublished manuscript.

"Soleil Impromptu" (trumpet, trombone, euphonium, tuba). 1990. Unpublished manuscript.

Suite in Folk Style (brass quartet). 1990. Unpublished manuscript.

Three Jazz Moods (brass ensemble). 1963. Unpublished manuscript. Commissioned by Howard Liva for the Purdue Brass Choir.

Percussion

"Shapes" (percussion ensemble). Unpublished manuscript. Recorded: Indiana University School of Music, 1988–89, no. 333.

Suite (Sweet) Louis (A Tribute to Louis Armstrong). 1971. Unpublished manuscript. Commissioned by the American Conservatory Percussion Ensemble.

Combinations

Ballade (F horn, alto saxophone, cello). 1967. Unpublished manuscript. Commissioned by Peter Gordon. Premiere, 1967.

Concerto for Fours (solo quartet [flute, cello, tuba, contrabass], tuba quartet, contrabass quartet, percussion quartet). 1980. Unpublished manuscript.

Contrasts (violin, cello, piano). 1976. St. Louis, Mo.: MMB Music, 1976. Commissioned by the Western Arts Trio. Contents: Passacaglia; A Song; Episodes (CEI/CCP); Kaleidoscope. Premiere, 1976. Recorded: Laurel LR-106.

"Duo for Clarinet and Cello." 1988. St. Louis, Mo.: MMB Music, 1988. Commissioned by Ronen Chamber Ensemble. Premiere, 1988. Recorded: Indiana University School of Music Program, 1990–91, no. 676.

"Homage à l'histoire" (clarinet, bassoon, trumpet, percussion, violin, double bass). 1994. n.p.: Dunsinane Music.

Jazz Suite for Sextet in Memory of Bob Thompson or *In Memoriam: Freedom* (trumpet, tenor saxophone, trombone, piano, double bass, drums). 1971. Unpublished manuscript. Recorded: Indiana University School of Music Program, 1995–96, no. 161.

"Modality, Tonality, and Freedom" (alto saxophone, five trumpets, four trombones, tuba, piano, double bass, drums). 1962. Unpublished manuscript. Commissioned by Jamey Aebersold.

Roots (violin, cello, piano). 1976. St. Louis, Mo.: MMB Music, 1976. Commissioned by the Beaux Arts Trio. Contents: Walpurgisnacht; Blues Waltz; Sorrow Song; Calypso Row; Finale. Premiere, 1976.

Roots II (violin, cello, piano). 1992. St. Louis, Mo.: MMB Music, 1992. Commissioned by the Beaux Arts Trio. Contents: Incantation; Dance in Congo Square; Sorrow Song; Boogie Woogie; Jubilee. Premiere, 1993. Recorded: Philips 438 866-2.

"Rouge et Noir" (flute, piano, double bass, drums). 1985. St. Louis, Mo.: MMB Music, 1985.

Singers of Songs/Weavers of Dreams: Homage to My Friends (cello, 17 percussion instruments). 1980. St. Louis, Mo.: MMB Music, 1980. Commissioned by Janos Starker. Contents: Miles; Sonny Rollins; Jimmy Yancey; Paul Robeson; Trane; Duke; Dizzy. Recorded: Golden Crest CRDG 4223; Laurel LR-817-CD.

Sonata for Brass Quintet and Piano. 1970. Unpublished manuscript. Premiere, 1972.

Sonata for French Horn and Jazz Quartet. 1986. St. Louis, Mo.: MMB Music, 1986.

Sonata for Jazz Violin and String Quartet. St. Louis, Mo.: MMB Music, 1987.

Sonata for Piano and String Quintet. 1971. Minneapolis: AAMOA Press, n.d. Commissioned by Helena Freire. Premiere, 1972. Recorded: AAMOA NS-7401; Silver Burdette 74-187-47.

Sonata for Tuba and String Quartet. 1971. St. Louis, Mo.: MMB Music, 1971. Commissioned by Harvey Phillips. Recorded: Golden Crest CRS-4122; Indiana University School of Music, 1990–91, no. 348.

Sonata for Violin, Cello, and Four Flutes. 1980. St. Louis, Mo.: MMB Music, 1980. Recorded: Indiana University School of Music Program, 1990–91, no. 289.

Suite for Cello and Jazz Trio (cello, piano, double bass, drums). n.p.: Dunsinane Music, n.d. Recorded: Liscio LAS-21793.

Suite for French Horn and Jazz Combo. 1986. St. Louis, Mo.: MMB Music.

Suite for French Horn, String Quartet, and Contrabass. 1985. St. Louis, Mo.: MMB Music, 1986.

Suite for Jazz Sextet. 1991. Also arranged for jazz ensemble under the title *Miami Suite.* Recorded: New World School of the Arts NWSA-001.

Suite for Tuba and String Quartet. Unpublished manuscript. Recorded: Golden Crest CRTS 4122.

Theme and Variations for Piano and String Quintet. 1971. St. Louis, Mo.: MMB Music, 1971.

"The Triplet Blues" (piano, drums, strings). Bowie, Md.: Bow-Bel Music, 1976.

STRING ORCHESTRA

Baker's Shuffle. 1970. Bowie, Md.: Creative Jazz Composers, 1976.

Black-Eyed Peas and Cornbread. 1970. Bowie, Md.: Creative Jazz Composers, 1976.

Blue Strings. 1970. Bowie, Md.: Creative Jazz Composers, 1976.

Blues. 1966. Bowie, Md.: Creative Jazz Composers, 1976. Recorded: Indiana University School of Music Program, 1983–84, no. 793; Jewels CD 87042; RCA Victor Red Seal CD 09026-68114-2.

The Jamaican Strut. 1970. Bowie, Md.: Creative Jazz Composers, 1976.

Little Princess Waltz. Bowie, Md.: Creative Jazz Composers, n.d.

Mod Waltz. 1970. Bowie, Md.: Creative Jazz Composers, 1976.

Slow Groove. 1970. Bowie, Md.: Creative Jazz Composers, 1976.

Sombertime. 1970. Bowie, Md.: Creative Jazz Composers, 1976.

Suite of Little Ethnic Pieces (string orchestra, jazz quartet). 1983. Unpublished manuscript.

The Sunshine Boogaloo. 1970. Bowie, Md.: Creative Jazz Composers, 1976.

Triplet Blues. 1970. Bowie, Md.: Creative Jazz Composers, 1976.

ORCHESTRA (CHAMBER OR FULL)

Images of Childhood. St. Louis, Mo.: MMB Music, 1994. Contents: Maypole; Lazy Summer Days; Hide and Seek; Follow the Leader.

Kosbro. 1973; revised 1975. New York: Associated Music, 1975. Commissioned by Paul Freeman. Premiere, 1974. Recorded: Albany TROY 104.

Shades of Blue. 1993. St. Louis, Mo.: MMB Music, 1993.

ORCHESTRA (CHAMBER OR FULL) WITH SOLOIST

Alabama Landscape (bass-baritone, orchestra). 1990. St. Louis, Mo.: MMB Music, 1990. Commissioned by Columbus Pro Musica. Premiere, 1991.

Le Chat qui pêche (orchestra, soprano, jazz quartet [alto/tenor saxophone, piano, double bass, drums]). 1974. New York: Associated Music, 1975. Commissioned by the Louisville Symphony Orchestra. Contents: Soleil d'Altamira; L'odeur de blues; Sons voiles; Guadeloupe-Calypso; Le Miroir noir. Premiere, 1974. Recorded: First Edition LS-751; Silver Crest CBD-69-6B.

Concert Piece for Viola and Orchestra. 1991. Unpublished manuscript. Premiere, 1991. Recorded: Indiana University School of Music Program, 1990–91, no. 548.

Concerto for Alto Saxophone and Orchestra. St. Louis, Mo.: MMB Music, 1989. Commissioned by Lee Konitz. Premiere, 1990.

Concerto for Bass Viol and Jazz Band (double bass, string quartet, solo violin, jazz ensemble). 1972. Unpublished manuscript. Commissioned by Gary Karr. Premiere, 1972.

Concerto for Brass Quintet and Orchestra. 1987. n.p.: Dunsinane Music, 1987.

Concerto for Cello and Chamber Orchestra. 1975. New York: Associated Music, 1975. Commissioned by Janos Starker. Premiere, 1975.

Concerto for Cello and Jazz Band. 1987. St. Louis, Mo.: MMB Music, 1987. Recorded: Liscio Recordings LAS-21793.

Concerto for Clarinet and Orchestra. 1986. Unpublished manuscript. Commissioned by Michael Limoli.

Concerto for Flute and Jazz Band (flute/alto flute, string quartet, jazz band). 1971. Unpublished manuscript. Commissioned by James Pellerite. Premiere, 1971. Recorded Laurel LR-125.

Concerto for Saxophone and Chamber Orchestra. 1987. n.p.: Dunsinane Music, 1989.

Concerto for Trombone, Jazz Band, and Chamber Orchestra. 1972. Unpublished manuscript. Commissioned by Thomas Beversdorf. Premiere, 1973.

Concerto for Trumpet, String Orchestra, and Jazz Band. St. Louis, Mo.: MMB Music, 1988. Commissioned by Dominic Spera.

Concerto for Trumpet, String Orchestra, Percussion, and Jazz Band. 1988. Unpublished manuscript. Recorded: Indiana University School of Music Program, 1987–88, no. 551; Laurel LR-115.

Concerto for Two Pianos, Jazz Band, Strings, and Percussion. 1976. St. Louis, Mo.: MMB Music, 1976. Commissioned by Webb-Hornibrook Duo. Premiere, 1977. Recorded: Laurel LR-115.

Concerto for Violin and Jazz Band. 1969. St. Louis, Mo.: MMB Music, 1969. Commissioned by Josef Gingold. Premiere, 1969. Recorded: Laurel LR-125.

Concertpiece for Trombone and Strings. 1991. St. Louis, Mo.: MMB Music, 1991.

Concertpiece for Viola (viola, orchestra). 1989. St. Louis, Mo.: MMB Music, 1989. Also arranged for viola and piano.

Ellingtones: A Fantasy for Saxophone and Orchestra. 1987. n.p.: Dunsinane Music, 1987. Commissioned by the New York Philharmonic. Premiere, 1987. Recorded: Blue Note n.n.

Jazz Suite for Clarinet and Symphony Orchestra: Three Ethnic Dances. 1992. St. Louis, Mo.: MMB Music, 1992. Recorded: Telarc CD-80409.

Levels: A Concerto for Solo Contrabass, Jazz Band, Flute Quartet, Horn Quartet, and String Quartet. 1973. Unpublished manuscript. Commissioned by Bertram Turetzky. Note: nominated for the Pulitzer Prize, 1973. Premiere, 1973.

Life Cycles (tenor, horn, string orchestra). 1988. St. Louis, Mo.: MMB Music, 1988. Also arranged for tenor, horn, and piano.

Parallel Planes (alto/soprano saxophone, orchestra). 1992. St. Louis, Mo.: MMB Music, 1992.

Piece for Brass Quintet and Orchestra. 1988. St. Louis, Mo.: MMB Music, 1988.

Reflections or *My Indianapolis* (jazz ensemble, orchestra). 1969. Unpublished manuscript. Commissioned by the Indianapolis Arts Council for the Indianapolis Summer Symphony. Premiere, 1969.

Sonata for Jazz Violin and String Quartet. 1987. Unpublished manuscript.

Two Improvisations for Orchestra and Jazz Combo (jazz trio [piano, double bass, drums], orchestra). 1974. New York: Associated Music, 1975. Contents: Harlem Pipes; Sangre Negro. Premiere, 1974.

BAND

Afro-Cuban Suite. 1954. Unpublished manuscript.

VOICE WITH INSTRUMENTAL ENSEMBLE

Fantasy (soprano, harp, brass ensemble). 1954. Unpublished manuscript.

Give and Take (soprano, flute/alto flute, oboe/English horn, viola, cello, percussion). 1975. St. Louis, Mo.: MMB Music, 1975. Commissioned by Edith Diggory. Contents: The Branch of a Green Tree; The Gift; The Funeral Is All; They Will Not Tell; An Almost Death; Canonization II. Premiere, 1975. Recorded: Laurel LR-115.

Songs of the Night (soprano, piano, string quartet). 1972. Unpublished manuscript. Commissioned by Rita Sansone. Contents: Rêve; Songs; Fragments; Kid Stuff; Poppy Flower; Borderline; Where Have You Gone?; Gethsemane; Religion; Now That He Is Safely Dead; End; Evening Song (solo piano). Premiere, 1972.

Through This Vale of Tears (tenor, piano, string quartet). 1986. St. Louis, Mo.: MMB Music, 1986. Commissioned by William Brown. Contents: Thou Dost Lay Me in the Dust of Death; If There Be Sorrow; My God, Why Hast Thou Forsaken Me?; Parades to Hell; Deliver My Soul; Sometimes I Feel Like a Motherless Child; Now That He Is Safely Dead. Premiere, 1986. Recorded: New World 80423-2.

SOLO VOICE

Abyss (soprano). 1968. Unpublished manuscript. Contents: Perception; Observation; Introspection; Penetration. Premiere, 1968.

The Black Experience (tenor). 1973. Unpublished manuscript. "Early in the Mornin'," "A Good Assassination Should Be Quiet," and "Status Symbol" in *Anthology of Art Songs by Black Composers* (New York: Edward B. Marks Music, 1977). Commissioned by William Brown. Contents: I Who Would Encompass Millions; The

Insurgent; Status Symbol; A Good Assassination Should Be Quiet; The Rebel; The Alarm Clock; Early in the Mornin'.

Five Settings for Soprano and Piano. 1969. Unpublished manuscript. Commissioned by Janice Albright.

"Men Shall Tell of the Lord" (soprano, piano). 1966. Unpublished manuscript.

Song Cycle (soprano, piano). Unpublished manuscript. Contents: If There Be Sorrow; The Smile; The Optimist; A Song; Parades to Hell. Recorded: Enharmonic ENCD 93-012.

Songs of Living and Dying (soprano, tenor, piano). 1988. Unpublished manuscript.

Witness: Six Original Compositions in Spiritual Style (baritone, double bass). 1990. St. Louis, Mo.: MMB Music, 1990. Commissioned by the Plymouth Music Series. Contents: We Has a Hard Time; Didn't My Lord Deliver Daniel; Death Is Riding; Sorrow Song; And He Never Said a Mumbalin' Word; My Lord, What a Morning. Premiere, 1991.

CHORAL MUSIC

"Any Human to Another" (SATB). 1973. Unpublished manuscript.

Catholic Mass for Peace or *Votive Mass for Peace* (SATB, jazz ensemble). 1969. Unpublished manuscript. Contents: Entrance Antiphon; Give Peace to Your People; Congregational Refrain; Great Amen; Recessional (Psalm 150). Premiere, 1969.

Five Songs to the Survival of Black Children (SATB unaccompanied). 1970. Unpublished manuscript. Commissioned by the Fisk Jubilee Singers. Contents: Now That He Is Safely Dead; Religion; Black Children; The Dream Boogie; If We Must Die. Premiere, 1970.

Four Biblical Tales in Spiritual Style (SATB, piano). 1993. St. Louis, Mo.: MMB Music, 1993. Contents: When I'm Dead; Golgatha; Witness; What a Morning.

"I Dream a World" (SATB). 1973. Unpublished manuscript.

Images, Shadows, and Dreams: Five Vignettes. 1993. n.p.: Dunsinane Music, 1993. Commissioned by the Meet the Composer/Reader's Digest Commissioning Program in partnership with the National Endowment for the Arts and the Lila Wallace–Reader's Digest Fund. Contents: Rent's Due Monday; The Nonagenarian; If There Be Sorrow; The Rebel; Let Me Tell You How To Meet the Day. Premiere, 1993. Recorded: Collins Classics 14762.

Lutheran Mass (SATB, jazz septet). 1967. Unpublished manuscript. Commissioned by the National Lutheran Campus Ministry. Contents: Prelude; Introit; Kyrie; Gloria; Gradual; Credo; Sanctus; Offertory; Agnus Dei; Nunc Dimitis; Postlude. Premiere, 1967.

Psalm 23 (SATB, organ). 1968. Unpublished manuscript. Commissioned by the United Christian Missionaries. Premiere, 1968.

"Thou Dost Lay Me in the Dust of Death" (SATB). 1966. New York: Associated Music, 1966. Also arranged for brass quartet. Note: originally part of *Psalm 22*.

DRAMATIC MUSIC

The Beatitudes (oratorio for SATB, soloists, narrator, jazz ensemble, string orchestra, dancers). 1968. Unpublished manuscript. Commissioned by the Christian Theological Seminary. Contents: Instrumental Prelude; Vocal Introduction; Blessed Are the Poor in Spirit; Blessed Are They That Mourn; Blessed Are the Meek; Blessed Are They That Hunger; Blessed Are the Merciful; Blessed Are the Clean in Heart; Blessed Are the Peacemakers; Blessed Are They Who Suffer Persecution; Blessed Are Ye When Men Shall Revile You; Instrumental Postlude.

Black America: To the Memory of Martin Luther King, Jr. (cantata for SATB, narrators, soloists, jazz ensemble, string orchestra). 1968. Unpublished manuscript. Contents: The Wretched of the Earth (Machinations, Missionaries, Money, Marines); Kaleidoscope; 125th Street; Martyrs: Malcolm, Medgar, Martin. Premiere, 1968.

The Frog Who Wanted to Sing (theater piece for storyteller, soprano, flute/piccolo/alto flute, bassoon/oboe, horn, bass trombone, percussion). 1989. Unpublished manuscript.

Modern Dance Suite. 1987. Unpublished manuscript. Commissioned by Bill Evans.

Psalm 22 (oratorio for SATB, narrators, jazz ensemble, string orchestra, dancers). 1966. Unpublished manuscript. Commissioned by the Christian Theological Seminary. Contents: Prelude; My God, My God; Yet Thou Art Holy; But I Am a Worm; Narration; I Am Poured Out Like Water; Thou Dost Lay Me in the Dust of Death; Narration; Deliver My Soul; Pastorale; I Will Tell of Thy Name; Yea, to Him Shall All the Proud of the Earth Bow Down; All the Ends of the Earth Shall Remember; Narration; Praise Him; Men Shall Tell of the Lord; Finale. Premiere, 1966.

Sangre Negro (ballet for jazz ensemble). 1974. Unpublished manuscript. Commissioned by Marina Svetlova. Premiere, 1974.

The Sun and the Moon (theater piece for storyteller, soprano, flute/piccolo/alto flute, bassoon/oboe, horn, bass trombone, percussion). 1989. Unpublished manuscript.

INCIDENTAL MUSIC

"Andy Jacobs' Campaign Song." 1972. Incidental television music. Commissioned by Andrew Jacobs Jr.

"The Black Experience." 1968. Incidental television music.

The Black Frontier. 1971. Incidental television series music. Contents: The New Americans; The Cowherders; The Buffalo Soldiers; The Exodusters.

Boochie. 1985. Incidental music for the play by Mari Evans.

"Brushstrokes." 1966. Television theme music.

"I Heard My Woman Call." 1969. Incidental music for a dramatic presentation adapted from Eldridge Cleaver's *Soul on Ice.* Premiere, 1969.

"Meet the Artist." 1970. Television theme music.

Promise and Performance. 1974. Documentary drama soundtrack.

"The Trial of Captain Henry Flipper." 1972. Incidental television music.

"A Walk with a Child" (voice, guitar). 1968. Unpublished manuscript. Note: music for use in Andrew Jacobs' 1968 Congressional campaign.

MULTIMEDIA

Concerto for Tuba, Jazz Band, Percussion, Choir, Dancers, Slides and Tape Recorders. 1975. Unpublished manuscript. Commissioned by Harvey Phillips. Premiere, 1975.

A Salute to Beethoven (piccolo, flute, oboe, clarinet, bassoon, horn, backstage flute choir, jazz ensemble, prerecorded tape). 1970.

Unpublished manuscript. Commissioned by Sidney Foster. Premiere, 1970.

A Song of Mankind (SATB, orchestra, jazz ensemble, rock band, vocal soloists, lights, and sound effects). 1970. Unpublished manuscript. Commissioned by Faith for a City, Inc. Note: Baker wrote only one of the seven movements, the remaining six are by other composers. Premiere, 1971.

JAZZ ENSEMBLE

[The following list of titles includes only works that were composed by the subject of the entry; it is not a list of recordings that were made by the subject. Although the composer may have made recordings of his own works, the list is not restricted to those recordings but in many cases includes performances by other artists of the composer's work. The list is made up of publication and discographical data, in cases where such information is available. Although no effort has been made to include documentation of the earliest recording of the works listed, the date of the earliest recording that is readily available has been given. —Ed.]

"Adumbratio." 1971. New York: Three Fifteen West Fifty-Third Street, 1971.

"The Aebersold Strut." 1982. Unpublished manuscript. Recorded: Laurel LR-505.

"Al-ki-hol." 1956. Unpublished manuscript.

"AlMaCo." 1982. Unpublished manuscript. Recorded: Laurel LR-505.

"Almost." 1973. Unpublished manuscript.

"An After Hours Lament." 1990. Unpublished manuscript. Recorded: Liscio Recordings LAS-31591.

"An Evening Thought." 1974. St. Louis, Mo.: MMB Music, n.d. Recorded: Laurel LR-503; Manna NR-16919.

"Anjisa." 1973. Unpublished manuscript.

"Apocalypse." 1964. Unpublished manuscript.

"April B." 1959. New York: Three Fifteen West Fifty-Third Street, 1970. Recorded: Indiana University School of Music Program, 1995–96, no. 559.

"April in August." 1996. Unpublished manuscript.

"At Twilight." 1996. Unpublished manuscript.

"Au demain." 1973. Unpublished manuscript.

"Aucon." 1973. Unpublished manuscript.

"Auev." 1973. Unpublished manuscript.

"Aujourd'hui." 1973. Unpublished manuscript.

"Aulil." 1973. Lebanon, Ind.: Studio PR, 1976. Also arranged for jazz septet. Recorded: Indiana University School of Music Program, 1993–94, no. 338.

"Autumn's Dreams." 1990. Glendale, Calif.: Walrus Music, n.d. Recorded: Liscio Recordings LAS-31591.

"Bash." 1972. Unpublished manuscript.

"Bebop Revisited." 1974. Unpublished manuscript. Recorded: Laurel LR-503.

"La belle fleur." 1964. Unpublished manuscript.

"Bily." 1974. Unpublished manuscript.

Bird (To the Memory of Charlie Parker). 1970. Unpublished manuscript. Contents: The Blues; In Beauty; Bird's Lady; Past-Present-Future.

"Birdsong." 1984. Unpublished manuscript. Also arranged for orchestra. Recorded: Indiana University School of Music Program, 1992–93, no. 606; Liscio Recordings LAS-31591.

"Black Man, Black Woman." 1969. Note: based on materials from "I Heard My Woman Call."

"Black Thursday." 1964. New York: Three Fifteen West Fifty-Third Street, 1970. Recorded: Indiana University School of Music Program, 1989–90, no. 587.

"Blues for Bird." 1972. Unpublished manuscript. Recorded: Indiana University School of Music Program, 1971–72, no. 128.

"De Boogie Man." 1973. Unpublished manuscript.

"Bossa Belle." 1973. Unpublished manuscript.

"Bougaloo." 1971. Unpublished manuscript.

"Bourne." 1984. Glendale, Calif.: Walrus Music, n.d. Recorded: Indiana University School of Music Program, 1986–87, no. 446.

"Brother." 1973. Glendale, Calif.: Walrus Music, n.d. Recorded: Indiana University School of Music Program, 1993–94, no. 305.

"Buck." 1975. Unpublished manuscript.

"Bus Ride." 1973. Unpublished manuscript.

"Cahaphi." 1982. n.p. Walrus Music, n.d. Recorded: Laurel LR-504.

"Calypso-Nova no. 1." 1970. New York: Three Fifteen West Fifty-Third Street, n.d. Also arranged for string orchestra.

"Calypso-Nova no. 2." 1971. Unpublished manuscript. Also arranged for string orchestra. Recorded: Indiana University School of Music Program, 1985–86, no. 146.

"Catalyst." 1966. Unpublished manuscript. Recorded: Indiana University School of Music Program, 1970–71, no. 424.

"Cattin'." 1971. Unpublished manuscript.

"CCP." Bowie, Md.: Creative Jazz Composers, n.d. Recorded: Indiana University School of Music Program, 1993–94, no. 606.

Celebration in Three Movements. 1992. Unpublished manuscript. Commissioned by the School of Law, Indiana University, in commemoration of their 150th anniversary. Recorded: Indiana University School of Music Program, 1992–93, no. 484.

Celebration Suite. Glendale, Calif.: Walrus Music, n.d. Contents: Sunburst; A Crystal Tear; Jam Session.

"CFB." 1972. Unpublished manuscript.

"Chariots." 1972. Unpublished manuscript.

"Le Chat qui pêche" (jazz ensemble). 1969. New York: Three Fifteen West Fifty-Third Street, n.d. Recorded: Silver Crest CBD-69-6B.

"Che." 1969. Unpublished manuscript. Recorded: Indiana University School of Music Program, 1970–71, no. 513.

"Check It Out." 1970. New York: Three Fifteen West Fifty-Third Street, n.d. Recorded: Canterbury n.n.

"Cinquatre." 1964. Unpublished manuscript.

"Clegre." 1973. Unpublished manuscript.

Coltrane in Memoriam. 1967. Unpublished manuscript. Contents: Lachrymose; Blues; Apocalypse. Recorded: Indiana University School of Music Program, 1995–96, no. 459.

"Cuzin' Ducky." 1973. Unpublished manuscript.

"Cuzin' Larry—The Champ." 1973. Unpublished manuscript.

"Cuzin' Lee." 1973. Unpublished manuscript.

"Dabd." 1973. Unpublished manuscript.

"Dakiap." 1973. Unpublished manuscript. Recorded: Indiana University School of Music Program, 1988–89, no. 196.

"Dave's Waltz." 1957. Unpublished manuscript.

"Digits." 1972. Unpublished manuscript.

"Do De Mi." 1965. Unpublished manuscript. Recorded: Indiana University School of Music Program, 1974–75, no. 382.

"A Dollar Short and a Day Late." 1964. Unpublished manuscript.

"Eclipse." 1996. Unpublished manuscript.

"Eros and Agape." 1969. Unpublished manuscript. Recorded: Indiana University School of Music Program, 1969–70, no. 303.

"Etc." 1972. Unpublished manuscript.

"Everybody's Song." 1996. Unpublished manuscript.

"The Felix Walk." 1973. Unpublished manuscript. Recorded: Indiana University School of Music Program, 1989–90, no. 317.

"The First Day of Spring." 1969. Bowie, Md.: Creative Jazz Composers, 1976. Also arranged for string orchestra. Recorded: Indiana University School of Music Program, 1970–71, no. 513.

"The Five M Calypso." 1984. Unpublished manuscript. Recorded: Indiana University School of Music Program, 1994–95, no. 210.

"Folklike." 1973. Lebanon, Ind.: Studio PR, 1977. Also arranged for jazz septet. Recorded: Sonet SNTF-849.

"Fuup Blues." 1973. Unpublished manuscript.

"Geo Rus." 1974. Unpublished manuscript.

"The Georgia Peach." 1973. Bowie, Md.: Creative Jazz Composers, 1978. Recorded: Indiana University School of Music Program, 1981–82, no. 530.

"Golgatha." 1976. Unpublished manuscript. Premiere, 1976.

"Green Minus Yellow." 1973. Unpublished manuscript.

"Groovin' for Diz." 1984. Unpublished manuscript. Recorded: Indiana University School of Music Program, 1986–87, no. 446.

"Harlem Pipes." 1973. Unpublished manuscript. Recorded: Indiana University School of Music Program, 1993–94, no. 236.

"Hello World." 1959. Unpublished manuscript.

"Herman's Theme." 1976. Lebanon, Ind.: Studio PR, 1977. Also arranged for jazz septet. Recorded: Indiana University School of Music Program, 1993–94, no. 606.

"HHHCCC." 1975. Lebanon, Ind.: Studio PR, 1977. Also arranged for jazz septet.

"Homage: Bartok, Bird and Duke." 1988. St. Louis, Mo.: MMB Music, 1988. Recorded: Indiana University School of Music Program, 1987–88, no. 580.

"Honesty." New York: Three Fifteen West Fifty-Third Street Corp., n.d. Recorded: Isis I-608; Milestone M-37027; Riverside 375/9375.

"Hoy Hoy." 1973. Unpublished manuscript.

"The I. U. Swing Machine." 1968. Unpublished manuscript. Recorded: Indiana University School of Music Program, 1975–76, no. 202.

"Illegal Entrance." 1996. Unpublished manuscript.

"Infinity." 1964. Unpublished manuscript.

"J Is for Loveliness." 1962. Unpublished manuscript. Recorded: Isis I-608.

"Jeanne Marie at the Picture Show." 1982. Rottenburg, Germany: Advance Music, n.d. Also arranged for brass quartet; orchestra. Recorded: Laurel LR-504.

"Just Before September." 1968. Unpublished manuscript.

"K.C.C." 1966. Unpublished manuscript. Recorded: Indiana University School of Music Program, 1970–71, no. 424.

"Kentucky Oysters." 1958. New York: Three Fifteen West Fifty-Third Street Corp., 1971. Recorded: Indiana University School of Music Program, 1982–83, 214; Riverside RLP-9341.

"Kirsten and Her Puppy Katie." 1996. Unpublished manuscript.

"Kirsten's First Song." 1990. Unpublished manuscript.

"Lacypso." 1974. Unpublished manuscript.

"Lerma Samba." 1982. Rottenburg, Germany: Advance Music, n.d. Also arranged for brass quartet; orchestra. Recorded: Indiana University School of Music Program, 1992–93, no. 259; Laurel LR-504.

"Let's Get It On." 1970. New York: Three Fifteen West Fifty-Third Street Corp., 1971. Recorded: Indiana University School of Music Program, 1970–71, no. 140.

"Light Blue, Dark Blue." 1962. Unpublished manuscript.

"Lima Beba Samba." 1982. Rottenburg, Germany: Advance Music, n.d. Also arranged for orchestra. Recorded: Laurel LR-504.

"The Little Princess." 1959. Bowie, Md.: Creative Jazz Composers, 1976. Recorded: Indiana University School of Music Program, 1969–70, no. 303.

"A Little Waltz." 1973. Unpublished manuscript.

"The Lone Ranger and the Great Horace Silver." 1957. Unpublished manuscript. Recorded: Indiana University School of Music Program, 1986–87, no. 760.

"Lorob." 1982. Unpublished manuscript. Recorded: Laurel LR-505.

Louis Armstrong in Memoriam. 1972. Unpublished manuscript. Commissioned by Grand Valley State College. Contents: Introduction; Genesis; Funeral March; The Creoles; 1928; Evolution; Louis/Life/Love. Premiere, 1973.

"Lumo." 1973. Unpublished manuscript.

"Lunacy." 1959. New York: Three Fifteen West Fifty-Third Street Corp., 1971. Originally titled "Stone Nuts." Recorded: Decca DL-74183.

"Lydian April." 1959. Unpublished manuscript. Recorded: Indiana University School of Music Program, 1981–82, no. 682.

"MA279 Boogaloo." 1970. New York: Three Fifteen West Fifty-Third Street Corp., 1971.

"Maba Tila." 1973. Lebanon, Ind.: Studio PR, 1976. Also arranged for jazz septet. Recorded: Indiana University School of Music Program, 1993–94, no. 187.

"Make a Joyful Noise." 1963. Unpublished manuscript.

"M'am." 1953. Unpublished manuscript.

"Mama Tu." 1973. Unpublished manuscript.

"Mauma." 1973. Unpublished manuscript.

Miami Suite. 1991. Glendale, Calif.: Walrus Music, n.d. Contents: Tippin'; Miami Nights; Sunfest. Recorded: New World School of Music NWSA-002.

"Mid-Evil." 1973. Unpublished manuscript.

"Le Miroir noir." 1974. Lebanon, Ind.: Studio 224, 1977. Also arranged for jazz septet. Recorded: Larrikin LRJ-066.

"Moments." Unpublished manuscript. Recorded: Manna NR-16819.

"Mon." 1973. Unpublished manuscript. Note: uses same tune as "L'odeur de blues" from *Le Chat qui pêche.* Recorded: Larrikin LRJ-066.

"Monkin' Around." 1962. Unpublished manuscript.

"A Morning Thought." 1973. Unpublished manuscript.

"Naptown Strut." Unpublished manuscript. Recorded: Larrikin RJ-066.

"Nina, Ever New." 1966. Unpublished manuscript.

"NJSO Calypso." Unpublished manuscript. Recorded: Liscio Recordings LAS-31591.

"None a Place Me Be." 1971. Unpublished manuscript.

"One for J. S." 1969. New York: Three Fifteen West Fifty-Third Street Corp., 1970. Recorded: Indiana University School of Music Program, 1984–85, no. 410.

"121 Bank." 1960. Unpublished manuscript. Recorded: Decca DL-79220.

"125th Street." New York: Three Fifteen West Fifty-Third Street Corp., n.d.

"Padospe." 1982. Rottenburg, Germany: Advance Music, n.d. Recorded: Indiana University School of Music Program, 1995–96, no. 281; Laurel LR-505.

"Passion." 1956. Unpublished manuscript. Originally titled "Sandra." Recorded: Indiana University School of Music Program, 1969–70, no. 566.

"Peace My Brother." 1966. Unpublished manuscript. Recorded: Indiana University School of Music Program, 1969–70, no. 139.

"Penick." 1970. New York: Three Fifteen West Fifty-Third Street Corp., 1971. Recorded: Canterbury n.n.

"Po' Ned." 1956. Unpublished manuscript.

Prelude. 1967. New York: Three Fifteen West Fifty-Third Street Corp., 1970.

"The Professor." 1966. New York: Three Fifteen West Fifty-Third Street Corp., 1971. Recorded: Indiana University School of Music Program, 1981–82, no. 682.

"Ramu." 1972. Bowie, Md.: Creative Jazz Composers, n.d. Recorded: Indiana University School of Music Program, 1993–94, no. 194.

"Rex." 1973. Unpublished manuscript.

"Le Roi." 1957. Unpublished manuscript. Recorded: Atlantic 1428; ESP-Disk 1059; Fermata FB-97.

"Roly Poly." 1968. New York: Three Fifteen West Fifty-Third Street Corp., 1970. Recorded: Indiana University School of Music Program, 1970–71, no. 79.

"R.S.V.P. Mr. Moody." 1982. Rottenburg, Germany: Advance Music, n.d. Recorded: Indiana University School of Music Program, 1995–96, no. 281; Laurel LR-504.

"Satch" (two saxophones, trumpet, trombone, drums, double bass, piano). 1976. Lebanon, Ind.: Studio PR, 1976.

"Save Me a Place." Unpublished manuscript. Recorded: Manna NR-16819.

"The Screemin' Meemies." St. Louis, Mo.: MMB Music, n.d. Recorded: Indiana University School of Music Program, 1995–96, no. 281; Silver Crest CBD-69-6B.

"Set" (two saxophones, trumpet, trombone, drums, double bass, piano). 1976. Lebanon, Ind.: Studio PR, 1976.

"The Seven League Boots." 1970. New York: Three Fifteen West Fifty-Third Street Corp., 1970.

"Shadows." 1966. Unpublished manuscript. Recorded: Indiana University School of Music Program, 1969–70, no. 566.

"Sharing the Way." Unpublished manuscript. Recorded: Manna NR-16819.

"Shima 13." 1973. Lebanon, Ind.: Studio PR, 1976. Also arranged for jazz septet. Recorded: Indiana University School of Music Program, 1982–83, no. 167.

"The Silver Chalice." 1966. Unpublished manuscript. Recorded: Indiana University School of Music Program, 1990–91, no. 147; Silver Crest CBD-69-6B.

"Simplicity." 1973. Unpublished manuscript.

"Soft Summer Rain." St. Louis, Mo.: MMB Music, n.d. Recorded: Blue Note BST-84328; Manna NR-16819; Silver Crest CBD-69-6B.

"Soleil d'Altamira." 1974. Unpublished manuscript.

"Son Mar." 1968. New York: Three Fifteen West Fifty-Third Street Corp., 1970. Recorded: Indiana University School of Music Program, 1984–85, no. 410; Silver Crest CBD-69-6B.

"Soul of a Summer's Day." 1969. Unpublished manuscript.

"The Soul of '76." 1975. n.p.: J. C. Penney Company, 1976. Commissioned by J. C. Penney.

"Soul Six." 1969. Unpublished manuscript. Note: based on materials from "I Heard My Woman Call." Recorded: Indiana University School of Music Program, 1971–72, no. 128.

"Spepai." 1972. Unpublished manuscript.

"Splooch." 1962. Unpublished manuscript.

"Steppin' Out." 1990. Unpublished manuscript. Recorded: Liscio Recordings LAS-31591.

"Stereophrenic." 1959. Unpublished manuscript. Recorded: Riverside RLP-9412.

"Stickin'." 1973. Unpublished manuscript.

"Suite from Black America." 1970. Unpublished manuscript. Note: based on materials from Black America. Recorded: Indiana University School of Music Program, 1969–70, no. 566.

"A Summer's Day in 1945" or "Summer 1945" (jazz ensemble, prerecorded tape). 1968. Unpublished manuscript.

"10/21/17." 1996. Unpublished manuscript.

"Terrible T." 1962. New York: Three Fifteen West Fifty-Third Street Corp., 1970. Recorded: Indiana University School of Music Program, 1992–93, no. 558.

"Thaddeus." Unpublished manuscript. Recorded: Indiana University School of Music Program, 1986–87, no. 310.

"That's the Way, Lord Nelson." 1968. Unpublished manuscript. Also arranged for jazz septet. Commissioned by James Nelson.

"Thing." 1959. Unpublished manuscript.

"This One's for Trane." 1980. Unpublished manuscript. Recorded: Laurel LR-503.

"Three for Malcolm." 1970. Unpublished manuscript. Recorded: Indiana University School of Music Program, 1969–70, no. 566.

Three Vignettes (four horns, jazz ensemble). 1968. Unpublished manuscript. Recorded: Indiana University School of Music Program, 1970–71, no. 296.

"To Dizzy with Love." 1988. Unpublished manuscript. Recorded: Liscio LAS-31591.

"To the Fore." 1996. Unpublished manuscript.

"A Tribute to Wes." 1972. Unpublished manuscript. Premiere, 1972.

"Truckin'." 1992. Glendale, Calif.: Walrus Music, n.d. Recorded: Indiana University School of Music Program, 1991–92, no. 471.

"Tuffy." 1973. Unpublished manuscript.

"25th and Martindale." 1973. Lebanon, Ind.: Studio 224, 1977.

"Two Faces of The Black Frontier." 1971. Unpublished manuscript. Note: based on materials from The Black Frontier. Recorded: Canterbury n.n.

"Uncla." 1973. Unpublished manuscript.

"Unclee." 1973. Unpublished manuscript.

"Velvet Rose." 1996. Unpublished manuscript.

"Verism." 1959. Unpublished manuscript.

"Vibrations." 1972. Unpublished manuscript.

"Vortex." 1962. Unpublished manuscript.

"W830007K." 1975. Lebanon, Ind.: Studio PR, 1976. Also arranged for jazz septet. Recorded: Indiana University School of Music Program, 1984–85, no. 410.

"Walpurgisnacht" (jazz ensemble). 1975. Unpublished manuscript.

"Walt's Barbershop." 1974. Bowie, Md.: Creative Jazz Composers, n.d. Note: uses same tune as "Guadeloupe-Calypso" from Le Chat qui *pêche.* Recorded: Indiana University School of Music Program, 1986–87, no. 185; Larrikin LRJ-066.

"The Waltz." 1957. Unpublished manuscript.

"War gewesen." 1959. Unpublished manuscript. Recorded: Decca DL-74183.

"Wellspring." 1995. Unpublished manuscript. Commissioned by Indiana University.

"Western Song," 1966. Unpublished manuscript.

"When?" 1972. Unpublished manuscript.

"Whew!" 1972. Unpublished manuscript.

"A Wind in Summer." 1971. Unpublished manuscript. Recorded: Indiana University School of Music Program, 1991–92, no. 506.

PUBLICATIONS

ABOUT BAKER
Dissertations

Hildreth, John. "The Keyboard Works of a Select Group of Black Composers." Ph.D. diss., Northwestern University, 1978.

Thomas, André Jerome. "A Study of the Selected Masses of Twentieth-Century Black Composers: Margaret Bonds, Robert Ray, George Walker, and David Baker." D.M.A. diss., University of Illinois at Urbana–Champaign, 1983.

Articles

Baker, David N., Lida M. Belt, and Herman C. Hudson, eds. "David Nathaniel Baker, Jr." In *The Black Composer Speaks,* 15–69. Metuchen, N.J.: Scarecrow Press, 1978.

Elaine, Karen. "The Cadenzas to David Baker's Concert Piece for Viola." *Journal of the American Viola Society* 7 (Spring 1991): 21–32.

DeMicheal, D. "Vortex: The Dave Baker Story." *Down Beat* 31 (December 17, 1964): 14–18.

Lockhart-Moss, Eunice, and Elaine Guregian. "David Baker: Jazz Advocate." *Instrumentalist* 41 (December 1986): 10–14.

Schuller, Gunther. "Indiana Renaissance." *Jazz Revue* 2 (September 1959): 48–50.

Slothurnmann, Jurg. "The Diverse David Baker." *Jazz Forum* 7 (1973): 46–50.

Wilkerson, Michael. "'In This for Love': Jazzman David Baker's Extraordinary Career." *Journal of the New York Brass Conference for Scholarships* no. 19 (1991): 16–20.

BY BAKER
Books and Monographs

Advanced Ear Training for Jazz Musicians. Lebanon, Ind.: Studio PR, 1977.

Advanced Improvisation. 2 vols. Chicago: Maher Publications, 1974. Reprint, Bloomington, Ind.: Frangipani Press, 1979.

Arranging and Composing for the Small Ensemble: Jazz/R&B/Jazz-Rock. Rev. ed. Bloomington, Ind.: Frangipani Press, 1985. Reprint, Van Nuys, Calif.: Alfred, 1988.

Bebop Jazz Solos: Correlated with Volumes 10 and 13 of Jamey Aebersold's Play-A-Long Book and Record Series. New Albany, Ind.: Jamey Aebersold, 1981.

The Black Composer Speaks, edited by David N. Baker, Lida M. Belt, and Herman C. Hudson. Metuchen, N.J.: Scarecrow Press, 1978.

Charlie Parker, Alto Saxophone. New York: Shattinger, 1978.

Contemporary Patterns. New York: Charles Colin, 1979.

Contemporary Techniques for the Trombone. 2 vols. New York: Charles Colin, 1974.

A Consortium of Opinion on Jazz Education, edited by David N. Baker. Bowie, Md.: Creative Jazz Composers, n.d.

A Creative Approach to Practicing Jazz: New and Exciting Strategies for Unlocking Your Creative Potential. New Albany, Ind.: Jamey Aebersold Jazz, 1994.

Ear Training Tapes for Jazz Musicians. 5 vols. Lebanon, Ind.: Studio PR, 1981.

How to Learn Tunes: A Jazz Musician's Survival Guide. New Albany, Ind.: Jamey Aebersold Jazz, 1997.

How to Play Bebop. 3 vols. Bloomington, Ind.: Frangipani Press, 1985. Reprint, Van Nuys, Calif.: Alfred, 1987.

The Humanities through the Black Experience, with Phyllis Rauch Klotman, Marian Simmons Brown, Robert Klotman, Roslyn Adele Walker, and Jimmy L. Williams. Dubuque, Iowa: Kendall/Hunt, 1976.

Improvisational Patterns: The Bebop Era. 3 vols. New York: Charles Colin, 1979.

Improvisational Patterns: The Blues. New York: Charles Colin, 1980.

J. J. Johnson, Trombone. New York: Shattinger, 1979.

Jazz Bass Clef Expressions and Explorations: A New and Innovative System for Learning to Improvise for Bass Clef Instruments and Jazz Cello. New Albany, Ind.: Jamey Aebersold Jazz, 1995.

Jazz Etudes: Correlated with Volumes 5 and 6 of Jamey Aebersold's Play-a-Long Book and Record Series. New Albany, Ind.: Jamey Aebersold, 1979.

Jazz Improvisation: A Comprehensive Method of Study for All Players. Rev. ed. Bloomington, Ind.: Frangipani Press, 1983.

Jazz Improvisation: Eine umfassende Methode für alle Instrumente. Rottenburg, Germany: Advance Music, n.d.

A Jazz Improvisation Method for Stringed Instruments. 2 vols. Chicago: Maher Publications, 1976.

Jazz Pedagogy: A Comprehensive Method of Jazz Education for Teacher and Student. Chicago: Maher Publications, 1979. Reprint, Van Nuys, Calif.: Alfred, 1989.

The Jazz Quiz Book, with Jeanne Baker. Bloomington, Ind.: Frangipani Press, 1984.

The Jazz Style of Cannonball Adderley: A Musical and Historical Perspective. Lebanon, Ind.: Studio PR, 1980.

The Jazz Style of Clifford Brown: A Musical and Historical Perspective. Lebanon, Ind.: Studio PR, 1982.

The Jazz Style of Fats Navarro: A Musical and Historical Perspective. Lebanon, Ind.: Studio PR, 1982.

The Jazz Style of John Coltrane: A Musical and Historical Perspective. Lebanon, Ind.: Studio PR, 1980.

The Jazz Style of Miles Davis: A Musical and Historical Perspective. Lebanon, Ind.: Studio PR, 1980.

The Jazz Style of Sonny Rollins: A Musical and Historical Perspective. Lebanon, Ind.: Studio PR, 1980.

Jazz Styles and Analysis: Alto Sax, edited by David N. Baker. Chicago: *Down Beat* Music Workshop Publications, 1975.

Jazz Styles and Analysis: Trombone. Chicago: Maher Publications, 1973. Reprint, Bloomington, Ind.: Frangipani Press, 1979.

Jazz Treble Clef Expressions and Explorations: A New and Innovative System for Learning to Improvise for Treble Clef Instruments and Jazz Violin. New Albany, Ind.: Jamey Aebersold Jazz, 1995.

Miles Davis: Trumpet. New York: Shattinger, 1978.

Modal and Contemporary Patterns. New York: Charles Colin, 1979.

Modern Concepts in Jazz Improvisation: A Comprehensive Method for All Musicians. A New Approach to Fourths, Pentatonics, and Bitonals. Van Nuys, Calif.: Alfred, 1990.

Modern Jazz Duets: For All Bass Clef Instruments. 2 vols. New York: Charles Colin, 1979.

Modern Jazz Duets: For All Trebel [sic] Clef Instruments. 2 vols. New York: Charles Colin, 1979.

The Monk Montgomery Electric Bass Method, edited by David N. Baker. Lebanon, Ind.: Studio PR, 1978.

A New Approach to Ear Training for the Jazz Musician. Lebanon, Ind.: Studio PR, 1976.

New Perspectives in Jazz: Report on a National Conference Held at Wingspread, Racine, Wisconsin, September 8–10, 1986. Washington, D.C.: Smithsonian Institution, 1990.

Techniques of Improvisation, Volume 1: A Method for Developing Improvisational Technique (Based on the Lydian Chromatic Concept by George Russell). Rev. ed. Chicago: Maher Publications, 1971.

Techniques of Improvisation, Volume 2: The II V7 Progression. Rev. ed. Chicago: Maher Publications, 1971.

Techniques of Improvisation, Volume 3: Turnbacks. Chicago: Maher Publications, 1971.

Techniques of Improvisation, Volume 4: Cycles. Chicago: Maher Publications, 1971.

Articles

"An Approach to Acquiring Facility with the Bebop Vocabulary through the Practice and Study of Bebop Compositions." *Jazz Player* 2 (February/March 1995): 59–61.

"The Battle for Legitimacy: 'Jazz' Versus Academia." *Black World* (November 1973): 20–27.

"The Bebop Major Scale." *Jazz Player* 1 (April/May 1994): 40–41.

"The Bebop Scales, Dominant and Major." *Jazz Educator* 17, no. 3 (1985): 8–11.

"Chord Substitutions and Bitonals. Part I: Non-Contextual Substitutions." *Jazz Player* 3 (December 1995/January 1996): 63, 79.

"Chord Substitutions and Bitonals. Part II: Contextual Substitutions." *Jazz Player* 3 (February/March 1996): 48–49.

"Creating Contrafacts and Using Them in Imaginative and Challenging Ways." *Jazz Player* 3 (April/May 1996): 17–19.

"Creating Contrafacts and Using Them in Imaginative and Challenging Ways, Part II." *Jazz Player* 3 (August/September 1996): 25–27.

"Creative Scale Practicing." *Jazz Player* 1 (June/July 1994): 20–21.

"Improvisation: A Tool for Musical Learning." *Music Educators Journal* 66 (January 1980): 42–51.

"Improvisational Techniques and Performance Practices Related to the Various Jazz Styles." In *100 Years of Jazz and Blues Festival,* 651. Brooklyn, N.Y.: Kings Majestic, 1992.

"Jazz Improvisation—The Weak Link." *Instrumentalist* (November 26, 1971): 21–24.

"A Periodization of Black Music History." In *Reflections on Afro-American Music,* edited by Dominique-René de Lerma. Kent, Ohio: Kent State University Press, 1973.

"Perspectives of John Coltrane, 1926–1967: Profile of a Giant." *NAJE Educator* 11 (February/March 1979): 10+.

"Playing on 'I Got Rhythm' Changes. Part I: Rhythm Changes for the Novice." *Jazz Player* 2 (April/May 1995): 39–40.

"Playing on 'I Got Rhythm' Changes. Part II: Traditional Approaches to Rhythm Changes." *Jazz Player* 2 (June/July 1995): 24–25.

"Playing on 'I Got Rhythm' Changes. Part III: Using Bebop Compositions as an Approach to Learning to Play Rhythm Changes." *Jazz Player* 2 (August/September 1995): 60–61.

"Playing on 'I Got Rhythm' Changes. Part IV: Expanding the Horizons of Playing 'I Got Rhythm' Changes." *Jazz Player* 2 (October/November 1995): 20–21.

"The Rhetorical Dimensions of Black Music: Past and Present." In *Black Communication: Dimensions of Research and Instruction,* edited by Jack L. Daniel. New York: Speech Communication Association, 1974.

"The String Approach in Jazz." *Orchestra News* (March 9, 1970): 5–6; (May 9, 1970): 8–9; (September 9, 1970): 10–11. Reprinted as "The String Player in Jazz," *Down Beat* 5 (March 5, 1970); (April 30, 1970); (May 28, 1970).

"Teaching Jazz." *Jazz Player* (December 1993): 6–7.

"Teaching Jazz." *Jazz Player* (February/March 1994): 44–45.

"A Technique for Learning Tunes: Melody and Changes." *Jazz Player* (August/September 1994): 58–59.

"A Technique for Learning Tunes: Melody and Changes, Part II." *Jazz Player* (October/November 1994): 42–43.

"A Technique for Learning Tunes: Melody and Changes, Part III." *Jazz Player* 1 (December 1994/January 1995): 55–56.

Regular contributions to *Down Beat.*

* * * * *

As composer, performer, and educator, David Baker stands among the front rank of American musicians of his generation. Equally well versed in jazz and Western concert music, he has created works in both styles and synthesized them in many works that are Third Stream (merging contemporary Western art music and jazz or vernacular musics).

A prolific composer, Baker has written more than 2,000 compositions, a fact made more remarkable because of the great range of material he has embraced. His works include five-minute jazz charts ("Kentucky Oysters," 1958; "Terrible T," 1962; "Bebop Revisited," 1974; "Birdsong," 1984; and countless others), chamber music for traditional and more unusual combinations, art and jazz-oriented songs (often arranged in cycles with texts by different authors on a central, unifying theme), and large-scale dramatic works, such as the oratorio *The Beatitudes* (1968), and a "jazz ballet," *Sangre Negro* (1974). He has also worked in electronic media, in works such as "Electric Stere-Opticon" for cello and electronic instruments (1975).

Baker grew up in Indianapolis, Indiana, where he began the study of music in the Indianapolis public schools. By his teens, he had settled on the trombone, and he was on his way toward a career in music by the time he graduated from Crispus Attucks High School (the only black high school in a still-segregated city), at the time a hothouse of black cultural achievement led by a remarkably strong faculty recruited from across the country. The composer still credits band director Russell W. Brown and his high school years generally as "major influences" on his subsequent development. Baker had been preceded at Attucks by such notables as J. J. Johnson and Wes Montgomery, and he recalls Slide Hampton among his classmates. Early contacts thus shaped his future.

Beginning in the late 1940s and through the early 1950s, he was performing in important groups as diverse as the big bands of Maynard Ferguson, Lionel Hampton, Quincy Jones, and Stan Kenton, and in small groups led by Wes Montgomery and Harold Land. Perhaps most important of all, he played in George Russell's seminal sextet. He also received knowledgeable tutelage in the craft of jazz trombone performance from such masters as Bobby Brookmeyer and J. J. Johnson. From contacts and experience gleaned within these groups and influential, early composition studies with Russell (a mentor-like figure for the young composer), John Lewis, Gunther Schuller, and William Russo, Baker quickly developed into a skilled arranger and composer. A 1953 accident forestalled his career as a trombonist, yet Baker responded by turning to a rigorous curriculum of cello studies with Leopold Teraspulsky and Jules Eskin. He has since pioneered the use of the cello in jazz.

Baker returned to his native state for further musical studies at Indiana University (B.Mus.Ed., 1953; M.Mus.Ed., 1954), receiving additional instruction from composer Bernard Heiden and, later, cellist Janos Starker within a rich musical environment that fostered Baker's manifold musical sensibilities. Following various teaching posts in Missouri, Indiana, and as a private instructor, he returned to Bloomington in 1966 a complete musician, writing a full-scale concert work utilizing jazz ensemble and orchestra, *Reflections* (*My Indianapolis*), in 1969. He has spent the past 30 years there, establishing one of the country's premiere jazz studies departments and encouraging younger generations of musicians with his seemingly endless compendium of experience. He has nurtured an incredible list of eminently successful students, both studio musicians and front-line artists, from the Brecker brothers to Robert Hurst. He has also taught countless others using a long list of pedagogical publications explaining the crafts of jazz composition, improvisation, and arranging. His role as a cultural leader has spawned countless important appointments, from the Indiana Arts Commission to the Folk Music and Jazz Advisory Panel of the U.S. Department of State to service as chairman of the Jazz, Folk, and Ethnic Advisory Panel of the National Endowment for the Arts.

Baker's vast experience is a key to his extraordinarily rich compositional style. His secure knowledge of the range of techniques and forms associated with Western art music reflects the fact that he credits Ives and Bartók among his primary influences. His compositional style encompasses sonatas (ten such works between 1966 and 1974 and others since, including neobaroque trio sonatas) and sonata forms (many concertos since the 1970s), on the one hand, and serial technique, used more as a coloristic device than a compositional mantra, on the other. Baker fuses diverse influences—Bach, Beethoven, and Brahms with blues, boogie-woogie, and bebop—into a highly personal yet always inviting style. A

piece such as his "Ethnic Variations on a Theme of Paganini" for violin (1976) is indicative of his flexible, fluid historiography. Much of the spirit of Baker's music stems from the vitality of its roots: African-American folk traditions (work songs, spirituals, and dance musics) and jazz in its many guises (from Jimmy Yancy to James Moody). Recent works such as *Roots II* for piano trio (1992) embody this spirit alongside earlier efforts. Although the folk source is often readily apparent in Baker's programs (many of his works are multimovement pieces with descriptive titles), ultimately the source itself is subsumed within Baker's creation, saturating the style of the music but not dominating the surface of the piece.

A recurring theme of Baker's work is homage, which is thoroughly understandable given his vocations as teacher and performer and his place in history. Certain figures stand out as particularly important in this regard. Surely paramount here is Duke Ellington (e.g., *Ellingtones: A Fantasy for Saxophone and Orchestra,* on a commission by the New York Philharmonic, one of Baker's most important works), around whom Baker's style departs in its own directions, reshaped by the singular voices of Louis Armstrong and Dizzy Gillespie, Sonny Rollins and John Coltrane. As with virtually every jazz artist since, bop innovator Charlie Parker also stands at the center of Baker's "bebop-and-beyond" approach to jazz training, composition, and performance practice. Parker figures prominently in *Birdsong* for orchestra and other pieces, in Baker's classroom teaching, and in his 21st-Century Bebop Band (a big band based at Indiana University devoted to keeping the bebop literature alive). Yet if other notables, such as Paul Robeson, Bessie Smith, and Dinah Washington, continue to tease Baker's muse, his inspirations, like his music, are not simply icon worship; rather, they grow from a fundamental, improvisatory approach to the craft of composition (e.g., "Improvisation" nos. 1 and 2 for unaccompanied violin, 1975). Baker's music demonstrates that he believes deeply in its many sources.

The variety of texts to which Baker has set his works ranges from biblical passages to poems by Langston Hughes and Arna Bontemps, Mari Evans and Solomon Edwards. *Through This Vale of Tears,* for tenor, string quartet, and piano (1986), illustrates this diversity, with psalm settings alternating with texts by Evans, Edwards, Carl Hines, and the Negro spiritual "Sometimes I Feel Like a Motherless Child." The cantata *Black America: To the Memory of Martin Luther King, Jr.* (1968) is a free mixture of texts reflecting on the slain leader.

In his long and productive career, Baker has demonstrated the rare ability to constantly change and revitalize his style without forsaking his "characteristic voice."

KENTUCKY OYSTERS (1958)

Written in 1958 for the George Russell Sextet and recorded on the group's album *Stratusphunk*, "Kentucky Oysters" is indicative of Baker's early work for jazz ensemble. In a bit of understatement, Russell called the piece "a good old funky, down-home blues in 3/4," and in his own analysis, the composer recalled that one observer at the recording session heard the work as "twenty-first century soul music," which may capture its essence more accurately.

In its mixture of blues harmonies with modal thinking and daring chord substitutions and with contrasts between duple and triple rhythmic groupings within a blues chorus structure, Baker retains the "down-home" funk of the blues in a rather progressive vehicle for improvisation. Thus, in this composition, Baker demonstrates early in his career the ability to fuse tradition with innovation (a blues, but in a triple meter continually reshaped by hemiola [two against three] patterns), vernacular materials (soul and funk), and concepts born of rigorous study (modal jazz) and practice (bebop).

The events of the piece, its "composition," grow as much from the notated "head" as from the five-chorus trombone solo by Baker at its center. The head provides the musical setting of the piece as well as its fundamental materials. These materials are systematically recalled in the solo, but they are not merely recomposed; rather, the solo is an organic continuation of the work, with its own integrity, growing both away from and toward the material around it.

The solo section is held together through the performer's progression from a low volume, restrained pace of rhythmic activity and harmonic exploration toward greater energy in nearly every parameter. Baker's linking of material across choruses (the ends of choruses two and three, and the middles of choruses three and four) unifies the composition beyond the simple level of chorus repetition, and his skillful placing of quotations from the head of the composition at the beginning of the second chorus and the end of the last effectively weaves together the loose-fitting fabric of solo improvisation with the sturdy material—a well-wrought, fertile head—at the composition's outset and conclusion.

SINGERS OF SONGS/WEAVERS OF DREAMS (1980)

Baker describes *Singers of Songs/Weavers of Dreams* for cello and 17 percussion instruments as an "homage to my friends." They include his longtime colleagues at Indiana University—cellist Janos Starker and percussionist George Gaber (for whom the work was written)—and seven prominent musicians of this century: Miles Davis, Sonny Rollins, Jimmy Yancy, Paul Robeson, John Coltrane, Duke Ellington, and Dizzy Gillespie. The seven brief movements are symmetrically arranged, the three longer middle movements being framed by four shorter movements in pairs. The opening movement, "Rollins," is scored for the battery of percussion instruments and described by the composer as being "inspired by Sonny Rollins' now standard 'St. Thomas.'" It recalls the carefree quality of the calypso, which is prominent in Rollins's style. The more enigmatic side of Miles Davis (the Davis of his mid-1960s group, for example) is effectively captured and reflected upon in the suite's second movement, with appropriately breathless cello lines accompanied by wind chimes. The powerful boogie-woogie piano style of Jimmy Yancy is caught in the third movement, a rhythmic tour de force with equally prominent and powerful blues riffs. The central movement, "Robeson," is the apex of the suite. Two spirituals are quoted as songs-without-words: "Go Down Moses" and, a Baker favorite, "Sometimes I Feel Like a Motherless Child." In this movement, the aesthetics of the spiritual are thrown into sharp relief. "Trane" juxtaposes *pizzicato* cello against timpani in what amounts to a quick sketch of Coltrane's early career, with the tenor saxophonist's famous "sheets of sound" confidently finding their way through unorthodox harmonies reminiscent of Thelonious Monk. The penultimate movement, "Duke," focuses on Ellington the orchestrator, ranging across a rich palette of harmonic colors cen-

tral to Ellington's language. The suite closes with the composer's evocation of the multifaceted personality "Dizzy" via bebop and Latin rhythms. Throughout, the percussionist acts as a one-man rhythm section, and the cellist wears many musical guises. These roles cross over the course of this 25-minute piece, as the composer exploits the melodic capabilities of the percussion instruments and the *pizzicato* cello as "the backbone of jazz," the bass.

Singers of Songs/Weavers of Dreams is a work intended for concert performance, notwithstanding the fact that it effectively captures the spirit of jazz and its roots.

THROUGH THIS VALE OF TEARS (1986)

Through This Vale of Tears is a song cycle for tenor, string quartet, and piano, composed for tenor William Brown. Its subject is the death of Dr. Martin Luther King Jr. and the sense of loss caused by his assassination. Contrasting texts include settings of verses from Psalm 22, a traditional spiritual, and modern African-American poetry. In the first and last movements, "Thou Dost Lay Me in the Dust of Death" and "Now That He Is Safely Dead," the composer reworks material from his cantata *Black America,* demonstrating a penchant for the critical re-elaboration that is central to Baker's compositional maturation. These opening and closing movements thus both frame this work and link it with its predecessor in his catalog. Both outer movements are based in the style of the baroque chorale setting, the former through the use of continuo-style writing, the latter as a manifestation of catharsis (a point of clarity at the very end emerging from within the hazy dream that precedes it). Yet these two movements are contrasted significantly in their texts, the first being a paraphrase from the psalm and the second a setting of a poetic eulogy by Carl Hines.

The five movements encased by these moments alternate other verses from the Psalm 22 text with the work of other contemporary poets. "If There Be Sorrow" sets the collection's most modern poetry, by Mari Evans, with appropriately disjointed music and craggy melodic lines atop dissonant harmony. The third ("My God, Why Hast Thou Forsaken Me?") and fifth ("Deliver My Soul") draw on the psalm text (verses one and 20 respectively) and capture qualities of the spiritual and gospel repertoires. They are thus among the most tradition-bound moments in the cycle. Yet typical of Baker's omnipresent, vernacular vision, "Deliver My Soul" "steps out" in moments of relaxation, featuring a waltz and prominent use of scat singing. The work's fourth and middle movement, "Parades to Hell," sets a text by Solomon Edwards; its aggressive character persuasively stands apart from the docile movements around it, drawing the listener's attention to Edward's powerful text (for example, "It's rough all day to roll a stone away, To let a stranger in who'll run off with your soul"). In the penultimate movement, Baker returns to "Sometimes I Feel Like a Motherless Child," but not as patently as in some of his other works, for here the sentiments of the text have especially powerful, symbolic meaning as the martyr and his followers both confront death.

ROOTS II (1992)

This work for piano trio (piano, violin, cello) is a reworking of *Roots* written in 1976, also for piano trio. The first and third movements, "Incantation" and "Sorrow Song," of the earlier work are reused in *Roots II*. Both versions were written for the Beaux Arts Trio, and the newer one was premiered by the trio at the Library of Congress in 1993. For the recording of the work, Baker wrote that there are many strands woven into this piece: "work songs, field hollers, blues, ragtime, boogie-woogie, rhythm & blues, spirituals, gospel songs, calypso, rock & roll, rap and of course jazz. . . . I made use of some of the musical features common to these varied styles, among them rhythmic preeminence, the spirit and attitude of the blues call and response, the ostinato, and certain musical forms, harmonic and melodic materials."

This five movement suite ("Incantation," "Dance in Congo Square," "Sorrow Song," "Boogie Woogie," and "Jubilee") can be viewed as a kind of history, progressing metaphorically from Africa to the New World to down the street, and from a distant past to the future. Although each movement connotes different times and places, the whole of the work grows from the various elements cited by the composer that unify their rich musical diversity.

The first movement is in ternary form (ABA') and is characterized by a persistent drone figure that moves between the tonic and subtonic (lowered leading tone) in E minor. The outer sections of the movement are marked by this drone figure (played by the piano), which serves as a framing device for the contrasting texture introduced in the B section. The violin and cello play an interpretation (through fragmentation) of the spiritual "Sometimes I Feel Like a Motherless Child" over the drone figure, setting a profoundly serious mood for the suite. The middle section (B) abandons the drone figure, creating contrast through a more active dialogue between the three instruments and moving more freely as melodic responsibilities are passed from one instrument to the next. A transition marks the return of the drone figure, and the movement closes in contemplative fashion, perhaps pointing to the conflict between the old world (Africa) and the new (America).

The second movement, "Dance in Congo Square," is inspired by the slave gatherings that took place in the Place Congo of pre–Civil War New Orleans and is in sectional form. It opens with a slow, arpeggiated piano introduction that creates a stylistic bridge between the first and second movements of the suite. The introduction is followed by a cello recitative (marked as such in the score) that introduces a C-major harmonic cycle (I–I^6–IV–ii–V$^{(7)}$–I). In the section that follows, this harmonic cycle functions as an ostinato over which the violin introduces the main theme of the movement—a calypso. The theme is then manipulated in a series of varied statements through which Baker suggests a joyful atmosphere. Yet his occasional, heavy use of dissonance suggests that this movement may carry a bittersweet subtext. The calypso, after all, is neither an African nor an American music but is imported from other slave cultures in the Caribbean.

The third movement functions as the work's centerpiece, summing up elements of the spirituals, laments, and shouts of the black church. Like the spirituals upon which it is based, "Sorrow Song," cast in an ABA form, is double-voiced, moaning and bittersweet. The melodic line is lyrical and long, and Baker makes use variously of call-and-response, unison, and soloistic textures. The rich and extended tertian sonorities are continually completed by

way of ascending arpeggios, which might be read as an appeal to a higher power—as an expression of faith.

The fourth movement, "Boogie Woogie," recalls, in a stylized and inventive manner, the energetic, highly rhythmic characteristics of the 1930s popular piano style after which it is named. While the motoric rhythms of the style are incorporated into the piano part of the movement, Baker's changes of meter at key points in the progression disrupt the normal rhythmic cycle of the style. In addition, the violin and cello parts are called upon to play very blues-influenced melodic materials, thereby shifting the style of the movement into a more hybrid space. This movement is another excellent example of Baker's ability to create allusions to several genres simultaneously.

The suite concludes with "Jubilee," a hopeful and celebratory movement in sectional form that derives its momentum from an upwardly arpeggiating figure in the piano part. This figure consists of alternating left- and right-hand open fifths that ascend through a three-octave range. The drive of the climbing effect is further strengthened by the introduction of a vibrant and energetic theme in the violin and cello parts. Later sections explore the theme through call-and-response and elaboration rather than through development of shorter motives. The piano abandons the arpeggiating figure in favor of a more melodic and dialogical role during the middle sections of the movement, only to return to the figure at the conclusion of the movement.

Roots II can be compared with *Singers of Songs* in order to appreciate prominent aspects of Baker's style and to note his development over the dozen years between the works. Both were written for specific performers and reflect prominent influences, but the later work is clearly a synthesis of the composer's thinking as it moved well beyond evocation and homage toward spiritual commentary and reflection.

REFERENCES

Baker, David. *Jazz Improvisation: A Comprehensive Method of Study for All Players*. Chicago: Maher Publications, 1969.

———. Liner notes, *Starker Plays Baker*. Laurel LR-117, 1981.

Baker, David, Lida M. Belt, and Herman C. Hudson, eds. *The Black Composer Speaks*. Metuchen, N.J.: Scarecrow Press, 1978.

Enright, Ed. "IU to Decide on Jazz Doctorate Program Proposal." *Down Beat* (January 1995): 58.

Ledbetter, Steven. "Three Different Ways to Be American." Liner notes, *Spring Music: Works by Baker, Rochberg, Rorem*, 2–4. Polygram/Philips 438 868-2.

Moore, Carman. "Baker, David (Nathaniel)." *New Grove Dictionary of American Music*, edited by Stanley Sadie, 1: 114. London: Macmillan, 1986.

Taylor, Billy. Liner notes, *Videmus: Works by T. J. Anderson, David Baker, Donal Fox, and Olly Wilson*. New World 80423-2, 1992.

Thomas, André Jerome. "A Study of the Selected Masses of Twentieth-Century Black Composers: Margaret Bonds, Robert Ray, George Walker, and David Baker." Ph.D. diss., University of Illinois, 1983.

JOHN ANDREW JOHNSON

BANFIELD, WILLIAM CEDRIC

Born in Detroit, Mich., March 24, 1961. **Education:** Detroit, Mich., public elementary school, began guitar studies, age 9; Cass Technical High School, 1975–79; New England Conservatory of Music, Boston, Mass., studied composition with George Russell, Mick Goodrich, and William Thomas McKinley, 1979–83, B.Mus., guitar performance, 1983; Tufts University, Medford, Mass., studied composition with T. J. Anderson, 1982–83; New England Conservatory, studied orchestration with Michael Gibbs, 1984; Boston University, studied composition with Theodore Antoniou, 1985–87, M.A., Theological Studies, 1988; University of Michigan-Ann Arbor, studied composition with Fred Lerdahl, Leslie Bassett, William Bolcolm, and William Albright, 1988–92, D.M.A., 1992; studied jazz arranging and composition with Patrick Hollenbeck, Theodore Antinou, Donal Fox. **Composing and Performing Career:** Detroit, Mich., played guitar in professional bands including Cool Breeze and The Sapphire, beginning age 12; Boston, Mass., founded Bill Banfield Quintet, 1980; Boston, Mass., B Magic Operations recording and production company, founder and operator, 1984–88; Detroit Metropolitan Orchestra, guest guitar soloist, 1984, 1989; Senegal, West Africa, conducted La Chorale des Martyrs de L'Ouganda (Senegalese Choir and Orchestra), 1988; University of Michigan-Ann Arbor, assistant musical director, *The People Could Fly,* 1989; Indiana University, Undine Smith Moore Collection, founder, 1993. **Teaching Career:** Boston, Mass., public schools, 1980–86; Tanglewood Music Festival, Tanglewood, Mass., music director, Days in the Arts program, 1984–88; Union United Church, Boston, minister of education, 1984–88; Boston Theological Institute, program coordinator, 1985–88; Young Artists Development Inc. (YADI), Boston, founder and director, 1985–88; Boston Music Community Center, 1986–88; University of Michigan-Ann Arbor, guitar instructor, 1988–89, jazz instructor, 1988–90; Ann Arbor, Mich., private instructor in composition, arranging, and guitar pedagogy, 1988–92; Hartford Biblical Studies Institute, Detroit, Mich., instructor, 1989–92; Indiana University-Bloomington, assistant professor, Department of Afro-American Studies, 1992–97; Indiana University/Purdue University at Indianapolis, professor of music, 1992–97; Afro-American Arts Institute, Indiana University, Soul Revue/Black Popular Arts Ensemble, director and composer-in-residence, 1992–97; Indiana University-Bloomington, composer-in-residence and director, Black Popular Arts, 1992–97; Plymouth Music Series of Minnesota, Minneapolis, Witness Series/Composer in Residence, 1993, 1995; visiting artist and scholar at various institutions including University of Michigan-Ann Arbor, 1994, Carleton College, 1995, St. Augustine College, 1995, Tufts University, 1995, University of Massachusetts-Amherst, 1995, University of Minneapolis, 1995, Butler University, 1996, Duke University, 1996, University of Akron, 1996; University of St. Thomas, St. Paul, Minn., endowed chair in the Humanities and Fine Arts, 1997–present. **Commissions:** Detroit Symphony, 1983; Union United Church, 1986; Second Baptist Church of Detroit, 1988; 4: (four factorial), 1991; Plymouth Music Series of Minnesota, 1992;

Thamyris, 1992; Akron Symphony Orchestra, 1993. **Memberships:** American Guild of Organists, National Advisory Council; ASCAP; College Music Society; Minnesota Composers Forum; National Association of Negro Musicians. **Honors/Awards:** Youth for Understanding, Chrysler Corporation Scholarship, 1978; Boston Foundation Artist Award, 1987; Polaroid Arts Grant, 1987; T. Jones Music and Arts Grant, 1987; Massachusetts Council of the Arts, Composers Recording Grant, 1988; Massachusetts Council of the Arts, Heritage Grant, 1988; Detroit Council of the Arts, Composers Grant, 1989; American Academy of Arts and Sciences composition award nomination, 1993; winner, Savannah Symphony American Symphony Orchestra League national search for black talent, 1993; American Music Center Copying Grant, 1994; National Endowment for the Arts recording grant, 1994; University of St. Thomas, Carleton College, McKnight Foundation Composers in Residence Fellowship, awarded by the American Composers Forum, 1995–96; Indiana University, Research Undergraduate School (RUGS) Research Grant, 1995; University of Utah, Spectrum Visiting Scholars Award, 1995; Technology Transfer Operations (TTO) Arts Recording/Scholarship Grant, 1995; Detroit Symphony/UNISYS award for *Essay for Orchestra,* 1995; Atlanta Symphony/National Black Arts Festival contest, finalist, 1994; Akron Symphony/NEA Recording Commission, 1995; Duke University/St. Augustine College William Grant Still Commission for Composition, 1995. **Mailing Address:** St. Thomas University, BEC9, 2115 Summit Ave., St. Paul, MN 55105.

MUSIC LIST

INSTRUMENTAL SOLOS
Oboe
"Gibbit." 1985; revised 1992. Unpublished manuscript. Note: originally entitled "Gibb It."

Bassoon
Two Tall Tales for Bassoon. 1992. Unpublished manuscript. Premiere, 1994.

Trumpet
Suite for Richard. 1990. Unpublished manuscript.

Guitar
"Balcones dela Luna" Unpublished manuscript.
"Belshazzar" (unaccompanied guitar). 1981. Unpublished manuscript.
"Hanaha" (unaccompanied guitar). 1981. Unpublished manuscript.
"Karla" (unaccompanied guitar). 1982. Unpublished manuscript.
"Song for Earl" (unaccompanied guitar). 1983. Unpublished manuscript.
"Song for Mic" (unaccompanied guitar). 1983. Unpublished manuscript.

Piano
"Fantasy." 1987. Unpublished manuscript.
"I V bVIII 5 b7 b7." 1982. Unpublished manuscript.

"A Little Look at Me." 1982. Unpublished manuscript.

"Mead 28." 1989. Unpublished manuscript.

"One Segment Samba." 1981. Unpublished manuscript.

"Reversed Roles." 1981. Unpublished manuscript.

"A Stroll in Lydian." 1981. Unpublished manuscript.

"Waggussyduke." 1989. Unpublished manuscript. Recorded: Innova 510.

"Warmly Embraced." 1980. Unpublished manuscript.

SMALL INSTRUMENTAL ENSEMBLE
Strings

"Bobby's Theme" (guitar quintet). 1985. Unpublished manuscript.

"Brooke" (guitar, string quartet). ca. 1985. Unpublished manuscript.

"Cone Tone: String Quartet no. 3." 1989. Unpublished manuscript. Recorded: Innova 510.

"Derwin E.: Six Minutes for String Quartet no. 1." 1983. Unpublished manuscript.

"El Dia de Derber: Wedding Suite for String Quartet and Piano." 1985. Unpublished manuscript. Premiere, 1985.

"Susan: String Quartet no. 2." 1985. Unpublished manuscript. Note: originally entitled "Song for Susan" or "String Quartet: Suite for Strings."

Woodwinds

Dance Like the Wind (woodwind quintet). 1995. Unpublished manuscript. Contents: She's Making Coffee; All Four in the Car; Dance Like the Wind. Recorded: Collins Classics 14762.

Combinations

"Brass Belly" (poet, piano, strings, flute, oboe/clarinet, alto saxophone, percussion). 1988. Unpublished manuscript.

"Can We All Get Along?" (piano, flute, clarinet, saxophone, percussion). 1992. St. Louis: MMB Music. Premiere, 1992.

"For Bass Wrapped in Pita Pocket with Ketchup, Mayo and a Dash of Hot Mustard" (four double basses, piano, percussion). 1991. Unpublished manuscript. Premiere, 1991.

"Four Persons" (oboe, clarinet, bassoon, piano). 1991. St Louis: MMB Music. Commissioned by 4: (four factorial). Recorded: Innova 510. Premiere, 1991.

"Spirituals" (piano, strings, flutes, clarinet, horn, trombone). 1988. Unpublished manuscript.

"Zola" (piano, violin, bass trumpet, flute, oboe, cello). 1988. Unpublished manuscript. Premiere, 1988.

FULL ORCHESTRA

Dream Realized/Nightmare Resolved: Symphony no. 2. 1992. St Louis: MMB Music. Notes: D.M.A. diss., University of Michigan–Ann Arbor, 1992; this work received a nomination for recognition in composition from the American Academy of Arts and Sciences in 1993. Premiere, 1993.

Essay for Orchestra. Unpublished manuscript. Premiere, 1995.

Fantasy for Orchestra on Themes from Shakespeare. 1989. Unpublished manuscript.

Four Songs for Five American Voices: Symphony no. 6. 1993. Unpublished manuscript. Commissioned by the Akron Symphony Orchestra. Contents: If Bernstein Wrote It . . . ; In an Ellington Mood; I'm DIZzy Over Miles; Someone Said Her Name Was Sarah. Premiere, 1994. Recorded: Telarc CD-80409.

Streams of Consciousness: Symphony no. 4. Unpublished manuscript. Premiere, 1996.

Symphony no. 1: *Brevities of Experience.* 1990. St. Louis: MMB Music. Premiere, 1992.

Symphony no. 5: *Five Shades of a Women in Black.* Boston: B Magic Music, 1993. Note: finalist in the National Black Arts Festival and Atlanta Symphony Orchestra competition, 1994.

ORCHESTRA (CHAMBER OR FULL) WITH SOLOISTS

Baroque Suite for Guitar and String Orchestra. 1987. Unpublished manuscript.

Delancey Street (tuba, orchestra). Unpublished manuscript. Premiere, 1994.

Heather (guitar, chamber orchestra). Unpublished manuscript. Also arranged for unaccompanied guitar and for guitar, flute, oboe, piano, violin, cello.

Jenny Festival for Guitar and Orchestra. 1989. Unpublished manuscript. Premiere, 1989.

Marsheila (voice, chamber orchestra). 1982. Unpublished manuscript. Also arranged for voice, string quartet, soprano saxophone, piano.

Moods and Colors: Concerto for Trombone and Orchestra. 1991. Unpublished manuscript.

96/66 Concerto for Guitar and Orchestra. ca. 1983; revised 1985. Unpublished manuscript. Note: originally entitled *96/66 Fantasy for Guitar and Orchestra.* Contents: Magdelena; Derry Alan; Stravinski; Lynne. Premiere, 1984.

Susej Moments for Guitar and String Orchestra. 1987. Unpublished manuscript.

Symphony no. 7: *Reveries, a Summer's Circle* (mezzo-soprano, chorus, orchestra). Unpublished manuscript. Premiere, 1997.

Three Movements and Themes on Shakespeare (speaker, orchestra). 1988. Unpublished manuscript.

Universal Love Concern (voice, chamber orchestra). Unpublished manuscript.

You Can Tell the World (soprano, orchestra). Unpublished manuscript. Premiere, 1992.

ORCHESTRA (CHAMBER OR FULL) WITH CHORUS

Guide Us through the Years (SATB, orchestra). 1988. Unpublished manuscript. Commissioned by the Second Baptist Church of Detroit to commemorate its 150th anniversary.

Job's Song: Symphony no. 3 (soprano, alto, tenor soloists, SATB, orchestra). 1992. Unpublished manuscript. Commissioned by Plymouth Music Series of Minnesota. Premiere, 1993.

Life Suite (children's choir, orchestra). 1995. Unpublished manuscript. Contents: Superstar; T.V.; The Door; The Leaves; Best Friends. Premiere, 1996.

Visions: Symphonic Songs for Orchestra and Double Chorus. 1988. Unpublished manuscript. Premiere, 1988.

CONCERT BAND

Concerto for Wind Symphony. 1995. Unpublished manuscript. Premiere, 1995.

The Seed: Fanfare for Wind Symphony. 1998. Unpublished manuscript. Premiere, 1998.

William Cedric Banfield; courtesy of the composer

SOLO VOICE

"All I Gotta Do" (high voice). 1984. Unpublished manuscript. Recorded: B Magic Operations.

"Desire: Langston Living among the Poets Unknown." 1992. Unpublished manuscript. Premiere, 1993.

"Harp Song" (high voice, harp). 1989. Unpublished manuscript.

The Prophetess (high voice). 1989. Unpublished manuscript. Contents: Job's Song; Love Song Bittersweet; God Bless Chocolate City and Its Vanilla Suburbs; The Children Are Dying. Recorded: Innova 510.

The Prophetess (II). 1992. Contents: Fret Not; Clean Hands; Whom Shall I Fear; A New Song. Premiere, 1992. Recorded: Innova 510.

"Psalm 100." Unpublished manuscript.

Spiritual Songs (tenor, cello). 1991. Unpublished manuscript. Contents: Were You There?; Soon; Hold On. Recorded: Innova 510. Premiere, 1992.

"Summer Lies" (soprano, violin). 1989. Unpublished manuscript.

CHORAL MUSIC

"Carols" (children's choir). Unpublished manuscript.

"Did You Say?" (SATB). ca. 1985. Unpublished manuscript. Premiere, 1987.

"Hear Ye the Lord" (SATB). ca. 1985. Unpublished manuscript.

"Lord Guide Us through the Years" (SATB). 1985. Unpublished manuscript.

"Psalm 50" (SATB). ca. 1985. Unpublished manuscript.

"Spiritual Anthem" (SATB, organ/piano). Unpublished manuscript.

"Steadfast Love: Psalm 118" (male chorus, strings). 1986. Unpublished manuscript. Commissioned by Union United Church.

"Steadfast Love: Psalm 138" (male chorus, strings, piano). 1989. Unpublished manuscript.

Three Short Prayers. Unpublished manuscript. Recorded: Indiana University School of Music, 1996–97, no. 60.

"A Voice" (SATB). ca. 1985. Unpublished manuscript.

DRAMATIC MUSIC

Eyes (musical). 1995. Unpublished manuscript. Premiere, 1995.

Fisherman's Dock (opera). 1997. Unpublished manuscript. Premiere, 1998.

Luyala (opera). 1997. Unpublished manuscript.

Momma Why? Questions of a Young American (opera). 1991. Unpublished manuscript. Premiere, 1991.

POPULAR SONG

"Are You Thinking about Me?" 1984. Unpublished manuscript. Recorded: B Magic Operations.

"Baby You." 1984. Unpublished manuscript.

"Be Thankful." Unpublished manuscript.

"Cassanova Beetle." Unpublished manuscript.

"Her Eyes." Unpublished manuscript.

"I Ain't Got No Sin." Unpublished manuscript.

"I Love You My Life" (baritone). 1990. Unpublished manuscript.

"I'm Searching." Unpublished manuscript.

"I'm Won." 1984. Unpublished manuscript. Recorded: B Magic Operations.

"Life Pushes On." Unpublished manuscript.

"Lix Calahan." Unpublished manuscript.

"Look Behind You." Unpublished manuscript.

"Love Forever." Unpublished manuscript.

"Love Grew." Unpublished manuscript.

"Love Is Thy Way" (voice, guitar). Unpublished manuscript.

"Love Is You." Unpublished manuscript.

"Love Will Be Forever." Unpublished manuscript.

"My Story of Love." Unpublished manuscript.

"Our Story of Love." Unpublished manuscript.

"Place in Mind." Unpublished manuscript.

"Pleasing Thought." 1979. Unpublished manuscript.

"Spanish Amor." Unpublished manuscript.

"Summer Memories." Unpublished manuscript.

"Trust." Unpublished manuscript.

"Unbeatable Team." Unpublished manuscript.

"Unmistakable You." 1985. Unpublished manuscript.

"A Voice inside My Head." Unpublished manuscript.

"Walk in the Newness of Life" (voice, guitar). Unpublished manuscript.

"Walking the Straight Line." Unpublished manuscript.

"Watermelon Rinds and Cherry Pits" (high voice). Unpublished manuscript.

"Written in Their Hearts." Unpublished manuscript.

JAZZ ENSEMBLE

[The following list of titles includes only works that were composed by the subject of the entry; it is not a list of recordings that were made by the subject. Although the composer may have made recordings of his own works, the list is not restricted to those recordings but in many cases includes performances by other artists of the composer's work. The list is made up of publication and discographical data, in cases where such information is available. Although no effort has been made to include documentation of the earliest recording of the works listed, the date of the earliest recording that is readily available has been given. —Ed.]

"Afghanastan" (saxophone, piano, guitar, double bass, drums). ca. 1980–85. Unpublished manuscript.

"Alderan" (saxophone, piano, guitar, double bass, drums). ca. 1980–85. Unpublished manuscript.

"And I Answered" (big band). Unpublished manuscript.

"And What Would You Like to Hear Little Lady?" (big band). 1995. Unpublished manuscript. Premiere, 1995.

"The Answer" (saxophone, piano, guitar, double bass, drums). 1979. Unpublished manuscript.

"B.B.B.B" (saxophone, piano, guitar, double bass, drums). ca. 1980–85. Unpublished manuscript.

"Back in Gear" (saxophone, piano, guitar, double bass, drums). ca. 1980–85. Unpublished manuscript.

"Bill's Blue" (big band). 1996. Unpublished manuscript. Premiere, 1998.

"Blues for Anne" (saxophone, piano, guitar, double bass, drums). 1992. Unpublished manuscript. Recorded: Atlantic Records 782373–2.

"Bostonian" (big band). 1979. Unpublished manuscript.

"Brooke" (saxophone, piano, guitar, double bass, drums). 1993. Unpublished manuscript.

"Brookes Way" (big band). 1997. Unpublished manuscript. Premiere, 1998.

"Buenos Dias Magdelena" (saxophone, piano, guitar, double bass, drums). ca. 1980–85. Unpublished manuscript.

"Calm as the Night" (saxophone, piano, guitar, double bass, drums). ca. 1980–85. Unpublished manuscript.

"Carla" (big band). 1983. Unpublished manuscript.

"Charley Brown Blues" (big band). Unpublished manuscript.

"Chelles Song" (saxophone, piano, guitar, double bass, drums). ca. 1980–85. Unpublished manuscript.

"Conceptual Vibes" (saxophone, piano, guitar, double bass, drums). ca. 1980–85. Unpublished manuscript.

"Confused Monk Blues" (big band). Unpublished manuscript.

"The Dark and Out Frankenstein" (saxophone, piano, guitar, double bass, drums). ca. 1980–85. Unpublished manuscript.

"Deena Dayna" (saxophone, piano, guitar, double bass, drums). ca. 1980–85. Unpublished manuscript.

"Derry Alan" (saxophone, piano, guitar, double bass, drums). 1993. Unpublished manuscript.

"The Dream Suite" (big band). 1980. Unpublished manuscript.

"Expressions" (saxophone, piano, guitar, double bass, drums). ca. 1980–85. Unpublished manuscript.

"A Feeling without Words" (saxophone, piano, guitar, double bass, drums). ca. 1980–85. Unpublished manuscript.

"Felipia" (saxophone, piano, guitar, double bass, drums). ca. 1980–85. Unpublished manuscript.

"El Fresco Hombre" (saxophone, piano, guitar, double bass, drums). ca. 1980–85. Unpublished manuscript.

"A Friend's Advice" (big band). 1984. Unpublished manuscript.

"Fritz" (saxophone, piano, guitar, double bass, drums). ca. 1980–85. Unpublished manuscript.

"Funking Left" (saxophone, piano, guitar, double bass, drums). ca. 1980–85. Unpublished manuscript.

"Grove Blues" (saxophone, piano, guitar, double bass, drums). ca. 1980–85. Unpublished manuscript.

"Hannatitus" (saxophone, piano, guitar, double bass, drums). ca. 1980–85. Unpublished manuscript.

"Happy" (big band). Unpublished manuscript.

"Her Embrace" (big band). 1990. Unpublished manuscript. Premiere, 1998.

"Her Rumpf" (big band). 1979. Unpublished manuscript.

"If I Should Ever See Your Face" (saxophone, piano, guitar, double bass, drums). ca. 1980–85. Unpublished manuscript.

"I'm Not Sure" (saxophone, piano, guitar, double bass, drums). ca. 1980–85. Unpublished manuscript.

"In Woa" (saxophone, piano, guitar, double bass, drums). ca. 1980–85. Unpublished manuscript.

"I've Got That Girl Feeling" (big band). Unpublished manuscript.

"Just a Note from Sam" (saxophone, piano, guitar, double bass, drums). 1988. Unpublished manuscript.

"Kufu" (saxophone, piano, guitar, double bass, drums). ca. 1980–85. Unpublished manuscript.

"Land of Bill" (saxophone, piano, guitar, double bass, drums). ca. 1980–85. Unpublished manuscript.

"Last Night She Had a Really Good Dream." (saxophone, piano, guitar, double bass, drums). 1992. Unpublished manuscript. Recorded: Atlantic Records 782373-2.

"A Leading Tone" (saxophone, piano, guitar, double bass, drums). ca. 1980–85. Unpublished manuscript.

"Linga Linga Linga" (saxophone, piano, guitar, double bass, drums). ca. 1980–85. Unpublished manuscript.

"Lisa" (saxophone, piano, guitar, double bass, drums). 1993. Unpublished manuscript.

"Little Eden" (saxophone, piano, guitar, double bass, drums). ca. 1980–85. Unpublished manuscript.

"Lobby Ballad" (saxophone, piano, guitar, double bass, drums). ca. 1980–85. Unpublished manuscript.

"Look Back" (saxophone, piano, guitar, double bass, drums). ca. 1980–85. Unpublished manuscript.

"Love Surprising" (saxophone, piano, guitar, double bass, drums). ca. 1980–85. Unpublished manuscript.

"Love Symphonie" (saxophone, piano, guitar, double bass, drums). ca. 1980–85. Unpublished manuscript.

"Love You More Each Day" (voice and big band). Unpublished manuscript.

"Loving Ways" (big band). Unpublished manuscript.

"Magdelene" (saxophone, piano, guitar, double bass, drums). 1993. Unpublished manuscript.

"Marcia" (saxophone, piano, guitar, double bass, drums). ca. 1980–85. Unpublished manuscript.

"Mic's Voice" (saxophone, piano, guitar, double bass, drums). ca. 1980–85. Unpublished manuscript.

"Mono Road" (saxophone, piano, guitar, double bass, drums). ca. 1980–85. Unpublished manuscript.

"Najje" (saxophone, piano, guitar, double bass, drums). ca. 1980–85. Unpublished manuscript.

"The No Melody Suite" (saxophone, piano, guitar, double bass, drums). ca. 1980–85. Unpublished manuscript.

"No Song" (saxophone, piano, guitar, double bass, drums). ca. 1980–85. Unpublished manuscript.

"Peaceful and Playful" (saxophone, piano, guitar, double bass, drums). ca. 1980–85. Unpublished manuscript.

"Poohs and Roos" (saxophone, piano, guitar, double bass, drums). ca. 1980–85. Unpublished manuscript.

"A Prayer" (big band). 1997. Unpublished manuscript. Premiere, 1998.

"Rachel" (saxophone, piano, guitar, double bass, drums). 1993. Unpublished manuscript.

"Responsibility" (saxophone, piano, guitar, double bass, drums). ca. 1980–85. Unpublished manuscript.

"Rita" (saxophone, piano, guitar, double bass, drums). ca. 1980–85. Unpublished manuscript.

"Rocket Ship/Midnight" (saxophone, piano, guitar, double bass, drums). ca. 1980–85. Unpublished manuscript.

"Rose" (saxophone, piano, guitar, double bass, drums). ca. 1980–85. Unpublished manuscript.

"Save It for Another Day" (saxophone, piano, guitar, double bass, drums). ca. 1980–85. Unpublished manuscript.

"Senorita Lopez" (saxophone, piano, guitar, double bass, drums). ca. 1980–85. Unpublished manuscript.

"She Made It Crystal Clear" (saxophone, piano, guitar, double bass, drums). 1995. Unpublished manuscript.

"Skip Skip Dobed Dayha" (big band). Unpublished manuscript.

"Song for George" (big band). 1996. Unpublished manuscript. Premiere, 1998.

"Spring Wishes" (big band). Unpublished manuscript.

"Straightline" (big band). 1983. Unpublished manuscript.

"Susan's Day" (saxophone, piano, guitar, double bass, drums). ca. 1980–85. Unpublished manuscript.

"Stroll through the Garden of Lydian" (saxophone, piano, guitar, double bass, drums). ca. 1980–85. Unpublished manuscript.

"Take the 'B' Train" (saxophone, piano, guitar, double bass, drums). ca. 1980–85. Unpublished manuscript.

"That Which I See in You" (saxophone, piano, guitar, double bass, drums). ca. 1980–85. Unpublished manuscript.

"The Third Movement" (big band). Unpublished manuscript.

"Three Late Night Discussions" (big band). 1996. Unpublished manuscript. Premiere, 1998.

"Tickle" (saxophone, piano, guitar, double bass, drums). ca. 1980–85. Unpublished manuscript.

"TIM (Time in Motion)" (saxophone, piano, guitar, double bass, drums). 1995. Unpublished manuscript.

"The Way I Feel" (saxophone, piano, guitar, double bass, drums). ca. 1980–85. Unpublished manuscript.

"What a Crazy Scene" (saxophone, piano, guitar, double bass, drums). ca. 1980–85. Unpublished manuscript.

"What You Bring to Mind" (voice, saxophone, piano, guitar, double bass, drums). ca. 1980–85. Unpublished manuscript.

"Williamstones" (saxophone, piano, guitar, double bass, drums). ca. 1980–85. Unpublished manuscript.

"The Woman in Me" (saxophone, piano, guitar, double bass, drums). ca. 1980–85. Unpublished manuscript.

"You Doubt My Love" (saxophone, piano, guitar, double bass, drums). ca. 1980–85. Unpublished manuscript.

"Your Love for Me" (voice and big band). Unpublished manuscript.

"You're the Sunshine after the Rain" (saxophone, piano, guitar, double bass, drums). ca. 1980–85. Unpublished manuscript.

PUBLICATIONS

BY BANFIELD

"The Aesthetic Thread." Paper presented at the Center for Afro-American Studies, University of Michigan–Ann Arbor, 1990.

"Artistic Theology." Paper presented at the American Academy of Religion, Wellesley College, Wellesley, Mass., 1987.

"The Black Aesthetic and the Dippin' Poole: The Source from Within." Paper and performance presented at Eastern Michigan University, Ypsilanti, Mich., 1992.

"Carter, Benny," "Carter, Ron," "Havens, Richie," "Hendricks, John," Terry, Clark," and "Williams, Joe." *Encyclopedia of African American Culture and History.* New York: Macmillan Publishing Company, 1991.

"Composer/Theologian: A View of the Aesthetic (A Prolegomena to Artistic Theology)." Paper presented at the Andover Newton School of Theology, Newton Centre, Mass., 1987.

"Cooper, Adu Augusta" and "Mitchell, Nellie B." *Black Women in the United States: An Historical Encyclopedia.* New York: Carlson Publishing, 1991.

"Ellington Colored Black, Brown, and Beige." Paper presented at a seminar on 20th-century music at the University of Michigan–Ann Arbor, 1989.

"James Cone and Cultural Perspective." Paper presented at the Boston University Conference on Multi-cultural Education, Boston, Mass., 1987.

Michigan Daily. Regular contributor, 1989–90.

"Mobilization and Cultural Creation: The Rise of African-American (AA) Consciousness (An Interpretation of AA History and Culture)." Paper presented at the University of Michigan–Ann Arbor, 1991.

"Rap: Expression of Diversity and Rebellion." Paper presented at the College Music Society Conference, San Diego, Calif., October, 1992.

"The Sass and the Cool—Sarah and Miles: Tribute to Staples of the Black Aesthetic." Paper presented at the Museum of African American History, Detroit, Mich., June 1992.

"Text Setting in Afro-American Popular Genres." Paper presented at the Inter-American Composition Workshop, Bloomington, Ind., July 1994.

What's the Right Note: Reflections on Black Contemporary Music. Bloomington, Ind.: Tichner Press, 1993.

* * * * *

William Cedric Banfield belongs to a vanguard of eclectic, young composers whose backgrounds, training, and creative output traverse traditional categories. While building on the achievements of such "elder statesmen" as Hale Smith, George Russell, and T. J. Anderson, Banfield's creative work strikes out in bold new directions. A college professor, Banfield has accrued a long list of accomplishments that clearly place him among the ranks of America's original compositional voices. His work has been widely recognized, having been performed by professional and university orchestras in the United States. Banfield's compositional output includes orchestral works, chamber music, tone poems, song cycles, jazz pieces, and ballets. His activities have earned distinguished awards, grants, commissions, and residencies. At the same time, he remains involved in jazz, gospel, and popular idioms by maintaining an active performance career as a jazz guitarist.

Banfield spent his formative years in Detroit, Michigan, in a middle-class family considered "old-siders," or black residents of long standing. On the young Banfield's insistence, his parents gave him a guitar at the age of eight. The energy of Detroit's vibrant black musical scene, especially the presence of Motown Records, provided the backdrop for Banfield's apprenticeship years. Growing up, he had formal guitar lessons, played woodwind instruments in elementary and middle school ensembles, performed for school functions, and sang in his church's gospel choir, which he also directed for a brief period. During these years, Banfield formed a number of ensembles that provided him valuable opportunities to experiment with composition and arranging. At Cass Technical High School, an important Detroit institution that produced such musical talents as Diana Ross, Ron Carter, and Greg Phillinganes, Banfield became consumed with formal musical studies and an active performance schedule (student and professional). In 1978, a Chrysler Corporation scholarship allowed him to study guitar in Acapulco, Mexico, under the auspices of the Mexican Federation of Musicians.

Continuing his musical education, Banfield studied at Boston's New England Conservatory of Music, earning a bachelor of music degree in guitar performance in 1983. At Boston University, he earned the degree of master of theological studies. While in Boston, he studied composition primarily with composers T. J. Anderson, William Thomas McKinley, and George Russell. Banfield also maintained an active musical career, founding a recording and production company called B Magic Operations that released several commercial recordings. He taught music at several institutions, including the Boston public schools, Boston Music Community Center, Tanglewood's Days in the Arts, and the YADI (Young Artists Development Inc.) school for performing arts, which he founded. Banfield completed his formal education in 1992 at the University of Michigan, where he studied with the composers Leslie Bassett, William Bolcom, and William Albright. While earning his doctorate at Michigan, he performed with and composed for local jazz and fusion groups around Ann Arbor and his native Detroit.

In 1992, Banfield joined the faculties of Indiana University's Afro-American Arts Institute and the music department at that university's Indianapolis campus, where he directed two performing groups. In 1997, he moved to the University of St. Thomas in St. Paul, Minnesota, as holder of an endowed chair in the Humanities and Fine Arts. Banfield's compositional output includes seven symphonies, concertos, stage works, music for chorus and string quartet, song cycles, and chamber works for various instruments. Banfield has earned numerous grants and awards and has held residencies at several institutions. In 1993 Banfield's *Symphony no. 2* received a nomination from the American Academy of Arts and Sciences.

Banfield's philosophy about the art-music composer's role in society reveals the breadth and complexity of his background. He sees himself as a "public ambassador for the arts," a position that compels him to create works that will "draw in new listeners and supporters" to what is commonly thought of as an elitist fringe of society. Banfield believes that the juxtaposition of the many styles that comprise the popular music scene today has prepared younger audiences for similar developments in art music.

LAST NIGHT SHE HAD A REALLY GOOD DREAM (1992)

"Last Night She Had a Really Good Dream" represents Banfield's compositional voice in jazz and jazz fusion. Written for the jazz fusion group Straight Ahead, a Detroit-based all female ensemble consisting of amplified violin, flute, keyboards, bass, and drums, the harmonic language of the work is primarily modal, and its rhythm is based on a Latin/world beat performed at a moderate tempo. Because of its scoring, it recalls the 1970s jazz fusion project of violinist Jean Luc Ponty, which received considerable attention during Banfield's formative years. "Last Night" is performed in three sections, which Banfield gives the usual jazz treatment: the entire melody is played, followed by soloists using the form as a basis for improvisation, and then a final and concluding return of the melody.

"Last Night" begins with a repeated one-bar ostinato bass figure accompanied by drums and, a few bars later, the piano. The tune proper introduces a plaintive but lyrical melody to join the ostinato figure, and the harmonies begin to shift between two chords. Overall, the head comprises three sections that are repeated throughout, distinguished primarily by their differing harmonic treatments. The eight-bar A section is modal; the B section, also eight bars, features a quick harmonic rhythm; and the unusual ten-bar C section is dominated by a pedal point in the bass and a sequential figure in the

melody, a strategy that, together with the increased volume of the passage, propels the listener into the next statement of the A section. This form is repeated during a piano solo (one chorus) and a violin solo (one chorus). The final statement of the melody consists of the A section only with an extended vamp, thus rendering the entire performance as an ABCABCABCA+vamp form. The combination of styles represented in "Last Night She Had a Really Good Dream"—jazz, fusion, pop, world beat, etc.—shows the side of Banfield's compositional voice that has been most influenced by Detroit's eclectic 1970s musical milieu.

SPIRITUAL SONGS (1991)

Spiritual Songs is a three-part song cycle, set for tenor and cello. The piece reflects Banfield's strong interest in both Christian theology and his African-American musical heritage. The absence of a piano part in the cycle gives the work an ethereal quality, yet Banfield's impressive command of his music's parameters allows him to charge key passages with expressiveness.

The first piece is a setting of the Negro spiritual "Were You There?" in which Banfield combines traditional and contemporary techniques. In this setting, three of the spiritual's five verses are treated with the melody rendered in its original state throughout much of the piece and the accompaniment and brief interludes rendered with greater freedom as the piece proceeds. It opens with the cellist knocking on the body of the instrument in a three-note gesture that seems to imply the text "were you there?" and at the same time invokes the image of Christ being nailed to the cross. Shortly thereafter, the cello moves into atonal, fluid passages consisting of double-stops, *pizzicato,* and *arco* figurations. The first verse is set to the melody (G major, very slow) against a pedal point (D) that lasts through the entire strophe. After a brief interlude that begins with the same "knocking" that opened the piece, the second verse begins with the repeat of the melody, unadorned, in the tenor with the cello moving in animated counterpoint. Another solo cello interlude follows, its musical rhetoric pushing the piece further into an atonalism that builds emotional intensity. The climax of this movement occurs in the third strophe with two gestures: first, the cello part carries the most agitated accompaniment yet presented; second, the verse is elongated because a cello solo is inserted into the middle of it, delaying the climax of the piece. After the final portion of the verse is delivered, the cello settles into figurations that flirt with tonality.

"Soon," the second piece in this cycle, is based on Andrae Crouch's gospel composition "Soon and Very Soon" (1976). A relaxed lyricism pervades the opening measures, which bear no relationship to Crouch's original. The arco (bowed, smooth) cello accompaniment—rolling eighth-note passages that move by leap and step—provides a gentle flow to the piece. In a surprising twist, the first direct quote of Crouch's piece is given in the cello part, which at times matches the lyrical quality of the vocal part. In fact, with the exception of well-crafted solo cello passages, this movement is primarily characterized by the way the vocal and cello parts complement each other in playful, interlocking dance.

"Hold On," the most rhythmically active of these pieces, like "Were You There?," is based on the Negro spiritual "Keep Your Hand on the Plow, Hold On." Banfield's background in popular music emerges as a central influence on this piece when the cello begins with a dramatic and funky ostinato figure (in E minor) that emphasizes a heavy backbeat and blue notes. This figure appears throughout the piece, but its almost march-like steadiness is occasionally offset by a rhythmically disjunct and atonal passage that unifies the piece with the rest of the cycle. Each strophe of the piece is distinguished by the particular textures of its cello accompaniment. The piece retains the strophic form of the original spiritual until the final measures. In the first half of the second verse, for example, the cellist shifts abruptly into pizzicato background figures that convey the impression and feel of a walking bass but in fact serve as a kind of countermelody to the vocal line. The third verse guides the listener into unstable but dramatic territory, the melody creating a feeling of the improvisatory work a gospel singer might perform near the climax of a performance. To this end, the accompaniment provides an expressive countermelody that seems to compete with yet never overtake the vocal line. The rolling arpeggios and lyrical singing style that conclude the piece recall the opening "Were You There?" and give unity to the cycle.

JOB'S SONG: SYMPHONY NO. 3 (1992)

The composer was inspired by the dramatic ethos of the Job story to write his third symphony, noting that "the story of Job is natural for dramatic setting, providing a colorful set of characters, . . . moods, conflicts and resolutions that are all translatable to musical setting." Scored for choir and orchestra, the symphony comprises a prelude, five movements, and a postlude—a series of loosely related sonic tableaux in which listeners are guided from one scene to the next by the trajectory of the poetic narrative of Job's story, truncated here because of its length. The symphony is largely through-composed, although two key figures and gestures presented near the beginning appear again toward the end of the piece.

The prelude begins with a plaintive violin motive that opens into a full string choir, the emotive, legato lines of which set the tone for the tragic circumstances in which the biblical character will find himself. When the chorus and orchestra enter with a theme to the text "Job was a man," the asymmetrical lengths of the phrases and the richly scored harmonies serve notice that the first movement is underway. Firmly settled in the orchestral rhetoric of the European tradition, the orchestration conjures up, for example, real and metaphorical storm scenes and suspenseful anticipation. As the story of Job unfolds, the listener is introduced to each of Job's tragedies as they are announced by the "messenger" chorus. With each disclosure of his growing worldly losses, the music tightens its grip. A particularly cogent moment comes when the first vocal soloist to be heard in the work delivers the ultimate blow to Job's list of woes: his family's death in a wind storm. Shortly thereafter, the character Job, a tenor, renders his first utterances in a paraphrase of a famous passage from Job 1:21: "Naked came I out of my mother's womb, and naked shall I return thither: the Lord gave, and the Lord hath taken away, blessed be the name of the Lord." Banfield scores Job as a tenor, and that strategy seems to convey both the vulnerability of the character's plight and the resolve of his faith in God. Dramatic contrast is particularly keen in the dialogue between God and Job, in which the voice of God is scored for full chorus (which earlier had delivered the narrative

prose of the story). The symphony ends with a brief but effective postlude, a restatement of the prelude's plaintive motive that brings the work to a satisfying close.

Job's Song: Symphony no. 3 began as a four-movement song cycle for voice and piano titled *The Prophetess* (1988). The symphonic version of the work, discussed here, was ultimately commissioned and premiered by the Plymouth Music Series of the Minnesota Chorus and Orchestra in 1994. Michael Anthony of the *Minneapolis Star Tribune* wrote that "Banfield's gifts as a composer and orchestrator are evident throughout his *Job's Song: Symphony no. 3.*"

FOUR SONGS FOR FIVE AMERICAN VOICES: SYMPHONY NO. 6 (1993)

The sixth symphony is the composer's "attempt to honor those artistic voices . . . whose personalities and music" had had an "impact on his life and art." Banfield's intent in the symphony, according to him, is to "bring to memory the musical presence of these great American Voices"—Leonard Bernstein, Duke Ellington, Miles Davis, Dizzy Gillespie, and Sarah Vaughan.

"If Bernstein Wrote It . . . ," the first movement, consists of a collage of brief orchestral poems that use discrete fragments of memorable Bernstein melodies, most notably "Maria" from the musical *West Side Story.* The piece opens majestically in what Banfield calls an "Americanesque landscape," recalling the orchestral writing not only of Bernstein but also of Copland and Barber. The soundscape shifts between lightly scored gestures that ebb and flow into more fully orchestrated passages or passages that move in syncopated rhythmic figures. The second movement, "In an Ellington Mood," utilizes a similar approach but employs much less repetition than the first movement. This movement is further differentiated by Banfield's strategy to undermine the authority of the melody through dominant accompaniment figures in the orchestra. Movement no. 3, "I'm DIZzy Over Miles," is described as a double trumpet concerto: trumpeters Miles Davis and Dizzy Gillespie are its inspiration. Banfield portrays their "voices" characteristically: stemless mute for Davis and nonmuted trumpet for Gillespie. This strategy works wonderfully. From the walking bass lines, jazz harmonies, and the subdued combinations of brass and woodwinds, Banfield succeeds in capturing the highly recognizable orchestral aesthetic of Gil Evans, made famous by Miles Davis's recordings of the 1950s. Each soloist improvises during the movement's opening measures, but throughout the remainder of the piece, each plays scored parts meant to give the impression of being improvised. As in the first movement, brief melodic fragments from Davis's composition "Four" and Gillespie's "A Night in Tunisia" make ephemeral appearances, each forming tangible yet fleeting references to each of these artists' voices. Furthermore, the entire soundscape of the third movement's climax recalls Bernsteinian orchestration. The symphony's final movement, "Someone Said Her Name Was Sarah," is meant to "pay homage to the sweet and lyrical facility of singer Sarah Vaughan." In truth, its connection to the singer is, perhaps, more abstract compared to the other movements. Indeed, more melodic than the other movements, the piece gradually moves from string orchestra to full orchestra, giving it a teleological feeling. Its conclusion, however, is quite anticlimactic, tapering off to a rare instance of Banfield ending on a conventional harmony: a C-major chord.

Symphony no. 6 was commissioned by the Akron Symphony, which premiered it on February 22, 1994. Donald Rosenberg of the *Cleveland Plain Dealer,* wrote that "[t]he work conjures up many qualities of the American voice in writing full of lush symphonic sonorities and jazzy interludes. The Symphony No. 6 is affectionate in its lyrical incorporation of quotes and its melding of idioms."

GUTHRIE P. RAMSEY JR.

BANKOLE, AYO

Born in Jos, Plateau State, Nigeria, May 17, 1935; died in Lagos, November 6, 1976. **Education:** Jos, Nigeria, earliest musical education from father, Theophilus Abiodun Bankole, organist, composer, and choirmaster of St. Peter's Church; Lagos, Nigeria, began music lessons on harmonium and piano with his grandfather, Akinje George, organist and choirmaster of the First Baptist Church, 1940; Baptist Academy, Lagos, graduated, 1954; Guildhall School of Music and Drama, London, studied composition with Guy Eldridge, organ with Harold Dexter and Alan Brown, 1957–60; obtained professional diplomas, 1958–61: Licentiate of the Trinity College, London (Piano Performance), Associate of the Royal College of Music, London (Piano), Licentiate of the Royal Academy of Music, London (Teacher's Diploma), Associate of the Royal College of Organists (ARCM), London, and the Graduate of the Guildhall School of Music and Drama (GGSM); Cambridge University, Clare College, London, studied organ, 1961–64, B.A. (music), 1964, M.A. (cantab), 1967; University of California–Los Angeles, studied ethnomusicology, 1964–66. **Composing and Performing Career:** Nigerian Festival of Arts competition series, participated for five years, 1949–54; Nigerian Broadcasting Service, staff member, 1954; Christ Church Cathedral, Lagos, assistant organist under composer T. K. Ekundayo Phillips, 1954–57; composed first major work, *Sonata no. 2: The Passion* for piano, 1956–59; Church of St. James-the-Less, South London, succeeded his Nigerian colleague, Akin Euba, as organist and choirmaster, 1957–61; Henry Wood Memorial Concerts, Royal Albert Hall, invited by Sir Malcolm Sergeant to play organ, 1961; Guildhall School of Music and Drama, London, organized mixed student choir for performances of his compositions, ca. 1957–61; Nigerian Broadcasting Corporation, Senior Music Producer, 1966–69; works recorded by Operation Music One of the Nigerian Broadcasting Corporation, 1967; published a dictionary of Nigerian musical instruments, 1974; Rivers State, Nigeria ethnomusicological field research, ca. 1970. **Teaching Career:** School of African and Asian Studies, University of Lagos, appointed Senior Lecturer in Music, 1969; Lagos, trained and directed various choirs, including Choir of Angels, 1970s; University of Nigeria, Nsukka, External Examiner, 1971; Ohio State University, Visiting Lecturer, 1971–72; Rivers State Council for Arts and Culture, Director of Music Seminar, 1974. **Commissions:** Nigerian Federal Government, 1973; Nigerian Federal Ministry of Information and the Nigerian Broadcasting Corporation, 1974. **Honors/Awards:** Nigerian Federal Government Scholarship, 1957; Clare College Organ Scholarship, 1961; Fellowship Award of the Royal College of Organists, ca. 1962–64; Rockefeller Foundation Fellowship, 1964–66; Fifth Congress of Soviet Composers, Moscow, Composer Elect, 1974.

MUSIC LIST

INSTRUMENTAL SOLOS
Piano
"Fugal Dance." 1959–60. Unpublished manuscript.

Nigerian Suite. 1959. London: Chappell & Co., 1961. Contents: Forest Rains: O ya ya K'a Konga; Orin fun osumare; October Winds; Warriors March.

Sonata no. 1: Christmas. ca. 1958. Unpublished manuscript.

Sonata no. 2: The Passion. 1959. Ile-Ife, Nigeria: University of Ife Press, 1977.

Sonata no. 3: Songs from Stories. 1959. Unpublished manuscript.

Sonata no. 4: English Winter Birds. ca. 1960–61. Unpublished manuscript.

Sonatina for Piano: Episode in the Life of a Newborn Baby. ca. 1959–61. Unpublished manuscript.

Variations, op. 10, no. 1. 1959. Unpublished manuscript.

Organ
Fantasia. ca. 1961–64. Unpublished manuscript.

Fugue. 1967. Ile-Ife, Nigeria: University of Ife Press, 1967.

Three Toccatas. 1964. Ile-Ife, Nigeria: University of Ife Press, 1978.

Toccata and Fugue. 1960. Ile-Ife, Nigeria: University of Ife Press, 1978.

SMALL INSTRUMENTAL ENSEMBLE
Organ Symphonia no. 1 (organ, drums, trumpet, trombone). 1961–64. Unpublished manuscript.

Organ Symphonia no. 2 (organ, drums, trumpet, trombone). 1961–64. Unpublished manuscript.

ORCHESTRA (CHAMBER OR FULL) WITH CHORUS
"Cantata no. 1: Baba se wa lomo rere (Father, make us good children)" (female chorus, chamber orchestra). 1959. Ile-Ife, Nigeria: University of Ife Press, 1967.

"Cantata no. 3: Jona" (soprano solo, speaker, drum, piano, *tambura*, orchestra). 1964. Unpublished manuscript.

"Cantata no. 4: FESTAC" (soloists, chorus, organ, orchestra that includes traditional Nigerian instruments). 1974. Unpublished manuscript.

SOLO VOICE
"Adura fun Alafia (Prayer for Peace)." 1969. Lagos, Nigeria: Precision Music Publishers, 1969.

"And Art Thou Come." 1964. Unpublished manuscript. Also arranged for chorus and piano.

"Keresimesi Odun de." 1960. Unpublished manuscript.

"Kristi, Ma Wole." 1958. Unpublished manuscript.

"Little Jesus, Gentle Jesus." 1964. Unpublished manuscript. Also arranged for chorus and piano.

"The Lord is My Shepherd" (female voice, organ). 1959. Unpublished manuscript.

"Ni owuro ojo keresimesi." 1959. Unpublished manuscript.

Ten Yoruba Songs. 1959–66. Unpublished manuscript.

Three Songs for Diana. 1971–72. Unpublished manuscript.

Three Yoruba Songs (baritone, piano). 1959. Ile-Ife, Nigeria: University of Ife Press, 1977. Contents: Iya; Ja itanna to ntan; Kiniun.

VOCAL MUSIC
"Canon for Christmas: Eyo, eyo, odun de o" (chorus, piano). 1964. Unpublished manuscript.

"Cantata: Ona ara" (chorus, soloists, organ, Yoruba musical instruments). 1970. Unpublished manuscript.

Christus Natus (chorus, piano). 1968. Unpublished manuscript.

"Death Be No More" (soprano soloist, chorus, ethnophonic instruments). 1972. Unpublished manuscript.

Four Yoruba Songs (chorus, piano). 1964. Unpublished manuscript. Contents: Adura mi (Little Ayo's Prayer); Ipinnu Rere (My Pledge); Adie funfun (The White Man); Eru o bomo Aje (The Son of a Witch Is Never Afraid).

"Fun mi ni 'beji (Give Me Twins)" (unaccompanied chorus). 1967. Unpublished manuscript.

"Keresimesi tun ma de o" (chorus, piano). 1968. Unpublished manuscript.

"Ore Ofe, Jesu Kristi (The Grace)" (unaccompanied chorus). 1967. Unpublished manuscript.

Requiem (chorus, organ). 1961. Ile-Ife, Nigeria: University of Ife Press, 1967.

"Salzburg Carol" (eight-part chorus, piano). 1964. Unpublished manuscript.

"Sweet, Sweet Jesus" (eight-part chorus, piano). 1966. Unpublished manuscript.

Three Part-Songs (female chorus). 1959. Ile-Ife, Nigeria: University of Ife Press, 1975. Contents: Orisa bi ofun ko si; Ile iwe nikan lo ri yungbayungba; Enikeni to ba gbe ara re ga.

DRAMATIC MUSIC

Ethnophony (mixed media with traditional African instruments). 1965. Unpublished manuscript.

Jona (cantata for narrator, chorus, dancers, and mixed media, including Indian *tambura*). 1965. Unpublished manuscript. Premiere, 1965.

Night of Miracles (opera). 1969. Unpublished manuscript.

PUBLICATIONS

ABOUT BANKOLE
Dissertations

Alaja-Browne, Afolabi. "Ayo Bankole: His Life and Work." M.A. thesis, University of Pittsburgh, 1981.

Ogunnaike, Anna. "Contemporary Nigerian Art Music: The Works of Bankole, Euba and Ekqueme." M.A. thesis, University of Lagos, Nigeria, 1986.

Articles

Euba, Akin. "Ayo Bankole: A View of Modern African Art Music through the Works of a Nigerian Composer." *Essays on Music in Africa,* vol. 1. Bayreuth, Germany: Iwalewa-Haus, University of Bayreuth, 1988.

BY BANKOLE

Bankole, Ayo, Judith Bush, and Sadek H. Samaan. "The Yoruba Master Drummer." *African Arts* 8, no. 2 (1975): 48–55.

The Dawners of Nigerian Musicology. Lagos, Nigeria: Department of African Languages and Literature, University of Lagos, 1973.

"Edo Musical Heritage." Research project with the Bendel State Council for Arts and Culture. Unpublished manuscript, 1974.

An Introduction to the Appreciation of the Problems of Synthesis in Modern Nigerian Music. Lagos, Nigeria: Department of African Languages and Literature, University of Lagos, 1970.

"The Music of the Rivers People." Research project with the Rivers State Council for Arts and Culture. Unpublished manuscript, 1975.

"Nigerian Musical Instruments: An Annotated Dictionary of Musical Instruments." Unpublished manuscript, 1974.

Sango Festival: An Ethnomusicological Study. Lagos, Nigeria: Department of African Languages and Literature, University of Lagos, 1971.

PRINCIPAL ARCHIVES

Iwalewa-Haus, University of Bayreuth, Bayreuth, Germany.

Library and Sound Archives, University of Pittsburgh, Pittsburgh, Pennsylvania.

* * * * *

Ayo Bankole was the most prodigious composer Nigeria had produced by the time of his death in 1976. His thorough music education, his virtuosity as an organist, and his facility as a composer served as a challenge to his contemporaries. According to Akin Euba, a Nigerian colleague and composer, Bankole was a significant African voice in modern art music, providing artistic models for the incorporation of indigenous musical concepts into concert music forms. He planted the seeds for this genre to grow in Africa, educating not only Africans but people in Europe and the United States, where Bankole spent important early years (1957–66) in the development of his musical career. His output reinforced the movement to establish Third World and other international composers who were working along the same lines as Africans to create new genres of art music.

Ayo Bankole, born on May 17, 1935, spent his early years with his musical family in the Plateau State of Nigeria at Jos; he belonged to the Yoruba ethnic group. At the age of five, he moved to the city of Lagos and began taking piano lessons at home with his grandfather, Akinje George. Ayo was preceded by two generations of church musicians who were trained in Western music through churches and mission schools, a common practice among Nigerian musicians at that time. Educated members of society who wished to be musicians were expected to concentrate on church music. His grandfather was organist and choirmaster of the First Baptist Church in Lagos; his father, Theophilus Abiodun Bankole, was an organist and choirmaster and his mother was also an active musician and music teacher at Queen's School in Ede. Thus, church music played an important role in his musical development and learning.

At a young age, Ayo began to achieve recognition as a budding musical talent, and by the time he was a teenager he was assisting his father as an organist at St. Peter's Church in Lagos. Ayo's father was among the first generation of pioneering Nigerian composers who began to write original hymns in which melodies were based on local song styles, language, and rhythms; they were played with Western instruments and used Western harmony. He formulated his own independent theory of composition in an unpublished book titled "Yoruba Music and Pentatonality" using the music of the Yoruba and its complex tonal language. His work left a deep impression on Ayo, whose compositions fusing Nigerian and European styles and instruments showed increasing emphasis on the Nigerian features during his short lifetime.

Ayo Bankole; courtesy of Max H. Brandt

After graduating from the Baptist Academy in Lagos in 1954, Ayo became a staff member of the Nigerian Broadcasting Corporation (NBC), where he made contact with Nigerian musicians and patrons. He greatly admired Fela Sowande, who later influenced him as both an organist and a composer. Sowande had begun to explore the possibility of writing keyboard and orchestral works—for example, his *African Suite* for strings—that employed melodies based on indigenous material. The efforts of composers such as Sowande gave inspiration to Nigerian composers who were to follow him, including Bankole, Euba, Lazarus Edwueme, Samuel Akpabot, and Adam Fiberesima.

Bankole was an organist at Christ Church Cathedral, Lagos, under T. K. Ekundayo Phillips, also a composer who conducted field research in interior villages to familiarize himself with the Yoruba music that served as models for his compositions and material for his book, *Yoruba Music*. It was during the time when Ayo was Cathedral organist (1954–57) that he began his first major work, the *Sonata no. 2: The Passion* (1956–59).

Bankole's student days in London and the United States (1957–66) mark the second of three periods in his life and musical development. He arrived in London in 1957 on a Nigerian government scholarship to study music at the Guildhall School of Music and Drama, where he succeeded Akin Euba, who then was returning to Nigeria.

At Guildhall, Bankole was enrolled in the Graduate Course, taking courses in composition, theory, piano, and organ. Studying composition with Guy Eldridge, he explored a range of contemporary styles and techniques while writing from a more conservative point of view, as in the tonal Toccata and Fugue for organ. He also became well-known for his organ performances within the various London colleges of music, and after four years he was a recipient of the prestigious Clare College organ fellowship, which enabled him to pursue studies at Cambridge University.

The young Bankole organized and trained a mixed choir, comprised of fellow students, to perform his compositions, many of which employed the Yoruba musical idiom and language. This opportunity spurred his creativity and contributed to his development of an individualistic style of composition in which elements of African and Western traditions are blended. Examples are *Four Yoruba Songs,* which include "Adura mi" ("Little Ayo's Prayer") written for his son Ayo, and Variations, op. 10, no. 1 for piano (1959), based on a Yoruba tune and written for his daughter, Femi Bankole.

The compositions that Bankole wrote during his student years demonstrated that he had developed compositional and technical skills that allowed him to write in many styles. However, throughout his life he was very practical about working with materials that were accessible to him or to other performers. Thus, his output of compositions in England included organ and piano pieces, choral works, and orchestra works that were technically oriented toward the performers and toward instruments available to him in Europe. His Toccata and Fugue and Requiem were conceived for European audiences. Later, when he returned to Nigeria, he adjusted his purpose and style to give his compositions more of an African identity in form, rhythm, and use of instruments.

During 1964–66, Bankole studied at the University of California–Los Angeles (UCLA), on a Rockefeller Foundation fellowship. This was a fruitful time for him as a composer. The UCLA Institute for Ethnomusicology, directed by Mantle Hood, fostered interaction among composers, performers, and ethnomusicologists and opened many compositional possibilities for Bankole, as demonstrated, for example, in *Ethnophony,* in which he makes creative application of principles of ethnomusicology and non-Western instruments. Bankole and Akin Euba, who was also studying at UCLA at that time, worked with Roy Travis, a composer known for including African and non-Western materials in his works. Bankole was devising a style founded on African music while expanding his knowledge of non-Western resources. His cantata *Jona,* sung in Yoruba, was composed for narrator, singers, dancers, and an innovative combination of instruments, including the Indian *tambura,* and was written and premiered in 1965 at UCLA.

In some sections of the piece, he experimented with improvisation; some sections were fixed and notated. Bankole increasingly felt a need to keep Nigeria's music vital and to seek inspiration in indigenous music for the development of a written art music. Both in London and the United States, he impressed audiences with his new idiom.

The third period of Bankole's life began with his return to Nigeria in 1966, when he was appointed a Senior Music Producer at the NBC (1966–69), after which he served as a Senior Lecturer of Music in the University of Lagos School of African and Asian Studies. At the NBC he was in close touch with the wide range of Nigerian music and began to expand his own horizons and his use of compositional materials. He wrote pieces using Nigerian stylistic features and musical instruments, primarily percussion, and an hourglass tension drum *iyaalu* ensemble; examples are the opera *Night of Miracles* (1969) and vocal works in the Yoruba language, such as "Fun mi ni 'beji" (Give Me Twins) for unaccompanied chorus (1967) and "Adura fun Alafia" (Prayer for Peace) for voice and piano (1969).

During the Civil War of the late 1960s, despite the disruptive and repressive environment of Nigeria, Bankole continued to produce compositions and performances that inspired and reinforced Nigerian cultural and artistic values. His aim was to provide materials relevant to Nigerian audiences in a style that local musicians could learn to perform while meeting the high standards of the art form. He trained children to read music, gave piano and voice lessons, and instructed choral groups for whom he composed songs, thereby exposing them to African and European music. His Choir of Angels was comprised of students of three secondary schools in Lagos. Bankole had always been interested in education, and so, with his experience at the NBC, he produced a series of radio programs intended to educate the Nigerian public about Western classical music by relating it to works by Nigerian composers and introducing the larger audience to African indigenous music. Listeners found that the ideas he injected into his programs were stimulating and informative. Among program titles in this series were "Talking about Folk Music in Nigeria," "The Symphony," and "The Pianoforte as an Instrument for Nigerian Music"; and there was discussion of works by Nigerian composers such as Fela Sowande and Akin Euba. An important benefit that arose from his efforts at the NBC was the federal sponsorship of a pilot project, initiated by Sowande, to record some of Bankole's works in 1967 under Operation Music One. This was a significant opportunity, considering the economic and political complications African composers face in having their works recognized in their own countries.

As a Lecturer in Music at the University of Lagos, Bankole obtained deeper knowledge of Nigerian music by conducting research, particularly in the Rivers State, which aided him in his compositions. He wrote several articles and papers, the first, in 1970, entitled "An Introduction to the Appreciation of the Problems of Synthesis in Modern Nigerian Music," in which he summarizes his own musical thought and the guiding principles that have sustained his musical convictions and style. He gives recognition in the article to Ransome-Kuti, the Nigerian composer whom he felt destined to follow. His other articles include "The Yoruba

Drummer" and an ethnomusicological study of the Sango festival. Carrying out his desire to promote Nigerian musical practices, he wrote a dictionary of Nigerian musical instruments.

Between 1971 and 1974, Bankole took on many special assignments. In 1973, he was commissioned to compose the anthem for the Second All-Africa Games, and in 1974 he was Composer Elect to the Fifth Congress of Soviet Composers in Moscow. In 1974, he was commissioned by the Federal Ministry of Information and the NBC to compose a work for the Second World Black and African Festival of Arts and Culture (FESTAC), which was his last completed work. Both he and his wife, Adetora, were murdered in their home several months before the festival took place in Lagos.

Ayo Bankole combined the roles of music educator, composer, performer, and musicologist in his career. Today his works are heard on radio and television and in churches and concert halls. The tragic circumstances of his death are still mourned in Nigeria, but he left a daughter, Femi, and a son, Ayo Bankole II, to whom he passed on his musical and compositional skills. As a composer, Bankole's aim was, first, to project his feeling of responsibility to his people and to Nigeria and, second, to condense the great achievement of its art music from the first creative experiments at the beginning of the 20th century when music was still dependent on Western Europe. His works represent his lifelong process of dedication to the synthesis of musical elements from both African and Western musical traditions. As one of Nigeria's most prolific composers, he has left a profound impression on the next generation of artists and laid a solid foundation for modern African art music. The richness of his legacy will not be forgotten.

SONATA NO. 2: THE PASSION (1956–59)

According to the composer, the Second Piano Sonata represents "a lament for the passion and crucifixion of Jesus Christ." In the first movement of this work, in sonata form, Bankole employs the repetition of a pedal tone in the bass as a unifying feature throughout the work. The first theme, a pentatonic motive, paints the night "they sought about for to kill him." The second theme grows from the first and is a melodic setting of the Yoruba phrase, "Jesu, Jesu, mo ki oo" (Jesus, Jesus, I greet you). A fresh theme, introduced in the development section, is a setting of "Jes Kristi igi oro" (Jesus Christ, O Painful Cross), the Yoruba passion song by the late J. J. Ransome-Kuti. Bankole reworks motivic material in its middle section, then demonstrates in the recapitulation his mastery of different textures and keys by recombining material from the exposition. In the opening of the first movement, the composer characteristically experiments with polytonal textures by employing bitonal effects and by combining chords (C-major and D-major triads) with a dominating bass pedal on *c*, which asserts the central tonality.

The second movement, in ternary form, also derived from classical models, is subtitled "And He Was Crucified." It begins with slow, chordal progressions (in A minor) that develop into a pentatonic melody. The B section of this ternary form, consisting of a fast scherzo, has complex meters and rhythms including sections in 18/8 and 12/8. It should be noted that 12/8 rhythms such as these are frequently used to create interesting asymmetrical rhythmic groupings within the context of African indigenous music.

The last movement, a rondo, features a melody with a lighter quality. Subtitled the "Song of Mary," it is based on the European hymn tune "St. Mary," which is presented in the first episode of the movement. The ABACA form of the rondo alternates fast and slow sections.

The sonata continues to be performed in the United States and Europe, and a recording from a London concert in 1990 can be found in the National Sound Archives in London.

THREE PART-SONGS (1959)

The *Three Part-Songs* for female octet illustrate the composer's use of harmony and choral counterpoint in his middle period. Written for the special choir he organized while he was at Guildhall School, the first two songs are unaccompanied and arranged for double choir, each in three parts. The third song is set for a single three-part choir with piano accompaniment.

In this work, the composer demonstrates his knowledge of the musical characteristics of the Yoruba language, a tone language in which the meaning of a word may be changed depending on the tonal patterns pronounced, distortion of syllable tones, and phrase intonations. The first song of the collection, "Orisa bi ofun ko si," (The Throat Is the Greatest of Gods), is a Yoruba saying meaning "man must eat to live," which is derived from a traditional Nigerian song. To some degree, the choice of certain pitches, the range, the rise and fall of intervals, and the use of selected sequences of repeated tones are meant to reflect speech patterns. However, the composer also takes into consideration musical factors, such as the parallelism among the parts that often occurs.

Similar compositional techniques can be found in the other two songs of the collection. The text of the second song, "Ile iwe nikan lo ri yungbayungba" (School Is the Only Enjoyable Place), is taken from a popular song in which women recollect their early school days. But Bankole gives it his own tune in two independent tonalities (E-flat and F) in the upper two voices. A rhythmic, Nigerian hand-clapping pattern appears in the accompaniment (scored for the four lower parts). The text for the third song, "Enikeni to ba gbe ara re ga" (for everyone who uplifts himself will be humbled, and he who humbles himself will be uplifted) is derived from Luke 14:11, but the musical setting is secular, with piano accompaniment based on dance rhythms. *Three Part-Songs* as well as other choral works such as "Ojo maa ro" (Rain Continues to Fall), are among his most popular works. These short, concise songs based on Yoruba rhythms have wide appreciation and are familiar to Nigerians throughout the country as well as abroad.

CANTATA NO. 4: FESTAC (1974)

The FESTAC cantata, one of Ayo Bankole's best-known works and probably the last completed composition before his death, summarizes his output. This work of medium length, with its Yoruba text, comprises 12 sections or numbers, nine for voice and instruments and three for instruments alone (the Overture, Instrumental Allegro, no. 3, and Instrumental Andante, no. 9). It is scored for four solo voices, choir, organ, orchestra (woodwinds, brass), and Nigerian instruments such as *sekere* (gourd rattle), two *agogo* (hand bells), small and large *ikoro* (slit drum), *iya ilu dundun* (mother drum of double-head tension drum family) and *gudugudu* (single-head kettle drum). In keeping with Yoruba indigenous music, the *iyaalu* (hourglass tension drum) is the lead instrument among the percussion and the only instrument that has a free improvisatory part.

The opening overture for trumpets and organ sets the mood (in C major), its theme reflecting the rhythmic organization of traditional African music as it alternates sections of duple and triple subdivisions of time. Complex rhythmic organization permeates the work, although a regular pattern of beats underlies the whole.

Three recurring melodies unify the piece. The first recitative for tenor, followed by a choral motet, is accompanied by an instrumental ostinato, and the second theme is also stated over an ostinato. The ostinato technique provides a stable referential basis against which the listener may follow the text. The theme of the third section appears as a flute melody over an instrumental interlude for Nigerian traditional instruments, with additional color added by the only free, improvisatory part, played on the *iyaalu*. The fourth section for chorus (in two parts with female voices against male voices) leads into a soprano recitative (section five) punctuated by the percussive sounds of the *sekere*. Section six is a passacaglia with a tenor aria based on the text of Psalm 14.

The eighth section and other portions of this cantata reflect Bankole's research on the Yoruba traditional art form of solo chanting, *ege* or *Oriki* (praise song). The chanting, superimposed over a choral recitative, is climaxed by the emergence of an instrumental and choral section in which the drumming, singing, and dancing that follow *Oriki* in traditional Yoruba ceremonies are reflected. The composer's adaptation of this chant, usually performed by priests, has aesthetic and symbolic value for the Yoruba who use *Oriki* as part of religious rituals and festivals to praise the spirits and ancestors and to solicit their support. Through the symbolic art of chanting and its use as a structural feature, the work also has spiritual meaning.

Section eleven, with its slower tempo, polytonal structure, and the introduction of a bass solo, features a change in texture and atmosphere. The choral fugue of the final section, based on a theme from an earlier work, "Ti Oluwa ni ile, cati ekan re" (The Earth Is the Lord's, and the Fullness Thereof), is announced by a trumpet fanfare. The work is brought to a close with a dynamic coda, in which all the elements and forces that have been used are, according to Afolabi Alaja-Browne, "woven into a convincing whole." It was commissioned in 1974 by the Nigerian Broadcasting Corporation in commemoration of the Second World Black and African Festival of Arts and Culture (FESTAC), where it was premiered five months after his death. The enthusiastic reception of works such as the FESTAC Cantata situated Bankole on the threshold of internationally recognized contemporary composers who also held a valid place in African culture.

REFERENCES

Alaja-Browne, Afolabi. "Ayo Bankole: His Life and Work," M.A. thesis, University of Pittsburgh, 1981.

Bankole, Ayo. Preface to Sonata no. 2 in C: The Passion, for piano. Ife Music Editions, no. 3. Ile-Ife, Nigeria: University of Ife Press, 1977.

———. Preface to Three Part-Songs for female choir. Ife Music Editions, no. 3. Ile-Ife, Nigeria: University of Ife Press, 1975.

———. Preface to Three Yoruba Songs for baritone and piano. Ife Music Editions, no. 6. Ile-Ife, Nigeria: University of Ife Press, 1977.

———. "Sango Festival, an Ethnomusicological Study." Lagos, Nigeria: University of Lagos, 1971.

Bankole, Ayo, Judith Bush, and Sadek H. Samaan. "The Yoruba Master Drummer." African Arts 8, no. 2, (1975): 48–55.

Ekwueme, Lazarus. "Concepts of African Musical Theory." *Journal of Black Studies,* 5, no. 1 (1974): 35–64.

Euba, Akin. "Ayo Bankole: A View of Modern African Art Music through the Works of a Nigerian Composer." *Essays on Music in Africa,* vol. 1. Bayreuth, Germany: Iwalewa-Haus, University of Bayreuth, 1988.

———. Personal interview, Los Angeles, Calif., October 1995.

Phillips, Ekundayo. *Yoruba Music.* Johannesburg: African Music Society, 1953.

CYNTHIA SCHMIDT

BARÈS, BASILE JEAN

Born in New Orleans, La., ca. January 9, 1845; died in New Orleans, September 4, 1902. **Education:** Studied piano as a youth with Eugène Prévost, conductor of the orchestras at the Théâtre d'Orléans and the French Opera of New Orleans; studied harmony and composition with C. A. Predigam. **Composing and Performing Career:** Achieved freedom at the end of the Civil War; Paris, played piano at the World's Fair, 1867; New Orleans, career as a pianist, a composer of popular dance music, and a Carnival bandleader.

MUSIC LIST

"Basile's Galop," op. 9. New Orleans: A. E. Blackmar, 1869.

"La Belle Créole: Quadrille des lanciers américains." New Orleans: A. Élie, 1866.

"Los campanillas." Unpublished manuscript.

"La Capricieuse: Valse de salon," op. 7. New Orleans: A. E. Blackmar, 1869.

"Les Cent gardes: Valse," op. 22. New Orleans: Louis Grunewald, 1874.

"La Coquette: Grande polka de salon." New Orleans: A. Élie, 1866.

"La Course: Galop brillant." New Orleans: A. E. Blackmar, 1866.

"La Créole: Polka mazurka." New Orleans: A. E. Blackmar, 1884.

"La Créole: Souvenir de la Louisiane, marche pour piano," op. 10. New Orleans: A. E. Blackmar, 1869.

"Delphine: Grande valse brillante," op. 11. New Orleans: Louis Grunewald, 1870.

"Élodia: Polka mazurka." New Orleans: Junius Hart, n.d.

"Exhibition Waltz." New Orleans: Louis Grunewald, 1884.

"Les Folies du carnaval: Grande valse brillante." New Orleans: A. E. Blackmar, 1866.

"Les Fusées musicales." ca. 1865. Note: unlocated.

"Galop du carnaval," op. 24. New Orleans: Louis Grunewald, 1875.

"Grande polka des chasseurs à pied de la Louisiane." New Orleans: [Basile/Tolti and Simon], ca. 1860.

"La Louisianaise: Valse brillante." New Orleans: A. E. Blackmar, 1884.

"Magic Bells." ca. 1865. Note: unlocated.

"Mamie Waltz," op. 27. New Orleans: Junius Hart, 1880.

"Mardi Gras Reminiscences: Waltz." 1884. New Orleans: A. E. Blackmar., n.d.

"Fifty Merry Lanciers," op. 21. New Orleans: Philip Werlein, 1873.

"Minuit: Valse de salon composée pour piano," op. 19. New Orleans: Henry Wehrmann, 1873.

"Regina: Valse pour le piano," op. 29. New Orleans: Louis Grunewald, 1881.

"La Séduisante: Grande valse brillante." New Orleans: A. E. Blackmar, 1866.

"Temple of Music: Polka Mazurka." New Orleans: A. E. Blackmar, 1871.

"Les Variétés du carnaval," op. 23. New Orleans: Louis Grunewald, 1875.

"Les Violettes: Valse," op. 25. New Orleans: Louis Grunewald, 1876.

"The Wedding: Heel and Toe Polka," op. 26. New Orleans: Louis Grunewald, 1880.

PUBLICATIONS

ABOUT BARÈS
Articles

Sullivan, Lester. "Composers of Color of Nineteenth-Century New Orleans: The History behind the Music." *Black Music Research Journal* 8, no. 1 (1988): 51–82.

Wyatt, Lucius R. "Six Composers of Nineteenth-Century New Orleans." *Black Music Research Journal* 10, no. 1 (1990): 125–140.

PRINCIPAL ARCHIVES

Amistad Research Center, Tulane University, New Orleans, Louisiana.

Archives and Special Collections, Xavier University of Louisiana, New Orleans, Louisiana.

* * * * *

Although he had a primarily local career, Basile Barès achieved some noteworthy accomplishments. In addition to being a piano star of the New Orleans music scene during Reconstruction, he composed several popular pieces. In fact, his first piece had been published and copyrighted by him while he was still enslaved. He also became a civil rights leader, a pattern shared by several local black composers of the time who, unlike Barès, had been free before the Civil War.

Barès's origins have long been hidden, perhaps even intentionally at one time, for he was unique among prominent New Orleans Creole composers of color in the 19th century for having been enslaved. He was born into the possession of the Frenchman Adolphe Périer and his wife, who owned his mother, Augustine Celestine; as a teenager, she had been brought to New Orleans as a slave from Martinique. His father, Jean Barès, was a French-born carpenter who immigrated to New Orleans in 1838 and eventually became a grocer, with a shop near the music store owned by the Périers. Basile grew up working amid the pianos and sheet music of what was one of the best stocked music stores in the city at the time.

By the time he was 16 years old, the young musician, who had been given free reign of the store and all its pianos by the childless Périers, had made himself into an adept pianist and aspiring composer. His first sheet music imprint, "Grande polka des chasseurs à pied de la Louisiane" for piano, is indeed a rare thing in American music history. The composer of the piece is given simply as "Basile," without a last name, but the piece traditionally has been attributed only to Basile Barès. It is perhaps not a remarkable work musically, save for a few chromatic bits and some interesting passage work at the extremes of the keyboard, but it certainly would have been an accomplishment for a 16-year-old. What makes this sheet music so unusual is that it is the work of a slave, published while he was still enslaved. Of Barès's contemporaries, only the more famous Thomas Green "Blind Tom" Bethune (1849–1908) also claimed that accomplishment. Further, contrary to law at the time, the copyright is assigned to the slave. This was no doubt inadvertent on the part of the registrar of copyright in New Orleans, but the implication in the lack of a last name for the copyright holder, "Basile," seems evident. Since there was no federal copyright office then, people sought copyright at their nearest federal district court; and New Orleans was a wide-open boomtown in which slaves, out and about on their own, were often mistaken for free black people and were not always asked for their passes, an almost inevitable outcome of the city's having the wealthiest free black population in the United States before the Civil War. After the War, nowhere in the local black press or in books in which Barès is mentioned is he ever identified as having been a slave. Nevertheless, the *New Orleans Tribune,* the first daily newspaper in the United States, does refer to him as "the self-made artist in all the strength of that expression." More than a decade later, in his *Music and Some Highly Musical People* (1878), James Monroe Trotter, himself a former slave, uses almost the same phrase, "self-made man," to describe Barès.

In addition to strong documentary evidence that Basile Jean Barès was a slave, which I presented in "Composers of Color of Nineteenth-Century New Orleans: The History behind the Music," there are strong internal musical similarities between the 1860 "Grande polka des chasseurs" by "Basile" and the first five pieces of sheet music by "Basile J. Barès," which appeared in 1866. All six pieces are in flat keys, and the left-hand patterns are strikingly similar, showing a tendency to go from the root to an inversion of the chord and to use octaves rather than single notes on the strong beat. Harmonically, although there is greater chromaticism in the later pieces, all six employ the chromatically diminished seventh chord as a favorite device. The highly sectional nature of the music, coupled with a uniform tempo within each piece, may be characteristic of other contemporary dance music, but the "feel" of the music has been reported by performers to be distinctive and uniform throughout the six pieces, with single-note melodies drawn comfortably from notes next to each other on the keyboard to form melodies consisting of five-finger patterns. All six pieces also display a fondness for octave melodies. In short, musical evidence alone points compellingly to the conclusion that the composers of "Grande polka des chasseurs" and of the five later pieces are one and the same.

Although some of Barès's earlier pieces contain a few indications of unfamiliarity with some aspects of conventional musical notation, he was not entirely self-taught. He studied piano with Eugène Prévost, the same Frenchman who had taught his fellow black New Orleanian Edmond Dédé, and he studied harmony and composition with C. A. Predigam. He also may have gained further training in Paris. After the Civil War, the widow Périer kept the music store, and Barès kept his old job there. He traveled several times to Paris on business for the Périer firm. On his first trip, in 1867, he played for four months at the International Exposition.

He had already been featured in the first concerts held by Creoles of color in New Orleans at the Théâtre d'Orléans at the end of the Civil War. His cohorts in this endeavor were the principal organizer, Victor-Eugène Macarty, who later helped desegregate the French Opera in New Orleans, and the conductor François-Michel-Samuel Snaër, organist at the Roman Catholic archbishop's chapel. Barès's participation was almost entirely at the piano,

Basile Jean Barès; courtesy of the University Archives and Special Collections Division of the Xavier University Library, New Orleans, Louisiana

although he was pressed into performing a small part in a play by French author Alexandre Dumas *père.* The young freedman performed not only his own works (including "Les Fusées musicales" and "Magic Bells") but also fantasies on themes from the operas *Robert le Diable* and *L'Africaine.* These fantasies have disappeared without a trace.

During Reconstruction, Barès, like Macarty, became involved in the issue of racial segregation at the French Opera. Throughout its history, the Opera had serious financial problems that left it open to the vagaries of shifting race relations. At once eager to keep the patronage of people of color and anxious about losing the larger support of increasingly color-conscious white Creoles, the Opera management vacillated throughout Reconstruction between strict enforcement of segregation in seating and laxness about it. Creoles of color staged a boycott that many of them believed precipitated the financial shortfall that caused the Opera to fail to pay its foreign singers at the end of the season. A benefit for the singers, at which Barès and other local black musicians performed together on the same stage with the white singers, played to great success before a large black audience, permitting the singers to return to France and dramatizing resistance to segregation.

Throughout the 1870s and 1880s, Barès developed an enviable interracial public following, even by the testimony of such a staunch white supremacist as local turn-of-the-century *littérateur*

Grace King. For a while, he was the most popular musician in town, and the sheet music of his highly decorative and scintillating piano dances became best sellers. He was most noted for performing at white Carnival balls, for which purpose he formed and led a "string band" (a wind band with the addition of strings—that is to say, a chamber orchestra). Between 1869 and the later 1880s, he secured publication of at least 19 piano pieces, including several associated with Carnival. Most of these were published by Louis Grunewald, in whose music store the composer worked for most of the 1870s. In 1880, Barès went to work at the store of Junius Hart, who also published some of his works. However, between the end of the 1880s, when he was still in his forties, and his death two decades later, no further works by Barès were published. Whether this was due to the absence of further composition, growing Jim Crowism, or changing tastes leading toward ragtime, jazz, and Tin Pan Alley may never be possible to determine.

LESTER SULLIVAN

GRANDE POLKA DES CHASSEURS À PIED DE LA LOUISIANE (CA. 1860)

Most of the compositions of Basile Barès bear French titles; only a few have English or Spanish names, the one Spanish title reflecting the unique identity of New Orleans as a city of the northern rim of the Caribbean, as a southern city of the United States, and as a capital of French culture in the Americas. Barès was fortunate in growing up in such an environment, for his opportunities for musical development were many. His music was greatly influenced by his early exposure to a high standard of performance and by the unusual course of his life, namely the good fortune of belonging to a musical family who encouraged his musical activities. Few African-American composers were able to compose and publish music while still held in slavery in the pre–Civil War South. Barès was born into slavery but escaped its worst vicissitudes through doors opened by his musical talents. His early musical training led to his success as a well-published composer of piano music for the dance and the salon.

The earliest extant piece by Barès is "Grande polka des chasseurs à pied de la Louisiane," written about 1860 and published in New Orleans. The French influence is obvious from the title and also from the sheet music cover, in which a dedication to a Captain St. Paul appears over the figure of a handsome, resolute soldier wearing elaborate epaulets and the baggy trousers of the Zouave uniform. The music is all one expects of a dance piece of the mid-to-late 19th century: its phrases are symmetrical in length, with each section of the piece being 16 measures long. The harmony is static within sections, even by dance music standards, only rarely going beyond an occasional dominant chord at the end of an eight- or 16-measure unit. This polka has five sections, each of which contains new material (ABCDE). The final section, in contrast to the other 16-measure sections, is a nine-measure coda that reprises the B section, which originally appeared in A-flat major (the only section to deviate from the home key of E-flat major).

Despite the formulaic left-hand pattern of dance music, quiescent harmony, and predictable form, the performer finds some surprises. The dynamic markings range from *pianissimo* to *forte*,

and pedal and articulation markings are given. The performer is required to execute grace notes, arpeggiated chords, tremolos, and octave shifts ending with *loco* ("return to original position"). Some engaging moments stand out from the otherwise placid harmonic fabric. In measure 20 and again in measure 76, a "hunting fifths" quotation appears in the left hand, creating an expressive dissonance against the E-flat major tonality of the right hand. Even more widespread is the use of the diminished seventh chords in the A and C sections, where Barès often moves from a tonic chord in first inversion to a diminished seventh chord and back within two measures; or he uses passing tones whose dissonance is emphasized by the octave right-hand melody. The dance form and texture of right-hand melody and left-hand accompaniment and Barès's use of the diminished seventh chord recall the dance music of Frédéric Chopin. Other reminders of Chopin are frequent octaves and chords in right-hand melodies and phrases ending with sixths or short neighbor-note figures. Chopin's music was an intrinsic part of French culture and would have been well known by the French community of New Orleans. (Indeed, Jules Fontana, Chopin's copyist, settled in New Orleans and probably disseminated some Chopin lore there.) Perhaps it is partly the Chopin influence that gives Barès's music its idiomatic pianistic feel, making it rewarding to play as well as to hear.

ANN SEARS

LES FOLIES DU CARNAVAL: GRANDE VALSE BRILLANTE (1866)

"Les Folies du carnaval: Grande valse brillante" is one of five dance pieces that Barès published in 1866. All of these pieces show a more accomplished, ambitious composer at work; they are longer, more compositionally interesting, and more difficult for the performer than are his earlier works. This example from 1866 has six sections, each based on new thematic materials (ABCDEF coda). In the key of D-flat, it moves to the subdominant (G-flat) and the relative minor (B-flat minor) as well as the dominant (A-flat). The waltz is announced via a long introduction with repeated octaves, like a trumpet call, and concludes with a lengthy coda that reprises materials from sections C, D, and A.

While "Les Folies du carnaval" has the symmetrical phrase structure typical of dance music, it is more interesting than many other dance pieces. The short modulation to B-flat minor, the occasional diminished chords used in a Chopinesque fashion, the octave textures often used in the melodies, and the frequent use of dotted rhythmic figures give this work a gracious flow and attractive character. Considerable virtuosity is required of the performer in this piece. There are both French and Italian influences at work in the instructions to the performer, as both French and Italian terms appear in the scores: *avec gaîté, tres lié, con gentillezza,* and more common terms such as *forzando* and *crescendo.* With "Les Folies du carnaval," Barès produced a piece in which the combination of his own rhythmic energy and lilting melody with traditional form and influence from other composers lifts it above the ordinary.

ANN SEARS

LA BELLE CRÉOLE: QUADRILLE DES LANCIERS AMÉRICAINS (1866)

"La Belle Créole" bears the dedication "à mon ami Eug. MA-CARTY," referring to Victor-Eugène Macarty, Barès's colleague in concerts at the Théâtre d'Orléans at the end of the Civil War. This is one of Barès's only pieces to hold a dedication of a personal nature. The work displays the same verve found in the composer's "Les Folies du carnaval." A bounding left-hand accompaniment with an extraordinary array of skips and repeated chords underpins melodies that contain copious grace notes, chords, and skips. The dynamic markings are *forte, fortissimo,* or *crescendo,* contributing to the bombastic character of this piece. The five figures of the quadrilles use a variety of time signatures (6/8 and 2/4) and keys (E-flat major, G-flat major, and B-flat major and minor); Barès's predilection for flat keys is apparent in this work.

ANN SEARS

LA SÉDUISANTE: GRANDE VALSE BRILLANTE (1866)

The music of "La Séduisante" reflects its provocative title, as does the beautiful woman pictured on the sheet music cover. Although subtitled "Grande valse brillante," this piece has a more intimate character than the other dance pieces Barès produced in 1866. The form of the piece is ABACDCABA, creating a large three-part structure, a compound ternary form. The A section has a lyric melody supported by a typical left-hand waltz accompaniment. The first measure is right-hand melody alone, an opening very different from his other dance pieces of 1866, which begin either with long, commanding introductions or immediately with the strongly rhythmic melodies that seem to be one of Barès's trademarks. The second half of the A section is more brilliant, as shown by the lyric melody repeated *fortissimo* and in octaves in the right hand and the rhythmic drive of hemiola in the B section. The sparkling character is further emphasized by the bass line in the second half of the B section, in which the left hand inserts a one-measure figure that is taken from the brass-band tradition of New Orleans. In a clever use of thematic material, Barès takes this figure and turns it into a bright melody in the C section. In the D section, Barès continues with the melodic nature in the left hand, in a dialogue in which its heroic figures (in octaves) interact with the right hand's more lyric single-voice texture. The coda, a series of single chords on the downbeat of each measure, finishes with a plagal cadence—an almost unheard-of harmonic event in dance and salon music for the piano. This is a long composition of carefully organized structure, with many repeated sections. Repeats are exact, even to exact measure numbers, suggesting that Barès expected these pieces to be used for dancing, rather than as stylized dances as did Chopin.

The remarkably melodic left hand in sections of this work as well as the changing character between sections (lyric to brilliant) make this one of Barès's most attractive pieces. Given the high level of inventiveness, it is very likely the last of the dance pieces of 1866, and it must have added to public appreciation of his gifts when he played it at the Louisiana Fair in 1866.

ANN SEARS

DELPHINE: GRANDE VALSE BRILLANTE (1870)

Written in 1870, "Delphine: Grande valse brillante" is dedicated to Mademoiselle Delphine Dolhonde, who was probably a patroness of Barès and his music. Like many of the other dances by Barès, this piece is in compound ternary form (ABACDCA coda) with an A section in the tonic and B and C sections modulating to the dominant. However, there are moments of musical imagination that set this unusually idiomatic piece apart from the innumerable dance pieces published in the mid- and late-19th century. The influence of Chopin continues to appear here; as Barès's career developed, he used Chopin's ideas ever more sensitively. A particularly delightful borrowing from Chopin is the extension of the second of four phrases within a section, in which Barès uses a three-measure series of chords sliding down by half-step to reach the dominant and extend the eight-measure phrase to ten. Often used by Chopin, this device suspends harmonic motion and creates musical tension in an expressive way. This "harmonic parenthesis," as it was called by Gerald Abraham, appears frequently in Chopin's mazurkas. Since Barès knew the works of Chopin and himself wrote at least three mazurkas, he may have learned this musical language from Chopin's music. We also see the influence of Chopin in Barès's tendency to build to the end of the phrase—in the thickening of texture, movement toward the extreme registers of the keyboard, expansion of volume, and harmonic closure—and in the sheer pianism of the writing. The ever increasingly idiomatic piano writing throughout Barès's career seems to have been influenced by a growing familiarity with Chopin's music. But Barès's individual stamp continues to appear as well, as evidenced by the left-hand "hunting fifths" of "Delphine," which appeared in his first published piece, "Grande polka des chasseurs à pied de la Louisiane," and by his continued delight with rhythmic ingenuity, which is revealed in the hemiola in the opening section of "Delphine." Virtuosity continues to be an important element, as in the cadenza-like introduction marked *grandiose* ("grandly") and *con velocità* ("with velocity") and in the rolled chords covering a tenth.

ANN SEARS

LA LOUISIANAISE: VALSE BRILLANTE (1884)

"La Louisianaise: Valse brillante" is one of two pieces Barès published in 1884, the last year in which he is known to have published any compositions. Although Barès was only 39 years old when "La Louisianaise" was published, it appears to represent a simplification of style. It eschews the virtuosic technique required for his earlier pieces, and it is in C major, a much simpler key for amateur readers than the flat keys Barès used so often early in his career. Although this piece is a compound ternary form, it does not contain an introduction, and the return of the initial ABA section is truncated to a restatement of the A section. Although Barès apparently intended the omission of his usual appellation *Grande,* a nod to Liszt appears in the alternating octaves in the coda, which could appear in any one of several Liszt études. The descending bass line of the opening phrase is reminiscent of Chopin, as are the series of grace notes that begin the B section, which could have been taken directly from Chopin's "Grande valse brillante in E-flat major," op. 18. Chopin's pianistic inspiration is also evident in Barès's frequent use of melodic and harmonic sixths, which provide a lyrical, almost vocal, character to this waltz. The mixture of sophisticated and naïve, derivative and original compositional techniques found in Barès's work through the early 1870s is missing here, even though this is an ingratiating, melodic piece; it is more conservative and less individual than his earlier work. However, the place of Barès as a composer is secure, based on the ebullient, effervescent group of pieces from 1866.

ANN SEARS

REFERENCES

Abraham, Gerald. *Chopin's Musical Style.* London: Oxford University Press, 1939.

Sullivan, Lester. "Composers of Color of Nineteenth-Century New Orleans: The History behind the Music." *Black Music Research Journal* 8, no. 1 (1988): 51–82.

Trotter, James M. *Music and Some Highly Musical People.* Boston: Lee and Shepard, 1878.

BARTHOLOMEW, DAVE LOUIS

Born in Edgard, La., December 24, 1920. **Education:** Edgard, La., McDonough #24 elementary school; New Orleans, La., Hoffman High School; studied trumpet with Peter Davis, composition with Henry Halloway and Abraham Maloone. **Military Service:** Army, Tech Seargent, played trumpet in the 196th Army Ground Force Band in France, 1942–46. **Composing and Performing Career:** New Orleans, performed as an amateur with many different ragtime bands; played professionally and toured internationally with the big bands of Jimmy Lunceford, Claiborne Williams, Ernie Fields, Papa Celestine, Joe Robicheaux, Clyde Kerr Sr., Fats Domino; played with Fats Pichon's band, 1938–42, led band, 1940–42; established and directed the Dave Bartholomew Big Band, 1946; Imperial Record Company, songwriter/arranger/producer, Artist and Repertoire director for many artists, including Fats Domino, ca. 1952–63. **Honors/Awards:** "The Fat Man" generated gold record, 1953; Smithsonian Institution Archives, Pioneer of Music, inductee, 1989; Capitol EMI-Music, Platinum Albums, 1991; Rock and Roll Hall of Fame, inductee, 1991; New Orleans Urban League, Honoree of the Year, 1995; Rhythm and Blues Foundation, Pioneer Awards, 1996; Louisiana Hall of Fame, inductee, 1997; National Black Music Hall of Fame, inductee, 1997; Songwriters's Hall of Fame, inductee, 1998. **Mailing Address:** 4732 Odin Street, New Orleans, LA 70126.

MUSIC LIST

[The following list of titles includes only works that were composed by the subject of the entry; it is not a list of recordings that were made by the subject. Although the composer may have made recordings of his own works, the list is not restricted to those recordings but in many cases includes performances by other artists of the composer's work. The list is made up of publication and discographical data, in cases where such information is available. Although no effort has been made to include documentation of the earliest recording of the works listed, the date of the earliest recording that is readily available has been given. —Ed.]

POPULAR SONGS

"A-1 in My Heart." Co-composer, Pearl King. Recorded, 1993: Bear Family 15673.

"Ah Cubanas." Recorded: Imperial 154660 1.

"Ain't Gonna Do It." Co-composer, Pearl King. Recorded, 1993: Bear Family 15541; Capitol 37350; Capitol 80184; Collectables 5630.

"Ain't It a Shame." Co-composer, Antoine "Fats" Domino. Recorded, 1993: Bear Family 15541; Capitol 80184.

"Ain't It Good." Co-composer, Antoine "Fats" Domino. Recorded, 1993: Bear Family 15541.

"Ain't That a Shame." 1955. Co-composer, Antoine "Fats" Domino. Recorded, 1996: Capitol 37350; Creole 161; SMS 2; MCA MCAD2 8001.

"All by Myself." Co-composer, Antoine "Fats" Domino. Recorded, 1993: Bear Family 15541; Capitol 137356.

"Another Mule." Recorded: Stateside 6036.

"Baby Please." Co-composer, Pearl King. Recorded, 1993: Bear Family 15541.

"Bad Habit." Recorded, 1991: Charly 273.

"Barrel House." Recorded, 1993: Bear Family 15541.

"Be My Guest." 1959. Co-composer, Antoine "Fats" Domino. Recorded, 1990: Creole 161; Curb D2-77378.

"Before I Grow Too Old." Co-composers, Antoine "Fats" Domino, Robert C. Guidry. Recorded, 1993: Bear Family 15541.

"Bells Are Ringing." Co-composer, Overton Lemon. Recorded, 1993: Bear Family 15673; Capitol 37350; Collectables 5630.

"Better Be on My Way." Recorded, 1993: Bear Family 15673.

"Big Beat." Co-composer, Antoine "Fats" Domino. Recorded: Bear Family 15541; Capitol 52326.

"Birds and Bees." Co-composer, Antoine "Fats" Domino. Recorded, 1993: Bear Family 15541.

"Blow Your Top." Co-composer, R. Harris. Recorded, 1993: Capitol 80184; EMI E2-80184.

"Blue Monday." 1955. Hollywood, Calif.: Commodore Music, 1957. Recorded, 1990: Bear Family 15541; Capitol 37350; Collectables 5630; Curb D2-77378.

"Blueberry Hill." Co-composer, Antoine "Fats" Domino. Recorded, 1990: Creole 161; Curb D2-77378; Delta 17087; MCA Soundtracks MCAC 11392; Prism 220.

"Blues." Co-composer, Pearl King. Recorded, 1996: Capitol 37350.

"Bo Weevil." Co-composer, Antoine "Fats" Domino. Recorded, 1993: Bear Family 15541; Capitol 80184.

"Boogie Woogie Baby." Recorded, 1993: Bear Family 15541.

"Brand New Baby." Recorded, 1993: Bear Family 15541.

"Bumpity Bump." Recorded, 1995: Collectables 5630.

"Bye Bye Baby." Co-composers, Antoine "Fats" Domino, Robert C. Guidry.

"Caldonia's Party." Recorded, 1995: Collectables 5630.

"Can't See for Lookin'." Recorded, 1993: Capitol 80184.

"Carnival Days." Recorded: Stateside 6036.

"Che Notte." Co-composers, Pearl King and Anita Steinman.

"Cinderella." Co-composer, Pearl King. Recorded: Imperial X5481.

"Come On." Co-composer, Pearl King. Recorded, 1995: Collectables 5630.

"Come on Little Baby." Co-composers, Edgar Blanchard, Edgar Porse.

"Cool One." Recorded: Imperial LP-9217.

"Country Boy." 1949. Recorded, 1991: Bear Family 15541; Charly 273.

"Country Gal." Recorded: Stateside 6036.

"Dance with Mr. Domino." Co-composer, Antoine "Fats" Domino. Recorded, 1993: Bear Family 15541.

"Dear Mary." Co-composer, Pearl King. Recorded, 1993: Bear Family 15673.

"Dedicated to Domino." Recorded: Capitol 37356.

"Detroit City Blue." Co-composer, Antoine "Fats" Domino. Recorded, 1993: Bear Family 15541; Capitol 37350.

"Do unto Others." Recorded, 1996: Capitol 36292; House of Blues 161301.

"Doin' the Ham Bone." Recorded, 1993: Capitol 80184.

"Don't Blame It on Me." Co-composer, Antoine "Fats" Domino. Recorded, 1993: Bear Family 15541.

"Don't Deceive Me." Co-composer, Antoine "Fats" Domino. Recorded, 1993: Bear Family 15541; Charly 1069.

"Don't Leave Me This Way." Co-composer, Antoine "Fats" Domino. Recorded, 1993: Bear Family 15541.

"Don't Marry Too Soon." Recorded, 1993: Capitol 80184; Specialty 2169.

"Don't You Hear Me Calling You." Co-composer, Antoine "Fats" Domino. Recorded, 1993: Bear Family 15541.

"Don't You Know I Love You." Co-composer, Antoine "Fats" Domino. Recorded, 1993: Bear Family 15541; Capitol 52326.

"Down the Road." Co-composer, S. Lewis. Recorded, 1991: Amazing 1024; Collectables 5630.

"Down Yonder We Go Ballin'." Co-composer, Pearl King. Recorded, 1995: Collectables 5630.

"Dreaming." Co-composer Antoine "Fats" Domino. Recorded, 1993: Bear Family 15541.

"Every Night." Co-composer, Antoine "Fats" Domino. Recorded, 1993: Bear Family 15541.

"Every Night about This Time." 1951. Co-composer, Antoine "Fats" Domino. Recorded, 1993: Bear Family 15541.

"Every Night, Every Day." Recorded: Imperial 1566311.

"The Fat Man." 1949. Co-composer, Antoine "Fats" Domino. Recorded, 1993: Bear Family 15541; Capitol 37350; Creole 161.

"Fats Domino Blues." Co-composer Antoine "Fats" Domino. Recorded, 1993: Bear Family 15541.

"Fats Frenzy." Co-composer Antoine "Fats" Domino. Recorded, 1993: Bear Family 15541.

"Four Winds." Co-composer, Pearl King. Recorded, 1996: Capitol 37350.

"44." Co-composer Antoine "Fats" Domino. Recorded, 1993: Bear Family 15541.

"Girl I Love." Co-composer, Antoine "Fats" Domino. Recorded, 1993: Bear Family 15541.

"Go On Fool." Co-composer, Dorothy Esther. Recorded: Bullseye Blues 9583.

"Goin' Back Home." Co-composer, Antoine "Fats" Domino. Recorded, 1993: Bear Family 15541.

"Goin' Round in Circles." Co-composer, Pearl King. Recorded, 1997: Bear Family 15961.

"Goin' to the River." Co-composer, Antoine "Fats" Domino. Recorded, 1993: Bear Family 15541; Capitol 37350.

"The Golden Rule." Recorded, 1991: Charly 273.

"Good Hearted Man." Co-composer, Antoine "Fats" Domino. Recorded, 1993: Bear Family 15541.

"Good Jax Boogie." Recorded, 1996: Capitol 37350.

"Good News." Recorded, 1993: Capitol 80184; EMI E2-80184.

"Good Times." Co-composer, Tommy Ridgley. Recorded: Imperial 1566371.

"Goodbye." Co-composer, Antoine "Fats" Domino. Recorded, 1993: Bear Family 15541.

"Gotta Call That Number." Recorded, 1997: Bear Family 15961.

"Great Big Eyes." Recorded, 1996: Capitol 37350.

"Gumbo Blues." Recorded, 1995: Collectables 5630.

"Hearts of Fire." Co-composer, Leone Richard. Recorded, 1997: Bear Family 15961.

"Hello Josephine." Co-composer, Antoine "Fats" Domino. Recorded: Atlantic 81751-4; Beat Goes On 241; Rhino R2-70657.

"Help Me." Recorded, 1993: Bear Family 15541.

"Helping Hand." Co-composer, Antoine "Fats" Domino. Recorded, 1993: Bear Family 15541.

"Hey La Bas." Recorded, 1993: Bear Family 15541.

"Hide Away Blues." Co-composer, Antoine "Fats" Domino. Recorded, 1993: Bear Family 15541.

"High Flying Women." Recorded, 1991: Charly 273.

"Honey Bee." Co-composer, Pearl King. Recorded, 1993: Bear Family 15673.

"Honey Chile." Co-composer, Antoine "Fats" Domino. Recorded, 1993: Bear Family 15541; Capitol 37356; Imperial X5407.

"Honky Tonk Trumpet." Recorded: Imperial 5835.

"How Can I Be Happy." Co-composer, Antoine "Fats" Domino. Recorded, 1993: Bear Family 15541.

"How Could You." Co-composer, Pearl King. Recorded: Imperial 154660 1.

"How I Feel." Co-composer, Pearl King. Recorded, 1993: Bear Family 15673.

"How Long (Must I Wait)." Recorded, 1997: Bear Family 15961.

"Howdy Podner." Recorded, 1993: Bear Family 15541.

"I Can't Go On." Co-composer, Antoine "Fats" Domino. Recorded, 1993: Bear Family 15541; Capitol 37356.

"I Can't Stop Loving You." Recorded, 1991: Amazing 1024.

"I Cried." Co-composer, Bobby Mitchell. Recorded, 1993: Bear Family 15541.

"I Don't Want to Be a Wheel No More." Recorded, 1997: Bear Family 15961.

"I Got Booted Blues." Recorded, 1993: Capitol 80184.

"I Hear You Knocking." Co-composer, Pearl King. Recorded, 1993: Bear Family 15541; Capitol 80184; Collectables 5630.

"I Just Cry." Co-composer, Antoine "Fats" Domino. Recorded, 1993: Bear Family 15541.

"I Just Want You." Co-composer, Robert C. Guidry. Recorded, 1996: Capitol 37350.

"I Know." Co-composer, Antoine "Fats" Domino. Recorded, 1993: Bear Family 15541.

"I Live My Life." Co-composer, Tommy Ridgley. Recorded: Imperial 1566371.

"I Lived My Life." Co-composer, Antoine "Fats" Domino. Recorded, 1993: Bear Family 15541.

"I Love Her." Co-composer, Antoine "Fats" Domino. Recorded, 1993: Bear Family 15541.

"I Love to Hold You." Co-composer, Bobby Mitchell. Recorded, 1997: Bear Family 15961.

"I Never Knew What Hit Me." Recorded, 1997: Bear Family 15961.

"I Still Love You." Co-composers, Antoine "Fats" Domino, Earl Palmer, Wilbur Watson. Recorded, 1993: Bear Family 15541.

"I Try So Hard." Co-composer, Pearl King. Recorded, 1997: Bear Family 15961.

"I Walk in My Sleep." Co-composer, Pearl King. Recorded, 1993: Capitol 80184.

"I Wanna Know." Co-composer, Pearl King. Recorded, 1993: Capitol 80184.

"I Want to Walk You Home." 1959. Co-composer, Antoine "Fats" Domino. Recorded, 1996: Capitol 37350; Creole 161.

"I Want You to Know." 1959. Co-composer, Antoine "Fats" Domino. Recorded, 1993: Bear Family 15541.

"I Wish I Knew." Co-composers, Robert C. Guidry, Lucky Millinder, L. Montgomery. Recorded, 1997: Bear Family 15961.

"I Would Like to Know." Co-composer, Bobby Mitchell. Recorded, 1997: Bear Family 15961.

Dave Louis Bartholomew; courtesy of the composer

"If I Could." Co-composer, B. Ford. Recorded, 1993: Bear Family 15541.

"I'll Be the Bee." Co-composer, A. C. Reed. Recorded, 1996: Capitol 37350.

"I'll Fiddle Why You Cry." Recorded, 1997: Bear Family 15961.

"I'll Never Be the Same." Recorded, 1991: Charly 273.

"I'm Gone." 1952. Co-composer, Leonard Lee. Recorded, 1993: Capitol 37350; Capitol 80184.

"I'm Gonna Be a Wheel Someday." Co-composer, Roy Hayes. Recorded, 1993: Bear Family 15541; Bear Family 15961; Capitol 80284; Capitol 37350.

"I'm in Love." Co-composer, Bobby Mitchell. Recorded, 1997: Bear Family 15961.

"I'm in Love Again." Co-composer, Antoine "Fats" Domino. Recorded, 1993: Bear Family 15541; Capitol 52326; Capitol 37350.

"I'm Slippin' In." Recorded, 1993: Bear Family 15673; Capitol 37350.

"I'm Walkin'." 1957. Co-composer, Antoine "Fats" Domino. Recorded, 1990: Bear Family 15541; Capitol 37350; Capitol 37356; Curb D2-77378.

"It Keeps Rainin'." Co-composers, Antoine "Fats" Domino, Robert C. Guidry. Recorded, 1993: Bear Family 15541; Capitol 37350.

"It Must Be Love." Co-composer, Antoine "Fats" Domino. Recorded, 1993: Bear Family 15541.

"It's Never Too Late." Co-composers, Antoine "Fats" Domino, Morrie Sanchez, Ed Thompson. Recorded: Mercury 72485.

"It's Too Late Now." Co-composers, Anthony Matthews, Cordell Thrower. Recorded, 1997: Bear Family 15961.

"It's You I Love." Co-composer, Antoine "Fats" Domino. Recorded, 1993: Bear Family 15541; Capitol 52326.

"I've Got My Fingers Crossed." Co-composer, Pearl King. Recorded, 1997: Bear Family 15961.

"I-Y I." Recorded, 1993: Capitol 80184.

"Jailbird." Recorded, 1995: Collectables 5630.

"Je suis encore amoureux." Co-composer, Antoine "Fats" Domino.

"Josephine." Co-composer, Antoine "Fats" Domino. Recorded: House of Blues 161301.

"Jump Children." Recorded, 1993: Capitol 80184; EMI E2-80184; Imperial 154660; Stateside 6036.

"Keeper of My Heart." Co-composers, Ruth Durand, Pearl King. Recorded, 1996: Capitol 37350.

"Korea Blues." Recorded, 1993: Bear Family 15541.

"La La." Co-composer, Antoine "Fats" Domino. Recorded, 1993: Bear Family 15541.

"Lavinia." Co-composer, Tommy Ridgley. Recorded, 1987: Black Top CD-BT-1037.

"Lawdy Lawdy Lord." Recorded, 1991: Charly 273.

"Lazy Woman." Co-composer, Antoine "Fats" Domino. Recorded, 1993: Bear Family 15541.

"Let the Four Winds Blow." Co-composer, Antoine "Fats" Domino. Recorded, 1990: Bear Family 15541; Capitol 37350; Capitol 80184; Curb D2-77378; SDS 2.

"Lil Liza Jane." Co-composer, Antoine "Fats" Domino. Recorded, 1993: Bear Family 15541.

"Lillie Mae." Recorded, 1995: Capitol 37350; Collectables 5630.

"Little Bee." Recorded, 1993: Bear Family 15541.

"Little Girls Sing Ding-a-Ling." Recorded, 1993: Capitol 37350; Capitol 80184; EMI E2-80184; Stateside 6036.

"Little Mama." Co-composer, Antoine "Fats" Domino. Recorded, 1993: Bear Family 15541.

"Little Mary." Co-composer, Antoine "Fats" Domino. Recorded, 1993: Bear Family 15541.

"Little School Girl." Co-composer, Antoine "Fats" Domino. Recorded, 1993: Bear Family 15541.

"Little Willie." Co-composer, Pearl King. Recorded, 1993: Capitol 80184.

"Love Me." Co-composer, Antoine "Fats" Domino. Recorded, 1993: Bear Family 15541.

"Magic Isles." Co-composer, Antoine "Fats" Domino. Recorded, 1993: Bear Family 15541.

"Man That's All." Co-composer, Antoine "Fats" Domino. Recorded, 1965: Paramount S-510.

"M'en revenant de guerre." Co-composers, Antoine "Fats" Domino, Robert C. Guidry.

"Messy Bessie." Recorded, 1991: Charly 273.

"The Monkey." 1985. Co-composer, Pearl King. Recorded, 1996: Capitol 37350; Stateside 6036.

"Monkey Business." Co-composer, Antoine "Fats" Domino. Recorded, 1965: Paramount S-510.

"Morning Star." Co-composer, James E. Crawford Jr. Recorded, 1993: Capitol 80184.

"Mother Knows Best." Recorded, 1991: Charly 273.

"Mr. Fool." Recorded, 1991: Charly 273.

"My Ding-a-Ling." 1952. Co-composer, Sam Rhodes. Recorded, 1991: Charly 273.

"My Girl Josephine." 1960. Co-composer, Antoine "Fats" Domino. Recorded, 1990: Bear Family 15541; Capitol 52326; Curb D2-77378.

"My Heart Is Bleeding." Co-composer, Pearl King. Recorded, 1993: Bear Family 15541.

"My Love for Her." Co-composer, Antoine "Fats" Domino. Recorded, 1993: Bear Family 15541.

"My Southern Belle." Co-composer, Pearl King. Recorded, 1997: Bear Family 15961.

"Natural Born Lover." Co-composer, Antoine "Fats" Domino. Recorded, 1993: Bear Family 15541.

"New Orleans Twist." Co-composers, Pearl King, Wardell Joseph Quezergue. Recorded, 1996: Capitol 37350.

"Nickel Wine." Recorded, 1991: Charly 273.

"No More Black Nights." Recorded: Imperial 1566311; Stateside 6036.

"No, No, No." Co-composer, Pearl King. Recorded, 1993: Bear Family 15541; Bear Family 15961.

"Nobody Knows." Recorded, 1961: Hi SHL-32004.

"Nothing But the Blues." Recorded, 1995: Collectables 5630.

"Nothing New." Co-composers, Antoine "Fats" Domino, Jack Jessup, Murphy Maddux Jr. Recorded, 1993: Bear Family 15541.

"Nothing Sweet as You." Co-composers, Bobby Mitchell, Earl Montgomery. Recorded, 1993: Bear Family 15961; Capitol 80184.

"Oh Ba-a-by." Co-composer, Antoine "Fats" Domino. Recorded, 1993: Bear Family 15541.

"Oh Whee." Co-composer, Antoine "Fats" Domino. Recorded, 1993: Bear Family 15541.

"Oh Yeah." Co-composer, Pearl King. Recorded, 1997: Bear Family 15961.

"An Old Cowhand from a Blues Band." Co-composer, Pearl King. Recorded: Stateside 6036.

"One Night." 1952. Co-composer, Pearl King. Recorded, 1993: Bear Family 15541; Capitol 37350; Capitol 80184; Collectables 5630.

"One Night of Sin." Co-composer, Pearl King. Recorded, 1956: Capitol C2-92861; Cotillion SD 9052; RCA 67452.

"One Night with You." Co-composers, Pearl King, Anita Steinman. Recorded, 1997: Intersound 9276.

"One of These Days." Co-composer, Antoine "Fats" Domino. Recorded, 1993: Bear Family 15541.

"Ooh La La." Recorded: Specialty SPCD-2169-2.

"People Are Talking." Co-composer, Pearl King. Recorded: Imperial 154660 1.

"Please Listen to Me." Co-composer, Pearl King. Recorded, 1995: Collectables 5630.

"Pony Tail." Recorded, 1993: Capitol 80184.

"Poor Boy." Co-composer, Pearl King. Recorded, 1993: Bear Family 15673.

"Poor Me." Co-composer, Antoine "Fats" Domino. Recorded, 1993: Bear Family 15541; Capitol 52326.

"Poppa Stoppa Theme Song." Recorded, 1996: Capitol 37350.

"Pyramid." Recorded, 1991: Charly 273.

"Queen of Hearts." Co-composer, Pearl King. Recorded, 1995: Collectables 5630.

"Railroad Station Blues." Recorded, 1991: EMI America E2-96738.

"Real Gone Lover." Co-composers, Ruth Durand, Joseph Robicheaux. Recorded, 1991: Amazing 1024; Collectables 5630.

"Real Thing." Recorded, 1993: Bear Family 15673; Capitol 80184.

"Rooster Song." Co-composer, Antoine "Fats" Domino. Recorded, 1993: Bear Family 15541.

"Rootin' and Tootin'." Co-composer, Pearl King. Recorded, 1995: Collectables 5630.

"Rose Mary." Co-composer, Antoine "Fats" Domino. Recorded, 1993: Bear Family 15541.

"Runnin' Wild." Recorded, 1993: Capitol 37350; Capitol 80184.

"Sail on Little Girl." Co-composer, Pearl King.

"Sailor Boy." Co-composer, Antoine "Fats" Domino. Recorded, 1993: Bear Family 15541.

"Second Line Jump." Co-composer, Antoine "Fats" Domino. Recorded, 1993: Bear Family 15541.

"She Keeps Me Wondering." Recorded, 1993: Bear Family 15673.

"She's Got Me Hook, Line and Sinker." Co-composer, Pearl King. Recorded, 1995: Collectables 5630.

"She's Gotta Wobble When She Walks." Co-composer, James Crawford Jr. Recorded, 1993: Capitol 80184.

"She's My Baby Blues." Co-composer, Antoine "Fats" Domino. Recorded, 1993: Bear Family 15541.

"Shrimp and Gumbo." Recorded: Imperial 1566311.

"Shu Rah." Co-composer, Antoine "Fats" Domino. Recorded, 1993: Bear Family 15541.

"Shufflin' Fox." Co-composer, Pearl King. Recorded: Imperial 154660 1.

"Sick and Tired." Co-composer, Christopher Kenner. Recorded, 1993: Bear Family 15541; Capitol 37350; Capitol 80184; Capitol 37356.

"Single Life." Recorded, 1993: Capitol 37350; Capitol 80184.

"Sister Lucy." Co-composer, Adolph Smith. Recorded, 1997: Bear Family 15961.

"Sittin' and Wonderin'." Recorded, 1996: Capitol 37350.

"64 Hours." Co-composer, Bobby Mitchell. Recorded, 1997: Bear Family 15961.

"Slow Down Little Eva." Co-composer, Roy Brown. Recorded, 1995: Capitol 544.

"Snatchin' Back." Recorded: Imperial 1566311; Stateside 6036.

"So Glad." Co-composer, Antoine "Fats" Domino. Recorded, 1993: Bear Family 15541.

"So Long." Co-composer, Antoine "Fats" Domino. Recorded, 1993: Bear Family 15541.

"Somebody New." Co-composer, Pearl King. Recorded: Imperial 156311.

"Someday." Co-composer, Pearl King. Recorded, 1996: Capitol 37350.

"Someday Bye and Bye." Recorded, 1993: Bear Family 15673.

"Something's Wrong." Co-composer, Antoine "Fats" Domino. Recorded, 1993: Bear Family 15541.

"Stack and Billy." Co-composer, Antoine "Fats" Domino. Recorded, 1993: Bear Family 15541.

"Swanee River Hop." Co-composer, Antoine "Fats" Domino. Recorded, 1993: Bear Family 15541; EMI America E2-96785.

"Sweet Home Blues." Recorded, 1991: Charly 273.

"Tell Me That You Love Me." Recorded, 1993: Bear Family 15541.

"Tennessee Slim." Co-composer, Pearl King. Recorded, 1993: Bear Family 15673.

"Texas Hop." Recorded: Imperial 1566311.

"That Certain Door." Recorded, 1993: Capitol 80184.

"That's Enough." Recorded, 1993: Bear Family 15673.

"That's How You Got Killed Before." Recorded, 1996: Capitol 37350.

"They Said It Couldn't Be Done." Co-composer, Pearl King. Recorded, 1993: Capitol 80184.

"Thinkin' 'bout My Baby." Co-composer, James Boone. Recorded, 1993: Capitol 80184.

"Thinking of You." Recorded, 1993: Bear Family 15541.

"Those Eyes." Co-composer, Robert C. Guidry. Recorded, 1993: Bear Family 15541.

"3 x 7 = 21." Recorded, 1993: Bear Family 15673; Capitol 37350; Capitol 80184.

"Tick of the Clock." Co-composer, Pearl King. Recorded: Capitol 544.

"Town Talk." Co-composer, Antoine "Fats" Domino. Recorded, 1993: Bear Family 15541.

"Toy Bell." Recorded, 1993: Capitol 37350; Capitol 80184.

"Troubles of My Own." Co-composer, Antoine "Fats" Domino. Recorded, 1993: Bear Family 15541.

"True Confession." Recorded, 1993: Bear Family 15541.

"Try Rock and Roll." Co-composer, Pearl King. Recorded, 1996: Bear Family 15961; Capitol 37350.

"Twins." Recorded, 1991: Charly 273.

"Twistin' the Spots." Co-composer, Antoine "Fats" Domino. Recorded, 1993: Bear Family 15541.

"Valley of Tears." Co-composer, Antoine "Fats" Domino. Recorded, 1993: Bear Family 15541; Capitol 80184; Capitol 37350; Capitol 52326.

"Wait and See." Recorded, 1993: Bear Family 15541; Capitol 52326.

"Walkin' to New Orleans." 1960. Co-composers, Antoine "Fats" Domino, Robert C. Guidry. Recorded, 1990: Bear Family 15541; Capitol 37350; Capitol 80184; Curb D2-77378.

"What a Party." Co-composer, Pearl King. Recorded, 1993: Bear Family 15541.

"What's That You Got." Recorded: Mercury 72485.

"When First We Met." Recorded, 1997: Bear Family 15961.

"When I See You." Co-composer, Antoine "Fats" Domino. Recorded, 1993: Bear Family 15541.

"When I Was Young." Co-composer, Antoine "Fats" Domino. Recorded, 1993: Bear Family 15541.

"When the Sun Goes Down." Recorded: EMI America E2-96738.

"Where Did You Stay." Co-composer, Antoine "Fats" Domino. Recorded, 1993: Bear Family 15541.

"Whole Lotta Loving." Co-composer, Antoine "Fats" Domino. Recorded, 1990: Bear Family 15541; Capitol 52326; Curb D2-77378.

"Why Fool Yourself." Recorded, 1993: Capitol 80184.

"Witchcraft." Co-composer, Pearl King. Recorded, 1993: Bear Family 15673; Capitol 37350; Capitol 80184.

"Without Love." Recorded, 1993: Bear Family 15673.

"Yeah, Yeah." Co-composer, Pearl King. Recorded: Stateside 6036.

"Yes, It's Me, and I'm in Love Again." Co-composer, Antoine "Fats" Domino. Recorded, 1993: Bear Family 15541; Phantom 253932; Ronn 8015.

"Yes, My Darling." Co-composer, Antoine "Fats" Domino. Recorded, 1996: Capitol 52326.

"You Ain't So Such a Much." Co-composer, Blanche Thomas. Recorded, 1993: Capitol 80184.

"You Are My Angel." Co-composer, Agnes Fortuna. Recorded, 1997: Bear Family 15961.

"You Better Go Home." Co-composer, Bob Hayes. Recorded, 1997: Bear Family 15961.

"You Can Pack Your Suitcase." Co-composer, Antoine "Fats" Domino. Recorded, 1993: Bear Family 15541; EMI America E2-96785.

"You Done Me Wrong." Recorded, 1993: Bear Family 15541.

"You Gave Me Love." Co-composer, James Crawford Jr. Recorded, 1995: Rounder 2139.

"You Left Me." Co-composer, Antoine "Fats" Domino. Recorded, 1993: Bear Family 15541.

"You Said You Love Me." Co-composer, Antoine "Fats" Domino. Recorded: See for Miles 455.

"Young School Girl." Co-composer, Antoine "Fats" Domino. Recorded, 1993: Bear Family 15541; Capitol 80184.

"You're Going to Be Sorry." Co-composer, Pearl King. Recorded, 1997: Bear Family 15961.

"Yours Truly." Recorded, 1996: Capitol 36292.

INCIDENTAL MUSIC

A Fine Mess. 1986. Incidental film music.
Roadhouse. 1989. Incidental film music.

PUBLICATIONS

ABOUT BARTHOLOMEW
Articles

McGee, David. "The Spirit of New Orleans." *Pro Sound News* 20, no. 7 (July 1998): 130, 128.

"Regal Records in New Orleans." *Cadence* 18 (March 1992): 25.

Sebastian, K. "Dave Bartholomew." *New Orleans Music* 3 (April 1992): 14–17.

* * * *

Dave Bartholomew, credited as one of the primary figures in the history of New Orleans–based rhythm and blues, has also been recognized as a leading contributor to the development of rock and roll during the 1950s and early 1960s. His career began as a performer and composer and continued in the recording studio, where he assumed duties as producer, arranger, composer, and recruiter for Imperial Records. Because of his position at Imperial Records, Bartholomew was able to influence and shape the sound ideals both of New Orleans rhythm and blues and of rock and roll. By the end of his career, Bartholomew had written or collaborated on thousands of songs and sold millions of records, and he continues to collect royalties today. In recognition of his achievements, he was inducted into the Smithsonian Institute Archives as a Pioneer of Music in 1989. Bartholomew was also inducted into the Rock and Roll Hall of Fame in 1991 and awarded a Rhythm and Blues Foundation Pioneer award by the Rhythm and Blues Foundation in 1996.

Bartholomew was born in Edgard, Louisiana, on December 24, 1920. He attended McDonough #24 elementary school and, after his family moved to New Orleans, continued his education at Hoffman High School. Influenced by his father, Louis Bartholomew, who played tuba in a New Orleans jazz band, Dave Bartholomew took an interest in music. He chose to play trumpet and studied with Peter Davis, Louis Armstrong's former teacher. By 1935, he began performing throughout Louisiana and Mississippi with Oscar "Papa" Celestin's band. He also performed with Marshall Lawrence's Brass Band, Toots Johnson's band, and Claiborne Williams's band in Donaldsonville.

He gained valuable experience while working with these bands and was able to join Fats Pichon's Band on the *SS Capitol,* a Mississippi River steamboat, from 1938 to 1941. In 1940, Fats Pichon left the band for an opportunity at the Absinthe House in New Orleans, and Bartholomew assumed leadership of the band until he was drafted into military service in 1942.

Military service proved to be invaluable for Bartholomew's musical development. He served in the 196th Army Ground Force (AGF) Band, which was stationed in France during World War II. During this time, he studied composition and arranging with Abraham Maloone and was also able to develop his musical abilities through constant performing. In retrospect, Bartholomew believes that his time in the military was "one of the best things that happened to me." He remained in the 196th AGF Band until his honorable discharge in 1946.

Upon returning to New Orleans in 1946, Bartholomew assembled the best players he could find, and his band quickly became the most popular club band in the city. He also began broadcasting a regular Sunday evening radio show for Dr. Daddy-O on WMRY. This wave of public interest in Bartholomew's band led to several early recordings of the band on the De Luxe label, including "She's Got Great Big Eyes (and Great Big Thighs)" and "Bum Mae." In addition to these recordings, Bartholomew's band was called upon to back up various other De Luxe artists. In 1949, Bartholomew's band recorded "Country Boy," his biggest record for De Luxe, with sales of about 100,000 copies in 1949.

By 1949, Bartholomew's band was playing a great deal of original material, and Lew Chudd, owner and president of Imperial Records, had occasion to hear the band perform at the Bronze Peacock Club in Houston. This performance piqued Chudd's interest in Bartholomew, and the two discussed the possibility of a future working relationship. Six months later, Chudd offered Bartholomew a position in New Orleans as a producer and recruiter for Imperial Records, and Bartholomew accepted.

Tommy Ridgley and Jewel King were the first artists to be recorded under Bartholomew's direction. Jewel King's "3 x 7 = 21" became the first in a long line of hits produced by Bartholomew. While Bartholomew also recorded such artists as Jesse Allen, Fats Mathews, Smiley Lewis, and Earl King, among others, it was the discovery of Antoine "Fats" Domino that catapulted Bartholomew and Imperial Records to national and international fame.

Domino contracted to record with Imperial Records, Bartholomew's band backed him, and "Detroit City Blue" and "The Fat Man" were released. By February of 1950, "The Fat Man" broke the *Billboard* rhythm and blues charts, and climbed to number two during a three-week run in the top ten. By 1953, the song had generated the first gold record for Bartholomew and Domino, selling more than a million copies. This initial success was followed by a string of hits including "Every Night about This Time" in 1951, "Goin' Back Home," which rose to number one on the *Billboard* rhythm and blues charts in 1952, and "Goin' to the River" in 1953.

By this time, the Bartholomew/Domino combination was attracting the attention of white audiences, and their songs were edging closer to the pop music charts. This success was due, in large part, to Bartholomew's careful writing and arranging as well as to his production values. The recordings of the mid-to-late 1950s are noteworthy for their clean, punchy quality and for the simple, straightforward style of the arrangements. Unison horn lines, simple chord progressions, and catchy melodies became hallmarks of the Bartholomew style. Bartholomew developed and defined the nature of his rhythm section, eventually achieving a tight, unified, rhythmically driven sound. This "big beat" approach stripped the music to its essential rhythmic drive, and the melody was then added to the groove. This type of rhythm-based arranging would come to have lasting effects on both rhythm and blues and rock and roll. Bartholomew recalls, "I always tried to keep things as simple as possible, and we always wanted something the kids could sing. I always kept a commercial mind and kept abreast of the market." The truth of his statements is evident in the succession of hits that Bartholomew and Domino continued to record into the early 1960s.

In 1955, "Ain't That a Shame" made the Billboard Pop Top Ten. It was the first song by a New Orleans rhythm and blues artist to break the white charts at that level, and it was followed by no less than 17 Hot 100 hits between 1956 and 1957. "I'm Walkin'," "Blue Monday," and the biggest hit of Domino's career, "Blueberry Hill," all made the *Billboard* Top Ten. Interestingly, Bartholomew did not feel that "Blueberry Hill" would do Domino justice and opposed the release. Twenty-five years later, Bartholomew said, "So who am I? The record is now at about thirty million sales." In 1959, the duo had two more Top Ten hits with "I Want to Walk You Home" and "Be My Guest." The last Top Ten hit for Bartholomew and Domino came in 1960 with "Walkin' to New Orleans."

The early 1960s signaled the beginning of the end of Bartholomew's productive career. While Domino still accounted for a number of modest hits through the early 1960s, none of his records climbed any higher than number 59 on the charts after 1962. Feeling the financial strain of these developments, Lew Chudd sold Imperial Records in 1963. Bartholomew then returned to maintaining his band and concertizing. He also participated in national and international tours with Fats Domino's Band. In 1967, he started his own record label with Domino, called Broadmoor, but never pursued it as anything more than a hobby. In 1981, Bartholomew released his own Dixieland album. So, the man who for the better part of two decades had helped to define and shape the sound of New Orleans–style rhythm and blues and rock and roll remained true to his roots and returned to them at the end of his career.

LORRAINE P. WILSON

THE FAT MAN (1949)

Because Bartholomew recorded so much material with Antoine "Fats" Domino and worked with him for such an extended period of time, it is possible to trace his compositional and stylistic development by examining the songs that resulted from this collaborative effort. The following works represent a chronological cross section of Bartholomew's work with Domino ranging from 1949 to 1960.

"The Fat Man" was recorded on December 10, 1949, and released in February of 1950. It was the first collaboration of Bartholomew and Domino and is also representative of Bartholomew's early recordings at Imperial Records. The song consists of two slightly different harmonic progressions, one for the introduction and the bridge, and the other for the verses and the solo.

Formally, the song consists of an introduction that utilizes two cycles of the first progression, followed by two verses paired together, each verse using one cycle of the second progression. A solo, using two cycles of the second progression, follows the verses. This solo leads back to the introductory material, presented as a bridge. The song concludes with a third verse. Because the first two verses were paired together, this last verse leaves the listener waiting for its counterpart.

The instrumentation for "The Fat Man" is carefully arranged. During the introduction, the piano has the lead and is accompanied by the bass, which plays only the root notes of the harmonic progression. A ride cymbal completes the instrumentation for the introduction. This texture is built upon as soon as the first verse begins. Here, the full trap set enters, the bass begins a walking line, and a horn section enters with a unison riff that outlines the harmonic progression. The solo features Domino's voice as the lead instrument. By utilizing his head voice, he approximates the sound of a muted trumpet with hints of a harmonica. Following this display of vocal flexibility, the instrumental texture is reduced to mirror that of the introduction, the bridge repeating the introductory material with alterations to the piano part. The bass line also remains active, walking the line rather than playing root notes as before. The final verse ends with a unison riff by the horns.

It is difficult to filter out Bartholomew's compositional and arranging talents from this recording. The vocal line is distorted, the ensemble is not balanced, and the sonic quality of the recording lacks clarity. Yet, when it is remembered that this is one of the early Bartholomew recordings and that the equipment available to him at that time was not nearly as sophisticated as it would be even five years after the original release of this song, it becomes clear that Bartholomew was limited by a lack of production experience and of equipment. "The Fat Man," however, does not suffer from poor writing or a lack of arranging skill. On the contrary, the song evidences many of the traits that came to define some of his biggest hits: simplicity of material, unison horn riffs, attention to ensemble color, and a solid, danceable groove.

TIMOTHY ROMMEN

BLUE MONDAY (1955)

"Blue Monday" was recorded on March 30, 1955, and released in December of 1955. Bartholomew wrote this song in rounded sectional binary form (AA'BA"), and the harmonic progressions are richer than those used in "The Fat Man." Heavy use of secondary dominants and seventh chords adds tonal color and a sense of motion to the progressions.

The song is initiated by a two-measure piano introduction that begins on an upbeat. This introduction immediately gives way to the first verse of the song. The B section of the song constitutes the refrain. After the first refrain, a saxophone solo takes the place of the vocal line and plays through the second verse. The voice resumes at the second refrain, and the song comes to an abrupt close at the end of the A" section.

The instrumentation is once again well planned and thoughtfully arranged. The solo piano introduction is followed by heavy, rhythmic chords played by the entire ensemble. This punchy sound serves to define the character of the song. The ensemble, fairly compact in size, features piano, a trap set, bass, and a saxophone section. Domino lays down a triplet feeling against the 4/4 meter, giving the song a swinging rhythmic base. These triplets are mirrored and emphasized by the ride cymbal used throughout the song. During the refrain, all the instruments pick up the triplets in a unified rhythmic gesture. This emphasizes the underlying rhythmic drive of the song and creates a climax at the return of the A" section. The saxophones are designated as riff instruments, playing a unison figure in support of the harmonic structure of the song.

The clarity of the recording, and especially of the cymbals, is marred only by the lack of definition in the bass line. Nevertheless, it is evident that Bartholomew was gaining access to ever-improving equipment and that he was, by now, completely comfortable in his role as producer. It is also evident that Bartholomew had recognized the salability of simplicity. No elaborate scoring or instrumentation intrudes upon the song, and, in contrast to the "The Fat Man," no time is devoted to bridges or long introductory passage-work. Bartholomew seems to have discovered how to give the public exactly what it desired to hear.

TIMOTHY ROMMEN

I'M WALKIN' (1957)

"I'm Walkin'" was recorded under Bartholomew's direction on January 3, 1957, and released in February of that year. Like "Blue Monday," it is in rounded binary form (AA'BA"). The simple harmonic structure of the song consists of tonic, subdominant, and dominant sonorities. A two-measure drum introduction sets the tempo and style, after which the vocal line carries one cycle of the song to completion. This is followed by a saxophone solo playing a full cycle as well. The vocal line is then repeated with small changes to the lyrics during the B section. Then comes a saxophone solo that fades out toward the end of the B section in order to complete the song.

The instrumentation is simple, yet effective. The vocal line is backed by piano, guitar, bass, trap set, and saxophone. The saxophone plays only during its own solos, and the guitar doubles the bass line almost throughout. The only individual line allotted to the guitar is a rhythmic motive that occurs during the first phrase of the B section. In addition to these instruments, hand claps support the sonic impact of the snare drum.

The Bartholomew touch is evident in the fact that the piano is quite far back in the mix, making the chordal triplets that Domino played sound more percussive. With the piano reduced to a percussive role, there is enough sonic room left for the guitar and bass to double one another at the octave without muddying the sound of the whole ensemble. The saxophone is able to solo over the top of the ensemble without competition from the piano. The vocal line is pushed into the foreground and hand claps are used to add an aggressive quality to the track. The saxophone dominates the ensemble like the vocal line; it is allotted two solos that counterbalance the two sung verses. The saxophone solos can be read as a response to the call of the vocal line. In this sense, "I'm Walkin'" can be interpreted as a song with two primary instruments: voice and saxophone.

Bartholomew's skill as writer and arranger is evident in the simple, catchy quality of the tune and in the transparent and balanced quality of the ensemble that he chose. His talent as a producer is evident in the fact that this song was recorded monaurally with a one-track recorder. The clarity, punch, and balance that he achieved in spite of these limitations are a tribute to his unique ability to hear important details and make necessary adjustments to achieve improved recording quality.

TIMOTHY ROMMEN

MY GIRL JOSEPHINE (1960)

"My Girl Josephine," written by Bartholomew and Domino, was recorded in July of 1960 and released in October of that year. This song consists of a single harmonic progression that is repeated for each verse. A four-measure drum introduction sets the shuffle character of the song and is followed by four verses of the vocal line, the fourth verse constituting a textual repeat of the first verse. After the fourth cycle through the harmonic progression, the vocal line gives way to a saxophone break, arranged for an ensemble of three saxophones. The saxophones complete one cycle of the progression and continue into a second cycle as the song fades out. The song ends before the second cycle is concluded, giving the piece a sense of continuing motion.

This arrangement shows Bartholomew's ability to create new textures. The ensemble consists of piano, bass, trap set, and guitar. Horns are not heard until the solo section of the song. The piano does not play the typical "Domino" triplets; instead, Domino plays a block chord on the second and fourth beats of every bar. As a result of this less active piano part, the guitar receives a more prominent role. The guitar does not double the bass line as it does in "The Fat Man," for example, but it joins the right hand of the piano in defining the harmonic structure of the song while adding a syncopated rhythmic motive that continues throughout the song. The entrance of the saxophones in the solo section comes as a mild surprise to the listener because they have not been heard up to this point, but their presence marks an effective climactic device that closes the song with a new sonic texture.

"My Girl Josephine" demonstrates the development of studio tools well. The use of reverb to create a sense of ambiance is the most notable of these. Bartholomew does not, however, compromise clarity in his application of reverb. He uses a rapid decay (causing the reverb to fade quickly) to maintain the punchy quality for which his recordings are known. The overall balance of the mix is also evidence of better equipment.

Bartholomew was able to write and produce hits between 1949 and 1962 because he was sensitive to market trends and public taste. This sensitivity led him to pursue simplicity in his compositions and arrangements. Yet not all of Bartholomew's recordings are reduced to the bare essentials. "Walkin' to New Orleans," for example, introduces a call-and-response pattern between the vocal line and a string section, and "Valley of Tears" incorporates a mixed chorus for added effect. The overall effectiveness of Bartholomew's compositions seems to stem from his ability to fashion simple, direct arrangements and record them with punch and sonic quality.

TIMOTHY ROMMEN

REFERENCES

Bartholomew, Dave. Personal interview with Lorraine P. Wilson, November 23, 1996.

Berry, Jason, Jonathan Foose, and Tad Jones. *Up from the Cradle of Jazz: New Orleans Music since World War II.* New York: Da Capo Press, 1992.

Broven, John. *Rhythm and Blues in New Orleans.* Gretna: Pelican Publishing House, 1983.

Hannusch, Jeff. *I Hear You Knockin': The Sound of New Orleans Rhythm and Blues.* Ville Platte: Swallow Publications, 1985.

BATISTE, ALVIN

Born in New Orleans, La., November 7, 1932. **Education:** Studied clarinet with Harold Battiste, 1947, Albert Narcisse, 1947–51; Graduated from Booker T. Washington High School, New Orleans, 1951; Southern University, Baton Rouge, La., studied clarinet with Huel Perkins, 1951–55, B.S., Music Education, 1955; Louisiana State University, Baton Rouge, La., studied composition with Kenneth B. Klause and clarinet with Paul Durksmire, M.Mus., clarinet performance/theory, 1969. **Military Service:** Served in the 333rd Army Reserve Band under Melville Bryant, 1953–65. **Composing and Performing Career:** New Orleans, worked as a freelance musician, beginning ca. 1952; founding member, American Jazz Quintet, 1955; Los Angeles, played with Ornette Coleman, 1956; toured the United States with Ray Charles, 1958; worked with Cannonball Adderley, contributing to *Lovers*, 1975; performed at the Montreux International Jazz Festival, 1977; recorded and performed with Billy Cobham, contributing to *Magic*, 1977; recorded and performed with John Carter's quartet, Clarinet Summit, 1981–91. **Teaching Career:** New Orleans Public School System, 1955–65; Southern University, 1965–86; director, Jazz and Louisiana Music Institute, 1990-present. **Honors/Awards:** National Endowment for the Arts Grant, 1972. **Mailing Address:** 2833 75th Avenue, Baton Rouge, LA 70807.

MUSIC LIST

[The following list of titles includes only works that were composed by the subject of the entry; it is not a list of recordings that were made by the subject. Although the composer may have made recordings of his own works, the list is not restricted to those recordings but in many cases includes performances by other artists of the composer's work. The list is made up of publication and discographical data, in cases where such information is available. Although no effort has been made to include documentation of the earliest recording of the works listed, the date of the earliest recording that is readily available has been given. —Ed.]

INSTRUMENTAL SOLOS
Clarinet
"Etude One for B-flat Clarinet." Baton Rouge, La.: Jazzstronauts, 1988.
"Etude Two for B-flat Clarinet." Baton Rouge, La.: Jazzstronauts, 1988.

Two Pianos
"Blues for Two Pianos." 1988. Baton Rouge, La.: Jazzstronauts, 1988.

SMALL INSTRUMENTAL ENSEMBLE
Woodwinds
"Beat Box" (three B-flat clarinets, one bass clarinet). Unpublished manuscript. Recorded: Black Saint BSR 0107.
"Clariflavors" (four clarinets). Baton Rouge, La.: Jazzstronauts, 1981. Recorded: India Navigation IN-1062.
"Duet for Two Clarinets." Baton Rouge, La.: Jazzstronauts, 1988. Note: may be played by B-flat soprano clarinet and bass clarinet; two B-flat soprano clarinets; E-flat soprano clarinet and E-flat clarinet.

Combinations
The Ayjala Suite (clarinet, piano, double bass). Baton Rouge, La.: Jazzstronauts, 1973. Recorded: Fantasy F9505.
"Duet for Clarinet and Bass Violin." Baton Rouge, La.: Jazzstronauts, 1988.
"Isola de Liri" (string quartet, jazz trio, clarinet). Baton Rouge, La.: Jazzstronauts, 1997.
Ode to Bechet (string quartet, jazz trio, clarinet). Baton Rouge, La.: Jazzstronauts, 1997.
"Picou" (clarinet, cello). New Orleans: Alvin Batiste, n.d. Recorded: India Navigation IN 1069CD.

ORCHESTRA (CHAMBER OR FULL) WITH SOLOISTS
Clean Air. Baton Rouge, La.: Jazzstronauts, 1971. Recorded: South Louisiana Music NR 12045.
The Kheri Hebs (clarinet, string orchestra). Baton Rouge, La.: Jazzstronauts, ca. 1972. Recorded: India Navigation IN-1065.
Musique d'Afrique Nouvelle Orleans, Suite no. 3 (clarinet, orchestra). Baton Rouge, La.: Jazzstronauts, 1973. Recorded: India Navigation IN-1065.
North American Idiosyncrasies (clarinet, piano, double bass, drums, orchestra). Baton Rouge, La.: Jazzstronauts, 1971.
Planetary Perspectives for Grass-Roots Players and Orchestra. Baton Rouge, La.: Jazzstronauts, 1994. Premiere, 1975.
Road Symphony. Baton Rouge, La.: Jazzstronauts, 1957.
Samba Dee. Baton Rouge, La.: Jazzstronauts, 1971.

BAND
Five Pieces for Brass Band. 1998. Unpublished manuscript.

SOLO VOICE
"My Reverie." ca. 1953. Baton Rouge, La.: Jazzstronauts.

VOICE WITH INSTRUMENTAL ENSEMBLE
"The Griot Is a Lady" (narrator, string quartet, jazz trio, clarinet). 1996. Baton Rouge, La.: Jazzstronauts, 1996.
"What Is Blackness" (narrator, clarinet, violin, piano). 1996. Baton Rouge, La.: Jazzstronauts, 1996.

CHORAL MUSIC
"Growing" (SATB, narrator, jazz trio, clarinet). 1995. Baton Rouge, La.: Jazzstronauts, 1995.

MULTIMEDIA
"Interiorlism" (clarinet, computer). New Orleans: Alvin Batiste, n.d.

INCIDENTAL AND COMMERCIAL MUSIC
A Bitter Glory. Baton Rouge, La.: Jazzstronauts, 1997. Music for the play by Dalt Wonk.

JAZZ ENSEMBLE
"Aerophonica." Recorded, 1988: India Navigation IN 1069CD.
"Banjo Noir." 1993. Recorded: Sony CT53314.

Alvin Batiste; courtesy of the composer

"Bat's Blues." 1993. Recorded: Sony CT53314; South Louisiana Music NR 12045.

"Bayou Magic." Recorded, 1988: India Navigation IN 1069CD.

"Broken Dreamer." Recorded: South Louisiana Music NR 12045.

"Bumps." Recorded: South Louisiana Music NR 12045.

"Capetown." Baton Rouge, La.: Jazzstronauts, ca. 1955.

"Centennial Celebration." Recorded: South Louisiana Music NR 12045.

"Chatterbox." Baton Rouge, La.: Jazzstronauts, ca. 1955.

"Clean Air." Recorded: South Louisiana Music NR 12045.

"The Clown." Baton Rouge, La.: Jazzstronauts, ca. 1953.

"Cochise." Baton Rouge, La.: Jazzstronauts, ca. 1955.

"The Endochrine Song." Recorded, 1988: India Navigation IN-1065.

"ESP." Recorded: South Louisiana Music NR 12045.

"Fluffy's Blues." Recorded, 1987: Black Saint BSR 0107.

"Ghetto Hero." Recorded: South Louisiana Music NR 12045.

"Give It Up or Tell Where It's At." Recorded: South Louisiana Music NR 12045.

"Imp and Perry." Recorded, 1988: India Navigation IN 1069CD; Sony CT53314.

"Jupiter Trek." Recorded: South Louisiana Music NR 12045.

"Kinshasa." 1993. Recorded: Sony CT53314.

"Late." 1993. Recorded: Sony CT53314.

"Morocco." Baton Rouge, La.: Jazzstronauts, ca. 1955.

"Mozartin'." Baton Rouge, La.: Jazzstronauts, ca. 1955. Recorded: Columbia CK 53177.

"Music Came." Recorded: South Louisiana Music NR 12045.

"My Little Star." Recorded: South Louisiana Music NR 12045.

"My Little Star Revisited." Recorded: South Louisiana Music NR 12045.

"Nigeria." Baton Rouge, La.: Jazzstronauts, ca. 1955.

"Ray's Segue." Co-composer, Ray Charles. Recorded, 1993: Sony CT53314.

"Rows." Recorded: South Louisiana Music NR 12045.

"Traveling to Eunice." Baton Rouge, La.: Jazzstronauts, 1952.

"Tutuman." Recorded, 1988: India Navigation IN 1069CD.

"Venus Flow." Recorded, 1988: India Navigation IN 1069CD.

"When the Saints." 1993. Recorded: Sony CT53314.

PUBLICATIONS

ABOUT BATISTE

Birnbaum, Larry. "Alvin Batiste." *Down Beat* 49, no. 10 (1982): 54–55.

BY BATISTE

How to Sell Jazz. Baton Rouge, La.: Jazzstronauts, 1988.

The Root Progression Process: Fundamental Principles of African American Music. Baton Rouge, La.: Jazzstronauts, 1997.

* * * * *

New Orleans rhythm and blues flourished during the 1950s, and this money-generating genre quickly absorbed a great deal of that city's creative energy. Yet, despite the pervasiveness of rhythm and blues, a small number of New Orleans-based musicians continued to explore the expressive possibilities of jazz. This community of musicians included, among others, Ellis Marsalis, Edward Blackwell, Harold Battiste, and Alvin Batiste. Batiste, a clarinetist who is a proficient performer of jazz, rhythm and blues, traditional New Orleans jazz, and classical music, and who has played and recorded with such musicians as Cannonball Adderley (*Lovers,* 1975) and Billy Cobham (*Magic,* 1977) and in John Carter's quartet, Clarinet Summit (*In Concert at the Public Theater,* 1991). He has also recorded solo albums, of which the most recent is *Late* (1993). Batiste is also a skilled composer who has written works for solo voice, chorus, jazz ensemble, string quartet, symphony orchestra, clarinet, and piano, and he is currently completing an opera. Batiste's compositions evidence a variety of stylistic influences, including those of his native New Orleans, African-American musical traditions (such as jazz, blues, and gospel), and music of West Africa (such as Ewe music), and he incorporates these divergent influences into a highly personal creative language.

Alvin Batiste showed early interest in music—following a jazz band around town on an Easter Sunday when he was only four or five years old—and was exposed to the rich and varied musical styles of New Orleans throughout his childhood. When Batiste was about 14, his father, Edgar Batiste, bought him a clarinet, but his creative energies were being absorbed by the study and practice of visual art. As a result, the clarinet at first remained virtually untouched. However, one day in 1947, Batiste heard Raymond Lewis (a cousin of Harold Battiste) play Charlie Parker's "Now's the Time" on tenor saxophone. This musical event radically changed his perception of music and increased his interest in it. Batiste recalls, "When that man started to play, my heart moved, and I knew right then I wanted to play." In fact, Batiste talked Harold Battiste into giving him a clarinet lesson that very day, and he applied himself with enthusiasm from that point on. Soon thereafter, he continued clarinet lessons with Albert Narcisse.

Batiste attended Booker T. Washington High School, where he benefited from the teaching of his band instructor, Doris D. Barthé, and began to be influenced by the music of Charlie Parker, John Coltrane, Sonny Rollins, Elvin Jones, Nat "King" Cole, Miles Davis, and Clifford Brown. After graduating from high school in 1951, Batiste entered the musical life of the city, freelancing in studio and live performance venues in and around New Orleans. In order to become a more versatile and marketable player, he learned to play the saxophone in addition to the clarinet. During the early 1950s, he played with Professor Longhair, Cannonball Adderley, the Duke Ellington Orchestra, Freddie Hubbard, and many other musicians and bands.

In 1951, Batiste entered Southern University (Baton Rouge, La.) and pursued a bachelor of science degree in music education, studying clarinet with Huel Perkins. This degree study exposed him to classical music and to the techniques of composing and arranging. By 1952, he began to pursue this interest seriously, concentrating primarily on jazz composition. In 1953, he enlisted with the 333rd Army Reserve Band, which was directed by Melville Bryant, and served with that unit until 1965. After graduating from college in 1955, he accepted a position with the New Orleans public school system, teaching band and elementary instrumental music for several schools at various locations. This position provided Batiste with ample opportunities to develop his transcribing, arranging, and writing skills, and he remained with the public schools until 1965.

In addition to teaching, Batiste continued to perform and record with various artists. He was a founding member of the American Jazz Quintet, which included Edward Blackwell and Ellis Marsalis, among others, and this group began playing some of his compositions (for example, "Imp and Perry" and "Mozartin'"). In 1956, Batiste played with Ornette Coleman, and in 1958, he toured with Ray Charles, establishing himself as one of the most respected, if not widely publicly recognized, clarinetists in the country.

In 1965, Batiste accepted a position as jazz instructor at Southern University, and his excellent work with the Southern University Jazz Ensemble led to a grant from the National Endowment for the Arts in 1972, which was awarded in order to assist him to develop a jazz music curriculum for public schools. That same year, Batiste spent eight weeks in Africa, where he visited several countries and studied many of the musical genres and cultural elements. As a result of this experience, he became interested in the interaction of different musics and cultures and was inspired to compose *Musique d'Afrique Nouvelle Orleans, Suite no. 3* (for clarinet and orchestra).

In 1969, Batiste earned a master of music degree in clarinet performance and composition from Louisiana State University. While enrolled, he studied clarinet with Paul Durksmire and composition with Kenneth B. Klause and developed an interest in combining classical and jazz elements for the resulting expressive possibilities. He also began to make a conscious distinction between the two arenas in which he actively engaged as a composer—the stage and the studio. He began to call his live and improvisatory work "spontaneous composition," while the materials that were worked out in his study came to be referred to by him as "meditative composition." His exceptional work at Louisiana State University prompted the inclusion of some of his compositions in the Louisiana Composer's Symposium of 1975. This symposium, sponsored by the New Orleans Philharmonic Orchestra, included the premiere of his *Planetary Perspectives for Grass-Roots Players and Orchestra*.

During the 1970s and early 1980s, Batiste continued to perform widely, participating in the Montreux International Jazz Festival in 1977 and performing with the Clarinet Summit from 1981 until 1991. He also founded his own record label/publishing house called Jazzstronauts. In 1986, Batiste resigned his position at Southern University and went into semiretirement. He spent the next four years composing and performing. In 1990, however, Southern University asked Batiste to return as director of the newly established Jazz and Louisiana Music Institute. He accepted this post and remains there as of this writing. In addition to his appointment at Southern University, Batiste has lectured and participated in symposiums and panels across the country and abroad. He has presented his works and ideas at institutions such as Yale University, Harvard University, the University of Michigan, the Harlem School for the Arts, Jackson State University, and the University of Bamako in Mali. His educational philosophy mirrors his approach to composition. Batiste asserts, "When you take African music as a foundation, you can teach any music on the planet, for it is based on universal principles."

His most recent compositions include "The Griot Is a Lady" (1996), for narrator, string quartet, jazz trio, and solo clarinet;

"Growing" (1995), for four-part chorus, narrator, jazz trio, and clarinet; and "What Is Blackness" (1996), for narrator, piano, clarinet, and violin. The poetry included in these works is drawn from the work of Batiste's wife, Edith Chatters. Batiste's career demonstrates his commitment to composition as well as his dedication to performance and education, and it exemplifies the concept of the "well-rounded musician." This musical breadth has earned him the respect of his colleagues and of his students, as well as the admiration of his audiences.

LORRAINE P. WILSON

BLUES FOR TWO PIANOS (1988)

A through-composed work in 4/4 time scored for two pianos, "Blues for Two Pianos" shows many of the musical influences that Batiste has incorporated into his style. It belongs to the body of his works that he designates as meditative compositions. A three-measure introduction precedes the opening motive, and once the motive has been stated, the melodic material is constantly developed until a varied restatement of the introductory material serves as a framing device at the conclusion of the work.

Batiste creates a highly complex rhythmic texture in "Blues for Two Pianos." The body of the work is based on constant 16th-note motion. This is achieved primarily through the two right-hand parts, where the motivic material is presented in an almost continuous 16th-note base rhythm. This rapid base rhythm provides a consistent texture within which Batiste explores sudden rests and syncopations. The rests, which occur at various point throughout the work, halt the 16th-note rhythm and introduce elements of surprise into the work. They also serve as points of articulation, breaking the work into several smaller sections. In the introduction and the conclusion of the work, Batiste utilizes triplets in order to add an additional layer of rhythmic complexity to these sections, enhancing their value as a frame for the body of the work. These elements give the work a sense of direction and provide additional means for the listener to organize the material during performance.

The melodic structure of "Blues for Two Pianos" is based primarily on scalar patterns and on a succession of short motivic cells. The relationship between the two right-hand parts is announced in the opening triplet gesture, where the two parts move in parallel perfect fourths. Subsequently, a large portion of the work is devoted to quartal textures. The left-hand parts operate within a more flexible relationship. Nevertheless, these parts are also frequently linked together by fourths and fifths. The resulting texture is measurably more horizontal than vertical in nature. The melodic emphasis is clearly placed on the right-hand parts, yet occasional, supporting countermelodies in slower rhythmic values are introduced into the left-hand parts. The work's harmonic structure, then, is determined through the individual lines rather than by a vertical stacking of voices. This linear activity, like the rhythmic points of articulation, gives the work a clear sense of direction.

The right-hand parts occasionally merge into unison passages, which break the insistent quartal relationship long enough to avoid monotony in the vertical texture. The melodic material also explores the expressive possibilities of blue notes. One of many examples of Batiste's use of blue notes is evident in measure six, where the opening group of 16th-notes comprises the pitches of *d, g, b*-flat, *c*-sharp, and *c*. The *c*-sharp adds a blue-note inflection to a figure that is built to sound pentatonic in nature. This combination of scale type and blue note lends the passage a distinct character that is evident in much African-American traditional and popular music. The blue inflection caused by the inclusion of *c*-sharp is explored in greater depth in the measures that follow.

Rhythmic complexity, quartal harmonies, blue notes, and constant variation and development of the melodic material characterize this work. The rhythmic complexity certainly draws from sub-Saharan African musical practices as well as from African-American sound ideals. In like fashion, the blue notes and constant variation can be linked to traditional African-American genres such as the spiritual. The quartal harmonies seem to be drawn from classical models. This integration of musical traits from diverse cultures and musical canons is typical of Batiste's commitment to exploring the possibilities of musical syncretism.

TIMOTHY ROMMEN

BAT'S BLUES (1993)

"Bat's Blues" was written for inclusion in Batiste's solo album titled *Late* (1993). This 12-bar blues is consciously modeled on late 1950s bebop style, as the theme is accompanied by a straightforward chord progression that is used throughout the entire song. In addition, the work follows the convention of stating the theme, breaking into various solos, and restating the theme. "Bat's Blues" showcases Batiste's virtuosity on his instrument, the B-flat clarinet, and the improvisatory material is a good example of what Batiste refers to as spontaneous composition.

Batiste recorded "Bat's Blues" with piano, bass, and drums. The recording is nine minutes and 20 seconds long and allows ample time for solos and exchanges between the parts. An introduction played by the piano, bass, and drums reveals the chord progression in F minor that becomes the basis for the remainder of the song. In its most basic functional realization, this progression can be diagrammed as follows: i–iv–V–i–iv–i–V–i. Yet the progression is modified with chord substitutions and chromatic inflections at almost every turn. The theme itself consists of a series of brief melodic figures, each of which begins on the seventh degree of the accompanying chord. In addition, each melodic figure encompasses a range of more than one octave, allowing for wide intervallic jumps and contributing to a sense that the melody is constructed of disjunct fragments. By creating this fragmentary feeling in the opening measures of the piece, Batiste prepares the listener for the introduction of a large variety of chord substitutions and chromatic materials in the solo sections. These more complex tonalities can then be interpreted as extensions of the disjunct opening gestures rather than as isolated events.

The introduction is followed by two statements of the theme on the clarinet. Between these two statements of the theme, there appear solos for clarinet, piano, bass, and drums, respectively. The solos for clarinet and piano are quite extended, each one playing out over nine cycles of the chord progression. The bass solo is, by comparison, of more modest proportions, coming to a close after four cycles of the progression. The drum solo is the shortest of all, absorbing a mere three cycles, after which the restatement of the theme begins. The thematic statements are mirrored by two varied restatements of the theme at the close of the piece.

"Bat's Blues" is an excellent reflection of Batiste's musical roots in the New Orleans jazz community, and it also illustrates his performative and improvisational abilities. The two works discussed in this essay reflect only a small sampling of the versatility and variety that Batiste develops in his compositions. For example, Batiste has worked with computer music and is currently working on projects that incorporate recited poetry; his treatment of larger ensembles is marked by the combination of classical and jazz forces. Batiste has said that a large part of composition involves "attuning or becoming attuned to your experience." The variety that is so evident in his compositions attests to both his rich experiences and to his successful "attuning" to them.

TIMOTHY ROMMEN

REFERENCES

Batiste, Alvin. Interview with Lorraine Wilson, August 29, 1996.

"Batiste, Alvin." In *The New Grove Dictionary of Jazz,* edited by Barry Kernfeld. London: Macmillan, 1988.

Berry, Jason, Jonathan Foose, and Tad Jones. *Up from the Cradle of Jazz: New Orleans Music since World War II.* New York: Da Capo, 1992.

Birnbaum, Larry. "Alvin Batiste." *Down Beat* 49, no. 10 (1982): 54–55.

BERRY, CHUCK

Born Charles Edward Anderson Berry in San Jose, Calif., October 18, 1926. **Education:** Began piano study at age seven; Wentzville and St. Louis, Mo., musical education in public schools studying guitar and saxophone, 1931–39; Sumner High School, encouraged by guitar teacher Julia Davis, sang in glee club, 1939–44. **Composing and Performing Career:** St. Louis, started with the Ray Banks Orchestra, ca. 1950; formed popular trio, 1952; Chicago, Ill., contract with Chess Records, 1955; recorded many hit singles for Chess, beginning with "Maybelline," 1955; toured widely in U.S. and abroad, 1955–61; after time in prison, 1961–63, made a comeback with "Nadine (Is That You?)" and "No Particular Place to Go," 1964; signed with Mercury Records, 1966; returned to Chess Records, 1970; number one pop hit with "My Ding-a-Ling," 1972; throughout his career has appeared on many television shows and in films, including *Rock, Rock, Rock,* 1956, *Mister Rock and Roll,* 1957, *Go Johnny Go,* 1959, and *American Hot Wax,* 1978; appeared in various concert films including, *The T.A.M.I. Show,* 1965, *Let the Good Times Roll,* 1973, and *Chuck Berry: Hail! Hail! Rock 'n' Roll,* 1987; autobiography published, 1987; continues to record occasionally and perform widely. **Honors/Awards:** "Johnny B. Goode" included on sampler of terrestrial music in *Voyager 2* space probe, launched in 1977; Rock and Roll Hall of Fame, charter inductee, 1986.

SELECTED MUSIC LIST

"Almost Grown." n.p.: Isalee Music, 1959. Recorded: Chess CHD3-80001; Chess CHD-92500; Elektra 61343; Instant CD 5035.

"Anthony Boy." n.p.: Isalee Music, 1958. Recorded: Chess CHD3-80001; Chess CHD-31260.

"Around and Around." n.p.: Isalee Music, 1958. Recorded: Chess CHD3-80001; Chess CHD-92500; Instant CD 5035; Instant CD INS 5016.

"Back in the USA." n.p.: Isalee Music, 1959. Recorded: Chess CHD3-80001; Chess CHD-92500; Epic BN 26176; Instant CD 5035.

"Beautiful Delilah." n.p.: Isalee Music, 1958. Recorded: Chess CHD3-80001; Chess CHD-92500; Instant CD 5035.

"Betty Jean." n.p.: Isalee Music, 1959. Recorded: Chess CHD3-80001.

"Bio." n.p.: Isalee Music, 1973. Recorded: Chess CHD3-80001; MCA Records CHC 91510.

"Brown-Eyed Handsome Man." New York: Arc Music, 1956. Recorded: Chess CHD3-80001; Chess CHD-92500; Epic BN 26176; Instant CD 5035.

"Bye Bye Johnny." n.p.: Isalee Music, 1960. Recorded: Chess CHD3-80001; Chess CHD-92500; Epic BN 26176; Instant CD 5035.

"Carol." n.p.: Isalee Music, 1958. Recorded: Chess CHD3-80001; Chess CHD-92500; Instant CD 5035; Instant CD INS 5016.

"Come On." New York: Arc Music, 1961. Recorded: Chess CHD3-80001; Chess CHD-92500; Instant CD 5035.

"Downbound Train." n.p.: Isalee Music, 1955. Recorded: Chess CHD3-80001; Chess 2CH-60028.

"Drifting Heart." New York: Arc Music, 1956. Recorded: Chess CHD3-80001; Chess CHD-9284; Chess 2CH-60028.

"Havana Moon." n.p.: Isalee Music, 1956. Recorded: Atco SD 38-118; Chess CHD3-80001; Chess CHD-92500; Chess CHD-9284.

"I Want to Be Your Driver." n.p.: Isalee Music, 1964. Recorded: Chess CHD-92500; Chess LP 1495; Rhino R2-70165.

"Jaguar and the Thunderbird." n.p.: Isalee Music, 1960. Recorded: Chess CHD3-80001.

"Jo Jo Gunne." n.p.: Isalee Music, 1958. Recorded: Chess CHD3-80001; Rhino 71062.

"Johnny B. Goode." n.p.: Isalee Music, 1958. Recorded: Chess CHD3-80001; Chess CHD-92500; Epic BN 26176; Instant CD 5035.

"Let It Rock." n.p.: Isalee Music, 1959. Recorded: Chess CHD3-80001; Chess CHD-92500; Instant CD 5035; Mercury 6463 044.

"Little Marie." n.p.: Isalee Music, 1964. Recorded: Chess CHD3-80001; Chess/MCA CHD-31261.

"Little Queenie." n.p.: Isalee Music, 1959. Recorded: Chess CHD3-80001; Chess CHD-92500; Chess CHD-92521; Instant CD 5035.

"Maybelline." n.p.: Isalee Music, 1955. Recorded: Chess CHD3-80001; Chess CHD-92500; Epic BN 26176; Instant CD 5035.

"Memphis." n.p.: Isalee Music, 1958. Recorded: Chess CHD3-80001; Chess CHD-92500; Epic BN 26176.

"Nadine (Is It You?)." New York: Arc Music, 1964. Recorded: Chess CHD3-80001; Chess CHD-92500; Instant CD 5035.

"No Money Down." n.p.: Isalee Music, 1955. Recorded: Chess CHD3-80001; Chess CHD-9284; Instant CD 5035.

"No Particular Place to Go." New York: Arc Music, 1964. Recorded: Chess CHD3-80001; Chess CHD-92500; Instant CD 5035.

"Oh Baby Doll." n.p.: Isalee Music, 1957. Recorded: Chess CHD3-80001; Chess CHD-92500; Mercury 6463 044.

"Promised Land." New York: Arc Music, 1964. Recorded: Chess CHD3-80001; Instant CD 5035.

"Reelin' and Rockin'." n.p.: Isalee Music, 1958. Recorded: Chess CHD3-80001; Chess CHD-92500; Epic BN 26176; Instant CD 5035.

"Rock and Roll Music." n.p.: Isalee Music, 1957. Recorded: Chess CHD3-80001; Chess CHD-92500; Instant CD 5035; Mercury 6463 044.

"Roll Over Beethoven." n.p.: Isalee Music, 1956. Recorded: Chess CHD3-80001; Chess CHD-92500; Instant CD 5035; MCA MCAD-6217.

"School Day." n.p.: Isalee Music, 1956. Recorded: Chess CHD3-80001; Chess CHD-9284; Chess CHD-92500.

"Sweet Little Rock 'n' Roller." n.p.: Isalee Music, 1958. Recorded: Chess CHD3-80001; Chess CHD-92500.

"Sweet Little Sixteen." n.p.: Isalee Music, 1958. Recorded: Chess CHD3-80001; Chess CHD-92500; Epic BN 26176; Instant CD 5035.

"Thirty Days" or "Forty Days." n.p.: Isalee Music, 1955. Recorded: Chess CHD3-80001; Chess CHD-92500; Instant CD 5035.

"Too Much Monkey Business." n.p.: Isalee Music, 1956. Recorded: Chess CHD3-80001; Chess CHD-92500; Epic BN 26176; Instant CD 5035.

"Tulane." n.p.: Isalee Music, 1969. Recorded: Chess CHD3-80001; Contour 6870638.

Chuck Berry; courtesy of the Frank Driggs Collection

"Wee Wee Hours." n.p.: Isalee Music, 1955. Recorded: Chess CHD3-80001; Chess CHD-9284; MCA MCAD-6217.

"You Can't Catch Me." n.p.: Isalee Music, 1955. Recorded: Chess CHD3-80001; Chess CHD-92500; Instant CD 5035; Instant CD INS 5016.

"You Never Can Tell." New York: Arc Music, 1964. Recorded: Chess CHD3-80001; Instant CD 5035.

PUBLICATIONS

ABOUT BERRY
Books and Monographs
De Witt, Howard A. *Chuck Berry: Rock 'n' Roll Music.* 2nd ed. Ann Arbor, Mich.: Pierian Press, 1985.

Reese, Krista. *Chuck Berry: Mr. Rock 'n' Roll.* London: Proteus, 1982.

Articles
Doering, C. "The Changing Sounds of Rock & Roll: Electric Guitar—A Brief History." *Rolling Stone* 363 (February 18, 1982): 61–62.

Fryer, Paul. "'Brown-Eyed Handsome Man': Chuck Berry and the Blues Tradition." *Phylon* 42, no. 1 (1981): 60–72.

Loder, Kurt. "The Rock and Roll Hall of Fame: The Music That Changed the World." *Rolling Stone* 467 (February 13, 1986): 49–50.

Lydon, Michael. "Chuck Berry." In *Rock Folk: Portraits from the Rock 'n' Roll Pantheon*, 1–23. New York: Carol Publishing Group, 1990.

Marsh, Dave. "Berry, Chuck." In *The New Rolling Stone Record Guide*, edited by Dave Marsh and John Swanson. 2nd ed. New York: Random House, 1983.

Sousa, L. M. "Chuck Berry: A Compendium." *OneTwoThreeFour: A Rock 'n' Roll Quarterly* 1 (Summer 1984): 56–62.

Tucker, Bruce. "'Tell Tchaikovsky the News': Postmodernism, Popular Culture, and the Emergence of Rock 'n' Roll." *Black Music Research Journal* 9 no. 2 (1989): 271–295.

Watson, A. "Rolling Stone Portraits: Chuck Berry." *Rolling Stone* 643 (November 12, 1992): 189+.

BY BERRY
Chuck Berry: The Autobiography. New York: Harmony Books, 1987.

PRINCIPAL ARCHIVES
Rock 'n' Roll Hall of Fame, Cleveland Ohio.

* * * * *

In the 1950s, Chuck Berry's songs exemplified the spirit, the lyric approaches, and the musical structure of rock 'n' roll music—a fusion of big band, country, blues, pop, and jazz. His evocative teen-oriented lyrics captured the imagination of the young public and placed him at the pinnacle of rock 'n' roll lyricists. His most famous compositions, among the more than 200 to his credit, are "Maybelline," "Roll Over Beethoven," "Johnny B. Goode," "School Day," "Rock and Roll Music," and "No Particular Place to Go." No other rock 'n' roll artist of the 1950s, black or white, wielded the influence on later music that Chuck Berry did. Among the many later recordings of his songs by other rock 'n' roll performers are Buddy Holly's "Brown-Eyed Handsome Man," Ronnie

Hawkins's "Forty Days" (retitled from "Thirty Days"), the Beach Boys' "Surfin' USA" (a reworking of "Sweet Little Sixteen"), Johnny Rivers's "Memphis," the Beatles' "Roll Over Beethoven," and the Rolling Stones' "Carol." Berry created the new musical language of rock 'n' roll and thus must be considered the principal founding father of the music.

Chuck Berry was involved in music from his childhood. He began piano study at age seven and obtained additional musical instruction in the public schools of Wentzville, Missouri, and St. Louis, where he studied the guitar and the saxophone and sang in the Sumner High School glee club. With his new facility on guitar, Berry learned to play the blues, country tunes, and popular ballads he had heard on radio. His two greatest musical influences were country and western music and Louis Jordan, whose sly and witty shuffle boogie-beat style of rhythm and blues shows up dramatically in Berry's approach to songwriting.

About 1950, Berry was playing in local bars to supplement his income from regular jobs, and he gradually began to develop his craft of songwriting, based mostly on blues structures that he enlivened and sped up, reflecting influences from Louis Jordan and country music. Much of his development on the guitar in the 1950s was as a result of instruction he received from Ira Harris, a jazz musician who taught him riffs that would help to make tunes swing. Said Berry, "Ira showed me many licks and riffs on the guitar that came to be the foundation of the style that is said to be Chuck Berry's." In the summer of 1952, Berry joined a combo at Huff's Garden in St. Louis.

From Huff's Garden, Berry advanced in 1953 to a much larger nightclub, the Cosmopolitan (or Cosmo) in St. Louis, where his performances were accompanied by pianist Johnnie Johnson and drummer Ebby Hardy. These sessions, in a club whose patrons were overwhelmingly African American, played a defining role in Berry's development as a musician and a composer, because in them, he mixed two vernaculars—country and western and rhythm and blues—and created a new syncretic music we now call rock 'n' roll. Said Berry, "the music played most around St. Louis was country-western, which was usually called hillbilly music, and swing. Curiosity provoked me to lay a lot of the country stuff on our predominately black audience and some of the club-goers started whispering, 'who is that black hillbilly at the Cosmo?' After they laughed at me a few times, they began requesting the hillbilly stuff and enjoyed trying to dance to it." Soon whites began flocking to the club to see this new phenomenon.

It was in this context that Berry developed as a composer, altering and revising songs with improvisations, adding verses, changing lyrics, and playing off the audience to see what would get applause. By the time he signed with Chess in 1955, he was ready to record the songs he was performing at the Cosmo Club.

Berry was almost fully formed as a composer and recording artist when he joined Chess. His first composition and recording for the label, "Maybelline," launched his career as a major rock 'n' roll star in 1955, the same year that rock 'n' roll began making its impact nationally and many months before Elvis Presley came on the scene. Berry was forced to share composing credits for "Maybelline" with Alan Freed and record distributor Russ Frato, since Chess had given each one-third of the royalties as payola (undercover or indirect payment) to help market the song.

Fast and beat-heavy songs with lyric themes relating to teenagers constitute the bulk of Berry's subsequent hit recordings. The songs celebrate youth culture and include "Roll Over Beethoven" (1956), "School Day" (1956), "Rock and Roll Music" (1957), "Sweet Little Sixteen" (1958), "Johnny B. Goode" (1958), and "Carol" (1958). On most of these songs Berry employs 12-bar blues progressions. The flip side of the single "Sweet Little Sixteen" features one of his most notable non-hit compositions, "Reelin' and Rockin'," which shows a heavy debt to Louis Jordan's 1949 hit "Saturday Night Fish Fry."

Berry has many instrumentals in his catalog, a result of recordings of between-song warm-ups of the session band. More formally recorded instrumentals are "Deep Feeling" and "Blue Feeling."

By 1959, Berry's recordings were less successful, and he was no longer the hit maker of earlier years. Two years of prison from 1961 through 1963 knocked him off the pop charts completely. But a comeback during the height of the British invasion produced such stellar songs as "Nadine (Is It You?)" (1964) and "No Particular Place to Go" (1964). But by the end of 1964, Berry's best work was behind him, and he had almost no success thereafter.

During the period from 1966 to 1969, Berry recorded for Mercury but produced nothing memorable. He returned to Chess in 1970, recording an album called *Back Home,* which showed little evidence that his songwriting skills were resuscitated. In 1972, in the United Kingdom, he recorded tracks for *The London Chuck Berry Sessions,* which was a combination of studio and live recordings. From the live portion of the album came his first number one pop hit, a ribald novelty, "My Ding-a-Ling." (Although he took songwriting credit, the song actually had been written and recorded by New Orleans bandleader Dave Bartholomew in 1952.)

Berry's last studio album for Chess was *Bio* in 1973. After that, his recording opportunities were exceedingly limited. With his creative years behind him, Berry toured worldwide on the strength of his legendary name, playing before large audiences with pick-up bands.

SELECTED WORKS

"Maybelline" was the song that launched Berry's recording career, but in terms of composition, it was not his most typical. It was based on a country song, "Ida Red," which had been recorded earlier by Bob Wills and also by the Louvin Brothers. Berry first started singing "Ida Red" when he was learning to play the guitar, and in 1953, while playing it at the Cosmo Club, Berry transformed it into "Maybelline." While singing "Ida Red," Berry would improvise and insert comical lines. The lyrics began to take on the cast of high school teen culture, revealing Berry's youth and recollection of his secondary school years. Musically, the song would change as Berry, singing a country song to a black audience, would add more drive and rhythm. When Berry brought the transformation to Chess, Willie Dixon told Berry that while the lyrics about "automobiles and racing" had that universal teen appeal, the song sounded too country and too much like "Ida Red." Berry added elements, primarily rhythmic, that changed the song into pure rock 'n' roll.

"School Day," a 12-bar blues, is more characteristic of Berry's compositions than "Maybelline." A product of Berry's memories of his own high school days, the song also exemplifies how the composer lyrically connected with the new rock 'n' roll audience by documenting a day in the life of a typical American teenager. Berry brilliantly incorporated breaks in the rhythm to evoke the changing makeup of the school day. In his biography, Berry says that rhyming took up the bulk of the time in composing the song. Thus, by having the lyrics already written and then using his guitar to pick the notes to accompany them, his melodies are spare and memorable. This is reflected in his entire body of work, the melodies of which are composed of few notes.

Berry created archetypes that embodied the spirit of rock 'n' roll, and "Johnny B. Goode" exemplifies that approach unlike any other of his songs. He originally wrote this song to exemplify his career, although the "Johnny" refers specifically to his piano accompanist, Johnnie Johnson. He worked, however, to make the song sound universal: originally describing Johnny B. Goode as a "colored boy," who "could play his guitar just like a-ringin'-a-bell," while recording the song, he changed the "colored boy" reference to "country boy" to make the song transcend race in appeal. But in his autobiography, he states that "colored boy" is what he really meant, saying "I imagine most black people naturally realize but I feel safe in stating that NO white person can conceive the feeling of obtaining Caucasian respect in the wake of a world of dark denial, simply because it is impossible to view the dark side when faced with brilliance. 'Johnny B. Goode' was created as all other things and brought out of a modern dark age." Berry seems to be saying here that the subtext of the song was the feeling of black pride and achievement, a sentiment that was not openly expressed in the 1950s.

"Johnny B. Goode" is a 12-bar blues in which once again Berry first wrote the lyrics and then picked out the melody on the guitar. A snippet of lyric in the song, "Deep down in Louisiana, close to New Orleans," uses one note, except for a little dip at the word "close." His technique was to stay on one note for a whole phrase. Different notes are used sparingly throughout "Johnny B. Goode," but the melody is riveting.

"Havana Moon" shows a side of Berry that he rarely explored, the Caribbean influence, which came to him through his contact with the Afro-Cuban population in New York. As recorded, Berry sang the song using a West Indian accent and gave this two-chord composition a calypso beat. The lyrics tell a story of a lovelorn Cuban sailor who stays up all night with a jug of rum, waiting for an American girl to arrive to take him to America, specifically to a New York City apartment. He, however, keeps drinking from the jug, and by morning he is passed out on the pier. (Berry apparently equated Cuban with West Indian.) He awakes too late, finding the girl on the boat disappearing beyond the horizon. In composing the song, Berry was influenced by Nat King Cole's "Calypso Blues." The song was recorded in 1956 and originally released as the flip side of a typical Berry rocker, "You Can't Catch Me." In 1964, a local radio station in Chicago, WVON, began playing the record again, which stimulated Chess to rerelease the song. It became a top ten R&B hit in Chicago but got few plays elsewhere. "Havana Moon" heavily influenced another R&B singer, Richard Berry, whose "Louie Louie" tells a similar story to a similar lilting beat.

REFERENCES

Berry, Chuck. *Chuck Berry: The Autobiography.* New York: Harmony Books, 1987.

Dixon, Willie, with Don Snowden. *I Am the Blues: The Willie Dixon Story.* New York: Da Capo, 1989.

ROBERT PRUTER

BETHUNE, THOMAS GREENE WIGGINS ("BLIND TOM")

Born Thomas Greene Wiggins near Columbus, Ga., May 25, 1849; died in Hoboken, N.J., June 13, 1908. **Education:** Showed musical aptitude from the age of four; allowed to play the piano of the family that owned him; informal instruction by the Bethune daughters and Mrs. Bethune, a former music teacher; Atlanta, Ga., studied with W. P. Howard, ca. 1865–66; New York, studied with Joseph Pozananski, ca. 1867. **Composing and Performing Career:** Exhibited throughout Georgia by his master, 1857; hired out to Perry Oliver for a tour through the South, 1858–61; forced to give benefit concerts for wounded Confederate soldiers, summer, 1861; toured throughout the United States, Canada, Europe, and South America, 1866–98; billed on the vaudeville circuit, 1890s; retired, 1898; made a final major concert tour, possibly on the Keith Circuit, 1904–05.

MUSIC LIST

COLLECTIONS

Plantation Melodies as Sung by Blind Tom, with His Original Accompaniments. n.p.: T. G. Bethune, 1881. Contents: Waggin' Up Zion's Hill; That Welcome Day; Come Along, Moses; Them Golden Slippers.

Specimens of Blind Tom's Vocal Compositions. 1867. Partial copy held at the Library of Congress.

INSTRUMENTAL SOLOS
Piano

"Academy Schottische." n.p.: W. P. Howard, 1864.

"The Battle of Manassas." Cleveland: S. Brainard's Sons, 1866.

"Blind Tom's March." Boston: Oliver Ditson & Co., 1851.

"Blind Tom's Mazurka." Boston: Oliver Ditson, ca. 1888.

"Blind Tom's Waltz," op. 2. Philadelphia: J. Marsh, 1854.

"Columbus March." Boston: Oliver Ditson, 1888.

"Concert Hall Polka." Boston: Oliver Ditson, 1888.

"Cyclone Galop." New York: William E. Ashnall, 1887.

"Daylight, a Musical Expression for the Piano." Cleveland: S. Brainard's Sons, 1866.

"General Howard's March." Philadelphia: J. March, 1865.

"Grand March Resurrection." Highlands, N.J.: E. Bethune, ca. 1901.

"March Lanpier Polka." New York: F. Blume, 1887.

"Oliver Gallop." New York: H. Waters, 1860. Recorded: Opus One 39; Desto DC-6445/7.

"The Rainstorm," op. 6. New York: J. L. Peters, 1865. Recorded: Challenge Productions CP-8206.

"Rêve charmant: Nocturne for Piano." [New York]: J. G. Bethune, 1881. Recorded: Challenge Productions CP-8206.

"Sewing Song: Imitation of the Sewing Machine." New York: W. A. Pond, ca. 1888. Recorded: Challenge Productions CP-8206.

"Virginia Polka." New York: H. Waters, ca. 1860. Recorded: Challenge Productions CP-8206.

"Water in the Moonlight." Chicago: S. Brainard's Sons, 1866. Recorded: Challenge Productions CP-8206.

"When This Cruel War Is Over." Philadelphia: J. Marsh, 1865.

SOLO VOICE

"I Wish Dear Jodie Would Come Home." In *Specimens of Blind Tom's Vocal Compositions.*

"The Man Who Mashed His Hand." In *Specimens of Blind Tom's Vocal Compositions.*

"The Man Who Snatched the Cornet Out of His Hand." In *Specimens of Blind Tom's Vocal Compositions.*

"The Man Who Sprained His Knee." In *Specimens of Blind Tom's Vocal Compositions.*

"Mother Wilt Thou Come and Cure Me?" In *Specimens of Blind Tom's Vocal Compositions.*

"Wilt Thou Bring My Baby Home?" 1881. Unpublished manuscript.

AS C. T. MESSENGALE

"Military Waltz." Bucyrus, Ohio: Guckert Music, 1899.

AS W. F. RAYMOND

"March Timpani." New York: F. Blume, ca. 1887. Recorded: Challenge Productions CP-8206.

AS FRANÇOIS SEXALINE

"Wellenklänge." New York: J. G. Bethune, 1882.

NOT VERIFIED

"Imitations of the Banjo" (improvisational music for piano); "Imitations of the Church Organ" (improvisational music for piano); "Imitations of the Douglas's Speech" (improvisational music for piano); "Imitations of the Dutch Woman and Hand-Organ" (improvisational music for piano); "Imitations of the Guitar" (improvisational music for piano); "Imitations of the Harp" (improvisational music for piano); "Imitations of the Music Box" (improvisational music for piano); "Imitations of the Scotch Bagpipes" (improvisational music for piano); "Imitations of the Scotch Fiddler" (improvisational music for piano); "Imitations of the Uncle Charlie" (improvisational music for piano); "The Man Who Got the Cinder in His Eye" (unpublished manuscript); "Mother, Dear Mother, I Still Think of Thee" (unpublished manuscript).

PUBLICATIONS

ABOUT BETHUNE
Books and Monographs

The Marvelous Musical Prodigy, Blind Tom, the Negro Boy Pianist, Whose Performances at the Great St. James and Egyptian Halls, London, and Salle Heartz, Paris, Have Created Such a Profound Sensation: Anecdotes, Songs, Sketches of the Life, Testimonials of Musicians and Savans, and Opinions of the American and English Press of "Blind Tom." Liverpool: Benson and Holme, 1867.

A Sketch of the Life of Thomas Greene Bethune. Philadelphia: Ledger Book and Job Printing Establishment, 1865.

Southall, Geneva H. *Blind Tom: The Post–Civil War Enslavement of a Black Musical Genius.* Vol. I. Minneapolis, Minn.: Challenge Productions, 1979.

———. *The Continuing "Enslavement" of Blind Tom, 1865–1887.* Vol. II. Minneapolis, Minn.: Challenge Productions, 1982.

Articles

A'Becket, John. "Blind Tom As He Is To-day." *Ladies Home Journal* 15 (September 1898): 13–14. Reprinted in *Black Perspective in Music* 4, no. 2 (1976): 184–188.

Abbott, E. "The Miraculous Case of Blind Tom." *Etude* 58 (August 1940): 517.

Andreu, Enrique. "Tragedia de un Beethoven Negro." *Revista Musical Chilena* (October/November 1947): 24–29.

Davis, Rebecca B. H.. "Blind Tom." *Atlantic Monthly* 10 (1862): 580–585. Reprinted in *Dwight's Journal of Music* 22 (1862): 250–252.

Pfaelzer, Jean. "Domesticity and the Discourse of Slavery: 'John Lamar' and 'Blind Tom' by Rebecca Harding Davis." *Esq: A Journal of the American Renaissance* 38, no. 1 (1992): 31–56.

"The Remarkable Case of the Late 'Blind' Tom: How an Imbecile Blind Negro Pianist Amazed Scientists and Musicians the World Over." *Etude* 26, no. 8 (1908): 532.

Robinson, Norborne T. N., Jr. "Blind Tom: Musical Prodigy." *Georgia Historical Quarterly* 51 (1967): 336–358.

Southall, Geneva H. "Blind Tom: A Misrepresented and Neglected Composer-Pianist." *Black Perspective in Music* 3, no. 2 (1975): 141–159.

Stoddard, Tom. "Blind Tom—Slave Genius." *Storyville* 28 (1970): 134–138.

Thornton, E. M. "The Mystery of Blind Tom." *Georgia Review* 15 (1961): 395.

———. "The Strange Case of Blind Tom." *Music Journal* 15 (November 1957): 16+.

Tutein, Anna Amalie. "The Phenomenon of 'Blind Tom'." *Etude* 37 (1918): 91–92.

Wright, Josephine, and Eileen Southern, comp. "Thomas Greene Bethune (1849–1908)." *Black Perspective in Music* 4, no. 2 (1976): 177–183.

* * * * *

Performing under the stage name of Blind Tom, Thomas Greene Bethune was well known as a pianist-composer during his concert career, which lasted approximately 45 years. He was one of the first African-American musicians to achieve an international reputation. Many 19th-century critics considered him a genius, and he composed more than 100 piano compositions reflecting the important stylistic developments in 19th-century piano literature. Tom's piano works are largely predictable salon pieces with a few striking pieces appearing here and there throughout his career: "The Battle of Manassas" (1866), "Rêve charmant: Nocturne for Piano" (1881); and "The Rainstorm" (1865). However, the individuality of these selected piano compositions distinguishes them from the legions of salon pieces that were published in the 19th century, assuring Tom a permanent place in American music.

Bethune was blind from birth, although he apparently could detect light and shadow. He was bought as an infant with his mother by Colonel James N. Bethune, a lawyer and politician

Thomas Greene Wiggins ("Blind Tom") Bethune; illustration appearing in Music and Some Highly Musical People *by James M. Trotter (1881)*

in Columbus, Georgia. When around age four his musical talent was recognized, Colonel Bethune's daughter Mary began to give him piano lessons. Blind Tom's publicity advertised him as a "natural untaught" pianist, but he had instruction throughout his career. Following the initial education he received from Bethune family members, tutors were hired to teach him new repertoire and to transcribe his compositions. He was also taken to hear other professional pianists and opera performances. Blind Tom's first public appearances as a pianist came in 1857, when he toured the state of Georgia under Bethune's supervision, then the southern states under Perry Oliver, a planter from Savannah, for whom Blind Tom's early piece, "Oliver Gallop," is probably named.

After his 1860 concerts in Baltimore, piano manufacturer William Knabe presented to him a grand piano bearing the inscription "a tribute to a genius." By age 11, he was invited to play a command performance for President James Buchanan. As an entertainer, he was compared favorably with renowned pianists such as Louis Moreau Gottschalk, as in the *New York Clipper* of October 7, 1865: "There is no use in talking about Gottschalk while Tom is around, for the latter holds the winning hand, and rakes down the pile every night." Hearing Bethune's piano playing influenced Edgar Stillman Kelley, composer and author of *Chopin the Composer,* to pursue a musical career, according to Louis C. Elson; and, according to Geneva Southall, novelist Willa Cather modeled the figure of Blind d'Arnault in *My Antonia* after Blind Tom, whom she heard play in Lincoln, Nebraska.

When the Civil War began, he was returned to the Bethune family, who continued to supervise tours through the South during the war years. Bethune's performances at that time were often benefit concerts to raise money for Confederate efforts. After the war his parents sued for custody, but, despite Emancipation and their hopes of equal treatment, the judicial system awarded custody to Colonel Bethune. He remained under the control of the Bethunes, first through an indenture contract (1864) and later through conventional business contracts. Following Colonel Bethune's death in 1883, his son John assumed Bethune's management; after John's death, his widow and Albert Lerché, her second husband, became his guardians. He continued to perform widely until 1904–1905 in concert halls and on the vaudeville circuit, in Canada, Europe, and the United States, and much of his music was copyrighted under Colonel Bethune's name. Bethune's blindness and other difficulties made it almost impossible for him to lead an independent life in 19th-century America. At the same time, it should be noted that the Bethune family may have had a more compelling interest in managing his career than their concern for his welfare. Court records show that early in Bethune's long career (1865) Perry Oliver had made $50,000 from concerts and paid Colonel James Bethune $15,000 for Bethune's services. His London concerts of 1866 alone, according to Southall, reportedly made $100,000 for his manager.

Bethune's reputation was made as a pianist and entertainer. Like many pianist-composers of the 19th century, he wrote most of his works to play at his own concerts; frequently, the published pieces were improvisations that had been transcribed by one of his tutors. His audiences had eclectic taste, and almost any genre of music was considered interesting. His programs, which later inspired John William "Blind" Boone, included pieces by composers such as Beethoven, Chopin, and Liszt; operatic potpourris; his own piano pieces and songs; improvisations, often on popular ballads and operatic arias; and his unique descriptive pieces, including, for example, "Imitation of the Music Box" and "The Battle of Manassas." Bethune's improvisatory feats impressed his audiences, especially when a member of the audience would spontaneously suggest the subject of the improvisation. Even more startling were his perfect reproductions of pieces he had heard perhaps only one time, including lengthy concert works, recitations, and songs in foreign languages. Audiences could select from his program of 82 works whatever they wanted to hear. At one point in his career, according to Donald Treffert, Bethune's managers claimed that his repertoire numbered more than 5,000 pieces.

Reports of his concerts invariably mentioned his unusual behavior on stage. For example, the *London Daily News* of July 23, 1866, commented that "his manners are eccentric, and he applauds himself even more loudly and delightedly than the audience applaud him." It is likely that he suffered from a form of autism, perhaps Savant Syndrome, which Treffert defines as "a condition in which persons with major mental illness or major intellectual handicap have spectacular islands of ability and brilliance that stand in stark, startling contrast to those handicaps."

Bethune's songs are usually strophic with short choruses supported by simple accompaniments, a style common to many of the parlor songs from the middle and late 19th century. He published several songs that were probably arrangements of spirituals he knew. They were described as *Plantation Melodies as Sung by Blind Tom, with His Original Accompaniments* and included titles such as "Waggin' Up Zion's Hill," "That Welcome Day," "Come Along, Moses," and "Them Golden Slippers." They tend to be in major keys and have hymn-like, chordal piano accompaniments doubling the melody line and rhythm of the vocal line. Some, however, show much more originality.

His piano compositions include dance pieces and marches; programmatic pieces like "The Rainstorm," op. 6; and character pieces after European models, such as "Rêve charmant: Nocturne for Piano."

WORKS ESSAY

"Wilt Thou Bring My Baby Home?" (1881) with its frequent dynamic changes, phrase-ending ornaments, and rubato, is unusual in that the verse is in common time and the chorus in 12/8, revealing the influence of certain opera arias (*cavatina* and *cabaletta*) of Donizetti, Bellini, and Rossini. The title of this song reveals Tom's acquaintance with flowery language, and the haunting text, written by Bethune, suggests the artist's view of the world. While the lines of text do not relate to each other logically, if viewed as a kaleidoscope of small pictures or events in his world, the poetry becomes meaningful and touching.

> Wilt thou bring my baby home? Now he is satisfied,
> Yes, he will be brought to you, And I will see him aft'r a
>   while.
> I thought I heard my mother singing and sitting there on the
>   steps,
> I think I see her with her sister Awaiting for the hack to
>   come.

These words show Bethune's concern about relationships and interactions with other people, and they may also be autobiographical. Do they tell how he felt about his continued separation from own mother and his parents' attempts to gain custody of their son? If so, its multiple meanings, musical and extra-musical, make this song a very important part of Bethune's compositional output.

"The Rainstorm," op. 6, was written at a very young age, possibly as early as 11 and certainly no later than 16, since the copyright of the earliest published version is 1865. Madame Anna Amalie Tutein, a piano tutor who taught Bethune works by Beethoven, Liszt, Chopin, and Mendelssohn, was moved by this early work to say: "Blind Tom's own compositions and improvisations were astonishingly interesting and often very beautiful. He played a piece called *The Rainstorm,* which was very suggestive and far from ordinary." The character (*barcarole*) and simple major harmonies of the opening theme do not reveal the drama of the music to come, but the subsequent texture, color, and pianistic effects contain the essential spirit of romantic piano music. The piece requires virtuosic technique, not only in sheer digital ability but also in its demand for tonal control and sophisticated pedaling. In ternary (three-part) form, like many character pieces, the A sections—the opening theme and its reprise at the end—represent the calm before and after the rainstorm. The B section depicts the rainstorm and is harmonically more complex (seventh chords, chromatic scale fragments, and a striking parallel tritone passage). Although, compositionally, "The Rainstorm" is much shorter and simpler and technically easier than Liszt's works, the sextuplet accompaniments, use of *crescendi* and *descrescendi* to mirror the wind, and chromatic scales representing the roll of thunder are reminiscent of Liszt's piano music, particularly the "Transcendental Etude no. 12 (Chasse-neige)."

Dedicated to William Steinway, under whose direction the Steinway firm became the preeminent American piano maker, "Rêve charmant: Nocturne for Piano" is the most effective of Bethune's character pieces. It is much more sophisticated than anything else he wrote in its melodic interest, harmonic motion, and the composer's use of texture to build an impressive closing climax. In its harmonic language, *cantabile* melody, and running accompaniment, the influences of Chopin and John Field are apparent. Following a slow, operatic introduction, the body of the piece begins with a running triplet accompaniment in the left hand and a slow, lyrical melody in the right hand (much like Field's Nocturne no. 5 in B-flat major or Chopin's Nocturne in A-flat major, op. 32, no. 2). The Chopin model may have also provided the inspiration for the two-against-three rhythmic figures produced by the melody and the accompaniment, the written-out decorative figures in the melody, and the modulations (key changes) that take place in the various sections. Bethune's "Programme," from which his audience could select what Bethune played during a performance, lists Chopin's "Funeral March" and several Chopin waltzes, so the influence of Chopin is not surprising. It is remarkable, however, that he was able to produce a piece of such length and with such developmental interest, a final statement of the main theme with such rich texture, and such a highly effective climax. "Rêve charmant" is the most musically satisfying of all his pieces and compares favorably with standard, better-known piano repertoire.

"The Battle of Manassas" is historically one of Bethune's most interesting pieces. Essentially a medley of familiar tunes, it describes the progress of the American Civil War's First Battle of Manassas (1861), an important and decisive victory for Confederate forces more commonly known today as the First Battle of Bull Run. As the war progressed and the poorly supplied Confederacy had few successes, Southern audiences enjoyed Bethune's musical reminder of the stubborn stand of Confederate troops and their commander General Thomas Jonathan "Stonewall" Jackson on the banks of Manassas Creek. This piece was a staple of Bethune's wartime concert programs and continued to be a crowd-pleasing part of his Southern program for many years. A grandson of General Bethune, N. T. Robinson, recalled: "Of all his compositions, his 'The Battle of Manassas' was the most popular. . . . What the musical cognoscenti thought of it, I do not know, but I do know that it was a knockout with the average audience." It is one of the earliest American piano pieces requiring the performer to produce "extra-musical" sounds such as clusters played in the low register of the piano with the palm of the hand to represent cannon, train sounds ("chu-chu-chu"), and whistles that represent the arrival of troops. The melodic material is composed of a series of melodies such as "Dixie," "The Girl I Left Behind Me," "The Star-Spangled Banner," and the "Marseillaise." An important part of our musical history and attractive to today's audiences, Bethune's music is well worth more frequent performances.

REFERENCES

Columbus Daily Enquirer, July 11, 1860.

Elson, Louis C. *The History of American Music.* New York: Macmillan, 1904.

London Daily News, July 23, 1866.

New York Clipper, October 7, 1865.

Robinson, Norborne T. N., Jr. "Blind Tom: Musical Prodigy." *Georgia Historical Quarterly* 51 (1967): 336–358.

Savannah Express, January 30, 1858.

Sears, Ann. 1988. "Keyboard Music by Nineteenth-Century Afro-American Composers." In *Feel the Spirit: Studies in Nineteenth-Century Afro-American Music,* edited by George R. Keck and Sherrill V. Martin, 135–155. Westport, Conn.: Greenwood Press.

Southall, Geneva. "Blind Tom: A Misrepresented and Neglected Composer-Pianist." *Black Perspective in Music* 3 (1975):141–159.

Southern, Eileen. *The Music of Black Americans: A History.* 2nd ed. New York: W. W. Norton, 1983.

Treffert, Darold A., M.D. *Extraordinary People: Understanding "Idiot Savants."* New York: Harper and Row, 1989.

Tutein, Anna Amalie. "The Phenomenon of 'Blind Tom'." *Etude* 37 (1918): 91–92.

ANN SEARS

BLAKE, ("BLIND") ARTHUR

Born Arthur Phelps, possibly in Jacksonville, Florida, ca. 1890–95; died in unknown place, possibly ca. mid-1930s. **Composing and Performing Career:** Little known about his early life; may have played guitar extensively in Florida, Georgia, and regional states; Detroit, Mich., and Chicago, Ill., performed and recorded 81 songs and instrumental pieces, 1926–32; toured with the show *Happy-Go-Lucky*, managed by his friend George Williams, 1929–late 1930 or 1931; professional associations with Gus Cannon, Johnny Dodds, Bertha Henderson, Gertrude "Ma" Rainey, Elzadie Robinson, Irene Scruggs, Charlie Spand, and Leola B. Wilson among others.

MUSIC LIST

[The following list of titles includes only works that were composed by the subject of the entry; it is not a list of recordings that were made by the subject. Although the composer may have made recordings of his own works, the list is not restricted to those recordings but in many cases includes performances by other artists of the composer's work. The list is made up of publication and discographical data, in cases where such information is available. Although no effort has been made to include documentation of the earliest recording of the works listed, the date of the earliest recording that is readily available has been given. —Ed.]

"Baby Lou Blues." Co-credited to Davis. Recorded, 1929: Biograph BLP-12050; Document Records DOCD-5027; Paramount 12918.

"Back Door Slam Blues." Recorded, 1928: Document Records DOCD-5026; Matchbox MSE 1003; Paramount 12710.

"Bad Feeling Blues." Recorded, ca. 1927: Biograph BLP-12003; Paramount 12497; Yazoo CD-1068.

"Black Dog Blues." Recorded, ca. 1927: Biograph BLP-12003; Paramount 12464; Yazoo CD-1068.

"Blake's Worried Blues." Recorded, ca. 1926: Biograph BLP-12023; Document Records DOCD-5024; Paramount 12442 or Broadway 5040.

"Blind Arthur's Breakdown." Note: issued under the name "Blind Arthur." Recorded, 1929: CPP/Belwin F3346GTXAT; Paramount 12892; Yazoo CD-1068.

"Bootleg Rum Dum Blues." Recorded, 1928: Biograph BLP-12003; Document Records DOCD-5025; Paramount 12695.

"Brownskin Mama Blues." Recorded, 1927: Biograph BLP-12003; Document Records DOCD-5024; Paramount 12606.

"Buck-Town Blues." Recorded, 1927: Biograph BLP-12003; Document Records DOCD-5024; Paramount 12464.

"C. C. Pill Blues." Recorded, 1928: Matchbox MSE 1003; Paramount 12634 or Broadway 5084; Yazoo CD-1068.

"Champagne Charlie Is My Name." Recorded, 1932: Biograph BLP-12037; Document Records DOCD-5027; Paramount 13137 or Crown 3357.

"Chump Man Blues." Co-credited to Davis. Recorded, 1929: CPP/Belwin F3346GTXAT; Paramount 12904; Yazoo CD-1068.

"Cold Hearted Mama Blues." Recorded, 1928: Document Records DOCD-5026; Matchbox MSE 1003; Paramount 12710.

"Cold Love Blues." Co-credited to Davis. Recorded, 1929: Biograph BLP-12050; Document Records DOCD-5027; Paramount 12918.

"Come on Boys, Let's Do That Messin' Around." Recorded, ca. 1926: Document DOCD-5216; Paramount 12413; CPP/Belwin F3346GTXAT; Yazoo CD-1068.

"Depression's Gone from Me Blues." Recorded, 1932: Biograph BLP-12037; Document Records DOCD-5027; Paramount 13137 or Crown 3357.

"Detroit Bound Blues." Recorded, 1928: Document Records DOCD-5025; Matchbox MSE 1003; Paramount 12657.

"Diddie Wa Diddie No. 2." Recorded, 1930: Biograph BLP-12050; Document Records DOCD-5027; Paramount 12994.

"Dissatisfied Blues." Recorded, 1932: Paramount 13115.

"Doggin' Me Mama Blues." Recorded, 1928: Biograph BLP-12050; Matchbox MSE 1003; Paramount 12673.

"Doing a Stretch." Co-credited to Taylor. Recorded, 1929: Biograph BLP-12037; Document Records DOCD-5026; Paramount 12810.

"Dry Bone Shuffle." Recorded, 1927: Biograph BLP-12037; Document DOCD-5062 or DOCD-5024; Paramount 1247.

"Early Morning Blues." Recorded, ca. 1926: Biograph 12031; Document DOCD-5150; Paramount 12387.

"Fightin' the Jug." Recorded, 1929: Biograph BLP-12037; Document Records DOCD-5026; Paramount 12863.

"Georgia Bound." Co-credited to Palmer. Recorded, 1929: CPP/Belwin F3346GTXAT; Paramount 12824; Yazoo CD-1068.

"Goodbye Mama Moan." Recorded, 1928: Biograph BLP-12037; Document Records DOCD-5025; Paramount 12634.

"Guitar Chimes." Note: issued under the name "Blind Arthur." Recorded, 1929: CPP/Belwin F3346GTXAT; Matchbox MSE 1003; Paramount 12892; Yazoo 1016;.

"Hard Pushing Papa." Recorded, 1939: Biograph BLP-12050; Paramount 12994; Yazoo CD-1068.

"Hard Road Blues." Co-credited to J. Mayo Williams. Recorded, 1927: Biograph 12031; Document Records DOCD-5024; Paramount 12583.

"Hey, Hey, Daddy Blues." Recorded, 1927: CPP/Belwin F3346GTXAT; Paramount 12606; Yazoo CD-1068.

"Hot Potatoes." Recorded, 1928: Document Records DOCD-5025; Matchbox MSE 1003; Paramount 12673.

"I Was Afraid of That—Part 2." Note: issued as "The Hokum Boys." Recorded, 1929: Biograph BLP-12050; Document Records DOCD-5026; Paramount 12882.

"Ice Man Blues." Co-credited to Davis. Recorded, 1929: Document Records DOCD-5026; Paramount 12904.

"Keep It Home." Recorded, 1929: Document Records DOCD-5026; Paramount 12964.

"Lonesome Christmas Blues." Recorded, 1929: Document Records DOCD-5027; Paramount 12867.

"Miss Emma Liza (Sweetness)." Recorded, 1932: Paramount 13115.

"New Style of Loving." Recorded, 1928: Document Records DOCD-5026; Matchbox MSE 1003; Paramount 12767.

"Night and Day Blues." Recorded, 1932: Paramount 13123.

"No Dough Blues." Recorded, 1928: Biograph 12031; Document Records DOCD-5025; Paramount 12723.

"Blind" Arthur Blake; courtesy of the Frank Driggs Colletion

"Notoriety Woman Blues." Co-credited to Davis. Recorded, 1928: Biograph 12031; Document Records DOCD-5026; Paramount 12754.

"One Time Blues." Recorded, ca. 1927: Biograph BLP-12037; Paramount 12479; Yazoo CD-1068.

"Panther Squall Blues." Recorded, 1928: Biograph 12031; Paramount 12723; Yazoo 1016.

"Poker Woman Blues." Recorded, 1929: Biograph BLP-12037; Paramount 12810; Yazoo 1015.

"Police Dog Blues." Co-credited to Lamoore. Recorded, 1929: CPP/Belwin F3346GTXAT; Paramount 12888; Yazoo CD-1068.

"Policy Blues." Recorded: CPP/Belwin F3346GTXAT.

"Ramblin' Mama Blues." Recorded, 1928: Document Records DOCD-5026; Matchbox MSE 1003; Paramount 12767.

"Rope Stretchin' Blues." Recorded, 1931: Paramount 13103.

"Rumblin' and Ramblin' Boa Constrictor Blues." Recorded, 1928: Document Records DOCD-5025; Matchbox MSE 1003; Paramount 12657.

"Sea Board Stomp." Co-credited to J. Mayo Williams. Recorded, 1927: Biograph 12031; Paramount 12583; Yazoo CD-1068.

"Search Warrant Blues." Co-credited to Davis. Recorded, 1928: Biograph BLP-12037; Document Records DOCD-5026; Paramount 12737.

"Skeedle Loo Doo Blues." Recorded, ca. 1926: Matchbox MSE 1003; Paramount 12413; Yazoo CD-1068.

"Slippery Rag (Rosey and Me)." Recorded, 1929: Biograph 12031; Document Records DOCD-5026; Paramount 12794 or Broadway 5080.

"South Bound Rag." Recorded, 1928: Document Records DOCD-5025; Matchbox MSE 1003; Paramount 12681.

"Southern Rag." Recorded, 1927: Biograph BLP-12037; Paramount 12565 or Broadway 5053; Yazoo CD-1068.

"Steel Mill Blues." Recorded, 1927: Document Records DOCD-5025; Paramount 12681.

"Stonewall Street Blues." Recorded, ca. 1926: Biograph 12031; Document Records DOCD-5024; Paramount 12431.

"Sun to Sun." Recorded, 1932: Paramount 13123.

"Sweet Jivin' Mama." Recorded, 1929: CPP/Belwin F3346GTXAT; Paramount 12964; Yazoo CD-1068.

"Sweet Papa Low Down." Recorded, 1928: Biograph BLP-12037; Paramount 12737; Yazoo CD-1068.

"Tampa Bound." Recorded, ca. 1926: Biograph BLP-12037; Document Records DOCD-5024; Paramount 12442 or Broadway 5040.

"That Lovin' I Crave." Recorded, 1928: Biograph BLP-12050; Document Records DOCD-5025; Paramount 12643.

"That Will Never Happen No More." Recorded, 1927: CPP/Belwin F3346GTXAT ; Paramount 12497; Yazoo 1012.

"Third Degree Blues." Recorded, 1929: Document Records DOCD-5027; Paramount 12867.

"Too Tight." Recorded, ca. 1926: Biograph 12031; Document Records DOCD-5024; Paramount 12431.

"Too Tight Blues No. 2." Recorded, 1929: Media 7 MJCD 801; Paramount 12824; Yazoo CD-1068.

"Tootie Blues." Recorded, 1928: Biograph BLP-12050; Document Records DOCD-5025; Paramount 12643.

"Wabash Rag." Recorded, 1927: Matchbox MSE 1003; Paramount 12597; Yazoo 1016.

"Walkin' across the Country." Co-credited to Davis. Recorded, 1928: Biograph 12031; Document Records DOCD-5026; Paramount 12754.

"West Coast Blues." Recorded, ca. 1926: Biograph 12031; CPP/Belwin F3346GTXAT ; Paramount 12387.

"You Gonna Quit Me Blues." Recorded, 1927: Matchbox MSE 1003; Paramount 12597; Yazoo CD-1068.

NOT VERIFIED

"Blue Getaway" (recorded, 1929; Paramount, unissued); "Fan Foot Woman" (recorded, 1929; Paramount, unissued); "Pop It Stomp" (recorded, 1929; Paramount, unissued).

PUBLICATIONS

ABOUT BLAKE
Books and Monographs

Bastin, Bruce. *Red River Blues: The Blues Tradition in the Southeast,* 40–43. Urbana: University of Illinois Press, 1986.

Grossman, Stefan. *Ragtime Blues Guitarists,* 91–129. New York: Oak, 1970.

Articles

Bakker, Dick M. "Blind Blake 26–32." *Micrography* 2 (February 1969): 10; 5 (August 1969): 12. (Discography; additions and corrections.)

Fanelli, André. "Blind Blake's Blues." *Blues and Swing Magazine* 1 (1971): 5–10.

Hanson, M. "Blues: Diddie Wa Diddie; Blind Blake's Ragtime Blues Classic." *Guitar Player* 24 (April 1990): 84–87.

Obrecht, Jas. "Blind Blake." *Blues Revue Quarterly* 7 (Winter 1993): 18–21.

———. "The King of Ragtime Guitar: Blind Blake and His Piano-Sounding Guitar." *Victrola and 78 Journal* 9 (Summer 1996): 15–19.

Vreede, Max E. "A Discography of Blind Blake." *Matrix* 19 (September 1958): 6–11; 33 (March 1961): 18; 35/36 (September 1961): 35. (Additions and corrections in last two issues.)

*   *   *   *   *

Blind Blake created and recorded many original compositions. His song lyrics are all on typical popular blues themes and do not display a special degree of poetic imagination. Slightly over a quarter of his pieces were in a ragtime form, including both songs and guitar instrumentals, some of the latter with spoken monologues. The remainder are blues, almost all with singing, but many of these are performed with fast ragtime rhythms or contain typical ragtime chord progressions. The same instrumental ideas and figures are duplicated in many of these pieces under different titles. A prototype East Coast bluesman, Blake was the first from this area to record, and his records were quite influential within the region. Not a major composer, Blind Blake's greatest strength was as a guitarist. Many of his songs are laced with dashes of humor.

For a prolific recording artist of such popularity, we know remarkably little about Blind Blake, not even his place and date of birth and death. We do not even know for certain whether Blake was a surname, his mother's name, a middle name, or a nickname, for some of his songs are credited to an Arthur Phelps. Record company advertising states that he came from Jacksonville, Florida, but this may simply have been his most recent home before he began his recording career in mid-1926. From then until 1932, when his career ended, we know that he lived in Chicago and Detroit, although there are reports of his appearances in many scattered parts of the South during this time. Nevertheless, his musical style and hints in his song lyrics suggest that he was originally from somewhere along the East Coast, most likely Florida or Georgia.

Although he is best known as a solo blues and ragtime singer and guitarist, Blind Blake accompanied many other singers on records and probably in personal appearances, including banjoist Gus Cannon, vaudeville blues singer Ma Rainey, pianist Charlie Spand, and gospel singer Daniel Brown. It seems quite likely that Blake spent part of his professional career in vaudeville theater, performing solo and as an accompanist to female singers.

Blake's melodies are not particularly remarkable, and he seems content to let listeners absorb the straightforward messages of his songs and marvel at his spectacular guitar playing. His strengths as a guitarist were speed, precision, a certain sense of harmonic complexity, and an ability to introduce variations in his playing. His most wide-ranging piece is "Police Dog Blues," but this is played in the very rare (for him) open E tuning that facilitates work higher on the neck of the guitar. Over 60 percent of his pieces were recorded in the C position of standard tuning, and most of the remainder were in G. With such limitations, it is not surprising that many of the same guitar figures and ideas reappear from one song to another.

SELECTED WORKS

"Early Morning Blues" (1926) was Blake's first solo recording and a big hit for him. It is a 12-bar blues played in the C position of standard tuning at a rather unaccustomed slow tempo in triplets. It exists in two versions, recorded about three months apart. The second version is almost identical to the first but somewhat more deliberate and precise in its execution, with a consequent slight loss of spontaneity. In any case, the similarity of the two versions indicates that the piece was rather carefully planned. The four lyric stanzas present a straightforward dialogue between Blake and his woman. She has returned home in the early morning to announce that she is leaving and refuses to tell where she spent the night. Blake responds with one of his more inspired lyric images, particularly startling coming from a blind man: "When you see me sleeping, baby, don't you think I'm drunk; I got one eye on my pistol and the other'n on your trunk." After a guitar chorus, he threatens to kill her if she tries to leave. Most, if not all, of his verses are traditional, a common characteristic of the initial recordings of self-accompanied blues singers, but Blake weaves them together so that they paint a clear picture of a scene of domestic conflict. His vocal line, mostly on the beat, is an undulating melody that spans an octave. The guitar line includes all seven steps of the scale (using both major and minor thirds and sevenths). In his introduction, guitar chorus, closing phrase, and some responses to vocal lines, he plays a prominent "blue" third achieved by the bending of a string. Most of his guitar figures are scalar phrases and arpeggios, conceived from basic chord positions, and most measures contain chord changes approximately every two beats, a common characteristic among East Coast folk

blues guitarists but rarer elsewhere. For example, the first full chorus of his first version contains the chord sequence shown in Example 1. The chord sequence in measures 8-11 is found widely in ragtime music. His second version of "Early Morning Blues" contains only minor variations at this point, mainly in the substitution of the V for the V^7 chord in some places.

Example 1. "Early Morning Blues," chord structure of first version

$$\text{I–I}^7 \mid \text{IV–V} \mid \text{I–V}^7 \mid \text{I–I}^7 \mid \text{IV} \mid \text{IV–V} \mid \text{I–V}^7 \mid \text{I–VI}^7 \mid \text{II}^7 \mid \text{V}^7\text{–V} \mid \text{I–V}^7 \mid \text{I–V}$$

"Southern Rag" (1927) is one of Blake's best ragtime pieces. It is played in the C position of standard tuning with the strings slackened about a half-step. It consists mostly of progressions (VI^7–II^7–V^7–I) played at a very rapid tempo, but no two of them are exactly alike. Blake constantly plays individual notes within chord positions formed by the left hand on the neck of the guitar, creating a clear sense of constantly varying melody. Most chords are played for two beats (half a measure), but some are extended for additional beats. Blake's picking in this performance includes alternating thumb on bass strings, thumb rolls, the thumb on the offbeat, bass runs played with the thumb, and syncopated treble notes played with fingers. Altogether it is an extraordinary performance of great virtuosity. It gives the impression that, at the time of recording, Blake largely put together guitar ideas and figures with which he was very familiar and which were highly polished from years of playing. His spoken monologue is most interesting as he paints a word picture of rural Southern life at harvest time. He calls this piece an "old Southern rag" and "Geechie music," and he speaks part of his monologue in the Geechie dialect of the Atlantic coastal islands stretching from northern Florida to South Carolina. If this is characteristic music of the area, it is not consistent with what has been collected there, which is almost entirely vocal and percussion music in the spiritual and worksong genres. Blake's piece may represent the surfacing of an underground tradition of secular instrumental music from the area, or perhaps it simply indicates his own popularity there where such music was otherwise not found.

"Chump Man Blues" (1929) is one of Blake's most distinctive 12-bar blues creations, thanks especially to the lovely guitar part played in the D position of standard tuning with the lowest string tuned down a full step to the tonic note. He picks with great accuracy in a fast duple rhythm with slightly accelerating tempo, occasionally substituting a three-note triplet for two eighth-notes. His guitar work mostly follows the basic chord positions (I–IV^7–V) behind his singing, answering his lines with an attractive figure (m3–M3–1–6–5–1). There is none of the harmonic complexity found in most of Blake's other recordings, suggesting that the guitar part was conceived more as a melody than as a harmonic pattern to be filled with note sequences. To emphasize, however, that he is still first and foremost an instrumentalist, Blake plays a guitar chorus between all five vocal stanzas, offering alternative and more complex lines to those he played behind his singing. His voice is plaintive, in keeping with the song's theme of a man who has been brought down by his love for a domineering woman. The text is quite straightforward in the manner of most popular commercial blues. Blake says he is going to jump in the river because his woman has "made me a chump." Then he simply proceeds to provide the background by stating how he loved her completely, how she threw him out and he begged her to take him back, that he knows she is no good but he still can't quit her, how she nags him, but that "she got a new quiver make a strong man lose his mind." It's not an outstanding poetic text, but the singing is effective and the guitar part excellent both as a performance and as a composition.

"That Lovin' I Crave" (1928), a 16-bar ragtime tune, is played in the G position of standard tuning at a moderately fast tempo. Blake plays rhythmic chords primarily to emphasize the song's harmonic structure, confining his picking mostly to the first string within the first three frets of the fingerboard. The basic chord structure is shown in Example 2. Blake's melody has the rather narrow range of a sixth (from the third above the tonic to the fifth below). The first eight bars are occupied by a rhymed couplet that carries the story line. The other eight contain a repeated refrain consisting of a four-line rhymed couplet and a final line that twice asks the question "Do you think that's right?" The singer complains that his woman is a whore who has taken advantage of his love: "For a long, long time I've been your slave; just because you got the kind of loving I crave." She throws his dinner at him, stays out half of the night, has other men while he sleeps in the back yard, and takes his last dime. In the opening stanza he threatens to jump in the lake, but after venting his litany of complaints, in the final stanza he settles for simply leaving her to her other men. The message and lyrics are fairly conventional, and the tune is mainly distinguished by its unusual structure and Blake's meticulous performance.

Example 2. "That Lovin' I Crave," chord structure

$$\text{I} \mid \text{V} \mid \text{I}^7 \mid \text{I} \mid \text{I} \mid \text{V} \mid \text{I}^7 \mid \text{I} \mid \text{I} \mid \text{I} \mid \text{I} \mid \text{VI}^7 \mid \text{II}^7 \mid \text{V}^7 \mid \text{I}^7 \mid \text{V}$$

REFERENCES

Balfour, Alan. Notes, *Blind Blake: The Complete Recorded Works in Chronological Order,* vols. 1–4. Document DOCD-5024/5025/5026/5027, 1991.

Bernstein, Joel. Notes, *Blind Blake, 1926–1930, "That Lovin' I Crave."* Biograph BLP-12050, 1975.

Calt, Steve, and Woody Mann. Notes, *Blind Blake, Ragtime Guitar's Foremost Fingerpicker.* Yazoo 1068, 1989.

Caplin, Arnold S. Notes, *Blind Blake, 1926–1930, "Bootleg Rum Dum Blues."* Biograph BLP-12003.

Dixon, Robert M. W., and John Godrich. *Blues and Gospel Records: 1902–1943,* 91–93. 3rd ed. Chigwell, Essex, England: Storyville, 1982.

Dyson, Ernest F. Notes, Blind Blake, Volume 2, 1926–1932, "Search Warrant Blues." Biograph BLP-12023.

Harris, Sheldon. *Blues Who's Who,* 415–417. New Rochelle, N.Y.: Arlington House, 1979.

DAVID EVANS

BLAKE, JAMES HUBERT ("EUBIE")

Born in Baltimore, Md., February 7, 1883; died in New York City, February 12, 1983. **Education:** Began organ lessons with Margaret Marshall, a neighbor, age four; studied music theory with local musician, Llewlyn Wilson; New York University, took Schillinger System composition courses, 1946. **Composing and Performing Career:** Baltimore, began to play professionally, age 15; wrote first piano rag, "Sounds of Africa" (later entitled "Charleston Rag"), 1899; New York, N.Y., joined cast of *In Old Kentucky,* 1902; Baltimore and Atlantic City, N.J., pianist at the Goldfield Hotel and other saloons, 1903, 1907–15; toured with a medicine show, then as accompanist for Madison Reed, 1910; formed songwriting partnership with Noble Sissle, 1915; first successful song, "It's All Your Fault," performed by Sophie Tucker, 1915; New York, N.Y., with Sissle, joined James Reese Europe's Society Orchestra, 1916; with Sissle, formed vaudeville act, the Dixie Duo, after World War I (1919); made numerous recordings as soloist and with his orchestra, 1917–30s; produced and toured with hit Broadway musical, *Shuffle Along,* 1921–23; toured with Sissle in Europe and the United States, 1925–27; collaborated with Sissle and other lyricists writing several Broadway and London shows, including *The Chocolate Dandies* and *Elsie,* 1920s and 1930s; wrote score for *Lew Leslie's Blackbirds of 1930,* 1930; toured as music director for USO productions, during World War II; retired from most professional activities, 1946; new career as touring ragtime artist and lecturer, 1960s; recorded *The Eighty-Six Years of Eubie Blake,* 1969; featured at the New Orleans Jazz Fest, 1969; Southern California and Newport Jazz Festivals, 1971; established own publishing and record company, Eubie Blake Music, 1972; performed at Jimmy Carter's White House Jazz Party, 1978; Broadway revue, *Eubie,* produced, 1978. **Honors/Awards:** Numerous awards from music and theater industries and from civic and professional organizations; Brooklyn College, honorary doctorate, 1973; Dartmouth College, honorary doctorate, 1974; New England Conservatory, honorary doctorate, 1974; Rutgers University, honorary doctorate, 1974; University of Maryland, honorary doctorate, 1979; America's Music and Entertainment Hall of Fame, inductee, 1979; Decoration for Distinguished Civilian Service, 1980; Presidential Medal of Honor, 1981; St. Peter's Church, New York City, marathon 24-hour jazz concert held in honor of his 100th birthday, 1983.

MUSIC LIST

PIANO

"Africana." 1907. Unpublished manuscript.

"Alma Yamero." 1917. Unpublished manuscript.

"The Baltimore Todolo." 1908. In *Sincerely Eubie Blake* (New York: Edward B. Marks, 1975). Recorded: Columbia C2S 847.

"Betty Washboard's Rag." 1978. Unpublished manuscript.

"Black Widow." Unpublished manuscript.

"Blue Classique." New York: Clarence Williams Music, 1934.

"Blue Thoughts." 1935. New York: Handy Brothers, 1935.

"Bolero." 1938. Unpublished manuscript.

"Brittwood Rag." 1911. In *Sincerely Eubie Blake* (New York: Edward B. Marks, 1975). Recorded: Columbia C2S 847.

"Bugle Call Rag." 1916. New York: Joseph W. Stern, 1916. Recorded: Victor 35533.

"Butterfly." 1946. Recorded: Stash Records ST 128.

"Capricious Harlem." 1937. Recorded: Columbia 34504; Stash Records ST 128.

"Charleston Rag." 1899. In *Sincerely Eubie Blake* (New York: Edward B. Marks, 1975). Original title, "Sounds of Africa." Recorded: Biograph BCD-112; Columbia C2S 847; Eubie Blake Music EBM-2; Quicksilver Records QSCD-9003.

"The Chevy Chase." 1914. New York: Joseph W. Stern, 1914. Recorded: Columbia C2S 847; Quicksilver Records QSCD-9003.

"Conversation." 1948. Unpublished manuscript.

"Corner of Chestnut and Low (in Baltimo')." 1903. Unpublished manuscript.

"Dicty's on Seventh Avenue." 1955. In *Giants of Ragtime* (New York: Edward B. Marks, 1971). Recorded: Eubie Blake Music EBM-1; Musical Heritage Society 416368A; Quicksilver Records QSCD-9003.

"Doodling Around." Unpublished manuscript.

"Eubie Dubie." Copyright, 1972. In *Sincerely Eubie Blake* (New York: Edward B. Marks, 1975). Co-composer, John Guarnieri. Recorded: Columbia C2S 847; Musical Heritage Society 416368A.

"Eubie's Boogie." 1941–42. Recorded: Columbia C2S 847.

"Eubie's Classical Rag." Copyright, 1972. In *Sincerely Eubie Blake* (New York: Edward B. Marks, 1975). Recorded: Columbia 34504; Stash Records ST 128.

"Eubie's Classical Rag no. 3." 1973. Unpublished manuscript.

"Eubie's E-flat Rag." 1976. Unpublished manuscript.

"La Fiesta." 1917. Unpublished manuscript.

"Fizz Water Rag." 1914. New York: Joseph W. Stern, 1914. Recorded: Eubie Blake Music EBM-1; Musical Heritage Society 416368A.

"The High Muck de Mucks." 1972. Unpublished manuscript.

"In an Indian Lodge." 1938. Unpublished manuscript.

"Just a Simple Little Old Blues (Blue Rag in Twelve Keys)." 1919. Recorded: Columbia C2S 847.

"Kitchen Tom." 1917. In *Sincerely Eubie Blake* (New York: Edward B. Marks, 1975). Recorded: Columbia C2S 847.

"Lady Beautiful." 1920. In *Original Classic Waltzes for Piano* (New York: Edward B. Marks, 1978).

"The Little Encore." Unpublished manuscript.

"March of the Senegalese." 1948. Unpublished manuscript.

"Melodic Rag." 1971. Recorded: Eubie Blake Music EBM-1.

"Moods of Harlem." 1937. Unpublished manuscript.

"Novelty Rag." 1932, revised 1971. Recorded: Eubie Blake Music EBM-1.

"Original Piano Tricks." 1962. Unpublished manuscript.

"Poor Archie." 1960. Unpublished manuscript.

"Poor Jimmy Green." 1904–05. In *Sincerely Eubie Blake* (New York: Edward B. Marks, 1975). Recorded: Columbia C2S 847; Quicksilver Records QSCD-9003.

"Poor Katie Red (Eubie's Slow Drag)." 1906. In *Sincerely Eubie Blake* (New York: Edward B. Marks, 1975). Recorded: Columbia C2S 847; Musical Heritage Society 416368A.

James Hubert "Eubie" Blake; collection of the Maryland Historical Society, Baltimore

"Rag Modern." 1951. Unpublished manuscript.

"Ragtime Piano Tricks." 1959. Unpublished manuscript.

"Ragtime Rag." 1959. Unpublished manuscript.

"Rain Drops." 1924. Recorded: Stash Records ST 128.

"Reverie." Unpublished manuscript.

"Rhapsody in Ragtime." 1973. In *Sincerely Eubie Blake* (New York: Edward B. Marks, 1975). Recorded: Eubie Blake Music EBM-5.

"Rose of Araby." 1928–30. Unpublished manuscript.

"Scherzo." 1948. Unpublished manuscript.

"Serenada." Unpublished manuscript.

"Six Shades of Blue." 1948. Unpublished manuscript.

"Slue Foot Nelson." 1973. Unpublished manuscript.

"Tickle the Ivories." 1928. Unpublished manuscript.

"Tricky Fingers." 1904, revised 1969. In *Giants of Ragtime* (New York: Edward B. Marks, 1971). Recorded: Columbia C2S 847; Musical Heritage Society 416368A; Quicksilver Records QSCD-9003.

"Troublesome Ivories." 1912. In *Giants of Ragtime* (New York: Edward B. Marks, 1971). Recorded: Columbia C2S 847; Musicmasters CD 20013.

"Valse Amelia." 1972. In *Original Classic Waltzes for Piano* (New York: Edward B. Marks, 1978).

"Valse Delma." 1972. In *Original Classic Waltzes for Piano* (New York: Edward B. Marks, 1978).

"Valse Eileen." 1972. In *Original Classic Waltzes for Piano* (New York: Edward B. Marks, 1978).

"Valse Erda." 1968. In *Original Classic Waltzes for Piano* (New York: Edward B. Marks, 1978).

"Valse Ethel." 1972. In *Original Classic Waltzes for Piano* (New York: Edward B. Marks, 1978).

"Valse Marion." 1972. In *Original Classic Waltzes for Piano* (New York: Edward B. Marks, 1978). Recorded: Stash Records ST 128.

"Valse Syncopation." Unpublished manuscript.

"Valse Vera." 1972. In *Original Classic Waltzes for Piano* (New York: Edward B. Marks, 1978).

"Violins." Unpublished manuscript.

"Waltz Please." Unpublished manuscript.

"Wild about Jazz." 1978. Unpublished manuscript.

SONGS

"Affectionate Dan." 1918. Notes: for *Happy Times*; not performed.

"Ain't Cha Coming Back, Mary Ann, to Maryland." 1919. New York: M. Witmark, 1919. Note: from *Shuffle Along*. Recorded: Pathé 22284.

"Ain't We Got Love." 1937. New York: Mills Music, 1937. Note: from *Swing It*.

"All of No Man's Land Is Ours." 1919. New York: M. Witmark and Sons, 1919. Co-composer, James Reese Europe.

"All the Wrongs You've Done to Me." 1924. Co-composer, Noble Sissle. Note: from *The Chocolate Dandies*.

"Al-Le-Lu (Old Noah's Ark)." 1925. Unpublished manuscript. Premiere, 1925.

"Alone with Love." 1952. Notes: for *Shuffle Along of 1952*; not performed.

"And So I Sorrow." 1954. Unpublished manuscript. Co-composer, Joshua Milton Reddie.

"And That Is You." 1947. Unpublished manuscript. Co-composer, Joshua Milton Reddie.

"Arabian Moon." 1932. Notes: for *Shuffle Along of 1933*; not performed.

"As Long as He's a Regular Guy." 1945. Unpublished manuscript.

"As Long as You Live." 1957. Co-composer, Arthur Porter. Recorded: Columbia C2S 847.

"At the Pullman Porter's Full Dress Ball." 1916. Unpublished manuscript. Premiere, 1916.

"Aunt Jemima's Divorce." 1930. Note: from *Lew Leslie's Blackbirds of 1930*.

"Baby Be Sweet." 1954. Unpublished manuscript.

"Baby Buntin'." 1923. New York: M. Witmark, 1923. Co-composer, Noble Sissle. Note: from *Elsie*. Premiere, 1923.

"Baby Mine." 1930. Note: from *Lew Leslie's Blackbirds of 1930*.

"Baltimore Blues." 1919. Unpublished manuscript. Premiere, 1919.

"Baltimore Buzz." 1921. New York: M. Witmark, 1921. Co-composer, Noble Sissle. Note: from *Shuffle Along*. Recorded: Stash Records ST 129.

"Bandana Days." 1921. New York: M. Witmark and Sons, 1921. Co-composer, Noble Sissle. Note: from *Shuffle Along, Shuffle Along of 1933,* and *Happy Times*. Recorded: Stash Records ST 129.

"Bandanaland." 1924. Co-composer, Noble Sissle. Note: from *The Chocolate Dandies*.

"Barber Shop." 1955. Notes: for *Irwin C. Miller's Brown Skin Models*; not performed.

"The Bass Fiddle Boogie Woogie." 1956. Unpublished manuscript.

"Be Yourself." 1950. Notes: for *Be Yourself*; not performed.

"Beautiful." Unpublished manuscript.

"Be-bop Blues." Unpublished manuscript.

"Bebopper's Anniversary." 1955. Notes: for *Hit the Stride*; not performed.

"Belong to Me." 1958. Unpublished manuscript.

"The Berries." 1930. Note: from *Lew Leslie's Blackbirds of 1930*.

"Black Bottomeroff." 1927. Notes: for *Teddy*; not performed.

"Blackbirds on Parade." 1930. Note: from *Lew Leslie's Blackbirds of 1930*.

"Blues, Why Don't You Leave Me Alone." 1937. Unpublished manuscript. Co-composer, Arthur Porter.

"Bonga-Boola." 1952. Note: from *Shuffle Along of 1952*.

"Boogie Woogie Beguine." 1945. Notes: for *Happy Times*; not performed. Recorded: Columbia 34504.

"Breakin' 'em Down." 1924. Co-composer, Noble Sissle. Note: from *The Chocolate Dandies*.

"Breakin' 'em In." 1932. Note: from *Shuffle Along of 1933*.

"Brown Skin." 1952. Note: from *Shuffle Along of 1952*.

"By the Sweat of Your Brow." 1937. New York: Mills Music, 1937. Note: from *Swing It*.

"Cabin Door." 1930. Note: from *Lew Leslie's Blackbirds of 1930*.

"The Cajun Dance." 1955. Notes: for *Hit the Stride*; not performed.

"Calling Romance." 1950. Notes: for *Be Yourself*; not performed.

"Carita Day." 1955. Notes: for *Irwin C. Miller's Brown Skin Models*; not performed.

"Castle of Love." ca. 1960. Unpublished manuscript.

"Chicago Loop." 1927. Notes: for *Teddy*; not performed.

"Chickens Come Home to Roost." 1932. Note: from *Shuffle Along of 1933*.

"Chocolate Dandies." 1924. Co-composer, Noble Sissle. Note: from *The Chocolate Dandies*.

"Christmas Is Coming." 1957. Unpublished manuscript.

"City Called Heaven." 1952. Note: from *Shuffle Along of 1952*.

"City Kept Girl." 1938. Unpublished manuscript.

"Cleo Zell My Creole Belle." 1921. Premiere, 1921.

"The College Song." 1958. Notes: for *Happy Times*; not performed.

"Come Along Children." 1958. Unpublished manuscript.

"Curse of the Blues." 1946. Unpublished manuscript. Co-composer, E. Blackman.

"Daddy Won't You Please Come Home" or "Low Down Blues." 1921. New York: M. Witmark, 1921. Co-composer, Noble Sissle. Note: from *Shuffle Along*.

"Dear Li'l Pal." 1923. Unpublished manuscript. Premiere, 1923.

"Dictionary." 1955. Notes: for *Irwin C. Miller's Brown Skin Models*; not performed.

"Dinah." 1930. Note: from *Lew Leslie's Blackbirds of 1930*.

"Dissatisfied Blues." 1930. Note: from *Lew Leslie's Blackbirds of 1930*.

"Dixie Ann in Afghanistan." 1940. Note: from *Tan Manhattan*.

"Dixie Moon." 1924. Co-composer, Noble Sissle. Note: from *The Chocolate Dandies*. Recorded: Columbia 34504; Columbia C2S 847.

"Doin' the Hepcat." 1952. Note: from *Shuffle Along of 1952*.

"Doin' the Mozambique." 1930. Note: from *Lew Leslie's Blackbirds of 1930*.

"A Dollar for a Dime." 1940. Note: from *Tan Manhattan*.

"Don't Cha Know." 1962. Unpublished manuscript.

"Don't Cheat on the Meat." 1955. Notes: for *Hit the Stride*; not performed.

"Don't Love Me Blues." 1923. Unpublished manuscript. Premiere, 1923.

"Don't Make a Plaything out of My Heart." 1958. Notes: for *Happy Times*; not performed.

"Don't Play the Mambo." 1955. Notes: for *Irwin C. Miller's Brown Skin Models*; not performed.

"Down Beat." 1939. Unpublished manuscript. Co-composer, Joshua Milton Reddie.

"Down in the Land of Dancing Pickaninnies." 1924. Note: from *The Chocolate Dandies*.

"Dreams Continue." 1959. Unpublished manuscript.

"Dumb Luck." 1924. Co-composer, Noble Sissle. Note: from *The Chocolate Dandies*.

"Dusting Around." 1932. Note: from *Shuffle Along of 1933*.

"Election Day." 1921. Co-composer, Noble Sissle. Note: from *Shuffle Along*.

"Elsie." 1923. New York: M. Witmark, 1923. Co-composer, Noble Sissle. Notes: for *Elsie*; not performed.

"Everybody's Struttin' Now." 1923. New York: M. Witmark, 1923. Co-composer, Noble Sissle. Note: from *Elsie*.

"Everything Reminds Me of You." 1921. New York: M. Witmark, 1921. Co-composer, Noble Sissle. Note: from *Shuffle Along*.

"Everything They Say about Love Is True." 1958. Notes: for *Happy Times*; not performed.

"Falling in Love." 1932. Note: from *Shuffle Along of 1933*.

"Farewell with Love." 1952. Note: from *Shuffle Along of 1952*.

"Fast Talk." 1954. Unpublished manuscript.

"Fate Is the Slave of Love." 1924. New York: Harms, 1924. Note: from *The Chocolate Dandies*.

"Firefly." 1936. Unpublished manuscript. Co-composer, Joshua Milton Reddie.

"Floradora Girls." 1920. Note: for a Schubert revue of 1920.

"The Gal from Baton Rouge." 1955. Notes: for *Hit the Stride*; not performed.

"Gee! I Wish I Had Someone to Rock Me in the Cradle of Love." 1919. Premiere, 1919. Recorded: Artrio-Angeles 8049; Warner Brothers 3267.

"Gee! I'm Glad That I'm from Dixie." 1919. New York: M. Witmark, 1919.

"Glory." 1932. Note: from *Shuffle Along of 1933*.

"Going Off the Deep End." 1950. Notes: for *Be Yourself*; not performed.

"Good Fellow Blues." 1921. Co-composer, Noble Sissle. Recorded: Biograph BLP-1012Q.

"Good Night, Angeline." 1919. New York: M. Witmark, 1919. Co-composers, James Reese Europe, Noble Sissle. Note: from *Shuffle Along*. Recorded: Warner Brothers 3267.

"Good-Bye My Honey I'm Gone." 1918. New York: Joseph W. Stern, 1918. Co-composer, James Reese Europe.

"Grand Street Boys." 1958. Unpublished manuscript.

"A Great Big Baby." 1940. Note: from *Tan Manhattan*.

"Green and Blue." 1937. New York: Mills Music, 1937. Note: from *Swing It*.

"Green Pastures." New York: Shapiro, Bernstein, 1930. Co-composer, Will Morrisey. Note: from *Lew Leslie's Blackbirds of 1930*.

"Gypsy Blues." 1921. New York: M. Witmark and Sons, 1921. Co-composer, Noble Sissle. Note: from *Shuffle Along*.

"Ham and Eggs." 1930. Note: from *Lew Leslie's Blackbirds of 1930*.

"Happy Times." 1958. Notes: for *Happy Times*; not performed.

"Harlem." 1930. Note: from *Lew Leslie's Blackbirds of 1930*.

"Harlem Bon Bon Baby." 1927. Notes: for *Teddy*; not performed.

"Harlem Hot House." 1952. Note: from *Shuffle Along of 1952*.

"Harlem Moon." 1933. Note: from *Shuffle Along of 1933*.

"Have a Good Time Everybody." 1924. Co-composer, Noble Sissle. Note: from *The Chocolate Dandies*.

"Heart's in Tune." 1952. Note: from *Shuffle Along of 1952*.

"Heaven Sent Wonderful You." 1937. Unpublished manuscript.

"Hep Cats Done Gone High Hat." 1955. Notes: for *Hit the Stride*; not performed.

"Here 'Tis." 1932. Note: from *Shuffle Along of 1933*.

"Here's to Your Country." 1958. Notes: for *Happy Times*; not performed.

"He's Always Hanging Around." 1919. Unpublished manuscript. Co-composer, Noble Sissle. Premiere, 1919.

"He's in the Calaboose Now." 1958. Unpublished manuscript. Co-composer, L. Henderson.

"Hit the Stride." 1955. Notes: for *Hit the Stride*; not performed.

"Hobble on the Cobble." 1955. Notes: for *Hit the Stride*; not performed.

"Hot Feet." 1958. Notes: for *Happy Times*; not performed.

"How to Play the Ole Banjo." 1930. Note: from *Lew Leslie's Blackbirds of 1930*.

"Huggin' and Muggin'." 1937. New York: Mills Music, 1937. Note: from *Swing It*.

"The Huskin' Bee." 1958. Notes: for *Happy Times*; not performed.

"The Juke Box Serenade." 1958. Notes: for *Happy Times*; not performed.

"I Ain't Gonna Give Nobody None of My Love." 1955. Unpublished manuscript.

"I Can't Get You Out of My Mind." 1964. Unpublished manuscript. Co-composer, Joshua Milton Reddie.

"I Guess the Cards Were Stacked Against Me." 1947. Unpublished manuscript.

"I Like to Walk with a Pal Like You." 1923. New York: M. Witmark, 1923. Co-composer, Noble Sissle. Note: from *Elsie*.

"I Love You So." 1927. Notes: for *Teddy*; not performed.

"I Wonder Where My Sweetie Can Be." 1925. Unpublished manuscript. Premiere, 1925.

"I Would Like to Know Why." 1926. Unpublished manuscript. Co-composer, Noble Sissle.

"If I Were You." 1936. Unpublished manuscript. Co-composer, Joshua Milton Reddie.

"If It Pleases You." 1955. Notes: for *Hit the Stride*; not performed.

"If It's Any News to You." 1932. Note: from *Shuffle Along of 1933*.

"If You've Never Been Vamped by a Brownskin." 1921. New York: M. Witmark, 1921. Co-composer, Noble Sissle. Note: from *Shuffle Along*. Recorded: Warner Brothers 3267.

"I'd Give a Dollar for a Dime." Recorded: Columbia 34504.

"I'll Find My Love in D-I-X-I-E." 1924. Co-composer, Noble Sissle. Note: from *The Chocolate Dandies*.

"I'm a Soprano." 1927. Notes: for *Teddy*; not performed.

"I'm Craving for That Kind of Love." 1921. New York: M. Witmark and Sons, 1921. Co-composer, Noble Sissle. Note: from *Shuffle Along*. Recorded: Stash Records ST 129; Warner Brothers 3267.

"I'm Just a Simple Girl." 1955. Notes: for *Irwin C. Miller's Brown Skin Models*; not performed.

"I'm Just Simply Full of Jazz." 1919. New York: M. Witmark and Sons, 1919. Note: from *Shuffle Along*. Recorded: Pathé 22284.

"I'm Just Wild about Harry." 1919. New York: M. Witmark and Sons, 1919. Co-composer, Noble Sissle. Note: from *Shuffle Along*. Recorded: Musical Heritage Society 416368A.

"I'm Setting a Trap." Notes: for *Cleo Steps Out*; not performed.

"I'm Setting a Trap to Catch You." 1936. Co-composer, Joshua Milton Reddie.

"Imitations of You." 1935. Unpublished manuscript.

"In Honeysuckle Time." 1919. New York: M. Witmark and Sons, 1919. Co-composer, Noble Sissle. Note: from *Shuffle Along*.

"In the Land of Sunny Sunflowers." 1932. Note: from *Shuffle Along of 1933*.

"It Ain't Being Done No More." 1935. New York: Handy Brothers, 1935. Co-composer, G. Irwin.

"It's Afro-American Day." 1969. Unpublished manuscript. Premiere, 1969.

"It's All Your Fault." 1915. Baltimore: Maryland Music, 1915.

"It's Grand to Be So Beautiful." 1935. Unpublished manuscript. Co-composer, Joshua Milton Reddie.

"It's Hard to Love Somebody When That Somebody Don't Love You." 1955. Notes: for *Hit the Stride*; not performed.

"It's Not Wrong to Have Fun." 1955. Notes: for *Hit the Stride*; not performed.

"It's the Gown That Makes the Girl That Makes the Guy." 1952. Co-composer, Joan Javits. Note: from *Shuffle Along of 1952*.

"It's the Youth in Me." 1936. Unpublished manuscript. Co-composer, Joshua Milton Reddie.

"I've the Lovin'es' Love for You." 1917. New York: Joseph W. Stern, 1918. Co-composer, James Reese Europe.

"Jassamine Lane." 1924. Co-composer, Noble Sissle. Note: from *The Chocolate Dandies*. Recorded: Musical Heritage Society 416368A.

"Jazzing Thunder Storming Dance." 1923. New York: M. Witmark, 1923. Co-composer, Noble Sissle. Notes: for *Elsie*; not performed.

"Jazztime Baby." 1924. Co-composer, Noble Sissle. Note: from *The Chocolate Dandies*.

"Jingle Step." 1923. New York: M. Witmark, 1923. Co-composer, Noble Sissle. Notes: for *Elsie*; not performed.

"Jive Drill." 1952. Note: from *Shuffle Along of 1952*.

"Jockey's Life for Mine." 1924. Co-composer, Noble Sissle. Note: from *The Chocolate Dandies*.

"John Saw the Number." 1944. Unpublished manuscript.

"Jubilee Brazilian." Co-composer, Joshua Milton Reddie. Notes: for *Cleo Steps Out*; not performed.

"Jubilee Tonight." 1960. Unpublished manuscript.

"The Juke Box Serenade." 1958. Notes: for *Happy Times*; not performed.

"Jump Steady." 1924. Co-composer, Noble Sissle. Note: from *The Chocolate Dandies*.

"Joshua Fit de Battle." 1932. Note: from *Shuffle Along of 1933*.

"Keep Your Chin Up." 1932. Notes: for *Shuffle Along of 1933*; not performed.

"Kentucky Sue." 1921. New York: M. Witmark, 1921. Co-composer, Noble Sissle. Notes: for *Shuffle Along*; not performed.

"King Tut's Tomb." Unpublished manuscript.

"A Kiss in a Cab." 1950. Notes: for *Be Yourself*; not performed.

"Labor Day Parade." 1932. Note: from *Shuffle Along of 1933*.

"Lady of the Moon." 1925. Co-composer, Noble Sissle. Note: from *Still Dancing*.

"Land of the Dancing Pickanninies." 1924. Note: from *The Chocolate Dandies*.

"Las Vegas." 1955. Notes: for *Hit the Stride*; not performed.

"Lenox Avenue Waltz." 1949. Unpublished manuscript.

"Let's Get Married Right Away." 1924. Note: from *Cochran's Revue of 1924*.

"Let's Wreck the Joint." 1955. Notes: for *Irwin C. Miller's Brown Skin Models*; not performed.

"Life Is Fine." 1949. Unpublished manuscript.

"Lonesome Man." 1933. Notes: for *Happy Times*; not performed.

"Lost in the Mountains." 1927. Notes: for *Teddy*; not performed.

"Love Chile." 1923. New York: M. Witmark, 1923. Co-composer, Noble Sissle. Notes: for *Elsie*; not performed.

"Love Like Ours." 1954. Unpublished manuscript.

"Love Will Find a Way." 1919. New York: M. Witmark and Sons, 1919. Co-composer, Noble Sissle. Note: from *Shuffle Along*. Recorded: Stash Records ST 129.

"Loving You the Way I Do." 1930. New York: Shapiro, Bernstein, 1930. Co-composers, Jack Scholl, Will Morrisey. Note: from *Hot Rhythm*.

"Lucinda Lee." 1962. Unpublished manuscript.

"Magic Little Words." 1962. Unpublished manuscript.

"Magnolia Rose." 1940. Note: from *Tan Manhattan*.

"Make Love to Me." 1956. Unpublished manuscript.

"Mammy's Little Choc'late Cullud Chile." 1919. New York: M. Witmark and Sons, 1919. Note: from *The Chocolate Dandies*.

"Manda." 1924. Co-composer, Noble Sissle. Note: from *The Chocolate Dandies*.

"Martin Luther King (Didn't the Angels Sing)." 1968. New York: Leo Feist, 1968.

"Memories of You." 1930. New York: Shapiro, Bernstein, 1930. Note: from *Lew Leslie's Blackbirds of 1930*. Recorded: Quicksilver QSCD 9003.

"Men Are Not Gods." 1947. Unpublished manuscript.

"Messin' Around." 1926. Unpublished manuscript. Co-composer, Noble Sissle. Premiere, 1926.

"Michi Mori San." 1919. Note: for a Schubert revue of 1919.

"Mirandy, That Gal of Mine." 1918. New York: Joseph W. Stern, 1918. Co-composer, James Reese Europe. Recorded: New World 260; Pathé Frère 22089-A.

"Miss Annabell." 1950. Unpublished manuscript.

"Mississippi Honeymoon." 1955. Notes: for *Irwin C. Miller's Brown Skin Models*; not performed.

"My Crinoline Girl." 1923. New York: M. Witmark, 1923. Co-composer, Noble Sissle. Note: from *Elsie.*

"My Flower of Love." 1927. Notes: for *Teddy*; not performed.

"My Handy Man Ain't Handy Any More." 1930. New York: Shapiro, Bernstein, 1930. Note: from *Lew Leslie's Blackbirds of 1930.* Recorded: Warner Brothers 3267.

"My Lady of the Mist." 1958. Notes: for *Happy Times*; not performed.

"My Little Dream Toy Shop." 1954. Unpublished manuscript. Co-composer, Joshua Milton Reddie.

"My Loving Baby." 1916. Unpublished manuscript.

"My Old Man's a Bouncer." 1955. Notes: for *Irwin C. Miller's Brown Skin Models*; not performed.

"My Vision Girl." 1920. New York: M. Witmark, 1921. Note: from *Midnight Rounders* and *Shuffle Along.*

"A National Love Song (Sweethearts Are We)." 1950. Unpublished manuscript.

"A New Building." 1955. Notes: for *Hit the Stride*; not performed.

"A New Star." 1955. Notes: for *Irwin C. Miller's Brown Skin Models*; not performed.

"Nileda." Notes: for *Cleo Steps Out*; not performed.

"A No Good Man Will Make a Good, Good Woman Bad." 1955. Notes: for *Hit the Stride*; not performed.

"Of Egypt's Queen." Notes: for *Cleo Steps Out*; not performed.

"Oh Baby." 1942. Unpublished manuscript.

"Oh, That Beautiful Bird of Paradise." 1924. Co-composer, Noble Sissle.

"Oh What a Baby." 1927. Notes: for *Teddy*; not performed.

"Oh Where Are You?" 1967. Unpublished manuscript.

"Old Fashioned Swing." Unpublished manuscript.

"Ole Man River Is Lonely Now." 1955. Notes: for *Irwin C. Miller's Brown Skin Models*; not performed.

"On My Ohio." 1953. Unpublished manuscript.

"On Patrol in No Man's Land." 1919. New York: M. Witmark and Sons, 1919. Co-composer, James Reese Europe. Note: from *Shuffle Along.* Recorded: New World Records NW 260; Pathé Frère 22089-B.

"One Hot Dog to a Customer." 1953. Unpublished manuscript.

"Oriental Blues." 1921. New York: M. Witmark, 1921. Note: from *Shuffle Along.* Recorded: Stash Records ST 129.

"Paris." Notes: for *Cleo Steps Out*; not performed.

"Pickaninny Shoes." 1920. New York: M. Witmark, 1921. Note: from *Shuffle Along.* Recorded: Stash Records ST 129.

"Playing Bingo." 1939. Unpublished manuscript. Co-composer, Joshua Milton Reddie.

"Readin', Ritin' an' Rhythm." 1936. Unpublished manuscript. Co-composer, Joshua Milton Reddie.

"Red River Blues." 1963. Unpublished manuscript.

"A Regular Guy." 1923. New York: M. Witmark, 1923. Note: from *Elsie.*

"Rock, Church, Rock." 1936. Unpublished manuscript. Co-composer, Joshua Milton Reddie.

"Rock's Song for Victory." 1958. Unpublished manuscript.

"Roll, Jordan." 1930. Note: from *Lew Leslie's Blackbirds of 1930.*

"The Rhythm of America." 1952. Note: from *Shuffle Along of 1952.*

"Run on the Bank." 1924. Co-composer, Noble Sissle. Note: from *The Chocolate Dandies.*

"Sand Flowers." 1923. New York: M. Witmark, 1923. Note: from *Elsie.*

"Saturday Afternoon." 1932. Note: from *Shuffle Along of 1933.*

"Say Hello to the Folks Back Home." 1940. Note: from *The Adelaide Hall Story.*

"See America First." 1915. Unpublished manuscript. Co-composer, Eddie Nelson.

"Seminole Trail." 1927. Notes: for *Teddy*; not performed.

"Señor Sam." 1947. Unpublished manuscript.

"Serenade Blues." 1922. Co-composer, Noble Sissle. Note: from *Shuffle Along.*

"Shack Town." 1955. Notes: for *Hit the Stride*; not performed.

"Sharing." 1956. Unpublished manuscript. Co-composer, B. Busey.

"She'll Say Bye Bye to You." 1955. Notes: for *Irwin C. Miller's Brown Skin Models*; not performed.

"Shuffle Along." 1921. New York: M. Witmark and Sons, 1921. Co-composer, Noble Sissle. Note: from *Shuffle Along.*

"Silver Wings in the Moonlight." 1955. Unpublished manuscript.

"Since Hannah from Savannah." 1930. Note: from *Lew Leslie's Blackbirds of 1930.*

"Sing and Dance Your Troubles Away." 1932. Note: from *Shuffle Along of 1933.*

"Sing Dance." 1958. Notes: for *Happy Times*; not performed.

"Sing Me to Sleep Dear Mammy." 1921. Co-composer, Noble Sissle. Note: from *Shuffle Along.*

"Sissle and Blake Cakewalk." 1958. Notes: for *Happy Times*; not performed.

"Somebody Else." Unpublished manuscript.

"A Song That's Got a Beat." 1956. Unpublished manuscript.

"The Sons of Old Black Joe." 1924. Co-composer, Noble Sissle. Note: from *The Chocolate Dandies.*

"Sore Foot Blues." 1932. Note: from *Shuffle Along of 1933.*

"Stage Door." 1955. Notes: for *Irwin C. Miller's Brown Skin Models*; not performed.

"Strange What Love Will Do." 1955. Notes: for *Irwin C. Miller's Brown Skin Models*; not performed.

"Sugar Babe." 1932. Note: from *Shuffle Along of 1933.*

"Supermarket." 1952. Note: from *Shuffle Along of 1952.*

"Swanee Moon." 1952. Note: from *Shuffle Along of 1952.*

"Sweet Talk." 1947. Unpublished manuscript.

"Swing Time at the Savoy." 1948. Unpublished manuscript.

"Sylvia." 1950. Unpublished manuscript. Premiere, 1950.

"Tahiti." 1924. Note: from *Cochran's Revue of 1924.*

"Take Down Dis Letter." 1924. Co-composer, Noble Sissle. Note: from *The Chocolate Dandies.*

"Take It Easy." 1953. Unpublished manuscript.

"Tan Manhattan." 1940. Note: from *Tan Manhattan.*

"Tears." 1954. Unpublished manuscript. Co-composer, Joshua Milton Reddie.

"Teddy." 1927. Notes: for *Teddy*; not performed.

"That Charleston Dance." 1924. Note: from *The Chocolate Dandies.*

"That Lindy Hop." New York: Shapiro, Bernstein, 1930. Note: from *Lew Leslie's Blackbirds of 1930.*

"That South Car'lina Jazz Dance." 1925. Unpublished manuscript. Co-composer, Noble Sissle. Premiere, 1925.

"That Was Me." Unpublished manuscript.

"There Are Some Things You Just Can't Tell." 1955. Notes: for *Hit the Stride*; not performed.

"There'll Always Be a Champ." 1955. Notes: for *Irwin C. Miller's Brown Skin Models*; not performed.

"There's a Million Little Cupids in the Sky." 1924. New York: Harms, 1924. Co-composer, Noble Sissle. Notes: for *The Chocolate Dandies*; not performed.

"There's One Lane That Has No Turning." 1926. Unpublished manuscript. Premiere, 1926.

"Thinking of Me." 1924. Co-composer, Noble Sissle. Note: from *The Chocolate Dandies*.

"Three Brave Men." 1927. Notes: for *Teddy*; not performed.

"The Three Wise Monkeys." 1925. Unpublished manuscript. Premiere, 1925.

"Thrill in Spain." 1955. Notes: for *Irwin C. Miller's Brown Skin Models*; not performed.

"Time Drags Along." 1947. Unpublished manuscript.

"Time Out for Love." 1952. Co-composer, Flourney E. Miller. Note: from *Shuffle Along of 1952*.

"To Hell with Germany." 1918. Unpublished manuscript. Premiere, 1918.

"Toussaint L'Overture." 1944. Unpublished manuscript. Co-composer, James P. Johnson.

"Trouble Seems to Follow Me Around." 1954. Unpublished manuscript. Co-composer, Joshua Milton Reddie.

"Truckin' on Down." 1935. Unpublished manuscript.

"Tweet Says (I've Got Nine Lives, Do You?)" 1960. Unpublished manuscript.

"Two Hearts in Tune." 1922. New York: M. Witmark, 1922. Co-composer, Noble Sissle. Note: from *Elsie*.

"'Twould Take a Gypsy Rose Lee." 1945. Unpublished manuscript.

"Uncle Tom and Old Black Joe." 1921. Co-composer, Noble Sissle. Note: from *Shuffle Along*.

"Under the Jungle Moon." 1930. Note: from *Lew Leslie's Blackbirds of 1930*.

"Up in the Clouds." 1927. Notes: for *Teddy*; not performed.

"Utterly Lovely." 1950. Notes: for *Be Yourself*; not performed.

"Vision Girl." 1920. Co-composer, Noble Sissle. Note: from *Midnight Rounders*.

"Voodoo Man." 1960. Unpublished manuscript.

"Waiting for the Whistle to Blow." 1932. Notes: for *Shuffle Along of 1933*; not performed.

"Wakin' Up the Folks Downstairs." 1930. Note: from *Lew Leslie's Blackbirds of 1930*.

"Walking the Dog." 1916. Co-composer, Noble Sissle. Notes: for *Ziegfeld's Follies of 1916*; not performed.

"Walking Home." 1927. Notes: for *Teddy*; not performed.

"Way Down in Dahomey." 1958. Notes: for *Happy Times*; not performed.

"We Are Americans Too." 1940. New York: Handy Brothers, 1941. Note: from *Tan Manhattan*.

"We Belong Together." 1930. Note: from *Lew Leslie's Blackbirds of 1930*.

"We Gotta Get Hitched, Baby." 1955. Notes: for *Hit the Stride*; not performed.

"Weary." 1940. Note: from *Tan Manhattan*.

"We're a Couple of Salesmen." 1932. Notes: for *Shuffle Along of 1933*; not performed.

"What a Great Great Day." 1918. Unpublished manuscript. Premiere, 1918.

"What Is Wrong with Me?" 1950. Notes: for *Be Yourself*; not performed.

"When a Carnation Meets a Red Red Rose." 1955. Notes: for *Irwin C. Miller's Brown Skin Models*; not performed.

"When a Crew Goes Out on a Cruise." Notes: for *Cleo Steps Out*; not performed.

"When Susie Simpkins Married Silas Green." Unpublished manuscript.

"When the Lord Created Adam." 1931. Unpublished manuscript.

"White Clouds." 1939. Unpublished manuscript. Co-composer, Joshua Milton Reddie.

"Who Said Blackbirds Are Blue." 1930. Note: from *Lew Leslie's Blackbirds of 1930*.

"Why Did You Make Me Care." 1925. Unpublished manuscript. Premiere, 1925.

"Wicked." 1927. Notes: for *Teddy*; not performed.

"Wintering in Florida." 1950. Unpublished manuscript.

"With You." 1923. New York: M. Witmark, 1923. Co-composer, Noble Sissle. Notes: for *Elsie*; not performed.

"Wonderful You." 1942. Unpublished manuscript.

"Won't Be Long Now." 1944. Unpublished manuscript.

"You Brought Me Love." 1956. Unpublished manuscript.

"You Can't Cash In on an Alibi." 1955. Notes: for *Hit the Stride*; not performed.

"You Can't Take the Rhythm Out of My Soul." 1958. Notes: for *Happy Times*; not performed.

"You Don't Look for Love." 1932. Notes: for *Shuffle Along of 1933*; not performed.

"You Got to Git the Gitting While the Gitting Is Good." 1955. Notes: for *Hit the Stride*; not performed. Recorded: Warner Brothers 3267.

"You Got to Have Koo Wah." 1932. Note: from *Shuffle Along of 1933*.

"You Ought to Know." 1924. New York: U. B. Noble Publishing/Crown Music, 1924. Co-composer, Noble Sissle. Note: from *The Chocolate Dandies*.

"You Spoke—I Never Heard a Word." 1950. Notes: for *Be Yourself*; not performed.

"You Were Born to Be Loved." 1947. Unpublished manuscript. Co-composer, Joshua Milton Reddie.

"You Were Meant for Me." 1923. New York: Harms, 1924. Co-composer, Noble Sissle. Note: from *London Calling* and *André Charlot's Revue of 1924*. Recorded: Columbia C2S 847.

"You're Calling Me, Georgia." 1927. Co-composers, W. B. Grossman, Eddie Nelson.

"You're Lucky to Me." 1930. New York: Shapiro, Bernstein, 1930. Note: from *Lew Leslie's Blackbirds of 1930*. Recorded: Quicksilver QSCD 9003; Stash Records ST 128.

"You're My Silver Symphony." 1950. Notes: for *Be Yourself*; not performed.

"You've Been a Good Little Mammy to Me." 1919. Unpublished manuscript. Premiere, 1919.

MUSICAL THEATER

Be Yourself. 1950. Note: unproduced.

The Chocolate Dandies. Originally titled *In Bamville.* Co-composer, Noble
    Sissle. Premiere, 1924.

Cleo Steps Out. Note: unproduced.

Elsie. Co-composer, Noble Sissle. Premiere, 1923.

Happy Times. 1958.

Hit the Stride. 1955. Co-composer, Flourney E. Miller.

Irwin C. Miller's Brown Skin Models. 1955. Co-composer, Flourney E.
    Miller.

Lew Leslie's Blackbirds of 1930. Premiere, 1930.

Shuffle Along. Co-composer, Noble Sissle. Premiere, 1921. Recorded: New
    World Records NW 260.

Shuffle Along of 1933. Premiere, 1932.

Shuffle Along of 1952. Premiere, 1952.

Swing It. Premiere, 1937.

Teddy. 1927. Note: unproduced.

Tan Manhattan. Premiere, 1940.

PUBLICATIONS

ABOUT BLAKE
Books and Monographs

Bolcom, William, and Robert Kimball. *Reminiscing with Sissle and Blake.*
    New York: Viking Press, 1973.

Carter, Lawrence T. *Eubie Blake: Keys of Memory.* Detroit: Balamp
    Publishing, 1983.

Rose, Al. *Eubie Blake.* New York: Schirmer Books, 1979.

Articles

Blesh, Rudi. "Little Hubie." In *Combo, USA: Eight Lives in Jazz.* London:
    Chilton Book Co., 1971; reprinted, New York: Da Capo, 1979.

Bolcom, William, and Robert Kimball. "The Words and Music of Noble
    Sissle and Eubie Blake." *Stereo Review* 29 (1972): 56–64.

Davies, J.R.T. "Eubie Blake: His Life and Times." *Storyville* 1, no. 6
    (1966): 19–20; continued as "Blake and Noble Sissle," 2, no. 7
    (1966): 12–13.

Doerschuk, B. "The Eubie Blake Story: A Century of American Music."
    Keyboard 8, no. 12 (1982): 52+.

King, Bobbi. "Eubie Blake, a Legend in His Own Lifetime." *Black
    Perspective in Music* 1, no. 2 (1973): 151–156.

Morath, Max. "93 Years of Eubie Blake." *American Heritage* 27 (1976):
    56–65.

Southern, Eileen. "Conversation with Eubie Blake: A Legend in His Own
    Lifetime." *Black Perspective in Music* 1, no. 1 (1973): 50–59.

PRINCIPAL ARCHIVES

Eubie Blake Collection, Maryland Historical Society, Baltimore, Maryland.

* * * * *

James Hubert "Eubie" Blake's contribution to the American musical theater of the 1920s was significant to the development of Broadway musicals. By drawing on the typical black musical of the previous decade, he demonstrated that a Broadway show could include a wide variety of disparate types of songs and still be suc-cessful. Blake's particular strength was that he was able to compose in a broad range of styles that combined and expanded upon those developed by both black and white composers of popular song during the first two decades of the 20th century. His ballads from the 1920s are in the latest Broadway style and demonstrate the same qualities as ballads by Gershwin and Youmans. His jazz-inspired songs, on the other hand, illustrate his familiarity with and ease of use of the black styles that had greatly influenced the direction of popular music beginning in the 1890s. The ragtime song, which developed from the coon song, was firmly established by the time Blake began composing his first songs. His use of harmony, how-ever, through the use of extended jazz chords, helped the genre to flourish in the jazz age and beyond. Through his relationship with James Reese Europe, who supplied dance music for Irene and Vernon Castle and white society balls, Blake absorbed the basic premise of new dances, including the turkey trot, fox trot, and maxixe, which he put to good use in his various shows. He also studied the structure and harmonic schemata of the Tin Pan Alley blues as he performed with the musicians of Europe's Tempo Club in the years before America's entry into World War I, and these were adapted for songs in his shows. Blake's music, particularly in the 1920s, was heard as the embodiment of the progress of the black artist during the Harlem Renaissance.

Although Blake was essentially self-taught as a pianist, he took lessons from a next-door neighbor, Margaret Marshall, who was an organist at a local church. She taught him to read music and play the organ for 25 cents a lesson. After practicing his assigned pieces, Blake would play them with the rhythms and syncopations he heard on neighborhood streets. Although his mother strongly disapproved of this kind of "street" music, he continued to impro-vise surreptitiously whenever it was possible. By age 15, Blake's technique was secure enough that he was hired to play popular songs of the day, including recent ragtime songs such as "Hello, Ma Baby," in Aggie Shelton's sporting house, where he could make up to 18 dollars a night. It was during this time that the young musi-cian honed his skills at playing ragtime piano pieces as well as per-forming as a singer. After three years at Shelton's house, he joined a medicine show, where he played a melodeon and buck-danced. In 1902, he joined a New York show, *In Old Kentucky,* where he again danced. On his return to Baltimore in 1903, he played at a saloon; his piano piece from that year, "Corner of Chestnut and Low (in Baltimo')," commemorates his employment there. During the next few years, Blake played at another sporting house and sev-eral saloons as well as in Atlantic City, where he met and became friends with James P. Johnson and Charles "Luckey" Roberts.

Blake's compositional legacy has been equaled by few com-posers of vernacular music in the 20th century. His earliest achieve-ments (with Noble Sissle) were with James Reese Europe. Blake began as a member of Europe's Society Orchestra; when Europe was called to active duty during World War I, Blake was left in charge of Europe's professional music business and the booking of the Society Orchestra and the Tempo Club's orchestras. Following the end of World War I, Sissle and Blake teamed up with the come-dians Miller and Lyles to produce the musical *Shuffle Along,* which became the unexpected sensation of Broadway in 1921. Late in life, Blake's name was once again before the public through his appearances on the "Tonight Show" with Johnny Carson. His performances of ragtime piano pieces helped spark the ragtime revival; and his reminiscences on television of his earlier career, as well as his interviews with William Bolcom and Robert Kimball in *Reminiscing with Sissle and Blake,* contributed both to the many honors bestowed on him and to the musical *Eubie* (1978). While Blake's fame in his later years was due to his performances of ragtime piano pieces, his central contribution to 20th-century popular music is as a composer in his own right.

From his earliest piano piece, "Sounds of Africa" (1899), published in 1921 as "Charleston Rag," Blake popularized black musical idioms for black and white audiences. His music reflects many influences, including the comic opera *Floradora* by the English composer Leslie Stuart and the work of the first generation of black popular composers (such as Will Marion Cook, Chris Smith, and "Luckey" Roberts) as well as white popular composers, whose music he had performed in Europe's orchestra. His partnership with Sissle was twofold: they were vaudeville performers, and they composed many songs. The 1921 success of *Shuffle Along* on white Broadway—a distinction that had eluded most previous all-black shows—established the team of Sissle and Blake as successful songwriters. By 1923, during the run of *Shuffle Along,* Sissle and Blake's fame was growing so quickly that they were invited to perform before the camera of movie pioneer Lee DeForest in one of his earliest experiments in sound film. Being offered an invitation to compose the songs for an all-white show, *Elsie,* was another sign of their increasing renown as a songwriting team.

In 1925, Sissle and Blake resumed touring engagements throughout the United States, France, and England. Sissle decided to remain in England in 1927, while Blake decided to resume his career as a composer in the United States. Their partnership was ended. For his next important show, *Lew Leslie's Blackbirds of 1930,* Blake teamed up with Andy Razaf and was reunited with Flournoy Miller, author of the book for the show. After the failure of a sequel to *Shuffle Along* in 1933, Blake returned to performing. He wrote several more musicals, but they did not achieve the success of his earlier works. During the 1940s and 1950s, he continued to write songs and piano rags, but his music did not catch the public's attention. It was only with the revival of ragtime in the late 1960s that he was "rediscovered." Blake's instrumental pieces are written for piano, the earliest in the tradition of Scott Joplin. Later pieces show Blake's mastery of stride piano style, and by the 1940s he was writing works like "Eubie's Boogie." After his study of the Schillinger System of Musical Composition at New York University in the late 1940s, Blake composed waltzes and other piano pieces not always associated with vernacular music. In all of these pieces, as in his other piano pieces, however, Blake's sense of melodic line is always flowing and convincing. While Blake's fame will always be associated first with the success of *Shuffle Along,* he should be viewed as a composer-performer who wrote many piano pieces and songs that traversed a wide variety of musical styles and genres, black and white.

SHUFFLE ALONG (1921)

Most of Blake's songs for *Shuffle Along* carry a joint authorship with Noble Sissle. It is clear from their subsequent careers, however, that

Blake was the driving force behind the music. His technique encompassed the many styles and genres of popular song heard during the 1920s. This variety is demonstrated by the score of their hit, *Shuffle Along.* In "Love Will Find a Way," Sissle and Blake wrote an up-to-date romantic ballad that still does not sound old-fashioned today. The verse, whose form is best described as AB, displays a harmonic palette of new tonal areas; at the words "Your love for me is heav'nly beacon," for example, the chord progression is raised to an unexpected key, which highlights the word "heav'nly." The music of the verse is conversational, with many repeated notes and scale-derived phrases. The A section repeats the same rhythmic phrase four times, each with slight variation and always starting on a different note. The B section is constructed from two longer phrases that lead the listener to the slower music of the refrain, which formally follows an AA' form. Here, Blake's scale-derived lines are disguised by large melodic skips, which give the impression of a disjunct melody to underscore the words "Love will find a way." This change of style, accompanied by an oom-pah bass and a less conversational melody, makes the refrain truly memorable. The lyrics are reflective of two lovers who have been separated, and "Love Will Find a Way" is a superb love song.

The title song, "Shuffle Along," reflects Blake's association with the ragtime pianists of Baltimore at the turn of the century. The style of the song is a syncopated ragtime song in which Blake has incorporated the stop-time effect that was used by Scott Joplin and others. "Shuffle Along" has a brief verse (AA') that suggests that the shuffle is "a step that's full of 'pep' and syncopation." The 32-bar refrain is also set as an AA' form. Its main feature is a short, repeated melodic phrase, which first appears in the verse and is sung to a variety of lyrics, including "shuffle along," "whistle a song," "sometimes a smile," and "right ev'ry wrong." In its early appearances, this phrase is followed by the stop-time silence, but by the middle of the A section, the music becomes continuous. In A', Blake begins as in the opening but varies the harmony of the second phrase. As the music becomes continuous once again, the refrain is brought to a close by a restatement of the opening phrases of the A section, this time without the stop-time silence. This musical connection splendidly ties both parts of the refrain together and brings it to a satisfying conclusion.

During the 1920s, many fox trot novelty songs were written, and Blake included several in *Shuffle Along.* "Baltimore Buzz" (1921) follows the usual pattern that was established by songs like Chris Smith's "Ballin' the Jack." The 12-bar verse, which combines ragtime syncopation with the rhythm of the fox trot, relates the Baltimore Buzz to other "raggy, draggy dances and prances." The refrain, 20 bars long, lacks the usual balance of these songs, since the first eight-bar phrase is answered by one 12 bars long. Blake, however, compensates for the extra bars by the use of an elision, so that the listener is carried along by the rising line to the climax of the song on the word "slide." The score of "Baltimore Buzz" is labeled as a "Novelty Fox Trot Song," and Blake sets the text in a long-short trochaic pattern, though each phrase ends with a syncopated short-long rhythm. The marchlike accompaniment, which is limited to three chords, establishes the dance as a variant of the fox trot, the most popular and long lasting of the new black-derived dances.

In contrast to his standard Broadway tunes, in *Shuffle Along* Blake includes a number of tunes that are representative of black popular song. Two numbers that created a sensation with audiences in 1921 were "If You've Never Been Vamped by a Brownskin, You've Never Been Vamped at All" and "I'm Craving for That Kind of Love." The latter combines a number of rhythmic patterns; most notable are a short-long iambic pattern (used for the words "kiss me," "press me," "whisper," and "honey") and a delayed, off-the-beat, equal pulse pattern for a variety of words—including the opening of the verse ("[beat] I'm wishing, [beat] and fishing," etc.) and the close of the chorus ("[beat] huddle me, [beat] cuddle me," etc.)—to establish the abandon that can be heard in the original cast recording made by Gertrude Saunders. Blake's melody here is quite limited in range, spanning just a little more than an octave. The many repeated phrases give an impression that Blake may have been thinking of a spiritual while he was setting this very secular text. While the harmonies of this song do not go beyond the basic chord progressions that one hears in many tunes of the period, its rhythmic vitality and repeated, syncopated melodic phrases add to a listener's impression that it represents yet a different style of song in *Shuffle Along*.

Although the blues were not yet fully established as part of the Broadway idiom in 1921, Blake included several in *Shuffle Along*. His blues do not adhere to the traditional 12-bar format but rather adapt various characteristics, such as blue notes and bass patterns, to establish the blues. One of his most successful songs in the genre is "Serenade Blues," which was not heard in the original production of *Shuffle Along* but was interpolated into later performances. The lyrics of the verse begin with a bow to W. C. Handy; the poetic scheme is unusual in that there are not always external rhymes, though some contain internal rhymes. Blake's setting of the text is idiomatic, breezy, and harmonically daring with unexpected whole-tone chords and lowered thirds and sevenths. While the bass does not follow the standard harmonic blues pattern, the chords of the verse still capture the quality of a blues. It is the refrain, however, that displays Sissle and Blake's compositional feat as they produce a musical gloss on Franz Schubert's well known "Ständchen." (They note in the credits that the words and music are by them "With apologies to the immortal FRANZ SCHUBERT.") Schubert's tune is syncopated and embellished, and his harmonies are extended beyond their original triads through the use of jazz-related chords. At the repeat of the refrain, the score notes, "use Schubert countermelody 2nd time only." In performance, the singer, Gertrude Saunders, continued with a repetition of the gloss while a second singer, perhaps one of the "boys" listed in the program, began singing Sissle and Blake's version of Schubert's original against the jazzy blues version. While the resultant duet sounds like two distinct parts, it is really a brilliant and unusual example of heterophony, where two versions of the same melody are heard simultaneously.

The musical numbers of *Shuffle Along*, in their varied styles, were enthusiastically received by the critics and audiences alike. By the end of 1921, an impressive number of the songs were recorded, usually as vocals but sometimes also as instrumental numbers. While the score was not published in its entirety, most of the songs were available individually to the public. One number in particular, "I'm Just Wild about Harry," remained in the public's consciousness long enough to be revived for the successful presidential campaign of Harry Truman.

JOHN GRAZIANO

BLAND, ED(WARD)

Born in Chicago, Ill., July 25, 1926. **Education:** DuSable High School, Chicago, studied clarinet with Eugene "Jug" Ammons, 1939; Englewood High School, Chicago, 1940; Sherwood School of Music, Chicago, studied clarinet with Angelo De Caprio, 1941–44; Wilson Junior College, Chicago, studied humanities with Joseph Axelrod, 1943–45; University of Chicago, studied form and analysis, counterpoint, musicology, and philosophy, instructors included Leonard B. Meyer, 1946–48; American Conservatory of Music, Chicago, studied composition with Jean Boyd, 1948–49; Chicago, studied composition privately with John Becker, 1954–56. **Military Service:** Treasure Island, San Francisco, Calif., U.S. Navy, Musician Third Class, played clarinet and baritone saxophone in the band, 1945–46. **Composing and Performing Career:** First composition, Trio for Flute, Clarinet, and Bassoon, 1944; co-produced *The Cry of Jazz,* with Nelam Hill, 1959; Vanguard Records, head of A&R, executive producer, and producer, 1974–78; composer and orchestrator for the films *A Soldier's Story,* 1984, *The House of Dies Drear,* 1985, and *A Raisin in the Sun,* 1988; composed or arranged for various artists, including Maya Angelou, George Benson, Country Joe and the Fish, Dizzy Gillespie, Lionel Hampton, King Harvest, Richie Havens, and Al Hirt; music has been performed at Lincoln Center and Carnegie Hall, New York, N.Y., and elsewhere in the United States and Europe; *The Music of Ed Bland* released on the Cambria label, 1986, re-released (with some different tracks) as *Urban Classical: The Music of Ed Bland,* 1994. **Teaching Career:** Bennington College, Bennington, Vt., composer-in-residence, 1980–84; visiting lecturer at colleges and universities, including California State University-Fullerton, University of Rhode Island, Baruch College of New York, N.Y., Montgomery College, Baltimore, Md., University of California-San Diego, State University of New York, Old Westbury, Long Island, N.Y., New School for Social Research, New York, N.Y., Long Island University, Brooklyn Campus, ca. 1980–83; Millersville College, Lancaster, Pa., composer-in-residence, ca. March 1981; Virginia Union University, Richmond, Va., composer-in-residence, ca. April 1981; Wisconsin Conservatory of Music, Milwaukee, ca. May 1982; Loyola Marymount University, Los Angeles, 1984–85; California State University-Pomona, lecturer, spring 1992. **Commissions:** Anti-Defamation League of B'nai B'rith, early 1950s; Madeline Tourtelot, 1957; Gail Hightower, 1979; Eberhardt Blum, 1980; Radio Bremen, János Négyesy, 1980; Quintet of the Americas, 1981; Universal Symphony, 1981; William Powell, 1982; New American Orchestra, 1984; János Négyesy and the New Cal Arts Twentieth Century Players, 1986; PBS Television Network, 1988; California Institute of the Art of Contemporary Music, 1989; eXindigo!!! Singers, 1991; Michele Zukovsky, 1992; Afro-American Chamber Ensemble, 1992, 1993; Delos Records, 1995. **Memberships:** American Composer Alliance; Broadcast Music Inc. (BMI); National Academy of Recording Arts and Sciences, New York Chapter, Board of Governors, 1979–80; American Federation of Musicians Local 47; American Music Center. **Honors/Awards:** Sherwood School of

Music Scholarship, Chicago, Ill., 1941–44; American Conservatory of Music, Chicago, Ill., scholarship, 1948–49; Commission for the White House Record Library, Presidential Commissioner, 1979–81; National Endowment of the Arts Recording Panel, panelist, 1988, 1989; American Academy of Arts and Letters, nominated as a candidate for annual awards in musical composition, 1994. **Mailing Address:** Osmund Music, Inc., P.O. Box 451112, Los Angeles, CA 90045-9998.

MUSIC LIST

INSTRUMENTAL SOLOS
Violin
"For Violin" (unaccompanied). 1980. New York: American Composers Alliance, 1980. Commissioned by Radio Bremen, János Négyesy. Recorded: Cambria CD 1026.

Cello
"Fragment for Cello" (unaccompanied). 1953. Unpublished manuscript.

Flute
"For Flute" (unaccompanied). 1980. New York: American Composers Alliance, 1980. Commissioned by Eberhardt Blum. Recorded: Cambria CD 1026; Cambria CD 1097; Serie INBA-SACM/CD Instituto de Bellas Artes de Mexico.
"For Flute no. 2" (unaccompanied). 1994. Unpublished manuscript. Note: adapted from "For Bassoon."
"For Flute no. 3" (unaccompanied). 1994. Unpublished manuscript. Note: adapted from "For Clarinet."

Oboe
"For Oboe" (unaccompanied). 1994. Unpublished manuscript. Note: adapted from "For Clarinet."

Clarinet
"For Bass Clarinet" (unaccompanied). 1994. Unpublished manuscript. Note: adapted from "For Bassoon."
"For Clarinet" (unaccompanied). 1953. New York: American Composers Alliance, 1980. Recorded: Cambria CD 1026.

Bassoon
"For Bassoon" (unaccompanied). 1979. New York: American Composers Alliance, 1980. Commissioned by Gail Hightower. Recorded: Cambria CD 1026.

Trumpet
"For Trumpet" (unaccompanied). 1994. Unpublished manuscript. Note: adapted from "For Clarinet."

Piano
"Classical Soul." 1992. Unpublished manuscript.
"Fragment for Piano." 1948. Unpublished manuscript.
"Piano Study no. 1." Los Angeles: Osmund Music, n.d.

Ed Bland; courtesy of the composer; photo by Helen Levitt

"Sketches Set Seven." 1987. Unpublished manuscript. Premiere: 1987. Recorded: Cambria CD 1026; Cambria CD 1097.

"Three Chaconnes in Blue." Los Angeles: Osmund Music, n.d.

ELECTRONIC MUSIC

"Cello/Tympani." 1953. Unpublished manuscript.

Music for a Global Village (five soloists, tape). Los Angeles: Osmund Music, n.d. Contents: Suite no. 1 (viola and tape); Suite no. 2 (flute and tape); Suite no. 3 (clarinet and tape); Suite no. 4 (violin and tape); Suite no. 4 (piano and tape).

String Quartet no. 2. 1951. Unpublished manuscript.

Trio no. 2 (three sound modules set as flute, clarinet, bassoon). 1950. Unpublished manuscript.

Trio no. 3 (three sound modules set as oboe, bassoon, trumpet). 1950. Unpublished manuscript.

SMALL INSTRUMENTAL ENSEMBLE

Strings

"Fragment for String Quartet." 1949. Unpublished manuscript.

Woodwinds

"Arion's Song" (Woodwind Quintet no. 2) or "Sketches Set Six." 1986. Unpublished manuscript. Premiere, 1994.

Woodwind Quintet no. 1 (The Jazz Quintet). 1981. New York: American Composers Alliance, 1981. Premiere, 1981. Commissioned by the Quintet of the Americas.

Brass

Brass Quintet (two trumpets, horn, trombone, bass trombone). 1981. Unpublished manuscript. Recorded, 1986: Cambria CD 1026.

Combinations

Clarinet Trio (clarinet, cello, piano). 1992. Unpublished manuscript. Commissioned by Michele Zukovsky.

Duet. Los Angeles: Osmund Music, n.d. Arranged for various pairs of instruments.

"For Viola and Four Others" (viola, flute, oboe, cello, piano). 1993. Unpublished manuscript.

"Magnetic Variations" (clarinet solo, flute, oboe, two percussion players, electric keyboards, electric violin, cello, Fender bass). 1982. Unpublished manuscript. Commissioned by William Powell. Premiere, 1983.

"Paean for an Endangered Planet" (flute, oboe, clarinet, bassoon, two percussion players, electric guitar, harp, electric keyboards, electric violin, electric viola, cello). 1989. Unpublished manuscript. Commissioned by the California Institute of the Art of Contemporary Music. Premiere, 1989.

"Passacaglia in Blue" (flute, clarinet, trumpet, trombone, two percussion players, electric keyboards, cello, double/Fender bass). 1988. Unpublished manuscript. Premiere, 1988.

Piano Trio. 1982. Unpublished manuscript.

"Primal Counterpoint" (flute, clarinet, trumpet, trombone, two percussion players, electric keyboards, cello, Fender bass). 1981. Unpublished manuscript. Commissioned by the Universal Symphony. Note: originally titled "Sketches Set Three."

"Romantic Soul" (soprano saxophone solo, flute, oboe, clarinet, percussion, electric guitar, harp, electric keyboard, cello). 1989. Unpublished manuscript.

"Sketches Set One" (clarinet, trumpet, trombone, timpani, two cellos). 1958. New York: American Composers Alliance, 1980. Recorded: Cambria CD 1026.

"Sketches Set Two" (clarinet, trumpet, trombone, cello). 1957. New York: American Composers Alliance, 1980.

Trio no. 1 (flute, clarinet, bassoon). 1944. Unpublished manuscript.

STRING ORCHESTRA

Partita for Strings. 1982. Unpublished manuscript.

CHAMBER ORCHESTRA

Piece for Chamber Orchestra (oboe, clarinet, trumpet, trombone, timpani, two violins, viola, cello, double bass). 1979. Unpublished manuscript. Recorded: Cambria CD 1026.

FULL ORCHESTRA

Grand Slam (small orchestra). 1993. Unpublished manuscript.

Let Peace Be Free. 1984. Unpublished manuscript. Commissioned by the New American Orchestra. Premiere, 1991.

Rambunctious Serenade (small orchestra). 1992. Unpublished manuscript. Commissioned by the Afro-American Chamber Ensemble.

ORCHESTRA (CHAMBER OR FULL) WITH SOLOISTS

Atalanta's Challenge (soprano saxophone, orchestra). 1988. Unpublished manuscript. Contents: The Oracle; The Race; The Golden Apples. Premiere, 1992.

Concerto for Electric Violin and Chamber Orchestra. 1986. Unpublished manuscript. Commissioned by János Négyesy and the New Cal Arts Twentieth Century Players.

Romantic Synergy (flute, two percussion players, electronic keyboards, strings). 1987. Unpublished manuscript.

DRAMATIC MUSIC

Assassins of the Soul (opera for two narrators, SATB chorus, clarinet, trumpet, trombone, percussion, piano, two cellos, dancers, TV monitors). 1997. Unpublished manuscript.

Dear Vera (dance). 1984. Unpublished manuscript.

Feeling Good (dance suite for flute and tape or computer). 1994. Unpublished manuscript.

New World Order (musical theater for SATB, percussion, and piano). 1991. Unpublished manuscript. Commissioned by the eXindigo!!! Singers.

White Satin (dance). 1983. Unpublished manuscript.

INCIDENTAL MUSIC

The Cool World. Film soundtrack. 1964.

Ganja and Hess. Film soundtrack. 1973.

The House of Dies Drear. Soundtrack for a television movie. 1985.

Jazz Suite (alto saxophone, drums, piano, double bass). 1989. Note: adaptation from the soundtrack for *A Raisin in the Sun.* Commissioned by PBS Television Network. Recorded, 1989: Delos 4020.

"JT." Incidental music for a television episode. 1971.

The Poetry of Maya Angelou. Incidental music to poetry of Maya Angelou. Contents: Burnt Umber; All Alone; Tell Me; I Will Last; Black Incense. Recorded, 1968: GWP 2001.

Reflections. Film score. 1957. Commissioned by Madeline Tourtelot.

A Soldier's Story. Film soundtrack. 1984.

To Live Together. Film score. 1950. Commissioned by the Anti-Defamation League of B'nai B'rith.

CONCERT BAND

Round Robin. Los Angeles: Osmund Music, (rental). Also arranged for various ensembles of wind instruments and for percussion octet.

JAZZ ENSEMBLE

[The following list of titles includes only works that were composed by the subject of the entry; it is not a list of recordings that were made by the subject. Although the composer may have made recordings of his own works, the list is not restricted to those recordings but in many cases includes performances by other artists of the composer's work. The list is made up of publication and discographical data, in cases where such information is available. Although no effort has been made to include documentation of the earliest recording of the works listed, the date of the earliest recording that is readily available has been given. —Ed.]

"Azure Blue." Recorded, 1977: Gateway GLSP 7025.

"Blue Cuchifrito." Recorded, 1969: GWP 5001.

"Bobby A." Recorded, 1975: Vanguard 79365.

"Casabah Melon." Recorded, 1969: GWP 5001.

"Chicken Giblets." Recorded, 1968: GWP 5001.

"Clabber Biscuits." Recorded, 1969: GWP 5001; Vanguard 79364; Vanguard 79381.

"Digital Display." Recorded, 1977: Vanguard 79389.

"Dirty Dude." Recorded, 1977: Gateway GLSP 7025.

"The Fly Fox." Recorded, 1969: GWP 5001.

"Get to That." Recorded, 1977: Gateway GLSP 7025.

"Gettin' Down." Recorded, 1977: Gateway GLSP 7025.

"Greasy Greens." Recorded, 1966: Glad Hamp 1011; Glad Hamp GH 2038; Milestone 9247.

"Grits and Gravy." Recorded, 1966: Prestige 7486.

"Guava Jelly." Recorded, 1968: RCA 3902.

"Keep It Greasy." Recorded, 1976: Vanguard 79366.

"King Cool." Co-composer, Lionel Hampton. Recorded, 1967: Glad Hamp 1011.

"Love Theme." Recorded, 1990: Delos 4020.

"Moody Magic." Recorded, 1977: Vanguard 79390.

"Old King Tut." Recorded, 1976: Vanguard 79366.

"Party Man." Recorded, 1977: Gateway GLSP 7025.

"Philomene." Recorded, 1976: Vanguard 79372.

"Pot Licka." Recorded, 1969: GWP 5001; Vanguard 79366.

"Radio Theme." Recorded, 1990: Delos 4020.

"Rutabaga Pie." Recorded, 1969: Gateway GLSP 7025; GWP 5001.

"Slew Foot." Recorded, 1977: Gateway GLSP 7025.

"Soul Mama." Recorded, 1977: Gateway GLSP 7025.

"Soul Time." Recorded, 1977: Gateway GLSP 7025.

"Stefanie." Recorded, 1975: Vanguard 79362; Vanguard 79366.

"Stomped and Wasted." Recorded, 1969: GWP 5001.

"Sun in Pisces." Recorded, 1976: Vanguard 79381.

"Sweet Stuff." Recorded, 1977: Gateway GLSP 7025.

"Turkey Fan." Recorded, 1969: GWP 5001.

"Turnip Tops." Recorded, 1969: GWP 5001.

"Walter's Theme." Recorded, 1990: Delos 4020.

POPULAR MUSIC

"Aldon B." Recorded, 1976: Vanguard 79371.

"Casanova Was a Girl/Cleopatra Was a Man."

"Chicken Scratch." Recorded, 1969: GWP 502; GWP 2041.

"Eddie A." Recorded, 1976: Vanguard 79371.

"Fly Vines." Recorded, 1969: GWP 001-Parts 1 and 2.

"A Gritty Nitty." Recorded, 1975: GWP 2041; Vanguard 79364.

"If You Grin You Are In." Recorded, 1963: Scepter 1920a.

"I'll Turn the Moon to Cottage Cheese."

"It's Good to Me."

"Juicy Lucy." Recorded, 1969: GWP 506.

"Loose and Juicy." Recorded, 1975: Vanguard 79364.

"Moonshot." Recorded, 1964: Columbia 4-43426; Columbia 2445.

"Mushroom Alley." Recorded, 1977: Vanguard 79388.

"Skunk Juice." Recorded, 1975: RCA 47-9634; Vanguard 79364.

"Toe Jam." Recorded, 1968: RCA 47-9634; Vanguard 79364.

PRINCIPAL ARCHIVES

Edward Bland Collection, Center for Black Music Research, Columbia College, Chicago, Ill.

*   *   *   *   *

Ed Bland is a remarkably versatile composer whose works reflect his diverse musical career. He attributes his musical influences to Duke Ellington, Art Tatum, and Igor Stravinsky, as well as African-American gospel music and West African drumming styles. His concert music draws on his experience as a jazz performer and as a composer, arranger, and producer in several popular music genres, including rock, pop, soul, rhythm and blues, country, and jazz.

As a child, Bland recalls that he was not overly impressed with the world of composing. When he was 11 years old, Bland's father interrupted a game of horseshoes to introduce him to the composer Ulysses Kay. As Bland recalls: "I politely and dutifully shook Kay's hands, while all the time wondering if and when I could escape back downstairs to resume horseshoes. . . . As I sauntered back down to the yard, I thought to myself, 'What a stupid thing for a grown man to do. Write music.'" But Bland became seriously interested in music the following year, when he heard his high school's concert band playing at an assembly. Later that year he began lessons on clarinet, studying with Angelo De Caprio among others. He worked primarily as a jazz musician playing clarinet and baritone saxophone.

Following graduation from Wilson Junior College (Chicago) in 1945 and a year of service in the navy, Bland attended the University of Chicago from 1946 to 1948. In 1948–49, Bland studied composition with Jean Boyd through a scholarship at the American Conservatory of Music in Chicago, and during 1954–56, he took private composition lessons with John Becker.

Although he was a successful jazz performer, Bland felt that the pop-song structure of jazz limited music's ability to express the range of African-American experience. While searching for a new medium, he heard Stravinsky's *Rite of Spring,* which proved to be a turning point. Bland states that he "was not only emotionally moved, but new musical possibilities leapt to mind, suggesting that the *Rite* was a beginning point and a partial model to use to create the extended forms needed to do justice to the Black Experience without sacrificing the vitality and swing of jazz." Bland's goal has been the incorporation of musical and verbal techniques from African-American culture into large-scale, written compositional forms. The most significant of these is the use of a pseudo-improvisational form on the orchestral rather than the soloistic level. Bland states that "like the jazz solo, the direction of the entire work would be problematic to the audience, making them wonder where the composition would go next." As a result, Bland's music has a sense of spontaneity and adventure, without necessarily relying on actual improvisation or jazz figurations.

A second element of African-American cultural interactions is found in Bland's use of "topping" (or "the Dozens"), the equivalent of a verbal jam session in which each competitor tries to top the other by hurling insults about one's family members. Bland uses an analogous musical form, which he describes as follows: "In my composing method, topping serves to delineate sections within the musical process, going from climax to climax. The formal problem, and thus the adventure, lasts until it is resolved at the end of the composition." The overall results are dynamic, unpredictable compositions stemming from a unique and personal voice.

Bland's output has varied considerably, ranging from electronic and tape music to concertos, chamber music, and instrumental solos. Generally, the concert music dates from pre-1960 or post-1979. In the interim, Bland composed, arranged, and produced numerous popular recordings. The early period includes four electronic and tape pieces (Trio no. 2 and Trio no. 3, 1950; String Quartet no. 2, 1951; and "Cello/Tympani," 1953), and three chamber works ("Fragment for String Quartet," 1949; and two works for combinations of clarinet, trumpet, trombone, cello, and timpani, "Sketches Set One," 1958, and "Sketches Set Two," 1957).

One of the most intriguing aspects of Bland's output is a series of solo instrumental explorations. Beginning with the "Fragment for Cello" and "For Clarinet" of 1953, Bland returned to the series with "For Bassoon" (1979), "For Flute" (1980), and "For Violin" (1980). He has made subsequent arrangements of these works for solo trumpet, oboe, and bass clarinet.

With these exceptions and a few works for piano solo, the later works are primarily compositions for larger ensembles. Most notable are two woodwind quintets, works for string and chamber orchestra, and two concertos (*Atalanta's Challenge* for solo soprano saxophone and orchestra, 1988; and Concerto for Electric Violin and Chamber Orchestra, 1986). Bland has also composed incidental music for television (*Jazz Suite* for the 1988 PBS television production of the play *A Raisin in the Sun*) and dance music (such as the suite *Feeling Good* for flute, tape, or computer, from 1994). In 1997, Bland composed an opera entitled *Assassins of the Soul.*

GAYLE SHERWOOD

SKETCHES SET SEVEN (1987)

Ed Bland's "Sketches Set Seven" was written in 1987 for piano solo. It continues the tradition of his earlier chamber works entitled "Sketches Set One" and "Sketches Set Two" (1958 and 1957 respectively) by presenting several concentrated, contrasting yet unified segments. "Sketches Set Seven" was premiered in 1987 by pianist Althea Waites at Merkin Hall, New York City.

The work is organized into five distinct sections. Characterized by unanticipated shifts in tempo, dynamics, register, and texture, the work's constant variety of sound creates a sense of spontaneity and excitement, exemplifying Bland's comparisons of his compositional style to an improvisation by a jazz performer.

Yet the work also has many features that unify it, including specific recurring thematic material. In each section, Bland presents a syncopated angular chromatic theme characterized by an opening atonal five-note motive, in diverse registral and textural arrangements. The effect is similar to that of a jazz improvisation in which a thematic motive recurs in different harmonic, melodic, and rhythmic figurations. Cluster chords also recur throughout the work, lending an architectural quality to the piece, in which the motive is constantly presented in a different light. Each section builds upon what has gone before, creating a cumulative effect. Apart from these general similarities, the sections of the work are organized symmetrically according to mood. Segments one, three, and five are more energetic than the others and make extensive use of counterpoint; segments two and four are slower and more lyrical, contrasting a melody against chordal accompaniment.

The first segment begins with the five-note motive in the lower register; it is subsequently presented in a variety of forms, relationships, and dynamics, and in an increasingly dense polyphonic texture. The segment ends with an octave statement of the motive and a sudden crashing cluster chord. Segment two offers an immediate contrast in mood while presenting thematic and textural continuity. In this segment, the theme is a straightforward hymnic melody that appears over an impressionistic, arpeggiated texture that alternates with octave statements. The introspective mood of the segment is interrupted by dense cluster chords reminiscent of segment one, recalled now as a syncopated harmonic progression. The third segment is a playful and pointillistic variation of the theme, its sparse Webernesque textures and extended ranges culminating in a registral dialogue between the right and left hands. As in segment one, this movement ends with a sudden staccato cluster chord, thus presenting yet another variation of that sonic element.

Segment four is perhaps the most reflective movement. Its lyrical melody is an unsyncopated version of the theme, set here to jazz harmonies. The jazz idiom is also invoked through call-and-response interplay between the right and left hands. In this section, the cluster chords are presented in softer dynamics and subtle syncopations. The final segment summarizes the preceding movements, combining a fiery tempo with intensified polyphony, octave thematic statements, cluster chords, call and response, and metrical shifting. It concludes with a final statement of the extended theme in the low register, which recalls the very opening of the work.

In its interplay of thematic, timbral, and textural variations, "Sketches Set Seven" embodies the thematic development and unpredictability of a compositional improvisation. At the same time, the cumulative form of each section and of the work as a whole epitomizes the progressive escalation of "topping." Bland creates five distinct yet unified miniatures with a minimum of material for a maximum overall effect.

GAYLE SHERWOOD

PIECE FOR CHAMBER ORCHESTRA (1979)

Piece for Chamber Orchestra is scored for oboe, clarinet, trumpet, trombone, timpani, and a small string section. Bland emphasizes rhythmic complexity throughout the approximately 15-minute work and also incorporates interesting dialogues between the various instruments. *Piece for Chamber Orchestra* is subdivided into very clear sections that are marked in the score by double bar lines and surrounding measures of silence. These distinct breaks divide the work into seven sections, each of which presents the performers with new challenges (both as an ensemble and individually).

The first section (mm. 1–91) serves as an introduction to the work, presenting the rhythmic and melodic ideas that form the basis for much of the material to follow. The rhythms are highly syncopated and the individual voices of the ensemble are independently conceived, thereby increasing the complexity of the musical events. The combination of these two factors makes for a work requiring a high level of technical ability on the part of each performer. It is difficult to point to any defining melodic theme in the opening section. It seems that the composer has replaced the function of melodic theme with identifiable, frequently recurring rhythmic cells. There are moments during which melody is isolated (for example, mm. 24–30). The melodies seem to be designed as bridges between sections of intense rhythmic activity rather than as themes around which the work is organized. The first section concludes with the first measure of silence in the work, a rest that, by its very uniqueness in the surrounding context, provides a strong point of articulation.

The second section of the work (mm. 92–215) begins with a melodic statement in the clarinet. Gradually the other instruments are added, thus creating a more stratified texture than in the first section. The woodwinds experiment with and develop the possibilities presented by the initial melody, while the other instruments add a strong rhythmic drive. This juxtaposition results in a complex and dense soundscape. The woodwinds are never free, however, to express their melodic discoveries unchallenged; throughout the section, the impression is of two groups of instruments in continual competition for sonic space, as they interrupt each other at every turn.

The third section (mm. 216–308) provides a strong contrast to the previous section. Here, Bland utilizes only the string section, exploring the possibilities of this reduced texture. This section offers in miniature what the previous section accomplished in large scale. The first violin is given a melodic role while the rest of the strings are primarily concerned with rhythmic ideas. This creates a dialogue between instruments similar to the one in the previous section.

The fourth and central section (mm. 309–406) reintroduces the entire ensemble into the texture, creating a section that is very dense as it uses most, if not all, of the instruments throughout. The rhythmic complexity rises to a higher degree, and, as is the case in the first section, thematic weight seems to be given to repeated rhythmic cells rather than to melodic motives.

Measures 407–543 comprise the fifth section, in which the composer has thinned the texture considerably by writing fewer notes for each instrument. Melodic ideas are emphasized, and the dialogue between instruments takes on a different character, as melodic material is passed back and forth in mutually supportive rather than competitive fashion (this is especially evident in the interaction between the violins and the woodwinds).

The sixth section (mm. 544–765) contains most of the techniques that were presented in more isolated fashion in the previous sections: stratified part writing, melodic dialogue between instruments, rhythmically oriented thematic material, and a wide range of textures. The result is a condensed impression of the process that has been carried out over the course of the work up to this point. At the conclusion of this section, there are four measures of silence—the longest moment of silence in the work and a point of articulation that immediately precedes the last section.

The final section (mm. 766–992) successfully binds together the rhythmic motives that open the work, re-emphasizing the interrelatedness of much of the rhythmic material that appears throughout. Bland also combines the two poles of texture that, to this point, have been kept rather compartmentalized by section: a rather dense texture, on one hand; and a more expansive, thinned-out texture, on the other. By integrating both of these extremes in the final section, Bland succeeds in reconciling the contrast between them.

Piece for Chamber Orchestra is extremely powerful, both in terms of rhythmic intensity and instrumental gesture. Bland's orchestration takes advantage of the chamber group's wide range of timbres and also creates interesting dialogues between the instruments. Jeannie Pool observes that "the work is dramatic, articulate, clear and provocative without being obtuse or inaccessible." This work has been recorded and performed by members of Speculum Musicae and the Group for Contemporary Music. In a review of the recording, Bruce M. Creditor comments that the piece is "a tour de force of instrumental virtuosity, of compositional intensity and focused energy, as well as richness of emotional expression."

TIMOTHY ROMMEN

FOR VIOLIN (1980)

"For Violin" was composed in 1980 and dedicated to János Négyesy. It is scored for solo violin and is approximately six minutes in duration. This work is a through-composed, post-tonal piece that retains an air of improvisatory freedom. In order to understand this work, it is helpful to think in terms of multiple layers of activity, three of which are explored here—melody, rhythm, and register.

The melodic material embodied in this work subdivides into three fairly distinct categories. The first category of material is characterized by angular, chromatic motion; the second is more lyrical; the third incorporates harmonies through the use of double stops. These categories also seem to serve relatively distinct functions within the work. The angular, chromatic material provides energetic and forceful passages that Bland intersperses between short sections of the more lyrical material. The lyrical materials give the work breadth and provide a contrast to the more aggressive material. The third category is the most flexible of the three. Bland uses double-stop harmonies to emulate both the angular and the lyrical material, offering a change of texture in the process. These melodic materials are made even more obviously distinct through the support of the rhythmic element.

The rhythmic character of the piece serves several functions as well. First, and most obviously, it provides the essential drive that animates the work. Second, it establishes a relationship with the melodic materials, mirroring the three categories described above. Thus, the angular, chromatic materials are supported by quick, disjunct rhythmic motives; the lyrical materials are always presented in slower, more evenly spaced rhythmic values; and the material based on double-stop chords is supported by rhythms that are suitable to the angular or lyrical type of material being presented.

The interaction between the various layers of melodic and rhythmic material helps to determine the character of the work. By juxtaposing short sections of these various materials, Bland achieves a sense of spontaneity in the music. The combining of rhythmic contrasts with melodic contrasts results in a powerful effect that permeates the work. In addition to the surface details of rhythmic and melodic function, however, Bland utilizes the element of register to good advantage as well.

Registral change, a very obvious element in this work, serves a dual function. On the one hand, it is used to maintain contrast within the work and to widen the range of pitch options. On the other hand, register is used to create dialogue. Restricted to a single instrument, the composer uses the wide registral compass of the violin in order to create and maintain a conversational quality within the work. While this layer of activity is not always in the foreground, the work revolves around a constant interplay between registral change and the juxtaposed melodic and rhythmic types.

The combination of these layers is, in fact, what makes this work interesting and engaging, and a sensitive performer can do much to enhance recognition of these layers. This work demonstrates Bland's ability to work within more limited timbral and registral parameters. "For Violin" has been recorded by János Négyesy and is included on a compilation of Bland's music published by Cambria Records.

TIMOTHY ROMMEN

REFERENCES

Creditor, Bruce M. Review, "The Music of Ed Bland," *Sonneck Society Bulletin* 16 no. 1 (1990): 42.

Pool, Jeannie. Liner notes to *Urban Classical: The Music of Ed Bland.* Cambria Master Recordings, CD-1026, 1994.

BONDS, MARGARET

Born in Chicago, Ill., March 3, 1913; died in Los Angeles, Calif., April 26, 1972. **Education:** Chicago, Ill., studied piano with her mother, a church organist and music teacher, with Martha Anderson at about age 5, and with T. Theodore Taylor at about age 8; studied piano and composition with Florence Price, then William Dawson, while attending Parker High School; Northwestern University, Evanston, Ill., studied with Emily Boettcher Bogue, B. Mus., 1933, M. Mus., 1934; Juilliard School, New York City, studied orchestration with Robert Starer, 1958–59, choral conducting with Abraham Kaplan, 1966; other teachers included Roy Harris, Emerson Harper, and Walter Gossett. **Composing and Performing Career:** Composed her first work, "Marquette Street Blues," at age 5; Canada and United States, active as solo and duo pianist, also working as accompanist for singer Etta Moten, and dancer Muriel Abbott, early 1930s; Chicago World's Fair, first black soloist with Chicago Symphony Orchestra, June 15, 1933; performed with the Chicago Women's Symphony Orchestra, October 11, 1934; recital at NAACP convention, 1934; New York City, soloist for concert on WNYC radio, May 23, 1941; New York City, formed piano duo with Gerald Cook, which toured and performed on radio, 1944; New York City, piano recital series on WNYC, 1944; appearances with New York City Symphony, and the Scranton Philharmonic, Scranton, Pa., 1950; New York City, made her Town Hall debut, February 7, 1952; New York City, first recitalist in Coffee Concerts, produced by Raoul Abdul, 1958; gave concert tours and lecture demonstrations throughout the country and the world, including Bahamas, Africa, and Russia, early 1960s. **Teaching Career:** Chicago, Ill., opened the Allied Arts Academy for ballet and music, early 1930s–1939; New York City, served as editor in music publishing house of Clarence Williams, 1939; New York, organized a black chamber society to encourage work of black musicians and composers, 1956; New York City, taught at the East Side Settlement House and the American Theater Wing; New York City, served on Music Committee to establish Harlem Cultural Community Center, 1962; Mount Calvary Baptist Church, Harlem, organized a sight-singing program, 1966; Los Angeles, Calif., worked with Inner City Cultural Center, taught at Inner City Cultural Center and worked with Inner City Repertory Theater, 1967–72. **Commissions:** Etta Moten, 1956; Laurence Watson. **Memberships:** National Association of Negro Musicians; Alpha Kappa Alpha; ASCAP. **Honors/Awards:** Rodman Wanamaker Award, honorable mention, 1931, prize, 1932; Honor Roll of Outstanding Negro Women, 1963; Women of the Century Award, 1964; ASCAP awards, 1964, 1965, 1966; Julius Rosenwald Fellowship; Roy Harris Fellowship; Northwestern University Alumni Merit Award, 1967.

MUSIC LIST

INSTRUMENTAL SOLOS
Cello
"I Want Jesus to Walk with Me." Unpublished manuscript. Premiere, 1964.

"Troubled Water." 1964. Unpublished manuscript.

Piano
"A Dance in Brown." Unpublished manuscript. Note: won Honorable Mention in the 1931 Wanamaker Competition.

Lillian M. Bowles: Twelve Easy Lessons for the Piano. Chicago, Ill.: Bowles Music, ca. 1939.

"Marquette Street Blues." ca. 1918. Unpublished manuscript.

Spiritual Suite. Unpublished manuscript. Contents: The Valley of Bones; The Bells; Group Dance.

"Three Sheep in a Pasture." ca. 1940. Unpublished manuscript.

"Troubled Water." New York: Sam Fox, 1967. Also published in *Black Women Composers: A Century of Piano Music, 1893–1990,* edited by Helen Walker-Hill (Bryn Mawr, Pa.: Hildegard, 1992). Recorded: Opus One No. 39; Cambria, CD 1097; Leonarda, CD-LE339.

SMALL INSTRUMENTAL ENSEMBLE
Quintet in F Major (piano quintet). 1933. Unpublished manuscript.

CHAMBER ORCHESTRA
Scripture Reading. Unpublished manuscript. Commissioned by Nicklauss Wyss.

FULL ORCHESTRA
Montgomery Variations. 1965. Unpublished manuscript. Contents: Jesus Walk with Me; Prayer Meeting; March; One Sunday in the South; Dawn in Dixie.

Peter and the Bells. Unpublished manuscript.

ORCHESTRA (CHAMBER OR FULL) WITH SOLOISTS
The Niles Fantasy (piano, orchestra). Unpublished manuscript.

ORCHESTRA (CHAMBER OR FULL) WITH CHORUS
Credo (SATB chorus, soprano, baritone, orchestra). 1967. Unpublished manuscript. Contents: I Believe in God; Especially Do I Believe in the Negro Race; I Believe in Pride of Race; I Believe in the Devil and His Angels; I Believe in the Prince of Peace; I Believe in Liberty; I Believe in Patience. Premiere, 1967.

Mass in D Minor (SATB, organ or orchestra). Unpublished manuscript. Premiere, 1959.

Standing in the Need of Prayer (soprano, SATB chorus, orchestra). 1970. Unpublished manuscript. Recorded: RCA Victor LSC-3183.

SOLO VOICE
"Available Jones." Unpublished manuscript.

"Be a Little Savage with Me." Unpublished manuscript.

"Beyond the End of the Trail." Unpublished manuscript.

"Birth." Unpublished manuscript.

"Bound." ca. 1950. Unpublished manuscript.

"Bright Star." Sherman Oaks, Calif.: Solo Music, 1968.

"Chocolate Carmencita." ca. 1940. Unpublished manuscript. Note: from *Tropics After Dark* .

Margaret Bonds; courtesy of the Northwestern University Archives

"Cowboy from South Parkway." ca. 1940. Unpublished manuscript. Note: from *Tropics After Dark*.

"Cue 10" or "Down and Out." ca. 1960. Unpublished manuscript.

"Diary of a Divorcee." ca. 1968. Unpublished manuscript.

"Don't Speak." ca. 1968. Unpublished manuscript.

"Down South in Dixie." ca. 1933. Unpublished manuscript.

"Empty Interlude." New York: Robbins, 1941.

"Fate Is a Funny Thing." Unpublished manuscript.

"Footprints on My Heart." Unpublished manuscript.

"Georgia" (voice and piano or orchestra). New York: Dorsey Brothers, 1939. Co-composers, Andy Razaf and Joe Davis.

"Hold the Wind." 1970. Unpublished manuscript.

"I'll Make You Savvy Somehow." ca. 1940. Unpublished manuscript. Note: from *Tropics After Dark*.

"I'm Going to Reno." ca. 1935. Unpublished manuscript.

"I'm So in Love." ca. 1937. Unpublished manuscript. Co-composer, Leonard Reed. Note: melody line only.

"I Shall Pass through the World." New York: Bourne, 1967. Also arranged for unaccompanied chorus.

"Joy." 1936. Unpublished manuscript.

"Lady by the Moon I Vow." ca. 1936. Unpublished manuscript.

"Let's Make a Dream Come True." Unpublished manuscript.

"Let's Meet Tonight in a Dream." Unpublished manuscript.

"Lonely Little Maiden by the Sea." ca. 1940. Unpublished manuscript. Note: from *Tropics After Dark*.

"Love Ain't What It Ought to Be." ca. 1935. Unpublished manuscript.

"Market Day in Martinique." ca. 1940. Unpublished manuscript. Note: from *Tropics After Dark*.

"The Moon Winked Twice." ca. 1941. Unpublished manuscript. Co-composers, Dan Burley and Dorothy Sachs.

"The Negro Speaks of Rivers" or "I've Known Rivers." 1941. New York: Handy Brothers, 1942. Also arranged for SATB. Recorded: Koch International Classics 3-7247-2 H1.

"The New York Blues." ca. 1938. Unpublished manuscript.

"No Good Man." Unpublished manuscript.

"The Pasture" (soprano). 1958. Unpublished manuscript. Premiere, 1959.

"Peachtree Street." 1939. New York: Dorsey Brothers, 1939. Co-composers, Andy Razaf and Joe Davis. Recorded: Decca 3501.

Pot Pourri. ca. 1968. Unpublished manuscript. Contents: Will There Be Enough; Go Back to Leanna; Touch the Hem of His Garment; Bright Star; No Man Has Seen His Face; Animal Rock 'n Roll.

"Pretty Flower of the Tropics." ca. 1940. Unpublished manuscript. Note: from *Tropics After Dark*.

"Radio Ballroom." ca. 1940. Unpublished manuscript. Co-composer, Andy Razaf.

"Rainbow Gold" (medium voice). New York: Chappell, 1956.

"Sea Ghost." Unpublished manuscript. Note: won Wanamaker Prize, 1932.

"Sin Weary." ca. 1938. Unpublished manuscript. Notes: from *Romey and Julie;* melody line only.

"The Singin' Mouse." ca. 1937. Unpublished manuscript. Note: melody line only.

"Sleep Song." Unpublished manuscript.

Songs of the Seasons. Unpublished manuscript. Contents: Poem d'automne; Winter-moon; Young Love in Spring; Summer Storm. Commissioned by Laurence Watson. Premiere, 1956.

"Spring Delight." Unpublished manuscript. Note: melody line only.

"Spring Will Be So Sad When She Comes This Year" (medium voice). 1940. New York: Mutual Music, 1941. Co-composer, Harold Dickinson.

"Stopping by the Woods on a Snowy Evening." 1963. Unpublished manuscript.

"Sweet Nothings in Spanish." ca. 1940. Unpublished manuscript. Note: from *Tropics After Dark*.

"Tain't No Need." Unpublished manuscript.

"That Sweet Silent Love." ca. 1937. Unpublished manuscript. Note: melody line only.

Three Dream Portraits. New York: G. Ricordi, 1959. Contents: Minstrel Man; Dream Variation; I, Too. Also published in *Anthology of Art Songs by Black American Composers* (New York: Edward B. Marks Music). Premiere, 1959. Recorded: University of Michigan SM0015; Koch International Classics 3-7247-2 H1.

"To a Brown Girl, Dead." Boston: R. D. Row, 1956. Commissioned by Etta Moten.

"Voo Doo Man." ca. 1940. Unpublished manuscript. Note: from *Tropics After Dark*.

"The Way We Dance in Chicago/Harlem." ca. 1940. Unpublished manuscript. Note: from *Tropics After Dark*.

"West Coast Blues." ca. 1938. Unpublished manuscript.

"What Lips My Lips Have Kissed." 1966. Unpublished manuscript.

"When the Dove Enters In." 1962. Unpublished manuscript.

"When the Sun Goes Down in Rhumba Land." ca. 1940. Unpublished manuscript. Note: from *Tropics After Dark*.

"Who Is That Man" (unaccompanied solo voice). 1963. Unpublished manuscript.

"You're Pretty Special." ca. 1941. Unpublished manuscript.

VOCAL ENSEMBLE

"African Dance" (duet). 1956. Unpublished manuscript.

CHORAL MUSIC

"Children's Sleep." New York: Carl Fischer, 1942. Note: originally written for voice solo in the children's operetta, *Winter Night's Dream*.

Fields of Wonder (TTBB). Unpublished manuscript. Contents: Heaven; Snake; Snail; Big Sur; Moonlight Night; Carmel; New Moon. Premiere, 1964.

"If You're Not There" (SATB). 1939. Unpublished manuscript.

"I'm Gonna Do a Song and a Dance" (unison chorus). Unpublished manuscript.

"Joy" (SAT chorus, string quartet, piano). 1954. Unpublished manuscript.

"No Man Has Seen His Face" (SATB). Unpublished manuscript.

"Praise the Lord." Unpublished manuscript. Premiere, 1965.

"Supplication" (SSAATTBB). ca. 1950. Unpublished manuscript.

DRAMATIC MUSIC

The Ballad of the Brown King: A Christmas Cantata (SATB chorus, tenor solo, piano). New York: Sam Fox, 1961. Contents: Of the Three Wise Men; They Brought Fine Gifts; Sing Alleluia; Mary Had a Little Baby; Now When Jesus Was Born; Could He Have Been an Ethiope?; Oh, Sing of the King Who Was Tall and Brown; That Was a Christmas Long Ago; Alleluia. Premiere, 1954.

Midtown Affair (musical). 1950s. Unpublished manuscript. Contents: You Give Me a Lift; Mist Over Manhattan; I Love the Lie I'm Living; My Kind of Man.

The Migration (ballet for piano and instrumental ensemble). Unpublished manuscript. Premiere, 1964.

Simon Bore the Cross (cantata for Easter). 1963. Unpublished manuscript.

Wings Over Broadway (ballet). Unpublished manuscript.

INCIDENTAL MUSIC

Clandestine on the Morning Line (piano). Unpublished manuscript. Incidental music to a stage play. Premiere, 1961.

Happy Hunting. 1956. Incidental music to a stage play.

Romey and Julie. Incidental music to a stage play.

Shakespeare in Harlem (chorus, vocalists, instrumental ensemble). 1959. Incidental music for a stage play by Langston Hughes. Premiere, 1959.

Tropics After Dark. 1940. Incidental music for the American Negro Exposition. Premiere, 1940.

Troubled Island. Incidental music to a play by Langston Hughes.

U.S.A. Incidental music to a stage play by John Dos Passos.

Winter Night's Dream. Incidental music to a stage play.

PERFORMING FORCES UNKNOWN

"The Price of a Love Affair." ca. 1957. Unpublished manuscript.

NOT VERIFIED

"Just a No Good Man" (solo voice); "Love's Running Riot in My Bones" (solo voice).

PUBLICATIONS

ABOUT BONDS
Dissertations and Theses

Burns, Pamela Teresa. "The Negro Spiritual: From the Southern Plantations to the Concert Stages of America." D.M.A. thesis, University of Alabama, 1993.

Floyd, Rosalyn Wright. "Afro-American Piano Music: Two Black American Female Composers." D.M.A. thesis, University of South Carolina, 1990.

Green, Mildred Denby. "A Study of the Lives and Works of Five Black Women Composers in America." D.M.E thesis, University of Oklahoma, 1975.

Harris, Charlene Diane. "Margaret Bonds, Black Woman Composer." Ph.D. diss., Bowling Green State University, 1976.

Hendricks, Melissa E. "An Analysis Including Discussion of Classical and Romantic Features from a Graduate Recital of Selected Piano Works by Mendelssohn, Ravel, and Bonds." M.M. thesis, Appalachian State University, 1995.

McCorvey, Everett David. "The Art Songs of Black American Composers." D.M.A. thesis, University of Alabama, 1989.

Patterson, Willis Charles. "A History of the National Association of Negro Musicians (NANM): The First Quarter, 1919–1943." Ph.D. diss., Wayne State University, 1993.

Stephenson, JoAnne. "*Tropics After Dark, Songs of the Seasons* and Other Unpublished Works of Margaret Bonds to the Poetry of Langston Hughes as Found in the James Weldon Johnson Collection." D.M.A thesis, University of Illinois at Urbana-Champaign, 1995.

Thomas, André Jerome. "A Study of the Selected Masses of Twentieth-Century Black Composers: Margaret Bonds, Robert Ray, George Walker, and David Baker." D.M.A. thesis, University of Illinois at Urbana-Champaign, 1983.

Articles

Brown, Rae Linda. "Florence B. Price and Margaret Bonds: The Chicago Years." *Black Music Research Bulletin* 12, no. 2 (1990): 11–14.

Green, Mildred Denby. "Margaret Bonds." In *Black Women Composers: A Genesis,* 47–53. Boston: Twayne Publishers, 1983.

Perry, Frank, Jr. "Margaret Allison Bonds (1913–1972)." In *Afro-American Vocal Music: A Select Guide to Fifteen Composers,* 51–56. Berrien Springs, Mich.: Vande Vere, 1991.

Tischler, Alice. "Margaret Allison Bonds." In *Fifteen Black American Composers: A Bibliography of Their Works,* 37–57. Detroit Studies in Musical Bibliography, no. 45. Detroit: Information Coordinators, 1981.

BY BONDS

"A Reminiscence." In *The Negro in Music and Art,* ed. Lindsay Patterson, 190–193. New York: Publishers Company, 1967.

* * * * *

Margaret Bonds's childhood home in Chicago was a mecca for a great variety of artistic personalities, especially composers, musical performers, and writers. Her mother, Estella C. Bonds, was a piano teacher at the Coleridge-Taylor Music School and also served as organist at the Berean Baptist Church. Her father, Monroe Majors, was a well-known physician and an author. Among the figures she knew growing up were Harlem Renaissance writers Langston Hughes and Countee Cullen and three musicians who would be important influences on her life and music: Abbie Mitchell, singer and actress; her husband, Will Marion Cook, composer and conductor; and Florence Price, composer and pianist. Through these personalities and others, including William Dawson and Noble Sissle, Bonds was drawn to African-American musical practices early in her career and received thorough training as well in Western European musical styles.

As a teenager, Bonds studied piano with Price and composition with Price and Dawson. From Mitchell and from German and French songs she learned subtleties of the art of text-setting. Bonds also came into direct contact with popular music by extracting parts for Price and copying parts for Sissle and Cook. About the latter, she wrote in "A Reminiscence": "Even now, when I write something for choir and it's jazzy and bluesy and spiritual and Tchaikovsky all rolled up into one, I laugh to myself, 'That is Will Marion Cook.'" Bonds joined the National Association of Negro Musicians (NANM) and became a charter member of the Junior Music Association. She performed in the youth department of the Chicago Music Association, served as an accompanist for singers (including Etta Moten), and accompanied rehearsals and performances for dancer Muriel Abbott. Bonds also achieved some success as a composer during this period, winning an honorable mention for "A Dance in Brown" for piano, in the 1931 Wanamaker Competition and, in the next year, another award in that competition for the song "Sea Ghost."

In May of 1933, Margaret Bonds presented her senior recital at Northwestern University; on the program were pieces by Franck, Debussy, Villa Lobos, and a two-piano version of John Alden Carpenter's Concertino for Piano and Orchestra.

On June 15, 1933, Margaret Bonds was the first black woman pianist to perform with the Chicago Symphony Orchestra. Bonds played Carpenter's Concertino; the orchestra was directed by Frederick Stock. Also on the program was Price's Symphony in E Minor. On October 12, 1934, Bonds played Price's Concerto in One Movement with the Chicago Women's Symphony, Ebba Sundstrum conductor. That year, too, Price's *Fantasie Nègro* was on the program given by Bonds for the convention of the National Association for the Advancement of Colored People (NAACP).

In the mid- to late-1930s, Bonds opened the Allied Arts Academy, a school for talented young students of music, dance, and art. The worsening depression of that decade, however, caused financial difficulties that forced the academy to close.

Bonds made a major change in her life, late in 1939, when she moved to New York City, which was to be her home for almost the next 30 years. She began working there as an editor and arranger in the publishing house of Clarence Williams and between 1939 and 1941 was successful in popular music circles. She collaborated with Andy Razaf and Joe Davis on "Peachtree Street" (1939), which was used in the movie version of *Gone with the Wind,* and on "Georgia" (1939). "Peachtree Street" and a later song, "Spring Will Be So Sad" (1941), were both recorded by Glenn Miller and Woody Herman.

While in New York, Bonds continued her professional development. During the 1958–59 academic year, she studied orchestration with Robert Starer and, in 1966, choral conducting with Abraham Kaplan in the Juilliard School of Music's Evening Division.

Bonds was active as a performer and teacher in New York City and in many other parts of the world. On May 23, 1941, she appeared as soloist in a WNYC broadcast of John Alden Carpenter's Concertino, with John Barnett conducting the WNYC orchestra. In 1944, she performed a two-piano piece with a former student, Gerald Cook, for WNYC. Bonds toured with Cook, Calvin Jackson (another of her protégés), and Frances Kraft Reckling in concert appearances and in nightclubs.

Her Town Hall recital debut in February 1952 received mixed reviews; the program included works by C.P.E. Bach, Beethoven, Liszt, Franck, Coleridge-Taylor, and Harris. When critic Raoul Abdul launched his Coffee Concerts in 1958, Bonds was invited to be the pianist in the first of a series of interracial recitals at the Little Theatre of St. Martin's Episcopal Church.

Among her travels was a tour of the college circuit in 1947, following a solo concert in Kimball Hall, Chicago. In the 1960s, she traveled to Africa and Russia and, in 1963, to Nassau, the Bahamas, and Bermuda for performances of her Christmas cantata, *The Ballad of the Brown King,* for which she had commissioned Langston Hughes to write the text.

Bonds was also actively involved in music education and cultural activities. She taught at the East Side Settlement House and the American Theater Wing, served as musical director of the White Barn Theater, and was on staff at Stage of Youth. In August 1962, Margaret Bonds was appointed chairman of the Music Committee mandated to assist Edward R. Dudley, Manhattan Borough President, in the establishment of a Harlem Cultural Community Center.

In 1967, Margaret Bonds moved to California. During the years from 1967 to 1972, she taught at the Inner City Cultural Center and served as a musical director of the Inner City Repertory Theater, both in Los Angeles. She died on April 26, 1972.

Margaret Bonds was highly respected as a composer in black music circles. Raoul Abdul said, "one is impressed with the high degree of musicality and fine craftsmanship in her work." A product of the Harlem Renaissance, she promoted the use of African-American idioms in art music. In her compositions, Bonds manifests this desire by combining elements of jazz, blues, and spirituals with European classical musical traditions. Throughout her life, Margaret Bonds also diligently worked for acceptance of black musicians; she was influential in breaking barriers to African-American artists. According to Hildred Roach, "both her productivity and the ideas used in her works have been far-reaching and commendable."

CREDO (1967)

Credo, a setting of a text by W.E.B. Du Bois, is dedicated to the memory of Abbie Mitchell and Langston Hughes. Scored for mixed (SATB) choir, soprano and baritone solos, and orchestra, the instrumentation is standard—strings, woodwinds in pairs plus contrabassoon, brass, harp, and percussion, including timpani, side drum, cymbals, and woodblock. A cyclic work, *Credo* consists of seven movements. The first, "I Believe in God," for choir and orchestra, opens with a pedal note (*a*) in the lower strings. On the text "I Believe in God," the choir sings a syncopated motive (see Ex. 1) in open perfect fifths. This rhythmic pattern unifies the entire composition. The chordal texture changes to fugal, with a subject outlining major chords; the opening section returns with a new text. The second movement, "Especially Do I Believe in the Negro Race," has a lilting, rhythmically complex melody for soprano solo, the melody colored with added tones (the lowered seventh, *g*-natural, of the key of A major). "I Believe in Pride of Race," the third movement (in D minor), is for men's voices and orchestra. Evident in this movement are hallmarks of Bonds's style: brief call-and-response figures typical of the blues; an ostinato figure in syncopated rhythm; descending chromatic lines in the bass; use of the Phrygian mode (a half-step between the first and second tones); parallel seventh chords; and motion of the vocal parts in parallel fourths and fifths.

Example 1. *Credo,* "I Believe in God," syncopated motive

Movement four, "I Believe in the Devil and His Angels," is built on the pedal note *d,* and the mixed choir, with divided basses, sings in speech-like phrases. Rhythmically complex, the fifth movement, "I Believe in the Prince of Peace" (in F major), is in three-part form (ABA) with the A section returning with new thematic material in the woodwinds. A coda begins with all the choral and orchestral forces, but gradually the dense texture fades to silence as the number and type of instruments are reduced. In the first measure of the sixth movement, "I Believe in Liberty," a syncopated ostinato figure, a pedal tone, and a boogie-woogie pattern appear. The baritone solo of the first part returns, harmonized, in the chorus, and a prominent rhythmic pattern (see Ex. 2) is recalled from the third movement. The conclusion of *Credo*, "I Believe in Patience," also reprises material, in this case the opening A-minor movement, with an added eight-measure introduction.

Example 2. *Credo*, "I Believe in Liberty," ostinato figure

Credo was premiered in 1967 in San Francisco by the McNeil Singers and an orchestra. In 1972, soon after Bonds died, Zubin Mehta conducted the Los Angeles Philharmonic in a performance of this work.

THREE DREAM PORTRAITS (1959)

Three Dream Portraits, settings of three texts by Langston Hughes, were written for two singers associated with the New York City Opera Company: "Dream Variation" for Adele Addison; "Minstrel Man" and "I, Too" for Lawrence Winters. In "Dream Variation," the text is set in two strophes, while the piano part is through-composed. In "Minstrel Man," the first part of each strophe is similar, but the second part differs. Another treatment of strophic form is used in "I, Too," where Bonds makes the principal structural melodic notes in the first strophe the basis of melodic extemporization in the second strophe—a technique widely used in jazz improvisation.

The first song of the set, "Minstrel Man," begins with a syncopated bass figure, an ostinato. It is based on triads, with prominent extended chord structures (altered seventh, ninth, eleventh, and thirteenth chords) often voiced in open spacing; the tonality changes from minor to major in the seventh measure.

The vocal part of "Dream Variation" begins with an ascending melody, similar to that of "Minstrel Man," with Bonds having veiled the tonal center. After the introduction, the tonic is not heard until the end of the first strophe, although even here quartal harmony (chords built on fourths) tempers the effect of its presence. Imagery is suggested by the use of an ascending scale pattern in the bass with the words "to fling my arms wide," by the character of the piano part with the word "dance," and by the repose of the accompaniment on the word "rest."

"I, Too" is highly unified. The piano introduction and postlude are almost identical, and rhythmically, both quarter- and eighth-note triplets are important in the structure of the vocal melody. Syncopation, as in Bonds's other works, is used very frequently. An example of word painting occurs in measure 15 on the word "laugh," with a brief staccato motive that appears in the introduction and postlude. A rhythmic ostinato using blues chords is

employed in measures 19–24 and 25–28, and characteristically, a descending chromatic line appears in the bass (at mm. 31–32).

The first performance of *Three Dream Portraits* was not given by the singers for whom they were written, but rather by tenor Lawrence Watson, who premiered them for a National Association of Negro Musicians concert given in May 1959 in Columbus, Ohio.

THE BALLAD OF THE BROWN KING (CA. 1954)

The Ballad of the Brown King is a Christmas cantata for SATB chorus, solo voices, and piano. Although the piece was originally scored for orchestra, the published version is a piano reduction. Langston Hughes, commissioned by Bonds, wrote the text, the subject of which is Balthazar, one of the Magi, who had dark skin. The first movement, "Of the Three Wise Men," is written for tenor solo and mixed chorus and begins with a piano introduction that contains a statement of the theme, which modulates from one key to another. Throughout the movement, the tonal center constantly shifts between these two keys/modes (F minor to A-flat major). In the postlude, the theme recurs in the tonic. Movement two, "They Brought Fine Gifts," is for mixed chorus. With a short introduction, this movement is through-composed and contains elements characteristic of Bonds's style: quartal harmony, chromatic voice leading, syncopation, improvisatory writing, and extended chords. Movement three, "Sing Alleluia," is for *a cappella* chorus in gospel style; it is melodically repetitious and enclosed within a narrow tonal range. It has the effect of being a prelude to the fourth movement, "Mary Had a Little Baby" for soprano and mixed chorus; this movement begins with a piano introduction that moves into a ternary form embracing a calypso rhythm (see Ex. 3). The final A section features the soprano solo and chorus, and the piano provides a two-measure conclusion.

Example 3. *The Ballad of the Brown King*, "Mary Had a Little Baby," calypso rhythm

The fifth movement, "Now When Jesus Was Born," for men's chorus in three parts (tenors *divisi*), begins with an introduction that contains material from the work's first movement, transposed and in augmentation, and followed by a binary (AB) song. In movement six, "Could He Have Been an Ethiope?" the theme from the first movement returns in the key of F minor. The movement is through-composed for baritone solo, soprano and tenor duet, and mixed chorus. The style is declamatory and the choral writing for voice pairs is in four-part harmony. The baritone solo makes use of the melodic motive from the tenor solo in the first movement. In movement seven, "Oh, Sing of the King Who Was Tall and Brown," after a 16-measure solo piano introduction, the women's chorus enters in three-part harmony (soprano *divisi*). The theme from the first movement returns in a piano interlude, and a pedal point on the dominant appears in the bass. Movement eight, "That Was a Christmas Long Ago" for mixed chorus, functions as a prelude to the movement that follows it, as did the third movement.

The four-measure piano introduction quotes measures 1–4 of the second movement; the vocal parts come from the first movement; the melody assigned to the soprano (mm. 5–8) corresponds to measures 9–12 of the first movement's tenor solo. Measures 5–8 of the alto, tenor, and bass are similar to the first movement's measures 36–39. In the final movement, "Alleluia," the style of the Negro spiritual prevails. In binary form, it is scored for mixed chorus with a duet for soprano and alto. The A section is in three-part harmony, with an alto solo followed by a duet for soprano and alto; the B section is in five-part harmony, with a bass ostinato on the tonic (*a*-flat), over which the melody is sung by the tenor. A piano interlude (mm. 37–52), repeats the choral materials from measures 21–36, and at measures 53–54 a motive from the first movement (mm. 45–46) is repeated. The movement ends with all voices singing the tenor melody of the B section.

The first performance of an early version of *The Ballad of the Brown King* took place on December 12, 1954, in New York City at the East Side Settlement House, with George McClain conducting the chorale. On December 11, 1960, on a television show entitled "Christmas U.S.A.," CBS broadcasted a performance of the complete work by the Westminster Choir of the Church of the Master in New York City. Sam Fox published the complete revised version in 1961.

TROUBLED WATER (1967)

This piece for solo piano can be seen as a set of variations on the spiritual "Wade in the Water" (the composer's subtitle is "Based on the spiritual 'Wade in the Water'"). The prevailing meter is triple, but there are three contrasting sections in duple time, the first only nine measures in length. At the beginning of the piece, the piano's left hand establishes a two-measure ostinato figure, which recurs in original or varied form throughout the piece. In the ninth measure the spiritual theme enters, and after two statements of it, a second, more florid theme enters, in octaves, accompanied by a fuller harmonization. Then the first duple-meter, contrasting section (*dolce, leggiero*) introduces a pentatonic theme that contains within it portions of the spiritual melody. With the return to triple meter, the main theme is restated, alternating between the inner line and the top line. The piano textures become still more florid and have the effect of extemporization. A bravura transition leads to the next section (E minor), in duple time. A riff-like rhythmic figure in open chords (fifths and fourths) and in parallel motion, which again quotes from the spiritual melody, has the effect of exploding into action and then receding into a series of long notes that serve as a transition to the next section. The opening section returns, with the ostinato decorated with a quick flourish and repeated twice before the main theme returns in a literal reprise. Restless harmonic activity (based on seventh and ninth chords) leads to the finale, in duple time, recalling the rhythmic figure of the earlier duple section, this time on a pedal note (*b*). An elongated statement of the main theme is made in octaves, high in the treble range of the keyboard, and supported by open chords (fifths and fourths) that give a bright texture to this fortissimo climax in broken chords.

This work was dedicated to Toy Harper, the wife of Emerson Harper, who had been one of Bonds's composition teachers. An eight-minute cello version was dedicated to cellist Kermit Moore.

REFERENCES

Abdul, Raoul. *Blacks in Classical Music: A Personal History.* New York: Dodd, Mead, 1977.

Berry, Faith. *Langston Hughes: Before and Beyond Harlem.* New York: Citadel Press, 1992.

Bonds, Margaret. "A Reminiscence." In *The Negro in Music and Art,* edited by Lindsay Patterson, 190–193. New York: Publishers Company, 1967.

Brown, Rae Linda. "Florence B. Price and Margaret Bonds: The Chicago Years." *Black Music Research Bulletin* 12, no. 2 (1990): 11–14.

Green, Mildred Denby. *Black Women Composers: A Genesis.* Boston: Twayne Publishers, 1983.

Hughes, Langston. *Chicago Defender,* November 26, 1949.

"Northwestern in New York." [Northwestern University] *Alumni Newsletter,* September, 1964.

Roach, Hildred. *Black American Music Past and Present.* 2nd ed. Malabar, Fla.: Krieger, 1992.

DEBORAH HAWKINS

BOONE, JOHN WILLIAM ("BLIND BOONE")

Born in Miami, Missouri, May 17, 1864; died in Warrensburg, Missouri, October 4, 1927. **Education:** Missouri Institute for the Education of the Blind, studied music with Enoch Donley, a fellow student, and later with the school music professor, 1872–75; Iowa State Teachers College, Cedar Falls, Iowa, studied with Mrs. M. R. Sampson, 1885. **Composing and Performing Career:** Columbia, Missouri, first professional concert, 1879; managed by John Lange Jr., 1879–1916; modeled his concert programs after those of Blind Tom after hearing him perform, 1880; formed the Blind Boone Concert Company, a troupe of five or six instrumentalists and singers; toured extensively in the United States, Canada, and Mexico, may have toured Europe twice, 1880–1927; made piano-roll recordings for QRS, 1912.

MUSIC LIST

INSTRUMENTAL SOLOS
Piano
"Aurora Waltz." Columbia, Mo.: Allen Music, 1907.
"Caprice de Concert, no. 1: Mélodies de nègres." St. Louis: Kunkel Brothers, 1893.
"Caprice de Concert, no. 2: Mélodies de nègres." St. Louis: Kunkel Brothers, 1893.
"Danse de nègres: Caprice de Concert, no. 3." St. Louis: Kunkel Brothers, 1902.
"Grand valse de concert," op. 13. Kansas City: J. W. Jenkins' Sons, 1893.
"The Hummingbird: Morceau de salon." Boston: O. Ditson, 1886.
"Josephine Polka." Cincinnati: John Church, 1891.
"Last Dream: Waltz." Columbia, Mo.: W. B. Allen, 1909.
"Love Fest: Waltz." Columbia, Mo.: W. B. Allen, 1913.
"Old Folks at Home: Grand Concert Fantaisie." St. Louis:, Kunkel Brothers, 1894.
"Serenade: Song without Words." Boston: O. Ditson, 1887.
"Southern Rag Medley, no. 1: Strains from the Alleys." Columbia, Mo.: Allen Music, 1908.
"Southern Rag Medley, no. 2: Strains from the Flat Branch." Columbia, Mo.: Allen Music, 1908.
"Sparks: Grand Galop de Concert." St. Louis: Kunkel Brothers, 1894. Also published in a version for piano four-hands.
"The Spring: Reverie for Piano." Boston: O. Ditson, 1885.
"Whippoorwill: Romance for Piano." Boston: White-Smith Publishing, 1891.
"Woodland Murmurs: A Spinning Song." Boston: O. Ditson, 1888.

SONGS
"Cleo: Waltz Song." Philadelphia: J. E. Ditson, 1886.
"Dat Mornin' in de Sky." Kansas City: Carl Hoffman, 1899.
"Dinah's Barbecue: Song and Breakdown." St. Louis: Kunkel Brothers, 1895.
"Georgia Melon." Columbia, Mo.: Allen Music, 1908.
"Melons Cool and Green: Plantation Song and Chorus." St. Louis: Drumheller-Thiebes Music Co., 1894.
"That Little German Band." St. Louis: Kunkel Brothers, 1894.

"Whar Shill We Go When de Great Day Comes?" New York: Willis Woodward & Co., 1892.
"When I Meet Dat Coon Tonight." New York: Willis Woodward & Co., 1892.
"You Can't Go to Gloria." St. Louis: Kunkel Brothers, 1893.

NOT VERIFIED
"Open de Window, Let de Dove Come In" (voice and piano).

PUBLICATIONS

ABOUT BOONE
Books and Monographs
Fuell, Melissa. *Blind Boone: His Early Life and Achievements.* Kansas City: Burton Publishing, 1915.

Dissertations
Batterson, Jack Alan. "Life and Career of Blind Boone." M.A. thesis, University of Missouri-Columbia, 1986.

Articles
Darch, R. "Blind Boone: A Sensational Missouri Musician Forgotten." *Bulletin of the Missouri Historical Society* 17, no. 3 (1961): 245+.
Gentry, N. T. "Blind Boone and John Lange Jr." *Missouri Historical Review* 34 (1940): 232+.
Harrah, Madge. "The Incomparable Blind Boone." *The Ragtimer* (July/Aug. 1969): 8–9.
———. "Wayne B. Allen: 'Blind' Boone's Last Manager." *The Ragtimer* (Sept./Oct. 1969): 10–15.
Parrish, W. "'Blind' Boone's Ragtime." *Missouri Life* 7, no. 5 (1979): 17+.
Sears, Ann. "John William 'Blind' Boone, Pianist-Composer: 'Merit, Not Sympathy Wins.'" *Black Music Research Journal* 9, no. 2 (1989): 225–247.
Swindell, Warren C. "John William 'Blind' Boone's Chicago Itinerary." *Black Music Research Journal* 12, no. 1 (1992): 113–125.

PRINCIPAL ARCHIVES
Library of Congress, Washington, D.C.
Center for Black Music Research, Columbia College Chicago.
Joint Collection, Western Historical Manuscript Collection, State Historical Society of Missouri, Elmer Ellis Library, University of Missouri, Columbia, Missouri.

* * * * *

Despite his long, prosperous concert career of nearly 40 years and his legacy of published music and piano rolls, John William "Blind" Boone and his music remain, for many musicians, an unheralded American success story. However, when the St. Louis music publishing firm of Kunkel Brothers published keyboard pieces and songs by Boone in the 1890s, he was a well-known artist and seasoned performer who, by age 35, had been touring with his own concert company for a decade. As a pianist-composer, Boone was one of a small,

John William "Blind" Boone; courtesy of the U.S. Library of Congress

select group of 19th-century African-American composers who wrote light concert pieces in addition to functional dance arrangements, sets of variations, and ceremonial music. Boone is further distinguished by his contributions to early ragtime, which are best illustrated by the piano rolls of his own pieces he made for QRS.

Boone experienced remarkably diverse environments and influences in his early years. Although blind from infancy, he was able to take advantage of every possible opportunity to advance his musical training. Sent by the Warrensburg townspeople to the Missouri Institute for the Education of the Blind in St. Louis, Boone acquired formal music training and supplemented it with trips to the "tenderloin" district, where he heard music of the vernacular traditions. Following his departure from school, he toured first with various exploitative agents, but soon his career took a more positive direction when in 1879 he met John Lange Jr. Boone's association

with Lange and his attendance at a concert by Blind Tom Bethune in 1880 began a new chapter in his musical development. Despite public skepticism, Lange gave up his own highly successful business endeavors to manage Boone's career and begin the Blind Boone Concert Company. The partnership between the two was highly unusual for the time. The Blind Boone Concert Company may well have been the first all-black company with a black manager, and Lange and Boone began their association with a contract that guaranteed Boone financial security. Realizing that Boone had not yet reached musical maturity, the far-sighted Lange arranged for additional training for Boone, which might have continued to 1896. During his lessons at Christian College, Boone learned more about classical technique, phrasing, and pedaling, and discovered the music of Bach, Beethoven, and Brahms. He also studied with Mrs. M. R. Sampson at Iowa State Teachers College in 1885.

The first concert of the Blind Boone Concert Company appears to have been on January 18, 1880, at St. Paul's Methodist Church in Jefferson City, Missouri, with a program modeled on Blind Tom's format, which came to be typical of Boone's programs for the next 30 years. In great demand and financially stable, the company normally toured from September until late June, performing six nights a week. Their success enabled them to do frequent benefits for schools, churches, and benevolent societies in the black community. In 1889 Boone married Lange's sister Eugenia, who often traveled with them during the touring season. As a performer, he developed programs that drew on his different musical interests. An evening's program would include a great variety of music, representing what H. Wiley Hitchcock has dubbed, "cultivated" and "vernacular." He usually opened with a hymn, followed by classical works by Beethoven, Chopin, or Liszt; frequently, he would play descriptive pieces, such as his famous "Marshfield Tornado" imitation, an improvisatory piece very likely patterned after Blind Tom's "The Battle of Manassas." He often improvised in ragtime style and sang his plantation songs to his own accompaniment. The company employed singers to sing popular repertoire of the day and present dramatic recitations. John Lange Jr. died on July 21, 1916, and, regrettably, the company never recovered from this loss. Facing ever-increasing competition from radio and movies and the threat of growing racism, the company gradually narrowed the range of its tours to the Midwest, and Boone began to report his farewell concert as early as 1921. His final concert actually took place shortly before his death in 1927. Although Boone lay in an unmarked grave for nearly 50 years, in 1971 the Columbia/Boone County Sesquicentennial Commission placed a tombstone on the graves of Boone and his wife Eugenia. Since 1976, the museum of Maplewood, owned and operated by the Boone County Historical Society, has housed Boone's restored Chickering piano in the Blind Boone Room.

Boone's career, his piano repertoire, and his compositions mirrored the diversity of his musical background; he felt perfectly at home in both the European tradition and the uniquely American styles he absorbed and synthesized in his own compositions. His early pieces show his familiarity with character pieces by 19th-century European composers in their titles: "The Hummingbird: Morceau de salon," "Serenade: Song without Words," "The Spring: Reverie for Piano," and "Woodland Murmurs: A Spinning Song." Musically these pieces reflect the forms and textures common in European salon music of the middle and late 19th century. Like many of Boone's dance pieces, they are primarily in sectional, rondo-like forms with long introductions and are essentially studies in texture and in register changes. Most of these character pieces date from the earlier years of his compositional career. However, his most individual works are those that reflect his growing awareness of his African-American heritage, his unique sense of humor, and his virtuosic, colorful approach to keyboard writing, such as "Caprice de concert, no. 2: Mélodies de nègres," "Old Folks at Home: Grand Concert Fantaisie," and "That Little German Band." These charming piano pieces and songs were written in the decade from the early 1890s to the turn of the century, when Boone's solo performing career and his concert company were at the peak of their success. Boone's final important compositional achievement was the publication of the "Southern Rag Medley, no.

1" and "Southern Rag Medley, no. 2," written in 1908–09, although the printed versions are probably only a skeleton of the ragtime improvisations that had so delighted his audiences for at least the previous decade. As the social and cultural history of the 19th and early 20th centuries is written, Boone should be noted as a pioneer, not only for the significant ragtime pieces he wrote but for his ability to create an extraordinarily successful career in spite of great obstacles and for serving as a positive role model for the artists who followed him. Musician, entrepreneur, and philanthropist, it is little wonder that he was eulogized by his contemporaries as one who, according to Batterson's "Life and Career of Blind Boone," "having reached the pinnacle of fame, wrote his name not in clay but on the hearts of men and women."

THAT LITTLE GERMAN BAND (1894)

Along with ragtime songs, Boone wrote plantation songs, spiritual settings, and comic songs, often with the text set in the dialect considered appropriate at the time. They are usually strophic songs with refrains that employ symmetrical phrases and simple harmony. Even though their musical language is somewhat predictable, these pieces convey genuine feeling. The piano accompaniments tend to double the vocal lines, with the right hand playing octaves and chords and the left hand often alternate octaves and chords. In general, Boone's accompaniments are richer in texture and more technically complex than much of the song literature published at the turn of the century. Boone's humorous "That Little German Band" is the most clever and witty of his songs. It tells the story of the roomer driven mad by the German band rehearsing next door, giving commentary on the presence and influence of German immigrants and their music in the Midwest. It is also a welcome contrast to the texts of the plantation and ragtime songs, which helped perpetuate the stereotypes of the late 19th century. The repetitions of the perky piano interlude paint the text well, as the singer complains that the constant rehearsal will eventually drive him to drink. The crisp, syncopated rhythms borrowed from ragtime, the accompaniment suggesting the instruments of the German band, and the sunniness of the major key (with abundant sixths and thirds) make this a very cheerful, funny song. In addition, it offers the singer great opportunities to be expressive with various instrument-imitations described in the refrain, which Boone undoubtedly embellished as he performed the song.

> The piccolo squeaks, the cornet shrieks,
> The bass drum falls in line,
> And then the flute, with a root toot toot!
> They've got the tune down fine.

This piece is certainly one of the works Boone alluded to when he talked of planning concert programs with music for every kind of listener, saying that he liked, according to William Parrish, "putting cookies on the lower shelf so that everyone can get at them."

OLD FOLKS AT HOME: GRAND CONCERT FANTAISIE (1894)

Boone's larger concert pieces are impressive, showing his pianistic writing at its best. Of this group, his favorite was probably "Old

Folks at Home: Grand Concert Fantaisie," dedicated to his "beloved manager John Lange." It often appeared on concert programs and is frequently mentioned in newspaper articles and reviews. Boone's choice of Stephen Foster's melody, "The Old Folks at Home," as a theme for a set of variations demonstrates his understanding of his diverse audience. During Foster's lifetime, "The Old Folks at Home" was one of his most popular songs. Indeed, according to Nicholas Tawa, by 1853 the noted critic John Sullivan Dwight was grumbling that this tune was "whistled and sung by everybody." Boone may have known some of the history of the song's performance. In 1852–53 it had been incorporated into early stage performances of "Uncle Tom's Cabin" and in 1853 had been sung by the celebrated African-American soprano Elizabeth Greenfield at concerts in London, which were arranged for her by Harriet Beecher Stowe. Everyone in Boone's audience would have been familiar with the melody and the nostalgic text that remembered happy times. However, it must have been especially poignant to the black audience of the 1890s, which faced economic difficulties and rising waves of racism.

Boone's piano composition is a set of variations framed by a long introduction and an octave-laden finale liberally sprinkled throughout with *cadenzas*. Among the variations is one with elaborate right-hand passagework, one with repeated 16th-note chords, and the requisite variation in a minor key. Boone follows the repetitive phrase structure and simple harmony of Foster's melody, which really contains only two phrases, simultaneously providing the listener the comfort of the familiar tune and variety in texture and mode. Boone seems to have aimed for the cultivated audience; in addition to requiring virtuosic technique and cadenzas, he instructs as follows: "To insure a refined and scholarly rendition of this piece, the artistic use of the pedal as indicated is imperative." He also includes metronome markings for the theme and several of its variations, and gives many indications for the fingering of passages, particularly the more technically demanding ones. Modeled after the European tradition of virtuosic piano variations, this work with its difficult octave passages, sweeping *arpeggios* (broken chords), and colorful use of the piano's high registers is clearly designed for the accomplished performer.

THE RAGTIME PIECES: SOUTHERN RAG MEDLEYS, NOS. 1 AND 2 (1908, 1909) AND WHEN I MEET DAT COON TONIGHT (1892)

The ragtime songs and rag medleys for piano are the pieces historians usually mention in connection with Boone, as his contributions in these genres are some of the early examples of published ragtime rhythm. His early song "When I Meet Dat Coon Tonight" contains a section marked "Dance," which has a recurring syncopated pattern common in ragtime (see Ex. 1).

Example 1.

Recorded for QRS in 1912 while his concert company was still under the management of John Lange and his concert career was flourishing, the medleys use familiar tunes: "Strains from the Alley" (no. 1) includes "Make Me a Pallet on the Floor"; and "Strains from the Flat Branch" (no. 2) uses "I'm Alabama Bound" and "Honey, Ain't You Sorry." Both medleys are notable for the blues influences they exhibit. "Southern Rag Medley, no. 1" uses a characteristic blues gesture, raised second scale step resolving to the third scale step. "Southern Rag Medley, no. 2" includes even more blue notes, a basic blues harmonic pattern, and boogie-woogie bass. Some ragtime historians, including Edward A. Berlin, think that the "I'm Alabama Bound" chorus of "Southern Rag Medley, no. 2" may be the first published example of boogie-woogie.

Although Boone played, published, and recorded ragtime, he left surprisingly little of it compared to his other published works. Perhaps through training and the demands of a concert career, say Blesh and Janis, the "spirit of ragtime was exorcised by an application of the sonata [read "classical"] treatment."

CAPRICE DE CONCERT, NO. 2: MÉLODIES DE NÈGRES (1893)

All of Boone's caprices use the sectional forms, simple harmonic schemes, and idiomatic piano writing found in his dance pieces. Here, the influence of Liszt's piano style on Boone's work is evident. Boone frequently played Liszt's works in concert, particularly the Hungarian Rhapsody, no. 5, and also incorporated many of Liszt's techniques into his own works, especially repeated octaves, dotted rhythms, octave-higher repetitions (as in the lyrical *meno mosso* sections), and broken and parallel octaves. Along with influences from Western European music, Boone's piano music contains unmistakably American elements. Immediately following the instructions in "Caprice de concert, no. 1: Mélodies de nègres" to be "refined and scholarly," the introduction uses rhythmic figures derived from ragtime.

American elements are even stronger in "Caprice de concert, no. 2: Mélodies de nègres," where the *bamboula* tune of the B section and the Afro-Caribbean rhythms underlying the A section's melody make this one of Boone's most rhythmically striking works. Given the rhythmic and register similarities of the D section of the "Caprice de concert, no. 2" to the second section of Louis Moreau Gottschalk's "The Banjo, Grotesque Fantasie, American Sketch," it is reasonable to assume that Boone must have known this Gottschalk work. He very likely also knew Gottschalk's "Souvenir de la Havane, grand caprice de concert" (1859) and "Bamboula: Danse de nègres," op. 2 (1844–45), which are based on music Gottschalk may have heard as a child in New Orleans. Boone may also have known the *bamboula* tune ("Quand patate le cuite na va mangé li!," or "When the tater's cooked, don't you eat it up!") as a folk song or dance tune spread by boatmen along the Mississippi River and its tributaries. All these influences combine to make "Caprice de concert, no. 2" Boone's most original and effective concert piece, one with a more complex form than many of the other light classical pieces of the 1890s: A B A^1 C D C A^1 A^2 B Coda.

As Boone repeats the A sections, he varies them with lively rhythmic variants and changes in texture and register, two of his favorite compositional devices. Like some of the classical composers whose music he favored, Boone often used material from the body of the piece in the coda. For example, in "Caprice de concert, no. 2" material from A^1 appears in the coda. The alternation of the European-inspired passagework in the C sections with the sections using American folk tunes and vernacular rhythms give this piece its individual voice and, better than anything else Boone wrote, shows his synthesis of the multiple musical influences active in late 19th-century America.

REFERENCES

Austin, William W. *"Susanna," "Jeanie," and "The Old Folks at Home:" The Songs of Stephen C. Foster from His Time to Ours.* 2nd ed. Urbana: University of Illinois Press, 1987.

Batterson, Jack Alan. "Life and Career of Blind Boone." M.A. thesis, University of Missouri-Columbia, 1986.

Berlin, Edward A. *Ragtime: A Musical and Cultural History.* Berkeley: University of California Press, 1980.

Blesh, Rudi, and Harriet Janis. *They All Played Ragtime.* 4th ed. New York: Oak Publications, 1971.

Fuell, Melissa. *Blind Boone: His Early Life and Achievements.* Kansas City, Mo.: Burton Publishing Company, 1915.

Hitchcock, H. Wiley. *Music in the United States: A Historical Introduction.* Englewood Cliffs, N.J.: Prentice Hall, 1988.

Parrish, William. 1979. "Blind Boone's Ragtime." *Missouri Life* 7, no. 5 (1979): 17–23.

Tawa, Nicholas E. *Sweet Songs for Gentle Americans: The Parlor Song in America, 1790–1860.* Bowling Green, Ohio: Bowling Green University Popular Press, 1980.

ANN SEARS

BOSCO, MWENDA JEAN

Born Mwenda wa Bayeke in Bunkeya village near Jadotville, Katanga, Belgian Congo, 1930; died near Lubumbashi, Zambia, September 22, 1991. **Education:** Mainly self-taught as a guitarist, beginning ca. 1946. **Composing and Performing Career:** Composed and recorded more than 150 titles, 1952–62; participated in the Newport Folk Festival, 1969; concertized throughout the 1970s; European concert tour, May to July 1982; concerts in Cape Town, South Africa, 1988. **Honors/Awards:** Osborn Award, Best African Artist of the Year, 1952.

MUSIC LIST

SONGS/GUITAR IMPROVISATIONS

"Baba Muko." Recorded, 1959: Gallotone CO 196.
"Bakikuowa Usiombe Kinga." Recorded, 1956: Gallotone CO 116.
"Bayeke." Recorded: Rounder 5061.
"Bembeliza Mapendo." Recorded, 1959: Gallotone CO 200.
"Bibi Cha Cha Cha." Recorded, 1960: Gallotone CO 203.
"Bibi Kunua." Recorded, 1956: Gallotone CO 156.
"Bibi Mpenzi." Recorded, 1955: Gallotone CO 80.
"Bibi Sofia." Recorded, 1956: Gallotone CO 149.
"Bibi Twende Kwetu." Recorded, 1956: Gallotone CO 138.
"Bibi Vasangushi Mtoto." Recorded, 1954: Gallotone CO 36.
"Bibi wa Oumba." Recorded, 1958: Gallotone CO 181.
"Bilombe Distingue." Recorded, 1962: Gallotone ASL 523.
"Bingina Mbiri." Recorded, 1956: Gallotone CO 143.
"Bombalaka." Grahamstown, South Africa: International Library of African Music, n.d. Recorded, 1952: Gallotone GB 1588T; Rounder 5061.
"Bosco Pishi." Recorded, 1955: Gallotone CO 102.
"Bulofua." Recorded, 1955: Gallotone CO 88.
"Bundugu bwa Mukizungu." Recorded, 1954: Gallotone CO 23.
"Bwana Alisema." Recorded, 1960: Gallotone CO 202.
"Bwivu." Recorded, 1956: Gallotone CO 142.
"Chaffeur Mulevi." Recorded, 1956: Gallotone CO 123.
"Cheka Mama." Recorded, 1955: Gallotone CO 80.
"Congo Inaendelea." Recorded, 1959: Gallotone CO 201.
"Ee Bibi ee Bwana." Recorded, 1954: Gallotone CO 24.
"Eshima." Recorded, 1960: Gallotone CO 205.
"Hutu wa Bwana Masasi." Recorded, 1959: Gallotone CO 195.
"Juu ya Franka." Recorded, 1962: Gallotone ASL 520.
"Kabumba, Part 1." Recorded, 1956: Gallotone CO 130.
"Kabumba, Part 2." Recorded, 1956: Gallotone CO 130.
"Kijana Moja." Recorded, 1956: Gallotone CO 133.
"Kilamuntu ana Penda." Recorded, 1956: Gallotone CO 152.
"Kipenza Wee." Recorded, 1962: Gallotone ASL 521.
"Kisqahili Inaachana." Recorded, 1959: Gallotone CO 198.
"Kitu Gani Kumulango." Recorded, 1954: Gallotone CO 25.
"Kitu Unapenda." Recorded, 1956: Gallotone CO 110.
"Kizeng Unakevea." Recorded, 1958: Gallotone CO 181.
"Kubisha Na Bakuba." Recorded, 1953: Gallotone GB 1790.
"Kubudongo." Recorded, 1954: Gallotone CO 38.
"Kucheza Mizuri." Recorded, 1956: Gallotone CO 149.

"Kufica kwa Mfalme." Recorded, 1956: Gallotone CO 123.
"Kufuata Mpenzi." Recorded, 1955: Gallotone CO 96.
"Kufwa." Recorded, 1958: Gallotone CO 190.
"Kuimba Ni Mawazo." Recorded: Rounder 5061.
"Kukumbuka Bayeke." Recorded, 1960: Gallotone CO 204.
"Kulia mi Nalia Maria." Recorded, 1954: Gallotone CO 34.
"Kulia Sousane." Recorded, 1959: Gallotone CO 197.
"Kulia Stephanie." Recorded, 1959: Gallotone CO 194.
"Kupendana Tuapendana." Recorded, 1955: Gallotone CO 81.
"Kupokelewa Vizuri." Recorded, 1955: Gallotone CO 81.
"Kutembea." Recorded, 1956: Gallotone CO 157.
"Kutembea kwa Wengi." Recorded, 1955: Gallotone CO 82.
"Kutembea Njiama." Recorded, 1955: Gallotone CO 101.
"Kutembea yu Sheko." Recorded, 1956: Gallotone CO 152.
"Kuturizana." Recorded, 1955: Gallotone CO 89.
"Kuvae Kula Kunwa." Recorded, 1954: Gallotone CO 25.
"Kuwowo Pasipo Kunwaza." Recorded, 1954: Gallotone CO 38.
"Kwabo." Recorded: Sonodisc CD CDS 6847.
"Kwenda ku Soko." Recorded, 1956: Gallotone CO 145.
"Kwimba Nako Nikuzuri." Recorded, 1956: Gallotone CO 126.
"Lizzie." Recorded, 1956: Gallotone CO 113.
"Magontwa Yatawisha." Recorded, 1960: Gallotone CO 205.
"Majengo sita kwenda." Recorded, 1952: Gallotone GB 1725 or Gallotone GB 1728.
"Mama Kilio-e." Recorded, 1952: Gallotone GB 1587 or Gallotone GB 1728.
"Mama Lillianne." Recorded, 1958: Gallotone CO 176.
"Mama Maria." Recorded, 1959: Gallotone CO 201.
"Mama na mwana." Recorded, 1952: Gallotone GB 1754.
"Mapendano Bosco." Recorded, 1956: Gallotone CO 113.
"Mara Mingi." Recorded, 1954: Gallotone CO 23.
"Mari Kiloko." Recorded, 1953: Gallotone GB 1789.
"Marianne." Recorded, 1958: Gallotone CO 193.
"Masanga" or "Masanga-njia." Grahamstown, South Africa: International Library of African Music, n.d. Recorded, 1952: Decca LF 1170 or Decca 1171; Gallotone GB 1586T or Gallotone GB 1700; Rounder 5061; Sonodisc CD CDS 6847.
"Masikitiko ya Mpenzi." Recorded, 1955: Gallotone CO 102.
"Masimango." Recorded, 1956: Gallotone CO 156.
"Mbele Yakuwina," Recorded, 1955: Gallotone CO 97; Rounder 5061.
"Miakaya Zaman." Recorded, 1958: Gallotone CO 177.
"Mtoko Kidogo." Recorded, 1954: Gallotone CO 26.
"Mtoto." Recorded, 1955: Gallotone CO 103.
"Muchoko wa Mukwazi Moja." Recorded, 1954: Gallotone CO 34.
"Mukabi." Recorded, 1953: Gallotone GB 1789.
"Mukini ja Coniense." Recorded, 1955: Gallotone CO 103.
"Mukisema na Bwana." Recorded, 1958: Gallotone CO 175.
"Mukwenu Wadima Madima." Recorded, 1954: Gallotone CO 41.
"Mungia." Recorded, 1956: Gallotone CO 157.
"Munongo Watwa." Recorded, 1956: Gallotone CO 145.
"Musana Bongo." Recorded, 1956: Gallotone CO 157.
"Mwàámi." Recorded, 1952: Gallotone GB 1781 B.
"Mwendo Tulikwenda." Recorded, 1954: Gallotone CO 26.

"Mwendo Wasipo Tayaki." Recorded, 1954: Gallotone CO 37.

"Na Kezengela Yo." Recorded, 1962: Gallotone ASL 523.

"Namlia-e." Recorded, 1952. Gallotone GB 158T.

"Nbele ya Kuenda mu Bar." Recorded, 1955: Gallotone CO 101.

"Ndumba." Recorded, 1954: Gallotone CO 41.

"Nimemukata." Recorded, 1955: Gallotone CO 88.

"Ninikukosea." Recorded, 1956: Gallotone CO 133.

"Njila Takwenda." Recorded, 1962: Gallotone ASL 519.

"Owa Bibi." Recorded, 1960: Gallotone CO 207.

"Paulina mubaya." Recorded, 1952: Gallotone GB 1728.

"Paulina-e." Recorded, 1952: Gallotone GB 1726.

"Pension." Recorded: Rounder 5061.

"Pilipili Yasipo Kula." Recorded, 1959: Gallotone CO 200.

"Pita Bakuone." Recorded, 1959: Gallotone CO 199.

"Pole Kwa Bwana." Recorded, 1960: Gallotone CO 206.

"Pole Pole njoa Mwendo." Recorded, 1954: Gallotone CO 39.

"Pole Pole ya Kuina." Recorded: Rounder 5061.

"Rudia Mpezi." Recorded, 1958: Gallotone CO 190.

"Sae Inapita." Recorded, 1954: Gallotone CO 24.

"Safari." Recorded, 1958: Gallotone CO 176.

"Safari Bunyeka." Recorded, 1958: Gallotone CO 188.

"Safari Mena Kwenda." Recorded, 1956: Gallotone CO 142.

"Safari ya Mupenzi." Recorded, 1962: Gallotone ASL 521; Rounder 5061.

"Sema Wazi." Recorded, 1960: Gallotone CO 206.

"Shangwe Mkubwa." Recorded, 1959: Gallotone CO 196.

"Shiku ya Kangua." Recorded, 1956: Gallotone CO 143.

"Siku Moja Nilikwenda." Recorded, 1956: Gallotone CO 111.

"Singa Tumbo Yawa." Recorded, 1954: Gallotone CO 41.

"Siwezi Kurudi Lucia." Recorded, 1959: Gallotone CO 197.

"Sokochomale zikita" or "Sokuchomale Jikita." Recorded, 1952: Gallotone GB 1587.

"Soya." Recorded, 1953: Gallotone GB 1790.

"Tajiri na Mali Yake." Recorded, 1959: Gallotone CO 199.

"Tambala Moja." Recorded, 1952: Gallotone GB 1586; Rounder 5061.

"Tembea Uwone." Recorded, 1954: Gallotone CO 36.

"Teresa walala." Recorded, 1952: Gallotone GB 1726.

"Tuende Turupi." Recorded, 1958: Gallotone CO 168.

"Tukianja Kulewa." Recorded, 1956: Gallotone CO 111.

"Tukienda Jadotville." Recorded, 1956: Gallotone CO 121.

"Tukizungumuza Wawili." Recorded, 1955: Gallotone CO 100.

"Turudi Nyumbani." Recorded, 1959: Gallotone CO 194.

"Tuwaeshimu Wazazi." Recorded, 1954: Gallotone CO 35.

"Uisfawye Matata Vasilo." Recorded, 1954: Gallotone CO 37.

"Ukifuki she Sikombiyo." Recorded, 1958: Gallotone CO 182.

"Ukinikuta Mubar." Recorded, 1954: Gallotone CO 39.

"Ukiwa na Maneno." Recorded, 1958: Gallotone CO 175.

"Unge Nikatala Mbele Bibi." Recorded, 1955: Gallotone CO 100.

"Uninikuta ku Meza." Recorded, 1956: Gallotone CO 138.

"Usafi." Recorded, 1958: Gallotone CO 182.

"Usichukie." Recorded, 1955: Gallotone CO 82.

"Usiseme Wongo." Recorded, 1955: Gallotone CO 96.

"Usitingizike." Recorded, 1959: Gallotone CO 198.

"Usitoke Nyumbani." Recorded, 1960: Gallotone CO 204.

"Usiwe Nasikitiko." Recorded, 1955: Gallotone CO 97.

"Uziwaze Mingi." Recorded, 1958: Gallotone CO 193.

"Vidawa." Recorded, 1958: Gallotone CO 168.

"Wa Bibi Zetu." Recorded, 1956: Gallotone CO 116.

"Wageni Wanafika." Recorded, 1955: Gallotone CO 98.

"Wakati Bali Kuowa." Recorded, 1956: Gallotone CO 115.

"Wakati Muli Owana." Recorded, 1956: Gallotone CO 121.

"Wakati Nilikupenda Rosa." Recorded, 1959: Gallotone CO 195.

"Wakati Nilikuwa Mtote." Recorded, 1956: Gallotone CO 115.

"Wakati Wa Kuowa." Recorded, 1960: Gallotone CO 202.

"Wakubwa Wazaman." Recorded, 1958: Gallotone CO 188.

"Walikwambia Poa Moto." Recorded, 1960: Gallotone CO 203.

"Wanga Walote." Recorded, 1956: Gallotone CO 110.

"Wapi Suzune." Recorded, 1962: Gallotone ASL 520.

"Watoto Wawili." Recorded, 1955: Gallotone CO 89; Rounder 5061.

"Watu Wapuzi." Recorded, 1955: Gallotone CO 98.

"Wauzaji wa Mankinga." Recorded, 1954: Gallotone CO 35.

"Wavijana." Recorded, 1958: Gallotone CO 177.

"Wezi Ni Wabaya." Recorded, 1960: Gallotone CO 207.

"Zamani Congo." Recorded, 1956: Gallotone CO 126.

PUBLICATIONS

ABOUT BOSCO

Kubik, Gerhard. Liner notes, *Mwenda Jean Bosco.* Museum Collection Berlin CD 21, 1997.

Roycroft, David. "The Guitar Improvisations of Mwenda Jean Bosco, Part I." *African Music Society Journal* 2, no. 4 (1961): 81–89.

_____. "The Guitar Improvisations of Mwenda Jean Bosco, Part II." *African Music Society Journal* 3, no. 1 (1962): 86–101.

* * * * *

Mwenda Jean Bosco can be counted as one of the most influential African guitarists and composers of the 1950s and early 1960s. Between the years 1952 and 1962, Bosco recorded more than 150 titles for the Gallotone Company in South Africa. From his native country, the Democratic Republic of Congo (then still under Belgian colonial administration), his music spread throughout the central and eastern regions of Africa, and his records had a considerable influence on the local music scenes. The popularity that his music achieved during the height of his career is evidenced by the numerous guitarists who began to imitate both his style of playing and his compositional techniques. Yet, while the most productive years of his career are well documented on vinyl, relatively little is known about the years that produced and followed that ten-year period in Bosco's life and career.

According to his own indications, Mwenda Jean Bosco was born Mwenda wa Bayeke in 1930 at Bunkeya village near Likasi (then Jadotville), Shaba Province (formerly Katanga), the Democratic Republic of Congo (at that time, Belgian Congo). He adopted his stage name "Jean Bosco" during his school years. Toward the end of the colonial era, it was fashionable among students to assign themselves names of famous personalities in the political and religious history of Europe. For this reason, one may encounter in central Africa an Alphonse de Lamartine, a Denfert Rochereau, and other such reincarnations. Later, under the impact of President Mobutu's ideology of "authenticity," Christian first

Mwenda Jean Bosco; courtesy of Moya A. Malamusi and Gerhard Kubik

names were generally prohibited. Bosco, no longer able to use his artist's name, simply reverted to Mwenda wa Bayeke, a name that was also status-enhancing because of the historical importance of the Bayeke clan. Bosco made the importance of his given name explicit, emphasizing his membership in the Bayeke clan and his genealogical relationship with the *mwàámi,* the king of the Bayeke, in conversations and in some of his songs.

As a boy, Bosco acquired a solid, Western education following the Belgian colonial model, and he became fluent in French. As a result, he found employment in Likasi (then Jadotville) when he was still a very young man, first in a bank, and later as an officer in the colonial administration. It is not known whether the young Bosco received any Western-style musical education. His father, however, was an organist (or perhaps rather a performer on the harmonium) in the local church. It is likely, then, that Bosco grew up in a musical environment. According to his own statement, Bosco began to play guitar at the age of about 16 (around 1946), at a time right after World War II that marked a point of departure for many central and east African guitarists of his generation. Within a few years, he developed a highly individual style that set his music and playing apart from that of other guitarist/composers. He also developed a healthy amount of confidence in his abilities during these years. On the day in 1952 when he met the ethnomusicologists Hugh and Peggy Tracey, he declared: "I am the best guitarist of Jadotville." What is certain is that when he met the Traceys in the streets of Likasi, his style was already fully developed.

The Traceys recorded eight of Bosco's songs, which were released that same year on the Gallotone label in South Africa. In 1952, as a result of the recordings he had made with the Traceys, Bosco received the first prize of the newly established Osborn Awards for the Best African Music of the Year. The jury was chaired by Hugh Tracey, who awarded the prize to Bosco for the instrumental version of his "Masanga." This exposure brought new opportunities Bosco's way. His name and photograph appeared in the *African Music Society Newsletter* (vol. 1, no. 6) in September 1953, where a note can be found on the establishment of the Osborn Awards along with the names of the prize winners in 1952. The Gallotone Company was also interested in recording more of Bosco's material. Thus, it became possible for him to pursue a full-time professional music career at the age of 22.

Mwenda Jean Bosco's music and that of other Katanga guitarists not only had an enormous impact on the development of new musical forms in central Africa, even in remote villages, but it also radiated into east Africa. Historically, Bosco's music falls into the category of the so-called Katanga guitar style. This term demarcates a type of finger-style guitar music of the 1950s that developed all along the Copperbelt mining area in Belgian Congo and Northern Rhodesia. It had a strong background in Luba, Lunda, and Bemba musical traditions. The term "Katanga guitar style" embraces a stylistic conglomerate characteristic of a distinctive time period, beginning in the mid-1940s, within which the most diverse individual forms and innovations became possible. Between 1946 and 1962, developments and mutations occurred prolifically, and the Katanga guitar style became immensely popular. Bosco's numerous recordings for Gallotone contributed to this popularity and helped to spread the style to remote areas of central and eastern Africa. Extensive touring and recording occupied much of Bosco's time and energy between 1952 and 1962, after which new developments in the music industry began to affect his success.

With the appearance of electric guitar music in the Congo around 1962, the acoustic finger guitar styles were increasingly marginalized within the industry. By the mid-1960s, Bosco was affected by that development as the record companies in Kinshasa, Brazzaville, and Nairobi—the main centers of the mass media in the region—changed their sales strategies and began exclusively to promote dance bands playing electric guitar music. Despite the negative impact of these developments on Bosco's career, he managed to accumulate considerable wealth from other sources of income during the 1970s. He managed a dance band called Super Shaba and also held a position at Gecamines, the state-owned mining company.

In the 1980s, Bosco became the focus of renewed European interest in Katanga guitar style. He was invited to travel to Europe for a concert tour, and from May until mid-July of 1982, he performed in various countries throughout the continent. At the con-

clusion of the tour, Bosco returned to Lubumbashi, and while his correspondence with several scholars remained active for a time, he gradually fell silent. Bosco was invited to concertize in South Africa during 1988, where he performed in Cape Town, but after that time, much information about Bosco receded into the realm of rumor and partial truth. No addresses or phone numbers were available to his contacts, and it was not until five years after his death, in a car accident in 1990 or 1991, that his European friends became aware of the sad news. An anthology of his music was released posthumously (Museum Collection Berlin CD 21).

SELECTED WORKS

All of Mwenda Jean Bosco's pieces are finished compositions, most of which have remained almost unchanged for decades; however, there is always a narrow but essential margin for variation or improvisation. When listening to Bosco's music, Western audiences often get the impression that the guitar, rather than the voice, is the solo instrument. David Rycroft has argued that "Bosco's choice of vocal notes is rather restricted and stereotyped. This seems to arise directly from the fact that his vocal lines are really a kind of descant, tethered to the cycle of harmonic progressions dictated by the guitar." However, African audiences as well as those who have studied guitar with Bosco, such as John Low, would not necessarily agree with this analysis, maintaining that the voice line contains the primary message. This general characteristic can be heard in four of Bosco's most influential songs: "Masanga-njia" (or "Masanga"; Bifurcation), "Bombalaka" (Alone), "Sokochomale zikita," and "Mwàámi" (King [of the Bayeke]), but is especially evident in "Sokochomale zikita."

A few aspects of Bosco's guitar style bear mention here. The beat is always in the bass notes of the guitar part, and chains of off-beat notes contribute to the complexity periodically formed in the treble notes or in the vocal part. These chains of off-beat syncopations can be heard clearly in the verses of "Bombalaka." In order to achieve this separation between treble and bass notes, Bosco almost always plays the right-hand guitar part with two fingers. The index finger sounds the upper strings, the thumb the lower ones.

The harmonic basis for the majority of Bosco's songs is a short cycle of two, three, or four bars, repeated throughout the piece. His style of playing is characterized by broken chords that are arpeggiated in various ways but always in an almost unbroken, motoric rhythm. This creates a sense of continuous motion throughout the work and is not dissimilar in effect to the sound generated by other instruments in Luba/Sanga culture, such as the *likembe* (a box-resonated lamellophone). An excellent example of this is "Mwàámi," which is based on the ubiquitous 12-pulse standard time-line pattern. Here, a progression between three rapidly alternating harmonic roots constitutes the cycle over which further melodic development takes place.

Bosco's style of playing is highly melodic and highly transparent. Rycroft has observed, "[D]escending scale passages in the treble seem to be one of Bosco's favorite devices." Bosco's habit of creating guitar parts that stand as both melody and accompaniment surely contributes to the manner in which his vocal lines work in and around the treble activity of the guitar. Of the four compositions considered here, this characteristic is most evident in

"Masanga-njia." In this song, Bosco uses two descending scale patterns, the first of which is halted before it reaches the tonic. The second descent completes the motion to the tonic and provides a balanced phrase.

The metric construction of Bosco's songs can most often be analyzed as polyrhythmic. He often operates with three independent lines (the voice, the treble, and the bass) and manipulates these in ways that create ambiguity (in foreign listeners) with regard to meter. This technique of obscuring the main beat is well illustrated in "Bombalaka." Rycroft has observed, "Bosco's rhythmic technique might be regarded as basically a form of syncopation . . . but one in which the main metrical framework is at times partially or completely obscured in favor of the off-set line or lines, which are often phrased in such a way as to pose as independent meters in their own right."

Bosco's lyrics integrate all the possibilities of ambiguity offered by the structure of the Kiswahili language. As a result, many of his texts contain multiple layers of meaning and encourage complex and varied readings. He often weaves into the text of his songs a bit of local news that does not necessarily have any relationship to the rest of the text. A good example of this is found in "Soko-chomale zikita," in which Bosco inserts a line of text that informs the audience that his relative Baba Jaques was imprisoned in the same year the song was composed.

As one of the most recorded and famous composer/performers of the Democratic Republic of Congo during the 1950s and 1960s, Bosco's compositions mark both the height and twilight of Katanga guitar style.

REFERENCES

Kubik, Gerhard. Liner notes, *Mwenda Jean Bosco.* Museum Collection Berlin CD 21, 1997.

Low, John. *Shaba Diary: A Trip to Rediscover the "Katanga" Guitar Styles and Songs of the 1950s and 1960s.* Vienna-Föhrenau: E. Stiglmayr, 1982.

Rycroft, David. "The Guitar Improvisations of Mwenda Jean Bosco, Part I." *African Music Society Journal* 2, no. 4 (1961): 81–89.

———. "The Guitar Improvisations of Mwenda Jean Bosco, Part II." *African Music Society Journal* 3, no. 1 (1962): 86–101.

GERHARD KUBIK

BRADFORD, ALEX E.

Born in Bessemer, Ala., January 23, 1927; died in Newark, N.J., February 15, 1978. **Education:** Began music lessons with Martha Belle Hall, a local teacher, at age four; Bessemer public schools, further music instruction; Snow Hill Normal and Industrial Institute, Hill, Ala., 1943–45. **Military Service:** U.S. Army tour of duty, 1945–47. **Composing and Performing Career:** Began performing on the vaudeville stage at age five; joined the Protective (Insurance) Harmoneers, at age 13; had his own radio show a year later; Chicago, worked with Roberta Martin, 1947; traveled with the Mahalia Jackson Singers, late 1940s; joined Willie Webb Singers, 1950; formed the all-male Bradford Specials, 1951; many of his compositions published and recorded by Roberta Martin, 1952–57; "I'm Too Close to Heaven" for Specialty records began a string of successful recordings under his own name, 1953; starred in Broadway production *Black Nativity*, 1961; toured through Europe, 1962–66; New York, established the Creative Movement Repertory Company and produced *Black Seeds of Music*. **Teaching Career:** Taught school as an ordained minister. **Memberships:** New Jersey Chapter of the National Convention of Gospel Choirs and Choruses, Inc., President, mid-1970s. **Honors/Awards:** National Black Music Council, 1 Million Award, 1953; Obie award, 1972.

MUSIC LIST

[The following list of titles includes only works that were composed by the subject of the entry; it is not a list of recordings that were made by the subject. Although the composer may have made recordings of his own works, the list is not restricted to those recordings but in many cases includes performances by other artists of the composer's work. The list is made up of publication and discographical data, in cases where such information is available. Although no effort has been made to include documentation of the earliest recording of the works listed, the date of the earliest recording that is readily available has been given. —Ed.]

COLLECTION

Alex Bradford Specials. Martin and Morris Gospel Star Song Book, no. 1. Chicago: Martin and Morris Music Studio, 1958.

SONGS

"After It's All Over." Chicago: Roberta Martin Studio, 1953. Arranger, Roberta Martin.

"All My Friends Got to Wait on Me." Los Angeles: Unichappell Music, 1963.

"All Power in His Hands." Los Angeles: Unichappell Music, 1963.

"Alone." New York: Blue Pearl Music, 1975.

"Angel on Vacation." Recorded: Vee Jay VJLP 5037.

"Ask Him Right Now." Newark, N.J.: Brad Pathway, 1971.

"At the End." Chicago: Roberta Martin Studio, 1953. Arranger, Roberta Martin.

"Baby Born Today." Recorded: Vee Jay D1-71780; Vee Jay NVG2-501; Vee Jay VJLP-8503.

"Band." Los Angeles: Blue Pearl Music, 1975.

"Be My Friend." Los Angeles: Cotillion, 1971.

"Because He Loves Me So." New York: Screen Gems-EMI, 1962.

"Big Man in the Sky." Recorded: Savoy DBL 7023.

"Big Wind a-Blowin'." New York: Screen Gems-EMI, 1959.

"Black Man's Lament." Recorded: Cotillion SD 061.

"Blessed Mother." Hollywood: Venice Music, 1965. Co-composer, Dorothy La Bostrie. Arranger, Kenneth Morris. Recorded: Specialty SPS-2152.

"Can't Trust Nobody." Recorded: Vee Jay VJLP 1069; Vee Jay VJLP 5037.

"Christ Is Born." Recorded: Vee Jay VJLP-8503; Vee Jay D1-74780; Vee Jay NVG2-501.

"Climbing up the Mountain." Recorded: TVP Records TVP-1035.

"Come On in the Room." Chicago: Roberta Martin Studio of Music, 1952. Arranger, Roberta Martin. Recorded: Kenwood KLP-489; Smithsonian Folkways 32426.

"Come On Let's Go." New York: Screen Gems-EMI, 1959.

"Creator of Love." n.p.: Lorena Music, 1966.

"Daniel Was a Praying Man." Recorded: Everest GS-67; Vee Jay VJLP 5037.

"Ding Dong Daddy Wants to Rock." Beverly Hills, Calif.: Longitude, 1961.

"Do It While You Can." Recorded: Cotillion SD 061.

"Do You Know Jesus?" Chicago: Roberta Martin Studio, 1953. Arranger, Roberta Martin. Recorded: Kenwood KLP-489.

"Don't Blame God." Recorded: Nashboro NA 27199.

"Don't Let Satan Turn You Around." Recorded: Specialty SPS-2143; Specialty SPCD-7042-2.

"Following Jesus." Newark, N.J.: Brad Pathway, 1975

"For Me." Chicago: Conrad Music Publishers, 1987.

"Friend Like Him." Los Angeles: Unichappell, 1977.

"Get High Everybody Drink Wine." Nashville, Tenn.: Acuff Rose, 1954. Co-composer or arranger, J. D. Miller.

"Get Your Heart Right with God." Newark, N.J.: Brad Pathway, 1969.

"Give Us Barrabas." Newark, N.J.: Brad Pathway, 1975.

"Glorious Glory." Chicago: Martin and Morris Music, 1951. Co-composer, Kenneth Morris.

"Glory Train." Recorded: Justin Time Records R2 79375.

"Go Away Satan." Los Angeles: Unichappell, 1963.

"Go Forth in the Name of the Lord." Chicago: Martin and Morris Music Studio, 1953. Arranger, Kenneth Morris.

"Go Where I Send Thee." Recorded: Vee Jay VJLP-8503; Vee Jay D1-74780; Vee Jay NVG2-501.

"The Goal." Newark, N.J.: Brad Pathway, 1969.

"God Is Good to Me." Chicago: Martin and Morris Music, 1952. Arranger, Kenneth Morris. Note: published as Alex E. Bradford Jr.

"God Leads His Dear Children Along." Recorded: Vee Jay VJLP 1069.

"God Never Sent a Soldier to Battle Alone." Chicago: Martin and Morris Music, 1960. Arranger, Kenneth Morris. Recorded: Savoy DBL 7023.

"God Searched the World." Recorded: Specialty SP 2108 (LP61); Specialty SPC-2133; Specialty SPCD-7042-2.

"Goin' On Through." Los Angeles: Cotillion, 1971.

"Goodnight Goodbye." Recorded: Cotillion SD 061.

"Got Everything I Need." Newark, N.J.: Brad Pathway, 1969.

Alex E. Bradford; Martin and Morris Music Company Records, Archives Center, NMAH, Smithsonian Institution; photo by Ian Middleton

"Hail the Saviour Prince of Peace." New York: Blue Pearl Music, 1977.

"Have Thine Own Way in My Life." Newark, N.J.: Brad Pathway, 1969.

"He Always Keeps His Promises." Recorded: Vee Jay VJLP 5037.

"He Is Such an Understanding God." Copyright, 1961. Arranger, Kenneth Morris. Recorded: Columbia ACS 8348; Columbia CL 1548; Columbia/Legacy CK 47335.

"He Leadeth Me." Chicago: Martin and Morris Music, 1960. Arranger, Kenneth Morris. Recorded: Savoy DBL 7023.

"He Lifted Me." Hollywood: Venice Music, 1954. Arranger, Kenneth Morris. Recorded: Specialty SPCD-7042-2; Specialty SPS-2143.

"He Made It Plain." Recorded: Everest GS-67; TVP Records TVP-1035.

"He Makes All My Decisions for Me." Chicago: Martin and Morris Music, 1959. Arranger, Kenneth Morris. Recorded: Savoy DBL 7023.

"He Stays in My Room." Recorded: Columbia/Legacy CK 47335; Columbia CS 8348.

"He Will Deliver Our Souls from Sin." Chicago: Roberta Martin Studio of Music, 1953. Arranger, Roberta Martin.

"He Won't Mind." New York: Pathway House of Music, 1957. Arranger, Kenneth Morris.

"He'll Be There." Chicago: Roberta Martin Studio of Music, 1952. Arranger, Roberta Martin.

"He'll Wash You Whiter than Snow." 1955. Recorded: Specialty SP 2108; Specialty SPC-2133; Specialty SPCD-7042-2.

"He's a Friend until the End." Los Angeles: Unichappell, 1954.

"He's a Light in Darkness." Chicago: Roberta Martin Studio of Music, 1952. Arranger, Roberta Martin.

"He's a Wonder." Chicago: Martin and Morris Music Studio, 1952. Arranger, Kenneth Morris. Recorded: Kenwood KLP-489.

"He's Everything to Me." Chicago: Martin and Morris Music, 1958. Arranger, Kenneth Morris. Recorded: Specialty SP-2108; Specialty SPC-2133.

"He's Got Enough Left Over." Recorded: Nashboro NA 27199.

"He's My Friend." Chicago: Martin and Morris Music, 1967.

"He's So Good to Me." Jackson, Miss.: Bess Music, 1954.

"Heaven Belongs to You (If You Live Right)." Recorded: Columbia/Legacy CK 47335; Columbia CS 8348.

"Help Me Lord Jesus." Los Angeles: Unichappell, 1962.

"Hiding Place." Recorded: Chess Records CH-9156.

"His Precious Love." Recorded: Savoy DBL 7023.

"Hold Out." Recorded: Savoy DBL 7023.

"Holy Ghost." Hollywood: Venice Music, 1955. Arranger, Kenneth Morris. Recorded: Specialty SPC-2133; Specialty SPCD-7015-2; Specialty SPCD-7042-2.

"Hour of Darkness." New York: Blue Pearl Music, 1977.

"How Can I Make It?" New York: Blue Pearl Music, 1977.

"Humble Me." New York: Pathway House of Music, 1957. Arranger, Frances Kraft Reckling.

"I Believe Every Word." Los Angeles: Unichappell, 1963.

"I Believe He's the Son of God." Newark, N.J.: Brad Pathway, 1963.

"I Can Call Him (He Always Answers Me)." Chicago: Martin and Morris Studio, n.d. Arranger, Kenneth Morris. Recorded: Columbia ACS 8348; Columbia CL 1548; Columbia/Legacy CK 47335.

"I Can Tell Him." Newark, N.J.: Brad Pathway, 1975.

"I Can't Leave God." Recorded: Chess Records CH-9156.

"I Can't Tarry." Hollywood: Venice Music, 1956. Arranger, Kenneth Morris. Recorded: Specialty SP 2108; Specialty SPC-2133; Specialty SPCD-7042-2.

"I Dare You." Hollywood: Venice Music, 1956. Arranger, Kenneth Morris. Recorded: Specialty SPCD-7042-2; Specialty SPS-2143.

"I Don't Care What the World May Do (I'm Going to Praise the Lord)." Chicago: Roberta Martin Studio of Music, 1953. Arranger, Roberta Martin. Recorded: Specialty SPCD-7042-2; Specialty SPS-2143.

"I Feel Like Going On." Recorded: Nashboro NA 27199.

"I Feel the Spirit." Hollywood: Venice Music, 1954. Arranger, Kenneth Morris.

"I Found a New Doctor." Recorded: Chess Records CH-9156.

"I Found the Answer." Recorded: Savoy DBL 7023.

"I Heard Him When He Called My Name." Chicago: Roberta Martin Studio, 1953. Arranger, Roberta Martin.

"I Know Better Now." Recorded: Chess Records CH-9156.

"I Know He Lives in Me." Chicago: Bowles Publishing House, 1952.

"I Know He'll Look Out for Me." Newark, N.J.: Brad Pathway, 1975.

"I Know I've Got to Leave Here." New York: Blue Pearl Music, 1977.

"I Lean on Him." Los Angeles: Unichappell, 1987.

"I Left My Sins Behind Me (Down at the Riverside)." Chicago: Martin and Morris, 1963. Recorded: Say Records LP 5023; TVP Records TVP-1035.

"I Love to Tell the Story." Los Angeles: Cotillion, 1971.

"I Made God a Promise." Recorded: Vee Jay VJLP 5037.

"I Met the Lord in Time." Newark, N.J.: Brad Pathway, 1969.

"I Must Tell Jesus." Recorded: Nashboro NA 27199.

"I Never Shall Forget." Recorded: Vee Jay VJLP 1069.

"I Tried Him." Los Angeles: Unichapell, 1963.

"I Want to Be at Rest with the Lord." Recorded: Vee Jay VJLP 5037.

"I Want to Be Like Jesus." Recorded: Chess Records CH-9156.

"I Want to Ride That Glory Train." Chicago: Martin and Morris Studio, 1960. Arranger, Kenneth Morris. Recorded: Columbia ACS 8348; Columbia CL 1548; Columbia/Legacy CK 47335.

"I Wasn't Gonna Tell Nobody." Los Angeles: Unichapell, 1953.

"I Won't Sell Out." Hollywood: Venice Music, 1954. Arranger, Kenneth Morris. Recorded: Specialty SP 2108; Specialty SPC-2133; Specialty SPCD-7015-2.

"I'd Be Baptized All Over Again." Nashboro Records NA4 7199.

"I'll Never Forget." Newark, N.J.: Brad Pathway, 1969.

"I'm Going to Work until the Day Is Done." Recorded: Savoy DBL 7023.

"I'm Holding On to His Hand." Los Angeles: Unichappell, 1964.

"I'm Leaning on Him." Chicago: Conrad Music Publishers, 1962.

"I'm Not Ashamed." Newark, N.J.: Brad Pathway, 1969.

"I'm Too Close to Heaven (to Turn Around)." 1952. Chicago: Roberta Martin Studio of Music, 1953. Arranger, Roberta Martin.

"I'm Tramping Trying to Make Heaven My Home." Chicago: Martin and Morris Music, 1957. Arranger, Kenneth Morris.

"I've Been Dipped in Water." Recorded: Nashboro 7145; Nashboro NA 27199; Savoy DBL 7023.

"I've Got a Job." Chicago: Martin and Morris Music, 1958. Arranger, Kenneth Morris. Recorded: Specialty SPCD-7015-2.

"I've Got a Robe." Newark, N.J.: Brad Pathway, 1969.

"I've Got to See Jesus, One of These Mornings." Chicago: Martin and Morris Music Studio, 1951. Arranger, Kenneth Morris.

"I've Gotta Go." Los Angeles: Cotillion, 1971.

"I've Spent a Lifetime." Los Angeles: Cotillion, 1971.

"If Anybody Asks You Who." Recorded: Vee Jay D1-74780; Vee Jay NVG2-501; Vee Jay VJLP-8503.

"If You Don't Want Me No More." Chicago: Conrad Music Publishers, 1951. Co-composer or arranger, Calvin Carter.

"If You Ever Needed the Lord." Chicago: Conrad Music Publishers, 1951.

"If You Let Him Be Your Friend." Los Angeles: Cotillion, 1963.

"In Everything I Do." Chicago: Conrad Music Publishers, 1963. Co-composer or arranger, Kenneth Morris.

"In Him I've Found Perfect Peace." Chicago: Martin and Morris Music Studio, 1953. Co-composer, Kenneth Morris.

"In My Darkest Hour." Nashville, Tenn.: Acuff Rose, 1954. Co-composer, J. D. Miller.

"In the Sweet By and By." Co-composer, Kenneth Morris.

"Is My Name on the Roll?" Chicago: Martin and Morris Music Studio, 1952. Co-composer, Kenneth Morris.

"Is This the Price to Pay?" Chicago: Conrad Music Publishers, 1957.

"It All Belongs to Him." Chicago: Martin and Morris Music, 1958. Arranger, Kenneth Morris. Recorded: Specialty SPCD-7015-2.

"It Makes Me Tremble." Recorded: Everest GS-67; Vee Jay VJLP 5037.

"It Takes a Good Man." Newark, N.J.: Brad Pathway, 1969.

"It Was Alone." New York: Blue Pearl Music, 1977.

"It's in My Mind." Chicago: Conrad Music Publishers, 1962.

"It's You." Los Angeles: MCA Duchess, 1957. Co-composer, Teacho A. Wiltshire.

"Jesus Is a Friend until the End." Chicago: Martin and Morris Music Studio, 1952. Arranger, Kenneth Morris.

"Jesus Is the Lover of My Soul." Recorded: Vee Jay VJLP 1069.

"Jesus Keep Me Near the Cross." Recorded: Savoy DBL 7023.

"Judas' Lament." New York: Blue Pearl Music, 1977.

"Just a Little Bit of Jesus." Recorded: Nashboro NA 27199.

"Just Another Name." Recorded: Cotillion SD 061.

"Just the Name Jesus." Hollywood: Venice Music, 1954. Arranger, Kenneth Morris. Recorded: Specialty SPCD-7042-2; Specialty SPS-2143.

"Just to Know I've Made It In." Recorded: Vee Jay VJLP 5037.

"Keep On Praying." Recorded: Chess CH-9156.

"Last Goodbye." Recorded: Black Label BLC 4020; TVP Records TVP-1035; Upfront UPF-202.

"Late Date." Los Angeles: Unichappell, 1967. Co-composers, Harold Cornelius, Manny Roberts.

"Lead Me Now." Recorded: Cotillion SD 061.

"Leak in the Building." Chicago: Martin and Morris Music Studio, 1960. Arranger, Kenneth Morris. Recorded: Savoy DBL 7023; Savoy ST-14069.

"Let God Abide." Chicago: Roberta Martin Studio, 1952. Recorded: Specialty SPS-2144.

"Let Me Call You Lover." Chicago: Conrad Music Publishers, 1987.

"Let the Heavenly Light Shine." Jackson, Miss.: Bess Music, 1955.

"Let the Lord Be Seen in You." Chicago: Conrad Music Publishers, 1963.

"Let Us All Go Back to the Old Landmark." Recorded: Smithsonian Folkways Records 32426.

"Let Us Praise the Lord." Chicago: Martin and Morris Music, 1953. Co-composer, Kenneth Morris.

"Let Your Conscience Be Your Guide." Recorded: Vee Jay VJLP 5037.

"Letter to the U.N." Los Angeles: Cotillion, 1971.

"Life's Candlelight." Hollywood: Venice Music, 1955. Arranger, Kenneth Morris. Recorded: Specialty SPCD-7015-2; Specialty SPCD-7042-2; Specialty SPS-2143.

"Lifeboat." Recorded: Specialty SP 2108 (LP61); Specialty SPC-2133 (CT82); Specialty SPCD-7042-2.

"A Lifetime Believing." Newark, N.J.: Brad Pathway, 1971.

"Little Bit of Jesus." Newark, N.J.: Brad Pathway, 1971.

"Lo, Is the Way." Chicago: Roberta Martin Studio, 1952. Arranger, Kenneth Morris.

"Look at the Blood." Newark, N.J.: Brad Pathway, 1975.

"Lord, I Want You to Humble Me." Chicago: Conrad Music Publishers, 1963.

"The Lord Jesus Is My All and All." Chicago: Martin and Morris Music Studio, 1951. Arranger, Kenneth Morris.

"The Lord Looks Out for Me." Recorded: TVP Records TVP-1035.

"Lord, Lord, Lord." Hollywood: Venice Music, 1954. Arranger, Kenneth Morris. Recorded: Black Lion BLP 12132/3; Shanachie 6005; Specialty SPCD-7042-2.

"The Lord Will Make a Way (Somehow)." Recorded: Columbia/Legacy CK 47335; Columbia/Legacy CK 57164; Nashboro NA 27199.

"The Lord's Prayer." Recorded: Columbia/Legacy CK 47335; Spirit Feel SF 1005.

"Lost Love." Berkeley, Calif: Cinnabar Music, 1964.

"Make the World Safe Again." Los Angeles: Cotillion, 1971.

"Marching Up to Zion." Nashville, Tenn.: Sony-ATV Songs, 1954.

"Money Won't Bring You Happiness." Newark, N.J.: Brad Pathway, 1975.

"Most Done Traveling." Recorded: Vee Jay D1-74780; Vee Jay NVG2-501; Vee Jay VJLP-8503.

"My Crown." Chicago: Martin and Morris Music Studio, 1953. Arranger, Kenneth Morris.

"My Freedom after a While." Los Angeles: Unichappell, 1963.

"My Heart Remembers What My Mind Must Forget." Chicago: Conrad Music Publishers, 1976.

"My Life Is Getting Sweeter." Los Angeles: Cotillion, 1971.

"My Lord Is Gonna Move This Wicked Race." Recorded: Savoy DBL 7023.

"My Reward Is in Heaven." Chicago: Martin and Morris Music Studio, 1953. Arranger, Kenneth Morris.

"My Soul Cries Thank You." Chicago: Conrad Music Publishers, 1963..

"My Way's Cloudy." Recorded: Vee Jay VJLP-8503; Vee Jay D1-74780; Vee Jay NVG2-501.

"Nobody Like Jesus." Los Angeles: Unichappell, 1962.

"Nobody Like the Lord." New York: Screen Gems-EMI, 1962.

"Nobody's Fault but Mine." Recorded: Savoy DBL 7023.

"Nothing but the Holy Ghost." Recorded: Everest GS-68; Vee Jay VJLP 5037.

"Now Lord." Jackson, Miss.: Bess Music, 1955.

"Oh Lord Remember Me." Jackson, Miss.: Bess Music, 1954.

"Oh Lord, Save Me." Hollywood: Venice Music, 1955. Arranger, Kenneth Morris. Recorded: Specialty SPCD-7015-2; Specialty SPCD-7042-2; Specialty SPS-2143.

"Oh My Good Lord." Los Angeles: Unichappell, 1963.

"On My Way Home." Chicago: Martin and Morris Music Studio, 1953. Arranger, Kenneth Morris.

"On That Day." Recorded: Nashboro NA 27199.

"Power Dump." Berkeley, Calif: Cinnabar Music, 1964.

"Pray to the Power of the Lord." Jackson, Miss.: Bess Music, 1959.

"Restore unto Me (the Joy of Thy Salvation)." Recorded: Columbia/ Legacy CK 47335.

"Right Now." Hollywood: Venice Music, 1954. Arranger, Kenneth Morris. Recorded: Specialty SPCD-7042-2.

"Said I Wasn't Gonna Tell Nobody." Chicago: Martin and Morris Music, 1960. Arranger, Kenneth Morris. Recorded: Mesa Records R2 79026; Columbia/Legacy CK 47335; Columbia/Legacy CK 67007.

"Second Hand Love." Chicago: Conrad Music Publishers, 1958.

"She Comes Because She's Concerned." Recorded: Smithsonian Folkways Records 32426.

"Since I Met Jesus." Chicago: Martin and Morris Music, 1953. Arranger, Roberta Martin. Kenwood KLP-489.

"Somebody Here Don't Believe in Jesus." Newark, N.J.: Brad Pathway, 1975.

"Somebody Touched Me." Recorded: Specialty SNTF 5002; Specialty SPC-2117; Specialty SPS-2143.

"Someone." Chicago: Martin Studio of Music, 1956. Arranger, Roberta Martin.

"Something Happened Today." Co-composer, Anthony O. Heilbut. Recorded: Cotillion SD 061.

"Steal Away." Hollywood: Venice Music, 1957. Arranger, Kenneth Morris. Recorded: Specialty SPCD-7015-2.

"The Storm Is Not Over." New York: Screen Gems-EMI, 1961.

"Sunday Mo'nin'." Los Angeles: Cotillion, 1971.

"Sweet Jesus." Beverly Hills, Calif.: Hill and Range Songs, 1961. Arranger, Kenneth Morris. Recorded: Columbia ACS 8348; Columbia CL 1548; Columbia/Legacy CK 47335.

"Taking Care of Business." Newark, N.J.: Brad Pathway, 1971.

"Ten Thousand Blessings." Chicago: Martin and Morris Music, 1959. Arranger, Kenneth Morris. Recorded: Savoy DBL 7023.

"That's God." Chicago: Conrad Music Publishers, 1976. Co-composer, Princess Stewart.

"There Are Days I'd Like to Be." New York: Blue Pearl Music, 1975.

"There's a Stranger in Town." Recorded: TVP-1035.

"They Came Out Shouting." Recorded: Everest GS-67; Vee Jay VJLP 5037.

"They Kicked Him Out (of Heaven)." Recorded: Black Lion BLP 12132/ 3; Timeless Records CD TTD 557; Vee Jay VJLP 1069.

"They've Got to Wait on Me." Recorded: Vee Jay VJLP 1069.

"Think." Recorded: Savoy DBL 7023.

"This May Be the Last Time." Recorded: Specialty SPCD-7042-2; Specialty SPS-2143.

"This Wonderful Savior." Recorded: TVP Records TVP-1035.

"Thy Word." Chicago: Martin and Morris Music Studio, 1953. Arranger, Kenneth Morris.

"Tiny Tim." n.p.: Vernal Music, 1959. Co-composer, Lavern Baker.

"Too Close to Heaven." 1953. Note: received a "1 Million Award" from the National Black Music Council. Recorded: Atlantic SD 8036; Rhino R2 70289; Specialty SPCD-7042-2; Specialty 5SPCD-4412-2.

"Too Late." Los Angeles: Unichappell, 1963.

"Try Him Today." Recorded: Nashboro NA 27199.

"Turn Away from Sin." Chicago: Martin and Morris Music Studio, 1953. Arranger, Kenneth Morris.

"Wait Till I Get You Home." Newark, N.J.: Brad Pathway, 1971.

"Waiting." Recorded: Cotillion SD 061.

"Walk through the Streets." Recorded: TVP Records TVP-1035.

"Walking up the King's Highway." Recorded: Vee Jay VJLP 1069.

"Walking with the King." Chicago: Martin and Morris Music, 1960. Arranger, Kenneth Morris. Recorded: Savoy DBL 7023.

"We Sure Do Need Him Now." Recorded: Vee Jay VJLP 1069.

"We're Marching to the City of God." Chicago: Roberta Martin Studio, 1953.

"What About You?" Los Angeles: Unichappell, 1963.

"What Did John Do?" Chicago: Martin and Morris Music, 1958. Arranger, Kenneth Morris. Recorded: Specialty SP 2108; Specialty SPC-2133; Specialty SPCD-7042-2.

"What Do You Know about Jesus?" Recorded: Savoy DBL 7023.

"What Folks Say about Me." New York: Pathway House of Music, 1959. Arranger, Kenneth Morris.

"What Have I Done to Thee?" Newark, N.J.: Brad Pathway, 1975.

"What Makes a Man Turn His Back on God?" New York: Pathway House of Music, 1959. Arranger, Kenneth Morris.

"What More Do You Want the Lord to Do?" Recorded: Savoy DBL 7023.

"When Jesus Comes." Chicago: Martin and Morris Music Studio, 1957. Arranger, Kenneth Morris. Recorded: Space 102.

"When My Time Comes." Recorded: Chess CH-9156; Chess CHD 9336.

"When the Power Comes." New York: Blue Pearl Music, 1975.

"When You Pray." Recorded: Everest GS-67; Vee Jay VJLP 5037.

"Where My Jesus Lives." New York: Screen Gems-EMI, 1960.

"Who Can I Blame?" Chicago: Martin and Morris Music Studio, 1953. Arranger, Kenneth Morris.

"Why Did I Do It?" New York: Blue Pearl Music, 1977.

"Without a God." Hollywood: Venice Music, 1956. Co-composer, Cleveland Carter. Arranger, Kenneth Morris. Recorded: Specialty SP 2108; Specialty SPC-2133; Specialty SPCD-7042-2.

"Without Your Love." Chicago: Conrad Music Publishers, 1976.

"Wonder of Knowing Jesus." New York: Blue Pearl Music, 1977.

"Wretch Like Me." Newark, N.J.: Brad Pathway, 1971.

"You Can't Make Me Doubt Him." Chicago: Martin and Morris, and New York: Pathway House of Music, 1963. Arranger, Kenneth Morris. Recorded: Columbia ACS 8348; Columbia CL 1548; Columbia/ Legacy CK 47335.

"You Must Have True Religion." Recorded: Savoy DBL 7023.

"You've Got to Bear the Consequence." Recorded: Columbia ACS 8348; Columbia CL 1548; Columbia/Legacy CK 47335.

PUBLICATIONS

ABOUT BRADFORD
Books and Monographs

Kilkenny, Niani, and Robert Selim, eds. *Too Close to Heaven: The Music of Professor Alex Bradford*. Washington, D.C.: Smithsonian Institution, National Museum of American History, 1987.

Thesis

Boyer, Horace Clarence. "The Gospel Song: A Historical and Analytical Survey." Master's thesis, University of Rochester, Eastman School of Music, 1964.

Articles

"Arms Royalty Suit Settled in Court." *Variety* 315 (July 4, 1984): 79+.

Boyer, Horace Clarence. "Chicago Gospel." *Black Music Research Bulletin* 12, no. 2 (1990): 4–8.

Haskins, J. "The Arts: Alex Bradford." *Now* 6 (1977): 48.

Heilbut, Anthony. "Professor Alex Bradford: 'The Singing Rage.'" In *The Gospel Sound: Good News and Bad Times*, 145–157. 3rd ed. New York: Limelight Editions, 1989.

Wilmer, Val. "Gospel Music: Interview with Alex Bradford." *Jazz Journal* 16 (July 1963): 13–14.

* * * * *

It was no surprise that gospel singer Alex Bradford spent the last part of his life on Broadway, for it is commonly agreed that he was a most theatrical and flamboyant gospel singer and one of the most talented. With a big and robust voice and possessing antics that had been developed from the age of four, Bradford could "take a house" at any time. If his singing did not arouse an audience, his marching, his pretense at washing clothes or of being held back by other singers as he attempted to surge forward—showing that he couldn't tarry—would have an audience on its feet in short order. And yet for all of his theatrics, Bradford was one of the most talented and celebrated musicians in the history of gospel, no others having possessed the talent to match that of this composer, singer, pianist, conductor, and actor. Bradford was the most important and popular composer of black gospel during the period 1952–58. His songs were recorded by the Roberta Martin Singers, Davis Sisters, Caravans, and several choirs.

Bradford was born in 1927 to Wilbur and Olivia Bradford in the small mining town of Bessemer, Alabama, the home of the first gospel jubilee quartets. His father was an ore miner and his mother a cook, seamstress, beautician, and "stage mother." He began piano and dancing lessons at age four and later that year appeared on stage in a vaudeville act. Within two years, he had joined a sanctified church because of the excitement of the frenzied service, the congeniality among the "saints" (members), and the overwhelming admiration of the congregation when he played and sang. His mother, however, ushered him back to the Baptist church as soon as his membership was discovered. By age 13, he had joined a children's gospel group, the Protective Harmoneers, and within a year had his own radio show on which he sang, played the piano, and presented other talented youth.

Bradford attended elementary and junior high school in Bessemer, but after a racial altercation, he was sent to New York to live with a relative and to complete school. In 1944, within months of his graduation from high school, he returned to Bessemer and his mother enrolled him in Snow Hill Institute, a prestigious African-American private school located approximately 160 miles from his hometown. An extremely bright student, Bradford excelled in history, English, and music, although he had no interest in European art music. He also led jam sessions in the latest blues hits and the latest songs of the gospel groups that visited Bessemer—groups such as the Kings of Harmony, the Swan Silvertones, the Famous Blue Jay Singers, Blind Arizona Dranes, and W. Herbert Brewster's Brewster Ensemble, featuring Queen Candice Anderson. In school, his teachers appointed him a teacher's assistant, and his classmates called him "Professor," a title he used throughout his career.

After graduating from Snow Hill, Bradford served a tour in the United States Army during World War II and upon his release in 1947 moved to Chicago, which was the center of gospel music performance and its industry. His ambition was to become a member of the Roberta Martin Singers, who, along with Mahalia Jackson, were the major recording stars of the gospel sound. Roberta Martin welcomed him to Chicago, presented him as a soloist on her concerts, and even permitted him to attend rehearsals of the Martin Singers, but she never invited him to become a member of the group or even to serve as a substitute member. However, Bradford did make several appearances with Robert Anderson and his singers and became friendly with Mahalia Jackson, traveling with her for a short time in the late 1940s as secretary and companion. While with Jackson, Bradford was invited to join the Willie Webb Singers. He accepted the invitation and recorded with them in 1950 on the Gotham label, singing the lead on his own arrangement of the 19th-century white Protestant hymn "Every Day and Every Hour." In 1951, he organized the all-male Bradford Specials, which recorded several sides of his compositions for the Apollo label. These recordings did not generate as much excitement as did his solo recording with the Willie Webb Singers, but they did bring him once again to the attention of Roberta Martin. In 1952, Bradford began to submit songs—mostly gospel ballads—to Martin for publication.

Over the next five years, the Roberta Martin Singers scored recording hits with six Bradford compositions: "After It's All Over," "Come On in the Room," "I'm Gonna Praise His Name," "Lo, Is the Way," "Since I Met Jesus," and "I'm Too Close to Heaven." And yet he was almost an unknown singer-composer outside of Chicago. While his name appeared on the sheet music for his songs published by Martin and Morris Music and the Roberta Martin Studio of Music, he remained under the shadow of the Chicago composers. This all changed when he became an instant celebrity after the release of "I'm Too Close to Heaven."

In 1953, the Bradford Specials recorded nine songs, all composed by Bradford. "I'm Too Close to Heaven" was selected as the first release, taking the gospel world by surprise with Bradford's gigantic husky voice, which could be as gentle as it was commanding. If the beauty of Bradford's rough voice and his ability to make it toss and turn at will was not satisfying enough, halfway through "I'm Too Close to Heaven" he inserts a real and pure high *c* in falsetto and immediately returns to his gruff baritone. His recording took the gospel world by storm, and he went on to record such hits as "Lord, Lord, Lord," "I Won't See Out," and "He'll Wash You Whiter than Snow," a duet with Sallie Martin, a colleague of Thomas Andrew Dorsey who is considered the "Mother" of African-American gospel music.

Just at the point in the late 1950s when Bradford's popularity began to wane, he was approached by Broadway producers to star in one of the earliest gospel musicals: *Black Nativity*, a Christmas gospel musical with book by Langston Hughes and music from relevant Negro spirituals and gospel songs, which opened on Broadway on December 16, 1961. The musical was highly successful and went on to have a run in London, after which Bradford toured in Europe for several years. On his return to the United States, he established the

Creative Movement Repertory Company, which produced *Black Seeds of Music.* In 1972, he returned to Broadway in *Don't Bother Me, I Can't Cope,* followed in 1975 by *Your Arms Too Short to Box with God,* the title taken from a sermon in *God's Trombones* by James Weldon Johnson. In the mid-1970s, he was active in the New Jersey Chapter of Thomas Andrew Dorsey's National Convention of Gospel Choirs and Choruses, Inc., and was preparing a revised version of *Your Arms Too Short to Box with God* when, on February 15, 1978, he died of a stroke in Newark, New Jersey.

COME ON IN THE ROOM (1952)

The lyrics of "Come On in the Room" are probably the wittiest written by Alex Bradford. Based on Mark 5:40–42, the text is concerned with the raising of the daughter of Jairus from the dead. The story begins while Jairus is listening to a sermon by Christ. As Christ is preaching, men come to inform Jairus that his 12-year-old daughter has died, and Jairus persuades Christ to accompany him to his home to raise the daughter. Upon reaching the home of Jairus, Christ "entereth in [the room] where the damsel was lying," and upon his saying "Damsel, I say unto thee, arise," the young girl comes to life.

Bradford treats the text as an invitation to enter the *prayer* room, in which Jesus becomes the doctor who writes prescriptions. The words of the chorus following verse one are:

He'll come in your room, He'll come in your room,
You take Jesus for your doctor,
The Bible your prescription
And He'll give you all of your medicine in the room.

In a succeeding chorus, Eugene Smith, the soloist on the 1952 Roberta Martin Singers recording, changes the third line to "He'll write His own prescription." Clearly, Bradford moved from paraphrases of the scriptures and prayer and praise text to personalized testimonies.

Unlike the majority of Bradford's songs recorded by the Roberta Martin Singers, "Come On in the Room" is not a slow ballad but a toe-tapping jubilee (moderately fast) song. Bradford employs a form in which the refrain is longer than the verse, comprising 12 bars (completely unrelated to the 12-bar form) while the verse has only eight. Each of the three four-bar phrases has a different melody, yielding a form of abc. The melody of the refrain, based on the major scale, has a contour that rises and falls in each phrase, with an occasional ascent to an octave above the beginning tone. It is the response of the choir that gives both the refrain and the verse cohesiveness. Using short rhythmic values, Bradford sets up a march-like response behind the long tones of the solo, suggesting a crowd marching into the prayer room. An added feature of the choral response is the modified "stop time" pauses—"Jesus" (rest) "Jesus" (rest)—and the return to six consecutive pulsations. Immediately, this event is repeated.

The verse, set to only eight bars of two equal phrases, carries forward the story of the song. Set for the soloist alone, it provides the one chord that is not a part of the ordinary gospel harmonic language. This chord (the vii) appears on the word "I" in the phrase "one day when I was a child." Because the next phrase is set to the

same music, the chord reappears at the same place. In a composition comprised of chords as simple as those of the blues (except the cadence, which employs a progression of altered chords made famous by Roberta Martin in the late 1940s), it is refreshing to have at least one chord out of the ordinary.

"Come On in the Room" was composed when Bradford was in the first phase of his celebrity. The song was immensely popular as soon as the recording of the Roberta Martin Singers was released and contributed to the belief that everything Bradford produced would turn to gold. Not only was it immediately adopted by church choirs (the simplicity of the song permitted singers and pianists to capture it from the recording), it was recorded by no less a group than Clara Ward and the Ward Singers, and the text resurfaced in the mid-1990s through a recording of the Mississippi Mass Choir but to a different melody.

I'M TOO CLOSE TO HEAVEN (TO TURN AROUND) (1952)

The success of "I'm Too Close to Heaven" was based as much on Bradford's performance as on his compositional talent. The song differs in several ways from the prototypical Chicago gospel song of the early 1950s, the peak of the Golden Age of Gospel. The greatest departure is the absence of a refrain or "burden" (the term some older gospel singers still use), the part of a composition that is usually considered the "hook." (Many songs are known only through their refrains; for example, in Charles Albert Tindley's "We'll Understand It Better By and By" and Thomas Andrew Dorsey's "Search Me, Lord," the verses are often omitted.) Bradford also deserted the established eight- or 16-bar form for the 32-bar American popular song form, and he does not introduce any new melodic twist or chords. Rather, it is the straightforward simplicity of the song that sets it apart.

The text is based on a variation of Luke 9:62: "And Jesus said unto him, 'No man, having put his hand to the plough, and looking back, is fit for the kingdom of God.'" Bradford replaces the plowing of the field with the climbing of a mountain, and "looking back" with "turning back." Providing a detailed record of what heaven must be like, the text states that he will journey on, for he doesn't want to "miss shaking hands with all my friends," that he can "almost see His face," and that he can "feel Him breathe on me." This casual and picturesque kind of speech had not been used by Tindley or Dorsey, masters of capturing the language of African-American Christians.

The song's two stanzas are set strophically (using the same music for both stanzas) in 32 bars, but not in the usual 8+8+8+8 format with a rhyme and melodic scheme of aaba, which is found in such popular songs as "Satin Doll" and "Body and Soul." Bradford has set the text to a poem of seven lines having a rhyme scheme of aabbccd, set musically into four large phrases with each pair of rhymes constituting a subphrase except the last. Retaining the eight-bar division, he employs a melodic scheme of aa (heavily altered) bc and a poetic scheme of abcd. For all practical purposes, the song is through-composed, since none of the material returns later in the song. This form is highly unusual in gospel music, especially since the gospel message is transmitted through repetition.

The published score of the song shows that Bradford made substantial changes in both melody and text between the time that the Roberta Martin Singers recorded the song in late 1952 and late 1953 when he recorded it. The song is published in 6/8 (rather than the "gospel rhythm" of 12/8 that would be employed in the late 1990s), and Bradford reduces the 37 bars published by Martin (one bar of music is omitted at the mid-point) to 32 for his recording. Since most gospel is performed as "heard" rather than as written, singers altered the published version to fit Bradford's performance.

Except in the last line of the song where the complete title of the song is stated, the melody of the song contains no memorable turn. In this last line, Bradford sets the words "I'm too close" and "to heaven" to the same music, while creating a different melody and harmony for the cadence "to turn around." While the printed version has a choral part throughout the song, Bradford's recorded version has the choir sing only on the last line of the song. The only harmony that departs from that of traditional gospel is the minor subdominant chord (the second of the three blues chords), which is used throughout the 32 bars.

"I'm Too Close to Heaven" was first recorded in 1952 by the Roberta Martin Singers but attracted little attention. Bradford's recording, however, became one of the most successful recordings of 1953. Not only did other gospel groups sing the song, but church choirs throughout the nation placed it in their repertoire. Bradford's recording sold more than a million copies and established him, as Heilbut tells us, as the "Singing Rage of the Gospel Age." The popularity of the song was ensured by almost simultaneous releases of recordings by the Davis Sisters, Bessie Griffin and the Caravans, the Staple Singers, and, later, Al Green.

LET GOD ABIDE (1952)

"Let God Abide," Bradford's most enduring composition, is based on the passage of scripture from the Holy Bible in which Christ admonishes his followers to "abide in me, and I in you" (John 15:4). The verse of this verse-refrain composition announces a number of qualifications which, if met, assure both the singer and listener that they are abiding in Christ: If you are a witness, if you've been converted, if you're sure you know Him and you let Him abide, the reward is an "answer to every problem." Set to a rhyme scheme of aaba, three of the four lines end with the words of the title.

The second part, the refrain, also employs a rhyme scheme of aaba; the text assures that a Christian will "always get the vic'try in ev'ry trial." The refrain incorporates three consecutive statements of the text "within your soul" (an instance of the beloved repetition), for it is understood that the Lord will "hear your call and he won't let you fall." The verse and refrain are of equal length. As in "I'm Too Close to Heaven" Bradford avoids the eight- or 16-bar form and instead sets the song in 64 bars, 32 to each section (12/8 meter would have reduced the number of bars to 16, the rhythmic division that the Roberta Martin Singers imply on their 1952 recording). The melody, based in A-flat major (the key of the song), is distinctive only in that it is so perfectly wedded to the rhythm of the semi-phrase "let God abide" that one is hardly aware that different pitches but the same rhythm are used for each semi-phrase. While each of the four phrases of the verse begins in the same rhythm and with the same ascending melodic gesture, few earlier melodic fragments reappear.

The chorus is less finely crafted, adhering to the convention in gospel of leaving one of the sections of a two-part song free of notated intricate rhythms, but the repetition of ideas substitutes for its weakness. The refrain opens with three statements of "within your soul," each with a different harmony in the choral part. The chorus enters on the subdominant chord, the second chord of the blues. (Since the song is in a major key, the major IV chord is used, but at its final statement it changes to the minor iv. This use of the major and minor subdominant in the same composition—even the same bar—appears three times.) The response is also distinctive for the parallel movement in all voices, a performance practice seldom notated.

While "Let God Abide" did not enjoy immediate success, its popularity grew slowly and strongly. From the recording of the Roberta Martin Singers and a slightly later one by Robert Anderson, the song eventually found its way into the standard repertoire of gospel. It has retained its popularity into the 1990s as both a solo and a choral selection, though it is seldom sung by soloists. This song, like other Bradford compositions, shows the influence of Roberta Martin, not Thomas A. Dorsey, in that there is much more concern for investigating new melodic turns and harmonies than was the practice of the latter. Bradford was one of the first composers whose work led to the change from the older-style gospel to that of the 1970s, where exotic harmonies and melodic turns played a more prominent role.

SINCE I MET JESUS (1952)

In "Since I Met Jesus," Alex Bradford reached his zenith. The song expresses the joy of one who has discovered Christ, has been blessed by Him, and feels a responsibility to publish the glad tidings. The two scriptural passages most closely associated with this song are John 4:28–29 and Mark 5:19–20. The first is concerned with the woman of Samaria who was asked by Christ for a drink of water and then was saved by him. Without his consent, she went into the city and told of his great works. The text from Mark is the story of a man possessed of so many unclean spirits that, when asked his name, he replied, "Legion: for we are many." Christ cleansed the man of the unclean spirits and told him, "Go home to thy friends, and tell them what great things the Lord hath done for thee, and hath had compassion on thee." Each of these healed persons went about declaring the goodness of the Lord. Bradford imagines that they began their story of healing with "Since I met Jesus there's a burning, O such a burning deep within," for this is the way he begins this song.

The text goes on to declare that the blessed have been inspired to "run on—hallelujah—to the end." With such a powerful text set to some of Bradford's most progressively beautiful music it is surprising that the song is not more popular with general audiences than it is. Yet, each time an audience hears the song in a sincere and well-crafted performance, it takes on a new life.

The song was published by Roberta Martin and recorded in late 1952. "Since I Met Jesus," published in the key of E-flat major, is written in the conventional refrain-verse format. Although true to the Bradford style, it forgoes the eight- or 16-bar form, opting instead for a verse of 32 bars and a refrain only half as long. As in other compositions with this unequal division, the compositional interest lies in the larger section. The melody of the verse opens with a leap of an octave and traverses every note of the traditional diatonic scale on its route downward to the end of the phrase. At mid-point, the melody soars up three tones above the octave and, though this is only the half-point of the song, this note, 12 tones above the beginning of the solo, is clearly the climax of the verse.

Strangely, the rhythm is not the most interesting element of the song, but rather the melody and the harmony. For example, in the second part of the verse there is a section that alternates between minor and major. A melodic and rhythmic pattern introduced rather innocently at the words "He changeth me from [day to day]" will return in the refrain and serve as the unifying rhythmic element for the first half of the chorus.

The chorus has been silent during the solo, but at the entrance of the refrain the chorus begins a battle with the soloist for prominence. While the soloist has interesting melodic fragments, it is the chorus that sets up the rhythmic continuity, although it is assigned only the tones of the supporting chord. Even these limited harmonic inflections of the chorus are made interesting by their rhythmic inflections. The choral response, marked by rhythmically punctuated articulations, serves not so much as a response as it does a separate melodic entity unto itself.

In addition to the Martin recording of the song, "Since I Met Jesus" was recorded by Bradford himself, Bessie Griffin and the Caravans, and Albertina Walker with the Caravans on the great California Shrine concert of 1955. Many gospel singers consider this song the finest example of the genius of Professor Alex Bradford.

REFERENCES

Boyer, Horace Clarence. *How Sweet the Sound: The Golden Age of Gospel.* Washington, D.C.: Elliott and Clark, 1995.

Heilbut, Anthony. *The Gospel Sound: Good News and Bad Times.* 3rd ed. New York: Limelight Editions, 1989.

Jackson, Irene V. *Afro-American Religious Music: A Bibliography and a Catalogue of Gospel Music.* Westport, Conn.: Greenwood Press, 1979.

HORACE CLARENCE BOYER

BRAXTON, ANTHONY

Born in Chicago, Ill., June 4, 1945. **Education:** Chicago public schools; began playing saxophone about age 12; Chicago Vocational High School, 1959–63; studied saxophone with Jack Gell, 1959–64; Wilson Junior College, Chicago, 1963; Roosevelt University, Chicago, liberal arts studies, including philosophy, 1966–68. **Military Service:** U.S. Armed Forces, member of army bands and organized own small groups, 1963–66. **Composing and Performing Career:** Chicago, performed with Muhal Richard Abrams, 1966, and performed and recorded with the Anthony Braxton Trio (later, as the Creative Construction Company) with Leroy Jenkins and Leo Smith, 1968–69; recorded unaccompanied saxophone album, *For Alto,* 1968; New York, N.Y., joined Circle, with Barry Altschul, Chick Corea, and Dave Holland, 1970–72; debut as leader at Town Hall and as soloist at Carnegie Hall, 1972; toured and recorded as soloist and with others, including the Art Ensemble of Chicago, Musica Elettronica Viva, and the Globe Unity Orchestra in Germany, throughout 1970s; continues to lead his own small groups to the present. **Teaching Career:** Mills College, Oakland, Calif., Darius Milhaud Associate Professor of Music, ca. 1985–90; Wesleyan University, Middletown, Conn., professor of music, 1990–present. **Memberships:** Association for the Advancement of Creative Musicians (AACM), 1966–present. **Honors/Awards:** *Swing Journal* Gold Disc awards, 1972, 1973; French Jazz Academy, Prix d'Oscar, 1973, 1976; *Stereo Review* Record of the Year, 1975; *Down Beat* 1976 Album of the Year, 1977; *Jazz Journal* Record of the Year, 1979; *Down Beat* Critics' Award, Clarinetist of the Year, 1980. **Mailing Address:** 36 Mansfield Terrace, Middletown, CT 06457.

MUSIC LIST

[The following list of titles includes only works that were composed by the subject of the entry; it is not a list of recordings that were made by the subject. Although the composer may have made recordings of his own works, the list is not restricted to those recordings but in many cases includes performances by other artists of the composer's work. The list is made up of publication and discographical data, in cases where such information is available. Although no effort has been made to include documentation of the earliest recording of the works listed, the date of the earliest recording that is readily available has been given.

Braxton's music can have four different types of titles: (1) standard word titles (rare), (2) composition number titles, (3) formulaic titles, and (4) graphic or pictorial titles. A sample of these can be found in Ronald M. Radano's New Music Figurations: Anthony Braxton's Cultural Critique (Chicago: University of Chicago Press, 1993), appendix A. A comprehensive list to 1989 appears in Anthony Braxton's Catalog of Works (Oakland, Calif.: Synthesis Music, 1989). Braxton's compositions are published by his own publishing company, Synthesis Music, Oakland, Calif.—Ed.]

INSTRUMENTAL SOLOS
Any Solo Instrument

Composition no. 14 or graphic title. 1970. Premiere, 1970.
Composition no. 77a-j or *Solo Music: Book Three* or formulaic titles. May be combined with *Compositions no. 8* and *26*. Recorded: no. 77c, g, New Albion NA023; no. 77b, e, d, Sound Aspects SAS 009.

Composition no. 99a-k or *Solo Music: Book Four* or graphic titles. 1978–83. Recorded: no. 99b, New Albion NA023.
Composition no. 106a-m or *Solo Music: Book Five* or graphic titles. 1982–85. May be performed with other solo music books. Recorded: no. 106a, c, d, j, New Albion NA023.
Composition no. 118a-l or *Solo Music: Book Six* or graphic titles. 1984–86. May be performed with other solo music books. Recorded: no. 118a, f, New Albion NA023.
Composition no. 119a-i or *Solo Music: Book Seven* or graphic titles. 1985–86. May be performed with other solo music books. Recorded: no. 199g, i, New Albion NA023.

Saxophone

Composition no. 8a-k or *Solo Music: Book One* or graphic and formulaic titles. 1966–69. May be performed with *Compositions no. 26* and *77*. Recorded: 8a, b, c, d, f, h, Delmark DS420-421.
Composition no. 26a-j or *Solo Music: Book Two* or graphic and formulaic titles. 1970–74. May be combined with *Compositions no. 8* and *77*. Recorded: no. 26f, New Albion NA023; no. 26e, i, Sound Aspects SAS 009.
Composition no. 120c (baritone saxophone). 1984. Note: solo materials extracted from Composition no. 120.
Composition no. 138a-d. Recorded: New Albion NA023.

Tuba

Composition no. 120e or graphic title. 1984. Note: music extracted from *Composition no. 120.*

Piano

Composition no. 5 or graphic title. 1968.
Composition no. 10 or graphic title. 1969.
Composition no. 30 or formulaic title. 1973. Premiere, 1975. Recorded: extracts, Finnadar SR 9011 or Westwind WW001.
Composition no. 31 or formulaic title. 1974. Premiere, 1975. Recorded: extracts, Finnadar SR 9011.
Composition no. 32 or formulaic title. 1974. Premiere, 1975. Recorded: extracts, Finnadar SR 9011.
Composition no. 33 or formulaic title. 1974. Premiere, 1975. Recorded: extracts, Finnadar SR 9011.
Composition no. 139 or graphic title. 1989. Recorded: Hat ART CD 6019.
Piano Piece 1. 1968.

Two or Four Pianos

Composition no. 16 or formulaic title (four pianos). 1971. Recorded: Musica MUS 2004.
Composition no. 95 or graphic title (two pianos). 1980. Notes: each pianist also plays melodica and zither; costumes required; choreography optional. Premiere, 1980. Recorded: Arista AL9559.

ELECTRONIC MUSIC

Composition no. 21 or formulaic title (recorded tape, with or without instruments). 1971. Recorded: Delmark DS 428.

Anthony Braxton; courtesy of the composer; photo by Bill Burkhart

Composition no. 34–36 or *Three Compositions* or graphic and formulaic titles (synthesizer, two instruments). 1974. Note: score in C.

Composition no. 38a-b (clarinet and synthesizer). 1974. Recorded: no. 38a, Arista AL4032.

Composition no. 50 or graphic title (two instruments, two synthesizers). 1975. Premiere, 1975.

SMALL INSTRUMENTAL ENSEMBLE
Strings

Composition no. 17 or formulaic title (string quartet). 1971. Premiere, 1979. Recorded: Sound Aspects SAS CD009.

Composition no. 18 or formulaic title (string quartet). 1971. Premiere, 1975.

Woodwinds

Composition no. 12 or formulaic title (woodwind quintet). 1969.

Composition no. 22 or graphic title (four soprano saxophones). 1971. Note: published version transcribed from recorded performance, London, 1971. Recorded: Freedom 400 112/3.

Composition no. 37 or graphic title (four saxophones). 1974. Recorded: Arista AL4032; Black Saint 120 1261/2/4.

Composition no. 129 or graphic title (five woodwinds). 1986. Premiere, 1988. Recorded: Sound Aspects SAS CD 023.

Brass

Composition no. 4 or graphic title (five tubas). 1968. Recorded: Freedom 400 112/113.

Composition no. 19 or graphic title (100 tubas). 1971. Note: marching music.

Composition no. 103 or graphic title (seven trumpets). 1983. Note: requires costumes, specially built risers, and special lighting.

Combinations

Composition no. 2 or formulaic title (four single-line instruments). 1968. Premiere, 1968.

Composition no. 3 or graphic title (eight single-line instruments, piano, two percussion). 1968. Premiere, 1969.

Composition no. 13 or formulaic title (four single-line instruments). 1970. Premiere, 1970.

Composition no. 15 or formulaic title (four instruments). 1970.

Composition no. 20 or formulaic title (two instruments). 1971. Premiere, 1971. Recorded: Delmark DS 428.

Composition no. 23a-p or graphic and formulaic titles (creative ensemble). 1971–74. Recorded: no. 23a, Arista AL4032.

Composition no. 29a-e or *Five Compositions* or graphic and formulaic titles (two wind instruments, piano). 1973–75. Note: score in concert pitch only.

Composition no. 40a-q or *Seventeen Compositions* or graphic and formulaic titles (creative ensemble). 1974–76. May be interlinked with *Compositions no. 6, 23,* and *69.* Recorded: no. 40n, Westwind WW001; nos. 40a, 40b, 40g, Antilles 422-848585-2.

Composition no. 43–44 or *Two Compositions for Quintet* or graphic and formulaic titles (one wind, one brass, double bass, piano, percussion). 1974.

Composition no. 46 or formulaic title (flute, oboe, English horn, clarinet, bass clarinet, horn, trumpet, trombone, bass trombone, tuba). 1971. Premiere, 1975.

Composition no. 47–48 or *Two Compositions for Quintet* or graphic titles (one wind, trumpet, trombone, and rhythm section). 1975.

Composition no. 52–54 or *Three Compositions for Quartet* or graphic titles (one single-line instrument, piano, rhythm section). 1976. Note: score in C.

Composition no. 59 or graphic title (two soloists, 13 instrumentalists). 1976. Premiere, 1977. Recorded: RCA Bluebird ND86579.

Composition no. 60–62 or *Three Duo Compositions* or graphic titles (one wind, piano). 1976.

Composition no. 64–68 or *Five Compositions* or graphic titles (two single-line instrumentalists, E-flat soprano saxophone, trombone, B-flat instrument, double bass, percussion). 1976–78. Premiere, no. 64–65, 1976. Recorded: no. 64–65, Moers Music NOMU 01036.

Composition no. 69a-q or *Seventeen Compositions* or graphic titles (creative ensemble). 1976–79. May be interlinked with *Compositions no. 6, 23,* and *40.* Recorded: no. 60b, c, f, Westwind WW001.

Composition no. 70 or graphic title (one wind, one brass, double bass, piano, percussion). 1976.

Composition no. 72a-h or *Eight Duet Compositions* or graphic and formulaic titles (one single-line instrument, double bass). 1977. Note: score available for two C instruments or B-flat/C, B-flat/B-flat, E-flat/C, E-flat/B-flat, and E-flat/E-flat instruments.

Composition no. 73 or graphic title (three single-line instrumentalists). 1977.

Composition no. 74a-e or graphic title (two multi-instrumentalists on single-line instruments; 74b for two flutes). 1976. Premiere, 1976. Recorded: no. 74a, b, Sackville 3016.

Composition no. 75 or graphic title (three instruments). 1976–77.

Composition no. 76 or graphic title (three instrumentalists, preferably multi-instrumentalists). 1977. Note: score in color. Recorded: Arista AB4181.

Composition no. 79–81 or *Three Compositions* or graphic titles (two woodwinds [preferably multi-instrumentalists], brass [preferably multi-instrumententalists], piano). 1977–78.

Composition no. 85–88 or *Four Duet Compositions* or graphic titles (one woodwind, double bass). 1978. Note: score in concert pitch, can be used by wind instrument in any key. Recorded: no. 88, Black Saint BSR 0106.

Composition no. 94 or graphic title (three instruments). 1980. Premiere, 1980.

Composition no. 98 or graphic title (four winds, two brass, piano). 1981. Premiere, 1981. Recorded: Hat ART CD 6062.

Composition no. 100 or graphic title (15 instruments). 1981. Premiere, 1981 or 1982.

Composition no. 101 or graphic title (one wind or brass multi-instrumentalist, piano). 1981. Premiere, 1982. Recorded: Black Saint BSR 0106; Dischi Della Quercia Q28015; Hat ART CD 6019.

Composition no. 107 or graphic title (two wind or brass multi-instrumentalists, piano). 1983. Premiere, 1984. Recorded: Hat ART CD 6019.

Composition no. 110a-d or *Four (Short) Quartet Pieces* or graphic titles. 1984. Recorded: no. 110a, c, d, Black Saint BSR 0086.

Composition no. 116 or graphic title (four instruments). 1984. Recorded: Black Saint Records BSR 0086.

Composition no. 121 or graphic title (two single-line instruments, piano, percussion). 1984. Premiere, 1985. Recorded: Leo CD LR 200-201.

Composition no. 122 or graphic title (two single-line instruments, piano, percussion). 1985. Recorded: Black Saint Records BSR 0106.

Composition no. 130 or graphic title (four instruments). 1986. Premiere, 1988.

Composition no. 131 or graphic title (upper voice for any wind instrument, piano; lower voice for double bass or wind instrument, percussion). 1986. Recorded: Black Saint BSR 0106.

Composition no. 146: Moogie and Stetson or graphic title (12 flutes, two sousaphones, percussion). 1989. Premiere, 1989.

Composition no. 147 or graphic title (three clarinets, chamber ensemble). 1989. Premiere, 1989.

CHAMBER ORCHESTRA

Composition no. 7 or formulaic title (six woodwinds, three trumpets, three trombones, two tubas, two string basses, two percussion). 1969.

Composition no. 41 or formulaic title. 1974. Premiere, 1977.

ORCHESTRA

Composition no. 24 or formulaic title. 1971.

Composition no. 27 or formulaic title. 1972. Premiere, 1975.

Composition no. 82 or graphic title (four orchestras). 1978. Recorded: Arista AL 8900.

Composition no. 137 or graphic title. 1988. Premiere, 1989.

CREATIVE ORCHESTRA

Composition no. 3 or formulaic title (five saxophones, four trumpets, four trombones, guitar, double bass, piano, percussion). 1974.

Composition no. 11 or graphic title (10–30 instruments). 1969.

Composition no. 25 (four multi-instrument reeds, four trumpets, trombone, two double basses, piano, two percussion, 112 bells, 100 balloons). 1972. Recorded: Ring 01024/5/6.

Composition no. 42 or *Introduction to Cell Structure and Language Design.* 1974.

Composition no. 45. 1975.

Composition no. 51 or graphic title. 1976. Recorded: Arista AL4080.

Composition no. 55 or graphic title. 1976.

Composition no. 56 or graphic title. 1976.

Composition no. 57 or graphic title. 1976.

Composition no. 58 or graphic title (creative marching orchestra). 1976.

Composition no. 71 or graphic title. 1977.

Composition no. 78 or *Introduction to Cell Structure and Language Design no. Two.* 1977.

Composition no. 83 or graphic title. 1977–78. Premiere, 1977.

Composition no. 89 or graphic title. 1979.

Composition no. 91 or graphic title. 1979.

Composition no. 92 or graphic title. 1979.

Composition no. 93 or graphic title. 1979.

Composition no. 112 or graphic title. 1983.

ORCHESTRA (CHAMBER OR FULL) WITH SOLOISTS

Composition no. 63 or graphic title (two soloists, chamber orchestra). 1976. Note: score transposed. Premiere, 1976. Recorded: Arista AL5002.

DRAMATIC MUSIC

Composition no. 120 or *Trillium-Dialogues A: After a Period of Change Zackko Returns to His Place of Birth* or graphic title (four-act opera with two interludes for six soloists, six instrumentalists, choir, large orchestra, dancers, slide projections). 1984. Note: includes instructions for stage design and costumes.

Composition no. 126 or *Trillium-Dialogues M: Joreo's Vision of Forward Motion* or graphic title (four-act opera with two interludes for six soloists, choir, solo piano, large orchestra, dancers, stage design, costumes). 1986. Note: includes instructions for stage design and costumes.

MULTIMEDIA

Composition no. 9 or formulaic title (four amplified shovels, one pile of coal, costumes, choreography). 1969.

Composition no. 28 or formulaic title (six musician, six dancers). 1973. Premiere, 1973.

Composition no. 49 or graphic title (1–20 musicians, with or without dancers). 1975. Premiere, 1975.

Composition no. 96 or graphic title (orchestra, four slide projectors). 1980. Premiere, 1981. Recorded: Leo LR169.

Composition no. 102 or graphic title (orchestra, puppet theater). 1982. Premiere, 1982.

Composition no. 105a-c or *Three Quartet Structures* or graphic titles (a: wind, double bass, piano, percussion; b: clarinet, double bass, piano, percussion; c: light structure). 1984.

Composition no. 113 or graphic title (soloist, large photograph, prepared stage). 1983. Note: two versions, one for any wind instrument, one for piano, percussion, and guitar.

Composition no. 120d or graphic title (soloist, dancer). 1984.

Composition no. 123 or graphic title or . . . *Shala Addresses the Concerns of the Guardsmen and Redirects Their Energies* (flute, slides, constructed environment). 1985. Notes: environment construction and design instructions included with score; includes choreographed movements for flute player.

Composition no. 125 or graphic title or . . . *'heh! Don't Fear This Guy— Bubba John Jack Is One of Us* (tuba or sousaphone, light show, constructed environment). 1986. Notes: environment design instructions included in score; can be done with or without choreographed movements for tuba player.

Composition no. 127 or graphic title (violin, E-flat saxophone, trombone, piano, dance ensemble). 1986. Notes: conductor required; can be performed with or without dancers. Premiere, 1986.

Composition no. 128 or graphic title (single-line wind instrument, two dancers). 1986. Note: body movement positions included in score. Premiere, 1986.

Composition no. 132: The Search for Ashmention's Loyalties or graphic title (two dancers, six B-flat saxophones or six clarinets or six E-flat sopranino saxophones, 16 or eight violins, 12 or six violas, eight or four cellos, six or two double basses, percussion, cathedral organ). 1986. Notes: requires the use of special headphone sets for the two conductors; special costumes and choreographed movements. Premiere, 1986.

ANY INSTRUMENTATION

Composition no. 6a-p or *Sixteen Compositions* or graphic and formulaic titles. 1966–72. Note: available in keys of C (treble and bass clef), B-flat, and E-flat.

Composition no. 84 or graphic title. 1978.

Composition no. 90 or graphic title. 1979. Premiere, 1979.

Composition no. 97a-j or *Kelvin System Structures* or formulaic titles. 1966–84.

Composition no. 104a-l or *Cobalt System Structures* or formulaic titles. 1966–84.

Composition no. 108a-d or *Four Pulse Track Structures* or graphic titles. 1984.

Composition no. 109 a-l or *Kaufman System Structures* or formulaic titles. 1966–84.

Composition no. 111 or *Environment Strolls.* 1970–84. Note: includes verbal instructions.

Composition no. 114 or graphic title. Recorded: Black Saint Records BSR 0086.

Composition no. 115 or graphic title. 1984. Recorded: Black Saint Records BSR 0086.

Composition no. 117 or graphic title. 1984.

Composition no. 120b or Zackko Ring or graphic title (preferably winds). 1984. Note: prelude, intermission, and postlude music for Composition no. 120.

Composition no. 124 or graphic title. 1985. Recorded: Black Saint Records BSR 0106.

Composition no. 126b or Joreo Ring or graphic title (preferably winds). 1986. Note: prelude, intermission, and postlude music for Composition no. 126.

PUBLICATIONS

ABOUT BRAXTON
Books and Monographs

De Craen, Hans, and E. Janssens. *Anthony Braxton Discography.* Brussels: New Think, 1982.

Heffley, Mike. *The Music of Anthony Braxton.* New York: Excelsior Publications, 1995.

Lock, Graham. *Forces in Motion: Anthony Braxton and the Meta-Reality of Creative Music.* New York: Quartet. Reprinted as *Forces in Motion: The Music and Thoughts of Anthony Braxton* (New York: Da Capo, 1988).

———, ed. *Mixtery: A Festschrift for Anthony Braxton.* Exeter: Stride Publications, 1995.

Radano, Ronald M. *New Musical Figurations: Anthony Braxton's Cultural Critique.* Chicago: University of Chicago Press, 1993.

Wachtmeister, Hans. *A Discography and Bibliography of Anthony Braxton.* Stocksund, Sweden: Blue Anchor, 1982.

Wilson, Peter. *Anthony Braxton: Sein Leben, seine Musik, seine Schallplatten.* Waakirchen, Germany: Oreos, 1993.

Dissertations

Heidbreded, Kevin F. "An Examination of Anthony Braxton's Improvisational and Compositional Language." Master's thesis, Bowling Green State University, 1985.

Radano, Ronald M. "Anthony Braxton and His Two Musical Traditions: The Meeting of Concert Music and Jazz." Ph.D. diss., University of Michigan, 1985.

Articles

"Anthony Braxton." In *Contemporary Musicians: Profiles of the People in Music.* Detroit: Gale Research, 1994.

Bley, Carla. "Vom Underground in dem Vordergrund." *Jazz Podium* 25, no. 12 (1976): 12–14; 26, no. 1 (1977): 11–14; 26, no. 2 (1977): 14–16.

Corbett, John. "Anthony Braxton: From Planet to Planet." In *Extended Play: Sounding Off from John Cage to Dr. Funkenstein,* 209–218. Durham, N.C.: Duke University Press, 1994.

Coudert, F. M. "Bilan de Braxton." *Jazz Magazine* 334 (December 1984): 69+.

Kleinert, G. "Disziplin der Improvisation: Anthony Braxton und Rova." *Jazz Podium* 38 (March 1989): 12–15.

Kostakis, Peter, and Art Lange. "Conversation with Anthony Braxton 3/31/76." *Brilliant Corners* no. 4 (Fall 1976): 53–99.

Kumpf, Hans H. "Jazz und Avantgarde." *Musik und Bildung* 9, no. 10 (1977): 521–525.

———. "Postserielle Musik und Free Jazz." In *Murr.* Herrenberg: Doring, 1976.

Laskin, D. L. "Anthony Braxton: Play or Die." *Ear Magazine* 14 (May 1989): 40–46.

Martinelli, Francesco. "Anthony Braxton: a Discography." *Nerosubianco* 3 (1995).

Radano, Ronald. "Braxton's Reputation." *Musical Quarterly* 72, no. 4 (1986): 503–522.

Rothbart, P. "Play or Die." *Down Beat* 49 (February 1982): 20+.

Shoemaker, B. "Anthony Braxton: The Dynamics of Creativity." *Down Beat* 56 (March 1989): 20–22.

Wilson, Peter Nicklas. "Die neue-alte? Kammermusikalitat im Jazz." *Musik und Bildung* 17, no. 2 (1985): 777–781.

———. "Ein Niemandsland zwischen E und U: Uber die Annaherung von Jazz und minimal music." *Musica* 39, no. 4 (1985): 360–365.

———. "Mit Arnold Schoenberg in Korea. Anthony Braxton: Musiker zwischen Afroamerica und Europa." *Musiktexte* 23 (1988): 40–43.

———. "Musikalische Systemphilosophie nach ihrem Ende: Anthony Braxton's musikalische Metaphysik." In *Jazz und Komposition.* Hofheim: Wolke, 1992.

———. "Zur Kompositionstechnik von Anthony Braxton." *Jazz Podium* 31 (August 1982): 4–7.

BY BRAXTON

Catalog of Works. Oakland, Calif.: Synthesis Music, 1989.

Composition Notes, Books A–E. 5 vols. Oakland, Calif.: Synthesis Music, 1988.

Tri-Axium Writings, Volumes 1–3. Oakland, Calif.: Synthesis Music, 1985.

*   *   *   *   *

One of the most compelling expressions of late 20th-century black musicianship appears in the work of composer-saxophonist Anthony Braxton. Since his emergence in American and European music circles in the late 1960s, Braxton has produced a series of adventurous approaches that at once embrace and exceed common conventions of performance, style, and genre. These experiments reflect a desire to radically revise artistic categories and boundaries in ways consistent with the instabilities and fragmentation commonly associated with postmodernism. At the same time, however, Braxton's belief in the transformative potential of music making goes against the grain of postmodernism's ironic and frequently cynical oppositions. His revisionist experiments are meant to enact patterns of social change in the spirit of racially minded civil rights initiatives. If one were to identify any pattern of consistency in Braxton's aesthetic, it is his activist commitment to radical artistic experiments that continually destabilize the norms of meaning and listening. What may be described as a "black experimental" practice brings together traditions of European artistic and social vanguardism with black civil rights action.

The foundation of Braxton's artistic approach took shape in the animated post–World War II environment of Chicago's South Side. During the 1950s and 1960s, black Chicagoans witnessed a veritable renaissance of artistic invention as innovations in blues, rhythm and blues, rock 'n' roll, gospel, and jazz challenged the authority of white mainstream practices in concert and popular music. Growing up in this fertile environment, Braxton responded to the many achievements in African-American music. In elementary school, he sang in a doo-wop group that performed along the lines of his boyhood idol, Frankie Lymon. He listened to blues and rhythm and blues favorites on the family radio and phonograph and sang in the local Baptist church. Turning to jazz as a teenager, he pursued the talent of local and national artists—Ahmad Jamal, Miles Davis, and John Coltrane. Ironically, however, this sense of racial pride prompted Braxton to challenge the musical dimensions that "blackness" commonly determined. By his mid-teens, he was listening widely across racial and musical lines and finding favorites in the work of Warne Marsh, Paul Desmond, Dave Brubeck, John Philip Sousa, and later, Arnold Schoenberg and John Cage. For Braxton, being a black artist meant testing the limits of one's creative potential without paying heed to the racialist conventions of American public culture. High-quality black music could take a variety of forms, its only constraint being the limits of one's imagination.

As a member of Chicago's activist arts collective, the Association for the Advancement of Creative Musicians (AACM), Braxton embarked on an individual search for ways of articulating the range of his "black aesthetic" and intellectual outlook. He did so ultimately by working from the achievements of African-American free jazz improvisers, whose radical experiments and commitment to civil rights politics had won wide respect in arts circles beginning in the early 1960s. At the same time, Braxton also searched for models in a variety of arenas, from the practices of white jazz musicians to the innovations of European concert composers. In the frequently atonal approaches of the latter, he identified modernity's extreme of progressive musical experiment, which ran parallel to the revisionism he had already witnessed in free jazz. Over the course of three decades, a body of creative work took shape that continually involved intersections of these two principal traditions in a series of radically hybrid inventions.

Braxton's compositions resist simple categorization. In each medium, he works to achieve a widely integrated and interconnected series of works. Within each, nonetheless, one can observe certain consistencies of approach and practice. Most commonly appearing on record, for example, are small-group works that feature two soloists (typically, Braxton and a trumpeter or trombonist) and a rhythm section of double bass, drums, and occasionally piano performing in contemporary styles that range from post-bop to march-inflected jazz to atonal chamber music. Other small-group works develop from a mix of improvised and composed approaches to create hybrids of atonal concert music and jazz. In most cases, Braxton's band members have demonstrated competence on one or more instruments. As "multi-instrumentalists," they extend the range of their expressive voices in order to fulfill Braxton's AACM-based aesthetic strategy of liberating the sounding potential of African-American artistry.

Braxton's works for large ensembles achieve a similar diversity of expression, while still acknowledging the stylistic approaches to which these ensembles commonly refer. The compositions for "creative orchestra" work from swing-band instrumental and per-

formance models and commonly feature a series of soloists improvising against a 4/4 swing rhythm. The arrangements themselves, however, frequently blur jazz and concert-music styles, and in some instances, they engage written segments and improvisational strategies—for example, sustained clusters or free metric areas—in which rhythmic propulsiveness is noticeably absent. Moreover, the works for orchestra and other large ensembles dramatically reveal Braxton's fascination with the pointillism and atonality associated with post-war serial composition. Yet, even within this medium, Braxton commonly introduces improvisational practices and qualities of nuance and inflection that derive from jazz. Finally, Braxton's repertory includes a body of unaccompanied saxophone works that, while typically improvised, appear in style and approach more closely linked to the concert performance procedures of European soloists. The works in this genre commonly generate many of the motivic elements that in turn inform his extended compositional corpus.

Further complicating the issue of artistic category is Braxton's interpretation of his works as parts of an interlinking compositional system. Put into place in the early 1970s, this system established relationships between components, elements, and procedures within various compositions that together represent what Braxton calls his core body of "principle [sic] material." This conception allows him to deny the oversimplified, disciplinary classifications of "jazz" imposed upon his work by public commentators, offering in their place a set of relationships that, Braxton claims, link to a larger program of musically based social change. The specifics of the musical-social linkages are difficult to discern, if only because the elements and guides to the system have also constantly changed over the course of their development. Perhaps the most notoriously controversial aspect of the system is the set of nonverbal picture titles that offer a kind of metaphoric commentary on all of Braxton's works. While the numbers, letters, and figures are meant to correspond to particulars within the compositions themselves, Braxton's choice not to outline the details of these correspondences suggest an intention to play up and parody the mystified images that frequently accompany discussions of his work in popular journalism.

Some of Braxton's best works achieve a sense of wonder and bafflement precisely because they successfully realize the vast hybridic character of late 20th-century experience. They push the limits of convention, both of jazz and concert music, by reworking standard practices and procedures in radically new ways or by drawing stylistic intersections that put into relief the artificiality of our own aesthetic categories and musical common sense. Braxton's solo works are particularly compelling in this regard. While drawing listeners into a diverting improvisational narrative, they open up new listening realities that, in their phrasing, motivic construction, and rhythmic character, often go against the assumptions the audience makes when listening to jazz. Moreover, the sometimes brutal assaults of abstraction that appear in both the compositions and solos seem to speak symbolically in Braxton's politically conscious art to the constructed character of the racial divide. By bringing together seemingly opposite racial-musical realms of "white" and "black," Braxton invigorates his art as he unseats conventional listening. His music gestures to the oppositions of America just as it reveals, in the spirit of W.E.B. Du Bois, the inevitability of racial engagement. If these art works do not fulfill a vanguardist program, they offer at the least inspired glimpses of a potential future, reworking racial ideology to formulate a new cultural common ground.

The four works discussed in this essay—*Composition 6e* (1968) for three multi-instrumentalists; *Composition 26b* (ca. 1971) for unaccompanied saxophone; *Performance 9/1/1979,* a "coordinate" of works for jazz quartet; and *Composition 165* for 18 instruments—range across three decades of artistic activity. In their breadth, they provide a sense of the many dimensions of Braxton's compositional practice, without implying a pattern of stylistic evolution. Many of the approaches and practices outlined here were already in place by the early 1970s; since then, Braxton has continued to work with them all. Accordingly, it is difficult to discern an overarching pattern of development, even as Braxton introduces new methods and orientations over the course of time.

The composition numbers correspond to nonverbal picture titles appearing on the specified album jackets and in Braxton's list of works. The name of the "coordinate" performance is taken from the title of Braxton's album (HatArt CD 6044).

COMPOSITION NO. 6E (1968)

Braxton calls *Composition no. 6e* "a platform for open-ended improvisation." It is a highly flexible set of constraints that orients group improvisation by three multi-instrumentalists. The work was composed in the summer of 1968 as a way of fostering an experimental collective procedure first outlined by Muhal Richard Abrams, Roscoe Mitchell, Joseph Jarman, and other AACM members. Yet, whereas AACM approaches typically maintained the interactive relations and stylistic character of post-bop and free jazz, Braxton and his principal collaborators, trumpeter Leo Smith and violinist Leroy Jenkins, pursued an improvisational practice that reinforced commitments to sound-color experiment as they retreated from standardized jazz instrumentation and four-beat rhythm accompaniment. Eschewing the virtuosity still common to AACM performances, Braxton's trio sought to position sound before the sound-makers. As AACM multi-instrumentalists, they created a course of diverse sonic textures that seemed to have little to do with the developmental, "narrative" approach associated with jazz improvisation.

In his five-volume compendium *Composition Notes,* Braxton explains that *Composition no. 6e* consists of four parts: "A1, A2, B, A1." The introductory material in A1 sets the basis for the extended improvisations in A2; in B, the ensemble moves into a "pointillistic section" of discrete segments that leads to a return to the introductory thematic material of A1. The recorded version from Braxton's first album, *Three Compositions of New Jazz* (1968), begins with an unaccompanied vocal segment (A1), featuring the three members of the trio. The atonal theme, which is sung slowly and, for the most part, in unison, reflects the musicians' fascination with post-war serial composition. Significantly, however, the trio's application of atonality represents something more than an obvious imitation of "serious composition." The untrained character of the musicians' voices and the allusions to children's songs (sung to the nonsense syllables "tra la la la") suggest that atonality here

serves to signify freedom from performance convention, and it is this dynamic that informs the entire work. Untrained "natural" articulations of atonal freedom represent a basic sound that orients the subsequent instrumental explorations. The amateurish singing quality particularly underscores the group's commitment to an aesthetic of anti-virtuosity through which the creative musician, liberated from modern jazz music's specializations, recovers its imagined origins in the primordial, black voice.

In part A2, collective instrumental engagements demonstrate a full flowering of the Braxton trio's extensions of "natural voice." Employing a battery of principal melodic instruments and percussion devices (what the AACM calls "little instruments"), the performers enact a range of voice-to-instrument transferences while intermittently interjecting fragments of the vocal theme. Over the course of the improvisation, they produce a kaleidoscope of constantly shifting instrumental and vocal combinations. These intersections of harmonica, police whistle, tambourine, kazoo, brake drum, snare drum, ratchet, penny whistle, and so on give coherence to the mix; the shifts in textural groupings give shape to spontaneous engagements in ways consistent with traditional jazz improvisation. By the midpoint of the nearly 20-minute performance, the improvisation grows increasingly sparse, suggesting that the open-ended part B begins here. As a collective improvisation, however, no clear line of demarcation is observable. New beginnings emerge organically and repeatedly, as ever-new instrumental combinations sustain a perpetual unfolding of ensemble expression.

In *Composition no. 6e,* the musicians seem at first to honor the jazz convention of a succession of instrumental solos repeatedly moving in and out of leadership roles. Braxton takes the first solo, introducing part A2, and Smith and Jenkins follow with their own statements. Braxton begins, playing a slow, languid alto saxophone solo colored with strong blues inflections that enhance the vocal quality of his instrumental sound. It is clear from this entry that he seeks to put forward a commanding presence. Despite undeniable virtuosity, however, Braxton performs in a way that ultimately undermines the work's development. While demonstrating a formidable and original voice, he appears detached, his solo playing fragmented and nearly static, in part because of the lack of a rhythmic accompaniment, yet even more so because his fiery playing works against conventional phrasing and development. Further, by constantly switching instruments, Braxton, and his cohorts in their turn, exacerbates the decentering of the soloist's role. He shifts from voice to alto saxophone to flute to clarinet and assorted "little instruments." Jenkins and Smith similarly involve various performance techniques, including rapid "fiddling," strumming, flutter-tonguing, overblowing, and open horn. Cast among the display of "little instruments," the soloist ultimately submits to the sonic clutter to engage a bounty of nondevelopmental coloristic dimensions. If these lead roles affirm the solo/accompaniment hierarchy of jazz, they do so while also presenting new, egalitarian modes of musical "conversation" that communicate Braxton's aesthetics of social liberation. By constructing a sonic world of endless possibility, the musicians realize the limitlessness of "black sound." They pay tribute in form to the conventions of African-American music making, only to abstract that background to convey new performative modes of black experience.

Braxton's early collective improvisations, then, build from the ethos and spirit of jazz to impart a new direction in African-American creative expression. Multivoiced textures, improvisation, "solos" that complicate subjectivity, and an ironic sense of collective engagement are at the heart of these works, effecting a precarious relationship with the norms of jazz performance. If the trio's improvisations reveal a traditional African-American commitment to storytelling and call-and-response metaphors, so do these "stories" equally pay tribute to the stasis of modernist nondevelopmental forms and to the qualities and conditions characterizing late 20th-century American life.

That these works received only limited notice inside and outside of African-American cultural circles—and then mainly within intellectual contexts—does not diminish their importance as emblems of a political utopianism associated with the Civil Rights movement.

COMPOSITION NO. 26B (CA. 1971)

Braxton's works for unaccompanied saxophone introduced a new genre of American improvised music, working from European concert repertory precedents and a few scattered experiments in jazz. Similar approaches also appeared in the work of AACM members (notably Roscoe Mitchell's *Congliptious*, 1968), but Braxton stands alone in raising the practice to a full-fledged mode of expression.

The "solo music," as Braxton calls it, commonly develops from elaborations on a small body of motivic material or set of stylistic approaches—rhythmic patterns, rapid-note figures, embouchure techniques, multiphonic textures, extreme-register distortions, and so on; these constitute the "languages" (or "language music") of the solo works. The elaborations take shape extemporaneously, although in many cases—as is the case in nearly all musical improvising—their execution also relies on stereotyped formulas. Stylistically, the solos feature procedures that complicate tonality and often suggest associations with atonal concert music. While the unaccompanied works can take nearly any length (recorded versions range from 19 seconds to over 20 minutes), they typically adhere to the five to ten-minute time conventions of contemporary jazz recordings. In their earliest incarnations, the solo compositions mimicked the static character of Braxton's ensemble works. Gradually, however, Braxton worked to articulate and amplify their formal markings to the point where they now represent his most formally conservative artistry—"conservative" in the sense that they rely on a clear statement of form and sense of progressive development as a means of sustaining improvisational practice.

Composition no. 26b is the second of ten works from Braxton's second book of unaccompanied alto saxophone music, composed during the years 1970–74. (The first book, *Composition no. 8,* consists of 11 works, a-k, composed from 1966 to 1969.) *Composition no. 26b* was composed for a performance at the Palace of Fine Arts in San Francisco in 1971 and has since been recorded on three albums: *Saxophone Improvisations Series F* (1972), *Live at Moers* (1974), and *Alto Saxophone Improvisations 1979* (1979). What defines all versions as the same work is the set of principal motivic materials and performance techniques (the "languages") from which Braxton builds each solo performance. Most recogniz-

able is the distinctive tremolo technique Braxton employs to introduce the slow melodic phrases at the beginning of each version. While melodically unrelated from performance to performance, the tremolo phrases play a common role: they serve as anticipatory statements leading to a second, contrasting section of coarse-textured rapid improvisation. These contrasts, in turn, often include a familiar cadential marker: overblown, highly chromatic, and extremely rapid descents to *d*-flat below middle *c*. The *d*-flat markers can appear at any point in the composition; Braxton employs them most commonly to specify endings of sections or, when played in rapid succession, the ending of the work.

After the opening statements, Braxton moves in each version to an expansive, virtuosic developmental section. Typically, he introduces these new sections first by elaborating on previous material. Sometimes this involves rapid succession of two contrasting ideas; other times, it may develop from an extended elaboration on a certain turn of phrase through sequence, variation, or other techniques. In all cases, however, Braxton ultimately brings his solo toward a section that highlights the tremolo technique. The three recorded versions each contain long sections of rapid-note repetitions that are similar to the tremolo idea. As these articulations shift pitch centers at intermittent, unpredictable intervals, they unseat tonal and phrase logic. In so doing, they create a sense of anticipation that prepares for a recapitulation and paraphrase of the original tremolo theme. The concluding statements extend the range of the original melodies as they set up the final *d*-flat cadential descents.

In the solo music and particularly in the versions of *Composition no. 26b,* Braxton ingeniously reworks materials and practices in order to construct a profoundly new species of art. The solo works do something more than merely cobble together stylistic references from concert music and jazz. They grow out of Braxton's practical experience as an analytically minded performer who consciously seeks ways of employing abstract, nontonal material in an improvisational context without relying on the formal, harmonic, and metric/rhythmic supports common to jazz. Braxton's stress on compositional logic over intuition and spontaneous playing helps sustain an approach that so frequently works from fragments and abstractions of jazz phrasing. Yet he still gives to his performances the same sense of freedom and excitement so frequently associated with modern black improvised music. In virtually all solo recordings and live performances, it is clear that Braxton is improvising, and, like any good soloist, he follows his intuitions on the spot. New figures and even mistakes can lead to extended digressions. As the rhythmic energy and momentum builds, he may then turn to the familiar techniques of overblowing and multiphonics common to the 1960s New York free style. To be sure, Braxton recognizes the importance of maintaining a sense of dynamism and motion in improvised music. Yet that energy derives less from swing per se than from a sense of timing that ultimately reflects his analytical perspective of form. A virtuoso performer, Braxton continually makes choices about what to play and what not to play—how long to develop an idea, when to follow an unanticipated pattern or idea, when to move on and what to move on to. His success in achieving momentum and flow arises from this same formal sense of purpose.

During the most successful unaccompanied solos, the listener is made aware of all of these performance complexities. In his 1974 version of *Composition no. 26b* (which appears as JMK-80/CFN-7 on the album, *Anthony Braxton: Solo at Moers New Jazz Festival*), for example, Braxton reveals the crux of his aesthetic: the performances appear saturated with the doublings of composition and spontaneity, rational order and intuition, pure abstraction and storytelling accessibility. With every turn of phrase, he exposes the edge of his revisionist tactics in ways that seem, at moments, to speak to new social possibilities, to new realities beyond the world as we know it.

As commodities appearing within the score-card rankings of jazz journalism, however, these performances played out the social contradiction of art and commerce as they revealed the weaknesses inherent to the conventional critical formulae. Whether praised ("1979") or dismissed ("Series F"), *Composition 26b* stood precariously between the vanguardism of black-arts social action and its co-optation within the standard narratives of jazz reportage.

PERFORMANCE 9/1/1979 (1971–79)

By the mid-1970s, Braxton had become increasingly concerned with the systematic implications of his "languages" and their relationship to his various compositions. This interest inspired a new dimension of creativity whereby the compositions themselves became, like the elements in each work, components of an extended, multi-compositional structure. *Compositions no. 30–33*, an aggregate of four piano works, and *Composition no. 25*, a sequence of discrete compositions for creative orchestra, are early recorded examples of a multiwork complex. *Performance 9/1/1979* represents a later stage of Braxton's development, during which he had grown even more conscious of the relationships between works. In *Performance 9/1/1979*, the individual compositions (*Compositions no. 69c, no. 69e, no. 69g, no. 40f, no. 69f, no. 23g,* and *no. 69h*) together make up a "master progression system," whose overarching sequence maps the contours of a larger composition-in-performance. Braxton's desire to plan his selections for a performance is hardly new. Yet, unlike many bandleaders, he perceives that his ensemble works in a systematic way. More than a pretentious imitation of academic system building, however, the multiwork schemes serve to arrest his most conspicuously "jazz" works from simple jazz categorization. While owing stylistically to post-bop practices, they find a place within aesthetic and compositional contexts that challenge the efficacy of jazz as a category. The system, then, serves not only to integrate jazz into Braxton's compositional aesthetic but also to protect all aspects of his aesthetics from the disciplines of conventional musical classification and representation.

Each of the seven works in *Performance 9/1/1979* develops from a particular compositional orientation that informs the manner of performance. (A diagram of the work is included in the album notes.) The first, third, sixth, and seventh works, for example, all feature an introductory theme leading to a sequence of solos against rhythm-section accompaniment. By varying the rhythmic character of each, Braxton encourages a variety of performing situations to take shape. The first, *Composition no. 69c*, maintains a stiff, quarter-note staccato rhythm in which each pulse is antici-

pated by a grace-note accent (a kind of flam). The third, *Composition no. 69g*, employs an extremely rapid (quarter note = 240), 24-bar head melody that winds through intricate figurations and a series of bop-based ascending eighth-note sequences. The sixth, *Composition no. 23g*, features a "gravallic basic" accompaniment, whose sparse, aperiodic, staccato accents (played in rhythmic unison by bass and drums) preclude swing playing. The seventh, *Composition no. 69h*, the performance's encore, is an example of Braxton's popular, march-style repertory. This particular rendition features arpeggiated melodies, drum rolls, stereotypical triplet rhythms, implied duple meter, and an altered rondo form (AABACADAA)—all march conventions.

The themes of the second, fourth, and fifth works (*Compositions no. 69e, 40f,* and *69f*, respectively), on the other hand, prepare for a series of diverse collective interactions. Braxton explains this sequence in his album notes. During the "language" interactions, the improvisers work collaboratively from the "line notation" (line drawings specifying general pitch contour). In "open improvisation," they "play in opposition. If one is going faster, the other might go slower; if one plays high, the other may play lower." "Collage improvisations," moreover, emerge from "a conscious decision to avoid connections. We are talking about total individualism in space." Near the ends of the improvisations, the quartet establishes a transition by alluding to the melody of the upcoming work. These "linkage dynamics" help to orient both the musicians and their listeners, while also enabling the group to perform without pauses between works.

The multicompositional structures, then, are significant to Braxton's creative development because they reflect a dramatic reconceptualization of the formal character of jazz performance. The procedures for drawing linkages between works show how Braxton had come to terms with jazz by modeling it in his own image. Removed from preexisting contexts, Braxton's "jazz" had taken on the character of his experimental system.

COMPOSITION NO. 165 (CA. 1989)

Composition no. 165 for 18 instruments is an example of Braxton's more recent work for large ensembles. A complex, extended work, it continues a line of concert-style compositions that reaches back to *Composition no. 3* for 11 instruments (1968). In instrumentation, *Composition no. 165* is nearly identical to Braxton's works for "creative orchestra." It features sections of trumpets, trombones, reeds (saxophones and doublings on conventional and unconventional instruments: bassoon, slide saxophone), together with a rhythm section that includes tuba and synthesizer. Stylistically, however, the work owes little or nothing to the big-band jazz repertory to which the creative-orchestra music typically relates. Rather, it seems more akin to small-group works such as *Composition no. 98*, which establishes a series of performative constraints that regulate free-style collective improvisation. Like *Composition no. 98*, too, performers work from a score consisting of several notations of varying specificity. At times, musicians play from conventional notation; other times, they work from nonpitched "line notations" that guide phrase contour and dynamics; still other times, they invent freely within established stylistic bounds and time constraints. Viewed together, these constraints give the performance a sense of discipline consistent with Braxton's overarching musical vision, just as their relationship to a general system of "language music" establishes the work's place within his sphere of composerly practice.

Serving as an informing feature throughout *Composition no. 165* are intermittent moments of sustained sound that supply consistency and order to an otherwise atonal and seemingly amorphous extended work. The 50-minute performance (written as a single movement) consists of groups of discrete temporal moments—pockets of sonic action—that are typically framed by brief periods of silence but that frequently overlap. In this respect, *Composition no. 165* recalls a practice common to the works of Morton Feldman (e.g., *Rothko Chapel*), where quiet clusters of sound are interspersed with areas of silence. The musical material in *Compositon no. 165* features sustained homophonic tonal clusters cut across with brief fragments of independent improvised lines played by one or more instrumentalists. Initially, these sustained clusters are played loud, frequently as rapid crescendos. Gradually, however, they give way to quieter, more open fields of sound, and eventually appear only intermittently, arising out of similarly brief improvisational exchanges between varying ensemble subgroups. Yet even when not heard, these clusters are implied, since they are what determine the compositional logic of contrasting temporal moments. In this way, they establish a kind of patterned phrasing from which varying groups of instrumental combinations appear and disappear in and out of the sound space. This readily discernible logic enables the listener to focus attention over the course of a 50-minute performance without the help of a musical score. As such, Braxton's guidelines work in ways not unlike the sectional markings heard traditionally in tonal music.

The commercial release of *Composition no. 165* follows a practice observable in the majority of Braxton's large body of recordings. The album includes a nonverbal picture-title as well as lengthy notes that introduce the work to listeners. Whereas, previously, Braxton's liner notes were notorious for their dramatic displays of scientific diagrams and technical language, his album notes from the mid-1980s on frequently have more accessible descriptions and representational titles, depicting familial or boyhood scenes in stick-figure animation. The picture-title of *Composition no. 165* includes a sunny landscape of green hills and vales in which two small stick figures appear, one performing and the other conducting. Curiously, Braxton's performance notes involve these images, revealing new intersections of music, text, and visual abstraction. Cast as a kind of children's tale, the notes center around two main characters, Ben and Johnathon, who are admiring cloud formations in the valley of "Norfolk." Moving on, the reader soon realizes that the visual images to which they refer are in fact metaphors for the sound forms appearing in the musical work. Rushing out of the forest when a thunderstorm arises, Ben and Johnathon take pause:

"Wait a minute," cried Ben—"look at that dark cloud formation—check it out, there's something out there I tell you."

"Come on, man," cried Johnathon, "there's no time for these games." . . . "No, listen . . . look at that formation and compare it to our charts. In *Composition no. 165* there are static and mutable cloud formations that drift in and out of the canvas of the music." . . . "Hey, even I recognized that cloud (chord)," said Johnathon. "Don't rush it," cried Ben, "it'll come in its own time. In *Composition no. 165,* moments float in and out of the sound space—yet there are target recognition states. This is a sequential event continuum that places equal emphasis on sound and space—the moments come, the moments go."

Braxton's notes are important extensions of his creative work as an artist and composer. The titles and their notes represent analogous forms of creativity, offering a kind of parallel performative action alongside his similarly provocative, experimental engagements. Braxton's shift away from abstract images and toward representational art and narrative form suggests an evolution in his manner of presentation. Yet it also reveals a consistency with his activist aesthetic observable since the 1960s. As an intersection of art and life, the visual and musical composite of *Composition no. 165* speaks to Braxton's commitment to enacting progressive social change. The arcane nature of his art forms are not meant to create distance from audiences but rather to jog normative listening in ways reminiscent of vanguardist practices across the modern era. As a trial requiring perseverance and commitment, listening and performing through the "sound map" of *Composition no. 165* and its various "principle sonic lanes" becomes a recipe for new social engagements toward a common progressive end, ones not without a discernibly Christian sense of resolution. The radical languages move beyond commonsense understanding toward a more profoundly "spiritual" awareness. As Ben concludes, "Thank heaven for hope and redemption. The phenomenon of manifestation is the greatest gift of all."

Composed in the late 1980s or early 1990s, *Composition no. 165* was premiered in 1992 by the University of Illinois Creative Music Orchestra under Braxton's direction.

REFERENCES

Braxton, Anthony. *Composition Notes, Books A–E.* 5 vols. Oakland, Calif.: Synthesis Music, 1988.

———. Liner notes, *Composition no. 165 for Eighteen Instruments.* New Albion 050.

———. Liner notes, *Performance 9/1/1979.* Hat ART CD 6044.

Heffley, Michael. *The Music of Anthony Braxton.* New York: Excelsior Press, 1995.

Lock, Graham. *Forces in Motion: Anthony Braxton and the Meta-reality of Creative Music: Interviews and Tour Notes.* London: Quartet, 1988. Reprinted as *Forces in Motion: The Music and Thoughts of Anthony Braxton* (New York: Da Capo, 1988).

Radano, Ronald M. *New Musical Figurations: Anthony Braxton's Cultural Critique.* Chicago: University of Chicago Press, 1993.

RONALD M. RADANO

BREWSTER, W(ILLIAM) HERBERT, SR.

Born in Somerville, Tenn., July 2, 1897; died in Memphis, Tenn., October 14, 1987. **Education:** Shelby County, Tenn., graduated high school, ca. 1919; American Baptist Theological Seminary, Nashville, Tenn., 1919–20; Roger Williams College, Nashville, 1920–22, B.A., 1922. **Composing and Performing Career:** East Trigg Baptist Church, Memphis, Tenn., pastor, 1925–87; Education Board of the National Baptist Convention, corresponding Executive Secretary; Shelby County General Baptist Association, Shelby County, Tenn., Dean; Brewster Theological Clinic, Memphis, founder and director, 1926–87; Brewster Ensemble, founder, mid-1940s; first gospel song to sell over 1 million copies, "Move On Up a Little Higher," published, 1946. **Honors/Awards:** Smithsonian Institution, Washington, D.C., retrospective of Brewster's works, 1982, 1984; W. H. Brewster Award, 1985.

MUSIC LIST

SONGS

[The following list of titles includes only works that were composed by the subject of the entry; it is not a list of recordings that were made by the subject. Although the composer may have made recordings of his own works, the list is not restricted to those recordings but in many cases includes performances by other artists of the composer's work. The list is made up of publication and discographical data, in cases where such information is available. Although no effort has been made to include documentation of the earliest recording of the works listed, the date of the earliest recording that is readily available has been given.—Ed.]

"Anywhere in Glory." n.p.: William Herbert Brewster, 1956. Arranger, Clara Ward.

"As an Eagle Stirreth in Her Nest." Los Angeles: MCA Duchess, n.d. Recorded: Reprise 2235.

"At the End of the Road." Chicago: Theodore R. Frye, 1952. Arranger, Virginia Davis.

"Bank in the Sky." Recorded: P-Vine PLP-9051.

"Book of the Seven Seals." Recorded: P-Vine PLP-9051.

"Bringing in the Sheaves." Los Angeles: Unichappell, 1952. Co-composers or arrangers, Virginia Davis, G. A. Minor, K. Shaw.

"Can You Tell Anything He Has Done for You?" Copyright, 1946. Arrangers, Virginia Davis, Josephine Daniels.

"Chapel." Los Angeles: MCA Duchess, 1955.

"Christian Race Track." New York: Screen Gems-EMI, 1961.

"Don't Wait Too Late." New York: Screen Gems-EMI, 1961.

"Faith That Moves Mountains." Philadelphia: Ward's House of Music, 1954. Arranger, Clara Ward.

"Farther On up the Road." Philadelphia: Ward's House of Music, 1953. Arranger, Berisford Shepherd. Recorded: Spirit Feel SF 1002.

"God's Amazing Love." Philadelphia: Ward's House of Music, 1954. Arranger, Berisford Shepherd. Recorded: Savoy MG 14026.

"Have Faith in God." Chicago: Theodore R. Frye, 1952. Arranger, Virginia Davis.

"He Died on Calvary." Chicago: Bowles Publishing House, 1947. Arranger, W. O. Hoyle.

"He Has a Way That's Mighty Sweet." Chicago: Theodore R. Frye, 1949. Arranger, Virginia Davis.

"He'll Fix It All." Chicago: Bowles Publishing House, 1950. Arranger, Virginia Davis.

"He'll Make It All Clear at Last." Chicago: Bowles Publishing House, 1947. Arranger, W. O. Hoyle.

"Here I Am I'll Go." New York: Screen Gems-EMI, 1962.

"He's Worthy." n.p.: Irving Music, 1967.

"The Hope of the World Is Jesus." Chicago: Theodore R. Frye, 1949. Co-composer, W. Herbert T. Brewster Jr. Arranger, Virginia Davis.

"How Far Am I from Canaan?" Chicago: Martin and Morris Music Studio, 1946. Arranger, Kenneth Morris. Note: in *The Garden of Prayer*.

"How I Got Over." Recorded: Shanachie/Spirit Feel 6011; Smithsonian/Folkways C-SF-40074.

"How Long, O Lord, How Long?" n.p.: W. Herbert Brewster, 1953. Arranger, Clara Ward.

"I Am Leaning and Depending on the Lord" or "God Hears a Prayer." Chicago: Martin and Morris Music Studio, 1941. Co-composer, Kenneth Morris. Arranger, Bobby Anderson.

"I Am Still on the Glory Road." Chicago: Theodore R. Frye, 1949. Arranger, Virginia Davis.

"I Found the Keys of the Kingdom." Chicago: Bowles Publishing House, 1952. Arranger, Virginia Davis.

"I Just Can't Afford to Fail My Jesus Now." Chicago: Theodore R. Frye, 1946. Arrangers, Virginia Davis, Josephine Daniels.

"I Know It Was Jesus." Chicago: Bowles Publishing House, 1952. Arranger, Virginia Davis.

"I Know the Lord Has Been with Me Each Step of the Way." Chicago: Bowles Music House, 1953. Co-composers, Juanita Brewster, Nina Daugherty, Dorothy Ford.

"I Know the Time and the Place." Chicago: Theodore R. Frye, 1946. Arrangers, Virginia Davis, Josephine Daniels.

"I Never Heard of a City like the New Jerusalem." Copyright, 1954.

"I Thank You, Lord." Chicago: Roberta Martin Studio of Music, 1945. Arranger, Queen C. Anderson. Recorded: Savoy SC 14104; Spirit Feel SF 1013.

"I Want the Lord to Smile on Me." Chicago: Bowles Publishing House, 1949. Arranger, Virginia Davis.

"I Want the Lord to Use Me." Chicago: Bowles Music House, 1946. Arranger, W. O. Hoyle.

"I Want to Get Closer to the Lord." Chicago: Bowles Music House, 1949. Arranger, Virginia Davis.

"I Was a Sinner." Los Angeles: MCA Duchess, 1955.

"I Will Kneel Down at the Cross." Copyright, 1959. Arranger, Virginia Davis.

"I Will Wait on the Lord." Chicago: Bowles Publishing House, 1947. Arranger, W. O. Hoyle. Recorded: Atlantic 890.

"I'll Be There." Copyright, 1946. Arranger, Virginia Davis.

"I'll Go On Through." Chicago: Bowles Music House, 1947. Arranger, W. O. Hoyle.

"I'll Never Forget How My Jesus Brought Me Through." Chicago: Bowles Publishing House, 1947. Arranger, W. O. Hoyle.

"I'll Press On." Chicago: Bowles Music House, 1949. Arranger, Virginia Davis.

"I'm Climbing Higher and Higher." Philadelphia: Ward's House of Music, 1954. Arranger, Berisford Shepherd. Recorded: Savoy 4055.

"I'm Getting Nearer to My Home." Chicago: Bowles Publishing House, 1949. Arranger, Virginia Davis.

"I'm Getting Richer." New York: Screen Gems-EMI, 1961. Arranger, Mary Wiley.

"I'm Going to Move Upstairs." Philadelphia: Ward's House of Music, n.d. Arranger, Mary Wiley.

"I'm Holding On." Chicago: Theodore R. Frye, 1952. Arranger, Virginia Davis.

"I'm Still on the Glory Road." Chicago: Theodore R. Frye, 1943. Arranger, Virginia Davis.

"I'm Your Humble Child (My Humble Prayer)." Chicago: Bowles Music House, 1946. Arranger, W. O. Hoyle.

"Jesus Is All." Chicago: Bowles Publishing House, 1949. Arranger, Virginia Davis. Recorded: Savoy 4013; Spirit Feel 1007.

"Jesus Knows and Will Supply My Every Need." Copyright, 1947. Arranger, W. O. Hoyle.

"Jesus the Perfect Answer." Chicago: Theodore R. Frye, 1949. Arranger, Virginia Davis.

"Just like an Eagle." Los Angeles: MCA Duchess, 1955.

"Just over the Hill." Chicago: Theodore R. Frye, 1949. Co-composer, William Herbert Brewster Jr. Arranger, Virginia Davis. Recorded: Apollo 221.

"Let Us Go Back to the Old Landmark." Chicago: Bowles Music House, 1949. Arranger, Virginia Davis. Recorded: Flying Fish FF-90368; Savoy 4033.

"Life Is Just One Step." Philadelphia: Savoy Music, 1961. Arranger, Mary Wiley.

"The Lord Gave Me Wings." Chicago: Bowles Publishing House, 1952. Arranger, Virginia Davis.

"Lord I've Tried." Chicago: Martin and Morris Music, 1945. Arranger, Kenneth Morris. Recorded: Aladdin 203; Savoy SL 14165; Savoy SL 14661, 14712.

"Make More Room for Jesus in Your Life." Chicago: Bowles Publishing House, 1947. Arranger, W. O. Hoyle.

"More of Jesus and Less of Me." Chicago: Bowles Publishing House, 1951. Arranger, Virginia Davis.

"Move On Up a Little Higher." Chicago: Bowles Publishing House, 1946. Arranger, W. O. Hoyle. Note: in *From Auction Block to Glory*. Recorded: Apollo 164; Spirit Feel SF 1011; Warner Brothers 9 45990-2.

"My Jesus Is All." Los Angeles: MCA Duchess, 1955.

"Oh Gabriel." Philadelphia: Clara Ward, 1955. Co-composer, Clara Ward. Arranger, James A. Jones.

"Oh Lord How Long." New York: Screen Gems-EMI, 1954.

"Oh What a Refuge." New York: Screen Gems-EMI, 1961.

"One Morning Soon (I Heard the Angels Singing)." Chicago: Bowles Publishing House, 1950. Arranger, Virginia Davis.

"Only the Crumbs." Copyright, 1954. Arranger, Berisford Shepherd.

"Our God Is Able" or "Surely, Our God Is Able" or "Surely God Is Able." Chicago: Theodore R. Frye, 1949. Arranger, Virginia Davis.

Recorded: Savoy 4017; Shanachie/Spirit Feel 6011; Warner Brothers 9 45990-2.

"Out on the Hill." Chicago: Theodore R. Frye, 1952. Co-composer, William Herbert Brewster Jr. Arranger, Virginia Davis.

"Packing Up." Copyright, 1957. Note: Clara Ward also claims authorship.

"Payday Someday." Copyright, 1958. Arranger, Virginia Davis.

"Peace Be Still." Chicago: Bowles Music House, 1949. Arranger, Virginia Davis. Recorded: Malaco MAL 6004 CD.

"Scatter Sweet Roses along Life's Way." Chicago: Bowles Publishing House, 1953.

"Shall I Crucify My Lord Again?" Los Angeles: Unichappell, 1952. Co-composer, Juanita Brewster.

"Sometime, Somewhere, Someday, Somehow." Chicago: Bowles Publishing House, 1953. Arranger, W. O. Hoyle.

"Speak to Me Jesus." Chicago: Bowles Music House, 1947. Arranger, W. O. Hoyle. Recorded: Smithsonian/Folkways C-SF-40074.

"The Sweet Rose of Sharon Is Blooming Today." Chicago: Bowles Music House, 1952. Arranger, Virginia Davis.

"Talk It Over with the Lord." Los Angeles: Unichappell, 1955.

"Tell the Angels." Chicago: Bowles Music House, 1950. Arranger, Virginia Davis.

"That's Enough for Me." Chicago: Theodore R. Frye, 1952. Arranger, Virginia Davis.

"These Are They." Chicago: Bowles Music House, 1949. Arranger, Virginia Davis. Note: in *The Garden of Prayer*. Recorded: Apollo 234.

"Treading the Wine Press Alone." Philadelphia: Ward's House of Music, 1955. Arranger, Dorothy Pearson.

"Weeping May Endure for a Night." Philadelphia: Ward's House of Music, 1954. Arranger, Dorothy Pearson.

"Whatever Else I Need." Chicago: Bowles Publishing House, 1949. Arranger, Virginia Davis.

"When I Shall Meet Him Face to Face." Chicago: Bowles Music House, 1946. Arranger, W. O. Hoyle.

"When They Crown Him." New York: Screen Gems-EMI, 1955. Co-composer or arranger, Clara Ward.

"When We Walk through the Water." Copyright, 1952. Arranger, Virginia Davis.

"Who So Ever Will." Philadelphia: Clara Ward, 1957. Co-composer or arranger, Clara Ward.

"Why Should I Doubt that God Hears Prayers?" New York: Screen Gems-EMI, 1961.

"Within Those Jasper Walls." Chicago: Bowles Publishing House, 1953. Arranger, W. O. Hoyle.

"The Wonderful Counselor Is Pleading for Me." Copyright, 1954. Arranger, Clara Ward.

DRAMATIC MUSIC

Deep Dark Waters (gospel drama).

From Auction Block to Glory (gospel drama). 1941. Premiere, 1941.

The Garden of Prayer (gospel drama).

The Rejected Stone (passion play).

Sowing in Tears, Reaping in Joy (gospel drama).

These Our Children (gospel drama).

Via Dolorosa (passion play).

W. Herbert Brewster Sr.; Bernice Johnson Reagon Files on the African American Sacred Music Tradition, Archives Center, NMAH, Smithsonian Institution

PUBLICATIONS

ABOUT BREWSTER
Books and Monographs

Crawford, Charles Wann. *The Robert R. Church Family: Interview with Reverend W. Herbert Brewster, July 6, 1983.* Memphis, Tenn.: Oral History Research Office, Memphis State University, 1983.

Reagon, Bernice Johnson. *Rememberings: William Herbert Brewster.* Washington, D.C.: Smithsonian Institution, National Museum of American History, Program in African American Culture, 1983.

Song Journey: A Retrospective of Gospel Music Composer Rev. William Herbert Brewster. Washington, D.C.: Smithsonian Institution, National Museum of American History, 1981.

Tribute: The Life of Dr. William Herbert Brewster. Memphis, Tenn.: Brewster House of Sermon Songs, Christian Literature and Dramatic Arts, 1983.

Articles

Boyer, Horace Clarence. "William Herbert Brewster: The Eloquent Poet." In *We'll Understand It Better By and By: Pioneering African American Gospel Composers,* edited by Bernice Johnson Reagon, 211–231. Washington, D.C.: Smithsonian Institution Press, 1992.

Heilbut, Anthony. "'If I Fail, You Tell the World I Tried': Reverend W. Herbert Brewster on Records." *Black Music Research Journal* 7 (1987): 119–126. (Reprinted in slightly varied form in *We'll Understand It Better By and By: Pioneering African American Gospel Composers,* edited by Bernice Johnson Reagon, 233–244. Washington, D.C.: Smithsonian Institution Press, 1992.)

———. "Reverend Brewster and the Ward Singers." In *The Gospel Sound: Good News and Bad Times,* 97–113. 3rd ed. New York: Limelight Editions, 1989.

Wiggins, William H., Jr. "William Herbert Brewster: Pioneer of the Sacred Pageant." In *We'll Understand It Better By and By: Pioneering African American Gospel Composers,* edited by Bernice Johnson Reagon, 245–251. Washington, D.C.: Smithsonian Institution Press, 1992.

BY BREWSTER

"Give the Negro a Chance." *Ever Ready Magazine* (1918).

The Old Landmark. Memphis, Tenn.: Bowles Music House and Rev. W. Herbert Brewster, 1949.

"Rememberings: An Interview Conducted and Edited by Bernice Johnson Reagon." In *We'll Understand It Better By and By: Pioneering African American Gospel Composers,* edited by Bernice Johnson Reagon, 185–209. Washington, D.C.: Smithsonian Institution Press, 1992.

* * * * *

Reverend William Herbert Brewster Sr. occupies a central position in the pantheon of early African-American gospel composers. Although Brewster's many vocations and avocations included editor and publisher, preacher, theologian, dramatist, teacher, organizer, Civil Rights leader, and administrator, he is remembered today as one of the early gospel period's most famous and prolific composers. Inextricably linked with the onset of recording and radio technology, Brewster claimed to have composed nearly 200 works, many composed specifically for traveling singing groups and famous gospel artists of the period. Of these songs, two were the first gospel songs to sell over a million copies in recordings: Mahalia Jackson's rendition of "Move On Up a Little Higher" (1946) and the Ward Singers' "Surely, Our God Is Able" (1950). Brewster songs helped to make careers for a new generation of gospel stars and, by extension, served as foundations for and standards within the soundscape of black gospel's Golden Era (1945–60).

Brewster was born into the systemic economic hardship of West Tennessee sharecroppers and tenant farmers in 1897, and his early education conformed to the calendrical cycles that governed the lives of African-American children in the rural South. Schooling took place during the months when there were no agricultural chores—chiefly the planting, cultivation, and harvesting of cotton and sorghum and of vegetables for the family table—to be done. Brewster's own education came from a combination of family tutoring and local church and subscription schools (schools that were also dependent on the local church but which used a combination of church offerings and sliding-scale pupil contributions to pay teachers). Secondary education and high school graduation came from a training school set up locally on the educational model of the schools at the Tuskegee Institute.

Brewster's call to preach came when he was 16 years old. According to his own writings and recollections in interviews, Brewster's approach to preaching and composing was grounded both in African-American folklore and oral tradition and in the dedicated study of the Bible and printed theological texts. Brewster's own story of his early salvation and preaching experiences is a study in this conflict that was to shape the rest of his career:

> I tried my best to get a sensible approach that was in my heart. When I became about ten and twelve, I had gone through the Bible. I had committed chapter after chapter, verse after verse, section after section, character after character. The old preacher couldn't do that. And he was preaching to me and a lot of things he would preach, I would know different because I had read it. . . . And all of that time I had an abiding faith in Jesus but they wouldn't accept that. They wanted me to cut up and stand on my head and jump benches like other kids who were doing that and [were] never heard from again. So when I finally reached the conclusion that the word of God is truth, that Christ is Christ and God is God, I had been on the mourner's bench so long that they thought I was a hard sinner, but I was a Christian. I had every equipment of Christianity. I believed the word as I read it. I knew it better than the preacher did. And I believed every word of it.

After coming to terms with his calling to be a preacher and getting his father's blessing, Brewster was a preacher and student in and around Memphis, where he attended a number of the Baptist religious colleges in the area, including LeMoyne Normal and the Howell Collegiate Institute, and studied theology, Shakespearean literature, theory of law, Greek, Latin, and Hebrew. After leaving the American Baptist Theological Seminary (Brewster was one of the first African Americans to attend), he studied Hebrew privately with a Jewish rabbi in Forrest City, Arkansas, and later received the bachelor of arts degree from Roger Williams College in Nashville in 1922.

In 1924, Brewster moved to the position he was to occupy for the rest of his life, that of pastor of the East Trigg Baptist Church in Memphis. In this position, he exhibited a commitment to community betterment and leadership that rivaled his commitment to music. In addition to his own continuing study of languages and literature, he began a school in the basement of his own church for the training of ministers, missionaries, and Christian workers in all church departments—and later even a medical clinic—at a time when segregation not only made funding difficult to obtain but also threatened the very idea of education for African Americans. He was active in the Civil Rights movement in its early stages, often using his songs and gospel dramas to comment on the problems and position of African Americans in the community, as in the case of "Move On Up a Little Higher." Brewster was called on to lead many early protest meetings, using music as a means of communication: "In order to get my message over, there were things that were almost dangerous to say, but you could sing it."

Brewster had an almost holistic approach to musical sound. From an early age, he could remember music being an integral part of family life, shaping and defining both the daily movements of the family and accompanying important community events. His early childhood was shaped by musical milestones: hearing his grandmother singing "Pilgrim of Sorrow" early one morning when he was about three, learning solfège and shape-note singing from his father, singing Methodist hymns from metered songbooks. One of Brewster's most interesting statements about his own early musical development outlines his theory that music can be divided into two categories and placed in two "songbooks"—one written by man and one written by God himself. Brewster remembered going out into the fields with his books and listening to bird songs, identifying and classifying birds by the musical sounds they produced:

Here was all of the music in the world. I would sometimes climb up in a tree, and get out on a limb and take my book and rest there against the tree and listen to the various birds. Then in the evening as the twilight came on, the night birds would tune up their hearts and you're talking about something! You would get a cooing of the doves, the chirping of the crickets, and you would hear the hooting of the owl. And all of those things came together; somehow or another, they blended. That was music!

Brewster's engagement with the African-American community carried over into his compositions. According to Brewster, the impetus for some of his most famous gospel songs originated with his observances of and experiences in the African-American South. His need to tell these experiences in music, coupled with the burgeoning careers of gospel artists in the 1940s and 1950s, pushed Brewster's productivity and influence to their highest levels during this period. Even after his compositional output declined in his later years, his songs remained cornerstones of an old-style repertoire that was continually referenced as the African-American gospel movement became more mainstream and continued to change and grow. Brewster songs such as "How Far Am I from Canaan?," "I'm Climbing Higher and Higher," "Payday Someday," and "How I Got Over," linked inextricably with emerging gospel stars, pro-

pelled him to a crossover status that compelled even white artists such as Elvis Presley to visit the East Trigg Baptist Church. Together with fellow Tennessean Lucie Campbell and composer/publishers such as Kenneth Morris, Sallie Martin, and Charles Tindley, Brewster used gospel music both as a musical means of worship and as a means of narrating and transforming the community.

MOVE ON UP A LITTLE HIGHER (1946)

"Move On Up a Little Higher," originally written in 1946 as a set song for one of his gospel pageants, highlights Brewster's engagement with and use of current events in composition. In addition to narrating the Christian's longing for a better place in the afterlife and the physical struggle to attain the reward of heaven, Brewster used the song as a means of exhorting the African-American community to take matters into its own hands in this life. Writing as he was at a difficult time in the early Civil Rights struggle, Brewster the lyricist had a point to make:

The fight for rights here in Memphis was pretty rough on the Black church. The lily white, the black and the tan were locking horns; and the idea struck me and I wrote that song "Move On Up a Little Higher." We'll have to move in the field of education. Move into the professions and move into politics. Move into anything that any other race has to have to survive. That was a protest idea and inspiration. I was trying to inspire Black people to move up higher. Don't be satisfied with the mediocre. Don't be satisfied. That was my doctrine.

Using a rhetoric rooted in the style of southern African-American preachers, Brewster's repetition and rhythmic setting of the lyrics place the song in the vamp, or cumulative, tradition, according to Horace Boyer. (Brewster's other early million-seller, "Surely God Is Able," provides another example of the vamp song.) A vamp, in this sense, is a harmonic and melodic section in which the music remains the same with the constant addition of new text and subtle but infrequent changes of rhythm, often in order to accommodate the constantly changing needs of the new text. In much the same way as an auctioneer at an auction, the composer uses this musical plateau to reinforce or elaborate a major point. Repetition becomes the device that causes the message to stick in the mind of the audience, becoming the strength of the performance, according to Boyer. In this case, "Move on up a little higher" alternates with a series of responses urging the listener to meet various biblical and familial figures: "Move on up a little higher/Meet Abraham and Isaac/Move on up a little higher/Meet the prophet Daniel," etc.

A characteristic of some printed gospel music is a seeming counterintuitiveness. The music looks more difficult than the singer makes it sound. The structure of "Move On Up a Little Higher" provides an interesting case of this visual difficulty and perhaps an insight into why musicians coming to the music for the first time might make this observation. Beginning with the chorus and following with the verses, Brewster arranges the song around the vamp section, seeming to compose from the center out, rather than allowing the vamp section to be improvised spontaneously, making the vamp section musically and textually the most important section of the song. The freedom given to the singer in "Move On Up a Little Higher" is not apparent from the printed page: although the vamp is physically longer than any other section, it flows seamlessly from the verses, closely following the structure of a good sermon and almost disappearing into the texture of the printed song. As noted by Boyer, the harmonic language in the song's vamp section slows to half the speed of that in the rest of the song, concentrating on tonic and dominant chords.

Brewster's songs are usually not harmonically difficult, using mostly tonic, dominant, and subdominant chords and written in the keys of C, F, B-flat, E-flat, and A-flat. Scholars have often stated that Brewster was primarily a lyricist, a point that Brewster himself reiterated on numerous occasions. In "Move On Up a Little Higher," however, we see that Brewster the lyricist paid close attention both to the needs and wants of the singers for whom he was writing and to the small musical details that made his melodies interesting. The melody frequently uses the Mixolydian mode rather than the major scale and has this small inflection printed in the original 1946 version of the song. In other words, working closely with singers and with his own knowledge of musical style, Brewster writes the structural nonchord tone that characterizes the Mixolydian mode (e-flat in the song's key of F major) in the places where it might characteristically be altered from e by the singer.

Mahalia Jackson's 1946 recording of "Move On Up a Little Higher" carries the distinction of being the first gospel recording to become a million seller, breaking that mark in 1947 after finding a wide crossover audience. Interestingly, the popularity of the song and the ownership conferred on Jackson by Brewster and by her enormous hit recording of it (Jackson also claims authorship, though the song is copyrighted to Brewster) prompted Brewster to compose "I'm Climbing Higher and Higher" for the Statesman Brother Quartet of Georgia: "It was a follow-up to 'Move On Up a Little Higher,' because Mahalia had taken it. They tried to get me to do something about it, but I said, 'I can't do that to Mahalia; if she wants it, let her take it, I can write a thousand.'"

FAITH THAT MOVES MOUNTAINS (1954)

Brewster the scholar and lyricist shows through in a genre of gospel songs in which he excelled and for which he is known, a style Boyer calls recitative and aria. Brewster often related his use of language in his sermons and his compositions to the natural flow of ordinary conversation: "I had a natural inclination toward oratory. I was trained like that. I still can't drop it all. I would divide my sermon up to include the practical side. But when I got ready to glorify God, everything from alpha to omega could be thrown in. If it's a flower, then let it bloom."

The structure of "Faith That Moves Mountains," an excellent example of Brewster's recitative and aria form, illustrates this divide. The basic form stresses a slower, often more serious section at the beginning of the song (the recitative), which gives way to a much faster, lighter chorus section (the aria). The choruses in Brewster's recitative and aria songs, however, usually contain more serious material and often continue and expand on the message or story of the recitative.

The recitative of "Faith That Moves Mountains" illustrates some basic principles of oratory often found in African-American religious practice. Supported by simple tonic and dominant chords in the key of C, the music is written in an unmetered and unpulsed style with the tempo designation "Very Slow." Characteristic of this style is the use of held tones, indicated by fermatas in the music, which allow the singer to melodically embellish these tones, illuminating or musically explaining the meaning of the text. This section is presented in a chant-like reciting style, referencing the old Baptist lining hymns that formed part of the musical landscape of Brewster's childhood. Rhythmic alteration and augmentation give the recitative a personal signature, linking the singer and the composer in an interactive creative process that is analogous to the processes of conversation.

Harmonic analysis of the chorus parts in the recitative section shows basic progressions of $I–vi^6–(IV)–V^7–I$ in two parallel halves, with the dominant seventh chord serving as a central connection for the two halves.

Brewster's "glorifying" section—the chorus—which is actually a ternary form within the larger song itself, introduces two new tempos and two new textual ideas. Chorus I begins a new, faster tempo and, more important, the metered section of the song. Although the harmonic language continues to mirror the basic progression of the recitative, Brewster uses chromaticism in the bass line to emphasize a momentary shift to minor (the raised dominant diminished seventh chord leads to the vi chord at the penultimate beat of the chorus's second phrase). The text, exhorting the believer to move through life by faith, leads directly into the second chorus.

Chorus II, taken at a tempo roughly double that of Chorus I, introduces new elements into the song. A call-and-response section leads to a vamp, linking this type of gospel song to the vamp song. The soloist begins rapid-fire declamation of biblical figures who, following from ideas introduced in Chorus I, played their roles in the biblical drama with blind trust in God, "by faith." Underneath this vamp by the soloist, the chorus keeps repeating the words "by faith," in plagal cadences, joining the soloist in a rush of naming until a final authentic cadence in the key of C brings closure. The song then returns to Chorus I, rounding out the form and closing the song.

Chorus II also introduces new harmonic territory, using an alteration of the lowered and natural third scale degree (e-flat and e) to provide color and emphasis. Interestingly, Brewster uses this technique only in the solo section, abandoning chromaticism with the return of a four-part chorale-style section to close Chorus II.

Recitative and aria form seems to be more closely linked with Brewster than with any other early gospel composer. "Faith That Moves Mountains," along with other songs that use this form, such as "I Never Heard of a City like the New Jerusalem" and the popular "How Far Am I from Canaan?" did not achieve the commercial successes of Brewster's songs in other gospel forms, but they illustrate Brewster's commitment to the written word like no others.

LORD I'VE TRIED (1945)

Brewster often composed songs in order to illustrate, within the context of religious music, points that taught lessons from everyday life. According to published interviews with the composer, one of his favorite songs, "Lord I've Tried" (referred to by Brewster as "Lord, I Tried"), came to him from experiences he had as a struggling young African-American preacher trying to hold his flock together financially. Brewster told the story of making a trip to see the banker after his church had been foreclosed, intending to pay off the loan himself to save the church. The banker refused to take his personal funds as payment, putting Brewster in an even more problematic position: "I just continued walking and praying. 'Lord, I have tried. This is your church. You take it and do what you want to do with it because I am finished. I don't know anything else to do or where to go.'" Brewster emphasizes in this story of composition that God led him to a person willing to help his church and school, but only after a number of dead ends and restarts: "God helps those who help themselves. And if you try, you can make it."

"Lord I've Tried" is composed in a form often called gospel (or Baptist) blues. Rather than the standard 12-bar formulation of the classic blues, the gospel blues form spans 16 bars. In contrast to a standard blues rhyme scheme of three lines (aab), the gospel blues uses a four-line poem (aaba), usually with a return of rhyming material from the first line to round out the form. "Lord I've Tried" is unusual in that the poem is constructed in a two-part paired rhyming scheme.

As in the classic blues, the lead part of gospel blues flows poetically over a constant harmonic structure complete with a turnaround section. Upon reaching the chorus, the harmonic structure changes only slightly, allowing for repetition by the lead of "Lord I've tried" over a more static chord progression sung by the responding chorus parts until the last two phrases, which return to the blues form.

"Lord I've Tried" was perhaps one of the first gospel blues to become widely known throughout the gospel music community. It was also the first Brewster song to have a major recorded version: the Soul Stirrers release of the song in October 1946. In addition to being a commercial success, this recording, according to Anthony Heilbut, became a standard by which gospel blues came to be measured.

FROM AUCTION BLOCK TO GLORY (1941)

In addition to being one of the most prolific composers of early gospel music, Brewster also composed and produced a number of gospel dramas. Produced for the 1941 meeting of the National Baptist Convention, *From Auction Block to Glory* crowns him as the father of this genre, according to William Wiggins. Dramatic presentations had long held a place in African-American religious expression, but Brewster's addition of specially composed music distinguished his gospel dramas from earlier models. Traditionally, musical numbers in these productions had been spirituals and hymns, selected according to their bearing on the dramatic thrust of the action and the ways in which the text complemented the script. Brewster, however, actually began his composing career writing songs for these plays.

According to Brewster, his purpose for writing these plays was multifold, but paramount was his goal of providing economical and Bible-based entertainment for his congregation: "Putting these plays on was a great help to me. It came near the time of the Depression, and people could not go anywhere. We would hold these plays for churches and give them half of the proceeds, and people would give those dimes and quarters and be there. A dime went a long way, you know."

Brewster composed and produced gospel dramas until the time of his death, using the East Trigg Baptist Church as a theater for these productions, which were held one Sunday in each month.

REFERENCES

Boyer, Horace Clarence. "William Herbert Brewster: The Eloquent Poet." In *We'll Understand It Better By and By: Pioneering African American Gospel Composers,* edited by Bernice Johnson Reagon, 211–231. Washington, D.C.: Smithsonian Institution Press, 1992.

Brewster, W. Herbert, Sr. "Rememberings: An Interview Conducted and Edited by Bernice Johnson Reagon." In *We'll Understand It Better By and By: Pioneering African American Gospel Composers,* edited by Bernice Johnson Reagon, 185–209. Washington, D.C.: Smithsonian Institution Press, 1992.

Heilbut, Anthony. "'If I Fail, You Tell the World I Tried': Reverend W. Herbert Brewster on Records." *Black Music Research Journal* 7 (1987): 119–126. (Reprinted in slightly varied form in *We'll Understand It Better By and By: Pioneering African American Gospel Composers,* edited by Bernice Johnson Reagon, 233–244. Washington, D.C.: Smithsonian Institution Press, 1992.)

————. "Reverend Brewster and the Ward Singers." In *The Gospel Sound: Good News and Bad Times,* 97–113. 3rd ed. New York: Limelight Editions, 1989.

Wiggins, William H., Jr. "William Herbert Brewster: Pioneer of the Sacred Pageant." In *We'll Understand It Better By and By: Pioneering African American Gospel Composers,* edited by Bernice Johnson Reagon, 245–251. Washington, D.C.: Smithsonian Institution Press, 1992.

JERRY CADDEN

BROOKS, SHELTON LEROY

Born in Amesburg, Ontario, Canada, May 4, 1886; died in Los Angeles, Calif., September 6, 1975. **Education:** Detroit, Mich., taught himself to play music on the family organ, ca. 1895–1900. **Composing and Performing Career:** Detroit, Mich., played as a cafe and theater pianist, age 16; Chicago, Ill., played piano and toured to other cities on the vaudeville circuit until the 1920s; New York, N.Y., starred in various Broadway shows including *Plantation Revue,* 1922, *Dixie to Broadway,* 1924, and *Blackouts of 1949.*

MUSIC LIST

"All Night Long." 1910. Chicago: Will Rossiter, 1912.

"At an Old-Time Ball." Chicago: Will Rossiter, 1913.

"The Cosey Rag." Chicago: Will Rossiter, 1911.

"The Darktown Strutters' Ball." 1917. New York: Leo Feist, 1917.

"Ev'ry Day." Chicago: Will Rossiter, 1918.

"Honey Gal." 1910. Unpublished manuscript.

"I Want to Shimmie." New York: Leo Feist, 1919.

"I Wonder Where My Easy Rider's Gone." 1913. Chicago: Will Rossiter, 1913.

"It Ruined Marc Anthony." Unpublished manuscript. Note: from *Canary Cottage.*

"Jean." 1911. Chicago: Will Rossiter, 1911.

"Oh You Georgia Rose." Chicago: Will Rossiter, 1912. Co-composers, Johnnie Watters, Bob Cole, W. R. Williams.

"Rufe Johnson's Harmony Band." 1914. New York: Maurice Abrahams Music, 1914.

"Some of These Days." 1910. Chicago: Will Rossiter, 1910.

"Tell Me Why You Want to Go to Paree." New York: McCarthy and Fisher, 1919.

"There'll Come a Time." 1911. Unpublished manuscript.

"Wake Up with the Blues." Unpublished manuscript. Note: from *Canary Cottage.*

"Walking the Dog." 1916. Chicago: Will Rossiter, 1916.

"You Ain't No Place but Down South." 1912. Dallas, Tex.: Chris Smith, 1912.

"You Ain't Talking to Me." Chicago: Will Rossiter, 1909.

MUSICAL THEATER

Canary Cottage. 1920. Co-composer, Earl Carroll. Premiere, 1920.

Miss Nobody from Starland (musical comedy). 1920. Premiere, 1920.

COLLECTIONS

Syncopated Ditties and Others. Chicago: Will Rossiter, 1913.

PUBLICATIONS

ABOUT BROOKS
Articles

Morgan, Thomas L., and William Barlow. "Shelton Brooks." In *From Cakewalks to Concert Halls: An Illustrated History of African*

American Popular Music from 1895 to 1930, 73–74. Washington, D.C.: Elliott and Clark, 1992.

Whitcomb, I. "Shelton Brooks Is Alive and Strutting." *Los Angeles Times Calendar* (May 18, 1969): 12.

BY BROOKS

"A Songwriter's Reminiscences." *Music Journal* 17 (1959): 26+.

* * * * *

During the 1910s and early 1920s, Shelton Brooks exemplified the more adventurous side of American popular music, especially the harmonically colorful and rhythmically syncopated features of ragtime music at its best. In fact, Brooks's most familiar songs, among them "Some of These Days" (1910) and "Darktown Strutters' Ball" (1917), resemble some of the sophisticated piano pieces composed by Joseph Lamb and James Scott about the same time. Yet Brooks was a one-of-a-kind figure, a ragtime composer whose music made use of strikingly modern blues sounds and a raunchy sound especially popular in an era in which people were beginning to rebel against Victorian mores.

Surrounded by music, Brooks grew up in a suburb of Windsor, Ontario, Canada, a comparatively short distance from Detroit. His parents were singers and organists. As a small boy, Shelton learned to operate an old organ owned by his family. His older brother worked the bellows because, according to Jack Burton's *Blue Book of Tin Pan Alley,* Shelton himself was at first too short to reach the instrument's pedals. After finishing high school, Brooks moved to the United States and for several years took whatever musical jobs he could find in and around Detroit. His first song, "You Ain't Talking to Me," was published in 1909 by Chicago musical entrepreneur William Rossiter. The following year, one of Brooks's best works, "Some of These Days," also appeared in print. The success of this lively number, combined with his skill as a musical comic, earned Brooks singing and piano-playing appearances throughout the eastern United States on the Keith and Orpheum vaudeville circuit. His novelty song "Walking the Dog" (1916) inspired a short-lived "jazz dance" craze, and the dance associated with it may even have anticipated the celebrated gyrations of dance sensation Josephine Baker, according to Maud Cuney-Hare.

Sometime after World War I, Brooks moved to New York City. There, and also on tour in other American cities, he won acclaim for several years for his work in a number of successful musical entertainments and revues. In 1922, for example, "The Darktown Strutters' Ball," as performed by Florence Mills in the *Plantation Revue,* made Brooks one of Broadway's brightest compositional stars. In 1924, he performed some of his own songs in the musical revue *Dixie to Broadway. New York Messenger* drama critic Theophilus Lewis singled Brooks out for praise, calling him "the bright spot in the show" and suggesting that he might surpass "the late Bert Williams, if he can find a producer who can keep him at work and give him his head."

During the later 1920s, however, Brooks's reputation and output as both songwriter and performer declined rapidly. Nevertheless, his best-known songs were recorded repeatedly during the 1930s and 1940s by Bing Crosby, Fats Waller, Benny Goodman, Sophie Tucker, Hoagy Carmichael, and Ella Fitzgerald. "The Darktown Strutters' Ball" remains one of the more familiar songs from the early years of the 20th century. In his later life, Brooks's public appearances were limited to a few "old-fashioned" shows, among them the *Blackouts of 1949,* and to special engagements before private organizations such as the Maple Leaf Club of Los Angeles. Brooks, who had continued to compose music for his own enjoyment until shortly before his death in 1975, spent the last years of his life in southern California.

Brooks, an erratic worker who improvised fluently, only occasionally wrote down the music he invented. Rather surprisingly, he wrote nothing for the stage, although several of his songs were used in Broadway shows. Moreover, Brooks seems to have drawn on personal experience in most or even all of his songs. Having toyed for several weeks with a melody he liked, for instance, he was unable to find suitable lyrics until—according to Jack Burton's *Blue Book of Tin Pan Alley*—he overheard two lovers quarreling in a Cincinnati restaurant. "Better not walk out on me, man!" the woman exclaimed. "For some of these days you're gonna miss me, honey." Grabbing a menu, Brooks jotted down the lyrics for "Some of These Days" while his coffee cooled. Another story has it that Midwestern saloons during Brooks's vaudeville days displayed signs reading "Open All Night Long." Tom Fletcher, in his *100 Years of the Negro in Show Business,* says that his song "All Night Long" may be associated with one of those signs. According to Sigmund Spaeth, "The Darktown Strutters' Ball" was supposedly "inspired by an actual social gathering attended by the composer" at the 1915 San Francisco International Exposition. If true, this story also suggests that Brooks worked slowly. Two years separated his visit to San Francisco from the publication of his best-known musical number.

Whatever his working methods, Brooks won praise for the liveliness and distinctive American flavor of his ragtime melodies. As Alec Wilder has pointed out, no one could ever confuse "Some of These Days" with "any composition emanating from London, Paris, Berlin, or Vienna." Brooks's compositions have a "vigor, novelty, and musical daring" not found in any other nation's popular music.

SELECTED WORKS

All of Brooks's published songs seem to have been composed between 1909 and 1915. All make use of ragtime rhythms and bluesy harmonies and contain touches of unexpected rhythmic and harmonic color. The chorus of "Darktown Strutters' Ball," for example, is much more highly syncopated than the choruses of contemporary ragtime numbers. Unlike the gentler music of Scott Joplin and the early songs of George Gershwin, this song appeals to listeners interested in more emphatic syncopations.

Unlike most of Brooks's other songs, however, "The Darktown Strutters' Ball" belongs to the coon-song tradition of the later 1890s and early 1900s. Earlier songs with lyrics about African-American get-togethers include Kerry Mills's "At a George Camp

Shelton Leroy Brooks; courtesy of Terry Parrish

Meeting" and, in a somewhat livelier vein, Will Marion Cook's "Darktown Is Out Tonight" (composed for *Clorindy, or The Origin of the Cakewalk,* one of the first all-black New York entertainments). By contrast, the lyrics of "Some of These Days" and "I Wonder Where My Easy Rider's Gone" (1913) are less minstrel-like in their language. These lyrics, all written by Brooks himself, concern the sadder side of life: gambling losses, disappointment in love, and other topics familiar to people down on their luck. Only words like "ain't" and names like "Lindy Lee" give "You Ain't Talking to Me" a touch of coon-song color.

"You Ain't Talking to Me," "Some of These Days," "The Darktown Strutters' Ball," and "I Wonder Where My Easy Rider's Gone" exemplify Brooks's style as a composer. The first of these opens with a touch of hoochy-koochy music, as do such "exotic" songs as "My Castle on the Nile" by Bob Cole and the Johnsons. Augmented triads over a drone bass in the introduction to "You Ain't Talking to Me" also create a bluesy mood that is quite different from the mood of most previous ragtime songs. Other blues touches include slightly surprising chords used to emphasize syncopated notes. One example of such emphasis, from "I Wonder Where My Easy Rider's Gone," (a diminished-seventh chord), occurs on the word "be" in the phrase "as crazy as can be" (see Ex. 1).

Example 1. *"I Wonder Where My Easy Rider's Gone"*

as can be
make some dough
A - bout that
I dreamed a–

Like other popular composers of his day, Brooks often used vamps or short instrumental interludes to introduce the verses or choruses of his songs. In "You Ain't Talking to Me" and "I Wonder Where My Easy Rider's Gone," the two-bar vamp before the verse is conventional in style and calls to mind similar vamps in hundreds of contemporary vaudeville songs. In "Some of These Days," however, the vamp before the chorus is replaced by three unsyncopated and rather solemn chords—a practice, as Nicholas Tawa tells us, that hearkens back to the innumerable waltz songs of the 1890s, including "After the Ball" by Charles Harris. In several of his songs, Brooks also wrote comparatively long choruses, anticipating the longer choruses of later composers such as Cole Porter.

The most striking musical feature of "You Ain't Talking to Me" and "I Wonder Where My Easy Rider's Gone," however, is the blues-like harmonies Brooks employs to give the choruses of these songs extra spice. In "You Ain't Talking to Me," the chorus begins not on the conventional tonic chord but on a D-major seventh, returning to the home key of F major by a roundabout route. A similar progression, known to musical analysis as a "circle-of-fifths"

series of chords, also appears in the opening of the chorus for "I Wonder Where My Easy Rider's Gone." Progressions like these create considerable harmonic tension and make Brooks's songs much more exciting than songs by most of his contemporaries. Added ninths in some chords also give "I Wonder Where My Easy Rider's Gone" a bluesy sound, as do sustained drones. We notice these sounds today especially in lines such as "That's why I'm so blue," but they occur throughout Brooks's works.

REFERENCES

Burton, Jack. *The Blue Book of Tin Pan Alley: A Human Interest Anthology of American Popular Music.* Watkins Glen, N.Y.: Century House, 1951.

Cuney-Hare, Maud. *Negro Musicians and Their Music.* Reprint, New York: G. K. Hall, 1996.

Fletcher, Tom. *100 Years of the Negro in Show Business.* New York: Burdge and Co., 1954.

Goldberg, Isaac. *Tin Pan Alley.* New York: Day, 1930.

Lewis, Theophilus. Review of *Dixie to Broadway. New York Messenger* 7 (January 1925): 18.

Morgan, Thomas L., and William Barlow. *From Cakewalks to Concert Halls: An Illustrated History of African American Popular Music from 1895–1930.* Washington, D.C.: Elliott and Clark, 1992.

Southern, Eileen. *The Music of Black Americans: A History.* New York: W. W. Norton, 1971.

Spaeth, Sigmund. *A History of Popular Music in America.* New York: Random House, 1948.

Tawa, Nicholas E. *The Way to Tin Pan Alley: American Popular Song, 1866–1910.* New York: Schirmer Books, 1990.

Wilder, Alec. *American Popular Song,* edited by James T. Maher. New York: Oxford University Press, 1972.

Woll, Allen. *Black Musical Theatre: From* Coontown *to* Dreamgirls. Baton Rouge: Louisiana State University Press, 1989.

MICHAEL SAFFLE

BROWN, JAMES

Born in Barnwell, Tenn., June 17, 1933. **Education:** Augusta, Ga., attended public school and sang in church choirs; Boys Industrial Institute, Rome, Ga., and Toccoa, Ga., 1950–52. **Composing and Performing Career:** Toccoa and Macon, Ga., performed in local nightclubs in the early 1950s; joined the Gospel Starlighters, led by Bobby Byrd, 1952; renamed the Famous Flames and playing R&B, signed with King Records, 1956; first single, "Please, Please, Please," released, 1956; toured extensively as James Brown and the Famous Flames Show, including performances at the Apollo Theatre, Madison Square Garden, and festivals throughout the world; recorded for Mercury, 1964; returned to King, 1965; appeared in concert film, *The T.A.M.I Show,* 1965; appeared on the *Ed Sullivan Show* and *Ready, Steady, Go,* 1966; signed with Polydor Records, 1971; scored the films *Black Caesar* and *Slaughter's Big Ripoff,* 1973; Atlanta, Ga., produced his own weekly syndicated television show, 1976; signed with TK Records, 1980; formed James Brown Productions and James Brown Enterprises, 1960s; cameo appearances in the films *The Blues Brothers,* 1980, and *Rocky IV,* 1985; continued to record occasionally and tour extensively, 1986–present. **Honors/Awards:** Charter inductee into the Rock and Roll Hall of Fame, 1986; Special Lifetime Achievement Grammy, 1992. **Mailing Address:** 1122 Greene Street, Augusta, GA 30933.

SELECTED MUSIC LIST

[The following list of titles includes only works that were composed by the subject of the entry; it is not a list of recordings that were made by the subject. Although the composer may have made recordings of his own works, the list is not restricted to those recordings but in many cases includes performances by other artists of the composer's work. The list is made up of publication and discographical data, in cases where such information is available. Although no effort has been made to include documentation of the earliest recording of the works listed, the date of the earliest recording that is readily available has been given. —Ed.]

"Ain't It Funky Now." n.p.: Golo Publishing, 1969. Recorded: Polydor 314 517 845-2 or Polydor 314 517 846-2; PolyGram 314 513 389-2; Starday-King 1092.

"Ain't That a Groove." n.p.: Dynatone Publishing, 1966. Co-composer, Nat Jones. Recorded: King 985; King 1018; Polydor 422-821 231-1 Y-1.

"Bring It Up." n.p.: Dynatone Publishing, 1966. Co-composer, Nat Jones. Recorded: King 1016; Polydor 422-821 231-1 Y-1.

"Cold Sweat." n.p.: Dynatone Publishing, 1967. Co-composer, Alfred Ellis. Recorded: King 1020; Polydor 2679 044; Scotti Bros. ZK 45164.

"Doing It to Death." n.p.: Dynatone Publishing, 1973. Recorded: Charly Groove CD Jam 1984 or Instant CD INS 5065; Polydor 849108; Rhino R2-71431.

"Don't Be a Dropout." n.p.: Dynatone Publishing, 1966. Co-composer, Nat Jones. Recorded: King 1016; Polydor 422-821 231-1 Y-1.

"Funky Drummer." n.p.: Dynatone Publishing, 1969. Recorded: Polydor 4054; Polydor 314 517 845-2 or Polydor 314 517 846-2; PolyGram CD 422 829 624-4 Y-1.

"Get It Together." n.p.: Dynatone Publishing, 1967. Co-composers, Bud Hobgood, Alfred Ellis. Recorded: King 1030; Polydor 422-821 231-1 Y-1.

"Get on the Good Foot." n.p.: Dynatone Publishing, 1972. Co-composers, Fred Wesley, Joseph Mims. Recorded: Charly Groove CD Jam 1984 or Instant CD INS 5065; HRB Records HRB 6212 or HRB Records 104; Polydor 2679 044.

"Get Up, Get Into It, and Get Involved." n.p.: Crited Music, 1970. Co-composers, Bobby Byrd, Ron Lenhoff. Recorded: Polydor 4054; PolyGram CD 422 829 624-4 Y-1.

"Get Up (I Feel Like Being Like a Sex Machine)." n.p.: Dynatone Publishing, 1970. Co-composers, Bobby Byrd, Ron Lenhoff. Recorded: King 1115 or Polydor 314 517 984-2; Polydor 511326; Polydor 849108.

"Good Good Lovin'." n.p.: Wisto Music, 1959. Co-composer, Albert Shubert. Recorded: King 683; Polydor 2679 044; Solid Smoke SSC 8023.

"Hot Pants." n.p.: Crited Music, 1971. Co-composer, Fred Wesley. Recorded: Blues Journey SSI 492; Polydor 2679 044; PolyGram CD 422 829 624-4 Y-1.

"I Can't Stand Myself (When You Touch Me)." n.p.: Dynatone Publishing, 1967. Recorded: King 1030; Polydor 422-821 231-1 Y-1.

"I Got a Bag of My Own." n.p.: Dynatone Publishing, 1972. Recorded: Polydor CF2-3004 or Polydor 2669 002 (2388 112-2488 113).

"I Got Ants in My Pants (And I Want to Dance)." n.p.: Dynatone Publishing, 1971. Recorded: HRB Records HRB 6212 or HRB Records 104; Polydor 422 829-624-1 Y-2 or Polydor 837 126-2.

"I Got the Feelin'." New York: Fort Knox Music/Trio Music, 1968. Recorded: HRB Records HRB 6212 or HRB Records 104; Polydor 2679 044; Solid Smoke SC-3.

"I Got You (I Feel Good)." New York: Fort Knox Music/Trio Music, 1965. Recorded: Duchesse CD 352061; King 946; Scotti Bros. ZK 45164.

"I'll Go Crazy." n.p.: Jadar Music, 1959. Recorded: King 683; Scotti Bros. ZK 45164; Solid Smoke 8006.

"It's a Man's, Man's, Man's World." n.p.: Dynatone Publishing/Clamike Music, 1964. Co-composer, Betty Newsome. Recorded: Duchesse CD 352061; Polydor 2679 044; Solid Smoke SC-3.

"It's a New Day." n.p.: Dynatone Publishing, 1971. Recorded: Polydor 4054; PolyGram CD 422 829 624-4 Y-1; Starday-King 1095.

"King Heroin." n.p.: Dynatone Publishing, 1972. Co-composers, Charles Bobbitt, Dave Matthews, Manny Rosen. Recorded: Polydor PD-5028 or Polydor 314 517 986-2.

"Let Yourself Go." n.p.: Dynatone Publishing, 1967. Co-composer, Bud Hobgood. Recorded: King 1016; Polydor 422-821 231-1 Y-1.

"Licking Stick, Licking Stick." New York: Fort Knox Music/Toccao Industries/Trio Music, 1968. Co-composers, Bobby Byrd, Alfred Ellis. Recorded: King 1115 or Polydor 314 517 984-2; Polydor PD 422 825 714-2; Polydor 422-821 231-1 Y-1.

"Lost Someone." n.p.: Jadar Music, 1961. Co-composers, Bobby Byrd, Lloyd Eugene Stallworth. Recorded: Duchesse CD 352061; King 743; Polydor CT-1-6340 or Polydor 422-823 275-1 Y-1 or Polydor 2391 539.

James Brown; courtesy of the Frank Driggs Collection

"Make It Funky." n.p.: Dynatone Publishing, 1971. Co-composer, Charles Bobbitt. Recorded: HRB Records HRB 6212 or HRB Records 104; Polydor 2679 044; Polydor PD-3003 or Polydor 314 517 983-2.

"Money Won't Change You." n.p.: Dynatone Publishing, 1966. Co-composer, Nat Jones. Recorded: King 1016; Polydor 422-821 231-1 Y-1.

"Mother Popcorn." n.p.: Dynatone Publishing, 1969. Co-composer, Alfred Ellis. Recorded: King 1063; Polydor 2679 044; Polydor PD 422 825 714-2.

"Papa Don't Take No Mess." n.p.: Dynatone Publishing, 1973. Co-composers, Fred Wesley, John Starks, Charles Bobbitt. Recorded: HRB Records HRB 6212 or HRB Records 104; Polydor 2679 044.

"Papa's Got a Brand New Bag." n.p.: Dynatone Publishing, 1965. Recorded: Blues Journey SSI 492; Duchesse CD 352061; Polydor 2679 044.

"The Payback." n.p.: Dynatone Publishing, 1973. Co-composers, Fred Wesley, John Starks. Recorded: HRB Records HRB 6212 or HRB Records 104; Polydor 2679 044; Solid Smoke SC-3.

"Please, Please, Please." n.p.: Jadar Music, 1956. Co-composer, Johnny Terry. Recorded: HRB Records HRB 6212 or HRB Records 104; Polydor PD 422 825 714-2; Solid Smoke SC-3.

"Rapp Payback." n.p.: Third World, 1980. Co-composers, D. Brown, H. Stallings. Recorded: Polydor 849108; Rhino R2-71003; TK Productions TK615 or Rhino Bros. R2 70569.

"Say It Loud (I'm Black and I'm Proud)." New York: Fort Knox Music/Trio Music, 1968. Co-composer, Alfred Ellis. Recorded: Duchesse CD 352061; HRB Records HRB 6212 or HRB Records 104; Polydor 2679 044.

"Soul Power." n.p.: Crited Music, 1971. Recorded: Polydor PD-3003 or Polydor 314 517 983-2; PolyGram 314 513 389-2.

"Super Bad." n.p.: Crited Music, 1970. Recorded: Polydor 2679 044; Polydor PD 422 825 714-2.

"Talkin' Loud and Sayin' Nothing." n.p.: Dynatone Publishing, 1970. Co-composer, Bobby Byrd. Recorded: HRB Records HRB 6212 or HRB Records 104; Polydor 2679 044; PolyGram CD 422 829 624-4 Y-1.

"There It Is." n.p.: Dynatone Publishing, 1972. Recorded: Polydor PD-5028 or Polydor 314 517 986-2.

"There Was a Time." n.p.: Golo Publishing, 1968. Co-composer, Bud Hobgood. Recorded: Polydor 517984; Polydor 849108; Rhino 70129.

"Try Me (I Need You)." n.p.: Jadar Music, 1958. Recorded: Charly Groove CD Jam 1984 or Instant CD INS 5065; Duchesse CD 352061; Solid Smoke 8006.

PUBLICATIONS

ABOUT BROWN
Books and Monographs
Brown, Geoff. *James Brown: Doin' It to Death.* London: Omnibus Press, 1996.
Rose, Cynthia. *Living in America: The Soul Saga of James Brown.* London: Serpent's Tail, 1991.

Dissertation
Kohl, Paul Robert. "Who Stole the Soul? Rock and Roll, Race, and Rebellion (Berry Gordy, Jr., James Brown)." Ph.D. diss., University of Utah, 1994.

Articles
Bloom, Steve. "Anything Left in Papa's Bag?" *Down Beat* 47, no. 9 (September 1980): 23–27.
Bowman, Rob. "Funk and James Brown: Re-Africanization, the Interlocked Groove and the Articulation of Community." Paper presented at the International Association for the Study of Popular Music, Havana, Cuba, October 7, 1994.
DeSilva, Earlston E. "The Theology of Black Power and Black Song: James Brown." *Black Sacred Music* 3, no. 2 (1989): 57–67.
Goldberg, Michael. "Wrestling with the Devil: The Struggle for the Soul of James Brown." *Rolling Stone* no. 549 (April 6, 1989): 36–37+.
Hazzard-Gordon, Katrina. "Dancing to Rebalance the Universe: African-American Secular Dance and Spirituality." *Black Sacred Music* 7, no. 1 (1993): 17–28.
Hirshey, Gerri. "James Brown: A Look at the High-Impact Career of the Godfather of Soul." *Rolling Stone* no. 585 (August 23, 1990): 98+.
Persson, Lennart. "The Story of James Brown: 'Sometimes I Feel So Good I Wanna Jump Back and Kiss Myself.'" *Feber* 2 (1990): 2–9.

BY BROWN
James Brown: The Godfather of Soul, with Bruce Tucker. New York: Macmillan, 1986.

PRINCIPAL ARCHIVE
Rock and Roll Hall of Fame, Cleveland, Ohio.

* * * * *

James Brown began his career as a conventional R&B songwriter, who took the gospel music of the church and secularized it with profane lyrics and elements from the blues. Typical was his very first hit, "Please, Please, Please." Most of his hits in the late 1950s and early 1960s were written to blues and gospel structures. By the mid-1960s, Brown was introducing extended vamps into the songs and complex syncopations and polyrhythms, describing this new music as funk. The changes he introduced into his music proved to be one of the most significant influences on popular music and on rhythm and blues in particular.

Brown and his R&B group the Famous Flames were signed to King Records in 1956, and their first recording, "Please, Please, Please," became a top five R&B hit and launched their career. Subsequent songs, many written by Brown, failed to bring the group any success. Discouraged, the Famous Flames disbanded, with Brown continuing on his own. (Later, Brown was backed for many years by a different Famous Flames group.) In 1958, Brown returned to the charts with a secularized gospel number, "Try Me," and once again, Brown could not immediately produce another hit. But by 1960, he began to generate regular hits, first with "I'll Go Crazy" and a remake of the Five Royales old hit, "Think." For the next two years, Brown recorded mainly ballads, notable among which was his song "Lost Someone" (1961).

In 1964, feeling constricted at King Records, he began recording for Mercury. He immediately produced the hit "Out of Sight," which suggested some of the polyrhythmic approaches that followed. Said Brown, "The horns, the guitar, the vocals, everything was starting to be used to establish all kinds of rhythms at once. On that record you can hear my voice alternate with the horns to create various rhythmic accents. I was trying to get every aspect of the production to contribute to the rhythmic patterns."

Brown rejoined King in 1965 after coming to an agreement over legal and creative differences. With the new creative freedom provided by King, Brown exploded with the new style of soul music. "Papa's Got a Brand New Bag" (which was more proto-funk than funk) was his first hit song in the top ten on the pop charts. An avalanche of hits quickly followed, bringing Brown's name into the consciousness of white America and making him the number one soul artist in the United States. Some of his notable compositions of the mid-1960s were "I Got You (I Feel Good)" (1965), which remains a part of the popular consciousness because of its use in numerous commercials, and two songs with remarkable propulsive drive: "Ain't That a Groove" (1966) and "Money Won't Change You" (1966). A ballad, "It's a Man's, Man's, Man's World" (1966), elicited several answer songs, notably "It's a Man's-Woman's World" and "It's a Man's, Man's World" by Irma Thomas and Big Maybelle, respectively.

Brown's orchestra grew with the addition of jazz and blues musicians—notably saxophonist Alfred "Pee Wee" Ellis, drummer John "Jabo" Starks, and tenor saxophonist Maceo Parker—and he brilliantly used their musical knowledge to build marvelous new compositions in the studio. A remarkable achievement for Brown was "Let Yourself Go" (1967), created in collaboration with Ellis and Starks. Said Jason Chervokas, "The song is a series of three highly arranged vamps. There are no chord changes at all, each vamp rolls over a single chord. There are two tightly swinging sections that ride on the kind of slashing guitar comping that is now synonymous with funk."

In the same year, Brown took his funk sound to a new level with a breathtaking composition entitled "Cold Sweat" (1967). Then came "Say It Loud (I'm Black and I'm Proud)" (1968), the black uplift song "Don't Be a Dropout" (1966), and his paean against drug addiction, "King Heroin" (1972). In 1969, Brown wrote and recorded several Popcorn dance records, and as his records became more radical and Africanized in their conception, his popularity began to wane among white Americans.

The year 1970 brought "Funky Drummer," which made only a minor dent in the pop charts but eventually became one of Brown's most influential compositions. Throughout the mid-1970s and 1980s—as classic soul gave way to funk, disco, techno, rap, and new jack swing—the composers of these new styles never forgot their debt to the pioneering funk of James Brown. The process of sampling, for example, in which rap performers incorporate snatches of sounds from other records to create an often dense undercurrent of sound for their raps (chanted vocals), became a force for the recapitulation of funk. Many sounds from the funk music of the late 1960s and early 1970s were resurrected. Thousands of rap records use samples from James Brown alone, and his most sampled composition is "Funky Drummer."

During 1970 and 1971, Brown at various times lost key members of his band and attracted others, at one key point naming his group the JBs. With this change, Brown's music underwent a metamorphosis, de-emphasizing horns for guitars. But the instabil-ity of his band in these years contributed to Brown's decline as a composer and a recording artist.

In 1974, Brown had one of the best years of his career, with three number one hits: "The Payback," "My Thang," and "Papa Don't Take No Mess." He also had two big sellers in the albums *The Payback* and *Hell,* which solidified Brown's preeminence as a funk composer. But 1974 also marked the last year in which Brown was known as a powerhouse entertainer, his decline signifying that soul music was receding into history. This decline was brought about in part by the complete disintegration of his band in 1975, after which his later records were recorded with studio musicians. As a result, he did not have help in composing his songs through interaction with a regular group of musicians. In 1979, Brown for the first time consented to be produced by someone other than himself, and his commercial and creative decline continued. His last major hit, "Living in America" (1985), introduced in the film *Rocky IV,* was neither written nor produced by him.

James Brown may have ceased to be a creative force by the mid-1980s, but his style of songmaking had a great influence on other artists, notably the self-contained urban black funk bands Kool and the Gang, Gap Band, Ohio Players, and George Clinton's Parliament/Funkadelic band. Jazz trumpeter Miles Davis developed a unique new style in the early 1970s, fusing jazz with the funk he heard from James Brown. Since the early 1980s, innumberable rap musicians have been inspired by James Brown's music and have employed his riffs in their music.

SELECTED WORKS

The song "Please, Please, Please," the starting point of Brown's recording career, became his signature song and routine closer. It represents his earliest musical influences and the R&B songwriting techniques he used in the early years of his popularity. Brown derived the song from an earlier blues song called "Baby Please Don't Go," which had been originally recorded in the 1940s by country blues guitarist and singer Big Joe Williams and in 1952 by the Orioles, whose hit version was the inspiration for Brown's transformation. Brown and the Flames discarded much of the melody and lyrics of "Baby Please Don't Go" and turned the song into one big vamp, similar to what occurs in the setting of a sanctified black church when the gospel song gets broken down into a vamp to rouse the religious frenzy of the congregation. Brown—who in his autobiography neglected to credit his co-writer, fellow Flames member Johnny Terry—related how the song came about: "The background vocals for ['Baby Please Don't Go'] included the word 'please' repeated several times. With that as a starting point, I wrote 'Please Please Please,' writing down the words and picking out the chords on the piano, but not writing down the chords. Then next day I taught the song to the group and worked out an arrangement by humming the solos. The first time we sang it in public the crowd went wild."

"Papa's Got a Brand New Bag" constituted the first stirrings of a new brand of rhythm and blues called funk. What made a song funk was the change in the emphasis of the beats. In R&B and soul, the emphasis is on beats two and four. But, as Brown related to music scribe Harry Weinger in the liner notes for *Star Time,* "You see, when you think of something, you pat your foot. That's on the downbeat. And you pat your hand in church, that's on the downbeat. See? So I put the music on the downbeat. And then it's on the one-and three, not two-and-four, in anticipation. That's what everybody felt. Now, right away, I got a new bag going." Thus, the lyrical subtext of "Papa's Got a Brand New Bag" was Brown's new funk music. The song was written on a series of blues changes but, as Chervokas notes, "instead of merely playing the changes, the band laid down a series of interlocking horn riffs with percussive horns, driven by a baritone sax, up in the forefront." Brown was trying to create in a recording the spontaneity of a live show, and he floated his vocals freely over the vamp and the changes. As recorded, however, the tempo was sluggish, and its time ran over seven minutes, which was unacceptable for a single release in those days. In a fateful decision, the record company edited the single down to less than three minutes, and the session tape was sped up to add more life and zip to the rendition. Here we see how two important elements in the making of a vernacular record—the process of composition through the interrelationship of the band in the studio and the post-production methods to change tempo and edit parts out of the performance—were part and parcel of a James Brown record production.

"Cold Sweat," from 1967, was Brown's preeminent achievement of the 1960s. Its composition reflects the collaborative efforts of the band at that time. Bandleader Alfred "Pee Wee" Ellis, who was a skilled jazz musician, related to journalist Harry Weinger the song's genesis: "James called me in to his dressing room after a gig. He grunted a rhythm, a bass line, to me. I wrote the rhythm down on a piece of paper. There were no notes. I had to translate it. I made some sort of graphic of where the notes should be." Ellis, who shares composing credit with Brown, created the jazz intervals in the horn section. Drummer Clyde Stubblefield devised a compelling, hesitating beat to the track. Brown took the lyrics from the 1962 song "I Don't Care" and applied them to this new creation. "Cold Sweat"—lyrics over rhythm with barely any chord changes—was recorded in just two takes. Introduced in this process was the practice in which Brown "yells" solos from members of the band, in this case Stubblefield, where he shouts "give the drummer some," and tenor saxophonist Maceo Parker, where he shouts, "Maceo, come on, now." Said Ellis, "The whole thing happened then, on the spot. The solos happened because James told them to play a solo. I didn't write any of them in. They guys looked to me when the changes were going to happen, and I got them from James." Subsequent Brown compositions usually always feature such solos.

"Cold Sweat" was unique in 1967 in that, although it was recorded in the studio, it had the feel of a live recording. But as good as the studio-created version of "Cold Sweat" was, it reached its apotheosis in the live version recorded at the Apollo Theater in 1968. In the live recording, "Cold Sweat" is presented in the context of one of the greatest live funk presentations ever recorded. Brown begins with "Let Yourself Go," segues with a vamp into an autobiographical interregnum (which was released as a hit single, "There Was a Time"), segues again into a bit of "I Feel All Right," and finally, after a dramatic shout by Brown of "hit it" to his band,

into "Cold Sweat." According to ethnomusicologist Rob Bowman, "Cold Sweat" "de-emphasized melody and harmony (i.e., no chord changes within sections of a song, near spoken lyrics) while privileging rhythm (both in qualitative and quantitative terms—i.e., employing more complex syncopated figures and using several different rhythm patterns at once creating . . . interlocked grooves). This reconstruction of Brown's music could be interpreted as de-emphasizing parameters favored by Euro-American society while privileging sub-Saharan African characteristics, in effect re-Africanizing the music."

The immediate "Cold Sweat" years, late 1960s and early 1970s, continued Brown's evolution away from conventional rhythm and blues to this radical Africanized sound, and it was always created in the studio. As Jabo Starks relates, "So many things that were done weren't written down, because you just couldn't. You couldn't write that *feel*. Many, many times we'd just play off each other, until James would say, 'That's It.'"

A typical Brown composition of the 1970s is "The Payback" (1974). Here is funk in its pure essence—declarative vocals, chanting, scratchy guitars, and downbeat drumming—and minimal singing and melody. The horns were down to one, Fred Wesley's saxophone. Brown had composed two film soundtracks the previous year and was working on another one for *Hell Up in Harlem*. In a collaborative head session with music director Wesley, guitarist Jimmy Nolen, and drummer Jabo Starks, Brown built the rhythm and vocal tracks in the studio. The lyrics were written to follow the action on the screen. In a later session, horns and background choruses were added. They took the final product to the film producer, who rejected it. Brown released the record anyway and sold a million copies.

In the 1970s, because of James Brown's influence, self-contained urban funk bands of African-American musicians and singers had begun to replace the standup vocal groups of that period, which had been endemic to the R&B scene for some two decades. In 1980, Brown updated "The Payback" in a new version called "Rapp Payback (Where Iz Moses)," which did not even make the pop charts. Such was the decline in Brown's fortunes.

REFERENCES

Bowman, Rob. "Funk and James Brown: Re-Africanization, the Interlocked Groove and the Articulation of Community." Paper presented at the International Association for the Study of Popular Music, Havana, Cuba, October 7, 1994.

Brown, James, with Bruce Tucker. *James Brown: The Godfather of Soul*. New York: Macmillan, 1986.

Chervokas, Jason. "Make It Funky! James Brown: How the Godfather of Soul Became the Father of Funk." *Goldmine* (May 26, 1995): 18–24+.

White, Adam, and Fred Bronson. *The Billboard Book of Number One Rhythm and Blues Hits*. New York: Billboard Books, 1993.

White, Adam, and Harry Weinger. "Are You Ready for Startime?" Liner notes, *Star Time*. Polydor 849 108–2, 1991.

ROBERT PRUTER

BURLEIGH, HARRY [HENRY] T(HACKER)

Born in Erie, Pa., December 2, 1866; died in Stamford, Conn., September 12, 1949. **Education:** Encouraged in music as a child; exposed to concert music at St. Paul's Episcopal Church; National Conservatory of Music, New York, studied voice with Christian Fritsch, harmony with Rubin Goldmark, counterpoint with John White and Max Spicker, music history with Henry T. Finck, and played double bass and timpani in the conservatory orchestra under Frank van der Stucken and Gustav Heinrichs, 1892–96; worked as copyist and often sang for conservatory director, Antonín Dvořák. **Composing and Performing Career:** St. George's Episcopal Church, New York, baritone soloist, 1894–1946; appeared briefly with the vaudeville troupe Black Patti's Troubadours, fall 1896; first song published, 1896; orchestra director for George Walker's and Bert Williams's *The Senegambian Carnival*, 1898; Temple Emanu-El, New York, choir member under Max Spicker and Kurt Schindler, 1900–1925; trained singers for *Shoo-Fly Regiment*, summer 1906; with Melville Charlton, helped Salem Tutt Whitney and J. Homer Tutt write the book and lyrics for *Bamboula*, 1920; toured in recital extensively, including at least two summer tours in Europe where he sang before royalty, 1896–1918; appeared with Booker T. Washington on fund-raising tours for Tuskegee Institute, 1900–1914; England, recital tour, 1908; gave lecture-recitals on spirituals 1916–1930s; G. Ricordi music publishers, editor, 1911 until retirement in 1946. **Teaching Career:** National Conservatory of Music, voice faculty, 1894–96; private teacher (composition and theory) and vocal coach beginning 1894; Marion School of Vocal Music, New York City, conducted music studio with Will Marion Cook, 1909–10; vocal students included Abbie Mitchell, Charlotte Wallace Murray, Ella Belle Davis, Carol Brice, Nell Pierce Hunter; students in music theory and composition included James Reese Europe, Carlette Thomas, Blanche K. Thomas, and Eva Jessye. **Memberships:** ASCAP, charter member, elected to board of directors, 1941. **Honors/Awards:** National Conservatory of Music tuition scholarship; Spingarn Medal, 1917; Atlanta University, honorary M.A., 1917; Howard University, Washington, D.C., honorary doctorate, 1920; Harmon Foundation Award, 1929.

MUSIC LIST

INSTRUMENTAL SOLOS
Violin
Southland Sketches. New York: G. Ricordi, 1916. Contents: Andante; Adagio ma non troppo; Allegretto Grazioso [*sic*]; Allegro. Recorded: (Allegretto Grazioso) Symposium 1140.

Piano
From the Southland. New York: William Maxwell, 1907. Contents: Through Moanin' Pines; The Frolic; In de Col' Moonlight; A Jubilee; On Bended Knees; A New Hidin' Place. Recorded: Premier PRCD 1041.

SOLO VOICE
"The Absent-Minded Beggar." ca. 1899. Unpublished manuscript.

"Achievement." New York: William Maxwell, 1905.

"Adoration." New York: G. Ricordi, 1921. Recorded: Centaur CRC 2252.

"And As the Gulls Soar!" New York: William Maxwell, 1905. Recorded: Centaur CRC 2252.

"Apart." New York: William Maxwell, 1905.

"Are You Smiling?" New York: G. Ricordi, 1928. Also arranged for choir.

"Before Meeting." New York: G. Ricordi, 1921.

"By the Pool at the Third Rosses." New York: G. Ricordi, 1916. Also arranged for TTBB and SSA. Premiere, 1916.

"Carry Me Back to the Pine Woods." New York: William Maxwell, 1909. Recorded: Centaur CRC 2252.

"Come with Me." New York: G. Ricordi, 1921.

"A Corn Song." New York: G. Ricordi, 1920.

"De Ha'nt." New York: G. Ricordi, 1921.

"The Dove and the Lily." New York: G. Ricordi, 1917. Recorded: Northeastern NR 252; Centaur CRC 2252. Premiere, 1917.

"Down by the Sea." New York: G. Ricordi, 1919.

"Dream Land." New York: William Maxwell, 1905.

"The Dream Love." New York: G. Ricordi, 1923.

"Dreams Tell Me Truly." New York: G. Ricordi, 1917.

"Eleven o'Clock (To Our Absent Brothers)." New York: G. Ricordi, 1926. Also arranged for TTBB.

"Elysium." New York: G. Ricordi, 1914. Recorded: Centaur CRC 2252.

"Ethiopia Saluting the Colors." New York: G. Ricordi, 1915. Premiere, 1915. Recorded: Columbia L. 1612; Northeastern NR 252-CD; Premier PRCD 1041.

"Exile." New York: G. Ricordi, 1922. Recorded: Northeastern NR 252-CD.

Five Songs on Poems by Laurence Hope. New York: G. Ricordi, 1915. Contents: Worth While; The Jungle Flower; Kashmiri Song; Among the Fuschias; Till I Wake. Recorded: Premier PRCD 1041; (Worth While; Among the Fuschias; Till I Wake) Albany 436 117-2.

"Fragments." New York: G. Ricordi, 1919.

"The Grey Wolf." New York: G. Ricordi, 1915. Also arranged for voice and orchestra. Recorded: Centaur CRC 2252.

"Hail to the King." New York: William Maxwell, 1906.

"Have You Been to Lons?" New York: G. Ricordi, 1920.

"He Met Her in the Meadow." New York: G. Ricordi, 1921. Also arranged for SATB, TTBB, SSA.

"He Sent Me You!" New York: G. Ricordi, 1915. Recorded: Centaur CRC 2252.

"Hearts." New York: G. Ricordi, 1915.

"Heigh-Ho!" New York: William Maxwell, 1904. Recorded: Centaur CRC 2252.

"His Word Is Love." New York: G. Ricordi, 1914.

"Ho, Ro! My Nut-Brown Maid." 1904. Unpublished manuscript.

"The Hour Glass." New York: G. Ricordi, 1914.

"I Lo'e My Jean." New York: William Maxwell, 1904.

"I Remember All." New York: G. Ricordi, 1919.

"I Want to Die While You Love Me." New York: G. Ricordi, 1919.

"I Wonder." New York: G. Ricordi, 1940.

"If Life Be a Dream." New York: William Maxwell, 1904.

"I'll Be Dar to Meet Yo'." New York: William Maxwell, 1905.

"In Summer." New York: G. Ricordi, 1917.

Harry [Henry] T. Burleigh; courtesy of the Associated Publishers, Incorporated

"In the Great Somewhere." New York: G. Ricordi, 1919.

"In the Wood of Finvara." New York: G. Ricordi, 1917. Premiere, 1916.

"It Was Nothing But a Rose." New York: William Maxwell, 1910.

"Jean." New York: William Maxwell, 1903. Recorded: Columbia A1779; NW 247.

"Just a Wearyin' for You." New York: William Maxwell, 1906.

"Just Because." New York: William Maxwell, 1906.

"Just My Love and I." New York: William Maxwell, 1904.

"Just You." New York: G. Ricordi, 1915. Also arranged for SSAA; TTBB a cappella with tenor solo. Recorded: NW 247.

"Keep a Good Grip on de Hoe." New York: William Maxwell, 1905.

"Listen to Yo' Guardian Angel." New York: G. Ricordi, 1920.

"The Little House of Dreams." New York: G. Ricordi, 1922.

"Little Mother of Mine." New York: G. Ricordi, 1917. Also arranged for SATB; SSA; TTBB. Recorded: Northeastern NR 252-CD.

"Love Found the Way." New York: G. Ricordi, 1922.

"Love Watches." 1920. New York: G. Ricordi, 1920. Recorded: Premier PRCD 1041.

"Love's Dawning." New York: William Maxwell, 1906.

"Love's Garden" (high voice). New York: William Maxwell, 1902.

"Love's Likeness." New York: G. Ricordi, 1927.

"Love's Pleading" (low voice). New York: William Maxwell, 1904.

"Lovely Dark and Lonely One." New York: G. Ricordi, 1935. Premiere, 1934. Recorded: Northeastern NR 252-CD; Premier PRCD 1041.

"Malay Boat Song." New York: William Maxwell, 1906.

"Mammy's Li'l Baby." 1903. New York: William Maxwell, 1903. Recorded: Classical Arts NR 252-CD.

"The Man in White." New York: G. Ricordi, 1917. Recorded: Centaur CRC 2252.

"Memory." New York: G. Ricordi, 1915.

"Myrra." New York: William Maxwell, 1909.

"Now Sleeps the Crimson Petal." 1908. New York: William Maxwell, 1908. Recorded: Centaur CRC 2252; Premier PRCD 1041.

"O Perfect Love." New York: William Maxwell, 1904.

"O Why Art Thou Not Near Me." New York: William Maxwell, 1904. Recorded: Centaur CRC 2252.

"Oh Love of a Day." New York: William Maxwell, 1905. Recorded: Centaur CRC 2252.

"Oh, My Love." New York: G. Ricordi, 1919. Recorded: Centaur CRC 2252.

"Oh!, Rock Me, Julie." New York: G. Ricordi, 1921. Recorded: Northeastern NR 252-CD.

"On Inishmaan: Isles of Aran." New York: G. Ricordi, 1917. Premiere, 1916.

"One Day." New York: William Maxwell, 1904. Recorded: Centaur CRC 2252.

"One Year: 1914-1915." New York: G. Ricordi, 1916. Premiere, 1916.

Passionale. New York: G. Ricordi, 1915. Contents: Her Eyes, Twin Pools; Your Lips Are Wine; Your Eyes So Deep; The Glory of the Day Was in Her Face.

"Passing By." New York: G. Ricordi, 1928. Also arranged for TTBB.

"Perhaps." New York: William Maxwell, 1906.

"Pilgrim." New York: William Maxwell, 1908.

Plantation Melodies Old and New (medium voice). New York: G. Schirmer, 1901. Contents: I Doan' Want Fu' t' Stay Hyeah No Longah; My Lawd's A-Writing Down Time; When de Debble Comes 'Round;

De Blackbird an' de Crow; My Merlindy Brown; Negro Lullaby; An Ante-Bellum Sermon.

"The Prayer." New York: G. Ricordi, 1915. Recorded: Argo 436 117-2; Centaur CRC 2252.

"The Prayer I Make for You." New York: G. Ricordi, 1921. Recorded: Centaur CRC 2252.

"Promis' Lan'." New York: G. Ricordi, 1917. Recorded: Premier PRCD 1041.

"Request." New York: William Maxwell, 1905.

"The Sailor's Wife." New York: G. Ricordi, 1917. Recorded: Centaur CRC 2252.

Saracen Songs. New York: G. Ricordi, 1914. Contents: Almona: Song of Hassan; O, Night of Dream and Wonder: Almona's Song; His Helmet's Blaze: Almona's Song of Yussouf to Hassan; I Hear His Footsteps, Music Sweet: Almona's Song of delight; Thou Art Weary: Almona's Song to Yussouf; This Is Nirvana: Yussouf's Song to Almona; Ahmed's Song of Farewell. Recorded: Premier PRCD 1041.

"Savior Divine." New York: William Maxwell, 1907.

"Since Molly Went Away." New York: William Maxwell, 1907. Recorded: Victor 64624.

"Sleep, Li'l Chile, Go Sleep." New York: Van Tilzer, 1902.

"The Soldier." New York: G. Ricordi, 1916. Recorded: Northeastern NR 252-CD.

"Somewhere." New York: William Maxwell, 1907.

"The Spring, My Dear, Is No Longer Spring." 1914. Recorded: Northeastern NR 252-CD.

"Tarry with Me, O My Savior." New York: William Maxwell, 1911.

"Tell Me Once More." New York: G. Ricordi, 1920.

"Three Shadows." New York: G. Ricordi, 1916. Premiere, 1917.

Three Songs. New York: G. Schirmer, 1898. Contents: If You But Knew; Life; A Birthday Song.

"Through Love's Eternity." New York: William Maxwell, 1906.

"Through Peace to Light." New York: William Maxwell, 1905.

"Thy Heart." 1902. New York: G. Schirmer, 1902. Recorded: Northeastern NR 252-CD.

"Tide." New York: William Maxwell, 1905.

"The Trees Have Grown So." 1923. New York: G. Ricordi, 1923. Recorded: Northeastern NR 252-CD.

Two Plantation Songs. New York: G. Schirmer, 1902. Contents: Ring, My Bawnjer Ring; You'll Git Dar in de Mornin'. Also arranged for SSA.

Two Poems by W. E. Henley. New York: G. Ricordi, 1914. Contents: Bring Her Again to Me; The Spring, My Dear Is No Longer Spring. Note: "Bring Her Again to Me" arranged for TTBB as "Bring Her Again, O Western Wind."

"Two Words." New York: William Maxwell, 1908.

"Under a Blazing Star." New York: G. Ricordi, 1918.

"The Victor." New York: G. Ricordi, 1919.

"Waiting." New York: William Maxwell, 1904.

"The Way o' the World." New York: William Maxwell, 1904.

"Were I a Star." New York: G. Ricordi, 1919. Premiere, 1919.

"You Ask Me If I Love You." New York: William Maxwell, 1907.

"The Young Warrior." New York: G. Ricordi, 1915. Premiere, 1916.

"Yours Alone." New York: William Maxwell, 1909.

CHORAL MUSIC

"Bethlehem" (SATB). New York: G. Ricordi, 1929.

"Cheyney" (SATB). Cheyney, Pa.: Cheyney College, 1929.

"Child Jesus Comes from Heav'nly Height" (SATB). New York: H. T. Burleigh, 1912.

"Christ Be with Me" (SATB). New York: G. Ricordi, 1929.

"The Christmas Bells" (unison). New York: Luckhardt and Belder, 1896.

"Come unto Me" (SATB). New York: William Maxwell, 1906.

"Dear Ol' NCC" (SATB). Durham, N.C.: North Carolina College, 1939.

"Ethiopia's Paean of Exultation" (SATB). New York: G. Ricordi, 1921.

"Fair Talladega" (SATB). Talladega, Ala.: Talladega College, 1927.

"Father to Thee" (SATB). New York: William Maxwell, 1904.

"A Fatuous Tragedy" (TTBB unaccompanied). New York: G. Ricordi, 1928.

"Greeting." 1936. Unpublished manuscript. Premiere, 1936.

"I Hope My Mother Will Be There" (SATB unaccompanied). New York: G. Ricordi, 1924. Premiere, 1924.

"In Christ There Is No East or West" (SATB unaccompanied). New York: H. T. Burleigh, 1940.

"The Last Goodbye" (mixed voices). New York: William Maxwell, 1907.

"The Lord's Prayer" (SATB). 1920. New York: G. Ricordi, 1921.

"Mattinata ('Tis the Day)" (SATB). New York: G. Ricordi, 1932.

"O Brothers, Lift Your Voices" (SATB unaccompanied). New York: G. Ricordi, 1924.

"O Southland" (TTBB unaccompanied). New York: G. Ricordi, 1914. Also arranged for SATB.

"The Promised Land" (SATB with soloist). New York: G. Ricordi, 1929. Also arranged for TTBB.

"The Reiland Amen" (SATB). New York: St. George's Church, 1924. Premiere, 1924.

"Responses for Vesper Services" (SATB). New York: St. George's Church, 1928. Premiere, 1928.

"Rockin' in de Win'" (SSAA). New York: William Maxwell, 1906. Also arranged for TTBB.

"Savior, Happy Would I Be" (SATB). New York: G. Ricordi, 1932.

"Silent Prayer (May the Words)" (SATB). New York: Congregation Emanu-El, 1935. Premiere, 1935.

"Six Responses" (SATB). New York: G. Ricordi, 1926. Premiere, 1926.

"Some Rival Has Stolen My True Love Away" (TTBB). New York: G. Ricordi, 1934.

"Southern Lullaby" (SATB with soprano solo, unaccompanied). New York: G. Ricordi, 1920.

"We Would See Jesus" (SATB). New York: William Maxwell, 1904.

"While Shepherds Watched Their Flocks" (SATB). New York: William Maxwell, 1904.

NOT VERIFIED

Six Plantation Melodies for Violin and Piano (1901); String Quartet (very likely unfinished).

PUBLICATIONS

ABOUT BURLEIGH
Books and Monographs

Simpson, Anne Key. *Hard Trials: The Life and Music of Harry T. Burleigh.* Metuchen, N.J.: Scarecrow Press, 1990.

Dissertations

Allison, Roland Lewis. "Classification of the Vocal Works of Harry T. Burleigh (1866–1949) and Some Suggestions for their Use in Teaching Diction in Singing." Ph.D. diss., Indiana University, 1966.

Carroll, Lucy Ellen. "Three Centuries of Song: Pennsylvania's Choral Composers 1681 to 1981." D.M.A. diss., Combs College of Music, 1982.

Harton-Brown, Connie Y. "African-American Influences in Selected Compositions by American Composers." M.A. thesis, Eastern Michigan University, 1993.

Snyder, Jean Elizabeth. "Harry T. Burleigh and the Creative Expression of Bi-Musicality: A Study of an African-American Composer and the American Art Song." Ph.D. diss., University of Pittsburgh, 1992.

Articles

Arvey, Verna. "Afro-American Music Memo." *Music Journal* 27 (November 1969): 68–69.

Hammond, Lily Hardy. "A Composer by Divine Right: Harry T. Burleigh." In *In the Vanguard of a Race.* New York: Council of Women for Home Missions and Missionary Education Movement of the United States and Canada, 1922.

Janifer, Ellsworth. "H. T. Burleigh Ten Years Later." *Phylon* 21 (1960): 144–154.

Marsh, John L. "Harry Thacker Burleigh: Hard Knocks and Triumphant Days." *Journal of Erie Studies* 9, no. 2 (1980): 28.

Murray, Charlotte. "The Story of Harry T. Burleigh." *Hymn* 17, no. 4 (1966): 104–111.

"Obituary of Harry Thacker Burleigh." *Journal of Negro History* 35 (January 1950): 104–105.

Overmyer, Grace. "Harry Thacker Burleigh." In *Famous American Composers,* 126–140. New York: Thomas Y. Crowell, 1944.

Snyder, Jean E. "A Great and Noble School of Music: Dvořák, Harry T. Burleigh, and the African-American Spiritual." In *Dvořák in America, 1892–1895,* 123–148. Portland, Ore.: Amadeus Press, 1993.

BY BURLEIGH

"The Negro and His Song." In *Music on the Air,* edited by Hazel Gertrude Kinscella, 186–189. New York: Viking Press, 1934.

"Some Pertinent Points Concerning Negro Spirituals." *Music Publishers Journal* 2 (November/December 1944): 26.

Collections of Spirituals and Folksongs

Bolton, Dorothy G. (comp.), and Harry Thacker Burleigh (arr.). *Old Songs Hymnal.* New York: Century, 1929.

Burleigh, Harry Thacker, ed. *Album of Negro Spirituals.* New York: G. Ricordi, 1917.

———. *Negro Folk Songs.* New York: G. Ricordi, 1921.

———, ed. *Negro Minstrel Melodies.* New York: G. Schirmer, 1909.

———. *Plantation Melodies Old and New.* New York: G. Schirmer, 1901.

———. *The Spirituals of Harry T. Burleigh.* Melville, N.Y.: Belwin-Mills, 1984.

PRINCIPAL ARCHIVES

Burleigh Collection, Erie County Public Library, Erie, Pennsylvania.

Burleigh Collection, Erie County Historical Society, Erie, Pennsylvania.

Burleigh Collection, Hampton Archives, Hampton University, Hampton, Virginia.

Burleigh Collection, St. George's Episcopal Church, New York City.

Burleigh Collection of Magazine Articles, Schomburg Collection, New York Public Library, New York City.

Harry Thacker Burleigh Memorial Center, Mercyhurst College, Erie, Pennsylvania.

* * * * *

Though he saw himself primarily as a singer, Harry T. Burleigh won recognition during the first quarter of the 20th century as an outstanding composer of art songs. Burleigh's songs display aspects of the late European romanticism that persisted through the first quarter of the century among many American art-song composers: syllabic setting of texts, modified-strophic and through-composed song forms, expressive wedding of text and tune, careful craftsmanship, increasing use of chromatic tones in the vocal line, and chromatically altered harmonies in his later songs. Burleigh's competence as a singer is reflected in the idiomatic vocalism of his melodies and the careful vocal interpretation they demand of the performer. His early songs exhibit primarily chordal accompaniments, but his later songs display contrapuntal movement in the piano that more actively engages the vocal line. As his songs increase in harmonic complexity, they demand more expertise of both singer and pianist.

Burleigh's mother, Elizabeth Waters Burleigh, who had studied at Avery College in Pittsburgh, performed art songs in Erie, Pennsylvania, musicales. She and her sister Louisa, who paid for the young Harry's first music lessons, encouraged him to pursue a career as a concert singer. Burleigh heard music by English, European, and American concert composers at St. Paul's Episcopal Church, the wealthy white congregation into which he was baptized at age two and where he was a charter member of the St. Paul's Boys' Choir. Hearing recitals in the community by visiting artists such as pianists Rafael Joseffy and Teresa Carreño and Italian tenor Italo Campanini also fed his determination to become a concert artist. The subscription lists of Erie citizens who contributed to his support when he left for New York show that by the age of 25 he had distinguished himself as a soloist in the local community. He left Erie for New York City to seek training as a professional concert singer.

His arrival at the National Conservatory in January 1892 placed Burleigh in the center of important events in American concert music. The faculty was comprised of many of the finest professional musicians in New York City, some of them internationally known. Though several of the Conservatory faculty, including Victor Herbert and Henry T. Finck, referred to Burleigh as one of Dvořák's composition students, Burleigh later reported that he was not advanced enough at that point to be in Dvořák's composition class. However, working as Dvořák's copyist gave him the opportunity to study Dvořák's scores and discuss composition methods with him. Dvořák's friendship with Brahms may have influenced Burleigh's view of Brahms's work as a standard for his own composition. In 1925 he referred to the harmonic methods of Brahms and Debussy as important models for composers.

Burleigh introduced Dvořák to the plantation songs and spirituals he had learned from his mother and grandfather, who had been a slave, and in return Dvořák encouraged Burleigh to compose. Dvořák's public affirmation of the artistic value of African-American music inspired Burleigh eventually to devote himself to "give those melodies to the world," by arranging the spirituals in art-song style. But his choral and solo arrangements of spirituals, published beginning in 1913 and 1916, respectively, were the result of his maturity as a composer. Their public success was assured not only by the beauty of the songs but also by Burleigh's solid reputation as an art-song composer, by his access to publication as an editor at G. Ricordi, and by the distinguished roster of international artists who were singing his secular art songs.

Burleigh's harmony teacher, Rubin Goldmark, a nephew of Viennese composer Karl Goldmark, was among Dvořák's composition students. A methodical, demanding taskmaster, Goldmark insisted that students master the principles of harmony in the Austro-German tradition. His own use of chromatically altered seventh and ninth chords in the style of Wagner, a Brahmsian preference for sweeping melody, and a rich contrapuntal texture are paralleled in Burleigh's mature songs.

Though he was described as a student of the folk music of many cultures, Burleigh seems not to have been in touch with the comparative musicologists of his time. These forerunners of today's ethnomusicologists examined recordings of music from cultures around the world, carefully measuring and comparing scale degree intervals, transcribing and describing the exotic sound of these musical artifacts. Rather than engage in this kind of detailed "armchair analysis," Burleigh participated as singer and as composer in the enthusiastic but only vaguely authentic appropriation of stereotypical musical gestures that suggested Arabic, Indonesian, Chinese, or East Indian music, with their exotic and often sensual associations.

Burleigh's recital career was significant in his development as a composer of art songs. He knew the song literature as a performer, and the range of styles in his own songs reflects the variety of songs a skilled performer selects in designing programs. His recitals typically began with German Lieder—songs by Beethoven, Schubert, Schumann, Grieg, and Franz—or sometimes an opera aria. Burleigh performed more songs by Samuel Coleridge-Taylor than by any other composer, as might be expected given their friendship and the impact of Coleridge-Taylor's example on African-American musicians. But in addition to the group of plantation melodies and musical theater pieces by his colleagues Will Marion Cook, J. Rosamond Johnson, and Alex Rogers, which distinguished his programs, he also sang songs by his Euro-American contemporaries—Walter Damrosch, Sidney Homer, Ethelbert Nevin, William Arms Fisher, Henry K. Hadley, Edward MacDowell, and others.

The stylistic development in Burleigh's songs reflects the tension between "high" and "low" culture as it was conceived of at this time. A number of his most popular songs, such as "Jean," "Little Mother of Mine," and "Just You," were described as ballads. A. Walter Kramer, an editor of *Musical America,* chided Burleigh for writing this kind of song. Although these lighter works sold well and were frequently programmed by recitalists and opera singers, an indication that Burleigh took the criticism seriously can be seen in his two settings of a text by James Weldon Johnson that appeared first in 1914 under the title "Elysium" and then the following year as "Your Lips Are Wine" in the song cycle *Passionale*. The latter setting (the text somewhat revised, by notes in Johnson's hand) is through-composed—a more intense, more vocally challenging song than the first, a "serious" art song. The proportion of ballads in Burleigh's output decreased in the later years as he focused on serious art songs and on arrangements of spirituals.

Burleigh's approximately 90 art songs and three song cycles, comprising an additional 16 songs, can be divided into three periods. The first eight songs, published from 1898 to 1903, are strophic or modified-strophic ballads of fluid melody, clear structure, expressive use of the lowered third and seventh step of the scale, frequent chord changes, and increasingly bold harmonic progressions, all of which were Burleigh trademarks.

The 31 secular songs published from 1904 through 1910 show more chromaticism, greater rhythmic and harmonic complexity, wider intervals in the melody, and greater variety in style. The ballad-style songs display great melodic and harmonic facility, and they often end with a climactic flourish. In this period, a number of shorter, more intense through-composed songs appear. These show careful musical expression of texts and harmonic exploration and foreshadow the songs of his most productive period, though they tend to be shorter and more restrained than the later songs.

The remainder of Burleigh's art songs, including the three cycles, were published from 1914 to 1935, the most productive period being 1914 to 1921. Beginning in 1917, the proportion of spiritual arrangements published began to overtake the number of art songs. The majority of the art songs of this period are through-composed, with the accompaniments demonstrating greater independence from the vocal lines. Wider, less predictable melodic intervals are associated with more frequent and sometimes abrupt modulation or tonal ambiguity. Extended and augmented chords show Burleigh's interest in French impressionism. Occasionally, portions of whole-tone scales or chords of the fourth appear, along with pungent dissonances and tonic seventh chords. Harmony in the ballads is more predictable than in the art songs, with chromaticism used primarily as ornamentation rather than to effect harmonic modulation.

Most of Burleigh's art songs give no overt indication of his African-American background in either their musical vocabulary or their texts. Like many of his colleagues, white and black, he set dialect verse on Southern themes by Paul Laurence Dunbar, James E. Campbell, Frank L. Stanton, Howard Weedon, and by his wife, Louise Alston Burleigh; but most of his song texts, including those written by African-American poets, are love lyrics expressing universal human experience. Among the exceptions are the four World War I songs ("The Young Warrior" [1915], "The Soldier" [1916], "One Year: 1914–1915" [1916], and "The Victor" [1919]); the pathetic plantation ballad "Sleep Li'l Chile, Go Sleep!" (1902); his setting of a Walt Whitman Civil War poem, "Ethiopia Saluting the Colors" (1915); and his last art song, Langston Hughes's "Lovely Dark and Lonely One" (1935). The Irish, Scottish, East Indian, and Persian themes common in the texts of

Burleigh's songs also appear in the songs of his contemporaries, and quite often they set the same texts.

Burleigh's "black aesthetic" (a term he probably would have rejected) was expressed partially in his insistence on artistic excellence as he conceived it. His belief that excellence in artistic expression by African-American artists could mitigate racial prejudice and bring social change foreshadowed the Harlem Renaissance, although throughout his career he firmly rejected the separatism that accompanied the more radical assertions of black pride. His life-long involvement in Euro-American concert traditions, his outspoken criticism of ragtime and jazz (though touches of ragtime appear in his piano sketches *From the Southland*), and his dislike of popularized versions of spirituals and of commercialized popular black music led some of his contemporaries as well as later critics to assume that Burleigh had capitulated to the demands of the white music establishment. This view does not account for the complex cultural background from which Burleigh's musical career developed nor does it reckon with some of the less public aspects of his work, such as his involvement well into the 1920s in training singers who performed in black musical theater productions.

Though Burleigh always demonstrated pride in his African-American artistic heritage, it is unlikely that he would have immediately concurred with the defiant tone of Langston Hughes's manifesto in his article, "The Negro Artist and the Racial Mountain": "If white people are pleased we are glad. If they are not, it doesn't matter. We know we are beautiful. And ugly too. The tom-tom cries and the tom-tom laughs. If colored people are pleased we are glad. If they are not, their displeasure doesn't matter either. We build our temples for tomorrow, strong as we know how, and we stand on top of the mountain, free within ourselves." The lyrics of many of his songs were written by African-American writers, but "Lovely Dark and Lonely One" presents the most overt expression of black pride and defiance of racial obstacles that can be found in any of the texts of Burleigh's art songs. His choice of Hughes's poem for his last art song suggests that his discomfort with black nationalism did not preclude his continuing engagement with questions of African-American identity and artistic integrity. It may also represent an acknowledgment of the intractability of racism, which persisted despite the artistic vitality which had characterized the Harlem Renaissance for more than a decade.

Often called a pioneer in arranging spirituals for concert performance, Burleigh must also be acknowledged as a path-breaker for his contribution as an American art song composer whose work found ready publication and wide public performance by many of the most distinguished international artists of the early 20th century. Though his art songs, like those of many of his contemporaries, have fallen out of use as the taste for a late Romantic sensibility declined, many of them merit reconsideration as valuable and enduring contributions to American art song repertoire.

SARACEN SONGS (1914)

In the *Saracen Songs*, set in the Persian desert, Burleigh creates a dramatic musical narrative with four characters: Almona and the three men who love her—Hassan, Yussouf, and Ahmed. The texts are taken from Frederick G. Bowles's 1912 collection by the same name. Although the seven songs do not yield a coherent plot, they relate to one another through their portrayals of vignettes of Almona's liaisons with each of the three men in roughly chronological sequence. The first two songs, "Almona (Song of Hassan)," and "O, Night of Dream and Wonder (Almona's song)," portray Almona's awakening to first love, and the succeeding four songs relate her turning to Yussouf. The cycle ends with "Ahmed's Song of Farewell," in which Ahmed rues his fatal attraction to Almona, whose beauty is sovereign in the desert.

Throughout the cycle, Burleigh uses gestures that may refer to Persian folk music characteristics or create a generalized Arabic flavor. The interval of a fourth occurs with significant frequency, perhaps referring to the particular intervallic (tetrachordal) structure of Arabic music. Motivic variations and sequences are also common (although they appear in many of Burleigh's songs). Pentatonicism and the minor mode, two characteristics often popularly associated at this time with "orientalism" are also employed, and the repetition of an ascending pentatonic "call" creates the predominant flavor of the piece.

The transparent harmony of "Almona" suggests Almona's youth and innocence. Burleigh's choice of the major mode underlines the brightness of the morning and Almona's wakening to first love. A *habanera* rhythm in the eight-measure prelude and the interlude between the two verses suggests the galloping Saracen horseman. The first half of each six-measure phrase of this modified-strophic song opens with the ascending pentatonic call, answered first by a disjunct descending sequence whose dotted rhythms echo the broken rhythm of the reined in horse. The second half of the second phrase quietly ends verse one. In verse two, the second phrase call moves to a climax a third higher than before, and the answer is extended by sequential repetitions of the tender summons, "Almona, 'tis morn, awake!" Underneath, the accompaniment recalls the ascending opening phrase, "Almona, Almona, awake!"

Burleigh dramatizes the romantic intensity of Almona's relationships with Hassan and Yussouf with increasingly intense dissonance and impressionistic color. The two-measure introduction to "O, Night of Dream and Wonder" reveals a graceful response (a rising-sixth motive) to Almona's phrases. The lingering unreality of her "night of dream and wonder" appears in the blurred tonality of adjacent falling fourths. With the realization of her new-found freedom and light ("My tent no more a prison" and "Love's sun hath truly risen"), the underlying G minor tonality is transformed to G major on "Love hath come at last!"

In "His Helmet's Blaze," Almona's agitation at the shimmering mirage of her new lover's approach calls forth Burleigh's boldest and most demanding harmonic ingenuity. An ascending series of augmented chords introduces Almona's breathless demand, a sequence of chromatic descents: "Be thou mine eyes! I cannot see; The vision dies; Who comes to me?" she exclaims in rising excitement as she recognizes "His horse's tread; His helmet's blaze; His lifted head," in a sequence of rising tritones. The melody climaxes in the cry, "Ah, day of days!" This brief "thirty seconds of ferocity and brilliance," as retired conductor James Sample has termed it, demands exquisite tuning from the singer and careful shaping so as to communicate delight rather than desperation.

In the fourth, fifth, and sixth songs, Almona and Yussouf reflect on the endurance of their love, its unforgettable beginning,

the obstacles that tested it, its passion and tenderness. In Almona's song of delight, "I Hear His Footsteps, Music Sweet," her opening "Ah" echoes the cry in "His Helmet's Blaze," but this is the luxuriant sigh of reminiscence not the breathless cry of anticipation. Once again the Saracen horse's hooves are heard in the accompaniment, and the disjunct falling fourths and the sway of the ascending eighth notes in Almona's melody suggest the nomadic movement of desert life, with a touch of the ornamentation typical of Arabic melody. In the second half of the song, she describes her love for Yussouf in images of sun and flame. The melody moves in a loosely inverted reflection of the first half of the song, creating an aural image of her recollection.

The fifth song, "Thou Art Weary," composes the still center of the cycle. One measure of rolled block chords introduces Almona's quiet welcome to Yussouf, home from the mountains. The rocking motion of her first two phrases ("Ah, my love but thou art weary, Thou hast ridden far and long") is once again mirrored in the loosely inverted contour of the third and fourth phrases of the first half of the song. Countermotives in the accompaniment create a sense of movement as she imagines his mountain journey. The first two phrases of the second half of the song echo the beginning, except that her declaration of love is emphatic, the dynamic *forte*, and, as in the first song, "Almona," it leads to a climax on "thou, most brave." Quiet returns as Almona affirms her devotion to Yussouf over lush but static chords.

In the sixth song, "This Is Nirvana," Yussouf recalls their first meeting, wondering if their love is a dream from which he might awaken. In the first two verses, which are in B-flat minor, the predominant melodic gesture is a rising fourth. The third verse, in which Yussouf exults in the reality of their love, shifts to a brighter key (C minor), then to a more triumphant one (D-flat major) for the climactic cry, "This is Nirvana! This is life!" The song concludes softly with a reference to the opening rising-fourth motive in the accompaniment, recalling the phrase, "Never forgotten that one day," now transformed to a more serene rising third, which leads to the final quiet reminiscence, "That one day!" on the D-flat major tonic and fifth.

The unintentional irony of the cry, "This is Nirvana!" which brings a Buddhist or Hindu image of perfect harmony into this Muslim world, seems to have escaped Burleigh and Bowles, the author of the verses, as well as all of their contemporary critics. Only in its most generalized usage is Nirvana appropriate in this context. But Burleigh's setting captures the intended meaning, the joyous affirmation of love fulfilled.

The final song, "Ahmed's Song of Farewell," the longest in the cycle, introduces a third, less happy suitor. Ahmed's love for Almona leads to death rather than to bliss, and the dark two-measure introduction in G minor suggests a march to the scaffold, though it is in 3/4 time. In his opening recitative, Ahmed speaks his farewell to twilight ("the hour beloved of Allah") to the Desert, to life and love, and to Almona. The anguish of his farewell to Almona is expressed in a falling augmented fourth interval in the voice.

In the middle section, which shifts to 4/4 time, Ahmed describes Almona's unattainable beauty in a passage of exquisite tonal lyricism before his anguished final lament. Burleigh chooses for the melodic motive of this section the opening phrase of the African-American spiritual "Somebody's Knocking at Your Door." As his use of "Marching through Georgia" in "Ethiopia Saluting the Colors" demonstrates, Burleigh frequently quoted snatches of known melodies, usually for their symbolic reference. In this case, however, it is the simple beauty of the melodic phrase, now in G major, presented over syncopated open chords in the piano, that makes Ahmed's description of Almona so effective. The first two statements of the motive, with the words "Never so stately a star/Rode the fair mansions of Heav'n," are exact quotations of the original theme. The third and fourth statements are sequential and varied.

The words "Matchless in beauty and grace" burst out in an exclamation that recalls the opening recitative and foreshadows the climactic "Mark, how a Saracen fell!" A sequential rising-fourth motive on the words "Perfect in body and soul" closes the verse, and a descending chromatic countermelody in the piano interlude leads to the return of the syncopated chords in the left hand that introduce the final verse.

A rhythmically extended version of the "Somebody's Knocking" motive suggests that the timelessness of Almona's spiritual and physical perfection is recognized by the heroes of the desert and by the Desert itself. But for Ahmed, the attraction is fatal, and the opening motive in 3/4 time underlies the end of each phrase ("Deserts shall dream of her face," and "Long as the ages shall roll"). The climax of the song ("Here in the heart of the hills, mark how a Saracen fell!") leads to the tortured "Love! how it stifles and kills" in a sharply disjunct line over *tremolo* in the left hand of the accompaniment. Again, on "how it stifles," Burleigh uses an augmented fourth or tritone interval in the melody to express emotional intensity.

The closing measures ("Ah, my Almona, farewell! My Almona") subside in a low range from *mezzo-forte* to *piano* over syncopated (diminished-seventh) chords in the piano before the final outburst of "Farewell!" which increases from *piano* to *forte* and is followed by a stentorian return of the opening funeral march motive in wide-spread octaves in both hands of the piano accompaniment. Then comes the final *fortissimo* cadence, suggesting the finality of an execution, in G major.

The demands the *Saracen Songs* make of both singer and pianist reflect Burleigh's study of serious art-song literature at this time and his familiarity with impressionistic and atonal harmonic practice of the early 20th century. He draws on a broad range of compositional devices to express the emotional intensity of the texts. Though he never approaches atonality, the expressive use of dissonance and non-traditional chords and harmonic progressions reflect dramatic purpose rather than conventional formulae.

In his Prefatory Note to the published score, W. J. Henderson, musical editor of the *New York Sun,* called the *Saracen Songs* "without question Mr. Burleigh's most ambitious and successful achievement." Two London reviewers quoted in Ricordi advertising flyers commented on the "Eastern character" of the cycle, which both felt was consistently maintained.

A. Walter Kramer lamented the inferior quality of the verse, but praised "the degree of excellence" in Burleigh's settings which transcended this liability. He commented that Burleigh "has not lagged behind in the onward race toward harmonic freedom." Anyone could "affect a modernistic style," but Burleigh's harmonic writing showed that he understood modern harmonic practice and used it convincingly.

The dramatic character of the *Saracen Songs* reflects Burleigh's fascination with opera and his familiarity with the works of Puccini, Wagner, and Verdi, which were being performed at the Metropolitan Opera house. Several well-known singers performed the cycle in 1915, including European baritone Christian Frederick Martens, Marie Steinway, and Marian Veryle. Kramer's observation that each of the songs in the cycle is "a *real song*" and could stand alone is borne out by the use of individual songs in recitals. Though the tessitura of the songs is best suited to mezzo-soprano and baritone voices, Boston tenor George Rasely named "Ahmed's Song of Farewell" among his "Ten Favorite American Songs," and this song was also a favorite of tenor Roland Hayes. The 1995 recording of the cycle by Hilda Harris and Arthur Woodley now makes all of the songs accessible to listeners.

ETHIOPIA SALUTING THE COLORS (1915)

Walt Whitman's poem portrays a Union soldier whose view of the war and of the world is suddenly transformed. Marching through the Carolinas in General Sherman's army, he meets an elderly slave woman who gives a human face and a life story to "Ethiopia," the anonymous race of Africans in America whose humanity he has not confronted before. Until their meeting, going off to war has consisted of color and excitement, the flourishes of fifes and drums, an adventure, an initiation into manhood. Similarly, for the woman, the progress of the soldiers from the North signals cataclysmic change in her world. She stands by the road throughout the day to greet them, and when the solider stops to talk with her, she recounts her memories of being captured by slave-catchers more than a century before, and brought from Africa to a lifetime of slavery in the South.

Burleigh's setting enhances the emotional depth in Whitman's portrayal of the profound effect that their meeting has on both characters. With his singer's love for opera, he creates a small operatic scene, weaving a series of motives that enrich the dramatic texture.

The army's march through the Carolina forest is portrayed in the introduction's beat of dissonant chords, over which a descending chord progression in the right hand introduces the soldier's angular pentatonic query in D minor: "Who are you, dusky woman, so ancient, hardly human, With your woolly white and turbaned head, and bare boney feet?" At the end of the second phrase ("Why rising by the roadside here do you the colors greet?"), the first snatches of Henry Clay Work's Civil War song "Marching through Georgia" break out over the marching chord ostinato, the bright C-sharp major motive suggesting the vivid, hypnotic call of the military parade. But as the soldier muses on his question again ("Who are you, dusky woman?"), Burleigh prepares for the soldier's epiphany in his harmonically unstable setting of the aside, "'Tis while our army lines Carolina's sands and pines." He moves through several major keys on "Forth from thy hovel door," then builds toward a climax through the phrase "Thou Ethiopia com'st to me," and finally resolves in B major with a return of the "Marching through Georgia" theme on the phrase "As under doughty Sherman I march tow'rd the sea."

The interlude preparing for the slave woman's response moves to the minor mode (the relative G-sharp minor). But as she recalls being wrenched from her parents' home, harmonic modulations reflect the disruption in her world. The transparent harmony and melodic line give a tone of reverie to the text, "A little child, they caught me, as the savage beast is caught." After a dramatic pause, the woman describes the traumatic slave ship passage over ominous rolled chords, and as the soldier takes in the grim reality of her story, the "Marching through Georgia" motive, now in the minor mode, becomes progressively more subdued.

The opening passage returns as the column moves off into the forest, but as the soldier reflects on the old woman standing silently by the road throughout the day, his perception has changed. Underlying the phrase "No further does she say, but lingering all the day," the chords in the right hand suggest the solemnity of a spiritual, while the marching chords and the martial motive in the left hand are muted. Though some of the word choices in Whitman's description of the slave woman connote the comic or the grotesque, there is in the music a suggestion that in the soldier's mind she has taken on the image of a queen reviewing her troops: "Her high-borne turban'd head she wags, and rolls her darkling eye, And court'sies to the regiments the guidons moving by." She salutes the colors, the Union flag, and the union of North and South and of the races. Though she curtsies, a gesture of respect, the innate dignity of her presence is acknowledged in the return of the military flourish in the accompaniment as the tempo picks up and the volume increases.

In the concluding section, the soldier wrestles with the questions raised by his encounter with this "fateful woman," and Burleigh's setting dramatizes his struggle with tremolo chords in the accompaniment. Over subdued chords in the final lines, he reflects thoughtfully on her story: "Are the things so strange and marvelous you see, or have seen?" By using the same descending minor-seventh interval in the concluding repetition of the phrase "or have seen," that he used for "sundered" in her account ("From my parents sundered"), Burleigh recalls the poignant reality which the soldier cannot escape. The song ends very quietly as the army moves off into the forest, the fife and the drums a distant echo.

This setting of Whitman's poem, published by G. Ricordi in 1915, was premiered by Herbert Witherspoon, whose performance was noted by the *New York Times,* the *Musical Courier,* and by A. Walter Kramer of *Musical America.* The *Times* commented that the song was "artistically conceived and skillfully executed" and that Witherspoon "sang it with a pathos that rang through with a poignant intensity." Kramer's review praised Burleigh's effective musical portrayal of the poem and the heroic scope of the setting: "The song is symphonically developed. . . . There are not a hundred pages by this country's composers that can rank with the final section beginning 'Are the things so strange.'" Later comments by Hiram K. Moderwell of the *Boston Evening Transcript* suggest that few of Burleigh's colleagues were attempting this dramatic, declamatory style: "The robust spirit that dictated 'Ethiopia Saluting the Colors' is one that is much needed to lift American song-literature from the deadly average of mediocrity which now holds it fast." Herbert Witherspoon, to whom the work was dedicated, listed it as one of his "Ten Favorite American Songs" in a survey by *Musical America.*

A favorite among basses and baritones, "Ethiopia Saluting the Colors" was recorded by bass Norman Allin in 1925 and by bass Eugene Brice in 1956. Two recent compact disc recordings are by mezzo-soprano Hilda Harris and by bass Oral Moses.

LITTLE MOTHER OF MINE (1917)

"Little Mother of Mine," published in 1917, exemplifies the ballads among Burleigh's output, which were among the most popular of his secular songs. It is a strophic song with an identical melodic setting of the two verses except for the final repetition of the phrase "O little mother of mine!" This short coda provides a climactic closure to the otherwise subdued, lyrical presentation. There is no refrain or contrasting middle section as is common in some other ballads. The author of the poem was confirmed as George S. Brengle, although the first sheet music publication attributed the text to Walter H. Brown, as did early pressings of John McCormack's recording (corrected in later pressings).

Even in the ballads, as this song illustrates, Burleigh rarely wrote an identical piano accompaniment to succeeding verses of a strophic song. Although in most cases the chords are repeated in corresponding measures of the second verse, varied spelling and spacing and somewhat thicker texture of the chords create a sense of progression. Where Burleigh departs from this pattern, it is with expressive intent. The text of the first verse recalls the mother singing quiet evening lullabies to her young son. In the second verse her son is changed; he is a man ("You'd hardly know that he was the lad You lull'd with your slumber song"). However, his love for his mother has not changed, and the harmony in the last half of the verse is also unchanged at the point at which the final cadence of the verse prepares for the four-measure coda.

Burleigh's settings of even the simplest melodies, including folk songs from other countries and from his African-American heritage, display active harmonic movement. Nearly every succeeding measure moves to a new chord. The exception to this pattern is significant in its sensitivity to the text of the song. There is no harmonic movement in verse one on the words "and the boy you lull'd to rest" and in verse two on "You lull'd with your slumber song." The pendular movement in the melody, which suggests a rocking motion, is reinforced by this static harmony, creating a subtle tonal reproduction of the text.

The overall melodic structure ascends and subsides in two arch-like patterns in each verse, the second half of each verse moving higher to the climax in the penultimate phrase of the verse. The predominantly stepwise movement of the melody contributes to the quiet, reflective mood, as does the half-note-quarter-note or half-note-two-eighth-note rhythmic pattern in 3/4 time, which tends to break into quarter-note sequences only in the climactic phrases. "Little Mother of Mine" illustrates the melodic lyricism that characterizes the ballads. It also has the rich harmonic foundation typical of all of Burleigh's songs, but with far less modulation, dissonance, and contrast than is common in the more intense art songs.

"Little Mother of Mine" was dedicated to Irish tenor John McCormack, who performed more than 20 of Burleigh's songs in his recitals. In 1914, McCormack used Burleigh's "Mother o'Mine" (Rudyard Kipling) as an encore, but Burleigh's songs were often listed in his programs, and frequently listeners singled them out for comment. In January 1917, McCormack sang "Three Shadows" to a crowd of 7,000 at the Hippodrome in New York City, and shortly after, he presented "Little Mother of Mine" to a sellout crowd there. Burleigh was one of the approximately 1,000 persons seated on the stage, and when the audience rose to applaud the song, McCormack urged the composer to come forward to receive the ovation. Burleigh declined but stated that McCormack "sang it wonderfully."

The *Evening Star* review of a performance of "Little Mother of Mine" by tenor John Finnegan in a March 4, 1918, recital in Lynn, Massachusetts, typifies its immediate reception: "One song was worth it all. . . . The heart-appealing 'Little Mother of Mine' by Burleigh was easily the distinctive number at the concert." In the October 3, 1918, *Musical Courier,* Francis Rogers listed "Songs the Soldiers Like." Negro spirituals claimed first position and "Little Mother of Mine" appeared among 50 other favorites. Clearly, McCormack's popular recordings helped to spread Burleigh's songs widely among the general American population, and this one spoke to the hearts of homesick soldiers in the trenches of Western Europe. No doubt those soldiers, too, appreciated McCormack's December 1919 recording of "The Victor," Burleigh's tribute to the soldiers returning from the war and to those who did not return.

"Little Mother of Mine" also illustrates the practical influence on a composer's work by the singers who made it known. A confirmed Anglophile, Burleigh was drawn to texts featuring English, Scottish, and Irish subjects even before McCormack performed his songs. But McCormack's Irish identity certainly influenced Burleigh to choose texts and song styles that he knew would appeal to his friend.

The influence of the performance of Burleigh's songs by McCormack and other famous singers is also seen in their voicing. Burleigh usually had a specific range and type of voice in mind for a particular song. In an undated letter most likely written in the 1940s to Mrs. N. W. Maise of Spelman College in Atlanta, he listed McCormack, George Hamlin, Oscar Seagle, Lawrence Tibbett, Roland Hayes, Mary Jordan, and Sophie Braslau among vocalists who "created a certain vogue for the type of songs I was writing." He comments further that these singers also influenced the voice range and tessitura of the songs he wrote: "That is why many of my songs are more suitable for tenor and contralto voices than for sopranos. I cannot imagine a soprano voice doing as good a job with 'Oh, My Love' as a tenor voice could do. 'Twas written for a tenor. I do not refer to the sentiment of the words but rather to the general tessitura of the composition."

Although McCormack helped to popularize this song, he was by no means the only singer who made it part of his repertoire. As Patricia Turner's discography indicates, this is probably the most-often recorded of Burleigh's secular songs. By 1949 it had been recorded by ten singers, including tenor Charles Harrison, baritone John Charles Thomas, and a choral group, the Yaarab Chanters of

Atlanta, Georgia, directed by Frank Cundell. The 1995 recording by bass-baritone Oral Moses is more easily accessible.

"Little Mother of Mine," like "Ethiopia Saluting the Colors" and the cycle *Saracen Songs,* demonstrates Burleigh's craftsmanship as a mature composer whose work brought him to a position of prominence among American concert songwriters and anticipated the profound impression his concert arrangements of spirituals would make in American musical culture.

LOVELY DARK AND LONELY ONE (1935)

With a text and a musical vocabulary that refer to distinctively African-American musical traditions, "Lovely Dark and Lonely One" is Burleigh's last published art song. Although his arrangement of "I Wonder" by Beatrice Fenner was published in 1940, no post-1935 art songs by Burleigh have been identified. By this time, Burleigh had been publishing arrangements of spirituals in art-song style for nearly 20 years and singing them in his recitals for 30, but few of his art songs reflect his African-American musical heritage. Even in his earliest songs, he sometimes used melodic and harmonic gestures that are today associated with jazz or blues performance, such as the lowered third and seventh steps of the scale, but he seemed to use these as expressive choices among a broad palette of tonal effects rather than to identify his work as African American. In "Lovely Dark and Lonely One," however, Burleigh moves to a new level in his integration of African-American and Euro-American musical vocabularies.

Despite Burleigh's lack of interest in the blues or in jazz as a means of personal expression, in his setting of "Lovely Dark and Lonely One," references to blues harmony reinforce the ironic sensibility of Hughes's poem. This is not a traditional blues lyric, and Burleigh makes no attempt to parallel the blues in form, meter, or chord progression; but he builds the harmonic and melodic structure on a succession of seventh and ninth chords that suggest blues harmony. This rich harmonic texture is combined with motivic gestures in the accompaniment, which create additional layers of expressive symbolism.

The first gesture is a rising interval of a sixth, which appears twice in the first measure: in the upper line in the left hand, anticipating and overlapping the prominent sixth in the right hand, which becomes the opening of a four-note melodic pattern with a falling *appoggiatura* on the first beat of the second measure. The rising sixth suggests aspiration, or reaching sunward, in the phrases "Bare your bosom to the golden sun" and "Open wide your arms to life." This motive reappears at the end of the song, this time with the rising sixth interval (now filled in) leading to the grace note (*appoggiatura*) in the penultimate measure and with the rising interval echoed in the left hand in contrary motion to the falling notes in the right hand.

In measures three and four, a three-note ascending chromatic motive in the inner right-hand voice of the accompaniment becomes the impetus for the singer's second melodic phrase, which rises stepwise on the words "Bare your bosom to the golden sun" from the fifth of the scale to the tonic and skips to the upper third step of the scale before resolving downward.

The tension in Hughes's poem between aspiration and the obstacles to its fulfillment is reflected in Burleigh's setting. Even the brightness of the open C-major chord on the phrase "Open wide your arms to life" is tempered by the lowered last note of the phrase, which prepares for the shift to a D-flat major tonality on "Whirl in the wind of pain and strife." The opening rising sixth motive in the accompaniment ends with a falling two-note gesture that creates a suspension (a delay in the resolution of tension in the harmony). This pattern is echoed throughout the song as the impulse sunward is countered by falling motives and suspensions, suggesting obstacles that test aspiration and delays that demand courage and persistence.

A third motive is introduced in the upper left-hand line on "afraid of light"; it parallels the voice at the interval of a sixth but creates a suspension at the end of the phrase. This pattern is repeated on "a child of right." In the following measure, on "Open wide your arms to life," the top-most line in the right-hand accompaniment introduces a related, four-note descending countermelodic motive, which is repeated, first at the octave, then in the new key of "Whirl in the wind of pain and strife."

The *molto expressivo* two-measure interlude in the piano leads to a series of suspensions that underlie the two repetitions of the word "wait," acting out and intensifying the meaning of the word. But embedded in the same measure as the final repetition of the word is the rising-sixth interval in the left hand, anticipating the return of the earlier challenge to "Open wide your arms to life." This time the melodic phrase with its melismatic flourish recalls the first phrase of the text, "Lovely dark and lonely one," which now functions as a closing refrain. The upper voice of the right-hand accompaniment repeats the falling four-note motive with its suspension, while the left hand begins each of the two measures with the ascending sixth interval, expressing both the buoyant hope and the persistent need for endurance in spite of the delayed realization of the dream. Burleigh's setting emphasizes the inherent paradox in Hughes's poem—the call to tenacious aspiration and the recognition that the dream may be deferred. The final phrase, "Bare your bosom to the sun," ascends stepwise in the vocal line through the interval of a sixth to the third step of the scale, an open-ended gesture echoed in the accompaniment. By concluding the song on the third step of the scale rather than on the tonic, Burleigh demonstrates the perpetual challenge and the unlimited potential in reaching for the sun.

Neither Hughes's poem nor Burleigh's setting employs stereotypical blues formulae in poetic verse form or harmonic progression, but both embody the emotional essence, the "existential tension," of the blues. In his autobiography, W. C. Handy quotes Burleigh as saying that the blues and the spirituals are "first cousins." Perhaps in this song Burleigh, who considered his arrangements of spirituals his most important work, comes closer to Cone's view that "the blues and the spirituals flow from the same bedrock of experience, and neither is an adequate interpretation of black life without the commentary of the other."

The persona addressed in the poem is invited in frankly sensual terms to "bare your bosom to the sun," to step forward naked to the light, absorbing the energy of the sun, reaching for the unattainable. In Burleigh's earlier settings (e.g., the *Saracen Songs*), sensuality is often expressed through an exotic sensibility. In Hughes's poem, the physical gesture, though natural and earthy, is

not seductive but defiantly vulnerable, a paradoxical triumph through surrender, accepting the inevitability of pain, claiming hope through persistent struggle. "Lovely Dark and Lonely One" represents both a culmination of Burleigh's development as a composer and a shift toward a clearer self-definition than in many of his earlier songs. The understated but cogent musical insight in Burleigh's setting suggests that his choice of this poem at the end of his career as an art-song composer serves as his own manifesto. Here, at age 69, he seems prepared to embrace and to declare his African-American identity in a more assertive tone through the medium of art song, claiming his ultimate identity as an African-American singer-composer.

REFERENCES

Aborn, Merton Robert. "The Influence on American Musical Culture of Dvorak's Sojourn in America." Ph.D. diss., Indiana University, 1965.

daBubna, Augusta. "The Negro on the Stage." *Theatre Magazine* 4 (April 1903): 96–98.

Burleigh, Harry T. Letter to Mrs. N. W. Maise. Private collection in the hands of Harry T. Burleigh II.

Cone, James H. *The Spirituals and the Blues.* New York: Seabury Press, 1972.

Duberman, Martin Bauml. *Paul Robeson.* New York: Alfred A. Knopf, 1988.

Evening Star. (March 5, 1918).

Finck, Henry T. *My Adventures in the Golden Age of Music.* New York: Funk and Wagnalls, 1926.

Gray, Leon Wilbur. "The American Art Song: An Inquiry into Its Development from the Colonial Period to the Present." 2 vols. Ed.D. diss., Columbia University, 1967.

Handy, W. C. *Father of the Blues: An Autobiography.* New York: Macmillan, 1941.

Henderson, W. J. "Prefatory Note" to *Saracen Songs* by Harry T. Burleigh. New York: G. Ricordi, 1914.

Hughes, Langston. "The Negro Artist and the Racial Mountain." *Nation* (June 23, 1926): 692–694.

Huneker, James. *Steeplejack.* New York: Charles Scribner's Sons, 1920.

James Weldon Johnson Manuscript Collection. Beinecke Library, Yale University.

Janifer, Ellsworth. "Harry T. Burleigh, Ten Years Later." *Phylon* 21 (1960): 144–154.

Kramer, A. Walter. "H. T. Burleigh: Composer by Divine Right and 'The American Coleridge-Taylor.'" *Musical America* (April 29, 1916): 25.

———. *Musical America* (August 8, 1914).

Moderwell, Hiram K. "'Deep River' Popularizes a Composer: The Rise and Progress of Harry T. Burleigh through His Negro Melodies into the Large Vogue of Song Recitals." *Boston Evening Transcript.* (March 10, 1917). Reprinted in *Black Perspective in Music* 2, no. 1 (1974): 75–79.

Musical America (October 16, 1915).

———. (November 20, 1915).

"New York Church Pays Tribute to Burleigh." *Musical America* (April 12, 1924): 21, 27.

New York Times (November 24, 1915).

Rogers, Francis. *Musical Courier* (October 3, 1918).

Sample, James. Personal communication. Meadville, Pa. April 10, 1991.

Simpson, Anne Kay. *Hard Trials: The Life and Music of Harry T. Burleigh.* Metuchen, N.J.: Scarecrow Press, 1990.

Snyder, Jean E. "Harry T. Burleigh and the Creative Expression of Bi-musicality: A Study of an African-American Composer and the American Art Song." Ph.D. diss., University of Pittsburgh, 1992.

"'Sweet Chariot' Inspired Anton Dvorak to Immortalize Negro Spirituals." *New York World Telegram* (Sept. 12, 1941).

Tomatz, D. "Rubin Goldmark, Post Romantic: Trial Balances in American Music." Ph.D. diss., Catholic University of America, 1966.

Turner, Patricia. *Dictionary of Afro-American Performers: 78 rpm and Cylinder Recordings of Opera, Choral Music and Song, c. 1900–1949.* New York: Garland, 1990.

Waters, Edward M. *Victor Herbert: A Life in Music.* New York: Macmillan, 1955.

JEAN E. SNYDER

CAMPBELL, LUCIE

Born in Duck Hill, Miss., April 30, 1885; died in Nashville, Tenn., January 3, 1963. **Education:** Memphis, Tenn., public schools; Kortrecht High School, Memphis, graduated, 1899; Rust College, Holly Springs, Miss., 1912–27, B.A., 1927; graduate work at the University of Chicago, Columbia University Teacher's College, New York, N.Y., Tennessee A&I College, Nashville; Tennessee State University, Nashville, M.A., 1951. **Teaching Career:** Carnes Grammar School, Memphis, 1899–1911; Booker T. Washington High School, Memphis, 1911–54; Women's Convention, Auxiliary of the Tennessee State Regulated Baptist Missionary and Education Convention, 1948–54; Tennessee A&I State College, Extension School Branch, beginning in 1951. **Composing and Performing Career:** National Sunday School and Baptist Young People's Union of the National Baptist Convention, music director, 1916–63; first composition, "Something Within," published, 1919; regularly introduced her compositions at the National Baptist Convention; "He Understands, He'll Say, 'Well Done,'" published, 1933. **Memberships:** Tennessee Educational Conference, president, 1941–46; Tennessee State Association of Teachers in Colored Schools, president, 1941–46; American Teacher's Association, vice president, 1944–45; National Policies Planning Commission of the National Educational Administration, consultant, 1946–56; Bluff County Teacher's League, president; National Baptist Choral Society, president; National Baptist Music Convention, vice president; Tennessee Negro Educational Association, president; Tennessee State Teacher's Association, president; West Tennessee Educational Congress, president. **Honors/Awards:** Received numerous awards from the National Baptist Convention; Alpha Phi Alpha Woman of the Year Award, 1957.

MUSIC LIST

COLLECTIONS

Lucie E. Campbell's Soul-Stirring Songs for All Religious Occasions: Sixty-four Pages of Soul-Stirring Songs as Sung and Recorded by National Singers. Memphis, Tenn.: L. E. Campbell and E.W.D. Isaac, 1952.

SONGS

[The following list of titles includes only works that were composed by the subject of the entry; it is not a list of recordings that were made by the subject. Although the composer may have made recordings of her own works, the list is not restricted to those recordings but in many cases includes performances by other artists of the composer's work. The list is made up of publication and discographical data, in cases where such information is available. —Ed.]

"Are They Equal in the Eyes of the Law?" Memphis, Tenn.: Campbell and Williams, 1919.

"Awake! for Thy God Reigneth." Copyright, 1949. Memphis, Tenn.: Lucie E. Campbell, n.d.

"Come, Lord Jesus, Abide with Me." Copyright, 1962. Memphis, Tenn.: Campbell and Williams, 1963.

"Come Ye Blessed of My Father." Memphis, Tenn.: Campbell and Williams, 1958.

"Even a Child Can Open the Gate." Memphis, Tenn.: Campbell and Williams, 1952.

"Footprints of Jesus." 1949. Memphis, Tenn.: Lucie E. Campbell, 1949. Recorded: Savoy MG-14038.

"God's Long Reach of Salvation." Memphis, Tenn.: Campbell and Williams, 1958.

"Going up the King's Highway" or "The King's Highway." Copyright, 1923. Memphis, Tenn.: Campbell and Williams, n.d. In *Inspirational Melodies* (Nashville, Tenn.: National BYPU Board, 1923).

"He Understands, He'll Say, 'Well Done.'" Copyright, 1933. Memphis, Tenn.: Campbell and Williams, 1950. Recorded: Savoy MG-14038; Smithsonian/Folkways C-SF-40074; Spirit Feel SF 1013; Vanguard R 923/CS.

"Heavenly Sunshine." Memphis, Tenn.: Campbell and Williams, 1923.

"His Grace Is Sufficient for Me." Memphis, Tenn.: Campbell and Williams, 1956.

"Holy Three in One." Memphis, Tenn.: Campbell and Williams, 1947.

"I Know I Won't Stop Singing (Jordan)." Memphis, Tenn.: Campbell and Williams, n.d.

"I Need Thee, Precious Lord." Copyright, 1948. Memphis, Tenn.: Campbell and Williams, 1949.

"I Want to Be Ready to Put on My Gospel Shoes." Copyright, 1940.

"In the Upper Room with Jesus." Copyright, 1946. Memphis, Tenn.: Campbell and Williams, 1947. Recorded: Musica Jazz 2MJP-1026; Savoy MG-14038; Shanachie/Spirit Feel 6011.

"Is He Yours." Copyright, 1933. Memphis, Tenn.: Campbell and Williams, n.d.

"Jesus Gave Me Water." Copyright, 1946. Memphis, Tenn.: Campbell and Williams, 1950. Recorded: Savoy MG-14038; Specialty SPC-2137.

"Jesus, Keep Me Humble." Memphis, Tenn.: Campbell and Williams, n.d.

"Just as I Am." Memphis, Tenn.: Campbell and Williams, 1947.

"Just to Behold His Face." Memphis, Tenn.: Campbell and Williams, 1941. Recorded: Savoy MG-14038.

"Look Away into Heaven." In *Spirituals Triumphant Old and New* (Nashville, Tenn.: Sunday School Publishing Board, National Baptist Convention, 1927).

"Looking to Jesus." Memphis, Tenn.: Campbell and Williams, 1947. Recorded: Savoy MG-14038.

"The Lord Is My Shepherd." Copyright, 1919. Memphis, Tenn.: Campbell and Williams, n.d. In *Gospel Pearls* (Nashville, Tenn.: Sunday School Publishing Board, National Baptist Convention, U.S.A., 1921).

"The Lord's Prayer." Memphis, Tenn.: L. E. Campbell, 1947.

"Love and Not Nails Held Him There." Memphis, Tenn.: Campbell and Williams, 1960.

"My Lord and I (on the Heavenly Road)." 1947. Memphis, Tenn.: Campbell and Williams, 1947. Recorded: Savoy MG-14038.

"My Savior." Memphis, Tenn.: Campbell and Williams, 1932.

"Nobody Else but Jesus." Copyright, 1923. Memphis, Tenn.: Campbell and Williams, 1951.

Lucie Campbell; Martin and Morris Music Company Records, Archives Center, NMAH, Smithsonian Institution

"Not Yours but You." Memphis, Tenn.: Campbell and Williams, 1947.

"Offertory Prayer." Memphis, Tenn.: Campbell and Williams, 1947.

"The Path through the Valley Leads Home." Memphis, Tenn.: Campbell and Williams, 1958.

"Please Let Your Light Shine on Me." Memphis, Tenn.: Campbell-Griggs Publishing, 1919.

"Praise Ye the Lord (Psalm 150)." Nashville, Tenn.: National Baptist Training Union Board, 1946.

"Room! Room!" Copyright, 1936. Memphis, Tenn.: Campbell and Williams, 1951.

"Signed and Sealed with His Blood (A Passport to Heaven)." Memphis, Tenn.: Campbell and Williams, 1962. Arranger, Lucie E. Campbell.

"A Sinner Like Me." Memphis, Tenn.: Campbell and Williams, 1952.

"Something Within." Memphis, Tenn.: Clarion Printing, 1919. Recorded: Savoy 45-4134; Savoy MG-14038; Smithsonian/Folkways C-SF-40074; Vanguard R 923/CS.

"Sometime Soon." Chicago: Martin and Morris, 1963. Arranger, Roberta Martin.

"The Story of Salvation Must Be Told (in Africa, China, and the Isles of the Sea)." Memphis, Tenn.: Campbell and Williams, 1960.

"There Is a Fountain." Memphis, Tenn.: Lucie E. Campbell, 1949. Recorded: Savoy 45-4134; Savoy MG-14038.

"They That Wait upon the Lord." Memphis, Tenn.: Campbell and Williams, 1952. Arranger, Lucie E. Campbell.

"This Is the Day the Lord Hath Made." Copyright, 1919. Memphis, Tenn.: L. E. Campbell, 1947.

"Touch Me, Lord Jesus." Memphis, Tenn.: Lucie E. Campbell, 1941. Recorded: Savoy MG-14038; Smithsonian/Folkways C-SF-40074.

"Tramping—Wanna Be Ready—Walk Children." Nashville, Tenn.: Lucie E. Campbell, 1940.

"Unto Thee, Thou Holy One." Memphis, Tenn.: Campbell and Williams, 1960.

"Welcome Chorus." Copyright, 1923. Memphis, Tenn.: Campbell and Williams, n.d.

"When I Get Home." Copyright, 1948. Memphis, Tenn.: Campbell and Williams, 1950.

PUBLICATIONS

ABOUT CAMPBELL
Books and Monographs

George, Luvenia A. *Lucie E. Campbell and the Enduring Tradition of Gospel Hymnody.* Washington, D.C.: Smithsonian Institution, National Museum of American History, Program in African American Culture, 1983.

Walker, Charles. *Miss Lucie.* National Baptist Great Personalities, no. 2. Nashville, Tenn.: Townsend Press, 1993.

Washington, William M., compiler and editor. *Miss Lucie Speaks: Addresses of Miss Lucie E. Campbell.* Nashville, Tenn.: C. R. Williams, 1971.

Articles

Boyer, Horace Clarence. "Lucie E. Campbell: Composer for the National Baptist Convention." In *We'll Understand It Better By and By: Pioneering African American Gospel Composers,* edited by Bernice Johnson Reagon, 81–108. Washington, D.C.: Smithsonian Institution Press, 1992.

Bradley, J. Robert. "Miss Lucie: The Legacy of the Woman and Her Music." In *The National Baptist Voice* 30–31 (1979): 1–10.

George, Luvenia A. "Lucie E. Campbell and the Enduring Tradition of Gospel Hymnody." In *The Songs of Lucie E. Campbell: Gospel Music Composer,* edited by Niani Kilkenny and Rebecca E. Curzon, 6–15. Washington, D.C.: Smithsonian Institution, National Museum of American History, 1984.

———. "Lucie E. Campbell: Baptist Composer and Educator." *Black Perspective in Music* 15, no. 1 (1987): 25–49.

———. "Lucie E. Campbell: Her Nurturing and Expansion of Gospel Music in the National Baptist Convention, U.S.A., Inc." In *We'll Understand It Better By and By: Pioneering African American Gospel Composers,* edited by Bernice Johnson Reagon, 109–119. Washington, D.C.: Smithsonian Institution Press, 1992.

Walker, Charles. "Lucie E. Campbell Williams: A Cultural Biography." In *We'll Understand It Better By and By: Pioneering African American Gospel Composers,* edited by Bernice Johnson Reagon, 121–138. Washington, D.C.: Smithsonian Institution Press, 1992.

* * * * *

After graduating from high school at age 14, Lucie Eddie Campbell began a teaching career that spanned 55 years in the Memphis, Tennessee, public schools. It is, however, as a composer of gospel hymns and as music director of the Sunday School and BYPU (Baptist Young Peoples Union) Congress—the teacher training and educational component of the National Baptist Convention, USA, Inc.—that her significance in the development of black gospel music has been defined. A self-taught musician, her unique manner of playing, or "plunking," the piano influenced a generation of church musicians in and around Memphis, who imitated her style.

Campbell was born on April 30, 1885, in Duck Hill, Mississippi, the youngest of nine children of Burrell and Isabella Wilkerson Campbell. Her father, an Illinois Central brakeman, was killed in a job-related accident shortly after her birth. Her mother moved the family to Memphis, where she worked as a laundress to support the family. An excellent student, the young Lucie Campbell won a penmanship award in elementary school and the top prize in Latin at Kortrecht High School; she graduated as class valedictorian in 1899.

In the first years after graduation, Campbell's outstanding contralto voice and her talent as a singer and as an accompanist rapidly brought her notice in music circles. By 1902, she directed music at the National Baptist Convention (a week-long meeting of Baptist Sunday School teachers and superintendents, who gathered to receive training, inspiration, and encouragement for their work in their local churches), which met that year in Memphis; by 1904, she served as organizer and president of the local Memphis Music Club; and by 1909, she taught youth choirs in local Baptist churches.

Before reaching age 20, Lucie Campbell had established a reputation as a respected musician who was beginning to exercise strong influence over black music in Memphis. Although she did not get a bachelor of arts degree until 1927, at age 42, she began teaching English and American history at Booker T. Washington High School in 1911. The author of Campbell's entry in *Historic Black Memphians* observes that she was to religious songs what W. C. Handy was to the blues; but to understand fully the position she occupies in the history of African-American sacred music, it is necessary to negotiate the milieu of her immediate world as it was defined by the structure of the black church. Campbell grew up in the period following the Civil War, when the isolation of blacks from the larger white American culture was an accepted reality: segregation, disenfranchisement, and discrimination were solidified and enforced by law. In the separate communities that resulted, the black church became the dominant institution of nurture and influence.

The National Baptist Convention of the United States of America (NBC) was organized in Atlanta, Georgia, on September 28, 1895, and in the following year, it established its National Baptist Publishing Board (NBPB), which led to the establishment of the National Sunday School and BYPU Congress to promote the materials and educational programs of the NBPB, which held its first assembly in Nashville, Tennessee, in 1906.

Lucie Campbell was named music director of the new Congress in 1916, in which position she joined with E.W.D. Isaac to publish songbooks that became widely used through the denomination, including the *Baptist Standard Hymnal* (1924), *Gospel Pearls* (1921), *Spirituals Triumphant Old and New* (1927), and *Inspirational Melodies* (n.d.).

Campbell's job as music director of the Congress was multifaceted, a position she largely defined by delineating her own "space," an important aspect of success and survival in the male-dominated Baptist denomination. As the author notes, Campbell, in her position as music director, "staged pre-Congress musicales, Friday night pageants and performances and directed the singing of huge choirs and immense audiences during the daily assemblages." Her behind-the-scenes activities included going early to cities where the Congress met to train the choir, select soloists, and construct a musical agenda of ensembles and performers to appear during the sessions. She wrote her songs with the Congress in mind, to inspire and uplift the masses in attendance, including material she deemed necessary for significant purposes. At the 1924 annual meeting in Cleveland, Ohio, for example, she introduced to the delegates the song "Welcome Chorus," in which she rallied support for the Congress, inspiring and informing the delegates by praising and identifying by name the leaders of the denomination. She further encouraged the purchase of products and literature from the new Sunday School Publishing Board, whose building was under construction in Nashville. The new edifice was named in memory of Dr. E. C. Morris, president of the National Baptist Convention from its organization in 1895 until his death in 1922.

In her personal life, Lucie Campbell had difficulty maintaining nonthreatening relationships with ministers in the churches where she held membership. She was an outstanding public speaker, a financially independent, well-educated woman of strong convictions who wanted things to proceed as she saw fit. A strict disciplinarian in the classroom, she was prone to express opinions fearlessly in churches in an era when women were not allowed to speak from the pulpit. Campbell became depressed when misunderstandings would escalate to a point beyond mediation; one of the churches from which she was dismissed forbade her songs to be sung there for many years.

In the 1940s, under the leadership of Campbell and its other renowned gospel songwriter, the Reverend W. H. Brewster, Memphis was beginning to establish itself as a gospel music center, bringing gospel choirs to local churches. In 1944, according to Sharon Stratton-Dobbins, Campbell "requested Thomas A. Dorsey to come to Memphis and head up the National Board meeting of the Gospel Choirs, Choruses and Singers Convention." Campbell's interest in the organization correlated with her desire to maintain high standards of gospel music performance. This was also an opportunity to advise and nurture young singers who sought her permission to perform at the National Baptist Convention and the Congress, a major venue for aspiring musicians. Her endorsement, or lack thereof, could make or break a singer.

In June 1954, Campbell retired from Booker T. Washington High School in Memphis, ending a 55-year career as an educator and civic and community activist; she had received many awards and earned high respect. In 1955, the Sunday School and BTU (Baptist Training Union) Congress observed its 50th Anniversary in a Golden Jubilee Session held in Atlantic City, New Jersey. One of the highlights of the celebration was a major address, "The Past of the Congress," delivered by Campbell, an honored founder who had seen the organization that was the source of inspiration for her music become one of the premier religious education institutions in the world. The extent of Campbell's influence on her protégés in the dissemination of gospel music is illustrated in the following account by J. Robert Bradley. On July 17, 1955, Bradley made his concert debut at Royal Festival Hall in London, with Campbell in attendance. As Bradley recalls, "at the end of the first part of the concert [I] broke all protocol, summoned Miss Lucie to the stage, introduced her to the audience, and sang 'Something Within' (1919) and 'Touch Me, Lord Jesus' (1941)." According to Bradley, "this was the *first time* Negro gospel music had been introduced in London or any part of Great Britain or Europe. . . . When the people [heard] Gospel Music written by Ms. Lucie Campbell, the audience began to feel the passionate, rhythmic swing and sway of the musical renditions, and power of The Holy Spirit . . . captured the soul and wafted it away to heaven."

On January 14, 1960, at 75 years of age, Lucie Campbell married the Reverend C. R. Williams, the executive director of the National Baptist Training Union Board, climaxing a friendship that had begun in 1902. Williams had been her business partner for many years, publishing some of her later songs through the BTU Board in Nashville.

GOSPEL HYMNS

During the period from 1919 to 1939, much of Campbell's music was owned and copyrighted by the BYPU Board and the Sunday School Publishing Board, the two governing bodies of the Congress. Composer Robert Holmes, a Campbell protégé, considers her songs composed during this early period to be hymns suitable for use in the denomination's hymnbooks. Her first hymn, "The Lord Is My Shepherd" (1919), a paraphrase of Psalm 23, appeared in *Gospel Pearls* (1921), a landmark compilation of 163 "familiar hymns and tunes."

Campbell's early hymns, influenced by the style of the Reverend C. A. Tindley, combine the traditional homophonic, four-part hymn format with features from Negro spirituals. Her lyrics, the strength of her songs, employ the strength of religious fervor, logic, and "human interest" that appealed to her audiences. "Something Within" (1919) was composed after watching a young blind man, Connie Rosemond, refuse to sing the blues on Memphis's famous Beale Street when offered money to do so. His statement ("I can't sing the blues . . . [because] I'm trying to be a Christian . . . and I've found the way out of darkness into light; I can't explain it, but there's something within me") was the inspiration for one of her best-loved hymns. "Something Within" was introduced by Rosemond at the 1919 session of the Congress in Newark, New Jersey.

"He Understands, He'll Say, 'Well Done'" (1933) is one of the best-known and best-loved hymns in the gospel literature. It has become a favorite funeral song in churches of all denominations; an early "crossover" gospel, it has been recorded by Lawrence Welk and Pat Boone and sung at the Grand Ole Opry in Nashville.

Religious pageants enjoyed great popularity in the African-American community during the 1930s, and Campbell, ever alert for stimulating musical events, produced several for the Congress. With her strong background as a teacher of English and history, she wrote original texts and integrated them with poems and passages from literature to create speaking parts with costumes. She combined this with huge choruses and soloists, spirituals, hymns, gospel songs, and anthems to create memorable spectacles, fondly recalled by participants to this day. Campbell usually produced pageants when the sessions were in Memphis, where her resources were greatest. Two of the titles are *Ethiopia at the Bar of Justice,* performed in 1933 and 1942, and *Patriotic Phantasy,* staged in 1959 with an original verse to "God Bless America," under which Campbell wrote, "with apologies to Irving Berlin."

"Just to Behold His Face" was a new gospel style for Campbell in 1941 and is the earliest example of writing in which she abandons the four-part homophonic structure of the hymn and places the solo on its own staff above a full piano accompaniment with heavy left-hand accents. The melody effectively underscores the lyric's statement of the Christian's goal: the reward of seeing Jesus at the end of life. This hymn is in 6/4, a meter that gospel scholar Horace Boyer identifies as the "gospel waltz, Miss Lucie's greatest contribution to gospel music." Singer Sallie Martin credited Campbell with "having the 'grace' to bring gospel music from the hymn books."

The decade of the 1940s was Campbell's most prolific; Library of Congress copyright deposits show 17 songs in the three-year period from 1946 to 1949. Her songs were now in such demand at the annual meetings and throughout the nation that she began publishing collections of them, as Books I-III of *Lucie E. Campbell's Soul-Stirring Songs for All Religious Occasions,* representative compilations of selections from the earliest to the most recent, 1919–47. The collections included music for special occasions such as Easter, parting hymns and offertories, responsive readings, and an Order of Service.

Anxious to show that she could be up-to-date and change with the times, Campbell's writing style began to show the freedom learned from the "Chicago Group" of Thomas A. Dorsey, Roberta Martin, and Sallie Martin. Two 1946 compositions were very popular: "In the Upper Room with Jesus," a favorite communion song,

and "Jesus Gave Me Water." The latter became even more popular in 1951 when it was recorded by Sam Cooke and the Soul Stirrers as a gospel single on Specialty Records.

ANTHEMS

Campbell's success as a composer of anthems during the 1940s was unprecedented. Bradley recalled: "She has had better results with anthems than anyone of our group. . . . Her first anthem was 'Praise Ye the Lord' (1946). . . . Over thirty thousand copies of [these were] sold, which is a record for present day anthems; 'Awake! for Thy God Reigneth' (1949) has sold nearly 20,000." The anthems are in the style of Western classical music, with metronome and dynamic markings, and tempo designations in Italian; they are written for "mixed voices," with recitatives, solos, and duets, and are similar to those in the *National Anthem Series* published by the National Baptist Publishing Board in 1906, which is still used in many churches today.

The 1950s were Campbell's second most prolific period of composing: 12 works were copyrighted between 1951 and 1959. Her lyrics became more introspective, based frequently on scriptural reference and inspirational sermons, with titles such as "A Sinner Like Me" (1952), based on the words of Apostle Paul to Timothy and Romans (1 Timothy 1:12; Romans 5:8) and "God's Long Reach of Salvation" (1954), "inspired by and dedicated to Dr. J. H. Jackson, the honored and beloved president of the National Baptist Convention." Typically, she offers insight into sources of her strength in songs such as "His Grace Is Sufficient for Me" (1956), based on II Corinthians 12:9.

Campbell's final compositions include three in 1960, one in 1962, and two published posthumously in 1963. "Unto Thee, Thou Holy One," a short anthem published in 1960, was sung at the pre-Congress Musicale program in Memphis the year before, and "The Story of Salvation Must Be Told (in Africa, China, and the Isles of the Sea)" (1960) bears the inscription, "Dedicated to our Foreign Mission Board and all who are interested in helping to evangelize the world." At the Congress in Denver, Colorado, in June 1962, Campbell, who had been ill, stumbled and fell coming offstage to direct a song, rendering her unable to attend a scheduled "Lucie E. Campbell Appreciation Day" testimonial in her honor. She was hospitalized in Denver, but never recovered after returning home, and died January 3, 1963, in Nashville.

Campbell's entire output was sacred music, with the exception of two patriotic songs composed in 1919: on the covers of "Please Let Your Light Shine on Me" and "Are They Equal in the Eyes of the Law?" is written "Words by Sergeant A. R. Griggs; Music by Lucie E. Campbell, Music Director, National SS and BYPU Congress." Even with secular music, she is identified with the black church. Thus, the criteria for gauging the significance of her music can be found in understanding the imperative of a woman whose creative energies were focused on the support and advancement of the black church in America, embodied for her in the National Baptist Convention, USA, and its auxiliary, the Sunday School and BYPU Congress. Her songs were composed for that specific audience, described by Charles Dinkins as a "vast educational enterprise, bringing together in one week of study, thousands of people from hundreds of churches and other organizations throughout the constituency of the National Baptist Convention, USA, Inc."

Campbell's music is distinguished chiefly for penetrating lyrics that relate to persons trying to make sense of their lives; she is described by Bradley as "a songwriter who wrote from the agony and ecstasy of her life's experience." Although Campbell was not a particularly prolific composer, there is a substantial variety of African-American sacred song forms in her music. Boyer has categorized them as follows: gospel lining-hymn, gospel ballad, gospel song, jubilee, and gospel waltz. Wendell Whalum observed that, while Campbell "was not as musically literate as some might have thought, she was a Memphis break-through in gospel music at a time when white gospel was the norm." Her ability to combine powerful lyrics with frequently memorable melodies allowed Lucie Campbell to achieve maximum effect with arguably minimal material. Confidently expressing the religious experience as she lived it and Christian doctrine as she understood it, such songs as "He Understands, He'll Say, 'Well Done'" and "Something Within" guarantee her lasting legacy. Her high musical standards and considerable organizational skills set the pace, tone, and environment of the Congress, which in turn influenced worship in churches far beyond her immediate environs. Campbell's singular importance can be assessed in the realization that the enthusiastic reception of her music by the National Baptist Convention was a major factor in the "high stakes" strategies of keeping the immense denomination together in critical periods of its history. The singularity of this legacy validates distinctive approaches for the consideration of her songs as a musical corpus of unique origin within the overall history of African-American gospel song, a genre whose rhetoric and semiology are still in the process of becoming standardized.

REFERENCES

Boyer, Horace Clarence. "Lucie E. Campbell: Composer for the National Baptist Convention." In *We'll Understand It Better By and By: Pioneering African American Gospel Composers,* edited by Bernice Johnson Reagon, 81–108. Washington, D.C.: Smithsonian Institution Press, 1992.

Bradley, J. Robert. "Fifty Years of Musical Service." In *The Sunday School Informer,* 14–15. Nashville, Tenn.: Sunday School Publishing Board, 1959.

———. "Miss Lucie: The Legacy of the Woman and Her Music." In *The National Baptist Voice* 30–31 (1979): 1–10.

———. Telephone interview with the author, July 26, 1997.

Dinkins, Charles L. "The Saga of the National Baptist Congress/Christian Education in the National Baptist Convention: Historical, the Present Situation, Projections." In *Utilizing Resources for Christian Education: 1980 Emphasis,* edited by Maynard P. Turner Jr., 21–57. Nashville, Tenn.: Townsend Press, 1980.

George, Luvenia A. "Lucie E. Campbell and the Enduring Tradition of Gospel Hymnody." In *The Songs of Lucie E. Campbell: Gospel Music Composer,* edited by Niani Kilkenny and Rebecca E. Curzon, 6–15. Washington, D.C.: Smithsonian Institution, 1983.

The Golden Hour Digest 1, no. 3 (April 1940).

Holmes Jr., Robert L. Interview with the author, Nashville, Tenn., July 27, 1983.

Jones Jr., Amos. *I Have Always Been in the Hands of God: The Life Story of J. Robert Bradley.* Nashville, Tenn.: Townsend Press, 1993.

King, D. E. Telephone interview with the author, July 13, 1983.

Martin, Sallie. Interview with the author, Chicago, August 19, 1983.

Memphis Pink Palace Museum. "Lucie E. Campbell: 1890–1963." In *Historic Black Memphians,* 16–17, Memphis: The Foundation, 1970.

Shelby Jr., Thomas H. Interview with the author, Washington, D.C., September 7, 1984.

Stratton-Dobbins, Sharon. "Gospel Music in Memphis: The Black Church's Heritage." In [Memphis] *Tri-State Defender* (February 16, 1980): 13–16.

Walker, Charles. *Miss Lucie.* Nashville, Tenn.: Townsend Press, 1993.

Whalum, Wendell. Telephone interview with the author, August 4, 1983.

LUVENIA A. GEORGE

CAPERS, VALERIE GAIL

Born in New York, N.Y., May 24, 1935. **Education:** Musical family: father, Alvin, a professional jazz pianist; brother, Robert (Bobby), played saxophone and flute in the Mongo Santamaria band; New York Institute for the Education of the Blind, began piano studies, age seven; Juilliard School of Music, New York, B.S., 1959, M.S., 1960. **Composing and Performing Career:** Began as composer, arranger for the Mongo Santamaria Afro-Cuban band; formed trio and made recording debut, 1967; appeared at numerous U.S. and European music festivals including Newport Jazz Festival, Kool Jazz Festival, Monterey and Mellon Jazz Festivals, Grande Parade International, Nice, France, North Sea Festival, The Hague, Netherlands; New York, performed regularly in local clubs; Carnegie Hall, conducted original Christmas jazz cantata, *Sing About Love*, 1978; St. Peter's Church, premiered "operatorio" *Sojourner*, 1981; frequent panelist, lecturer, clinician, and performer at conferences. **Teaching Career:** Hunter College, New York, summer 1959 and 1960; Manhattan School of Music, New York, 1968–75; High School of Music and Art, New York, fall 1971; Bronx Community College of the City University of New York, Department of Music and Art, full professor, 1985–95, chairman, 1987–95. **Commissions:** All-City Chorus of New York City, 1976; New Music Consort, 1985; Smithsonian Institution, 1987. **Honors/Awards:** New York City Creative Arts Public Service Award, 1974; National Endowment for the Arts grant, 1976; City University of New York Research Foundation grant, 1983; *Essence* magazine, "Woman of Essence" in Music, 1987; Bronx Borough President's Award for outstanding artistic contributions to community, 1992; National Endowment for the Arts Special Project, 1994–95; Honorary degree, Doctor of Fine Arts, Susquehanna University, 1996; International Women in Jazz inductee, 1997; Jazz Heritage award, 1997.

MUSIC LIST

PIANO SOLO

Portraits in Jazz. 1976; revised and published Valcap Music, 1998. Contents: Ella Scats the Little Lamb; Waltz for Miles; Sweet Mister Jelly Roll; The Monk; Blues for the Duke; A Taste of Bass; Billie's Song; Mr. Satchmo; Canción de Havana; Bossa Brasilia; Blue-Bird; Cool-trane. Note: 5, 6, and 7 in *Black Women Composers: A Century of Piano Music, 1893–1990*, edited by Helen Walker-Hill (Bryn Mawr, Pa.: Hildegard, 1992). Recorded: nos. 7 and 12, Leonarda CD-LE339.

INSTRUMENTAL ENSEMBLE

Escenas Afro-Cubanas. 1985. Unpublished manuscript. Contents: Canción Callejera; Homenaje; Descarga. Note: written for New Music Consort.

SOLO VOICE WITH INSTRUMENTAL ENSEMBLE OR ORCHESTRA

Song of the Seasons (voice, piano, cello). 1987. Unpublished manuscript. Contents: Spring; Summer; Autumn; Winter. Commissioned by the Smithsonian Institution. Premiere, 1987.

CHORAL MUSIC

"Christmas Is Love." Unpublished manuscript.

Duke Ellington Suite (chorus and jazz trio). 1984. Unpublished manuscript. Commissioned by the All-City Chorus of New York.

The Gift of Song. 1982. Unpublished manuscript. Contents: You; A Love Letter; Farmchild's Lullaby; We Wear the Mask; The Gift of Song. Commissioned by CUNY Research Grant.

"In Praise of Freedom" (chorus, instrumental ensemble). 1976. Unpublished manuscript. Commissioned by the All-City Chorus of New York.

"Psalm 150" (chorus, jazz ensemble). 1980. Unpublished manuscript. Commissioned by the All-City Chorus of New York.

Sing About Love (Christmas cantata with jazz ensemble and orchestra). 1974. Unpublished manuscript. Commissioned by New York City Creative Artists Public Service. Recorded: ("Out of All He's Chosen Me") Columbia CK 66670.

DRAMATIC MUSIC

Sojourner ("operatorio" for chorus and jazz ensemble). 1981. Unpublished manuscript. Note: composed through a grant from the National Endowment for the Arts. Premiere, 1981.

JAZZ ENSEMBLE

"Ah Ha." n.p.: Mongo Music.

"Blue Monday." Bronx, N.Y.: Valcap Music.

"Chili Beans." n.p.: Mongo Music.

"La Gitana." n.p.: Mongo Music.

"Hey Stuff." Bronx, N.Y.: Valcap Music.

"Kenne's Soul." Bronx, N.Y.: Valcap Music.

"Little David Swings." Bronx, N.Y.: Valcap Music.

"Odyssey." Bronx, N.Y.: Valcap Music. Recorded, 1995: Columbia CK 66670.

"Organum." Recorded, 1982: KMArts, KMA 1907-B.

"The Ring Thing." 1993. Note: jazz treatment of Richard Wagner's *The Ring of the Nibelung*.

"Sabrosa." Bronx, N.Y.: Valcap Music.

"Sarai." n.p.: Mongo Music.

"El Toro." n.p.: Mongo Music. Recorded, 1990: Fantasy/OJC OJCCD-490-2.

"Winter's Love." Note: Bossa nova based on Wagner love themes.

PUBLICATIONS

ABOUT CAPERS
Articles

Palmer, Robert. "Concert: Valerie Capers." *New York Times* (December 20, 1978): C21.

Southall, Geneva Handy. "In Celebration of Black Women Composers." Program notes for fourth annual "Music of Black Composers" program at Smithsonian Institution, Washington, D.C., May 15, 1988.

"Students Pack Blind Teacher's Jazz Class." *New York Amsterdam News* (June 16, 1962): 25.

"Valerie Capers, Composer, Plans Piano Performances." *New York Times* (January 22, 1986).

Wilson, John S. "An Imaginative Approach." *New York Times* (July 2, 1973).

———. "Jazz: By Valerie Capers." *New York Times* (February 28, 1981).

———. "Valerie Capers to Conduct Her Jazz-Based Cantata." *New York Times* (December 17, 1978): sect. 1, 100.

BY CAPERS

"Tenor Madness: John Coltrane: Bringing Verismo to Jazz." *Village Voice* 31 (June 24, 1986): T8.

PRINCIPAL ARCHIVES

Clipping file at New York Public Library Music Division, Lincoln Center.

* * * * *

The music of Valerie Capers is admired by musicians as diverse as soprano Kathleen Battle, with whom she shared a program at Riverside Church in 1993, and Wynton Marsalis, who appears with her on her third jazz album, the 1995 CD *Come On Home* produced by Columbia/Sony on its Legendary Pioneers of Jazz series. The New Music Consort, the All-City Chorus of New York City, the Smithsonian Institution, the City University of New York Research Foundation, and the National Endowment for the Arts are among the institutions from whom she has received grants and commissions. These honors testify to the importance of her musical contributions. Her jazz compositions reflect her eclectic background and have brought a fresh imaginative approach to the standard jazz forms and instrumentations. In such extended works as her cantata *Sing About Love,* and her opera/oratorio *Sojourner,* she has carried on and expanded the legacy of Duke Ellington's and Mary Lou Williams's large-scale sacred jazz works in classical forms.

The path to these accomplishments has not been without obstacles. At the age of six, Capers was blinded by a streptococcus infection that damaged her optic nerve. She was sent to the New York Institute for the Education of the Blind in the Bronx where she received an excellent education and learned to read and write Braille fluently. She demonstrated musical ability at an early age. When she was 11, she began classical piano lessons at the Institute with Elizabeth Thode, an exacting but inspirational teacher. Caper's love of opera also began at the Institute, where she heard recordings and studied the Braille librettos of operas by Verdi, Puccini, and Mozart.

Capers' home and family background were no less important in her musical education. She remembers a large record collection including Beethoven's *Fifth Symphony,* Tchaikovsky's *Nutcracker Ballet,* and works by Rachmaninoff, Grieg, Bing Crosby, Duke Ellington, and Count Basie. Her mother, a civil service worker for the New York Department of Hospitals, liked to play the piano, and there was always a large stack of sheet music on the piano. Her father, Alvin Capers, a postal employee, was also a professional jazz pianist and a friend of Fats Waller. Her parents sacrificed to provide for their children's musical education, and Valerie's younger brother Bobby, who later played saxophone and flute with Mongo Santamaria's Afro-Cuban band, attended the High School of Music and Art.

After graduating from the Institute in 1953 as valedictorian of her class, she was advised by her teacher to take a year to prepare for college, during which she practiced eight to ten hours a day. She was offered scholarships at both the Juilliard School of Music and Barnard College. Capers was the first blind student to receive the bachelor's degree from Juilliard and finished her master's degree there in 1960.

Capers was then urged by her brother Bobby to explore her African-American musical roots in the jazz idiom. Because the jazz discipline is so different from the classical, she found it necessary to put aside classical playing for a couple of years. Her brother and other jazz musicians such as Artie Jenkins taught her chord changes. She systematically made up exercises for herself and played LP recordings by Sonny Rollins, John Coltrane, and others at slow speed, memorizing the music, then transposing it. It was two to three years before she tried her first gig at Kenny's on Boston Post Road. Around this time Bobby also asked her to compose pieces for Mongo Santamaria's band, beginning with "El Toro," which was recorded on Santamaria's *Live at the Village Gate* album and performed on television. This led to more pieces: "La Gitana," "Chili Beans," and "Ah Ha," which was used for a dance sequence in the movie *Made in Paris,* starring Louis Jourdan and Ann-Margret. By 1973, Capers' jazz piano style had evolved so that a review in the *New York Times* lauded her "strong, positive attack" and "big, brash chords that swung with tremendous force."

As a performer, Capers has appeared as soloist in Mozart piano concertos with the Bronx Arts Ensemble Orchestra and the Strawberry Music Festival in Malibu, California, and has performed with jazz greats Dizzy Gillespie in the "Jazz in America" television series, with Billy Taylor in "An American Sampler" concert series at the Whitney Museum in New York, with Marian McPartland in her "Piano Jazz Series" on radio, and with Mongo Santamaria, Donald Byrd, Slide Hampton, Max Roach, and Ray Brown, to mention only a few. Her trio has performed at the Monterey Jazz Festival, Newport Jazz Festival, the Kool Jazz Festival, North Sea Jazz Festival in The Hague, Holland, and the Grand Parade de Jazz in Nice, France. She has taught music at the Manhattan School of Music, Hunter College, and the Bronx Community College of the City University of New York, where she developed a model jazz curriculum and served as Chair of the Department of Music and Art from 1987 until her retirement in 1995.

In 1974 a New York City Creative Arts Public Service Award supported her first large-scale jazz work, *Sing About Love,* a two and one-half hour Christmas cantata that has received numerous performances. This work demonstrated Capers' ability to compose extended jazz works in which different idioms—bebop, Latin, gospel, blues—are combined to form a satisfying whole. In 1976 she was awarded a National Endowment for the Arts grant to compose *Sojourner* for which she coined the term "operatorio" since it has aspects of both oratorio and opera. Here she again used jazz elements with skill and perception in an extended form with classical formal elements.

Other works by Capers include *Portraits in Jazz* (1976), a set of 12 piano teaching pieces; *Song of the Seasons* (1987), a song cycle on her own text in classical art song idiom; *The Gift of Song* (1982),

Valerie Gail Capers; courtesy of Helen Walker-Hill

five non-jazz settings of Paul Laurence Dunbar poems for chorus; "Psalm 150" (1980) for chorus; "In Praise of Freedom" (1976), a choral and jazz ensemble setting of Martin Luther King Jr.'s March on Washington speech; and *Duke Ellington Medley* (1984) for chorus and jazz trio.

Many of Capers' compositions have appeared on her jazz albums—"Organum" on *Affirmation* (1982), and "Odyssey" on *Come on Home* (1995). She continues to write in the popular song genre, most recently "Always You" (1995). "The Ring Thing" and "Winter's Love," a pop song in the style of bossa nova, both composed in 1993, celebrate her long-standing passion for the operas of Richard Wagner, culminating in a 1992 visit to the Bayreuth Festival in Germany. Indeed, Wagner is not without influence on Capers' composition. "The Ring Thing," a five-minute jazz piece, quotes themes from the opera cycle *The Ring of the Nibelung* in a high-spirited satire. It is just one of the many ways—as composer, performer, teacher, and administrator—through which Valerie Capers creates a bridge between the European classical and the African-American jazz traditions.

SING ABOUT LOVE (1974)

While completing *Sing About Love* in 1974, Capers was mourning the tragic death of her beloved brother and mentor, Bobby Capers. As she resolved to compose music that would make a difference in the lives of other people and that would be connected to her African-American heritage, she was inspired by the universal and enduring popularity of Handel's *Messiah*, composed at a time when he was losing his sight.

Sing About Love tells the Biblical Christmas story with both traditional Biblical texts and the composer's own words. The cantata movements are in a variety of forms and styles: classical European, blues, swing, Latin, jazz, jazz solos, and gospel. Mary's solo "Out of All He's Chosen Me" is in popular song style. "Calling of the Council" employs salsa and blues. Herod's counselor sings a gospel solo full of fiery preaching and testifying. The chorus "God of Ancient Israel" is in Lutheran chorale style (with a slight blues inflection). "No Room at the Inn" is a bossa nova. After the conclusion of the story and the final chorus, a meditative instrumental "Interlude" evokes Bach's "Air for the G String." The original chorus, "Sing About Love," concludes the work in joyous gospel style. The various styles are well-suited to the mood of each particular piece, the sequence of contrasting styles and instrumentation contribute to the overall dramatic structure of the work, and the juxtapositions of these seemingly incompatible idioms are skillfully constructed.

The instrumentation, both the choice of instruments and how they are used, is equally well-crafted. When combined, the orchestral strings and jazz ensemble enhance each other. Instrumental solos and small groupings, vocal and choral sounds and textures, are alternated to optimal effect. In "No Room at the Inn," the bossa nova is introduced by the piano, bass, Latin percussion, and three flutes—a totally unexpected and original sound.

The tonal language of the movements also varies according to stylistic idiom. The Prologue begins with a movement for full orchestra that contains biting contemporary dissonances, in which the angel Gabriel announces to Mary her future in declamatory vocal style. In the following number, the brass and rhythm sections

open a duet between Gabriel and Mary in jazz vocal style with jazz harmonies. The final section of the Prologue, the solo "Out of All He's Chosen Me," sung by Mary in popular song style, simplifies the harmonies still further. The remaining movements continue to vary their tonal language to reflect both idiom and the psychological development of the narrative. Herod's fevered "Soliloquy" is the most atonal movement of the cantata. It begins with a long, tonally ambiguous solo for bass clarinet followed by a dark and sinuous duet between Herod and the bass clarinet. This duet becomes progressively more dissonant and culminates, with the chorus, strings, and timpani improvising eerie unpitched and glissando sounds to echo his delusion, when Herod decrees that all male children two years and under must die. The movement ends with an atonal cluster in the winds and screams by the chorus. After this climactic and violent moment, the consonant diatonic harmonies of the unaccompanied chorale, "God of Ancient Israel," provide stunning contrast and emotional consolation. Later in the work, "Quiet Night," with its soothing jazz harmonies and alto saxophone solo, and the following haunting "Interlude for Strings" in baroque aria style similarly contrast with the chromatic dissonance of the triumphant choral and instrumental "Glory." The audience is thereby given an opportunity to meditate upon the events of the narrative. This, in turn, prepares and contrasts with the upbeat gospel rhythms and harmonies of the joyful finale, "Sing About Love," in which the audience joins with clapping.

In 1969, Capers was invited by John Motley, conductor of the All-City Chorus of New York, to compose a Christmas piece for his choir. "Sing About Love," a five-minute work in semi-gospel style, was performed that Christmas. A year later Capers received a Creative Arts Public Service Grant to write a larger composition suitable for community presentation. *Sing About Love* was expanded to a two and one-half hour cantata and was first performed in 1974 at Central Presbyterian Church in New York City with a 20-voice chorus and 22-piece orchestra conducted by Miss Capers. The following season the work was performed at Cuyahoga Community College in Cleveland, Ohio. A fourth performance of *Sing About Love* occurred at Carnegie Hall on December 18, 1978, by the New York Jazz Repertory Company, conducted by Capers. Guest performers were Slide Hampton on trombone, Mongo Santamaria on congas, and Donald Byrd and Nat Adderly on trumpet. Other performances of the cantata have been given at Clark Atlanta University in Georgia in 1991 and at the College of New Rochelle, New York, in 1993.

Each performance of the cantata has met with enthusiastic critical acclaim. After the 1978 performance at Carnegie Hall, the *New York Times* stated, "Miss Capers proved her talent as an adept writer in several idioms, but more importantly, she demonstrated a rare ability to make disparate elements cohere compositionally . . . 'Sing About Love' was first-class jazz writing . . . it should be performed every Christmas."

PORTRAITS IN JAZZ (1976)

The 12 piano pieces in Capers' collection *Portraits in Jazz* are intended to be pedagogical in the spirit of Robert Schumann's *Album for the Young*. The technical difficulty varies from easy to considerable, and the pieces are meticulously fingered and marked.

Further instruction is provided by the composer's dedication of each piece to a great jazz musician whose spirit it is intended to evoke and by prefaces by the composer with remarks about construction or style. The duration of the entire set is 20 to 25 minutes, but the separate pieces can also be effectively programmed in small groups.

The first, "Ella Scats the Little Lamb," marked "Bright and Spirited," arranges the familiar nursery tune "Mary Had a Little Lamb" in Ella Fitzgerald's scat-singing style over a steady left-hand bass continuo in half notes. "Waltz for Miles" is a simple melodic tribute to Miles Davis's style of phrasing and his warm impressionistic harmonies. The ragtime-style "Sweet Mister Jelly Roll" pays homage to Jelly Roll Morton in which the left hand plays a simplified stride bass, with typical oom-pah skips and repeated chords.

"The Monk," written in the keyboard style of Thelonius Monk, features open fifths and sevenths, biting seconds, off-balance accents, cluster chords, and a quote from Monk's "Straight No Chaser." "Blues for the Duke" is reminiscent of Duke Ellington's early style. In traditional 12-bar blues form, the harmonic structure is based on chords on the first, fourth, and fifth tones of the key. According to the composer's preface, this blues can be thought of as a theme with two variations and a return to the opening theme.

"A Taste of Bass" is dedicated to bassist Ron Carter, whose solos and rhythm work influenced the generation of bass players who followed him. The first section is a miniature bass solo for the left hand, followed by a quarter-note walking bass line characteristic of the supportive rhythmic and harmonic role of the bassist in a jazz ensemble. The seventh piece, "Billie's Song" is a simple, one-page ballad dedicated "in fondest memory" to Billie Holiday and evoking the warmth and poignancy of her style.

In "Mr. Satchmo," written in the style of the old New Orleans street bands in which Louis Armstrong began his career, the right-hand interjections imitate Armstrong's early trumpet playing. "Canción de Havana," rather than an illustration of a particular musician's style, is an example of the Afro-Cuban idiom and is dedicated to Mongo Santamaria. It includes a passage of *guaguanco* music, which combines flamenco and Western African influences. "Bossa Brasilia," a variant of the Brazilian bossa nova, which strongly influenced American popular music and jazz during the 1960s, is characterized by a two-measure rhythmic pattern in 4/4 time and tricky combined rhythms. "Blue-Bird" contains subtle rhythmic complexities and an extended bebop melodic line with off-beat accents characteristic of Charlie "Bird" Parker. It is a modern "chromatic blues" that includes frequent chord changes and expanded harmonies.

In the last piece, "Cool-trane," the most difficult and the most harmonically adventurous, the right hand creates a melodic line similar to a saxophone solo. The title is a word play on the name of John Coltrane, and the piece closes with a quote from his "Cousin Mary."

SONG OF THE SEASONS (1987)

This song cycle for soprano, cello, and piano was commissioned by the Smithsonian Institution to demonstrate Capers' versatility. The texts, written by the composer, were inspired by the economy and imagery of *haiku,* the Japanese poetic form. The work is divided into four songs, "Spring," "Summer," followed immediately (*attacca*) by "Autumn," then "Winter." The second and last songs each change mood before they end, in anticipation of the next season.

These songs are not in the jazz or popular song idioms usually associated with Capers, but rather in a late romantic art song style. The harmonic language is tonal, with lush harmonies and florid piano figuration. The influence of Wagner is heard not only in the unexpected shifts of key and evasions of resolution but also in the freely floating, semi-declamatory vocal melodic line. The cello functions both as a partner with the voice in contrapuntal duet or imitative dialogue and as the melodic solo line in introductions and transitory interludes. When played *pizzicato,* it shares the accompanying role of the piano, whose arpeggiations and repeated chords provide harmonic color, sustain motion, and fill out the texture. In the third song, "Autumn," and part of the last, "Winter," the cello is silent and the piano assumes the function of melodic counterpoint with the voice.

The lyrics of the first song, "Spring," extol the typical spring emblems—melting snows, cherry blossoms, returning birds, and hope "of splendid dreams and things to be." In 6/8 meter, vocal and cello lines lilt in predominantly quarter-eighth rhythm, with large, expansive melodic contours and a wide pitch span. Its three sections are centered on E-flat major, A-flat major, and D-flat major, respectively.

"Summer," a love song, begins with a short cello introduction in A minor. The indication is *Moderato ed espressivo,* and the chordal piano accompaniment is gently pulsated. The song explores several tonalities before ending in A-flat major, its mood shifting from the fulfillment of "warm days," "hot summer skies," and "two people but a single heart" to the "fading summer days" that "whisper of what used to be" and "just a memory." Just before the change to the anticipation of "Autumn," the piano shifts to a static, whole-note chord progression, foretelling the opening of the last song, "Winter." Although "Summer" ends with a conclusive cadence in A-flat, the next song begins without a break and maintains the same tempo and the same gently syncopated accompaniment. Its lyrics depart, however, from the love theme to depict colors of fall, the fruits of harvest, and labor's rest, for "autumn is the promise kept." As noted above, the cello is absent, not to return until the melting of the snows of winter. The conclusion of "Autumn" (in B-flat major), sets up the opening of the next song (in the relative G minor).

"Winter" changes mood radically, with a piano introduction of slow, static, whole-note chords, inspired, according to the composer, by the hollow open chords in Schubert's "Der Doppelgänger" from his song cycle *Schwanengesang.* When the soprano enters, it intones the first phrase on one note in her low register: "Late at night as I peer into the dark and endless winter sky." The starkness of this initial statement sets up the next breathtaking phrase, "I listen to the rain," with its soaring leap to high *a.* Recollections of times past summon the accompaniment motives of previous songs, and in an atonal transitional passage of almost suspended time, the stage is set for the triumphant return of "Spring."

Unity in the song cycle is established by the obvious anticipations of following seasons in "Summer" and "Winter" and by the recall of previous material in the concluding song. Key relationships also tie the songs together, as they cadence first in D-flat major, then A-flat major, B-flat major, and finally again D-flat major. A less perceptible unity is provided by similar rhythmic and melodic motives among the songs. The first and last songs end with climactic thrice-repeated short motives separated by rests and accompaniment figures: "'tis spring," three times in the first, and "tomorrow," three times in the last. A short melodic motive of four rising scale steps is found in all four songs: in "Spring" at "My heart cries out"; in "Summer" at "The fields were green"; in the opening phrase of "Autumn," to almost the same words: "The fields of green"; and at the close of "Winter" at "The time has past." In addition, the opening melodic line of "Summer" recurs in "Autumn." These melodic and rhythmic recollections are not obvious but, nevertheless, operate on a subliminal level to unite the songs. The cycle is a worthy and very accessible addition to the growing repertory of songs for voice with cello and piano.

Dedicated to D. Antoinette Handy, *Song of the Seasons* was premiered May 3, 1987, at the Smithsonian Institution in Washington, D.C., by soprano Mereda Gaither-Graves with Capers as pianist and John Robinson on cello. The ten-minute work has subsequently been performed at the Bronx Community College by soprano Elizabeth Henreckson-Farnum, with Sylvia Eversole, pianist, and John Robinson, cellist.

SOJOURNER (1981)

Capers considers her most innovative work to be her "operatorio" on the life of Sojourner Truth. She coined the term to indicate a form more concise than an opera, consisting primarily of music rather than theater and employing elements of both opera and oratorio.

This work for chorus, soloists, and jazz ensemble, which lasts slightly under an hour, is organized into three parts and built around episodes in the life of Sojourner Truth, the 19th-century freed slave who became a powerful and eloquent orator in the struggle for emancipation and the rights of blacks and women. The narrative takes place in two time levels: actual time and remembered, or disjunct time. Actual time corresponds to the work's setting in a small Midwestern town that serves as a frame for the first and last sections. Remembered time includes previous events and non-sequential recollections and reflections by Sojourner on her past.

In actual time, the arrival of Sojourner is awaited by the townspeople, some of whom object that "We don't want her here!" and others who eagerly welcome her. Before she appears in the town, however, we are taken back to several episodes from her life. The first event is from her childhood in New York, when she was sold at the age of seven as a throw-in with an auction of sheep. In the second section she remembers her parents, Papa Baumfree and Mama Betts, and the man she married. In the third part, the New York law freeing slave children born after 1799 is proclaimed, and she prays for guidance. The Lord instructs her to travel the countryside with the message of freedom and gives her the name Sojourner Truth. She arrives in the small Midwestern town of the opening scene and speaks her message despite confrontations and a near riot.

This story unfolds in a variety of musical sections, some of them transitory and connected through the narrative flow and others set off as fully developed, independent units. The scenes in the town flow continuously from solo voices in declamatory style to choral interjections to instrumental interludes. Part I culminates in an extended and energetic choral and instrumental jazz number, marked "swinging," in which the townspeople welcome Sojourner.

Part II, in which Sojourner is sold, begins with an instrumental piece in Latin-Caribbean style marked "mambo." The Caribbean rhythms and instrumentation are carried over into the auction scene where each bid is delivered in mambo rhythm. Part II continues with Sojourner's recollections of her past, in which her parents appear and sing to her. The vocal lines are partly declamatory and partly *arioso,* with interjections by solo instruments— string bass and alto saxophone. A striking effect is achieved by the inclusion of the Lord's Prayer sung by Sojourner: each of its phrases is intoned on one note and followed by questions and further recollections in combinations of melody and speech. The final phrase of the prayer concludes Part II.

In Part III, the law that frees slaves in New York is proclaimed and explained by the chorus. The vocal lines are delivered in speech, supported by instrumental background. Then the instruments fall silent and a piece in the style of a spiritual, for chorus and soloist, begins; Sojourner laments her confusion and calls upon the Lord. Four members of the chorus improvise overlapping independent lines in "a moaning and beseeching manner," and Sojourner's plea is answered by the Lord in a recitative replete with classical declamation, harmonies, cadences, and instrumental punctuation.

The finale of Part III returns to the small town, with the town band playing a Salvation Army-style march and the crowds challenging Sojourner in half-spoken shouts and cries. She delivers a monologue consisting of passages from her most memorable speeches underscored by an instrumental background that includes an eloquent single melodic line played by the alto saxophone. The last chorale-style instrumental accompaniment leads into the choir's concluding phrase, which also concludes the work: "Truth is eternal and truth is love."

Sojourner, while continuing Scott Joplin's legacy in his opera *Treemonisha* of combining classical operatic and African-American elements, does indeed represent a new form in its brevity and its combination of traditional and novel formal elements, classical and African-American idioms, and real and remembered time. It broadens the possibilities for dramatic expression while avoiding the necessity of large and expensive stage production and is a welcome model for the many other composers drawn to the medium of opera.

Sojourner has been staged several times: by Duane Jones for Opera Ebony in 1985 and again in 1986 with Loretta Holkam in the title role; by Hope Clark for Opera Ebony in 1988 with soprano Elvira Green; and by Von Washington at Calvin College Fine Arts Center in Grand Rapids, Michigan, in 1990 with soprano Claritha Buggs. The work was commissioned in 1976 by the National Endowment for the Arts for the Bicentennial year, but due to illness, Capers was not able to finish it until several years later. Its premiere was a concert performance at St. Peter's

Church in New York City in February 1981, with Elvira Green in the title role, Capers at the piano, and John Robinson conducting.

REFERENCES

Capers, Valerie. Personal interview with the author, October 12, 1990.

———. Personal interview with the author, November 11, 1995.

Palmer, Robert. "Concert: Valerie Capers." *New York Times* (December 20, 1978): C21.

Wilson, John S. "An Imaginative Approach." *New York Times* (July 2, 1973).

———. "Jazz: By Valerie Capers." *New York Times* (February 28, 1981).

———. "Valerie Capers to Conduct Her Jazz-Based Cantata." *New York Times* (December 17, 1978): sect. 1, 100.

HELEN WALKER-HILL

CARTER, ROLAND

Born in Chattanooga, Tenn., May 4, 1942. **Education:** Chattanooga, Tenn., attended public schools, 1948–60; piano study with Alma Stoval, 1948–60; Howard High School, music classes with Edmonia Simmons, 1958–60; Hampton University, Hampton, Va., B.S. in music education, 1964; New York University, New York., N.Y., M.A. in music education, 1966; further study at New York University, 1966; Catholic University of America, Washington, D.C., 1970; Aspen Choral Institute, Aspen, Colo., 1973; private study with Emerson Myers (piano), 1970, John Nelson (conducting), 1974, Hugh Ross (choral studies), 1968–70. **Composing and Performing Career:** Crusader Male Chorus of Hampton, assistant director, accompanist, arranger, 1962–79, director, 1980–89; Hampton, Va., Peninsula Youth Symphony, director, 1974–80; Choir Directors and Organists Guild of the Hampton University Ministers' Conference, assistant director, 1963–79, director, 1980–89; accompanist and coach for Marilyn Thompson, 1982–present; Chattanooga Choral Society for the Preservation of Negro Spirituals, director, 1989–present; Chattanooga, First Baptist Church, director of music, 1992–present; Chattanooga, Tenn., Mar-Vel Publishers, founder and chief executive, 1978-present. **Teaching Career:** Hampton University, Hampton, Va., Summer Music Institute for High School Students, 1964–69, director, 1966–69; Hampton University, director of choral music, 1965–88, chair, 1986–89; University of Tennessee at Chattanooga, music department faculty, 1989–present, department head, 1989–95. **Commissions:** Hampton University, 1968, 1978; Ric-Charles Choral Ensemble and the New Jersey Council for the Arts, 1988; Martin St. Baptist Church, Raleigh, N.C., 1988; Alfred St. Baptist Church, Alexandria, Va., 1989; National Association of Negro Musicians, 1994. **Honors/Awards:** Maclellan Foundation fellowship, Chattanooga, 1965–66; National Association of Negro Musicians, Distinguished Musician Award, 1974, Musician of the Year, Eastern region, 1981; Hampton University, Lindback Award for Distinguished Teaching, 1982; University of Tennessee at Chattanooga, ALPHA Society, 1992; University of Tennessee at Chattanooga College of Arts and Sciences, Excellence in Service award, 1992; Black Music Caucus of MENC, National Award, 1994; **Mailing Address:** Department of Music, University of Tennessee at Chattanooga, 615 McCallie Avenue, Chattanooga, TN 37403.

MUSIC LIST

ORCHESTRA (CHAMBER OR FULL) WITH CHORUS
Hold Fast to Dreams (soprano solo, SATB, orchestra). 1978. Chattanooga, Tenn.: Mar-Vel Music, n.d. Commissioned by Hampton University for the inauguration of William Harvey as president.
Lift Ev'ry Voice and Sing (SSAATTBB, brass band or keyboard, orchestra). Chattanooga, Tenn.: Mar-Vel Music, n.d.

CHORAL MUSIC
"Anniversary Hymn." 1988. Unpublished manuscript. Commissioned by Martin St. Baptist Church, Raleigh, N.C.

Five Choral Responses (SATB unaccompanied). Chattanooga, Tenn.: Mar-Vel Music, n.d.
"A Hampton Portrait: Prologue" (SSAATTBB, organ, horn, timpani). 1968. Chattanooga, Tenn.: Mar-Vel Music, n.d. Commissioned by Hampton Institute for its centennial. Premiere, 1968.
"How Beautiful Are the Feet" (soprano solo, SATB). 1989. Chattanooga, Tenn.: Mar-Vel Music, n.d. Commissioned by Alfred St. Baptist Church, Alexandria, Va.
"I Dream a World" (SATB). 1994. Chattanooga, Tenn.: Mar-Vel Music, n.d. Commissioned by the National Association of Negro Musicians for their 75th Anniversary.
"No Room in the Inn" (bass solo, SSAATTBB). Chattanooga, Tenn.: Mar-Vel Music, 1988.
Psalm 23 (soprano solo, SATB unaccompanied). 1988. Chattanooga, Tenn.: Mar-Vel Music, n.d. Contents: I Shall Not Want; Aria; The Shadow of Death; I Shall Dwell. Commissioned by Ric-Charles Choral Ensemble of Plainfield, N.J., and the New Jersey Council for the Arts.
"You Must Have That True Religion" (SSAATTBB unaccompanied). New York: Lawson-Gould Music, 1982.

* * * * *

Roland Carter's biographical sketch in a 1995 concert program concluded, "Carter maintains a fervid schedule, constantly traveling throughout the United States as a highly sought-after conductor, lecturer, choral clinician, and publisher." This rather stock statement encapsulates a large part of the important work of this composer: writing choral music and informing audiences about it, telling people about the music of other African-American composers, and conducting and premiering his works in a variety of settings. Carter has combined this portion of his work with the life of a college professor teaching choral music, conducting, applied piano, and theory/composition, often while discharging duties as department head. His importance, therefore, is neither strictly as a composer nor as an educator but truly as a "composer-educator."

A product of the segregated public school system of Chattanooga, Tennessee, Carter began music study at age six and first appeared as a pianist for his Sunday school at age eight. At Chattanooga's Howard High School, he was influenced by Edmonia Simmons, a graduate of Hampton University (formerly Hampton Institute) in Hampton, Virginia, and former pupil of R. Nathaniel Dett. According to Carter, Simmons saw to it that he began his collegiate music education at Hampton "by physically taking me there and depositing me on the steps of the music building. . . . I could not have attended the University of Chattanooga [now the University of Tennessee at Chattanooga] upon finishing high school in the early 1960s, but there was a certain pride in returning there as music department head in 1989."

Like many other composers and musicians, Carter received formal musical training at Hampton while also participating in the musical life of the church and the university. For Carter, because of the influences of Edmonia Simmons and of his own years at

Hampton as student and professor, "The spirit of Dett [who taught there from 1913 to 1932] was never far away. Alumni longed to hear his arrangements. I felt him looking over my shoulder as I taught and directed the choir." Carter has pursued his study of Dett's compositions throughout his career and has been featured in lectures, recitals, and other presentations concerned with Dett's *oeuvre*. Carter cites two major influences at Hampton: his work with Charles Flax, choral director of the University Church, and—though largely self-taught as a composer—his study with Noel Da Costa, professor of theory and composition.

It may be said that Roland Carter's compositions are truly *Gebrauchsmusik*—music for use—often with an African-American flavor. His compositional output has developed through his fulfillment of commissions for specific occasions, as well as from the need for music within his own practice as a university professor, choral ensemble director, and church musician. Five such commissions are "A Hampton Portrait: Prologue" (1968), *Hold Fast to Dreams* (1978), *Psalm 23* (1988), "How Beautiful Are the Feet" (1989), and "I Dream a World" (1994).

SELECTED WORKS

Roland Carter's *oeuvre* consists of original choral compositions and arrangements of spirituals for solo and ensemble. The works described below exemplify his original compositions and share the common characteristic of being composed for some combination of mixed voices, usually with at least one section for solo voice.

"A Hampton Portrait: Prologue," Carter's first commission, sets a text by Albert Berrian and was commissioned by Hampton University in 1968 for its centennial year. Scored for double mixed chorus, organ, horn, and timpani, the music mirrors mood changes in the text and captures the rising and falling of the sea through dynamics, voicing, and accompaniment. The recurring repetition of the opening phrase, "You stand where the land and sea meet" (Hampton is located on the Chesapeake Bay inlet), sung at increasing dynamic levels, leads to a triumphant close.

"Hold Fast to Dreams" is another Hampton University commission, written for the 1978 inauguration of William Harvey as its 12th president. Scored for mixed chorus (SATB), soprano solo, and orchestra, "Hold Fast to Dreams" has been performed by several choruses in the southeastern United States. The eight-minute work, with text by Langston Hughes, opens with chorus and orchestra moving among three ideas: (1) a veiled instrumental reference to the phrase "[if you] wanna' get to heaven" from the spiritual "Hold On," (2) robust singing of the opening phrase, "Hold fast to dreams," and (3) a dreamlike orchestral interlude. The first stanza of the poem is developed through this succession of ideas, ending with the mutation of the command "hold fast" into a jubilant "hold on" in B-flat major, a verbal suggestion of the influence of the spiritual "Hold On."

The soprano solo that comprises the contrasting middle section of the work begins with a statement of the phrase "first in the heart is the dream," accompanied by an underlying syncopation that eventually gives way to flowing triplets in the strings. As in the first section, one key area (C minor) is fully explored, giving way again to B-flat minor as the chorus returns to the opening mood with another reference to the spiritual "Hold On," this time pre-

sented in a more direct manner. The chorus joins the syncopated accompaniment of the orchestra, building to a climax with repetition of the phrase "Hold on!"

Psalm 23 was Carter's 1988 response to a commission from the Ric-Charles Choral Ensemble of Plainfield, New Jersey. An unaccompanied SATB motet with soprano solo, the four sections are "I Shall Not Want," "Aria" (He Makes Me to Lie Down), "The Shadow of Death," and "I Shall Dwell." *Psalm 23* reflects the definition of "motet" by employing a sacred text, and, with the exception of the solo soprano aria, each section requires contrapuntal entrances of singers, who often sing independent melodies.

The section "I Shall Not Want," which opens in C major, is a setting of only this phrase and its predecessor, "The Lord is my shepherd." It builds contrapuntally from the lowest to the highest voice, with an immediate segue into the "Aria," a soprano solo in 5/4 meter. The 24-measure aria treats the text "He makes me to lie down," ending with "he restoreth my soul." The aria has a sparse, wordless choral accompaniment, with a flowing, through-composed melody centering in the key of E major.

The third section, "The Shadow of Death," opens with a bass ostinato on the tonic and dominant tones (*d* and *a*) of D minor, followed by the other voices entering together, each with a more or less independent melody. The melodies finally move together into four-part harmony and cadence in the dominant at "thou art with me," reentering from soprano to bass on "thy rod and thy staff." All voices join in a recitative in D minor, "thou preparest a table," with 16th-note text painting on the word "runneth." Octave leaps on "surely goodness and mercy" lead to a cadence in G major, preparing for the conclusion of the composition ("And I Shall Dwell") in C major with a return to the melody, key, and harmony of the opening section.

"How Beautiful Are the Feet" was written in 1989 on commission from the Alfred St. Baptist Church of Alexandria, Virginia. It is dedicated to the pastor of the church, Dr. J. D. Peterson, on his 25th anniversary of service. Based on the biblical texts Romans 10:15 and Isaiah 52:7, this SATB anthem with soprano solo and keyboard accompaniment represents a departure for Carter from works that reference the African-American experience. In this straightforward, five-minute work in A minor, the chorus and keyboard alternate phrases in the opening bars, developing the question from Romans, "How shall they preach?" The solo begins in measure 12, supported initially by the keyboard, then by the chorus, echoing the title phrase of the song. In both unison and in parts, the men's and women's sections salute the dedicatee with calls of "steadfast," "committed," and "compelled." After a brief return to the anthem's opening, "How Beautiful Are the Feet" closes with an appropriate phrase, "How shall they preach, except they are called."

"I Dream a World" is a six-minute setting of the well-known poem by Langston Hughes for SATB chorus (with some parts added, *divisi*) and piano, with slight textual adaptations for gender inclusiveness. Commissioned for and premiered at the 75th Anniversary of the National Association of Negro Musicians in Dallas in 1994, "I Dream a World" represents Carter's exploration of undulating quintal and quartal harmonic accompaniment (using intervals of fourths and fifths), which gives way at times to quotations

Roland Carter; courtesy of Ed Duling

of the Negro spirituals "We Shall Overcome," "O Freedom," and "I've Been 'Buked." After the briefest introduction, the chorus hums an altered version of "I've Been 'Buked," moving to a statement of the title phrase starting in the basses. The key center is E minor as the chorus explores the text, with sections of the chorus often presenting brief independent melodies, echoes at the ends of phrases, and staggered entrances. As the basses and tenors sing "A world where all people . . . ," the piano sings out "We Shall Overcome." As the work builds in volume in four-part harmony to a climax on "I dream of such a world where all will overcome," the keyboard makes reference to the opening of the spiritual "O Freedom." The piece closes quietly with a brief reprise of the hummed opening and ends on the urgent words, "Our world!"—a confirmation in reply to the poet's dream.

REFERENCES

Carter, Roland M. Personal conversations with the author, August 4 and August 29, 1995.
———. Telephone conversation with the author, August 22, 1995.
Program notes, *Vocal Music of William Grant Still.* Southeast Center for Education in the Arts, University of Tennessee, Chattanooga, July 11, 1995.

ED DULING

CHARLES, RAY

Born Ray Charles Robinson in Albany, Ga., September 23, 1930. **Education:** Musically self-taught in early childhood; completely blinded by glaucoma, age six; State School for the Deaf and Blind, St. Augustine, Fla., learned piano, trumpet, clarinet, alto saxophone, and organ, 1937–45. **Composing and Performing Career:** Jacksonville, Fla., began playing in nightclubs at age 15; moved to Seattle, Wash., at age 18; Seattle, played with his own group, the McSon Trio, 1948–50; first studio recording, "Confession Blues," 1949; toured the U.S. as a solo act with Lowell Fulson, 1950–52; formed his own band and accompanied singers such as Ruth Brown, 1953; first number one hit, "I Got a Woman," released 1954; acted in the movies *Ballad in Blue,* 1966, and *The Blues Brothers,* 1980; subject of PBS television documentary, *Ray Charles: The Genius of Soul,* 1992. **Honors/Awards:** Grand Prix du Disque Award, Best Jazz Vocal Album, 1958; *Down Beat* International Critics Poll, Best New Star, Male Singer, 1958; *Down Beat* Readers Poll, R&B Personality of the Year, 1958, 1959; received 12 Grammy Awards: four in 1960, one each in 1961, 1962, and 1963, two in 1966, and one each in 1975, 1990, and 1993; *Down Beat* International Critics Poll, Best Male Singer 1961–64, 1968, 1969, 1973; *Down Beat* Readers Poll, Best Male Vocalist, 1963, 1964, 1968, 1969; *Swing Journal* Best Male Singer, 1964–66, 1969–72; Paris, commemorative coin issued in his honor, 1965; Hollywood Radio/TV Society, International Broadcasting Award, 1966; U.S. House of Representatives, resolution in his honor introduced, 1966; City of Los Angeles, Calif., Ray Charles Day, June 8, 1967; Florida A&M University, Tallahassee, Fla., honorary degree in music, 1967; Sickle Cell Disease Research Foundation, National Chairman, 1967; *Playboy* Jazz and Pop Hall of Fame, inductee, 1968; American Academy of Achievement, Golden Plate Award, 1975; National Association for Sickle Cell Disease, Man of Distinction, 1975; American Music Conference, National Music Award, 1976; Beverly Hills Lodge of B'nai B'rith, Beverly Hills, Calif., Man of the Year Award, 1976; *Playboy* Music Award Readers Poll, Best Jazz Male Vocalist, 1976; Songwriters Hall of Fame, inductee, 1976; Georgia Music Hall of Fame, inductee, 1978; Shaw University, Raleigh, N.C., honorary doctorate, 1978; Hollywood Boulevard "Walk of Fame" Star, 1981; NAACP Image Awards, Hall of Fame Award and Best R&B Male Vocalist, 1983; John F. Kennedy Center for the Performing Arts, honoree, 1986; Republic of France, Commander of Fine Arts and Letters, 1986; Rock and Roll Hall of Fame, inductee, 1986; Grammy Lifetime Achievement Award, 1988; Clio Award, Best Male Performer, 1990; University of South Florida, Tampa, honorary doctorate, 1990; Florida Artists Hall of Fame, inductee, 1992; National Medal of Arts, 1993; American Foundation for the Blind, Helen Keller Personal Achievement Award, 1994; Johnson Publishing's Black Achievement Awards, Lifetime Achievement Award, 1994; Horatio Alger Award, 1995; Occidental College, Los Angeles, Calif., honorary doctorate, 1996; Rhythm and Blues Hall of Fame, honorary life chairman. **Mailing Address:** Ray Charles Enterprises, 2107 W. Washington Blvd., Los Angeles, CA 90018.

MUSIC LIST

POPULAR SONGS

[The following list of titles includes only works that were composed by the subject of the entry; it is not a list of recordings that were made by the subject. Although the composer may have made recordings of his own works, the list is not restricted to those recordings but in many cases includes performances by other artists of the composer's work. The list is made up of publication and discographical data, in cases where such information is available. Although no effort has been made to include documentation of the earliest recording of the works listed, the date of the earliest recording that is readily available has been given. —Ed.]

"Ain't That Love." Recorded, 1951: Atlantic 7 82310-2; Rhino 72859.

"All to Myself (Alone)." Recorded, ca. 1950: Charly Records CDCD 2002; Ebony CD 8001/CD 8002; Star Line SLC-61118.

"Baby, Let Me Hold Your Hand" or "Oh, Baby." Recorded, 1949: Charly Records CDCD 2002; Ebony CD 8001/CD 8002; Rhino 72859.

"A Bit of My Soul" or "A Bit of Soul." Recorded: Atlantic 7 82310-2; Atlantic 8094.

"Blackjack." Recorded, 1954: Atlantic 7 82310-2; Rhino 72859; Rhino/Atlantic 71667.

"Blue Funk." Recorded, 1989: Atlantic 81951.

"Blue Genius." Recorded, 1989: Atlantic 81951.

"Blues Is My Middle Name" or "Some Day." Recorded, 1949: Drive CD 3233; Ganton House ONN 37.

"Booty-Butt" or "Boody Butt." Recorded, 1971: Rhino 72859.

"Brightest Smile in Town." Recorded, 1963: DCC Compact Classics GSZ 1027; Rhino 72859.

"But on the Other Hand Baby." Co-composer, Percy Mayfield. Recorded, 1961: Rhino 72859.

"Charlesville." Recorded, 1961: Atlantic 1369; Atlantic 81951.

"Chitlins with Candied Yams." Recorded, 1966: ABC ABCS-590X.

"Come Back Baby." Recorded, 1954: Atlantic 7 82310-2; Rhino 72859.

"Confession Blues." Recorded, 1949: Charly Records CDCD 2002; Ebony CD 8001/CD 8002; Rhino 72859.

"Cosmic Ray." Recorded, 1989: Atlantic 81951.

"Dawn Ray." Recorded, 1956: Atlantic 81731.

"Don't You Know." Recorded, 1953: Atlantic 7 82310-2; Rhino 72859.

"A Fool for You." Note: instrumental version titled "Sweet Sixteen Bars." Recorded, 1954: Atlantic 7 82310-2; Atlantic 1289; Rhino 72859; Rhino/Atlantic 71667.

"From the Heart." Recorded, 1966: ABC ABCS-590X; DCC 38.

"Funny (but I Still Love You)." Recorded, 1952: Atlantic 7 82310-2; Rhino/Atlantic 71667.

"The Genius after Hours." Recorded, 1961: Atlantic 1369; Atlantic 81951.

"Hallelujah, I Love Her So." Recorded, 1956: Atlantic 81951; Atlantic 7 82310-2; Rhino 72859.

"Hard Times (No One Knows Better Than I)." Recorded, 1950: Atlantic 7 82310-2; Rhino/Atlantic 71667.

"Here Am I" or "Here I Am" or "Let's Have A Ball" or "By Myself" or "All Alone Again." Recorded, 1949: Rhino R471722.

"Hey Someday." Recorded, 1980: Drive CD 3233; Ganton House ONN 37.

"Honey, Honey." Recorded, 1949: Design SDLP-245; Royal Collection RC 83154.

"Hornful Soul." Recorded, 1950: Atlantic 81731; Rhino/Atlantic 71667.

"Hot Rod." Recorded, 1959: Atlantic 1289; Atlantic 81732-2.

"I Believe to My Soul." Recorded, 1959: Atlantic 7 82310-2; Rhino 72859; Rhino/Atlantic 71667.

"I Can Make It through the Day." Recorded: Rhino 72859; Tangerine/ABC Records ABCX 765/TRC.

"I Chose to Sing the Blues." Co-composer, Holliday. Recorded: Rhino 72859.

"I Got a Woman" or "I've Gotta Woman." Recorded, 1954: Atlantic PR 439; Atlantic 7 82310-2; Atlantic 1289; Rhino 72859.

"I Had a Dream." Co-composer, Harper. Recorded, 1951: Atlantic 7 82310-2.

"I Want to Know." Recorded, 1951: Atlantic 7 82310-2.

"If I Give You My Love." Recorded, 1954: Ebony CD 8001/CD 8002; International Award Series AKS-243; Rhino R471722.

"If It Wasn't for Bad Luck." Co-composer, James Lewis. Recorded: ABC Records ABCS-695; Rhino 72859.

"It's Alright." Recorded, 1951: Atlantic 7 82310-2.

"Joy Ride." Recorded, 1956: Atlantic 81731.

"Jumpin' in the Morning." Recorded, 1951: Atlantic 7 82310-2.

"Kissa Me, Baby." Recorded, ca. 1950: Rhino 72859; ZETA Records ZET 707.

"Leave My Woman Alone." Recorded, 1951: Atlantic 8054; Atlantic 7 82310-2; Rhino 72859.

"Let's Go." Recorded, 1960: DCC 38; Rhino 72814.

"Light Out of Darkness." Recorded: Gitanes Jazz/Verve 314 519 703-2.

"Love on My Mind." Recorded, 1950: Atlantic 81951; Rhino/Atlantic 71667.

"Mary Ann." Recorded, 1951: Atlantic 7 82310-2.

"Misery in My Heart" or "Going Down to the River" or "Givin' It Up" or "I'm Going to Drown Myself." Recorded, ca. 1950: Coronet CX-173; Spinorama S-141.

"Mister C." Recorded, 1960: DCC 38; Rhino 72814.

"My Baby! (I Love Her, Yes I Do)." Recorded, ca. 1959: Rhino 72859.

"Nobody Cares." Recorded, 1950: Atlantic 7 82310-2; Rhino/Atlantic 71667.

"Questions." Recorded, 1980: Atlantic SD 19281.

"Ray's Blues." Recorded, 1950: Atlantic 7 82310-2; Fat Boy 325; Rhino/Atlantic 71667; ZETA ZET 707.

"Ray's Segue." Co-composer, Alvin Batiste. Recorded, 1993: Sony CT53314.

"Rockhouse, Parts 1 and 2." Recorded, 1956: Atlantic 7 82310-2; Rhino 72859; Rhino/Atlantic 71667.

"Rocking Chair Blues." Recorded, 1949: Charly Records CDCD 2002; Drive CD 3233.

"Sentimental Blues." Recorded: Charly Records CDCD 2002; Ebony CD 8001/CD 8002.

"She's on the Ball." Recorded, ca. 1950: Drive CD 3233; Ganton House ONN 37.

"The Snow Is Falling" or "Snowfall" or "I Used to Be So Happy." Recorded, ca. 1950: Premiere PM 2005; Royal Collection RC 83154.

"St. Pete Florida Blues" or "St. Pete's Blues" or "Done Found Out" or "I Found My Baby There." Recorded, 1947: Rhino R471722.

"The Sun's Gonna Shine Again." Recorded, 1950: Atlantic 7 82310-2; Rhino/Atlantic 71667.

"Tell All the World about You." Recorded, 1951: Atlantic 7 82310-2.

"Tell Me How Do You Feel." Co-composer, Percy Mayfield. Recorded, 1951: Atlantic 8054; Atlantic 7 82310-2.

"Tell Me What You Want Me to Do." Recorded, 1996: Qwest/Warner Bros. 9 46107-4.

"That's Enough." Recorded, 1951: Atlantic 7 82310-2.

"Them That Got." Recorded, ca. 1959: Rhino 72859.

"Then We'll Be Home." Recorded, 1975: Crossover CR 9005.

"This Little Girl of Mine." Recorded, 1955: Rhino 72859.

"Understanding." Recorded, 1968: Rhino 72859.

"Walkin' and Talkin'" or "Talkin' 'Bout You" or "Tell Me, Baby." Recorded, 1947: Atlantic 1289; ZETA Records ZET 707.

"What Have I Done?" or "Ray Charles' Blues." Recorded: Ebony CD 8001/CD 8002; Star Line SLC-61118; ZETA Records ZET 707.

"What Kind of Man Are You?" Recorded, ca. 1957: Atlantic 7 82310-2.

"What Would I Do without You?" Recorded, 1950: Atlantic 7 82310-2; Rhino/Atlantic 71667.

"What'd I Say?" or "What I Say." Recorded, 1959: Atlantic 7 82310-2; Atlantic 1289; Rhino 72859; Valentine GJ-1.

"Who You Gonna Love?" Recorded, ca. 1959: Atlantic n.n.

"Why Did You Go?" Recorded, 1947: Ebony CD 8001/CD 8002; Mainstream MRL 310.

"Wondering and Wondering." Recorded, 1947: Ebony CD 8001/CD 8002; Fat Boy 325; ZETA Records ZET 707.

"X-Ray Blues." Recorded, 1950: Atlantic 81951; Rhino/Atlantic 71667.

"You Be My Baby." Co-composers, Doc Pomus, Mort Shuman. Recorded, 1963: Atlantic 7 82310-2; Atlantic 8029; Atlantic 8054; Atlantic CS 8054.

INCIDENTAL MUSIC

Black Rodeo. 1972. Film soundtrack.

Warnung vor einer heiligen Nutte. 1971. Film soundtrack.

PUBLICATIONS

ABOUT CHARLES
Articles

Albertson, Chris. "Ray Charles." *Stereo Review* 51 (February 1986): 55–59.

Booth, Stanley. "Ray Charles Tells the Truth." *Pulse!* 166 (December 1997): 34–40, 132.

Cartier, J. "Ray, Charles, 'The genius, aveugle comme la fortune.'" *MUS* 96 (March 1962): 12–16.

Cooke, J. "Ray Charles: In Person." *Jazz Monthly* 9 (July 1963): 6–8.

"Dix jours avec Ray Charles: Sa tournée en France." *Jazz Hot* 178 (July–August 1962): 24–27; 179 (September 1962): 28+.

Fong-Torres, Ben. "Ray Charles (Interview)." *Rolling Stone* 126 (January 18, 1973): 28–36.

———. "Rolling Stone: The Interviews—Ray Charles." *Rolling Stone* 641 (October 15, 1992): 56–58.

Gardner, Barbara. "The Bright Night World of Ray Charles." *Down Beat* 27, no. 14 (1960): 20–22.

Ray Charles; courtesy of Qwest Records; photo by Mark Hanauer

George, N. "Ray Charles and Soul." *Jazz Podium* 39 (April 1990): 3–5.

Goddet, L. "Ray Charles pas à pas." *Jazz Hot* 329 (July–August 1976): 8–12.

Guralnick, Peter. "Ray Charles." In *The Rolling Stone Illustrated History of Rock & Roll,* 130–134. 3rd ed. New York: Random House, 1992.

Lattes, P., and P. Nahman. "Un roi à Paris." *Jazz Magazine* 7 (December 1961): 39–41.

Levenson, Jeff. "What'd I Say—A Conversation with Ray Charles." *Down Beat* 56, no. 1 (1989): 16–19.

Lydon, Michael. "Ray Charles." In *Boogie Lightning,* 187–229. New York: Dial, 1974.

Masson, J. R. "Le retour de Ray Charles." *Jazz Magazine* 9 (June 1963): 20–27.

Morrison, A. "Ray Charles." *Jazz Journal* 13 (December 1960): 3–6.

Postif, F. "Marjorie Hendricks, David Newman, et John Hunt nous aident a mieux connaître les véritables débuts de Ray Charles." *Jazz Hot* 170 (November 1961): 14–17.

"Ray Charles: Widening the Range." *Jazz Podium* 43 (September 1994): 10–12.

"Ray Charles regne a cinq jours sur Paris." *Jazz Magazine* 7 (December 1961): 26–35.

Soporek, W. "Ray Charles: 'There's Nothing Like the Real Thing'." *Jazz Forum* 94 (1985): 44–48.

Tenot, F. "Lumières sur Ray Charles." *Jazz Magazine* 6 (December 1960): 36–40.

———. "La semaine éblouissante." *Jazz Magazine* 9 (July 1963): 30–32.

Tronchot, J. "Ray Charles." *Jazz Hot* 167 (August 1961): 16–20.

Weber, Bruce. "Rolling Stone Portraits." *Rolling Stone* 643 (November 12, 1992): 83–92.

Welding, Pete. "Ray Charles: Senior Diplomat of Soul." *Down Beat* 44, no. 9 (1977): 12–15, 46.

Wexler, Jerry, and David Ritz. "The Chairman of the Board." *Rolling Stone* 650 (February 18, 1993): 50–52.

BY CHARLES

Brother Ray: Ray Charles' Own Story, with David Ritz. New York: Dial, 1978. Updated ed., New York: Da Capo Press, 1992.

"Ray Charles Story." *Jazz Magazine* 275 (May 1979): 36–39+.

* * * * *

Ray Charles is an innovator, adapter, and a study in musical fusion. His career stretches from working small nightclubs, where he covered Charles Brown and Nat "King" Cole tunes, to international fame and recognition as one of the greats in popular music. Along the way, Charles absorbed the many genres of music to which he was exposed, fusing together unique and powerful hybrid styles. His influences are diverse, including the music he heard in his childhood church (Shiloh Baptist Church in Greenville, Florida), country music, classical music, jazz, and rhythm and blues. Ray Charles' ability to combine the best of each is what makes his music unique. His lifelong experimentation with sound—whether it be a band without a drummer (the McSon Trio), adding female back-up vocalists to his band (the Raelettes), or incorporating novel instruments into his recordings (such as a Wurlitzer electric piano)—has continually pushed his music to new heights. Ray

Charles, as attested to by his enormous success, is truly one of the giants of African-American popular music.

Charles possessed a predilection for music from an early age—"I was born with music inside me," he has stated—and he began to play the piano before he lost his sight at the age of six because of untreated glaucoma. Charles treated his desire to learn to play music like he did the loss of his sight—not as an obstacle to be overcome but an opportunity to gain some form of expertise. As a child, his nickname was "Mechanic," earned as a result of his fascination with engines and motors. That unquenchable desire to unravel the inner dynamics of various phenomena led him to acquire certain skills uncommon for a blind person—driving a car and piloting a plane, for example—but even more important, it convinced him that music was a system with ascertainable rules. Gaining command of those principles was, for Ray Charles, like gaining control over his blindness, the result of proceeding, in Robert Palmer's words, "straightforwardly, with a firm, squarely centered sense of personal direction and a highly evolved and sensitive sonar."

Charles' intensive musical education (studying composition and acquiring proficiency in piano, trumpet, clarinet, alto saxophone, and organ), begun when he was eight years old at the State School for the Deaf and Blind in St. Augustine, Florida, was augmented by his familiarity with a wide range of musical forms, either through firsthand experience or by listening to recordings. All forms of music fascinated Ray Charles, from gospel to Glenn Miller to the Grand Ole Opry.

Another crucial quality of Charles' musical training was the stress laid upon instrumental competence and adaptability. "Musically," he said, "I was raised during a time of absolutely no compromise: Either you could play your instrument or you couldn't." To this day, the most telling remark ever made to him about his music was when the bandleader Lucky Millinder dismissed his application to join his band by stating, "You don't got what it takes." Charles left school at the age of 15 and spent the rest of his teens as a professional musician in Florida and in the state of Washington, perfecting the skills Millinder felt he lacked. At the core of any form of musical competency, Charles feels, must be a command of the blues. "Show me a guy who can't play the blues, and I'm through with him before he can get started. If you can't get nasty and grovel down in the gutter, something's missing."

Despite that devotion to down-home emotionalism, Ray Charles initially established his reputation not by playing the kind of blues one would associate with his rural roots but by the urbane and less overtly lowdown style that took root in Los Angeles and is most intimately associated with what Peter Guralnick has called the "sophisticated cocktail swing" performed by Charles Brown and Nat "King" Cole. For some time, as he forged his own unique manner, Charles patterned himself after these players, Cole in particular, whose work combined certain qualities he admired—"jazz improvisation, pretty melodies, hot rhythms, and an occasional taste of the blues." Jack Lauderdale of Swing Time Records, one of the many savvy entrepreneurs who sought out and recorded African-American performers during this period, signed Charles in 1949 and released his first single, "Confession Blues." He joined the touring company of another of Lauderdale's performers, guitarist/singer Lowell Fulson, who had topped the charts in 1950 with "Every Day I Have the Blues." Playing with him afforded Charles his first opportunity to create arrangements and strengthened his devotion to the road and the need to perfect his material in front of live audiences before committing it to a recording.

In 1952, Charles signed with Atlantic Records and in 1953 began to lead his own band. In 1954, he had his first number one hit, "I Got a Woman," which was recorded and released by Atlantic Records. For the next five years, Atlantic executives Ahmet Ertegun and Jerry Wexler permitted Charles to record as many different kinds of music with as many different kinds of ensembles as he wished. This also proved to be the principal period during which Charles composed, for whenever he did not like the material sent to him by Atlantic, he was forced to write music, more from necessity than inspiration. Charles routinely downplays his abilities ("I like to think I'm a half-ass composer. I ain't no Duke Ellington, but I *can* write"), but he did write some of his most successful recordings, including "Don't You Know" (1953), "Blackjack" (1954), "Come Back Baby" (1954), and "Rockhouse, Parts 1 and 2" (1956).

In 1959, Charles left Atlantic for ABC Paramount Records and remained with the company until 1973, producing some of the finest material of his career—particularly the albums *Modern Sounds in Country and Western Music, Vols. 1 and 2* (1962, 1963) and *Genius plus Soul Equals Jazz* (Impulse, 1961).

Ahmet Ertegun's brother, Nesuhi, coordinated the jazz portion of Atlantic's catalog, and he paired Charles with Milt Jackson of the Modern Jazz Quartet on two successful albums of expressive small ensemble blues: *Soul Brothers* (1957) and *Soul Meeting* (1958). By 1959, Charles had taken the manner of performance heard in "I Got a Woman" to new heights. Two factors that led to his band's pronounced degree of sophistication were his ceaseless road schedule and the stern, at times autocratic manner in which he conducted his band. Several key members of that ensemble included Marcus Belgrave on trumpet, David "Fathead" Newman on alto and tenor saxophone, and Hank Crawford on baritone saxophone. Possibly even more important to the sound of Charles' band than these musicians was the trio of female singers called the Raelettes. When Charles contracted Margie Hendrix, Darlene MacRae, and Pat Mosley to join him, the trio was known as the Cookies and had been backing vocalist Chuck Willis. They had engaged in call-and-response patterns with him on one of his most popular recordings, a version of "C. C. Rider." Of them, Charles states, "I could have had four men and formed a regular all-male gospel quartet. . . . Instead, I wanted the flavor of a man's voice—my voice—set against women. I hadn't heard anyone do that with popular music before, and I really didn't care whether it was an old idea or a new one; I just knew that was what I was searching for."

From the start of his career, Ray Charles has been drawn to jazz and to this day seeks out musicians from that domain above all others as members of his band. He is attracted to jazz players because of their ability to play charts precisely and to range across various genres of music: "If I found cats who could play jazz, I could fix it so they could play my other little items—the rhythm-and-blues things. If a guy can handle jazz, that means he's a good musician, and it's easy for him to switch over to less complicated

styles." While good musicianship is important to Charles, he disdains the kind of haughtiness discernible on the part of some performers, that brand of "cool" that falsely allows them to feel superior to their audience. Charles believes that the public's tastes must be respected: "People give you their bread and are entitled to some kind of musical return on their dollar. I don't mean you got to give them *exactly* what they want. But you do have to keep them in mind."

Consequently, the kind of jazz that Charles recorded retains an unpretentious feel and lends itself more to dance than does most post-bebop jazz. This is due, in large part, to Charles' focus on rhythmic and melodic patterns rather than on technical virtuosity. This rhythmic focus is, most likely, directly related to the fact that for many years his concerts were held in dance halls rather than in concert arenas. In addition, the jazz that Charles recorded is heavily influenced by blues, and thus, it often revolves around a relatively simple chord progression. Few of the technical innovations that followed in the wake of bebop appear in his music. His themes are intensely melodic, often structured around a simple yet quotable riff, and they stress variation over ornate development. What stands out about his jazz playing, whether as pianist or saxophonist, is his relaxed approach: the deft, unaffected manner with which he synchronizes gospel, blues, and jazz elements.

Ray Charles' innovative nature is clearly evident in his approach to music. His vast musical abilities are summed up well in the words of Jerry Wexler, one of his producers: "I realized that the best thing I could do with Ray Charles was leave him alone. . . . It was a privilege to watch him work, to see how he—and American music, for that matter—evolved through his own unique instincts." In short, Ray Charles possesses both the instincts and the talent necessary to relate his musical ideas to those found in other styles and, from the interaction among them, to create new and innovative styles. Wexler also offers this insight into the importance of Charles' career: "Ray Charles took care of it all: simultaneously, he was a bopper, a bluesman, a gospel shouter, and the initiator of a back-to-the-roots jazz/soul movement. Ray saw past categories and played what he felt."

Ray Charles' influence on other performers was significant and wide reaching. First, the emotionalism of his voice—the fierce intensity with which he projected lyrics—influenced some indirectly; others, such as British artist Joe Cocker, copied it emphatically. Second, he influenced other performers by his infusion of gospel stylings into popular music. Others had done so to some extent, but Charles' emphatic adoption of call-and-response patterns for both his vocals and the instrumentalists who supported him was epochal. Third, the manner in which Charles "crossed over" from the black-identified to the more wide-ranging pop charts set a precedent for subsequent African-American performers, both in the fact of Charles' accomplishment and the manner in which he frequently performed material not specifically identified with the African-American musical tradition. This pattern is most notable in the successful country recordings of the early 1960s. Lastly, he has been influential by the manner in which he acted as a cultural entrepreneur, specifically in the running of the Tangerine label, which he established as a portion of his contract with ABC-Paramount after he left Atlantic Records.

I GOT A WOMAN (1954)

"I Got a Woman," recorded and released in 1954, was composed while Charles and Renald Richard, his bandleader at the time, were traveling from South Bend, Indiana, to Nashville, Tennessee. They were listening to a gospel station on the car radio (tuned in, Richard believes, to an Alex Bradford recording), when something about the underlying groove of the song attracted their interest. At first, the two men began to sing secular lyrics over the sacred text, creating a parody on the genre. Engaged by the results of this lighthearted exercise, Charles asked his partner to work on the material. Overnight, Richard fleshed out a first draft of the lyrics to which Charles quickly added the melody and orchestration.

This song not only solidified Charles' career but also encapsulated his mature style. Due in part to the blending of rhythm and blues with gospel, "I Got a Woman" replaced the more urbane style of his earlier work with a high degree of exuberance—a level of emotional energy that, while novel to the mainstream pop-music market of the time, was within the experience of African Americans who had grown up in the church. For Charles, the distinction between sacred and secular music was inconsequential: "I'd always thought that the blues and spirituals were close—close musically, close emotionally—and I was happy to hook 'em up."

The landmark quality of "I Got a Woman" is customarily attributed to the amalgamation of sacred and secular genres, yet this was not an uncommon phenomenon in African-American popular music. What stands out as much as or more than Charles' righteous vocalizing is his integration of the vocals with the accompanying ensemble. Each phrase of text is accompanied only by the rhythm section, allowing Charles to bring in the piano and the horn section as call-and-response instruments between phrases. As Wexler observes: "The band laid out except for the rhythm section while Ray sang a phrase. At the end of the phrase, he filled in on piano, like Lloyd Glenn or Amos Milburn, but here's the kicker: Ray's band doubled the piano figure, voiced to Ray's prescription." This treatment of the horn section prefigures the call-and-response patterns that Charles subsequently wrote for his backing vocalists, the Raelettes.

The form of the song is strophic. A brief introduction is followed by two verses, a tenor saxophone solo, a bridge, and a final verse. The harmonic progression used for the verses can be diagrammed as follows: I V I (IV) I—IV V^7—I IV—I V^7 I (IV) I (V^7). Each phrase (designated by dashes) absorbs eight bars of music, making for a very straightforward, danceable progression of 32 bars.

Charles' careful attention to orchestration is evident in his treatment of the bridge that immediately follows the saxophone solo. The bridge is orchestrated to provide an aural break from the insistent rhythmic patterns that prevail throughout the first part of the song. Here, Charles' lyrics are not accompanied at all. Rather, the entire band punctuates the vocal phrases with chords between lines of text. This bridge serves to create a heightening of tension as the listener comes to expect an imminent return to the original texture. Charles indeed returns to the original rhythms and brings the song to a close after a final verse.

The exuberance, some might even say spirited raggedness, of the song might, in part, have resulted from the fact that Charles' producers, Ertegun and Wexler, did not record the material in their studio in New York. Rather, they laid down the track at the Georgia Tech radio station WGST in Atlanta. The spit-and-polish sharpness customary on Atlantic releases gave way to a performance that, in Robert Palmer's words, "pressed the ecstasies of black church music into the service of a Dionysian sensuality." Although the lyrics generated some letters attacking Charles for desecrating God's word, less noticed or discussed at the time was that Charles successfully treated his band as a unified ensemble in order to obtain powerful answers to his driving calls.

WHAT'D I SAY (1959)

"What'd I Say" had its beginnings on the stage, growing out of an unplanned addition to the playlist. Caught short at the end of a performance with 15 minutes to fill, Charles extemporized the identifying riff and subsequent call-and-response between himself and the Raelettes. So captivated was the audience by this serendipitous combination of elements that Charles refined the initial spontaneous outburst over a number of weeks and then committed it to vinyl. The resulting recording is noteworthy for several reasons. First, Charles plays a Wurlitzer electric piano, a novel lead instrument in 1959. Second, the rhythmic structure, as Robert Palmer has observed, conveys a distinctly Latin feel. This is created by the interplay that occurs between the syncopations of drummer Milt Turner and Charles' piano figurations. Third, Charles uses several layers of call-and-response technique in the song.

A basic 12-bar progression forms the harmonic context of the song, and it can be diagrammed as follows: I IV I V^7 IV I (V^7). The song opens with an introduction of the progression by the electric piano. The drummer then enters, adding a distinctly Latin feel. The first level of call-and-response lies in Charles' treatment of the solo voice against the instrumental accompaniment. The first line of each verse is sung without accompaniment, after which the instruments re-enter, playing their customary parts. This continues for three verses, after which Charles takes a brief solo (12 bars). Thereafter, two more verses are sung in the same fashion.

At this point, another level of call-and-response is introduced into the texture. The first line is sung as before, and the accompaniment resumes underneath the vocal line, this time with the addition of the horn section. Rather than playing with the rhythm section, however, the horns echo Charles' vocal phrases during the latter portion of each verse. Two verses are sung with this double layer of call-and-response patterns. At this point, the song abruptly breaks off, and the listener hears a lively interaction among the musicians in the studio. Lively, that is, until Charles gets the attention of everyone and resumes the song.

A third level of call-and response is now introduced. The Raelettes are used in direct call-and-response, immediately repeating in unison every note that Charles sings. This dialogue between Charles and the Raelettes serves as a new treatment of the first line of the verse. After this new opening section of the verse, the accompaniment resumes and the Raelettes join the horns in call-and-response. This configuration of call-and-response patterns is repeated three times, each time with new improvisatory openings to the verses.

"What'd I Say" was the first of Charles' songs to top one million units in sales, and Charles' clear exploitation of call-and-response technique points to his continued integration of African-American spirituality within his music. One can imagine that his secularization of certain aspects of gospel services provided, as did the public oratory of preachers in the Civil Rights movement, one of the few opportunities through which mainstream America could appreciate the complexity of African-American spirituality.

ROCKHOUSE, PARTS 1 AND 2 (1956)

The first of Charles' popular instrumentals, "Rockhouse, Parts 1 and 2," appeared in 1956 and reached both the rhythm and blues and the pop charts. (The work was divided into two parts because it would not fit on a single side of a 45 rpm record.) It is a danceable piece that features a well-defined, memorable theme that is immediately announced by the piano. The theme encompasses a falling octave and is played over a basic blues progression that can be diagrammed as I–IV–I–V–IV–I. Charles' orchestration is once again very important to the overall flow of the piece. After the initial statement of the theme, Charles restates the theme with additional help from the horns, which punctuate the theme with staccato chords. This instrumentation remains intact for a repetition of the theme. At this point, instead of giving solos to various band members, Charles performs several interesting but unadventurous variations on the theme. He works his way through three of these improvisatory variations before returning to a statement of the original theme, again with the support of the horn section. Then, a saxophone solo by David "Fathead" Newmann absorbs two full cycles of the chord progression. A fourth variation on the theme by the piano is followed by a final restatement of the original theme, once again assisted by the horn section. A fade-out brings the piece to a close.

One hears many of the individual styles that have influenced Charles' career in this song, and one can imagine that "Rockhouse" would have met with the approval of his first music teacher, a local store owner and pianist, Wylie Pittman, on whose lap Charles would sit and absorb the blues and boogie woogie. Taken as a whole, "I Got A Woman," "What'd I Say," and "Rockhouse" demonstrate that Ray Charles' career has fused together and, in turn, brought to a mass audience a diverse body of styles and influences. As he has stated, "When I look at my career as a musician, I see that I believe in accumulation. I never really gave anything up, except the Nat Cole and Charles Brown imitations. Everything else I developed I just threw on top of the pile."

REFERENCES

Bradley, Lloyd. *Soul on CD: The Essential Guide.* London: Kyle Cathie, 1994.

Charles, Ray, and David Ritz. *Brother Ray: Ray Charles' Own Story.* Updated ed., New York: Da Capo Press, 1992.

Dawson, Jim, and Steve Propes. *What Was the First Rock 'n' Roll Record?* Boston: Faber and Faber, 1992.

George, Nelson. *The Death of Rhythm and Blues.* New York: Plume Books, 1988.

Guralnick, Peter. "Ray Charles." In *The Rolling Stone Illustrated History of Rock & Roll,* 130–134, 3rd ed. New York: Random House, 1992.

Palmer, Robert. Liner notes, *Ray Charles, The Birth of Soul: The Complete Atlantic Rhythm & Blues Recordings, 1952–1959.* Atlantic 7 83210-2, 1991.

Russell, Tony. *Blacks, Whites, and Blues.* New York: Stein and Day, 1970.

Wexler, Jerry, and David Ritz. *Rhythm and the Blues: A Life in American Music.* New York: Alfred A. Knopf, 1993.

DAVID SANJEK

CLEVELAND, JAMES EDWARD

Born in Chicago, Ill., December 5, 1931; died in Los Angeles, Calif., February 9, 1991. **Education:** Self-taught in voice and piano; studied piano informally with Roberta Martin, 1943–44. **Composing and Performing Career:** Chicago, sang with the Thorne Gospel Crusaders, 1946–54; "Grace Is Sufficient" composed for Thorne Gospel Crusaders, 1947; Chicago and Detroit, sang with the Caravans, led by Albertina Walker, 1954–57, the Gospelaires, the Roberta Martin Singers, Mahalia Jackson, and the Meditation Singers of Detroit, 1957–59; Detroit, Prayer Tabernacle Church, co-founder and director of music; Voices of Tabernacle choir, founder and director; New Bethel Baptist Church, directed Radio Choir; Gospel Chimes, founder, 1959; Los Angeles, Southern California Community Choir, founder and director, 1967–91; Gospel Music Workshop of America, founder and president, 1968–91; Detroit; served as musical director for Aretha Franklin's album *Amazing Grace*, 1972; Los Angeles, Cornerstone Institutional Baptist Church, founder and pastor, 1970–91. **Honors/Awards:** Grammy Awards, 1974, 1975; National Association of Negro Musicians Award, 1975; National Association for the Advancement of Colored People, Image Award, 1976; *Billboard,* Trend-Setter Award; *Ebony,* Arts Award; Hollywood Walk of Fame, honored with a star, 1983; Temple Bible College, honorary doctorate.

MUSIC LIST

COLLECTIONS

The Best of James Cleveland: The Best in Gospel Songs. Compiled and edited by Sallie Martin and Kenneth Morris. Chicago: Martin and Morris, 1965.

The James Cleveland Songbook. Elizabeth, N.J.: Savgos Music, 1979.

SONGS

[The following list of titles includes only works that were composed by the subject of the entry; it is not a list of recordings that were made by the subject. Although the composer may have made recordings of his own works, the list is not restricted to those recordings but in many cases includes performances by other artists of the composer's work. The list is made up of publication and discographical data, in cases where such information is available. Although no effort has been made to include documentation of the earliest recording of the works listed, the date of the earliest recording that is readily available has been given. —Ed.]

"Ain't No Way Unless You've Been Born Again." New York: Screen Gems-EMI, 1968.

"Ain't That Good News." Hollywood, Calif.: Rand C. Music/Venice Music, 1959. Arranger, Kenneth Morris. Recorded: Savoy MG 14343.

"All of These Things." New York: Screen Gems-EMI, 1974.

"All That I Am." New York: Screen Gems-EMI, 1966.

"All the Way from Heaven." Los Angeles: Frazier-Cleveland, 1964. Arranger, Thurston G. Frazier. Recorded: Savoy 14085.

"All Things Bright and Beautiful." New York: Screen Gems-EMI, 1974.

"And That's Good Enough for Me." Los Angeles: Unichappell, 1988. Co-composer, Karl R. Tarleton.

"Anyhow." Newark, N.J.: Savoy Music, n.d. Recorded: Savoy MG 14405; Kirkelig Kulturverkstad FXCD 116.

"As Long as There's God." In *The James Cleveland Songbook.* Recorded: Savoy DBL 7009.

"Beside the Crystal Sea." New York: Screen Gems-EMI, 1967.

"Beyond the Dark Clouds." Chicago: Martin Studio of Gospel Music, 1960. Arranger, Kenneth Woods Jr.

"Blessed Quiet." New York: Screen Gems-EMI, 1951.

"Blood." New York: Screen Gems-EMI, 1963.

"Breakthrough." New York: Bridgeport Music, 1991. Recorded: King James KJ 8507.

"By the Grace of God." In *The James Cleveland Songbook.* Recorded: Savoy SL 14412.

"Call Him Up and Tell Him What You Want." Chicago: Martin and Morris Music Studio, 1954. Arranger, Kenneth Morris.

"Cast All Your Cares on Him." Chicago: Martin Studio of Gospel Music, 1960. Arranger, Roberta Martin.

"Child of the King." New York: Screen Gems-EMI, 1971.

"Christ Is the Answer." Los Angeles: Frazier-Cleveland, 1962. Arranger, Thurston G. Frazier. Recorded: Savoy SC 5003 or Savgos RI 5003; I AM Records 4013-2-M.

"Christian's Prayer." Los Angeles: Frazier-Cleveland, 1966.

"Count Your Blessings." Chicago: Martin and Morris Music, 1952. In *The Best of James Cleveland.* Arranger, Kenneth Morris. Recorded: Savoy 14296; Word 7109664601.

"Deep Down in My Heart." Chicago: Martin and Morris Music, 1961. In *The Best of James Cleveland.* Arranger, Kenneth Morris.

"Dream Is Still Alive." Los Angeles: James Cleveland Music, 1988. Co-composer, Hidle Brown Barnum.

"Every Day." New York: Screen Gems-EMI, 1952.

"Every Now and Then." Chicago: Roberta Martin Studio of Music, 1956. Arranger, Roberta Martin. Recorded: Mankind NMI 29001; Nashboro NAC-2-7,291.

"Everybody's Comin' on the Lord's Side." In *The James Cleveland Songbook.* Recorded: Savoy SL 14445.

"Ezekiel Saw the Wheel (Big Wheel)." Chicago: Martin and Morris Music, 1958. Arranger, Kenneth Morris.

"First Day of My Life." New York: Screen Gems-EMI, 1974.

"Give It Back." New York: Screen Gems-EMI, 1967.

"God Is a Good God." Copyright, 1961. Arranger, Kenneth Morris.

"God Is in the Blessing Business." Los Angeles: Frazier-Cleveland, 1966. Arranger, Kenneth Morris. Recorded: Savoy 14131.

"God Specializes." Co-composer, Kenneth Morris. Recorded: Savoy ST 14069; Spire SP 5508; Suffolk Marketing SMI 2-20G.

"God Won't Put No More on You (than You Can Bear)." In *The James Cleveland Songbook.* Recorded: Savoy SL 14425.

"God's Going to Set His Children Free." New York: Screen Gems-EMI, 1968.

"Good Enough for Me." Chicago: Martin and Morris Music, 1960. In *The Best of James Cleveland.* Arranger, Kenneth Morris. Recorded: HOB HBD 3511; Nashboro NAC-2-7291.

"Good News the Chariot's Coming." Chicago: Martin and Morris Music, 1958. Arranger, Kenneth Morris.

"Grace Is Sufficient." 1947. Chicago: Martin and Morris Music, 1958. Arranger, Roberta A. Martin. Recorded: Savoy SGL 7022; Savoy SL 14262.

"The Grace of God." Recorded: Savoy SL 14494; Savoy SGL 7090.

"Great Day (God's Gonna Build Up the Zion Wall)." In *The James Cleveland Songbook.* Recorded: Savoy SL 14445; Savoy SL 14732.

"Had It Not Been for Him." Chicago: Roberta Martin Studio of Music, 1960. Arranger, Kenneth Woods Jr. Recorded: Savoy SL 14489.

"Have You Any Rivers?" Chicago: Martin and Morris Music, 1958. Co-composer, Kenneth Morris.

"Have You Ever Seen a Man Like Jesus." Chicago: Martin and Morris Music Studio, 1955. Arranger, Kenneth Morris.

"He Brought Me Out (Hal-le-lu-jah)." Chicago: Roberta Martin Studio, 1961. Arranger, Roberta Martin. Recorded: Nashboro NAC-2-7291.

"He Cares for Me." Chicago: Martin and Morris Music Studio, 1955. Arranger, Kenneth Morris.

"He Chose Me." Jackson, Miss.: Savgos Music, 1980.

"He Comes to See about Me." Chicago: Roberta Martin Studio of Music, 1959. Arranger, Roberta Martin.

"He Done It All." New York: Screen Gems-EMI, 1971.

"He Never Forgets His Own." Chicago: Martin and Morris Music Studio, 1955. In *The Best of James Cleveland.* Arranger, Kenneth Morris.

"He Will Provide." New York: Screen Gems-EMI, 1964.

"He Won't Fail." Chicago: Roberta Martin Studio of Music, 1960. Arranger, Roberta Martin.

"Heart and Soul." In *The James Cleveland Songbook.* Recorded: Savoy DBL 7014.

"Heaven, That Will Be Good Enough for Me." Los Angeles: Frazier-Cleveland, 1965. Arranger, Kenneth Morris. Recorded: Savoy 14103.

"He'll Fight Your Battles." Los Angeles: MCA Duchess, 1962.

"He'll Fill Every Space in Your Life." Chicago: Martin and Morris Music, 1952. Arranger, Kenneth Morris.

"He'll Make a Way." New York: Screen Gems-EMI, 1965.

"He'll Make It Alright." New York: Screen Gems-EMI, 1970.

"He'll Make You Happy." Chicago: Roberta Martin Studio of Music, 1956. Arranger, Roberta Martin.

"He'll Work a Wonder." Chicago: Roberta Martin Studio of Music, 1956. Arranger, Roberta Martin.

"He's a Shelter." New York: Screen Gems-EMI, 1964.

"He's All Right with Me." Newark, N.J.: Savoy Music, 1960. Arranger, Kenneth Morris. Recorded: Savoy MG 14045.

"He's Always There." In *The James Cleveland Songbook.* Recorded: Savoy SL 14494.

"He's Done Something for Me." Chicago: Roberta Martin Studio of Music, 1961. Arranger, Roberta Martin.

"He's Everything You Need (Come Rain or Shine)." Chicago: Roberta Martin Studio of Music, 1959. Arranger, Roberta Martin.

"He's Real (Twenty-Four Hours of the Day)." Chicago: Martin and Morris Music, 1959. Arranger, Kenneth Morris.

"He's So Good." Los Angeles: Frazier-Cleveland, 1962. Arranger, Thurston G. Frazier. Recorded: Savoy SC 5003 or Savgos RI 5003.

"He's the Joy of My Salvation." Los Angeles: Frazier-Cleveland, 1965. In *The Best of James Cleveland.* Arranger, Kenneth Morris. Recorded: Savoy SCD 14096.

"He's Using Me." 1955. Chicago: Roberta Martin Studio of Music, 1955. Arranger, Roberta Martin. Recorded: Savoy SGL 7072.

"Hold Me Jesus." Chicago: Roberta Martin Studio of Music, 1959. Arranger, Roberta Martin.

"I Am Pressing On (Trying to Get Home)." Chicago: Martin and Morris Music Studio, 1957. Arranger, Kenneth Morris.

"I Call Jesus My Rock." New York: Screen Gems-EMI, 1952.

"I Can Depend on Him." New York: Screen Gems-EMI, 1968.

"I Can Feel Him Moving." New York: Screen Gems-EMI, 1975.

"I Can Get a Prayer Through." Jackson, Miss.: Savgos Music, 1976.

"I Can't Stop Loving God." Los Angeles: Frazier-Cleveland, 1965. In *The Best of James Cleveland.* Arranger, Kenneth Morris. Recorded: Savoy SCD 14096.

"I Can't Turn Around." New York: Screen Gems-EMI, 1974.

"I Don't Need You Around." Los Angeles: Unichappell, 1967. Co-composer, Karl R. Tarleton.

"I Feel the Holy Spirit." New York: Screen Gems-EMI, 1968.

"I Get a Blessing Every Day." Chicago: Martin and Morris Music, 1980. Arranger, Kenneth Morris. Recorded: Priority RU 37707.

"I Know the Lord Will Bless You." Chicago: Martin and Morris Music, 1964. In *The Best of James Cleveland.* Arranger, Kenneth Morris.

"I Never Knew Such Joy Before." Chicago: Martin and Morris Music Studio, 1956. In *The Best of James Cleveland.* Arranger, Kenneth Morris.

"I Promised the Lord." New York: Screen Gems-EMI, 1968.

"I Saw the Lord." Jackson, Miss.: Savgos Music, 1979.

"I Stood on the Banks of Jordan." Los Angeles: Frazier-Cleveland Co., 1964. In *The Best of James Cleveland.* Arranger, Kenneth Morris. Recorded: Savoy SGL 7089; Malaco MAL 2007; Savoy SCD 14096.

"I Want to See Him for Myself." Los Angeles: James Cleveland Music, 1985. Co-composer, Charles Wesley May.

"I Will Follow My Dream." Jackson, Miss.: Savgos Music, 1976.

"I Won't Be Cast Away." Jackson, Miss.: Savgos Music, 1981.

"I Won't Turn Back." In *The James Cleveland Songbook.*

"If You Have the Faith." In *The James Cleveland Songbook.* Recorded: Savoy SGL 7080.

"If You Just Believe." In *The James Cleveland Songbook.*

"If You Want to See Jesus." Chicago: Martin and Morris Music, 1958.

"If You Want to See the Lord." Chicago: Martin and Morris Music Studio, 1954. Co-composer and arranger, Kenneth Morris.

"If You're Not Going My Way." Los Angeles: Frazier-Cleveland, 1967.

"I'll Do What You Want Me to Do." New York: Screen Gems-EMI, 1973.

"I'll Keep On Holding to His Hand." Chicago: Roberta Martin Studio of Music, 1961. Arranger, Roberta Martin.

"I'm Determined." Chicago: Roberta Martin Studio of Music, 1953. Arranger, Roberta Martin. Recorded: HOB HBD-3535.

"I'm Going to Trust Him." New York: Screen Gems-EMI, 1962.

"I'm His Child." Chicago: Roberta Martin Studio of Music, 1961. Arranger, Roberta Martin. Recorded: HOB HBD 3530.

"I'm His, He's Mine." Los Angeles: Frazier-Cleveland, 1964. Arranger, Thurston G. Frazier. Recorded: Savoy SL 14544.

James Edward Cleveland; courtesy of the James Cleveland Trust

"I'm in Christ." Chicago: Roberta Martin Studio of Music, 1955. Arranger, Kenneth Woods Jr.

"I'm on the Lord's Side." New York: Screen Gems-EMI, 1967.

"I'm Saved by the Blood." New York: Screen Gems-EMI, 1963.

"I'm Still Saying 'Yes' to the Lord." Chicago: Martin and Morris Music Studio, 1953. Arranger, Jeanette Sims.

"In My Heart." In *The James Cleveland Songbook.* Recorded: Savoy DBL 7014.

"It All Belongs to My Father." Los Angeles: Frazier-Cleveland, 1962. Arranger, Thurston G. Frazier. Recorded: Savoy SC 5003 or Savgos RI 5003.

"It Keeps Me Happy All Day Long." Chicago: Martin and Morris Music, 1964. Arranger, Kenneth Morris.

"It Was the Blood." Chicago: Roberta Martin Studio of Music, 1961. Arranger, Roberta Martin.

"It's Mighty Hard." New York: Screen Gems-EMI, 1967.

"It's Mighty Nice." New York: Screen Gems-EMI, 1965.

"I've Found a Friend." Los Angeles: Frazier-Cleveland, 1967.

"I've Found Him." Chicago: Roberta Martin Studio of Music, 1958. Arranger, Roberta Martin.

"I've Got a New Born Soul (Since the Holy Ghost Took Control)." 1954. Chicago: Roberta Martin Studio of Music, 1954. Arranger, Roberta Martin.

"I've Got You Baby." Los Angeles: Unichappell, 1968. Co-composer, Karl R. Tarleton.

"Jesus I'll Never Forget." Los Angeles: Frazier-Cleveland, 1963. Co-composer, Andraé Edward Crouch. Recorded: Rhino R2 70289.

"Jesus Is Always There." New York: Screen Gems-EMI, 1967.

"Jesus Paid It All." Chicago: Theodore R. Frye, 1951. Co-composer and arranger, Virgina Davis.

"Jesus Will." Chicago: Martin and Morris Music, 1960. In *The Best of James Cleveland.* Arranger, Kenneth Morris. Recorded: HOB HBD 3511.

"Jesus Will Bring Things Out Alright." Los Angeles: Frazier-Cleveland, 1962. Co-composer, Alfred Bolden. Arranger, Thurston G. Frazier. Recorded: Savoy SC 5003 or Savgos RI 5003; Word 7019664601 or EK 67449.

"Just How Much We Can Bear." New York: Bridgeport Music, 1991.

"Just Like He Said He Would." Newark, N.J.: Savoy Music, 1960. Arranger, Kenneth Morris. Recorded: Savoy MG 14045; A&M Records 75021-8530-2.

"Keep Looking Up." Chicago: Roberta Martin Studio of Music, 1955. Arranger, Roberta Martin.

"Learn How to Walk by Faith." New York: Screen Gems-EMI, 1965.

"Leave It There." New York: Screen Gems-EMI, 1963.

"Let Him in Today." In *The James Cleveland Songbook.* Recorded: Savoy SGL 7089.

"Let It Shine." New York: Screen Gems-EMI, 1972.

"Let Jesus Lead You." New York: Screen Gems-EMI, 1963.

"Let the Church Roll On." New York: Screen Gems-EMI, 1972.

"Life Can Be Beautiful." Los Angeles: Frazier-Cleveland, 1965. In *The Best of James Cleveland.* Arranger, Kenneth Morris. Recorded: CGI 51416 1173 2 or A&M 31454 0088 2; Savoy SCD 14096.

"Listen the Lambs Are Crying." Chicago: Roberta Martin Studio of Music, 1960. Arranger, Roberta Martin.

"Little Talk with Jesus." New York: Screen Gems-EMI, 1962.

"Looking for a Witness." New York: Screen Gems-EMI, 1971.

"Looking for You and Me." New York: Screen Gems-EMI, 1967.

"Lord, Do It (for Me)." Los Angeles: Frazier-Cleveland, 1967. Arranger, Kenneth Morris. Recorded: HOB HBD 3508; HOB HBD 3511; HOB HBD 3537.

"Lord Don't Leave Me." Chicago: Martin Studio of Gospel Music, 1960. Arranger, Roberta Martin. Recorded: Savoy SGC 7971; HOB HBD 3530.

"Lord, Help Me to Hold Out." Chicago: Planemar Music Co., 1974. Recorded: Malaco MALC 9; I AM Records 4013-2-M; Savoy SCD 7059.

"Lord, I'll Go." New York: Screen Gems-EMI, 1964.

"Lord, I'm Willing to Go." Chicago: Costoma Publishing, 1965.

"The Lord Is My Life." In *The James Cleveland Songbook.* Recorded: Savoy SL 14425.

"The Lord Is Standing Up (on the Inside of Me)." Chicago: Martin and Morris Studio, 1955. Arranger, Kenneth Woods Jr.

"The Lord Will Provide." Chicago: Martin and Morris Music, 1958. Arranger, Kenneth Morris. Recorded: Savoy SL 14533.

"Low Down the Chariot." Los Angeles: Unichappell, 1968.

"Malachi 3:10 (Try Jesus)." Chicago: Martin and Morris Music, 1960. Arranger, Kenneth Morris. Recorded: HOB HBX 2110; Nashboro NAC-2-7291; HOB HBD-3527.

"The Man, Jesus (How I Love Him Yes I Do)." Chicago: Roberta Martin Studio of Music, 1954. Arranger, Roberta Martin.

"May the Lord God Bless You Real Good." Elizabeth, N.J.: Savgos Music, 1977. Arranger, Kenneth Morris. In *The James Cleveland Songbook.*

"More Love to Thee." New York: Screen Gems-EMI, 1969.

"My God Can Do Anything." Los Angeles: Frazier-Cleveland, 1964. In *The Best of James Cleveland.* Arranger, Kenneth Morris. Recorded: Savoy SCD 14096.

"My Job Is Working for Jesus." Chicago: Martin and Morris Music, 1959. In *The Best of James Cleveland.* Arranger, Kenneth Morris.

"My Lord's Prayer." New York: Screen Gems-EMI, 1968.

"My Soul Looks Back and Wonders." Hollywood, Calif.: Rand C. Music/ Venice Music, 1959. Arranger, Kenneth Morris. Recorded: Shanachie 6005.

"No Cross, No Crown." Los Angeles: Frazier-Cleveland, 1964. In *The Best of James Cleveland.* Arranger, Kenneth Morris. Recorded: CGI 51416 1173 2 or A&M 31454 0088 2; Savoy SCD 14096.

"No Trouble at the River." Chicago: Martin and Morris Music Studio, 1955. Arranger, Kenneth Morris.

"Nobody Like You." New York: Screen Gems-EMI, 1962.

"Nothing but a God." Chicago: Roberta Martin Studio of Music, 1955.

"O Lord, I Surrender to Thee." Chicago: Martin and Morris Music Studio, 1955. Arranger, Kenneth Morris.

"O Lord, Stand by Me." Chicago: Roberta Martin Studio of Music, 1952. Arranger, Roberta Martin.

"Oh How I Love Jesus." Chicago: Martin and Morris Music Studio, 1955. In *The Best of James Cleveland.* Arranger, Kenneth Martin.

"Oh Lord, I'm Satisfied." New York: Screen Gems-EMI, 1961.

"Oh the Joy." Jackson, Miss.: Savgos Music, 1983.

"Oh the Lord Saved Me." New York: Screen Gems-EMI, 1968.

"One More River to Cross." Chicago: Martin and Morris Studio, 1955. In *The Best of James Cleveland.* Arranger, Kenneth Morris.

"One More Time." Chicago: Martin and Morris, 1981. Arranger, Kenneth Morris. Recorded: Black Label BLCD 4006; HOB HBDE 3502; HOB HBD 3511.

"One Step at a Time." Chicago: Bowles Publishing House, 1960. Co-composer, Sallie Martin. Arrangers, Sallie Martin, Kenneth Woods Jr. Recorded: Nashboroo NAC-2-7291.

"Our God." New York: Screen Gems-EMI, 1974.

"Picked Up the Pieces." New York: Screen Gems-EMI, 1970.

"Promise to Meet Me There." Chicago: Martin and Morris Music, 1953. Arranger, Kenneth Morris.

"The Promises of God." New York: Screen Gems-EMI, 1968.

"The Push Is On." New York: Screen Gems-EMI, 1973.

"Rock My Soul." Chicago: Roberta Martin Studio of Music, 1958. Arranger, Roberta Martin. Recorded: Savoy MG 14336.

"Saved." Chicago: Roberta Martin Studio of Music, 1955. Arranger, Roberta Martin. Recorded: Shanachie 6005.

"Sell Out (to the Master Right Now)." Chicago: Martin and Morris Music Studio, 1954. In *The Best of James Cleveland.* Arranger, Kenneth Morris. Recorded: Rhino R2 70289.

"Shine on Me." Chicago: Martin and Morris Music, 1954. Arranger, Kenneth Morris. Recorded: Savoy DBL 7020; Savoy SCD 14076.

"Sign of the Judgement." New York: Screen Gems-EMI, 1968.

"Since I Met Him." Chicago: Roberta Martin Studio of Music, 1960. Arranger, Roberta Martin.

"Soldiers in the Army (Onward Christian Soldiers)." Chicago: Martin and Morris Music, 1956. In *The Best of James Cleveland.* Arranger, Kenneth Morris. Recorded: Savoy SGL 7067.

"Somebody Touched Me, It Must Have Been the Hand of the Lord." In *The James Cleveland Songbook.* Recorded: Savoy SL 14491.

"Someday (I'm Goin' to Put on My Golden Shoes)." Chicago: Martin and Morris Music, 1958. Arranger, Kenneth Morris.

"Stop Giving Your Man Away." New York: Chevis Publishing, n.d. Co-composer, Laura Lee.

"The Sun Will Shine Afterwhile." Los Angeles: Frazier-Cleveland, 1964. In *The Best of James Cleveland.* Arranger, Kenneth Morris. Recorded: CGI 51416 1173 2 or A&M 31454 0088 2.

"Sweet Jesus." New York: Screen Gems-EMI, 1966.

"Take Me to the Water." In *The Best of James Cleveland.* Arranger, Kenneth Morris. Copyright, 1956. Recorded: CGI 51416 1179 2.

"Take Them and Leave Them There." Chicago: Martin and Morris, 1964. In *The Best of James Cleveland.* Arranger, Kenneth Morris.

"Tell Me What I Can Do." Los Angeles: Unichappell, 1967.

"Thank You Jesus for My Journey." New York: Screen Gems-EMI, 1974.

"That's Just Like the Lord." Chicago: Martin and Morris Music, 1961. Arranger, Kenneth Morris.

"That's What a God Is For." Chicago: Martin and Morris Music Studio, 1956. Arranger, Kenneth Morris.

"That's What He's Done for Me." Los Angeles: Frazier-Cleveland, 1962. Arranger, Thurston G. Frazier.

"That's What I Like about Jesus." Los Angeles: Frazier-Cleveland, 1966. Arranger, Kenneth Morris. Recorded: Savoy MG 14131.

"That's What My God Can Do." Los Angeles: Frazier-Cleveland, 1965.

"There's a Man (on the Other Side of Jordan)." Chicago: Roberta Martin Studio of Music, 1955. Arranger, Roberta Martin.

"There's Gonna Be a Fire." New York: Screen Gems-EMI, 1967.

"There's No Condemnation." Chicago: Martin and Morris Music, 1958. In *The Best of James Cleveland.* Arranger, Kenneth Morris.

"They Don't Like It." Los Angeles: Frazier-Cleveland, 1967.

"They That Wait on the Lord." Jackson, Miss.: Savgos Music, 1978.

"Touch Me." In *The James Cleveland Songbook* and *Angelic Gospelodium Songbook* (Chicago: Martin and Morris, 1979). Arranger, Kenneth Morris. Recorded: Savoy DBL 7009; Savoy SGL 7089; Malaco MALC 9.

"Touched by His Hand." Recorded: Savoy SL 14425.

"Trouble in My Way." Chicago: Roberta Martin Studio of Music, 1955. Arranger, Kenneth Woods Jr. Recorded: Savoy 14322.

"Trust Him." Los Angeles: Frazier-Cleveland, 1962. Arranger, Thurston G. Frazier. Recorded: Savoy SL 14104; Savoy SC 5003 or Savgos RI 5003.

"Try Me and See." Jackson, Miss.: Savgos Music, 1981.

"Trying to Make a Hundred." Chicago: Roberta Martin Studio of Music, 1955. Arranger, Roberta Martin.

"Two Wings." Los Angeles: Frazier-Cleveland, 1965. Arranger, Kenneth Morris. Recorded: King James KJ 8506; CGI 51416 1173 2 or A&M 31454 0088 2; CGI 51416 1179 2.

"Walk On by Faith." Chicago: Martin and Morris Music Studio, 1962. Arranger, Roberta Martin. Recorded: Antilles 91236-1.

"Was the Blood." Los Angeles: Unichappell, n.d.

"We Don't Do That Anymore." New York: Screen Gems-EMI, 1968.

"What a Mighty God We Serve." Chicago: Martin and Morris Music, 1961. Arranger, Roberta Martin.

"What Do You Know about Jesus? (He's Alright)." Los Angeles: Frazier-Cleveland, 1963. Arranger, Thurston G. Frazier.

"Where's God?" Jackson, Miss.: Savgos Music, 1981.

"While I Have a Chance." Chicago: Martin and Morris Music, 1954. In *The Best of James Cleveland.* Arranger, Kenneth Morris.

"Whole Truth." New York: Screen Gems-EMI, 1967.

"Why." New York: Screen Gems-EMI, 1966.

"Why Do I Love Him?" Chicago: Martin and Morris Music, 1958. Arranger, Kenneth Morris.

"Why Not Do It Today?" Chicago: Sally Martin's House of Music, 1972. Note, arranger, Kenneth Woods Jr. Recorded: Savoy SL 14278.

"With a Made Up Mind." In *The James Cleveland Songbook.* Recorded: Savoy SL 14489.

"Witness for My Lord." New York: Screen Gems-EMI, 1971.

PUBLICATIONS

ABOUT CLEVELAND
Thesis

Casey, M. E. "The Contributions of James Cleveland." Thesis, Howard University, 1980.

Articles

"Cleveland, James." *Current Biography Yearbook* (1985).

Heilbut, Anthony. "The Crown Prince of Gospel: James Cleveland." In *The Gospel Sound: Good News and Bad Times,* 205–219. 3rd ed. New York: Limelight Editions, 1989.

Jackson, D. "James Cleveland Sings the Horn off the Devil (Interview)." *Village Voice* 24 (April 16, 1979): 73–74.

"James Cleveland, Top U.S. Gospel Artist." *Sepia* (May 1965): 54–59.

* * * * *

The two most important years in the history of the African-American gospel choir were 1932 and 1968. In 1932, Thomas Andrew Dorsey, considered the "father" of African-American gospel music, and a small coterie of gospel singers in and around Chicago organized the National Convention of Gospel Choirs and Choruses, Incorporated; in 1968, James Cleveland and a group of gospel singers from across the United States organized the Gospel Music Workshop of America. While Dorsey's convention pledged to organize gospel choirs and teach them the new black church music, Cleveland's workshop was committed to creating a singing community of gospel choirs and shaping them into professional singers. Cleveland was a prolific composer, composing over 1,000 songs, more than 20 of which have become gospel music standards. Like his chief model, he had the ability to write and sing in the everyday language of his audience. His subject matter and the simplicity of his musical material struck a resonant chord with the gospel-music-loving public.

It is no coincidence that Cleveland, like Dorsey, organized a gospel choir convention—though Cleveland called his a workshop—for he came under the influence of Dorsey at the age of eight and for the next 52 years, step by step, duplicated all of Dorsey's musical activities.

James Edward Cleveland was born in Chicago, Illinois, on December 5, 1931. He graduated from the Douglass Grammar School and is reported to have attended DuSable High School. Cleveland had little interest in formal education but was totally committed to the Junior Choir at Chicago's Pilgrim Baptist Church, which he joined at the age of eight. From his first rehearsal with the choir, Cleveland was completely dedicated to the type of music that the director, Thomas Andrew Dorsey, taught the choir. Pilgrim was the center of gospel music in Chicago, and Chicago was the center of gospel music in the world. Dorsey's friends—Theodore R. Frye, who assisted Dorsey in the organization of the gospel choir at Pilgrim seven years earlier; Roberta Martin, pianist for the choir for a short time in the 1930s; Mollie Mae Gates, director of the gospel choir at Metropolitan Community Church; and Kenneth Morris, organist at the First Church of Deliverance—often attended rehearsals and assisted Dorsey in teaching new songs. Cleveland was overwhelmed by these musicians and absorbed every nuance of the music. Possessing an extraordinary musical ear from an early age, he quickly and accurately learned all of the songs of the Junior Choir as well as those of all the gospel groups in Chicago. He taught himself to play the piano and at every opportunity attended Reverend Lucy Smith's All Nations Pentecostal Church where her granddaughter, "Little" Lucy Smith, three years younger than he, played "gospel" organ for the services. Cleveland and "Little" Lucy became friends and exchanged musical ideas and skills at the piano (Smith was studying piano with her stepmother, Roberta Martin). "Little" Lucy introduced Cleveland to the Roberta Martin Singers, who later played an important part in his musical development.

At age 15, Cleveland joined the Thorne Gospel Crusaders, remaining with them for the next eight years. As a lead singer of the group, he strained to reach high notes and, in the absence of sound systems, sang at louder levels than his vocal cords could accommo-

date. This vocal strain resulted in a throaty and gravelly quality that increased with the years. Cleveland began composing during his tenure with the Thornes and by age 16 had composed "Grace Is Sufficient," which was later recorded by the Roberta Martin Singers.

In 1954, Cleveland joined Albertina Walker's Caravans as pianist, arranger, and soloist. During his three years with the Caravans, Cleveland composed such gospel standards as "I've Got a New Born Soul" (1954), "He's Using Me" (1955), and "I Never Knew Such Joy Before" (1956). Throughout the mid-1950s, he traveled between Chicago and Detroit, maintaining an active career in each city and working with several groups simultaneously. With the Reverend Charles Craig, one of the first singers of gospel's Golden Age (1945–60) to switch from singer to preacher, and the Reverend Leslie Bush, he helped found the Prayer Tabernacle Church, for which Craig was pastor, Bush his assistant, and Cleveland the director of music. Cleveland organized and directed a 100-voice choir that became the sensation of Detroit. His success with the Voices of Tabernacle, as the choir was called, led the Reverend C. L. Franklin, pastor of the New Bethel Baptist Church and father of fledgling gospel singer Aretha Franklin, to ask Cleveland to develop and direct his Radio Choir. During his tenure at New Bethel, Cleveland tutored Aretha in piano and accompanied her during the early stages of her gospel career.

From 1957 until 1959, Cleveland was the pianist and musical arranger for the Meditation Singers of Detroit (the group in which singer and actress Della Reese honed her talents before switching to popular music in 1954). In 1959, he organized the Gospel Chimes, whose membership included at various times Dorothy Norwood, Imogene Green, Jessy Dixon, and Bishop Claude Timmons. In 1960, Cleveland made several appearances with the Gospel All Stars of Brooklyn, New York.

In the same year, while the Gospel Chimes were conducting a revival (a series of nightly concerts) at the First Baptist Church in Nutley, New Jersey, Cleveland combined the church's gospel choir with his singers. Relinquishing his position at the piano to the Reverend Lawrence Roberts, pastor of the church, Cleveland stood before the choir, as a minister before his congregation, and cajoled them into the kind of passionate delivery associated with Pentecostal singers; he coaxed a comparable response from the congregation. This style of gospel choral singing was perfected by 1963; that year's recording of the 19th-century white gospel hymn "Peace, Be Still" illustrates the mature Cleveland vocal style. Cleveland crooned the verses of songs, occasionally inserting a "sanctified" holler, and "preached" the refrains. His "hard gospel" technique of singing at the extremes of his register evoked a sharp contrast with the rich falsetto he often employed. He was particularly fond of the vamp (repeated short nonmelodic segments of one or two bars) over which he would extemporize variations. He liked a treble sound and dispensed with the bass voice in the gospel choir, forcing male singers, tenors and basses, to sing four or five tones higher than typical soprano-alto-tenor-bass arrangements normally required. The treble sound, with the male singers at the top of their register, was one of passion, energy, and emotion and was quickly adopted by gospel choirs around the nation. Cleveland preferred the call-and-response treatment of choral singers over the direct or "in-concert" style, allowing nonsingers to join in without embarrassment.

In 1964, at the invitation of Annette May Thomas, gospel-singing daughter of the renowned Brother Joe May, who became his personal manager, Cleveland relocated to Los Angeles. He organized the Southern California Community Choir in 1967 and continued to record "in service" (live) albums of his and other gospel songs.

The organization of the Southern California Community Choir inspired Cleveland to assemble a group of gospel singers to consider the formation of a convention of gospel choirs that would promote new music, organize choirs in churches previously loath to permit this music into their sanctuaries (Catholic, Presbyterian, and some branches of African American Methodist), and seek a higher level of artistic standards than was customary in gospel choirs at that time. In August 1968, Cleveland and these gospel singers organized the Gospel Music Workshop of America, with Cleveland as president, a position he held until his death. By 1973, when the Gospel Music Workshop of America (GMWA) was firmly established, each large town in the United States had a chapter to which Cleveland would make periodic visits in order to teach new songs and techniques and critique the work of local choirs. GMWA held annual conventions that lasted one week, each year in a different location. Since many members of GMWA would schedule their vacations to coincide with the convention, attendance at these gatherings was large. Each year's convention resulted in a recording of the outstanding groups participating, with Cleveland leading one or two songs.

In 1972, Aretha Franklin, the former gospel singer now known as the "Queen of Soul," was persuaded to record an album of gospel music. She secured Cleveland as her musical director and recorded the album *Amazing Grace* with the choir of her father's church. The recording, Franklin's first gospel recording since 1958, captured her and Cleveland in their most comfortable and inspiring circumstance: extraordinary instrumentalists, an energetic choir, and a full and responsive audience. This recording, which has sold over 2 million copies to date, introduced Cleveland to the popular music world. Major engagements followed the release of the album, and Cleveland went on to direct a choir with Quincy Jones in the television production of "Roots," to direct a gospel choir for the Ray Charles and Cleo Lane recording of George Gershwin's opera *Porgy and Bess,* to star with Natalie Cole in the television special "In the Spirit," which was filmed in Northampton, England, for Granada Television (BBC), to direct choirs for the films *The Blues Brothers* and *The Idolmaker,* and to make several appearances at Carnegie Hall.

None of these activities and honors, according to Cleveland, matched the joy he felt in November 1970 when he organized and assumed the pastorate of the Cornerstone Institutional Baptist Church of Los Angeles. Beginning with 60 charter members, membership had grown to 7,000 in 1984 when Cleveland led his congregation into a new $1,500,000 structure that contained an altar made of marble stone imported from Italy and a unique cross made of 800 red and white lights.

In the gospel world, Cleveland enjoyed a success unparalleled since that of Mahalia Jackson, who in her day was the most famous gospel musician since Dorsey. Cleveland was part of a triumvirate—made up of Cleveland, Edward Smith, and the Reverend Lawrence Roberts—that possessed unusual abilities to bring people together and promote a product, as Dorsey before him had also done. As in the Dorsey triumvirate—where Sallie Martin had the business acumen to make money, Theodore R. Frye had the showmanship to call attention to the group, and Dorsey possessed the talent—Edward Smith, Cleveland's longtime manager, created opportunities to make money, the Reverend Lawrence, gospel music producer for Savoy Records, served as conduit to the people, and Cleveland provided the talent. Like Dorsey, Cleveland played the piano, sang, composed, organized choirs and a gospel choir convention, and, finally, became a preacher.

Cleveland received every award in gospel music and was recognized as the leader of the gospel world from the 1970s until his death. He was awarded an honorary doctorate by Temple Bible College and received the first Trend-Setter Award from *Billboard* magazine, *Ebony* magazine's Arts Award, and the Achievement Award from the National Association of Negro Musicians. He was invited, along with the Southern California Community Choir, Andraé and Sandra Crouch, and Shirley Caesar, to perform in concert at the Sultan's Pool amphitheater in Jerusalem. Hollywood recognized Cleveland on August 12, 1983, when he was awarded a star on the Hollywood Walk of Fame. Cleveland died of heart failure in Los Angeles on February 9, 1991.

GRACE IS SUFFICIENT (1947)

The hymn "Amazing Grace" is so popular in gospel music that any gospel song including the word "grace" in its title receives more than passing curiosity, which is what happened with "Grace Is Sufficient" when the 1958 recording of the song by the Roberta Martin Singers was released. It was met with widespread acclaim. Published in the same year it was recorded by the Roberta Martin Singers, the song captures the essence of the prayers of supplication: in the text, Cleveland celebrates the answer to his requests of the Lord. The title was taken from words of Christ as recorded in II Corinthians 12:9 by Saint Paul, who, after having prayed three times for relief from "a thorn in his flesh," finds relief when Christ responds: "My grace is sufficient for thee."

In the key of B-flat major in 6/8 meter, the song is in verse and refrain form; the verse comprises eight bars, and the chorus is twice as long. A verse with fewer bars than the refrain is not exceptional in African-American gospel, especially when the composer considers the refrain the more important of the two, as was the case with "Grace Is Sufficient." The 16 bars of the refrain are divided into four phrases of four bars each, with a poetic rhyme scheme of abab. The third phrase of the refrain is an exact repetition of the first, while the second and fourth phrases begin with the same words ("His Grace") but end with different rhyming words.

Although the poetry of the refrain is set in an abab scheme, its melody has a scheme of abac. The melody of the first phrase, divided into two subphrases of two bars each, begins on a sustained note (*d*), which is repeated before descending to the tonic (*b*-flat). The second subphrase, composed of only two tones, begins with a sustained tone on *e*-flat and is followed by another sustained tone on *d,* a half step lower. The second phrase is more active than the first but still uses only three notes: *b*-flat, *c,* and *d.* On the Roberta Martin Singers recording, the second phrase displays the parallelism of voice movement first made popular in gospel during the 1950s.

The third phrase, a repetition of the first, leads directly to the final phrase, which is as active as the second. Beginning on the same tone as in the second phrase (*c*), the final phrase ascends to *e*-flat before descending to the tonic (*b*-flat), only to be interrupted by several articulations on *c* before its final articulation on *b*-flat. Only four tones (*b*-flat, *c*, *f*, and *e*-flat) are employed in the melody. While Cleveland's refrain is melodically economical, the composition portrays a simple elegance.

Although there is no separate piano score in the published version, the Roberta Martin Singers recording has an active accompaniment of repeated chords, triplet figures, and eighth-note "runs" provided by Martin on piano and "Little" Lucy Smith on organ. Harmony in this composition is no more sophisticated than is needed to support the lyrics. The I, IV, and V chords provide the basic harmony for the refrain. The slow harmonic motion of the refrain—ten of the 16 bars involve only one harmony—lends authority to the words of Christ.

The verse ("grace woke me up this morning," "grace will make you love your enemies," "grace will comfort lonely hours") is half as long as the refrain, but it is much more harmonically and rhythmically active. Set in four phrases of two bars each, the four-line text has a scheme of abcb. Expressed through a melodic scheme of abcd, the verse evokes the elegantly simple but wordy early compositions of Dorsey. For example, the three stanzas, without repetition of text, cover several areas. The first stanza addresses the role of grace in daily activities; the second is concerned with grace and living the Christian life, while the third discusses grace and Christ. Whereas the text of the refrain was set to only four notes, that of the verse occupies six: the first six notes of the B-flat major scale (*b*-flat, *c*, *d*, *e*-flat, *f*, and *g*).

The first phrase of the verse begins on the tonic note (*b*-flat), ascending a third and then returning to *b*-flat. The second phrase begins a fifth above (on *f*) and gently descends to *b*-flat, at which point the verse divides into two large parts with a sustained note on *c*. The climax of the verse is reached in the third phrase as the melody begins on *g*, six notes higher than the tonic, and then slowly descends back down to *b*-flat. The final phrase, beginning on a high *f*, quickly descends to the tonic, bringing the verse to a close. The melodic climax found in the third phrase is combined with a harmonic climax, as Cleveland sets the word "enemies" to a vii/vii chord (the chord often used by classical composers to introduce a cadenza—an improvised section to show the virtuosity of the soloist). This chord is usually followed by the tonic chord in an inversion. While this chord does not appear in the published score, it is prominent on the recording of the Roberta Martin Singers.

The use of triplet figures, the subdivision of the beat, and long note values cooperate to produce an active rhythmic foundation for the melody and harmony. Each of the phrases begins with a long rhythmic value (dotted quarter or less) and is followed immediately by a series of shorter note values (eighth notes).

"Grace Is Sufficient" was the most successful Cleveland composition recorded by the Roberta Martin Singers, though they recorded more than ten of his compositions, each successful to a degree. There are two interesting historical footnotes to this composition: it was never recorded by Cleveland; and, though it was not recorded by the Roberta Martin Singers until 1958, Cleveland composed the song in 1947 at the age of 16.

HE'S USING ME (1955)

"He's Using Me," composed in 1955, is the first indication of Cleveland's fascination with lyrics that, like many of Dorsey's, abandon literary paraphrases of the scriptures in favor of the colloquial language of the "downtrodden and disinherited." His use of the vernacular in his compositions and commentary reached such popularity in the 1960s that audiences demanded interjected sermonettes during his musical performances. The seeds of what was to become known as "songs and sermonettes" began to sprout as early as 1953 in such phrases as "when I suffer all night long, giving up the right for wrong," and "when you see me do my best, when you see me stand the test," which appear in "He's Using Me."

Like all of his songs, except those set only in refrains, "He's Using Me" is organized in the verse and refrain form. It is in the key of A-flat major with a meter of 4/4. While there is no scriptural quotation in the text, it is based on Matthew 5:35–40, in which Christ assures his disciples that when he was hungry, thirsty, a stranger, naked, sick, and in prison, they came to his rescue. Upon inquiry into the time they responded to those situations Christ replied: "Inasmuch as ye have done it unto one of the least of these my brethren, ye have done it unto me." To exploit the use of Christians as Christ surrogates, Cleveland uses the refrain to show instances in which he was used thus by Christ: "He's using my hands to do His will, He's using my feet to climb the hill. He's using my eyes that I might see some good in others, same as me; He's using my voice to bring sight to the blind; He's using me in His own good time."

It is the verse, however, that became the popular part of the song and, consequently, it was always sung before the refrain. Consisting of 12 bars, it bears several resemblances to the blues. Like the blues, the text is cast in three lines with a rhyme scheme of aab; and also like many blues, "He's Using Me" employs single lines composed of two subphrases that constitute one complete phrase (e.g., "when you see me walking right, when you see me talking right," which corresponds to a blues line: "my man don't love me, treats me awful mean"). The comparison extends to the repetition of the melody in the second phrase but ceases at that point. Using all seven tones of the A-flat major scale, the key of the song, Cleveland assigns a melody to each of the subphrases that differs slightly at the beginning but ends in the same way.

The melody of the verse is supported by an F-minor chord in alternation with a C-major chord with an added major seventh (*c-e-g-b*). The presence of F-minor and its dominant, C-major, results in tonal ambiguity for eight bars; it is not until the third phrase and the words "oh, oh, oh, oh, God's using me" that the home key of A-flat major is established through the cadential progression I–V–I–IV–I–V–I. The cadential melody ascends scalewise from *a*-flat up to *e*-flat, but, after each scale degree is articulated, the melody reaches back to its lower neighboring tone before ascending to the next higher note (e.g., *a*-flat, *g*, *a*-flat; *b*-flat, *a*-flat, *b*-flat; etc.). Therefore, a five-note melody is expanded into 11 notes.

Cleveland uses an unusual style of call-and-response; the response is not a diminution of the call or an independent commentary on the call but a complete repetition of the text: solo—"when you see me walking right," chorus—"when you see me walking right." This treatment, which is applied to the text in the first two phrases, is replaced in the third phrase as Cleveland textually brings the two parts together. The third phrase, cadential in melody and harmony, is harmonically new to gospel though not original with Cleveland, having been used by such composers as Raymond Rasberry, "Little" Lucy Smith, and James Herndon (pianist for Albertina Walker's Caravans).

The refrain, concerned textually with examples of how God uses Christians, comprises 17 bars divided into four phrases, each with four bars except the fourth, which includes an additional bar that elongates the cadence. The text is set in four lines and, like the verse, each line is composed of two phrases ("He's using my hands to do his blessed will, He's using my feet to climb the hill"). Cleveland chose the little-used technique of placing the rhyme within the sentence (will-hill) but with no rhymes between the four lines. This yields an overall rhyme scheme of abcd, the same through-composed form as for the melodic and harmonic scheme.

The melody of the refrain revolves around the axis of the home key of A-flat. Each of the phrases begins either above or below the tonic note, *a*-flat, but for emphasis resolves to the tonic at crucial melodic points. Cleveland brings back the final phrase of the verse as the final phrase of the refrain as a unifying element.

Each of the phrases, except the fourth, uses gospel's primary chords, I–IV–V (tonic, subdominant, dominant), with the vi and V/V inserted before the dominant chord at the midpoint of the refrain. The first phrase is supported by the IV chord in its major structure for the first bar and the same chord in its minor structure for the second bar, closing the phrase with the tonic chord. The second phrase begins on the vi chord, moves to the V/V, and closes on the V chord, while the third phrase moves from the tonic chord to the subdominant, ending with an incidental augmented sixth chord in preparation for the cadential phrase (m. 24), beginning this time on an inversion of the tonic chord.

As in the verse, call-and-response treatment is assigned to the text of the refrain. The rhythm throughout the refrain is designed to create a martial affect and to promote the idea of forward motion (physical "use" by the Lord). There is no syncopation in the composition.

Cleveland came into prominence as a composer after Alex Bradford had reigned as the most popular figure in Chicago and the gospel world for five years. As a pianist, singer, composer, and group leader, Cleveland was expected to follow the compositional lead of Bradford. Cleveland, however, chose not to imitate Bradford, instead returning to the early compositional and textual style of Dorsey. His simplicity of musical material, supporting a text that not only resonated the concerns of African-American Christians but also their language, is largely responsible for his celebrity.

LORD, HELP ME TO HOLD OUT (1974)

Job, generally acknowledged as the most patient man in the Bible, has long served as the model of patience for African-American Christians, who, when all else fails, find the wisdom and courage to utter his famous phrase, "all the days of my appointed time will I wait, till my change come" (Job 14:14). Countless gospel songs have been composed in honor of this paragon of long suffering and patience. From "all my appointed time, gonna wait till my change come," the early sanctified refrain of the 1920s, through Robert Anderson's "Prayer Changes Things" of 1947 to the 1953 composition of Dorothy Love Coates, ("He May Not Come When You Want Him but) He's Right on Time," Job has been enlisted to assure Christians that, according to God's plan, even the good must suffer. Job was once again the subject of an extremely popular gospel song in 1974 when James Cleveland, with Harold Smith and the Majestics of Detroit, released Cleveland's "Lord, Help Me to Hold Out."

The song became an instant hit for three reasons: the text was composed of very few words and much repetition; it had a sing-along melody that was simple and rhythmically catchy; and Cleveland delivered the solo as if he were a minister rousing his congregation on a Sunday morning. This song, like "Soon and Very Soon (We Are Going to See the King)," a 1976 composition by Andraé Crouch, is so close to the "Jubilee" Negro spiritual of the late 19th century that most listeners felt they knew the songs, although, in fact, both were new. What they both possessed was that familiar melodic strain, perfect marriage of text and melody, and predictable, though interesting, rhythm that fell easily on the ear and tongue. As a result of these attributes "Lord, Help Me to Hold Out" immediately entered gospel's standard repertoire, where it remained into the 1990s.

In "Lord, Help Me to Hold Out," Cleveland looked backward at the same time as he insisted on being current, for while he used the conventional form of verse and chorus for the design of the song, he added a vamp at the end, over which the soloists might improvise variations. Set in the key of A-flat major, with a meter signature of 4/4, the refrain, always sung first in performance, is assigned 16 bars while the verse is set to eight. Textually, Cleveland returns to the two-statement, four-line structure of the Negro spiritual in which the principal idea, captured in the title, is stated three times and, for the sake of variety, a different fourth line is added. The fourth line acts in one of three ways: it comments on the activity of the title line, poses questions or answers to illuminate the title line, or completes a statement or question. "Lord, Help Me to Hold Out" is an example of the third variety, for although the title line is repeated three times, the idea of the song is not complete until the fourth line ("until my change come") is added. This completion of the statement is reminiscent of such spirituals as "I Want to Be Ready," "My Lord, What a Morning," and "Give Me That Old Time Religion" ("Give me that old time religion, it's good enough for me"). Poetically, then, the refrain has a rhyme scheme of aaab, though the first three lines are, in fact, not rhyme but repetitions.

While the poetry of the refrain fits into a rhyme scheme of aaab, the melodic scheme is abac. Set to the first five notes of the A-flat major scale (*a*-flat, *b*-flat, *c*, *d*-flat, *e*-flat), the melody also draws upon the lowered third degree (*c*-flat) in the first phrase as it moves scalewise from the *a*-flat, the tonic, to *c*-flat and back down to *a*-flat. The entire phrase is delivered on the tonic chord, though parallel ascending chords are insinuated into this harmony. The second phrase, based on the dominant chord, unifies the refrain, for while it begins on a different tone from the first phrase (*b*-flat), it retains the melodic contour and harmony of the first phrase, which, in its original embodiment, is repeated as the third phrase.

The fourth phrase, completely different from phrases one through three, provides the "hook" in the refrain. While the melody of the first three phrases ascends, that of the fourth phrase descends. The parallel chords of the first three phrases are present again in the final phrase, providing an additional element of unity.

Equally as important as the unifying elements of melody and harmony is a refreshingly ordered rhythm that characterizes each phrase of the refrain. In each of the first three phrases, a long value (whole note) tied to two shorter values in the next bar and followed by quarter-note triplets to complete the third bar, are again followed by a whole note in the fourth bar. The fourth phrase has the rhythmic essence of the other three phrases but with slight changes.

The verse, much less popular than the refrain and often omitted in performances of the song, offers little to the overall composition, though its text provides the rationale for the request in the title. Composed of four lines, the verse has a rhyme scheme of abcb, distributed over eight bars. In contrast to the refrain, the melody of the verse is through-composed, with a scheme of abcd. Beginning on the third scale degree above the tonic note (c) the melody skips between a-flat, c, and e-flat, before it comes to a close on the tonic, a-flat. Harmonically, the entire phrase is delivered on the tonic chord. The relative angularity of the first phrase is characteristic also of phrases two and three.

In contrast to the angularity of the first three phrases, the fourth phrase is conjunct (scalewise), with the exception of a skip of a third at the cadence. It begins, like phrases one and two, on the third scale degree (c), ascends to the fifth scale degree, and descends again in conjunct motion to the third scale degree before it comes to a close with a skip downward to the tonic note. Unlike the slow harmonic motion of the other phrases, the final phrase employs four different harmonies.

The "special chorus," an extra chorus altered in such a way that the soloist is obliged to improvise, fell out of popularity in the 1960s, replaced by the vamp, although the vamp was not usually included in the published versions of songs. Cleveland was one of the first to include the vamp in a published version of a song with "Lord, Help Me to Hold Out." While he does not include the soloists' variations, he offers one of the first published versions of the vamp, which, while retaining the same chord tones, exchanges voice parts throughout the chorus (the "exchangeable" vamp). Cleveland adds a two-bar vamp with a text of "Lord, help me to hold out" over the tonic and the lowered-seventh major chord (g-flat, b-flat, d-flat, f-flat), with the tonic chord occupying the first bar while the lowered-seventh occupies the second. The first few statements of the vamp are distributed so that the sopranos sing a-flat, while the altos are assigned the e-flat and the tenors the c. In the next several statements, the sopranos are given the c, the altos the a-flat, and the tenors the e-flat. In the final statements, the sopranos have ascended to the e-flat and the altos to the c, while the tenors are on a high a-flat. With his rapid-fire delivery and uncanny ability to build a story through a vamp, Cleveland was able with this vamp to effect a climax that is almost unparalleled in gospel.

During the last 20 years of his life, Cleveland was almost totally occupied with the supervision of the Gospel Music Workshop of America and found little time for composition. The gospel world was honored that he would compose yet another song that so perfectly captured his—and their—compositional style. "Lord, Help Me to Hold Out" was the most popular of Cleveland's final compositions.

WALK ON BY FAITH (1962)

By 1962, James Cleveland had established a reputation as a composer and a singer; he had recorded his first album with the choir of the First Baptist Church of Nutley, New Jersey, and had coached such famous singers as Aretha Franklin and Della Reese. Yet when Roberta Martin called and asked for a new song, Cleveland found it difficult to deny her. Included in the last portfolio of songs that Cleveland composed at the request of Roberta Martin was "Walk On by Faith." Like a large number of Cleveland compositions, this song is based on a scriptural passage, II Corinthians 5:6–7— "Therefore we are always confident, knowing that, whilst we are at home, in the body, we are absent from the Lord: For we walk by faith and not by sight." Quoting no other part of the passage save the title, used as an internal subrefrain in the composition, he textually proposes a number of situations that cannot be resolved unless one would "walk by faith."

Set in the key of E-flat major with a meter signature of 6/4, this work once again employs the conventional verse and refrain form. The verse and refrain each contain ten bars and each concludes with the same material, textually, melodically, harmonically, and rhythmically. The verse, always sung first in performances of the song, is divided into four lines of two bars each. The fourth line contains, according to theorist Leon Stein, "repetition of the last member," since the last line is repeated exactly as stated immediately before, adding an additional two bars to the final phrase (2+2+2+4).

Cleveland made no attempt at rhyming in the verse, resulting in a rhyme scheme of abcd, though the melody uses a more traditional form of abcb. The first phrase begins on a high e-flat, repeats that tone three times, and then begins a descent down to g. The second phrase employs the same melodic contour as the first, beginning on c and finally descending six notes to the tonic, e-flat. This melody is assigned a rhythm of alternating long and short values. While the third phrase is a repetition of the first phrase, the fourth, which, like the second phrase, begins on c and descends to e-flat, is cast in a rhythm of alternating quarter-note and half-note pulses (short-long), ending with four quarter-notes on an arpeggio of the E-flat chord (e-flat, g, b-flat, e-flat). Each of the four phrases ends with a long note value.

Characteristically, the harmonies supporting the melody of the verse are the primary chords of folk music, I–IV–V. The final phrase, however, introduces the one chord that in each Cleveland composition lifts the harmony out of the ordinary. In bars 7 and 9 (a repeat of bar 7), Cleveland inserts a minor iv chord before the dominant (V) that leads to the tonic.

In the text of the refrain, Cleveland revives an older gospel textual device of naming the days of the week and assigning an activity, prayer, or blessing to each of the days. The refrain begins, "On Monday walk on, on Tuesday walk on." Although Cleveland cites only two days of the week, it was enough to resurrect memories of the days when singers listed days from Monday to Sunday, warning people of the necessity of constant worship or rehearsing blessings they received on each day of the week. The remainder of the text assures listeners that Jesus can "see way down the road" and all one needs to do is "walk on by faith" to receive the benefit of His blessings.

While the verse is delivered by a solo voice (the printed version assigns most of the song to four-part harmony, though Roberta Martin used a soloist on her recording), with the chorus joining in on the last line, the refrain alternates between call-and-response and direct (all singing together) delivery. Composed of four lines, in which the soloist sings the first part of the line while the chorus completes the statement, the refrain, like the verse, has a poetic scheme of abcd. The first phrase begins on the fifth degree of the E-flat major scale (*b*-flat) with the soloist leaping up a third to the *d*, with the same melodic contour, and returns again to the *b*-flat only to leap up to the *e*-flat. The soloist, joined by the entire ensemble, then begins a melodic ascent from *c* (above the *b*-flat) up to a high *g*, providing the climax of the refrain. Unusual in African-American gospel, the song uses all seven notes of the scale.

The third phrase ascends once again to the high *g* before descending a third below the tonic, *e*-flat. The final phrase of the refrain is the same as that of the verse. The third phrase provides the harmonic interest in the refrain, for it includes the vi7/V and the V7/vi chords, both of which are used in such a way that the entire refrain suddenly takes on a harmonically adventurous flair.

Despite the absence of syncopation and a vamp, and while using all seven tones of the diatonic scale, Cleveland was able to create a work that appealed to choirs around the country. Although Cleveland never recorded the song, it entered gospel's standard repertoire and remained popular in the 1990s.

REFERENCES

Boyer, Horace Clarence. *How Sweet the Sound: The Golden Age of Gospel.* Washington, D.C.: Elliott and Clark, 1995.

Heilbut, Anthony. *The Gospel Sound: Good News and Bad Times.* Rev. ed. New York: Limelight Editions, 1985.

Jackson, Irene V. *Afro-American Religious Music: A Bibliography and a Catalogue of Gospel Music.* Westport, Conn.: Greenwood Press, 1979.

HORACE CLARENCE BOYER

CLINTON, GEORGE

Born in Kannapolis, N.C., July 22, 1940. **Composing and Performing Career:** Newark, N.J., organized vocal group, the Parliaments, and recorded their first single, "Poor Willie," 1956; Detroit, Mich., played area clubs and auditioned for Motown, recorded several tracks, but nothing ever released, 1963; first successful recording, "I Wanna Testify," 1967; Detroit, Mich., house writer for Motown, ca. 1967; the Parliaments renamed Parliament, 1968; formed Funkadelic, 1969; Parliament signed with Casablanca Records and recorded three albums, mid-1970s; *Mothership Connection,* several million copies sold, 1976; recorded on Warner Brothers label, 1976; title track from *One Nation under a Groove* reached number 28 on the pop charts, 1978; pursued various solo projects; signed with Capitol Records, 1982; joined Paisley Park label, 1989; played on Lollapalooza tour, summer 1994. **Honors/Awards:** Cleveland, Ohio, with Parliament-Funkadelic, inducted into the Rock and Roll Hall of Fame, 1997; N.A.A.C.P. Image Award Hall of Fame, inductee, 1997.

MUSIC LIST

[The following list of titles includes only works that were composed by the subject of the entry; it is not a list of recordings that were made by the subject. Although the composer may have made recordings of his own works, the list is not restricted to those recordings but in many cases includes performances by other artists of the composer's work. The list is made up of publication and discographical data, in cases where such information is available. Although no effort has been made to include documentation of the earliest recording of the works listed, the date of the earliest recording that is readily available has been given. —Ed.]

"Acupuncture." Co-composers, DeWayne McKnight, Walter Walters. Recorded, 1983: Uncle Jam 2K-39168.

"Adolescent Funk." Co-composers, Bernie Worrell, Michael Hampton. Recorded, 1978: Priority Records P4 53873; Warner Brothers CDGR 101.

"Agony of Defeat." Co-composers, Ron Dunbar, Donnie Sterling. Recorded, 1980: Casablanca/FilmWorks 842 623-2; Casablanca NBL5-7249; Casablanca NBLP 7249.

"Ahh, the Name is Bootsy, Baby." Co-composer, Bootsy Collins. Recorded, 1995: Rykodisc 90323.

"Alice in My Fantasies." Co-composer, Grace Cook. Recorded, 1974: Westbound WB 1001; Westbound W-208.

"All Sons of Bitches." Co-composer, Belita Woods. Recorded, 1995: Hot Hands 087426.

"All Your Goodies are Gone (The Loser's Seat)." Co-composers, Clarence Haskins, William Nelson. Recorded, 1967: Casablanca 7842 619-2; Casablanca NB 9003; F-Punk F-PR34; Revilot 211.

"America Eats Its Young." Co-composers, Bernie Worrell, Harold Beane. Recorded, 1972: Westbound WBCD-2020; Westbound W2-221; Westbound 2WB-2020.

"Aqua Boogie (A Psychoalphadiscobetabioaquadoloop)." Co-composers, Bernie Worrell, Bootsy Collins. Recorded, 1974: Casablanca 422-822 637-1 M-1; Casablanca 422 842 621-4.

"As Good as I Can Feel." Recorded, 1969: Westbound 2WB-C 1111; Westbound SEW2-005.

"Atmosphere." Co-composers, Garry Shider, Bernie Worrell. Recorded, 1975: Westbound WB-CD215; Westbound WC-215; Westbound W-215.

"Atomic Dogs." Co-composers, Garry Shider, David Spradley. Recorded, 1982: Capitol 4XL 9765; Capitol CDP 7 96266 2.

"Baby I Owe You Something Good." Recorded, 1969: Westbound 2WB-C 1111; Westbound SEW2-005.

"Baby That's a Groove." Co-composers, Eddie Holland, Lamont Dozier. Recorded, 1966: Stephanye Records n.n.

"Balance." Co-composer, Bernie Worrell. Recorded, 1972: Westbound WBCD-2020; Westbound W2-221; Westbound 2WB-2020.

"Be My Beach." Co-composers, Bernie Worrell, Bootsy Collins. Recorded, 1975: Westbound WB-CD215; Westbound WC-215; Westbound W-215.

"Better by the Pound." Co-composer, Grace Cook. Recorded, 1969: Westbound 2WB-C 1111; Westbound SEW2-005; Westbound WB-CD215; Westbound WC-215; Westbound W-215.

"Better Days." Recorded, 1978: Essential ESDLP 185.

"The Big Bang Theory." Co-composers, Donnie Sterling, Ron Dunbar. Recorded, 1979: Casablanca 842 622-2.

"Big Footin'." Co-composers, Clarence Haskins, Garry Shider. Recorded, 1975: Casablanca 422 836 700-4; Casablanca NBLP 7014.

"The Big Pump." Co-composer, Prince. Recorded, 1993: Paisley Park/Warner Brothers 9 25518-2; Paisley Park PRO-A-6537.

"Biological Speculation." Recorded, 1969: Westbound 2WB-C 1111; Westbound SEW2-005; Westbound WBCD-2020; Westbound W2-221; Westbound 2WB-2020.

"Body Language." Recorded, 1980: Casablanca/FilmWorks 842 623-2; Casablanca NBL5-7249; Casablanca NBLP 7249.

"Bodyguard." Recorded, 1985: Capitol C4-96356; Capitol 4XT 12417; Capitol ST-12417.

"The Bomb." Recorded, 1974: Casablanca 422-822 637-1 M-1.

"Bootsy (What's the Name of This Town?)." Co-composer, Bootsy Collins. Recorded, 1993: Paisley Park/Warner Brothers 41057; Rykodisc 90323.

"Bootzilla." Co-composer, Bootsy Collins. Recorded, 1995: Rykodisc 90323.

"Bop Gun (Endangered Species)." Co-composers, Garry Shider, Williams Colins. Recorded, 1974: Casablanca 422-822 637-1 M-1; Casablanca 7084; Casablanca 824 5012; Casablanca NBLP 7084.

"Breakdown." Co-composers, Ruth Copeland, Clyde Wilson. Recorded, 1967: Aurific Records MMCS 0605; Deep Beats 23; F-Punk F-PR34; Invictus Is-9095.

"Bullet Proof." Recorded, 1985: Capitol C4-96356; Capitol 4XT 12417; Capitol ST-12417.

"Butt-to-Buttresuscitation." Co-composer, Eddie Hazel, Bernie Worrell. Recorded, 1976: Westbound W-227.

"Can You Get Me That." Recorded, 1971: Westbound WB-CD-2007; Westbound SEW 002; Westbound W-218.

"Can You Get to That." Co-composer, Ernie Harris. Recorded, 1969: Paisley Park Records 4-25994; Paisley Park Records I-25994; Paisley Park Records 9 25994-2; Westbound 2WB-C 1111; Westbound SEW2-005.

"Can't Shake It Loose." Co-composers, Sidney Barnes, Ray McCoy, James Jackson. Recorded, 1966: Westbound 55; Westbound 2WB-C 1111; Westbound SEW2-005.

"Can't Stand the Strain." Co-composer, Eddie Hazel. Recorded, 1973: Paisley Park Records 4-25994; Paisley Park Records I-25994; Paisley Park Records 9 25994-2; Westbound WB-CD 2022.

"Catch a Keeper." Co-composers, Donnie Sterling, Sylvester Stewart. Recorded, 1983: Uncle Jam 2K-39168.

"Chant (Think It Ain't Illegal Yet)." Recorded, 1978: Warner Brothers BSK 3209.

"Children of Production." Co-composers, Bootsy Collins, Bernie Worrell. Recorded, 1976: Casablanca (422) 842 620-2; Casablanca NBLP 57034; Casablanca NBLP 7034; Casablanca CALD 5002.

"Chocolate City." Co-composers, Bootsy Collins, Bernie Worrell. Recorded, 1974: Casablanca 422-822 637-1 M-1; Casablanca 422 836 700-4; Casablanca NBLP 7014.

"Cholly (Funk Gettin' Ready to Roll)." Co-composers, Bootsy Collins, Walter Morrison. Recorded, 1978: Warner Brothers BSK 3209.

"The Chong Show." Recorded, 1978: Essential ESDLP 185.

"The Cinderella Theory." Co-composer, Joseph Fiddler. Recorded, 1989: F-Punk F-PR34.

"Clone Communicado." Recorded, 1993: AEM 25651.

"Colour Me Funky." Co-composer, J. S. Theracon. Recorded, 1979: Casablanca 842 622-2.

"Comin' Round the Mountain." Co-composer, Grace Cook. Recorded, 1978: Priority Records P4 53873; Warner Brothers CDGR 101.

"Common Law Wife." Recorded, 1993: AEM 25671.

"Computer Games." Co-composer, Walter Morrison. Recorded, 1982: Capitol 4XL 9765; Capitol CDP 7 96266 2.

"Cool Joe." Recorded, 1985: Capitol C4-96356; Capitol 4XT 12417; Capitol ST-12417.

"Cosmic Slop." Co-composer, Bernie Worrell. Recorded, 1969: Paisley Park Records 4-25994; Priority Records P4 53873; Warner Brothers CDGR 101; Westbound 2WB-C 1111; Westbound WB-CD 2022.

"Crush It." Co-composer, Bootsy Collins. Recorded, 1980: Casablanca/FilmWorks 842 623-2; Casablanca NBL5-7249; Casablanca NBLP 7249.

"Cryin' Has Made Me Stronger." Co-composer, Ruth Copeland. Recorded: Invictus Records SMAS 9802.

"Deep." Co-composers, Bootsy Collins, J. S. Theracon. Recorded, 1978: Casablanca 422 842 621-4.

"Do Fries Go with That Shake?" Recorded, 1986: Capitol CDP7 96267; Capitol 4CT 12481.

"Do That Stuff." Recorded, 1974: Casablanca 422-822 637-1 M-1; Casablanca (422) 842 620-2; Casablanca NBLP 57034; Casablanca NBLP 7034; Casablanca CALD 5002.

"Dog Star." Co-composer, DeWayne McKnight. Recorded, 1995: Hot Hands 087426.

"Don't Be Sore at Me." Co-composers, G. Thomas, P. Lewis. Recorded, 1967: Casablanca 7842 619-2; Casablanca NB 9003; F-Punk F-PR34'; Revilot 211.

"Don't You Wish You Had (What You Had When You Had It?)." Co-composer, Ruth Copeland. Recorded: Deep Beats 22; Invictus Records SMAS 9802.

"Dopey Dope Dog." Co-composers, Daddy Freddy, Lige Vurry. Recorded, 1995: Hot Hands 087426.

"Double Uh-Oh." Recorded, 1985: Capitol C4-96356; Capitol 4XT 12417; Capitol ST-12417.

"Dr. Funkenstein." Co-composers, Bootsy Collins, Bernie Worrell. Recorded, 1976: Casablanca (422) 842 620-2; Casablanca NBLP 57034; Casablanca NBLP 7034; Casablanca CALD 5002.

"Electric Pygmies." Recorded, 1985: Capitol C4-96356; Capitol 4XT 12417; Capitol ST-12417.

"Electric Spanking of War Babies." Co-composers, Bob Bishop, Walter Morrison. Recorded, 1981: Charly Records CDGR 102; Priority P2 53874; Warner Brothers XBS 3482.

"Electro-Cuties." Co-composers, Ron Ford, J. Ali. Recorded, 1981: Charly Records CDGR 102; Priority P2 53874; Warner Brothers XBS 3482.

"Every Little Bit Hurts." Recorded, 1994: AEM Record Group 25761-2.

"Everybody Is Going to Make It This Time." Co-composer, Bernie Worrell. Recorded, 1972: Westbound WBCD-2020; Westbound W2-221; Westbound 2WB-2020.

"Everything Is on the One." Co-composers, Bootsy Collins, Bernie Worrell. Recorded, 1976: Casablanca (422) 842 620-2; Casablanca NBLP 57034; Casablanca NBLP 7034.

"Fantasy Is Reality." Co-composers, Bernie Worrell, L. Ware. Recorded, 1977: Casablanca CALD 5002.

"Field Maneuvers." Recorded, 1979: Charly Groove CDGR 103; Warner Brothers 3371.

"Fifi." Co-composer, DeWayne McKnight. Recorded, 1995: Hot Hands 087426.

"Fish, Chips and Sweat." Co-composer, B. Nelson, Eddie Hazel. Recorded, 1967: Revilot 207; F-Punk F-PR34; Westbound 2WB-C 1111; Westbound SEW2-005.

"The Flag Was Still There." Co-composers, Tracey Lewis, Steven Boyd, Phelps Collins. Recorded, 1993: Paisley Park/Warner Brothers 9 25518-2; Paisley Park PRO-A-6537.

"Flashlight." Co-composers, Bootsy Collins, Bernie Worrell. Recorded, 1974: Casablanca 7084; Casablanca 824 5012; Casablanca NBLP 7084; Casablanca 422-822 637-1 M-1.

"Flatman and Bobbin." Recorded, 1994: AEM Record Group 25761-2.

"Follow the Leader." Co-composer, Rakim. Recorded, 1995: Hot Hands 087426.

"Foot Soldier (Star-Spangled Funky)." Co-composer, Jim Vitti. Recorded, 1979: Charly Groove CDGR 103; Warner Brothers 3371.

"Freak of the Week." Co-composers, P. Bishop, DeWayne McKnight. Recorded, 1979: Charly Groove CDGR 103; Warner Brothers 3371.

"Free Alterations." Co-composer, Darryl Clinton. Recorded, 1982: Capitol CDP 7 96266 2.

"Free Your Mind and Your Ass Will Follow." Co-composers, Eddie Hazel, Ray Davis. Recorded, 1970: Westbound WB-CD-2001; Westbound W-217 (0698).

"The Freeze (Sizzleanmean)." Co-composer, DeWayne McKnight. Recorded, 1979: Casablanca 842 622-2.

"French Kiss." Co-composers, DeWayne McKnight, Steve Washington, Andre Williams. Recorded, 1989: F-Punk F-PR34.

"Friday Night, August Fourteenth." Co-composers, Billy Nelson, Eddie Hazel. Recorded, 1970: Westbound WB-CD-2001; Westbound W-217 (0698).

"Funk Gets Stronger." Co-composer, Michael Hampton. Recorded, 1981: Charly Records CDGR 102; Priority P2 53874; Warner Brothers XBS 3482.

George Clinton; courtesy of Sony 550 Music; photo by TAR

"Funk It Up." Recorded, 1978: Essential ESDLP 185.

"A Funkadelic the One and Only Blackbyrd Period." Recorded, 1978: Essential ESDLP 185.

"Funkentelechy." Co-composer, Bootsy Collins. Recorded, 1977: Casablanca 7084; Casablanca 824 5012; Casablanca NBLP 7084.

"Funkin' for Fun." Co-composers, Garry Shider, Glen Goins. Recorded, 1976: Casablanca (422) 842 620-2; Casablanca NBLP 57034; Casablanca NBLP 7034.

"Funkin' for My Mama's Rent." Recorded, 1978: Essential ESDLP 185.

"Funky Dollar Bill." Co-composers, Eddie Hazel, Ray Davis. Recorded, 1969: Paisley Park Records 4-25994; Paisley Park Records I-25994; Paisley Park Records 9 25994-2; Westbound 2WB-C 1111; Westbound WB-CD-2001.

"Funky Kind." Co-composer, Joseph Fiddler. Recorded, 1996: Music/Epic 57144.

"Funky Woman." Co-composer, Bernie Worrell. Recorded, 1970: Aurific Records MMCS 0605.

"Gamin' on Ya." Co-composers, Bootsy Collins, Bernie Worrell. Recorded, 1976: Casablanca CALD 5002; Casablanca (422) 842 620-2; Casablanca NBLP 57034; Casablanca NBLP 7034.

"Generator Pop." Co-composers, Garry Shider, David Spradley. Recorded, 1983: Uncle Jam 2K-39168.

"Get Dressed." Co-composer, Bootsy Collins. Recorded, 1991: Capitol CDP 7 96266 2.

"Get Off Your Ass and Jam." Recorded, 1975: Westbound WB-CD215; Westbound WC-215; Westbound W-215.

"Get Satisfied." Co-composers, Michael Payne, Tracey Lewis. Recorded, 1993: Paisley Park/Warner Brothers 9 25518-2; Paisley Park PRO-A-6537.

"Get Your Funk On." Co-composer, Dale Spradley. Recorded, 1996: Music/Epic 57144.

"Gettin' to Know You." Co-composer, Garry Shider. Recorded, 1976: Casablanca (422) 842 620-2; Casablanca NBLP 57034; Casablanca NBLP 7034.

"Give Up the Funk (Tear the Roof off the Sucker)." Co-composers, Bootsy Collins, Bernie Worrell. Recorded, 1974: Casablanca 422-822 637-1 M-1; Casablanca NBLP 7042.

"Go for Yer Funk." Recorded, 1978: Essential ESDLP 185.

"Good Old Music." Co-composers, the Funkadelics. Recorded, 1967: Revilot RV-223; F-Punk F-PR34; Westbound WB-CD-2000; Westbound W-216; Lax Records JWT 37087.

"Good Thoughts, Bad Thoughts." Co-composer, Grace Cook. Recorded, 1974: Westbound WB 1001; Westbound W-208.

"Good to Your Earhole." Co-composers, Grace Cook, Clarence Haskins. Recorded, 1975: Westbound WB-CD215; Westbound WC-215; Westbound W-215.

"The Goose (That Laid the Golden Egg)." Co-composers, Ernie Harris, Eddie Hazel. Recorded, 1967: Casablanca 7842 619-2; Casablanca NB 9003; Revilot RV-214; Revilot 207; F-Punk F-PR34.

"Groovallegiance." Co-composers, Walter Morrison, Bernie Worrell. Recorded, 1978: Warner Brothers BSK 3209.

"Handcuffs." Co-composers, Glen Goins, McLaughlin. Recorded, 1975: Casablanca 824 502-2; Casablanca 7022.

"Hard as Steel." Recorded, 1996: Music/Epic 57144.

"Hardcore Jollies." Co-composer, Bernie Worrell. Recorded, 1978: Priority Records P4 53873; Warner Brothers CDGR 101.

"Hare Krishna." Co-composer, Ruth Copeland. Recorded: Deep Beats 22; Invictus Records SMAS 9802.

"He Dance Funny." Co-composer, Wes Boatman. Recorded, 1989: MCA MCAD-42048.

"Help Scottie, Help (I'm Tweaking and I Can't Beam Up)." Co-composers, Tracey Lewis, DeWayne McKnight. Recorded, 1995: Hot Hands 087426.

"Hey Good Lookin'." Recorded, 1986: Capitol CDP7 96267; Capitol 4CT 12481.

"Hey Mama." Recorded, 1967: Rick-Tic Records n.n.

"High in My Hello." Co-composer, Steve Washington. Recorded, 1993: Paisley Park/Warner Brothers 9 25518-2; Paisley Park PRO-A-6537.

"Hit It and Quit It." Co-composers, Billy Nelson, Garry Shider. Recorded, 1969: Westbound 2WB-C 1111; Westbound SEW2-005; Westbound WB-CD-2007; Westbound SEW 002; Westbound W-218.

"Holly Wants to Go to California." Co-composer, Bernie Worrell. Recorded, 1979: Charly Groove CDGR 103; Warner Brothers 3371.

"Hollywood Squares." Co-composer, Bootsy Collins. Recorded, 1995: Rykodisc 90323.

"Hooray." Co-composer, Dave Spradley. Recorded, 1989: MCA MCAD-42048.

"How Do Yeaw View You?" Co-composers, Bootsy Collins, Bernie Worrell. Recorded, 1969: Westbound 2WB-C 1111; Westbound SEW2-005; Westbound W-227.

"Hydraulic Pump." Co-composers, Sylvester Stewart, Jimmy Giles, Ron Ford. Recorded, 1983: Uncle Jam 2K-39168.

"I Ain't the Lady (He Ain't the Tramp)." Recorded, 1995: Hot Hands 087426.

"I Bet You." Co-composers, Pat Lindsey, Sidney Barnes. Recorded, 1970: Westbound WB-CD-2000; Westbound W-216; Lax Records JWT 37087.

"I Call My Baby Pussycat." Co-composers, Billy Nelson, Eddie Hazel. Recorded, 1967: Aurific Records MMCS 0605; Invictus Is-9077; Revilot 207; F-Punk F-PR34; Westbound 2020.

"I Can Feel the Ice Melting." Co-composer, Vivian Lewis. Recorded, 1967: Casablanca 7842 619-2; Casablanca NB 9003; Revilot 207; F-Punk F-PR34.

"I Can Move You (If You Let Me)." Co-composers, Bootsy Collins, Bernie Worrell, Cordell Mosson. Recorded, 1974: Casablanca 7842 619-2; Casablanca NB 9003.

"I Envy the Sunshine." Recorded, 1993: AEM 25671.

"I Got a Thing for You Daddy." Co-composer, Ruth Copeland. Recorded, 1969: Deep Beats 22; Invictus Records 7303.

"I Misjudged You." Co-composers, Clarence Haskins, Ernie Harris. Recorded, 1975: Casablanca 422 836 700-4; Casablanca NBLP 7014.

"I Owe You Something Good." Recorded, 1975: Westbound WB-CD215; Westbound WC-215; Westbound W-215.

"I Wanna Know If It's Good to You." Co-composers, Eddie Hazel, Billy Nelson, Clarence Haskins. Recorded, 1969: Westbound 2WB-C 1111; Westbound SEW2-005; Westbound WB-CD-2001; Westbound W-217 (0698).

"(I Wanna) Testify." Co-composer, Deron Taylor. Recorded, 1967: Casablanca 7842 619-2; Casablanca NB 9003; Revilot 207; F-Punk F-PR34.

"Ice Melting in Your Heart." Recorded, 1994: AEM Record Group 25761-2.

"Icka Prick." Co-composer, Garry Shider. Recorded, 1981: Charly Records CDGR 102; Priority P2 53874; Warner Brothers XBS 3482.

"I'd Rather Be with You." Co-composer, Bootsy Collins. Recorded, 1995: Rykodisc 90323.

"If Anybody Gets Funked Up." Co-composer, G. Cooper. Recorded, 1996: Music/Epic 57144.

"If It Don't Fit (Don't Force It)." Co-composers, Bernie Worrell, Garry Shider. Recorded, 1975: Casablanca 422 836 700-4; Casablanca NBLP 7014.

"If True Love." Co-composer, Tracey Lewis. Recorded, 1993: Paisley Park/ Warner Brothers 9 25518-2; Paisley Park PRO-A-6537.

"If You Don't Like the Effects, Don't Produce the Cause." Co-composer, Garry Shider. Recorded, 1969: Westbound 2WB-C 1111; Westbound SEW2-005; Westbound WBCD-2020; Westbound W2-221; Westbound 2WB-2020.

"If You Got Funk, You Got Style." Co-composers, Bootsy Collins, Bernie Worrell. Recorded, 1978: Priority Records P4 53873; Warner Brothers CDGR 101.

"I'll Bet You." Co-composers, Pat Lindsey, Sidney Barnes. Recorded, 1966: Paisley Park Records 4-25994; Paisley Park Records I-25994; Paisley Park Records 9 25994-2; Westbound 2WB-C 1111; Westbound SEW2-005.

"I'll Stay." Co-composer, Grace Cook. Recorded, 1974: Westbound WB 1001; Westbound W-208.

"I'll Wait." Co-composer, Eddie Hazel. Recorded, 1967: Atco 45-6675; Revilot 207; F-Punk F-PR34.

"I'm Never Gonna Tell It." Co-composer, Bernie Worrell. Recorded, 1976: Westbound W-227.

"In the Cabin of My Uncle Jam (P Is the Funk)." Recorded, 1993: AEM 25651.

"Intense." Recorded, 1986: Capitol C2-96267.

"Into You." Co-composers, Walter Morrison, Bootsy Collins. Recorded, 1978: Warner Brothers BSK 3209.

"I've Been Watching You (Move Your Sexy Body)." Co-composers, Garry Shider, Glen Goins. Recorded, 1976: Casablanca (422) 842 620-2; Casablanca NBLP 57034; Casablanca NBLP 7034.

"Jimmy's Got a Little Bit of Bitch in Him." Co-composer, Grace Cook. Recorded, 1969: Westbound 2WB-C 1111; Westbound SEW2-005; Westbound WB 1001; Westbound W-208.

"A Joyful Process." Co-composer, Bernie Worrell. Recorded, 1969: Westbound 2WB-C 1111; Westbound SEW2-005; Westbound WBCD-2020; Westbound W2-221; Westbound 2WB-2020.

"Just Say Ding (Databoy)." Co-composers, Tracey Lewis, DeWayne McKnight. Recorded, 1995: Hot Hands 087426.

"Kibbles and Bits." Recorded, 1995: Hot Hands 087426.

"Kickback." Recorded, 1993: Paisley Park/Warner Brothers 9 25518-2; Paisley Park PRO-A-6537.

"Kredit Kard." Co-composer, Michael Payen. Recorded, 1989: Paisley Park 2-25994.

"The Landing." Recorded, 1977: Casablanca CALD 5002.

"Let Me Be." Recorded, 1975: Casablanca 422 836 700-4 Casablanca NBLP 7014.

"Let's Get Funky." Co-composer, Joseph Fiddler. Recorded, 1996: Music/ Epic 57144.

"Let's Make It Last." Co-composer, Eddie Hazel. Recorded, 1973: Westbound WB2022; Westbound WB223; Westbound WB-CD 2022.

"Let's Play House." Co-composers, Bootsy Collins, Walter Morrison. Recorded, 1980: Casablanca/FilmWorks 842 623-2; Casablanca NBL5-7249; Casablanca NBLP 7249.

"Let's Take It to the People." Co-composers, Garry Shider, Eddie Hazel. Recorded, 1976: Westbound W-227.

"Let's Take It to the Stage." Co-composers, Bootsy Collins, Garry Shider. Recorded, 1969: Westbound 2WB-C 1111; Westbound SEW2-005; Westbound WB-CD215; Westbound WC-215; Westbound W-215.

"Liquid Sunshine." Co-composers, Linda Brown, Jim Vitti, Bob Bishop. Recorded, 1978: Casablanca 422 842 621-4.

"Little Man." Co-composer, Tracey Lewis. Recorded, 1967: F-Punk F-PR34; Revilot RV-214.

"Livin' the Life." Co-composers, Bernie Worrell, Billy Nelson. Recorded, 1970: Aurific Records MMCS 0605.

"Long Way Round." Co-composer, Walter Morrison. Recorded, 1980: Casablanca/FilmWorks 842 623-2; Casablanca NBL5-7249; Casablanca NBLP 7249.

"Look at What I Almost Missed." Co-composer, Vivian Lewis. Recorded, 1967: Revilot 217; Revilot 207; F-Punk F-PR34.

"Loose Booty." Co-composer, Harold Beane. Recorded, 1969: Westbound 2WB-C 1111; Westbound SEW2-005; Westbound WBCD-2020; Westbound W2-221; Westbound 2WB-2020.

"Lunchmeataphobia." Co-composer, Bernie Worrell. Recorded, 1978: Warner Brothers BSK 3209.

"Maggot Brain." Co-composer, Eddie Hazel. Recorded, 1971: Warner Brothers BSK 3209; Westbound WB-CD-2007; Westbound SEW 002; Westbound W-218.

"Manopener." Co-composer, Bernie Worrell. Recorded, 1989: MCA MCAD-42048.

"Man's Best Friend/Loopzilla." Recorded, 1982: Capitol 4XL 9765; Capitol CDP 7 96266 2.

"March to the Witch's Castle." Recorded, 1973: Westbound 2022.

"Martial Law (Hey Man, Smell My Finger)." Co-composers, William Bryant III, Kerry Gordy. Recorded, 1993: Paisley Park/Warner Brothers 9 25518-2; Paisley Park PRO-A-6537; Paisley Park 0-41214.

"Mathematics." Co-composer, DeWayne McKnight. Recorded, 1996: Music/Epic 57144.

"Maximumisness." Co-composers, Bootsy Collins, Bill Laswell. Recorded, 1993: Paisley Park/Warner Brothers 9 25518-2; Paisley Park PRO-A-6537.

"May We Bang You?" Co-composers, Bootsy Collins, Phelps Collins, J. S. Theracon. Recorded, 1979: Casablanca 842 622-2.

"Michelle." Recorded, 1978: Essential ESDLP 185.

"Miss Lucifer's Love." Co-composer, Clarence Haskins. Recorded, 1972: Westbound WBCD-2020; Westbound W2-221; Westbound 2WB-2020.

Mix Master Suite. Contents: Startin' from Scratch; Counter Irritant; Nothin' Left to Do but Burn. Recorded, 1986: Capitol C2-96267.

"Mommy, What's a Funkadelic?" Recorded, 1970: Westbound WB-CD-2000; Westbound W-216; Lax Records JWT 37087.

"Moonshine Heather (Takin' Care of Business)." Recorded, 1970: Aurific Records MMCS 0605.

"Mothership Connection (Star Child)." Co-composers, Bootsy Collins, Bernie Worrell. Recorded, 1974: Casablanca 824 502-2; Casablanca 7022; Casablanca 422-822 637-1 M-1; Casablanca CALD 5002.

"Motor Booty Affair." Co-composers, Garry Shider, Ron Ford. J. S. Theracon. Recorded, 1978: Casablanca 422 842 621-4.

"Mr. Wiggles." Co-composers, Bootsy Collins, Michael Hampton. Recorded, 1978: Casablanca 422 842 621-4.

"Music for My Mother." Co-composers, Billy Nelson, Eddie Hazel. Recorded, 1967: Revilot 207; F-Punk F-PR34; Westbound 2WB-C 1111; Westbound SEW2-005; Westbound WB-CD-2000.

"My Automobile." Co-composer, Clarence Haskins. Recorded, 1970: Aurific Records MMCS 0605.

"Nappy Dugout." Co-composers, Garry Shider, Cordell Mosson. Recorded, 1973: Westbound WB2022; Westbound WB223; Westbound WB-CD 2022.

"A New Day Begins." Recorded, 1967: Atco 45-6675; Revilot 207; F-Punk F-PR34.

"New Doo Review." Co-composer, Ron Ford. Recorded, 1980: Casablanca/FilmWorks 842 623-2; Casablanca NBL5-7249; Casablanca NBLP 7249.

"New Spaceship." Recorded, 1996: Music/Epic 57144.

"Nice." Recorded, 1989: MCA MCAD-42048.

"Night of the Thumpasorus People." Co-composers, Garry Shider, Bootsy Collins. Recorded, 1977: Casablanca CALD 5002; Casablanca 824 502-2; Casablanca 7022.

"No Compute." Co-composer, Garry Shider. Recorded, 1973: Westbound WB2022; Westbound WB223; Westbound WB-CD 2022.

"No Computer." Recorded, 1974: Paisley Park Records 4-25994; Paisley Park Records I-25994; Paisley Park Records 9 25994-2.

"No Head Backstage Pass." Co-composer, Ron Bykowski. Recorded, 1975: Westbound WB-CD215; Westbound WC-215; Westbound W-215.

"(Not Just) Knee Deep." Recorded, 1979: Charly Groove CDGR 103; Warner Brothers 3371.

"Nubian Nut." Co-composers, David Spradley, Lane Strickland. Recorded, 1983: Capitol 4XT 12308; Capitol SDT-12308.

"Oh, I." Co-composers, Garry Shider, Rodney Curtis. Recorded, 1981: Charly Records CDGR 102; Priority P2 53874; Warner Brothers XBS 3482.

"One Fun at a Time." Co-composer, Walter Morrison. Recorded, 1982: Capitol CDP 7 96266 2.

"One Nation under a Groove." Co-composers, Garry Shider, Walter Morrison. Recorded, 1978: Warner Brothers BSK 3209.

"One of Those Funky Thangs." Co-composer, Ray Banks. Recorded, 1978: Casablanca 422 842 621-4.

"One of Those Summers." Co-composer, Walter Morrison. Recorded, 1983: Uncle Jam 2K-39168.

"Our Love (Is in the Pocket)." Co-composers, R. McCoy, J. Jackson. Recorded: Revilot RV-201.

"P. E. Squad." Co-composers, Garry Shider, Linda Brown. Recorded, 1978: Warner Brothers BSK 3209.

"P-Funk (Wants to Get Funked Up)." Co-composers, Bootsy Collins, Bernie Worrell. Recorded, 1974: Casablanca 422-822 637-1 M-1; Casablanca 824 502-2; Casablanca 7022.

"Pack of Wild Dogs." Co-composers, Andre Williams, Mike Clark. Recorded, 1995: Hot Hands 087426.

"Paint the White House Black." Co-composers, Barrett Strong, Norman Whitfield, William Bryant, Kerry Gordy. Recorded, 1993: Paisley Park/Warner Brothers 9 25518-2; Paisley Park PRO-A-6537; Paisley Park 0-41214.

"Party Boys." Recorded, 1958: APT n.n.

"Party People." Co-composers, Bootsy Collins, Garry Shider. Recorded, 1979: Casablanca 842 622-2.

"Peek-a-Groove." Co-composer, Ron Ford. Recorded, 1980: Casablanca/FilmWorks 842 623-2; Casablanca NBL5-7249; Casablanca NBLP 7249.

"Picture This." Co-composers, William Bryant, Kerry Gordy. Recorded, 1993: Paisley Park/Warner Brothers 41057.

"Pin the Tail on the Funky." Co-composer, Bootsy Collins. Recorded, 1979: Casablanca 842 622-2.

"Pinocchio Theory." Co-composer, Bootsy Collins. Recorded, 1995: Rykodisc 90323.

"Placebo Syndrome." Co-composer, Billy Nelson. Recorded, 1977: Casablanca 7084; Casablanca 824 5012; Casablanca NBLP 7084.

"Pleasures of Exhaustion (Do It Till I Drop)." Recorded, 1985: Capitol C4-96356; Capitol 4XT 12417; Capitol ST-12417.

"Poor Willie." Recorded, 1958: APT n.n.

"Pot Sharing Tots." Co-composer, Walter Morrison. Recorded, 1982: Capitol CDP 7 96266 2.

"Presence of a Brain." Co-composer, Garry Shider. Recorded, 1974: Casablanca 7842 619-2; Casablanca NB 9003.

"Promentalshitbackwashpsychosis Enema Squad (The Doo Doo Chasers)." Co-composers, Garry Shider, Linda Brown. Recorded, 1978: Warner Brothers BSK 3209.

"Psychoticbumpschool." Co-composer, Bootsy Collins. Recorded, 1995: Rykodisc 90323.

"Pump Up and Down." Co-composers, Jimmy Giles, Ron Ford, Sylvester Stewart. Recorded, 1995: Westbound 097.

"Pumpin' It Up." Co-composers, Bob Bishop, Garry Shider, Ron Ford. Recorded, 1983: Uncle Jam 2K-39168.

"Pumpin' You Is So Easy." Co-composers, Jimmy Giles, Ron Ford, Sylvester Stewart. Recorded, 1995: Westbound 097.

"Pussy." Co-composers, Billy Nelson, Eddie Hazel. Recorded, 1972: Westbound WBCD-2020; Westbound W2-221; Westbound 2WB-2020.

"Put Love in Your Life." Co-composer, Vivian Lewis. Recorded, 1970: Invictus 7302.

"Qualify and Satisfy." Co-composers, Eddie Hazel, Billy Nelson. Recorded, 1969: Westbound 2WB-C 1111; Westbound SEW2-005; Westbound WB-CD-2000; Westbound W-216; Lax Records JWT 37087.

"R and B Skeletons in the Closet." Recorded, 1986: Capitol C2-96267.

"Rat Kissed the Cat." Recorded, 1994: AEM Record Group 25761-2.

"Red Hot Mama." Co-composers, Eddie Hazel, Bernie Worrell. Recorded, 1967: Revilot 207; F-Punk F-PR34; Westbound 2WB-C 1111; Westbound WB 1001; Westbound W-208.

"Rhythm and Rhyme." Co-composers, J. Pandy, D. Galea, D. Hope. Recorded, 1993: Paisley Park/Warner Brothers 9 25518-2; Paisley Park PRO-A-6537.

"Ride On." Co-composers, Bootsy Collins, Bernie Worrell. Recorded, 1975: Casablanca 422 836 700-4; Casablanca NBLP 7014.

"Rite Bewitched." Co-composer, Tracey Lewis. Recorded, 1989: Paisley Park 2-25994.

"Rock the Party." Co-composer, Olivia Ewing. Recorded, 1996: Music/Epic 57144.

"Roto-Rooter." Co-composer, Bootsy Collins. Recorded, 1995: Rykodisc 90323.

"Rumpofsteelskin (You're a Fish and I'm a Water Sign)." Co-composer, Bootsy Collins. Recorded, 1978: Casablanca 422 842 621-4.

"Send a Gram." Recorded, 1978: Essential ESDLP 185.

"Sexy Ways." Co-composer, Grace Cook. Recorded, 1974: Paisley Park Records 4-25994; Paisley Park Records I-25994; Paisley Park Records 9 25994-2; Westbound WB 1001; Westbound W-208.

"Sick 'em." Recorded, 1995: Hot Hands 087426.

"Side Effects." Co-composers, Bootsy Collins, A. Kilson. Recorded, 1975: Casablanca 422 836 700-4; Casablanca NBLP 7014.

"Sir Nose D'Voidoffunk (Pay Attention B3M)." Co-composers, Bootsy Collins, Bernie Worrell. Recorded, 1977: Casablanca 7084.

"Sloppy Seconds." Recorded, 1996: Music/Epic 57144.

"Smokey." Co-composer, Garry Shider. Recorded, 1978: Priority Records P4 53873; Warner Brothers CDGR 101.

"So Called Friends." Co-composers, Sidney Barnes, Taylor. Recorded, 1968: Revilot Records n.n.

"Some More." Co-composer, Ernie Harris. Recorded, 1970: Westbound WB-CD-2001; Westbound W-217 (0698).

"Some Next Shit." Co-composer, Michael Payne. Recorded, 1995: Hot Hands 087426.

"Some of My Best Jokes Are Friends." Recorded, 1985: Capitol C4-96356; Capitol 4XT 12417; Capitol ST-12417.

"The Song Is Familiar." Co-composers, Bootsy Collins, Bernie Worrell. Recorded, 1975: Westbound WB-CD215; Westbound WC-215; Westbound W-215.

"Soul Mate." Co-composer, Grace Cook. Recorded, 1978: Priority Records P4 53873; Warner Brothers CDGR 101.

"Standing on the Verge of Getting It On." Co-composer, Grace Cook. Recorded, 1969: Westbound 2WB-C 1111; Westbound SEW2-005; Westbound WB 1001; Westbound W-208.

"Stuffs and Things." Co-composer, Grace Cook. Recorded, 1969: Westbound 2WB-C 1111; Westbound SEW2-005; Westbound WB-CD215; Westbound WC-215; Westbound W-215.

"Summer Swim." Co-composer, Walter Morrison. Recorded, 1996: Music/Epic 57144.

"Super Stupid." Co-composers, Eddie Hazel, Tawl Ross, Billy Nelson. Recorded, 1971: Paisley Park Records 4-25994; Paisley Park Records I-25994; Paisley Park Records 9 25994-2; Westbound WB-CD-2007.

"Supergroovalisticprosifunkstication." Co-composers, Bootsy Collins, Bernie Worrell, Garry Shider. Recorded, 1975: Casablanca 824 502-2; Casablanca 7022.

"Take Your Dead Ass Home." Co-composers, Glen Goins, Bernie Worrell, Garry Shider. Recorded, 1976: Westbound W-227.

"Tales of Kidd Funkadelic." Co-composer, Bernie Worrell. Recorded, 1976: Westbound W-227.

"Tales That Wag the Dog." Co-composers, Tracey Lewis, Derrick Rossen. Recorded, 1995: Hot Hands 087426.

"T.A.P.O.A.F.O.M." Co-composer, D. Barsha. Recorded, 1996: Music/Epic 57144.

"That Was My Girl." Co-composer, Sidney Barnes. Recorded, 1972: Westbound WBCD-2020; Westbound W2-221; Westbound 2WB-2020.

"Theme from the Black Hole." Co-composers, Bootsy Collins, J. S. Theracon. Recorded, 1974: Casablanca 422-822 637-1 M-1.

"There I Go Again." Co-composers, Joe Harris, Joe Fiddler. Recorded, 1989: F-punk F-PR34.

"There Is Nothing Before Me but Thang." Co-composers, Ernie Harris, Eddie Hazel, Bernie Worrell. Recorded, 1970: Aurific Records MMCS 0605.

"Think Right." Recorded, 1993: AEM 25651.

"This Is the Way We Funk with You." Co-composers, Bernie Worrell, Eddie Hazel, Glen Goins. Recorded, 1977: Casablanca CALD 5002.

"Thrashin." Recorded, 1985: Capitol C4-96356; Capitol 4XT 12417; Capitol ST-12417.

"Throw Your Hands Up in the Air." Co-composers, Jimmy Giles, Ron Ford, Sylvester Stewart. Recorded, 1995: Westbound 097.

"Time." Co-composer, Tracey Lewis. Recorded, 1967: Revilot RV-223; Revilot 207; F-Punk F-PR34.

"Together." Co-composers, Bootsy Collins, Bernie Worrell. Recorded, 1975: Casablanca 422 836 700-4; Casablanca NBLP 7014.

"Too Tight for Light." Recorded, 1994: AEM Record Group 25761-2.

"Trash-a-Go-Go." Recorded, 1973: Westbound WB2022; Westbound WB223; Westbound WB-CD 2022.

"Trombipulation." Co-composer, Bootsy Collins. Recorded, 1980: Casablanca/FilmWorks 842 623-2; Casablanca NBL5-7249; Casablanca NBLP 7249.

"Uncle Jam." Co-composers, Garry Shider, Bootsy Collins, Bernie Worrell. Recorded, 1979: Charly Groove CDGR 103; Warner Brothers 3371.

"Uncut Funk." Recorded, 1974: Casablanca 422-822 637-1 M-1.

"Underground Angel." Co-composer, S. Boyd. Recorded, 1996: Music/Epic 57144.

"Undisco Kidd." Co-composers, Bootsy Collins, Bernie Worrell. Recorded, 1969: Casablanca CALD 5002; Westbound 2WB-C 1111; Westbound SEW2-005; Westbound W-227.

"Unfunky UFO." Co-composers, Bootsy Collins, Garry Shider. Recorded, 1975: Casablanca 824 502-2; Casablanca 7022.

"Up for the Down Stroke." Co-composers, Bootsy Collins, Bernie Worrell, Clarence Haskins. Recorded, 1974: Casablanca 422-822 637-1 M-1; Casablanca 7842 619-2; Casablanca NB 9003; Casablanca NBLP 7042.

"Up, Up, Up and Away." Recorded, 1994: AEM Record Group 25761-2.

"U.S. Custom Coast Guard Dog." Recorded, 1995: Hot Hands 087426.

"Vital Juices." Recorded, 1969: Westbound 2WB-C 1111; Westbound SEW2-005.

"Wake Up." Co-composers, Bernie Worrell, James Wesley Jackson. Recorded, 1972: Paisley Park Records 4-25994; Paisley Park Records I-25994; Paisley Park Records 9 25994-2; Westbound WBCD-2020.

"Wars of Armageddon." Co-composers, Tawl Ross, Bernie Worrell, Ramon Fullwood. Recorded, 1971: Westbound WB-CD-2007; Westbound SEW 002; Westbound W-218.

"Way Up." Co-composer, Foley McCreary. Recorded, 1993: Paisley Park/ Warner Brothers 9 25518-2; Paisley Park PRO-A-6537.

"We Hurt Too." Recorded, 1972: Westbound WBCD-2020; Westbound W2-221; Westbound 2WB-2020.

"What Comes Funky." Co-composers, Bootsy Collins, Bernie Worrell. Recorded, 1975: Casablanca 422 836 700-4; Casablanca NBLP 7014.

"What Is Soul?" Recorded, 1970: Westbound WB-CD-2000; Westbound W-216; Lax Records JWT 37087.

"What You Been Growing." Co-composer, Ernie Harris. Recorded, 1967: Revilot 217.

"Whatever Makes Baby Feel Good." Co-composer, Eddie Hazel. Recorded, 1974: Casablanca 7842 619-2; Casablanca NB 9003.

"Who in the Funk Do You Think You Are?" Recorded, 1978: Essential ESDLP 185.

"Who Says a Funk Band Can't Play Rock?" Co-composers, Walter Morrsion, Michael Hampton. Recorded, 1978: Warner Brothers BSK 3209.

"A Whole Lot of B. S." Co-composer, Bernie Worrell. Recorded, 1969: Westbound 2WB-C 1111; Westbound SEW2-005.

"Why Should I Dog U Out?" Co-composers, Joe Fiddler, Dwayne McKnight. Recorded, 1989: F-Punk F-PR34.

"Wizard of Finance." Recorded, 1977: Casablanca 7084; Casablanca 824 5012; Casablanca NBLP 7084.

"You and Your Folks, Me and My Folks." Co-composers, Judie Jones, Bernie Worrell. Recorded, 1969: Westbound 2WB-C 1111; Westbound SEW2-005; Westbound WB-CD-2007; Westbound SEW 002; Westbound W-218.

"You Can't Miss What You Can't Measure." Co-composer, Sidney Barnes. Recorded, 1973: Westbound WB2022; Westbound WB223; Westbound WB-CD 2022.

"You Hit the Nail on the Head." Co-composers, Clarence Haskins, Bernie Worrell. Recorded, 1972: Westbound WBCD-2020; Westbound W2-221; Westbound 2WB-2020.

"You Scared the Lovin' Outta Me." Co-composer, Glen Goins. Recorded, 1978: Priority Records P4 53873; Warner Brothers CDGR 101.

INCIDENTAL MUSIC

"Black People." 1995. For the motion picture *Panther.* Recorded: Mercury 314 525 479-4.

"Brainscan." 1994. For the motion picture *Brainscan.* Recorded: Sony Music Entertainment CK 64267.

"Demon Warriors/Mortal Combat." 1997. For the motion picture *Mortal Kombat.* Recorded: TVT 8200-4.

"The End." 1997. For the motion picture *Beverly Hills Ninja.* Recorded: EMI 7243-8-55204-2-6.

"Erotic City." 1994. For the motion picture *PCU.* Recorded: Fox 07822-11017-4.

"Goro vs. Art." 1997. For the motion picture *Mortal Kombat.* Recorded: TVT 8200-4.

"The Shag-adelic Austin Powers Medley." 1997. For the motion picture *Austin Powers: International Man of Mystery.* Recorded: Hollywood HR-62112-4.

"Stomp." 1994. For the motion picture *PCU.* Recorded: Fox 07822-11017-4.

"A Taste of Things to Come." 1997. For the motion picture *Mortal Kombat.* Recorded: TVT 8200-4.

"We Can Funk." 1990. Co-composer, Prince. For the motion picture *Graffiti Bridge.* Recorded: Paisley Park 27493.

PUBLICATIONS

ABOUT CLINTON
Articles

Brower, W. A. "George Clinton: Ultimate Liberator of Constipated Notions." *Down Beat* 46 (April 5, 1979): 16–18.

Corbett, John. "Brothers from Another Planet: The Space Madness of Lee 'Scratch' Perry, Sun Ra, and George Clinton." In *Extended Play: Sounding Off from John Cage to Dr. Funkenstein,* 7–24. Durham, N.C.: Duke University Press, 1994.

———. "George Clinton: Every Dog Has His Day." In *Extended Play: Sounding Off from John Cage to Dr. Funkenstein,* 144–154. Durham, N.C.: Duke University Press, 1994.

———. "George Clinton: The Hair of the Dog." In *Extended Play: Sounding Off from John Cage to Dr. Funkenstein,* 277–292. Durham, N.C.: Duke University Press, 1994.

Fricke, David. "George Clinton." *Rolling Stone* 587 (September 1990): 74–77.

Goldberg, Michael. "George Clinton: The Return of Dr. Funkenstein." *Rolling Stone* (June 23, 1983): 46+.

Lanier, J. "The Future: Apocalypse How? (How the World Will End According to Musicians and Others)." *Spin* 11 (November 1995): 76–78+.

Stern, Chip. "Parliament Funkadelic." *Musician Player and Listener* 17 (March/April 1979): 31–37.

———. "The Serious Metafoolishness of Father Funkadelic, George Clinton." In *The Rock Musician.* New York: St. Martin's Press, 1993.

Vickers, T. "A Journey to the Center of Parliament/Funkadelic." *Rolling Stone* 220 (August 26, 1976): 20–21.

* * * * *

In the mid 1960s, the African-American visual artist Romare Bearden adopted collage as his primary medium of expression. Symbolically acknowledging the multiplicity of subjects and sources that make up black cultures in the diaspora, Bearden's art simultaneously embraced the energy of the turbulent decade and sought to commemorate disappearing rituals of community often associated with a rural Southern past. While the musical art of George Clinton was rarely pastoral in mode, by the late 1960s, he too had embraced a kind of collage as key to the rejuvenation of black popular musics. Continuing a process begun by James Brown—the paring down of black popular music to its rhythmic core—Clinton's compositions articulated an ethic of black cultural revitalization. By working with all the available materials—psychedelic rock, rhythm and blues, gospel, soul, and, to a lesser extent, jazz and blues—Clinton created a highly idiosyncratic but extremely vital body of work. He became, arguably, the only individual in the African-American musical tradition to define and create a whole new genre, that of funk. His vibrant eclecticism led not only to the creation of some of the most infectious African-American music ever written but also to the establishment of an interesting fan base. The message of revitalization central to his compositions seemed to attract followers as much as his compelling musical package. Clinton's subsequent reputation continues to exist at the intersection between musical form and cultural ideology. In the 1980s, he became a godfather, of sorts, to the variety of musics associated with hip hop; the strength of his reputation and this genealogy is best measured, perhaps, by his being arguably the most "sampled" of rhythm and blues performers.

Very little is known about Clinton's early musical education. It is likely that he was largely an autodidact working from the record collections of family members. Somewhat impressionistically, Clinton described his beginnings to John Corbett: "The first thing I can remember I was about five years old. My father had just come back from the service. The war was over, everybody was talking about atomic bomb. I can remember the blackouts, big searchlights all over the sky at night. And in the daytime you couldn't see the sky for rows and rows of planes. I mean, it literally had a *top* on it, all day, everyday. . . . I was right away into music. . . . Then Frankie Lymon popped up with his little hit record 'Why Do Fools Fall in Love?' and that was it." The emphasis here is on a musical education that is informal and largely a response to the world around him. He never really attached himself to a particular instrument; his path to becoming a composer was largely the development of an encyclopedic knowledge of popular musical styles.

Clinton was no overnight sensation. His struggle in the music business from 1955 through 1968 and his entrepreneurial instinct were crucial preparation for his diverse musical accomplishments. He started the Parliaments vocal group when he was only 13 years old and kept the group active for nearly 15 years, enduring a variety of personnel changes and lack of commercial recording success. He supplemented his income with a variety of factory jobs and ran his own hair salon in Newark, New Jersey. While there is no question about his musical professionalism, what is distinctive about Clinton's development is his relationship to black aspiration and sense of community. He combined this emergent ethic with a knowledge of the mechanics of popular music recording: writing, collaborating, producing, and marketing. Jobs with Jobete Music (Motown's publishing branch), Golden World, Ric Tic, and Revilot Records exposed Clinton to all aspects of the production process. He gathered a variety of musicians around him in the late 1960s and early 1970s (most importantly, bassist William "Bootsy" Collins and classically trained keyboardist Bernie Worrell), establishing an extremely productive musical collective, and he is firmly rooted in the experience of black urban populations in the post–World War II period.

While George Clinton continues to be an active composer, performer, and producer, the period from 1968 to 1983 gives the best sense of his accomplishments. That period is the heyday of the "Parliafunkadelicment Thang," a loose confederation of 20 to 30 musicians who produced music primarily (but not exclusively) under the labels "Parliament" and "Funkadelic." Almost every composition on a Parliament or Funkadelic album was a collaboration, but even acknowledging the substantial contributions of Bernie Worrell, George Clinton was the guiding intellectual and artistic force behind the music.

The music of Parliament was grounded in rhythm and blues and made for dancing. Influenced by James Brown, Sly Stone, and a long line of black vocal groups (of which the earlier Parliaments were clearly a part), Parliament laid down explosive rhythm tracks that urged audiences to get out of their seats and move. The 1970s marked an important reemergence of black dance music, culminating by mid-decade in the disco phenomenon. Clinton is an obvious instigator of that reemergence, but his importance as a composer and pop-culture icon is due to the expressive depth he brought to a music that, by design, was somewhat limited in formal complexity. *The Mothership Connection* (1975), Parliament's (and Clinton's) landmark recording, introduces a complex imaginative cosmology in which blacks are central figures in an emergent (and perhaps past) "space civilization." Thus Clinton brings to dance music a kind of ritual theater replete with role playing and dastardly villains. The limitations of this music are not its basic repetitiveness or the fact that it is derivative but rather the absence of the social experience of the club or dance floor and the emotional experience of the often outrageous Parliament "live" performance. While the music of an opera might be appreciated without its libretto, Clinton's Parliament productions were so rooted in the collective (and performed) psyche of black urban populations (and often that of disaffected whites) that without the social interaction of the live performance of club dance floor, however good the groove, something often seems missing.

In Funkadelic, Clinton found a space in which he could explore the full range of his musical interests, which included the Beatles, Jimi Hendrix, and a variety of psychedelic rockers, especially the Detroit bands MC5 and the Stooges. The goal of Funkadelic's music was fundamentally the same as that of Parliament: to get people to dance. But Funkadelic's compositions eventually led to more explicit politics than the science fiction-based elaborations of mid-1970s Parliament. Albums such as *Maggot Brain* (1971) alluded to Vietnam, civil rights, urban violence, and the intransigency of white racism. The soul-inflected music of Parliament—which often highlighted James Brown-influenced horn punctuations—often gave way in Funkadelic to strong electric guitar solos (especially by Eddie Hazel and Gary Shider), complete with requisite feedback, synthesizers, drum machines, and a variety of rattles, bells, and whistles. Compositions associated with Funkadelic are chaotic, with almost complete disregard for categories or genres.

The strength of Clinton's personality and vision shines through all of the 1970s recordings, regardless of whether or not they carried the Parliament or Funkadelic name. Indeed, the overwhelming force of his personality renders these distinctions moot: they are worth drawing only insofar as they help elaborate Clinton's sometimes paradoxical goals as a composer. On the one hand, Clinton's music encourages the listener to give way to the body and indulge unconditionally in the limited hedonism often associated with 1970s American culture. On the other hand, Clinton consciously asserted the necessity of reflecting on the character of the culture in which one finds oneself. "Think!," he insisted, "it ain't illegal yet." The best of Clinton's compositions productively maintain the tension in this paradox, asserting unconditionally the value of black culture in the post–Civil Rights era ("Pure Funk") while rearticulating in new terms the necessity of change ("One Nation under a Groove").

UP FOR THE DOWN STROKE (1974)

This album is exemplary of George Clinton as a composer, especially the version of his musical collective known as Parliament. This critically acclaimed album contains eight compositions, with Clinton credited with seven of them.

Clinton's Parliament compositions are highly functional music with a clear purpose: to make people want to dance. As in other American art forms, form follows function. In *Up for the Down Stroke,* form is a collage of popular musical genres and styles with Clinton taking the rhythm and blues exemplified by James Brown and Sly Stone and making a number of important changes. Some of the compositions on the album are five to seven minutes in length—a clear violation of the formula that brought such success to Motown and Stax records—which is prescient of an important sociological shift in American listening habits and a shift to elaborate performance concepts in popular music. In the title song "Up for the Down Stroke," R&B conventions are reversed. Strong vocals, often the vehicle for nonsense lyrics, have been central to the success of the tradition, but in Clinton's reformulation of it, vocals, complete with a powerful horn section, are simply one expression of significant musical ideas. Melody remains with the vocals but takes somewhat of a back seat to a very heavy bass line. The goal of getting people to dance is further advanced by the percussiveness of the ever-present horns. Even the keyboards contribute short, repetitive figures and seem to contribute more to the construction of relatively independent rhythmic structures than to the definition of the melody.

Other compositions on the album continue the process of redefining "voice" in R&B. "Testify" is a complete reworking of the earlier 1967 Parliament hit. This new version places the horns in the dominant communication role, with the vocals sounding almost slurred. Despite Clinton's distinct lack of interest in vocal virtuosity, the end result is never unsatisfying. He seeks to displace vocal precision (tight harmonies, perfect pitch and tone) in order to highlight the "groove," the prominent bass lines, and the repetition of short melodic figures that, with the addition of a lyric, sound like slogans. In "The Goose," there is a subtle parody of Motown performance styles, especially of the Temptations. The piece is a slow shuffle, neither ballad nor blues, and the clarity of its pop vocals is replaced with layered electric guitars, loose vocal counterpoint, vaguely synthesized sounds, and a prominent drum box. The overall effect—seen in many of the compositions on the album—is almost of "white noise." These compositions are suggestive of an enthusiastic house party; the specificity of a single voice in counterpoint with backup singers is displaced by the hum of the crowd.

In "Whatever Makes Baby Feel Good," vocals surrender the clarity of the line by trailing off toward the ends of phrases and are slightly distorted in the production process. The effect is reminiscent of the Beatles' *Sgt. Pepper's Lonely Hearts Club Band* and is suggestive of the ways in which composition and production are wholly integrated processes for Clinton. It is not likely that the vocal distortions would be notated on sheet music; nor would one simply reproduce the sounds written on staff paper. George Clinton the composer does not exist without George Clinton the producer.

Thematically, *Up for the Down Stroke* is a typical Parliament concoction, emphasizing as it does a sexual hedonism, a commitment to "getting together," and a sometimes paradoxical critique of excessive materialism ("All Your Goodies Are Gone" and "The Goose"). The politics or ideological content of Clinton's Parliament compositions always seem indirect, with content clearly secondary to formal devices meant to get people to dance. Of course, dance itself may be understood as political gesture, an aesthetic of pleasure in a post–Civil Rights, Watergate period of American culture. Compared to Clinton's compositions for Funkadelic, however, these compositions seem calculated to affect the body rather than the mind.

ONE NATION UNDER A GROOVE (1978)

This 1978 effort for Funkadelic is arguably the highlight of George Clinton's career as a composer. There is significant maturity here (and strategic immaturity, too). The album reached number one on the black music charts and number 28 on the pop music charts, and it is consistently identified by critics as a high point of 1970s pop music. It is an encyclopedia of pop and black music styles, but it possesses a compelling thematic unity and an urbane intellect. *One Nation,* more than any other Clinton album, is made up of nine distinct parts (all collaborations) and deserves to be approached as a single composition of operatic scope and ambition.

One Nation begins with an R&B anthem of the same name, repeating the formula that had worked so well since the late 1960s: loose, even anarchic vocals sung in counterpoint to a powerful horn section, drums and drum machine, stunning bass lines, and keyboard—all collaborating to make of the composition and performances something akin to pure rhythm. The lyrics (and horns) pay direct homage to James Brown ("Can I get it on my good foot/ good god"). Little respect is paid to the exigencies of mainstream pop, all the parts violating the conventions of "hit radio": sentimental content, rhythm secondary to melody or the "hook," and three minutes or less in length. "Groovallegiance" begins with a rhythm that is reminiscent of Afro-Caribbean musics; before the composition ends, it points to gospel and doo-wop in its vocal improvisations. "Who Says a Funk Band Can't Play Rock?" is a stunning and respectful mimicking of the whitest of 1970s rock music. Hard edged (and humorously self-indulgent) electric guitar solos are prominent. In "Promentalshitbackwashpsychosis Enema Squad (The Doo Doo Chasers)," Clinton offers up his best "talking song" since "Chocolate City" and points forward to the emergence of hip hop. "Into You" recalls the best of soul balladry, and "Cholly (Funk Gettin' Ready to Roll)" returns to the Sly Stone/James Brown intersection that began the album. Three additional compositions complete the album, but they mark an important shift, and before discussing them, it is important to describe the thematic unity of the album.

One Nation under a Groove is cultural criticism and, consciously or unconsciously, Clinton has significant command of the jeremiadic and satirical modes often adopted by African-American speakers. As did Frederick Douglass, David Walker, and other early African-American creative intellectuals, Clinton adopts prominent public democratic language and transforms it to make it fit his own uses. Phrases such as "one nation under a groove," "do you promise to funk?" "we shall all be moved," and "pledge a groovallegiance to the funk," both humorous and deadly serious, signify on language associated with declarations of equality and justice and, at the same time, their continued negation in American history. Clinton constantly returns to this language to advance his themes: the repressiveness of categories, the crime of disunity, and the revitalizing possibilities in African-American culture. The "one nation" of the title refers simultaneously to a democratic polity and a cultural sphere where differences are to be celebrated and not regulated. (This universalizing instinct in the music is somewhat paradoxical. Some commentators have noted that there is a black nationalism at work, too; it is sophisticated and expansive, however, and not exclusive. Those who are willing to recognize black culture's accomplishments and dignity are welcome, regardless of background.) There is also a sophomoric humor often at work in the cultural criticism that is surprisingly engaging. In "The Doo Doo Chasers," Clinton utilizes a repetitive obsession with scatology (like the eighteenth-century English novelists) to promote his criticism of the thoughtlessness of public discourse, not wholly inappropriate for the post-Watergate era. However, the songs are not really arguments. They are most effective in amusing and encouraging converts; for the non-Clinton acolyte, the humor (and music) is likely received as typical of the very things it sets out to critique.

The verbal jabs and scatological humor disappear in the final three compositions of *One Nation,* which are wholly instrumental (with the exception of some muttering and crowd noise). Long guitar solos and meditative dance grooves replace the occasionally aggressive rhetoric, and there is a kind of theory-and-practice feel to this division of the album. Clinton seems to suggest that, consciousness-raising aside, the importance of music lies in the opportunities it provides for transcendence, however temporary. The first six tracks theorize on the possibilities in a musical culture and on education not bound by limited categories—a position also articulated by Duke Ellington and Charles Mingus—while the final three tracks provide direct access to the experiences of a music not bound by racial, institutional, or traditional divisions. In *One Nation under a Groove,* by refining and revising its central tenets—that blackness is not pathological, that rhythm and community are connected, and that movement (as in dance or in the crossing of a border) can be thought—Clinton defines himself as one of the most interesting American composers of the latter half of the 20th century.

REFERENCES

Corbett, John. *Extended Play: Sounding Off from John Cage to Dr. Funkenstein.* Durham, N.C.: Duke University Press, 1994.

Fernando Jr., S. H. *The New Beats: Exploring the Music, Culture, and Attitudes of Hip Hop.* New York: Anchor, 1994.

Jebsen, Peter. "The P. Funk Timeline." *Goldmine* (January 25, 1991): 42+.

JAMES C. HALL

COATES, DOROTHY LOVE

Born Dorothy McGriff in Birmingham, Ala., January 30, 1928. **Composing and Performing Career:** Birmingham, Ala., played piano for her church at age ten; sang with a family group, the McGriff Singers, and with the Royal Travelers as a teenager; joined the Original Gospel Harmonettes, an all-female group, 1946; the group performed her works, recorded regularly, and made successful appearances until it was disbanded, 1959; reorganized the Harmonettes, 1961; toured and performed at major gospel festivals including the Newport Jazz Festival, 1961, and Jazzfest in New Orleans, 1997.

MUSIC LIST

COLLECTIONS

Gospel Harmonettes Specials, compiled and edited by Sallie Martin and Kenneth Morris. Chicago: Martin and Morris Music, ca. 1959.

Martin and Morris Gospel Star Song Book, no. 2. Chicago: Martin and Morris Music, 1959.

Songs by Dorothy Love Coates: As Sung by the Gospel Harmonettes. Birmingham, Ala.: The Dorothy Love Coates Singers, 197?.

SONGS

[The following list of titles includes only works that were composed by the subject of the entry; it is not a list of recordings that were made by the subject. Although the composer may have made recordings of her own works, the list is not restricted to those recordings but in many cases includes performances by other artists of the composer's work. The list is made up of publication and discographical data, in cases where such information is available. Although no effort has been made to include documentation of the earliest recording of the works listed, the date of the earliest recording that is readily available has been given. —Ed.]

"After a While." Recorded: Savoy SL 14466.

"Ain't Goin' There." Nashville, Tenn.: Sony-ATV Songs, 1955.

"All over This World." Los Angeles: Renleigh Music, 1967.

"Am I a Soldier?" Recorded: Everest GS-71; Specialty SPC 2141; Specialty SPCD-7205-2.

"Born Again." Nashville, Tenn.: Sony-ATV Songs, 1970.

"By Myself." Recorded: Savoy MG-14050.

"Calvary." Recorded: Nashboro Records NB 7118; Savoy SL 14570.

"Camp Meeting." Chicago: Conrad Music Publishers.

"Carry Me Home." Chicago: Conrad Music Publishers.

"The Chariot." New York: Embassy Music, 1969. Recorded: Nashboro CD 4508-2.

"A Child of God." Recorded: Savoy SL 14570.

"The Christian Army." In *Songs by Dorothy Love Coates.* Recorded: Okeh OKS 14125.

"A City Built Four Square." Recorded: Savoy SC 14500.

"Come in This House." In *Songs by Dorothy Love Coates.*

"Come On and Go with Me." New York: Embassy Music, 1969. Recorded: Nashboro CD 4508-2.

"Count Your Blessings." Chicago: Conrad Music Publishers, 1964. Arranger, Kenneth Morris.

"Dark Day in Jerusalem." New York: Embassy Music, 1969. Recorded: Nashboro CD 4508-2.

"Don't Forget about Me." Chicago: Conrad Music Publishers, 1976.

"Don't You." Chicago: Martin and Morris, 1959. Arranger, Kenneth Morris. Recorded: Savoy SC 14500.

"Elijah." In *Gospel Harmonettes Specials.* Recorded: Shanachie 6004.

"Ever Since I Met Him." Recorded: Savoy MG-14050.

"Every Day Will Be Sunday (By and By)." Recorded: Nashboro CD 4508-2; Specialty SPC 2141; Specialty SPCD-7056-2; Specialty SPCD-7205-2.

"Everybody's Talking about Heaven." Nashville, Tenn.: Sony-ATV Songs, 1955.

"Everything Goes Back to the Dust." New York: Screen Gems-EMI, 1962. Recorded: Savoy MG-14050.

"Everything Must Go Back." New York: Screen Gems-EMI, 1961.

"The Finishing Line." Chicago: Martin and Morris, 1959. Arranger, Kenneth Morris.

"Get Away Jordan." Recorded: Specialty SPCD-7017-2; Specialty SPCD-7056-2; Specialty SPCD-7205-2.

"Give Me Strength." Los Angeles: Renleigh Music, 1967.

"God Rose in a Windstorm." Chicago: Meek Gospel Music, 1995.

"God's Goodness (You Don't Know How Good God Is to Me)." Chicago: Martin and Morris, 1958. Arranger, Kenneth Morris. In *Gospel Harmonettes Specials.*

"Gospel Train." Los Angeles: Renleigh Music, 1967.

"The Great Coronation." Los Angeles: Renleigh Music, 1967.

"The Handwriting on the Wall." Recorded: Okeh OKS 14125.

"He Cares." Recorded: Savoy SL 14570.

"He Died." Chicago: Conrad Music Publishers, 1964.

"The Healer." Chicago: Conrad Music Publishers, 1964. Arranger, Kenneth Morris.

"Heaven." In *Songs by Dorothy Love Coates.* Recorded: Savoy SL 14466; Specialty SPC 2141; Specialty SPCD-7205-2.

"Heaven (I've Heard So Much about It)." Nashville, Tenn.: Excellorec Music, 1969. Arranger, Kenneth Morris. Recorded: Nashboro CD 4508-2; Nashboro N-7132.

"Heaven Is a Beautiful Place." Chicago: Conrad Music Publishers, 1964.

"Heaven's My Final Goal." New York: Screen Gems-EMI, 1963.

"He's Alright with Me." New York: Embassy Music, 1971.

"He's Calling Me." Hollywood, Calif.: Venice Music, 1955. Arranger, Kenneth Morris. In *Gospel Harmonettes Specials.* Recorded: Specialty SPC-2144; Specialty SPCD-7017-2; Specialty SPCD-7205-2.

"He's Got Everything You Need." In *Songs by Dorothy Love Coates.* Recorded: Nashboro CD 4508-2.

"He's Helping Me." Recorded: Savoy SL 14466.

"He's Real to Me." Chicago: Conrad Music Publishers, 1963.

"He's Right on Time." Hollywood, Calif.: Venice Music, 1953. Arranger, Kenneth Morris. In *Gospel Harmonettes Specials.* Recorded: Specialty SPC-2134; Specialty SPCD-7205-2; Warner Bros. 9 45990-2.

"Holding On and Won't Let Go." New York: Embassy Music, 1968.

"How Much More." New York: Screen Gems-EMI, 1963.

"Human Bondage." In *Songs by Dorothy Love Coates*. Recorded: Okeh OKS 14125.

"I Must Tell Jesus." Chicago: Conrad Music Publishers, 1976.

"I Shall Know Him." Hollywood, Calif.: Venice Music, 1953. Arranger, Kenneth Morris. Recorded: Specialty SPC 2141; Specialty SPCD-7205-2.

"I Wish You Could Have Been There." In *Songs by Dorothy Love Coates*.

"I Won't Let Go." Recorded: Nashboro CD 4508-2; Nashboro N-7132.

"I Wouldn't Mind Dying." Hollywood, Calif.: Venice Music, 1955. Arranger, Kenneth Morris. Recorded: Specialty SPC 2141; Specialty SPCD-7017-2; Specialty SPCD-7205-2.

"If I Had My Way." Recorded: Columbia G 31086-88.

"(If You Don't Believe) That's Alright with Me." Nashville, Tenn.: Excellorec Music, 1972. Arranger, Kenneth Morris. Recorded: Nashboro N-7132.

"I'll Be with Thee." Hollywood, Calif.: Venice Music, 1955. Arranger, Kenneth Morris. Recorded: Okeh OKS 14125.

"I'll Make It." Recorded: Savoy MG-14050; Savoy SC 14500.

"I'm Glad He Found Me." Recorded: Savoy SC 14500.

"I'm Holding On and I Won't Let Go of My Faith." In *Songs by Dorothy Love Coates*.

"I'm on My Way." In *Songs by Dorothy Love Coates*. Recorded: Nashboro CD 4508-2.

"I'm Thankful." New York: Screen Gems-EMI, 1961.

"In That Morning." In *Songs by Dorothy Love Coates*. Recorded: Okeh OKS 14125.

"It's Going to Rain." New York: Screen Gems-EMI, 1963.

"It's Praying Time." In *Songs by Dorothy Love Coates*.

"I've Got to Make It." New York: Embassy Music, 1971.

"Jesus." Los Angeles: Renleigh Music, 1967.

"Jesus, I Love You." Recorded: Savoy SC 14500.

"Jesus Laid His Hand on Me." Hollywood, Calif.: Venice Music, 1955. Arranger, Kenneth Morris. In *Gospel Harmonettes Specials*. Recorded: Specialty SPC-2134; Specialty SPCD-7205-2.

"Joyous Tidings." Recorded: Savoy MG-14050.

"Kingdom of Babylon Is Falling Down." Recorded: Savoy SC 14500.

"Let Me Ride." Newark, N.J.: Savoy Music, 1959. Arranger, Kenneth Morris.

"Let the Holy Ghost Come." Aurora, Ill.: Joni Music Publishing, 1966.

"Let's Come in the House." Recorded: Savoy MG-14050.

"Lord, Don't Forget about Me." Hollywood, Calif.: Venice Music, 1955. Arranger, Kenneth Morris. In *Gospel Harmonettes Specials*. Recorded: Specialty SPC 2141; Specialty SPCD-7205-2.

"Lord, I'll Go." Ann Arbor, Mich.: Stone Funk Publishing, 1971. Co-composer, Lucy Evans.

"Lord, I'm Trying." Recorded: Savoy SL 14466.

"Lord, Tell Me When." New York: Embassy Music, 1969. Recorded: Nashboro CD 4508-2.

"Lord, You've Been Good to Me." Recorded: Nashboro 7138.

"Love Lifted Me." Recorded: Nashboro 7080.

"Mother Told God." Recorded: Savoy MG-14050.

"My Father's Children." New York: Screen Gems-EMI, 1963.

"Ninety-Nine and a Half." Hollywood, Calif.: Venice Music, 1956. Arranger, Kenneth Morris. In *Gospel Harmonettes Specials*. Recorded: Specialty SPC-2134; Specialty SPCD-7017-2; Specialty SPCD-7205-2.

"No Hiding Place." Hollywood, Calif.: Venice Music, 1954. Co-composer, Evelyn Starks; arranger, Kenneth Morris. Recorded: Specialty SPC-2134 ; Specialty SPCD-7017-2; Specialty SPCD-7205-2.

"Now I'm Ready." Chicago: Conrad Music Publishers.

"One Day." Recorded: Columbia G 31086-88.

"One Morning Soon." Hollywood, Calif.: Dorothy Love and Venice Music, 1952. Arranger, Kenneth Morris. Recorded: Specialty SPC-2134; Specialty SPCD-7205-2.

"Open the Door." Recorded: Savoy SC 14500.

"Packin' Up." Recorded: Shanachie/Spirit Feel 6011.

"Power of the Holy Ghost." Recorded: Savoy SL 14466.

"Pray for Deliverance." New York: Screen Gems-EMI, 1963.

"Prayer for a Change." Los Angeles: Renleigh Music, 1967.

"Prayin' Time." Recorded: Okeh OKS 14125.

"Remember Me, Oh Lord." New York: Embassy Music, 1971.

"Rest for the Weary." Recorded: Specialty SPCD-7017-2.

"The Righteous on the March." Chicago: Conrad Music Publishers, 1964.

"Separation Line." New York: Embassy Music, 1969. Recorded: Nashboro CD 4508-2.

"Sign of Time." Los Angeles: Renleigh Music, 1967.

"So Many Falling by the Way Side." New York: Embassy Music, 1969. Recorded: Nashboro CD 4508-2.

"So Many Years." Newark, N.J.: Savoy Music, 1960. Arranger, Kenneth Morris.

"Standing on the Rock." Recorded: Savoy SL 14570.

"Step Back." Chicago: Martin and Morris, 1960. Arranger, Kenneth Morris. Recorded: Savoy SC 14500.

"Step by Step." Chicago: Conrad Music Publishers, 1964.

"Stop, Take a Little Time to Pray!" Nashville, Tenn.: Excellorec Music, 1970. Arranger, Kenneth Morris. Recorded: Nashboro 7088; Nashboro N-7132.

"The Strange Man." Recorded: Columbia/Legacy C2K 57160; Columbia/Legacy CK 57163; Word 7019603602.

"Stranger in the City." Chicago: Crest-Mate Music, 1978.

"Thankful." Recorded: Savoy MG-14050.

"That's Enough." Hollywood, Calif.: Venice Music, 1956. Arranger, Kenneth Morris. In *Gospel Harmonettes Specials*. Recorded: Specialty SPC-2134; Specialty SPCD-7017-2; Specialty SPCD-7205-2.

"That's the Kind of God He Is." Recorded: Savoy SL 14466.

"These Are the Days." Recorded: Savoy SL 14466; Savoy SAV 7095.

"They Won't Believe." Recorded: Nashboro 7080; Nashboro N-7132 .

"'Till I Get Back There." Recorded: Savoy MG-14050.

"'Till My Change Comes." In *Songs by Dorothy Love Coates*. Recorded: Nashboro CD 4508-2; Nashboro NAC-7269.

"Trouble." Recorded: Shanachie 6004.

"The Walls of Jericho Must Come Down." In *Gospel Harmonettes Specials*.

"We'll See Who's a Winner at the Finishing Line." New York: Embassy Music,. 1970.

"When I Reach My Heavenly Home." Hollywood, Calif.: Venice Music, 1952. Co-Composer, Evelyn Starks; arranger, Kenneth Morris. Recorded: Specialty SPC-2134; Specialty SPCD-7205-2.

"When They Ring Those Golden Bells." Los Angeles: Renleigh Music, 1967.

"Where Shall I Be?" Hollywood, Calif.: Venice Music, 1953. Arranger, Kenneth Morris. Recorded: Savoy SL 14570; Specialty SPC-2134; Specialty SPCD-7205-2.

Dorothy Love Coates (top) and the Original Gospel Harmonettes; courtesy of Fantasy Records

"Who Art Thou?" Recorded: Everest GL-71.

"Without You." Chicago: Conrad Music Publishers, 1976.

"Work On." New York: Embassy Music, 1971.

"You Better Run." Recorded: Specialty SPC-2134; Specialty SPCD-7205-2.

"You Brought Me from a Long Way." Chicago: Conrad Music Publishers, 1987.

"You Can't Hurry God." Chicago: Anne-Rachel Music.

"You Must Be Born Again." In *Gospel Harmonettes Specials.* Recorded: Everest GS-71; Specialty SPC 2141; Specialty SPCD-7205-2.

"You've Been Good to Me." Chicago: Conrad Music Publishers, 1965. Arranger, Kenneth Morris.

PUBLICATIONS

ABOUT COATES
Dissertations

McAllister, Anita Bernadette. "The Musical Legacy of Dorothy Love Coates: African American Female Gospel Singer, with Implications for Education and Theater Education." Ed.D., Kansas State University, 1995.

Articles

Heilbut, Anthony. "'I Won't Let Go of My Faith': Dorothy Love Coates." In *The Gospel Sound: Good News and Bad Times,* 159–186. 3rd ed. New York: Limelight Editions, 1989.

BY COATES

As editor and researcher. *A Salute to Historic Black Women.* Empak "Black History" Publication Series, vol. 1. Kankakee, Ill.: Empak Enterprises, 1984.

* * * * *

Dorothy Love Coates, also known during her career as Dorothy Love, ranks among the most important post-World War II American gospel artists. A performer, musical entrepreneur, and composer, Coates has won praise for her original music and lyrics as well as for her vigorous interpretations of gospel standards.

Coates was born Dorothy McGriff, but throughout her life, her family and friends called her "Dot." When she was six years old, her father, a Baptist minister, left Birmingham, abandoning his family in order to preach in the North. Shortly afterward, the young girl's parents were divorced. Coates's mother, however, continued to encourage Coates's interest in music, and by the age of ten, the girl had learned to play the piano well enough to accompany services at the Baptist Church she and her mother attended regularly. Her mother even organized a family music ensemble, the McGriff Singers; later, the young Coates sang with that group and, for a while, with the Royal Travelers. Coates also grew up singing hit songs by African-American artists, such as Duke Ellington. Among her musical idols were Mahalia Jackson, whom she heard sing in nearby storefront churches, and the celebrated Georgia Lee Stafford, "Songbird of the South."

In the early 1940s, Coates quit high school to work. About the same time, she married Willie Love, himself a gospel singer and

member of the Fairfield Four, but they soon separated. Then, in 1946, Coates joined the Original Gospel Harmonettes, an all-female group consisting of Vera Kilb, Mildred Miller Howard, Odessa Edwards, Willie Mae Newberry, and pianist Evelyn Starks. Unfortunately, Coates's career with the Harmonettes was twice interrupted. In 1948, she contracted pneumonia while pregnant with her daughter Cassandra. Born with several severe medical problems, Cassandra required constant attention for more than a year after she was born. Thus Coates was unable to work with the Harmonettes after RCA Victor offered them a recording contract the following year. Coates rejoined the Harmonettes in 1951, the year in which the group switched to Specialty Records. Their first two releases with Specialty, "I'm Sealed" and "Get Away Jordan," established them as a prominent gospel ensemble. Throughout the next seven years, the group primarily performed music written or arranged by Coates. In his book *The Gospel Sound,* Tony Heilbut calls the Harmonettes "dignified accompanists" to the "spiritual dynamo" that was Coates.

In 1959, an exhausted Coates "retired" from the Harmonettes and married Carl Coates, then the bass singer and manager of the Sensational Nightingales, another gospel group. In 1961, Dorothy Coates rejoined and reorganized the Harmonettes and later led them on several successful tours of the United States.

During the 1960s, Coates crusaded with Martin Luther King Jr. and other activists on behalf of African-American rights. As a result of her activities, she was jailed at least once. James Cleveland's song "We Are the Soldiers of the Army," made popular by the Harmonettes, became an anthem of Civil Rights campaigners and was recorded by a number of other ensembles. Among the other and later successes of the Harmonettes was a 1991 compact-disc reissue of their greatest hits. Writing for *Down Beat* magazine, critic Dan Ouellette captured the spirit of Coates's performing style when he praised her "incredible contralto" voice and said her performances carried her and her listeners "wailing, shouting and hollering . . . into another world."

Coates's musical performances cannot be separated from the music she composed and arranged, much of it for her own performances with the Harmonettes. As both creative artist and performer, she demonstrated sober but intense, even passionate devotion to gospel traditions even as she modified and modernized some of those traditions through words and music. Her lyrics make use of many traditional devices, including the wandering couplets of old-fashioned hymns. Almost all of her own compositions and arrangements are deceptively simple in style, leaving plenty of room for the interpolations that most gospel artists think nothing of adding and that Coates herself mastered early in her career.

As a singer, Coates was simple and powerfully sincere, occasionally rough-edged, sometimes even hoarse. Her religious conviction was unmistakable. As an artist, she "lived out her righteousness to the full," says Viv Broughton in his book, *Black Gospel,* "commanding a special sort of respect from black audiences." In performance, she avoided the clowning, costumes, and outrageous hairdos favored by gospel groups such as the Caravans. In contrast, Coates and the Harmonettes dressed modestly, even plainly, and the rest of the group performed with marked restraint. Coates herself, however, was anything but restrained, either vocally or physically. She was an innovator in making gospel music "move" on stage, and her vigorous gestures were copied and expanded on by her rivals. Throughout the 1950s, all over the country "young women and men began moving like [Coates]," says Heilbut, extending the boundaries of "emotional expression [in gospel music] from vocal to physical contortions" and "allowing the vocally weak but athletically gifted a new opportunity to shine."

Coates's lyrics are also innovative and have won her admirers. In a verse she added to the lyrics of "Get Away Jordan," for example, she wrote

> When my feet get cold, my eyes shut,
> Body has been chilled by the hands of death,
> Tongue glued to the roof of my mouth,
> Hands, they're folded across my breast.

With these words, Coates made death seem physically imminent in a way gospel song texts had never done before. A decade or so later, Coates drew on the Civil Rights movement in her lyrics, describing Satan and his minions as "throwing their rocks and hiding their hands." As guitarist Jo Jo Wallace has put it, Coates says "something in every line." Unfortunately, according to Heilbut, the lyrics and music Coates wrote for "Get Away Jordan" and other Harmonettes hits "made a lot of money for many artists, including the white Statesmen Quartet," but not for Coates. Later, in her publishing ventures with Conrad Music and other firms, she was somewhat more commercially successful.

Coates never abandoned her principles in order to make money. She steadfastly refused to sell the rights to several of her most successful songs even though in her later years she complained bitterly of exploitation and about the general indifference to Christian music. One of her complaints was about soul music, which won acclaim while gospel artists were struggling to be heard. Such singers "take a simple, gospel beat, change the words, and the world goes wild," she is quoted in Heilbut's book as saying. As a performer, though, Coates seems to have shed her resentments and given all she had to her listeners. She once described the "saints" who sing gospel music as "saved, sanctified and filled with the Holy Ghost." "Sanctified folks," she added, "can shout for days." Her career testifies to the sincerity of these convictions and her own religious faith.

SELECTED WORKS

Coates's work as a composer consists today, in printed form, of music that was mostly arranged, edited, or at least "cleaned up" by other artists, especially gospel composer Kenneth Morris. Some of her numbers show the influence of other gospel artists, including William Herbert ("Bill") Brewster. Only occasionally does Coates use comparatively complex harmonic and rhythmic patterns in her melodic lines and accompaniments. Of course, what she writes is merely an indication, an outline, of the kind of music she herself performed throughout her career.

Consider, for instance, Coates's book of gospel compositions, which was published in about 1957 or 1958 under the title *Gospel Harmonettes Specials*. This book consists of ten numbers, all of them carrying the attributions "Words and Music by Dorothy

Love" and "Arr. by Kenneth Morris." All ten songs are scored for a gospel group or choir of four to six parts and a lead singer. All are in many ways original in style, but all reflect gospel-music styles widespread in the United States in the 1950s.

The first number in the *Gospel Harmonettes Specials* collection, "Elijah," opens with a modified call-and-response pattern. The lead singer's part begins with the words "God said He would send," sung to a triadic, call-to-battle motive also characteristic of many Brewster motives. Then, on the words "down fire," Coates's chorus joins with simple, sustained (subdominant and tonic) chords. By making a call-and-response pattern into a complete and uninterrupted phrase, Coates begins the chorus of this musical number in a rousing manner. To establish contrast in the two verses that follow, she gives the lead singer a mildly syncopated melody designed to be sung over a sustained series of accompanying chords. In the 18th century, a melody accompanied by such chords would have been called an "accompanied recitative," and Coates adds the performance direction "sing recitatively" to the beginning of both verses. Only with the third chorus does Coates finally make use of a conventional call-and-response pattern: here, the lead begins with an unaccompanied melodic motive set to the words "Oh Lord." This is followed by several chords set to the same words and sung by the rest of the ensemble.

In "He's Calling Me" syncopation is almost entirely absent, although one word ("eternally") is repeatedly presented with a prolonged third syllable, creating a mild ragtime effect. Of greater interest is Coates's occasional use of the lowered seventh scale step as a harmonic "color" note. In the second statement of the phrase "God's calling me," part of the opening chorus call-and-response, Coates uses the note *b*-flat to give the music a momentarily less cheerful, more bluesy sound. A slightly different phrase appears later in the number, this time set to the words "He's calling me" and "He called my name," and this time the *b*-flat also appears in the choral response. (The C-major dominant ninth chord shown in Example 1 gives the music greater interest and variety.)

Example 1. "He's Calling Me"

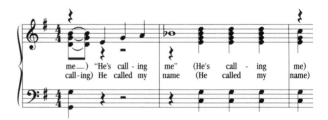

Sometimes Coates uses triplets to give a number greater rhythmic variety. In "Don't You," published in 1959, the words "I want to" in the phrase "I want to walk" are set to eighth-note triplets. Then, while the lead singer holds "walk," the rest of the chorus responds "Don't you" in a syncopated eighth-note, dotted-quarter-note accompaniment pattern. Later in the same number, the phrase "thanks to the Father and the Son" is sung by the entire ensemble in block chords set in a ragtime rhythm pattern before the lead singer's line returns to more eighth-note triplets and the entire call-and-response pattern begins again.

The *Gospel Harmonettes Specials* book was published about 1957 or 1958, before Coates "retired" temporarily from public performances. "You've Been Good to Me," a number written by Coates and distributed by Martin and Morris in the mid-1960s, is starker in sound and makes greater use of contrasts between major and minor chords than the other works in the collection. Written in C major, "You've Been Good to Me" contains a number of C-minor triads that give the music a slightly uneasy feeling. In the phrase "And Lord, You've sure been good to me," the words "sure" and "to" are accompanied by minor chords, the words "Lord," "been," and "me" by major chords. Minor thirds in otherwise major music are commonplace in gospel numbers, but Coates's sudden shift from an *e*-flat on "sure" to an *e*-natural an octave away on "been" is unusually effective and emotionally unsettling. Also effective is Coates's restrained use of such effects; never again in "You've Been Good to Me" does the same harmonic pattern reappear. Instead, subsequent *e*-flats are used to color other kinds of chords (including subdominant F-major triads, or as passing tones above dominant G-major seventh chords).

REFERENCES

Boyer, Horace Clarence. "Dorothy Love Coates." In *New Grove Dictionary of American Music.* London: Macmillan Press, 1986.

Broughton, Viv. *Black Gospel: An Illustrated History of the Gospel Sound.* New York: Blandford Press, 1985.

Heilbut, Tony. *The Gospel Sound: Good News and Bad Times.* New York: Simon and Schuster, 1971.

Oliver, Paul. "Gospel." In *The New Grove Gospel, Jazz, and Blues: With Spirituals and Ragtime.* New York: W. W. Norton, 1986.

Ouellette, Dan. Review of *The Best of Dorothy Love Coates. Down Beat* 59 (1992): 36.

Reagon, Bernice Johnson. *We'll Understand It Better By and By: Pioneering African American Gospel Composers.* Washington, D.C.: Smithsonian Institution Press, 1992.

MICHAEL SAFFLE

COLE, ROBERT ALLEN ("BOB")

Born in Athens, Ga., July 1, 1868; died in the Catskills, N.Y., August 2, 1911. **Education:** Studied music as a child, playing various instruments; Atlanta, may have attended high school. **Composing and Performing Career:** Toured on the vaudeville circuit, 1890s; first songs published, 1893; formed the All-Star Stock Company, 1894; performed with Black Patti's Troubadors, 1896–97; wrote and toured with *A Trip to Coontown,* 1897–1900; began lifelong association with Johnson brothers, producing numerous shows and songs, ca. 1897; wrote and starred in *The Shoo-Fly Regiment,* 1906–08, and *The Red Moon,* 1909–10.

MUSIC LIST

SONGS

"Ada, My Sweet Potater." New York: Joseph W. Stern, 1908. Co-composers, J. Rosamond Johnson, Joe Jordan. Note: from *The Red Moon.*

"Ain't Dat Scan'lous." New York: Joseph W. Stern, 1901. Co-composer, J. Rosamond Johnson.

"All Chinks Look Alike to Me." 1897. Co-composer, William "Billy" Johnson. Note: from *A Trip to Coontown.*

"The Animals' Convention." New York: Joseph W. Stern, 1904. Co-composer, J. Rosamond Johnson. Note: from *Huckleberry Finn.*

"As Long as the World Rolls On." 1908. Co-composers, J. Rosamond Johnson, Joe Jordan. Note: from *The Red Moon.*

"At Jolly Cooney Isle." 1896–97. Note: from *At Jolly Coon-ey Island.*

"Belle of Avenue A." 1896–97. Note: from *At Jolly Coon-ey Island.*

"Big Indian Chief." New York: Joseph W. Stern, 1904. Co-composer, J. Rosamond Johnson. Note: from *An English Daisy.*

"The Big Red Shawl." 1908. Co-composers, J. Rosamond Johnson, Joe Jordan. Note: from *The Red Moon.*

"The Black Four Hundred's Ball." New York: Howley, Haviland, 1896. Note: from *At Jolly Coon-ey Island.*

"Black Gal Mine." 1896–97. Note: from *At Jolly Coon-ey Island.*

"Bleedin' Moon." 1908. Co-composers, J. Rosamond Johnson, Joe Jordan. Note: from *The Red Moon.*

"Christening of a Little Black Coon." New York: Howley, Haviland, 1897.

"Colored Aristocracy." New York: Brooks and Denton, 1896.

"Come My Love and Go With Me." 1906. Co-composer, J. Rosamond Johnson. Note: from *Shylock and Co., Bankers.*

"Come out, Dinah, on the Green." New York: Howley, Haviland, 1901. Co-composer, J. Rosamond Johnson. Note: from *Sleeping Beauty and the Beast.*

"Comic Song." 1896–97. Note: from *At Jolly Coon-ey Island.*

"Como le Gusta (How Do You Like Me)." New York: Joseph W. Stern, 1904.

"Congo Love Song." New York: Joseph W. Stern, 1903. Co-composer, J. Rosamond Johnson.

"Conjure Man." New York: Joseph W. Stern, 1901.

"Coontown Frolique." 1897. Co-composers, J. Rosamond Johnson, Joe Jordan. Note: from *The Red Moon* and *A Trip to Coontown.*

"The Coontown Regiment." 1897. Co-composers, J. Rosamond Johnson, Joe Jordan. Note: from *The Red Moon* and *A Trip to Coontown.*

"Coola-Woo-La." 1908. Co-composers, J. Rosamond Johnson, Joe Jordan. Note: from *The Red Moon.*

"The Countess of Alagazam." New York: Joseph W. Stern, 1904.

"Cupid's Ramble; or, Cupid's Blind They Say." New York: Joseph W. Stern, 1903. Co-composer, J. Rosamond Johnson. Note: from *Nancy Brown.*

"Cupid Was an Indian Pickaninny." 1908. Co-composers, J. Rosamond Johnson, Joe Jordan. Note: from *The Red Moon.*

"Dem Golden Clouds." New York: Brooks and Denton, 1896.

"Don't Butt In." New York: Joseph W. Stern, 1901. Co-composer, J. Rosamond Johnson. Note: from *The Supper Club.*

"Don't Tell Tales Out of School." 1908. Co-composers, J. Rosamond Johnson, Joe Jordan. Note: from *The Red Moon.*

"Don't Wake Him Up Let Him Dream." New York: Joseph W. Stern, 1904.

"Down to Coney Island." 1896–97. Note: from *At Jolly Coon-ey Island.*

"Everybody Wants to See the Baby." New York: Joseph W. Stern, 1903.

The Evolution of Ragtime. 1903. New York: Edward B. Marks, 1903 (Echoes of the Day; The Spirit of the Banjo; Sounds of the Times). Co-composer, J. Rosamond Johnson. Contents: Voice of the Savage; Echoes of the Day; Essence of the Jug; Darkies Delights; The Spirit of the Banjo; Sounds of the Times. Note: from *Mother Goose; A Little Bit of Everything.*

"The Famous Black Moguls." 1908. Co-composers, J. Rosamond Johnson, Joe Jordan. Note: from *The Red Moon* and *A Trip to Coontown.*

"Father's Got a Job." New York: Joseph W. Stern, 1906.

"Fishing." New York: Joseph W. Stern, 1904. Co-composer, J. Rosamond Johnson.

"Fly-Fy-Fly." New York: Brooks, Denton, 1895.

"For All Eternity." 1897. Co-composers, J. Rosamond Johnson, Joe Jordan. Note: from *The Red Moon* and *A Trip to Coontown.*

"4-11-44." 1897. Co-composer, William "Billy" Johnson. Note: from *A Trip to Coontown* and *At Jolly Coon-ey Island.*

"Gimme de Leavin's." New York: Joseph W. Stern, 1904. Note: from *Alabama Blossom.*

"He Handed Me a Lemon." New York: Joseph W. Stern, 1906.

"Here's a Hoping These Few Lines Find You Well." 1897. Co-composer, William "Billy" Johnson. Note: from *A Trip to Coontown.*

"Honey Does You Love Your Little Man." 1896–97. Note: from *At Jolly Coon-ey Island.*

"Hottentot Love Song." ca. 1906. Co-composer, J. Rosamond Johnson. Note: from *Marrying Mary.*

"La Hoola Boola." New York: Howley, Haviland, ca. 1897. Co-composer, William "Billy" Johnson. Note: from *A Trip to Coontown.*

"Hottentot Love Song." 1906. Co-composer, J. Rosamond Johnson. Note: from *Marrying Mary.*

"How a Monocle Helps the Mind." 1904. Co-composer, J. Rosamond Johnson. Note: from *In Newport.*

"I Ain't Gwinter Work No Mo'." New York: Joseph W. Stern, 1900. Co-composer, J. Rosamond Johnson. Note: from *The Belle of Bridgeport.*

"I Ain't Had No Lovin' in a Long Time." 1908. Co-composers, J. Rosamond Johnson, Joe Jordan. Note: from *The Red Moon.*

The songwriting team of Bob Cole, James Weldon Johnson, and his brother J. Rosamond Johnson (from left to right); photo courtesy of Jewell Plummer Cobb (niece of Bob Cole)

"I Can Stand for Your Color, But Your Hair Won't Do." 1897. Co-composer, William "Billy" Johnson. Note: from *A Trip to Coontown.*

"I Can't Think of Nothin' in the Wide, Wide World But You." New York: Joseph W. Stern, 1907. Co-composer, J. Rosamond Johnson. Note: from *The Shoo-Fly Regiment.*

"I Don't Want to Be No Actor Man." In *Song Successes Introduced by Peter F. Dailey in the New Successful Comedy "Champagne Charlie"* (New York: Joseph W. Stern, 1901). Co-composer, J. Rosamond Johnson. Note: from *Champagne Charlie.*

"I Must o' Been a Dreamin'." New York: Morse Music, 1900. Note: from *A Trip to Coontown* and *The Belle of Bridgeport.*

"I Want My Chicken." 1908. Co-composers, J. Rosamond Johnson, Joe Jordan. Note: from *The Red Moon.*

"I Wonder What Is That Coon's Name?" 1897. Co-composer, William "Billy" Johnson. Note: from *A Trip to Coontown* and *A Reign of Error.*

"If Adam Hadn't Seen the Apple." New York: Joseph W. Stern, 1908. Note: from *The Shoo-Fly Regiment.*

"I'm Thinkin' 'bout You, Honey, All the Time." Co-composer, J. Rosamond Johnson.

"In Dahomey." 1897. Co-composer, William "Billy" Johnson. Note: from *A Trip to Coontown.*

"In Gay Ballyhoo." 1903. Co-composer, J. Rosamond Johnson. Note: from *Nancy Brown.*

"In Shin Bone Alley." Chicago: Will Rossiter.

"The Italian Man." 1897. Co-composer, William "Billy" Johnson. Note: from *A Trip to Coontown.*

"I've Got Troubles of My Own." 1900.

"I've Lost My Teddy Bear." 1908. Co-composers, J. Rosamond Johnson, Joe Jordan. Note: from *The Red Moon.*

"A Jolly Old Rube." 1897. Co-composer, William "Billy" Johnson. Note: from *A Trip to Coontown.*

"The Katy-Did, the Cricket and the Frog." New York: Joseph W. Stern, 1903. Note: from *Nancy Brown.*

"Leave It to Bill." New York: Joseph W. Stern, 1914.

"Life Is a Game of Checkers." New York: Joseph W. Stern, 1908. Co-composers, J. Rosamond Johnson, Joe Jordan. Note: from *The Red Moon.*

"Lindy." New York: Joseph W. Stern, 1903. Co-composer, J. Rosamond Johnson. Note: from *In Newport.*

"Louisiana Lize." New York: Joseph W. Stern, 1899. Co-composer, J. Rosamond Johnson. Note: from *The Belle of Bridgeport.*

"The Luckiest Coon in Town." New York: Howley, Haviland, 1899. Co-composer, William "Billy" Johnson. Note: from *A Trip to Coontown.*

"Ma Chicken." 1897. Co-composer, William "Billy" Johnson. Note: from *A Trip to Coontown.*

"Ma Mississippi Belle" or "My Mississippi Belle." New York: Joseph W. Stern, 1903. Co-composer, J. Rosamond Johnson. Note: from *The Belle of Bridgeport* and *Nancy Brown.*

"Magdaline, My Southern Queen." 1900. New York: Joseph W. Stern, 1900. Co-composer, J. Rosamond Johnson. Note: from *The Belle of Bridgeport* and *Nancy Brown.*

"The Maid from Tokio." New York: Howley, Haviland and Dresser, 1902. Co-composer, J. Rosamond Johnson.

"The Maid of Timbuctoo." New York: Joseph W. Stern, 1903. Co-composer, James Weldon Johnson. Note: from *Whoop-Dee-Doo.*

"The Maiden with the Dreamy Eyes." New York: Joseph W. Stern, 1901. Co-composer, J. Rosamond Johnson. Note: from *The Little Duchess.*

"Man, Man, Man." New York: Joseph W. Stern, 1904.

"Mandy Won't You Let Me Be Your Beau." New York: Joseph W. Stern, 1902.

"Mary Was a Manicure." 1904. Co-composer, J. Rosamond Johnson. Note: from *In Newport.*

"Meet Me at the Gin Spring." 1897. Co-composer, William "Billy" Johnson. Note: from *A Trip to Coontown.*

"Mexico." New York: Joseph W. Stern, 1904.

"Miss Arabella Jones." 1897. Co-composer, William "Billy" Johnson. Note: from *A Trip to Coontown.*

"My Angemima Green." New York: Joseph W. Stern, 1902.

"My Castle on the Nile." New York: Joseph W. Stern, 1901. Co-composer, J. Rosamond Johnson. Note: from *Champagne Charlie; In Dahomey; The Sons of Ham.*

"My Indian Maid." 1908. Co-composers, J. Rosamond Johnson, Joe Jordan. Note: from *The Red Moon.*

"My Lulu San." New York: Joseph W. Stern, 1905.

"My One and Only." New York: Joseph W. Stern, 1906. Co-composer, J. Rosamond Johnson. Note: from *Shylock and Co., Bankers.*

"No Coons Allowed!" New York: Howley, Haviland, 1899. Co-composer, William "Billy" Johnson. Note: from *A Trip to Coontown.*

"Nobody But You." 1904. Co-composer, J. Rosamond Johnson. Note: from *In Newport.*

"Nobody's Lookin' but the Owl and the Moon." In *Song Successes Introduced by Peter F. Dailey in the New Successful Comedy "Champagne Charlie"* (New York: Joseph W. Stern, 1901). Co-composer, J. Rosamond Johnson. Note: from *Sleeping Beauty and the Beast.*

"Octette to Bacchus." 1903. Co-composer, J. Rosamond Johnson. Note: from *Nancy Brown.*

"Oh You Georgia Rose." Chicago: Will Rossiter, 1912. Co-composers, Johnnie Watters, Shelton Brooks, W. R. Williams.

"Old Kentucky Home." 1897. Co-composer, William "Billy" Johnson. Note: from *A Trip to Coontown.*

"On the Gay Luneta." New York: Joseph W. Stern, 1907. Co-composer, James Reese Europe. Note: from *The Shoo-Fly Regiment.*

"On the Road to Monterey." New York: Joseph W. Stern, 1909. Note: from *The Red Moon.*

"Parthenia Took a Likin' to a Coon." Chicago: Will Rossiter, ca. 1904.

"Peggy Is a New Yorker Now." 1904. Co-composer, J. Rosamond Johnson. Note: from *In Newport.*

"Phoebe Brown." 1908. Co-composers, J. Rosamond Johnson, Joe Jordan. Note: from *The Red Moon.*

"Pickaninny Days." 1908. Co-composers, J. Rosamond Johnson, Joe Jordan. Note: from *The Red Moon.*

"Picken on a Chicken Bone." 1897. Co-composer, William "Billy" Johnson. Note: from *A Trip to Coontown.*

"A Preposessing Little Maid." New York: Joseph W. Stern, 1904. Note: from *An English Daisy.*

"Red Hots." 1896–97. Note: from *At Jolly Coon-ey Island.*

"Red Moon." 1908. Co-composers, J. Rosamond Johnson, Joe Jordan. Note: from *The Red Moon.*

"Roaming Around the Town." New York: Joseph W. Stern, 1905. Co-composer, J. Rosamond Johnson.

"Run, Brudder Possum, Run." 1900. Co-composers, J. Rosamond Johnson, Joe Jordan. Note: from *The Red Moon* and *The Rogers Brothers in Central Park.*

"Sambo." 1908. Co-composers, J. Rosamond Johnson, Joe Jordan. Note: from *The Red Moon.*

"Sambo and Dinah." New York: Joseph W. Stern, 1904. Note: from *Humpty Dumpty.*

"Save It for Me." New York: Joseph W. Stern, 1903. Note: from *Nancy Brown.*

"Scandal." 1904. Co-composer, J. Rosamond Johnson. Note: from *In Newport.*

"Since You Went Away." New York: Joseph W. Stern, 1900. Co-composer, J. Rosamond Johnson.

"Society." 1900–02. Note: from *The Sons of Ham.*

"The Soldier Is the Idol of the Nation." New York: Joseph W. Stern, 1900. Co-composer, J. Rosamond Johnson. Note: from *Nancy Brown.*

"The Spirit of the Banjo." New York: Joseph W. Stern, 1903. Co-composer, J. Rosamond Johnson.

"Strollin' Along the Beach." New York: Joseph W. Stern, 1902. Co-composer, J. Rosamond Johnson. Note: from *The Little Duchess.*

"Sugar Babe." New York: Globe Music, 1909. Co-composer, J. Rosamond Johnson. Note: from *The Shoo-Fly Regiment.*

"Susanna." 1907. Co-composer, J. Rosamond Johnson. Note: from *The Husband.*

"Sweet Salomaa." New York: Joseph W. Stern, 1901. Co-composer, J. Rosamond Johnson. Note: from *The Little Duchess.*

"Sweet Savannah." 1897. Co-composer, William "Billy" Johnson. Note: from *A Trip to Coontown.*

"The Sweetest Gal in Town." 1908.

"Tell Me, Dusky Maiden." 1901. New York: Howley, Haviland and Dresser, 1901. Co-composer, J. Rosamond Johnson. Note: from *Sleeping Beauty and the Beast.*

"That Certain Party." New York: Joseph W. Stern, 1902.

"There's a Warm Spot in My Heart for You, Babe." New York: Howley, Haviland, 1897. Co-composer, William "Billy" Johnson. Note: from *A Trip to Coontown.*

"There's Always Something Wrong." New York: Joseph W. Stern, 1907. Co-composer, J. Rosamond Johnson. Note: from *The Shoo-Fly Regiment.*

"There Is Something about You That I Love, Love, Love." New York: Joseph W. Stern, 1904.

"The Three Little Kinkies." 1896–97. Note: from *At Jolly Coon-ey Island.*

"To-da-lo Two Step." 1908. Co-composers, J. Rosamond Johnson, Joe Jordan. Note: from *The Red Moon.*

"Trio from Atilla." 1897. Co-composer, William "Billy" Johnson. Note: from *A Trip to Coontown*.

"A Trip to Coontown." 1897. Co-composer, William "Billy" Johnson. Note: from *A Trip to Coontown*.

"Two Bold Bad Men." 1897. Co-composer, William "Billy" Johnson. Note: from *A Trip to Coontown*.

"Two Eyes." 1903. New York: Joseph W. Stern, 1903. Co-composer, J. Rosamond Johnson. Note: from *Nancy Brown*.

"Under the Bamboo Tree." New York: Joseph W. Stern, 1902. Note: from *Sally in Our Alley* and *Nancy Brown*.

"The Way to Kiss a Girl." 1897. Co-composer, William "Billy" Johnson. Note: from *A Trip to Coontown*.

"The Wedding of the Chinee and the Coon." New York: Howley, Haviland, 1897.

"When I Am Chief of Police." 1904. Co-composer, J. Rosamond Johnson. Note: from *In Newport*.

"When the Band Plays Ragtime." New York: Joseph W. Stern, 1902. Co-composer, James Weldon Johnson. Note: from *The Supper Club*.

"When the Chickens Go to Sleep." 1897. Co-composer, William "Billy" Johnson. Note: from *A Trip to Coontown*.

"Who Do You Love?" New York: Joseph W. Stern, 1906. Co-composer, J. Rosamond Johnson.

"Why Don't the Band Play?" New York: Joseph W. Stern, 1904. Co-composer, J. Rosamond Johnson. Note: from *The Belle of Bridgeport*.

"Wildfire Dance." 1908. Co-composers, J. Rosamond Johnson, Joe Jordan. Note: from *The Red Moon*.

"Women." 1904. Co-composer, J. Rosamond Johnson. Note: from *In Newport*.

"Won't You Be My Little Brown Bear?" New York: Joseph W. Stern, 1907. Note: from *The Shoo-Fly Regiment*.

"Won't Your Mamma Let You Come Out and Play." New York: Joseph W. Stern, 1906. Co-composer, J. Rosamond Johnson. Note: from *Shylock and Co., Bankers*.

"You'll Have to Choose Another Baby Now." New York: Howley, Haviland, 1897.

"You're All Right Teddy." New York: Joseph W. Stern, 1904. Co-composer, J. Rosamond Johnson. Note: Republican campaign song.

"Zel, Zel, Arabian Love Song." New York: Joseph W. Stern, 1905.

MUSICAL THEATER

At Jolly Coon-Ey Island: A Merry Musical Farce. 1896–97. Co-composer, William "Billy" Johnson. Premiere, 1896.

The Belle of Bridgeport. Co-composers, James Weldon Johnson, J. Rosamond Johnson. Premiere, 1900.

Cooney Dreamland (musical comedy). Premiere, 1904.

Coontown Carnival. 1900. Note: unproduced.

Humpty Dumpty. Co-composers, James Weldon Johnson, J. Rosamond Johnson. Premiere, 1904.

In Newport (musical comedy). Co-composers, James Weldon Johnson, J. Rosamond Johnson. Premiere, 1904.

The King of Spades (musical comedy). 1900. Note: unproduced.

Kings of Koon-Dom. Co-composer, William "Billy" Johnson. Premiere, 1898.

The Red Moon (operetta). 1908-09. Co-composers, Joe Jordan, J. Rosamond Johnson. Premiere, 1909.

The Shoo-Fly Regiment (musical comedy). 1905–07. Co-composer, J. Rosamond Johnson. Premiere, 1905.

A Trip to Coontown. 1897–1901. Co-composer, William "Billy" Johnson. Premiere, 1898.

AS WILL HANDY

"Oh, Didn't He Ramble?" 1902.

PUBLICATIONS

ABOUT COLE
Articles

Berlin, Edward A. "Cole and Johnson Brothers' 'The Evolution of Ragtime.'" *Current Musicology* 36 (1983): 21–39.

Danner, P. "Return with Us Now: *Soundboard*'s Featured Facsimile—'Under the Bamboo Tree' by Bob Cole." *Soundboard* 17 (1990): 53–55.

Morgan, Thomas L., and William Barlow. "Bob Cole and the Johnson Brothers." In *From Cakewalks to Concert Halls: An Illustrated History of African American Popular Music from 1895 to 1930.* Washington, D.C.: Elliot and Clark, 1992.

Riis, Thomas L. "Bob Cole: His Life and Legacy to Black Musical Theater." *Black Perspective in Music* 13, no. 2 (1985): 135–150.

BY COLE

"The Negro and the Stage." *Colored American Magazine* 4, no. 3 (1902): 301–306.

* * * * *

Bob Cole was a remarkable man of the musical theater—composer, lyricist, vaudeville performer, writer of skits, producer, director, and stage manager. Probably his greatest successes resulted from his decade-long collaboration (1900–11) with the brothers James Weldon and, especially, James Rosamond Johnson. Many of their popular songs became sensations, and many of their theatrical productions solidified the careers of dozens of black musicians and performers. Thomas Riis has described Cole as "important, perhaps even critical, to the development of black musical theater."

Robert Allen Cole Sr. was a carpenter and well-known political figure in the black community of Athens, Georgia, when his son Bob was born shortly after the beginning of Reconstruction. The oldest of six children, Bob studied music at an early age and learned to play the piano, banjo, guitar, and cello. At the age of 15, however, he was forced to leave town after injuring the son of a former town mayor. After hiding out in Florida, young Cole managed to rejoin his family when they moved to Atlanta; there he finished high school but never went on to college. Later, Cole earned his living in Florida, New Jersey, Illinois, and New York as a musician and vaudeville entertainer. For seven years, he played the part of a hobo called Willy Wayside with Sam T. Jack's traveling Creole Show, an all-black, male-and-female minstrel entertainment. In 1895–96, Cole served as the show's writer and stage manager.

Will Rossiter of Chicago brought out Cole's first songs: "Parthenia Took a Likin' to a Coon" and "In Shin Bone Alley." Three years later, four "genuine Negro songs" by Cole appeared in print; these included "Colored Aristocracy" and "Dem Golden Clouds," already staples in the repertories of several entertainment organizations. As early as 1894, Cole organized his own show, the All-Star Stock Company, which toured New England. All-Star boasted one of the first all-black casts on Broadway and included performers such as Irving Jones, Sylvester Russell, and Sam Lucas and his wife. Later, Cole himself performed with Black Patti's Troubadors. One of the skits he wrote for that revue, "Coon-ey Island," featured two of his more familiar songs: "4-11-44" (later used in *A Trip to Coontown*) and "The Black Four Hundred's Ball." Unable to find work after breaking with Black Patti's Troubadours, Cole was forced for a while to publish songs under the pseudonym "Will Handy." Even today that name is linked with "Oh, Didn't He Ramble?"

On September 27, 1897, *A Trip to Coontown,* the first all-black American musical show, opened in South Amboy, New Jersey. Written by Cole, the show became a resounding popular success and toured the United States before closing in 1900. Around the time he conceived the show, Cole met and became partners with the Johnson brothers, and he continued to work with J. Rosamond Johnson until his own death in 1911. Together, Cole and the Johnsons produced more than 150 songs, many of them intended for the New York stage. Among the Broadway shows that featured Johnson and Cole numbers were *The Belle of Bridgeport* (1900), *Sleeping Beauty and the Beast* (1901), *Sally in Our Alley* (1902), *Nancy Brown* (1903), and *In Newport* (1904). Another collaboration between Cole and Rosamond Johnson was "La Hoola Boola," considered by some the model for Yale University's "Hoola Boola" fight song.

Cole's final theatrical ventures, *The Shoo-Fly Regiment* (1906–08) and *The Red Moon* (1909–10), were critical successes. *The Shoo-Fly Regiment* boasted a cast consisting of veteran entertainers such as Tom Brown, Sam Lucas, and Anna Cooke, and for a time James Reese Europe directed both its orchestra and its chorus. The show's "military" plot, actually a send-up of the Spanish-American War, calls to mind other contemporary hits, among them George M. Cohan's *Little Johnny Jones* (1904).

In some respects, *The Shoo-Fly Regiment* represented a radical break from previous all-black entertainments. First, according to Allen Woll's 1991 study of black musical theater, "all [of its] male leads were [depicted as] brave, educated, and patriotic, a far cry from the shuffling stereotypes of minstrel origin." Second, according to Reid Badger's biography of James Reese Europe, *Shoo-Fly* "broke the taboo against having serious love scenes in black shows." James Weldon tells how if anything approaching a love duet was introduced in a musical comedy [prior to *The Shoo-Fly Regiment*], it had to be broadly burlesqued. "The reason behind this taboo lay in the belief that a love scene between two Negroes could not strike a white audience except as ridiculous. . . . The superiority stereotype [was] that Negroes . . . mate . . . in some sort of minstrel fashion. . . . [In *The Shoo-Fly Regiment*] coloured performers in New York experienced for the first time release from the restraining fears of what a white audience would stand for; for the first time they felt free to do on the stage whatever they were able to do."

By 1902, Cole seems to have become increasingly aware of the intertwined significance of racial and theatrical issues in his life,

since in that year he wrote an article about "The Negro and the Stage" for the *Colored American Magazine* in which he expressed concern over racial stereotyping and enthusiasm for the future of black actors in United States theaters. As Allen Woll puts it, "Cole believed that blacks should strive for excellence in artistic creation and must compete on an equal basis with whites. His musicals, therefore, had to rival those of white composers and lyricists, and thus demonstrate that the Negro was capable of matching whites in all realms of cultural production."

Unfortunately, Cole's optimism was incapable of sustaining him physically. In the spring of 1911, he collapsed unexpectedly, due perhaps to paresis brought about by advanced syphilis. Several months later, during a visit with his family to a Catskills resort, Cole apparently took his own life by drowning. A good deal of controversy sprang up over his death, and rumors flew thick and fast. What precisely happened to him will probably never be known.

During his career, Cole transformed himself from vaudeville and minstrel comic who also wrote coon songs into a sophisticated theatrical composer and performer. In collaboration with the Johnson brothers, Cole increasingly produced songs that left behind the racial and musical stereotypes of the 1890s. The lyrics he and the Johnsons wrote for numbers like "Under the Bamboo Tree" and "My Castle on the Nile" have been called "cute, sentimental, romantic, and at times melancholy," while their musical content has been described as harmonically rich, sonorous, and technically more difficult and polished than other products of the time.

To some extent, the improvements in Cole's later works may have been due to Rosamond Johnson's superior musical training and keyboard skills. Nevertheless, according to Riis, Cole's own "keen sense of what would work on stage must also have guided the writing of these new pieces." It is often difficult to tell a Cole song from a Rosamond Johnson song, or vice versa. In many cases, Cole may have collaborated with one or both of the Johnsons on the words and music of the songs published under his own name.

Representative compositions by Bob Cole include "4-11-44," "The Wedding of the Chinee and the Coon," "Under the Bamboo Tree," and "My Castle on the Nile." The first and earliest of these songs, "4-11-44," is quite different from the rest. Its melody is rhythmically stiff and jerky, although entirely unsyncopated in ragtime terms, and its dismal story revolves around a black man who has an unfortunate dream about playing craps according to a "four-eleven-forty-four" system and who loses all he has. The undemanding piano accompaniment harks back to the days of Stephen Foster, and the dotted rhythms of both verse and chorus are in the tradition of "Zip Coon." Other early, racially stereotypical Cole songs, such as "The Wedding of the Chinee and the Coon," are of interest today primarily because of their offensive lyrics. In his "Wedding," however, Cole introduces touches of ragtime syncopation as well as "Oriental" pentatonic sounds.

"Under the Bamboo Tree" and "My Castle on the Nile" seem to have been written by a different composer—and, to some extent, were. The title page of "My Castle on the Nile" identifies Rosamond Johnson as composer; his brother Weldon and Cole himself receive credit only for the song's lyrics. Nevertheless, the two works resemble each other closely. Both songs are noteworthy for their lovely tunes, touches of textual and musical irony, and a melancholy mood far removed from the abrasive racism of songs like "4-11-44." Ragtime rhythmic figures are scattered throughout both songs, but the songs themselves are less bouncy than the more recent numbers of Shelton Brooks and George T. Cohen.

Both "Under the Bamboo Tree" and "My Castle on the Nile" open with piano introductions featuring drone basses, and the introduction to "My Castle" also contains a hint of hoochy-koochy music. Directions such as "Moderato" and "not fast," however, suggest a gentler and more wistful performance style. The lyrics of both songs are about longing for something better. In "My Castle," a poor man yearns after wealth, represented (half humorously) by a palace with "inlaid diamonds on de flo[or]" and "a baboon butler at my do[or]." In "Under the Bamboo Tree," a "royal Zulu from Matabooloo" woos a "dusky maid" and begs her to become his queen. Conventional in its two-verse-and-chorus structure, "My Castle" is remarkable chiefly for the loveliness and "singability" of its well-known melody. The same holds true for "Under the Bamboo Tree," certainly one of the most famous American popular songs of all time. So famous did Cole's music and lyrics become that, in his "Fragments of an Agon," T. S. Eliot drew on "Under the Bamboo Tree" in order to satirize modern Anglo-American taste. In this song, the drone bass continues throughout the chorus, supporting a catchy melody that many people no longer associate in any way with "colored" music. "Under the Bamboo Tree" is subtly unconventional, however, in that it employs three verses instead of two, and the delicate polish of its piano accompaniment is also unusual.

Cole's reputation as a composer has recently been strengthened through careful studies of his music by Thomas Riis and other scholars of the African-American stage. Earlier critics were more inclined to slight his songs. Alec Wilder, for instance, was quoted in 1948, in Sigmund Spaeth's *History of Popular Music in America*, as saying that there was nothing unusual about "Under the Bamboo Tree" except "in comparison to the other songs of that period." On the other hand, James Weldon Johnson held Cole's work in high esteem. In his *Black Manhattan*, for example, Johnson praised *The Red Moon*—a show he played no part in writing—for its well-constructed book and well-written score.

Today, Cole's reputation remains unfocused. In *Scandalize My Name*, a study of anti-black sentiments in American popular song, Sam Dennison speaks of the "condescending, sniggering attitude" of "cannibal" songs like "Under the Bamboo Tree," with its "chorus of inane babbling." Dennison also deplores the racial content of Cole's lyrics for "If Adam Hadn't Seen the Apple," a novelty song that Dennison claims "twists the doctrine of original sin into a ludicrous tangle of conjecture." True, Cole was neither theologian nor poet. But he was also no racist. Instead, he was an entertainer who sought to amuse his audiences and an innovator who did a great deal to improve the lot of African-American entertainers during the early years of the twentieth century. Few of us today can listen to a sensitive performance of "My Castle on the Nile" without coming to realize that everyone, no matter what his race or place in life, has aspirations similar to our own.

REFERENCES

Badger, Reid. *A Life in Ragtime: A Biography of James Reese Europe.* New York: Oxford University Press, 1995.

Berlin, Edward A. "Ragtime Songs." In *Ragtime: Its History, Composers, and Music,* edited by John Edward Hasse, 70–78. New York: Schirmer Books, 1985.

Dennison, Sam. *Scandalize My Name: Black Imagery in American Popular Music.* New York: Garland Publishing, 1982.

Johnson, James Weldon. *Black Manhattan.* New York: Alfred A. Knopf, 1930.

Riis, Thomas L. "Bob Cole: His Life and Legacy to Black Musical Theater." *Black Perspective in Music* 13, no. 2 (1985): 135–150.

———. *More than Just Minstrel Shows: The Rise of Black Musical Theatre at the Turn of the Century.* Brooklyn: Institute for Studies in American Music, 1992.

Spaeth, Sigmund. *A History of Popular Music in America.* New York: Random House, 1948.

Tawa, Nicholas E. *The Way to Tin Pan Alley: American Popular Song, 1866–1910.* New York: Schirmer Books, 1990.

Wilder, Alec. *American Popular Song: The Great Innovators, 1900–1950,* edited by James T. Maher. New York: Oxford University Press, 1972.

Woll, Allen. *Black Musical Theatre: From "Coontown" to "Dreamgirls."* Baton Rouge: Louisiana State University Press, 1989.

MICHAEL SAFFLE

COLEMAN, ORNETTE

Born Randolph Denard Ornette Coleman in Fort Worth, Tex., March 29, 1930. **Education:** Fort Worth, public schools; primarily self-taught in music, began playing alto saxophone, age 14; began playing tenor saxophone during last year of high school; Los Angeles, Calif., studied music theory textbooks on his own while working as an elevator operator, 1950s; Lenox, Mass., attended Lenox School of Jazz along with Don Cherry at instigation of John Lewis, 1959; taught himself to play violin and trumpet, 1962–65. **Composing and Performing Career:** During high school, formed own rhythm and blues group and appeared with other groups in local clubs; moved to New Orleans, La., 1948; returned to Texas, by 1950; performed and toured with various groups including "Red" Connors, the Silas Green from New Orleans Show, and Clarence Samuels; toured with "Pee Wee" Crayton's rhythm and blues band, 1950; left Crayton's band to live in Los Angeles, 1950–52; returned to Fort Worth, ca. 1952; played only rarely with different groups, including the Jazz Messiahs, 1957, and the Bley Quintet, 1958; first albums released for Contemporary, *Something Else: The Music of Ornette Coleman,* 1958, and *Tomorrow Is the Question,* 1959; New York, N.Y., quartet including Don Cherry (trumpet), Billy Higgins (drums), and Charlie Haden (double bass), debuted at the Five Spot Café, 1959; influential recordings for Atlantic released, including *The Shape of Jazz to Come* and *Change of the Century*; *Free Jazz* released, 1960; Town Hall concert, 1962; Atlantic contract severed, withdrew from performing to practice and study, 1962–65; began writing music for "classical" ensembles including string quartet, woodwind quintet, and symphony orchestra; unconventional style on trumpet and violin led to denunciations by prominent jazz musicians including Miles Davis and Charles Mingus upon his return to active performing, 1965; toured Europe to critical acclaim with stops in London, Stockholm, Paris, Rome, and Berlin, 1965–66; began playing with his son, Denardo Coleman (drums), then age ten, debuting on the album *The Empty Foxhole,* 1966; produced soundtrack for the film *Who's Crazy,* 1966; performed at London's Albert Hall, 1968; recorded *Skies of America* with London Philharmonic, 1972; performed with Ornette Coleman Septet, 1970s; toured Europe, Nigeria, and Morocco, 1972–73; founded Prime Time, initially a quintet with two electric guitars, bass, and drums, 1975; film *Ornette: Made in America,* directed by Shirley Clarke, 1984; Hartford, Conn., week-long Coleman festival presented by Real Art Ways, 1985; "Song X" began a Coleman revival, recorded with guitarist Pat Metheny, 1985, on tour, 1986; Weill Recital Hall, Carnegie Hall, New York, two retrospective concerts, "Ornette Coleman Celebration," 1987; returned to London for performance, 1987; recorded album *Virgin Beauty* featuring Grateful Dead guitarist Jerry Garcia, 1988; own imprint, Harmolodic Records, with Verve, 1994; Lincoln Center, featured in week-long festival, "? Civilization," 1997; released more than 60 albums during career. **Commissions:** Conrad Rooks, ca. 1965; Tufts University; Brooklyn Academy of Music, 1983; Fromm Foundation and Harvard University, 1986. **Honors/Awards:** *Down Beat* Awards: New Star Award (now Talent Deserving Wider

Recognition), Critics Poll, 1960, Record of the Year (*At the Golden Circle* vol. 1), 1966, Jazzman of the Year, 1966, 1971–72, alto saxophone, Critics Poll, 1967, 1972–74, 1986–87, Hall of Fame, 1969, Readers' poll, 1972–74, Record of the Year (*Song X*), Readers Poll, 1986, Critics Poll, 1987, Electric Jazz Group, Ornette Coleman and Prime Time, Critics Poll 1987, 1988, 1990, Record of the Year (*In All Languages*), Critics Poll, 1988, Reissue of the Year (*Beauty Is a Rare Thing*), Critics Poll, 1994, Jazz Album of the Year (*Sound Museum: Hidden Man*), Critics Poll, 1997, Jazz Artist of the Year, Critics Poll, 1998; *Melody Maker,* Musician of the Year, 1966; Guggenheim Fellowship, 1967, 1974; National Endowment for the Arts, American Jazz Master, 1984; University of Pennsylvania, honorary doctorate, 1989; California Institute of the Arts, honorary doctorate, 1990; Boston Conservatory of Music, honorary doctorate, 1993; John D. and Catherine T. MacArthur Fellowship, 1994; Rex Foundation, Ralph S. Gleason Award, 1996; Jazz Journalists Association, Artist of the Year, 1996, 1997; American Academy of Arts and Letters, inductee, 1997; Republic of France, named an officer in the French Order of Arts and Letters, 1998; Critics Choice Jazz Awards, Top Musician, 1998; The New School for Social Research, honorary doctorate; *Rolling Stone,* Jazz Artist of the Year. **Mailing Address:** c/o Harmolodic Inc., 103 E. 125th St., New York NY 10035.

MUSIC LIST

COLLECTIONS

A Collection of the Compositions of Ornette Coleman, edited and transcribed by Gunther Schuller. New York: MJQ Music, 1961. Contents: Bird Food; Chronology; The Face of the Bass; Focus on Sanity; Forerunner; Free; Lonely Woman; Peace; Una Muy Bonita.

A Collection of 26 Ornette Coleman Compositions. New York: MJQ Music, 1968. Contents: Beauty Is a Rare Thing; Bird Food; Blues Connotation; C. and D.; Change of the Century; Chronology; Congeniality; Cross Breeding; Ecars; Enfant; Eos; Eventually; The Face of the Bass; Focus on Sanity; Folk Tale; Forerunner; Free; Kaleidoscope; Lonely Woman; Mapa; Peace; Ramblin'; R.P.D.D.; T. and T.; Una Muy Bonita; W.R.U.

JAZZ ENSEMBLE*

[The following list of titles includes only works that were composed by the subject of the entry; it is not a list of recordings that were made by the subject. Although the composer may have made recordings of his own works, the list is not restricted to those recordings but in many cases includes performances by other artists of the composer's work. The list is made up of publication and discographical data, in

---

* Prime Time was a varied jazz ensemble of six to nine players. Instrumentation consists of the following: alto saxophone/trumpet/violin, one or two guitars, two electric basses, and two drum players; or saxophone/violin/trumpet, guitar, keyboards, acoustic and electric bass, drums, tablas/percussion, voice, and bass/keyboards; or saxophone/violin/trumpet, drums/keyboard/percussion, drums, two bass guitars, and three guitars —Ed.

cases where such information is available. Although no effort has been made to include documentation of the earliest recording of the works listed, the date of the earliest recording that is readily available has been given. —Ed.]

"A Capella for Three Wise Men and a Sage" (trumpet/violin, two basses, drums).

"The Adjuster" (alto/tenor saxophone/trumpet/violin, trumpet, bass, drums). Recorded, 1976: Artist House (unissued).

"Africa Is the Mirror of All Colors" (alto/tenor saxophone/trumpet/violin, trumpet, bass, drums). New York: Phrase Text Music. Also arranged for Prime Time ensemble. Recorded, 1987: Caravan of Dreams CDP 85008; Harmolodic/Verve 314 531 915-2.

"Air Ship" (alto saxophone, two guitars, two drum players). 1979. New York: Phrase Text Music. Recorded: Antilles 2001.

"Airborne" (alto saxophone, tenor saxophone, bass, drums). New York: Phrase Text Music. Recorded, 1968: Blue Note CDP 7 84356 20.

"The Alchemy of Scott La Faro" (alto saxophone, pocket trumpet, bass, drums). New York: Phrase Text Music. Recorded, 1961: Atlantic 1572; Atlantic 7 90978-2.

"All My Life" (voice, alto saxophone, tenor saxophone, pocket trumpet, trumpet, bass, two drum players). Recorded, 1971: Columbia KC 31061.

"Alpha" (alto saxophone, trumpet, piano, bass, drums). Berkeley, Calif.: Contemporary Music. Recorded, 1958: Contemporary C3551; Original Jazz Classics CD 163-2.

"Angel Voice" (alto saxophone, trumpet, piano, bass, drums). Berkeley, Calif.: Contemporary Music. Recorded, 1958: Contemporary C3551; Original Jazz Classics CD 163-2.

"The Anthem" (alto saxophone/violin, trumpet/Indian flute, tenor saxophone/clarinet, bass, drums). 1969. New York: Phrase Text Music. Recorded: Impulse AS-9187 (unissued).

"Antiques" (alto saxophone, bass, drums). New York: Phrase Text Music. Recorded, 1965: Blue Note CDP 7 84225 2; Jasrac EJC-802.

"Architect" (alto saxophone, bass, drums). Recorded, 1962: ESP 1006 (unissued).

"The Ark" (alto saxophone, bass, percussion). Also arranged for alto/tenor saxophone/trumpet/violin, bass, drums. Recorded, 1962: ESP 1006.

"The Art of Love Is Happiness" (Prime Time ensemble). 1987. New York: Phrase Text Music. Recorded: Caravan of Dreams CDP 85008; Harmolodic/Verve 314 531 915-2.

"Asa" (Prime Time ensemble). Recorded, 1978: (unissued).

"Asia" (Prime Time ensemble). Recorded, 1982: Antilles (unissued).

"Atavism" (alto saxophone, musette, bass, drums). Recorded, 1968: (unissued).

"Bach Prelude" (Prime Time ensemble). New York: Harmolodic Music. Note: based on composition by J. S. Bach. Recorded, 1995: Harmolodic/Verve 314 527 483-2.

"Badal" (Prime Time ensemble). New York: Harmolodic Music. Recorded, 1995: Harmolodic/Verve 314 527 483-2.

"Ballad" (alto saxophone, bass, drums). Recorded, 1965: Polydor 623 246/247.

"Be with Me" (Prime Time ensemble). Recorded, 1982: Antilles (unissued).

"Beauty Is a Rare Thing" (alto saxophone, pocket trumpet, bass, drums). New York: Phrase Text Music, 1961. Recorded, 1960: Atlantic 1353.

"Bells and Chimes" (violin, tenor saxophone, bass, drums). Recorded, 1968: Impulse 9178.

"Bhudda's Blues" (musette, bass, drums). Recorded, 1967: (unissued).

"Biosphere" (Prime Time ensemble). 1987. New York: Phrase Text Music. Also arranged for alto saxophone, piano, bass, drums. Recorded: Caravan of Dreams CDP 85008; Harmolodic/Verve 314 531 915-2; Harmolodic/Verve 314 531 657-2.

"Bird Food" (alto saxophone, trumpet, bass, drums). New York: MJQ Music, 1960. Recorded, 1959: Atlantic 1327-2; Atlantic 81341-2.

"The Black House" (alto saxophone, tenor saxophone, trumpet, two bass, two drummers). Recorded, 1977: Artists House (unissued).

"The Blessing" (alto saxophone, trumpet, piano, bass, drums). Berkeley, Calif.: Contemporary Music. Recorded, 1958: Contemporary C3551; Inner City 1007; MUSIDISC 500542; Original Jazz Classics CD 163-2.

"Blues Always" (alto/tenor saxophone/trumpet/violin, trumpet, bass, drums). Recorded, 1960: Atlantic (Japan) P-10085A.

"Blues Connotation" (alto saxophone, pocket trumpet, bass, drums). New York: Phrase Text Music, 1961. Recorded, 1960: Atlantic 1353; Atlantic 1558.

"Blues Misused" (alto saxophone, guitar, piano, bass, drums). Recorded, 1962: ESP 1006 (unissued).

"Bourgeois Boogie" (Prime Time ensemble). Copyright, 1988. New York: Harmolodic Music. Recorded: CBS RK 44301.

"Brings Goodness" (alto saxophone, trumpet, bass, drums). Recorded, 1960: Atlantic 7 90978-2; Atlantic (Japan) P-10085A.

"Broad Way Blues" (alto saxophone, tenor saxophone, bass, drums). New York: Phrase Text Music. Recorded, 1968: Blue Note CDP 7 84287 2; Blue Note CDP 7243 8 2337 2 5.

"Broken Shadows" (alto saxophone, trumpet/Indian flute, tenor saxophone/clarinet, bass, drums). 1969. New York: Phrase Text Music. Recorded: Impulse AS-9187.

"C. and D." (alto saxophone, trumpet, bass, drums). New York: MJQ Music. Recorded, 1961: Atlantic 1378; Atlantic SD1558.

"Change of the Century" (alto saxophone, trumpet, bass, drums). New York: MJQ Music, 1960. Recorded, 1959: Atlantic 1327-2; Atlantic 781341-2.

"Chanting" (Prime Time ensemble). Copyright, 1988. New York: Harmolodic Music. Recorded: CBS RK 44301.

"Check-Out Time" (alto saxophone, tenor saxophone, bass, drums). New York: Phrase Text Music. Recorded, 1968: Blue Note 84356.

"Check Up" (alto saxophone, pocket trumpet, bass, drums). New York: Phrase Text Projections. Recorded, 1961: Atlantic 1588.

"Children's Books" (alto saxophone, bass, drums). Recorded, 1962: ESP 1006 (unissued).

"Chippie" (alto saxophone, trumpet, piano, bass, drums). Berkeley, Calif.: Contemporary Music. Recorded, 1958: Contemporary C3551; Original Jazz Classics CD 163-2.

"Chronology" (alto saxophone, cornet, bass, drums). New York: MJQ Music, 1961. Recorded, 1959: Atlantic 1317-2; Atlantic 19238-2.

"The Circle with a Hole in the Middle" (alto saxophone, cornet, bass, drums). New York: Phrase Text Music. Recorded, 1959: Atlantic 1572; Atlantic 7 90978-2.

"City Living" (Prime Time ensemble). Also arranged for alto saxophone, piano, bass, drums. Recorded, 1982: CDP 85001; Harmolodic/Verve 314 531 657-2.

Ornette Coleman; courtesy of Verve/Polygram; photo by Austin Trevett

"Civilization Day" (alto saxophone, tenor saxophone, pocket trumpet, trumpet, bass, two drummers). Recorded, 1971: Columbia KC 31061.

"The Clergyman's Dream" (alto saxophone, bass, drums). Recorded, 1965: Polydor 623 246/247.

"Cloning" (alto saxophone, trumpet, bass, drums). New York: Phrase Text Music. Also arranged for Prime Time ensemble. Recorded, 1987: Caravan of Dreams CDP 85008; Harmolodic/Verve 314 531 915-2.

"C.O.D." (alto saxophone/trumpet/violin, tenor saxophone, bass, drums). Recorded, 1968: Impulse 9178.

"Comme il faut" (alto saxophone/violin, trumpet/Indian flute, tenor saxophone/clarinet, bass, drums). 1969. New York: Phrase Text Music. Recorded: Impulse AS-9187.

"Compassion" (alto saxophone, pocket trumpet, bass, drums). Berkeley, Calif.: Composers Music. Recorded, 1959: Contemporary M3569; Contemporary S-7569; Original Jazz Classics CD 342-2.

"Compute" (Prime Time ensemble). Recorded, 1982: Caravan of Dreams CDP 85001.

"Congeniality" (alto saxophone, cornet, bass, drums). New York: MJQ, 1961. Recorded, 1959: Atlantic 1317-2; Atlantic 19238-2.

"Country Town Blues" (alto saxophone, tenor saxophone/pocket trumpet, trumpet, bass, two drummers). Recorded, 1971: Columbia FC 38029.

"Cross Breeding" (tenor saxophone, pocket trumpet, bass, drums). New York: Phrase Text Music, 1961. Recorded, 1962: Atlantic 1394; Rhino R2 71455.

"Crossroads" (alto saxophone, trumpet, piano, bass, drums). Recorded, 1958: Improvising Artists IAI 37.38.52.

"Cyber Cyber" (alto saxophone, piano). New York: Harmolodic Music. Recorded, 1996: Harmolodic/Verve 314 537 789-2.

"Dawn" (alto saxophone, pocket trumpet, bass, drums). New York: Phrase Text Music. Recorded, 1965: Blue Note CDP 7 84224 2; Blue Note CDP 7243 8 23372 2 5.

"Dee Dee" (alto saxophone/violin/trumpet, bass, drums). New York: Phrase Text Music. Recorded, 1965: Blue Note CDP 7 84224 2; Blue Note CDP 7243 8 23372 2 5.

"Desert Players" (Prime Time ensemble). Copyright, 1988. New York: Harmolodic Music. Note: Recorded with Jerry Garcia. Recorded: CBS RK 44301.

"The Disguise" (alto saxophone, trumpet, piano, bass, drums). Berkeley, Calif.: Contemporary Music. Recorded, 1958: Original Jazz Classics CD 163-2.

"DNA Meets E=MC2" (Prime Time ensemble with original quartet). Commissioned by Tufts University.

"Don't Know" (alto/tenor saxophone, trumpet, bass, drums). Recorded, 1976: Artist House (unissued).

"Don't You Know by Now" (two vocalists, alto saxophone, piano, bass, drums). New York: Harmolodic Music. Recorded, 1996: Harmolodic/Verve 314 531 657-2.

"Doughnut" (alto saxophone, bass, percussion). Recorded, 1962: ESP 1006; Polydor 623 246/247.

"Dream Talking" (Prime Time ensemble). Recorded, 1978: (unissued).

"Earth Souls" (Prime Time ensemble). Recorded, 1978: (unissued).

"Earth Souls/Meta" (alto saxophone, drums). Note: composed for White House Jazz Festival. Recorded, 1978: (unissued).

"Ecars" (tenor saxophone, pocket trumpet, bass, drums). New York: Phrase Text Music, 1962. Recorded, 1961: Atlantic 1394; Rhino R2 71455.

"Elizabeth" (alto saxophone, tenor saxophone, pocket trumpet, trumpet, bass, two drummers). Recorded, 1971: Columbia FC 38029.

"Emotion Modulation" (trumpet, violin, two basses, vocals, drums). Recorded, 1968: private tape, Royal Albert Hall concert.

"The Empty Foxhole" (trumpet, bass, drums). New York: Phrase Text Music. Recorded, 1966: Blue Note 84246; Blue Note CDP 7243 8 28982 2 1.

"Endangered Species" (alto saxophone, guitar/guitar synthesizer, bass, drums, drums/percussion). New York: Phrase Text Music. Co-composer, Pat Metheny. Recorded, 1985: Geffen GHS 24096.

"Endless" (alto saxophone, pocket trumpet, bass, drums). Berkeley, Calif.: Composers Music. Recorded, 1959: Contemporary M3569; Contemporary S-7569; Original Jazz Classics CD 342-2.

"Energy, Mind, and Matter" (alto/tenor saxophone/trumpet/violin, trumpet, bass, drums). Recorded, 1976: Artist House (unissued).

"Enfant" (tenor saxophone, pocket trumpet, bass, drums). New York: Phrase Text Music, 1962. Recorded, 1961: Atlantic 1394; Rhino R2 71455.

"Eos" (tenor saxophone, pocket trumpet, bass, drums). New York: Phrase Text Music, 1962. Recorded, 1961: Atlantic 1394; Rhino R2 71455.

"European Echoes" (alto saxophone, bass, drums). New York: Phrase Text Music. Also arranged for Prime Time ensemble; jazz quartet. Recorded, 1965: Artists House AH-1; Blue Note CDP 7 84224 2; Harmolodic/Verve 314 531 657-2; Harmolodic/Verve 314 531 916-2.

"Eventually" (alto saxophone, cornet, bass, drums). New York: MJQ Music, 1964. Recorded, 1959: Atlantic 1317-2; Atlantic 19238-2.

"The Face of the Bass" (alto saxophone, trumpet, bass, drums). New York: MJQ Music, 1961. Recorded, 1959: Atlantic 1327-2; Atlantic 781 3 41-2.

"Faces and Places" (alto/tenor saxophone/trumpet/violin, bass, drums). New York: Phrase Text Music. Recorded, 1965: Blue Note 4224/4225.

"Faithful" (alto saxophone, bass, drums). New York: Phrase Text Music. Recorded, 1966: Blue Note 84246; Blue Note CDP 7243 8 28982 2 1.

"Falling Stars" (trumpet/violin, bass, drums). Recorded, 1965: Polydor 623 246/247.

"Family Reunion" (Prime Time ensemble). New York: Harmolodic Music. Recorded, 1995: Harmolodic/Verve 314 527 483-2.

"Faxing" (alto saxophone, piano). New York: Harmolodic Music. Recorded, 1996: Harmolodic/Verve 314 537 789-2.

"Feet Music" (alto/tenor saxophone/trumpet/violin, trumpet, bass, drums). New York: Phrase Text Music. Also arranged for Prime Time ensemble. Recorded, 1987: Caravan of Dreams CDP 85008; Harmolodic/Verve 314 531 915-2.

"The Fifth of Beethoven" (alto saxophone, trumpet, bass, drums). New York: Phrase Text Music. Recorded, 1960: Atlantic 1572; Atlantic 7 90978-2.

"First Take" (double quartet: two trumpets, alto saxophone, bass clarinet, two basses, two drummers). New York: Phrase Text Music. Note: this composition represents the first realization of *Free Jazz*. Recorded, 1960: Atlantic 1364-2; Rhino R2 75208.

"Focus on Sanity" (alto saxophone, cornet, bass, drums). New York: MJQ Music, 1961. Recorded, 1959: Atlantic 1317-2; Atlantic 19238-2.

"Folk Tale" (alto saxophone, pocket trumpet, bass, drums). New York: Phrase Text Music, 1961. Recorded, 1960: Atlantic 1353.

"Forerunner" (alto saxophone, trumpet, bass, drums). New York: MJQ Music, 1960. Recorded, 1959: Atlantic 7 81341-2; Atlantic 1327-2.

"Forgotten Children." (trumpet, two basses, drums). ca. 1968. Note: concert in Royal Albert Hall.

"Forgotten Songs" (alto saxophone, tenor saxophone, bass, drums). Recorded, 1970: Flying Dutchman FDS-123.

"Fou amour" (Prime Time ensemble: alto saxophone, two guitars, bass, two drummers). New York: Harmolodic Music. Also arranged for jazz quintet. Recorded, 1975: Harmolodic/Verve 314 531 916-2.

"Free" (alto saxophone, trumpet, piano, bass, drums). Also arranged for alto saxophone, trumpet, bass, drums. Recorded, 1958: Atlantic 1327-2; Inner City 1007; MUSIDISC 500542.

Free Jazz (double quartet: two trumpets, alto saxophone, bass clarinet, two basses, two drummers). New York: MJQ Music. Recorded, 1960: Atlantic 1364-2; Rhino R2 75208.

"Freeway Express" (trumpet, bass, drums). New York: Phrase Text Music. Recorded, 1966: Blue Note 84246; Blue Note CDP 7243 8 28982 2 1.

"Friends and Neighbors" (violin, tenor saxophone, bass, drums). Recorded, 1970: Flying Dutchman FDS-123.

"The Garden of Souls" (alto saxophone, tenor saxophone, bass, drums). New York: Phrase Text Music. Recorded, 1968: Blue Note 84287; Blue Note CDP 7 84287 2.

"Giggin'" (alto saxophone, pocket trumpet, bass, drums). Berkeley, Calif.: Composers Music. Recorded, 1959: Contemporary M3569; Contemporary S-7569, Original Jazz Classics CD 342-2.

"The Golden Number" (trumpet, bass). Recorded, 1976: A&M Horizon SP-727.

"Good Girl Blues" (alto saxophone, tenor saxophone, bass, drums, piano, electric guitar, voice, woodwind quintet). Recorded, 1972: Columbia FC 38029.

"The Good Life" (alto saxophone, tenor saxophone, trumpet, bass, drums). Recorded, 1972: (unissued).

"Good Old Days" (alto saxophone, bass, drums). New York: Phrase Text Music. Recorded, 1966: Blue Note 84246; Blue Note CDP 7243 8 23372 2 5; Blue Note CDP 7243 8 28982 2 1.

"Growing Up" (alto saxophone/trumpet, tenor saxophone, bass, drums). Recorded, 1969: Impulse 45-275.

"Guadalupe" (Prime Time ensemble). New York: Harmolodic Music. Recorded, 1995: Harmolodic/Verve 314 527 483-2.

"Haight Ashbury" (alto saxophone, two basses, drums). 1968. Note: concert in Royal Albert Hall.

"Happy Fool" (alto saxophone, bass, drums). Recorded, 1965: Polydor 623 246/247.

"Happy Hour" (Prime Time ensemble). Copyright, 1988. New York: Harmolodic Music. Recorded: CBS RK 44301.

"Happy House" (alto saxophone, tenor saxophone, pocket trumpet, trumpet, bass, two drum players). Recorded, 1971: Columbia FC 38029.

"Harlem's Manhattan" (tenor saxophone, pocket trumpet, bass, drums). New York: Phrase Text Music. Recorded, 1961: Atlantic 1572; Atlantic 7 90978-2.

"Harloof" (alto saxophone/trumpet/violin, guitar, bass, drums). Recorded, 1974: (unissued).

"Harlowe" (alto saxophone, guitar, bass, drums). Recorded, 1974: (unissued).

"Harmolodic Bebop" (Prime Time ensemble). Recorded, 1983: Caravan of Dreams CDP 85001.

"Healing the Feeling" (Prime Time ensemble). Copyright, 1988. New York: Harmolodic Music. Recorded: CBS RK 44301.

"Him and Her" (alto saxophone, two guitars, two drum players). 1979. New York: Phrase Text Music. Recorded: Antilles 2001.

"Holiday for a Graveyard" (alto saxophone, two basses, drums). Note: written for John Coltrane's funeral. Recorded, 1967: Flying Dutchman FDS-104.

"Home Grown" (Prime Time ensemble: alto saxophone, two guitars, bass, two drummers). New York: Harmolodic Music. Also arranged for jazz quartet and jazz quintet. Recorded, 1975: Harmolodic/Verve 314 531 657-2; Harmolodic/Verve 314 531 916-2.

"Honeymooners" (Prime Time ensemble). Copyright, 1988. New York: Harmolodic Music. Recorded: CBS RK 44301.

"House of Stained Glass" (alto saxophone, piano). New York: Harmolodic Music. Recorded, 1996: Harmolodic/Verve 314 537 789-2.

"Humpty Dumpty" (alto saxophone, pocket trumpet, bass, drums). Berkeley, Calif.: Contemporary Music. Recorded, 1960: Atlantic 1353.

"I Don't Love You" (alto saxophone, bass, drums). Recorded, 1962: ESP 1006 (unissued).

"If I Knew as Much about You (As You Know about Me)" (Prime Time ensemble). New York: Harmolodic Music. Recorded, 1995: Harmolodic/Verve 314 527 483-2.

"In All Languages" (alto/tenor saxophone/trumpet/violin, trumpet, bass, drums). New York: Phrase Text Music. Also arranged for Prime Time ensemble. Recorded, 1982: Caravan of Dreams CDP 85008; Harmolodic/Verve 314 531 915-2.

"Invisible" (alto saxophone, trumpet, piano, bass, drums). Berkeley, Calif.: Contemporary Music. Recorded, 1958: Contemporary C3551; Original Jazz Classics CD 163-2.

"Is It Forever" (alto saxophone, tenor saxophone, bass, drums, piano, electric guitar, vocal, woodwind quintet). Recorded, 1972: Columbia FC 38029.

"Jayne" (alto saxophone, trumpet, piano, bass, drums). Berkeley, Calif.: Contemporary Music. Recorded, 1958: Contemporary C3551; Original Jazz Classics CD 163-2.

"Job Mob" (alto saxophone, two guitars, two drum players). 1979. New York: Phrase Text Music. Recorded: Antilles 2001.

"Joy of a Toy" (alto saxophone, pocket trumpet, bass, drums). New York: Phrase Text Projections. Recorded, 1960: Atlantic 1588.

"Jump Street" (alto saxophone, two guitars, two drum players). 1979. New York: Phrase Text Music. Recorded: Antilles 2001.

"The Jungle Is a Skyscraper" (alto saxophone, tenor saxophone, trumpet, bass, drums). Recorded, 1971: Columbia KC 31061.

"Just for You" (alto saxophone/trumpet, cornet/tenor saxophone, bass, drums). New York: Phrase Text Music. Recorded, 1959: Atlantic 1572; Atlantic 7 90978-2; Blue Note 84356.

"Kaleidoscope" (alto saxophone, pocket trumpet, bass, drums). New York: MJQ Music. Recorded, 1960: Atlantic 1353.

"Kartham Place" (Prime Time ensemble). Recorded, 1982: Antilles (unissued).

"Kathelin Gray" (alto saxophone, guitar/guitar synthesizer, bass, drums, drums/percussion). New York: Phrase Text Music. Also arranged for Prime Time ensemble. Co-composer, Pat Metheny. Recorded, 1985: Geffen 9 24096-2; Geffen GHS 24096; Harmolodic/Verve 314 527-483-2.

"La Capella" (Prime Time ensemble). New York: Harmolodic Music. Recorded, 1995: Harmolodic/Verve 314 527 483-2.

"Latin Genetics" (alto/tenor saxophone/trumpet/violin, trumpet, bass, drums). 1982. New York: Phrase Text Music. Also arranged for Prime Time ensemble. Recorded: Caravan of Dreams CDP 85008; Harmolodic/Verve 314 531 915-2.

"Law Years" (alto saxophone, tenor saxophone, trumpet, bass, drums). 1971. New York: Phrase Text Music. Recorded: Columbia KC 31061.

"The Legend of Bebop" (alto saxophone, pocket trumpet, bass, drums). New York: Phrase Text Music. Recorded, 1960: Atlantic 1572; Atlantic 7 90978-2.

"Let's Play" (trumpet, two basses, drums). Recorded, 1968: Flying Dutchman FDS-123.

"Light House" (alto saxophone, tenor saxophone, pocket trumpet, trumpet, bass, two drummers). Recorded, 1971: (unissued).

"Listen Up" (Prime Time ensemble). 1987. New York: Phrase Text Music. Recorded: Caravan of Dreams CDP 85008; Harmolodic/Verve 314 531 915-2.

"Little Symphony" (alto saxophone, pocket trumpet, bass, drums). New York: Phrase Text Projections. Recorded, 1960: Atlantic 1588.

"Local Instinct" (Prime Time ensemble). New York: Harmolodic Music. Recorded, 1995: Harmolodic/Verve 314 527 483-2.

"Lonely Woman" (alto saxophone, pocket trumpet, bass, drums). New York: Phrase Text Music, 1961. Recorded, 1959: Atlantic 1317-2; Atlantic 19238-2; Elektra Nonesuch 979163-2.

"Long Time No See" (alto saxophone, two basses, drums). New York: Phrase Text Music. Also arranged for jazz quintet. Premiere, 1968. Recorded, 1970: Flying Dutchman FDS-123; Geffen 24096.

"Lorraine" (alto saxophone, pocket trumpet, bass, drums). Berkeley, Calif.: Composers Music. Recorded, 1959: Contemporary M3569; Contemporary S-7569, Original Jazz Classics CD 342-2.

"Love and Sex" (alto saxophone, two basses, drums). 1967. Recorded: private tape, Village Theatre concert.

"Love Call" (alto saxophone/trumpet/violin, tenor saxophone, bass, drums). 1968. New York: Phrase Text Music. Recorded: Blue Note 84356.

"Love Eyes" (alto saxophone, tenor saxophone, trumpet, bass, drums). Recorded, 1972: (unissued).

"Love Words" (alto saxophone, two guitars, two drum players). 1979. New York: Phrase Text Music. Recorded: Antilles 2001.

"Macho Woman" (Prime Time ensemble: alto saxophone, two guitars, bass, two drummers). New York: Harmolodic Music. Also arranged for jazz quartet; jazz quintet. Recorded, 1975: Harmolodic/Verve 314 531 657-2; Harmolodic/Verve 314 531 916-2.

"Man on the Moon" (alto saxophone/trumpet, tenor saxophone, bass, drums). Co-composer, Emanuel Ghent. Recorded, 1969: Impulse 45-275.

"Mapa" (tenor saxophone, pocket trumpet, bass, drums). New York: Phrase Text Music, 1962. Recorded, 1961: Atlantic 1394; Rhino R2 71455.

"McB" (alto saxophone, trumpet, piano, bass, drums). Berkeley, Calif.: Contemporary Music. Recorded, 1958: Original Jazz Classics CD 163-2 (unissued).

"Meta." (Prime Time ensemble). Recorded, 1978: (unissued).

"Midnight Sunrise" or "Music from the Cave" (alto saxophone, clarinet, and Master Musicians of Morocco playing nontempered reed and string instruments and different sized drums). New York: Phrase Text Music. Recorded, 1973: A&M CD 0807; A&M SP-722.

"Miguel's Fortune" (Prime Time ensemble). New York: Harmolodic Music. Recorded, 1995: Harmolodic/Verve 314 527 483-2.

"Mind and Time" (alto saxophone, pocket trumpet, bass, drums). Berkeley, Calif.: Composers Music. Recorded, 1959: Contemporary M3569; Contemporary S-7569, Original Jazz Classics CD 342-2.

"A Minor Augment" (Prime Time ensemble). Recorded, 1982: Antilles (unissued).

"Mob Job" (alto saxophone/violin, guitar/guitar synthesizer, bass, drums, drums/percussion). New York: Phrase Text Music. Also arranged for jazz quartet. Recorded, 1985: Geffen GHS 24096; Harmolodic/Verve 314 531 657-2.

"Monk and the Nun" (alto saxophone, pocket trumpet, bass, drums). 1959. New York: Phrase Text Projections. Recorded, 1959: Atlantic 1588.

"Monsieur Allard" (alto saxophone, piano, bass, drums). Copyright, 1996. New York: Harmolodic Music. Recorded: Harmolodic/Verve 314 531 657-2.

"Moon Inhabitants" (alto saxophone, trumpet, bass, drums). New York: Phrase Text Music. Recorded, 1960: Atlantic 1572; Atlantic 7 90978-2.

"Morning Song" (alto saxophone, bass, drums). New York: Phrase Text Music. Recorded, 1965: Blue Note CDP 7 84225 2; Jasrac EJC-802.

"Mothers of the Veil" (alto/tenor saxophone/trumpet/violin, trumpet, bass, drums). New York: Phrase Text Music. Also arranged for Prime Time ensemble. Recorded, 1987: Caravan of Dreams CDP 85008; Harmolodic/Verve 314 531 915-2.

"Motive for Its Use" (alto saxophone, pocket trumpet, bass, drums). Recorded, 1960: Atlantic (Japan) P-10085A.

"Mr. and Mrs. Dream" (alto saxophone, trumpet, tenor saxophone, two basses, two drummers). Recorded, 1977: Artists House (unissued).

"Mukami" (alto saxophone/trumpet/violin/ bassoon, two guitars, bass, two drummers). Recorded, 1977: Artists House (unissued).

"Music Always" (alto saxophone, cornet, bass, drums). Recorded, 1959: Atlantic 7 90978-2; Atlantic (Japan) P-10085A.

"Music News" (Prime Time ensemble). 1987. New York: Phrase Text Music. Recorded: Caravan of Dreams CDP 85008; Harmolodic/Verve 314 531 915-2.

"Name Brain" (alto saxophone, trumpet, tenor saxophone, two basses, two drummers). Recorded, 1977: Artists House (unissued).

"New York" (alto saxophone, tenor saxophone, bass, drums). Recorded, 1968: Impulse 9178.

"News Item" (Prime Time ensemble). Recorded, 1982: Antilles (unissued).

"Night Plans" (alto saxophone, piano). New York: Harmolodic Music. Recorded, 1996: Harmolodic/Verve 314 537 789-2.

"Night Worker" (alto/tenor saxophone/trumpet/violin, trumpet, bass, drums). Recorded, 1976: Artist House (unissued).

"OAC" (Prime Time ensemble). New York: Harmolodic Music. Recorded, 1995: Harmolodic/Verve 314 527 483-2.

"Old Gospel" (alto saxophone, trumpet, piano, bass, drums). Recorded, 1967: Blue Note BST 84262; Blue Note CDP 7243 8 233722 5.

"Old Wives Tales" (Prime Time ensemble). Recorded, 1982: Antilles (unissued).

"Open to the Public" (alto saxophone/trumpet/violin, tenor saxophone, bass, drums). 1968. New York: Phrase Text Music. Recorded: Blue Note 84356.

"P. P. (Picolo Pesos)" (alto saxophone, piano, bass, drums). New York: Harmolodic Music. Recorded, 1996: Harmolodic/Verve 314 531 657-2.

"Passion Cultures" (alto saxophone, piano). New York: Harmolodic Music. Recorded, 1996: Harmolodic/Verve 314 537 789-2.

"Peace" (alto saxophone, cornet, bass, drums). New York: Phrase Text Music, 1961. Recorded, 1959: Atlantic 1317-2; Atlantic 19238-2.

"Peace Warriors" (alto/tenor saxophone/trumpet/violin, trumpet, bass, drums). 1987. New York: Phrase Text Music. Also arranged for Prime Time ensemble. Recorded: Caravan of Dreams CDP 85008; Harmolodic/Verve 314 531 915-2.

"Play It Straight" (alto saxophone, bass, drums). Recorded, 1962: ESP 1006 (unissued).

"Poise" (alto saxophone, pocket trumpet, bass, drums). Berkeley, Calif.: Contemporary Music. Recorded, 1960: Atlantic 1353.

"Police People" (Prime Time ensemble). Recorded, 1982: Antilles (unissued).

"Race Face" (alto saxophone, tenor saxophone, trumpet, two basses, two drummers). Recorded, 1977: Artists House (unissued).

"Rainbows" (trumpet, tenor saxophone, bass, drums). 1968. Recorded: Impulse 9178.

"Ramblin'" (alto saxophone, trumpet, bass, drums). New York: MJQ Music, 1960. Recorded, 1958: Atlantic 7 81341-2; Atlantic 1327-2; Improvising Artists IAI 37.38.52.

"Refills" (alto saxophone/trumpet, piano). New York: Harmolodic Music. Recorded, 1996: Harmolodic/Verve 314 537 789-2.

"Rejoicing" (alto saxophone, pocket trumpet, bass, drums). Berkeley, Calif.: Composers Music. Recorded, 1959: Contemporary M3569; Contemporary S-7569, Original Jazz Classics CD 342-2.

"The Riddle" (alto saxophone, bass, drums). New York: Phrase Text Music. Recorded, 1965: Blue Note CDP 7 84225 2; Jasrac EJC-802.

"Rock the Clock" (trumpet/violin, musette/tenor saxophone, bass, drums). Recorded, 1971: Columbia KC 31061.

"Round Trip" (alto saxophone, tenor saxophone, bass, drums). New York: Phrase Text Music. Recorded, 1968: Blue Note CDP 7 84287 2; Blue Note CDP 7243 8 23372 2 5.

"R.P.D.D." (alto saxophone, pocket trumpet, bass, drums). New York: Phrase Text Music, 1962. Recorded, 1961: Atlantic 1378.

"Rubber Gloves" (alto saxophone, tenor saxophone, bass, drums). Recorded, 1972: Columbia FC 38029.

"Sadness" (alto saxophone, bass, drums). New York: Phrase Text Music. Recorded, 1962: ESP 1006; Polydor 623 246/247.

"School Work" (alto saxophone, tenor saxophone, trumpet, bass, drums). Recorded, 1971: Columbia FC 38029.

"Science Fiction" (poet, alto saxophone, tenor saxophone, pocket trumpet, trumpet, bass, two drummers). 1966. New York: Phrase Text Music. Recorded, 1971: Columbia KC 31061.

"Script Trip" (Prime Time ensemble). Recorded, 1982: Antilles (unissued).

"Search for Life" (Prime Time ensemble). New York: Harmolodic Music. Recorded, 1995: Harmolodic/Verve 314 527 483-2.

"See-Thru" (Prime Time ensemble). Recorded, 1983: CDP 85001.

"Sex Spy" (tenor saxophone, bass). Recorded, 1977: Artist House AH-6; Caravan of Dreams CDP 85001; Harmolodic/Verve 314 531 917-2; Polygram CD 531917.

"Sex Spy II" (Prime Time ensemble). Recorded, 1982: Antilles (unissued).

"Silence" (alto saxophone, bass, drums). Recorded, 1965: Polydor 623 246/247.

"Singing in the Shower" (Prime Time ensemble). Copyright, 1988. Note: recorded with Jerry Garcia. New York: Harmolodic Music. Recorded: CBS RK 44301.

"Sleep Talk" (alto saxophone, two guitars, two drum players). 1979. New York: Phrase Text Music. Recorded: Antilles 2001.

"Sleep Talking" (alto saxophone/trumpet/violin/bassoon, two guitars, bass, two drummers). Recorded, 1977: Artists House (unissued).

"Snowflakes and Sunshine" (trumpet/violin, bass, drums). New York: Phrase Text Music. Recorded, 1965: Blue Note CDP 7 84225 2; Jasrac EJC-802.

"Soap Suds" (tenor saxophone, bass). Recorded, 1977: Artist House AH-6; Harmolodic/Verve 314 531 917-2; Polygram CD 531917.

"Some Day" (trumpet, bass). Recorded, 1977: Artist House AH-6; Harmolodic/Verve 314 531 917-2; Polygram CD 531917.

"Some Other" (alto saxophone, pocket trumpet, bass, drums). Recorded, 1960: Atlantic (Japan) P-10085A.

"Something to Listen To" (alto saxophone, tenor saxophone, bass). Recorded, 1973: (unissued).

"Song X" (alto saxophone, guitar/guitar synthesizer, bass, drums, drums/percussion). New York: Phrase Text Music. Also arranged for jazz quintet. Recorded, 1985: Geffen GHS 24096.

"Song X Duo" (alto saxophone, guitar). New York: Phrase Text Music and Pat-Meth Music. Co-composer, Pat Metheny. Recorded, 1985: Geffen 9 24096-2.

"Sound Amoeba" (alto saxophone, tenor saxophone, trumpet, two basses, two drummers). Recorded, 1977: Artists House (unissued).

"Sound Gravitation" (violin, bass, drums). New York: Phrase Text Music. Recorded, 1966: Blue Note 84246; Blue Note CDP 7243 8 28982 2 1.

"Sound Is Everywhere" (Prime Time ensemble). New York: Harmolodic Music. Recorded, 1995: Harmolodic/Verve 314 527 483-2.

"Sound into That" (trumpet, guitar, bass, drums). Recorded, 1974: (unissued).

"Sound Manual" (alto/tenor saxophone/trumpet/violin, trumpet, bass, drums). 1987. New York: Phrase Text Music. Also arranged for Prime Time ensemble. Recorded: Caravan of Dreams CDP 85008; Harmolodic/Verve 314 531 915-2.

"Sound Museum" (alto saxophone/violin, piano, bass, drums). New York: Harmolodic Music. Recorded, 1996: Harmolodic/Verve 314 531 657-2.

"Space Church (Continuous Services)" (alto/tenor saxophone/trumpet/violin, trumpet, bass, drums). 1987. New York: Phrase Text Music. Also arranged for Prime Time ensemble. Recorded: Caravan of Dreams CDP 85008; Harmolodic/Verve 314 531 915-2.

"Space Jungle" (alto saxophone/violin, trumpet/Indian flute, tenor saxophone/clarinet, bass, drums). 1969. New York: Phrase Text Music. Recorded: Impulse AS-9187.

"Spelling the Alphabet" (Prime Time ensemble). Copyright, 1988. New York: Harmolodic Music. Recorded: CBS RK 44301.

"The Sphinx" (alto saxophone, trumpet, piano, bass, drums). Berkeley, Calif.: Contemporary Music. Recorded, 1958: Contemporary C3551; Original Jazz Classics CD 163-2.

"Stopwatch" (alto saxophone, piano, bass, drums). New York: Harmolodic Music. Recorded, 1996: Harmolodic/Verve 314 531 657-2.

"Story Teller" or "Storyteller" (alto saxophone, bass, drums). Recorded, 1962: ESP 1006 (unissued).

"Story Tellers." 1987. New York: Phrase Text Music. Recorded: Caravan of Dreams CDP 85008; Harmolodic/Verve 314 531 915-2.

"Story Writing" (alto saxophone/violin, piano). New York: Harmolodic Music. Recorded, 1996: Harmolodic/Verve 314 537 789-2.

"Straight Line in a Circle" (Prime Time ensemble). Recorded, 1982: Antilles (unissued).

"Strange as It Seems" (alto saxophone, trumpet, piano, bass, drums). Recorded, 1967: Blue Note BST 84262.

"Street Blues" (Prime Time ensemble). New York: Harmolodic Music. Recorded, 1995: Harmolodic/Verve 314 527 483-2.

"Street Woman" (alto saxophone, tenor saxophone, pocket trumpet, trumpet, bass, two drummers). 1971. New York: Phrase Text Music. Recorded: Columbia KC 31061.

"T. and T." (alto saxophone, pocket trumpet, bass, drums). New York: Phrase Text Music, 1964. Recorded, 1961: Atlantic 1378.

"Tears Inside" (alto saxophone, pocket trumpet, bass, drums). Berkeley, Calif.: Composers Music. Recorded, 1959: Contemporary M3569; Contemporary S-7569, Original Jazz Classics CD 342-2.

"Theme from a Symphony: Variation One" (Prime Time ensemble). Also arranged for jazz quintet. Recorded, 1976: A&M CD 0807.

"Theme from a Symphony: Variation Two" (Prime Time ensemble). Also arranged for jazz quintet. Recorded, 1976: A&M CD 0807.

"Three Ways to One" (alto saxophone, piano). New York: Harmolodic Music. Recorded, 1996: Harmolodic/Verve 314 537 789-2.

"Three Wise Men and the Saint" (violin, two basses, drums). ca. 1968. Note: concert in Royal Albert Hall.

"Three Wishes" (Prime Time ensemble). Copyright, 1988. New York: Harmolodic Music. Note: Recorded with Jerry Garcia. Recorded: CBS RK 44301.

"The Time Is Now" (alto saxophone, trumpet, piano, bass, drums). Berkeley, Calif.: Contemporary Music, 1958. Recorded, 1958: Original Jazz Classics CD 163-2 (unissued).

"Times Square" (alto saxophone, two guitars, two drum players). 1979. New York: Phrase Text Music. Recorded: Antilles 2001.

"To Know What to Know" (Prime Time ensemble). Recorded, 1982: Antilles (unissued).

"To See and to Hear My Love" (alto saxophone/trumpet/violin, tenor saxophone/musette, bass, drums). Recorded, 1973: (unissued).

"To Us" (alto saxophone, pocket trumpet, bass, drums). Recorded, 1960: Atlantic (Japan) P-10085A.

"Today, Yesterday, and Tomorrow" (Prime Time ensemble). 1987. New York: Phrase Text Music. Recorded: Caravan of Dreams CDP 85008; Harmolodic/Verve 314 531 915-2.

"Tomorrow" (alto saxophone, trumpet/flute, tenor saxophone/clarinet, bass, drums). 1969. New York: Phrase Text Music. Recorded: Flying Dutchman FDS-123.

"Tomorrow Is the Question!" (alto saxophone, pocket trumpet, bass, drums). Berkeley, Calif.: Contemporary Music. Recorded, 1959: Contemporary M3569; Contemporary S-7569, Original Jazz Classics CD 342-2.

"Tone Dialing" (Prime Time ensemble). New York: Harmolodic Music. Recorded, 1995: Harmolodic/Verve 314 527 483-2.

"Toy Dance" (alto saxophone, tenor saxophone, bass, drums). New York: Phrase Text Music. Recorded, 1968: Blue Note CDP 7 84287 2.

"Trigonometry" (alto saxophone, guitar/guitar synthesizer, bass, drums, drums/percussion). New York: Phrase Text Music and Pat-Meth Music. Co-composer, Pat Metheny. Recorded, 1985: Geffen GHS 24096.

"Trouble in the East" (alto saxophone/violin, trumpet/Indian flute, tenor saxophone/clarinet, bass, drums). 1969. New York: Phrase Text Music. Recorded: Impulse AS-9187.

"Turnabout" (alto saxophone, pocket trumpet, bass, drums). Berkeley, Calif.: Composers Music. Recorded, 1959: Contemporary M3569; Contemporary S-7569; Original Jazz Classics CD 342-2.

"Tutti" (alto saxophone/trumpet/violin, guitar, bass, drums) Recorded, 1974: (unissued).

"Una Muy Bonita" (alto saxophone, trumpet, bass, drums). New York: MJQ Music, 1960. Recorded, 1959: Atlantic SP 1558; Atlantic 7 81341-2; Atlantic 1327-2.

"Unknown Artist" (Prime Time ensemble). Copyright, 1988. New York: Harmolodic Music. Recorded: CBS RK 44301.

"Unknown Races" (alto saxophone/tenor saxophone, trumpet, bass, drums). Recorded, 1972: (unissued).

"Video Games" (alto saxophone, guitar/guitar synthesizer, bass, drums, drums/percussion). New York: Phrase Text Music. Recorded, 1985: Geffen GHS 24096.

"Virgin Beauty" (Prime Time ensemble). Copyright, 1988. New York: Harmolodic Music. Recorded: CBS RK 44301.

"Voice Poetry" (Prime Time ensemble: alto saxophone, two guitars, bass, two drummers). New York: Phrase Text Music. Recorded, 1975: Artists House AH-1; Harmolodic/Verve 314 531 916-2.

"W.R.U." (alto saxophone, pocket trumpet, bass, drums). New York: Phrase Text Music, 1964. Recorded, 1961: Atlantic 1378.

"We Now Interrupt for a Commercial" (violin, tenor saxophone, bass, drums). New York: Phrase Text Music. Note: in LP version, the voice of Mel Furman was overdubbed. Recorded, 1968: Blue Note CDP 7 84287 2.

"What Is the Name of That Song?" (alto saxophone, two guitars, two drum players). 1979. New York: Phrase Text Music. Recorded: Antilles 2001.

"What Reason" (alto saxophone, piano, bass, drums). 1996. New York: Harmolodic Music. Recorded: Harmolodic/Verve 314 531 657-2.

"What Reason Could I Give?" (voice, alto saxophone, tenor saxophone, pocket trumpet, trumpet, bass, drums). 1971. New York: Phrase Text Music. Recorded: Columbia KC 31061.

"When Will I See You Again?" (Prime Time ensemble). New York: Harmolodic Music. Recorded, 1995: Harmolodic/Verve 314 527 483-2.

"When Will the Blues Leave?" Berkeley, Calif.: Contemporary Music. Recorded, 1958: Improvising Artists IAI 37.38.52; Original Jazz Classics CD 163-2.

"Who Do You Work For?" (alto saxophone/violin, trumpet/flute, tenor saxophone/clarinet, bass, drums). 1969. New York: Phrase Text Music. Recorded: Impulse AS-9187 (unissued).

"Without Name or Number" (alto/tenor saxophone/trumpet/violin, trumpet, bass, drums). Recorded, 1976: Artist House (unissued).

"Woman of the Veil" (alto saxophone/trumpet, piano, bass, drums). New York: Harmolodic Music. Recorded, 1996: Harmolodic/Verve 314 531 657-2.

"The Word Became Music" (alto saxophone, tenor saxophone, trumpet, bass, drums). Recorded, 1972: (unissued).

"Word for Bird" (alto/tenor saxophone/trumpet/violin, trumpet, bass, drums). 1987. New York: Phrase Text Music. Also arranged for Prime Time ensemble. Recorded: Caravan of Dreams CDP 85008; Harmolodic/Verve 314 531 915-2.

"Writing in the Streets" (alto saxophone/trumpet/violin/bassoon, two guitars, bass, two drummers). Recorded, 1977: Artists House (unissued).

"Written Word" (alto saxophone, tenor saxophone, pocket trumpet, trumpet, bass, two drummers). Recorded, 1971: (unissued).

"Yesterday, Today, and Tomorrow" (alto saxophone/trumpet/violin, piano, bass, drums). New York: Harmolodic Music. Recorded, 1996: Harmolodic/Verve 314 531 657-2.

"Ying Yang" (Prime Time ensemble). New York: Harmolodic Music. Recorded, 1995: Harmolodic/Verve 314 527 483-2.

"Zig Zag" (alto saxophone, bass, drums). New York: Phrase Text Music. Recorded, 1966: Blue Note 84246; Blue Note CDP 7243 8 23372 2 5; Blue Note CDP 7243 8 28982 2 1.

INSTRUMENTAL SOLOS
Violin
"Trinity." 1986. Recorded: What Next Recordings WN 005.

Cello
"City Minds and Country Hearts." 1963.

Mandolin
"Notes Talking." 1986.

SMALL INSTRUMENTAL ENSEMBLE
Strings
"Dedication to Poets and Writers" (string quartet). Recorded, 1962: ESP 1006-2.

"Saints and Soldiers" (string quartet). Recorded, 1967: Bluebird 6561-2-RB; RCA LSC-2982.

"Space Flight" (string quartet). Recorded, 1967: Bluebird 6561-2-RB; RCA LSC-2982.

Woodwinds
"Forms and Sounds" (wind quintet, trumpet). Note: with trumpet interludes performed by Ornette Coleman. Recorded, 1967: Bluebird 6561-2-RB; Polydor 623 246/247; RCA LSC-2982.

"Titles" (woodwind quintet). Co-composer, F. A. Chambers.

Combinations
"The Sacred Mind of Johnny Dolphin" (double string quartet, trumpet, percussion). 1983. Commissioned by the Brooklyn Academy of Music. Premiere, 1983.

"In Honor of NASA and Planetary Soloist" (string quartet and wind soloist performing on oboe, English horn, and *mukhavina*). 1986. Commissioned by the Fromm Foundation and Harvard University for the Kronos Quartet and Joseph Celli.

"Prime Design/Time Design" (for amplified string quartet and electric drum set). 1983. Note: dedicated to Buckminster Fuller. Recorded: Caravan of Dreams CDP 85002.

ORCHESTRA (CHAMBER OR FULL) WITH SOLOISTS
Skies of America. 1972, revised 1983. New York: Phrase Text Music. Contents: Part I: Skies of America; Native Americans; The Good Life; Birthdays and Funerals; Dreams; Sounds of Sculpture; Holiday for Heroes; All of My Life; Dancers; The Soul within Woman; The Artist in America; Part II: The New Anthem; Place in Space; Foreigner in a Free Land; Silver Screen; Poetry; The Men Who Lived in the White House; Love Life; The Military; Jam Session; Sunday in America. Recorded: Columbia KC 31061; Columbia KC-31562; Columbia CG 33669.

Sun Suite of San Francisco. Recorded, 1968: Impulse (unissued).

DRAMATIC MUSIC
Architecture in Motion (ballet). 1990s.

INCIDENTAL AND COMMERCIAL MUSIC
"Ballad/Joan." 1991. Note: from the film soundtrack *Naked Lunch*. Recorded: Milan 73138 35614-2.

Box Office. Film soundtrack.

"Bugpowder." 1991. Note: from the film soundtrack *Naked Lunch*. Recorded: Milan 73138 35614-2.

Chappaqua Suite. Film soundtrack (unused). Contents: Part I, Part II, Part III, Part IV. Commissioned by Conrad Rooks. Recorded, 1965: CBS 62 896/97.

"Cloquet's Parrots." 1991. Note: from the film soundtrack *Naked Lunch*. Recorded: Milan 73138 35614-2.

Communication Explosion. 1968. Film soundtrack.

"Intersong." 1991. Note: from the film soundtrack *Naked Lunch*. Recorded: Milan 73138 35614-2.

"Midnight Sunrise." 1991. Note: from the film soundtrack *Naked Lunch*. Recorded: Milan 73138 35614-2.

Population Explosion. 1966. Documentary film soundtrack.

Run. 1971. Film soundtrack.

Who's Crazy: Part One and Part Two (alto saxophone/trumpet/violin, bass, drums). Soundtrack for unreleased film. Contents: (Part one) January; Sortie le coquard; Dans la neige; The Changes; Better Get Yourself Another Self; The Duel, Two Psychic Lovers and Eating Time; (Part two) The Mis-used Blues (The Lovers and the Alchemist); The Poet; The Wedding Day and Fuzz; Fuzz, Feast, Breakout, European Echoes, Alone and the Arrest. Recorded, 1966: Atmosphere (France) IRI 5006/5007.

"Writeman." 1991. Note: from the film soundtrack *Naked Lunch.* Recorded: Milan 73138 35614-2.

PUBLICATIONS

ABOUT COLEMAN
Books and Monographs
Litweiler, John. *Ornette Coleman: A Critical Biography.* London: Quartet, 1990.
———. *Ornette Coleman: A Harmolodic Life.* New York: William Morrow, 1992.
McRae, Barry. *Ornette Coleman.* London: Apollo, 1988.
Wild, David, and Michael Cuscuna. *Ornette Coleman, 1958–79: A Discography.* Ann Arbor, Mich.: Wild Music, 1980.
Wilson, Peter Niklas. *Ornette Coleman: Sein Leben, seine Musik, seine Schallplatten.* Schaftlach, Germany: Oreos, 1989.

Thesis
Cogswell, Michael Bruce. "Melodic Organization in Four Solos by Ornette Coleman." Master's thesis, University of North Texas, 1989.

Articles
Balliett, Whitney. "Ornette." In *Jelly Roll, Jabbo and Fats: Nineteen Portraits in Jazz,* 187–197. New York: Oxford University Press, 1983.
Block, Steven. "Organized Sound: Pitch-Class Relationships in the Music of Ornette Coleman." *Annual Review of Jazz Studies* 6 (1993): 229–252.
Blome, Rainer. "Pitch-Class Transformations in Free Jazz." *Music Theory Spectrum* 12, no. 2 (1990): 181–202.
Blumenthal, Bob. "Ornette: An Experimental Music That Has Aged Gracefully." *Jazz Magazine* 1, no. 3 (1977): 39–42.
Buhless, Gunter. "Charlie Parker—Ornette Coleman—Vergleichund Deutung." *Hi-Fi Stereophonie* 15, no. 4 (1976): 386–392; 15, no. 6 (1976): 628–631.
Davis, Francis. "There's No Success Like Failure, and Failure's No Success at All: Ornette Coleman's Permanent Revolution." In *In the Moment: Jazz in the 1980s,* 133–146. New York: Oxford University Press, 1986.
Endress, Gudrun. "Ornette Coleman." In *Jazz Podium: Musiker über sich selbst,* 182–189. Stuttgart, Germany: Deutsche Verlags-Anstalt, 1980.
Feather, Leonard. "Ornette Coleman: Harmolodic Master Explores the Perils of Self-Expression." *Down Beat* 48 (July 1981): 16–19, 62–63.
Giddins, Gary. "Harmolodic Hoedown." In *Rhythm-a-ning: Jazz Tradition and Innovation in the '80s,* 235–249. New York: Oxford University Press, 1985.
———. "Ornette Coleman, Continued." In *Riding on a Blue Note: Jazz and American Pop,* 179–189. New York: Oxford University Press, 1981.
Goldberg, Joe. "Ornette Coleman." In *Jazz Masters of the Fifties,* 228–246. Rev. ed. New York: Macmillan, 1983.
Gordon, Robert. "The Los Angeles Underground." In *Jazz West Coast: The Los Angeles Jazz Scene of the 1950s,* 189–199. New York: Quartet, 1986.
Gumplowicz, Phillipe. "Qu'est-ce qu'une identité musicale? L'exemple du free jazz." *Revue d'esthétique* 19 (1991): 152–164.

Hartman, Charles O. "Ornette Coleman: The Shapes of Jazz." In *Jazz Text: Voice and Improvisation in Poetry, Jazz, and Song,* 57–74. Princeton, N.J.: Princeton University Press, 1991.
Hentoff, Nat. "Ornette Coleman." In *The Jazz Life,* 222–248. New York: Dial Press, 1961.
Jost, Ekkehard. "Ornette Coleman." In *Free Jazz,* 44–65. Graz, Austria: Universal Edition, 1974.
———. "Zur jüngsten Entwicklung des Jazz." In *Die Musik der sechziger Jahre.* Mainz, Germany: B. Schott, 1972.
———. "Zur Musik Ornette Colemans." *Jazzforschung* 2 (1970): 105–124.
Kumpf, Hans H. "Ornette Coleman." In *Postserielle Musik und Free Jazz,* 26–29 Herrenberg, Germany: Döring, 1976.
Lange, Art. "Ornette Coleman and Pat Metheny: Songs of Innocence and Experience." *Down Beat* 53 (June 1986): 16–19, 53.
Litweiler, John. "Ornette Coleman: The Birth of Freedom." In *The Freedom Principle: Jazz after 1958,* 31–58. New York: William Morrow, 1984.
Mandel, Howard. "Ornette Coleman: The Color of Music." *Down Beat* 54 (August 1987): 16–19.
———. "Ornette Coleman: The Creator as Harmolodic Magician." *Down Beat* 45 (October 1978): 17–19, 53–56.
Porter, Lewis. "The Blues Connotation in Ornette Coleman's Music: With Some General Thoughts on the Relation of Blues to Jazz." In *Proceedings of the First International Conference on Jazz Studies,* edited by Francesco Gerosa. Bologna, Italy: University of Bologna, 1988.
Roggeman, Willy. "Ornette Coleman." In *Free en Andere Jazz—Essays,* 55–66. Nieuwe Nijghboeken, vol. 26. The Hague, Netherlands: Nijgh Van Ditmer, 1969.
Rockwell, John. "Free Jazz, Body Music, and Symphonic Dreams." In *All American Music: Composition in the Late Twentieth Century,* 185–197. New York: Knopf, 1983.
Spellman, A. B. "Ornette Coleman." In *Black Music: Four Lives,* 79–150. New York: Schoken Books, 1970.
Taylor, Arthur R. "Ornette Coleman." In *Notes and Tones: Musician-to-Musician Interviews,* 32–41. Rev. ed. New York: Da Capo Press, 1982.
Troupe, Quincy. "Ornette Coleman: Going Beyond Outside." In *The Jazz Musician,* edited by Mark Rowland and Tony Sherman, 25–46. New York: St. Martin's Press, 1994.
Williams, Martin. "Ornette Coleman: Innovation from the Source." In *The Jazz Tradition,* 235–248. 2nd rev. ed. New York: Oxford University Press, 1993.
———. "Ornette Coleman in Concert." In *Jazz Masters in Transition, 1957–69,* 282–284. Rev. ed. New York: Da Capo Press, 1980.
———. "Ornette Coleman in Stockholm." In *Jazz Masters in Transition, 1957–69,* 203–205. Rev. ed. New York: Da Capo Press, 1980.
———. "Rehearsing with Ornette." In *Jazz Masters in Transition, 1957–69,* 54–57. Rev. ed. New York: Da Capo Press, 1980.
Wilson, Peter Niklas. "Harmolodics: Theorie, Wahnsystem, Worthulse? Versuch zur Syntax und Asthetik der Musik Ornette Coleman." In *Darmstädter Jazzforum 89.* Hofheim, Germany: Wolke, 1990.

BY COLEMAN
"Harmolodic—Highest Instinct: Something to Think About." Available on www.harmolodic.com/thinkabout.html, cited April 21, 1997.
"Prime Time for Harmolodics." *Down Beat* 50 (July 1983): 54–55.

* * * * *

Ornette Coleman's primary contribution to the art of jazz has been to question conventions and reinterpret the fundamental building blocks of music: sound, melody, rhythm, harmony, and structure. His compositions are musical experiments built to examine and test these parameters by placing his band members into unfamiliar musical territory in which expression attempts to overcome convention. The results of these experiments have opened new avenues to ensemble interaction and have demanded new strategies of listening that have forever altered the shape of jazz. Coleman's 1960 recording *Free Jazz* gave its name and impetus to an entire movement in avant-garde jazz that helped dismantle the boundary between jazz as popular entertainment and jazz as art. While the relentless sincerity of his music making won a number of supporters instantly, others rejected his music as pure charlatanism. After 40 years of recording, many of his compositions have come to be accepted in the core repertory of jazz. Yet Coleman has continued to experiment, such that critics in the early 1990s were just as split over his aesthetic merits as were their predecessors in the 1960s. Regardless of the listener's bias, however, one aspect of Coleman's art remains true: his recordings and ideas have asserted a powerful influence that has fundamentally altered the way musicians, critics, and audiences alike listen to jazz. As bassist Charlie Haden has said, "Ornette has influenced almost every musician who is making any kind of contribution to the art form."

Coleman's search for expressive freedom prompted him to discard or distort many standard conventions that he felt limited the expressive range of bebop: regular harmonic patterns or "changes," motivic variation, tempered intonation, and traditional compositional forms. His departures from accepted practice led to accusations of amateurism, poor intonation, and inferior technique.

Coleman's music addresses a defining issue in Western aesthetics: the balance between technique and expression. One end of this aesthetic spectrum posits technique as the *sine qua non* of expression and virtuosity as the fundamental basis of excellence. The other pole suggests that technique is an impediment to emotion, a barrier between the artist and experience. While Coleman's reputation might seem concordant with the latter view, Coleman is both an expressionist and a virtuoso. He places technique at the service of expression. In his music, technique functions as a means of communication rather than as an access point for the listener. While Coleman's technical control and facility certainly increased after he gained more regular musical employment, even his early recordings reveal a musician in command of his instrument. As Charles Hartman explains: "The issue [of freedom] centers not on escape, but on the liberation of certain aspects of the music from rule-governed regularity, so as to make them variable, and so potentially expressive. What can be significantly varied can make meaning." This privileging of expression guided the development of Coleman's aesthetic system and compositional technique, now known as Harmolodics.

Born in 1930, Coleman did not get his first horn until his midteens. He never received formal music instruction, a fact that undoubtedly contributed to his independent and original musical conceptions. A quick learner, Coleman was working professionally in less than a year. No recordings of Coleman's earliest style have survived, but his professional résumé and personal recollections reveal that he was a member of the bebop underground within the southwest rhythm and blues network. Coleman made a modest living playing R&B, but his compositional interests moved in the direction of Charlie Parker's stylistic innovations. While his improvisations were already outside the norm, at this time Coleman used standard harmonic patterns with bebop substitutions in his solos and compositions. Never very successful as a sideman, he was often forced to take non-music jobs to earn even a meager living. Working as an elevator operator in Los Angeles, Coleman studied music theory texts on his own during his free time. He also formed a woodshedding/rehearsal ensemble to test his compositions and theoretical concepts. The result of these self-study strategies was what Gunther Schuller has described as "a radically new concept and style, seemingly from a combination of musical intuition born of southwestern country blues and folk forms, and his misreadings—or highly personal interpretations—of the theoretical texts." Since finding this musical voice in the late 1950s, Coleman has changed his basic improvisational style and compositional approach little.

While most jazz composers found commercial success and notoriety through performance, Coleman's first break came about because of his compositional skills. Members of Coleman's Los Angeles woodshedding group invited bassist and recording artist Red Mitchell to a rehearsal. Impressed with Coleman's tunes but not his playing, Mitchell arranged for Coleman to audition his tunes for Lester Koenig, owner of Contemporary Records. Koenig not only bought seven tunes for $25 each but asked Coleman to assemble a group and record them, resulting in the album *Something Else!* (1958). His next break came when members of the Modern Jazz Quartet, including pianist John Lewis, heard Coleman playing at a Los Angeles club. Lewis, who would describe Coleman as "doing the only really new thing in jazz since the innovation in the mid-forties of Gillespie, Parker, and Monk," helped bring Coleman to Atlantic Records for his third album, *The Shape of Jazz to Come*. With Atlantic's backing, Lewis sent Coleman and his trumpeter, Don Cherry, to the Lenox (Massachusetts) School of Jazz in 1959. The enthusiastic critical response that Coleman received on the East Coast led directly to his now famous engagement at the Five Spot Café, which ballooned from two weeks to two and a half months, polarized the jazz community, and precipitated his permanent move to New York.

Coleman's work demands a broader understanding of the term "composer." Chief among his compositional decisions is the formation and training of his ensembles. His 1987 recording *In All Languages* reveals the impact of such ensemble chemistry through contrasting performances by his original quartet with those of his Prime Time ensemble of seven musicians. Such side-by-side listening not only helps unravel the complex polyphony of the electric band but demonstrates the wide variance allowed within the compositional structure. Some pairs of recordings differ in length by as much as a third. Although Coleman's sporadic work history has made many of his ensembles short-lived, each new band propels Coleman's work into a new realization of his aesthetic. Out of his woodshedding group in Los Angeles, Coleman formed a quartet of

Cherry, bassist Charlie Haden, and drummer Billy Higgins. Successive versions of the quartet have included (in order of appearance): Ed[ward] Blackwell (drums), Scott La Faro (bass), Bobby Bradford (trumpet), Jimmy Garrison (bass), Charlie Moffett (drums), Ornette Denardo Coleman (drums), Dewey Redman (tenor saxophone), and Elvin Jones (drums). By the time of Coleman's self-financed Town Hall concert in 1962, he worked with only a trio, including Moffett and bassist David Izenzon.

While Coleman's creative activity has been continuous, his public performing and recording activities have been cyclic. In 1963 and 1964, Coleman withdrew from public performance, maintaining an active salon of avant-garde music in his home, Artists House, and teaching himself violin, trumpet, and guitar. By learning new instruments, Coleman escaped the clichés of his own alto saxophone-based virtuosity and sequential patternings as well as the pedagogical traditions of not only jazz but Western music altogether. His goal was to perform "without memory." In particular, Coleman's violin performances established a new gestural vocabulary of emotion. His raw instrumental sounds transformed the social dynamics of his ensembles: "When I play alto, I have control, but when I play trumpet or violin, it frees the group." His return to public performance at the Village Vanguard in 1965, using these new instruments, created a sensation, but Coleman has continued to perform in New York only on rare occasions. When Coleman left for a successful European tour in late 1965, he began a relationship with the European avant-garde jazz community that has continued to enjoy the majority of his public performances. In 1966, Coleman began recording with his son, Denardo, on drums. In the 1970s, Coleman found new inspiration in Moroccan music, rock, and pop. Beginning in 1975, his first recordings with a new electric band, Prime Time, exhibit nonstop improvising and a wealth of melodic creativity. More recent Prime Time recordings show increased group interplay among the two electric guitars, two electric basses, and two drummers who complement Coleman in the ensemble. Beginning in the 1980s, Coleman found additional inspiration by recording albums with prominent collaborators, including guitarist Pat Metheny (*Song X,* 1985), Grateful Dead guitarist Jerry Garcia (*Virgin Beauty,* 1988), and East German pianist Joachim Kühn (*Colors,* 1997). In the 1990s, he began working with pianists again after shunning the chordal instrument since the early 1960s.

Coleman has recorded for well over 30 different companies during his career, providing some indication of his tense and mutually suspicious relationship with the music industry. At odds with company officials over the balance between artistic integrity and commercial potential, he did not find a suitable contractual agreement until 1994, when Verve offered Coleman his own imprint, Harmolodic Records. Further improving his professional situation, his son, Denardo, who joined Prime Time around 1977, has increasingly taken over the management of Coleman's career. The 1990s therefore have witnessed a dramatic increase in Coleman's activities: performances, new recordings, and re-releases of earlier albums on compact disc. In July 1997, for example, New York's Lincoln Center featured Coleman in a week-long festival entitled "? Civilization" that included elaborate performances of the multimedia show *Tone Dialing,* and his symphony, *Skies of America.* The Web site of Harmolodic Records, www.harmolodic.com, contains information on Coleman's numerous activities as well as historical notes and even essays by Coleman himself.

HARMOLODIC THEORY (BEGUN CA. 1950) AND LONELY WOMAN (1959)

At the core of Coleman's music is his theory of Harmolodics. According to Coleman, in the absence of standard chord changes, Harmolodics addresses the question, "What do you play after you play the melody?" Like other 20th-century theories of composition, Harmolodics seeks to assure freedom of expression through a disciplined and structured system of artistic creation that undercuts convention. When Coleman invoked artistic freedom to release his music from a dependence on convention, Harmolodics filled the resultant void and gave order to his compositions. A synthesis of the terms *harmonic, movement,* and *melodic,* it has been explained by Coleman concisely as the phrase "all parts are equal."

First mentioned in Coleman's liner notes to his 1972 recording of *Skies of America,* the term "Harmolodics" or "Harmolodic theory" encompasses both the technical and the philosophical approach propelling Coleman's music making. The origins of this approach extend back at least to the 1950s during Coleman's period of self-study and exploration in Los Angeles. Like all of Coleman's theoretical vocabulary, Harmolodics reflects an unconventional, highly personal, even idiosyncratic reading of traditional terminology filtered through his musical philosophy. More praxis than rule, the term eludes precise definition and allows for flexible reinterpretation depending on its particular musical realization. The theory is not an immutable law but rather a tentative hypothesis or critical position that demands further questioning. Harmolodics contains an imperative for change, evidenced by Coleman's many works, varied influences, and ensemble formats. Even the identity of his work is in flux as successive renditions of Coleman's compositions differ in much more than just improvised content.

The continuous development, frequent accretions, and changing emphasis of the theory have led to several conflicting interpretations. Building on Coleman's explanations of the orchestral writing in *Skies of America,* some critics, such as Schuller, have associated Harmolodics with parallel iterations of melodic material in multiple transpositions or clefs that create a form of polymodal organum. Coleman's own 1983 article for *Down Beat* magazine, entitled "Prime Time for Harmolodics," failed to clarify his ideas precisely and led to the unfortunate and inaccurate association of the term exclusively with his electric band, Prime Time.

Harmolodic theory involves the balance and interplay primarily between melody, harmony, and rhythm, but also dynamics, speed, time, tempo, duration, form, phrase, instrumentation, and purpose. While bebop asserted a clear hierarchy of these musical parameters, Harmolodic theory disrupts their relationships. The bebop composer built a head melody that fit a pre-established chord pattern or set of harmonic "changes," usually within a 12-bar blues or 32-bar song form. Furthermore, bebop performance usually followed a standard format: introduction (optional), melody, solo choruses, recapitulation of the melody, and coda (optional), all grounded firmly within permutations of the harmonic and rhythmic pattern underlying the melody. For the bebop composer, form begets harmony, which begets melody, which begets improvisation. Coleman, in contrast, made rhythm, harmony, and melody "all equal," effectively raising the status of rhythm and especially melody from a derivative aspect of harmony to the level of parallel organizing principles. According to Coleman, "The pattern for the tune will be forgotten, and the tune itself will be the pattern."

Among his most influential works, "Lonely Woman" was, according to Coleman, the first fully Harmolodic composition he recorded. The work's disruption of bebop practice is evident immediately in the absence of a recurring solo-chorus structure. Coleman likewise inverts the rhythmic relationship between the faster subdivisions of a bebop melody and its slower, pulsing accompaniment. In "Lonely Woman," the melody floats in slow, lyric shapes, while the rhythm section flies at a blistering pace. A low *d* pedal point in the bass underlies much of the melody and suggests a stable pitch center. This center is neither tonal nor modal, however, as such a point of gravitational repose in a traditional scale is defined as much by the notes it excludes as those it includes. Coleman's melody excludes very little—each of the 12 chromatic pitches appears in the ensemble mix, and every pitch but *e*-flat appears in the melody itself. But *d* clearly lies at the core of Coleman's melody, as *c*-sharp resolves to *d* at the end of each 15-bar phrase.

Despite many critics' accusations, Harmolodic theory is not random, but studied, intentional, and tightly organized. Coleman's first pupil, trumpeter Don Cherry, described it as "a profound system based on developing your ears along with your technical proficiency." Critic Ekkehard Jost borrows the term "motivic chain association" from experimental psychology to capture a sense of the stream-of-consciousness practice of Harmolodics. Jost's analyses of Coleman's solos in transcription reveal the intricate relationships being explored between rhythm, melody (motive), and harmony. In these analyses, Jost posits a mutating stream of tonal centers akin to modal improvisation. In contrast to the static center of modal improvisation, however, Coleman's music flows from one modal space to the next, turning on the harmonic implications of the melody. Coleman's primary bassist, Charlie Haden, has described this approach as "a constant modulation." Yet Coleman does not feel the compulsion to affirm the transient pitch center of these modulations with cadential punctuation. His gestures are often cut short, modulating yet again, even before they have been fully realized.

Harmolodics does not ignore traditional harmonic practice. In fact, Coleman claims to have known he had found something only after he discovered that he could make mistakes. As Cherry has explained, "We have to know the chord structure perfectly, all the possible intervals, and then play around it. If I play a *c* and have it in my mind as the tonic, that's what it will become. If I want it to be a minor third or a major seventh that had a tendency to resolve upward, then the quality of the note will change." Cherry's remark helps explain Coleman's flexible approach to intonation as emotionally expressive. As a wind player, Coleman is not bound to the tempered scale of the piano keyboard. For him, intonation is not absolute but determined by harmonic context. Since Coleman's harmonic context is determined by thought and expression rather than cadence or accompaniment, Coleman can play sharp or flat "in tune."

Listening provides the key to Coleman's music. Coleman advises that the listener "follow the idea of melody and listen to the many different ways the idea can affect the melody." Of course, "melody" for Coleman encompasses an unusually broad, polyphonic sense of the word that can include bass lines, accompaniments, countermelodies, and so on, brought together in a single "unison" of emotional expression. As Cherry suggests above, Harmolodics is a performance strategy based on listening. Listening enables Coleman's ideal of "unison" or spontaneous "free group improvisation." "I realized," Coleman has said, "that if I changed the harmonic structure or the tempo structure while someone else is doing something, they couldn't stay there, they'd have to change with me."

While Harmolodics is ostensibly a technical term, in practice it becomes a philosophy. Coleman attempts to make all musical styles equal, dissolving the boundaries between jazz, folk, country, rock, pop, and classical musics. Coleman's Harmolodic ensembles are also remarkable for their consistent ability to bridge issues of race in America: not only does his music appeal to diverse audiences, but throughout his career both blacks and whites have been members of his bands. Coleman's recordings with the Joujouka musicians of Morocco crossed national, ethnic, and spiritual boundaries as well. Continuous change, the dissolution of category, and the disruption of hierarchy have become more than musical processes for Coleman. By adding the subtitle "A Harmolodic Life" to his critical biography, John Litweiler suggests that, for Coleman, Harmolodics is more than an inert technical procedure. The word has explicit philosophical and spiritual overtones. Coleman's essay "Harmolodic—Highest Instinct" (published on the World Wide Web) draws parallels between music and life: rhythm, for example, is described as "oxygen for the notes." Under sections entitled "Music for Humanity," "A Cornerstone for the World," and "The Highest Instinct," Coleman explains that his music attempts to escape categories of class, style, and time, as a model for society: "I think of my music as having some sort of healing quality, like religion or medicine. There's a lot of emotional love that's closer to religion in music. . . . Harmolodic is the best title to describe my music. . . . You can think Harmolodically."

FREE (1958)

Featured as the second cut on Coleman's 1959 recording for Atlantic entitled *Change of the Century,* "Free" is "well-explained by the title," according to Coleman: "Our *free* group improvising is well demonstrated here. Each member goes his own way and still adds tellingly to the group endeavor. There was no predetermined chordal or time pattern. I think we got a spontaneous, free-wheeling thing going here." Yet, this was not the first recording of the piece: "Free" was recorded as early as 1958 during Coleman's Hilcrest Club gig as a member of the Paul Bley Quintet. There is much in common between the two performances of "Free." These constants hint at the exact nature of Coleman's composition and help define the parameters of the work. The elements that change, on the other hand, presumably define the realm of "free group improvisation."

Possibly even more difficult to define than Harmolodics, Coleman's many-faceted use of the word *free* presents obstacles to the understanding of his music. For critics and historians who value innovation over tradition, *free* implies a welcome act of revolution. Preceded by albums with such grandiose marketing titles as *Something Else! Tomorrow Is the Question!* and *The Shape of Jazz to Come,* Coleman entered the New York City jazz scene as an unwitting invader—a revolutionary to be celebrated as a hero or vilified as a musical rogue. His supporters, such as critic Martin Williams, took Coleman's abstract theories as evidence of jazz having escaped its roots in the entertainment industry. For them, Coleman's approach was the intellectual equal to avant-garde classical music and thus assured jazz of a place in the canon of Western art. His detractors dismissed Coleman's version of freedom from chord changes as the misconceptions of a dilettante, hence the many accusations of poor technique and bad intonation. Intense competition also fueled animosity. By the 1960s, the New York jazz scene had already begun to shrink. The big bands of the swing era had all but disappeared, and jobs were increasingly difficult to find. A musical outsider wherever he went, and lacking the hard-earned credentials of an established sideman, Coleman was seen by many as a threat. If the "New Thing," as his music was labeled, took over, even more musicians would lose their livelihood. Others interpreted Coleman's cry for "freedom" in relation to the racial tensions characterizing the United States at this time. For LeRoi Jones (Imamu Amiri Baraka), the honks, moans, and raw emotionalism of Coleman's plastic saxophone derived from the down-home blues aesthetic of the rural South, lending credence to the existence of a powerful and nationalistic black cultural aesthetic.

Each of these interpretations is valid on certain levels. Lost, however, is Coleman's compositional ingenuity, building on the past innovations of bebop artists such as Charlie Parker while engineering a new focus on group interaction and musical discourse. Rather than a radical break, the two performances of "Free" reveal that Coleman did not divorce the jazz tradition; "Free" is not a rejection of the past but a reinterpretation of jazz reaching back to its roots in New Orleans. As Coleman states in the liner notes to the album *Change of the Century,* "the idea of group improvisation is not at all new; it played a big role in New Orleans' early bands." Likewise, the listener can still perceive in "Free" the vestiges of the bebop and modal jazz traditions that Coleman struggles to extend and develop.

Each performance of "Free" begins with an unconventional realization of a standard jazz device, the head melody. Structured in the traditional four-times-eight-bar AABA phrase structure of the 32-bar song form, Coleman's melody also takes advantage of a bebop tendency to improvise over the B section or bridge. Since each A section repeats the same undulating phrase, the precomposed melodic idea of "Free" totals a mere eight bars. Expanding from the developments of modal jazz, Coleman establishes a multivalent pitch center of *f* without specifying scale or chord. In "Free," the harmonic environment is just as subject to improvisational change as melody and rhythm. Unlike bebop and modal jazz, Coleman's free jazz contains no pre-established chord pattern. To emphasize this independence from harmonic structure, Coleman reduces or eliminates the keyboard part in his ensemble. The Paul Bley Quintet recording of "Free" includes Bley on piano, but as the idiomatic harmonic patterning of the piano would clash with Coleman's Harmolodic conception, Bley sits out for the majority of the piece, entering late in the work for a brief and primarily unaccompanied solo. By late 1959 and *Change of the Century,* Coleman had removed the piano from his group entirely, forming a unique quartet of alto saxophone, trumpet (Don Cherry), bass (Charlie Haden), and drums (Billy Higgins).

The second recording of "Free" represents a much more successful realization of Coleman's ideal of free group improvisation. In the Bley version, the Harmolodic ideal of equality among the voices is distorted by the conventional procession of solo voices with accompaniment. The head melody of the Bley version, for example, features a fast-paced saxophone/trumpet duet with subordinate bass and drums accompanying on the bridge. The second recording allows the bass and drums a greater melodic role—the pair lends punctuation throughout while taking over the bridge completely; the traditional roles of tune and accompaniment begin to break down, allowing the four instrumental voices to separate into independent melodies. While each player falls under the aural spotlight at some point, often the textures could be described as duets, trios, and quartets. Approaching Coleman's goal of a polyphonic "unison," the second version uses a greater variety of textures and tempos, thus communicating a broader range of emotional states. In the drum and bass duet over the bridge, for example, Higgins and Haden suddenly adopt a slow, nonmetrical sense of time in radical contrast to the virtuosic bebop pace of the A sections. For the remainder of the performance, each of the four musicians switches back and forth independently between rhythmic feelings: 4/4, 2/4, 1/1 and an atmospheric, nonmetrical feel. Some of Cherry's and Coleman's melodies are blistering and angular, while others are languid and sonorous. Incorporating time, rhythm (beat and tempo), and speed, Coleman's "three-dimensional" understanding of rhythm gives his performance a fluidity of expression that escapes representation in the simple mathematical denominators of Western notation. His solo centers predominantly on *f* with frequent departures as he cycles through a series of motivic shapes that often reflect but never quote the head melody verbatim. Higgins and Haden perform both driving percussion lines and soloistic melodic gestures.

FREE JAZZ (1960)

On December 21, 1960, Coleman recorded a landmark composition that would have a profound effect on the avant-garde and lend its name to an entire movement within improvisational music. In many ways, *Free Jazz* is simply an extension of the conversational group aesthetic established by the work of Coleman's quartet, but the raw experimental nature of this octet/double quartet performance was new. Rather than an extension of the nightclub, Atlantic's recording studio became a laboratory in which the results of Coleman's structural manipulations could be preserved on tape. The experiment could be experienced and analyzed by listeners only after the album was pressed. *Free Jazz* helps mark a fundamental shift in jazz economics from nightly club dates to recording sessions and festival events.

As a composer, Coleman's role has often been that of a teacher, communicating his ideas to other musicians and training them to realize these ideas in performance. Despite a willingness to experiment among his players, overcoming years of training and experience to explore the New Thing presented real challenges. To combat these habituated musical responses, Coleman frequently manipulates the social and textural parameters of his ensembles in order to place his musicians into unfamiliar territory. These new sonic environments allow for new musical solutions. Eliminating the piano from his quartet was one such attempt to create space for new ideas; forming an improvisational octet was another. By doubling the size of his ensemble, literally using two quartets instead of one, Coleman released his performers from their traditional roles. Certainly, Charlie Haden and Scott La Faro knew how to function as the bassist in a jazz combo, but what role did an improvisational bassist play as one of two bass players within a jazz octet? The answer to this question permitted new sounds to emerge. For *Free Jazz,* Coleman engaged two bassists, two trumpeters (Don Cherry and Freddie Hubbard), and two drummers (Billy Higgins and Ed Blackwell), and mirrored his own role with avant-garde rival Eric Dolphy. Dolphy played several wind instruments but selected bass clarinet for the *Free Jazz* session. Coleman organized his players into two groups with himself, Cherry, La Faro, and Higgins recording on the left stereo channel and Dolphy, Hubbard, Haden, and Blackwell on the right. With the exception of Dolphy and Hubbard, each of these musicians had played or was currently playing with Coleman's quartet.

The first take resulted in a 17-minute performance, while the second produced the 37-minute album *Free Jazz* released in 1961. The album was not edited, spliced, or manipulated in any way, except for an awkward studio fade that facilitated the need to flip the album. Recent compact disc versions have eliminated the fade and reunited *Free Jazz* with its "First Take." The similarities between the takes reveal the core of Coleman's composition. Both takes alternate between predetermined "composed" material and group improvisation. The preset material takes three basic forms: frenetic running scales, sustained chords or chorales, and unison melody. While the pitches and voicings of the chorales and melodies seem predetermined, their pacing is not. The runs communicate an emotional state, yet the pitches themselves are improvised. Each short segment of composed material introduces a soloist who leads the group's improvisation. The order of soloists remains the same for both takes: Dolphy, Hubbard, Coleman, Cherry, Haden, La Faro, Blackwell, and Higgins. Coleman appears to lead or cue the arrival of the composed sections. While their order is set, their timing and duration are not. This flexible deployment of composed material became a fundamental technique in free jazz and avant-garde music. The extended melody introducing Coleman's solo appears to be the overall theme of the composition as reflections of this tune appear in many of the wind passages, especially those of Dolphy and Coleman. The melody's five asymmetrical phrases contain a wealth of motivic material for Harmolodic development.

Both takes begin with an outburst of free runs and chaotic virtuosity resolving into sustained chords that fade into Dolphy's solo. Like all of the set passages in *Free Jazz,* the opening does not aspire to a uniform or clean presentation but introduces each of the collective instrumental timbres and launches the work with driving intensity. Dolphy's solo sets up an aggressive, extroverted persona;

as Coleman later commented, he sounds "as if he was playing all the instruments behind him." Like each of the soloists, Dolphy sometimes slips into bebop phrasing. His first-take solo is ecstatic and full of virtuosic runs, while his second take begins as an extension of the opening chorale. As Dolphy solos, the three remaining wind players join in, comment, and exit. Generally speaking, the second version evidences both a greater variety of time and texture as well as a more successful integration of the ensemble into a single unit. The first take, however, exhibits many of the most exciting solo passages. One change between the two versions is the greater dynamic range of the second performance. Despite its improvisational core, *Free Jazz* was certainly rehearsed.

Each musician performs not as an independent solo voice but as a member of the ensemble. Several fundamental musical strategies enable this group interaction, including repetition, variation, and quotation. Dolphy and Hubbard, for example, frequently set up repeating ostinato accompaniments that threaten to dominate the soloist. Coleman and Cherry build chains of motivic variations and relations. Cherry's "solo," in particular, often takes the form of a duet with Coleman. One of the clearest exchanges of motivic material occurs between the bassists: Haden closes his solo with a descending set of strummed harmonics, and La Faro quotes this gesture to begin his solo.

In many ways, the simplified textures and nonpitched effects make the last four solos of *Free Jazz* the most accessible to the listener. Haden's solo is a complete composition unto itself, with its own thematic cohesion and dramatic trajectory. Higgins' and Blackwell's supporting cymbal work seems perfectly attuned to the Eastern-inspired sound of Haden's solo effort. Yet these rhythm section instrumentalists seem most prone to falling back on jazz convention: La Faro's virtuosity is remarkable, but he refuses to discard chord changes. Haden's accompaniment to the blues-based harmonies of La Faro's solo takes on an ironic hue, as does the swing pattern that Blackwell uses to accompany Higgins. The rhythm players seem to accept the composer's invitation to "play" with aspects of the jazz tradition.

Free Jazz delivered unprecedented challenges to its listeners, yet it offered unusually rich rewards. Repeated listenings present new perspectives and new insights into Coleman's work. The reproduction of Jackson Pollock's "White Light" on the album cover of *Free Jazz* presents an appropriate visual metaphor, and indeed, Coleman himself compares his music to the abstract expressionist's paintings: "There is a continuity of expression, certain continually evolving strands of thought that link all my compositions together."

Not surprisingly, critical response to *Free Jazz* was split into groups of supporters and detractors. In January 1962, two *Down Beat* magazine reviewers wrote opposing evaluations: Pete Welding gave the work five out of five stars, while John A. Tynan gave it a rare zero, saying, "If nothing else, this witch's brew is the logical end product of a bankrupt philosophy of ultraindividualism. . . . 'Collective improvisation—' Nonsense." Writing with 30 years of hindsight, another *Down Beat* critic, Bill Shoemaker, observes, "It is precisely that *Free Jazz* was created, not spewed out by rote, that it was a musical proposition so overtly grappled with, and played with, by the musicians, that it lives, and not merely endures as history."

SKIES OF AMERICA (1972)

Ornette Coleman generally has refrained from making overt political statements about his music, letting his performances speak for themselves. His music communicates powerful emotional states but refrains from pictorial representation or narrative. One exception to this rule, however, is his symphony *Skies of America,* which uses ominous meteorological images to comment on discrimination and inequality in the United States. Coleman's inspiration for the work came from his own experiences with racial injustice:

> I grew up in Texas, in the South, where there was lots of discrimination, lots of problems for minorities. Sometimes the sun is shining and beautiful on one side of the street, and across the street, just maybe three feet apart, there'd be big balls of hail and thunderstorms, and that reminded me of something that happened with people. In America you see them all enjoying themselves and next moment they're all fighting. They're the same way as the elements. When I titled that piece, it was to let me see if I could describe the beauty, and not have it be racial or any territory. In other words, the sky has no territory; only the land has territory. I was trying to describe something that has no territory.

Coleman's musical vision responds not only to his personal experience as an African American but to the barriers that impede many groups in the United States. Another source of this musical imagination in *Skies* was a night Coleman spent on a Crow Indian reservation in Montana:

> I participated in their sacred rites, and it made me think about the many different elements existing in America, in relation to its causes, purpose and destiny. For some reason, I got that feeling from the sky. I feel that everything that has ever happened in America, from way before the Europeans arrived, is still intact as far as the sky is concerned.

Whether because of its discomforting social commentary or its unusual combination of style and instrumentation (a jazz ensemble with a symphony orchestra), *Skies of America* has suffered through a checkered performance and recording history that has prevented Coleman from fully realizing his compositional idea.

With recording time limited by budgetary constraints, Coleman was forced to trim the Columbia recording of *Skies of America* with the London Philharmonic Orchestra down to 41 and a half minutes in length. Its American premiere, on July 4, 1972, less than two months after the recording session, lasted nearly 54 minutes. A 1983 performance in Coleman's hometown of Fort Worth, Texas, stretched to an hour and a half. Further distorting the recording, the rules of Britain's music union prevented Coleman's quartet from performing; only Coleman himself plays on the recording. According to Litweiler, Columbia Records failed to support Coleman's project but used the artist for the prestige his name added to their roster. Rather than release Coleman's symphony on their classical label, Columbia released it through their jazz division. Adding insult to injury, Columbia arbitrarily divided the album into 21 short bands with impressionistic titles, ostensibly to encourage radio play. Coleman, who has spoken out against the commercialism of the music industry throughout his career, had a different explanation: "Basically, they were trying to keep it from having the image of a symphony. I realize now that it was another social-racial problem."

The performance history of *Skies of America* only reinforces the urgency of its vision—a social world without boundaries or categories. To break down these boundaries, Coleman depends on the equalizing force of his Harmolodic theory. He also turns to another favorite technique, introducing a coloristic twist in instrumentation. *Skies of America* violates one of the most time-honored boundaries in Western culture by combining classical music's most prestigious ensemble, the symphony orchestra, with a jazz band. By mixing these ensembles, Coleman attacks the boundary between literate and oral musics—the divide between printed notation and improvisation. Coleman solos over approximately one-half of the composition as the orchestra takes on the symbiotic role of his quartet. The orchestral musicians are also invited to make improvisational decisions during performance, regarding the octaves in which to realize their notated passages.

The sound of *Skies of America* provides the best working definition of Harmolodic theory. Rather than a philosophy in progress, the piece demonstrates that Coleman's Harmolodic concept was fully formed by 1972. Although the symphony is organized into coordinated sections, the independent tempi of the voices (especially timpani and drums) and the layered, polyphonic melodies demonstrate Coleman's principle of musical equality. Rather than instruct the orchestra players in the precepts of free improvisation, Coleman uses a notational device both to preserve the melody as the generative compositional resource and to escape the confines of traditional harmony. By writing identical melodies into each of the player's scores regardless of the transposition or clef of the instrument being played, Coleman creates a radical "unison" in which the shape and rhythm of the melody is preserved while its modal identity is skewed. A brief dance-like canon of Part I, band 3, "The Good Life," reveals this technique in action: first the strings state the melody, then the winds, and finally the brasses. As each section enters and states the same tune in conflicting transpositions, the number and complexity of modal flavors multiplies, creating what Gary Giddins calls "a fresh harmonic approach that had both the density of clusters and the spaciousness of multiple keys." This compact, yet expansive writing creates a mass of atmospheric sound that fits Coleman's sonic imagery well: "I wanted the sound of the orchestra to create a very clear earth and sky sound as much as the feeling of night, stars and daylight." Unlike Coleman's capricious jazz quartet themes, the image melodies of *Skies of America* form enormous tapestries of unbroken sound, while the asymmetric patterns of rising and falling intervals provides a sense of momentum and emotional drama.

The two parts of the symphony are structural inverses of one another. While Coleman refrains from improvisation until the very end of Part I, he solos during all of Part II except the very end. Harmolodic sonorities are used throughout the symphony and help form a cohesive whole. The dramatic thrust of the work gives Part II a much wider variety of polyphonic textures: the final section of Part II includes, for example, as many as seven simultaneous and independent voices, while Coleman's unaccompanied alto saxophone is the only voice on band 17, "The Man Who Lived in the White House." In contrast to the congested polymodal harmony of the orchestral sections, Coleman's unaccompanied solo sounds almost reactionary. Despite the freely improvised character of the timpani and the jazz-inspired patterns of the drum set, the Columbia recording fails to truly integrate the jazz and classical idioms. A performance of the work with Coleman's full quartet or Prime Time ensemble would overcome many of the problems of blend and balance to produce a richer synthesis.

The critical reception of *Skies of America* has been mixed; some jazz critics consider it Coleman's masterpiece in the classical genre, while others, particularly classical critics, are suspicious of the work's heterophonous disunity and self-indulgent grandeur. Writing of the 1997 Lincoln Center performance by the New York Philharmonic and the Prime Time septet, *New York Times* critic Bernard Holland suggests that this piece is an apt metaphor for America: "Loud and garish, teeming with complexity yet unashamedly naive, alternately exciting and boring, [it] overloads the senses and goes on too long. . . . More negotiating table than melting pot. Every faction longed for communication . . . the irreconcilable differences in cultures, styles, traditions, procedures, not to mention sound colors, meter and rhythm, described the character of *Skies of America*. But maybe benign disunity is what Mr. Coleman had in mind." In his book *All American Music,* John Rockwell offers a more sympathetic assessment: "There are, certainly, moments of naïveté and clumsiness in the conception, arrangement and execution of this fresco. But the overall impact is Ivesian in scope and in spirit, too. Very few first efforts are so powerful as this."

REFERENCES

Blumenfeld, Larry. "Verve to Imprint Harmolodics." *Down Beat* 61 (October 1994): 11.

Coleman, Ornette. "Harmolodic—Highest Instinct: Something to Think About." Available from www.harmolodic.com/thinkabout.html; cited April 21, 1997.

———. Liner notes, *Change of the Century.* Atlantic 81341.

———. Liner notes, *Naked Lunch.* Milan 73138 35614–2.

———. Liner notes, *Skies of America.* Columbia 31061.

———. "Prime Time for Harmolodics." *Down Beat* 50 (July 1983): 54–55.

Giddins, Gary. "Harmolodic Hoedown." In *Rhythm-a-ning: Jazz Tradition and Innovation in the '80s,* 235–249. New York: Oxford University Press, 1985.

———. "Ornette Coleman, Continued." In *Riding on a Blue Note: Jazz and American Pop,* 179–189. New York: Oxford University Press, 1981.

Haden, Charlie, John McDonough, and John Litweiler. "Pro and Con: Thirty Years of Free." *Down Beat* 59 (January 1992): 29–31.

Hartman, Charles O. "Ornette Coleman: The Shapes of Jazz." In *Jazz Text: Voice and Improvisation in Poetry, Jazz, and Song,* 57–74. Princeton, N.J.: Princeton University Press, 1991.

Holland, Bernard. "Sharing a Gig of Benign Collisions." *New York Times* (July 10, 1997): B1, B4.

Jones, LeRoi [Imamu Amiri Baraka]. *Black Music.* New York: William Morrow, 1967.

———. *Blues People.* New York: William Morrow, 1963.

Jost, Ekkehard. *Free Jazz.* Graz, Austria: Universal Edition, 1974.

Litweiler, John. "Ornette Coleman: The Birth of Freedom." In *The Freedom Principle: Jazz after 1958,* 31–58. New York: William Morrow, 1984.

———. *Ornette Coleman: A Harmolodic Life.* New York: William Morrow, 1992.

Palmer, Robert. Liner notes, *Ornette Coleman, Beauty Is a Rare Thing: The Complete Atlantic Recordings,* Rhino R2 71410.

Rockwell, John. "Free Jazz, Body Music, and Symphonic Dreams." In *All American Music: Composition in the Late Twentieth Century,* 185–197. New York: Knopf, 1983.

Schuller, Gunther. "Coleman, Ornette." In *New Grove Dictionary of Jazz,* vol. 1, edited by Barry Kernfeld, 229–231. New York: St. Martin's Press, 1994.

Shoemaker, Bill. "Free Jazz." *Down Beat* 56 (September 1989): 72, 74.

Spellman, A. B. "Genesis of the New Music—III: Ornette Coleman," *Evergreen Review* no. 47 (June 1967): 78–80.

Tynan, John A. "Free Jazz." *Down Beat* 56 (September 1989): 72.

Williams, Martin. Liner notes, *The Shape of Jazz to Come.* Atlantic 1317.

———. "Ornette Coleman: Innovation from the Source." In *The Jazz Tradition,* 235–248. 2nd rev. ed. New York: Oxford University Press, 1993.

MARK CLAGUE

COLERIDGE-TAYLOR, AVRIL

Born as Gwendolen Coleridge-Taylor in South Norwood, England, March 8, 1903; died in East Sussex, England, December 21, 1998; a.k.a. Peter Riley. **Education:** Trinity College of Music, London, studied piano with Agnes Winter, voice with Norman Notley, orchestration and composition with Gordon Jacob and Alec Rowley, 1916–19; studied conducting under Ernest Read, 1931, also with Sir Henry Wood, and Albert Coates. **Composing and Performing Career:** Wrote first composition at age 12; performed recitals with her brother, Hiawatha, and with flutist Joseph Slater, ca.1916–19; Royal Albert Hall, London, formal debut as conductor, 1933; London, founded the Coleridge-Taylor Musical Society and Choir, 1945, and the Coleridge-Taylor Symphony Orchestra, 1946–51; South Africa, conducted two concerts with the South African Broadcast Corporation orchestra, and appeared in recitals, lectures and concerts of the municipal orchestras of Cape Town and Durban, 1952–57; guest conductor, BBC Symphony Orchestra, London Symphony Orchestra; founder and conductor of the Malcolm Sargent Symphony Orchestra, 1971; musical director and conductor for T. C. Fairbairn's production of *Hiawatha* and his ballet *The Fire Spirits,* 1946–50; wrote the "Ceremonial March" marking the independence of Ghana, 1957. **Honors/Awards:** won scholarship to study composition and piano at Trinity College of Music, 1915.

MUSIC LIST

INSTRUMENTAL SOLOS
Violin
Romance. 1945; revised 1964. Unpublished manuscript.

Flute
"Crépuscule d'une nuit d'été." Unpublished manuscript.
"Idylle," op. 21. 1921. London: Rudall, Carte, 1923.
"Impromptu in A Minor (Romance de Pan)," op. 33. 1922. Unpublished manuscript.
"A Lament," op. 31. Unpublished manuscript.

Piano
"Caprice." 1931; revised 1978. Unpublished manuscript.
My Garden. Unpublished manuscript. Contents: Evening Song; The Weeping Flower; The Garden Pool; All Lovely Things.
"Nocturne" (piano or harpsichord). 1978. Amersham, Bucks, England: Halstan, 1978.
"Pastorale." 1949. Unpublished manuscript. Note: inscribed "Avril Coleridge-Taylor for Peter Riley."
"Rhapsody for Pianoforte: Per Adua ed Astra," op. 174. ca. 1943. Unpublished manuscript.
"Traümerei." 1978. Unpublished manuscript.

STRING ORCHESTRA
Pastoral Suite. Unpublished manuscript. Note: inscribed "Peter Riley and Avril Coleridge-Taylor."

CHAMBER ORCHESTRA
All Lovely Things. 1964. Unpublished manuscript.

FULL ORCHESTRA
Ceremonial March. 1957. Unpublished manuscript. Commissioned for Ghana's Independence Celebration, 1957.
Comet Prelude. 1952. Unpublished manuscript.
Danse Extatique. Unpublished manuscript.
From the Hills. 1935. Unpublished manuscript.
In Memoriam, op. 176. 1945. Unpublished manuscript. Note: Largo movement also arranged for piano.
Spring Magic. Unpublished manuscript.
Sussex Landscape, op. 27. 1940. Unpublished manuscript. Also arranged for piano.
To April. 1931. Unpublished manuscript. Premiere, 1931.
Valse Caprice. Unpublished manuscript. Note: radio broadcast, ca. 1937.

ORCHESTRA (CHAMBER OR FULL) WITH SOLOISTS
Concerto in F Minor for Piano and Orchestra. 1936; revised 1970, 1973. Unpublished manuscript. Premiere, 1943.

ORCHESTRA (CHAMBER OR FULL) WITH CHORUS
Historical Episode (Symphonic Impression), op. 29 (SATB, boy soprano, solo piano, orchestra). 1942. Unpublished manuscript.
Wyndore (wordless SATB, piano or orchestra). 1936. London: J. and W. Chester, 1936. Premiere, 1937.

SOLO VOICE
"The Apple Tree." 1923. Unpublished manuscript.
"April," op. 5 (38). London: Edwin Ashdown, 1924.
"The Butterfly." Unpublished manuscript.
"Can Sorrow Find Me?" London: Cary, 1938.
"The Entranced Hour," op. 8 (37). London: Edwin Ashdown, 1923.
"Green Is My Garden." 1941. Unpublished manuscript.
"I Can Face It, Lord." 1971. Unpublished manuscript.
"I Heard a Blackbird Singing." 1950. Unpublished manuscript.
"In This Quiet Hour." 1937. Unpublished manuscript.
"It Was the Lovely Moon." 1936. Unpublished manuscript.
"Love's Philosophy" (tenor/soprano). 1936. Unpublished manuscript.
"The Monkey Puzzle." 1931. Unpublished manuscript.
"Nightfall," op. 43. 1922. Unpublished manuscript.
"Regret." 1939. Unpublished manuscript.
"The Rustling Grass," op. 32. London: Edwin Ashdown, 1923.
"The Sea" (baritone). 1923. Unpublished manuscript.
"Sleeping and Waking," op. 45. 1922. New York: Galaxy, 1939.
"A Spring Song." 1930. Unpublished manuscript.
"Twilight." 1936. Unpublished manuscript.
"Where'er My Bitter Teardrops Fall." 1924. Unpublished manuscript.
"Winds." 1933. Unpublished manuscript.

VOICE WITH INSTRUMENTAL ENSEMBLE
God's Remembrance (soprano, harp, violin, viola, cello). 1970. Unpublished manuscript.

VOCAL DUET OR TRIO

"O'er All the Hill-Tops." London: Augener, 1957.

CHORAL MUSIC

"All Is Beauty" (2 parts, female voices). London, Augener, 1951.

"A Child's Song" (unison). London: Ascherberg, Hopwood and Crew, 1948.

The Green Pastures (TTBB, optional piano accompaniment). 1956. Unpublished manuscript. Contents: De Blin' Man Stood on de Road an' Cried; My Lord's A'Writin' All de Time; You Better Min'; Joshua; Rise an' Shine.

"Star of Ghana" (unison with piano). London: Keith Prowse, 1959.

"Through the Sunny Garden" (2 parts, female voices). London: Adam and Charles Black, 1949.

DRAMATIC MUSIC

The Golden Wedding (ballet). Unpublished manuscript.

AS GWENDOLEN COLERIDGE-TAYLOR

"Apple Blossom," op. 44 (solo voice). 1922. Unpublished manuscript.

"The Dreaming Water Lily," op. 56 (solo voice). London: Edwin Ashdown, 1930.

"Goodbye Butterfly," op. 1 (solo voice). London: Augener, 1917.

"Mister Sun," op. 2 (solo voice). London: Ascherberg, Hopwood and Crew, 1921.

"Reverie," op. 26 (solo voice) 1921. Unpublished manuscript.

"Silver Stars," op. 3 (solo voice). London: Ascherberg, Hopwood and Crew, 1924.

"Who Knows?" op. 4 (solo voice). London: Ascherberg, Hopwood and Crew, 1922. Also arranged for voice and orchestra.

AS PETER RILEY

"Concert Etude" (piano). ca. 1948. Unpublished manuscript.

Fantasie (violin, piano). 1949. Unpublished manuscript.

"Fantasie Pastorale" (flute). 1933. Unpublished manuscript.

Just As the Tide Was Flowing (piano). 1948. Unpublished manuscript. Contents: Berceuse; Nocturne.

Meditations I and II (piano). Unpublished manuscript. Contents: Lento; Andante tranquillo.

The Peace Pipe (bass/baritone solo, chorus, orchestra). 1949. Unpublished manuscript.

"The Shepherd" (vocal solo or duet). 1948. Unpublished manuscript.

"Tears, Idle Tears" (solo voice). 1952. Unpublished manuscript.

Two Short Pieces for Piano. Unpublished manuscript. Contents: Allegro; Lento.

NOT VERIFIED

"Cradle Song" (solo voice); "Impromptu," op. 9 (piano); "In September" (vocal duet or trio); "Interlude" (piano); *The Snow Goose Suite* (full orchestra); *Suite romantique* (full orchestra); "Threnody," (piano).

PUBLICATIONS

BY COLERIDGE-TAYLOR

The Heritage of Samuel Coleridge-Taylor. London: Dobson Books, 1979.

"The Music of Coleridge-Taylor." *Sound* (April 1947).

"My Father and His Music." *Fanfare* (1948).

"Samuel Coleridge-Taylor." *Music and Musicians* (August 1975): 6–7.

PRINCIPAL ARCHIVES

Boosey and Hawkes Hire Library, London, England.

* * * * *

Avril Coleridge-Taylor, the daughter of the Anglo-African composer Samuel Coleridge-Taylor, is the composer of more than 80 works. The London firm of Boosey & Hawkes is the primary repository for her output, which includes pieces for violin, flute, piano, voice, and orchestras of various configurations. During her career of four decades (1931–60s), she stands out as one of the few active women composers.

Avril Coleridge-Taylor, born in South Norwood in 1903, was given the name Gwendolen at birth. Her early musical talent was nurtured by a close relationship with her father, the composer Samuel Coleridge-Taylor, whose tragic and untimely death when Gwendolen was nine years of age robbed her not only of a loving father but also of an invaluable mentor. An obituary in the *Penge and Anerley News* on September 7, 1912, noted: "The composer's little daughter had learnt one of the Fairy Ballads, 'Big Baby Moon,' and she sang it for me, with her father accompanying at the piano. But then father and daughter were such chums, and the two often sang together the themes of new works as they were evolved."

The sudden death of Samuel Coleridge-Taylor left the family unprovided for, perhaps accounting for the brevity of Gwendolen's formal musical education. At age 12, after a short time at the Guildhall School of Music, she wrote her first composition and won a scholarship to Trinity College of Music. She attended Trinity from 1916 to 1919, studying piano with Agnes Winter, voice with Norman Notley, and composition with Gordon Jacob and Alec Rowley. During these years, she collaborated with her brother Hiawatha in performances of works composed by her father. She also performed in recitals with flutist Joseph Slater, a collaboration that inspired the *Idylle,* op. 21, and *Impromptu in A Minor (Romance de Pan)* for flute and piano. Other works from these years include songs for voice and piano written in a popular style, a genre in which she continued to write throughout her career. Her last song, *I Love All Beauteous Things,* dates from 1975.

Gwendolen Coleridge-Taylor was married in 1924 and divorced about 1929 or 1930. Seeking new direction and purpose, Coleridge-Taylor changed her name to Avril and began working on her first orchestral work, *To April,* which was performed in the summer of 1931. This event marked her first public appearance as a conductor and prompted her to study conducting under the guidance of Ernest Read, Sir Henry Wood, and Albert Coates. Her formal debut as a conductor took place in Royal Albert Hall, London, in 1933, after which she frequently appeared in the dual role of conductor and composer, performing her own compositions along with those of her father. She premiered her *Wyndore,* for wordless chorus and orchestra (1936), with the Birkenhead Philharmonic Society on February 16, 1937. According to the com-

Avril Coleridge-Taylor; courtesy of Daniel Labonne (artistic director, Samuel Coleridge-Taylor Society) and Nigel Dashwood; photo by Alexander Hedderwick

poser's notes, *Wyndore* was performed subsequently by the Crystal Palace Choral and Orchestral Society in 1938 and in Boston in 1939, 1948, and 1953.

During the 1940s, Coleridge-Taylor married Bruce Somes Charlton and together they founded the Coleridge-Taylor Musical Society, which incorporated the Coleridge-Taylor Symphony Orchestra. Later, the name of the society was changed to the New Era Concert Society, and financial difficulties eventually caused its dissolution. Her second marriage also ended in divorce.

During this same period, Avril Coleridge-Taylor adopted the pseudonym Peter Riley, under which name the following works, among others, appeared: "Concert Etude" (piano), "Pastorale" (piano), *Two Short Pieces for Piano, Just As the Tide Was Flowing* (piano), "Fantasie Pastorale" (flute and piano), "Fantasie" (violin and piano), *The Peace-Pipe* (baritone solo, chorus, and orchestra, with text from Longfellow's "Hiawatha"), and the *Pastorale Suite* (string orchestra). From 1946 to 1950, Coleridge-Taylor served as musical director of T. C. Fairbairn's productions of Samuel Coleridge-Taylor's *Hiawatha*. Her *The Peace-Pipe* (1949), one of three additional scenes for *Hiawatha*, was commissioned by Fairbairn for use in a dramatic production.

In 1952, Coleridge-Taylor traveled to South Africa and conducted two concerts with the South African Broadcasting Corp. orchestra, featuring works by various composers and her own Piano Concerto in F Minor. She remained in South Africa five years, giving recitals and lectures and participating in concerts given by the municipal orchestras of Cape Town and Durban. Her *Ceremonial March,* composed to celebrate the independence of Ghana on March 6, 1957, was performed during the January 10, 1957, visit of England's Prime Minister, Harold MacMillan.

In the years following her return to England, Coleridge-Taylor served as guest conductor of the BBC Orchestra and of various London and provincial orchestras and choral societies; organized and conducted in an annual music festival in Sussex during the years 1964–66; and founded in 1971 the Malcolm Sargent Symphony Orchestra. Compositions from the period 1964–1978 include *In Memoriam* for orchestra (1967), *God's Remembrance* for voice and chamber ensemble (1970), "Sussex Landscape" (1964) and "Träumerei" for piano (1978), and "Nocturne" for harpsichord (1978).

Several of Coleridge-Taylor's compositions were inspired by her personal experiences or by historical events: *To April* received its impetus in the aftermath of her first divorce, although it is not autobiographical and represents no specific events; *Historical Episode* was inspired by General MacArthur's campaign in the Philippines; and *Wyndore* and *Sussex Landscape,* which feature folk-like pentatonic melodies, modal-sounding harmonies, use of seventh and ninth chords, and compound meters, by the English countryside. Coleridge-Taylor's fondness for juxtaposing colorful, nonrelated harmonies is evident in some of her earliest works (such as the "Reverie" for cello and piano) and continues into later works such as *God's Remembrance,* where abrupt harmonic changes mark important structural points in the piece. Her melodies are often constructed of small melodic units developed from single motives; this technique yields works based on related themes or in which later themes grow out of earlier ones.

Coleridge-Taylor is the author of one book, *The Heritage of Samuel Coleridge-Taylor,* which is a valuable source of information about her father and herself. She has also contributed writings to various journals and news publications.

REVERIE, OP. 26 (1921)

The "Reverie" for cello and piano exists only in manuscript, and the circumstances that inspired its composition are unknown. The work consists of a light-spirited, song-like melody for the cello enhanced by a simple piano accompaniment, gently rhythmic and somewhat accented on the second beat of each measure. It is a three-part form (ABA) with a coda; the outer sections are in triple meter, while the middle section changes to duple mater.

In this early work, Avril Coleridge-Taylor already displayed the fondness for chromatic, unstable harmony within a tonal idiom that would be evident in her later works. Unexpected harmonic turns aided by an imaginative use of irregular or melodic phrases of different lengths give the music a mercurial, or searching, quality characteristic of reverie or daydreaming. By contrast, the melodies themselves are tightly constructed from several short melodic fragments, or motives. The resulting web of inner motivic relationships (like internal rhyme in lines of poetry) draws the melodic phrases together, imposing order upon the unpredictable harmony and irregular phrasing and betraying an underlying seriousness of purpose.

After a calmly lyrical beginning in G major, the music begins striving toward two different keys (E minor or D major), but it never reaches either key. In the last phrase, which acts as something of a harmonic climax, the initial chord (V/V) that seems headed for a new key (D major) is diverted by means of unexpectedly chromatic harmonies to an equally unexpected pitch level (the dominant of A minor).

The second section, *Poco agitato,* is divided into two subsections, each in different keys; in the last subsection, the expected harmonic goal fails to materialize. The music trails off distractedly and dwindles to a halt on a single whole note played by the piano. Another whole note follows, but it is not clearly legible and cannot be identified with certainty. The music of the first section returns with no further preparation.

CONCERTO IN F MINOR FOR PIANO AND ORCHESTRA (1936)

The Concerto in F Minor is in three movements, *Allegro maestoso, Adagio,* and *Allegro deciso,* with the second and third dedicated respectively to the memories of Edward Elgar and Samuel Coleridge-Taylor.

In a program note, critic Russell Palmer observed that owing to the equality of the piano and orchestra, the work is more aptly described as a symphony in which the piano is integral to the structure rather than as a concerto in which the piano figures in a starring role.

The first movement contains some of the features of sonata form, including an opening motive in F minor, two lyrical themes in contrasting keys, a middle section that occupies itself with motives from the first of those themes, a recapitulation of the opening motive and the first of the two themes, and a cadenza followed by an ending section or coda.

On the other hand, the composer's use of tonality makes this movement a very free form, and this freedom is evident from the very first notes. The opening motive begins, not solidly in F minor, as one would expect, but with a dramatically unstable effect produced by an E-flat minor triad figure in the horns against a tremolo *f* in the timpani. The piano, entering with a flourish of octaves, takes up the final portion of the orchestral figure and directs the tonality to the home key of F minor (m. 16). Two major themes form the substance of the movement, but neither is in the home key of F minor. The first theme (in D-flat major) is first stated by the piano (m. 19), then loudly and grandly by the strings and woodwinds with the piano contributing an exultant, thickly chordal accompaniment (m. 38). The second theme in A-flat major is begun by the orchestra (m. 50) and then assumed by the piano. This theme does not receive the same elaborate treatment as the first, and it is not restated in the recapitulation.

Coleridge-Taylor's unusual and free use of key is most conspicuous where it blurs the boundary between the first and second large sections (exposition and development). Ordinarily, development sections are sizable enough to balance the exposition and recapitulation sections, and they avoid the keys of the exposition. However, the rather lengthy passage following the second theme (mm. 65–88) remains close to A-flat, D-flat, and F minor—the keys of the exposition. The tonal shift to C-sharp minor (m. 88) is not so radical as it first appears, since it is really the parallel minor of D-flat, the key of the first theme; and it occurs so late in the proceedings that a development section beginning here would be too short to balance the outer sections, comprising only the 31 measures remaining before the beginning of the recapitulation (m. 129). Another noteworthy feature of this section is the introduction of a new theme (m. 106), which brings about the return to F minor.

The recapitulation begins with the same motive that opened the movement, followed by the first theme in its grandiose form. A short unmeasured cadenza (m. 170) contains much pianistic figuration but no thematic material. The coda uses the new melodic material introduced near the end of the development. A strong cadential gesture (m. 197) momentarily establishes a new key in which a derivation of the first theme appears (derived from m. 22) and then returns to F minor for the final cadence.

The *Adagio* movement is an ABA form with a lyrical main melody in F minor that begins with a three-note upbeat. The middle section features inversions of motives from the melody of the A section. Just before the reappearance of the A section, the main theme from the first movement appears in the oboe part. This theme, now taken up by the piano, is combined with the second movement's original theme, played by the orchestra. The final cadence, avoiding the more traditional dominant-tonic gesture, leads from the key a third below the tonic (D-flat) to the tonic (F minor).

The fiery final movement contains rhythmic features reminiscent of Samuel Coleridge-Taylor's Violin Concerto, Ballade in A Minor and *Bamboula*. It opens with rapid, brilliant scale passages in the orchestra punctuated by sharp chordal interjections from the piano. A centrally located piano cadenza leads to a section in 3/4, still for piano alone and marked *tranquillo cantabile;* a graceful, attractive melody is accompanied by dance-like accompaniment figures. This new melody is taken up, in the *più mosso* section that follows, by a solo clarinet accompanied by the strings. The opening material returns in even more virtuosic form, followed by another dance-like passage and a reprise of the orchestra's opening brilliant scale passages. Progress to a climactic conclusion is interrupted by an off-stage trumpet solo, accompanied only by timpani, a poignant memorial to Samuel Coleridge-Taylor. A gradual crescendo then draws orchestra and piano together for the movement's triumphant conclusion.

The Concerto in F Minor was first performed in 1943 in Aberdeen, Scotland, by pianist Frank Laffitte and the Coleridge-Taylor Symphony Orchestra, under the direction of the composer. Subsequent performances took place in London, Melbourne, Johannesburg, and more recently in a concert devoted to the music of Avril and Samuel Coleridge-Taylor at Bexhill-on-Sea on Sunday, April 8, 1973. The latter performance was by pianist Irene Kohler and the Malcolm Sargent Symphony Orchestra, under the direction of the composer.

FANTASIE FOR VIOLIN AND PIANO (1949)

Written under the pseudonym Peter Riley, the Fantasie for Violin and Piano is a dramatic work in which the two instruments create a dialogue. Each section of the work's ABA form is divided into two subsections, with violin cadenzas marking these subdivisions in the first A and the B sections. The A and B sections are characterized and shaped by different keys, themes, and types of motivic development. Each section builds to a high point with the largest climax in the final section, giving the entire piece a sense of forward motion. The upbeat beginning of both A sections contributes to this forward propulsion.

The A section has two main themes, both strongly rhythmic gestures in C major. Though both themes have their own distinct melodic patterns, they are related by means of their opening motives: the first, a stepwise, three-note ascending motive in dotted rhythm; the second, a stepwise three-note descending motive in even eighth notes. The combined pitches of the two motives fill the interval from C to G. The pitch pattern of the first theme undergoes a succession of alterations that gradually bring about its transformation into the second theme. The relationship between the two themes is further emphasized near the end of the A section where the dotted rhythm of the first theme reappears with the descending three-note motive of the second theme. By recalling the first theme at this point and in this way, the composer ensures that the connection between the themes will not be missed.

The B section employs a new theme in E minor. (Even this theme has the stepwise, three-note motive embedded in it.) The theme of the B section undergoes alterations in rhythm rather than in pitch, appearing in various forms in both the piano and violin parts. A violin cadenza leads to a reprise of the beginning of the B section an octave higher. The section culminates in a climactic double-stop passage that ushers in the return to the first A theme in C major.

In the final section, the moderately fast first theme is shortened while the more animated second theme is repeated. The piano augments the section's quickening tempo and growing intensity with a thicker texture that includes 32nd-note broken chord figures; the violin reciprocates with a greater density of 16th-note motives. This constitutes the work's most powerful climax, bringing it to a close.

GOD'S REMEMBRANCE (1970)

This work for soprano, harp, violin, viola, and cello is a setting of a poem from Francis Ledwidge's *Songs of the Fields*. The poem speaks of youth, old age, and death, using the seasons as metaphors and drawing upon images from nature such as birds, the wind, and the sea, and suggesting that the promise of life is created by the mind of God and fades with His forgetfulness.

The music is through-composed in three sections, with the first stanza of the poem being used in each of the first two sections, and the second stanza, in the third. The sections are separated by instrumental interludes and further distinguished musically by the introduction of new motivic material in each section. Although no music is repeated, there is a subtle resemblance in the last section's vocal line, at the words "and he remembered me as something far in old imagination," to the sung first line of the first section. A comparison of these two passages shows similarities in rhythm, in the syllabic, almost monotone recitation, and in melodic contour.

The music is elegiac in tone, with a predominance of slow tempos. Its texture consists of short motives woven together rather than in long lyrical phrases. The instrumental parts are permeated by a two-note motive representing sighing or yearning, which first appears in the instrumental introduction as long notes (dotted half notes) for the harp. The motive is passed to the violin where it quickens (quarter notes) and reappears when the voice first enters, embedded in the harp's accompanying chordal figure (m. 27). This chordal figure reappears as accompaniment to a still quicker eighth-note version of the motive in the violin part, which motive takes on a dual significance when it becomes integrated into a bird-call motive (m. 59–60) and continues to figure in the remainder of the piece until, a few measures from the end, it reappears in the harp's accompanying chordal figure. The bird call receives one last reprise, drawing the listener directly into the act of remembrance, heightening the sense of nostalgia and loss created by the poem.

Throughout the work, instrumental parts sometimes introduce melodic material that is taken up by the voice and some-times take over elements of the vocal line. Certain melodic patterns appearing in the voice or string parts also appear as chordal sonorities in the harp part (triads with an added sixth, segments of the whole tone scale). The instruments are used with a fine sense of their idiomatic capabilities, with many colorful flourishes appearing in the harp part and eloquent and powerful melodies in the strings.

The piece is rich in its use of word painting, portraying poetic ideas by means of harmonic and melodic figures. The words "death shook his lean bones," for example are accompanied by an upward sweep in whole tones from the harp and tremolos for the strings; and following the words "I heard a blackbird whistle half his lay," melodic figures suggestive of birdsong appear in the violin and viola parts. On the words "a mighty breath," the viola and cello create an oscillation of E minor and C major, like inhaling and exhaling; and turbulent 16th-note figurations accompany the words "singing upon the wind" and "like a sparking star drowned in the lavender of evening sea." The juxtaposition of remote harmonies (A-flat major and E minor) is used to underscore the meaning of the word "with distance."

Colorful juxtaposition of non-related harmonies underscores the importance of key words in the text, creates disruptions that serve to separate the sections of the music, and sometimes seems to function as a metaphor for the forgetfulness of which the poem speaks.

REFERENCES

Coleridge-Taylor, Avril. "The Music of Coleridge-Taylor." *Sound* (April 1947).

———. "My Father and His Music." *Fanfare* (1948).

———. *The Heritage of Samuel Coleridge-Taylor.* London: Dobson Books, 1979.

Fuller, Sophie. "Avril [Gwendolen] Coleridge-Taylor." In *The New Grove Dictionary of Women Composers,* edited by Julie Anne Sadie and Rhian Samuel, 126–127. London: Macmillan, 1994.

Sayers, W. C. Berwick. *Samuel Coleridge-Taylor, Musician: His Life and Letters.* London: Augener, 1927.

VICTORIA VON ARX

COLERIDGE-TAYLOR, SAMUEL

Born in Holborn, England, August 15, 1875; died near Croydon, England, September 1, 1912. **Education:** Began violin study with his grandfather, Benjamin Holman, around the age of five; studied violin with Joseph Beckwith, ca. 1881–88; British School, Croydon, studied singing with Herbert A. Walters, ca. 1884–88; Royal College of Music, London, studied composition with Charles Villiers Stanford, violin with Henry Holmes, piano with Algernon Ashton, organ with Walter Alcock, and harmony with Charles Wood, 1890–97. **Composing and Performing Career:** First published composition, "To Thee O Lord," 1891; first concert of works performed, 1893; Salle Érard, London, joint recital with Paul Laurence Dunbar, 1896; Conservatory Orchestral Society, director, 1898–1906; Westmorland Music Festival, conductor, 1901; Kendal Festival, director, ca. 1902–04; organized Coleridge-Taylor Symphony Concerts, 1902–05; Rochester Choral Society, conductor, 1902–07; Handel Society, West London, conductor, 1904–12; toured United States, 1904 (with stops in Boston, Washington, D.C., Chicago, New York, Philadelphia), 1906 (with stops in Washington, D.C., Baltimore, Pittsburgh, St. Louis, Chicago, Milwaukee, Detroit, Toronto, Boston, and Connecticut), 1910 (attended the Norfolk [Connecticut] Music Festival); founded String Players Club, 1906; Blackheath, Brockley, Lewiswan Orchestral Society, president, 1907–09, conductor, 1909–12; Central Croydon Choral Society, conductor, 1909–10; New Symphony Orchestra, subconductor, 1910–12. **Teaching Career:** Croydon Conservatory, 1895–1912; Trinity College of Music, London, professor of music, 1903–12; Crystal Palace School of Art and Music, professor of theory and harmony, 1905–12; Guildhall School, 1910–12. **Commissions:** Committee of the Three Choirs Festival, 1898, 1899; North Staffordshire Musical Festival, 1899; Royal Choral Society, 1900; Leeds Musical Festival, 1901; Sheffield Musical Festival, 1902; Herbert Beerbohm Tree, 1900, 1901, 1906, 1908, 1911; Samuel Coleridge-Taylor Choral Society, 1904; Mr. and Mrs. Carl Stoeckel, 1910, 1911. **Honors/Awards:** Royal College of Music, composition scholarship, 1893–97; Leslie Alexander Prize for Composition, 1895, 1896.

MUSIC LIST

INSTRUMENTAL SOLOS
Violin
Ballade in C Minor, op. 73. 1907. London: Augener, 1909. Premiere, 1907.

"Deep River." Boston: Ditson, 1911.

Four African Dances, op. 58. 1902. London: Augener, 1904. Premiere, ca. 1902.

Gipsy Suite, op. 20. 1898. London: Augener, 1900. Contents: Lament and Tambourine; A Gipsy Song; A Gipsy Dance; Waltz. Recorded: Marco Polo 8.223516.

Hiawatha Sketches, op. 16. London: Augener, 1897. Contents: A Tale; A Song; A Dance. Premiere, 1896.

Romance, op. 59, no. 2. 1905. London: Augener, 1905.

Six Easy Pieces with Piano Accompaniment. London: Augener, 1920.

Sonata in D Minor for Violin and Piano, op. 28. 1899. London: Hawkes, 1917. Recorded: Columbia L-1396/7.

Suite de pièces, op. 3 (violin, piano or organ). 1895. London: Schott, 1895. Contents: Pastorale; Cavatina; Barcarolle; Contemplation.

Two Romantic Pieces, op. 9. 1896. London: Augener, 1896. Contents: Lament; Merry-Making. Premiere, 1896.

"Valse-caprice," op. 23. 1898. London: Augener, 1898.

Cello
Variations in B Minor. London: Augener, 1918. Premiere, 1907.

Clarinet
Sonata for Clarinet and Piano in F Minor. ca. 1893. Unpublished manuscript. Note: manuscript missing.

Piano
African Suite, op. 35. 1898. London: Augener, 1898. Contents: Introduction; A Negro Love Song; Valse; Danse nègre. Premiere, 1898.

"Barcarolle." London: Schott, 1915.

Cameos, op. 56. 1904. London: Augener, 1904.

"Cavatina." London: Schott, 1915.

Forest Scenes: Five Characteristic Pieces for Pianoforte, op. 66. 1907. London: Augener, 1907. Contents: The Lone Forest Maiden; The Phantom Lover Arrives; The Phantom Tells His Tale of Longing; Erstwhile They Ride, The Forest Maiden Acknowledges Her Love; Now Proudly They Journey Together Towards the Great City.

"Lament." London: Augener, 1900.

"Meditation." New York: Associated Music Publishers, 1915. Also arranged for carillon.

"Menuet." London: Augener, 1917.

Minnehaha Ballet Music, op. 82, no. 2. London: Hawkes and Son, 1925. Contents: Laughing Water; The Pursuit; Love Song; The Homecoming.

"Moorish Dance," op. 55. 1904. London: Augener, 1904.

"Nourmahal's Song and Dance," op. 41. 1900. London: Augener, 1900.

"Papillon." London: Augener, 1908. Recorded: Da Camera Magna SM 93144.

Scènes de ballet, op. 64. 1906. London: Augener, 1906.

Six Negro Melodies. Boston: Oliver Ditson, 1905. Contents: At the Dawn of Day; Warrior Song; Deep River; Don't Be Weary, Traveler; Sometimes I Feel Like a Motherless Child; They Will Not Lend Me a Child.

Three Cameos, op. 56. London: Augener, 1904.

Three Humoresques, op. 31. 1897. London: Augener, 1898. Also arranged for orchestra.

Three Silhouettes, op. 38. 1899. London: Ashdown, 1904. Contents: Valse, Tambourine; Lament.

Three-Fours: Valse-Suite, op. 71. 1909. London: Augener, 1909.

Twenty-Four Negro Melodies, op. 59, no. 1. 1904. Boston: Oliver Ditson, 1905. Contents: At the Dawn of Day (Loko ku ti ga); The Stones Are Very Hard (Maribye ma nonoha ngopfu); Take Nabandji (Thata Nabandji); They Will Not Lend Me a Child (A ba boleki

mwana!); Song of Conquest (Ringendjé); Warrior's Song; Olaba;
The Bamboula (African Dance); The Angels Changed My Name;
Deep River; Didn't My Lord Deliver Daniel?; Don't Be Weary
Traveler; Going Up; I'm Troubled in Mind; I Was Way Down A-
Yonder (Dum-a-lum); Let Us Cheer the Weary Traveler; Many
Thousand Gone; My Lord Delivered Daniel; Oh, He Raise a Poor
Lazarus; Pilgrim's Song; Run, Mary, Run; Sometimes I Feel Like a
Motherless Child; Steal Away; Wade in the Water. Premiere (three
pieces), 1904. Recorded: Orion ORS-78205/306; "The Angels
Changed My Name," Musical Heritage Society MHS 7035.

Two African Idylls. London: Augener, 1904.

Two Impromptus. London: Augener, 1911.

Two Moorish Tone-Pictures, op. 19, no. 1. 1897. London: Augener, 1897.
Contents: Andalla; Zarifa.

Two Oriental Valses. London: Forsyth, n.d. Contents: Haidée; Zuleika.

Piano, Four Hands
Valse. London: E. Ashdown, 1928. Recorded: Music & Arts CD 737.

Organ
Album. London: Augener, n.d. Note: two volumes.

Interlude. In *The Modern Organist,* vol. 3. York, England: Banks Music, ca.
1982.

Three Impromptus, op. 78. 1911. London: A. Weekes, 1911.

Three Short Pieces. London: Novello, 1898. Contents: Melody; Elegy;
Arietta.

SMALL INSTRUMENTAL ENSEMBLE
Strings
Fantasiestücke, op. 5 (string quartet). 1895. London: Augener, 1921.
Contents: Prelude; Serenade; Humoresque; Minuet and Trio;
Dance. Premiere, 1895.

Quartet for Strings in D Minor, op. 13. 1896. Unpublished manuscript.
Note: manuscript missing.

Combinations
Five Negro Melodies (violin, cello, piano). Boston: Oliver Ditson, 1906.
Contents: Sometimes I Feel Like A Motherless Child; I Was Way
Down A-Yonder; Didn't My Lord Deliver Daniel?; They Will Not
Lend Me a Child; My Lord Delivered Daniel.

"I Was Down A-Yonder" (violin, cello, piano). Boston: Oliver Ditson,
1906.

Nonet in F Minor, op. 2 (piano, clarinet, bassoon, horn, two violins, viola,
cello, double bass). 1895. Unpublished manuscript. Premiere,
1895.

Quintet for Clarinet and Strings in F-sharp Minor, op. 10. 1895.
Leipzig: Breitkopf und Härtel, 1895. Premiere, 1895. Recorded:
Chantry ABM-23; Koch International Classics 3-7056-2H1;
Spectrum SR-127.

Quintet for Piano and Strings in G Minor, op. 1 (piano, string quartet).
ca. 1893. Unpublished manuscript. Premiere, 1893.

Trio in E Minor (violin, cello, piano). 1893. Unpublished manuscript.

STRING ORCHESTRA
Four Novelletten, op. 52 (string orchestra, tambourine, triangle). 1902.
London: Novello, 1903. Also arranged for violin and piano.

FULL ORCHESTRA
Ballade in A Minor, op. 33. 1898. London: Novello, 1898. Commissioned
by Three Choirs Festival, Glouston, England. Also arranged for
piano solo. Premiere, 1898. Recorded: Argo 436 401-2.

The Bamboula: Rhapsodic Dance, op. 75. 1910. London: Hawkes and Son,
1911. Commissioned by Mr. and Mrs. Carl Stoeckel for the
Norfolk [Connecticut] Music Festival. Premiere, 1911. Recorded:
EMI EL 270145.

Ethiopia Saluting the Colours: Concert March for Orchestra, op. 51. 1902.
London: Augener, 1902.

Four Characteristic Waltzes, op. 22. 1898. London: Novello, 1899. Also
arranged for piano solo. Contents: Valse bohèmienne; Valse
rustique: Tempo di valse; Valse de la reine; Valse mauresque.
Premiere, 1898. Recorded: Marco Polo 8.223516; Pearl CD 9965;
RCA Victor 27225/6, B.8378/9.

From the Prairie: Rhapsody. London: Boosey, n.d. Premiere, 1911.

Hemo Dance: Scherzo, op. 47, no. 2. 1900. London: Novello, 1900. Also
arranged for violin and piano.

Hiawatha Ballet, op. 82, no. 1. London: Boosey, 1919. Contents:
Hiawatha's Wooing; The Wedding Feast; The Famine; Bird Scene
and Conjurer's Dance; The Departure; The Reunion in the Last of
the Hereafter.

Idyll, op. 44. London: Augener, ca. 1922. Also arranged for violin and
piano.

Overture to the "Song of Hiawatha," op. 30, no. 3. 1899. London: Novello,
1899. Premiere, 1899. Recorded: Marco Polo 8.223516.

Petite suite de concert, op. 77. 1911. London: Boosey and Hawkes, 1911.
Contents: La caprice de Nannete; Demande et réponse; Un sonnet
d'amour; La tarantelle frétillante. Also arranged for piano solo, two
pianos, and violin and piano. Recorded: HMV ESD7161; Koch
International Classics 3-7056-2H1; Marco Polo 8.223516; Pearl
CD 9965; Odeon PSXLP 30123.

Rhapsodic Dance, no. 2. New York: Boosey and Hawkes, n.d. Note: based
on the "Moorish Dance" for piano.

Romance of the Prairie Lilies. London: Boosey and Hawkes, 1931.
Recorded: Marco Polo 8.223516.

Scenes from an Everyday Romance, op. 41, no. 1. 1900. London: Novello,
1900. Also arranged for piano solo. Premiere, 1900.

Solemn Prelude, op. 40, or *A Solemn Rhapsody.* 1899. London: Novello,
1899. Also arranged for piano solo. Commissioned by the
Committee of the Three Choirs Festival. Premiere, 1899.

Symphonic Variations on an African Air, op. 63. 1906. London: Novello,
1906. Also arranged for piano solo. Note: based on "I'm Troubled
in Mind." Premiere, 1906. Recorded: Argo 436 401-2.

Symphony in A Minor, op. 8. 1896. Unpublished manuscript. Premiere,
1896.

Toussaint l'Ouverture, op. 46. 1901. London: Novello, ca. 1901. Premiere,
1901.

ORCHESTRA (CHAMBER OR FULL) WITH SOLOISTS
Ballade in D Minor, op. 4 (violin, orchestra or piano). 1895. London:
Novello, 1895. Premiere, 1903.

Concerto in G Minor for Violin and Orchestra, op. 80. 1911. London:
Metzler, 1912. Commissioned by Mr. and Mrs. Carl Stoeckel.
Premiere, 1911.

Fantasiestück in A Major (cello, orchestra). Premiere, 1907.

Samuel Coleridge-Taylor; courtesy of Jeffrey Green

Keep Me from Sinking Down: Slow Movement on a Negro Melody (violin, orchestra). Unpublished manuscript. Premiere, 1911.

Legend from the Concertstück, op. 14 (violin, orchestra). 1893. London: Augener, 1897.

Romance in G Major, op. 39 (violin, orchestra). 1899. London: Novello, 1900. Premiere, 1899.

The Shoshone's Adieu (medium voice, orchestra). London: Boosey, 1904.

Zara's Ear-Rings, op. 7 (medium voice, orchestra). Unpublished manuscript. Premiere, 1895.

ORCHESTRA (CHAMBER OR FULL) WITH CHORUS

Five Choral Ballads, op. 54 (baritone solo, SATB, orchestra). 1904. London: Breitkopf und Härtel, 1904. Contents: Beside the Ungathered Rice He Lay (SATB); She Dwells by Great Kenhawa's Side (SSA); Loud He Sang the Psalm of David (SATB); The Quadroon Girl (baritone solo, SSA); In Dark Fens of the Dismal Swamp (SATB). Commissioned by the Samuel Coleridge-Taylor Choral Society. Premiere, 1905.

Kubla Khan: Rhapsody, op. 61 (mezzo-soprano solo, SATB, orchestra). 1905. London: Novello, 1905. Premiere, 1906.

Meg Blane: A Rhapsody of the Sea, op. 48 (mezzo-soprano solo, SATB, orchestra). 1902. London: Novello, 1902. Commissioned by the Sheffield Musical Festival. Premiere, 1902.

SOLO VOICE

African Romances, op. 17 (medium voice). 1897. London: Augener, 1897. Contents: An African Love Song; A Prayer; A Starry Night; Dawn; Ballad; Over the Hills; How Shall I Woo Thee? Recorded: "Dawn," Rococo 5291.

"Ah Sweet, Thou Little Knowest" (high voice). London: Ricordi, 1904.

"Ah Tell Me, Gentle Zephyr" (medium voice). Unpublished manuscript.

"The Arrow and the Song" (medium voice). ca. 1893. Unpublished manuscript. Premiere, 1893.

"At Candle Lightin' Time" (high or low voice). ca. 1896. Cincinnati, Ohio: John Church, 1909.

"A Birthday" (high voice). London: Metzler, 1909. Also arranged for voice and orchestra.

"The Bridal Day: I Hear the Flutes" (medium voice). New York: Arthur P. Schmidt, 1918.

"The Broken Oar" (medium voice). ca. 1893. Unpublished manuscript. Premiere, 1893.

"Comfort," op. 42, no. 4 (low voice). London: Novello, 1900.

"The Corn Song" (medium voice). ca. 1896. London: Boosey, 1897. Also arranged for voice and orchestra.

"A Dance of Bygone Days" (medium voice). Unpublished manuscript.

"The Delaware's Farewell" (medium voice). Unpublished manuscript.

"Dimple-Chin." (medium voice). Unpublished manuscript.

"The Easter Morn" (medium voice). London: Boosey, 1904. Also arranged for medium voice, violin, cello, and organ.

"Eulalie" (medium voice). London: Boosey, 1904.

"An Explanation" (medium voice). Boston: Arthur P. Schmidt, 1914.

Five Fairy Ballads. London: Boosey, 1909. Contents: Sweet Baby Butterfly; Alone with Mother; Big Lady Moon; The Stars; Fairy Roses. Also arranged for voice and orchestra. Recorded: "Big Lady Moon," Prelude Records PRS 2505.

"Five-and-Twenty Sailormen" (medium voice). New York: John Church, 1910.

"Genevieve" (high voice). New York: William Maxwell, 1905.

"The Gift Rose" (high voice). Boston: Oliver Ditson, 1907.

"The Guest" (medium voice). 1911. London: Augener, 1914.

"If I Could Love Thee" (high voice). New York: William Maxwell, 1905.

"I'm Troubled in Mind" (medium voice). London: Boosey and Hawkes, 1928.

In Memoriam: Three Rhapsodies, op. 24 (low voice). 1898. London: Augener, 1898. Contents: Earth Fades, Heaven Breaks on Me; Substitution; Weep Not, Beloved Friends. Premiere, 1977.

"The Island of Gardens" (medium voice). London: Boosey and Hawkes, 1911.

"A Lament" (medium voice). London: Ricordi, 1906.

"Life and Death" (medium voice). London: Augener, 1914. Recorded: HMV B-9451; Parnassus PAR 1009.

"The Links o' Love" (low voice). New York: John Church, 1910.

"Love Is Like the Roses" (low voice). New York: Arthur P. Schmidt, 1918.

"A Lovely Little Dream" (medium voice). New York: Schirmer, 1909. Also arranged for strings and harmonium or organ.

"Love's Mirror: Song for Michelmas Day" (medium voice). 1897. London: Augener, 1916.

"Love's Passing" (low voice). New York: William Maxwell, 1905.

"Love's Questionings" (medium voice). London: Keith, Prowse, 1904.

"Low Breathing Winds" (high or medium voice). London: Augener, 1914.

"My Algonquin" (medium voice). Philadelphia: Theodore Presser, 1909.

"My Doll" (medium voice). London: Boosey, 1910.

"My Lady" (medium voice). London: Augener, 1916.

"O Mistress Mine" (medium voice). London: Winthrop Rogers, 1906.

"The Oasis" (medium voice). London: Augener, 1898. Note: music based on "We Strew These Opiate Flowers," from *Part-Songs,* op. 21, for SSA.

"Oh Sweet, Thou Little Knowest" (medium voice). London: Ricordi, n.d.

"Once Only" (medium voice). London: Winthrop Rogers, 1906.

"Our Idyll" (medium voice). London: Augener, 1906. Note: music based on "A June Rose Bloomed" for SSA.

"The Parting Glass" (narrator, piano). Unpublished manuscript. Premiere, 1912.

"Prithee, Tell Me" (medium voice). Unpublished manuscript.

"Scottish." London: Augener 1917.

"She Rested by the Broken Brook" (high voice). Boston: Oliver Ditson, 1906. Recorded: EMI HLM.7037; HMV HQM-1176 and HMV DA-1778.

Six American Lyrics, op. 45 (contralto or baritone). 1901. London: Novello, 1903. Contents: O Thou, Mine Other Stronger Part; O Praise Me Not; Her Love; The Dark Eye Has Left Us; O Ship That Saileth; Beat, Beat, Drums.

Six Little Songs for Little Folks, op. 19. no. 2 (medium voice). 1898. London: Boosey, 1898. Contents: Sea-Shells; A Rest by the Way; A Battle in the Snow; A Parting Wish; A Sweet Little Doll; Baby Land.

Six Songs, op. 37 (low voice). 1898. London: Novello, 1899. Contents: You'll Love Me Yet; Canoe Song; A Blood-Red Ring Hung Round the Moon; Sweet Evenings Come and Go, Love; As the Moon's Soft Splendour; Eleänore. Premiere, 1898 (nos. 1–4 only). Recorded:

"Eléanore," L'Oiseau-Lyre SOL-324; Columbia DB-2083; Gramophone D-3730.

Six Sorrow Songs, op. 57 (low voice). 1904. London: Augener, 1904. Contents: Oh What Comes over the Sea; When I Am Dead, My Dearest; Oh, Roses for the Flush of Youth; She Sat and Sang Away; Unmindful of the Roses; Too Late for Love. Premiere, 1904. Recorded: "Unmindful of the Roses," Pearl CD 9965; "When I Am Dead, My Dearest," HMV B-572.

"Solitude" (high voice). 1893. London: Augener, 1918. Premiere, 1893.

"Song of the Nubian Girl" (medium voice). London: Augener, 1905.

Songs of Sun and Shade (high voice). London: Boosey, 1911. Contents: You Lay So Still in the Sunshine; Thou Hast Bewitched Me, Beloved; The Rainbow Child; Thou Art Risen, My Beloved; This Is the Island of Gardens. Recorded: Columbia FB-3031 (no. 4); HMV B-8285 (nos. 2 and 5); HMV E-414 (no. 4); Pearl CD 9965 (nos. 2 and 5).

"Sons of the Sea" (medium voice). London: Novello, 1910. Recorded: HMV C-2728; Pearl CD 9965.

The Soul's Expression: Four Sonnets by Elisabeth Barrett Browning, op. 42 (low voice). 1900. London: Novello, 1900. Contents: The Soul's Expression; Tears; Grief; Comfort. Premiere, 1900.

Southern Love Songs, op. 12 (high voice). 1896. London: Augener, 1896. Contents: My Love: A Spanish Ditty; Tears: A Lament; Minguillo; If Thou Art Sleeping, Maiden; Oh! My Lonely Pillow: Stanzas to a Hindu Air.

"A Summer Idyll" (high voice). London: Boosey, 1906.

"Tell, O Tell Me" (high or medium voice). London: Augener, 1915.

"Thou Art" (medium voice). Philadelphia: Presser, n.d.

"The Three Ravens" (medium voice). London: Boosey, 1897.

Three Song-Poems, op. 50 (low voice). 1903. New York: Boosey, 1905. Contents: Dreaming for Ever; The Young Indian Maid; Beauty and Song.

Three Songs, op. 29 (high voice). 1899. London: Augener, 1899. Contents: Lucy; Mary; Jessy.

Three Songs of Heine (medium voice). London: Augener, 1918. Contents: My Pretty Fishermaiden; Thy Sapphire Eyes; I Hear the Flutes and Fiddles.

"Toujours, l'amour" (medium voice). Unpublished manuscript.

Two Songs, op. 81. 1912. London: Boosey, 1920. Contents: Waiting; Red o' the Dawn.

Two Songs (medium voice). London: Augener, 1916. Contents: My Lady; Love's Mirror.

"Until" (medium voice). Boston: Oliver Ditson, 1908.

"The Vengeance" (medium voice). Unpublished manuscript.

"Viking Song" (low voice). Boston: Oliver Ditson, 1914. Also arranged for SA.

"The Violet Band" (high voice). New York: William Maxwell, 1905.

"A Vision" (medium voice). Philadelphia: Theodore Presser, 1905.

"We Watched Her Breaking through the Night" (medium voice). Unpublished manuscript. Also arranged for SSA.

"Why Does Azure Deck the Skies?" (medium voice). Unpublished manuscript.

VOCAL ENSEMBLE

"Keep Those Eyes" (soprano, tenor, piano). London: Novello, 1903.

"Lift Up Your Heads" (SATB soli, organ). London: Novello, 1892.

CHORAL MUSIC

"All Are Sleeping, Weary Heart" (TTBB). London: Curwen, 1910.

"All My Stars Forsake Me," op. 67, no. 1 (SATB unaccompanied). London: Augener, 1905.

"Beauty and Truth" (SA). London: Curwen, 1912.

"Break Forth into Joy" (tenor solo, SATB, organ). London: Novello, 1892.

"By the Lone Seashore" (SATB). London: Novello, 1910.

"By the Waters of Babylon" (soprano, contralto, tenor, bass, SATB, organ). London: Novello, 1899.

"Dead in the Sierras," op. 67, no. 2 (SATB unaccompanied). London: Augener, 1905.

"Drake's Drum" (SA). London: Curwen, 1906.

"Encinctured with a Twine of Leaves" (SSA). London: Novello, 1908.

"The Evening Star" (SATB). London: Novello, 1911. Recorded: Audio House AHS-30F75.

"The Fair at Almachara" (SATB unaccompanied). London: Augener, 1905.

"Fall on Me Like a Silent Dew" (SA). London: Curwen, 1912.

"In Thee, O Lord, Have I Put My Trust" (SATB). London: Novello, 1891.

"Isle of Beauty" (SATB). London: Augener, 1920.

"Jesu, the Very Thought of Thee." In *The Methodist Sunday School Hymnal* (New York: Methodist Book Concern, 1911).

"A June Rose Bloomed" (SSA). London: Augener, 1906.

"Land of the Sun," op. 15 (SATB). ca. 1897. London: Augener, ca. 1897.

"The Lee-Shore" (SATB). London: Novello, 1912.

"Little Boy Blue" (unison). London: Boosey and Hawkes, 1923.

"The Lord Is My Strength" (SATB, organ). London: Novello, 1892.

"Loud Sang the Spanish Cavalier" (TTBB). London: Curwen, 1910.

Morning and Evening Service, op. 18 (SATB, organ). 1890. In *Parish Choir Book* (London: Novello, 1899), nos. 5, 7, 9, 10, 14. Contents: Te Deum; Benedictus; Jubilate; Magnificat; Nunc dimittis.

"Now Late on the Sabbath Day" (SATB). London: Novello, 1901.

"O Mariners, Out of the Sunlight" (TTBB). London: Curwen, n.d.

"O Who Will Worship the Great God Pan?" (TTBB). London: Curwen, 1910.

"O Ye That Love the Lord" (SATB, organ). London: Novello, 1892.

"Oh, the Summer" (SA). London: Curwen, 1911.

"The Pixies" (SSA). London: Novello, 1908.

Part-Songs, op. 21 (SSA). 1898. London: Augener, 1898. Contents: We Strew These Opiate Flowers; How They So Softly Rest. Premiere, 1898. Also arranged for piano solo.

"Prayer for Peace, April 1911" (unison). 1911. London: Curwen, 1911.

"Sea-Drift: Rhapsody," op. 69 (SSAATTBB unaccompanied). 1908. London: Novello, 1908.

"The Sea-Shell" (SATB). London: Curwen, 1911.

"Song of Proserpine" (SATB). London: Novello, 1912.

"Summer Is Gone" (SATB). London: Curwen, 1911.

Te Deum in F Major (SATB, organ). 1890. Unpublished manuscript. Note: later became part of *Morning and Evening Service*.

"To Thee O Lord." London: Novello, 1891.

"What Can Lambkins Do?" (SSA). London: Novello, 1908.

"What Thou Hast Given Me?" (SATB). 1901. London: Weekes, n.d.

"Whispers of Summer" (SATB). London: Novello, 1910.

DRAMATIC MUSIC

The Atonement, op. 53 (sacred cantata for soprano, contralto, tenor, baritone, SATB, and orchestra). 1903; revised 1904. London:

Novello, 1903; 1904 (revision). Contents: Prelude; Gethsemane; Prayer of the Holy Women and Apostles; Pontius Pilate; Calvary. Premiere, 1903.

The Blind Girl of Castél-Cuillé, op. 43 (cantata for soprano, baritone, SATB, and orchestra). 1901. London: Novello, 1901. Commissioned by the Leeds Musical Festival. Premiere, 1901.

Bon-Bon Suite, op. 68 (cantata for baritone, SATB, orchestra). 1908. London: Novello, 1908. Contents: The Magic Mirror; The Fairy Boat; To Rosa; Love and Hymen; The Watchman; Say, What Shall We Dance? Premiere, 1909.

The Death of Minnehaha, op. 30, no. 2 (cantata for soprano, baritone, SATB, orchestra). 1899. London: Novello, l899. Contents: Ever Thicker; And the Foremost Said; Forth into the Empty Forest; Gitchie Manito; Give Your Children Food; Minnehaha; And the Lovely Laughing Water; Hark, She Said; Wahonomin; Then He Sat Down; Then They Buried Minnehaha; For Her Soul; Farewell, Said He; To the Land of the Hereafter. Commissioned by the North Staffordshire Musical Festival of 1899. Note: part 2 of *Scenes from the Song of Hiawatha.* Premiere, 1899. Recorded: HMV C2210/13.

Dream Lovers, op. 11 (operatic romance for soprano, mezzo-soprano, tenor, bass, SATB, and orchestra). 1898. London: Boosey, 1898. Contents: Prelude; Duet: Is the Red Rose?; Trio: You May Go from Bleak Alaska; Song: Long Years Ago; Song: Pray Tell Me; Solo and Chorus: I'm a Wealthy Wand'ring Wight; Quartet: Long, Long the Labour. Premiere, 1898.

Endymion's Dream, op. 65 (opera in one act for soprano, tenor, SATB, and orchestra). 1909. London: Novello, 1910. Premiere, 1910.

The Gitanos (cantata-operetta for soprano, two mezzo-sopranos, two contraltos, SSA, and piano). 1898. London: Augener, 1898.

Hiawatha's Departure, op. 30, no. 4 (cantata for soprano, tenor, baritone, SATB, and orchestra). 1900. London: Novello, 1900. Contents: Spring Had Come (soprano); From His Wand'rings; At Each Other Look'd the Warriors; True Is All Iagoo Tells Us; By the Shore of Gitche Gumee; All the Air Was Full of Freshness; From the Brow of Hiawatha (soprano); Beautiful Is the Sun (baritone); Then the Generous Hiawatha; Still the Guests; And They Said Farewell. Commissioned by the Royal Choral Society. Note: part 3 of *Scenes from the Song of Hiawatha.* Premiere, 1900.

Hiawatha's Wedding Feast, op. 30, no. 1 (cantata for tenor, SATB, and orchestra). 1898. London: Novello, 1899. Contents: You Shall Hear How Pau-Puk-Keewis; Then the Handsome Pau-Puk-Keewis; He Was Dress'd in Shirt of Doe-Skin; First He Danc'd a Solemn Measure; Then Said They to Chibiabos; Onaway, Awake, Beloved (tenor); Thus the Gentle Chibiabos; Very Boastful Was Iagoo; Such Was Hiawatha's Wedding. Note: part 1 of *Scenes from the Song of Hiawatha.* Premiere, 1898. Recorded: Angel S-35900; Arabesque Recordings 8005; Brunswick 35003-A; Columbia C-1931/4; HMV ASD-467; HMV ESD7161.

A Tale of Old Japan, op. 76 (cantata for soprano, contralto, tenor, bass, SATB, and orchestra). 1911. London: Novello, 1911. Commissioned by Mr. and Mrs. Carl Stoeckel. Premiere, 1911.

Thelma, op. 72 (opera in three acts). 1908. London: Aschererg-Hawkes, ca. 1908. Premiere, "Prelude" only, 1910.

INCIDENTAL MUSIC

"The Clown and the Columbine" (narrator, violin, cello, piano). Unpublished manuscript. Note: accompaniment to the poem. Premiere, 1912.

Faust, op. 70 (orchestra). 1908. London: Boosey, 1909. Contents: Dance of the Witches: Brocken Scene; The Four Visions: Helen, Cleopatra, Messalina, Margaret; Dance and Chant; The Devil's Kitchen; A King There Lived in Thule; Menuet des folles, by Berlioz; Ballet des sylphes, by Berlioz. Incidental music to the play of Goethe. Commissioned by Herbert Beerbohm Tree. Premiere, 1908.

The Forest of Wild Thyme, op. 74 (orchestra). 1911. London: Boosey, 1911. Contents: Scenes from an Imaginary Ballet; Three Dream Dances; Intermezzo; Your Heart's Desire; Little Boy Blue (female voices); Come In; Dreams, Dreams (unison children's voices); Christmas Overture. Incidental music to a play. Commissioned by Herbert Beerbohm Tree. Recorded: "Intermezzo," "Christmas Overture," and "Three Dream Dances," Pearl CD 9965; "Christmas Overture," Columbia 9137; "Intermezzo," JB-8113; "Three Dream Dances," Victor 27230/1.

Herod, op. 47, no. 1 (orchestra). 1900. London: Augener, 1901. Contents: Processional; Breeze Scene; Dance; Finale. Incidental music to the play of the same name. Commissioned by Herbert Beerbohm Tree.

Nero, op. 62 (orchestra). 1906. London: Novello, 1907. Contents: Prelude; Intermezzo: Singing Girl's Chorus; Eastern Dance; First entr'acte; Second entr'acte: Poppea; Processional March. Incidental music to the drama of Stephen Phillips. Commissioned by Herbert Beerbohm Tree. Premiere, 1906.

Othello, op. 79 (orchestra). 1911. London: Metzler, 1912. Contents: Dance; Children's Intermezzo; Funeral March; The Willow Song; Military March. Incidental music to a play. Commissioned by Herbert Beerbohm Tree. Recorded: Boosey and Hawkes 4273/4; Marco Polo 8.223516; Pearl CD 9965.

St. Agnes' Eve (orchestra). 1910. London: Hawkes, n.d. Contents: That Ancient Beadsman Heard the Prelude Soft; Her Maiden Eyes Divine; Prophyro, Now Tell Me Where Is Madeline. Incidental music to a play. Premiere, 1910.

Ulysses, op. 49 (orchestra). 1901. London: Novello, 1902. Incidental music to a play by Stephen Phillips. Commissioned by Herbert Beerbohm Tree. Premiere, 1902.

The War God. Unpublished manuscript. Incidental music to the play of Israel Zangwill. Premiere, 1911.

PUBLICATIONS

ABOUT COLERIDGE-TAYLOR
Books and Monographs

Coleridge-Taylor, Avril. *The Heritage of Samuel Coleridge-Taylor.* London: Dobson Books, 1979.

Coleridge-Taylor, Jessie. *A Memory Sketch; or, Personal Reminiscences of My Husband, Genius and Musician, S. Coleridge-Taylor, 1875–1912.* London: John Crowther, 1943.

Sayers, W. C. Berwick. *Samuel Coleridge-Taylor, Musician: His Life and Letters.* London: Cassell, 1915.

Self, Geoffrey. *The Hiawatha Man: The Life and Work of Samuel Coleridge-Taylor.* Aldershot, Hants, England: Scolar Press, 1995.

Thompson, Jewel Taylor. *Samuel Coleridge-Taylor: The Development of His Compositional Style.* Metuchen, N.J.: Scarecrow Press, 1994.

Tortolano, William. *Samuel Coleridge-Taylor: Anglo-Black Composer, 1875–1912.* Metuchen, N.J.: Scarecrow Press, 1977.

Dissertations

Batchman, John Clifford. "Samuel Coleridge-Taylor: An Analysis of Selected Piano Works and an Examination of His Influence on Black American Musicians." Ed.D. diss., Washington University, 1977.

Braithwaite, Coleridge Alexander. "A Survey of the Lives and Creative Activities of Some Negro Composers." Ed.D. diss., Teachers College, Columbia University, 1952.

———. "The Achievements and Contributions to the History of Music by Samuel Coleridge-Taylor, Colored English Musician." B.A. thesis, Harvard University, 1939.

Carter, Nathan M. "Samuel Coleridge-Taylor: His Life and Works." D.M.A. thesis, Peabody Institute of the Johns Hopkins University, 1984.

Phillips, Theodore Dewitt. "The Life and Musical Compositions of Samuel Coleridge-Taylor." M.Mus. thesis, Oberlin College, 1935.

Thompson, Jewel Taylor. "Samuel Coleridge-Taylor: The Development of His Compositional Style." Ph.D. diss., University of Rochester, Eastman School of Music, 1981.

Articles

Abdul, Raoul. "Coleridge-Taylor: 100 Years Later." In *Blacks in Classical Music,* 26–28. New York: Dodd, Mead, 1977.

Antcliffe, Herbert. "Some Notes on Coleridge-Taylor." *Musical Quarterly* 8 (1922): 180–192.

de Lerma, Dominique-René. "Black Composers in Europe: A Works List." *Black Music Research Journal* 10 (1990): 275–334.

Evans, Marjorie. "I Remember Coleridge." In *Under the Imperial Carpet: Essays in Black History, 1780–1950,* edited by Rainer Lotz and Ian Pegg, 32–41. Crawley, Sussex, England: Rabbit Press, 1986.

Green, Jeffrey. "'The Foremost Musician of His Race': Samuel Coleridge-Taylor of England, 1875–1912." *Black Music Research Journal* 10, no. 2 (1990): 233–254.

———. "Perceptions of Samuel Coleridge-Taylor on His Death (September 1912)." *New Community* 22, no. 2 (1985): 321–325.

Green, Jeffrey, and Paul McGilchrist. "Samuel-Coleridge Taylor: A Postscript." *Black Perspective in Music* 14, no. 3 (1986): 259–266.

Haynes, Elizabeth Ross. "Samuel Coleridge-Taylor." In *Unsung Heroes,* 127–149. New York: Dubois and Dill, 1921.

Janifer, Ellsworth. "Samuel Coleridge-Taylor in Washington." *Phylon* (Summer 1967): 185–196.

McGilchrist, Paul, and Jeffrey Green. "Some Recent Findings on Samuel Coleridge-Taylor." *Black Perspective in Music* 13, no. 2 (1985): 151–178.

Richards, Paul. "Africa in the Music of Samuel Coleridge-Taylor." *Africa* 57, no. 4 (1987): 566–571.

Sprigge, S. S. "Copyright and the Case of Coleridge Taylor." *English Review* (February 1913): 446–453.

BY COLERIDGE-TAYLOR

"Preface." In *Twenty-Four Negro Melodies.* Boston: Oliver Ditson, 1905.

PRINCIPAL ARCHIVES

Royal College of Music, London, England
Tree Collection, Boston Public Library, Boston, Mass.

*   *   *   *   *

At the time of his death in 1912, Samuel Coleridge-Taylor was just beginning to enjoy substantial fame as a composer. Several of his compositions had brought him attention early in his career, but he now had the respect and admiration of accomplished contemporaries such as Sir Arthur Sullivan, Sir Edward Elgar, Gustav Holst, and Ralph Vaughan Williams. He was regularly receiving commissions from outstanding music organizations and was in demand as a conductor, teacher, and adjudicator. He had made successful tours of the United States, and several choral societies there had been named for him. Coleridge-Taylor was a prolific composer and had written more than 150 works by 1912. Yet, he had not reached the zenith of his musical abilities, for he was still a young craftsman who was continuing to explore possibilities for the expression of his musical ideas. It is clear, however, that he had an impact upon and a place among the musicians and audiences of his day and that his works were performed for years after his death.

The son of a black physician from Sierra Leone and a British mother from London, England, Coleridge-Taylor was trained and educated in the schools of England and lived all of his life in the English town of Croydon. Belonging to a small racial minority, he suffered many social prejudices but married an English woman who had been a fellow student at the Royal College of Music. Exposure to the cultures of his father's race was obtained through his own reading and research, attendance at the annual London concerts of the Fisk Jubilee Singers, the establishment of friendships with outstanding blacks in America, and three visits to the United States—in 1904, 1906, and 1910.

Music study began for Coleridge-Taylor at age seven, when he was discovered by Joseph Beckwith, the conductor of a local orchestral society and of the orchestra at the Croydon Theatre. For seven years he was under the tutelage of Beckwith and developed facility on his child-size violin. At age 15, Coleridge-Taylor was sponsored as a student at the Royal College of Music by Colonel Herbert A. Walters, the honorary choirmaster of St. George's Presbyterian Church of Croydon. He selected the violin as his major and the piano as a minor instrument.

As Coleridge-Taylor showed signs of becoming an outstanding violinist, he also exhibited unusual ability in composition. His Te Deum was written during his first year of college, and a series of his anthems was published by Novello in 1891 and 1892. These anthems were brought to the attention of Sir George Grove, Director of the Royal College, and arrangements were made for Coleridge-Taylor to major in composition with Dr. Charles Villiers Stanford. With composition as his major, he developed rapidly as a composer.

In March 1892, he competed for one of the nine open scholarships at the college and was successful: "Now you are a scholar and before the world," wrote Sir George Grove to the budding composer. On October 9, 1893, he presented a concert of chamber music at the Small Public Hall, Croydon. Five of the six items on the program were his own compositions, including the songs "Solitude," "The Broken Oar," and "The Arrow and the Song"; the Sonata for Clarinet and Piano in F Minor; and the Quintet for Piano and Strings in G Minor, op. 1. The performers were fellow students from the Royal College, and Coleridge-Taylor himself played the piano parts.

On July 5, 1895, Coleridge-Taylor appeared on a student concert as the composer of Nonet in F Minor, op. 2, for piano, clarinet, bassoon, horn, two violins, viola, cello, and double bass. The performance of the Nonet was well received and focused the eyes of music critics upon the composer. That same year and the year after, Coleridge-Taylor added to his growing list of academic triumphs by winning the Lesley Alexander Prize for composition. Thereafter, many college concerts included one of his compositions, and to each, the press gave encouraging commendation.

A significant friendship developed at this time with Paul Laurence Dunbar, the African-American poet. Coleridge-Taylor's fame had spread to America, and his career was being followed with much interest by cultured men of the black race. Dunbar was among those who were attracted; and when he visited England in 1896 to give public readings of his poems, he made it a point to meet the rising musician. As a result, a joint recital of the works of both men was given at the Salle Érard. Coleridge-Taylor's contributions were nine new songs, five *Fantasiestücke* for string quartet, his *Hiawatha Sketches,* op. 16, for violin and piano, and settings of the Dunbar lyrics "The Corn Song" and "At Candle Lightin' Time," and the *African Romances,* op. 17.

Coleridge-Taylor completed his work at the Royal College in 1897 and thereafter continued his career in earnest. Early in 1898 he received a commission from the Three Choirs Festival and presented to them his Ballade in A Minor, for orchestra. During this time, collaborations with Dunbar continued, resulting in their *Dream Lovers,* a small but interesting operetta. Coleridge-Taylor's *African Suite,* for piano, also inspired by one of Dunbar's poems, was published the same year (1898). Also in 1898, Coleridge-Taylor resumed work on *Hiawatha,* which he had begun while he was in college. After many revisions, *Hiawatha's Wedding Feast* was performed on November 11, 1898, with great success, elevating Coleridge-Taylor to even greater fame.

The principal work of 1899 was the second part of *Hiawatha, The Death of Minnehaha*; and the third part, *Hiawatha's Departure,* was completed and performed on March 22, 1900. The entire evening was devoted to a single work, performed by a choir and orchestra of a thousand people, before an enormous audience, in the largest concert room in the United Kingdom. It was received with tremendous enthusiasm.

During 1900, music organizations from the United States began to contact the young composer, resulting in the successful tours of 1904, 1906, and 1910, which included visits to New York, Washington, Chicago, Baltimore, Philadelphia, Pittsburgh, Boston, Detroit, St. Louis, Milwaukee, and Norfolk (Connecticut). The United States Marine Band was secured for his visit to Washington, D.C., where he was received at the White House by President Theodore Roosevelt. During these visits, he also met Booker T. Washington, Harry T. Burleigh, violinist Fritz Kreisler, George W. Chadwick, and Horatio Parker, among other notables.

The Jubilee Singers of Fisk University in Nashville, Tennessee, toured England on more than one occasion in the late 1890s. Coleridge-Taylor attended some of their concerts and was deeply affected by the singing. The melodies struck a responsive chord in him, and thereafter he began collecting Negro melodies and including some of them in his works. He read the famous book by W.E.B. Du Bois, *The Souls of Black Folk,* and became especially interested in his race and heritage. This dedication and identification with his race spurred a new trend in his musical thinking and influenced his further development as a composer. In his works, he began to place emphasis upon rhythm through the use of off-beats, anticipated beats, delayed beats, heterometric rhythm (two or more meters together), polyrhythms, and cross-rhythms. Solo-chorus alternations and partially lowered third and seventh scale degrees also found their way into his writing. The titles of his works also reflected these new leanings: *African Suite* (1898), *Twenty-Four Negro Melodies Transcribed for Piano* (1904), *Toussaint l'Ouverture* (1901), *Ethiopia Saluting the Colours* (1902), *Four African Dances* (1902), and *Symphonic Variations on an African Air* (1906).

Coleridge-Taylor also wrote incidental music for various romantic plays produced at His Majesty's Theatre (London), receiving commissions from the producer Sir Herbert Beerbohm Tree for *Herod, Ulysses, Othello, Nero,* and *Faust.* He later arranged orchestral suites from these musical plays.

Coleridge-Taylor had been trained to follow the techniques of the great masters, and he used these techniques to establish himself in the music world. His melodies were very lyrical and expressive, and his musical ideas were expressed in definable forms that were most often stamped by elements of his own individuality. The harmonies were rich with nonharmonic material that hinted at the trend toward expanded chromaticism. Exciting orchestration was an earmark of the Coleridge-Taylor style, and rhythm became more energetic and driving with each phase of his development. He was a student of counterpoint, but he used basically homophonic texture with only brief segments of contrapuntal writing.

Coleridge-Taylor's style was his own; for unlike Sir Edward Elgar, Ralph Vaughan Williams, Gustav Holst, and other contemporaries, he moved beyond the limits of English and European traditions and embraced the musical idioms of a culture that had not yet been recognized as a serious musical source. While his life was tragically short, he nevertheless left a legacy that assures him an honored place among outstanding composers.

BALLADE IN A MINOR (1898)

On the recommendation of Sir Edward Elgar, Coleridge-Taylor received a commission in early 1898 to write a work for the Three Choirs Festival at Gloucester, where one of the oldest of the great annual English musical gatherings took place. The result was a work for full orchestra, the Ballade in A Minor, op. 33. Its premiere on the evening of September 12, 1898, with the composer conducting, was greeted by a storm of applause.

The Ballade is based on four alternating themes presented and developed in a modified rondo form (ABABA). A haunting melody, the first theme in a minor key moves stepwise within the interval of a major third. The related second theme covers a broader tonal range and uses contrasting phrases and sequences. The third theme, am were his own compositions, including the songs "Sol- The Broken Oar," and "The Arrow and the Song"; the r Clarinet and Piano in F Minor; and the Quintet for l Strings in G Minor, op. 1. The performers were fellow from the Royal College, and Coleridge-Taylor himself e piano parts.

July 5, 1895, Coleridge-Taylor appeared on a student s the composer of Nonet in F Minor, op. 2, for piano, clar- oon, horn, two violins, viola, cello, and double bass. The nce of the Nonet was well received and focused the eyes critics upon the composer. That same year and the year eridge-Taylor added to his growing list of academic tri- y winning the Lesley Alexander Prize for composition. r, many college concerts included one of his composi- l to each, the press gave encouraging commendation. significant friendship developed at this time with Paul Dunbar, the African-American poet. Coleridge-Taylor's spread to America, and his career was being followed with erest by cultured men of the black race. Dunbar was ose who were attracted; and when he visited England in give public readings of his poems, he made it a point to rising musician. As a result, a joint recital of the works of was given at the Salle Érard. Coleridge-Taylor's contribu- e nine new songs, five *Fantasiestücke* for string quartet, his *Sketches,* op. 16, for violin and piano, and settings of the yrics "The Corn Song" and "At Candle Lightin' Time," *frican Romances,* op. 17.

eridge-Taylor completed his work at the Royal College in thereafter continued his career in earnest. Early in 1898 d a commission from the Three Choirs Festival and pre- them his Ballade in A Minor, for orchestra. During this laborations with Dunbar continued, resulting in their *overs,* a small but interesting operetta. Coleridge-Taylor's *uite,* for piano, also inspired by one of Dunbar's poems, shed the same year (1898). Also in 1898, Coleridge-Tay- ed work on *Hiawatha,* which he had begun while he was . After many revisions, *Hiawatha's Wedding Feast* was per- n November 11, 1898, with great success, elevating Col- ylor to even greater fame.

e principal work of 1899 was the second part of *Hia- he Death of Minnehaha*; and the third part, *Hiawatha's* , was completed and performed on March 22, 1900. The ning was devoted to a single work, performed by a choir stra of a thousand people, before an enormous audience, est concert room in the United Kingdom. It was received endous enthusiasm.

ring 1900, music organizations from the United States contact the young composer, resulting in the successful 904, 1906, and 1910, which included visits to New York, on, Chicago, Baltimore, Philadelphia, Pittsburgh, Bos- oit, St. Louis, Milwaukee, and Norfolk (Connecticut). ed States Marine Band was secured for his visit to Wash- .C., where he was received at the White House by Presi- odore Roosevelt. During these visits, he also met Booker gton, Harry T. Burleigh, violinist Fritz Kreisler, George wick, and Horatio Parker, among other notables.

The Jubilee Singers of Fisk University in Nashville, Tennessee, toured England on more than one occasion in the late 1890s. Coleridge-Taylor attended some of their concerts and was deeply affected by the singing. The melodies struck a responsive chord in him, and thereafter he began collecting Negro melodies and including some of them in his works. He read the famous book by W.E.B. Du Bois, *The Souls of Black Folk,* and became especially interested in his race and heritage. This dedication and identification with his race spurred a new trend in his musical thinking and influenced his further development as a composer. In his works, he began to place emphasis upon rhythm through the use of off-beats, anticipated beats, delayed beats, heterometric rhythm (two or more meters together), polyrhythms, and cross-rhythms. Solo-chorus alternations and partially lowered third and seventh scale degrees also found their way into his writing. The titles of his works also reflected these new leanings: *African Suite* (1898), *Twenty-Four Negro Melodies Transcribed for Piano* (1904), *Toussaint l'Ouverture* (1901), *Ethiopia Saluting the Colours* (1902), *Four African Dances* (1902), and *Symphonic Variations on an African Air* (1906).

Coleridge-Taylor also wrote incidental music for various romantic plays produced at His Majesty's Theatre (London), receiving commissions from the producer Sir Herbert Beerbohm Tree for *Herod, Ulysses, Othello, Nero,* and *Faust.* He later arranged orchestral suites from these musical plays.

Coleridge-Taylor had been trained to follow the techniques of the great masters, and he used these techniques to establish himself in the music world. His melodies were very lyrical and expressive, and his musical ideas were expressed in definable forms that were most often stamped by elements of his own individuality. The harmonies were rich with nonharmonic material that hinted at the trend toward expanded chromaticism. Exciting orchestration was an earmark of the Coleridge-Taylor style, and rhythm became more energetic and driving with each phase of his development. He was a student of counterpoint, but he used basically homophonic texture with only brief segments of contrapuntal writing.

Coleridge-Taylor's style was his own; for unlike Sir Edward Elgar, Ralph Vaughan Williams, Gustav Holst, and other contemporaries, he moved beyond the limits of English and European traditions and embraced the musical idioms of a culture that had not yet been recognized as a serious musical source. While his life was tragically short, he nevertheless left a legacy that assures him an honored place among outstanding composers.

BALLADE IN A MINOR (1898)

On the recommendation of Sir Edward Elgar, Coleridge-Taylor received a commission in early 1898 to write a work for the Three Choirs Festival at Gloucester, where one of the oldest of the great annual English musical gatherings took place. The result was a work for full orchestra, the Ballade in A Minor, op. 33. Its premiere on the evening of September 12, 1898, with the composer conducting, was greeted by a storm of applause.

The Ballade is based on four alternating themes presented and developed in a modified rondo form (ABABA). A haunting melody, the first theme in a minor key moves stepwise within the interval of a major third. The related second theme covers a broader tonal range and uses contrasting phrases and sequences. The third theme,

"Eleänore," L'Oiseau-Lyre SOL-324; Columbia DB-2083; Gramophone D-3730.

Six Sorrow Songs, op. 57 (low voice). 1904. London: Augener, 1904. Contents: Oh What Comes over the Sea; When I Am Dead, My Dearest; Oh, Roses for the Flush of Youth; She Sat and Sang Away; Unmindful of the Roses; Too Late for Love. Premiere, 1904. Recorded: "Unmindful of the Roses," Pearl CD 9965; "When I Am Dead, My Dearest," HMV B-572.

"Solitude" (high voice). 1893. London: Augener, 1918. Premiere, 1893.

"Song of the Nubian Girl" (medium voice). London: Augener, 1905.

Songs of Sun and Shade (high voice). London: Boosey, 1911. Contents: You Lay So Still in the Sunshine; Thou Hast Bewitched Me, Beloved; The Rainbow Child; Thou Art Risen, My Beloved; This Is the Island of Gardens. Recorded: Columbia FB-3031 (no. 4); HMV B-8285 (nos. 2 and 5); HMV E-414 (no. 4); Pearl CD 9965 (nos. 2 and 5).

"Sons of the Sea" (medium voice). London: Novello, 1910. Recorded: HMV C-2728; Pearl CD 9965.

The Soul's Expression: Four Sonnets by Elisabeth Barrett Browning, op. 42 (low voice). 1900. London: Novello, 1900. Contents: The Soul's Expression; Tears; Grief; Comfort. Premiere, 1900.

Southern Love Songs, op. 12 (high voice). 1896. London: Augener, 1896. Contents: My Love: A Spanish Ditty; Tears: A Lament; Minguillo; If Thou Art Sleeping, Maiden; Oh! My Lonely Pillow: Stanzas to a Hindu Air.

"A Summer Idyll" (high voice). London: Boosey, 1906.

"Tell, O Tell Me" (high or medium voice). London: Augener, 1915.

"Thou Art" (medium voice). Philadelphia: Presser, n.d.

"The Three Ravens" (medium voice). London: Boosey, 1897.

Three Song-Poems, op. 50 (low voice). 1903. New York: Boosey, 1905. Contents: Dreaming for Ever; The Young Indian Maid; Beauty and Song.

Three Songs, op. 29 (high voice). 1899. London: Augener, 1899. Contents: Lucy; Mary; Jessy.

Three Songs of Heine (medium voice). London: Augener, 1918. Contents: My Pretty Fishermaiden; Thy Sapphire Eyes; I Hear the Flutes and Fiddles.

"Toujours, l'amour" (medium voice). Unpublished manuscript.

Two Songs, op. 81. 1912. London: Boosey, 1920. Contents: Waiting; Red o' the Dawn.

Two Songs (medium voice). London: Augener, 1916. Contents: My Lady; Love's Mirror.

"Until" (medium voice). Boston: Oliver Ditson, 1908.

"The Vengeance" (medium voice). Unpublished manuscript.

"Viking Song" (low voice). Boston: Oliver Ditson, 1914. Also arranged for SA.

"The Violet Band" (high voice). New York: William Maxwell, 1905.

"A Vision" (medium voice). Philadelphia: Theodore Presser, 1905.

"We Watched Her Breaking through the Night" (medium voice). Unpublished manuscript. Also arranged for SSA.

"Why Does Azure Deck the Skies?" (medium voice). Unpublished manuscript.

VOCAL ENSEMBLE

"Keep Those Eyes" (soprano, tenor, piano). London: Novello, 1903.

"Lift Up Your Heads" (SATB soli, organ). London: Novello, 1892.

CHORAL MUSIC

"All Are Sleeping, Weary Heart" (TTBB). London: Curwen, 1910.

"All My Stars Forsake Me," op. 67, no. 1 (SATB unaccompanied). London: Augener, 1905.

"Beauty and Truth" (SA). London: Curwen, 1912.

"Break Forth into Joy" (tenor solo, SATB, organ). London: Novello, 1892.

"By the Lone Seashore" (SATB). London: Novello, 1910.

"By the Waters of Babylon" (soprano, contralto, tenor, bass, SATB, organ). London: Novello, 1899.

"Dead in the Sierras," op. 67, no. 2 (SATB unaccompanied). London: Augener, 1905.

"Drake's Drum" (SA). London: Curwen, 1906.

"Encinctured with a Twine of Leaves" (SSA). London: Novello, 1908.

"The Evening Star" (SATB). London: Novello, 1911. Recorded: Audio House AHS-30F75.

"The Fair at Almachara" (SATB unaccompanied). London: Augener, 1905.

"Fall on Me Like a Silent Dew" (SA). London: Curwen, 1912.

"In Thee, O Lord, Have I Put My Trust" (SATB). London: Novello, 1891.

"Isle of Beauty" (SATB). London: Augener, 1920.

"Jesu, the Very Thought of Thee." In *The Methodist Sunday School Hymnal* (New York: Methodist Book Concern, 1911).

"A June Rose Bloomed" (SSA). London: Augener, 1906.

"Land of the Sun," op. 15 (SATB). ca. 1897. London: Augener, ca. 1897.

"The Lee-Shore" (SATB). London: Novello, 1912.

"Little Boy Blue" (unison). London: Boosey and Hawkes, 1923.

"The Lord Is My Strength" (SATB, organ). London: Novello, 1892.

"Loud Sang the Spanish Cavalier" (TTBB). London: Curwen, 1910.

Morning and Evening Service, op. 18 (SATB, organ). 1890. In *Parish Choir Book* (London: Novello, 1899), nos. 5, 7, 9, 10, 14. Contents: Te Deum; Benedictus; Jubilate; Magnificat; Nunc dimittis.

"Now Late on the Sabbath Day" (SATB). London: Novello, 1901.

"O Mariners, Out of the Sunlight" (TTBB). London: Curwen, n.d.

"O Who Will Worship the Great God Pan?" (TTBB). London: Curwen, 1910.

"O Ye That Love the Lord" (SATB, organ). London: Novello, 1892.

"Oh, the Summer" (SA). London: Curwen, 1911.

"The Pixies" (SSA). London: Novello, 1908.

Part-Songs, op. 21 (SSA). 1898. London: Augener, 1898. Contents: We Strew These Opiate Flowers; How They So Softly Rest. Premiere, 1898. Also arranged for piano solo.

"Prayer for Peace, April 1911" (unison). 1911. London: Curwen, 1911.

"Sea-Drift: Rhapsody," op. 69 (SSAATTBB unaccompanied). 1908. London: Novello, 1908.

"The Sea-Shell" (SATB). London: Curwen, 1911.

"Song of Prosperine" (SATB). London: Novello, 1912.

"Summer Is Gone" (SATB). London: Curwen, 1911.

Te Deum in F Major (SATB, organ). 1890. Unpublished manuscript. Note: later became part of *Morning and Evening Service.*

"To Thee O Lord." London: Novello, 1891.

"What Can Lambkins Do?" (SSA). London: Novello, 1908.

"What Thou Hast Given Me?" (SATB). 1901. London: Weekes, n.d.

"Whispers of Summer" (SATB). London: Novello, 1910.

DRAMATIC MUSIC

The Atonement, op. 53 (sacred cantata for soprano, contralto, tenor, baritone, SATB, and orchestra). 1903; revised 1904. London:

Novello, 1903; 1904 (revision). Contents: Prelude; Gethsemane; Prayer of the Holy Women and Apostles; Pontius Pilate; Calvary. Premiere, 1903.

The Blind Girl of Castél-Cuillé, op. 43 (cantata for soprano, baritone, SATB, and orchestra). 1901. London: Novello, 1901. Commissioned by the Leeds Musical Festival. Premiere, 1901.

Bon-Bon Suite, op. 68 (cantata for baritone, SATB, orchestra). 1908. London: Novello, 1908. Contents: The Magic Mirror; The Fairy Boat; To Rosa; Love and Hymen; The Watchman; Say, What Shall We Dance? Premiere, 1909.

The Death of Minnehaha, op. 30, no. 2 (cantata for soprano, baritone, SATB, orchestra). 1899. London: Novello, l899. Contents: Ever Thicker; And the Foremost Said; Forth into the Empty Forest; Gitchie Manito; Give Your Children Food; Minnehaha; And the Lovely Laughing Water; Hark, She Said; Wahonomin; Then He Sat Down; Then They Buried Minnehaha; For Her Soul; Farewell, Said He; To the Land of the Hereafter. Commissioned by the North Staffordshire Musical Festival of 1899. Note: part 2 of *Scenes from the Song of Hiawatha*. Premiere, 1899. Recorded: HMV C2210/13.

Dream Lovers, op. 11 (operatic romance for soprano, mezzo-soprano, tenor, bass, SATB, and orchestra). 1898. London: Boosey, 1898. Contents: Prelude; Duet: Is the Red Rose?; Trio: You May Go from Bleak Alaska; Song: Long Years Ago; Song: Pray Tell Me; Solo and Chorus: I'm a Wealthy Wand'ring Wight; Quartet: Long, Long the Labour. Premiere, 1898.

Endymion's Dream, op. 65 (opera in one act for soprano, tenor, SATB, and orchestra). 1909. London: Novello, 1910. Premiere, 1910.

The Gitanos (cantata-operetta for soprano, two mezzo-sopranos, two contraltos, SSA, and piano). 1898. London: Augener, 1898.

Hiawatha's Departure, op. 30, no. 4 (cantata for soprano, tenor, baritone, SATB, and orchestra). 1900. London: Novello, 1900. Contents: Spring Had Come (soprano); From His Wand'rings; At Each Other Look'd the Warriors; True Is All Iagoo Tells Us; By the Shore of Gitche Gumee; All the Air Was Full of Freshness; From the Brow of Hiawatha (soprano); Beautiful Is the Sun (baritone); Then the Generous Hiawatha; Still the Guests; And They Said Farewell. Commissioned by the Royal Choral Society. Note: part 3 of *Scenes from the Song of Hiawatha*. Premiere, 1900.

Hiawatha's Wedding Feast, op. 30, no. 1 (cantata for tenor, SATB, and orchestra). 1898. London: Novello, 1899. Contents: You Shall Hear How Pau-Puk-Keewis; Then the Handsome Pau-Puk-Keewis; He Was Dress'd in Shirt of Doe-Skin; First He Danc'd a Solemn Measure; Then Said They to Chibiabos; Onaway, Awake, Beloved (tenor); Thus the Gentle Chibiabos; Very Boastful Was Iagoo; Such Was Hiawatha's Wedding. Note: part 1 of *Scenes from the Song of Hiawatha*. Premiere, 1898. Recorded: Angel S-35900; Arabesque Recordings 8005; Brunswick 35003-A; Columbia C-1931/4; HMV ASD-467; HMV ESD7161.

A Tale of Old Japan, op. 76 (cantata for soprano, contralto, tenor, bass, SATB, and orchestra). 1911. London: Novello, 1911. Commissioned by Mr. and Mrs. Carl Stoeckel. Premiere, 1911.

Thelma, op. 72 (opera in three acts). 1908. London: Aschererg-Hawkes, ca. 1908. Premiere, "Prelude" only, 1910.

INCIDENTAL MUSIC

"The Clown and the Columbine" (narrator, violin, cello, piano). Unpublished manuscript. Note: accompaniment to the poem. Premiere, 1912.

Faust, op. 70 (orchestra). 1908. London: Boosey, 1909. Contents: Dance of the Witches: Brocken Scene; The Four Visions: Helen, Cleopatra, Messalina, Margaret; Dance and Chant; The Devil's Kitchen; A King There Lived in Thule; Menuet des folles, by Berlioz; Ballet des sylphes, by Berlioz. Incidental music to the play of Goethe. Commissioned by Herbert Beerbohm Tree. Premiere, 1908.

The Forest of Wild Thyme, op. 74 (orchestra). 1911. London: Boosey, 1911. Contents: Scenes from an Imaginary Ballet; Three Dream Dances; Intermezzo; Your Heart's Desire; Little Boy Blue (female voices); Come In; Dreams, Dreams (unison children's voices); Christmas Overture. Incidental music to a play. Commissioned by Herbert Beerbohm Tree. Recorded: "Intermezzo," "Christmas Overture," and "Three Dream Dances," Pearl CD 9965; "Christmas Overture," Columbia 9137; "Intermezzo," JB-8113; "Three Dream Dances," Victor 27230/1.

Herod, op. 47, no. 1 (orchestra). 1900. London: Augener, 1901. Contents: Processional; Breeze Scene; Dance; Finale. Incidental music to the play of the same name. Commissioned by Herbert Beerbohm Tree.

Nero, op. 62 (orchestra). 1906. London: Novello, 1907. Contents: Prelude; Intermezzo: Singing Girl's Chorus; Eastern Dance; First entr'acte; Second entr'acte: Poppea; Processional March. Incidental music to the drama of Stephen Phillips. Commissioned by Herbert Beerbohm Tree. Premiere, 1906.

Othello, op. 79 (orchestra). 1911. London: Metzler, 1912. Contents: Dance; Children's Intermezzo; Funeral March; The Willow Song; Military March. Incidental music to a play. Commissioned by Herbert Beerbohm Tree. Recorded: Boosey and Hawkes 4273/4; Marco Polo 8.223516; Pearl CD 9965.

St. Agnes' Eve (orchestra). 1910. London: Hawkes, n.d. Contents: That Ancient Beadsman Heard the Prelude Soft; Her Maiden Eyes Divine; Prophyro, Now Tell Me Where Is Madeline. Incidental music to a play. Premiere, 1910.

Ulysses, op. 49 (orchestra). 1901. London: Novello, 1902. Incidental music to a play by Stephen Phillips. Commissioned by Herbert Beerbohm Tree. Premiere, 1902.

The War God. Unpublished manuscript. Incidental music to the play of Israel Zangwill. Premiere, 1911.

PUBLICATIONS

ABOUT COLERIDGE-TAYLOR
Books and Monographs

Coleridge-Taylor, Avril. *The Heritage of Samuel Coleridge-Taylor*. London: Dobson Books, 1979.

Coleridge-Taylor, Jessie. *A Memory Sketch; or, Personal Reminiscences of My Husband, Genius and Musician, S. Coleridge-Taylor, 1875–1912*. London: John Crowther, 1943.

Sayers, W. C. Berwick. *Samuel Coleridge-Taylor, Musician: His Life and Letters*. London: Cassell, 1915.

Self, Geoffrey. *The Hiawatha Man: The Life and Work of Samuel Coleridge-Taylor*. Aldershot, Hants, England: Scolar Press, 1995.

Thompson, Jewel Taylor. *Samuel Coleridge-Taylor: The Development of His Compositional Style*. Metuchen, N.J.: Scarecrow Press, 1994.

Tortolano, William. *Samuel Coleridge-Taylor: Anglo-Black Composer, 1875–1912*. Metuchen, N.J.: Scarecrow Press, 1977.

* * * * *

Dissertations

Batchman, John Clifford. "Samuel Coleridge-Taylor: An Analysis of Selected Piano Works and an Examination of His Influence on Black American Musicians." Ed.D. diss., Washington University, 1977.

Braithwaite, Coleridge Alexander. "A Survey of the Lives and Creative Activities of Some Negro Composers." Ed.D. diss., Teachers College, Columbia University, 1952.

———. "The Achievements and Contributions to the History of Music by Samuel Coleridge-Taylor, Colored English Musician." B.A. thesis, Harvard University, 1939.

Carter, Nathan M. "Samuel Coleridge-Taylor: His Life and Works." D.M.A. thesis, Peabody Institute of the Johns Hopkins University, 1984.

Phillips, Theodore Dewitt. "The Life and Musical Compositions of Samuel Coleridge-Taylor." M.Mus. thesis, Oberlin College, 1935.

Thompson, Jewel Taylor. "Samuel Coleridge-Taylor: The Development of His Compositional Style." Ph.D. diss., University of Rochester, Eastman School of Music, 1981.

Articles

Abdul, Raoul. "Coleridge-Taylor: 100 Years Later." In *Blacks in Classical Music*, 26–28. New York: Dodd, Mead, 1977.

Antcliffe, Herbert. "Some Notes on Coleridge-Taylor." *Musical Quarterly* 8 (1922): 180–192.

de Lerma, Dominique-René. "Black Composers in Europe: A Works List." *Black Music Research Journal* 10 (1990): 275–334.

Evans, Marjorie. "I Remember Coleridge." In *Under the Imperial Carpet: Essays in Black History, 1780–1950*, edited by Rainer Lotz and Ian Pegg, 32–41. Crawley, Sussex, England: Rabbit Press, 1986.

Green, Jeffrey. "'The Foremost Musician of His Race': Samuel Coleridge-Taylor of England, 1875–1912." *Black Music Research Journal* 10, no. 2 (1990): 233–254.

———. "Perceptions of Samuel Coleridge-Taylor on His Death (September 1912)." *New Community* 22, no. 2 (1985): 321–325.

Green, Jeffrey, and Paul McGilchrist. "Samuel-Coleridge Taylor: A Postscript." *Black Perspective in Music* 14, no. 3 (1986): 259–266.

Haynes, Elizabeth Ross. "Samuel Coleridge-Taylor." In *Unsung Heroes*, 127–149. New York: Dubois and Dill, 1921.

Janifer, Ellsworth. "Samuel Coleridge-Taylor in Washington." *Phylon* (Summer 1967): 185–196.

McGilchrist, Paul, and Jeffrey Green. "Some Recent Findings on Samuel Coleridge-Taylor." *Black Perspective in Music* 13, no. 2 (1985): 151–178.

Richards, Paul. "Africa in the Music of Samuel Coleridge-Taylor." *Africa* 57, no. 4 (1987): 566–571.

Sprigge, S. S. "Copyright and the Case of Coleridge Taylor." *English Review* (February 1913): 446–453.

BY COLERIDGE-TAYLOR

"Preface." In *Twenty-Four Negro Melodies*. Boston: Oliver Ditson, 1905.

PRINCIPAL ARCHIVES

Royal College of Music, London, England
Tree Collection, Boston Public Library, Bost

* * * * *

At the time of his death in 1912, Samue beginning to enjoy substantial fame as compositions had brought him attentior now had the respect and admiration of ac ies such as Sir Arthur Sullivan, Sir Edwar Ralph Vaughan Williams. He was regula from outstanding music organizations ar ductor, teacher, and adjudicator. He ha the United States, and several choral named for him. Coleridge-Taylor was a written more than 150 works by 1912. zenith of his musical abilities, for he w who was continuing to explore possibilit musical ideas. It is clear, however, that h a place among the musicians and audie works were performed for years after hi

The son of a black physician fron mother from London, England, Coleri educated in the schools of England an English town of Croydon. Belonging tc suffered many social prejudices but m who had been a fellow student at the Exposure to the cultures of his father's his own reading and research, attenda concerts of the Fisk Jubilee Singers, th ships with outstanding blacks in Amer United States—in 1904, 1906, and 19

Music study began for Coleridge he was discovered by Joseph Beckwith orchestral society and of the orchestra a seven years he was under the tutelage c facility on his child-size violin. At age sponsored as a student at the Royal Co Herbert A. Walters, the honorary choir byterian Church of Croydon. He selec and the piano as a minor instrument.

As Coleridge-Taylor showed sig ing violinist, he also exhibited unusual Te Deum was written during his first ye his anthems was published by Novello anthems were brought to the attention tor of the Royal College, and arrange eridge-Taylor to major in compositior Stanford. With composition as his maj a composer.

In March 1892, he competed for arships at the college and was successf and before the world," wrote Sir Geo composer. On October 9, 1893, he pre music at the Small Public Hall, Croyd in a major key and with syncopated rhythm, is a lively contrast to its two predecessors and conveys a lighter and happier mood. These characteristics are continued by the fourth theme.

Coleridge-Taylor's lyrical melodies recur often in varied form. The first theme, for example, is sometimes transposed and otherwise developed and embellished, in one instance assuming the form of a mini-development section. The other themes also appear in various transpositions, and throughout the work, contrast of the themes in a basic homophonic texture is emphasized. An introduction and coda frame the main body of the work.

The harmonic language of the Ballade is basically traditional but embellished with nonharmonic tones, chromatic chords, and borrowed chords. These additional materials enrich and expand the work's texture.

An essential element in the success of the Ballade is its rhythmic vitality. The intensity of rhythms and variety of tempos are distinctive. In the eight-measure first theme, for example, the effect of accelerated tempo is achieved through diminution of the first phrase in the second. This device is used with almost every restatement of that theme. The contrast of two against three and the use of the triplet in 2/4 meter are persistent rhythmic characteristics, as is melodic syncopation. Tempos range from very fast to moderate or slow, and dynamics fluctuate from differing levels of *forte* to *piano*.

Standard orchestral forces are increased by four horns, two trumpets in F, and alto, tenor, and bass trombones. Percussion, however, includes only timpani and cymbals. The strings, which carry the greatest weight of all the orchestral forces, share the presentation and development of important thematic ideas with the winds and brass, which also provide strong harmonic support. Several orchestral techniques are notable: (1) the various instruments take turns in introducing the main themes, and contrasting instrumental colors emphasize the individuality and character of each theme; (2) successive restatements of the A theme appear in higher or lower registers and so bring freshness and brightness in contrast to the somberness of the initial statement; and (3) the tone colors of strings, woodwinds, and brasses interlock, overlap, become superimposed upon, and enclose one another.

The arresting character of the Ballade's opening theme, the ingenious economy of the use of material throughout, the unexpected transitions, and the richness and balance of the orchestration combined to rouse the premiere audience to great enthusiasm. The composer of promise who had gone to Gloucester on September 12 returned to London the next day a recognized master of his art.

DANSE NÈGRE (1898)

Inspired by writings of Paul Laurence Dunbar, the *African Suite,* for piano, consists of four movements entitled: "Introduction," "A Negro Love Song," "Valse," and "Danse nègre." The composer transcribed the fourth movement for orchestra, and it became one of his earliest orchestral works that was consciously directed to the representation of Negro life and culture. Thus, "Danse nègre" has come to stand alone in the repertoire as a single and complete work.

"Danse nègre" is a spirited dance that is presented in a hybrid form that bears characteristics of both sonata and ternary designs. As distinguished from sonata form, "Danse nègre" draws the listener's attention immediately with an upbeat flourish, dynamic

chords, and a *tremolo* embellishment; presents its themes in unorthodox ways; and divides its development section into two sections, each in a definable form, the first exploring motives based on material presented in the closing section of the exposition, the second introducing a new theme altogether, which is repeated three times. The recapitulation brings the return of theme A and theme D, transposed, the latter of which was introduced in the development section.

The broad tonal scheme of the movement presents elements of novelty that depart from the standard tonal relationships of the classical sonata. Distantly related keys and keys from the flat side of the primary tonic (D major) intensify the contrast of themes and sections and assist in delineating the form.

The rhythmic structure of the work is based on motives taken from the primary theme, and the subsidiary themes and bridge passages find their *raison d'être* in these motivic cells. Rhythmic and motivic continuity, intensified by dynamic accents and contrasting tempos, is an important element in a piece of tremendous energy and drive. Surprisingly, considering the work's title, syncopation plays only a small role in the rhythmic structure, occurring only as a counter-rhythm to theme C, for a brief seven measures in the horns and trombones.

A prominent feature of "Danse nègre" is its colorful orchestration, in which the composer uses woodwinds in pairs, adds a piccolo, and assigns these instruments significant roles in the introduction of the main themes. Additionally, recalling concertogrosso technique, the composer contrasts blocks of sound, placing a smaller group of instruments against the full orchestra and presenting interesting changes of color throughout.

"Danse nègre" is an early attempt to fuse Negro idioms with classical form. Although the thematic material was original, its conception was found in Coleridge-Taylor's increasing familiarity with and adaptation of Negro folk music. The work has been performed on several orchestral programs in recent years and is a part of Columbia Records Black Composers Series.

HIAWATHA'S WEDDING FEAST (1898)

Hiawatha's Wedding Feast, composed in 1898, is Part I of what later became a musical trilogy on Henry Wadsworth Longfellow's epic poem, *The Song of Hiawatha.* The Longfellow poem is a detailed account of the wedding celebration of the American Indian hero, Hiawatha, and the Indian maiden, Minnehaha. The lengthy epic poem with lines of eight syllables each (a poetic meter that consistently placed cadences on the weak beat), the unusual Indian names (Pau-Puk-Keewis, Yenadizzi, Chibiabos), and the primitive slant of the overall plot all fascinated the composer; and he accepted each one as a challenge to his creative abilities. A careful matching of pitches with words, a meticulous placement of climactic points, and novel approaches for the many lines of the same length were all necessary to avoid the ever-present threat of monotony and countless repetitions.

Coleridge-Taylor's setting of the poem as a continuous choral narrative, with one solo number and orchestral accompaniment, is noted for its beautiful, well-defined melodies, of which several appear again and again in colorful developments and transformations. It is in the presentation and development of these themes, designed to make them readily accessible to development, that Coleridge-Taylor's creativity becomes evident. The first theme is initially presented as a fanfare by the flutes and trumpets, and with its numerous appearances it behaves much like a reminiscence motive in the work overall. It is marked by wide leaps (a perfect fifth up, an octave down, a perfect fourth up) which are contrasted with predominantly descending stepwise motion at the end. The perfect intervals give this theme a primitive flavor that corresponds with the plot of the epic. The second theme is characterized by scalewise movement, contrasting thereby with the first theme. In all, seven main themes are introduced by men's and women's voices that alternately enter and exit in various combinations. The texture thickens and thins as unison voices contrast with the four-part chorus in alternating homophonic and contrapuntal textures. The sixth theme is the aria "Onaway, Awake Beloved," which is the only aria in the work. Written for tenor solo, "Onaway" momentarily adds contrast by replacing temporarily the declamatory style of choral narrative that has dominated the text setting.

In *Hiawatha's Wedding Feast,* tone painting is frequent: key words and phrases in the text are given special treatment, with disjunct motion selected for words or phrases expressing deep emotion and stepwise motion used for descriptive passages. The "frenzied gestures" of Pau-Puk-Keewis's dance are depicted by rushing eighth and 16th notes, and the octave leaps in the vocal parts describe the "wild tossing of sand in the air surrounding him." The moving lines of the different voice parts suggest "great snow drifts, landscapes, and leaping dunes."

The form of the work is shaped by the many lines of the text. Akin to a short opera in concert form, it is a multisectional work that consists of alternating choruses and interludes. The choruses are one-part forms that are extended by phrase repetition or sequence and by orchestral interludes that serve as codettas or transitions to new sections. The choruses are brought back in succeeding sections with different texts and with changes in mode, rhythm, or other elements appropriate for the particular time and event in the plot. A declamatory homophonic style is predominant, with occasional use of contrapuntal and imitative writing. The music is continuous and its phrases are marked by feminine endings. The work's one aria is a strophic song with a three-part design.

Hiawatha's Wedding Feast has a rich and variable tonal scheme, and a rich harmonic color and expanded tonality pervade almost every phrase. The music often moves quickly from one key area to another, employing changes of key with changes of phrase. The aria begins in one key and ends in an unrelated key a half step away.

The rhythmic character of the work is one of its most interesting characteristics, with the following treatments contributing to its rhythmic appeal. (1) Coleridge-Taylor uses a rhythmic pattern that has been traditionally associated with Indian culture (half note followed by two quarter notes), establishing an "ethnic" character for the unfolding of the choral narrative. (2) The lines of the poem are in trochaic meter, and the phrases all have feminine endings. (There is only one masculine ending in all of the 1,048 measures.) In addition, the phrases begin on various beats of the measure, such irregularity giving novelty and freshness to each chorus. (3) The dotted-quarter note followed by the eighth or its diminution or augmentation appears consistently in the rhythmic

design of each theme. This rhythmic figure heightens the effect of the trochaic meter and lends interest to the overall rhythmic scheme. (4) Syncopation appears at several points in the accompaniment and is subtly present in the feminine endings of all the phrases of the various choruses.

For this Indian legend, the orchestra serves as a musical narrator of events in the plot and a commentator on the action. Sudden contrasts in dynamics and tempos further dramatize the subjective and emotional content of the music. The orchestra's accompanimental role is diversified in that it establishes mood and harmonic background, supplies rhythmic and melodic counterpoint to the voices, provides interludes between the choruses, introduces and develops themes, effects key changes, and knits the work together as a whole.

Hiawatha's Wedding Feast presented something novel and quite striking to the British audience of 1898. On the evening of the premiere every seat was taken, and people were standing in the corridors. When Sir Charles Stanford took the baton and the trumpets gave out the simple but arresting opening subject, the interest of the audience was secured; and it increased as the curious rhythmic plan of the work unfolded. The unusual melodic design, the rapid transitions from rhythm to rhythm and from key to key, the unexpected orchestral effects, the descriptive effect of the writing, and the singability of the whole had a broad sweep of appeal. When the last strains of the orchestra died away, Coleridge-Taylor was recalled again and again. The next morning he awakened to find himself indeed famous, every London paper devoting considerable space, in words of praise, appreciation, and congratulations, to *Hiawatha's Wedding Feast.* The work was performed many times during the composer's lifetime, often with the composer conducting, and several times after his death. The tenor aria from that work, "Onaway, Awake Beloved," is a part of the Columbia Records Black Composers Series.

TWENTY-FOUR NEGRO MELODIES (1905)

In connection with his first visit to the United States in 1904, Coleridge-Taylor was invited by the Oliver Ditson Company to arrange for publication of an album of Negro folk songs for the piano. The response to the request was *Twenty-Four Negro Melodies Transcribed for the Piano.* Profoundly impressed by *The Souls of Black Folk* by W.E.B. Du Bois, Coleridge-Taylor attempted to represent in his opus the main currents of native Negro music from regions of both Africa and America.

In the foreword, Coleridge-Taylor explained that the melodies were not merely arranged but were harmonized and altered in other respects to suit the purpose of the book. He felt that the original melodies were beautiful but wanted to do for these Negro melodies what Brahms had done for Hungarian folk music, Dvořák for Bohemian, and Grieg for Norwegian. The plan he adopted was that of theme with variations. The actual melody in every case was inserted at the head of each piece as a motto so that his treatment could be clearly recognized and not confused with any idea of "improving" the original material.

Of the 24 melodies, four came from Southeast Africa ("At the Dawn of Day," "The Stones Are Very Hard," "Take Nabandji," and "They Will Not Lend Me a Child"), two from South Africa

("Song of Conquest" and "Warrior's Song"), one from West Africa ("Olaba"), one from the West Indies ("The Bamboula"), and 16 from America ("The Angels Changed My Name," "Deep River," "Didn't My Lord Deliver Daniel?" "Don't Be Weary Traveler," "Going Up," "I'm Troubled in Mind," "I Was Way Down A-Yonder," "Let Us Cheer the Weary Traveler," "Many Thousand Gone," "My Lord Delivered Daniel," "Oh, He Raise a Poor Lazarus," "Pilgrim's Song," "Run, Mary, Run," "Sometimes I Feel Like a Motherless Child," "Steal Away," and "Wade in the Water"). The sources of these melodies were *Les Chants et les contes des Ba Ronga,* a collection by M. Henri Junod; *New Jubilee Songs,* a collection of songs sung by the Fisk Jubilee Singers and compiled by Theodore Seward; *Jubilee and Plantation Songs,* published by Oliver Ditson; *Afro-American Folk Songs,* a collection by Henry Edward Krehbiel; and Mrs. Victoria Randall, a family friend who supplied the West African melody, "Olaba." Coleridge-Taylor thought the African melodies were more martial and free in character, and the American melodies, more personal and tender.

Although he arranged each of the melodies as a theme with variations, the treatments are also suggestive of other forms. Four categories are discernible among the transcriptions: theme with sectional variations, theme with continuous variations, theme and variations in a three-part design, and theme and variations in rondo style. The original melodies and their character are preserved in the presentation of each motto, with ten in fast tempo, ten in moderate tempo, and four in slow tempo. All are in their original keys—13 in a major key and 11 in minor.

Whereas the melodies are simple in their harmonic implications, Coleridge-Taylor did not hesitate to draw upon his musical intuitiveness to broaden their harmonizations. Rhythmic devices include two-against-three relationships, mixed meters, and rhythmic motives in the form of a chant or drum roll. Grace notes, rolled chords, octave passages, arpeggiation, and *tremolo* appear prominently and frequently.

Five transcriptions in particular give some insight into Coleridge-Taylor's variation technique. "At the Dawn of Day" is a three-part design in which the contrasting middle section has been created through the composer's segmentation and repetition of thematic fragments at changing pitch levels (sequence). In "Deep River," several dissimilar two-measure segments based on the main theme are presented in succession in a variety of key areas, with intervals expanded, rhythms modified, and major and minor modes alternated. Three of the four variations (1, 3, and 4) of "I'm Troubled in Mind" have fixed structures and melodies. The harmonization and style of accompaniment of each are decisively altered so that there are changes of mood and character. The second variation is free in its melodic contour, length, mode, and harmonic style—an episode in the course of the series. "I Was Way Down A-Yonder (Dum-a-lum)" has two highly contrasting thematic elements—one lyrical, the other rhythmical. Variation takes place in both parts as they alternate, with the entire piece resembling rondo form. From the outset and continuing throughout, part B of this double theme forms a harmonic ostinato as well. In "Wade in the Water" the variations follow each other uninterruptedly, connections between them being made through chordal elisions at the ends of phrases. Melodic and rhythmic motives are used in various guises and combinations, and the transcription as a whole is rhapsodic and improvisatory in style.

Although the 24 transcriptions of this opus are authentic melodies of a people with whom Coleridge-Taylor was developing new and important personal relationships, it does not appear that his intent was to accent or dramatize their ethnic character. Rather, his compositional approach was to give them a new interpretation and permanence as music literature, since the melodies are extended and explored in ways that demonstrate their adaptability to classical idioms and principles.

REFERENCES

Sayers, W. C. Berwick. *Samuel Coleridge-Taylor, Musician: His Life and Letters.* London: Cassell, 1915.

Thompson, Jewel Taylor. *Samuel Coleridge-Taylor: The Development of His Compositional Style.* Metuchen, N.J.: Scarecrow Press, 1994.

JEWEL T. THOMPSON

COLTRANE, JOHN

Born in Hamlet, N.C., September 23, 1926; died in Huntington, Long Island, N.Y., July 17, 1967. **Education:** Musical family, father played violin and sang, mother was church pianist and sang in choir; High Point, N.C., public schools; began studying clarinet, age 12, and alto saxophone a few years later; Philadelphia, Pa., Ornstein School of Music, studied saxophone and music theory, 1942; Granoff Studios, studied composition, 1951. **Military Service:** Hawaii, played in United States Navy band, 1945–46. **Composing and Performing Career:** Philadelphia, Pa., played alto and tenor saxophone with various groups including Joe Webb Blues Band, King Kolax, Eddie "Cleanhead" Vinson, and Jimmy Heath, 1945–48; toured with Dizzy Gillespie, 1949–51, Earl Bostic, 1952–53, and Johnny Hodges, 1953–55; recording debut with Gillespie's band; joined Miles Davis Quintet, 1955–57, 1958–60; performed and recorded with many artists including Donald Byrd, Don Cherry, Paul Chambers, Tadd Dameron, Red Garland, and John Griffin; recording debut as band leader, 1957; played in Thelonious Monk's quartet, July–December 1957; Jazz Gallery, New York, N.Y., debut with his own quartet, 1960; recorded extensively with this group, 1960–65; played and recorded in different groups with various artists including Rashied Ali, Art Davis, Steve Davis, Eric Dolphy, Jimmy Garrison, Roy Haynes, Billy Higgins, Elvin Jones, McCoy Tyner, Reggie Workman, and Alice McLeod Coltrane, 1960s. **Honors/Awards:** *Down Beat* International Critics Poll, voted number one in four categories: new star, tenor saxophone, miscellaneous instruments (soprano saxophone), and new combo, 1961; *Down Beat* International Critics Poll, voted number one on tenor saxophone, number two on miscellaneous instruments (soprano saxophone), 1964; *Down Beat* Reader's Poll, voted Jazzman of the Year, number one on tenor saxophone, Record of the Year, elected to the Hall of Fame, 1965.

MUSIC LIST

[The following list of titles includes only works that were composed by the subject of the entry; it is not a list of recordings that were made by the subject. Although the composer may have made recordings of his own works, the list is not restricted to those recordings but in many cases includes performances by other artists of the composer's work. The list is made up of publication and discographical data, in cases where such information is available. Although no effort has been made to include documentation of the earliest recording of the works listed, the date of the earliest recording that is readily available has been given. —Ed.]

"Africa." Recorded, 1961: Impulse IZ 9361-2; Impulse MCAD-42001; MCA MCAD-8028.

"After the Crescent." Recorded, 1965: Impulse IZ 9346-2; Impulse 120.

"After the Rain." Recorded, 1963: Impulse IZ 9346/2; Impulse AS-42; Impulse GRP-3-119.

"Alabama." Recorded, 1963: Impulse AS-50; Impulse GRP-3-119.

"Amen." Recorded, 1965: Impulse AS 9211; Impulse 167.

Ascension, Part 1 and 2. Recorded, 1965: Impulse AS-95; Impulse GRD2-113.

"Ascent." Recorded, 1965: Impulse AS 9211; Impulse 167.

"Attaining." Recorded, 1965: Impulse AS 9211; Impulse 167.

"Bass Blues." Recorded, 1957: Original Jazz Classics OJCCD-189-2; Prestige LP 7123; Prestige 24003.

"Bessie's Blues." Recorded, 1964: Impulse AS-66; Impulse GRP-3-119; Red Baron 64602.

"Big Nick." Recorded, 1962: GRP 9872; Impulse AS-9223-2.

"Blue Train." Recorded, 1957: Astor Place 4003; Blue Note 1577.

"Blue Valse." Recorded, 1965: Charly 87; Esoldun (France) 2119.

"Blues Minor." Recorded, 1961: Enemy 136; Impulse AS-6; Impulse MCAD-42001; JA Records JA 1243D.

"Blues to Bechet." Recorded, 1960: Atlantic 1382; Rhino/Atlantic 71984.

"Blues to Elvin." Recorded, 1960: Atlantic 1382; Rhino/Atlantic 71984.

"Blues to You." Recorded, 1960: Atlantic 1382; Rhino/Atlantic 71984.

"Brazilia." Recorded, 1965: Black Label 8012; Impulse AS-85.

"By the Numbers." Recorded, 1957: Blue Note 1577; Original Jazz Classics 394; Prestige 7378.

"Call." Recorded, 1966: Impulse (unissued).

"Central Park West." Recorded, 1960: Rhino 1419; Rhino/Atlantic 71984.

"Chasin' Another Trane." Recorded, 1961: Impulse IZ 9361/2; Impulse MCAD-39136l; Impulse 128.

"Chasin' the Trane." 1961. Recorded, 1961: GRP 119; Impulse AS-9325; Impulse 39136.

"Chronic Blues." Recorded, 1957: Original Jazz Classics 020; Prestige 7105.

"Compassion." Recorded, 1966: Impulse AS 9110; Impulse MCAD-39139; Impulse GRP 118.

"Consequences." Recorded, 1966: Impulse AS 9110; Impulse MCAD-39139; Impulse GRP 118.

"Cosmos." Recorded, 1965: Impulse 21462 or GRP 146.

"Count Down." Recorded, 1958: Atlantic 1311; Rhino 90462; Rhino/Atlantic 71984.

"Cousin Mary." Recorded, 1958: Atlantic 1311; Rhino 90462; Rhino/Atlantic 71984.

"Crescent." Recorded, 1964: Impulse AS-66; Impulse GRP-3-119; JA Records JA 1243D.

"Dahomey Dance." Recorded, 1961: Rhino 1373; Rhino/Atlantic 71984.

"Darkness." Recorded, 1966: Impulse (unissued).

"Dear Lord." Recorded, 1965: Impulse IZ 9346-2; Impulse GRP-3-119.

"Dearly Beloved." Recorded, 1965: Impulse 167.

"The Drum Thing." Recorded, 1964: Astor Place 4003; GRP 200; Impulse AS-66.

"Dusk Dawn." Recorded, 1965: Impulse IZ 9345-2.

"Equinox." Recorded, 1960: Rhino 1419; Rhino/Atlantic 71984.

Evolution, Part 1 and 2. Recorded, 1965: Impulse 146.

"Excerpt." Recorded, 1962: Impulse (unissued).

"Exotica." Recorded, 1960: Blue Note 93901; DCC Compact Classics DCC 014; Del Rack DRZ 903.

"Expression." Recorded, 1967: CMP CMP-CD-35; Evidence 222193; Impulse GRP-131.

"The Father and the Son and the Holy Ghost." Recorded, 1966: Impulse AS 9110; Impulse MCAD-39139.

"Fifth House." Recorded, 1959: Atlantic 1354; Rhino 1354; Rhino/Atlantic 71984.

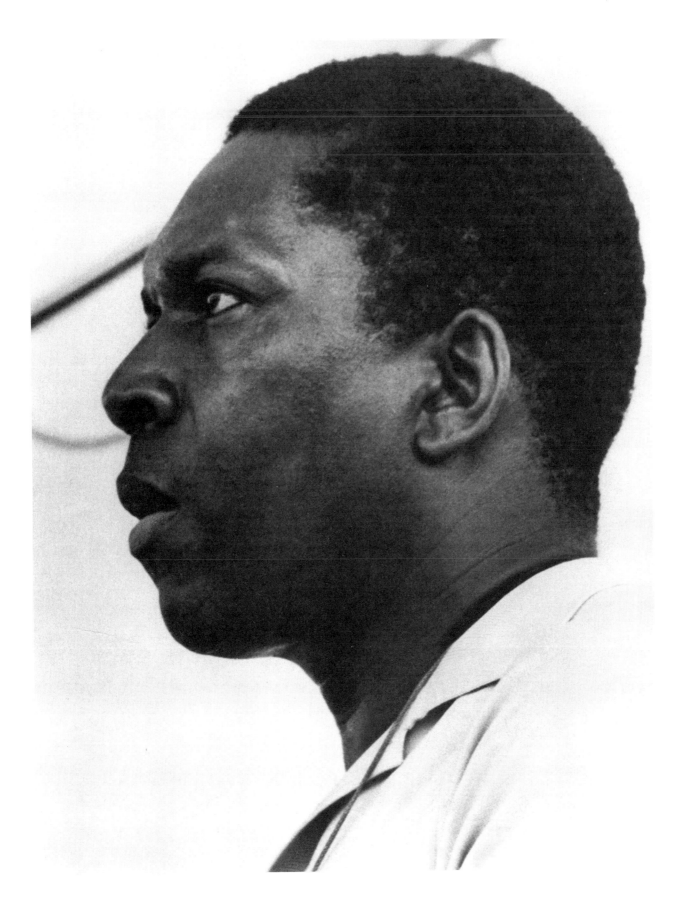

John Coltrane; courtesy of the Frank Driggs Collection; photo by Joe Alper

"Giant Steps." Recorded, 1959: Atlantic 1311; DIW 401; Rhino 90462; Rhino/Atlantic 71984.

"Goldsboro Express." Recorded, 1958: Original Jazz Classics 415; Prestige 7353.

"Grand Central." Recorded, 1959: EmArcy 834588; JVC 20456; Mercury MG 20449.

"Harmonique." Recorded, 1959: Rhino 1354; Rhino/Atlantic 71984.

"Impressions." Recorded, 1961: Astor Place 4003; Impulse IZ 9361/2; Impulse IZ 9346/2; Impulse GRP-3-119.

"India." Recorded, 1961: Astor Place 4003; Impulse AS-9223-2; Impulse AS-42.

"John Paul Jones." Recorded, 1956: Jazz West LP7.

"Joy." Recorded, 1965: Impulse GRP 118.

"Jupiter." Recorded, 1967: Impulse GRP-110; Soul Note 121287-2.

"Just for the Love." Recorded, 1956: Blue Note CDP 0777 7 99175 2 5.

"Kaleidoscope." Recorded, 1967: Impulse (unissued).

"Lazy Bird." Recorded, 1957: Blue Note 1577; MCA MCAD-42122; Original jazz Classics 841.

"Lead Us On." Recorded, 1966: Impulse (unissued).

"Leo." Recorded, 1966: Impulse GRP-110; Impulse 102; Soul Note 121287-2.

"Liberia." Recorded, 1960: Rhino 1419; Rhino/Atlantic 71984.

"Like Sonny" or "Simple Like." Recorded, 1959: Blue Note 9390; JA Records JA 1243D; Red Baron 64602; Rhino 1354; Rhino/Atlantic 71984.

"Living Space." Recorded, 1965: Impulse GRP-3-119.

"Locomotion." Recorded, 1957: Blue Note 1577.

"Lonnie's Lament." Recorded, 1964: GRP 200; Impulse AS-66.

"Love." Recorded, 1966: Impulse AS 9110; Impulse MCAD-39139; Impulse GRP 118.

A Love Supreme: Part I (Acknowledgement), Part II (Resolution), Part III (Pursuance), Part IV (Psalm). Recorded, 1964: Impulse AS-77.

"Manifestation." Recorded, 1966: Impulse AS-9223-2; MCA MCAC2-4132.

"Mars." Recorded, 1967: Impulse GRD-110.

"Meditations." Recorded, 1965: Impulse A-9110.

"Miles' Mode." Recorded, 1961: GRP 119; Impulse IZ 9361/2; Impulse AS-9223-2; Impulse 5883.

"Moment's Notice." Recorded, 1957: Blue Note 1577; DIW 401.

"Mr. Day" or "One and Four." Recorded, 1960: Blue Note 93901; Owl R2-79245; Rhino 1382; Rhino/Atlantic 71984; Roulette B2-93901.

"Mr. Knight." Recorded: Rhino 1382; Rhino/Atlantic 71984.

"Mr. P. C." Recorded, 1958: Atlantic 1311; JA Records JA 1243D; Rhino 90462.

"Mr. Syms." Recorded, 1960: Atlantic 1382; Rhino/Atlantic 71984.

"Naima." Recorded, 1959: Astor Place 4003; Atlantic 1311; Impulse IZ 9361/2; JA Records JA 1243D; Rhino/Atlantic 71984.

"Neptune." Recorded, 1962: Impulse (unissued).

"Nita." Recorded, 1956: Blue Note CDP 0777 7 99175 2 5.

"None Other." Recorded, 1967: Impulse (unissued).

"Not Yet." Recorded, 1962: Impulse (unissued).

"Number Eight." Recorded, 1967: Impulse (unissued).

"Number Five." Recorded, 1967: Impulse (unissued).

"Number Four." Recorded, 1967: Impulse (unissued).

"Number One." Recorded, 1967: Impulse GRP-131.

"Number Seven." Recorded, 1967: Impulse (unissued).

"Number Six." Recorded, 1967: Impulse (unissued).

"Number Two." Recorded, 1967: Impulse (unissued).

"Offering." Recorded, 1967: Impulse GRP-131; Impulse GRP-3-119; Impulse 169.

"Ogunde." Recorded, 1967: Impulse AS-9223-2; Impulse GRP-131.

"Olé." Recorded, 1961: Rhino 1373; Rhino/Atlantic 71984.

"Om." Recorded, 1965: Impulse 4131; Impulse 39118.

"One Down, One Up." Recorded, 1965: Black Label 8012; Impulse IZ 9346/2.

"One Up and One Down." Recorded, 1963: Ozone 21.

"Peace on Earth." Recorded, 1966: Impulse 102.

"Pristine." Recorded, 1957: Bethlehem 5001.

"The Promise." Recorded, 1963: Impulse AS-9223-2; JA Records JA 1243D; MCA MCAD 42122.

"Psalm." Recorded, 1964: Impulse AS77.

"Pursuance." Recorded, 1964: Impulse AS77.

"Resolution." Recorded, 1964: Impulse AS77.

"Reverend King." Recorded, 1966: Impulse AS-9148.

"Rockin.'" Recorded, 1963: Impulse (unissued).

"Satellite." Recorded, 1960: Astor Place 4003; Rhino 1419; Rhino/Atlantic 71984.

"Saturn." Recorded, 1967: Impulse GRP-110.

"Selflessness." Recorded, 1965: Impulse GRD2-113.

"Serenity." Recorded, 1966: Impulse AS 9110; Impulse MCAD-39139; Impulse GRP 118.

"The Sleeper." Recorded, 1959: EmArcy 834588.

"Slowtrane." Recorded, 1957: Original Jazz Classics 394; Prestige 7378; Prestige 11005.

"Some Other Blues." Recorded, 1959: Atlantic 1354; JA Records JA 1243D; Rhino/Atlantic 71984.

"Song of Praise." Recorded, 1965: Black Label 8012; Impulse AS-85.

"Spiral." Recorded, 1958: Atlantic 1311; Rhino 90462.

"Spiritual." Recorded, 1961: Impulse AS-9325; Impulse MCAD-39136; JA Records JA 1243D.

"Straight Street." Recorded, 1957: Original Jazz Classics 020; Prestige 7105.

Suite. Contents: Prayer and Meditation: Day; Peace and After; Prayer and Meditation: Evening; Affirmation; Prayer and Meditation: 4 A.M. Recorded, 1965: Impulse GRD3-119; Impulse MVCI 23057 or Impulse MCVI 23065.

"Sunship." Recorded, 1965: Impulse 167.

"Syeeda's Song Flute." Recorded, 1958: Atlantic 1311; Rhino 90462.

"To Be." Recorded, 1967: Impulse GRP-131.

"Trane's Slo Blues." Recorded, 1957: Original Jazz Classics 131; Prestige PRST 7581.

"Traneing In." Recorded, 1957: Original Jazz Classics 681; Original Jazz Classics OJCCD-189-2; Pablo 2308-227; Prestige 24003.

"Transition." Recorded, 1965: Delmark DE 463; Impulse 124.

"Tunji." Recorded, 1962: Impulse 5883.

"26-2." Recorded, 1960: Rhino 1419; Rhino/Atlantic 71984.

"Two, Three, Four." Recorded, 1962: Impulse (unissued).

"Up 'gainst the Wall." Recorded, 1962: Impulse AS-42; Soul Note 121287-2.

"Venus." Recorded, 1967: Impulse GRD-110; Soul Note 121287-2.

"Vigil." Recorded, 1965: Impulse AS-9106; Impulse 124.

"Village Blues." Recorded, 1960: Rhino 1354; Rhino/Atlantic 71984.

"Welcome." Recorded, 1965: Impulse AS-9106; Impulse GRP-3-119; Impulse 107.

"Wise One." Recorded, 1964: GRP 200; Impulse AS-66; Impulse 107.

"Your Lady." Recorded, 1963: Altenburgh NAI-105; Impulse 33109.

COLLECTIONS

Jazz Improvisation: Transcriptions of John Coltrane's Tenor Solos for All Instrumental Musicians. Tokyo, Japan: Nichion Publishing, 1978.

The Music of John Coltrane. Milwaukee, Wisc.: Hal Leonard Publishing, 1991. Note: saxophone part with chord symbols.

The Works of John Coltrane, Volumes 1–10. edited by Andrew White. Washington, D.C.: Andrew's Musical Enterprises, 1975.

PUBLICATIONS

ABOUT COLTRANE
Books and Monographs

Baker, David. *The Jazz Style of John Coltrane: A Musical and Historical Perspective.* Lebanon, Ind.: Studio 224, 1980.

Cole, Bill. *John Coltrane.* New York: Schirmer Books, 1976.

Daverat, Xavier. *John Coltrane.* Paris: Editions du Limon, 1995.

Davis, Brian. *John Coltrane Discography.* Hockley, England: B. Davis and R. Smith, 1976.

Filtgen, Gerd, and Michael Ausserbauer. *John Coltrane: Sein Leben, seine Musik, seine Schallplatten.* Gauting-Buchendorf, Germany: Oreos, 1983.

Fraim, John. *Spirit Catcher: The Life and Art of John Coltrane.* West Liberty, Ohio: Great House, 1996.

Fujioka, Yasuhiro, with Lewis Porter and Yoh-Ichi Hamada. *John Coltrane: A Discography and Musical Biography.* Metuchen, N.J.: Scarecrow Press, 1995.

Gerber, Alain. *Le cas Coltrane.* Marseille: Parentheses, 1985.

Jepsen, J. G. *A Discography of John Coltrane.* Denmark: Karl Emil Knudsen, 1969.

Nisenson, Eric. *Ascension: John Coltrane and His Quest.* New York: Da Capo, 1993.

Porter, Lewis. *John Coltrane: His Life and Music.* Ann Arbor, Mich.: The University of Michigan Press, 1998.

Putschögl, Gerhard. *John Coltrane und die afroamerikanische Oraltradition.* Jazzforschung/Jazz Research, vol. 25. Graz, Austria: Akademische Druck, 1993.

Priestley, Brian. *John Coltrane.* London: Apollo, 1987.

Simpkins, Cuthbert Ormond. *Coltrane: A Biography.* Philadelphia: Herndon House, 1975.

Thomas, J. C. *Chasin' the Trane: The Music and Mystique of John Coltrane.* New York: Doubleday, 1975.

Wild, David Anthony. *The Recordings of John Coltrane: A Discography,* 2nd ed. Ann Arbor, Mich: Wildmusic, 1979.

White, Andrew. *Trane 'n Me: A Semi-autobiography: A Treatise on the Music of John Coltrane.* Washington, D.C.: Andrew's Musical Enterprises, 1981.

——. *A Treatise on Transcription.* Washington, D.C.: Andrew's Music, 1978.

Theses and Dissertations

Angelos, Blake Jason. "Concepts and Styles in the Music of Miles Davis and John Coltrane from the Years 1958 through 1967." Master's thesis, Arizona State University, 1992.

Cole, William S. "John Coltrane and Sonny Rollins: What Else Is There to Say?" University of Pittsburgh, 1970.

Cole, William Shadrack. "The Style of John Coltrane, 1955–1967." Ph.D. diss., Wesleyan University, 1974.

Davis, John. "John Coltrane: The Message." Master's thesis, California State University, Dominguez Hills, 1994.

DeLaney, Richard Evans. "The Development of Melodic and Rhythmic Structure in the Style of John Coltrane." Master's thesis, University of Rochester, 1978.

Grey, DeSayles R. "John Coltrane and the 'Avant-Garde' Movement in Jazz History." Ph.D. diss., University of Pittsburgh, 1986.

Hester, Karlton Edward. "The Melodic and Polyrhythmic Development of John Coltrane's Spontaneous Composition in a Racist Society." Ph.D. diss., City University of New York, 1990.

Kernfeld, Barry. "Adderley, Coltrane and Davis at the Twilight of Bebop: The Search for Melodic Coherence (1958–59)." Ph.D. diss., Cornell University, 1981.

Kofsky, Frank Joseph. "Black Nationalism and the Revolution in Music: Social Change and Stylistic Development in the Art of John Coltrane and Others, 1954–1967." Ph.D. diss., University of Pittsburgh, 1973.

Millett, Les. "Improvisation and Structure: The Music of John Coltrane." Master's thesis, San Jose State University, 1988.

Porter, Lewis. "John Coltrane's Music of 1960 through 1967: Jazz Improvisation as Composition." Ph.D. diss., Brandeis University, 1983.

Putschögl, Gerhard. "Kontinuität und Transformation der schwarzen Oraltradition in den U.S.A.: Eine ethnohermeneutische Annäherung an die Musik John Coltranes." Ph.D. diss., University of Frankfurt, 1992.

Reed, Roxanne, R. "A Love Supreme: A Look at Spiritual Motivation for Transcendence in the Life of John Coltrane." Master's thesis, Bowling Green State University, 1992.

Robinson, Bill. "John Coltrane: Giant Steps." Master's thesis, Hofstra University, 1980.

Williams, Charles. "John Coltrane (1926–1967), Saxophonist and Composer: The Evolution of the Man, His Music and His Influence upon Young Jazz Musicians." Master's thesis, University of Puget Sound, 1974.

Articles

Carno, Zita. "The Style of John Coltrane." *Jazz Review* (October 1959): 17–21; (November 1959): 13–17.

DeMichael, D. "John Coltrane and Eric Dolphy Answer the Jazz Critics." *Down Beat* (April 12, 1967): 20–23.

Demsey, David. "Chromatic Third Relationships in the Music of John Coltrane." *Annual Review of Jazz Studies* 5: 145–180.

Gerber, Alain. "Huit Faces de Coltrane." *Jazz Magazine* (June 1972): 14–17; (July 1972): 25–31.

Horricks, Raymond. "John Coltrane: A Love Supreme." *Profiles in Jazz: From Sidney Bechet to John Coltrane,* 253–255. New Brunswick, N.J.: Transaction Publishers, 1991.

Hunt, D. C. "Coleman, Coltrane and Shepp: The Need for an Educated Audience." *Jazz and Pop* (October 1968): 18–21.

Ioakimidis, D. "Sonny Rollins et John Coltrane." *Jazz Hot* (December 1962): 30–34.

Jost, Ekkehard. "John Coltrane 1965–1967." *Free Jazz,* 2nd edition, 84–104. Graz, Austria: Universal Edition, 1981.

———. "John Coltrane and Modal Playing." *Free Jazz,* 2nd edition, 17–43. Graz, Austria: Universal Edition, 1981.

Kernfeld. Barry. "Two Coltranes." *Annual Review of Jazz Studies* 2 (1983): 7–66.

Kofsky, Frank. "A Different Drummer: John Coltrane and the Revolution in Rock." In *Black Nationalism and the Revolution in Music,* 185–197. New York: Pathfinder Press, 1970.

———. "John Coltrane and Albert Ayler." In *Black Nationalism and the Revolution in Music,* 173–183. New York: Pathfinder Press, 1970.

———. "John Coltrane and the Black Music Revolution." In *Black Nationalism and the Revolution in Music,* 155–171. New York: Pathfinder Press, 1970.

———. "Revolution, Coltrane, and the Avant-garde." *Giants of Black Music.* New York: Da Capo, 1980.

Mortara, A. "John Coltrane: La maturazione di uno stile." *Music Jazz* (May 1961): 10–14.

Polillo, A., and G. C. Testoni. "Impressioni su Coltrane." *Music Jazz* (January 1963): 10–14.

Porter, Lewis. "John Coltrane's *A Love Supreme*: Jazz Improvisation as Composition." *Journal of the American Musicological Society* 38 (1985): 593–621.

Postif, F. "John Coltrane: Une Interview." *Jazz Hot* (January 1962): 12–14.

Santucci, U. "Jazz and microstruttura and John Coltrane." *Music Jazz* (July–August 1963): 12–17.

Walker, M. "John Coltrane." *Jazz Monthly* (August 1966): 11–13; (September 1966): 30–31; (October 1966): 23–24; (November 1966): 29–31.

Weinstein, Norman. "John Coltrane: Sounding the African Cry for Paradise." In *A Night in Tunisia: Imagining of Africa in Jazz,* 60–72. Metuchen, N.J.: Scarecrow Press, 1992.

Williams, Martin. "John Coltrane: A Man in the Middle." *Down Beat* (December 14, 1967): 15–17. Reprinted in *The Jazz Tradition,* 197–206. New York: Oxford University Press, 1970.

BY COLTRANE

"Coltrane on Coltrane," with D. DeMichael. *Down Beat* (October 24, 1963): 18–19.

* * * * *

John Coltrane rates among those few artists who had profound influences and conveyed inspiration on many different levels. He gained historical significance by pioneering numerous approaches to improvisation for generations of musicians, by breaking ground for new forms of musical organization, and by creating a variety of styles through the exploration of different worlds of music. His legacy reaches far beyond the area of music and, by so doing, spreads impulses in many cultural fields and directions. This represents an outstanding achievement in African-American music. A crucial component of Coltrane's contribution is the accomplishment of a reappraisal of the traditional functional role of music in black culture as a central focus, a major source of information and fundamental value orientation.

A central aspect of Coltrane's cultural significance is his reappropriation and innovative transformation of structures and elements of traditional black music. On the one hand, he applied highly complicated and advanced tonal and harmonic systems; on the other, he persistently investigated the conceptual and expressive potential of the black oral culture. Exhausting the totality of this tradition, both the religious and the secular, he succeeded in recreating the essence of old ritual structures in contemporary forms. His study of African and Asian music cultures, a further opening toward non-Western sources of orientation, can be interpreted as a deepening of this fundamental method: a particular approach toward the historically and geographically most remote origins and prototypes of black music. This provided a certain "visibility" of the continuum of black music and lent a historical perspective that was of invaluable importance in the development of black self-awareness and in the search for a "unique black identity" during the cultural emancipation of the sixties. Significantly, the notion of a "black cultural unity" and the vision of a liberated black culture, demonstrated in the symbolic forms of Coltrane's music, became a primary source of inspiration and reference point for the "New Black Poetry" of the sixties and early seventies (Amiri Baraka: "The Evolver," 1968; Michael Harper: "Dear John, Dear Coltrane," 1970, etc.).

In order to grasp the particular nature of Coltrane's work, it is important to consider his musical achievements as vehicles of his spiritual message, his cultural and religious notions, his vision of creative human life, and his social philosophy. His social behavior as a musician and his conscientious striving to complete tasks obligated by his own conception as an artist add credence to this notion. From this perspective, Coltrane's pioneering holistic approach toward music and life opened not only new aesthetic dimensions but also set new ethical standards in the jazz world, standards that conspicuously corresponded to the "solidarity"—and "inner strength"—principles of the "new black consciousness" of the sixties. Coltrane himself defined his attitude and his goals in a quote that appears in the liner notes to the album *Meditations*: "My goal in meditating on this [force for unity in life] through music . . . is to uplift people, as much as I can. To inspire them to realize more and more of their capacities for living meaningful lives. Because there is certainly meaning to life."

The musical world to which Coltrane was exposed in his parental home and the education he received during his childhood and youth were of decisive importance for the late stages of his musical development and work as a composer. Both of his grandfathers were preachers, and his family was strongly involved in the activities of the church, including the music. As a young man, he was surrounded by the whole spectrum of black religious music, including sermons as well as gospel singing. At age 16, he moved to Philadelphia; while there, he deepened his studies on the alto saxophone and took classes in music theory at the Ornstein School of Music. In 1951, he continued his studies, now including composition, at the Granoff School of Music. In Philadelphia, Coltrane also became familiar with the secular styles of black music, including the blues and R&B. During this time, he played in various bebop and R&B bands, including Eddie "Cleanhead" Vinson's band, where he switched to tenor saxophone (1947–48); Earl Bostic's band (1952–53); Dizzy Gillespie's big band, with which he had his record debut in 1949; and Johnny Hodges' ensemble (1953–55). The Miles Davis Quintet, which Coltrane joined in 1955, was the first band of which he was a member that had a determining influence on the stylistic direction and conceptual development of jazz.

Another turning point in Coltrane's life and musical development, on a different level and even more decisive than his joining the Miles Davis Quintet, was the spiritual awakening that opened up to him an entirely new dimension of creativity and awareness. As he stated in the liner notes of *A Love Supreme,* "During the year 1957, I experienced, by the grace of God, a spiritual awakening which was to lead me to a richer, fuller, more productive life. At that time, in gratitude, I humbly asked to be given the means and privilege to make others happy through music. I feel this has been granted through His grace."

Among the multiple musical influences to which Coltrane was exposed, the cooperative periods with Miles Davis (1955–57 and 1958–60) and Thelonius Monk (1957) certainly had the strongest and most lasting effect. In the ensembles of both musicians, he collected information and gained invaluable experience that was crucial to his further development. Both musicians, each in his own way, stimulated Coltrane to explore new ways of thinking. With Monk, it was primarily the unorthodox treatment of musical forms and a bold sense of harmony. Miles was mostly responsible for stimulating Coltrane to recognize, and effectively use, the freedom of simplicity—especially on the level of melody.

During his stay with Monk's group, Coltrane produced his first record under his own name (*Blue Train*); two of the recorded pieces contain elements and structural tendencies that presage his development in the following years. The theme of "Blue Train," a medium-tempo blues, consists of a simple two-bar riff pattern (repeated six times). "Moment's Notice," which is based on a complicated harmonic scheme with dense harmonic rhythm, has six bars of an ostinato riff pattern at the end of its AA' form. Among the "riff-type tunes" whose themes are conspicuously based on repetitious riff patterns, there are many blues compositions ("Mr. P. C.," "Cousin Mary") and other pieces like "Dahomey Dance." Generally, Coltrane's use of the riff pattern, with its static harmony and clear horizontal melodic tendency, already points toward modal structures. This is supported by the fact that Coltrane used it as a composing element various times during his modal period (late 1960–65), most prominently in the suite *A Love Supreme.*

While Coltrane's almost obsessive quest for exploring the possibilities of functional harmony reached its peak in 1959 with the recording of his composition "Giant Steps," his new, and in certain respects, contrary stylistic orientation toward horizontal creation became manifest around 1959, in his improvisations on Davis's modal compositions "So What" and "Flamenco Sketches." During this time Coltrane worked almost exclusively with his Classical Quartet, which included McCoy Tyner (piano), Jimmy Garrison (bass), and Elvin Jones (drums).

Remarkably, the first decisive steps toward composing with structural elements based on modes (i.e., scales rather than chord progressions) were taken during his reconstruction of the Rodgers and Hammerstein waltz, "My Favorite Things." His idiosyncratic arrangement and instrumentation bestowed on this tune an entirely new quality and atmosphere. More importantly, the original AAB form was dissolved or transformed in favor of an order determined by the dominating elements of scale improvisation and ostinato riff patterns. The possibility for the unlimited expansion by the soloists upon each of the two improvising scales (E minor and G major) gave way to new concepts of structural freedom that implied open-ended form. At the same time, the eight-bar unit was established in Coltrane's modal music as an organizing principle. The contemporary use of the soprano saxophone in "My Favorite Things" represented a decisive initial step in the process of admitting to jazz timbres and other musical elements of African and Asian cultures.

Coltrane's concern for musical structure and organization grew immensely during his modal and postmodal periods. Conspicuously, its most distinct expression is found within the improvisational structures of his solos and his communication with the ensemble, that is, within the context of the live repertoire. Prominent among compositions featuring this concern for musical structure and organization over time are "My Favorite Things" (1960–66), the up-tempo tune "Impressions" (1961–65), and the ballad "Naima" (1959–66). In order to adequately understand the value of the compositional craft that is manifested in this music, it should be considered as oral composition, that is, the process of composing or music-making in which the musical development takes place by means of the spontaneous interaction of the group members based on oral communication as opposed to notated scores. With the thematic material and the formal basis of Coltrane's modal tunes often amounting to an absolute minimum, his ingenious sense and skill in construction is most clearly demonstrated by systematic development upon coherent structural and dynamic elements over extremely long periods of time (up to 30 minutes) by utilizing smaller units. Though veiled by abstraction and stylistic transformation mechanisms, the architecture and the aesthetic characteristics of Coltrane's modal music nevertheless clearly exhibit fundamental adaptations of the organizational principles and expressive features that are deeply rooted in black oral traditions such as the chanted sermon or gospel singing.

This radical departure from jazz conventions severely confounded many critics and listeners whose musical and cultural understanding did not provide sufficient preparation for these practices and who therefore refused to accept the "New Black Music." Behind the negative comments denigrating Coltrane's music (and that of others) as "chaotic," "monotonous," "hysterical," or as "anti-jazz" were often hidden old repressive behavior patterns based on ethnocentric prejudices. If Coltrane's reception had been ambivalent in the fifties, its polarization into enthusiastic followers and fierce opponents sharpened drastically during the sixties. His increasingly uncompromising attitude was philosophically and religiously motivated and characterized by an unrelenting quest for constant stylistic renewal: "There is never any end," he told Leonard Feather in an interview for an October 1964 *New York Post* article. "There are always new sounds to imagine, new feelings to get at and always there is the need to keep purifying these feelings and sounds, so we can see more and more clearly what we are. In that way, we can give to those listening the essence, the best of what we are." This idea was coupled with his natural confidence that "eventually the listeners move right along with the musicians."

With his album entitled *A Love Supreme* (1964) Coltrane enjoyed a degree of success and recognition that is very rare in the jazz world. The four movements of the suite are closely linked by a motive and can be considered Coltrane's most consummate composition. Representing the culmination of his conceptual thinking and by stylistic characteristics worked out during the modal period, its last part, "Psalm" played in "free meter," already foreshadows Coltrane's future development.

Other pioneers of "Free Black Music," such as Ornette Coleman and Cecil Taylor, had already made the emancipatory step away from metric restrictions, but it was Coltrane whose explorations of rhythmic structural possibilities in free meter exhibited a strong inclination toward black religious vocal traditions, specifically the soloistic chant in cantillation style, known as "free meter gospel song." Coltrane uses cantillation style in three types of compositional form, as follows: (1) covering an entire composition, including theme and improvisation ("Song of Praise," 1965); (2) appearing only in the thematic parts surrounding the improvisations and codas ("Brazilia," 1965); and (3) covering rhythmically independent movements of a larger composition that are interchanged with metrically structured parts (Suite, 1965). A remarkable innovative feature of this genre is the enormous spectrum of atmospherical levels for which it makes room, thus allowing for instantaneous transitions between extremely different, seemingly opposed modes of emotional expression and musical activity.

During this last (postmodal) period, we find a drastic intensification of previous developments in the form of a major shift in the hierarchical arrangement of musical parameters. Elements of sound unambiguously dominate the nature and determine the course of Coltrane's postmodal music. The possibilities of these further explorations in sound are heavily dependent on the new freer, rhythmic conceptions and on highly intense forms of collective interaction. The universal meaning of sound in this music mirrors Coltrane's philosophical notion, as stated by his wife, Alice, that "sound was the first manifestation in creation before music." Others of Coltrane's substantial innovations are a new functional treatment of the established instruments, the addition of numerous smaller percussive instruments (*zanza*, bells, etc.) that primarily serve the purpose of adding colors, and occasionally an increase in instrumentation (several horns, drums, two basses, etc.) to achieve a broad, multi-directional sound with a strong and flexible rhythmic-percussive basis. Whatever the spiritual influences from East Indian sources on compositions like "Om" ("All possible sounds that man can make vocally," he says) may have been, they meet with the traditional black notion of music as a "healing" cathartic power and of sound as a central cultural force.

GIANT STEPS (1959)

There is some ambivalence about the stylistic classification of "Giant Steps." On the one hand, it still belongs to the bebop/hardbop vein in the idiomatic style of the improvisations and its rather conventional structure-theme (repeated)/Coltrane solo/Tommy Flanagan piano solo/Coltrane short solo—all on the chord-changes of the theme/theme repeated. On the other hand, the harmonic principles on which the composition is based clearly go far beyond standard bebop harmony, thus fully blasting its restrictions. For Coltrane, who had been obsessed with exploring the possibilities of functional harmony in jazz compositions, Giant Steps was an ultimate step in the completion of his search of multi-chordal structures.

As innovative and original as Coltrane's harmonic concept appeared to be in the context of late fifties' jazz harmony, there were clear precedents for it in the music of the Romantic era of European classical music and, to a certain extent, even in the tradition of jazz interpretations of Broadway songs. David Demsey claims, for instance, that "three nineteenth-century songs by Hugo Wolf provide models which are similar to Coltrane's thirds pieces [the harmonic organization of this genre of pieces is based on the equal division of the octave into three parts by major thirds, thus creating three equal key areas] with respect to chromatic third relationships which form thirds cycles." In the jazz tradition, the most interesting precursor is offered in the harmonic progressions of the "bridge" of Richard Rodgers' composition "Have You Met Miss Jones?" (1937). Beyond this historical backdrop, one source provides a singularly definitive influence on Coltrane's harmonic concept in "Giant Steps": Nicolas Slonimsky's *Thesaurus of Scales and Melodic Patterns*. It contains distinctive patterns to which the melody and particularly the harmonic progressions of the B section of "Giant Steps" exhibit a direct connection.

Coltrane's first use of the harmonic concept of chromatic third relations served as a foundation for sophisticated patterns of improvisation; that is, as a means of creating harmonic color and variation and, by superimposing new progressions, of melodically exhausting further vertical possibilities in a set of given standard chords. This is demonstrated in Coltrane's improvisations on "Limehouse Blues" (1959) and "Double Clutching" (1958). In the former, the improvised lines reveal the use of the division of the octave into both three and four parts.

The idea of chord substitution as enrichment of harmonic color undoubtedly also gave rise to Coltrane's reharmonization of Davis's "Tune Up," which was recorded with the title "Countdown" on the same day as "Giant Steps" and published on the same LP. The understanding of the system of harmonic substitution applied here (as it is in later contrafacts reharmonized by Coltrane, such as "Fifth House" on the structure of "What Is This Thing Called Love" or "Satellite" on the structure of "How High the Moon") is indispensable to understanding the genealogy of "Giant Steps." In addition to creating a new melody, Coltrane enriches the first three four-bar sections of the 16-bar "Tune Up" form by inserting a set of additional cadences, thus producing a dense harmonic rhythm of one chord every second beat (at the tempo of quarter note = 352, this results in an extremely rapid change of chords).

The function of the chromatic major third principle in "Giant Steps" differs sharply from that in "Countdown." Instead of being applied merely for harmonic decoration (re-harmonization), it becomes the foundation of the entire composition, the constructive principle on which the coherence and logic of "Giant Steps" is built.

The conceptual dominance of harmony is used by Coltrane to bestow structural unity on the thematic presentation concerning all levels of musical organization. Most remarkably, the rhythmic structure of the melody shows absolute congruence with the harmonic rhythm. In other words, every note becomes harmonized. As a result, the melodic rhythm underlines the importance of the target chords of each phrase, which are the only chords with a four-beat duration and played with anticipatory off-beats (mm. 3, 7, 9, 11, 13, 15). The theme of "Giant Steps," in its concise 16-bar form, represents a composition of distinctive and complex construction, highly inventive and carefully organized with a compelling logic.

One of Coltrane's major motives for composing "Giant Steps" was to create a kind of virtuosic etude to systematically train a complete (technical) mastery of the harmonic progressions of the piece. However, the resulting enriched harmonic variety and color, and the apparent gain in harmonic flexibility, turned out to be restrictive to improvisational flexibility (as the reiterative, somewhat clichéd patterns in the improvisations show) and in certain respects a hindrance toward creativity. For this reason, Coltrane later refrained from the composed ensemble conception of "Giant Steps" and used this harmonic system without the restrictions that the conventional formal structure with its determined harmonic rhythm imposed on his melodic creativity. Said Coltrane in a 1960 *Down Beat* article, "I haven't completely abandoned this approach, but it wasn't broad enough. I'm trying to play these progressions in a more flexible manner now."

For many musicians, arrangers, and composers, "Giant Steps" became an important reference point, an etude for practicing and an inspiration for the creative use of harmony according to "chromatic thirds."

IMPRESSIONS (1961)

The numerous live recordings of "Impressions" offer the clearest documentation of Coltrane's stylistic progress in oral composition during his modal period, which rests upon the principles of organization, communication strategies, and the use of structural patterns and expressive characteristics. Moreover, it seems that a large number of stylistic innovations originated in Coltrane's experiments with this tune. A scholarly examination of "Impressions" should actually commence within Coltrane's improvisations on "So What" in the Davis ensemble. The theme and the improvisations of Coltrane's tune are built on the same formal and tonal structure: a 32-bar AABA-scheme (with the Dorian scale as a basis for improvisation in the A sections and a chromatic shift to E-flat Dorian in the B section). From this perspective, "Impressions" represents a certain continuation of "So What," which ended in the final performance on July 28, 1965, in Paris. Coltrane gave the Davis tune a new theme, and the vehement departure from the original conceptual features of the Davis quintet's interpretation is a direct result of Coltrane's new stylistic approaches, with special regard to his very close cooperation with the rhythm section: by force of the collective creation of new strategies of oral communication and oral composition, the Classical Quartet turned "Impressions" into a musical construction that, in spite of maintaining its common formal basis, had very little in common with the former performances of "So What."

A 1995 live recording from Stockholm provides an excellent example of well-conceived solos and comprehensive large structure in Coltrane's band. Its advanced development represents a mature mastery and coordination of modal style and a highly experienced, calculated, and effective usage of a variety of techniques and strategies. The crucial significance of teamwork within the Coltrane group becomes highly evident here. The multiple functions of drummer Elvin Jones contribute significantly to the constructive processes. Coltrane's closest stimulating partner playing a second solo instrument that simultaneously supports all other activities in the group, Jones makes rhythm a central component in Coltrane's music.

In the Stockholm performance, the quartet displays a subtractive approach to instrumentation and texture which, in its basic format, represents many "Impressions" documents. After the theme is stated, pianist McCoy Tyner takes the first solo; during Coltrane's solo, Tyner drops out after three choruses; then, after the fifth chorus, bassist Jimmy Garrison drops out. This sequence is crucial to the nature of the increase of dynamic level taking place in Coltrane's solos: he is working from a medium level of expressive energy in the beginning, increasing in stages toward climaxes of varying intensity and nature, and culminating in the vehemently expressive episodes of the final 10–12 choruses. This process is based on a steady intensification of the interaction between the rhythmic/percussive and the melodic/sound elements that unfold in the Coltrane-Jones duo, starting from the sixth chorus.

During this process, the 32-bar chorus scheme remains intact. Except for the second and the sixth choruses, which Coltrane initiates with rising sequences of "honk" formulae, the chorus action rises out of shout-like phrases that become increasingly vehement, repetitive, and rhythmically complex in the second half of the solo. Interestingly, during the first choruses, these initial phrases regularly lead to intensified activities in the second half of the chorus. From the seventh chorus onward, these voice-like statements already constitute the peak phases of each chorus unit.

As a distinct indicator of structural change within a chorus, "honk" formulae appear several times at the beginning of the B section. In their strongly contrasting effect, they underline the formal and tonal division of the chorus scheme. A sequential use of such formulae, which is of special structural interest, starts in the third chorus. Together with Jones's simultaneously originating asymmetrical accent patterns (5+5+3+3+3+3+3+3+4=32 followed by 3+3+3+3+3+2+2+1=20), it produces a first major climax in Coltrane's solo. Conspicuously, Jones's typical asymmetrical groupings coincide with chord accents that McCoy Tyner executes at the piano.

In the choruses that follow, there appear similar culminating phases which originate either simultaneously between the musicians or in a stimulating-reactive fashion. Both cases—in which Coltrane's highly expressive sound articulation ("screaming") and repetitive statements coincide with or subtly stimulate the intense playing of Jones—confirm the idea that the basis of the compositional concept applied here is the traditional African-American system of oral communication. A "screaming" and "honking" formula with strong internal contrast of pitch shift (register leap) and tone color, which Coltrane plays throughout chorus 11, serves as a terminating factor in many other solos, thereby being used as a method of formal order.

Coltrane's last performance of "Impressions" (1965) reveals a further development in all aspects of oral composition. Most strikingly, the freer creation of structural design is based on the dominance of sound parameters and the communicative potential of the performers. As a consequence, the chorus unit loses its significance as a determinant of structural coherence; many formulaic unities show an overlap between various parts of different choruses. This freer use of elements and treatment of form represented, ironically, an increase in control in all aspects of musical production, the result of a sovereign mastery of form, hard training, and disciplined routine. This approach to music making is clearly manifested in the multiple, extended, and highly differentiated ways in which paraphrase is applied to increase tension. The most impressive example of the process of "repetitive variation" takes place in the last formulaic unity (a structurally coherent unity in which particular formulaic patterns are developed or worked out). An initial "sound phrase" (vocal or instrumental passages with no clear content or pitch structure, in which the parameter of sound is prevalent), which is centered around *b*-flat, is turned by systematic gradual permutation into a pattern circling around *c*". Remarkably, in spite of the rather free yet highly controlled development and the "form-dissolving" tendencies, this section still shares the most elementary principles of construction with all other versions of "Impressions": the musicians strictly observe the 4/4 meter (though it appears quite often only as an abstract framework) and the fundamental 32-bar chorus scheme.

A LOVE SUPREME (1964)

With his suite *A Love Supreme,* John Coltrane created a work that became highly inspirational for musicians and audiences. Its spiritual message opened a new dimension of cultural meaning in jazz music. The four movements—"Acknowledgement," "Resolution," "Pursuance" and "Psalm"—"suggest a kind of pilgrim's progress in which the pilgrim acknowledges the divine, resolves to pursue it, searches, and eventually celebrates what has been attained in song," says Lewis Porter. Since the "Psalm" represents in a unique manner the musical/wordless recitation of Coltrane's religious poem (which appears on the LP cover) and speaks his "literary legacy" of *A Love Supreme,* it assumes a special position in the suite.

A second studio recording of *A Love Supreme* is lost. There is proof of only one live recording, which was made in July 1965 at a festival in Antibes, France, and published on record. A comparison of the studio and the live versions reveal, with all their differences, the elementary common conceptual basis of John Coltrane's musical thought. Generally speaking, the concert version maintains a level of high intensity throughout, thus forfeiting some of the studio version's logic and differentiation. A third recording of *A Love Supreme,* made in Tokyo in 1978 by the Elvin Jones group as *Dear John Coltrane,* shows only evidence of the first two movements.

Exhibiting an elaborate and well-balanced application of the various material and formative principles of the preceding years, *A Love Supreme* in many respects represents the conclusive "magnum opus" of Coltrane's modal period. The composed parts and their interrelationship, and the construction of Coltrane's solos, stand out clearly and in logical order. The dynamic build-up rises from the rather restrained first part through an intensification and an increase

in tempo in the second, toward the culminating and fastest third part, after which the slow "free-meter" recitations of the last part form a solemn finish. Tonally, both the thematic material and the improvisations of the first three parts and the recitations of the "Psalm" share as a common foundation (and a strong factor of coherence) the pentatonic minor scale (1-lowered 3–4–5-lowered 7). In addition, there are various motivic relationships, the most obvious and important of which exists between the initial theme of "Acknowledgement" (played by the bass) and the theme of "Pursuance." The relationship of the tonal centers also shows a systematic order; they shift from *f* in the first part down a major second to *e*-flat in the second, up a fifth to *b*-flat in the third, and up a major second to *c* in the fourth. On the basis of these connecting elements, the differently structured frames of reference of the four parts offer a wide spectrum of emotional levels and improvisational approaches.

"Acknowledgement" begins with a fanfare-like statement from Coltrane; the characteristic intervallic structure (fourths) of this initial signal is clearly related to the pentatonic scale. The well-conceived, uncomplicated construction prepares the atmosphere, sets the pace, and presents the central melodic idea. As the performance progresses, an ostinato bass emerges, and the drums join the mix with an Afro-Latin rhythm. This leads to a solo by Coltrane.

The ostinato represents the nucleus from which a considerable amount of motivic and melodic material is developed. Pentatonically oriented, this material is used by Coltrane to develop his solo, which is divided into five parts and is used several times as a starting point for variations. The solo's increasing intensity resembles the procedure used in "Impressions," insofar as several structural units build up internally to moments of culmination, leading to a final climax.

In the last section, in which tension is released, Coltrane plays the initial bass pattern in all 12 keys, following this display of virtuosity with a repetitive chanting of the words "A Love Supreme," joined by Garrison. (The chanting is omitted in the live version.) With bass and drums executing a fade, "Acknowledgement" ends as it began, following the "fanfare"; the circle is closed in that the bass is playing unaccompanied at the very end.

The bass's introduction to the theme of "Resolution" brings about a smooth, organic transition from "Acknowledgement" and stresses the "suite" character of the work. As Garrison plays an extensive solo, the bass is used to connect, disconnect, prepare parts, or simply produce a contrast to the mighty sound of the full ensemble. The 24-bar theme of "Resolution," which is comprised of three repeated eight-bar sections, is played twice with an insertion of 16 bars of improvised tenor saxophone. This results in a thematic statement of 64 bars. The repeated sections are distinguished by their endings, a feature found often in traditional black music: the melodic shape is characterized by gradual descent and four long held notes, which are approached by a melodic pattern also characteristic of traditional black music. During Coltrane's solo, repetitive variation is not used until choruses five and ten, which serve as climax choruses and which mark a structural difference to parts I and III, in which the improvisations begin with this principle of melodic construction.

The theme of "Pursuance" is made up exclusively of transpositions of the central cell of "Acknowledgement." Though "Pursuance" is a minor blues in B-flat, Coltrane's 16-chorus improvisation also exhibits rooting in the F-minor pentatonic scale. The traditional 12-bar scheme is treated in a rather abstract and free manner here. During the last choruses, especially, Coltrane deviates considerably from the basic tonality by using chromatic material, moving to different tonal centers, and becoming increasingly flexible in his melodic construction. Interestingly, no matter how long, short, or complex in tonality Coltrane's phrases are, the eighth note as central rhythmic unit is not abandoned except for the climaxes in choruses 3, 4, 8, 15, and 16. These are dominated by "screams" on the notes *a*-flat" and *f*", which can be interpreted as a "blue third" and its tonic.

The "Psalm" opens an aesthetic dimension that differs widely from that of the first three parts. The saxophone's melody is a transformation of Coltrane's poem "A Love Supreme" into music, word for word, as if sung. Structuring coherent spoken lines musically, on a pentatonic scale, Coltrane begins with an ascending phrase, then "recites" on one note using neighboring tones, and finishes with a descending phrase. Whereas, in the beginning passages, the note *g* (a fifth above the tonic) serves as the recitation note, in later sections higher notes (the seventh or the octave) are used. For the recurring phrase "Thank you, God," Coltrane applies a short melodic formula. In this "declamation without words" the principle of dynamic increase mentioned above is also manifested to a limited extent. The use of declamation and of formulae confirm Coltrane's affinity to, and concern with, the black oral traditions, especially the religious.

Due probably to its stylistic uniqueness, the live version of "Psalm" (also played in free meter) shares the fewest common features with the studio version. With no direct reference to the poem, Coltrane plays a theme with a contour vaguely reminiscent of the first phrase of the studio version, which he varies extensively. His improvisation consists of five sections, in each of which a basic formula becomes increasingly abstract through continuous variation. During these processes, the ensemble develops a collective sound, which increases, during each section through kinetic intensity, density of activity, and Coltrane's expressive power.

The suite *A Love Supreme* had a kind of reception that is very rare in the jazz world. Marking Coltrane's position as the spiritual leader of the new movement and conveying a religious message, it carried strong symbolic meaning. It was voted Record of the Year in the 1964 *Down Beat* critic's poll and received numerous other awards.

REFERENCES

Baker, David. *The Jazz Style of John Coltrane: A Musical and Historical Perspective.* Lebanon, Ind.: Studio 224, 1980.

Coltrane, Alice. *Jazz and Pop* 9, no. 68 (1968): 123–124.

Coltrane, John. Liner notes, *A Love Supreme.* Impulse A-77, 1965.

———. Liner notes, *Meditations.* Impulse A-9110, 1965.

Coltrane, John, and Don DeMichael. "Coltrane on Coltrane." *Down Beat* (September 29, 1960): 26–27.

Demsey, David. "Chromatic Third Relations in the Music of John Coltrane." *Annual Review of Jazz Studies* 5 (1991): 145–180.

Feather, Leonard. "Coltrane Shaping Musical Revolt." *New York Post* (Sunday, October 18, 1964): 54.

Hentoff, Nat. Liner notes, *Meditations.* Impulse A-9110, 1965.

———. Liner notes, *Om.* Impulse 9140, 1966.

Jaffe, Andrew. *Jazz Theory.* Dubuque, Iowa: Wm. C. Brown, 1983.

Jost, Ekkehard. *Free Jazz: Stilkritische Überlegungen zum Jazz der 66er Jahre.* Mainz: Schott, 1975.

Porter, Lewis R. "John Coltrane's Music of 1960 through 1967: Jazz Improvisation as Composition." Ph.D. diss., Brandeis University, 1983.

Porter, Lewis R., and Michael Ullman. *Jazz: From Its Origins to the Present.* Englewood Cliffs, N.J.: Prentice Hall, 1993.

Putschögl, Gerhard. *John Coltrane und die afroamerikanische Oraltradition.* Jazzforschung/Jazz Research, vol. 25. Graz, Austria: Akademishe Druck, 1993.

Slonimsky, Nicolas. *Thesaurus of Scales and Melodic Patterns.* New York: Charles Scribner's Sons, 1947.

GERHARD PUTSCHÖGL

COOK, WILL MARION

Born William Mercer Cook in Washington, D.C., January 27, 1869; died in New York, N.Y., July 20, 1944. **Education:** Oberlin Conservatory, Ohio, studied violin, 1884–88; Berlin, Germany, studied violin, 1888–ca. 1889; National Conservatory of Music, New York, studied under director Antonín Dvořák, John White, and others, 1895. **Composing and Performing Career:** Washington, D.C., debut as concert violinist, 1889; appointed director of new orchestra with C. A. Fleetwood as manager and Frederick Douglass as president, 1890; Casino Roof Garden, New York City, *Clorindy, or The Origin of the Cakewalk*, first major black show at a major theater, 1898; musical director and composer for the George Walker/Bert Williams company, including the shows *In Dahomey, In Abyssinia, In Bandanna Land*, 1899–1908; Buckingham Palace, performed for King George V of England, 1903; musical *The Southerners* with white cast and black chorus produced on Broadway, 1904; took Ernest Hogan's troupe, the Memphis Students, to Europe, 1905; collaborated on many musicals, including *The Traitors* and *Darkeydom*, 1912–15; Carnegie Hall, participated as performer and composer in the Clef Club Orchestra concert, 1912; organized and toured widely with the New York Syncopated Orchestra (a.k.a. Southern Syncopated Orchestra, American Syncopated Orchestra, Will Marion Cook Syncopated Orchestra), which included Sidney Bechet, Tom Fletcher, Abbie Mitchell, and Will Tyers, 1918; returned to U.S., 1920, toured with Clef Club orchestras; promoted concerts by performers such as Georgette Harvey, Fletcher Henderson, Paul Robeson; Times Square Theater, New York, N.Y., sponsored "Negro Nuances" concert series, 1924; collaborated with Will Vodery for musical *Swing Along*, 1929. **Teaching Career:** Music advisor, teacher, coach, and patron of many New York musicians. **Memberships:** Founding member, American Society of Composers, Authors and Publishers (ASCAP), 1914.

MUSIC LIST

PIANO

"Clorindy March and Two Step." New York: M. Witmark and Sons, 1898.

"Creole Dance." New York: M. Witmark and Sons, 1898.

"Cruel Papa." New York: Joseph W. Stern, 1914

"Lotus Blossoms." New York: John H. Cook, 1904.

SONGS

"After All I've Been to You." Note: from *The Traitor*.

"Any Old Place in Yankee Land Is Good Enough for Me." New York: Gotham-Attucks Music, 1908. Note: from *Bandanna Land*.

"As the Sunflower Turns to the Sun." New York: Gotham-Attucks Music, 1904. Note: from *The Southerners; The Girl from Dixie*.

"Bon Bon Buddy." New York: Gotham-Attucks Music, 1907. Note: from *Bandanna Land*.

"Brown-Skin Baby Mine." New York: G. Schirmer, 1902. Note: from *In Dahomey*.

"By-gone Days Are Best." New York: Joseph W. Stern, 1900. Note: from *The Casino Girl; Mrs. Black Is Best*.

"Caboceer's Entrance." New York: Will M. Cook, 1902. Note: from *In Dahomey*.

"Cannibal King." New York: Will M. Cook, 1903.

"Colored Girl from Vassar." New York: Harry von Tilzer, ca. 1900. Note: from *Jes' Lak White Fo'ks*.

"Cruel Daddy." New York: Joseph W. Stern, 1915.

"Czar of Dixie Land." New York: Joseph W. Stern, 1901. Note: from *In Dahomey*.

"Dainty." New York: A. Payne, 1909.

"Daisy Deane." New York: John H. Cook, 1904. Note: from *The Southerners*.

"Dandy Dan." New York: John H. Cook, 1904. Note: from *The Southerners*.

"Darktown Barbecue." New York: John H. Cook, 1904. Note: from *The Southerners*.

"Darktown Is Out Tonight." New York: M. Witmark and Sons, 1898. Note: from *Clorindy, or The Origin of the Cakewalk*.

"Dar's Mah Mindy." Chicago: Will M. Cook, 1907.

"Dat's All, Ragtime Girl." Note: from *The New Yorkers*.

"Dinah." New York: Gotham-Attucks Music, 1907. Note: from *Bandanna Land*.

"Down de Lover's Lane: Plantation Croon." New York: G. Schirmer, 1900. Note: from *The Traitor; Jes Lak' White Fok's; The Sons of Ham; The Casino Girl*.

"Dreamin' Town." New York: John H. Cook, 1904. Also known as "Mandy Lou." Note: from *Darkydom; The Southerners*.

"Ducky Wucky." New York: Will M. Cook, 1930.

"Evah Dahkey Is a King" or "Evah Nigger Is a King." New York: Harry von Tilzer Music, 1902. Also slightly revised and published in the *New York American and Journal*, 1902. Note: from *Jes' Lak White Fo'ks*.

"Ev'ry Body Loves." New York: Will M. Cook, 1925.

"Exhortation: A Negro Sermon." New York: G. Schirmer, 1912. Note: from *Bandanna Land*.

"An Explanation." New York: G. Schirmer, 1914.

"Gal o' Mine." New York: Artmusic, 1918.

"The Ghost Ship: The Slave Ship." New York: Will M. Cook, 1929. Note: from *Darkydom; My Friend from Georgia*.

"Girl from Vassar." New York: Joseph W. Stern, 1901. Note: from *Jes Lak' White Fok's; In Dahomey*.

"Good Evenin': A Real Native Southern Negro Melody." New York: Harry von Tilzer Music, 1902. Note: from *The Southerners; In Dahomey*.

"Harlem Band." New York: Will M. Cook, 1929.

"Harlem Is Hell." Washington, D.C.: Will M. Cook, 1932.

"Hot Foot." New York: Joseph W. Stern, 1901.

"Hottest Coon in Dixie." New York: M. Witmark and Sons, 1898. Note: from *Clorindy, or The Origin of the Cakewalk*.

"Hurrah for Captain Kidd." New York: Harry von Tilzer Music, 1902. Note: from *In Dahomey*.

"I Want to Live and Die in Dixie Land." New York: Empire Music, 1915. Note: from *Darkydom*.

"If the Sands of All the Seas Were Peerless Pearls." New York: Jerome Remick, 1914.

Will Marion Cook; Photographs and Prints Division, Schomberg Center for Research in Black Culture,
The New York Public Library, Astor Lenox and Tilden Foundation

"In Bandanna Lan'." New York: Gotham-Attucks Music, 1907. Note: from *Bandanna Land*.

"In de Evenin'." New York: Harry von Tilzer Music, 1910.

"It's Allus de Same in Dixie." New York: John H. Cook, 1904. Note: from *The Southerners*.

"Jewel of the Big Blue Nile." New York: John H. Cook, 1908. Note: from *Darkydom; In the Jungles*.

"Julep Song." New York: York Music, 1904. Note: from *The Southerners*.

"Jump Back, Honey, Jump Back." New York: M. Witmark and Sons, 1898. Note: from *Clorindy, or The Origin of the Cakewalk*.

"Just a Little Bit of Heaven Called Home." New York: Metro-Goldwyn-Mayer, 1934.

"Just the Same." New York: Gotham-Attucks Music, 1907. Note: from *Bandanna Land*.

"Kinky." New York: Gotham-Attucks Music, 1908. Note: from *Bandanna Land*.

"Leader of the Colored Aristocracy." New York: Harry von Tilzer Music, 1902. Note: from *In Dahomey*.

"Let's Save the U.S.A., to Hell with Over There (Over Here)." New York: Will M. Cook, 1941.

"A Little Bit of Heaven Called Home." New York: G. Schirmer, 1933.

"The Little Gypsy Maid." New York: Harry von Tilzer Music, 1902. Note: from *The Wild Rose*.

"Love in a Cottage Is Best." New York: M. Witmark, 1898. Note: from *Clorindy, or The Origin of the Cakewalk*.

"Love Is the Tend'rest of Themes." New York: Howley, Haviland, 1896.

"Love Looks Not at Estate." Brooklyn: Will M. Cook, 1904. Note: from *Jes' Lak White Fo'ks*.

"Love Me with a Tiger Love." New York: Harry von Tilzer Music, 1910. Note: from *The Deacon and the Lady*.

"Lover's Lane." Note: from *The Traitor*.

"Lulu." New York: Gotham Music, 1905.

"Maggie Magee." New York: John H. Cook, 1905.

"Mammy." New York: Artmusic, 1916. Note: from *Darkydom*.

"Mammy's 'Lasses Candy Chile." New York: Maurice Shapiro, 1909. Note: from *Cohan and Harris' Minstrels*.

"Molly Green." New York: Harry von Tilzer Music, 1902. Note: from *In Dahomey*.

"My Alabama Dan." Washington, D.C.: Will M. Cook, 1912.

"My Lady." New York: G. Schirmer, 1914.

"My Lady Frog." New York: Harry von Tilzer Music, 1902. Note: from *In Dahomey*.

"My Lady Nicotine." New York: Harry von Tilzer Music, 1910. Note: from *Darkydom*.

"My Lady's Lips Am Like de Honey." New York: G. Schirmer, 1915. Note: from *Darkydom*.

"My Little Irish Canary." New York: Howley, Dresser, 1904.

"On Emancipation Day." New York: Harry von Tilzer Music, 1902. Note: from *Clorindy, or The Origin of the Cakewalk; In Dahomey*.

"Oo! Oo!! Oo!!! It's Very Strange." New York: John H. Cook, 1908.

"Parthenia Johnsing." New York: John H. Cook, 1904. Note: from *The Southerners*.

"Pensacola Mooch." New York: Harry von Tilzer Music, 1910.

"Possum Am de Best Meat After All." New York: Joseph W. Stern, 1901.

"Rain Song." New York: G. Schirmer, 1912. Also arranged for men's chorus.

"Red Red Rose." New York: Gotham-Attucks Music, 1908. Note: from *Bandanna Land; The Man from Bam'*.

"Returned." New York: Harry von Tilzer Music, 1902. Note: from *In Dahomey*.

"Romance." New York: Joseph W. Stern, 1900. Note: from *The Casino Girl*.

"She's Dancing Sue." New York: Harry von Tilzer Music, 1902. Note: from *In Dahomey*.

"Slumber Song." New York: John H. Cook, 1904. Note: from *The Southerners*.

"Society." London: Keith, Prowse, 1903. Note: from *The Sons of Ham; In Dahomey*.

"Spread de News." Brooklyn: Will M. Cook, 1904. Note: from *Jes' Lak White Fo'ks*.

"Springtime." New York: G. Schirmer, 1914.

"Squirrel Song." New York: John H. Cook, 1904. Note: from *The Southerners*.

"A Summah Night." New York: Harry von Tilzer Music, 1906.

"Sweet Dreams, You Can't Come Back." New York: Cook and Rogers, 1911.

"Swing Along." 1902. New York: G. Schirmer, 1912. Also arranged for men's chorus. Note: from *The Southerners; In Dahomey*.

"That'll Be All Right Baby." New York: Spaulding and Gray, 1896.

"There's a Place in the Old Vacant Chair." New York: Gotham Music, 1905.

"Until Then." New York: Gotham-Attucks Music, 1907. Note: from *Bandanna Land*.

"Ups and Downs." New York: Will M. Cook, 1927.

"The Vassar Girl." New York: Will M. Cook, 1904.

"We're Marching On." West Medford, Mass.: George Broome, 1896.

"We's a Comin'." New York: Will M. Cook, 1904. Note: from *Jes' Lak White Fo'ks*.

"What Makes Me Love You the Way I Do." New York: Cook and McPherson, 1902.

"What Would You Be a' Doing." New York: Harry von Tilzer Music, 1902. Note: from *The Wild Rose*.

"Whatever the Hue of Your Eyes." New York: Joseph W. Stern, 1900. Note: from *The Casino Girl*.

"Where the Lotus Blossoms Grow." New York: John H. Cook, 1904. Note: from *The Southerners*.

"Who Dat Say Chicken in Dis Crowd." New York: M. Witmark and Sons, 1898. Note: from *Clorindy, or The Origin of the Cakewalk*.

"Whoop'er Up with a Whoop La! La!" 1908. New York: Harry von Tilzer Music, 1910. Note: from *The Boys and Betty; Just Forgot*.

"Wid de Moon, Moon, Moon." New York: G. Schirmer, 1907. Note: from *In Zululand*.

MUSICAL THEATER

Abyssinia or *In Abyssinia* (musical comedy). Co-composer, Bert Williams. Premiere, 1906.

Bandanna Land or *Bandana Land* (musical comedy). Premiere, 1908.

Clorindy, or The Origin of the Cake Walk (musical comedy). Premiere, 1898.

Darkydom or *Darkeydom* (musical revue). Co-composer, James Reese Europe. Premiere, 1915.

In Dahomey (musical farce). London: Keith, Prowse, 1903. Premiere, 1902.

In the Jungles (musical comedy). 1906. Co-composer, Alex C. Rogers.

In Zululand. 1907. Co-composers, Joe Jordan, James T. Brymn. Premiere, 1907.

Jes' Lak White Fo'ks or *Jes' Lak White Folks* (musical playlet). 1899. Note: much of the music for this show was later re-worked into *The Cannibal King.* Premiere, 1900.

A Lucky Coon (musical show). 1898–99. Premiere, 1898.

My Friend from Georgia. 1906–07. Co-composer, Joe Jordan. Premiere, 1906.

Negro Nuances (musical comedy). 1924. Co-composer, James P. Johnson. Premiere, 1924.

St. Louis 'Ooman (folk opera). 1929. Note: unproduced.

The Sons of Ham (musical comedy). 1900–02. Premiere, 1900.

The Southerners (musical). 1904. Premiere, 1904.

Swing Along. Premiere, 1929.

The Traitor (musical comedy). 1913–14. Premiere, 1913.

Uncle Eph's Christmas (musical comedy). 1899. Premiere, 1899.

PUBLICATIONS

ABOUT COOK
Book
Riis, Thomas, ed. *The Music and Scripts of In Dahomey.* Madison, Wisc.: A-R Editions, 1996.

Dissertation
Carter, Marva Griffin. "The Life and Music of Will Marion Cook." Ph.D. diss., University of Illinois, 1988.

Articles
Green, J. "*In Dahomey* in London in 1903." *Black Perspective in Music* 11, no. 1 (1983): 22–40.

BY COOK
"Clorindy, or The Origin of the Cakewalk." *Theater Arts* 31 (1947): 61+. Reprinted in *Readings in Black Music,* edited by Eileen Southern. 2nd ed. New York: W. W. Norton, 1983.

PRINCIPAL ARCHIVES
Moorland-Springarn Research Center, Howard University, Washington, D.C.

Music Division, Library of Congress, Washington, D.C.

* * * * *

At the turn of the century, Will Marion Cook was considered to be the most original composer among his contemporaries. Respected for his pioneering achievements in popular songwriting, black musical comedy, and syncopated orchestral music, Cook dramatically transformed these genres during his lifetime. As one who helped to advance the careers of many musicians, his most notable proteges were Duke Ellington, Margaret Bonds, and his student Eva Jessye. Cook's compositions were published by reputable firms, performed for international audiences, and recorded on major labels.

Cook's goal seems to have been a career as a concert violinist. He studied the instrument at the Oberlin Conservatory, beginning in 1884. He gave recitals there and in Washington, D.C., his birthplace. By 1888, he went to Berlin, Germany, for study with the leading European violinist of the late nineteenth century, Joseph Joachim, a friend of Johannes Brahms. Cook was immersed in Western concert music through his years in Berlin: chamber music, including that played by the string quartet of his teacher; vocal music, sung by singers such as Amalie Joachim and Lillian Nordica in Italian opera; and orchestral music conducted by Hans von Bülow, Artur Nikisch, Anton Seidl, and other leading artists of the day.

After returning from Berlin in 1890, Cook continued to concertize but also took up orchestral conducting, beginning with an orchestra named after Cook and formed in Washington, D.C. The orchestra's president was Frederick Douglass, whose grandson Joseph Douglass was one of the violinists. This group distinguished itself, according to the *New York Age,* "as an untried experiment in Afro-American annals" and was the city's first orchestra to introduce the saxophone. Later, Cook was to use his conducting skills with the Nashville Students, subsequently called the Memphis Students, who made a European tour in 1905, and with the New York Syncopated Orchestra, which performed a mixed repertoire of early jazz and classical music. This ensemble, with its name changed to the Southern Syncopated Orchestra, toured the United States and Europe in 1918–19.

Besides performing and conducting activities, Cook began to turn to composing. He went to New York City in 1895 and attended the National Conservatory of Music, where he studied briefly with Antonín Dvořák. This Bohemian composer challenged Americans to discontinue emulating European models and to forge a new path based on the indigenous musics of America. This viewpoint undoubtedly gave Cook strong impetus to create music based on African-American idioms. Another force that directed him along this path was the burgeoning black musical theater. He first worked with singer/manager Bob Cole as arranger and director and, in 1898, began a collaboration with poet Paul Laurence Dunbar. Their first work was a ragtime operetta, *Clorindy, or The Origin of the Cakewalk,* which made theatrical history as the first all-black musical comedy to appear on Broadway. It introduced syncopated song and dance to Broadway, where they continue to be basic elements in musical theater to this day. Later collaborations were *Jes' Lak White Fo'ks* (1899) and *The Cannibal King* (1901).

In 1899, Cook married soprano Abbie Mitchell, who frequently performed in his shows and continued to do so after their separation in 1908.

The first decade of the twentieth century was very productive for Cook, especially with shows that featured the vaudeville team of Bert Williams and George Walker. The most successful of their musical comedies was *In Dahomey* (1902), the first full-length musical written and performed by blacks to be presented on Broadway, on a London stage, or at Buckingham Palace.

For James Reese Europe's Clef Club Orchestra's Carnegie Hall concert in 1912, Cook not only performed as a violinist but also contributed three of his own works, "Swing Along," "Exhortation," and "Rain Song." Several stage works were produced in the 1920s, when Cook returned to the United States after the Southern

Syncopated Orchestra disbanded. Among them was *Swing Along* (1929), with Will Vodery.

In his works, Cook made use of the compositional techniques employed by both black and white composers of his day. In addition to songs based on African themes, ethnic humor, and Negro stereotypes, he also wrote songs about love, patriotism, nostalgia, and the more universal common themes in songs written by whites who were not minstrel composers. Cook stood out among his peers in his consistent use of syncopation and chromaticism, which was a significant deviation from the standard popular songs of the period. He also made use of secondary dominants, augmented sixths, and nonharmonic tones with great technical skill. His choral writing sometimes included climactic effects similar to those found in the operetta finales of the day.

Will Marion Cook was a musical genius whose valuable contributions should not be overlooked when examining the history of black musical comedy and orchestral jazz ensembles.

SWING ALONG! (1902)

This song was the opening chorus of the first act of *In Dahomey*. It reflected Cook's racial pride and his optimism about African-Americans' pursuit of social justice. He boldly proclaims that the race should "swing along" in spite of "White folks watchin' an' seein' what you do." He uses two syncopated ideas that shift in key, meter, and mood. "Swing Along" is structured in an ABBA'B'A" form with the first two sections consisting of 16 measures of related four-measure phrases separated by a modulating metric-changing interlude between the first two sections. Fourteen measures of the second A are interrupted by a bluesy harmonic variation of the B refrain. The final A is extended by a climactic coda.

As proof of the increased commercial success of this work, in 1912, after its historic, critically acclaimed Clef Club Concert at Carnegie Hall, G. Schirmer chose to publish "Swing Along" in several editions for chorus, solo voice, and orchestra. Three years later, Cary B. Lewis, of the *Chicago Defender,* indicated that "Swing Along" stamped Cook's "individuality and ranked him as the champion of racial composers." The piece became a standard, programmed by every first-class college glee club in the United States for at least fifty years.

THE LITTLE GYPSY MAID (1902) AND BROWN-SKIN BABY MINE (1902)

One of Cook's most popular songs was written with two textual settings—one with a white subject and the other, a black subject. In 1902, the charming ballad "Little Gypsy Maid" was interpolated into *The Wild Rose,* which starred Marie Cahill. It was later recast with dialect lyrics by Cook and Cecil Mack (a.k.a. Cecil McPherson) and retitled "Brown-Skin Baby Mine." This version was popularized by Abbie Mitchell and included in the London performance and publication of *In Dahomey* in 1903. In that same year, a third version of the song, which retained the "Brown-Skin Baby Mine" title but altered the lyrics from dialect to standard English, was published by G. Schirmer.

The romantic association with love and nature is born out in the comparative lyrics of the two textual versions. The gypsy maid is compared to several other flowers and becomes metaphorically "a wildflower of the forest shade"; but no other fair flower can compare with brown-skin baby mine. Harry B. Smith and Cecil Mack created the lyrics to the gypsy version, while Cook and Mack created the brown-skin lyrics. This latter version conveyed a more positive New-Negro image of a dark-skinned female, which was distinctly different from the stereotypic coon-song variety.

The subtle charm of the song lies in its wide use of ornamental *appoggiaturas* and syncopated rhythms that help unite the verse and the chorus, the placement of the syncopated rhythms reinforcing the effectiveness of the *appoggiaturas.* It is written in a 32-bar strophic sentimental verse-and-chorus structure with a 12-bar introduction. Its harmonic color is heightened by a prominent use of secondary dominant progressions.

"Brown-Skin Baby Mine" was one of Cook's most widely favored ballads. According to Jeffrey Green, it was particularly well received as performed by Abbie Mitchell during the London tours of *In Dahomey.*

RED RED ROSE (1908)

"Red Red Rose," one of Cook's few art songs with universal appeal, was sung by his wife in *Bandanna Land* (1908). The lyrics by Alex Rogers poetically search for the red rose that holds the secret of his love: "If you are not my love O! red, red rose/Then won't you tell me just which red rose knows." The prominent piano accompaniment provides the romantic atmosphere for the song as it varies in dynamic levels, tempi, and driving octaves that increase the drama. This art song begins with a four-measure introduction followed by a 32-measure verse-refrain form and concluded by a two-measure extended ending. The accompaniment mirrors the vocal line an octave lower, with syncopated chords punctuating the melodic verse. A dramatic metric change from a simple meter (4/4) to a compound meter (12/8) ushers in the refrain. This rhythmic shift enhances the search for love's rose by broadening the pace and introducing triplet accompanimental figurations during the refrain for a heightened dramatic effect.

In style, Cook's "Red Red Rose" is similar to an earlier favorite of the day, "The Holy City," by Stephen Adams. In these two songs, many of the accompanimental procedures are the same, including the use of triplet figurations to heighten the tension and a dynamic use of octaves in the bass to deepen the drama. Both songs also use the same key schemes: both are in B-flat major; but "The Holy City" contains a D major section, while "Red Red Rose" has a D-flat major segment. "Red Red Rose" is an example of one of Cook's most beautiful song melodies.

Reviews of "Red Red Rose" cited it far above the ordinary and complimented Abbie Mitchell's clear, trained soprano performance as exhibiting unusual sweetness and good quality.

ON EMANCIPATION DAY (1902)

Cook and Paul Laurence Dunbar wrote "On Emancipation Day" for the finale of *In Dahomey*. A march song, it is masterfully built on a minimum of material, with melodic chromaticism prominent from the initial measure of the introduction to the song's conclusion. It consists of an 8-bar introduction, 36-bar verse, and 32-bar chorus. The song is built on a motive that occupies its first two measures (see Ex. 1). Supported by a marchlike bass, this two-measure motive is modified and extended to four measures at the chorus. A syncopated accompaniment figure adds zest. The verse and chorus are related in that, in the verse, a rhythmically active measure is followed by an inactive measure, while in the chorus, the reverse occurs. The song is structurally well balanced in that melodic climaxes occur midway through the verse, at its conclusion, and midway through the chorus, all strongly supported harmonically.

Example 1. "On Empancipation Day," mm. 1–2

On E - man-ci - pa - tion day,_____

"On Emancipation Day" stands out as one of Cook's most successful "ragtime" songs, saturated with syncopated rhythm both in its vocal melody and its piano accompaniment. This song of emancipation excels in its "development" of a small musical idea, its rhythmic energy, its artfully crafted climactic structure, and its use of harmonies just beyond the ordinary. Cook wrote instrumental versions of this song within the overture to *In Dahomey* and as a solo piano march and two step.

"On Emancipation Day" received enthusiastic coverage from the press; its cakewalking finale especially made a tremendous impact upon British audiences.

REFERENCES

Carter, Marva Griffin. "The Life and Music of Will Marion Cook." Ph.D. diss., University of Illinois, 1988.

Green, Jeffrey. "*In Dahomey* in London in 1903." *Black Perspective in Music* 11, no. 1 (1983): 22–40.

Johnson, James Weldon. *Along This Way: The Autobiography of James Weidon Johnson.* New York: Viking Press, 1933. Reprinted, New York: Viking Press, 1968.

New York Age, September 27, 1890:1.

Riis, Thomas L. *Just Before Jazz: Black Musical Theater in New York, 1890–1915.* Washington D.C.: Smithsonian Institution Press, 1989.

———. *The Music and Scripts of In Dahomey.* Madison, Wisc.: A-R Editions, 1996.

Unidentified clipping ["Red Red Rose"]. Held in the *In Bandanna Land* folder, Harvard Theatre Collection, Harvard College Library, Cambridge, Massachusetts.

MARVA GRIFFIN CARTER

CORDERO, ROQUE

Born in Panama City, Panama, August 16, 1917. **Education:** Studied clarinet, viola, violin as child; began writing popular songs at an early age, turned to formal composition, age 17; Escuela de Artes y Oficios, Panama City, studied with Máximo Boza, 1931–35; private study with Pedro Rebolledo, 1934–36, Herbert de Castro, 1936–41; University of Panama, studied with Myron Schaeffer, 1941–43; University of Minnesota–Minneapolis, studied conducting with Dimitri Mitropoulos, 1943–46; Hamline University, St. Paul, Minn., studied composition and counterpoint with Ernst Krenek, 1943–47, B.A. magna cum laude, 1947; Berkshire Music Center, Tanglewood, Mass., studied conducting with Stanley Chapple, summer 1946; National Orchestral Association, New York, N.Y., studied conducting with Leon Barzin, 1947–49. **Composing and Performing Career:** Banda del Cuerpo de Bomberos de Panamá [fire brigade band of Panama], played clarinet, 1933–43; founded the Orquesta de la Unión Musical, 1938; Orquesta Sinfónica de Panamá, played viola, 1941–43; University of Minnesota Orchestra, Minneapolis, viola, 1943–47; toured widely as lecturer, conductor, and consultant, beginning 1957; Orquesta Nacional de Panamá, conductor, 1964–66; often served as guest conductor throughout Central and South America. **Teaching Career:** Escuela de Artes y Oficios, Panamá, 1941–43; Conservatorio Nacional de Música de Panamá (now Instituto Nacional de Música de Panamá), 1950–66, director, 1953–64; Latin American Music Center, Indiana University–Bloomington, Assistant Director, 1966–69; Illinois State University, Normal, Ill., 1972–1987. **Commissions:** Dimitri Mitropoulos, 1949; Minneapolis Civic Orchestra, 1958; Elizabeth Sprague Coolidge Foundation, 1959; Serge Koussevitzky Music Foundation, 1961; Adolfo Odnoposoff, 1963; Third Music Festival of Caracas, 1965; Hamline University A Cappella Choir, 1966; University of Alabama, 1967; Universidad Católica de Chile, Santiago, 1968; Second Music Festival of Guanabara, 1970; National Institute of Culture and Sports of Panama, 1971; National Institute of Tourism, Panama, 1974; Illinois State University, 1974, 1980, 1981; National Endowment for the Arts, 1976; Kennedy Center, Washington, D.C., 1978; Illinois Arts Council, 1983, 1987; Linda Hirt, 1985; Cincinnati Symphony Orchestra, 1994; Peoria Symphony Orchestra, Peoria, Ill., 1996. **Memberships:** Delegate to the International Music Council of UNESCO, 1961–66, 1968. **Honors/Awards:** Institute of International Education, New York, N.Y., 1943–44; Mitropoulos scholarship to Hamline University, 1943–47; Berkshire Music Center, Tanglewood, Mass., scholarship, summer 1946; Panamanian Government grant, 1946–48; Reichhold Contest, Detroit, Mich., Honorable Mention, 1947; Guggenheim Fellowship, 1949; Panama, Ricardo Miró Award, 1953; Caracas, Venezuela, Caro de Boesi Award, 1957; Panama, decorated with the Orden de Vasco Núñez de Balboa, 1958; Universidad de Chile, honorary professor, 1963; Hamline University, Doctor of Humane Letters, 1966; Koussevitzky International Recording Award, 1974; San José, Costa Rica, Chamber Music Award, 1977; Panamá, Gran Cruz de la Orden de Vasco Núñez de Balboa, 1982; Illinois State University, Outstanding Teacher Award, 1983; Illinois State University, Distinguished Professor, 1983. **Mailing Address:** Music Department, Illinois State University, Normal, IL 61790-5660.

MUSIC LIST

INSTRUMENTAL SOLOS
Violin
Dos piezas cortas (Two Short Pieces for Violin and Piano). 1945. New York: Peer International, 1960. Premiere, 1945.

Doble concierto sin orquesta (Double concerto without orchestra) (violin, piano). 1978. Unpublished manuscript. Commissioned by the Chairman's National Commission on Blacks in the Performing Arts at the Kennedy Center, Washington, D.C. Premiere, 1979.

"Rapsodia Panameña" (unaccompanied violin). 1988. Unpublished manuscript. Premiere, 1990.

Sonatina for Violin and Piano. 1946. New York: Peer International, 1962. Premiere, 1947.

Viola
Tres mensajes breves (Three Short Messages). 1966. New York: Peer International, 1970. Premiere, 1967.

Cello
"Soliloquios no. 6" (unaccompanied cello). 1992. Unpublished manuscript. Premiere, 1993.

Sonata for Violoncello and Piano. 1963. New York: Peer International, 1970. Commissioned by Adolfo Odnoposoff. Premiere, 1966.

Double Bass
"Soliloquios no. 5" (unaccompanied double bass). 1981. Unpublished manuscript. Commissioned by Illinois State University, 1981. Premiere, 1983.

Guitar
Cinco mensajes para cuatro amigos. 1983. Paris: Editions Salabert, 1985. Contents: Para Alirio Díaz; Para Miguel Alcázar; Para Ana María Rosado; Para Ernesto Bitetti; Para Alirio Díaz. Premiere, 1984. Recorded: Albany Records Troy 087.

Tres preludios para guitarra (Three Preludes for Guitar). 1988. Ancona, Italy: Bérben Edizioni musicali, 1989. Premiere, 1989.

Flute
"Soliloquios no. 1" (unaccompanied flute). 1975. New York: Peer International, 1977. Premiere, 1976.

Clarinet
"Soliloquios no. 3" (unaccompanied clarinet). 1976. New York: Peer International, 1980. Premiere, 1977.

Saxophone
"Soliloquios no. 2" (unaccompanied alto saxophone). 1976. New York: Peer International, 1977. Premiere, 1976.

Percussion
"Soliloquios no. 4" (unaccompanied percussion). 1981. Unpublished manuscript. Premiere, 1981.

Harp
"Tres veces 13" (unaccompanied harp). 1997. Unpublished manuscript.

Piano
Five Miniatures. 1944. Unpublished manuscript.
Five New Preludes. 1983. Unpublished manuscript. Premiere, 1984.
Nine Preludes. 1947. Unpublished manuscript. Premiere, 1948.
"Nostalgia." 1943. Unpublished manuscript. Premiere, 1944.
"Preludio para la cuna vacía." 1943. Unpublished manuscript. Premiere, 1944.
Sonata breve. 1966. New York: Peer International, 1970. Premiere, 1967.
Sonata for Piano. 1985. Unpublished manuscript. Commissioned by Linda Hirt. Premiere, 1986.
Sonatina rítmica. 1943. New York: Peer International, 1954. Recorded: Sonopress ECHO-295. Premiere, 1944.
Tres meditaciones poéticas. 1995. Unpublished manuscript. Premiere, 1995.
Tres piececillas para Alina. 1978. Unpublished manuscript. Premiere, 1979.
Variations for the Second Miniature. 1944. Unpublished manuscript.

Two Pianos
"Duo 1954." 1954. New York: Peer International, 1965. Premiere, 1954. Recorded: Centaur Records CRC-2171; Organización de los Estados Americanos OEA-003.
Rhapsody for Two Pianos. 1945. Unpublished manuscript. Premiere, 1946.

SMALL INSTRUMENTAL ENSEMBLE
Strings
Danza en forma de fuga (string quartet). 1943. Unpublished manuscript. Also arranged for string orchestra. Premiere, 1950.
String Quartet no. 1. 1960. New York: Peer International, 1969. Commissioned by the Elizabeth Sprague Coolidge Foundation. Premiere, 1961.
String Quartet no. 2. 1968. New York: Peer International, 1976. Commissioned by University of Alabama. Premiere, 1969.
String Quartet no. 3. 1973. Unpublished manuscript. Note: received the Chamber Music Award, San José, Costa Rica, 1977. Premiere, 1977.
String Quartet no. 4. 1983. Unpublished manuscript. Commissioned by the Illinois Arts Council. Premiere, 1987.
Three Permutations 3 (violin, cello, double bass). 1984. Unpublished manuscript. Premiere, 1987.

Woodwinds
3 Miniminiatures for Ernst (flute, clarinet). 1985. Unpublished manuscript. Premiere, 1985.
Mensaje breve (clarinet, bassoon). 1958. Unpublished manuscript.
Mensaje breve (flute, oboe, clarinet, bassoon). 1957. Unpublished manuscript. Premiere, 1957.
"Variations and Theme for Five" (woodwind quintet). 1975. New York: Peer International, 1976. Premiere, 1976.

Brass
"Música para cinco metales (Music for Five Brass)" (brass quintet). 1980. Unpublished manuscript. Commissioned by Illinois State University. Premiere, 1981.

Combinations
Circunvoluciones y móviles (Circumvolutions and Mobiles). 1967. Unpublished manuscript.
Dodecaconcerto (flute, English horn, clarinet, alto saxophone, bassoon, horn, trumpet, trombone, percussion, violin, viola, cello). 1990. New York: Peer International (rental). Recorded: North/South Recordings N/S R 1003.
Four Messages: For Flutes and Piano (flute, alto flute, piccolo, piano). 1992. Unpublished manuscript. Recorded: La Música en el Caribe II-Edición Sonora FCCOO/2CD. Premiere, 1992.
Paz, Paix, Peace (harp solo and four trios: flute, English horn, bass clarinet; alto flute, clarinet, bassoon; violin, viola, cello; viola, cello, double bass). 1969. New York: Peer International (rental). Premiere, 1970.
Permutaciones 7 (piano, clarinet, trumpet, timpani, violin, viola, double bass). 1967. New York: Peer International, 1973. Premiere, 1969. Recorded: Sony Music PTD 1442–96.
Petites mobiles (bassoon, trios of woodwinds and brass, percussion, strings). 1983. Unpublished manuscript. Premiere, 1984.
Poetic Nocturne of the Min River (four flutes, two alto flutes, bass clarinet, percussion). 1981. Unpublished manuscript. Premiere, 1981.
Quinteto (flute, clarinet, violin, cello, piano). 1949. New York: Peer International, 1967. Premiere, 1957. Recorded: Albany Records Troy 153; Turnabout/Vox TV-S 34505.
Serenatas (flute, clarinet, viola, harp). 1987. Unpublished manuscript. Contents: Preludio; Notturno a due; Scherzino giocoso; Notturno a tre; Moto perpetuo. Commissioned by the Illinois Arts Council. Premiere, 1989.

STRING ORCHESTRA
Adagio trágico. 1955. New York: Peer International, 1972. Premiere, 1955.
Elegy. 1973. New York: Peer International, 1979. Premiere, 1977.
Movimiento sinfónico. 1946. New York: Peer International (rental). Premiere, 1947.

CHAMBER ORCHESTRA
Momentum jubilo (Fanfare) (brass, percussion, strings). 1973. New York: Peer International (rental). Premiere, 1973.
Ocho miniaturas (Eight Miniatures for Small Orchestra). 1943; revised 1948. New York: Peer International (rental). Contents: Marcha grotesca; Meditación; Pasillo; Danzonete; Nocturne; Mejorana; Plegaria; Allegro final. Premiere, 1950. Recorded: Columbia M-32784; Fanfare 3534.

FULL ORCHESTRA
Capricho interiorano. 1939. New York: Peer International (rental). Premiere, 1942.
Centennial Symphonic Tribute. 1997. Unpublished manuscript. Commissioned by Peoria Symphony Orchestra, Peoria, Ill. Premiere, 1997.
Cinco mensajes breves para orquesta. 1959. New York: Peer International (rental). Commissioned by Minneapolis Civic Orchestra. Premiere, 1959.

Roque Cordero; courtesy of the composer

Introducción y allegro burlesco. 1950. Unpublished manuscript.
    Commissioned by Dimitri Mitropoulos. Premiere, 1955.
Obertura de salutación. 1980. Unpublished manuscript. Premiere, 1987.
Obertura Panameña no. 2 (Panamanian Overture no. 2). 1944. New York:
    Peer International (rental). Premiere, 1946.
Rapsodia campesina. 1953. Unpublished manuscript. Note: received the
    Ricardo Miró Award, 1953.
*Sinfonía con un tema y cinco variaciones (no. 3) (Symphony with One Theme
    and Five Variations, no. 3).* 1965. New York: Peer International
    (rental). Commissioned by the Third Music Festival of Caracas.
    Premiere, 1966.
Seis móviles para orquesta (Six Mobiles for Orchestra). 1975. New York: Peer
    International (rental). Commissioned by Illinois State University.
    Premiere, 1975.
Symphony no. 1 in E-flat. 1945. New York: Peer International (rental).
    Note: received honorable mention in the Reichhold Contest,
    Detroit, 1947. Premiere, 1955.
Segunda sinfonía (Symphony no. 2). 1956. New York: Peer International,
    1972. Premiere, 1957. Note: received the Caro de Boesi prize at the
    Second International Music Festival of Caracas, 1957. Recorded:
    Louisville Orchestra LOU-765.
Symphony no. 4 (*Panamanian*). 1986. New York: Peer International
    (rental). Premiere, 1987.

ORCHESTRA (CHAMBER OR FULL) WITH SOLOISTS

Concertino for Viola and String Orchestra. 1968. Unpublished
    manuscript. Commissioned by Universidad Católica de Chile,
    Santiago, Chile.
Concerto for Piano and Orchestra in E Minor. 1944. Unpublished
    manuscript. Premiere, 1955.
Concerto for Violin and Orchestra. 1962. New York: Peer International,
    1969. Published in reduction for violin and piano. Commissioned
    by the Serge Koussevitzky Music Foundation. Note: received the
    Koussevitzky International Recording Award, 1974. Premiere,
    1965. Recorded: Columbia M-32784.
Mensaje fúnebre: In memoriam Dimitri Mitropoulos (clarinet, string
    orchestra). 1961. New York: Peer International (rental). Premiere,
    1967.
Música veinte (Music Twenty). (two soprano soloists, two alto soloists,
    baritone solo, chamber orchestra). 1970. New York: Peer
    International, 1972. Commissioned by the Second Music Festival
    of Guanabara. Premiere, 1970.

CONCERT BAND

Brisas marinas. 1933. Unpublished manuscript. Note: withdrawn by the
    composer. Premiere, 1933.
Fanfarria jubilosa (brass, woodwind, percussion). 1994. Unpublished
    manuscript. Commissioned by the Cincinnati Symphony
    Orchestra. Recorded: Illinois State University Wind Symphony,
    1996–97. Premiere, 1995.
Fantasía crepúsculo. 1933. Unpublished manuscript. Note: withdrawn by
    the composer. Premiere, 1934.
Obertura Panameña no. 1. 1935. Unpublished manuscript. Note:
    withdrawn by the composer. Premiere, 1937.
Poema sinfónico Napoleón. 1936. Unpublished manuscript. Note:
    withdrawn by the composer. Premiere, 1936.

Reina de amor (The Spirit of Panama). 1937. Unpublished manuscript.
    Note: received the National Prize of Panama, 1937.

VOCAL ENSEMBLE

"Aleluya" (three voices). 1961. Unpublished manuscript. Premiere,
    1961.
"Canon no. 1" (three voices). 1961. Unpublished manuscript. Premiere,
    1961.

CHORAL MUSIC

Dos pequeñas piezas corales (Two Short Choral Pieces) (unaccompanied
    SATB). 1966. New York: Peer International, 1970. Contents:
    Canción de mar; Motivo bañado de luna. Commissioned by the
    Hamline University A Cappella Choir. Premiere, 1967.
Patria: Poema para declamador y coro (narrator, SATB). 1944. Unpublished
    manuscript. Premiere, 1958.
Psalm 113 (SATB). 1944. Unpublished manuscript.

DRAMATIC MUSIC

Ballet Folklórico (ballet). 1974. Unpublished manuscript. Commissioned
    by the National Institute of Tourism, Panama. Premiere, 1974.
Cantata para la paz (Cantata for Peace) (baritone solo, SATB chorus,
    orchestra). 1979. New York: Peer International (rental).
    Commissioned by the National Endowment for the Arts.
Sensemayá (ballet for mixed chorus, drum). 1950. Unpublished
    manuscript. Premiere, 1950.
Setetule (ballet). 1956. Unpublished manuscript.

INCIDENTAL MUSIC

An Mar Tule (chamber ensemble). 1971. Incidental film music.
    Commissioned by the National Institute of Culture and Sports of
    Panama.

PUBLICATIONS

ABOUT CORDERO
Books and Monographs
Filós Gooch, Priscilla. *El piano en las obras de Roque Cordero.* Panamá:
    Compañia de Seguros Chagres, 1985.

Dissertations
Brawand, John Edward. "The Violin Works of Roque Cordero." D.M.A.
    thesis, University of Texas at Austin, 1985.
De Dobay, Thomas Raymond. "A Stylistic Analysis of Selected Short
    Works by Roque Cordero." M.M. thesis, Indiana University, 1971.
Engle, Susan Stancil. "A Harmonic Analysis and Comparison of Selected
    Twelve-Tone Compositions of Krenek and Cordero." M.M. thesis,
    Indiana University, 1969.
Ennett, Dorothy Maxine. "An Analysis and Comparison of Selected Piano
    Sonatas by Three Contemporary Black Composers—George
    Walker, Howard Swanson, and Roque Cordero." Ph.D. diss., New
    York University, 1973.
Filós Gooch, Priscilla. "The Piano in the Works of Roque Cordero."
    D.M.A. thesis, Indiana University, 1974.
Greaves, Earl S. "Structural Elements in Selected Works of Roque
    Cordero." M.M. thesis, Southern Illinois University, 1977.

Articles

Chase, Gilbert. "Composed by Cordero." *Américas* 10, no. 6 (1958): 7–11.

Orrego-Salas, Juan. "Roque Cordero, un músico de América." *Zig-Zag* no. 2879 (1960): 60–61.

Sider, Ronald Ray. "Central America and Its Composers: A Panamanian Giant." *Inter-American Music Bulletin* 77 (1970): 12–14.

———."Roque Cordero: The Composer and His Style Seen in Three Representative Works." *Inter-American Music Bulletin* 61 (1967): 1–17.

BY CORDERO

"Actualidad musical en Panamá." *Buenos Aires Musical* 12, no. 197 (October 1957): 5.

"Análisis de *Circunvoluciones y móviles*." *Heterofonía* 2, no. 8 (1969): 14–17.

Curso de solfeo. Panamá: Departamento de Bellas Artes y Publicaciones, Ministerio de Educación, 1956; Buenos Aires: Ricordi Americana, 1963.

"Dodecafonismo vs. nacionalismo?" *Clave* 6, no. 5 (1957): 13.

"The Folkmusic of Panama." *New Grove Dictionary of Music and Musicians,* edited by Stanley Sadie, 14: 151–154. London: Macmillan, 1980.

"La Música en Centroamérica y Panamá." *Journal of Interamerican Studies* 8, no. 3 (1966): 411–418.

"Música y educación." *Tierra y Dos Mares* 20 (1964): 3.

"Nacionalismo versus dodecafonismo?" *Revista Musical Chilena* 13, no. 67 (1959): 28–38.

"El público y la música viva." In *Music in the Americas,* edited by George List and Juan Orrego-Salas, 57–63. Bloomington: Indiana University Press, 1967.

"Raquel Boldorini." *Latin American Music Review* 3, no. 2 (1982): 244–246.

"Relaciones de la educación musical con los conservatorios." *Revista Musical Chilena* 18, no. 87/88 (1964): 63–67.

"Remembranzas de Roque Cordero." *Revista Lotería Panamá* no. 368 (September–October 1987): 15–25. Reprinted in *Panameños Ilustres* (1988): 154–173.

"Vigencia del músico culto." In *América Latina en su música.* Guadalajara, Mexico: Editorial Siglo 21, 1978.

* * * * *

Panamanian composer, conductor, educator, and musical diplomat Roque Cordero considers himself artistically "Panamanian" but not "nationalistic." As his country's first internationally acclaimed composer of serious concert music, he carries the dual burden of proving his competence in established European genres and presenting to the world of art music the musical flavor of Panama's indigenous vernacular styles. Both represent long-spanning traditions of which he is firmly a part. Cordero's cultural perspective lies somewhere between Central and North America, between classical and vernacular music, and between his dual role as music maker and music administrator.

Cordero's early musical training included clarinet, viola, and violin lessons. At the same time he experimented with composing popular songs in local styles. He began his musical studies within an environment of fluctuating isthmus politics. Panama became essentially an occupied territory when Bunau-Varillo's Zone Treaty, signed into effect in 1904, granted sovereign power to the United States in Panama, thereby generating resentment and internal conflict. But the interaction of four main groups—mestizos, Antilleans, Indians, and Zonians (Americans living within the canal zone)—enriched Panama's cultural environment. Despite conflict in the isthmus of Panama, the United States was a symbol of unlimited educational and economic possibilities.

During the 1930s and 1940s, when Panama suffered an economic depression, many ambitious students, including Cordero, enrolled in universities and conservatories in the United States. He began studying music education at the University of Minnesota–Minneapolis. Shortly thereafter, a mutual acquaintance arranged for the young composer to meet the legendary conductor Dimitri Mitropoulos. Upon recognizing the budding talent in Cordero's first large orchestral work, titled *Capricho interiorano* (1939) and based on rhythms and melodies of the native Panamanian *mejorana,* Mitropoulos recommended that Cordero complete his training with Austrian composer and composition teacher Ernst Krenek at Hamline University in St. Paul. With Krenek, Cordero studied orchestration and Palestrinian counterpoint from 1943 to 1947. In 1946, Cordero was still studying with Ernst Krenek, playing viola with the University of Minnesota Orchestra in Minneapolis, and finishing his last year of conducting studies with Dimitri Mitropoulos. In April of that year, Mitropoulos conducted the Minneapolis Symphony Orchestra in the premiere of Cordero's *Obertura panameña no. 2 (Panamanian Overture no. 2).* A few months later, Cordero traveled to the Berkshire Music Center at Tanglewood, Massachusetts, to study conducting with Stanley Chapple during the summer months before his last year of college. Amid all of this musical activity and a growing reputation, Cordero completed the Sonatina for Violin and Piano, his first completely serial work.

After completing his conducting, composition, and music education studies at the University of Minnesota and at Hamline University, in St. Paul, Minnesota, Cordero returned to Panama. While serving as director of the Conservatorio Nacional de Música de Panamá, he overhauled public school music education. At the same time, as conductor of the Orquesta Nacional de Panamá, he revived the National Symphony and raised national standards of quality for Panamanian musicians. He wrote articles on Panamanian folk music and published a widely used theory text book, *Curso de solfeo.* Though Cordero's formidable accomplishments as music educator, conductor, and scholar have been internationally recognized, he is perhaps best known as a composer.

Cordero's compositions blend two opposing musical ingredients: dodecaphony, a systematic approach to composing with all 12 tones, and elements of earthy Panamanian folk musics. He often draws upon the vibrant and angular melodies, asymmetrical rhythms, and changing meters of Panama's indigenous dances, the *tamborito* and *mejorana.* He communicates intense emotion within the framework of European classical forms such as the sonata, concerto, and symphony. Many characteristics of Cordero's music can be traced to the conflict between Central American and European culture in the 1930s and 1940s.

Panamanians in the 1930s saw a growing conflict between a nationalistic school of "exotic regionalism" and advocates of the increasing explorations of late-19th-century European romanticism. As the compositional advances of modernism in the United States and Europe came to be known among Panamanian musicians, more progressive members of the artistic community there began to criticize musical nationalism as stylistically inferior. Cordero, always a musical diplomat, avoided these debates and made a career blending elements of the two aesthetics. His music was not national, Cordero stated, but personal, and the personal could include musical elements of one's native land. According to Gilbert Chase, Cordero remarked, "what is needed is to find the *essence* of our nationalism in the melodies and rhythms of our typical songs and dances, in order to create from them a *personal* art, which, precisely because it *is* personal, will be Panamanian without having to 'beat the drum' to proclaim its nationality."

Early on, Cordero began writing in a nationalistic idiom that blends modern techniques with vernacular styles. His first major success, the carnival march *Reina de amor* for concert band (1937), reflected the "Spirit of Panama" (the English title of the piece) in such a vivid way as to gain Cordero positive recognition in both Latin and North America. This syncretic sensibility is reflected in pieces such as *Capricho interiorano* for orchestra (1939), *Sonatina rítmica* for piano (1943), *Obertura panameña no. 2* for orchestra (1944), *Ocho miniaturas* for chamber orchestra (1943; revised 1948), and *Rapsodia campesina* for orchestra (1953). One of these works, *Ocho miniaturas,* is a colorful piece and exemplary of his early style. Framed between an introduction and a coda, both bursting with vitality, the remaining six of the eight miniatures alternate between meditative calm ("Meditación," "Nocturne," and "Plegaria") and lively, energetic Latin dances ("Pasillo," "Danzonete," and "Mejorana").

After years of experimenting with polytonality, increasingly chromatic harmony, and atonal melodies, Cordero gained international recognition in the 1950s and 1960s with pieces that employed free use of 12-tone serialism and an intense level of personal expression. In particular, his studies in the 1940s with Austrian composer Ernst Krenek stimulated experiments in 12-tone composition. This syncretic sesibility is reflected in pieces such as Sonatina for Violin and Piano (1946), *Segunda sinfonía* (Symphony no. 2) (1956), and Concerto for Violin and Orchestra (1962) represent this later style. In the 1960s, Cordero refined his use of serial methods while placing more emphasis on subtle instrumental timbres and the development of complex rhythmic layering. Nevertheless, the general characteristics of his style remain firmly intact. During this time, his professional activity included posts as professor and director of the music conservatory in Panama City, touring engagements as lecturer, competition jurist, and conductor, and an appointment as delegate to the International Music Council of UNESCO.

Since the 1950s, prominent awards, commissions, performances, and recordings have propelled him to the forefront of Central American composers. Though interest in musical nationalism in Panama declined in the 1950s, Cordero continued to display the "personal" in his mature works. Cordero was among a number of Latin-American composers who gained international

recognition in the 1960s. Like Alberto Ginastera, Heitor Villa-Lobos, Mario Davidovsky, and Juan Orrego Salas, he received support in the United States. Growing interest in Latin-American music led to the establishment of the Latin American Music Center at Indiana University in 1966, and Cordero immigrated permanently to the United States in that year to assume the position of associate director. In 1972, Cordero accepted a teaching position at Illinois State University in Normal, Illinois, where he remained pedagogically and compositionally active until his retirement from teaching in 1987.

SONATINA RÍTMICA (1943)

Sonatina rítmica, for solo piano, is an important early example of Cordero's compositional skill and stylistic originality. It was the first piece he wrote while studying with Krenek and demonstrates his skill in composing energetic and percussive piano music. He refined this ability in later works for piano, such as "Duo 1954" for two pianos. Many of Cordero's mature works have their roots in *Sonatina rítmica.*

Sonatina rítmica demonstrates Cordero's commitment to composing almost exclusively within the confines of classical forms. The sonatina presents three short movements in sonata-allegro, ternary, and rondo forms. The two fast dance-like outer movements frame the central, lyrical slow movement. Linear, angular melodies underscore the strongly rhythmic drive of the work. During this period, prior to his adoption of the 12-tone method, Cordero favored a basically traditional, yet harmonically advanced, approach to composition. Cordero maintained rhythmic vitality through extensive use of accents, syncopation, hemiolas, frequently changing meters and tempos, and repeated-note patterns.

The opening movement is marked *Presto con furia* (fast with fury). Repeated "hammering" notes announce a metrically irregular, monophonic first theme and the movement's tonal center of E. The piece progresses in irregular meter, alternating mostly between 6/16, 9/16, 3/16, and 6/16 (the sequence of the first four measures) with strategically placed accents and hemiola effects within the angular line of perpetual 16th notes emphasizing the metric irregularity. The more chordal, syncopated second theme, less aggressive, provides appropriate contrast to the driving, linear first theme. Both themes are expanded and altered through sequential patterns and modulations in a conventional development section. Following an extended recapitulation, the movement accelerates to an exciting conclusion. Throughout the movement, constant dynamic contrast creates an atmosphere of high drama.

The second movement, lyrical and in ternary form (ABA), favors a transparent, two-voiced texture. The slow and expressive melody, in alto range, carries the movement with its smooth, expansive, string-like legato line. An accompanying line of single tones appears in the upper register, with the left hand crossed over the right and the tonal center of the movement alternating between G major and G minor. The gentle, singing, two-voiced polyphony created by the interaction of the two lines moves forward with few meter changes and with increased chromaticism underscoring the climax in the middle section. Following a contrasting middle section, the opening 13 measures are repeated at the end. After a static and unresolved six-measure coda, a brief window of calm moves without pause into the lively third movement, a rondo.

Like the opening movement, the bold rondo finale (ABACA) centers around the pitch *e* and contains many references to rhythms from the Panamanian dance known as the *mejorana* (see Ex. 1). A *mejorana* rhythm characterizes the opening flourish and the entire A section. (In the instrumental version of this traditional dance, a violin usually plays the *mejorana* melody, which alternates between compound and duple meters.) In this movement, the meter alternates between compound (6/8) and triple (3/4). The right hand plays wide-leaping phrases that can be seen as idiomatic for, or referential to, *mejorana*-inspired violin playing. The rondo form is characterized by contrasting sections of new material followed by returning thematic material presented in distant keys. The composer creates an overall feeling of continuity and closure by incorporating cyclic restatements of the first movement's main theme—with its memorable single-note linear melody divided between the hands—in the middle section of this third movement.

Example 1. *Mejorana* rhythm

Sonatina rítmica represents Cordero's free tonal period, which combines late-romantic harmonic language with Latin-inspired angular melodies and rhythmic drive. His consistent adherence to classical forms demonstrates a dedication to balanced structure. Comparisons to the "primitive" style typical of European piano music in the 1920s by composers such as Béla Bartók and Igor Stravinsky seem valid due to the percussive nature of the piano writing in the first and the third movements. However, scholars writing on Cordero's music have emphasized that European modernist techniques were not his only influences. His style also stemmed from an awareness of native vernacular music in Panama and international trends of folkloristic nationalism. Highly idiomatic piano writing makes this work a rewarding challenge for pianists.

SONATINA FOR VIOLIN AND PIANO (1946)

Cordero's Sonatina for Violin and Piano shows the composer working for the first time in the 12-tone idiom. It demonstrates Cordero's command of classical forms; the three movements are presented as sonata-allegro, binary, and rondo forms, all of which are based on a single 12-tone row that is used freely throughout the work. The sonata-allegro first movement opens with a slow introduction characterized by an initial solo violin statement of the tone row on which the piece is based. Frequent meter changes enhance the improvisatory feeling in the free-sounding violin part. Typical rhythmic and melodic characteristics of the Panamanian national dance *tamborito* are evident in this introduction, such as the syncopated anticipation of the first beat (see Ex. 2). The chordal piano accompaniment supports the rhapsodic violin

opening and adds intensity until the exposition bursts forth. Through the repetition of melodic and harmonic patterns, ostinato textures occur frequently, and often a complete presentation of the row is divided between the violin and the piano. The presentations of the row are structured within a loose arch form in which the order of the themes and row presentations are reversed in the recapitulation. For example, the exposition presents the first theme as the prime row and the second theme as its retrograde, while the recapitulation presents the second theme (retrograde) followed by the first theme (prime). Thus, without referring to a tonal center, Cordero achieves a feeling of resolution by returning to the prime form of the row. In addition, by repeating the prime-retrograde pairing he presented in the exposition, Cordero implies the characteristic tonic-dominant conflict inherent in the classical sonata form.

Example 2. *Tamborito* rhythm

The second movement opens with a solo violin two-phrase statement in two 12/8 measures of free-sounding rhythm. These two phrases, with an implied tempo *rubato,* present the inversion and transposition of the row on which this movement is based. The broad, descending phrases, which recur as a brief, introspective coda at the conclusion of the movement, frame the rest of the lyrical section. Intense violin playing, emphasized by mostly high-register events and ascending double-stops, averts attention from the conventional binary form and complex transformation of the row. The second movement provides a moment of meditative calm before it launches into the third movement, a rondo, which arrives energetically.

The rondo features a dance-like compound meter, lively tempo, *tamborito* rhythms (represented by eighth notes tied across barlines to anticipate the down beat), and rhythms derived from the *tamborito* (see Ex. 2). The initial theme of the movement, based on the *mejorana* rhythm, is countered by the slower (*melancólico*) middle section. The rondo is a symmetrical arch form (ABACABA) in which many technical demands are made on the violinist, who must negotiate a variety of playing techniques such as staccato, *pizzicato,* various accents, octave doublings, and rapid bowings. The interval of the seventh is emphasized throughout, and complex rhythms full of accents, syncopations, hemiolas, and imitative counterpoint between the players propel the movement toward its conclusion. Large melodic leaps and sharply articulated playing by both pianist and violinist make this a dazzling yet modestly virtuosic finish.

Cordero's tendency toward communicative and referential music, even in the 12-tone idiom, indicates that dodecaphony is merely a compositional technique and not a musical style. The composer's cultural eclecticism, though certainly not restricted to his early works, is found here in the blending of 12-tone techniques with Latin-inspired dance music. Other folk-music techniques utilized in the Sonatina for Violin and Piano, especially in the first and third movements, include *habanera* rhythms, syncopation, the Cuban *tresillo,* and the simultaneous or successive presentation of compound and triple meters. Many of the compositional elements presented in the youthful Sonatina and other works of his early dodecaphonic period reached maturity in the large-scale orchestral works of the 1950s and 1960s.

SEGUNDA SINFONÍA (SYMPHONY NO. 2) (1956)

In 1956, Cordero entered a composition competition for Latin-American composers sponsored by the José Angel Lamas Institution of Caracas, Venezuela, in 1956. Cordero completed his dodecaphonic *Segunda sinfonía* (Symphony no. 2) in just eight weeks, and after submitting it under a pseudonym, he won the Caro de Boesi award. The prize included 5,000 dollars and a premiere performance in Caracas on April 6, 1957, with Carlos Chávez conducting the Orquesta Sinfónica de Caracas.

The approximately 25-minute, one-movement *Segunda sinfonía* has been referred to by the composer as a compound sonata form in which the development section contains an embedded sonata form. Suggesting the dimensions of a multi-movement sonata cycle, the work is divided into well-balanced sections. The symphony can at times sound tonal, chromatic, or serial. The two main 12-tone rows on which the piece is based are used freely throughout the work, with certain motives being associated with each of the rows. The ascending melodic leap of a fifth, played by the trumpets and trombones, becomes a unifying motive heard throughout the piece. The major themes that result from various dissections of the two rows and the motivic development of these major themes are memorable—main motives remain in the ear after only one hearing of the work. The introduction presents the easily recognizable first row, which is usually heard in its untransposed form. The first theme of the exposition features the second row, while the following second theme again draws on material from the first row. This second theme, played by the violins, displays rhythmic characteristics of the *tamborito.*

Cordero has been praised for his orchestration, and the orchestration of the *Segunda sinfonía* shows why this is so. From the opening brass fanfare, the colorful capabilities of conventional orchestral instruments are exploited, and the power of the orchestration embellishes broad neoromantic melodies with complex polyrhythms, extreme ranges, alternation between *tutti* and chamber sections, and textural and timbral effects. Frequent soloistic treatment of individual instruments within the orchestra highlights the work's compositional detail.

Ostinato patterns and elements from Panamanian dances add another richly detailed level to the symphony's solid formal and technical structure. Many of the work's ostinato patterns derive from the Afro-Panamanian and Colombian dance known as the *cumbia.* The work's forward-moving energy comes from frequent use of melodic and rhythmic ostinato patterns—a device Cordero favors in other works as well. At times, the extensive repetition of an ostinato or a drone-like figure can give the impression of a temporary tonal center, with these ostinatos deriving from major thematic material, such as that of the beginning of the recapitulation. Here the ascending *pizzicato* pattern in the strings accompanies solo instruments from the brass and reed sections and the snare drum. This timbral combina-

tion creates a particularly poignant moment in the work. Drawing on the many thoughtful, static, suspended passages that preceded it, the symphony's unusually subdued conclusion softly fades away.

The premiere of the work took place as part of the Second International Music Festival, and the Caracas festival became a scene of conflict between nationalists and dodecaphonists. This fact makes it all the more significant that Cordero's *Segunda sinfonía*—a work that seamlessly combines the two extremes—was celebrated by critics and audiences. It is both strongly visceral and emotionally introverted and has been praised widely for its expression of a wide range of emotions including what Gilbert Chase refers to as "affirmation and spiritual triumph."

After the work's successful premiere in Caracas, Cordero's symphony had its United States premiere as part of the First Inter-American Music Festival one year later, on April 18, 1958, in Washington, D.C., with Howard Mitchell conducting the National Symphony Orchestra. Again, Cordero received a warm, appreciative ovation from the audience, suggesting that the modernist work communicated to a broad public. Cordero is quoted by Gilbert Chase as having remarked that his music was "the expression of thoughts that can be understood only through the medium of sound . . . an art of expression." The successful performance of this work in the United States led to institutional support for the composer, such as grants and commissions from the Guggenheim, Elizabeth Sprague Coolidge, and Koussevitsky foundations.

CONCERTO FOR VIOLIN AND ORCHESTRA (1962)

Three years after Cordero began composing the Concerto for Violin and Orchestra in 1958, he received a commission from the Serge Koussevitsky Music Foundation, and he completed the concerto in 1962 after more than a year of diligent work.

The approximately 30-minute violin concerto finds Cordero continuing his exploration of the challenges of absolute music, again in the concerto form. (He had begun exploring concerto form with his piano concerto of 1944.) The demanding but idiomatic solo part, which requires almost continuous playing on the part of the violinist, calls for full technical control of large leaps, double-stops, left-hand *pizzicati,* harmonics, complex rhythms, lengthy and rapid 16th-note passages (often in extreme registers), and interpretive powers of intimate expression. Organized around a single 12-tone row, the three movements are set in the characteristic forms of Cordero's earlier works: modified sonata-allegro, ternary, and rondo forms. The first three notes of the tone row, in its various transformations, become a primary motive of the first movement. This trichord's first interval, a major seventh, is also prominent throughout the work. The treatment of the row tends to favor dividing the 12 pitches between the violin and the orchestra, often allowing the accompanying body to complete the statement of the soloist, and vice versa.

The first movement is formally organized in a three-part structure that resembles a conventional sonata form of exposition-development-recapitulation. After the opening, unaccompanied *Largo*—a violin solo based on the row's first seven notes—the central, fast section (*Allegro strepitoso*) begins with the aggressive orchestra playing the concluding five notes of the row, with new themes emerging through various transformations of the original row. The second theme, which was presented initially by the flutes, is a retrograde of the prime row. Ostinato accompaniments and rich counterpoint thicken the texture and propel the musical action forward, and an abridged, written-out cadenza follows a quasi-development section. After a fiery climax, the conclusion of the first movement returns to the opening solo statement, this time including the first eight notes of the row. Resolution is achieved as the orchestra calmly completes the row by playing its last four notes.

The slow three-part second movement (*Lento*) is more introspective and private than the emotionally charged first movement. Drawing pitch materials freely from the original tone row, the slow movement explores rich color combinations within a thinner texture, favoring mostly lower strings and winds as a modified chamber ensemble within the large orchestra. The conclusion of the movement combines unusual but haunting timbres featuring violin harmonics and clarinets in a low register.

The third movement finale (*Allegro vigoroso*), an energetic rondo, features a dance-like theme with some rhythms from the Panamanian *tamborito*. It opens with a forceful timpani ostinato that is clearly related to the first four notes of the original row. The rondo alternates between intense, passionate *tutti* sections and virtuosic solo sections. A subtle, effective orchestration features a wide range of textural contrasts, dynamic outbursts, and passages of deep emotional intensity. Careful orchestral balance spotlights the soloist, particularly the forceful and driving finale passages.

The concerto, dedicated to the memory of Serge and Natalie Koussevitsky, had its premiere at the Third Inter-American Music Festival in Washington, D.C., in 1965. In 1974, Columbia Records recorded Cordero's Concerto for Violin and Orchestra for the Black Composers Series with soloist Sanford Allen, conductor Paul Freeman, and the Detroit Symphony Orchestra. For this recording, the composer and performers won the Koussevitsky International Recording Award. Consistent with his other works in the 12-tone idiom, Cordero's violin concerto has supreme power of communication, as audiences and critics alike have agreed.

REFERENCES

Béhague, Gerard. *Music in Latin America: An Introduction.* New Jersey: Prentice Hall, 1979.

Chase, Gilbert. "Composed by Cordero." *Inter-American Music Bulletin* 7, no. 4 (1958): 1–4.

Cordero, Roque. "The Folkmusic of Panama." *New Grove Dictionary of Music and Musicians,* edited by Stanley Sadie, 14: 151–154. London: Macmillan, 1980.

Sider, Ronald Ray. "Roque Cordero: The Composer and His Style Seen in Three Representative Works." *Inter-American Music Bulletin* 61 (1967): 1–17.

AMY C. BEAL

CROUCH, ANDRAÉ

Born in Los Angeles, Calif., July 1, 1942. **Education:** San Fernando, Calif., public school system through high school; San Fernando, Calif., attended Valley Junior College; Los Angeles, Calif., attended Life Bible College. **Composing and Performing Career:** Began playing for church services when he was 11; formed COGICS (Church of God in Christ Singers); formed the Disciples, 1965; first major commercial success with the Disciples, *Take the Message Everywhere,* 1969. **Honors/Awards:** Numerous awards from the music and recording industries, including Grammy Awards in 1975, 1978, 1979, 1995; Berklee College of Music, Boston, honorary doctorate, 1997.

MUSIC LIST

COLLECTIONS

Andraé. Burbank, Calif.: Manna Music, 1972.

Andraé Crouch. Burbank, Calif.: Manna Music, 1971.

Andraé Crouch and the Disciples Keep On Singin'. Newbury Park, Calif.: Lexicon Music, 1971.

Andraé Crouch Choral Series. Burbank, Calif.: Manna Music, n.d.

The Andraé Crouch Songbook: 40 Favorite Andraé Crouch Songs. Newbury Park, Calif.: Lexicon Music, 1976.

The Best of Andraé: Andraé Crouch and the Disciples. Newbury Park, Calif.: Lexicon Music, 1975.

Finally: Songs of Andraé Crouch. Newbury Park, Calif.: Lexicon Music, 1982.

Just Andraé: Arrangements for Youth Choirs. Newbury Park, Calif.: Lexicon Music, 1973.

No Time to Lose. Newbury Park, Calif.: Lexicon Music, 1984.

Songs of Andraé Crouch and the Disciples. Newbury Park, Calif.: Lexicon Music, 1979.

Soulfully. Newbury Park, Calif.: Lexicon Music, 1972.

Take Me Back. Newbury Park, Calif.: Lexicon Music, 1975.

This Is Andraé Crouch. Vol. 1. Burbank, Calif.: Manna Music, 1969.

SONGS

[The following list of titles includes only works that were composed by the subject of the entry; it is not a list of recordings that were made by the subject. Although the composer may have made recordings of his own works, the list is not restricted to those recordings but in many cases includes performances by other artists of the composer's work. The list is made up of publication and discographical data, in cases where such information is available. Although no effort has been made to include documentation of the earliest recording of the works listed, the date of the earliest recording that is readily available has been given. —Ed.]

"All I Can Say (I Really Love You)." In *Take Me Back.* Recorded: CGI Records 51416 1135 2; Light Records LS 5784; Light Records LS-5637-LP.

"All That I Have." Recorded, 1991: CGI Records 51416 1010 4; Light Records 7-115-74062-3.

"All the Way." In *Finally: Songs of Andraé Crouch.* Recorded: Light Records SPCN 7-115-710759; Light Records 51416 1037 2; Light Records 7-115-74063-1.

"Along Came Jesus." In *Andraé Crouch and the Disciples.* Recorded: Light Records LS-5546.

"Always Remember." In *No Time to Lose.* Recorded: Light Records LS-5863; Pinebrook PB-2128.

"Believe in His Holy Name." Recorded: Light Records LS 5598.

"Bless His Holy Name (Psalm 103)." 1973. Newbury Park, Calif.: Lexicon Music, 1978. In *Just Andraé, The Best of Andraé, The Andraé Crouch Songbook,* and *Songs of Andraé Crouch and the Disciples.* Recorded: Light Records 7-115-74062-3; Light Records 51416 1038 2; Light Records 51416 1156 2.

"The Blood Will Never Lose Its Power." Burbank, Calif.: Manna Music, 1966. In *This Is Andraé Crouch.* Arranger, Dick Bolks. Recorded: SMI SMIC-30AS.

"Bringing Back the Sunshine." Recorded, 1991: CGI Records 51416 1010 4; Light Records LS-5763; Light Records 7-115-74062-3.

"The Broken Vessel." Burbank, Calif.: Manna Music, 1968. In *This Is Andraé Crouch.* Arranger, Dwight Elrich.

"Can't Nobody Do Me Like Jesus." Recorded: Light Records SPCN 7-115-710759; Light Records 51416 1052 2; SMI SMIC-30AS.

"(The) Choice." Co-composers, Gregory (Blaine) Eckler, James Felix. Recorded, 1982: A&M 161053; Light Records 51416 1037 2; Light Records 7-115-74063-1.

"Come On Back My Child." In *Just Andraé.* Recorded: Light Records LS 5598.

"Come On, Come On." Brentwood, Tenn.: Birdwing Music, n.d.

"Don't Give Up." Recorded, 1996: Warner Bros. BSK 3513.

"Don't Let This Moment Pass You By." Brentwood, Tenn.: Birdwing Music, n.d.

"Dreamin'." Recorded, 1991: CGI Records 51416 1010 4; Light Records 7-115-74062-3; Light Records 51416 1156 2.

"Everlasting Joy." Co-composer, Sandra E. Crouch. Northridge, Calif.: Sanabella Music, n.d.

"Everybody's Got to Know." In *Finally: Songs of Andraé Crouch.* Recorded: Light Records LS 5784; Warner Bros. BSK 3513.

"Everything Changed." In *Soulfully, The Best of Andraé,* and *The Andraé Crouch Songbook.* Recorded: Light Records E1-60071; Light Records 51418 1038 4; Light Records 51416 1038 2.

"Everywhere." In *Andraé.*

"Finally." In *Finally: Songs of Andraé Crouch.* Recorded: Arrival 3089-2; Light Records 51416 1037 2; Light Records 7-115-74063-1.

"Gathering." N.p.: Crouch Music, n.d.

"Give It All Back to Me." Recorded, 1994: Qwest Records 9 45432-2; Star Song G2724382008521.

"God Loves the Country People." In *Just Andraé.* Recorded: Light Records LS 5598.

"Got Me Some Angels." In *No Time to Lose.* Recorded: Light Records LS 5863; K-Tel International 251-2.

"Hallelujah Gospel Theme." Brentwood, Tenn.: Birdwing Music, n.d.

"Hallelujah I Am Free." Pacific City, Ore.: Manna Music, n.d.

"Handwriting on the Wall." Co-composers, Patrick Henderson, Marvin Winans. Recorded, 1996: Warner Bros. BSK 3513.

"He Included Me." New York: SIMCO, 1967. Arranger, Kenneth Morris.

"He Never Sleeps." In *Andraé.*

"He Proved His Love to Me." In *Soulfully.* Recorded: Light Records LS-5581.

"He Washed My Sins Away." Brentwood, Tenn.: Birdwing Music, n.d.

"He's Coming to Take Me Away." Brentwood, Tenn.: Birdwing Music, n.d.

"He's Gone, He's Back." Co-composers, James Horner, Sandra E. Crouch.

"He's Waiting." In *Finally: Songs of Andraé Crouch.* Co-composers, Alfred and Linda McCrary. Recorded: Light Records LS 5784; Light Records 60170.

"Heaven (One of These Days I'm Going There)." Newbury Park, Calif.: Lexicon Music, n.d.

"Heaven Belongs to You." Co-composer, Sandra E. Crouch.

"His Truth Still Marches On." In *No Time to Lose.* Recorded: Light Records LS 5863.

"Hollywood Scene." Co-composer, David Z. Williams. Recorded, 1996: Warner Bros. BSK 3513.

"How Sweet It Is to Know the Lord." In *This Is Andraé Crouch.*

"I Can't Keep It to Myself." Recorded: Warner Bros. BSK 3513.

"I Come That You Might Have Life." In *Soulfully, The Best of Andraé,* and *The Andraé Crouch Songbook.* Recorded: Light Records E1-60071; Light Records LS-5678; Light Records 51416 1038 2.

"I Didn't Think It Could Be (Somebody Told Me)." In *Andraé, The Best of Andraé,* and *The Andraé Crouch Songbook.* Recorded: SMI SMIC-30AS; Light Records 51416 1038 2; Light Records 51416 1052 2.

"I Don't Know Why (Jesus Loved Me)." Newbury Park, Calif.: Lexicon Music, 1972. In *Andraé Crouch and the Disciples, The Best of Andraé, The Andraé Crouch Songbook,* and *Songs of Andraé Crouch and the Disciples.* Recorded: Light Records 51416 1038 2; Light Records 51416 1052 2; Light Records 51416 1156 2.

"I Find No Fault in Him." Burbank, Calif.: Manna Music, 1966. In *This Is Andraé Crouch.*

"I Just Love My Jesus." In *Andraé.*

"I Just Want to Know You." Recorded: Light Records LSX 5717; Light Records 51416 1055 2; Light Records 51416 1036 2.

"I Love Him Because He First Loved Me." In *This Is Andraé Crouch.*

"I Love Walkin' with You." Recorded, 1996: Warner Bros. BSK 3513.

"I Must Go Away." In *Andraé Crouch and the Disciples.* Recorded: Light Records LS-5546.

"I Shall Never Let Go His Hand." In *This Is Andraé Crouch.*

"I Surrender All." Co-composer, W. S. Weeden. Recorded: Arrival 620-2; Light Records SPCN 7-115-710759; Light Records 51416 1036 2.

"I'll Be Good to You, Baby (A Message to the Silent Victims)." Recorded, 1996: Warner Bros. BSK 3513.

"I'll Be Thinking of You." Recorded, 1993: Light Records 51416 1055 2; Light Records 7-115-74060-7; Light Records 51416 1156 2.

"I'll Never Forget." In *This Is Andraé Crouch.* Recorded: Light Records LS-5504-LP.

"I'll Still Love You." In *Take Me Back.* Recorded: CGI Records 51416 1010 4; CGI Records 51416 1135 2; Light Records 7-115-74062-3.

"I'm Coming Home, Lord." In *Andraé Crouch and the Disciples, The Best of Andraé,* and *The Andraé Crouch Songbook.* Recorded: Accord 4N-7177; Light Records E1-60071; Light Records 51416 1038 2.

"I'm Gonna Keep On Singing." Newbury Park, Calif.: Lexicon Music, 1971. In *Andraé Crouch and the Disciples, The Best of Andraé,* and *The Andraé Crouch Songbook.* Recorded: Light Records 7-115-74060-7; Light Records 51416 1038 2; Light Records 51416 1156 2.

"I'm in Love." Brentwood, Tenn.: Birdwing Music, n.d.

"I've Got Confidence." Newbury Park, Calif.: Lexicon Music, 1969. In *Andraé Crouch and the Disciples, The Best of Andraé, The Andraé Crouch Songbook,* and *Songs of Andraé Crouch and the Disciples.* Recorded: Light Records 7-115-74060-7; Light Records 51416 1038 2; Light Records 51416 1156 2.

"I've Got It." In *Andraé.*

"I've Got the Best." Recorded, 1993: Arrival 3089-2; Light Records 51416 1037 2; Light Records 7-115-74063-1.

"I've Got Jesus." Recorded: Accord 4N-7177.

"If Heaven Never Was Promised to Me." In *Just Andraé, The Best of Andraé,* and *The Andraé Crouch Songbook.* Recorded: Light Records E1-60071; Light Records LS-5748; Light Records 51416 1038 2.

"If I Was a Tree (The Highest Praise)." Recorded: Light Records LSX 5717; Light Records 51416 1036 2.

"It Ain't No New Thing." In *Take Me Back.* Recorded: CGI Records 51416 1135 2; Light Records 51416 1037 2; Light Records 7-115-74063-1.

"It Will Never Lose Its Power." Los Angeles: Frazier-Cleveland, 1962. Arranger, Thurston G. Frazier.

"It Won't Be Long." Newbury Park, Calif.: Lexicon Music, 1972. In *Soulfully, The Best of Andraé, The Andraé Crouch Songbook,* and *Songs of Andraé Crouch and the Disciples.* Recorded: Light Records 7-115-74060-7; Light Records 51416 1038 2; Light Records 51416 1052 2.

"It's Gonna Rain." Recorded: Light Records 51416 1037 2; Light Records 7-115-74063-1; Light Records 51416 1156 2.

"It's Not Just a Story." In *Just Andraé.* Recorded: Light Records LS 5598; Light Records SPCN 7-115-710759.

"Jesus (Every Hour He'll Give You Power)." Newbury Park, Calif.: Lexicon Music, 1971. In *Andraé Crouch and the Disciples, The Best of Andraé,* and *The Andraé Crouch Songbook.* Recorded: Light Records E1-60071; Light Records LS-5748; Light Records 51416 1038 2.

"Jesus, Come Lay Your Hand on Me (Luke 7:36–50)." In *No Time to Lose.* Recorded: Light Records LS 5863.

"Jesus I'll Never Forget." Co-composer, James Cleveland. New York: Screen Gems-EMI, 1963.

"Jesus Is Lord." Co-composer, Patrick Henderson. Recorded, 1993: Light Records 51416 1037 2; Light Records 7-115-74063-1; Arrival 3089-2.

"Jesus Is the Answer." Newbury Park, Calif.: Lexicon Music, 1973. In *The Best of Andraé, The Andraé Crouch Songbook.* Co-composer, Sandra E. Crouch. Recorded: CGI Records 51416 1145 2; Light Records 51416 1052 2; Light Records 51416 1156 2.

"Just Like He Said He Would." Newbury Park, Calif.: Lexicon Music, 1974. In *The Best of Andraé, Take Me Back,* and *The Andraé Crouch Songbook.* Recorded: CGI Records 51416 1135 2; Light Records 51416 1145 2; Light Records 51416 1156 2.

"Leave the Devil Alone." In *Soulfully.* Recorded: Light Records LS-5581.

"Let's Worship Him." In *Finally: Songs of Andraé Crouch.* Co-composers, Abraham Lopez Laboriel and Lyn M. Laboriel. Recorded: Arrival 3089-2; Light Records 7-115-74063-1; Light Records 51416 1037 2.

"Let the Same Spirit." Brentwood, Tenn.: Birdwing Music, n.d. Recorded, 1993: Light Records 51416-1054-2.

"Life." Brentwood, Tenn.: Birdwing Music, n.d.

Andraé Crouch; courtesy of Qwest Records; photo by David Roth

"Livin' This Kind of Life." In *No Time to Lose.* Recorded: Light Records LS 5863.

"Lookin' for You." Recorded, 1993: Arrival 3089-2; Light Records 51416 1037 2; Light Records 7-115-74063-1.

"Lord, Don't Lift Your Spirit from Me." In *This Is Andraé Crouch.*

"Lord Is My Light." Co-composer, Michael Omartian. Recorded, 1994: Qwest Records 9 45432-2.

"Lord, You've Been Good to Me." In *Just Andraé.* Recorded: Light Records LS 5598.

"Lullaby of the Deceived (II Timothy 3:13)." In *Just Andraé.* Recorded: Light Records LS 5598.

"Masquerade." Co-composers, Victoria Hill McCall, James Everette Lawrence, and Martin Marshall McCall.

"Maybe God Is Tryin' to Tell You Somethin'." Los Angeles: Warner Chappell, n.d. Co-composers, David Francis Del Sesto, Quincy D. Jones, William D. Maxwell. Recorded, 1986: Qwest Records 25356-1.

"My Peace I Leave with You." Brentwood, Tenn.: Birdwing Music, n.d.

"My Tribute (To God Be the Glory)." Newbury Park, Calif.: Lexicon Music, 1971. In *Andraé Crouch and the Disciples, The Best of Andraé, The Andraé Crouch Songbook,* and *Finally: Songs of Andraé Crouch.* Recorded: CGI Records 51416 1177 2; CGI Records 51426 1125 2 or Light Records 51416 1125 2; Light Records 51416 1156 2.

"No Time to Lose (I Wanna Be Ready)." In *No Time to Lose.* Recorded: Light Records LS 5863.

"Nobody." Co-composer, Lon Christian Smith. Brentwood, Tenn.: Birdwing Music, n.d.

"Nobody But You." Co-composer, Jessy D. Dixon. Brentwood, Tenn.: Birdwing Music, n.d.

"Oh, I Need Him." Newbury Park, Calif.: Lexicon Music, 1969. In *Soulfully, The Best of Andraé,* and *The Andraé Crouch Songbook.* Recorded: Light Records E1-60071; Light Records LS-5678; Light Records 51416 1038 2.

"Oh, It Is Jesus (Luke 8:43–48)." In *No Time to Lose.* Recorded: Light Records LS 5863; Pinebrook PB-2128.

"Oh Saviour." In *Take Me Back.* Recorded: CGI Records 51416 1135 2; Light Records 51416 1037 2; Light Records 7-115-74063-1.

"One Way." In *Andraé.*

"Perfect Peace." In *Songs of Andraé Crouch and the Disciples.* Recorded: Arrival 3089-2; Light Records 51416 1036 2; Light Records 51416 1156 2.

"Please Come Back." Recorded: Light Records 51416 1055 2; Light Records 51416 1037 2; Light Records 7-115-74063-1.

"Polynesian Praise Song (I Love You)." In *Songs of Andraé Crouch and the Disciples.* Recorded: CGI Records 51416 1010 4; Light Records 7-115-74062-3.

"Praise God, Praise God." Recorded: Light Records LSX 5717; Light Records 51416 1036 2.

"Praises." Newbury Park, Calif.: Lexicon Music, 1975. In *The Best of Andraé, Take Me Back,* and *The Andraé Crouch Songbook.* Recorded: CGI Records 51416 1135 2; Light Records 51416 1055 2; Light Records 7-115-74062-3.

"Quiet Times." In *Songs of Andraé Crouch and the Disciples.* Recorded: Arrival 3089-2; Light Records 51416 1055 2; Light Records 7-115-74062-3;

"Revive Us Again." Co-composers, William P. Mackey, John J. Husband. Recorded: Arrival 30132; Light Records LSX 5717; Light Records 51416 1036 2.

"Right Now." In *No Time to Lose.* Recorded: Arrival 421-2; Light Records LS 5863.

"Running for Jesus." Brentwood, Tenn.: Birdwing Music, n.d.

"Satisfied." In *Soulfully, The Best of Andraé,* and *The Andraé Crouch Songbook.* Recorded: Arrival 620-2; Light Records E1-60071; Light Records 51416 1038 2.

"Save the People." Recorded, 1996: Warner Bros. BSK 3513.

"Say a Little Prayer." Brentwood, Tenn.: Birdwing Music, n.d.

"Say So." Recorded, 1994: Qwest Records 9 45432-2; Warner Alliance 9 45771-2; Warner Brothers WBC-4180.

"Somebody Somewhere Is Prayin' (Just for You)." In *No Time to Lose.* Recorded: Light Records LS 5863.

"Someday I'll See His Face." In *This Is Andraé Crouch.*

"Soon and Very Soon (We Are Going to See the King)." 1976. In *Songs of Andraé Crouch and the Disciples.* Recorded: CGI Records 51416 1090 2; Light Records 7-115-74060-7; Light Records 51416 1156 2.

"A Strong Foundation." Co-composer, Stevie Wonder.

"Sweet Communion." In *Finally: Songs of Andraé Crouch.* Recorded: CGI Records 51416 1010 4; Light Records 60170; Light Records 7-115-74062-3.

"Sweet Love of Jesus." In *Take Me Back.* Recorded: Light Records 7-115-74059-3; Light Records 7-115-74060-7; CGI Records 51416 1135 2.

"Take a Little Time." In *Andraé Crouch and the Disciples, The Best of Andraé, The Andraé Crouch Songbook,* and *Songs of Andraé Crouch and the Disciples.* Recorded: Light Records 51416 1036 2; Light Records 51416 1038 2; Light Records 51416 1156 2.

"Take Me Back." Newbury Park, Calif.: Lexicon Music, 1973. In *The Best of Andraé, Take Me Back,* and *The Andraé Crouch Songbook.* Recorded: CGI Records 51416 1135 2; Light Records 51416 1038 2; Light Records 51416 1156 2.

"Tell Them." 1975. Newbury Park, Calif.: Lexicon Music, 1975. In *The Best of Andraé, Take Me Back, The Andraé Crouch Songbook,* and *Songs of Andraé Crouch and the Disciples.* Recorded: CGI Records 51416 1135 2; Light Records 51416 1036 2; Light Records 51416 1038 2.

"Thank You Lord." Downers Grove, Ill.: Lexicon Music, n.d.

"That's What It's All About." Recorded: Light Records LS 5598.

"That's Why I Needed You." In *Finally: Songs of Andraé Crouch.* Recorded: Arrival 3089-2; CGI Records 51416 1010 4; Light Records 7-115-74062-3.

"There Is a Name." In *Andraé.*

"There Is Power in the Blood." Co-composer, Lewis E. Jones. Recorded: Light Records LSX 5717; Light Records SPCN 7-115-710759; Light Records 51416 1036 2.

"There's No Hatred." Brentwood, Tenn.: Birdwing Music, n.d.

"They Shall Be Mine." In *Take Me Back.* Recorded: Light Records 51416 1055 2; Light Records 7-115-74060-7; CGI Records 51416 1135 2.

"This Is Another Day." Recorded, 1982: Light Records 51416 1037 2; Light Records 7-115-74063-1; Light Records 51416 1036 2; Light Records 51416 1156 2.

"Through It All." 1971. Burbank, Calif.: Manna Music, 1971. In *Andraé.* Arranger, Dwight Elrich or Robert J. Hughes. Recorded: Light

Records 7-115-74060-7; Light Records 51416 1038 2; Light Records 51416 1156 2.

"Touch Me." Recorded, 1991: Arrival 3089-2; CGI Records 51416 1010 4; Light Records 7-115-74062-3.

"Try Me One More Time." In *Soulfully.* Recorded: Light Records LS-5581.

"Until Jesus Comes." N.p.: Crouch Music, n.d.

"Waiting for the Son." Recorded, 1996: Warner Bros. BSK 3513.

"We Are Not Ashamed." In *Finally: Songs of Andraé Crouch.* Recorded: Arrival 3089-2; CGI Records 51416 1010 4; Light Records 7-115-74062-3.

"We Expect You." Brentwood, Tenn.: Birdwing Music, n.d.

"We Love It Here." Recorded, 1994: Qwest Records 9 45432-2.

"We Need to Hear from You." Recorded, 1991: CGI Records 51416 1010 4.

"Well Done." Recorded: Light Records LSX 5717; Light Records 51416 1036 2.

"What Does Jesus Mean to You?" In *Just Andraé.* Co-composer, William Thedford. Recorded: Light Records LS 5598.

"What Makes a Man Turn His Back on God." In *Andraé.*

"What Ya Gonna Do?" Newbury Park, Calif.: Lexicon Music, 1971. In *Andraé Crouch and the Disciples.* Recorded: Light Records LS-5546.

"Why." Brentwood, Tenn.: Birdwing Music, n.d.

"Wonderful Counsellor." Brentwood, Tenn.: Birdwing Music, n.d.

"You Ain't Living." In *Just Andraé.* Recorded: Light Records LS 5598.

"You Can Depend on Me." In *Take Me Back.* Recorded: CGI Records 51416 1125 2 or Light Records 51426 1125 2; CGI Records 51416 1135 2; Light Records 7-115-74063-1.

"You Can Make It." Co-composer, Lenny Macaluso. Brentwood, Tenn.: Birdwing Music, n.d.

"You Don't Have to Jump No Pews (I've Been Born Again)." Recorded: Light Records 51416 1036 2; Light Records 51416 1156 2; Light Records SPCN 7-115-710759.

"You Don't Know What You Are Missin'." In *Soulfully.* Recorded: Light Records LS-5581; Light Records 51416 1052 2; Light Records 51416 1156 2.

"You Gave to Me." Recorded, 1982: Light Records LSX 5717; Light Records SPCN 7-115-710759; Light Records 51416 1036 2.

"You're the Only One." Co-composer, Keith Gordon Green. Brentwood, Tenn.: Birdwing Music, n.d.

PUBLICATIONS

ABOUT CROUCH
Books and Monographs
Hartley, Al. *On the Road with Andraé Crouch.* Spire Christian Comics. Old Tappan, N.J.: F. H. Revell, 1977.

Mainse, David. *The Andraé Crouch Story.* Springfield, Mo.: Turning Point, 1976.

Dissertations
Booth, John David. "The Music of Andraé Crouch and the Disciples." Master's thesis, New Orleans Baptist Theological Seminary, 1974.

Jenkins, Keith Bernard. "The Rhetoric of Gospel Song: A Content Analysis of the Lyrics of Andrae Crouch." Ph.D. diss., Florida State University, 1990.

Articles
Butler, D. W. "Gospel: The First Word in American Music." *ASCAP in Action* (Fall 1980): 40–43.

Doerschuk, Bob. "Backstage with Andraé Crouch." *Contemporary Keyboard* 5 (August 1979): 6+.

"Gospeler Crouch Ignores Critics with New Sounds." *Billboard* 87 (April 5, 1975): 31.

Salvo, P. "Andraé Crouch, New King of Pop Gospel." *Sepia Magazine* 25, no. 12 (1976): 50.

"Soul Sauce." *Billboard* 88 (November 13, 1976): 52.

"Spirit." *People Weekly* 44, no. 17 (1995): 103.

"WB Tries to Break Crouch Via Regular Commercial Avenues." *Variety* 304 (October 21, 1981): 89.

Wix, K. "Making a Joyful Noise." *Cash Box* 52 (July 8, 1989): 6–8.

BY CROUCH
Through It All: A Biography, with Nina Ball. Waco, Tex.: Word Books, 1974.

* * * * *

Andraé Crouch belongs to a vital tradition of gospel song composers that spans the entire 20th century and whose ranks include Rev. Charles Albert Tindley, Lucie Eddie Campbell, Thomas A. Dorsey, and Rev. William Brewster. Crouch synthesized key elements of the popular secular styles of his day with the conventions and forms of gospel music, creating a style that was appealing to a wide audience. Exerting extensive influence on subsequent gospel trends, Crouch is among the most important innovators of the contemporary gospel music style. In the 1960s and 1970s, along with fellow Californians Edwin Hawkins and the Hawkins Family Singers and James Cleveland, Crouch helped to establish Los Angeles (where he was born in 1942) and San Francisco as important centers for black gospel music. Moreover, Crouch's affiliation with the Church of God in Christ (COGIC), a primarily black pentecostal denomination, has helped to perpetuate his gospel-music innovation within its many churches. Crouch's early work can be viewed as the church's answer to the Motown Sound: self-consciously assimilationist yet true to its roots in black vernacular culture. Young, white Christians of the Jesus Movement formed an important part of Crouch's audience. Crouch aggressively sought to reach listeners beyond the traditional audience base of black gospel music not only with his compositional style but also with polished recordings that sometimes included jazz sidemen, non-traditional performance venues, and a successful mix of evangelical zeal and promotional expertise.

Like other musicians in the gospel tradition, Crouch began his apprenticeship in the Christ Memorial COGIC of Pacoima, California, a pentecostal church pastored by his father, the Rev. Benjamin Crouch. According to his parents, Crouch's earliest musical experiences included singing in a trio at Sunday School with his elder brother Benjamin and his twin sister Sandra. At age nine, he began to play piano by learning the melodies of hymns, such as "What a Friend We Have in Jesus." He developed rapidly and by age 11 was playing for his father's worship services. Later, he formed a group called the COGICS, an acronym for the denomination in which the group was based. Although Crouch was educated formally in the San Fernando, California, public schools and at Valley Junior College and Life Bible College in Los Angeles, the musical activities in his father's church appear to have provided his most important artistic outlets. These experiences provided a solid foundation for Crouch's later activities, within which his compositional talents would flourish. In fact, Crouch once credited his father for his broad, flexible attitude toward gospel composition by heeding his father's musical counsel: "If you have to hymn it, hymn it. If you have to rock it, rock it. If you have to funk it, funk it." Crouch's compositional output certainly spans these musical practices; his output attracted a racially diverse audience "through a 'split-compositional' personality," says gospel scholar Horace Boyer, that shifted between and blended traditional and contemporary gospel styles. Thus, Crouch's blend of light rock, soul, and pop, combined with the influence of traditional hymns and anthems, found a diverse religious audience.

Crouch's split-compositional personality was clearly evident early in his career. In 1965, he formed Andraé Crouch and the Disciples, the recording and touring activities of which provided Crouch with his primary compositional vehicle. Over the years, the group has included in its ranks Sherman Andrus, Billy Thedford, Sandra Crouch, Tramaine Davis Hawkins, and Danniebelle Hall. This ensemble's first recording, the album *Take the Message Everywhere* (Light Records LS-5504-LP), features the mixture of original compositions, arrangements, and performance practices that would mark the "Crouch sound": arrangements of the Negro spiritual "Wade in the Water," Thomas Dorsey's "Precious Lord, Take My Hand," and the hymn "No, Not One!," as well as several of his own compositions, including "The Blood Will Never Lose Its Power," a piece that would later be canonized in standard denominational hymnals. Each of the selections on *Take the Message Everywhere* demonstrates not only how Crouch had absorbed a broad slate of musical forms (including hymns, anthems, pop-rock, and light soul) but also how the boundaries separating the activities of composition, arranging, and performance practice blur in the gospel tradition. "I'll Never Forget," one of the original compositions on the album, features Crouch's groundbreaking synthesis of diverse musical elements. The song's simple harmonic language, its "shuffle-beat" in compound meter, its lyric content, and Crouch's use of standard gospel instrumentation—organ, piano, tambourine, bass, and drums—are all reminiscent of hymns and of traditional gospel music. What places the work in the "contemporary" realm, however, is Crouch's use of jazz harmonies and the inclusion of a harp in the instrumentation. Other works on the album use a wide range of techniques and instruments atypical of traditional gospel, including pop-rock beats, understated unison vocal lines that also feature elements of doo-wop, and scoring for instruments that range from vibraphone to symphony orchestra. Crouch continued to mix idioms over the next three decades, and his efforts were met with much popular success: Andraé Crouch and the Disciples appeared on television broadcasts such as the Tonight Show, performed at the Hollywood Bowl, and toured before appreciative audiences throughout the United States and abroad.

After a ten-year hiatus from recording, during which he concentrated on his family, church, and producing projects for others, Crouch released *Mercy* on the Qwest label in 1994. The project won Crouch his sixteenth Grammy the next year and demonstrated his continuing experimentation with eclectic idioms with his use of rhythms of African and other "world" musics.

SELECTED WORKS

Four works from the late 1960s and early 1970s present clear examples not only of Crouch's distinctive compositional voice but also the musical and stylistic parameters of contemporary gospel music. These pieces—"The Blood Will Never Lose Its Power," "Through It All," "Bless His Holy Name," and "My Tribute"—like the hymns that inspired them, are verse-chorus structures (AB) or some variation thereof; thus, each is a suitable frameworks for spontaneous improvisation.

"The Blood Will Never Lose Its Power" (1966), for example, published when Crouch was still a teenager, comprises a 32-bar form: 16 bars for the verses and 16 for the chorus (or refrain). A typical performance (usually congregational) would feature the two verses first and then repeated choruses (AABB), although the printed score does not make this designation. Crouch's original recording of the piece, however, presents the AABB form, and congregations have followed that outline.

"Through It All" (1971) is also a 32-bar piece, containing three 16-bar verses and a chorus of the same length. Convention dictates that performers follow the AABABB form featured on Crouch's recording and not the basic verse-chorus structure represented in the printed score.

"Bless His Holy Name" and "My Tribute," however, depart from the 32-bar pattern. "Bless His Holy Name" (1973), is a 16-bar song that divides evenly into two eight-bar sections of a simple chorus that may be repeated continuously:

> Bless the Lord,
> O my soul,
> And all that is within me,
> Bless His holy Name.
> He has done great things,
> He has done great things,
> He has done great things,
> Bless His holy Name.

"My Tribute" (1971) is a ballad with three sections—a chorus with two musically different verses (ABC)—which still lends itself to repetition and improvisation, especially in the eight-bar refrain (chorus). The harmonies of these pieces contain little chromaticism or elaborate chords. Instrumentalists on the recordings, however, take liberties with the scores, adding a richer harmonic language, improvisatory fills, highly expressive accompanying passages, extended cadences, modulations, and special codas, or "tags," to heighten their emotional content.

Crouch's instrumentation itself represents an important development in gospel music. He employed a variety of instruments (e.g., organ, acoustic and electric guitars, vibraphone, tambourine, electric bass, drums, electric keyboards, synthesizers, strings, and horns) to achieve a unique sound that shifts between the traditional gospel style represented in "The Blood Will Never Lose Its Power" and the more pop-oriented style of "My Tribute" and "Through It All."

In the same way, the melodic aspect of Crouch's printed scores provides only a sketch for what typically happens during a performance. The melodies, for example, are written in a straightforward fashion that only hints at the syncopation and vocal fills that performers routinely add. The melodies proceed, for the most part, in stepwise motion with occasional skips, such as the sequential passage in the chorus of "My Tribute." Vocal ranges are narrow, rarely spanning more than an octave and usually falling within the range of a fifth. Although all of these songs are routinely performed as congregational hymns, the original recordings (with the exception of "Bless the Lord") feature solo vocal lines on the verses and vocal ensembles singing in three- and four-part harmony on the choruses. The background vocals are usually sung in a toned-down but full-throated gospel style. By way of contrast, the vocal solos on "My Tribute," "Through It All," and "The Blood Will Never Lose Its Power" are presented in a staid, almost crooned style, though with some improvisatory elements that depart from the score.

The primary rhythmic interest of these pieces lies mostly in the performative aspects of the recordings. The written scores are in simple meter with the exception of "The Blood," which is in 3/4 time. As with other parameters of these compositions, the original recording—not the score—has held greater influence in determining how these pieces have been performed. The shuffling subdivision of the beat in "The Blood," for example, while intermittently present in the bass line of the written piano part, is usually played throughout the entire piece in performance, as the recording illustrates.

Finally, Crouch's lyrics are quite traditional, avoiding direct reference to specific political situations or social commentary. His lyrics represent personal reflections or testimonies of the benefits of Christian living (e.g., "Through It All" and "The Blood Will Never Lose Its Power") or worship and adoration (e.g., "My Tribute" and "Bless His Holy Name"). These attributes, together with what contemporary audiences perceive as important innovations in compositional and performance practice, explain the enthusiastic reception of Crouch's music into the American church's canon of best-loved compositions. They also confirm Crouch's position as one of the most important sacred song writers of his generation.

REFERENCES

Boyer, Horace Clarence. "A Comparative Analysis of Traditional and Contemporary Gospel Music." In *More Than Dancing*, edited by Irene V. Jackson, 127–146. Westport, Conn.: Greenwood Press, 1985.

Broughton, Viv. *Black Gospel: An Illustrated History of the Gospel Sound.* London: Penguin Books, 1989.

Cleveland, J. Jefferson, and Verolga Nix, eds. *Songs of Zion.* Nashville, Tenn.: Abingdon Press, 1981.

Crowe, Jerry. "Meet Pastor Crouch." *Los Angeles Times* (September 21, 1995): sect. F, 1–2.

Doerschuk, Bob. "Backstage with Andrae Crouch." *Contemporary Keyboard* 5 (August 1979): 6+.

Heilbut, Anthony. *The Gospel Sound: Good News and Bad Times.* New York: Simon and Schuster, 1971. Reprint, Garden City, N.Y.: Limelight Editions, 1987.

Monroe, Steve. "Mercy." *American Visions* 9, no. 4 (August/September 1994): 48.

GUTHRIE P. RAMSEY JR.

CUNNINGHAM, ARTHUR

Born in Piermont, N.Y., November 11, 1928; died in Nyack, N.Y., March 31, 1997. **Education:** Tappanzee Public School, Piermont, N.Y.; began piano study with Mary Riker, 1935–39; Metropolitan Music School, New York, N.Y., studied piano with Anne Dodge, theory with Sam Morgenstern, theory and composition with Wallingford Riegger, and jazz piano with Johnny Mehegan and Theodore ("Teddy") Wilson, 1941–45; Juilliard School of Music, studied choral conducting and arranging with Peter Wilhowsky, composition with Peter Mennin and Henry Brant, music theory, and timpani, summers 1945, 1946; Fisk University, Nashville, Tenn., studied theory and composition with John W. Work III, piano with William Duncan Allen, music with John Ohl, 1947–51, B.A., music education, 1951; Juilliard School of Music, studied composition with Henry Brant, theory with Francis Goldstein, film and television scoring with Norman Lloyd, composition and literature with Peter Mennin, film scoring with Alex North, and choral studies with Margaret Hillis, Robert Shaw, and Peter Wilhowsky, 1951–52; Columbia University Teachers College, studied conducting with Vernon Church, composition with Howard Murphy, 1955–57, M.A., theory and conducting, 1957, doctoral study, 1957–58. **Military Service:** Special Services of U.S. Army, Entertainment Specialist, composer for band, musical revues, and television, 1953; toured as bassist in an army-sponsored jazz trio, 1953–55. **Composing and Performing Career:** Began improvising and composing as a child; first performed his own works in public at age seven, 1935; performed professionally on electric bass in jazz and rock ensembles, 1936; organized, trained, composed, and arranged for his own 13-piece jazz band, 1940; composed first concert music pieces, 1942; continued to write for jazz groups throughout high school and college years; WNYC radio, performed own works, 1941–45; St. Mark's Church, New York, N.Y., concert of his works performed, 1951; supplied his own 18-piece jazz band with new works, 1953; Atlanta, Ga., Festival of Contemporary Music with Robert Shaw and the Atlanta Symphony Orchestra, music director and arranger, 1968; bassist with Mabel Mercer, Ronnie Graham, Bill McCutcheon, McLean Stevenson, Tommy Leonetti, Emme Kemp, Kate Davidson, and Maynard Ferguson; conductor of his own works in the 1970s; music research coordinator and narrator for television documentary "Exiles," 1989; European tour with stops in Paris and The Hague, 1992. **Teaching Career:** New York, N.Y., Broadway vocal coach for several shows, including *A Chorus Line, Follies, Company,* and *Promises, Promises*; piano teacher, beginning 1957; St. Lawrence University, guest lecturer, ca. 1969. **Commissions:** Karamu House, 1953; Joy Barker, 1960; Lee Bellaver, 1965; Unitarian Church, Pomona, N.Y., 1965; Grench Shoe Manufacturers, 1968; Hudson Valley Choral Group, 1968; Symphony of the New World, 1968; National Theater Company, 1969; Natalie Hinderas, 1969; Earl Madison, 1969; Arthur Davis, 1969, 1972; Robert Jones and the Laurentian Singers, 1971; Ortiz Walton, 1971; Robert Jones, 1972; Edward Pierson, 1972; Cheyney State College, 1973; Cary McMurran for the Peninsula Symphony Orchestra, 1974; Tom Everett for the Harvard

Symphony Band, 1976; David Harrington for the Kronos String Quartet, 1978; David Harrington, 1978; government of Spain, 1992; Rockland County Symphony, 1993; New York Philharmonic Brass Quintet, 1995. **Memberships:** ASCAP; American Music Center; American Federation of Musicians (Local 291); Actors Equity; Manhattan Association of Clubs and Cabarets; Rockland County Symphony Orchestra, board of directors; Rockland Center for the Arts, board of directors; Edward Hopper House, board of directors; Helen Hayes Performing Arts Center, advisory board; Finklestein Memorial Library, advisory board; Columbia Teachers College, board, 1994–97. **Honors/ Awards:** ASCAP awards and grants, 1972, 1992; National Endowment for the Arts grant, 1974; Pulitzer Prize nominations for *Concentrics,* 1969, and *Night Song;* Rockland County Executive Award, Lifetime Contribution to the Arts, 1990; Columbia University Teachers College, Distinguished Alumnus Award, 1992; Seville, Spain, World's Fair Good Will Ambassador, 1992.

MUSIC LIST

INSTRUMENTAL SOLOS
Viola

"Sketch." 1981. Unpublished manuscript. Premiere, 1981.

Cello

"Ecclatette." 1969. Nyack, N.Y.: Cunningham Music, 1975.
    Commissioned by Earl Madison for the 1970 Tchaikovsky
    Competition. Premiere, 1988.
"Serenade." 1950. Unpublished manuscript. Premiere, 1950.

Double Bass

Dance Suite. ca. 1990. Unpublished manuscript. Premiere, 1990.
"Early Elephants." ca. 1990. Unpublished manuscript. Premiere, 1990.
"Golden." 1988. Unpublished manuscript.
"Ora." 1990. Unpublished manuscript.

Oboe

"Minakesh (Conjurer of Good or Evil)." 1969. Unpublished manuscript.
    Also arranged for solo cello and strings; contralto-vocalise and
    piano. Premiere, 1969.

Saxophone

"Periwinkle." 1989. Unpublished manuscript. Premiere, 1989.

Horn

"First Light" (horn unaccompanied). 1988. Unpublished manuscript.

Organ

"Organ Prelude." 1965. Unpublished manuscript. Commissioned by the
    Unitarian Church, Pomona, N.Y. Premiere, 1965.

Piano

Beginners Piano Book. 1964. Unpublished manuscript.

"Blue Bending." 1988. Unpublished manuscript. Premiere, 1988.

"Blue Bridge." 1987. Unpublished manuscript. Premiere, 1987.

"Engrams." 1969. Bryn Mawr, Pa.: Theodore Presser, 1978. Commissioned by Natalie Hinderas. Premiere, 1969. Recorded: CRI-CD 629; Desto 7102/3.

"Four Shadows." 1950. Unpublished manuscript. Premiere, 1950.

"Lilac." 1987. Unpublished manuscript.

"Phoenix." 1987. Unpublished manuscript. Premiere, 1988.

"Quarter Moon." 1989. Unpublished manuscript. Premiere, 1989.

"Sille." 1988. Unpublished manuscript.

Sixty Piano Pieces. 1965. Unpublished manuscript.

Piano, Four Hands

Two Haitian Play Dances (piano, four hands). 1951. Unpublished manuscript. Premiere, 1951.

SMALL INSTRUMENTAL ENSEMBLE
Strings

"Basis" (four double basses). 1968. Unpublished manuscript. Note: excerpted from original version of *Concentrics.* Premiere, 1971.

"Covenant" (cello, double bass). 1972. Commissioned by Arthur Davis. Unpublished manuscript.

"Jill Ellen" (guitar, violin, viola, cello). 1975. Unpublished manuscript. Also arranged as a "solo guitar blues hoe down." Premiere, 1975.

"Line Drive" (string quartet). 1978. Unpublished manuscript. Commissioned by David Harrington for the Kronos String Quartet.

"Mimosa" (violin, viola, cello). 1989. Unpublished manuscript. Premiere, 1989.

"Sundown Song" (violin, viola, cello). 1989. Unpublished manuscript. Premiere, 1989.

"Trinities" (cello, two double basses). 1969. Unpublished manuscript. Commissioned by Arthur Davis. Premiere, 1969.

Trio for Violin, Viola, and Violoncello. 1968. Unpublished manuscript. Note: excerpted from original version of *Concentrics.*

Two Inventions (two double basses). 1952. Unpublished manuscript. Also arranged for two bassoons.

"Two World Suite" or "Strut" (six double basses). 1971. Unpublished manuscript.

Woodwinds

"Septet" (piccolo, flute, clarinet, bass clarinet, English horn, bassoon). 1968. Unpublished manuscript. Note: excerpted from original version of *Concentrics.*

Brass

Rag Concerto: A Cultural Soundscape (trumpet, horn, trombone, tuba). 1995. Unpublished manuscript. Commissioned by the New York Philharmonic Brass Quintet.

Percussion

"Octet" (timpani, snare drum, tambourine, suspended cymbal, triangle, güiro, maracas, claves, bass drum, five temple blocks, four timbales). 1968. Unpublished manuscript. Note: excerpted from original version of *Concentrics.*

Combinations

"Fragment" (three horns, three trumpets, three trombones, five temple blocks, maracas, claves, tambourine, cymbal, snare drum, three timpani, bass drum). 1968. Unpublished manuscript. Note: excerpted from original version of *Concentrics.*

Perimeters (flute, clarinet, vibraphone, double bass). 1965. Unpublished manuscript. Contents: Arc; Radius; Circumference; Diameter. Premiere, 1965.

Swatches (piano, bass, saxophone). 1989. Unpublished manuscript. Contents: Tweed; Haitian Cotton; Twill; Velvet; Ramie; Dotted Swiss; Chord Du Roy; Silk; Peau de Sole; Linen; Herringbone; Satin; Pumpkin. Premiere, 1989.

Trio for Flute, Viola, and Bassoon. 1952. Unpublished manuscript. Premiere, 1952.

"Whistle Stops" (saxophone, bass, piano). 1989. Unpublished manuscript. Premiere, 1989.

STRING ORCHESTRA

Omnus. 1968. Unpublished manuscript. Note: excerpted from original version of *Concentrics.*

FULL ORCHESTRA

Concentrics. 1968; revised 1989. New York: Theodore Presser, (rental). Commissioned by the Symphony of the New World. Note: nominated for a Pulitzer Prize, 1969. Contents (1989): Dissidents; Reflection 1; Dialogue; Reflection 2; Septet; Reflection 3; Fragments; Circuits; Nonet; Reflection 4. Premiere, 1969.

Lights across the Hudson. 1956. Unpublished manuscript. Premiere, 1957.

Night Lights. 1955. Unpublished manuscript.

Theatre Piece. 1965–66. Unpublished manuscript. Premiere, 1968.

ORCHESTRA (CHAMBER OR FULL) WITH SOLOISTS OR CHORUS

Adagio for Oboe and Strings. 1995. Unpublished manuscript. Also scored for clarinet, strings; clarinet, piano. Premiere, 1996.

Adagio for String Orchestra and Oboe. 1954. Unpublished manuscript. Premiere, 1954.

Dialogue for Piano and Chamber Orchestra. 1966. Bryn Mawr, Pa.: Theodore Presser, 1967. Premiere, 1967.

Dialogue for Piano and Orchestra. 1967; revised 1987. Bryn Mawr, Pa.: Theodore Presser, 1987.

Dim Du Mim (Twilight) (English horn or oboe, chamber orchestra). 1969. Unpublished manuscript. Premiere, 1971.

Litany for the Flower Children (SATB, orchestra/rock). 1972. Unpublished manuscript. Commissioned by Robert Jones. Premiere, 1972.

Lullabye for a Jazz Baby (trumpet, orchestra). 1969. Bryn Mawr, Pa.: Theodore Presser, 1975. Based on original piano version of *Harlem Suite.* Premiere, 1970. Recorded: Desto 7107.

Night Bird (soprano, jazz quintet, chamber orchestra). 1978. Unpublished manuscript. Premiere, 1978.

Sun Bird (guitar, contralto, chamber orchestra). 1974. Unpublished manuscript. Commissioned by Cary McMurran for the Peninsula Symphony Orchestra. Premiere, 1975.

Suncatcher (four soloists, chorus, orchestra). 1992. Unpublished manuscript. Premiere, 1992.

Arthur Cunningham; courtesy of Kate Davidson Cunningham

The Walton Statement or Concerto for Double Bass (double bass, piano or orchestra) 1971. New York: Theodore Presser, 1971. Commissioned by Ortiz Walton. Premiere, 1980.

BAND

Almost Home. Unpublished manuscript. Premiere, 1988.

Crispus Attucks. 1976. Unpublished manuscript. Commissioned by Tom Everett for the Harvard Symphony Band. Premiere, 1976.

I'm Impressed. Unpublished manuscript. Premiere, 1988.

SOLO VOICE

"Born a Slave." ca. 1972. Unpublished manuscript. Commissioned by Edward Pierson. Premiere, 1972.

"Call His Name." 1972. Unpublished manuscript. Premiere, 1972.

"Everywhere I Go." 1961. Unpublished manuscript.

"Jabberwocky" (soprano). 1960. Unpublished manuscript. Commissioned by Joy Barker. Premiere, 1960.

"The Leaden-Eyed" (soprano). 1956. Unpublished manuscript. Premiere, 1960.

"Prometheus" (bass-baritone). 1964; revised 1965; orchestrated 1967. New York: Theodore Presser. Later titled "The Prince." Premiere, 1964.

"Song of Songs." 1951. Unpublished manuscript. Premiere, 1951.

"Starfield." 1988. Unpublished manuscript.

"This Love Is True Love." 1961. Unpublished manuscript.

"Turning of the Babies in the Bed" (baritone). 1951. Unpublished manuscript. Premiere, 1951.

VOICE WITH INSTRUMENTAL ENSEMBLE

Four Songs (soprano, piano, cello). 1965. Unpublished manuscript. Contents: Purple Grapes, Green Figs, and Mulberries; Asleep My Love; I Do Wander Everywhere; Lovers and Madmen. "I Do Wander Everywhere" commissioned by Lee Bellaver. "Asleep My Love" arranged for cello, flute, and viola, or flute and cello as "Thisby Dying." Premiere, 1965.

Two Songs (soprano, cello, piano). Premiere, 1969.

CHORAL MUSIC

"Amen, Amen" (SATB). 1965. Unpublished manuscript. Premiere, 1965.

"Casey Jones: The Brave Engineer" (SATB). 1968. New York: Shapiro and Bernstein, 1968. Co-composer, Julian Work.

"Christmas Lullabye" (SATB, tenor solo). ca. 1982. Unpublished manuscript. Premiere, 1982.

"The Cossack" (SATB). 1964. Unpublished manuscript.

"Fifty Stars" (SA). 1963. Unpublished manuscript.

Four Choral Works. ca. 1988. Unpublished manuscript. Contents: Blessed Be Our House (SATB); This Is Our Day (SATB); This Is Our Day (SSAA); Carry On (SATB). Premiere, 1988.

"From Where I Stand" (SATB unaccompanied). 1950; revised 1964. Unpublished manuscript.

"Fruitful Trees More Fruitful Are" (SATB with organ prelude). 1965. Unpublished manuscript. Commissioned by the Unitarian Church, Pomona, N.Y. Premiere, 1965.

"The Garden of Phobos" (SATB unaccompanied). 1968. Unpublished manuscript. Commissioned by the Hudson Valley Choral Group. Premiere, 1969.

"The Gingerbread Man" (SATB). 1953. Unpublished manuscript. Commissioned by Karamu House, Cleveland, Ohio. Also arranged for TTBB. Premiere, 1953.

"Harlem Suite Choral." 1971. Unpublished manuscript. Commissioned by Robert Jones and the Laurentian Singers. Premiere, 1971.

"He Met Her at the Dolphin" or "Holiday" (SATB). 1963. New York: Remick and Witmark, 1964. Premiere, 1963.

"Hymn of Our Lord at the Last Supper" (SATB). 1962. Unpublished manuscript. Premiere, 1962.

"In the Year Seventeen" (SATB). 1965. Unpublished manuscript. Commissioned by the Unitarian Church, Pomona, N.Y. Premiere, 1965.

"Into My Heart" (SATB). 1964. Unpublished manuscript.

Jubilee Songs. 1971. Bryn Mawr, Pa.: Theodore Presser, 1972. Contents: Honey Brown (TTBB); Timber (SATB); We Gonna Make It (SATB); Lord Look Down (SATB). "Honey Brown" and "Timber" published separately; "We Gonna Make It" and "Lord Look Down" published as *Two Prayers*. Premiere, 1971.

"Lead Us Still and Guide Us" (SATB, organ). 1965. Unpublished manuscript. Commissioned by the Unitarian Church, Pomona, N.Y. Premiere, 1965.

"Let the Day Begin" (SA). 1964. Unpublished manuscript.

"The Loveliest of Trees" (SATB). 1964. Unpublished manuscript.

"Pale Moons Rise in Endless Calm" (SATB). 1955; revised 1964. Unpublished manuscript.

"Ring Out Wild Bells" (SATB, children's voices). 1965. Unpublished manuscript. Premiere, 1965.

"Sing Children Sing" (SATB). 1964. Unpublished manuscript.

"Standing in the Light" (SATB). 1989. Unpublished manuscript. Premiere, 1989.

"Sunday Stone" (SATB, piano or organ). 1973. Bryn Mawr, Pa.: Theodore Presser, 1974. Premiere, 1973.

"Then the Cricket Sings" (SATB, solo voice). 1957; revised 1964. Unpublished manuscript. Premiere, 1957.

"The West Wind" (SATB). 1962. Unpublished manuscript.

"When I Was One and Twenty" (SATB). 1963. Unpublished manuscript.

"With Rue My Heart Is Laden" (SATB). 1964. Unpublished manuscript.

DRAMATIC MUSIC

Ballet (string quartet with jazz quartet). 1968. Unpublished manuscript. Commissioned by Grench Shoe Manufacturers. Premiere, 1968.

Harlem Suite (ballet for SATB, solo voices, piano, electric bass, drums, orchestra, and dancers). 1969–74. Bryn Mawr, Pa.: Theodore Presser, 1972. Contents: A Little Love (SATB, soprano and bass soloists, piano); World Goin' Down (SATB, soprano and alto soloists); Sunday in de Evening (SA divisi, piano); Lenox (SATB, narrator, piano); Mundy Man (SATB and piano or SATB, orchestra, harmonica); Lullaby for a Jazz Baby (orchestra); Sugar Hill (piano); Pataditas (piano, orchestra); Harlem Is My Home; Hinkty Woman (SATB, tenor solo). Premiere, 1971. Recorded: Desto DC-7107.

His Natural Grace or *Louey, Louey* (one-act rock opera). 1968. Unpublished manuscript. Premiere, 1968.

Night Song (soloists, SATB, orchestra). 1973. New York: Theodore Presser, 1974. Commissioned by the Cultural Studies Program of Cheney State College, Marc Liebler, director. Contents: I. Utumbuizo (SATB, orchestra, quadraphonic tape, four narrators); II. Kai: De Hoppuhgras' an de Ant (baritone, gospel quartet); De Milkmaid

(SATB, strings); Didn' 'e Roll (TTBB); Baby Chile (SSAA); Don'cha Know (SATB, strings); III. Night Men (renamed "Night People") (TTBB, brass); When You Wake (SA, orchestra).

Ostrich Feathers (children's musical play for piano and improvising combo, electric bass, drums, vibraphones, guitar). 1964. New York: Theodore Presser, rental. Premiere, 1965.

Patsy Patch and Susan's Dream (rock musical for children). 1963. Unpublished manuscript. Premiere, 1963.

Rooster Rhapsody (narrator, orchestra, rock quartet, sound effects). 1975. Theme copyright, 1974; piece completed 1975. Bryn Mawr, Pa.: Theodore Presser, n.d. Premiere, 1975.

Shango. 1969. Incidental music for African instruments. Unpublished manuscript. Commissioned by the National Theatre Company. Premiere, 1969.

String and Jazz Quartet Ballet. 1968. Unpublished manuscript. Premiere, 1968.

Sunshine, the Beauty Part. 1963. Musical show with improvised piano accompaniment. Unpublished manuscript. Premiere, 1963.

Violetta or *Violets and Phospher* (soprano, tenor, baritone, and bass soloists, string quartet, string octet). 1964. Unpublished manuscript.

PUBLICATIONS

ABOUT CUNNINGHAM
Dissertations

Ellis, John. "Arthur Cunningham: A Brief Biography and an Analysis of His Use of Jazz and Serialism in *Engrams* (1969)." D.M.A. diss., Manhattan School of Music, 1991.

Mitchell, Roberta Sue. "*Suncatcher*: A Study of the Creativity of Arthur Cunningham." Ed.D. diss., Columbia University Teacher's College, 1993.

Oliver, Christine Evangeline. "Selected Orchestral Works of Thomas J. Anderson, Arthur Cunningham, Talib Rasul Hakim, and Olly Wilson: A Descriptive Study." Ph.D. diss., Florida State University, 1978.

Articles

Tischler, Alice. "Arthur Cunningham." In *Fifteen Black American Composers: A Bibliography of Their Works*, 79–105. Detroit Studies in Musical Bibliography, no. 45. Detroit: Information Coordinators, 1981.

BY CUNNINGHAM

"Curriculum Re-Evaluation of the Serious Music Student." Unpublished typescript. Held in the Black Music Collection, Indiana University Music Library, Bloomington, Indiana.

"Notes from My Journal." Unpublished typescript. Held in the Black Music Collection, Indiana University Music Library, Bloomington, Indiana.

Studies for Singing the Blues. New York: Theodore Presser, 1974.

* * * * *

Working diligently and away from the spotlight, Arthur Cunningham quietly became one of the most prolific and performed composers of his generation. He composed over 140 classical works, including full-scale symphonic and choral pieces, and he claimed that one composition, *Lullabye for a Jazz Baby*, had received more than 1,000 performances. In the mid-1970s, his *Harlem Suite* and *Jubilee Songs* topped sales at Theodore Presser. His very first orchestral commission, *Concentrics* (1968), was nominated for a Pulitzer Prize in 1969, and a revised orchestration was featured at four concerts by the New York Philharmonic under the direction of Zubin Mehta in 1989.

Arthur Cunningham's creative activity resists simple classification or summary. His struggles to escape the limitations of racism and its social expectations are in many ways emblematic of the struggles of black composers in the United States in general and black classical composers in particular. Unlike those of mainstream composers, the works of black composers are immediately politicized as representative not only of the individual artist but of the race as a whole. While jazz inspired much of Cunningham's musical activity, the social imperatives of this prototypical black genre also became a burden for him at times. Although Cunningham taught piano and worked as a jazz pianist and bassist to earn a living, his true vocation was composition. From the 1950s through the 1960s, he spent every moment of his spare time studying and composing classical music in near seclusion, hidden from the skepticism of colleagues and the continual rejections of New York's classical music performers and publishers.

As a child prodigy, Cunningham found generous support for his music studies; yet after his student days were finished, he discovered that opportunities for the professional black composer were difficult to find. While a youth, his skill at improvisation had earned him tuition-free instruction at the Metropolitan Music School in New York. Even his first year as an undergraduate had been paid for in full by a group of New York professionals, including Kurt Weill, Richard Rodgers, Oscar Hammerstein, Dwight Wiman, Irving Berlin, and Langston Hughes. Hughes had added a stipulation to the tuition grant, so despite Cunningham's desire to attend Juilliard, he was required to attend Fisk University in order to learn more about his African heritage. According to the composer, Fisk's all-black student life came as a shock. As a child, Cunningham had grown up in a remarkably integrated environment among the kaleidoscope of New York's races and religions. His education had been carefully controlled and shielded, and so he was innocently unaware of racial discrimination and the struggle for civil rights.

While Cunningham considered himself to be an African American and has been seen as such by others, his biographers have emphasized a diverse ancestry including African, Irish, Scottish, and Native American roots. This diffusion of Cunningham's racial identity is remarkable when viewed against his compositions, which reveal a consistent and focused core of African and African-American sounds and subjects: *Two Haitian Play Dances* (1951), "Prometheus" (1964, later retitled "The Prince"), *Harlem Suite* (1969–74), *Shango* (1969), *Jubilee Songs* (1971), "Lenox" (1972), "Harlem Is My Home" (1972), "Born a Slave" (1972), *Crispus Attucks* (1976), and *Rag Concerto: A Cultural Soundscape* (1995). His music is frequently bitingly political, and one of his works has been deemed too controversial for performance: *Night Song* (1973) was rejected by its commissioning agency (the Cultural Studies Program of Cheyney State College) because of its bold use of texts stemming from the debates on slavery just prior to the U.S. Civil War. The work has never been performed.

As a composer, Cunningham refused to limit himself to any single source of musical inspiration. Although never simply an eclectic bricolage, his music contains elements borrowed from romantic music, serialism, jazz, rock, and the gospel tradition. A poem he wrote in the early 1970s serves as his artistic credo. Reprinted frequently, this poem has appeared on record jackets and in the *New York Times* and was even chosen by the United Nations as the official poem for World Children's Day.

Let Others Dream
What They Dream
I Dream
Music
I Am A Source Person
My Body
Its Height Width Length and Color
Is My House
The Earth
The Universe
My Place
Call Me What You Will
Call My Music
Music.

The opportunity to express his music, however, did not come easily. The aesthetics of 20th-century classical music require that each composer realize her or his own unique musical voice. Unlike the classical composers of the Harlem Renaissance, who used tonal harmony to engage the broadest possible listening public, Cunningham, like many other composers (both black and white) writing after World War II, was forced to confront the aesthetic judgment of an increasingly academic establishment in the form of publishers and critics. Tonal music had become passé and an emblem of naïveté. Serial music was in vogue and demanded an antitraditional stance and individualistic experimentation. Cunningham's development as a classical composer can be viewed as the struggle to distance himself from both the classical musical tradition, on the one hand, and social patterns of racial discrimination, on the other. To find his unique musical voice and thus earn a place in contemporary classical music, he had to go beyond the imitative exercises and traditional harmony he had practiced during his schooling and challenge the limitations placed on him by a charged racial culture. Aspiring to the elite realm of "classical" or "art" music, black composers like Cunningham threatened a carefully constructed and historically reinforced white cultural hegemony that presided over the United States.

For Cunningham, this battle to find his compositional voice became a conflict between his professional jazz activities and his dreams of writing classical music. After playing a Cole Porter tune while on tour as an Army musician, Cunningham had been told by a white member of the audience to "play his own kind of music," that is, music written by blacks, not by whites. Sometimes jazz appeared to Cunningham to be a trap—a music that fulfilled certain racist expectations of his largely white paying audience and a

music he was forced to play in order to earn a living. In the 1950s, jazz had not yet been accepted as art: black jazz musicians were not yet "composers" in the sense that they received little respect and, all too often, little money in proportion to their creative capacities. *Concentrics* (1968) is Cunningham's attempt to escape the social stigma attached to jazz and to depict his conflict with American society by embracing 20th-century avant-garde techniques. Ironically, it would be a return to jazz that would allow Cunningham finally to synthesize his classical and jazz experiences into a unique and rich music all his own. Written in 1969, his piano work "Engrams," commissioned by Natalie Hinderas, realizes this new compositional voice through a deep synthesis of the substance of jazz with serial technique.

Cunningham began to explore the intersection of his jazz and classical personae as a guest lecturer at St. Lawrence University. According to John Ellis, he discussed the topic of the "separation of my jazz world and my classical world . . . and how these two things were living and going down two separate roads." The response of the students to his music and ideas was so overwhelmingly positive that Cunningham felt inspired once again to write a classical work for the piano—an instrument for which he feared writing because of his strong associations between the piano, his jazz career, and more traditional harmonic thinking.

For Cunningham, the fundamental conflict between jazz and classical musics centered around harmony. While the swing-era jazz with which he had grown up was firmly rooted in traditional harmony, 20th-century aesthetics required composers of classical music to explore nontonal harmonies. Until *Concentrics,* Cunningham's nontonal strategies had always involved creating his own vocabulary of chords and avoiding tonal gestures: "I had this great fear of leading tones because they kept forcing me back into the diatonic system." In "Engrams," Cunningham resolved this problem through a two-stage compositional process. First, he drafted the entire work in three or four days, using a strict application of Schoenberg's 12-tone technique. Then, he spent three or four more days going back through the work, adding freely composed material and changing pitches to fit the dictates of his ear and musical intuition. These "aberrations," as Cunningham called them, masked the original row and allowed its modal and tonal implications to speak. Tone clusters, which become more frequent and insistent as the piece progresses, counteract the pull of tonal gravity and prevent any incipient modality or harmony from becoming established.

Cunningham's self-proclaimed compositional approach focuses on structure and substance, form and philosophy. Although he avoided traditional forms such as the sonata and the rondo, all of Cunningham's works exhibit an architectural strength of nearly blatant clarity reinforced by textural changes. An observer of life, he frequently chose geometric models from outside music: "The structure of a stone, the structure of a crystal could be the structure of a piece. It helps the piece to have a fresh sound." This approach to enlivening tradition with innovation also enriches his jazz and gospel works; the preface to his *Jubilee Songs,* for example, indicates his intention to "continue that tradition and spirit of the jubilee song and to extend its boundaries to include contemporary compositional techniques."

Other hallmarks of his style include pitch clusters, asymmetry, serial technique, a concern for instrumental color, a penchant for brass and percussion, meticulous performance directions, the use of extended instrumental technique, a concise nondevelopmental treatment of musical material, a flexible and constantly shifting conception of time and meter, and a sensitivity to overall length. Cunningham's penchant for the dramatic helps communicate his social philosophy of music to his audience: "I always try to weave into the piece some sort of statement about living." Toward the end of his life, Cunningham became increasingly concerned about the audience and emphasized the playful aspects of his music "to make the spirit and the life of the listener lift up a bit."

CONCENTRICS (1968, REVISED 1989)

Much of Arthur Cunningham's music is highly personal and even autobiographical. *Concentrics,* an extended composition for large orchestra, results both structurally and spiritually from Cunningham's experience as a participant in one of the first black composers symposia—the Festival of Contemporary Music in Atlanta, 1968. The black conductor Paul Freeman had invited Cunningham to attend the event in the company of many highly respected and much more experienced black composers such as George Walker, T. J. Anderson, and Ulysses Kay. In contrast, Cunningham had never heard even one of his orchestral compositions performed. The Atlanta Symphony's performance of his *Theatre Piece* at one of the conference's reading sessions was his first. Still a young composer, Cunningham had attended the conference with high expectations and hopes of learning much from his illustrious colleagues.

While the recognition of his peers and the opportunity to hear his orchestral music performed was an incredibly positive experience for him, as Cunningham remembers it, the angry racial politics that saturated this meeting made him physically ill. Held during the height of racial protests of the 1960s, the symposium's activities centered around politics. Cunningham stunned the participants when he naively but sincerely asked, "When are we going to start talking about music?" While he desired practical knowledge about how to become a successful composer, his peers were already successful, published composers who had a different agenda. The conference participants drafted a position paper that stated that the signers were, according to Cunningham, "black men who composed black music for black people." While Cunningham, who had already composed black nationalist music ("Prometheus," 1965, and *Harlem Suite,* 1969–74) signed the statement, he later had powerful misgivings and asked that his name be removed. He substituted a new personal philosophy: "I write music. Period!"

Alienated and disappointed, Cunningham nevertheless left the symposium inspired and determined to write the best music he had ever composed in order to validate his newfound philosophy. An article about the symposium that quoted Cunningham appeared in *Newsweek* and prompted an offer for his first classical commission. The resultant work, *Concentrics,* depicts the turmoil and miscommunication not only of the conference but within U.S. society as a whole at this time. According to the composer, "[*Concentrics*] is . . . a portrait of a 20th-century human." That this sketch is a self-portrait was revealed by Cunningham when he said to Sue Mitchell, in an interview for her dissertation, that, "[The

symposium] was like the explosion that triggered off all the other parts of my life into one composition; all of the racial attitudes, the historical attitudes are all in one piece."

To answer and impress his critics, Cunningham used a variety of 20th-century compositional techniques that stressed intellectual rigor and formal complexity. *Concentrics* was, in fact, his first work written outside of a predominantly tonal system. The work opens with an ironically titled "Dialogue" in which a trio of solo violin, viola, and cello perform a fugue, but this fugue has been transformed by aleatoric or chance elements to illustrate schism and disjunction. Cunningham wrote this section by first composing a traditional fugue in which the voices precisely imitate one another—a model of communication, unity, and understanding. Next, he discarded the initial subject and physically cut the remaining manuscript paper (the episodes of the fugue) into 9- or 10-measure segments, put the fragments into a paper bag, and mixed them by shaking, finally picking out scraps at random and notating them into his score. Thus, the traditional order of the fugue was destroyed, its origins and structure lost, and musical chaos ensued. In the revised 1989 orchestration, Cunningham named this first section "Dissidents"—a depiction of the Atlanta conference that he described to Sue Mitchell as "a trialogue [a dialogue among three] of dissonant voices, everyone trying to say something but no one ever intending to communicate." After 32 measures, the solo cello, marked "freely (rebel)" in the score, breaks away from the cacophonous trio. It seems likely that the cello part portrays the composer's autobiographical experience of the conference.

Cunningham divided his single-movement work into 11 sections that often alternate between sections termed "Micro Unit Pod Support Systems" and "Source Concept/Reflections." It concludes with a cadenza for solo cello. The full orchestra is rarely heard, as Cunningham distills the ensemble into smaller groups, allowing decisive shifts in instrumentation to delineate his architectonic structure. These sections function as independent and exclusive cells of musical development that comment upon and argue with one another. In section D, for example, the snare drum performs what Cunningham terms "the rhythm of life" to reflect and inspire the short calls of the woodwinds. Section E, in contrast, uses only the strings, which perform a complex linear tapestry of more lyrical gestures. *Concentrics'* form mirrors the composer's stream-of-consciousness process in which blocks of "wandering sounds," often in the brass, serve as a background for a series of instrumental soliloquies, dialogues, and outbursts. Cunningham circumnavigates traditional harmonic practice by using cells of pitches as harmonic and melodic resources, but the work does not use 12-tone rows or other serial devices. While the composer has attempted to inhibit his own instincts toward organic unity, ideas originating from the opening "rebellious" cello solo nevertheless saturate the work as a whole.

In many ways, section G, a double quartet of string basses, marks the psychological climax of the piece. In his *New York Times* review of the 1989 performance, John Rockwell singled out this segment as "a dazzlingly played section for double basses alone." Following a cacophonous percussion segment, the basses open with an eerie, almost subliminally quiet chord of string harmonics. Cunningham, who himself is a professional bassist, experimented here with a variety of extended performance techniques, including sliding the thumb up and down the fingerboard under the string while bowing to produce waves of *glissandi*. He even releases the bassists from traditional notation, asking them to improvise pitches, durations, and rhythms. Thus, this octet of the orchestra's least soloistic instrument is allowed to shine as an independent, creative voice. Cunningham saw this gesture as emblematic of the need to allow the forgotten or discarded voices of society to speak as equals. (His concerto for double bass, *The Walton Statement,* would bring this ideal to fruition.)

Concentrics ends with an unmeasured and unaccompanied reprise of the cello's introductory solo, now marked "impatiently" and "wildly." A *tutti* strike by the full orchestra silences the cadenza, but the snare drum's "rhythm of life" trails off into infinity. Cunningham explained that this gesture represents his contention that the concentric circles of an individual's impact on society continue to affect everyone and everything else like ripples in an infinite pond: "the waves of energy are endless in time and space. They never ever stop." Cheered by its first Lincoln Center audience, hailed by critics, commercially published, and nominated for a Pulitzer Prize, *Concentrics* proved to be of great importance to Cunningham's career, as his opportunities for performances, publications, and commissions radiated from its premiere.

ENGRAMS (1969)

Cunningham viewed "Engrams" as the pivotal composition in his development as a composer and called it "a reflection of myself . . . a biographical sketch of a person being right on the edge of starting to reconcile his European training with his jazz feelings." Prior to this work, Cunningham lived and thought in two mutually exclusive sonic worlds: jazz and classical. "I had done it," observed Cunningham in conversation with John Ellis. "I had edited myself and presented myself to the world two different ways . . . because I had bought into the idea of the music being separate. [By synthesizing the classical and jazz idioms,] I was shaking off that kind of bondage." His title—"Engrams"—describes this process of musical synthesis and catharsis, yet only after the piece was completed and Cunningham realized the work's pivotal significance did he apply the title. The word "engram," which comes from biology and describes a theoretical mechanism of memory function, means something very personal to the composer. In his view, engrams are "tiny bits of information that rest within us in our very bones and form the essence of who we are."

"Engrams" was written in a white heat of inspiration in a total of seven days. The piece begins tentatively and in an extremely low register, which, Cunningham felt (as reported in Ellis), represented "that search way down into the person so that it could start from an absolute beginning." The frequent return to this lowest register within the piece reminds the listener of the distance traveled in the composer's journey of personal discovery.

As described in the composer essay, the final form of "Engrams" is the culmination of a two-stage compositional process of atonal creation followed by tonally inspired "aberrations." The dissertation by John Ellis, one of Cunningham's piano students, clearly identifies the original form of the tone row in "Engrams" as *e-b-c-a-b*-flat-*a*-flat-*e*-flat-*d-f*-sharp-*c*-sharp-*g-f.* Saturated with tonal implications (ascending half-steps, perfect fifths, perfect fourths, and

a single tritone), this row breaks with the composer's earlier nontonal strategies, which resisted these intervals. Interestingly, the few areas of the finished piece in which the intact row has survived the composer's recompositional tinkering are, in fact, the sections most closely associated with jazz. In measure 47 and similar passages in measures 95 and 143, Cunningham marks the row using a sudden acceleration and a single-line melody in parallel octaves evocative of Charlie Parker and Dizzy Gillespie's collaborative experiments in virtuosity. "The row . . . lent itself beautifully to that kind of angular, boppish kind of way of writing," observed Cunningham to Ellis. The composer has even sublimated the harmonic pillars of the 12-bar blues form by using only three transpositions of the row: Prime (tonic, mm. 1–94), P5 (up a fourth, mm. 95–124), and P7 (up a fifth, mm. 125–141), followed by a return to Prime (mm. 142–end).

"Engrams" grows smoothly out of the developments in bebop in the 1940s and free jazz in the 1960s but does more than simply borrow an affective veneer of jazz; "Engrams" adopts the substance rather than simply the style of jazz. The jazz influence in this work refers to a specific practice of abstracted jazz that was championed on the piano by players such as Bud Powell and Lennie Tristano, two artists whom Cunningham greatly admired and whose practices and tendencies he imitated in "Engrams." Cunningham's frequent use of nonfunctional quartal and quintal harmonies (such as in measures 85 and 86) owes a debt to both Powell and to Schoenberg. Cunningham's synthesis of jazz and classical technique is so complete that the work never stumbles into an awkward jazz cliché or caricature, nor does Cunningham's treatment of Schoenberg's 12-tone technique become sterile intellectual dogma. He has adopted the Viennese master's goal of the erasure and subsequent rehabilitation of the subjective self, creating the opportunity to escape his own fears of jazz and traditional harmony and thus realize his unique personal voice. "Engrams" displays modernist traits from both jazz and classical music with a remarkable vitality and an arresting personal drama.

"Engrams" explores new territory, but the composer also observed that the work is the "child of *Concentrics.*" In both works, the composer used a stream-of-consciousness writing strategy, an approach in which musical material forms and dissolves without undergoing traditional development. To give himself a blank slate on which to inscribe this stream of musical ideas, Cunningham does not use key or time signatures. With the immediacy of an improvisation, the composer could add individual notes or change rhythms during the process of composition without need for metric adjustments or artificial corrections. "It's like waves of sound thought," noted Cunningham, "flecks of information floating around in there constantly. It tries again and again to lift up and to fly." Brought to the fore by register and resonant octave doublings, the singing melodies of "Engrams" produce this striving quality through their emphasis on half steps. Cunningham often places the row's half steps in the uppermost voice as neighbor notes that reach up and fall back over the course of each phrase.

A shared sense of drama also helps link "Engrams" to *Concentrics.* As Ellis has noted, "Engrams" spins forward in ever-faster formal segments. Beginning in measure 125, a brief reminder of the slow, delicate opening with its motivic eighth-note pairs and yearning half steps sets up the return of the bebop-inspired virtuosity that drives the work to a close. An impressive showpiece, "Engrams" has been in the touring repertoire of such outstanding pianists as Natalie Hinderas and Leon Bates. Writing about Hinderas's recording of the work, Howard Klein concluded in his *New York Times* review that, "Cunningham's *Engrams* is an inventive stream of unconsciousness whose name suggests a process of self-analysis used in the mystic cult of Scientology. The inner life of the piece, however, compels attention as the music grows from chaos to order, from despair to triumph."

LULLABYE FOR A JAZZ BABY (1969)

Lullabye for a Jazz Baby, for solo trumpet and orchestra, reveals the more whimsical, humorous side of Cunningham's music. "*Jazz Baby* is fun, a lot of fun," admitted the composer. The work is actually just one of nine scenes for the theater by Cunningham and is entitled *Harlem Suite.* The set was written, according to its dedication, "because of a deep personal feeling and out of gratitude to the people who live in that part of New York City known the world over as Harlem. May this city within a city continue to be, as it has been for me, one of the great 'source places' of America." *Harlem Suite* began as a series of brief piano sketches, including "Lullabye," written for pianist Natalie Hinderas in 1966. It bears a dedication to André Kostelanetz because the conductor suggested, on hearing the composer play the original piano vignettes, that the "Lullabye" would make a wonderful orchestral work. In fact, only the bluesy lullaby theme, originally played by the harp in measures 25–46, derives from the earlier piano work. Cunningham also borrowed the Mendelssohn-like *scherzo* (m. 126ff) from another of his piano works, entitled "Sugar Hill."

Sugar Hill, the affluent section of Harlem around 155th Street, is the setting for the programmatic aspects of *Lullabye for a Jazz Baby.* Cunningham chose this location since "all of the stars lived there, the prize fighters and the big time musicians, because at that time 'sugar' meant 'money.'" The piece opens with a baby alone in a crib. The baby's feet, portrayed by the use of brushes on the snare drum, patter erratically in an irregular 5/8 meter as if stumbling on a soft mattress. The solo trumpet enters almost immediately using a wah-wah mute to sound the coos, cries, and questionings of a baby who, according to the performance directions, "doesn't want to go to sleep." The trumpet writing is based on the playing of Rex Stewart, a trumpet soloist for Duke Ellington's orchestra from 1934 to 1945, who carried on the traditions of "Bubber" Miley and "Cootie" Williams by using a wah-wah mute and his original half-valve technique to make the trumpet seem to "talk" to his audience.

Beginning at section A, the child's parents begin a series of increasingly desperate attempts to get their child to sleep. First, they sing a lullaby, here played by the harp and marked "tenderly" in the score. Unfortunately, this angular and bluesy lullaby not only "indicates where the baby is coming from sociologically," as Cunningham remarks, but its hip 3/8 + 5/8 meter seems to spur the baby on to yet more restless antics. The trumpet continues to coo, and its rising smear in measure 43 seems but a sly request to get out of the crib and play. Soon, the lullaby theme shifts to the strings and marimba as the tempo picks up. A rich *glissando* in the harp ushers in a "serenade/foxtrot" section that evokes the luscious string writing, woodwind harmonies, and fills of Hollywood musical film scores. To depict the recalcitrant baby, Cunningham gives the trumpet soloist latitude "all the way through to do whatever he or she wants to do." Then 16 years old, trumpeter Jon Faddis established much of the baby's character in his performance for the work's premiere recording made in 1970 by the Oakland Symphony Youth Orchestra under the direction of Robert Hughes. Because of Faddis's interpretation, it has become traditional for the trumpeter to solo over the changes of the serenade section. Yet the soloist is still more of an actor than a jazzer and must stay in character. Cunningham warns that "the trumpet solos should have the humor and wit of a little baby in the crib." After two "solo" choruses, the brass section enters with a four-to-the-bar rock theme that, although syncopated and faster still, evokes the Hollywood sound through its lyrical section harmonies. A final cinematic gesture, a rising chromatic line in the strings, invigorates the harmonies and exhausts the tension to bring the serenade section to a close.

Next, the lullaby theme reappears in one of Cunningham's favorite textures, the clarinet trio, formed here with a bass clarinet, an A clarinet, and a B-flat clarinet. Oblivious to the lullaby theme, the baby continues to thwart its parents' wishes. The percussion section portrays the clicks, jingles, and pops of the baby playing with its toys. A *caesura* (pause) indicates that yet another attempted lullaby has failed, and the ensuing *scherzo* seems to signify a new approach—to wear the baby out and into an exhausted slumber. The spirited 5/8 patter meter of the opening returns as the strings enter *pianissimo* and the texture builds in energy and volume to include the full ensemble. A descending chromatic line in the trombones and horns in measures 153–155 intones Cunningham's homage to the orchestral writing of Duke Ellington. As the *scherzo* fades away, the lullaby theme returns yet again to complete its task, and the gentle coos of the baby reappear in the trumpet. Cunningham's flair for creative performance indications is evident in the parent's goodnight kisses. The composer asks the brass players to pucker and kiss their mouthpieces to produce convincing sounds of affection. The baby resists sleep one more time as the coda's Charleston-inspired rhythms recall the alert vitality of the *scherzo*. The parents forcefully refuse with a *tutti* "hit" by the orchestra that depicts a brisk "spank," *sforzando* and accented. Orchestral "hits" that appear earlier in the work are played softly and represent "gentle love pats," according to the composer. A final falling smear from the trumpet, ends the piece as the jazz baby finally yields and, miraculously, falls off to sleep.

Choreographed by the Alvin Ailey American Dance Theater in 1983, *Lullabye for a Jazz Baby* has also been performed by orchestras such as the Cleveland Symphony, Detroit Symphony, Baltimore Symphony, Rochester Philharmonic, Buffalo Philharmonic, and Syracuse Symphony, and it was even featured on a radio broadcast by the Grand Rapids Symphony in 1989. Cunningham has claimed that *Lullabye* has received well over 1,000 performances worldwide. The work's clarity of form and traditional blues-inspired harmonies make it an effective piece for the teaching of musical analysis.

NIGHT SONG (1973)

Commissioned by Cheyney State College, in Cheyney, Pennsylvania, to celebrate the bicentennial of the United States, the oratorio *Night Song* delivers an overt political message by chronicling the slave experience in the United States. It tells the story of an African family that was wrenched from its native land, culture, and language and sold into slavery on the Eastern seaboard. For Cunningham, this family represents the fundamental, if somewhat traditional, building blocks of society—its wisdom from the past (the father as guide), current needs (the mother as unifying force), and hope for the future (the son and daughter as the leaders and progenitors of the future). By the close of the work, Cunningham has broadened the scope of this nuclear African family to represent the human family as a whole. Blurring the boundaries of geography, history, religion, and race, *Night Song* celebrates diversity within the context of an all-encompassing human family.

To tell the story of the human family, Cunningham uses the power of language as a narrative device employing a process that he terms "lingual modulation." Over the course of the work's three movements, he uses a progression of languages to depict the various legs of the journey of enslaved Africans to North America, shifting from Swahili to the composite tongues of Gullah and Geechie, and finally to English. While Swahili and English represent the lingua francas of Africa and the United States respectively, Gullah and Geechie are regional dialects from the Eastern Sea Islands and the coastal regions of South Carolina that mix African and English elements. The initial clash between these languages comes early in the first movement when an American slave trader shouts in English and drowns out a quartet singing in Swahili. The slavetrader's English sounds a disrespectful violence on the Swahili-speaking people. For the English text, Cunningham has quoted from a pre–Civil War document justifying slavery and published in the *American Literary Messenger* of 1858. Rather than a triumphal celebration of the bicentennial, Cunningham's historical trajectory uncovers this unflattering passage from America's past: "We assert that in all countries and at all times there must be a class of hewers of wood and drawers of water who must always of necessity be the substratum of society. We affirm that it is best for all that this class be formed of a race upon whom God himself has placed a mark of physical and mental inferiority." The nature of this mark becomes clear as the scene shifts dramatically to the auction blocks where slaves are being sold and the auctioneer shouts, "Blacks, blacks to be sold. Blacks valuable as slaves."

The actors in Cunningham's drama are the words themselves. As the text of *Night Song* shifts from Swahili to English, for example, the word "work" becomes an agent of social power. In the first movement, Cunningham describes the Swahili work ethic as a function of personal debt: "If you owe me something, you must work for me." When used by the English-speaking slaveholders, however, this "work" ethic is no longer based on personal debt but on racial inferiority: "You work because you are black," noted the composer. Language in *Night Song* thus encodes, preserves, and even generates history. The slaveholder's abuse of words, however, forces the audience to confront and question its own linguistic heritage. For the slaveholders, language becomes a weapon—a tool of enforcement and dehumanization. For Cunningham, the recitation of this offensive text in the context of art music encourages a new awareness within the audience that makes change possible. Throughout the remainder of the work, language strives toward

freedom by granting the power to cope, the power to resist, and the power to build a better future.

The second movement contains five independent choral pieces that can be performed apart from *Night Song,* either individually or as a set with or without orchestra. Only sections two and five use the orchestra at all, and in section five the strings simply double the voices. Entitled "Kai" (Truth), the second movement focuses on the adaptation of language as a metaphor for the mental resilience of enslaved Africans. Set in Gullah and Geechie, much of the movement is intelligible as an English dialect. Language becomes one of the slaves' tools for combating slavery—in Cunningham's words, a "survival technique," permitting the slaves to talk, laugh, cry, and sing. As in the autobiography of Frederick Douglass, Cunningham's *Night Song* portrays language as the key to self-determination—an expression of social power that can even unlock the chains of bondage.

As Gullah and Geechie mix English and Swahili into a powerful new combination, the music of the second movement also blends the African and European traditions into a new sonic and political tool. While the first movement uses pentatonic and other African-inspired scales in the European-based form and style of "an early motet," the second movement takes a more historical approach, highlighting the rich choral harmonies of the African-American gospel tradition with its calls, responses, claps, and shouts derived from the slaves' ring shout. The first three of the movement's five sections retell African-American folk tales, while the final two become increasingly devotional in character. In section one, "De Hoppuh-gras' [Grasshopper] an de Ant," the baritone soloist's tale is punctuated by his own hand claps. Soon a male choir (TTBB) enters in the style of an "old time gospel quartet" and begins repeating, commenting, and signifying on the baritone's narrative. Cunningham proudly admits that for section three, "Didn' 'e Roll," the story of an escaping slave, and section four, "Baby Chile," the story of the naming of the baby Jesus, he borrowed harmonies and the formal conception from the music of the Wings Over Jordan Choir, an African-American gospel choir. Section five reveals Cunningham's more experimental nature, as its first 73 measures use only the text of its title, "Don'cha Know," repeated 147 times. The composer employed staggered breathing and a huge *crescendo* to produce a continuous wall of shimmering choral sound and an energetic dramatic shape out of just three words. Understatement provides the movement's ultimate message as the choir whispers the words, "Don'cha know ah [I] got freedom on my mind." By this time, the three original words, "Don'cha know," have taken on a spiritual and affirmative dimension—their intense repetition has generated a devotional state of affirmation that evokes synonyms such as "Amen" or "Praise God."

Cunningham suggested to the author that today, the third movement, "Night Men," should be renamed "Night People" in order to bring the originally intended sense into agreement with contemporary usage. His original text for this final movement uses the imagery of light and dark, day and night as metaphors for an embattled American national consciousness plagued by discrimination, emptiness, and hopelessness: "Faceless, cipher-men building a new nation with no eyes. Invisible in the night. Shadow men. Nowhere men. Hollow men." Cunningham's words seem to echo T. S. Eliot's poem, *The Hollow Men,* yet with a more hopeful conclusion. Using light imagery, the movement tropes upon the issue of skin color and racial consciousness as a new day dawns and the sopranos and altos sing, "When you wake, sing a day song." The light of day reveals a diverse and colorful nation made strong by the trials of night. The full chorus enters and asks, "How far have we come? How far must we go to see how good it would feel to touch the sweet sound of the sun, to feel free?" Full of optimism and the ideals of universal brotherhood, the composer turns skeptical in the final line and asks for only a modest beginning—freedom for even just "one day in the year."

REFERENCES

Cunningham, Arthur. Telephone interviews by the author, June 20, 22, and 24, 1996.

Ellis, John. "Arthur Cunningham: A Brief Biography and an Analysis of His Use of Jazz and Serialism in *Engrams* (1969)." D.M.A. diss., Manhattan School of Music, 1991.

Klein, Howard. "Overdoing 'Benign Neglect'?" *New York Times* (March 7, 1971): 1+.

Mitchell, Roberta Sue. "*Suncatcher*: A Study of the Creativity of Arthur Cunningham." Ed.D. diss., Columbia University Teachers College, 1993.

"New Sounds in Atlanta." *Newsweek* 71, no. 13 (March 25, 1968): 98–101.

Rockwell, John. "Philharmonic with Goode in Schumann Concerto." *New York Times* (November 4, 1989): sect. 1, 12.

MARK CLAGUE

DA COSTA, NOEL G.

Born in Lagos, Nigeria, December 24, 1929. **Education:** Brought to the United States, age 11; New York, N.Y., studied violin with Dr. Barnabas Istok, 1941–50; studied poetry with Countee Cullen during secondary school; Queens College, City University of New York, studied composition, theory, and conducting, 1948–52, B.A., 1952; Juilliard School of Music, New York, N.Y., studied choral conducting, 1953–54; New York, N.Y., Columbia University, 1954–56, M.A. in theory and composition, 1956; Manhattan School of Music, studied violin and orchestral music, 1954–56; Florence, Italy, Conservatorio Cherubini, studied composition with Luigi Dallapiccola and violin with Antonio Abussi, 1958–60; Siena, Italy, conducting seminars at the Accademia Chigiana, summers, 1958–60; Waltham, Mass., Brandeis University, studied music theory and composition, 1966–67. **Composing and Performing Career:** Performed as violinist with orchestras accompanying Broadway musicals, such as *Promises, Promises,* and various operas and ballets, 1968–70; performed as violinist with the Symphony of the New World, 1971–79; John F. Kennedy Center for the Performing Arts, Washington, D.C., "Counterpoint" performed by the Hampton Institute Choir, 1973; New York, N.Y., Triad Chorale, music director, 1973–86; Carnegie Hall, *Two Songs for Julie-Ju* performed by Betty Lane and Wayne Saunders, 1974; Boston, Symphony Hall, *Primal Rites for Solo Drummer and Orchestra,* premiered by Max Roach and the Boston Pops Esplanade Orchestra, 1983. **Teaching Career:** Hampton Institute, Hampton, Va., 1961–63; Queens and Hunter Colleges, City University of New York, 1963–66; Rutgers The State University, New Brunswick, N.J., 1970–present. **Commissions:** New York State Arts Council and the Symphony of the New World, 1976; National Center of Afro-American Artists and the Massachusetts Council on the Arts and Humanities, 1983. **Memberships:** Society of Black Composers, vice-president, 1973–79; Bloomingdale House of Music, board member, 1989–91; West Side Arts Coalition, New York, N.Y., member. **Honors/Awards:** Columbia University, Seidl Fellowship, 1955–56; Fulbright Fellowship, 1958–60; National Association of Negro Musicians, Distinguished Achievement Award, 1983. **Mailing Address:** 250 West 94th Street, New York, NY 10025.

MUSIC LIST

INSTRUMENTAL SOLOS
Violin
Jes' Grew no. 1: Chant Variations for Violin (violin, electric piano). 1973. New York: Atsoc Music, n.d. Contents: Chant; I Thought I Heard Buddy Bolden Say; In Two/Six Over Eight. Premiere, 1973. Recorded: CRI SD 514.

"Magnolia Blue." 1975. New York: Atsoc Music, n.d.

Set of Dance Tunes for Solo Violin. 1978. Unpublished manuscript. Contents: Walk Around; Brudder Bones; Neumedia; Little Diamond/Bird on the Wing; Jigs; New Orleans-Clog; Walk-Off-Clog Blues.

Six Etudes for Jazz Violin. 1990. Unpublished manuscript.

Cello
Five Verses with Vamps. 1968. New York: King's Crown Music Press, Columbia University Press, 1976. Premiere, 1970. Recorded: CRI SD 514.

Two Pieces for Unaccompanied Cello. 1973. New York: Atsoc Music, n.d. Premiere, 1973.

Double Bass
In Space (double bass unaccompanied). 1972. New York: Atsoc Music, 1972. Contents: Take Off; Earth Song; Space Walking; Changes. Premiere, 1973.

Flute
"Improvisation, Flute, no. 1" (flute unaccompanied). 1964. New York: Atsoc Music. Recorded: Eastern ERS-513.

"Silver-Blue." 1964. New York: Atsoc Music, 1964. Recorded: Eastern ERS-513.

Three Short Pieces for Alto Flute (alto flute unaccompanied). 1966. New York: Atsoc Music, n.d. Recorded: Eastern ERS-513.

Oboe
"Moods for Solo Oboe." 1978. Unpublished manuscript.

Trumpet
"Broadway Mall Fanfare" (trumpet unaccompanied). 1986. Unpublished manuscript.

"Central Park Boathouse Fanfare" (trumpet unaccompanied). 1990. Unpublished manuscript.

"Gabriel's Tune for the Last Judgment" (trumpet unaccompanied). 1970. New York: Atsoc Music, n.d.

Passages. 1966. New York: Atsoc Music, n.d.

Trombone
Four Preludes for Trombone and Piano. 1973. New York: Atsoc Music, 1984. Premiere, 1973. Recorded: CRI SD 514.

Street Calls. 1970. New York: Atsoc Music, n.d.

Piano
"Extempore Blue." 1969. New York: Atsoc Music, n.d. Premiere, 1974.

"Old Raritan Variations." 1989. Unpublished manuscript.

Two Pieces for Piano. 1971. New York: Atsoc Music, n.d. Contents: Clave Tune; Blue Tune.

Organ
"Chilí-lo." 1971. New York: Atsoc Music, n.d. Premiere, 1973. Recorded: Adama Records 1.

"Maryton (Hymn Tune Variations)." 1955. New York: Atsoc Music, n.d.

Spiritual Set for Organ. 1974. Melville, N.Y.: H. W. Gray, 1977. Contents: Invocation; Affirmation; Spiritual: Round about the Mountain; Praise. Premiere, 1974. Recorded: Adama Records 1.

Triptich for Organ: Prelude, Processional, Postlude. 1972. New York: Atsoc Music, 1973. Premiere, 1972.

SMALL INSTRUMENTAL ENSEMBLE
Strings
"Still Music no. 1" (two violins). 1965. New York: Atsoc Music, n.d.

Woodwinds
Woodwind Quintet. 1957. Unpublished manuscript.
Soundpiece for Woodwind Quintet. 1956. New York: Atsoc Music, n.d.
    Contents: Song; Interlude; Jump.

Brass
"Fanfare Rhythms" (four trumpets or trumpet choir, percussion). 1970.
    New York: Atsoc Music, n.d.
"Psalm Tune Variations" (brass quintet). 1959. New York: Atsoc Music, n.d.

Percussion
"Ishwara Drum Beat" (two bass drums). 1988. Unpublished manuscript.

Combinations
"Blue Mix: A Composition in the Form of a Chart" (solo double bass/
    Fender bass, cello, double bass, percussion). 1970. New York: Atsoc
    Music, n.d.
"Chime Tones" (horn, vibraphone, chimes). 1973. New York: Atsoc
    Music, n.d. Premiere, 1974.
"Epigrams" (solo viola, flute, clarinet, bass clarinet, bassoon, vibraphone,
    piano). 1965. New York: Atsoc Music, n.d. Recorded: Eastman
    School of Music, 1988–89.
"In the Circle" (four electric guitars, Fender bass, percussion). 1970. New
    York: Atsoc Music, n.d.
"Lydian Moods" (guitar, double bass). 1978–79. Unpublished manuscript.
Occurrence for Six (flute, clarinet, bass clarinet, tenor saxophone, trumpet,
    double bass). 1966. New York: Atsoc Music, n.d.
"Riff Time" (violin, cello, piano, percussion). 1972. New York: Atsoc
    Music, n.d.
"Spaces" (trumpet, double bass). 1966. New York: Atsoc Music, n.d.
"Statement and Responses" (flute, oboe, clarinet, bass clarinet, trumpet,
    trombone, tuba, viola, cello, double bass). 1966. New York: Atsoc
    Music, 1966.
"Time Patterns" (bassoon, harpsichord). 1990–91. Unpublished
    manuscript.
Ukom Memory Songs (organ, percussion). 1981. New York: Atsoc Music.
    Contents: Awakening; Where Has the Woman Gone?; Statement,
    Proverb, Restatement; Proverb 2; Men's Song Riffs; Proverb 3;
    Dance to Thirds. Premiere, 1997. Recorded: Adama Records 1.

CHAMBER ORCHESTRA
Still Music no. 2. 1967. Unpublished manuscript.

FULL ORCHESTRA
Blue Memories. Unpublished manuscript.
Expression in Six Moods. 1983. Unpublished manuscript. Note: withdrawn
    by the composer.
Quietly . . . Vamp It and Tag It. 1971. New York: Atsoc Music, n.d.

ORCHESTRA (CHAMBER OR FULL) WITH SOLOISTS
Generata (organ, chamber string orchestra). 1958. Unpublished
    manuscript. Recorded: Adama Records 1.

Primal Rites (solo drummer, orchestra). 1983. Unpublished manuscript.
    Commissioned by the National Center of Afro-American Artists
    and the Massachusetts Council on the Arts and Humanities.
    Premiere, 1983.

ORCHESTRA (CHAMBER OR FULL) WITH CHORUS
Ceremony of Spirituals (soprano, soprano/tenor saxophone, orchestra,
    chorus). 1976. Unpublished manuscript. Commissioned by the
    New York State Arts Council and the Symphony of the New World.
    Premiere, 1977.

SOLO VOICE
"Beyond the Years" (soprano). 1973. New York: Atsoc Music, n.d.
    Premiere, 1974.
Blues Lyrics (bass baritone). 1989–90. Unpublished manuscript.
Dream Thoughts (tenor). 1982. Unpublished manuscript. Contents:
    Dream Dust; Dreams; The Dream Keeper.
"My People" (mezzo-soprano). 1974. New York: Atsoc Music, n.d.
"Prayer of Steel" (baritone). 1975. New York: Atsoc Music, n.d. Premiere,
    1963.
Two Songs (soprano). 1956. New York: Atsoc Music, n.d. Contents: Sleep;
    Dustbowl.
Two Songs for Julie-Ju (soprano). 1972. New York: Atsoc Music, n.d. In
    Anthology of Art Songs by Black American Composers, edited by
    Willis Patterson (Melville, N.Y.: Edward B. Marks, 1977).
    Contents: Such a Pretty Black Girl Is My Julie-Ju; It's Time to Sleep
    and Dream. Premiere, 1974. Recorded: University of Michigan
    Records SM 0015.
"Vocalise" (soprano unaccompanied). 1972. New York: Atsoc Music, n.d.

VOICE WITH INSTRUMENTAL ENSEMBLE
The Cocktail Sip (soprano, mezzo-soprano, alto, tenor, baritone, bass-
    baritone, chorus). 1958. New York: Atsoc Music, n.d.
The Confession Stone (soprano, SSA trio, flute, oboe, clarinet, bassoon,
    horn, trumpet, viola, cello, double bass, piano). 1969. New York:
    Atsoc Music, n.d. Premiere, 1969.
Five Epitaphs (soprano, string quartet). 1956. New York: Atsoc Music,
    n.d. Contents: For a Poet; For My Grandmother; For Paul
    Laurence Dunbar; For a Lady I Know; If You Should Go.
    Premiere, 1956.
Four Glimpses of Night (baritone, flute, clarinet, bass clarinet, tenor
    saxophone, trumpet, piano, percussion). 1964. New York: Atsoc
    Music, n.d. Contents: Eagerly Like a Woman Running to Her
    Lover; Night Is a Curious Child; Peddling from Door to Door;
    Night's Brittle Song. Premiere, 1965.
Four Haiku Settings (soprano, piano, percussion). 1964. New York: Atsoc
    Music, n.d. Contents: The First Firefly; As I Picked It Up; Fleeing
    the Hunter; Suddenly You Light. Premiere, 1972.
In the Landscape of Spring (mezzo-soprano, flute, oboe, clarinet, bass
    clarinet, horn, trumpet, viola, cello, double bass, vibraphone,
    percussion). 1962. New York: Atsoc Music, 1962. Contents: In the
    Landscape of Spring; Sitting Quietly, Doing Nothing; The Blue
    Mountains. Also arranged for soprano, flute, clarinet, percussion,
    piano. Premiere, 1965.
"In the Quiet Of" (soprano, viola, vibraphone). 1985. Unpublished
    manuscript.

Noel G. Da Costa; courtesy of the composer

"The Last Judgment" (SSA, speaker, piano, percussion). 1964. New York: Atsoc Music, n.d.

November Song (concert scene for soprano, saxophone, violin, piano). 1974. New York: Atsoc Music, n.d.

"Time . . . On and On" (soprano, tenor saxophone, violin, prerecorded electronic sounds). 1971. New York: Atsoc Music, n.d.

CHORAL MUSIC

"Counterpoint" (double chorus, SSATB quintet, organ or two pianos). 1970. New York: Atsoc Music, n.d. Premiere, 1973.

"Five/Seven" (SSA, organ). 1969. New York: Atsoc Music, n.d.

"Harriet and the Promised Land" (boys choir, trumpet, saxophone, percussion). 1983. Unpublished manuscript.

"I Have a Dream" (SATB, organ). 1971. New York: Atsoc Music, n.d. Premiere, 1973.

I See the Moon (children's two-part chorus, piano). 1955. New York: Atsoc Music, n.d. Contents: I See the Moon; The Moon, It Shines as Bright as Day; How Many Miles to Babylon.

"I'm So Glad Trouble Don't Last Alway" (SAATBB unaccompanied). 1963. New York: Atsoc Music, n.d. Premiere, 1966.

"Leaf in the Wind" (male chorus, hand percussion). 1983. Unpublished manuscript.

"Let Down the Bars o Death" (SSATB unaccompanied). 1957. New York: Atsoc Music, n.d. Premiere, 1962.

"Little Lamb" (SATB unaccompanied). 1952. New York: Atsoc Music, n.d. Premiere, 1952.

"O God of Light and Love" (SATB, organ). 1971. New York: Atsoc Music, n.d. Premiere, 1972.

"Tambourines" (children's chorus, piano, Fender bass). 1970. n.p.: United Church Press, 1970.

". . . Through the Valley . . ." (SATB unaccompanied). 1969. New York: Atsoc Music, n.d. Premiere, 1972.

Two Prayers of Kierkegaard (children's chorus, organ). 1966. New York: Atsoc Music, n.d. Contents: Be Near to Us; Oh Grant That We May Hear.

Two Shaker Songs (SATB unaccompanied). 1964. New York: Atsoc Music, n.d.

DRAMATIC MUSIC

Babu's Juju (children's cantata for soprano, children's chorus, three percussionists). 1974. New York: Atsoc Music, n.d. Premiere, 1974.

The Cocktail Sip (opera in one act). 1958. Unpublished manuscript.

The Confession Stone (cantata). 1969. Unpublished manuscript.

The Dreamer beyond the Garden Gate (mixed media theater work for actress, chorus, solo dancer, off-stage voice, percussion). 1991. Unpublished manuscript.

Generations (narrator, dancers, chorus, percussion). 1985. Unpublished manuscript.

The Knee-High Man (children's cantata for boy soprano, boy alto, narrator, children's chorus, flute, piano, percussion). 1973. New York: Atsoc Music, n.d. Also arranged with chamber orchestra accompaniment. Premiere, 1973.

Maxims from Satchel Paige (three narrators, percussion, piano). 1989. Unpublished manuscript.

The Second Sermon on the Warpland (solo voices, narrator, chorus, piano). 1988. Unpublished manuscript.

Sermon on the Warpland (tenor, baritone, narrator, chorus, piano, organ). 1979. Unpublished manuscript.

The Singing Tortoise (children's cantata for soprano, baritone, narrator, children's chorus, flute, piano, percussion). 1971. New York: Atsoc Music, n.d. Also arranged with chamber orchestra accompaniment. Premiere, 1973.

Wakeupworld (three singers, rapper, two dancers, percussion). 1991. Unpublished manuscript.

INCIDENTAL MUSIC

The Big Picture. 1978. Documentary film soundtrack.

Fun House (soloists, chorus, instrumental ensemble). 1968. New York: Atsoc Music, n.d. Note: incidental music to a play by George Bass.

Frances Steloff: Memoirs of a Bookseller. 1986. Documentary film soundtrack.

The Transformation of Mabel Wells. 1975. Film soundtrack.

A Trio for the Living (soloists, chorus, organ). 1966. New York: Atsoc Music, n.d. Note: incidental music to a play by George Bass.

PUBLICATIONS

ABOUT DA COSTA
Dissertations

Laidman, Janet Loretta. "The Use of Black Spirituals in the Organ Music of Contemporary Black Composers as Illustrated in the Works of Three Composers." Ed.D. diss., Columbia University Teachers College, 1989.

Articles

McDaniel, Lorna. "Transmission Process in Ukom Memory Songs by Noel Da Costa." New York: Society for Ethnomusicology, 1981.

"Noel G. Da Costa." In The Black Composer Speaks, edited by David N. Baker, Lida M. Belt, and Herman C. Hudson, 70–92. Metuchen, N.J.: Scarecrow Press, 1978.

* * * * *

Noel Da Costa combines African, American, and Caribbean modes of expression with abstract compositional techniques, subjecting the distinctive sounds of African drumming, jazz riffs, gospel and spirituals, field hollers, and black preaching to rigorous serial procedures and using formal designs based on ostinatos and vamps. These techniques result in a highly individual and personal method of composition. Da Costa has long been fascinated with the juxtaposition of compositional craft, the demands of a compositional system, and the creativity of the performer in the realization of musical ideas. In his opinion, the contrasting ideals of the total control of integral serialism and the freedom of improvisation are two faces of the same coin. In both, the composer releases a degree of determination over the finished product. Da Costa demonstrates in his music that the collaboration between the inspiration and technical skills of both the composer and the performer can result in works of high artistic merit and truth. Da Costa's music has been performed at the Kennedy Center in Washington, D.C., and Lincoln Center, Carnegie Hall, and the Brooklyn Academy of Music in New York City. His work in the Society of Black Composers and ASCAP Young

Composer Grants program, his youth education programs with the Baltimore Symphony, and his teaching at Hunter College in New York City and at Rutgers University in New Brunswick, New Jersey, highlight his dedication to supporting young composers and encouraging the development of American music.

Originally from Lagos, Nigeria, Da Costa's family moved to the West Indies when he was three years old, where they lived in Jamaica, Barbados, Antigua, and Trinidad. Relocating to New York when he was 11, Da Costa attended junior high school in Harlem. There he studied French and English with the poet Countee Cullen, who instilled in him an appreciation of the qualities and sounds of words in various poetic structures. In music class, he learned to sing the spirituals that later infused his work. The music of Harlem—jazz, blues, gospel—was a significant influence on the developing tastes of the young man. The music on the radio, in the streets, in concert halls, and in churches formed what Da Costa later referred to as an "unconscious memory" that, combined with the vestiges of African music and culture in the West Indies, provided a wealth of vernacular and traditional "snatches, motives and patterns" upon which he continues to draw. He found that his family's travels throughout the West Indies and finally to New York made him sensitive to the vocal inflections of the different island and urban dialects, a pervasive aspect of his compositions.

After earning a B.A. in music theory, composition, and conducting at Queen's College in New York, Da Costa continued his training in violin and conducting at Juilliard and the Manhattan School of Music. He was awarded the Seidl Fellowship in composition at Columbia University where Otto Luening, Jack Beeson, and Henry Cowell were his professors.

His Seidl Fellowship in composition from Columbia was followed by a Fulbright Fellowship to study with Luigi Dallapiccola in Florence. His experience in Italy proved to be invaluable. Dallapiccola shared with Da Costa his appreciation and knowledge of the works of Webern, an emphasis on the discipline of learning craftsmanship through technical exercises, and the exposure to an Italianate sense of lyricism and feeling for repetition as an expressive device.

Growing up in Harlem listening to radio broadcasts of jazz, blues, and, on Sunday mornings, the various black college choirs singing spirituals, Da Costa grew to appreciate the spiritual as the fertile beginning of the vital black contribution to American musical culture. As a professor at Hampton Institute in Virginia and as a conductor, he arranged and conducted several spirituals for choral performances, and he later incorporated aspects of the spiritual's musical style—the melodic inflections, the quality of vocal sounds, the emotional intensity of rhythmic variation—into his instrumental as well as his choral pieces.

Da Costa's output includes instrumental and vocal solos, chamber pieces, and large-scale choral works and orchestral compositions. His fondness for the use of timbral structures—contrasting instrumental colors—is evident in the non-traditional combinations of many of his chamber ensembles. "Blue Mix: A Composition in the Form of a Chart" (1970), written for the jazz bassist Ron Carter, is scored for solo double bass/Fender bass, cello, double bass, and percussion; "Epigrams" (1965) contrasts the sounds of the viola, flute, clarinet, bass clarinet, bassoon, vibraphone, and piano; and "Chime Tones" (1973) utilizes the resonant

qualities of the horn, vibraphone, and chimes to create a trance-like fusion of sounds that suspends time. For Da Costa, orchestration is closely tied to melody: the nature of the initial melodic gestures may suggest the medium, or the instrumentation may become apparent through working out the motives.

Da Costa's compositions reflect a current of personal experience that has strengthened as his ability has matured. His earlier works, "Little Lamb" (1952; on the poetry of William Blake) and *Five Epitaphs* (1956; on the poetry of Countee Cullen), are written in a tonal/modal style that reveals his search for a systematic basis for the treatment of spirituals. The works discussed more in depth here represent the composer's ability to incorporate seemingly unlikely, if not incompatible, concepts and techniques developed through his study with Dallapiccola, writing music of transparent textures and dynamic rhythms that are absorbed into a serialized, yet free-sounding, 12-tone idiom. *Occurrence for Six* (1966), for example, employs dodecaphonic procedures, symmetrical structures, and improvisation.

The works of the late 1960s and early 1970s display a developing facility for incorporating aspects of jazz and blues into his style. Interest in African heterophonic singing traditions resulted in freer treatment of dissonance in *Ceremony of Spirituals* (1976). Through the work of his sister, ethnomusicologist Lorna McDaniel, Da Costa was exposed to the rhythmic intricacies of African drumming techniques and traditions. The synthesis of these techniques with his ongoing awareness of the rhythmic and improvisatory possibilities inherent in American vernacular traditions represent a new facet of his personal style. *Ukom Memory Songs,* for organ and percussion (1981), incorporates layers of communicative drum patterns and inflections as experienced through the filter of African-American culture. Throughout his career, Da Costa has continued to develop the blending of methods from the European tradition with the music, gestures, principles, and feeling of African and American cultural expressions.

OCCURRENCE FOR SIX (1966)

In *Occurrence for Six* (scored for flute, clarinet, bass clarinet, tenor saxophone, trumpet, and double bass), Da Costa explores aspects of improvisation as well as the systematic use of serialism for both motivic and structural purposes, using a 12-tone row that divides into two six-note cells (hexachords). This work in eight movements shows the influence of his study with Dallapiccola. Da Costa treats the row freely, allowing notes to return in some phrases before the entire row has sounded, usually in the form of 16th notes or grace notes. His melodies are derived from the content of the two hexachords. The first hexachord (*c*-sharp-*c*-*b*-*a*-*g*-*b*-flat) forms a uniform intervallic scheme that functions as a substructure in the first four movements. The diminished octave (or major seventh) between *c*-sharp and *c* begins the first, third, and fourth movements, and inverted (minor second), it ends the second. The notes of the second hexachord (*e*-*f*-sharp-*d*-*e*-flat-*a*-flat), though not as systematically utilized, provide the material for the openings of the fifth through eighth movements.

In the first movement, the entry of each instrument on a single note builds clusters of sevenths that alternate between the two hexachords. Da Costa uses a similar technique in the fourth movement, which oscillates between the vertical construction of the tonal clusters and the linear movements of short solos for the bass clarinet. Dynamically, the first movement forms an arch, building to a *sforzando* climax with the instruments playing in their upper ranges in contrast, the fourth movement, built of *sforzando* clusters, inverts the dynamic structure with a *mezzo-piano* section at measures 20-24.

The second and fifth movements are solos for the flute and trumpet, respectively. Both are in the nature of impromptus, with a spontaneous, improvisatory quality that the composer achieves by writing melodic phrases of irregular length, with octave displacements among the notes of the hexachord. The composer exploits the timbral possibilities of each instrument, contrasting notes at the extremes of their ranges and asking for glissandos, flutter tonguing, and a wide range of dynamic changes. The alternation between the pitches *c* and *c*-sharp at the end of the second movement forms a link to the opening of the third.

The third movement is structured by the interplay between instruments. Here, Da Costa spins one long melody that migrates from one voice to another and that is set in relief against one or two held notes. Dynamics, rhythm, and timbre provide marked contrast at each entry. A more subtle use of tone color is seen in the sixth movement, with its "delicate, Webern-like exchange of timbres," as Da Costa himself has noted. The melodic material is mainly in the clarinet, but the initial pitch of each instrument forms the retrograde of the row.

In the seventh movement, the interval of the second that opens the second hexachord is expanded into a ninth and forms the principal motivic material. This motive, essentially a two-note idea filled in by glissandos or ornamented by escape notes, appoggiaturas, and grace notes, is sometimes extended into a three- and four-note succession of ninths, or seconds, or their inversions, sevenths. While Da Costa uses the same techniques as in the rest of *Occurrence for Six,* the sparse texture (unaccompanied, extremely brief solo statements) and interspersed silences produce a quality of spontaneity and simplicity.

In the A section of the last movement, a ternary form (ABA), Da Costa directs the instrumentalists, following nonmetrical flourishes of overlapping versions of the basic set, to improvise on an assigned portion of the set, beginning with the trumpet. When all of the instrumentalists have entered and begun their improvisation, the B section begins. The trumpet plays the B material, consisting of three tranquil notes, either *c-b-c*-sharp or *c*-sharp-*b-c*, directed to be sustained at differing rhythmic note values, each separated by a fermata; upon the trumpet's entrance, the other instruments conclude their improvisations and enter on the B material one by one. An extended solo bass improvisation based on the original row leads to a return of the fantasia-like A section.

Written during the winter of 1966, while Da Costa was teaching at Hunter College, *Occurrence for Six* was not composed with specific performers in mind; it was later performed at the Brooklyn Academy of Music, with Tania Léon conducting.

CEREMONY OF SPIRITUALS (1976)

This composition for soprano, tenor and soprano saxophone, chorus, and orchestra was commissioned by the New York State Arts Council and the Symphony of the New World. In it, as in Da

Costa's *Spiritual Set for Organ* (1974), the composer interprets the music, behaviors, and emotions of the traditional African-American religious experience. After attending a traditional Baptist church in Wilmington, Delaware, Da Costa was inspired to compose *Spiritual Set,* based on the form and freedom of the service. In *Ceremony of Spirituals,* he develops a similar organizational concept. The form of the movements, and the manner in which the thematic material evolves, is governed by its analogy to the Baptist church service, which begins with pre-service "devotions": intonations of the "old songs," sometimes alternating with and sometimes accompanying prayers led by an elder or deacon of the church. This is followed by the service proper. Music frames the focal point of the religious event: the sermon, a truly interactive part involving the preacher, choir, and congregation in questions, responses, shouts, and song, all of which contribute to a collective emotional experience.

A different spiritual serves as the thematic basis of each of the three movements: "You Hear the Lambs a-Cryin'," "Two Wings," and "I'm Troubled in Mind." The composer uses a combination of tonal and atonal, rhythmically free and highly articulated material in the first movement, which begins with a rich, muted D-minor passage for the low strings and winds. Analogous to the low rumble of praying, foot-tapping, organ music, and singing, there are scattered fragments of motives that are later heard to be based on the ornamented version of the spiritual melody "You Hear the Lambs a-Cryin'," finally sung by the choir at the end of the movement.

Da Costa, while composing for a large orchestra, writes sensitively, never calling for more than a *forte* dynamic marking, using muted brass, dividing not only the winds but also the violas, cellos, and basses, and using extensive syncopated tam-tam and gong ostinatos marked *mezzo-piano.* Halfway through this movement, a dramatic moment occurs when the tenor saxophone (taking the lead in the role of the church elder) plays a cadenza-like passage. Da Costa directs the performer to freely improvise on a melodic contour, which is graphically notated.

The soprano soloist links the first and second movements, singing a wordless, improvised melisma based on scripted bends, blue notes, and glissandos, and then smoothly segues into the melodic material of the second spiritual, "Two Wings," followed by a rhythmic choral response. The instruments of the full orchestra enter gradually, building to a vamp section that is analogous to the repetitive rhetorical phrases of the preacher, the shouts of the congregation, and the musical interpolations of the organist and choir; the vamp intensifies the harmonic, rhythmic, and textual ideas. The saxophone begins improvising over a series of "sound backgrounds" (aleatoric passages of short motives performed freely by the orchestra and chorus). In the third "sound background," the soprano soloist enters, the orchestra and chorus are cut off, and an improvisational interplay between the saxophone and soprano elides into the third movement.

The saxophonist, now playing soprano saxophone, is given the melody "I'm Troubled in Mind." Rather than giving it a somber treatment, Da Costa, continuing the church association, in which the part of the service after the sermon emphasizes personal faith and dedication, sets the spiritual in a manner that suggests serenity and peace. The chorus is then given the melodic material, weaving in and out of consonant and dissonant sonorities, and the texture gradually contracts, ending quietly with muted brass, percussion, and low strings and winds.

Ceremony of Spirituals had its world premiere at Carnegie Hall in 1977, performed by the Symphony of the New World with the Howard University Choir. It was also performed at the Kennedy Center, Washington, D.C., by the same choir with the National Symphony Orchestra.

UKOM MEMORY SONGS (1981)

Ukom Memory Songs, composed for the composer's sister, organist and ethnomusicologist Lorna McDaniel, is a by-product of McDaniel's field research in the Ukom drum music and songs and their role in the tribal culture in Nigeria. Da Costa was fascinated by the vocality of the *Ukom Nkwa* (Ukom drum ensemble) and its ability to imitate speech tones, as well as by its complex rhythms, which use syncopation, hemiola, polyrhythms, and asymmetrical meters. In his compositions, the concept of communication and language is important. The *Ukom Nkwa,* comprised of ten miniature tuned drums, a large drum, and split-log drum, is played by two drummers—a master drummer and receiver soloist—on opposite sides of the drum row in a call-and-response style.

Da Costa's composition, in four sections connected by drum "proverbs," or improvisations, follows the three-day funeral ceremony that ensures a soul's entry into ancestorhood. The concept of improvisation is important and valid to Da Costa when the potential of a musical idea goes beyond the capabilities of musical notation and is particularly appropriate in this piece, which attempts to approximate the sense of an oral tradition. In the first movement, "Awakening," the organ plays a fanfare on a solo trumpet stop, and the composer directs the drummer to respond to the rhythm and melodic form of the tonal vocabulary. The proverbs themselves are the improvised musical realizations of the memorial speeches that "privilege"—are tailored and directed to—the guests attending the ceremony (or the audience in a Western-tradition performance). An important element of *Ukom Memory Songs* is that privilege; while striving to capture the sense of the Ukom tradition practiced among the Igbo, Da Costa wants to filter the interpretation of that tradition through the African-American experience.

In the second movement, "Where Has the Woman Gone?" based on a multilinear Ukom song, the organ improvises on two six-beat phrases, following a two-voice contrapuntal section that contrasts with the seven- and five-beat phrases in the drum row and the three-beat phrases in the large drum. The third movement, "Men's Song Riffs," based on a circular dance pattern, combines an intensely expressive, dissonant single chord with chromatic inflections, a hypnotic repetitive rhythmic pattern accompanied by bells, and a chanting melody comprised of short chromatic motives. In the last movement, "Dance to Thirds," the theme, made up of parallel thirds, alternates with an interpretation of the thematic material by the drummers, mirroring the function of the tuned drums in ceremonial use.

This work, recorded in 1981 by Lorna McDaniel, organ, and Newman Baker, drums, had its premiere concert performance in July 1997 at the American Guild of Organists Region III Conference in Washington, D.C., with Mickey Thomas Terry, organ, and Roberta Washington and Joseph Connell, drums.

KIMBERLYN MONTFORD

DAOUD, RAGEH

Born in Cairo, Egypt, November 23, 1954. **Education:** Cairo Conservatoire, preparatory and secondary education, studied piano with Rachel Salib, 1963–71; Cairo Conservatoire, studied piano with Ettore Puglisi, composition with Gamal Abdel-Rahim, 1971–77, B.Mus., 1977; Vienna Academy of Music, studied composition with Thomas Christian David and Francis Burt, 1981–88; Graduate Diploma, 1987; Magister Artium, 1988. **Composing and Performing Career:** First acknowledged composition, 1978; one to three new works each year, 1982–present; Hanager Center Chamber Orchestra of Egyptian Ministry of Culture, conductor, 1993–present. **Teaching Career:** Cairo Conservatoire, teaching/research assistant to Gamal Abdel-Rahim, 1978–81; Cairo Conservatoire, Associate Professor of Composition, 1988–present. **Honors and Awards:** Prize of Artistic Creation of the Ministry of Culture, 1990; Alexandria Film Festival prize, 1991; Film Critics Association prize, 1992. **Mailing Address:** Cairo Conservatoire, Avenue of the Pyramids, Giza, Egypt.

MUSIC LIST

INSTRUMENTAL SOLOS
Cello
Nocturne for Cello and Piano. 1989. Unpublished manuscript.

Flute
Suite for Alto Flute Solo. 1992. Unpublished manuscript.
Suite for Flute and Piano. 1992. Unpublished manuscript.

Oboe
Three Pictures for Oboe and Piano. 1987. Unpublished manuscript.

Piano
Nocturne for Piano. 1989. Unpublished manuscript.
Sonata for Piano. 1978. Unpublished manuscript. Premiere, 1996.

Two Pianos
"Three Children's Pictures for Two Pianos." 1987. Unpublished manuscript.

SMALL INSTRUMENTAL ENSEMBLE
Strings
Four Dances for String Quartet. 1982. Unpublished manuscript.
String Quartet. Unpublished manuscript.

Woodwinds
Quartet for Woodwinds. 1985. Unpublished manuscript. Premiere, 1986.

Combinations
Fantasy for Harp, Cello, and Percussion. 1982. Unpublished manuscript.
Trio for Piano, Violin, and Cello. 1987. Unpublished manuscript. Premiere, 1987.
Quartet for Flute, Oboe, Clarinet, and Bassoon. 1985. Unpublished manuscript.

STRING ORCHESTRA
Four Pieces for String Orchestra. 1981. Unpublished manuscript.
Fugue for String Orchestra. 1981. Unpublished manuscript.
Meditation for String Orchestra. 1986. Unpublished manuscript.
Portrait no. 1 for String Orchestra. 1986. Unpublished manuscript.
Portrait no. 2 for String Orchestra. 1987. Unpublished manuscript.
Rhapsody for String Orchestra. 1988. Unpublished manuscript.

FULL ORCHESTRA
Egyptian Glimpse for Orchestra. 1978. Unpublished manuscript.

ORCHESTRA (CHAMBER OR FULL) WITH SOLOISTS
Fantasy for Woodwinds and String Orchestra. 1983. Unpublished manuscript.
Passacaglia for Lute, Organ, and String Orchestra. 1993. Unpublished manuscript.
Rhapsody for Flute, Violin, and Orchestra. 1992. Unpublished manuscript.
Takassim for Clarinet and Orchestra. 1984. Unpublished manuscript.

ORCHESTRA (CHAMBER OR FULL) WITH CHORUS
Requiem for Choir and Orchestra. 1990. Unpublished manuscript.
Thirty Songs for Children and Small Orchestra. 1991. Unpublished manuscript.

SOLO VOICE
"Lied for Alto and Piano." 1984. Unpublished manuscript.
"Lied for Soprano and Piano." 1978. Unpublished manuscript.

VOICE WITH INSTRUMENTAL ENSEMBLE
"Der neue Ankommende: Lied for Alto, Bass Clarinet, and Vibraphone." 1986. Unpublished manuscript.

* * * * *

One of Egypt's leading composers, Rageh Daoud belongs to the third generation of modern Egyptian composers, which consists of those born between 1950 and 1970. An advocate of what Nigerian composer, pianist, and scholar Akin Euba has termed "intercultural music," he assimilates into his compositions ideas taken from both the Arabic and Western worlds. He lives in a culture where the performer and improviser have traditionally been more important than the composer (in the Western European sense of the term), and as a teacher, he is in a position to influence the directions that his students may take as they develop into Egypt's next generation of composers.

As a child, Daoud was exposed to both Arabic music and to European classical music. One decisive early influence upon him was his father, a professional writer and journalist who was also an excellent amateur singer of Egyptian art and folk music. It was his father who made it possible for Daoud and his four siblings to study music seriously. Daoud was particularly attracted at a young age to European piano music, showing his talents early in life by playing harmonic improvisations on the keyboard.

In 1963, Daoud entered the Cairo Conservatoire as a secondary school student to study piano. In the 1970s, in the Conservatoire proper, he continued his piano studies and began taking composition classes with Gamal Abdel-Rahim. In 1977, he became one of the first students to graduate from the Conservatoire with a diploma in musical composition. A turning point in his career took place in 1981, when a scholarship from the Egyptian government enabled him to undertake graduate studies in composition at the *Hochschule für Musik und Darstellende Kunst* in Vienna (hereafter referred to as the *Hochschule*). He and his wife, Mauna Ghoneim, were the first two graduates of the Cairo Conservatoire to be admitted to a foreign music graduate school without being required to do any remedial work at the undergraduate level. After receiving his master's and doctoral degrees in composition from the *Hochschule,* he returned to Egypt late in 1988 to pursue his career as a professor of composition at the Cairo Conservatoire. One of Daoud's most significant achievements came in 1993, when he founded the chamber orchestra of the Hanager Center of the Egyptian Ministry of Culture. As conductor of this group, he is now in a position to promote contemporary Egyptian orchestral music.

Although his first professional compositions date from 1978, Daoud's initial development as a composer took place between 1971 and 1977, when he became one of Gamal Abdel-Rahim's first composition students. With Abdel-Rahim, Daoud studied the traditional Arabic modes, the music of 20th-century composers such as Bartók and Stravinsky, and compositional techniques, including the art of motivic development. His three earliest compositions reflect his interest in experimenting with various mediums (solo piano, song, and orchestra) and large-scale forms.

Daoud's years in Vienna (1981–88) provided him with the opportunity to further develop his knowledge of Western music, to gain familiarity with the 12-tone technique and with developmental procedures, and to write 17 of his 28 compositions to date, including several for unusual instrumental combinations (for example, Fantasy for Harp, Cello, and Percussion; and "Der neue Ankommende: Lied for Alto, Bass Clarinet, and Vibraphone").

By the time of his return to Egypt in 1988, Daoud had settled on a style of writing in which his melodies were derived from the Egyptian modes. In his more mature works, the harmonies are derived from his melodies, and the music is chromatic, dissonant, and contrapuntal. Finally realizing that large-scale forms do not appeal to the Egyptian concert-going public, he has gravitated increasingly toward small-scale forms (e.g., ternary) and rhapsodic forms (fantasy, nocturne, and rhapsody). He has also focused more on chamber music recently, both because it is easier to get high-quality performances in Egypt and because the Cairo Symphony Orchestra prefers to limit itself to the standard Western repertory. While he believes that the forms, ensembles, and electronic sound resources of the Western world should be further investigated by Egyptian composers, he has become increasingly convinced that some musical ideas should not be taken from the Western world, particularly elements such as melody and rhythm or methodological concepts such as the 12-tone technique. During recent years, Daoud has spent much of his time composing film music, for which he was awarded several prizes (1991–92). A recent creation, the Passacaglia for Lute, Organ, and String Orchestra is the first composition in which Daoud has used a traditional Egyptian instrument, the *oud.*

SONATA FOR PIANO (1978)

Written soon after he had completed his studies with Gamal Abdel-Rahim, the Sonata for Piano is one of the longest and most ambitious solo piano works written by an Egyptian composer to date and is his first major composition. Dedicated to his composition teacher, it comprises an opening movement in sonata form, a slow middle movement, and a concluding fast movement in rondo form. The 93-measure exposition (first presentation of themes) of the first movement is divided into two sections, an *allegretto animato* (mm. 1–44) and an *andante* (mm. 45–93). The main theme, in 6/8 meter, is a conjunct (step-wise), lyrical four and one-half measure melody that ascends from the tonic note *b*-flat to *f,* then gradually descends to an inconclusive ending on *g*-flat. Supported by a simple chordal accompaniment, this main theme is stated three times during the exposition, in each case with greater intensity. The initial statement is marked *piano,* while the second, a fifth lower (on *g*-flat), is to be played *mezzo-forte.* The third statement returns to the original pitch level and is to be more emphatically rendered as demonstrated by the *forte* dynamic level and the doubling of the theme in octaves. Rapid chromatic scales follow, rendered over a slightly slower arpeggiated accompaniment. The *andante* section introduces a new melody (conjunct) that is stated initially with a chordal accompaniment and later with quicker arpeggios surrounding it. A shift to 2/4 meter marks the beginning of another new idea, one whose most distinguishing feature is a stepwise descent outlining a tritone (three whole steps) from *g*-flat to *c.*

The 39-measure development section (mm. 94–132) is based entirely on the main theme, which is altered from previous statements in two significant ways: the ascending fifth is filled in chromatically and, later, a descending whole step is expanded to an augmented second, an interval characteristic of many Arabic modes. A final distinctive feature is the contrapuntal texture, which contrasts with the homophonic texture of the opening and closing sections. As each imitative statement of the theme enters four notes lower than the previous one, the intensity increases due to a gradual crescendo and a progressively denser texture. An unexpected *subito piano* (immediately soft) phrase is followed by more varied statements of the theme, as well as by motivic development based on the opening measure of this idea.

The recapitulation (restatement of the themes) begins with a literal restatement of the first 30 measures of the exposition. Beginning with the return of the *andante* section, much of the material is restated a fifth higher, helping to bring the first movement to an effective and dramatic close.

The second movement, in ternary form, has opening and closing sections that are somewhat rhapsodic in style. The opening section consists of five short phrases, all of which are one measure in length, with the exception of the more expansive fourth phrase in two measures. The emphasized pitches, (*c-d*-flat-*e*-flat-*e* and *g*-flat-*g-a-b*-flat) indicate that the mode is a variant of an Arabic mode (*saba zamzama*).

Rageh Daoud; courtesy of the Commission for Educational and Cultural Exchange between the U.S.A. and the A.R.E. (The Binational Fulbright Commission)

In the middle section, a more regular *Lento* tempo is established (quarter note = 46 beats per minute). This portion of the movement is unified throughout by a left-hand ostinato that is initially stated on *f* and varied and transposed to other pitch levels. The melody in this section shows the composer's predilection for two favorite Arabic intervals, the minor second and the augmented second (for example, *f-g*-flat and *g*-flat-*a*). The concluding section of the movement takes the opening rhapsodic material and expands upon it.

The third and final movement of the sonata is an energetic rondo in seven sections (ABACABA'). In the A section, the tritone (*f-b*) is prominent in both the melody and the chords and is heard on the downbeats of many measures. The B section differs from this main section in that it is more conjunct and *legato* in style and is performed more softly and slowly.

The centerpiece of the rondo is the C section, which is approximately twice as long as any of the other sections of the movement. It is clearly distinguished from the rest of the movement by its asymmetrical rhythmic units (four measures of 3+3+2+2, one measure of 3+2+3+2+2, two measures of 3+2, and four measures of 3+3+2). After returning to duple meter, the remaining portion of the section develops motives from earlier parts of the movement; the most significant of these ideas, which is derived from the opening four notes of the rondo theme, is stated 18 times and emphasized by a crescendo to *fortissimo*.

Although the first three A sections of the movement correspond closely to one another, the composer surprises the listener near the end by restating the rondo theme on different pitch levels. The entire sonata appears to be Daoud's most Western and least Arabic work. It differs from his other compositions in its multiplicity of themes, its less intricate motivic development, and its large-scale form.

The Sonata was composed in 1978, but the entire work was not premiered until March 1996, when it was given a highly acclaimed performance in Cairo by Russian pianist Maja Narimamize.

FOUR PIECES FOR STRING ORCHESTRA (1981)

This set of four pieces effectively exploits the coloristic possibilities of the string orchestra in a variety of homophonic and contrapuntal textures. There are frequent meter shifts and tempo changes and the melodic material is highly chromatic. Three of the four pieces are in three-part form, while the second functions as a transition from the vigorous first piece to the contemplative third. In the concluding work, the main theme of the first returns in dramatic form.

The *Four Pieces for String Orchestra* were composed during a time of Daoud's transition from his country to the unfamiliar surroundings of Vienna. The overall fast-slow-fast structure of this work is somewhat unusual for Daoud, who generally prefers to compose single-movement pieces with numerous contrasting sections rather than a cycle of miniatures.

The first piece is played primarily *forte* and in a *marcato* (emphasized) style. The texture is homophonic throughout, with the violas, cellos, and basses providing harmonic support beneath the melody of the first (and occasionally the second) violins. The movement consists of three sections, each with its own distinctive melody.

The first section (mm. 1–13) is based on a scale constructed of two four-note groups: one group contains a half-step framed by whole steps on either side of it (*c-d-e*-flat-*f*), and the other consists of an augmented second surrounded by two half-steps (*f-g*-flat-*a-b*-flat). The harmonies clash against one another and often form dissonances with the melody. One prominent feature is the irregular groups of two and three eighth notes, which are presented in alternation as the music shifts between 4/4, 3/4, and 5/8 meter.

The most important material is found in the middle section (mm. 14–45), which is more than twice the length of the opening and closing parts of the movement. Here, open fifths support a new melody in duple meter. The climax is reached in mm. 29–40, where a syncopated, descending scale (featuring an augmented second) appears. Soon, for several measures the violins move in parallel intervals (major sevenths) over a span of more than an octave. Toward the end of the section, the second melody is restated, in octaves, by a divided first violin section.

The first piece ends in a subdued manner, with a new melodic idea that has a tritone between its second and third notes. In 9/8 meter with one 11/8 measure in the middle, this melody is stated first in the violas, then in the cellos, as the upper strings play a final chord (*b*-flat-*c*-sharp-*f*-sharp) that is dissonant against the melody. The second piece is a short interlude that continues to use this last idea on a different pitch level (transposed up a fourth).

The third piece introduces a highly expressive, four-measure *cantabile* melody in the muted strings. It is in a *Lento* tempo with shifts between 6/8, 7/8, and 8/8 meters. The melody is very chromatic, and the first 13 notes of the piece use 11 of the 12 notes in a chromatic scale. Reaching its peak fairly early (on the fifth note), the melody is stated initially in the violas and imitated in the cellos while the violas continue with a countermelody. For the third statement, the melody is divided between the two violin parts and altered through octave displacement, changing rhythms, fragmentation, and repeated open chords (fifths or fourths). This is followed by three statements by the second violins of a variant of the melody, one of which is imitated in the second violins before being transferred to other pitches. The movement ends with the original form of the melody.

The fourth and final piece is in three sections. The first of these (mm. 1–14) is highly percussive and dissonant, with the meter moving among 4/4, 3/4, and 5/4 and a dialogue taking place between the lower strings. The second section (m. 15–40) begins with a sudden change to a slow-moving, *cantabile* melody that is initially stated by the cellos and basses and imitated by the violas five measures later. This melody is then varied and the note values halved as it is introduced and imitated by the first and second violins and by the violas and cellos. The intensity increases as the piece begins its third section (mm. 41–69). A climax is effected through a dramatic return of the main theme of the first movement, which is stated twice and followed by a descending scale (featuring an augmented second). The closing, third statement of the melody is once again played in octaves by divided first violins, and the piece ends with a heavily accented (*sforzando*) chord (of a perfect fifth with a dissonant major second).

Because they are technically less demanding than most of his music, the *Four Pieces for String Orchestra* have been performed more frequently and in more countries than Daoud's other compositions. The first performances were given by the Cairo Conservatoire Orchestra during 1984 in Cairo, Bonn, and Prague. In 1985, the Egyptian Musical Youth Orchestra also performed the work in England, Canada, and Poland. Written in highly accessible style that appeals to most listeners, the *Four Pieces* were received enthusiastically by audiences on all of these occasions.

QUARTET FOR WOODWINDS (1985)

Written during the middle of the composer's stay in Vienna, the Quartet for Woodwinds is a one-movement work in seven sections (ABCB'A'BC). Rather than conceiving of this as a rondo or some other Western form, however, Daoud views this quartet as a free form that juxtaposes three different emotional moments (A, B, and C). It reflects Daoud's preoccupation with counterpoint, changing meters, and motivic development; and its instrumentation (flute, oboe, clarinet, and bassoon) is rare among the repertory of Egyptian music.

In the A section, the listener is thrown off guard by constantly shifting meters in an *adagio* tempo and by subtle syncopations and motives that begin on weaker beats (6/8, 4+3/8, 9/8, etc.). The two-phrase melodic line has as prominent intervals the perfect fourth and the tritone and is made up of the repetition of short motivic ideas within different rhythmic contexts. The interludes between entries continue the counterpoint by extensive motivic development. The entire A section is heavily imitative throughout.

The B section is an *allegro* in duple meter. It has a *staccato* melody derived from the opening section, which focuses on tritones. The section begins with the melody in octaves between the clarinet and bassoon, laid out in two asymmetrical phrases. Later, presented in the flute, this melody is accompanied by a more conjunct countermelody that is divided equally between the oboe and clarinet parts.

A second transformation of the opening theme dominates the slow C section (*adagio molto,* duple meter). This theme—similar to the opening idea of a descending tritone and an ascending half step—has a gradually ascending contour and an active countermelody. One hears the theme stated successively in the flute, the clarinet, and the oboe, again with accompanying countermelodies.

The remaining sections of the quartet are either exact or modified restatements of the first three sections described above. While the fourth section returns to the B material, it differs from the original B section in that it uses highly dissonant, *staccato* arpeggios (outlining a tritone) to reach a climax. The abbreviated return to the A section uses the motivic ideas of the opening measures, arranged somewhat differently. More subdued than the previous section, this A section uses several different instrumental combinations to create nearly continuous duets. The sixth section is exactly the same as the original B section. The final section is equivalent to the first 19 measures of the previous C section, but with a soft, *legato* coda added in which the outer parts move in contrary motion to an open fifth.

Although it has only been performed on two occasions, audiences have responded well to the Quartet for Woodwinds because of its juxtaposition of three different emotional states. The world

premiere was given in Vienna in 1986, the Egyptian premiere took place in Cairo in 1996.

TRIO FOR PIANO, VIOLIN, AND CELLO (1987)

The Trio for Piano, Violin, and Cello is one of the composer's most significant works. Through its use of melodic intervals derived from Arabic modes, Egyptian rhythmic patterns, motivic development, and counterpoint, this composition summarizes what Daoud learned from Gamal Abdel-Rahim and from his studies at the *Hochschule* in Vienna. This one-movement trio falls into three sections (fast-slow-fast), with the last section being essentially a condensed reiteration of the opening one (ABA').

A six-note motive is the basis of the entire work. Including several melodic intervals common to many Arabic modes—minor third, minor second, tritone—it is stated by the piano in each of the first three measures, with a variation in the third, and reaches an augmented triad on the tonal center in the fourth. A dialogue between piano and strings ensues, as the instrumental textures become more complex, and there are many changes in instrumentation in the reiteration of the opening 19 measures. The sequential statement of the unifying motive and its variant follows, which concludes the A section of this three-part composition.

The B section is distinguished from the previous material through its use of still more complex textures, different rhythmic patterns, and more intricate transformations of the unifying motive. Beginning in an *adagio* tempo, the muted strings and piano state a variant of the unifying motive in 6/8 meter. A highly dissonant variant in four-part counterpoint (violin, right-hand piano, cello, left-hand piano), with each part entering a half-measure after the previous one, leads to a slow (*andante con moto*) passage that introduces two new transformations of the unifying motive. Unfolding in a series of five-measure phrases, this slow section is in 7/8 meter and uses for its bass line the *dor hindi* rhythmic mode (3+2+2).

Twenty-five measures after the beginning of the slow section, Daoud introduces a melody that is essentially a backward and inverted statement of the idea presented in the second transformation of the previous slow section. Initially presented in the violin and imitated by the cello, with rhythmic variants, this backwards, inverted melodic variant is reiterated in both hands of the piano part as the music gathers in intensity. One of the most interesting passages in the entire work appears as three simultaneous versions of a four-note motive based on the unifying idea of a tritone. The concluding portion of the B section contains the most dramatic moment in the trio. Beginning with a return to an *adagio* tempo, it accelerates to a faster pace (*allegro con fuoco*) as increasing attention is paid to close intervals.

The A' section of the trio is essentially a restatement of measures 14 through 48 of the A section with some changes in rhythm and pitch. During the final 11 measures of the piece, Daoud returns to a more recognizable version of the unifying motive, which he restates numerous times to bring the composition to an effective close.

The 1987 world premiere of Daoud's Trio was held at the Society of Austrian Composers in Vienna, and its first Egyptian performance was given in Cairo in 1990. In both the Western and the Arabic worlds, it has been viewed by the composer's colleagues and former teachers to be one of the finest chamber works written by an Egyptian composer to date.

REFERENCES

El-Kholy, Samha. *Nationalism in Twentieth-Century Music.* Kuwait: Alam Al Maarifa, 1992. (In Arabic)

Robison, John O. "Intercultural Music in Modern Egypt: The Third Generation." *Intercultural Music,* vol. 3, edited by Akin Euba and Cynthia Tse Kimberlin. Bayreuth: E. Breitinger, forthcoming.

JOHN O. ROBISON

DAVIS, ANTHONY CURTIS

Born in Paterson, N.J., February 20, 1951. **Education:** Studied classical piano as a child; Princeton, N.J., elementary school, grades 1–4; State College, Pa., public school, grades 5–9; Torino, Italy, American School, grades 10–11; Exeter, N.H., Exeter Preparatory School, grades 11–12; New Haven, Conn., Yale University, B.A., in music, 1975. **Composing and Performing Career:** First composition, "Waltz for Piano," 1966; New Haven, worked with a number of musicians espousing the principles of the Association for the Advancement of Creative Musicians, ca. mid-1970s; co-founded the free-jazz group Advent, 1973; worked with trumpeter Leo Smith's band, New Delta Ahkri, 1974–77; New York, performed with violinist Leroy Jenkins' trio, 1977–79; co-leads a duo and quartet with flutist James Newton, since 1978; works with the octet Episteme, formed 1981; New York City Opera, premiered *X: The Life and Times of Malcolm X,* 1986; Opera Theater of St. Louis, premiered *Under the Double Moon,* 1989; American Music Theater Festival, premiered *Tania,* 1992; composed music for Broadway production of Tony Kushner's *Angels in America,* 1993. **Teaching Career:** Yale University, Lecturer, Music and Afro-American Studies, 1981–82; Cornell University, Senior Fellow, Society for the Humanities, 1987; Yale School of Music, Visiting Professor of Composition, 1990, 1993, 1994; University of California, San Diego, Visiting Professor of Music, 1995; Harvard University, Visiting Lecturer in Afro-American Studies, 1992–96; Northwestern University, Visiting Artist, 1997. **Commissions:** Houston Symphony Orchestra, 1982; Brooklyn Philharmonic, 1983; Molissa Fenley and Dancers, 1983; Ursula Oppens, 1983; San Francisco Symphony, 1984; The Kitchen Center, 1985; Laura Dean Dancers and Musicians, 1985; Massachusetts Institute of Technology, 1987; American Composers Orchestra, 1988; Kansas City Symphony, 1988, 1997; Opera Theater of St. Louis, 1989; Dora Ohrenstein, 1990; Carnegie Hall, 1991; Chanticleer, Musica Sacra, and the Dale Warland Singers, 1991; Chamber Music America, 1991; American Music Theater Festival, 1992; Bravo Festival, 1992; St. Luke's Chamber Orchestra, 1992; Ralph Lemon, 1994; Atlanta Committee for the Olympic Games Cultural Olympiad, 1995; Penn State University, 1995; String Trio of New York, 1995; Lyric Opera of Chicago, 1997. **Honors/Awards:** McDowell Colony, Peterborough, New Hampshire, 1991; Scholar-in-Residence, Rockefeller Foundation, Study and Conference Center, Bellagio, Italy, 1993. **Mailing Address:** 5139-B Renaissance Avenue, San Diego CA 92122.

MUSIC LIST

INSTRUMENTAL SOLOS
Violin
Sonata for Violin and Piano. 1991. New York: G. Schirmer, 1991. Commissioned by Carnegie Hall. Premiere, 1991.

Clarinet
"Parenthetically." 1986. New York: G. Schirmer, 1998.

Vibraphone
"FMW." Unpublished manuscript. Recorded: MPS 68267.

"A Walk through the Shadow." Unpublished manuscript. Also arranged for piano and for jazz ensemble, both published by G. Schirmer, 1981. Recorded: MPS 68267.

Piano
"Beyond Reason." 1979. Unpublished manuscript. Recorded: India Navigation IN-1047.

"Five Moods from an English Garden." 1978. Unpublished manuscript. Recorded: India Navigation IN-1047.

"Lady of the Mirrors." Unpublished manuscript. Recorded, 1980: India Navigation IN-1047.

"Locomotif no. 1." Unpublished manuscript. Recorded, 1978: Red Records VPA 134; Red Records RR 123100.2.

"Man on a Turquoise Cloud." Unpublished manuscript. Recorded, 1980: India Navigation IN-1047.

"Middle Passage." New York: G. Schirmer, 1983. Commissioned by Ursula Oppens. Premiere, 1983. Recorded: Gramavision Records 18-8807; Gramavision Records GR 8401; Music and Arts CD-862.

"On an Azure Plane." Unpublished manuscript. Recorded: Red Records VPA 134.

"A Proposition for Life." Unpublished manuscript. Recorded, 1984: Gramavision 18-8807; Gramavision Records GR 8401.

"Waltz for Piano." 1966. Unpublished manuscript.

"Wayang no. 4." or "Under the Double Moon." Unpublished manuscript. Also arranged for vibraphone and for jazz ensemble (the latter published by G. Schirmer, 1981). Recorded: India Navigation IN-1047.

Two Pianos
"Wayang no. 6." 1985. New York: G. Schirmer, 1985. Commissioned by Laura Dean Dancers and Musicians. Premiere, 1985.

SMALL INSTRUMENTAL ENSEMBLE
Brass
Brass Quintet no. 1. 1991. New York: G. Schirmer, 1991. Commissioned by Chamber Music America for the Saturday Brass Quintet. Premiere, 1992.

Combinations
song was sweeter even so (computer, chamber ensemble). 1987. New York: G. Schirmer, 1987. Commissioned by the Massachusetts Institute of Technology. Premiere, 1987.

"Still Waters, no. 3" (flute, piano, cello). 1982. New York: G. Schirmer. Recorded: Gramavision GR 8201.

CHAMBER ORCHESTRA
Litany of Sins. 1992. New York: G. Schirmer, 1992. Commissioned by the St. Luke's Chamber Orchestra. Premiere, 1992.

FULL ORCHESTRA
Esu Variations. 1995. New York: G. Schirmer. Commissioned by the

Atlanta Committee for the Olympic Games Cultural Olympiad for the Atlanta Symphony Orchestra. Premiere, 1995.

Jacob's Ladder. 1997. Unpublished manuscript. Commissioned by the Kansas City Symphony Orchestra.

Notes from the Underground. 1988. New York: G. Schirmer, 1988. Commissioned by the American Composers Orchestra. Premiere, 1988.

Still Waters. 1982. New York: G. Schirmer, 1982. Commissioned by the Houston Symphony Orchestra. Premiere, 1983.

ORCHESTRA (CHAMBER OR FULL) WITH SOLOISTS

Maps (violin, orchestra). 1988. New York: G. Schirmer, 1988. Commissioned by the Kansas City Symphony. Premiere, 1988. Recorded: Gramavision 18-8807-4.

Wayang no. 5 (piano, orchestra). 1985. New York: G. Schirmer, 1985. Commissioned by the San Francisco Symphony. Premiere, 1984. Recorded: Gramavision 18-8807.

SOLO VOICE

"In This House of Blues" (voice, clarinet, piano). 1994. New York: G. Schirmer, 1994.

VOICE WITH INSTRUMENTAL ENSEMBLE

"In the Beginning of Light, of Time Passing" (voice, flute, clarinet, trombone, piano, violin, cello, double bass, percussion). New York: G. Schirmer, 1986.

"It Was" (soprano, chamber ensemble). 1992. New York: G. Schirmer, 1992. Commissioned by the Bravo Festival and Erie Mills. Premiere, 1992.

"Lost Moon Sisters" (soprano, violin, piano, percussion; revised version for soprano and nine instruments). 1990; revised 1991. New York: G. Schirmer, 1990; revised 1991. Commissioned by Dora Ohrenstein. Premiere, 1990. Recorded: original version, CRI CD 654.

"Some Springs." New York: G. Schirmer, 1986.

CHORAL MUSIC

"Voyage through Death to Life upon These Shores." 1991. New York: G. Schirmer, 1991. Commissioned by Chanticleer, Musica Sacra, and the Dale Warland Singers. Premiere, 1991.

DRAMATIC MUSIC

Amistad (opera). 1997. New York: G. Schirmer, 1997. Commissioned by Lyric Opera of Chicago. Premiere, 1997.

Dance (ballet). 1994. New York: G. Schirmer, 1995. Commissioned by Ralph Lemon for the José Limón Dancers. Premiere, 1995.

Hemispheres (ballet). 1983. New York: G. Schirmer, 1983. Contents: Esu at the Crossroads; Little Richard's New Wave; Ifa: The Oracle, Esu the Trickster; A Walk through the Shadow; Clonetics. Commissioned by Molissa Fenley and Dancers. Premiere, 1983. Recorded: Gramavision Records R2-79428.

Tania (opera in two acts). 1992. New York: G. Schirmer, 1992. Commissioned by the American Music Theater Festival. Premiere, 1992.

Under the Double Moon (opera in two acts). 1989. New York: G. Schirmer, 1989. Commissioned by the Opera Theater of St. Louis. Premiere, 1989.

X: The Life and Times of Malcolm X (opera in 3 acts). 1985. New York: G. Schirmer, 1986. Commissioned by The Kitchen Center. Premiere, 1985 (excerpt), 1986. Recorded: Gramavision Records R2-79470.

INCIDENTAL AND COMMERCIAL MUSIC

Angels in America: Millennium Approaches. 1993. Incidental music for the Tony Award winning show by Tony Kushner. Premiere, 1993.

Angels in America: Perestroika. 1993. Incidental music for Tony Award winning show by Tony Kushner. Premiere, 1993.

A Man around the House. 1980. Incidental film music.

Miraj. 1983. Incidental film music.

Painting in the Dark. 1981. Incidental music for a documentary on Steve Hannock, the artist.

Return from Space. 1989. Commercial music for the documentary on the NASA space program.

JAZZ ENSEMBLE

[The following list of titles includes only works that were composed by the subject of the entry; it is not a list of recordings that were made by the subject. Although the composer may have made recordings of his own works, the list is not restricted to those recordings but in many cases includes performances by other artists of the composer's work. The list is made up of publication and discographical data, in cases where such information is available. Although no effort has been made to include documentation of the earliest recording of the works listed, the date of the earliest recording that is readily available has been given. —Ed.]

"African Ballad." Recorded, 1978: India Navigation IN-1036.

"Andrew." Recorded, 1978: India Navigation IN-1036.

"Behind the Rock." Also for solo piano. Recorded, 1978: India Navigation IN-1036.

"Estraven" (violin, cello, piano, percussion). Recorded, 1978: Sackville Records 3020.

"The Fugitive of Time." Recorded: India Navigation 1056.

"Graef" (violin, cello, piano, percussion). Recorded, 1978: Sackville Records 3020.

"Happy Valley Blues" (violin, guitar, piano, double bass). 1995. New York: G. Schirmer. Recorded: Music and Arts 994. Commissioned by the String Trio of New York.

"Hocket in the Pocket." Recorded, 1980: India Navigation IN 1041.

"Lethe" (violin, cello, piano, percussion). Recorded, 1978: Sackville Records 3020.

"Locomotif no. 6." 1976. Recorded: Douglas NBLP 7046.

"Madame Xola" (violin, cello, piano, percussion). Recorded, 1978: Sackville Records 3020.

"Of Blues and Dreams" (violin, cello, piano, percussion). Also for solo piano. Recorded, 1978: Sackville Records 3020.

"Past Lives." Also for solo piano. Recorded, 1980: India Navigation IN 1041.

"Persephone" (piano, flute, violin, trombone, drums, vibraphone, bass). Recorded: Gramavision 8205.

"Simultaneity I" (flute, cello, piano). 1989. Recorded: Gramavision R2 79441.

"Song for the Old World." Recorded, 1978: India Navigation IN-1036.

Anthony Curtis Davis; courtesy of American International Artists; photo by Ray Block

"Still Waters for Septet" (wind ensemble). 1983. Commissioned by the Brooklyn Philharmonic. Premiere, 1983. Recorded: Blue Mesa Moon 8612.

"Sudden Death." Recorded, 1980: India Navigation IN 1041.

"Undine" (wind ensemble). New York: G. Schirmer, 1985. Recorded: Mesa Blue Moon 8612.

"Variations in Dream-Time." Recorded, 1982: India Navigation 1056.

"Wayang no. 1." Recorded: Moers Music MOMU 01048.

"Wayang no. 2" (flute, violin, cello, trombone, piano, percussion, double bass). New York: G. Schirmer, 1981. Written for Episteme. Recorded, 1981: Gramavision GRC 8101.

"Whose Life?" (flute, piano, cello). Recorded, 1989: Gramavision R2 79441.

PUBLICATIONS

ABOUT DAVIS
Articles

Davis, Francis. "Anthony Davis's New Music." In *In the Moment: Jazz in the 1980s,* 3–28. New York: Oxford University Press, 1986.

———. "New Music Traditionalist." *Down Beat* 49 (January 1982): 21–23, 68.

Giddins, Gary. "Composers Ascendant." In *Rhythm-a-ning: Jazz Tradition and Innovation in the 80's,* 59–63. New York: Oxford University Press, 1985.

LaFare, Kenneth. "Poles Apart: Are American Composers Becoming Entrenched in Opposing Camps?" *Musical America* 108, no. 5 (1988): 31–33.

Strickland, Edward. "Anthony Davis." In *American Composers: Dialogues on Contemporary Music,* 71–86. Bloomington: Indiana University Press, 1991.

———. "From Malcolm X to the Unknown Planets: An Interview with Anthony Davis." *Fanfare* 11, no. 2 (1987): 325–35.

Zabor, R. "Funny, You *Look* like a Jazz Musician." *Village Voice* 24 (July 1979): 72+.

* * * * *

In a *Time* magazine cover article, critic Jack E. White called Davis "a master" who, in his most provocative work to date (1986), the opera *X,* "stunned his critics [with] a fierce, modernist, free-tonal piece." As both composer and pianist, Davis demonstrates bold ideas for music's future informed by a profound respect for and knowledge of its past. With every premiere, he continues to produce exciting work. Few figures on the American music scene are as active as he.

Davis was reared within a culturally active family. Following elementary school in Princeton, New Jersey, and State College, Pennsylvania, he spent his high school years at the American School in Torino, Italy, and at Exeter Academy in New Hampshire. Davis entered Yale University for his college studies, taking the B.A. in music in 1975. While at Yale, he began working as a jazz pianist around New Haven with trombonist George Lewis in the group Advent and with trumpeter Leo Smith in the New Delta Ahkri band. Davis returned to his *alma mater* in the early 1980s to teach piano and Afro-American studies, the first of several important teaching appointments he has held (work at Cornell, the University of California, San Diego, and Harvard, along with a return to Yale and a brief tenure at Northwestern University in the 1990s, followed). Davis continues to balance an active teaching career with a busy performing schedule and prolific compositional output.

In the mid-1970s, Davis emerged on the New York loft scene as a prominent new voice in a duo with flutist James Newton (from 1978) and in the influential ensemble Episteme (knowledge), founded by Davis (from 1981). With musical influences as diverse as Duke Ellington, the Association for the Advancement of Creative Musicians (AACM), and Thelonious Monk, the strength of Davis's style stems both from his sure-handed command of his instrument and an ability to grapple with larger social issues and spiritual pursuits.

His musical rhetoric is polyglot. In his compositions, the sound of the Balinese gamelan crosses with late 19th-century European harmonies and with the blues; free jazz sometimes gives way to soul and funk; and a new-age eclecticism suggests an art gallery environment. Davis's orchestra, like his keyboard, seems to function as a canvas on which his music unfolds. The *Zeitgeist* that fostered the dramatic works of John Adams, Philip Glass, and Steve Reich has played a significant part in shaping his style, though his work is markedly different from theirs. Unlike these composer-performers, he continues to return to improvisation as a means of generating new expression. There is a stream-of-consciousness quality in some of his works, but control and shape underlie them.

Most of Davis's early work grew out of his experience as an improviser in jazz combos in which there were equally fluent performers. Examples of his jazz albums are *Of Blues and Dreams* (1978) and the solo piano effort *Lady of the Mirrors* (1980). As a sideman, Davis was active as a co-composer on a number of other recordings, for example, early on with Leo Smith on his *Reflectivity* (1974) and Oliver Lake on *Life Dance of Is* (1978). Along with his work with Anthony Braxton, Steve Lacy, and others, these collaborations all grew out of the improvisations of virtuoso musicians capable of performing and composing simultaneously. Early in his career, Davis saw himself as part of a tradition of composer-pianists that includes, among others, Scott Joplin, Jelly Roll Morton, James P. Johnson, Duke Ellington, Fats Waller, Theolonious Monk, Bud Powell, and Cecil Taylor. However, he has also commented on the role of European art music in his work, claiming to openly appropriate it for use in his own African-American-based works.

Davis has produced a number of works for prominent concert artists such as soprano Dora Ohrenstein ("Lost Moon Sisters") and pianist Ursula Oppens ("Middle Passage"); groups such as the St. Luke's Chamber Ensemble (*Litany of Sins*), the Kansas City Symphony (*Maps,* a violin concerto for co-commissioner Shem Guibbory), and the American Composers Orchestra (*Notes from the Underground*); and choral ensembles such as Chanticleer, the Dale Warland Singers, and Musica Sacra, which jointly commissioned "Voyage through Death to Life upon These Shores." In 1991, he received a commission from Carnegie Hall for a violin sonata for its International American Music Competition.

Davis's four operas are among his most important compositions: *X: The Life and Times of Malcolm X* (New York, 1986), on the life of black activist Malcolm X, with a libretto by the composer's cousin Thulani Davis; *Under the Double Moon* (St. Louis, 1989), a science-fiction thriller concerning telepathic twins, based on his wife Deborah Atherton's book; *Tania* (Philadelphia, 1992), on the kidnapping of heiress Patty Hearst; and *Amistad* (Chicago, 1997), detailing a 19th-century slave revolt, again on a text by Thulani Davis.

A statement made by Davis about *X* is indicative of his approach to composition. Quoted in an article by Gerald Seligman, he says: "This opera is the piece where I have felt freest about drawing upon my own experience, even back to the days when I was an improviser playing in groups and doing Charles Mingus's music, which I haven't felt free to do in my other work. To me it's a test of the theory that one can create an American music that still embraces this whole wide span of tradition, and that can be integrated into an organic whole."

LOCOMOTIF NO. 6 (1976)

Davis's "Locomotif no. 6" grows directly from the New York loft scene of the 1970s, recorded among nights of furious activity at saxophonist Sam Rivers's place in May 1976. Twenty-two performances capturing the work of some 60 musicians were released as a five-record set, *Wildflowers,* on Douglas Records the following year. Davis's piece was written while the composer was a member of trumpeter Leo Smith's group, New Delta Ahkri, which also included such important figures as Oliver Lake (alto saxophone), Wes Brown (bass), and Paul Maddox and Stanley Crouch (drums).

The six-minute piece, while not featuring the composer's piano stylings as prominently as in some of his other recordings, is a powerful work in its collective energy. While Smith and Lake are featured, the title surely reflects the propulsion of the rhythm section, utilizing a pair of drummers. While a later vestige of Ornette Coleman's "free jazz" or "new thing" could describe the overall style of the music, ultimately such labels seem anachronistic. The music is "new" ca. 1976, thus integrating the cultural awareness trends of the later 1960s (toward the AACM and the Art Ensemble of Chicago) in the musicians' almost dramatic approach to their instruments, mindful of tradition yet appreciating the fundamental role of innovation in stylistic evolution.

Davis provides much room for the musicians to explore their own voices, and "Locomotif no. 6" bears down hard with "collective improvisation" of the earliest jazz used as a means to new ends, a means for organizing the improvisational enterprise freely yet providing room for each soloist to explore his own "space" within the composition. Dissonances are difficult to recognize as such since the music is saturated with close harmonies. Rhythms cross in unorthodox ways in addition to the results produced when two (or more) orthodox rhythms are juxtaposed for often unusual spans of musical time.

Time is indeed crucial to the piece, since the audience has little idea of beginning-middle-end through conventional formal markers; and one suspects that the New York audience was somehow a partner in the enterprise, in the close space of the loft setting, where performer and audience are nearly one. While the music stands as recorded, and withstands repeated hearings, ultimately the music is of the moment, like a wildflower, fresh yet fleeting.

Perhaps the most remarkable aspect of Davis's composition is that repeated hearings of the piece cause differing reactions, while the initial message persists. That is part of virtually any listening experience, but here it becomes a subtext of the piece itself.

LADY OF THE MIRRORS (1980)

Lady of the Mirrors is the title of an album of five solo piano compositions, written at different times and in different places, which Davis released in 1980: "Beyond Reason," "Lady of the Mirrors," "Five Moods from an English Garden," "Under the Double Moon," and "Man on a Turquoise Cloud." Davis demonstrates the remarkable range of his interests over the span of these pieces and his ability to achieve his stated aim: "a conception of a larger, more fertile imaginative universe."

"Beyond Reason," written in 1979, explores the earliest of keyboard techniques via the use of a melodic *passacaglia* (melody repeated throughout the composition) above a pedal in the bass, with the harmonies completed by the pianist's remaining fingers. As the composer explains in the liner notes, "Lady of the Mirrors," is quasi-programmatic: a dancer is imagined "through an environment of refracted or distorted light, like broken glass. You never see the lady; you only see her reflection." These images are reflected musically through the use of ever-changing motivic moments, where for various spans of time new ideas become prominent and are investigated, only to be discarded for others.

"Five Moods from an English Garden (for Vasili Kandinsky)" was written in Munich in the spring of 1978 and reflects upon the work of the expressionist artist. The first of its "moods" is clearly recognizable as containing birdcalls, while the others are more abstract. The third mood recurs as a linking device between sections, yielding something like a *rondo* form as the piece unfolds. In his discussion, Davis refers to the harmony, pointing out that keys are not necessary to establish hierarchy; rather, harmonic moments can serve this end.

The ideas developed in "Under the Double Moon" ("Wayang no. 4") link it with several other works. Davis wrote five pieces on the subject of the *wayang,* the Balinese shadow puppet theater, of which only nos. 1 and 4 exist as solo piano compositions (the others are scored for various groups). A point of unity within the collection as a whole—musical shadows (as in "Lady of the Mirrors")—is found here. But "Under the Double Moon" also refers to the work by science fiction novelist Deborah Atherton, on which Davis based his second opera. At the time of this recording, however, the novel had not yet been completed. Nevertheless, the composer had worked out a four-movement dance suite (of which the movement recorded here is the opening) entitled *Suite for Another World,* cast in the distant Bali of *wayang.* Imaginary scrims and shadows play on the listener's emotions as the music moves between notated sections of repose and more lively improvisational excursions. Within each section, the rhythms remain consistently enigmatic, as unpredictable as the compositional mirror Davis uses to refract those scrims and shadows.

The collection's final movement, "Man on a Turquoise Cloud (for Edward Kennedy Ellington)," is refracted in other directions, toward Ellington's compositional colors (a "turquoise" blues) and toward his often overlooked piano stylings, a particularly poignant manner of bringing Davis the composer and pianist together.

X: THE LIFE AND TIMES OF MALCOLM X (1985)

In Anthony Davis's *X: The Life and Times of Malcolm X,* the three acts of Thulani Davis's libretto, based on a scenario story by the composer's brother, Christopher Davis, span Malcolm X's lifetime: Act I (1931–45), with three scenes about his Lansing, Michigan, boyhood, wild youth in Boston, and time in prison; Act II (1946–63), moving to 125th Street in Harlem and concluding with Malcolm Little's cathartic conversion to Islam under the tutelage of Elijah Muhammad; Act III (1963–65), covering the event-filled last years of Malcolm's life, with the continuation of his ministry for the Nation of Islam followed by the revelations discovered on his visit to Mecca and his assassination at Harlem's Audubon Ballroom.

The nearly three-hour work has a cast of five principals, 11 additional roles, and a vocal ensemble accompanied by a chamber orchestra (in the original production, Davis's group, Episteme, also performed). The opera takes the form of a series of unfolding, shifting musico-dramatic vignettes, Davis having drawn upon his wide-ranging stylistic resources to compose music evocative of the various biographical moments of the social activist's life.

In the notes for the premiere recording, Francis Davis (no relation) refers to the work's "unsentimental mix of lush melodic lines with complex rhythmic patterns (drawn from Asian, African, and African-American sources), vocal lines that can be both 'painterly' and abstract." Indeed, this juxtaposition of a sense of "composedness" vs. spontaneity threads its way through the *X* score, yielding startling, even unsettling sounds that somehow remain convincing at every turn.

Perhaps the most convincing aspect of the work is the striking manner in which it recreates the era of its subject; as Mary Lou Humphrey has observed, "swing, scat, modal jazz and rap, the libretto's emulation of contemporaneous literary styles, help recreate the 'sound' of Malcolm's era." But the leader's odyssey traverses much ground, and his story is replete with heavy baggage, both black-and-white and black-on-black. Francis Davis recognized this aspect of the work: "Because of its volatile subject matter, this is an opera that makes incredible demands of its singers, who must convince us to accept the work's interpretations of characters about whom we might have our own preconceptions."

Of his decision to write the opera, the composer told Gerald Seligman, "One thing that disturbed me about modern opera is its distance. I wanted to do something political, something people would have to think about, that would be powerful and have a story to tell." While the work may be a personal odyssey for its creators, the completed art work contains its own esthetic world, realistically depicting its subject, yet also standing alone in its own operatic space.

Andrew Porter wrote of *X* that "Davis in his approach disciplines the jazz musician's fondness for extended self-expression. He here makes virtuosity serve specific dramatic ends. His score is constantly impressive for its metric, rhythmic, and harmonic control of structures and pacing. . . . [A]n 'ordinary' operagoer will be able to respond readily to the music of 'X.' The vocal lines are eloquent. The choral writing is vivid."

Davis's first opera, *X* was heard publicly first as a work-in-progress at the conference "Opera in America" in New York in December 1983. Its first act was produced in workshop form by the American Music Theater Festival in Philadelphia in 1984. In 1985, there were three performances of excerpts by the Springfield (Massachusetts) Symphony, followed by additional portions of the work in performance at the Brooklyn Academy of Music. The first complete performance of the opera was given in Philadelphia in October of the same year. As *X: The Life and Times of Malcolm X,* the work received its world premiere at the New York City Opera on September 28, 1986, and a recording of this production was released in 1992.

Most critics would agree that with *X,* a seminal achievement in 20th-century opera, Davis ensured himself a long career. While not all critics appreciated the work's approach to its topic, differing opinions seem inevitable given the highly personal messages that Malcolm X spoke and continues to speak. The opera has become a benchmark against which Davis's later works are measured. At the same time, the score's great variety and vitality and the widely recognized sophisticated manner in which it deals with its volatile subject have yielded a critical palette that encourages Davis's audience to hear, and pay close attention to, his next works. The liner notes accompanying a 1991 recording of the composer's "Middle Passage" (1983) by pianist Ursula Oppens perhaps best summarized the critical situation of the opera to date: "Davis's propulsive *X* brilliantly reflects the vitality of Malcolm X's life and persona." On this, most critics agree.

LOST MOON SISTERS (1990)

In "Lost Moon Sisters," a 13-minute concert aria for soprano, keyboards, violin, marimba, and vibraphone, Davis continues to demonstrate his ability to effectively shape dramatic space toward the text, the music, and their aggregate. Written for Dora Ohrenstein and included on her album, *Urban Diva,* the text was of her choosing: "Ave," a 1971 poem by Diane di Prima.

"Urban diva" is perhaps a fitting metaphor for Davis's piece. It is at once a return to the loft atmosphere in which pop styles and jazz dominate a contemporary musical community equally schooled in Babbitt, Glass, Cage, and Ives. The work grows from what is often termed "new music," not jazz or academic *per se,* but a free mixture of both. As in so many of Davis's works, neither improvisation nor fully notated composition determines the style of the piece.

In "Lost Moon Sisters," there are moments of kinship to Ives's songs, especially in passages where certain words of di Prima's angular text are set off in sharp relief, and others in which more contemporary sources are evoked. Ohrenstein reflected on the dreamy landscape of di Prima's text, calling it "an oracle; it possesses restorative power," and Davis captures this anachronistic quality in his use of the mallet instruments.

As in virtually all of Davis's works, in "Lost Moon Sisters" there seems to be a personal subtext close to the surface that never detracts from the music's overall diversity. This may take the form of an ongoing musical dialogue with a text, an improvisatory musing on a series of related motives, a playful repartee with musical ghosts, or a dogged grappling with larger social issues. For Davis, the music comes forth first, yet the sincerity of his utterances is all the more convincing due to the depth of their roots.

REFERENCES

Davis, Anthony. Liner notes, *Lady of the Mirrors*. India Navigation IN-1047, 1980.

Davis, Francis. Liner notes, *X: The Life and Times of Malcolm X*. Gramavision Records R2-79470, 1992.

Firestone, Ross. Liner notes, *Wildflowers 2: New York Jazz Loft Sessions*. Casablanca/Douglas Records NBLP 7046, 1976.

Humphrey, Mary Lou. "Davis, Anthony." In *New Grove Dictionary of Opera*. London: Macmillan, 1992.

Kernfeld, Barry. "Davis, Anthony." In *New Grove Dictionary of American Music*. London: Macmillan, 1986.

Liner notes, *American Piano Music of Our Time*. Music and Arts CD699, 1991.

Ohrenstein, Dora. Liner notes, *Urban Diva*. Composer's Recordings Inc. CRI CD 654, 1990.

Porter, Andrew. Review of *X*. *New Yorker* (October 28, 1985): 84–87.

Seligman, Gerald. "The Road to X: Anthony Davis Talks About His Opera on the Life and Times of Malcolm X, Seen This Month at New York City Opera." *Opera News* 51 (September 1986): 28–30.

White, Jack E. "The Beauty of Black Art: Free of Old Constraints, African Americans Spark a Stunning Cultural Movement." *Time* (October 10, 1994): 66–73.

JOHN ANDREW JOHNSON

DAVIS, GUSSIE LORD

Born in Dayton, Ohio, December 3, 1863; died in Whitestone, N.Y., October 18, 1899. **Education:** Nelson Musical College, Cincinnati, Ohio, forced to take only private lessons while working in the college as a janitor, ca. 1880. **Composing and Performing Career:** Played piano at the Bergen Star Concerts in the 1880s; moved to New York, N.Y., worked as a "Tin Pan Alley" composer, ca. 1886–99; toured the United States with the Davis Operatic and Plantation Minstrels, late 1880s–1890s; joined Bob Cole's All-Star Stock Company, 1894.

MUSIC LIST

"Ain't I Your Home Boy No More?" New York: Howley, Haviland, 1896.

"All's Quiet along the Potomac Tonight." New York: F. A. Mills, 1898.

"And the Court Adjourned." New York: Howley, Haviland, 1896.

"At the Board of Trade." New York: Hitchcock Music Stores, 1895.

"Baby's Beneath the Snow." Cincinnati: George Propheter, 1888.

"Baby's Laughing in Her Sleep." Cincinnati: George Propheter, 1886.

"Because I Loved Her Too." New York: William C. Dunn, 1899.

"Beyond Pardon, beyond Recall." New York: Spaulding and Gray, 1894.

"The Black Twin Brother of Mine." New York: Howley, Haviland, 1898.

"Blue-Eyed Etta Waits for Me." New York: C. A. Hitchcock, ca. 1893.

"Blue Skies Waiting Somewhere." New York: Howley, Haviland, ca. 1898.

"The Bridegroom That Never Came." New York: T. B. Harms, 1897.

"The Bridge Is Washed Away." New York: Howley, Haviland, 1898.

"The Bright Side of Life." New York: M. Witmark and Sons, 1896.

"Bye and Bye." New York: K. Dehuchoff, 1898.

"The Cabin on the Mississippi Shore." Cincinnati: J. C. Groene, 1884.

"Chimes of de Golden Bells." New York: James Stillman, 1893.

"The Choir Singer; or, Gone, but Not Astray." New York: James Stillman, 1894.

"Christmas in the Old Home." New York: Howley, Haviland, 1898.

"Climb up de Ladder to de Clouds." New York: Hitchcock and McCargo, 1890.

"Come Back Papa Dear." New York: Hitchcock Publishing, 1897.

"Coming through the Mail." New York: B. W. Hitchcock, 1893.

"The Coon That I Suspected." Cincinnati: John Church, 1895.

"The Court House in de Sky." New York: George Propheter, 1887.

"Dance, Pickaninnies, Dance." New York: Hitchcock Music Stores, 1895.

"The Dear Folks at Home." Cincinnati: John Church, 1881.

"Delia Moore." Brooklyn: Charles W. Held, 1894.

"Did My Last Letter Go Astray?" New York: Hitchcock Music Stores, 1889.

"Dig Away, Dempsy, Dig Away." New York: Howley, Haviland, 1898.

"Do the Old Folks Miss Me?" Cincinnati: George Propheter, 1887.

"Don't Forget to Send for Me." New York: Spaulding and Gray, 1895.

"Don't Hide Your Sweet Face from Me." Cincinnati: George Propheter, 1886.

"Don't Let Her Fall." New York: Howley, Haviland, 1897.

"Don't Move Mother's Picture." Cincinnati: George Propheter, 1887.

"Don't You Miss It on Your Life." New York: John Church, 1895.

"Don't You See That Bright Light?" New York: T. B. Harms, 1890.

"Drifting from Each Other." Cincinnati: George Propheter, 1886.

"Drifting in Poverty Row" or "Down in Poverty Row." New York: Joseph W. Stern, 1896.

"Ever since Melinda Struck the Town." New York: Howley, Haviland, 1895.

"Fair Virginia from Virginia." New York: Howley, Haviland, 1899.

"Fairies Watch Our Little Darling." New York: Hitchcock Music Stores, 1888.

"Faithful Bright Eyes." New York: Hitchcock and McCargo, 1890.

"Fascinating Glance." New York: Hitchcock Music Stores, 1889.

"The Fatal Wedding." New York: Spaulding, Kordner, 1893.

"Fighting Life's Battle Alone." Boston: White-Smith Music, 1897.

"The Gal I Love Loves Me." Chicago: Will Rossiter, 1896.

"The Gal That Stole Miss Liza Jackson's Bean." New York: Hitchcock Music, 1896.

"Get On Your Sneak Shoes, Children." New York: New York Music, 1894.

"The Girl He Didn't Get." New York: Spaulding and Gray, 1895.

"The Girl I Loved Best." Chicago: Will Rossiter, 1896.

"The Girl I Promised to Wed." New York: Spaulding and Gray, 1895.

"The Girl Who Left a Happy Home for Me." New York: Spaulding and Gray, 1894.

"Give Me a Penny." Cincinnati: Newhall and Evans, 1888.

"Give Me Your Answer Today." n.p.: Butterick, 1894.

"Give My Love to Mother Dear." New York: Willis Woodward, 1891.

"Go Where Duty Calls You." Cincinnati: John Church, 1895.

"Good Bye, Old Home, Good Bye." New York: George Propheter, 1887.

"Have Pity Judge, She's My Mother." New York: Hamilton S. Gordon, 1897

"He Carved His Mother's Name upon the Tree." New York: Feist and Frankenthaler, 1898.

"He Found Her in the City." New York: Howley, Haviland, 1899.

"He Is Coming to Us Dead." New York: F. A. Mills, 1899.

"He Will Return to Me." New York: Hitchcock Music Stores, 1889.

"Her Choice." New York: James I. Horton, 1895.

"The Hermit." New York: George Propheter, 1888.

"Hoist up the White Sails." Cincinnati: John Church, 1895.

"Hold Out Dat Light!" Brooklyn: Charles W. Held, 1891.

"Hold Your Temper, Casey." New York: Spaulding and Gray, 1894.

"Home on a Furlough." New York: Howley, Haviland, 1898.

"Honey, Don't You Shake Me." New York: M. Witmark and Sons, 1895.

"How Can We Part?" Cincinnati: George Propheter, 1888.

"I Am Thinking of Home Tonight." Cincinnati: J. C. Groene, 1884.

"I Don't Need You Never No More." New York: Howley, Haviland, 1897.

"I Guess He Knows the Secret Now." New York: Spaulding and Gray, 1894.

"I Just Got a Message from Mars." New York: Howley, Haviland, 1896.

"I Know That Some Day You'll Forget Me." Cincinnati: George Propheter, 1886.

"I Loved Her First." Chicago: Will Rossiter, 1898.

"If Only I Could Blot Out the Past." New York: Hamilton S. Gordon. 1896.

"If They Write That I'm Forgiven, I'll Go Home." New York: Howley, Haviland, 1896.

"I'll Bring It Home to You All the Time." New York: Spaulding and Gray, 1895.

"I'm the Father of a Little Black Coon." New York: George Propheter, 1897.

Gussie Lord Davis; from the collection of David A. Jasen

"In a Little Fisher Village." New York: T. B. Harms, 1897.

"In the Baggage Coach Ahead." New York: Howley, Haviland, 1896.

"Irene Good Night." Cincinnati: George Propheter, 1886.

"I've Been Hoodoo'ed." New York: Spaulding and Gray, 1894.

"Just a Sort a Hangin' Round." New York: Howley, Haviland, 1898.

"Just Ask If He's Forgotten Her." New York: George L. Spaulding, 1897.

"Just beneath the Coffin Lid." New York: Howley, Haviland, 1899.

"Just Outside the Millionaire's Door." New York: James Stillman, 1896.

"Just Set a Light." New York: Howley, Haviland, 1897.

"Just 13." Cincinnati: John Church, 1895.

"Kiss Me Mother, I'm So Sleepy." Cincinnati: George Propheter, 1886.

"The Kiss of a True Wife." New York: Hitchcock and McCargo, 1890.

"A Kiss Was the Cause of It All." New York: Spaulding and Gray, 1895.

"The Ladies of Old." Cincinnati: George Propheter, 1886.

"The Last Fight I Was In." Cincinnati: George Propheter, 1886.

"The Last Kiss Grandmother Gave Me." New York: Willis Woodward, 1893.

"Lay Me Close beside My Mother's Grave." New York: George Propheter, 1888.

"Let All of Us Stay at Home." New York: D. F. Henessey, 1896.

"The Light House by the Sea." Cincinnati: J. C. Groene, 1886.

"Like Echoes of Harp Strings." New York: Hitchcock Music Stores, 1892.

"Little Footsteps in the Snow." Cincinnati: George Propheter, 1886.

"The Little Wife I Left Behind." New York: Howley, Haviland, 1899.

"Make Up and Be Lovers Again." New York: I. Prager, 1893.

"Mamma, Does You Love Your Honey?" New York: Spaulding and Gray, 1894.

"Maxims That I Heard When a Boy." New York: Alberto Heman, 1891.

"McCarthy, the Pride of the Force." New York: George Propheter, 1887.

"McGriffin's Home Run." New York: Willis Woodward, 1891.

"Meet Me at the Mill." Cincinnati: George Propheter, 1886.

"The Mermaid's in Love with Me; or, The Bottom of the Sea." New York: James Stillman, 1893.

"The Midway in the Moon." New York: Spaulding and Gray, 1895.

"Mine Alone." New York: Spaulding and Gray, 1895.

"Mother's the Girl for Me." Cincinnati: John Church, 1895.

"Mother's Words Were True." New York: C. H. Ditson, 1891.

"My Creole Sue." New York: Hamilton S. Gordon, 1898.

"My Sailor Lad's Return." New York: George Propheter, 1887.

"The Mystery of the Village." New York: New York Music, 1894.

"Nearing the Harbor." New York: T. B. Harms, 1887.

"'Neath the Maples Long Ago." Cincinnati: George Propheter, 1886.

"Nettie, Are You Lonely?" New York: B. W. Hitchcock, 1892.

"Never Speak to Me Again." Cincinnati: George Propheter, 1887.

"Nigger, You Won't Go." New York: Howley, Haviland, 1898.

"The Night Father Sent Kate Away." New York: M. Witmark and Sons, 1896.

"De Noble Game of Craps." New York: Howley, Haviland, 1898.

"The Old Church Bells Are Silent." Cincinnati: J. C. Groene, 1884.

"The Old Church Door." New York: E. T. Paull Music, 1898.

"The Old Easy Chair by the Fire." New York: James Stillman, 1892.

"An Old-Fashioned Valentine." New York: James Stillman, 1894.

"Once in a While I See Her." Cincinnati: Charles A. Brutting, 1897.

"One Little Word." New York: Hamilton S. Gordon, 1899.

"Only a Bowery Boy." New York: New York Music, 1894.

"Only a Nigger Baby." New York: Howley, Haviland, 1898.

"Parted at the Altar." Unpublished manuscript.

"Parted by the Sea." Boston: Charles D. Blake, 1889.

"The Pastor's Resignation." New York: Spaulding and Gray, 1895.

"The Patch on My Dear Brother's Pants." Cincinnati: John Church, 1881.

"Picture 84." New York: New York Music, 1894.

"Play on the Stage Every Day." New York: B. W. Hitchcock, 1892.

"The Postman's Welcome Call." New York: James I. Horton, 1895.

"Pretty Blue-Eyed Rose." Cincinnati: George Propheter, 1886.

"Pretty Katie Daley." New York: B. W. Hitchcock, 1892.

"The Reason Bess Went Away." New York: Cruger Brothers, 1894.

"The Rector's Daughter, Nell." St. Louis: Brokaw Music, 1896.

"Sadie's a Lady." New York: Hamilton S. Gordon, 1896.

"Secrets of the Heart." Cincinnati: George Propheter, 1886.

"Send Back the Picture and the Ring." New York: New York Music, 1896.

"Send for the Wanderer." New York: James Stillman, 1892.

"The Sexton Will Never Know." New York: Broder and Schlam, 1897.

"She Haunts Me in My Dreams." Cincinnati: George Propheter, ca. 1886.

"She Waited at the Altar in Vain." New York: Hamilton S. Gordon, 1897.

"She's So Much Like Her Mother." New York: Joseph W. Stern, 1897.

"The Ships in the Harbor Today." New York: B. W. Hitchcock, 1892.

"Since Hannah's Done Learned to Ride a Wheel." New York: Hitchcock Music Stores, 1895.

"Since Nancy Goes to Dancing School." New York: Spaulding and Gray, 1895.

"Sing Again the Sweet Refrain; or, Far from the Old Folks at Home." New York: Spaulding and Gray, 1894.

"The Soldier and Sweetheart That Never Returned." New York: Howley, Haviland, 1899.

"A Story the Villagers Tell." New York: Haviland, 1899.

"Sweet Eily McShane." New York: M. Maetzler, 1891.

"Sweet Norine." New York: Feist and Frankenthaler, 1899.

"Take Care of the Old Folks." Cincinnati: George Propheter, 1886.

"Telephone the News on High." New York: Hitchcock Music Stores, 1889.

"Tell Me If He's True." New York: B. W. Hitchcock, 1892.

"That Strange Coon." Cincinnati: George Propheter, ca. 1886.

"There'd Never Be No Trouble If They'd Kidnapped a Coon." New York: Howley, Haviland, 1899.

"There's Always a Home for You." New York: W. B. Gray, 1899.

"There's No One Like Mother to Me." Cincinnati: J. C. Groene, 1886.

"Too Late." Chicago: National Music, 1895.

"Trusting Only You." New York: Howley, Haviland, 1895.

"'Twas a Sad Trip Coming Back." New York: Spaulding and Gray, 1895.

"Twilight by the Mill." New York: George Propheter, 1887.

"Uncle Eph." Cincinnati: George Propheter, 1886.

"Up Dar in de Sky." Cincinnati: George Propheter, 1886.

"The Village Inn; or, That Old Violin." New York: Hitchcock Music Stores, 1888.

"Vows at the Altar." New York: New York Music, 1894.

"Wait Till the Tide Comes In." New York: George Propheter, 1887.

"Walk for the Golden Crown." New York: Hitchcock Music Stores, 1899.

"The Wanderer's Dream of Home." New York: I. Prager, 1899.

"We Never Meet, 'Tis Better So." New York: Howley, Haviland, 1897.

"We Sat beneath the Maple on the Hill." Cincinnati: F. W. Helmick, 1880.

"We Were Comrades." Cincinnati: Newhall and Evans, 1888.

"Wedded at Last." New York: M. Witmark and Sons, 1894.

"We'll Meet Tonight after Eight." Cincinnati: Ilsen, 1896.

"When Africa and Ireland Go to War." New York: Howley, Haviland, 1898.

"When I Do the Hoochy-Coochy in de Sky." New York: T. B. Harms, 1896.

"When Nelly Was Raking the Hay." Cincinnati: J. C. Groene, 1884.

"When Old Peter Reads You His Riot Act." New York: Willis Woodward, 1891.

"When the Cuckoo Goes to Sleep." Cincinnati: George Propheter, 1886.

"When the Mighty Ship Begins to Roll." New York: W. B. Gray, 1888.

"When the Sun Sets by the Sea." New York: George Propheter, 1887.

"When the Troops Come Home." New York: Howley, Haviland, 1898.

"When They Straightened All the Colored Peoples Hair." New York: Spaulding and Gray, 1894.

"Whenever There's a Woman in the Case." New York: James Stillman, 1892.

"Where the Swallows Nest." New York: Hitchcock Music Stores, 1889.

"White Sails Come Again." New York: C. H. Ditson, 1891.

"Who's Been Here Since I've Been Gone?" Chicago: Will Rossiter, 1898.

"Why Did I Ever Learn to Love You?" Cincinnati: George Propheter, 1886.

"Why Don't You Write a Letter Home?" New York: Howley, Haviland, 1898.

"Why Don't You Write Me a Letter?" New York: George Propheter, 1889.

"The Wrecker's Child." Cincinnati: John Church, 1889.

"Yes, Yes Indeed." Cincinnati: Ilsen, 1896.

"You're Alright, but You Must Stay Out." New York: Howley, Haviland, ca. 1898.

"You're It." New York: W. B. Gray, 1898.

PUBLICATIONS

ABOUT DAVIS
Articles

Kearns, William K. "From Black to White: A Hillbilly Version of Gussie L. Davis's 'The Fatal Wedding.'" *Black Perspective in Music* 2, no. 1 (1974): 29–36.

Southern, Eileen. "In Retrospect: Gussie Lord Davis (1863–1899), Tin Pan Alley Tunesmith." *Black Perspective in Music* 6, no. 2 (1978): 188–230.

Wright, Josephine R. "A Checklist of the Published Compositions of Gussie Lord Davis in the Whittlesey File at the Library of Congress." *Black Perspective in Music* 6, no. 2 (1978): 194–199.

* * * * *

In spite of a short life and even shorter career, Gussie Davis became one of America's more important composers of 19th-century popular song. Among his successes are "The Fatal Wedding," "Only a Bowery Boy," "Parted at the Altar," and his most familiar number, "In the Baggage Coach Ahead." Davis is best known for composing ballads that combined humor with pleasant melodies; for example, "In the Baggage Coach Ahead" was one of late 19th-century America's most popular songs and is still occasionally performed today.

Little is known of Davis's early life except that he was a quiet, unobtrusive individual who grew up in poverty and never finished high school. Excluded from the Nelson Musical College of Cincinnati because he was black, Davis agreed to work as a janitor in exchange for a monthly salary of $15 and private lessons. In 1880, while playing piano in a vaudeville show, he managed to bring out his first song, "We Sat beneath the Maple on the Hill," by giving a publishing firm $20 in exchange for royalties. The song sold well, and Davis rather unexpectedly found himself launched as a creator of popular favorites. Another song, "When Nelly Was Raking the Hay," was dedicated by Davis to Wallace King, a well-known tenor, and it appeared in 1884. Still another, "The Light House by the Sea" (1886), proved so successful that soon afterward Davis was able to move to New York City and establish himself as a "Tin Pan Alley" songwriter. There he became a protégé of James E. Stewart, who almost certainly helped him secure contracts with several prestigious publishing houses.

Davis flourished in New York. His fame as a balladeer became so great that a contest was set up one Sunday evening at Manhattan's Wallach Theater between Davis and James Thornton, another composer of popular songs. Helena Mora, a beautiful vaudeville artiste, sang "Send Back the Picture and the Ring" by Davis and "It Don't Seem like the Same Old Smile" by Thornton (the last number virtually forgotten today). A standing-room-only audience greeted the works of both composers with enthusiasm, and no real winner was declared. The story, however, filled newspaper columns for days afterward, according to the vaudeville star Tom Fletcher. In 1895, though, Davis won second prize in a contest sponsored by the *New York World* to uncover the "ten best songwriters in the United States." His entry, the same song selected for the competition against Thornton, brought Davis $500 in gold and additional publicity. The following year, "In the Baggage Coach Ahead" sold more than a million copies and made Davis one of the two or three best-known songwriters in the world.

But Davis did not depend for all of his income on song writing. Throughout the late 1880s and 1890s, he organized his own company, the Davis Operatic and Plantation Minstrels, and took them on tour shortly before his death. He also performed in concert with Bob Cole and other African-American celebrities. Nor did Davis aspire only to popular success; an opera, entitled *King Herod,* was drafted by him but apparently never finished. In 1899, however, his show *A Hot Old Time in Dixie* was successfully launched on a national tour. His sudden death in October of that year left his partner, Tom McIntosh, responsible for the remaining performances.

As a composer, Davis could be described as a talented opportunist; at least this is one way of understanding his career. Unquestionably, he was a man who wrote ballads that combined pleasant melodies with sentimental texts. Almost all of Davis's songs devolve on hackneyed melodramatic situations, and many of them make use of racial stereotypes offensive to many Americans even before the turn of the century. In one of his 1880s numbers, for example—a mock spiritual entitled "Up Dar in de Sky"—Davis created what Sam Dennison has called "a travesty of black music without the remotest propinquity for the real thing." Dennison also considers another of Davis's songs, the successful "When I Do the Hoochy-Coochy in de Sky," a "nonpareil insult to the black religious experience." The lyrics to this last number include the words "I know you coons will stare/When I fly up through the air,/When I bid all of you black chromos good bye;/I will raise a big sensation with the white population,/When I do the hoochy-coochy in de sky!"

There is, however, a different way of understanding Davis's place in musical history. Unlike some black composers, he unquestionably catered to prejudiced white tastes. Yet most of his songs, "In the Baggage Coach Ahead" among them, sound today like send-ups of the sentimental ballads so popular with refined white music lovers of the 1880s and 1890s. Praising Davis for composing "the greatest tear-jerker[s] of the time," the ragtime pianist James P. Johnson called some of his works "white-style ballads," and in *Black Manhattan,* James Weldon Johnson went further: according to him, Davis became before his death "a typical New York writer, whose songs have not the slightest relation to the south or even to the Negro." Davis, therefore, can also be understood as a talented tunesmith with a penchant for catering to every possible taste, black or white. Or, as Jack Burton has it, Davis "aimed his tunes at the tear glands of the public."

SELECTED WORKS

"The Fatal Wedding" (1893), one of Davis's tear-jerkers, is set to words by the popular singer William Windom. "The Fatal Wedding" opens with an 11-bar introduction that manages to combine

the theme of the "Wedding March" from Mendelssohn's incidental music to *A Midsummer Night's Dream* with something that sounds like the opening instrumental solo from "Let the Merry Bells Ring Round" in Handel's *L'Allegro.* In other words, Davis pulled out "classical" stops in order to captivate his listeners. At bar 12, however, the music suddenly switches from duple to triple meter, and the verse of Davis's own "excellent" Bowery-waltz tune begins.

A very few measures later, an appropriately sentimental reference to C major (the subdominant chord in the tonic key of G major) at the words "a moonlight winter's night" leaves behind the cheerful mood of the introduction and suggests the pathos that is to come. Like other turn-of-the-century ballads, "The Fatal Wedding" has several long verses followed by a repeated and shorter chorus and a coda that serves also as a vamp. Its only unusual feature is the presence of three verses; most contemporary songs had, at most, two. Much of the effect of Davis's song is in the words of Windom's text: an abandoned mother interrupts a wedding in progress because "the bridegroom is my husband, sir, and this [the baby she's holding] our little child." Alas! the infant is already dead from exposure, but the errant father confirms the truth of his abandoned wife's words when, "before the break of day," he too dies, and by his own hand. As Sigmund Spaeth has pointed out, though, not even the "monumental silliness" of Windom's words damages "the song's appeal to a public that doted on vicarious infidelity, sudden death, and artificial melodrama in general."

"In the Baggage Coach Ahead" (1896) features two extraordinarily long verses, written by Davis himself, followed by a shorter chorus. The piece employs no musical quotations, and Davis's almost inevitable waltz tune is genteel in style and mood. The story is luridly melodramatic: a young father, criticized by several passengers because his child is disturbing them during a railway journey, gives a heartbreaking answer to their callous questions: "Where is its mother, go take it to her,"/This a lady then softly said,/"I wish that I could" was the man's sad reply,/"But she's dead, in the coach ahead."

The rest of Davis's output draws on different traditions, including those of the coon song ("Up Dar in de Sky," 1886) and the temperance ballad ("Fighting Life's Battle Alone," 1897). Numbers like "Up Dar," however, contain no real ragtime features and, in fact, predate by several years such trend-setting numbers as Ernest Hogan's 1896 sensation "All Coons Look Alike to Me" or the gentler, more ironic songs of Bob Cole and the Johnson brothers. "Fighting Life's Battles Alone," for instance, opens with a slow piano introduction in duple time. In no way unusual, this introduction nevertheless incorporates the circle-of-fifths progressions associated at the turn of the century not only with the sentimental song but with the German (i.e., the "cultivated") musical tradition. The melody of the verse that follows contains a number of arpeggiated figures, suggesting a slowish military march. All these features can also be found in temperance songs of the 1870s and 1880s, as can the switch to triple meter at the chorus. "Fighting Life's Battles," however, is about feminine virtue, not abstinence from drink. The lyrics, written by William H. Gardner, are as saccharine as some of Davis's own. Although her "sweet dreams of home" have "flown," the maiden narrator's honor, carefully nurtured in her childhood by Mother, enables her to "still withstand the tempter, While she battled life alone."

REFERENCES

Burton, Jack. *The Blue Book of Tin Pan Alley: A Human Interest Anthology of American Popular Music.* Watkins Glen, N.Y.: Century House, 1951.

Cuney-Hare, Maud. *Negro Musicians and Their Music.* Washington, D.C.: Associated Publishers, 1936.

Dennison, Sam. *Scandalize My Name: Black Imagery in American Popular Music.* New York: Garland Publishing, 1982.

Fletcher, Tom. *100 Years of the Negro in Show Business.* New York: Burdge, 1954.

Hasse, John Edward, ed. *Ragtime: Its History, Composers, and Music.* New York: Schirmer Books, 1985.

Johnson, James Weldon. *Black Manhattan.* New York: Alfred A. Knopf, 1930.

Spaeth, Sigmund. *A History of Popular Music in America.* New York: Random House, 1948.

Tawa, Nicholas E. *The Way to Tin Pan Alley: American Popular Song, 1866–1910.* New York: Schirmer Books, 1990.

MICHAEL SAFFLE

DAWSON, WILLIAM LEVI

Born in Anniston, Ala., September 26, 1899; died in Montgomery, Ala., May 2, 1990. **Education:** Tuskegee Institute, Ala., studied instrumental performance with Frank L. Drye and harmony with Carter Simmons, 1914–21; Washburn College, Topeka, Kans., studied composition with Henry V. Stearns, 1921–22; Horner Institute of Fine Arts in Kansas City, Mo., studied composition with Carl Busch and Regina G. Hall, 1922–25, B.Mus., 1925; American Conservatory of Music, Chicago, Ill., studied composition with Adolph Weidig, M.Mus. in composition, 1927; Chicago Musical College, studied composition with Thornvald Otterstrom and Felix Borowski, ca. 1930–31; Eastman School of Music, Rochester, N.Y., completed additional graduate work. **Composing and Performing Career:** Toured the Redpath Chautaqua Circuit in New England as trombonist and tenor, 1921; Kansas City, performed as jazz trombonist in various ensembles, 1922–26; first trombone for the Chicago Civic Orchestra, 1926–1930; Tuskegee Institute, began conducting the Tuskegee Choir, 1932; New York City, conducted the Tuskegee Choir at opening of Radio City Music Hall, December 27, 1932; invited to perform at the White House by President Herbert Hoover, 1933; participated in birthday festivities for President-elect Franklin D. Roosevelt, 1933; Academy of Music in Philadelphia, Philadelphia Orchestra under Leopold Stokowski premiered *Negro Folk Symphony*, 1934; traveled to western Africa where he studied native music of several countries, 1952–53; retired from Tuskegee Institute, 1955; sent to Spain as choral conductor by the U.S. Department of State, July–August 1956; Nashville, Tenn., invited to conduct the Fisk University Choir, 1958–59; continued activity as guest conductor and lecturer; Atlanta University Complex, served as a consultant, 1970; Chicago, Ebenezer A.M.E. Church, choir director. **Teaching Career:** Kansas Vocational College, Topeka, Kans., director of music, 1921–22; Lincoln High School, Kansas City, Kans., director of music, 1922–25; Tuskegee Institute, established the school's music curriculum as head of school of music, 1931–55. **Commissions:** Columbia Broadcasting System, 1940. **Honors/ Awards:** Chicago Daily News Prize for Contest of Band Directors, 1929; two Rodman Wanamaker prizes, 1930; third Wanamaker prize, 1931; Tuskegee Institute in Alabama, honorary doctorate, 1955; University of Missouri at Kansas City, Alumni Achievement Award, 1963; Third Annual Workshop on Afro-American Music, Atlanta, Ga., honoree, 1974; elected to Alabama Arts Hall of Fame, 1975; American Choral Directors Association Award, 1975; Lincoln University, Lincoln, Pa., honorary Doctor of Laws, 1978; Alabama Coalition for the Arts and Humanities at Alabama State University, Alabama Fine Arts Award, 1980; Marshall Bartholomew Award, 1981; Ithaca College, Ithaca, N.Y., honorary Doctor of Music, 1982; Heinecke Award, 1983; inducted into Alabama Hall of Fame, 1989; honored again by American Choral Directors Association at Southern Division Convention, March 1990; honorary plaque from Georgia State University; University of Michigan School of Music, citation for distinguished contributions to the understanding of African-American folk song.

MUSIC LIST

INSTRUMENTAL SOLOS
Violin

Sonata for Violin and Piano. 1927. Unpublished manuscript. Recorded: Westminster W-9633.

Piano

"Interlude." Unpublished manuscript.

SMALL INSTRUMENTAL ENSEMBLE

Trio in A Major (piano, violin, cello). 1925. Unpublished manuscript.

FULL ORCHESTRA

Negro Folk Symphony. 1932; revised 1952. Delaware Water Gap, Pa.: Shawnee Music, 1965. Note: originally titled Symphony no. 1 in E-flat Major. Contents: The Bond of Africa; Hope in the Night; O Le' Me Shine. Premiere, 1934. Recorded: Decca DL 710077; MCA Records MCAD2-9826A; Musical Heritage Society 513912A.

Negro Work Song. 1940. Unpublished manuscript. Commissioned by Columbia Broadcasting System for American School of the Air.

Scherzo. 1930. Unpublished manuscript. Note: won Wanamaker Prize, 1930.

ORCHESTRA (CHAMBER OR FULL) WITH CHORUS

Break, Break, Break. 1928. Unpublished manuscript.

SOLO VOICE

"Forever Thine." Tuskegee, Ala.: Music Press of Tuskegee Institute, 1920.

"Go to Sleep" (low voice). Chicago: H. T. FitzSimons, 1926. Also arranged for SATB, SSA, and TTBB chorus.

"Jump Back, Honey, Jump Back." Kansas City, Mo.: Wunderlichs Piano Co., 1923.

"Out in the Fields." Chicago: Gamble Hinged Music, 1929. Also arranged for voice and orchestra, SATB and piano or orchestra, and SSAA unaccompanied. Recorded: Desto DC-7107.

CHORAL MUSIC

"Before the Sun Goes Down" (SATB). Park Ridge, Ill.: Kjos Music, 1978.

"Feed-a My Sheep" (SATB). Tuskegee, Ala.: Music Press of Tuskegee Institute, 1971. Also arranged for TTBB and SSAA.

"Lovers Plighted" (SATB). Unpublished manuscript. Note: won Wanamaker Prize, 1931.

"The Rugged Yank" (TTBB). Chicago: Gamble Hinged Music, 1930. Note: originally titled "The Mongrel Yanks: A Yankee Is a Mixture of Many Races," op. 6. Also arranged for male voice and piano.

"Slumber Song" (SATB). Tuskegee, Ala.: Music Press of Tuskegee Institute, 1974. Also arranged for SSA, SA, and TTBB.

William Levi Dawson; courtesy of Hawkins Studio, Tuskegee, Alabama

PUBLICATIONS

ABOUT DAWSON
Book
Spady, James G., ed. *William L. Dawson: A Umum Tribute and a Marvelous Journey.* Philadelphia: Creative Artists' Workshop, 1981.

Dissertations and Theses
Johnson, David Lee. "The Contributions of William L. Dawson to the School of Music at Tuskegee Institute and to Choral Music." Ed.D. thesis, University of Illinois at Urbana-Champaign, 1987.

Macmillan, William Robert. "The Choral Music of William Dawson." D.A. thesis, University of Northern Colorado, 1991.

Malone, Mark Hugh. "William Levi Dawson: American Music Educator." Ph.D. diss., Florida State University, 1981.

Shingles, Samuel D. "William Levi Dawson: The Man and His Music." M.M. thesis, Bowling Green State University, 1994.

Thompson, Jacqueline Kay. "William Levi Dawson (b. 1898) and an Analysis of His *Negro Folk Symphony* (1932; rev. 1952)." M.M. thesis, Conservatory of Music, University of Missouri, Kansas City, 1979.

Articles
Brown, Rae Linda. "William Grant Still, Florence Price, and William Dawson: Echoes of the Harlem Renaissance." In *Black Music in the Harlem Renaissance: A Collection of Essays,* edited by Samuel A. Floyd Jr., 71–86. Westport, Conn.: Greenwood Press, 1990.

Haberlen, John B. "William Dawson and the Copyright Act (A Victim of Arrangers)." *Choral Journal* 23, no. 7 (1983): 5–8.

Malone, Mark Hugh. "William Levi Dawson and the Tuskegee Choir." *Choral Music* 30 (August 1990): 17–19.

Perry, Frank, Jr. "William Levi Dawson." In *Afro-American Vocal Music: A Select Guide to Fifteen Composers,* 34–38. Berrien Springs, Mich.: Vande Vere Pub., 1991.

Tischler, Alice. "William Levi Dawson." In *Fifteen Black American Composers: A Bibliography of Their Works,* 107–123. Detroit Studies in Musical Bibliography, no. 45. Detroit: Information Coordinators, 1981.

BY DAWSON
"Interpretation of the Religious Folk-Songs of the American Negro." *Etude* 73 (March 1955): 11, 58, 61.

* * * * *

The distinguished career of William L. Dawson spanned nearly eight decades, during which time he became one of the 20th century's most respected African-American composers. Along with William Grant Still and Florence Price in the 1930s, Dawson played a role in establishing an orchestral tradition based on African-American folk idioms. His *Negro Folk Symphony* (1932) was both a crystallization of Harlem Renaissance ideals and a distillation of his passion for African-American folk music. Dawson's orchestral music occupies a modest but significant niche in his musical *oeuvre;* it was his role as a composer, arranger, and conductor of African-American vocal music (especially spirituals) that brought him sustained international acclaim.

Dawson was born in the town of Anniston, Alabama, at the end of a generation of African-Americans that had experienced or witnessed profound social setbacks. The demise of Reconstruction, the implementation of the "separate but equal" policy of *Plessy vs. Ferguson,* and the proliferation of "Jim Crow" laws sounded a death knell for optimistic efforts at assimilation in the decades immediately following the Civil War. In this nadir in cultural morale, Booker T. Washington proposed social policies that aimed to inspire and empower African Americans, an undertaking that would profoundly affect the aspirations of young William Dawson.

In 1881, Washington founded his own school, which later became Tuskegee Institute, and Dawson enrolled as a young teenager determined to follow the self-help mantra of its founder and president. Though Tuskegee was renowned for its "industrial education" curriculum, Dawson found ample opportunities to cultivate his musical talents during his student years. He began to nurture a burgeoning interest in African-American folksong, which would soon become the foundation of his compositional aesthetic. He played trombone in the band, sang in the choir, and studied piano and composition; his first copyrighted piece, the song "Forever Thine" (1920), was written while he was a Tuskegee student.

After completing his studies at Tuskegee in 1921, Dawson moved to Topeka, Kansas, and then to Kansas City, Missouri, where he taught at Lincoln High School in Kansas City, Kansas, and pursued a bachelor of music degree at the Horner Institute of Fine Arts, Kansas City, Missouri. Dawson's Trio for Piano, Violin, and Cello was performed at his graduation from Horner Institute in 1925; however, he was not able to acknowledge the applause for the piece or receive his diploma during the commencement ceremonies; a Euro-American student accepted it for him because of the school's segregationist policies.

In addition to his teaching duties and his musical studies, Dawson became absorbed in the city's flourishing jazz scene. He prospered as a professional trombonist in several of the city's jazz ensembles. Outside the musical realm, Dawson expanded his awareness of the new forces that were shaping the fabric of African-American cultural life in the 1920s. These currents were centered upon the activities of the Harlem Renaissance, which were not geographically restricted to the New York City area. While staying at the colored YMCA in Kansas City, Dawson made the acquaintance of two men who would become intrinsically connected with these currents: Roy Wilkins, then a young journalist, who would later become the executive director of the NAACP; and Aaron Douglass, a native Kansan whose paintings based on African and African-American folk themes would make him the most celebrated visual artist of the Harlem Renaissance.

With his move to Chicago in 1926, Dawson continued to expand his musical horizons, which by now encompassed jazz, concert, and religious musics. Like Kansas City, Chicago teemed with first-rate jazz musicians, including Louis and Lillian Armstrong, Johnny Dodds, and Earl "Fatha" Hines; Dawson occasionally performed with these artists as either a trombonist or bassist. On a more regular basis, he performed in Jimmy Noone's Apex Orchestra and with "Doc" Cook and the 14 Doctors of Syncopation (with whom he made several recordings). He supplemented his study of concert music at several institutions in Chicago and received advanced tutelage in Germany at the Hamburg conservatory. In addition to these activities, Dawson served as the music director of the choir at the Ebenezer A.M.E. Church—one of Chicago's largest—and began to publish numerous spiritual arrangements.

While Dawson was preparing music for the World's Fair of 1933, Robert R. Moton, Booker T. Washington's successor as president of Tuskegee Institute, invited him to return to Tuskegee to establish a music school. Dawson accepted and proceeded to select a 12-member faculty, almost all of whom had studied at prestigious American conservatories. He also established a 50-member glee club in preparation for a celebration of the school's 50th anniversary. On December 27, 1932, national attention was focused upon Dawson as a result of the Tuskegee Choir's performance at the opening of New York's Radio City Music Hall, where the group was held over for six weeks. Critical response was overwhelmingly favorable, and one typical review stated that the choir under Dawson ranked "among the truly great choral organizations of the musical world." The next 25 years of Dawson's life would be spent at Tuskegee; after his departure, he served as a guest conductor and musical ambassador at venues throughout the United States and around the world.

Dawson's vocal music, primarily for large ensembles, forms the core of his compositional output. He achieved lasting fame with his arrangements of spirituals (a lifelong endeavor), but he also set to music the poetry of Alfred Tennyson (*Break, Break, Break,* 1928) and Elizabeth Barrett Browning ("Out in the Fields," 1929). Dawson's major contributions to the orchestral repertoire are Scherzo (1930), *Negro Folk Symphony* (1932; revised 1952), and *Negro Work Song* (1940), all composed while he was a relatively young man. Works for smaller instrumental combinations include a Trio for Piano, Violin, and Cello (1925), a Sonata for Violin and Piano (1927), and an "Interlude" (n.d.) for solo piano.

The rubric conventionally assigned to Dawson's musical style is "neoromantic," but this label perhaps confines his influences too narrowly to the European concert tradition and disregards important contemporary movements, especially jazz. For the most part, Dawson's harmonic language is tonal, tinged by moments of dissonance and extended chromaticism. The primacy Dawson accorded to African-American folksong forms the foundation of his approach to musical texture. His text settings generally allow for the clearest possible declamation, even within the context of dense contrapuntal activity. Registral extremes are rarely exploited; instead Dawson relies on various groups and combinations of instruments to achieve textural variety. Dawson's fascination with rhythm dates from his early stints in jazz ensembles, and his subtle use of syncopation and shifting meters is especially noteworthy. A visit to West Africa in 1952 prompted him to investigate the relationship between African-American and African rhythms and led to a revision of the *Negro Folk Symphony* in the same year.

Inspired by the cultural achievements of African Americans in the decades immediately following the Civil War, Dawson endeavored to bring the folk music of his youth to the concert hall. His music embodies the aesthetic ideals of Dvořák and the Harlem Renaissance intellectuals, both of whom hoped for a tradition of concert music based on African-American folk idioms. The premiere of the *Negro Folk Symphony* in 1934 hailed Dawson as one of the most significant American composers of his generation, although in later years he established a reputation as a first-rank composer and conductor of choral music. His enthusiastic advocacy of African-American concert music resonated with audiences and critics from the age of Booker T. Washington through the post–Civil Rights era.

NEGRO FOLK SYMPHONY (1932; REVISED 1952)

The *Negro Folk Symphony* is Dawson's response to the complex and often conflicting stylistic innovations of American music in the 1930s. As Southern has said, Dawson's immediate musical goal was to "write a symphony in the Negro folk idiom, based on authentic folk music but in the same form used as the composers of the [European] romantic-nationalist school."

Written in the key of E-flat major, the work consists of three movements, each with programmatic subtitles. The first and third movements are in sonata form, and the second movement is a loosely structured ABA song form. The symphony is unified by a pentatonic "missing link" or leading motive, which appears periodically throughout the piece. The motive symbolizes the "link [that] was taken out of a human chain when the first African was taken from the shores of his native land and sent to slavery," according to the composer. The themes of the symphony, which recur throughout, are taken from the body of Negro spirituals.

The first movement, "The Bond of Africa," begins with a slow introduction (*Adagio,* 4/4 time) in which the leading motive is stated in a "call" by the solo horn over tremolo strings. The "response" is provided by a trochaic (long-short) rhythmic idea in the winds and low brass. The first theme is announced by a solo horn and then extended by the clarinets. A transitional section based on the leading motive is followed by the oboe's presentation of the second theme, which is based on the spiritual "Oh, M' Littl' Soul Gwine-a Shine." New musical material subsequently appears in the strings and then in the entire orchestra—a heavily accented, almost percussive passage that suggests "the clapping of hands and patting of feet." A development section expands fragments of the two main themes and the leading motive; the passages featuring the leading motive are highlighted by sudden and dramatic changes in tempo (from *allegro* to *adagio*) and *fortissimo* dynamics. The presentation of themes in the recapitulation is similar to that of the exposition, with the "clapping and patting" passage functioning as a transition linking the themes. The movement concludes with a brief coda.

The second movement (*Andante,* 4/4), "Hope in the Night," begins with three strokes from the gong, suggesting the Trinity. The main theme of the A section (in B minor) is stated by the English horn and accompanied by a gently plodding ostinato in the harp. The atmosphere of the middle B section is more upbeat, beginning with a spirited, rhythmic theme in the oboes. After an extended development of this theme, a change of mood is foreshadowed by a presentation of the leading motive, followed by alternating short sections of the first and second themes. The final A section commences with a change in tempo to the original *andante,* and shortly thereafter, the full orchestra engages in a grandiose restatement of the theme of the A section. The movement subsides with a series of *crescendos* and *decrescendos* and finally dissolves amidst three pulses of the gong over the steady pulse of the tenor drum (tom-tom).

The final movement (*Allegro con brio*, 2/2), "O Le' Me Shine," is in sonata form. The two themes of the exposition are both based on the spirituals, "O Le' Me Shine, Lik' a Mornin' Star" (first theme) and "Hallelujah, Lord I Been Down into the Sea" (second theme). The first theme, whose melodic contour closely resembles that of the leading motive, is spun out by the woodwinds; the second theme is stated by the oboe. The two themes are reworked during the development, where the composer employs call-and-response figures and rhythmic augmentation. The sequence of themes in the recapitulation mirrors that of the exposition. After the ensuing coda, the symphony concludes with the melody of "O le' me shine lik' a mornin' star" dramatically proclaimed by the brass.

The *Negro Folk Symphony* was performed by the Philadelphia Orchestra under Leopold Stokowski at the Philadelphia Academy of Music on November 14, 15, and 17, 1934, and at Carnegie Hall in New York City on November 20, 1934. The New York audience received the work enthusiastically, as did a majority of the critics. Reviewers, while noting that the symphony was a momentous cultural achievement, criticized what they felt to be too obvious a debt to Dvořák. Olin Downes of the *New York Times* stated that the symphony had some superb moments but was weakened by "conventional passages of symphonic padding." As expected, critics with allegiance to the Harlem Renaissance rendered favorable responses. *The Crisis* declared that the "folk music of the symphony still lives among the Negro people [Dawson] knows." Alain Locke wrote that the work demonstrated "mastery of the full resources of the modern orchestra," and that Dawson's symphony, along with the works of Still and Price, hailed the inauguration of an African-American orchestral tradition.

INTERLUDE

"Interlude," for piano, is Dawson's only surviving composition for solo piano; it is a work in the tradition of the 19th-century character (or salon) pieces of Schubert, Schumann, Brahms, and Chopin. Despite the brevity of the piece (only about five pages), it is a dense work that unwinds at a leisurely pace with detailed expressive markings in almost every measure. It is reminiscent of an improvisatory exercise that surprisingly becomes a composition, dividing neatly into four discrete sections demarcated by changes in tempo.

The first section of the work, marked *Lento* (72 beats per minute) and set in a waltz-like triple meter, gives the vague impression of a dance in which the music stops and starts quite frequently. It is filled with arppegiated chords, short motives, and halting phrases.

At the beginning of the next section, the tempo increases slightly (80 beats per minute). A subtle rhythmic tension is present here, due in part to the rhythmic pattern of two-against-three, divided between the hands. The nebulous tone of the piece is effected by melodic phrases that end inclusively, with harmonic suspensions outlined by arpeggios replacing a clear cadential sequence.

The piece gains additional momentum in its third section (84 beats per minute), and the fluctuating harmonies and rhythmic tension continue to increase the sense of instability. The work becomes more virtuosic as sequences of octaves in the left hand are added. Finally, tonal resolution arrives as the section ends on a D major chord.

The final section of the piece begins in a manner similar to the first but rapidly moves toward closure. The composer initiates a drive toward the final cadence, with elaborate scale passages in the right hand played over octaves and diminished chords in the left; this frenzy of musical activity halts momentarily on a climactic chord (A-flat ninth). A return to the musical texture of the beginning rounds out the musical form, which concludes with a final cadence. The sonority of the final chord (B-flat major seventh) provides the expected completion but with a touch of dissonance, leaving the listener with expectations yet to be fulfilled.

BREAK, BREAK, BREAK (1928) AND OUT IN THE FIELDS (1929)

Dawson created choral settings of texts by two English-language poets: "Break, Break, Break" (poetry by Alfred Tennyson) and "Out in the Fields" (poetry attributed to both Elizabeth Barrett Browning and Louise Imogen Guiney). A discussion of Dawson's arrangements of these two works for orchestra and chorus (SATB) follows, though Dawson arranged *Out in the Fields* for several different combinations of voices and instruments.

Tennyson's poem is a tribute to Arthur Hallam (also the subject of "In Memoriam A.H.H.") and is a celebration of life that evolves from the melancholy of death. The first image of the poem is a mourner contemplating the loss of a friend as waves break upon a seashore (stanza 1). The shouts of a fisherman's son playing with his sister and the singing of a young sailor interrupt this reverie as the mourner begins to remember the joyous sounds of life (stanzas 2 and 3) and accept the friend's death (stanzas 3 and 4).

Dawson's setting (C major, 4/4) commences with a 16-measure instrumental introduction divided into four sections. The first and third sections of the introduction are marked *Grave* and share similar motivic material; the second and fourth sections are marked *Allegro* and have analogous melodic and rhythmic constructions. The tempo *Allegro* precedes the first vocal incantation, "Break, Break, Break." The first three words of the poem are boldly set in whole-note chords, which form a striking sequence of harmonies (C major–A major–F-sharp minor). These chords are accompanied by a flurry of chromatic scales. As the section closes with a strong (C major) cadence on the word "sea," the meter of the piece changes to 12/8 and continues through the next musical section; Dawson utilizes this technique of overlapping metrical changes with strong cadences throughout the composition. Beginning with the stanza's third line, the vocal texture shifts from homophonic to polyphonic, perhaps suggesting the myriad thoughts described by the poet. The music of the first stanza closes on another strong (E major) cadence.

The second stanza (*Andante*) begins with a tenor solo that is soon followed by a bass solo, both depicting joy from the perspectives of the fisherman's boy and the sailor lad. The full chorus is employed for the final line of the stanza, "That he sings in his boat on the bay" (which concludes in the key of G major).

The third stanza is a contrast of musical moods. The section begins with the voices entering in pairs; tenor and bass, then soprano and alto ("And the stately ships go on . . ."). The tempo is *Moderato,* the key is A major, and the meter is a gently rocking 6/8. Another tenor solo introduces the third line of the stanza,

"But O for the touch of a vanished hand," then the vocal texture returns to a full chorus alternating between polyphony and homophony. Overall, this section is solemn and hymn-like, reaching a momentary resolution on a somber chord (B-flat minor). The vocal texture then returns to imitative polyphony, climaxing on the word "voice," and quickly dying away.

A piano cadenza, which grows out of a *decrescendo* from the previous section, provides an instant of relief before the start of the final section of music. The last stanza begins as the first (*Allegro*) with the three-note motive "Break, Break, Break." The second half of the stanza gradually builds to a climax on a tense, unstable chord (F-sharp diminished) at the word "back." An *a cappella* passage in which the chorus reiterates the words "never, never come back to me" fades to a *pianissimo* chord, which is overlaid with arpeggios reminiscent of the piano cadenza that began the section.

Out in the Fields (E-flat major, 4/4) is dedicated to Dawson's wife Cornella. The text describes the poet's awareness of God's presence in nature. The piece begins in a tranquil mood, tempo *Moderato*. After a two-measure introduction, the full chorus enters ("The little cares that fretted me"). The gentle ambiance of this first section is underscored by short melodic ideas (mostly two-measure phrases) set in vocal homophony and doubled by accompanying instruments.

The second section begins with a tempo change (*Presto*), and the tone of the poem shifts from tranquillity to a resoluteness. This change of tone is enhanced by snappy entrances of paired voices (soprano and alto, then tenor and bass), and the spirit of the section is intensified through heavily accented (*sforzando*) emphasis on the phrase "cast away" and poignant chromaticism in both the melody and harmony.

The final section of the piece reverts to the tempo of the first section (*Moderato*), but the music here is forceful. The broad, *cantabile* melody is often doubled by the winds and strings, and the closing passage is a chorale-like setting of the poem's title, a pious testament to God and nature.

REFERENCES

Brown, Rae Linda. "William Grant Still, Florence Price, and William Dawson: Echoes of the Harlem Renaissance." In *Black Music of the Harlem Renaissance: A Collection of Essays,* edited by Samuel A. Floyd, Jr., 71–86. Westport, Conn: Greenwood Press, 1990.

Butcher, Harold. "The Dawson Folk Symphony." *The Crisis* (February 1935): 47–48.

Dawson, William. *Negro Folk Symphony.* Leopold Stokowski and the American Symphony Orchestra. MCA Records, VC 81056. Reissue of Decca Gold Label Series records, DL 10077, Stereo DL 710077, 1978.

Downes, Olin. "Stokowski Gives American Works." *New York Times* (November 21, 1934): 22.

Locke, Alain. *The Negro and His Music,* Washington, D.C.: Associates in Negro Folk Education, 1936. Reprint, New York: Arno Press and the *New York Times,* 1969.

Southern, Eileen. *The Music of Black Americans.* 2nd ed. New York: W. W. Norton, 1983.

Spady, James G., ed. *William L. Dawson: A Umum Tribute and a Marvelous Journey.* Philadelphia: Creative Artists' Workshop, 1981.

WILLIE STRONG

DÉDÉ, EDMOND

Born in New Orleans, La., November 20, 1827; died in Paris, France, January 4, 1901. **Education:** New Orleans, La., studied violin with Constantin Debergue, director of the local Philharmonic Society, and Ludovico Gabici, director of the St. Charles Theater orchestra; studied counterpoint and harmony with Eugène Prévost, conductor of the orchestras at the Théâtre d'Orléans and the French Opera of New Orleans, and with Charles Richard Lambert, conductor of the Philharmonic Society; Paris, studied violin with Jean-Delphin Alard and composition with Jacques-François Fromental Halévy, 1857. **Composing and Performing Career:** Grand Théâtre, Bordeaux, France, conductor, ca. 1860; Théâtre de l'Alcazar orchestra, director, 1865–69, 1872; Grand Orchestra, Arcachon, director, 1869; Folies Bordelaises, Bordeaux, director, 1885–89; Concerts Delta, Bordeaux, director, 1870–72; Marseilles, 1873–76; Bordeaux-Bastide, 1880–85; Paris, composer, 1891–93; New Orleans, returned to give concerts over several months, 1893–94. **Memberships:** French Society of Authors, Composers, and Editors of Music, by mid-1880s; Société des Jeunes-Amis, ca. 1893; Society of Dramatic Authors and Composers in Paris, full member, by 1894.

MUSIC LIST

INSTRUMENTAL SOLOS
Piano
"Mirliton fin de siècle: Polka originale." Paris: E. Fromont, 1891.

"Mèphisto masqué: Polka fantastique." Paris: Bathlot et Hèraud, 1889. Also arranged for orchestra. Recorded: Columbia MT 34533.

"Mon sous off'cier: Quadrille brillant." Bordeaux: E. Philibert, 1877.

"El pronunciamento (la conspiration): Marche espagnole." Paris: Bathlot et Hèraud, 1886.

SMALL INSTRUMENTAL ENSEMBLE
"Rêverie champêtre: Fantasie" (violin and cello or flute and bassoon, piano). Paris: Author, 1891.

FULL ORCHESTRA
Arcadia ouverture. Note: manuscript lost.

Chicago: Grand valse à l'américaine. Paris: E. Fromont, 1891. Also arranged for piano.

Le Palmier ouverture. Note: manuscript lost. Premiere, 1865.

Symphony: *Quasimodo.* ca. 1865. Note: manuscript lost.

Sylvia ouverture. Note: manuscript lost.

SOLO VOICE
"Les Adieux du coursier: Chant dramatique oriental." Paris: E. Fromont, 1888.

"C'est la faute à Colas." Paris: L. Couderc, 1881.

"Comme une soeur." Paris: F. Guillemain, 1887.

"La Conspiration des amoureux: D'après le Pronunciamento Marche espagnole." Paris: Bathlot et Hèraud, 1887.

"Cora la bordelaise." Bordeaux: E. Philibert, 1881.

"L'Ermitage ou l'hospice de St. Vincent de Paul à Pouy près Dax (Landes): Romance religieuse." Bordeaux: E. Philibert, 1865.

"Françoise et Cortillard." Bordeaux: E. Philibert, 1877.

"Le Garçon troquet: Chanson-type." Paris: Raymond Viel et Masson, 1887.

"J'la connais!" Paris: Chez Duhem, 1884.

"La Klephte: Chant dramatique oriental." Paris: E. Fromont, 1888.

"La Malagaise: Seguedille." Paris: E. Fromont.

"Le marin de la France: Chansonnette de bord." Bordeaux: E. Philibert, 1865.

"Mon pauvre coeur: Mélodie." New Orleans: n.p., 1852.

"Mon sous off." Bordeaux: E. Philibert, 1876.

"Une noce en musique: Chansonnette comique." Paris: Bathlot et Hèraud, 1889.

"Ous'qu'est mon toréador?" Paris: Bathlot et Hèraud, 1889.

"Patriotisme." Note: manuscript lost.

"Quasimodo!" Bordeaux: E. Philibert, 1865.

"Rosita: Cancion sevillanne." Paris: J. Poulalion, 1890.

"Le serment de l'Arabe: Chant dramatique." Bordeaux: E. Philibert, 1865. Note: reprinted in *Music and Some Highly Musical People,* by James M. Trotter, 53–59. New York: Johnson Reprint Corp., 1968.

"Si j'étais lui" (Should I Be He). New Orleans: A. E. Blackman, ca. 1893.

"Titis: Débardeurs et grisettes." Paris: Smite, 1876.

"Tond les chiens, coup'les chats: Duo burlesque." Paris: Puigellier et Bassereau, 1893.

VOCAL ENSEMBLE
"Kikipatchouli et Kakaoli: Duo chinois" (vocal duet). Paris: G. Ondet, 1891.

CHORAL MUSIC
"La Journée champêtre." Paris: E. Fromont, 1890.

DRAMATIC MUSIC
L'Abile de la chouette: Féerie (dramatic piece). Note: manuscript lost.

Ables (ballet). Note: manuscript lost.

L'Anneau du diable: Féerie (dramatic piece in three acts). 1880. Note: manuscript lost.

L'Anthropophage (operetta in one act). 1880. Note: manuscript lost.

Après le miel (opéra comique). 1880. Note: manuscript lost.

Une aventure de Télémaque (opera). Note: manuscript lost.

Battez aux champs: Cantate dédiée à L. M. l'Empereur Napoléon III (cantata). 1865. Unpublished manuscript.

Le Sultan d'Ispahan (opera). ca. 1886. Note: manuscript lost.

PUBLICATIONS

ABOUT DÉDÉ
Articles

LaBrew, Arthur R. "Edmond Dédé (dit Charentos), 1827–1901." *Afro-American Music* 1 (1984): 69–83.

Sullivan, Lester. "Composers of Color of Nineteenth-Century New Orleans: The History behind the Music." *Black Music Research Journal* 8, no. 1 (1988): 51–82.

Edmond Dédé; Louisiana Collection, Amistad Research Center, Tulane University

Wyatt, Lucius R. "Six Composers of Nineteenth-Century New Orleans." *Black Music Research Journal* 10, no. 2 (1990): 125–140.

PRINCIPAL ARCHIVES
Bibliothèque Nationale, Paris, France.

* * * * *

Edmond Dédé stands out from most of his fellow 19th-century Creole composers of color of New Orleans in having developed a career outside the United States. Much associated with the Belle Époque in France, he composed successfully in both Bordeaux and Paris. Responding to the demands of major European metropolitan musical centers, he wrote in a far greater range of forms than the usual piano scores of post-Civil War New Orleans, from solo and chamber music to orchestral and operatic scores. Further, his success abroad provided the proponents of African-American rights in the United States with an instructive example of black accomplishment to trumpet in Reconstruction-era newspapers.

Edmond Dédé's parents were free Creoles of color who had immigrated to New Orleans around 1809 from the French West Indies. His father became *chef de musique* of a local militia unit and was the boy's first teacher. Dédé's first instrument, befitting the son of a bandmaster, was the clarinet, but he soon developed into a violin prodigy, studying violin, counterpoint, and harmony under both white and black teachers. His black violin teachers, Constantin Debergue and Charles Richard Lambert, were both conductors of the local Philharmonic Society founded by free Creoles of color sometime in the late antebellum period. This was the first nontheatrical orchestra in the city and even included some white musicians among its 100 instrumentalists, an extremely large aggregation for the time.

At the age of 21, in 1848, Dédé moved to Mexico, as did many other New Orleans free Creoles of color after the Mexican War, probably in reaction to changes in race relations in New Orleans. There he met virtuoso pianist Henri Herz and dramatic soprano Henriette Sontag, who were on extended concert tours of the Americas. Illness eventually drove Dédé back to New Orleans in 1851. The next year, his *mélodie,* "Mon pauvre coeur," appeared. It is the oldest surviving piece of sheet music by a New Orleans Creole of color. Like most antebellum imprints of music by local blacks, it probably was published by the composer himself. After the Civil War, most such works were published by the white proprietors of the leading local music stores.

Dédé supplemented his income from music with work as a cigarmaker, as did a number of local musicians. By 1857, he had saved enough money to book passage to Europe. He arrived with an introduction to Adolphe Adam, who in turn recommended him to Jacques-François Halévy. Although Dédé's teachers in Paris, both Halévy and Jean-Delphin Alard, worked at the Conservatoire, it remains unclear whether Dédé actually attended there. It was during this time, according to the anonymous critic of *L'Artiste de Bordeaux* of 1886–87, that Dédé became associated with "that wanton music which was destined to make the celebrity of [Jacques] Offenbach."

About 1860, Dédé went to Bordeaux, where he first worked as conductor of the orchestra at the prestigious old Grand Théâtre.

New Orleans and Bordeaux were once closely related, and trade and other connections were still strong between the two at the time Dédé went there. Quite a few Louisiana Creoles of color, including musicians and *littérateurs,* had settled there in the 1850s and 1860s in order to escape first the growing sentiment at home against free blacks and later the Civil War and its aftermath. Photographs of Dédé indicate that his African ancestry was more pronounced than that of many Creoles of color of New Orleans, where racial mixing was a way of life. In 1864, he married a Frenchwoman, Sylvie Anna Leflet; when the marriage was announced in black-interest newspapers in both New Orleans (*Tribune*) and New York (*National Anti-Slavery Standard*), much was made of his African appearance. He and Sylvie later had a son, Eugène Arcade Dédé, who also became a composer.

After leaving the Grand Théâtre and except for brief stints in Algiers and Marseilles and his last years in Paris, Dédé spent most of his career in Bordeaux as a theater orchestra conductor at the Théâtre de l'Alcazar and the Folies Bordelaises, where the light music of the *café-concert* held sway. During his Bordeaux period, he wrote about 150 dances, 95 songs, and six string quartets, as well as ballets, *ballets-divertissements,* operettas, *opéras-comiques,* and overtures, most of which have not been uncovered. Among the overtures is *Le Palmier,* which was performed by black New Orleanians on August 22, 1865, making it one of the few of his orchestral pieces ever to be played in the United States. In addition to writing all of this theatrical music, much of which may yet survive in Bordeaux, Dédé produced an unpublished cantata, *Battez aux champs: Cantate dédiée à L. M. l'Empereur Napoléon III* (1865), which was deposited at the Bibliothèque Nationale in Paris and may have been submitted as a contest piece. This variety and volume of output contrasts sharply with the production of the New Orleans black composers who remained at home, where piano dances and piano-accompanied songs prevailed.

By the mid-1880s, Dédé had a Paris publisher and membership in the French Society of Authors, Composers, and Editors of Music. The anonymous critic of *L'Artiste de Bordeaux* of 1886–87 stated that "there is not a resident of Bordeaux who does not know Dédé and has not heard and applauded him. Several generations have hummed his gayest refrains!" The composer's quadrilles were found to be "animated," his waltzes "intoxicating and passionate." "Not a day passes," *L'Artiste* reported, "that he does not write some page. Composition is for him a veritable need." Dédé was found to be "a composer of merit" with "an astonishing facility," in most of whose works were to be found "exquisite passages, full of grace and freshness."

By 1894, Dédé was a full member of the Society of Dramatic Authors and Composers in Paris. The only piece by him that appears ever to have been available on a commercial recording is one that was written during this period: "Mèphisto masqué: Polka fantastique" for orchestra (1889) is included on *Turn of the Century Cornet Favorites.* The piece was orchestrated by Gunther Schuller for this recording, substituting a euphonium for the ophicleide and eliminating the parts for four mirlitons (French kazoos). Even in this altered form, it remains an exemplar of light-hearted and cleverly orchestrated entertainment music of the sort that must have helped make Dédé's reputation in the musical whirl of the Belle Époque.

Dédé returned to New Orleans only once, in 1893, when he was in his mid-sixties. (Claims that he returned to the Crescent City in 1865 are based on a garbled report of a concert including music by Dédé held there in May, which was carried by the New York *National Anti-Slavery Standard* four months after the fact, on August 12, 1865. The *New Orleans Tribune* article of May 11, 1865, reporting on the same concert, correctly does not indicate the composer's presence.) In 1893, Dédé's Paris publisher had just released his new comic vocal duet, the latest piece now held by the Bibliothèque Nationale. Dédé was on his way home to visit relatives in New Orleans when, during a rough crossing, the ship on which he was traveling was disabled. In the confusion, his Cremona violin was lost. The passengers were taken aboard a steamer to Galveston, where the parents of pioneering black music historian Maude Cuney-Hare were among those who entertained Dédé during the two-month layover.

For several months after arriving in New Orleans, Dédé concertized widely, even garnering some attention from *L'Abeille,* the last major French-language organ of white Creole New Orleans. He was assisted at these concerts by local black musicians and, once, by the white music critic of *L'Abeille,* a notable case of musical interracialism during the era of increasing Jim Crowism. The fare consisted mostly of pieces for violin with piano accompaniment, including a paraphrase on *Rigoletto* by his old teacher Jean-Delphin Alard. Dédé introduced two new songs. "Si j'étais lui" (Should I Be He) was published locally by A. E. Blackmar and is reproduced in slightly incomplete form in the *Afro-American Music Review* of 1984 by Arthur LaBrew, who received a copy from the late Louisiana Creole folk-song authority Camille Nickerson. Her father, William J. Nickerson, teacher of Jelly Roll Morton, played with Dédé on one of these New Orleans programs. Dédé regarded the other song, "Patriotisme," as his farewell to New Orleans; in it, he laments his destiny to live far away because of "implacable prejudice" at home.

Grateful for receiving honorary membership in the Société des Jeunes-Amis, a leading local social group composed mostly of Creoles of color of antebellum free background, but weary of the inconveniences and indignities of racial segregation, Dédé returned to France in 1894. He died in Paris in 1901. It is unclear whether he completed his magnum opus, the opera *Le Sultan d'Ispahan,* which may have been inspired by his stay in Algeria. Some writers maintain that the opera was incomplete when Dédé died. LaBrew, however, finds an announcement for an upcoming performance at the Bordeaux Grand Théâtre in 1886. If Dédé's work "Le Serment de l'Arabe" is indeed an aria from this opera, as at least one researcher has speculated, then the work must have been fairly long in preparation, because the song is included by Trotter in 1878.

LESTER SULLIVAN

MON PAUVRE COEUR: MÉLODIE (1852)
"Mon pauvre coeur: Mélodie" fits comfortably into the category of parlor song: the poetry is heavily sentimental, even maudlin at times; the accompaniment is secondary to the vocal melodic line; and both vocal and accompanying parts employ simple harmonic language and rhythmic figures. The four-measure introduction is

in E minor, yet the verse begins in the key of G major. This harmonic pattern is perfectly acceptable text setting for the first verse, which begins "When I see you, oh! my blond Creole! on the balcony." It is not very convincing for the beginning of the third verse, which has quite a different mood: "I have suffered too much, I no longer have any hope in the future." However, this song distinguishes itself from a great number of parlor songs with moments of interest and individuality. For example, "Mon pauvre coeur" is in a minor key, with different music used for the introduction and the interlude or postlude music. The simple accompaniment occasionally uses triplet figures in the right-hand chords against duple figures in the vocal line. Dédé wrote lovely vocal lines that are easy to sing and attractive to the listener, and he instructs the singer to sing *andante appassionato,* a strong directive for a parlor song. His instructions in the piano part, such as *suivez* (follow; i.e., follow the singer), or *expressivo* [*sic*], demonstrate his familiarity with vocal performance traditions. Not all the phrases are symmetrical; indeed, within the short 24 measures of this piece, the introduction is followed by phrases of four, six, and four measures in length. This piece suggests that musical traditions in New Orleans were rather sophisticated much earlier than in many other centers of American musical life.

ANN SEARS

LE SERMENT DE L'ARABE: CHANT DRAMATIQUE (1865)
"Le serment de l'Arabe: Chant dramatique" (The Oath of the Arab: Dramatic Song) is the most fascinating of all the music by Dédé that is easily available to performers and scholars in the United States. Clearly, Dédé was responding to the enormous French interest in Egypt, Lebanon, and the Arab world, which came about during the 19th century as a result of Napoleon's disastrous Egyptian campaign of 1798, the French presence in Algeria in the 1830s, and, later, the construction of the Suez Canal under Ferdinand de Lesseps, 1859–69. The text is a far cry from much of the sentimental song literature published in 19th-century America, for this poetry is heroic and masculine, conjuring up the exotic life of the nomadic Arabs:

> One day in his tent, I recall, my father made me swear on the Koran death to the lions. Thus having placed his bloodied hands on my forehead, his soul flew off to other regions. Today how my arm can handle a weapon, how my hate has grown as the child has grown. When a roar at the Douar [a group of Arab tents arranged in a circle] gives the alarm, happy then I leave under the burning sun. By the Houris of the holy Prophet, by all powerful Allah, master of the universe, is there a more noble game, is there a more beautiful feast than a lion hunt in our vast desert?

There has been speculation that this composition may have been intended as an aria from a lost opera, *Le Sultan d'Ispahan.* Although that cannot be proven at present, musically, such conjectures are well founded. The initial impression of this piece, when performed as it appears in Trotter's book, is that of an opera aria with piano transcription in place of orchestral accompaniment.

Like an aria in which a character gets a chance to shine brighter than the story for a few moments and explicate his character, this piece is full of action, even though it is only 63 measures long. It merits its subtitle of "Dramatic Song." The eight-measure introduction in C minor has *tremolo* octaves in the right hand and dotted eighth- and 16th-note figures in octaves in the left hand; both figures are common in operatic accompaniments and are easily transcribed for piano accompaniments. When the body of the piece begins, the tonal architecture—from C minor to E-flat major, C major, and finally back to C minor—follows the narrative of the poem. In measures 9-25, the Arab's father dies and the oath is sworn. The tonality is C minor and the accompaniment provides an ascending chromatic scale as the soul flies off. The influence of Giuseppe Verdi is apparent here, with the vocal melody doubled in a low register of the accompanying orchestra. In measure 16, triplet figures imply movement of the lions like the tiger so eloquently described in Haydn's *The Creation,* although here the triplet figures descend as the lions are hunted. At measure 25, the song moves to E-flat major as the Arab sings of his strength and happiness at hearing the roar of the lion and beginning the hunt. The bass line repeats a fragment of the dotted rhythm which appears in the voice part. At measure 41, the song modulates to C major, moving into a 3/4 section marked *Allegro brillante.* Containing some of the highest notes of the piece on the word "Lions," this section describes the glory of the hunt. Murmurs of Italian opera appear again in the thirds paralleling the voice in the accompaniment. The piece concludes in measures 59 through 63 with a coda in C minor built around descending C-minor scales in left-hand tremolos. This work is written well for the voice, with long lyrical lines in a range nicely designed for a dramatic baritone. It deserves revival by performers and leads the scholar to hope that an entire opera by Dédé will be found.

ANN SEARS

CHICAGO: GRANDE VALSE À L'AMÉRICAINE (1892)

This work, published in 1892, appears to be a piano arrangement of the original orchestral version published in 1891 by the Parisian publisher Fromont. It is dedicated to Dédé's cousin, Samuel A. Armstrong, of New Orleans. The cover and title indicate that Dédé may have been looking toward the World's Columbian Exposition of 1893, which was held in Chicago. Small pictures representative of exhibits to come appear on the cover: American Indians, the Sphinx representing the Egyptian Pavilion, cherubs hovering over symbols of art and music, and, most prominent, a stylized figure of a draped woman wearing a star in her hair and holding a lighted torch clearly representing the Statue of Liberty. Designed in 1884, lighted with electric arc lamps in 1885, and dedicated in the harbor of New York in 1886 with a poem by Emma Lazarus, this "new colossus" on the sheet music cover shows that Dédé was in touch with political and cultural matters in his homeland. It is ironic that he showed the symbol of liberty on his music and saluted Chicago

in his title yet felt that he must emigrate to France in order to have a successful professional career.

Although the dedication, the title, and cover page make this piece American, musically "Chicago" is a Eurocentric dance piece in 3/8 meter, somewhat unusual for a waltz, as is its introduction and coda in C minor, with the body of the piece in C major. The form of the piece may be denoted as ABCBDCD with an introduction and coda and an interlude between section D and the restatement of section C, which is comprised of material from the introduction. The introduction, interlude, and coda are in C minor; sections A and B are in C major; and the first statement of sections C and D are in G major. The reprise of the C and D sections after the interlude is in the tonic (C major) rather than the dominant key (G major) of their original statements. This is somewhat unusual in dance music; normally, the sections are repeated in their original keys. A more detailed analysis of the valse reveals some uneven phrase lengths, a clue that this piece was written later in the 19th century, when the waltz had liberated dance music from the necessity to always provide even numbers of phrases and measures in order to have figure dances such as cotillions and quadrilles fit the music properly.

Evidence that this is a transcription from orchestral music abounds. For example, there are many measures of doubled octaves in the melody, tremolo chords (often used to transcribe sustained chords in the strings to the keyboard), two-measure phrases repeated in different octaves and at different dynamic levels to reflect orchestration, and long passages of repeated notes and chords (played with facility on strings or by woodwinds but often difficult on the piano). While it is charmingly melodic dance music, "Chicago" does not show the fire and lyric line of Dédé's vocal music. Piano transcriptions hardly ever do orchestral music justice, and this piece would undoubtedly be more effective in Dédé's original orchestral setting.

ANN SEARS

REFERENCES

L'Artiste de Bordeaux series 2, no. 3 (1886–87): 1.

Fabre, Michel. Letter to Robert E. Skinner, April 11, 1997. Held in Archives and Special Collections, University Library, Xavier University, New Orleans, Louisiana.

LaBrew, Arthur R. "Edmond Dédé (dit Charentos), 1827–1901." *Afro-American Music* 1 (1984): 69–83.

Sullivan, Lester. "Composers of Color of Nineteenth-Century New Orleans: The History behind the Music." *Black Music Research Journal* 8, no. 1 (1988): 51–82.

Trotter, James M. *Music and Some Highly Musical People.* Boston: Lee and Shepard, 1878.

Turn of the Century Cornet Favorites. Gerard Schwartz, cornet, Columbia Chamber Ensemble, Gunther Schuller, conductor. Columbia MT 34553, 1977.

DETT, R(OBERT) NATHANIEL

Born in Drummondville (now Niagara Falls), Ontario, October 11, 1882; died in Battle Creek, Mich., October 2, 1943. **Education:** Oliver Willis Halstead Conservatory, Lockport, N.Y., studied piano, 1901–03; Oberlin Conservatory of Music, Oberlin, Ohio, studied composition and organ with George W. Andrews, piano with George Carl Hastings, B.Mus., 1903–08; Oberlin Conservatory, studied with Karl Gehrkens, summer 1913; Columbia University, New York, N.Y., studied with Peter Dykema, 1915; American Conservatory of Music, Chicago, Ill., and Northwestern University, Evanston, Ill., attended classes, summer 1915; Harvard University, Cambridge, Mass., studied with Arthur Foote, 1919–20; Fontainebleau, France, studied with Nadia Boulanger, summer 1929; Eastman School of Music, Rochester, N.Y., studied piano with Max Landow and composition with Bernard Rogers and Howard Hanson, 1931–32, M.Mus., 1932. **Composing and Performing Career:** Played piano at church as a boy; Mt. Zion Baptist Church, Oberlin, Ohio, directed choir, 1903–08; Hampton Institute, Hampton, Va., developed the choir, directing their concerts on tours of the United States and Europe, 1913–31; Carnegie Hall, New York, N.Y., Hampton Institute Choir concert, 1928; conducted concerts of his own works; Bennett College, Greensboro, N.C., developed and toured with the chorus, 1937–42; Battle Creek, Mich., directed USO Women's Army Corps chorus and community chorus, 1943. **Teaching Career:** Lane College, Jackson, Tenn., 1908–11; Lincoln Institute, Jefferson City, Mo., 1911–13; Hampton Institute, 1913–31; Sam Houston College, Austin, Tex., summer 1936; Bennett College, 1936–42; Virginia State College, Petersburg, Va., and Northwestern University, guest lecturer, 1941. **Memberships:** National Association of Negro Musicians, president, 1924–26. **Honors/ Awards:** Harvard University, Francis Boott Prize and Bowdoin Prize, 1920; Howard University, Washington, D.C., honorary doctorate, 1924; Oberlin Conservatory, honorary doctorate, 1926.

MUSIC LIST

COLLECTION

The Collected Piano Works of R. Nathaniel Dett. Evanston, Ill.: Summy-Birchard, 1973. Contents: Cinnamon Grove Suite; Eight Bible Vignettes; Enchantment; In the Bottoms: Characteristic Suite; Magnolia; Tropic Winter.

INSTRUMENTAL SOLOS
Violin
"Ramah." 1923. Boston: Boston Music, 1923.

Piano
"After the Cakewalk." 1900. Williamsport, Pa.: Vander Sloot Music, 1900.
"Cave of the Winds March." 1902. Niagara Falls, N.Y.: S. C. Fragard, 1902.
Cinnamon Grove Suite. 1928. New York: John Church, 1928. Contents: Moderato molto grazioso; Adagio cantabile; Ritmo moderato e con sentimento; Quasi gavotte. Recorded: "Adagio cantabile," Victor 17912.

Concert Waltz and Ballad. by 1919. Unpublished manuscript.
"Cotton Needs Pickin'." 1924. Unpublished manuscript. Premiere, 1924.
Eight Bible Vignettes. New York: Mills Music, 1941–43. Contents: Father Abraham; Desert Interlude; As His Own Soul; Barcarolle of Tears; I Am the True Vine; Martha Complained; Other Sheep; Madrigal Divine. Premiere, "Father Abraham," 1942. Recorded: New World Records 367-1/2.
Enchantment. 1922. New York: John Church, 1922. Contents: Incantation; Song of the Shrine; Dance of Desire; Beyond the Dream. Premiere, 1923.
"Fair Weather." 1926. Bryn Mawr, Pa.: Theodore Presser, 1926.
In the Bottoms: Characteristic Suite. 1913. Chicago: Clayton F. Summy, 1913. Contents: Prelude; His Song; Honey—Humoresque; Barcarolle—Morning; Dance—Juba. Premiere, 1913. Recorded: Desto 7102/3; CRI CD 629; Music and Arts CD 737; New World Records 367-1/2; Philips 9500-096.
Inspiration Waltzes. 1903. London: Richard A. Saalfield, 1903.
Magnolia. 1912. Evanston, Ill.: Summy-Birchard, 1973. Contents: Magnolias; The Deserted Cabin; My Lady Love; Mammy; The Place Where the Rainbow Ends. Recorded: New World Records NW 367-2.
"March Negre." Unpublished manuscript. Premiere, 1915.
"My Agnes from Niagara." 1909. Niagara Falls, N.Y.: S. C. Fragard, 1909.
"Nepenthe and the Muse." 1922. New York: John Church, 1922.
Sonata no. 1 in F Minor. by 1924. Unpublished manuscript.
Sonata no. 2 in E Minor. by 1925. Unpublished manuscript.
Tropic Winter. 1938. Chicago: Clayton F. Summy, 1938. Contents: The Daybreak Charioteer; A Bayou Garden; Pompons and Fans; Legend of the Atoll; To a Closed Casement; Noon Siesta; Parade of the Jasmine Banners.

SMALL INSTRUMENTAL ENSEMBLE
Strings
String Quartet. New York: Southern Music, ca. 1974.

FULL ORCHESTRA
American Sampler. 1937. Unpublished manuscript. Premiere, 1937.

ORCHESTRA (CHAMBER OR FULL) WITH CHORUS
Music in the Mine (chorus, orchestra). 1916. Unpublished manuscript. New York: G. Schirmer, 1916. Premiere, 1922.

SOLO VOICE
"Churning Song." 1903. Unpublished manuscript.
"Go On, Mule!" 1918. New York: J. Fischer and Bro., 1918.
"God Understands" (medium voice). 1926. New York: John Church, 1926.
"Hymn to Parnassus." 1942. New York: Mills Music, 1942.
"Iorana: Tahitian Maiden's Love Song" (medium voice). 1935. Chicago: Clayton F. Summy, 1935.
"Lead Gently, Lord, and Slow." 1929. New York: John Church, 1929.
"Magic Moon of Molten Gold." 1919. New York: John Church, 1919.
"My Day." 1929. New York: John Church, 1929.

"O Lord, the Hard-Won Miles." 1934. New York: G. Schirmer, 1934.

"Oh, the Land I'm Bound For" (low voice). New York: John Church, 1923.

"Open Yo' Eyes." 1923. Bryn Mawr, Pa.: Theodore Presser, 1923.

"The Soul of America Defend!" 1942. New York: Mills Music, 1942.

"A Thousand Years Ago or More." 1919. New York: John Church, 1919.

"The Voice of the Sea." 1924. New York: John Church, 1924.

"Were Thou the Moon." 1924. New York: John Church, 1924.

"The Winding Road." 1923. Bryn Mawr, Pa.: Theodore Presser, 1923.

CHORAL MUSIC

"America the Beautiful" (SATB). 1918. New York: J. Fischer and Bro., 1918. Premiere, 1918.

"As by the Stream of Babylon" (soprano solo, SATB unaccompanied). 1933. New York: G. Schirmer, 1933.

"As Children Walk Ye in God's Love" (soprano solo, SATB; or tenor solo, TTBB). 1930. New York: G. Schirmer, 1930.

"Ascapezzo" (women's chorus). 1940. New York: J. Fischer and Bro., 1940. Premiere, 1940.

"Ask for the Old Paths" (tenor solo, SATB unaccompanied). 1941. New York: Mills Music, 1941. Recorded: Mark Custom Recording Service ACDA 89MC-1.

"Ave Maria" (baritone solo, SATB unaccompanied). 1930. New York: G. Schirmer, 1930.

The Chariot Jubilee (tenor solo, SATB, organ or piano). 1919. New York: John Church, 1919. Also arranged for tenor solo, SATB, and orchestra. Premiere, 1920. Recorded: Audio House AHS 30F75.

"City of God" (SATB). 1941. New York: J. Fischer and Bro., 1941.

"Hampton, My Home by the Sea" (SATB). 1914. Hampton, Va.: Hampton Institute Press, 1914.

"Hew Down the Tree" (contralto solo, SSAA unaccompanied). 1940. Chicago: Hall and McCreary, 1940.

"Juba" (SATB). 1934. Chicago: Clayton F. Summy, 1934. Premiere, 1934.

"The Lamb" (SSA unaccompanied). 1938. New York: J. Fischer and Bro., 1938.

"Let Us Cheer the Weary Traveler." New York: John Church, 1926.

"Now Rest Beneath Night's Shadows" (SSAA unaccompanied). 1938. New York: J. Fischer and Bro., 1938.

"O Holy Lord" (SSAATTBB). 1916. New York: G. Schirmer, 1916. Recorded: Richsound Records RSSW 02091.

"So We'll Go No More A-Roving" (SSAA unaccompanied). 1940. New York: J. Fischer and Bro., 1940.

DRAMATIC MUSIC

The Ordering of Moses: Biblical Folk Scenes (oratorio for SATB soli, SSAATTBB chorus, piano/organ or orchestra). 1931–32. New York: J. Fischer and Bro. Originally titled *Sacred Cantata for Soli, Chorus, and Orchestra.* Note: M.Mus. thesis, Eastman School of Music, 1932. Premiere, 1937. Recorded: Silver Crest TAL 42868; Unique Opera Records UORC 113.

PUBLICATIONS

ABOUT DETT
Books and Monographs

Gray, Arlene E. *Listen to the Lambs: A Source Book of the R. Nathaniel Dett Materials in the Niagara Falls Public Library, Niagara Fall, N.Y.*

Ridgeway, Ontario: Smith-Davidson, 1984.

———. *Supplementary Materials 2 for the Dett Project: E. W. Brydges Public Library, Niagara Falls, N.Y.* Crystal Beach, Ontario: A. E. Gray, 1986.

McBrier, Vivian Flagg. *R. Nathaniel Dett, His Life and Works, 1882–1943.* Washington D.C.: Associated Publishers, 1977.

Pope, Marguerite. *A Brief Biography of Dr. Robert Nathaniel Dett.* Hamilton Bulletin, 42, no. 1, Hampton, Va.: Hampton Institute Press, 1945.

Simpson, Anne Key. *Follow Me: The Life and Music of R. Nathaniel Dett.* Composers of North America, no. 10. Metuchen, N.J.: Scarecrow Press, 1993.

Spencer, Jon Michael, ed. *The R. Nathaniel Dett Reader: Essays on Black Sacred Music.* Durham, N.C.: Duke University Press, 1991.

Dissertations

Braithwaite, Coleridge Alexander. "A Survey of the Lives and Creative Activities of Some Negro Composers." Ed.D. diss., Teachers College, Columbia University, 1952.

Burns, Pamela Teresa. "The Negro Spiritual: From the Southern Plantations to the Concert Stages of America." D.M.A. thesis, University of Alabama, 1993.

Fansler, Terry Lee. "The Anthem in America: 1900–1950." Ph.D. diss, University of North Texas, 1982.

Jackson, Raymond Thompson. "The Piano Music of Twentieth-Century Black Americans as Illustrated Mainly in the Works of Three Composers." Ph.D. diss., Juilliard School of Music, 1973.

McBrier, Vivian Flagg. "The Life and Works of Robert Nathaniel Dett." Ph.D. diss., Catholic University of America, 1967.

Miles, Debra Ann. "An Analysis of Robert Nathaniel Dett's *In the Bottoms.*" M.Mus. thesis, North Texas State University, 1983.

Spencer, Jon Michael. "The Writings of Robert Nathaniel Dett and William Grant Still." Ph.D. diss., Washington University, 1982.

Wilson, J. Harrison. "A Study and Performance of *The Ordering of Moses* by Robert Nathaniel Dett." D.M.A. thesis, University of Southern California, 1970.

Articles

"Dett, R. Nathaniel, 1882–1943." In *Black Music in the Harlem Renaissance,* edited by Samuel A. Floyd Jr., 189–195. Westport, Conn.: Greenwood Press, 1990.

De Lerma, Dominique-René. "Dett and Engel: A Question of Cultural Pride." *Black Perspective in Music* 1, no. 1 (1973): 70–72.

Downes, Olin, D. L. Bicknell, and F. Yeiser. "Dr. Dett's Outstanding Contribution for 1937: His Oratorio *The Ordering of Moses.*" *Southern Workman* (October 1937): 303–310.

Levy, Alan H. "Composers Who Happened to be African American: Music and Memory in the Lives of R. Nathaniel Dett and Henry T. Burleigh." *Mid-America* 74, no. 1 (1992): 5.

Perry, Frank, Jr. "R. Nathaniel Dett." In *Afro-American Vocal Music: A Select Guide to Fifteen Composers,* 13–18. Berrien Springs, Mich.: Vande Vere, 1991.

Ryder, Georgia A. "Harlem Renaissance Ideals in the Music of Robert Nathaniel Dett." In *Black Music in the Harlem Renaissance,* edited by Samuel A. Floyd Jr., 55–70. Westport, Conn.: Greenwood Press, 1990.

Composer Edmund Thornton Jenkins, author and scholar Benjamin Brawley, and R. Nathaniel Dett (from left to right); courtesy of Jeffrey Green

Spencer, Jon Michael. "R. Nathaniel Dett's Views on the Preservation of Black Music." *Black Perspective in Music* 10, no. 2 (1982): 133–148.

Stanley, May. "R. N. Dett, of Hampton Institute, Helping to Lay the Foundation for Negro Music of Future." *Musical America* 28 (July 1918): 17+. (Reprinted in *Black Perspective in Music* 1, no. 1 [1973]: 64–69.)

BY DETT
Articles

"As the Negro School Sings." *Southern Workman* 56 (July 1927): 304–305.

"The Emancipation of Negro Music." *Southern Workman* 47 (April 1918):

172–176.

"From Bell Stand to Throne Room." *Etude* 52 (February 1934): 79–80. (Reprinted in *Black Perspective in Music* 1, no. 1 [1973]: 73–81.)

"John W. Work." *Southern Workman* 54 (1925): 438.

"A Musical Invasion of Europe." *Crisis* 37 (1930): 405–407, 428.

"Musical Standards." *Etude* 15, no. 323 (1920).

"Negro Music." Typescript. (Note: this essay won the Bowdoin Literary Prize, Harvard University, 1920.)

"Negro Music." In *The International Cyclopedia of Music and Musicians,* edited by Oscar Thompson, 1243–1246. 6th ed. New York: Dodd, Mead, 1952.

"The Song of Seven." Held in the Dett Archival Collection, Collis P.

Huntington Memorial Library, Hampton University.
[Note: These articles are all reprinted in *The R. Nathaniel Dett Reader: Essays on Black Sacred Music,* edited by Jon Michael Spencer (Durham, N.C.: Duke University Press, 1991).]

Collections of Poetry
Album of a Heart. Jackson, Tenn.: Mocowat-Merser, 1911.

Collections of Spirituals and Folksongs
The Dett Collection of Negro Spirituals, edited by R. Nathaniel Dett. 4 vols. Chicago: Hall and McCreary, 1936.
Negro Spirituals, edited by R. Nathaniel Dett. London: Blanford Press, 1959.
Religious Folk-Songs of the Negro as Sung at Hampton Institute, edited by R. Nathaniel Dett. Hampton, Va.: Hampton Institute Press, 1927.

PRINCIPAL ARCHIVES
Dett Archival Collection, Collis P. Huntington Memorial Library, Hampton University, Hampton, Virginia.

* * * * *

R. Nathaniel Dett received national attention for his skills and artistry as a piano recitalist and international acclaim as a choral conductor. His success in these pursuits rested largely on the performance of his own works. However, the particular significance of Dett as an African-American composer-arranger was established and validated by his devotion to the presentation and preservation of music and musical idioms of the African-American culture, for which he was also an articulate spokesman. His several piano suites were frequently performed (Percy Grainger was one of Dett's champions), as were his numerous original and arranged works for chorus. He was one of the most successful composers of his generation who worked carefully to use African-American folk music in Western European forms.

Dett's mother was Canadian, his father American, and both were musical. His first home was in a community of former slaves, Drummondville, Ontario, where he was born on October 11, 1882. It was there that he was provided his earliest musical experiences. He grew up hearing his grandmother singing spirituals, and his parents encouraged him in his piano lessons. By the time he was an adolescent, he was performing publicly as a pianist around Niagara Falls, New York, where his family had moved in 1893. While living in the United States, he and his older brother Samuel attended school in Niagara Falls, Ontario. Before Dett was 20 years old, his first publication, a ragtime piano solo titled "After the Cakewalk," was issued. In 1901, he began a two-year course of study at the Halstead Conservatory of Music, in Lockport, New York, some 20 miles from his home. There he studied piano with the director, Oliver Willis Halstead, who was a demanding teacher.

Immediately afterward, Dett was enrolled at the Oberlin Conservatory of Music (Ohio), where he studied piano, organ, voice, composition, and music theory. He directed a church choir there as well. Throughout his college years, he had many opportunities to perform as piano soloist and accompanist and to conduct. It was a concert experience, however, that made one of the strongest impressions on his musical thinking: a performance of Dvořák's "American" String Quartet. It called up his memories of the folk music he had first heard sung by his grandmother as well as other kinds of black folk music, and this response informed and vitalized his musical concepts for the remainder of his life.

On graduation from Oberlin in 1908, Dett accepted a position at Lane College in Jackson, Tennessee, instead of pursuing the goal of becoming a concert pianist, which some of his professors had hoped he would undertake. His next academic post was at Lincoln Institute in Jefferson City, Missouri. In both institutions he had many piano students, and as a choral conductor, raised standards considerably. Dett remained at Lincoln Institute for two academic years from 1911 to 1913 and then left to take over the already well-established chorus of Hampton Institute, in Hampton, Virginia. In characteristic fashion, he brought the choir to even greater levels of achievement and acclaim. During his years at Hampton Institute, 1913–31, the longest tenure of any position he held, he concertized extensively as a soloist and received positive reaction to his own piano music, some of which was always on his program and was being published. He was responsible for founding a community chorus in 1914 to foster good relations between the Institute and the community at large. Dett carried on this kind of activity enthusiastically in many of the places he worked. As choir director at Hampton Institute, he emphasized the importance of spirituals and wrote many arrangements and original works based on them for his choir, which made U.S. and European tours under his direction.

An outspoken proponent of the traditional music of black Americans, Dett stated: "We have this wonderful folk music—the melodies of an enslaved people, who poured out their longings, their griefs, and their aspirations in one great universal language." He also took action on his words by serving as one of the organizers of the National Association of Negro Musicians in 1919; he was president of the association from 1924 to 1926.

The extent to which Dett further articulated his concepts and voiced his opinions about black music and related issues may be found in his essays, program notes, interviews, and book reviews, in which, according to Jon Michael Spencer, "he makes very clear his high regard for and love of the spiritual and offers reasons for his concerns about its future." His thoughts are stated at length in his four-part essay "Negro Music" (1920), for which he received the Bowdoin Literary Prize at Harvard. Some of his theses are reiterated in prefaces to *Religious Folk-Songs of the Negro as Sung at Hampton Institute* (1927) and his four groups of songs in *The Dett Collection of Negro Spirituals* (1936). In both publications, the songs are presented in traditional harmonizations, although a few in the Hampton collection are enhanced by Dett, as in "Dust and Ashes." In doing this, he followed a practice begun as early as 1874, according to Thomas Fenner, the editor of the first edition of the Hampton collection entitled *Cabin and Plantation Songs as Sung by the Hampton Students.*

While preparing these collections and composing and arranging additional material for chorus or solo voice, Dett created settings for several spirituals in the form of motets, a fine example being "Let Us Cheer the Weary Traveler" (1926). He had already composed a more extended work, *The Chariot Jubilee* for chorus, solo, and orchestra (1919), based on the spiritual "Swing Low,

Sweet Chariot." The composer remarked in 1936 that, to his knowledge, *The Chariot Jubilee* was the "first attempt to develop the spiritual into an oratorio form," although it is not a dramatic narrative and was published as a motet.

Dett was forced to resign from Hampton in 1931, presumably because of differences between himself and the college's president. He was cut short of a pension benefit by one year. He moved his family to Rochester, New York, in order to attend the Eastman School of Music for graduate study, and arrangements were made for him to spend a second year there. He became an active member of the Rochester musical community, in part through directing a community chorus, and attracted the admiration and respect of leading members of the Eastman faculty, including Dr. Howard Hanson, its director. His master's thesis, *The Ordering of Moses,* was not premiered until 1937 at the Cincinnati May Festival. Its extraordinary success generated other notable performances. Renewed interest in the work may be attributed to the heightened cultural awareness of black Americans that developed with and was nurtured by the Civil Rights movement in the 1960s.

After living for five years in Rochester, Dett moved to Austin, Texas, to serve as a visiting professor at Sam Houston College for a period of a few months. In 1936, he joined the faculty at Bennett College in Greensboro, North Carolina. He left there in 1942 with the hope of finding more time for composition. To that end, and to have a steady income, he joined the United Services Organization (USO) in early 1943 and was assigned to its Battle Creek, Michigan, base. His principal duties were directing a Women's Army Corps chorus, and once more he organized a community chorus. His activities in this latest of his careers were abruptly ended when he suffered a heart attack. Approximately a month later, he suffered a fatal heart attack, shortly before his 61st birthday.

Memorial services for Dett were held in many communities, particularly in Oberlin and Niagara Falls and at Hampton Institute. Obituaries appeared in newspapers around the country. There was general agreement that the work of Dett as composer-arranger, conductor, and pianist had made a significant contribution to musical life in the United States and to the acceptance and importance of African-American folk music as basic to the development of American music in the 20th century.

IN THE BOTTOMS: CHARACTERISTIC SUITE (1913)

In prefaces and forewords to many of his scores, Dett was careful to specify what he intended to convey in those works. He stated that two of his piano suites, *Magnolia Suite* (1912) and *In the Bottoms* (1913), are of "that class of music known as 'Program music' or 'music with a poetic basis,'" and further, "As it is quite possible to describe the traits, habits, and racial peculiarities without using the vernacular, so is it similarly possible to musically portray racial peculiarities without the use of national tunes or folk-songs." *In the Bottoms: Characteristic Suite* has "five numbers giving pictures of moods or scenes peculiar to Negro life in the river bottoms of the Southern sections of North America." The pieces are "Prelude," "His Song," "Honey—Humoresque," "Barcarolle—Morning," and "Dance— Juba." The notes for this work are meant to indicate the "intimate" relationship of the program to the music. The mood of each piece is described, but there is relatively little comment on musical features.

Pianistically, the suite is characterized by contrasting and rapidly shifting textures and registers of the keyboard, repeated accompaniment patterns, and chromatic scalar and chordal melodic embellishments. The primary features of this suite include repetition of melodic motives and harmonic patterns, short diatonic melodies, predominantly homophonic textures, frequent, sharp contrasts in dynamic levels, syncopation (especially in the pattern eighth note/quarter note/eighth note), and *rubato* tempos. Concerning syncopation, Dett noted in his comments about the fourth piece, "Barcarolle," that "The rhythmic figure [16th note/ eighth note/16th note] which forms the theme . . . is in reality the rhythmic motif of the whole Suite."

In the "Prelude," "the heavy chords represent the heavy shadows, and the open fifths the peculiar hollow effect of the stillness." (This is one of the very few references in Dett's notes in the score to the correlation of the music with programmatic elements.) In the first section of this three-part form (ABA), the theme is stated twice, the open fifths doubled in the first statement and played by the left hand, in the same register, in the second statement. The repetition of the statement is varied by the accompaniment of broken-octave chromatic descending scales and ascending broken chords. That scale figure is shortened to one measure (from two) in the return of the A section, which concludes with an extended progression to the dominant and a slow unfolding of the D-major tonic chord, from the lowest *d* on the keyboard to the *d* above the treble staff. In the B section, "the syncopated melody which occurs is the 'tumming' of a banjo, which music is, however, only incidental to the gloom." The pentatonic melody reflects a folk source and is stated first in single notes, then in octaves, with the harmony expanding to octaves in both hands. The dynamic level remains *piano* throughout the section; the return of the A section *fortissimo,* in double octaves, insists on the "gloom."

The main theme of "His Song" (*patetico*) is structured in the form of the refrain of a spiritual—aa'ab, each a four-measure phrase. The overall form of the movement is again three-part (ABA). The theme is stated twice in the first A section, shifting two octaves lower in the second statement and unaccompanied in two phrases. The b phrase, a descending harmonic minor scale, forms the basis of the theme of section B. In the approach to a sustained augmented-sixth chord on *b*-flat preceding the sustained dominant (*a*), there is a call-and-response pattern before the return of section A in D major, *forte* and *maestoso.* The last statement of the a phrase is in the original D minor, in the bass, and unaccompanied. The tritone *g-c*-sharp, which "resolves" to the tonic note *d* in that phrase, may be part of the reason for the composer's note that the piece has "a weird melody [that] seems to strangely satisfy a nameless yearning of the heart."

"Honey—Humoresque," in two-part form, begins in a capricious mood, *allegretto,* and moves to a slower, more flexible tempo in the second part. The rhythmic pattern eighth note/quarter note/eighth note is pervasive and varied, and tonal excursions from the key of F major are by the third relation, to A minor and D-flat. This piece is "after a poem, 'A Negro Love Song,' by Paul Laurence Dunbar," and "the intimation here is one of coquetry."

The picture of the "Barcarolle" that Dett describes is "the pleasure of a sunshiny morning on the Father of Waters." The form of the "Barcarolle" is two-part, AB A'B', with the repeats being varied from their first statements. Of all the movements in the suite, this is the most reminiscent of a 19th-century salon piece, with the theme of section A ornamented by sweeping chromatic scales and chordal figures and the theme of section B, in octaves, set off by chordal patterns in both hands. Underlying the florid, Chopinesque melodies is the basic barcarolle pattern (see Ex. 1). As noted earlier, Dett cited the 16th-note/eighth-note/16th-note figure as "the rhythmic motif of the whole Suite."

Example 1. "Barcarolle," *In the Bottoms,* barcarolle rhythm

Dett described "Juba" as "probably the most characteristic number of the Suite, as it portrays more of the social life of the people." This movement is also perhaps the most popular of his many compositions. The "juba" is a patting dance in which the dancers stamp on the ground and then pat their hands twice (see Ex. 2a). The work is in rondo form—ABACAD, the final section functioning as a coda. The "patting" rhythm always accompanies the main theme of the dance, but it gives way to 16th-note octaves in scales in section B and, with a folk-like melody in the bass clef played by the right hand in section C, to a modified inversion of that rhythm (see Ex. 2b).

Example 2. "Juba," *In the Bottoms*
a. Juba rhythm

b. Variation of Juba rhythm

The composer noted that "The orchestra [for the dance] usually consists of single fiddler . . . [who] does the impossible in the way of double stopping and bowing." This suggests to the pianist something about his or her approach to the performance of "Juba," but Dett stressed that the dance must not be played *"too fast."*

Dett often performed *In the Bottoms,* for which he received enthusiastic reviews as both composer and pianist. His friend Percy Grainger also included it in his recitals or played "Juba" as an encore, always with great effect.

LET US CHEER THE WEARY TRAVELER (1926)

"Let Us Cheer the Weary Traveler" is "A Negro Spiritual in the form of a short unaccompanied motet for mixed voices." The melody is found in *Religious Folk Songs of the Negro as Sung at Hampton Institute.* During his time at the Institute, Dett edited this collection, considering the songs as actual hymns and grouping them by theme—"admonition," "death of Christ," "pilgrimage," "tribulation," and so on. Dett's attitude toward and concern for perpetuating folk music is expressed at some length in his foreword to the collection. This statement is representative: "Folk-songs, then, quite aside from their music value, are of inestimable worth because of the light which they throw upon those individualizing elements in the character of the race that produced them."

In the eight-measure refrain of "Let Us Cheer the Weary Traveler," soprano and bass sing the first two lines of the verse, at the octave, with inner voices harmonizing. The tenor doubles the soprano in the third line, and the last line is in four-part harmony. The refrain is then repeated in a contrapuntal texture. The verse, also contrapuntal, with call-and-response figures, may be sung by four solo voices (*ad lib.*) or by the full chorus, and the direction is given to sing in a "reciting" (*recitando*), simple style. This contrasts with the *marcato* (marked) articulation of the refrain. The refrain returns, a literal repeat of its first statement. Instead of an immediate repetition of the refrain, however, the verse follows, set as before and again with the option of solo voices or full choir. The second statement of the refrain returns, and the piece ends with an extended, broad setting of "Along the heavenly way," the last line of the refrain. The form is AA'BABA' coda. The tempo marking is *Moderato molto maestoso* (moderately, with great majesty), and this setting, in its contrasts of homophonic and contrapuntal textures and the vigor of its melody, convincingly exhorts the listener to "cheer the weary traveler."

THE ORDERING OF MOSES: BIBLICAL FOLK SCENES (1931–32)

Dett described *The Ordering of Moses* as a "Biblical Folk Scene for Soli, Chorus, and Orchestra." The text is based on scripture and folklore compiled and set to music by the composer. There are five solo parts: Miriam (soprano), Moses (tenor), the Voice of Israel (alto), the Voice of God (baritone), and the Word (baritone). The solos for men's voices are usually in recitative style, except when they are based on the spiritual melody "Go Down, Moses," the principal unifying source of the work's thematic material. Solos for women's voices are more lyrical. The ranges of the choral voices are demanding, two octaves for the soprano and bass, and almost two octaves for the alto (a 13th) and tenor (a 14th). The choral writing is highly varied, with homophonic textures prevailing, relatively few unison passages, and several contrapuntal phrases. The extremes of the ranges are used tellingly, especially at climactic moments, and choral sections are often divided.

While 22 numbers are indicated in the score, the movement of the action is uninterrupted, from despondency to triumph. After the opening instrumental prelude, which begins with a melodic figure in the solo cello derived from the spiritual's refrain, a solo baritone (the Word) sings the opening line of the spiritual. There is a plea to God for deliverance from bondage—"And unto God they sorely cried." He looked down on them "with respect." God speaks to Moses, telling him to lead his people to the promised land—"Go down, Moses, Way down in Egypt's land." Moses questions his worthiness, and God replies, "Now therefore go and I will be thy mouth; I will instruct thee what thou shalt say." The "Meditation of Moses" follows. For orchestra alone, it is highly chromatic, with the augmented triad alone and seventh, ninth, and eleventh chords favored. Melodic figures are derived from the spiritual, and contrasting orchestral textures, with solo winds and brass, are featured.

The Word declaims, "And when Moses smote the water, The children all passed over. . . . The sea gave way."

The next two sections may be seen as tone poems: "March of the Israelites through the Red Sea" —with wordless chorus singing "Ah"—and "The Egyptians Pursue"—without voices. Ostinato patterns support the vigorous forward motion of these sections. In the "March," Dett's approach to the possibilities of choral color is very evident: first altos, then tenors, with basses joining in, and then full chorus in unison, in double and triple octaves; the men's chorus is then divided into four parts, and in conclusion, the full chorus is in six parts, with sopranos and basses divided.

A call by solo baritone and response by chorus—"And when they reached the other shore, O hallelujah, They sang a song of triumph o'er, O hallelujah"—leads to "I will praise Jehovah," sung by Moses. Miriam, introduced by baritone solo as "gifted with prophecy," sings "Come let us praise Jehovah." The women's voices of the chorus accompany her with an ostinato pattern (see Ex. 3) in the most lyrical number of the work (*Allegretto grazioso*), an aria in C major. Moses adds his praise. The conclusion of *The Ordering of Moses* is an extended setting of the spiritual "He Is King of Kings," which also includes variants of "Go Down, Moses." Moses and Miriam again sing Jehovah's praise, and the chorus proclaims "Praise the Great I Am" before the orchestra's final *presto* flourish.

Example 3. *The Ordering of Moses,* ostinato pattern

The instrumental sections of the work are intended to convey both mood—the "Prelude" and "Meditation of Moses"—and dramatic action—"March of the Israelites" and "The Egyptians Pursue." The latter two movements, describing the successful exodus of the Jews into the Promised Land, constitute the turning point of this extended choral work. From the initial lament to Moses "smoting" the water, the tonal center moves from F minor to B-flat major, with many excursions along the way. This first section is followed by the "March" in D-flat major, then in A major (one of the many instances of the third relation, favored by Dett), to A minor for the pursuit, and briefly back to F minor. Miriam's C-major aria leads to the triumphant "King of Kings," in F major.

The Ordering of Moses is an oratorio, although that term is not used in the vocal score. It was written in 1931–32 when Dett was working for his master's degree at the Eastman School of Music, and it fulfilled the thesis requirement for the degree. The first performance, however, was given not in Rochester but in Cincinnati, at the prestigious May Festival in 1937. Dett evidently made several revisions of the score between the time of its completion and the premiere. Reaction by the audience and critics was enthusiastic, and several other performances followed. Dett's treatment of the text, with its intermingling of scripture and folklore, and his skillful synthesis of African-American with European musical techniques demonstrate his sensitivity to and mastery of

melodic, harmonic, rhythmic, and formal practices of both traditions. *The Ordering of Moses* is one of his most, if not *the* most, significant achievements as a composer.

ENCHANTMENT (1922)

Dett wrote that his piano suite *In the Bottoms* gave "pictures of moods or scenes peculiar to Negro life." *Enchantment,* written almost a decade later (1922) and more technically demanding, is subtitled "A Romantic Suite for the Piano on an Original Program." Not intended as pictorial, as were the movements in the earlier suite, its program can be considered "psychological." The theme of the program is a soul's search for the unattainable. Titles of the four pieces are "Incantation," "Song of the Shrine," "Dance of Desire," and "Beyond the Dream." "Romantic" is a key word in describing this suite, which has much of the character of salon music. The term "fantasy pieces," too, seems apt. The suite demonstrates Dett's ease in treating late-19th-century harmonic practice—highly chromatic, yet grounded firmly in tonality. Thematic motives grow out of diatonic scales and chords, often chromatically embellished. Formal patterns are two-part, three-part, and rondo. No metronome marks are given, so the performer must judge basic tempos for each work, three of which require frequent to constant *rubato* tempos.

The music has a brooding, sometimes obsessive quality, with extensive use of augmented chords and diminished seventh and ninth chords and much repetition, often literal, of melodic motives and harmonic and rhythmic patterns.

In "Incantation" (marked *Agitato*), *rubato* tempos and fluctuating dynamic levels, often from measure to measure, prevail. Dett usually works in four-measure phrases, but phrase lengths tend to be more irregular here than in many of his compositions, with three-, five-, and seven-measure phrases. The form is three-part (ABA'), with the return of the A section much varied from its first occurrence. "Incantation" is in C-sharp minor, the A section being in the relative major key of E. The return of the A section begins in E major and moves through chords by half-step and tritone progressions to an arpeggio flourish of a *g*-sharp eleventh chord, signaling the return of C-sharp minor, but first in the major mode. The climax of the piece begins with a restatement of the A section theme, which is then followed by a chord progression over the dominant, comprised of repeated octave chords in sextuplets for both hands. A coda, *presto* and *prestissimo,* with an octave figure based on the theme and a rapidly ascending chord progression, leads to the final, plagal cadence, *allargamente.* The B section, relatively short, alternates a ponderous progression of four chords (I, II, V, I) with rapidly moving scale figures. The second A section, with more juxtapositions of tempo and keyboard textures than in the first, might be seen, according to Dett, as the soul's yielding "to an overpowering impulse of the moment to utter an Incantation before the shrine of an unknown goddess."

"Song of the Shrine" is monothematic, the theme in two four-measure phrases from which essentially all melodic motives and scalar and chordal embellishments are derived. There is relatively little tonal motion, the most frequent being from the key center E-major to its relative C-sharp minor. The span of the melody is almost two octaves, and its character is plaintive, the tempo marking being *Lento con molto espressione.* Melodic statements grow in intensity, from the single-note presentation to the theme in harmonized octaves and more rapid ornamentation in the right hand. With a change of meter, from cut time to 6/4, the longer notes are extended by one beat, which makes the theme more emphatic. This is the climax of the piece—perhaps, as Dett writes, when the soul hears a "voice of molten melody Singing love that may not be." After this passage, the texture lightens, and over 25 measures the piece subsides to the final E-major chord, *pianissimo.* There is some ambiguity about the form of the "Song of the Shrine." It can be analyzed as two-part, the second part beginning with an ornamented theme at Tempo I (m. 39), or as three-part, the second again beginning at measure 39 and the third beginning at measure 55 after the climax. However viewed, the theme as it is interwoven throughout the work creates a sense of strong unity.

Con moto is the tempo indication of "Dance and Desire," which contrasts greatly with the preceding "Song of the Shrine." Six short principal thematic motives are variously related and juxtaposed over a steady, driving rhythm in duple time. Syncopation animates two of those motives, all of which are usually in two- or four-measure phrases. The formal organization of the piece is a rondo, in which the main themes of "Incantation" and "Song of the Shrine" are parodied. ("In the urge of the music the Incantation mingles with the now mocking Song of the Shrine.") There are abrupt and frequent key changes and shifts in tonal centers, and chord progressions are often parallel. Contrary motion between right and left hands is frequently used. The piece builds to a climax through rhythmic complexity (including three eighth notes against four 16ths and five 16ths against two eighth notes), sustained loud dynamic level, more *marcato* articulation, and octaves staggered between left and right hands. The effect is of a toccata.

The concluding number of *Enchantment,* "Beyond the Dream," marked *Andante patetico,* is the most lyric and reflective of the suite. The expansive main theme, extending over almost two octaves, has a vocal quality and employs hemiola. The second theme, in an inner voice, is a chromatic-scale figure also using hemiola. The form is two-part, with a transition between the two parts serving almost as a cadenza. The two-measure head motive of the main theme is the basis for the thematic motives, and agitated chord motion is parallel. In the second part, the accompaniment varies from the first part, and the themes themselves move in different key areas. In the conclusion of the work, the pace slows, chords are extended over two measures, an ascending chromatic line based on the second theme, in hemiola, rests on the tonic note *a,* and the tonic chord unfolds in single notes, from the lowest *a* on the keyboard to the highest, over the span of seven measures. The soul remains with "the still unsatisfied longing for the unattainable."

Dett's idiomatic writing for the piano indicates a high level of sensitivity to the instrument's coloristic possibilities, including chord voicings from two notes to 12 and more, filigree patterns based on scales and chords, articulation, changes in dynamic level from very gradual to very abrupt, and contrasts of registers. The kinds of demands he makes on the performer attest to his own technical achievements as a pianist.

The suite was dedicated to Percy Grainger "in appreciation," and Grainger's interest in Dett's music is an indication of the regard held for Dett in the musical community. There seems to be little current performance of *Enchantment,* while there is some of *In the Bottoms.* Given broader-based musical tastes in the closing years of the 20th century, a revival of interest in Dett's piano music is due.

REFERENCES

Dett, R[obert] Nathaniel. "The Development of the Negro Spiritual." In *The Dett Collection of Negro Spirituals,* 4: 3–4. Chicago: Hall and McCreary, 1936.

_____. "Negro Music." In *The International Cyclopedia of Music and Musicians,* 1st ed., edited by Oscar Thompson, 1243–1246. New York: Dodd, Mead, 1939.

_____, ed. *Religious Folk-Songs of the Negro as Sung at Hampton Institute.* Hampton, Va.: Hampton Institute Press, 1927.

Dett, R[obert] Nathaniel, and Charles H. Flax. Program notes. Recital program of Dett and Flax, Philadelphia, Pa., February 24, 1931. Original held by Walter Moss Jr., Philadelphia, Pa.

Fenner, Thomas P. "Preface to the First Edition (1874)." In *Religious Folk-Songs of the Negro as Sung at Hampton Institute,* edited by R. Nathaniel Dett, v-vi. Hampton, Va.: Hampton Institute Press, 1927.

Floyd, Samuel A., Jr. "Music in the Harlem Renaissance: An Overview." In *Black Music in the Harlem Renaissance,* edited by Samuel A. Floyd Jr., 1–27. Westport, Conn.: Greenwood Press, 1990.

Johnson, James Weldon, ed. *The Book of American Negro Poetry.* Rev. ed. New York: Harcourt, Brace and World, 1959.

McBrier, Vivian Flagg. "The Life and Works of Robert Nathaniel Dett." Ph.D. diss., Catholic University of America, 1967.

_____. *R. Nathaniel Dett, His Life and Works, 1882–1943.* Washington, D.C.: Associated Publishers, 1977.

Moton, Robert R. "Preface to Edition of 1909." In *Religious Folk-Songs of the Negro as Sung at Hampton Institute,* edited by R. Nathaniel Dett, ix. Hampton, Va.: Hampton Institute Press, 1927.

Ryder, Georgia A. "Harlem Renaissance Ideals in the Music of Robert Nathaniel Dett." In *Black Music in the Harlem Renaissance,* edited by Samuel A. Floyd Jr., 55–70. Westport, Conn.: Greenwood Press, 1990.

Simpson, Anne Key. *Follow Me: The Life and Music of R. Nathaniel Dett.* Metuchen, N.J.: Scarecrow Press, 1993.

Southern, Eileen. *The Music of Black Americans: A History.* 2nd ed. New York: W. W. Norton, 1983.

Spencer, Jon Michael. "R. Nathaniel Dett's Views on the Preservation of Black Music." *Black Perspective in Music* 10, no. 2 (1982): 133–148.

Stanley, May. "R. N. Dett, of Hampton Institute, Helping to Lay the Foundation for Negro Music of Future." *Musical America* 28 (July 1918): 17+.

GEORGIA A. RYDER

DICKERSON, ROGER DONALD

Born in New Orleans, La., August 24, 1934. **Education:** New Orleans, public schools; studied piano performance with Miriam Panalle, 1942–48; studied counterpoint, harmony, and orchestration with Wallace Davenport, a relative who played trumpet with Lionel Hampton, Duke Ellington, Count Basie, and Ray Charles; Dillard University, New Orleans, B.A. *cum laude,* 1955; Indiana University at Bloomington, studied composition with Bernard Heiden and orchestration with Thomas Beversdorf, M.M., 1957; Akademie für Musik und Darstellende Kunst, Vienna, Austria, studied composition with Karl Schiske and Alfred Uhl, 1959–62. **Military Service:** U.S. Army, Specialist 3rd Class, 1957–59; Fort Chaffee, Ark., 1957, Heidelberg, Germany, 1957–59. **Composing and Performing Career:** New Orleans, began composing in elementary school; played jazz and blues professionally in college; toured with Joe Turner and "Guitar Slim," summers, 1951–54; Fort Smith, Ark., played double bass with the Fort Smith Symphony Orchestra, 1957; Heidelberg, Germany, composed and arranged for USAREUR (United States Army in Europe) Headquarters Company Band, 1957–59; New Orleans, performed extensively in French Quarter, 1962–present; compositions performed by New Orleans Symphony and other groups, 1962–present; Institute for Services to Education, Washington, D.C., Program Associate/Consultant in Humanities, 1979. **Teaching Career:** private teaching, composition and piano, 1962–present; Xavier University of Louisiana, New Orleans, adjunct professor, 1979–82; Southern University at New Orleans, adjunct professor, 1979–85, associate professor and coordinator of music in the Division of Fine Arts, 1985–present; Dillard University, New Orleans, Lecturer in Music, 1986–present. **Commissions:** New Orleans Symphony, 1973; Rockefeller Foundation, 1973; New Orleans Bicentennial Commission/New Orleans Chapter, Links, Inc., 1976; Loyola University Chorale, New Orleans, 1979; Richard Baruch, 1983. **Memberships:** ASCAP, 1965; Creative Arts Alliance of New Orleans (CAANO), co-founder, 1975; Phi Mu Alpha Sinfonia, 1977; Mayor's Task Force on Arts Policy for the City of New Orleans, 1978; Mayor's Advisory Board for Arts and Cultural Affairs for the City of New Orleans, 1979; Louisiana State Division of the Arts grant committee, 1981. **Honors/Awards:** Dillard University Scholarship, 1951–55; Dave Frank Award (Werlein's for Music), 1955; Louisiana Out-of-State Scholarship, 1956–57; Fulbright Fellowship, 1959–60, 1960–61; John Hay Whitney Fellowship, 1964; American Music Center Award, 1972, 1975; New Orleans Bicentennial Commission Certificate, 1977; New Orleans, Citation of Achievement and key to the city, 1977; New Orleans Recreation Department (NORD), Louis Armstrong Cultural Development Fund Memorial Award, 1977; Masons Enterprises of New Orleans, Outstanding Musicianship Award, 1977; Special Commendation, City Council of New Orleans, 1978; National Distinguished Achievement Award in the Arts, Links, Inc., 21st National Assembly, Chicago, 1978; Austin, Tex., key to the city, 1978; Institute for Services to Education (ISE), Washington, D.C., beginning 1978; annual ASCAP Awards, 1978–82; University of New Orleans, Marcus-Christian Award, 1979; University of New Orleans, artist-in-residence, 1979; National Endowment for the Arts grant in composition, 1980; Kennedy Center for the Performing Arts, National Black Music Colloquium, composer-honoree, 1980; Louisiana State Arts Council, music panelist, beginning 1981; New Orleans Arts Council Board, 1981–82; National Endowment for the Arts, panelist, beginning 1984; Institute for Minority Nationalities, People's Republic of China, honorary doctorate, 1990. **Mailing Address:** c/o ASCAP, ASCAP Building, One Lincoln Plaza, New York, NY 10023.

MUSIC LIST

INSTRUMENTAL SOLOS
Trumpet
"Movement for Trumpet and Piano." 1960. New York: Southern Music, n.d. Premiere, 1960.

Piano
Sonatina for Piano. 1956. New York: Southern Music, 1980. Premiere, 1956.

Organ
Chorale Prelude ("Das neugeborne Kindelein"). 1956. Boston: E. C. Schirmer, 1966. Premiere, 1971.

SMALL INSTRUMENTAL ENSEMBLE
Strings
Music for String Trio. 1957. Unpublished manuscript.
String Quartet. 1956. New York: Southern Music, n.d. Premiere, 1957.

Woodwinds
Quintet for Wind Instruments. 1961. New York: Southern Music, n.d. Premiere, 1961.
Variations for Woodwind Trio (flute, clarinet, bassoon). 1955. Unpublished manuscript. Premiere, 1956.

Percussion
"Prekussion" (triangle, wood blocks, large cymbal, tambourine, bass drum, tom tom, side drum, castanets, timpani, piano). 1954. Unpublished manuscript. Premiere, 1954.

STRING ORCHESTRA
Ten Concert Pieces for Beginning String Players. 1973. New York: Southern Music, 1977. Contents: Cathedral Bells; Jubilee; Angelic Chorus; Dance; Mysteries; Song; Parade of the Dragons; An American Village; Figures in Space; The Machine Age. Commissioned by the youth string program of the New Orleans Symphony through a Rockefeller Foundation grant. Premiere, nos. 1, 5, 7, and 9, 1973.

FULL ORCHESTRA
Concert Overture for Orchestra. 1957. New York: Southern Music (rental). Note: master's thesis. Premiere, 1965.

Orpheus an' His Slide Trombone (orchestra, narrator). 1974–75. New York: Southern Music, n.d. Premiere, 1975.

ORCHESTRA (CHAMBER OR FULL) WITH SOLOISTS

New Orleans Concerto (soprano soloist, piano, orchestra). 1976. New York: Southern Music, n.d. Commissioned by New Orleans Bicentennial Commission/New Orleans Chapter, Links, Inc. Premiere, 1977.

ORCHESTRA (CHAMBER OR FULL) WITH CHORUS

A Musical Service for Louis (A Requiem for Louis Armstrong) (orchestra, optional mixed chorus). 1972. New York: Southern Music, 1973. Commissioned by the New Orleans Symphony. Premiere, 1972.

CONCERT BAND

Essay for Band. 1958. New York: Southern Music, n.d. Premiere, 1958. Recorded: Northern Arizona University NAUWS 003.

JAZZ ENSEMBLE

"Fugue 'n Blues" (trumpets, trombones, saxophones, rhythm section, solo flute). 1959. Unpublished manuscript. Premiere, 1959.

SOLO VOICE

"Music I Heard" (soprano). 1956. Unpublished manuscript. Premiere, 1956.

"The Negro Speaks of Rivers" (soprano). 1961. Note: vocal line can be played by flute or oboe. Premiere, 1969.

CHORAL MUSIC

"African-American Celebration" (soprano, SATB unaccompanied). 1984. Unpublished manuscript. Premiere, 1984.

"Fair Dillard" (SATB unaccompanied). 1955. Unpublished manuscript. Premiere, 1955.

"Psalm 49" (SATB, three timpani). 1979. New York: Southern Music, n.d. Commissioned by the Loyola University Chorale, New Orleans. Premiere, 1979.

PUBLICATIONS

ABOUT DICKERSON
Articles

Johnson, Clifford V., and Carolyn Fitchett-Bins, eds. *A Discussion Guide for the* New Orleans Concerto *Film.* Washington, D.C.: Institute for Services to Education, 1978.

Tischler, Alice. "Roger Dickerson." In *Fifteen Black American Composers: A Bibliography of Their Works,* 125–133. Detroit: Information Coordinators, 1981.

Wyatt, Lucius R. "Roger Dickerson, Composer." *Black Music Research Newsletter* 6, no. 2 (1984): 3–5.

Film Documentary

New Orleans Concerto. New York: Jim Hinton, 1978.

BY DICKERSON

"Introduction." In *New Orleans Blues,* Marty Most. New Orleans: Maurice Martinez, 1964.

PRINCIPAL ARCHIVES

Roger Dickerson Collection, Amistad Research Center, Tulane University, New Orleans, La.

* * * * *

Roger Dickerson's importance as a composer lies in the fact that he speaks with his own voice, one that is an amalgam of his two distinct worlds of music: one personal and subjective—the informal (jazz) tradition of his native New Orleans; the other impersonal and objective—the formal (classically oriented) tradition inculcated by his graduate experiences at Indiana University School of Music and his strong European training at the Akademie für Musik und Darstellende Kunst in Vienna. These two worlds, the formal and the informal, come from the same source, spirit, consciousness; and with him, there are no contradictions between these two streams of music, rather, they both feed on each other. Dickerson has excelled in both traditions. As Roscoe Lee Browne has said, when you hear his music, "you are aware [that] someone with [a] passionate intellect has written it."

From an early age, Dickerson was exposed to a musical environment in both his family and his neighborhood in New Orleans. According to Dickerson, nearly everyone in the community had a piano. From age 8 to 14, he studied the piano with Miriam Panalle. At two nearby elementary schools, McDonogh 37 and Wicker, his talent was nurtured and his participation in the many available musical activities was supported. Since the piano was not used in the band, he learned to play other instruments. He began with the French horn and proceeded throughout high school and into college to learn the double bass, the baritone horn, alto saxophone, trombone, and tuba, thereby laying the groundwork for his understanding of instrumentation and orchestration.

In addition to his school music experiences, he had been listening to the music in the streets of New Orleans, which had an alluring appeal to the developing young musician. He was instrumental in forming a band with some of the fellow students in the neighborhood, including his life-long friend Ellis Marsalis. A relative by marriage, Wallace Davenport, who played with Lionel Hampton, Duke Ellington, Count Basie, and Ray Charles, made some small arrangements for the neighborhood group of youngsters and taught Dickerson how to transpose and orchestrate. The young group played in the community and later at dances at the YMCA and St. Katherine's Church Hall, both located close to the neighborhood. Eventually, the group was called Roger Dickerson and the Groovy Boys. Others of the professional musicians in the close-knit area assisted the young musicians by loaning them their instruments, including the double bass and saxophones. Among them were Lee Allen, a tenor saxophone player, and Roy Brown of "Good Rocking Tonight" fame, who was a next-door neighbor of Dickerson's mother.

The neighborhood was a beehive of musical activity both in the schools and in the streets. Close by was the internationally famous club, the Dew Drop Inn, where all the major jazz artists who came to New Orleans would perform and where, as a high school and college student, Dickerson himself performed.

Roger Donald Dickerson; courtesy of the composer

In high school, Dickerson attended two of the premiere African-American schools in New Orleans: one, the private and now defunct Gilbert Academy, operated by the Congregational Church; the other, McDonogh 35 Senior High School. At Gilbert Academy, Dickerson and Marsalis were members of a jazz group promoted by a dynamic educator, Maxine Holtry, who became one of Dickerson's prime motivators.

Following high school, Dickerson won a scholarship to Dillard University (New Orleans) and in 1955 became an honors graduate with a bachelor of arts degree in music. While at Dillard, Dickerson had the musical support and encouragement of two individuals who sustained his interest in becoming a composer: Dr. Melville Bryant, who was the head of Dillard's music department and for whom Dickerson made some arrangements for his Army Reserve band; and David Buttolph, who was a former student of Hindemith and who informally guided Dickerson in his compositional efforts. Buttolph also served as a contact with the New Orleans Symphony, which later premiered a number of Dickerson's works. At Dillard, Dickerson studied piano briefly with the distinguished concert pianist and composer, George Walker.

Dickerson began his formal studies in composition in 1955 with Bernhard Heiden at Indiana University's School of Music. In addition to composition, Dickerson studied score reading with Heiden, orchestration with Thomas Beversdorf, and other theoretical studies with Charles Kent and William Christ. While there, Dickerson became a musical cohort of distinguished African-American jazz artist and composer David Baker and music educator and jazz connoisseur Bernard Holly. Dickerson's thesis for his master of music degree in composition at Indiana was *Concert Overture for Orchestra* (1957).

Works that demonstrate Dickerson's individuality and independence, his nationalistic bent, and his particular musical ancestry are a piece for big band, "Fugue 'n Blues" (1959), premiered by the 33rd Army Band in Heidelberg, Germany; "The Negro Speaks of Rivers" (1961), for high voice and piano (optional flute or oboe and vocal line), on a popular text of Langston Hughes; and "African-American Celebration" (1984), for *a cappella* choir. These three works also demonstrate his affinity for both formal and informal works and his tendency toward stylistic integration in logical, coherent works based on his belief that for him, both composed and improvised music come from the same source—spirit consciousness.

In 1965, the New Orleans Symphony, in residence at Tulane University in New Orleans, premiered *Concert Overture for Orchestra* as part of a symposium for composers. At this premiere, the work was recorded and a live broadcast for the Voice of America was made. This collaboration of Dickerson, the New Orleans Symphony, and its conductor Werner Torkanowsky was the first of a long line of fruitful experiences the composer enjoyed with this musical organization. The compositions Dickerson composed for the orchestra include *Concert Overture for Orchestra* (1965), *A Musical Service for Louis* (1972), *Orpheus an' His Slide Trombone* (1975), and *New Orleans Concerto* (1976), and he arranged for the orchestra, with Electric Soul Train and jazz orchestra, *Many Rivers to Cross* (1970).

Immediately after completing his master's degree in 1957, Dickerson went back to his reserve army status to retain his rank of

Specialist 3rd Class and was then drafted into the army. He did his basic and advanced training at Fort Chaffee Military Base in Arkansas, where he performed with and arranged for the 449th Army Band and composed for it his *Essay for Band* (1958). While at Fort Chaffee, Dickerson also played double bass with the Fort Smith (Arkansas) Symphony Orchestra. At the end of basic training, he received orders to report to Heidelberg, Germany, where he was assigned to the USAREUR Headquarters Band.

At the end of his military service, Dickerson received a Fulbright Fellowship. With it, he spent the years 1959–62 studying composition at the Akademie für Musik und Darstellende Kunst in Vienna, Austria, with Alfred Uhl and Karl Schiske. Throughout his stay in Vienna, Dickerson studied piano with Frau Professor Brunnhauser. By now fluent in the German language (all classes at the Akademie were held in German), Dickerson immersed himself in this musical capitol, which claimed three symphony orchestras and two opera houses. Through his activities in this musical city and other European locations, especially his yearly visits to Italy, Dickerson became fascinated with European visual art. "In reverse, as the visual artists had come to music for their inspiration," he said, "I went to the visual artist for my sustenance, my inspiration or influence—from them, I reached a level of consciousness beyond the [common]: a precious profundity about our reality." While at the Akademie, Dickerson met such national and international figures as Willi Apel, Paul Hindemith, Zubin Mehta, Raoul Abdul, Cannonball Adderly, and the African-American composer Howard Swanson. Dickerson readily admits the dynamic influence of Swanson—personally, professionally, and artistically—on his own musical life and art.

Many of the young musicians, artists, and composers at this period felt that New York was the focal point for a serious career as an artist. Although Dickerson considered living there, he felt more strongly that his musical life, career, and composition should be rooted in his own unique cultural heritage. Therefore, in 1962, after his sojourn in Vienna, Dickerson decided to return to New Orleans and re-immerse himself in the rich musical life of his native city, where he feels, his "place in the sun" can be nourished, regenerated, and fulfilled. In New Orleans, Dickerson renewed his lifelong friendship with such outstanding musicians as Ellis Marsalis (patriarch of the musical Marsalis clan), Allen Toussaint, and the visual artist John Scott, among others, who shared his feelings about the indigenous and unique cultural quality of their native city. As he told me, "There is a cultural sun in New Orleans—the whole cultural phenomenon of New Orleans would continue to nourish and sensitize my soul and spirit—the city for me is a cultural oil field."

In New Orleans, Dickerson was a catalyst for and co-founder and first president of the Creative Artists Alliance of New Orleans (CAANO). CAANO's membership included a group of artists who believed that New Orleans could be the source and center of their creative life. The organization would act as a resuscitation for aesthetic and personal consciousness and as a "transfertilization" of creative perceptions and processes. Dickerson has commented that this New Orleans period was a "glorious time in my life."

One member of this group was Werner Torkanowsky, conductor of the New Orleans Symphony (1963–77), a treasured musical colleague, a respected personal friend, and a promoter of

Dickerson's works. Through the influence and efforts of Tor-kanowsky, Dickerson received premieres of five of his large works for orchestra. Torkanowsky felt that the orchestra should be rooted in the culture that it serves and that it has the responsibility of performing the works of native composers. In fact, all of Dickerson's music, published or not, has been performed.

Dickerson is presently working on a large-scale work based on New Orleans culture in the 1940s, and he continues to be involved in the musical and cultural life of his beloved city. His musical life is enhanced by his performance and teaching. In addition to extensive private instruction of composition, arranging, orchestration, piano, voice, and music theory, he serves as associate professor and Coordinator of Music in the Department of Fine Arts and Philosophy at Southern University at New Orleans (SUNO). Teaching and working with young people hold a special place in Dickerson's world of music—a strong concern for the personal worth of each individual student. He has refined his musical thought and philosophy on music to a fine point. Succinctly, Dickerson made this summation: "I cannot deny who I am. . . . I can only be my experience."

SONATINA FOR PIANO (1956)

The Sonatina for Piano is in three movements in fast-slow-fast format, the two outer movements in the key area of E-flat and the middle in B-flat. Each of those movements begins in those keys, and in the course of each there is modulation to a number of different keys, with highly chromatic writing. The structural plan in each movement is ABA, and, as is customary in sonatina form, there are only short sections of thematic development.

The first movement has two basic thematic ideas, the first melody having a well-defined curve, the second, a more disjointed character. The second theme is followed by a short development section that prepares for the return of the first theme, and the closing section contains a reprise of the second theme.

The impressionistic second movement, à la Debussy, contains an eight-measure melodic idea that is stated twice. Resonant harmonies accompany a melodic line that appears in the key of B-flat. An abrupt modulation to the key of C ushers in the B section, where there appear three short, improvisation-like variations on the theme. Through chromatic alteration, there is a smooth return to the A section, which is in the key of B-flat; the repeat of the A section, which follows, is exactly the same as the first.

The energetic and fast final movement contains two main germinal ideas, each complementary of the other and each extended, expanded, and developed. The overall form is ABA' coda.

The Sonatina was written when the composer was 22 years old, but it remained unpublished until 1980. In the interim, however, the work was performed frequently by a number of pianists. In January 1980, it was featured as part of the National Black Music Colloquium and Competition. A year later, the International American Music Competitions, sponsored by Carnegie Hall and the Rockefeller Foundation, selected the Sonatina as one of the required competition numbers.

"Sonatina . . . showed a freshness of approach and some imagination. The work is pianistic," wrote Sidney Dalton in the Nashville Tennessean of November 5, 1956. Louis Nicholas, in the same paper, wrote that "Sonatina . . . disclosed a pleasant well-made composition which showed a very valuable sense possessed by the composer—the knowledge of when to stop!"

AFRICAN-AMERICAN CELEBRATION (1984)

"African-American Celebration," for a cappella choir with soprano solo, was composed for and dedicated to the Afro-American Pavilion of the 1984 Louisiana World Exposition. Because the official name for the Pavilion was "I've Known Rivers," after the first line of Langston Hughes' poem of the same name, Dickerson penned in the score of this short but effective work the following words, which refer to the Hughes poem: "Celebration of Life! Great rivers, rivers of life, Celebrate Black American life, oh yes, Black life. We celebrate life! Celebration of life! Afro-American culture, Black American life. Black life, great gifts, with pride we celebrate life, oh yes! We celebrate with pride. Oh great gifts to the world and to America. Oh yes great gifts! We stand as a catalyst for true democracy. We break ground today to celebrate great culture, great gifts. African-American culture, African-American gifts. Celebration of Life! We celebrate our great spirit. Great rivers of life. Celebrate, my Lord. Our rich contributions!"

The entire work derives from and is based on its opening six-note motive, which sets the text "Celebration of life" in equal eighth notes. Throughout the work, this germinal idea is found whenever the text "Celebration of Life" is stated. The repetition of melodic and rhythmic motives serves as a unifying and an organizing principle in this opus. Although references are made to the African-American spiritual, the work has more of the qualities of a patriotic song, a song of inspiration or of pride, than those of the spiritual.

The solo voice plays the role of a song leader and an inspirer of participation, recalling the call-and-response device so often present in African-American folk music. The final statement of the work, "our rich contributions," is performed by the soloist ad libitum.

Dickerson has captured the spirit of celebration in this compact work. The importance of nuances, shadings, articulation of color tones, word painting, contrasts between chorus and soloist, and the vitality of its rhythmic cells all contribute to the work's expressiveness. This little gem, one of Dickerson's most integrated and well-knit works, evokes very successfully the spirit of an African-American celebration.

STRING QUARTET (1956)

The String Quartet, in three movements, recalls the string quartets of Bartók. The first movement is in rounded binary form (introduction ABA' coda). The movement progresses by way of expansion and elaboration of its thematic material; and it is polythematic (two or more themes) and atonal (without a tonal center), although there are sporadic references to tonality or areas that resemble tonality. The movement begins with a short four-measure introduction by the full quartet, after which the first violin states the first theme with underlying support from the other instruments. This thematic material is tossed about from part to part, closely followed by material that makes use of syncopation and double-stop passages that are exchanged between the first and second violins and the viola and cello. Solo parts are to be played espressivo, and there are sections in which pizzicato (plucking) and arco (with the bow) alternate. Modified statements of the first theme are found sporadically as the movement progresses. Alternate phrasings, with the first and second violins appearing on the beat and the viola and cello off the beat, appear in syncopated exchanges throughout the movement.

The contrasting second theme is heard first in the violins, supported by chordal accompaniment in the other instruments. The second theme is then played by the viola, followed, after a brief episode, by the first and second violins an octave apart. After several excursions into related but modified thematic material, the first theme reappears, and a short call-and-response passage is played by the first violin and viola.

Activated by a syncopated entrance, the first-theme material is developed in alternating on-beat and off-beat patterns, first by the first violin and cello, then by the second violin and viola, and next by the cello and viola, accompanied by violins playing trills or *pizzicato*. The first violin plays an extended first theme that abounds in double stops and is augmented by strongly accented syncopated beats in the viola and cello. Then comes an energetic fugal coda, in which the viola and violins build the dynamic level throughout the last 18 measures of the movement.

The form of the second movement is ABA', following very closely the traditional scheme for the slow movement of the sonata form. It begins as a contrapuntal series of contrasts between a subject and countersubject, first between the first violin and viola, then viola and cello, and finally the cello and second violin. After this opening exchange, the subject and countersubject become motivic in character. At the *più mosso*, new material is stated—a descending melodic/rhythmic fragment that is exchanged among the voices. The first violin plays a rhythmically augmented version of this material; at the finale of the section, the ensemble plays with full intensity (marked *fff*). A short cadenza, played first by the viola and second violin (marked *ad lib.*), serves as a bridge to a return of the original subject of the second movement (see Ex. 1).

Example 1. String Quartet, second movement, mm. 1–4

At the return of the original tempo (A'), abridged statements of the original idea return with the second violin playing the subject and the first violin, the countersubject. Fragmented exchanges of the original musical idea continue among all the members of the quartet through the remainder of the movement. The cello makes reference to a fragment from the *più mosso* or second theme. The movement ends quietly (*ppp*) with moody exchanges between all the voices.

The third movement begins in a tranquil manner with the cello in the role of soloist. It is a rondo (ABA'B'A), marked *Allegro*, with a slow introduction, marked *Lento placido*, and a corresponding concluding *Andante sostenuto*. In the *Allegro*, the bouncy A theme is tossed around first by the first violin, then the second violin and viola; the cello responds with the beginning of the theme after another full statement by the first violin. The jagged but dissonant and contrapuntal texture of the first theme is balanced by an expressive and smooth B theme played alternately by the first violin, second violin, viola, and cello. The return of the first theme (A') is slightly altered from the first statement; in addition, the cello, which played only the beginning of the theme in the first A section, now answers the first violin with a full statement. The B' section begins with the cello rather than the first violin. Throughout the section, the cello plays rhythmic variations on the theme while the other instruments carry on dialogues with each other. The first violin opens the final section with a statement of the theme followed by a quick response from the viola. A continuous dotted rhythmic pattern by the second violin, viola, and cello ensues, and the final climactic statement gradually builds collectively to a sustained *fortissimo*. As the movement began with a slow and calm tempo and mood (*Lento placido*), so it ends (*Andante sostenuto*), using thematic material from the B theme.

A MUSICAL SERVICE FOR LOUIS (A REQUIEM FOR LOUIS ARMSTRONG) (1972)

A Musical Service for Louis, for orchestra and optional chorus, approximately 15 minutes in length, is based on an ever-present three-note motive that appears in various guises throughout the composition. Toward the end of the work there appears a second persistent, reiterated melodic and rhythmic pattern that grows in loudness and intensity, then subsides in three final statements by an off-stage trumpet—the work's single direct reference to Louis Armstrong.

This one-movement work begins with the establishment of the somber and serene mood of the dirge. The opening statement of the motive is heard in the first five measures of the work as it is played in unison by the first violin, first trombone, and the first horn in F. This generative motive operates much in the manner of the famous four-note opening motive in Beethoven's Symphony no. 5. As this section progresses, the strings play short bluesy turns while the harp and piano glide idiomatically along, adding to the serene quality of the section. Points of color evoke blues and jazz, but the writing is generally not based in African-American idioms.

At measure 50, marked *pesante* for the trombones and tuba, the tempo changes. Introduced by the violins and violas in another bluesy turn, this section becomes more accented and rhythmic in all the parts, as it prepares for the second major part of the work, which appears to be a "dance" section. Measures 50 to 58 serve as a musical bridge to the following section at measure 60, which is marked "faster."

The dance section recalls the traditional New Orleans jazz funeral of which the "second line" (the dancers—the followers of the first line) is a characteristic feature. At this point the chorus, accompanied by snare drum, tambourine, third trumpet, and eventually all the trumpets, augmented by hand clapping ("with feeling"), add a distinct orchestral color. At measure 75, the additional color of the jazz drum set (ride cymbals, drums, and hi-hat) blends into the ensemble and continues through the remainder of the dance section.

After the movement gets under way, the feeling of collective improvisation abounds in force, with syncopated ragtime-like rhythms alternating between the various choirs of the orchestra. At various points, the piece "swings" in response to the composer's notation, "free playing permitted, 'swinging' as written rhythms." The drive and intensity of the dance section abruptly ends in measure 111.

At this break, the trombones return with an inverted variation of the motive in a slow tempo. Adding color to the musical texture of the work, the clarinet, trumpet (vibrato), trombones (muted), bassoons, horns, violins and violas, solo violin, English horn, and first and second violins (*con sordino*) display jazzy turns, bent notes, slides and scoops (*glissandi*), and blue notes, eventually anticipating the tritone outlined in the final three statements of the motive (see Ex. 2). Alternating with these color schemes are the somber tones of the various choirs as they enrich the overall sonority and blend of the orchestra.

Example 2. *A Musical Service for Louis,* mm. 193–196

A persistent melodic and rhythmic pattern begins in measure 153. This ostinato persists through the final three statements of the motive by the off-stage trumpet. The chorus joins the orchestral forces on the neutral vowel "Ah," which is doubled variously by the horns and the trumpets. The opening motive of the work returns, sung by the chorus and again doubled by either the horns or the trumpets. Finally, the work's dignified character gives way to a two-measure spot of jubilation—a joyful shout, a happy relaxation.

In a final statement of the ostinato, first in the strings, then in the full orchestra and chorus, the persistent melodic and rhythmic pattern returns and is sounded three times before the memorable final statements by the off-stage trumpet. This final trumpet solo, which is to be played vibrato "*à la* Louis," intimating that the legacy of Louis Armstrong should live forever, and accompanied only by the cellos and double basses that play from *piano diminuendo poco a poco* to *ppp*, is a dignified musical memorial to a celebrated artist and musician.

Torkanowsky, the musical director and conductor of the New Orleans Symphony, the organization that performed the premiere of *A Musical Service for Louis,* had this to say of the work: "Roger Dickerson has given us a dignified musical memorial. . . . The orchestra [New Orleans Symphony] is an altogether appropriate setting for this piece, and we are pleased that Roger Dickerson's composition has turned out so well. It's music that is very playable, will be enjoyed by the audience, and at the same time the piece has important historic significance. What is more fitting than the major music organization in the city of Louis'

birth, performing what is probably the first original work dedicated to the memory of this great jazz composer and trumpeter." This work was commissioned by Torkanowsky and the New Orleans Symphony, assisted by a grant from the National Endowment for the Arts.

Of a May 22, 1981, performance of *A Musical Service for Louis,* critic Frank Gagnard stated, "Dickerson's sometimes astringent alternating layers of dirge, lamentation, and up tempo blues remain arresting and very much an expression of the composer's own sensibility. . . . [H]is work is a personal expression of loss and appreciation."

Rhodes Spedale wrote in 1982 that Dickerson's music "is a form of personal, individual expression and creativity. . . . [It is] very much a creative statement of Dickerson, the individual." Indeed, Dickerson is adamant against categorization and classification in relation to his musical compositions and his role as a musician and composer.

Fellow musician Lucius R. Wyatt quotes from critics of *A Musical Service for Louis, Orpheus an' His Slide Trombone,* and the *New Orleans Concerto:* "Mr. Dickerson has achieved a personal style, which while American and clearly 20th century makes a distinctive and valuable musical statement." Critic Bill Trotter wrote that *A Musical Service for Louis* "is a melodramatic work, but the sincerity of its inspiration makes it a genuinely moving experience. . . . Dickerson is clearly a composer of uncommon gifts." Dickerson's String Quartet, the Sonatina for Piano, and the *Concert Overture for Orchestra* are early works that revealed the composer's promise.

REFERENCES

Browne, Roscoe Lee. Interview by Frank Gagnard. [New Orleans] *Times-Picayune* (March 18, 1975): sect. 2, 4.

Dalton, Sydney. "Patton Recital Demonstrates His Brilliance." *Nashville Tennessean* (November 5, 1956).

Dickerson, Roger. Interview with the author, August 6, 1995.

———. Program notes, *A Musical Service for Louis: A Requiem.* New Orleans Symphony, Werner Torkanowsky conducting. March 7, 1972.

Gagnard, Frank. "'Symphony in Black' Rewarding but Overextended." [New Orleans] *Times-Picayune/States-Item* (May 26, 1981).

———. "A Musical Service for Louis." [New Orleans] *Times-Picayune* (March 9, 1972).

Nicholas, Louis. "Cathedral Singers Opening Concert Called Pleasing." *Nashville Tennessean* (November 5, 1956).

Scarbrough, Ken. "With Humility and Piety, Roger Dickerson Serves the City, Students and the Human Spirit," *Scholastic* 122, no. 8 (April 1981): 22–24.

Spedale, Rhodes. "Roger Dickerson: Personal Expression in Music." *New Orleans Magazine* (June 1982).

Trotter, Bill. "EPO Concert: 2 Successes, 1 Failure." *Greensboro* [N.C.] *Record* (July 14, 1975).

Wyatt, Lucius. "Roger Dickerson, Composer." *Black Music Research Newsletter* 6, no. 2 (1984): 3–5.

MALCOLM J. BREDA

DIXON, WILLIE JAMES

Born in Vicksburg, Miss., July 1, 1915; died in Burbank, Calif., January 29, 1992. **Education:** Elementary school, Vicksburg. **Composing and Performing Career:** Moved to Chicago, Ill., and hoboed around the country, 1926–29; Vicksburg, Miss., worked in local spiritual groups, 1929–32; Chicago, pursued boxing career, 1936; learned string bass and began singing with guitarist and pianist Leonard "Baby Doo" Caston, 1938; formed, performed, and recorded with the Five Breezes, 1939–41, the Four Jumps of Jive, 1945–46, and the Big Three Trio, 1946–52; worked as producer, composer, arranger, musician, and A&R representative for various recording labels, most notably Chess Records, 1952–56, 1959–69, and Cobra Records, 1956–59; founded Ghana Music Publishing Company, 1957; organized the American Folk Blues Festival with Memphis Slim, early 1960s; various television appearances during the 1960s and 1970s; formed the Chicago Blues All Stars and toured the United States and Europe, late 1960s and 1970s; founded Yambo/Spoonful recording label complex, 1969; appeared in British film *Chicago Blues,* 1970; founded Blues Factory/Soul Productions, a talent, recording, and production company, ca. 1970–74; appeared in film *Out of the Blacks into the Blues,* 1972; autobiography published, 1989. **Honors/Awards:** *Blues Unlimited* readers' poll, Best Blues Bassist, 1973; *The Reader* pop poll, Chicago Blues Artist of the Year, 1973; Grammy Award for *Hidden Charms* album, 1988; Rock and Roll Hall of Fame inductee, 1994.

SELECTED MUSIC LIST

[The following list of titles includes only works that were composed by the subject of the entry; it is not a list of recordings that were made by the subject. Although the composer may have made recordings of his own works, the list is not restricted to those recordings but in many cases includes performances by other artists of the composer's work. The list is made up of publication and discographical data, in cases where such information available. Although no effort has been made to include documentation of the earliest recording of the works listed, the date of the earliest recording that is readily available has been given. —Ed.]

"Back Door Man." New York: Hoochie Coochie Music, 1960. Recorded: Blues Encore CD-52026; Chess CHD2-16500; Columbia/Legacy CK-53627.

"Bring It On Home." New York: Hoochie Coochie Music, 1963. Recorded: Chess CHD2-16500; Chess CD-1-15; Ovation OVD/ 1433.

"Crazy for My Baby" or "Crazy about You Baby." New York: Hoochie Coochie Music, 1954. Recorded: Blues Encore CD-52026; Chess CHD2-16500; MCA Records CHC-9353.

"Diddy Wah Diddy." New York: Arc Music/Hoochie Coochie Music, 1955. Co-composer, Ellas McDaniel. Recorded: Chrysalis 2; PRT 4009; Rhino R2-75777.

"Down in the Bottom." New York: Hoochie Coochie Music, 1961. Recorded; Chess LPS-1469; Chess 5908; Disky BV Kwest 5156; Vanguard 79178.

"Easy Baby." New York: Conrad Music/Hoochie Coochie Music, 1958.

Recorded: Bullseye Blues 9569; Bullseye Blues 9581; Capricorn 9 42012-2.

"Evil (Is Going On)." New York: Hoochie Coochie Music, 1954. Recorded: Chess CHD2-16500; Chess 9340; One Way 29219; Zillion 2611192.

"Hidden Charms." New York: Hoochie Coochie Music, 1958. Recorded: Chess CHD2-16500; Chess CHD-93001; Columbia/CBS PC-9987; Warner Brothers 45903.

"I Ain't Gonna Be Your Monkey Man." New York: Hoochie Coochie Music, 1949. Co-composer, Leonard Caston. Recorded: Columbia 30166; Columbia/Legacy CK-46216.

"I Ain't Superstitious." New York: Hoochie Coochie Music, 1961. Recorded: Chess CHD2-16500; Columbia/Legacy CK-53627; MCA CHD-9351.

"I Am the Blues." Copyright, 1969. New York: Hoochie Coochie Music/ Arc Music, n.d. Recorded: Chess 4553; Columbia/CBS PC-9987.

"I Can't Quit You Baby" or "Can't Quit You, Baby." Copyright, 1956. New York: Hoochie Coochie Music, n.d. Recorded: Capricorn 9 42012-2; Chess CHD2-16500; Columbia/Legacy CK-53627.

"I Just Want to Make Love to You" or "Airwave Jungle." New York: Hoochie Coochie Music, 1954. Recorded: Chess CHD2-16500; MCA Records CHC-9353; Varese Sarabande VSD-5234.

"I'm Ready." Copyright, 1954. New York: Hoochie Coochie Music, n.d. Recorded: Chess CHD2-16500; Chess CD-1012; Def American Recordings 4-26795.

"(I'm Your) Hoochie Coochie Man." New York: Hoochie Coochie Music, 1954. Recorded: Chess CHD2-16500.

"Little Red Rooster" or "The Red Rooster." Copyright, 1961. New York: Hoochie Coochie Music, n.d. Recorded: Chess CHD2-16500; Columbia/Legacy CK-53627; Evidence Music ECD 26063-2.

"Mellow Down Easy." Copyright, 1954. New York: Hoochie Coochie Music, n.d. Recorded: Chess CHD2-16500; Chess CHD-9292; Country Music Foundation CMF-024-CD.

"My Babe." Copyright, 1955. New York: Hoochie Coochie Music, n.d. Recorded: Blues Encore CD-52026; Chess CHD2-16500; Evidence Music ECD 26052-2.

"My Love." New York: Arc Music/Hoochie Coochie Music, 1957. Recorded: Capricorn 9 42012-2.

"My Love Will Never Die." n.p.: Armel Music, 1952. Recorded: Capricorn 9 42012-2; Columbia/CBS PC-9987; Dr. Horse Sweden H-804.

"Pain in My Heart." New York: Hoochie Coochie Music, 1951. Recorded: Blues Encore CD-52026; Checker 851; Chess CHD2-16500.

"Pretty Thing." New York: Hoochie Coochie Music, 1955. Recorded: Chess CHD2-16500; Ichiban ICH-1060-CD; MCA 19502.

"The Same Thing." Copyright, 1964. New York: Hoochie Coochie Music, n.d. Recorded: Chess CHD2-16500; Columbia/Legacy CK-53627; Mobile Fidelity Sound Lab MFCD-872.

"The Seventh Son." Copyright, 1955. New York: Hoochie Coochie Music, n.d. Recorded: Chess CHD2-16500; Columbia/Legacy CK-53627; Evidence ECD 26063-2.

"Shake for Me." Copyright, 1961. New York: Hoochie Coochie Music,

(content)

Willie James Dixon; courtesy of the Frank Driggs Collection

West Side, gave the group its first work. The following year, the Five Breezes began recording for RCA. The group broke up in 1941, however, and in 1945, Dixon formed the Four Jumps of Jive and recorded for Mercury. This group soon broke up as well, and Dixon rejoined Caston to form the Big Three Trio in 1946. The group (bassist Dixon, pianist Caston, and guitarist Bernardo Dennis) was basically a lounge combo that mixed jazz, vocal harmonies, boogie-woogie, and a touch of blues—a sound established by Dixon's predecessor groups. When the Big Three Trio disbanded in 1952, they had been winding down for some time as the harder blues sounds and doo-wop groups were becoming more and more popular with African-American audiences.

Dixon began working as a session player for the Chess brothers in 1948, when he played on a Robert Nighthawk session. By the time the Big Three broke up, Dixon was working full-time in the studio. Soon he was producing and writing as well as playing in sessions.

The first artist with whom Dixon had success at Chess was Eddie Boyd. The song "Third Degree," released in 1953 and written for Boyd, demonstrated Dixon's ability to write brooding ballads, and this national hit led to more successful Chess recordings, including his "(I'm Your) Hoochie Coochie Man" which, written for Muddy Waters, went to number three on the R&B chart in 1954. Dixon penned two other hits for Muddy that year: "Just Make Love to Me" and "I'm Ready." With Chess's other blues giant, Little Walter, Dixon wrote the huge hit "My Babe" (1955), which became one of his most recorded songs. For a three-year interlude in the late 1950s, Dixon worked for a West Side label, Cobra, where he wrote some of the best songs that Otis Rush ever recorded, including "I Can't Quit You Baby."

From 1959 to 1961, Dixon worked with Memphis Slim (Peter Chatman), performing and touring the United States and abroad. Several albums recorded in New York for Prestige came out of this pairing, namely *Willie's Blues, Memphis Slim and Willie Dixon, The Blues Every Which Way,* and *At the Village Gate.*

In the early 1960s, Dixon was back at Chess. There he wrote some of the most penetrating songs in Howlin' Wolf's repertoire, including "Spoonful" (which became one of his most valuable copyrights), "Back Door Man," "Little Red Rooster," "Down in the Bottom," and "Wang Dang Doodle." He had another big hit in 1962 when Bo Diddley placed "You Can't Judge a Book by Its Cover" on both the pop and R&B charts. By the 1960s, Dixon's songs were moving beyond the world of Chess-recorded blues artists: Sam Cooke did a soulful and sly version of "Little Red Rooster"; the Rolling Stones took the same song and turned it into a rock song; and Johnny Rivers had a pop hit with "The Seventh Son" in 1965. Soon, hundreds of other rock acts were performing and recording Dixon's songs, and he was quickly becoming a legend in his own time.

By the time Koko Taylor took "Wang Dang Doodle" to the top of the charts in 1966, the type of blues recorded by Chess was beginning to fade. In 1969, Dixon left Chess to establish his own recording company. On a succession of small labels, he acted as administrator, chief songwriter, and producer. Dixon also formed a band of his own, the Chicago Blues All Stars, as a backing and touring band. In 1970, Columbia recorded an album of songs by the All Stars, *I Am the Blues,* featuring nine of Dixon's most famous songs. This recording brought his name before a new and different generation of fans and launched Dixon again as an active recording and touring artist. Three more albums in the 1970s were recorded: *Peace* on his own Yambo label and *Catalyst* and *What Happened to My Blues?* for Ovation.

Dixon moved to Southern California in 1983 and there released two more albums for Pausa: *Mighty Earthquake and Hurricane* and *Backstage Access.* He also began composing and producing songs for movie soundtracks, contributing a new song for *The Color of Money* and producing Bo Diddley's new version of "Who Do You Love" for the soundtrack of *La Bamba.* For Capitol, he released the album *Hidden Charms* in 1988.

In his later years, Dixon found that his songs were becoming a part of the repertoire of British rock groups, but not always with proper attribution to him and, by extension, royalties for him. For example, the British rock group Led Zeppelin recorded the following Dixon songs without naming Dixon as whole or part writer: "Bring It on Home" and "You Need Love" (recorded as "Whole Lotta Love"). Litigation by Dixon's management corrected this situation and brought him much-needed income, which he used in part to set up the Blues Heaven Foundation, a nonprofit corporation whose purpose is to further education and awareness of the blues as a musical form by providing funds for scholarships and the purchase of musical instruments for schools. The foundation also provides legal help for blues artists and composers who need it in obtaining earned royalties and better treatment from record companies. After Dixon's death in 1992, his widow continued the work of the Blues Heaven Foundation.

SELECTED WORKS

Dixon has always composed songs that he felt could be sung and recorded by all sorts of artists. For example, "Violent Love" was recorded by Dixon's Big Three Trio and by Otis Rush, and "Wang Dang Doodle" was recorded by Dixon, by Howlin' Wolf, and by Koko Taylor. But he also approached the composition of many of his songs with the idea of tailoring them to the type of personality and emotional demeanor of a specific recording artist.

Muddy Waters's recording of Dixon's "(I'm Your) Hoochie Coochie Man" represents Dixon's tailored songwriting method and defines his classic, lyrical approach to the 12-bar blues form. The subject matter was designed to fit the persona of Muddy Waters, who was a formidable and dangerous-looking man. In his early compositions, such as "Louisiana Man," Waters made reference to "hoodoo" (a vernacular African-American term for the Afro-Haitian "voodoo"), which, combined with foreboding and deep vocal textures, resulted in an ominous and scary sound.

In this spirit, Dixon composed "Hoochie Coochie Man," also for Waters. Dixon's philosophy in composing was to keep the lyrics and the tune simple so that its appeal would be obvious to anyone. Like many blues songs, it was composed in part by applying riffs to a series of declarative lyrics. Dixon taught Waters the song by showing him the riff "Da-da-da-da-Da" and alternated it with the lyrics, for example, "The gypsy woman told my mother/Da-da-da-da-Da/Before I was born/Da-da-da-da-Da/You got a boy child coming/Da-da-da-da-Da/He's gonna be a sonuvagun." This is really a sophisticated blues technique called stop-time, in which the lyric line is followed by a defined melody played by the answering band. Dixon, if not the originator of this technique, made it famous.

"Hoochie Coochie Man" was a breakthrough for Dixon's composing career as well. Its success in the market convinced Chess that Dixon's songs were commercially viable and that Dixon was an important asset to the company. He continued to write songs related to African-American mythology, notably "The Seventh Son" (1955) for Willie Mabon and "I Ain't Superstitious" (1961) for Howlin' Wolf.

In 1955, "My Babe," as recorded by Little Walter, became the first Dixon composition to become a number-one hit on the national R&B charts. Dixon wrote the song—which in fact is not a blues—with blues singer Little Walter in mind. The melody actually came from an old folk gospel song entitled "This Train Don't Take No Gamblers," which Dixon had produced about Reverend Ballinger the previous year. Dixon played bass on "My Babe" and coached the other musicians in its performance. "My Babe" became one of Dixon's most valuable copyrights, as it was recorded hundreds of times by blues and rock artists.

"I Can't Quit You Baby," as recorded by Otis Rush, is a minor key traditional blues written with Rush in mind. Knowing that Rush was in a morose condition over a conflict with his girlfriend, Dixon wrote a song to which he knew Rush could personally relate. The song, recorded while Dixon was working at Cobra Records in 1956, became a top ten R&B hit. Years later, the British rock group Led Zeppelin included "I Can't Quit You Baby" on their first album.

Dixon wrote "Wang Dang Doodle" in 1951, reportedly for Howlin' Wolf. Shortly after writing the song, he recorded it himself with a vocal group, the Dells, in the background. "Wang Dang Doodle" consists of eight lines of lyrics, all sung on the same chord, that build to a chorus. It owes its structure to gospel, reflecting Dixon's work singing in gospel groups when he was a youth.

In "Wang Dang Doodle," Dixon early broke away from the strict 12-bar blues format. According to journalist Jeff Lind, Dixon later said, "Most cats used to play the Delta 12-bar blues, but I found that I couldn't always tell the story properly in 12-bars. Then I started messin' with 18, 24, and even 30-bar blues, which gave me enough time to convey the message I was trying to convey."

In 1960, Howlin' Wolf recorded what many thought was the definitive version of "Wang Dang Doodle," featuring one-note guitar answers to the vocal lines. According to Dixon, Wolf thought that the song was "too old-timey, sound like some old levee camp number." The line that particularly bothered him was the stereotyping phrase "Tell Automatic Slim and Razor-Toting Jim." In 1966, Koko Taylor recorded the song with a less aggressive attack and a minor key hook. It became the number one song on R&B radio in Chicago, reportedly selling 100,000 copies in the city alone.

REFERENCES

Dixon, Willie, with Don Snowden. *I Am the Blues: The Willie Dixon Story.* New York: Da Capo, 1989.

Lind, Jeff. "From Vicksburg to Blues Heaven: The 77 Year Odyssey of Willie Dixon." *Discoveries* 87 (August 1995): 30–33.

ROBERT PRUTER

DORSEY, THOMAS ANDREW

Born in Villa Rica, Ga., July 1, 1899; died in Chicago, Ill., January 23, 1993. **Education:** Born into musical family; Atlanta, Ga., Carrie Steele Orphanage School, 1909–13; studied with local pianists, including Edward "Eddie" Heywood Sr. and local teacher Mrs. Graves, ca. 1913–16; Wendell Phillips High School, Chicago, Ill., 1916; Chicago School of Composition and Arranging, ca. 1919–21. **Composing and Performing Career:** Atlanta, Ga., performed at various social events and in local saloons, ca. 1910–16; Chicago, Ill., played piano in saloons and with various bands, beginning 1916; first sacred piece, "If I Don't Get There," appeared in *Gospel Pearls* collection, 1921; played with Will Walker's Whispering Syncopators, 1922–23; Paramount Record Company, arranger and agent, ca. 1922–28; became coach and accompanist for blues singer Ma Rainey, 1924; organized, arranged, and wrote for five-piece Wild Cats Jazz Band, to accompany and tour with Rainey, ca. 1924–26; toured and recorded with various other performers including Charlie Jackson, Bertha "Chippie" Hill, Big Bill Broonzy, and Hudson "Tampa Red" Whitaker as the Hokum Boys, late 1920s; Ink Williams' Chicago Music Publishing Company, arranger, ca. 1928; Brunswick Recording Company, arranger, 1928–32; National Baptist Convention, Chicago, well-received performance of "If You See My Savior," 1930; Ebenezer Baptist Church, Chicago, organized Ebenezer Chorus with Theodore Frye, 1931; Chicago Gospel Choral Union, Inc., co-founder with Frye and Magnolia Lewis Butts, 1931; Thomas A. Dorsey Gospel Songs Music Publishing Company, founder, 1932; National Convention of Gospel Choirs and Choruses, Inc., co-founder with Sallie Martin, 1932; "Take My Hand, Precious Lord" composed, 1932; Pilgrim Baptist Church, Chicago, choir director, 1932–83; toured worldwide with Gospel Choral Union, 1932–44; DuSable High School, Chicago, promoted first gospel concert to charge admission, 1936; accompanist for Mahalia Jackson, ca. 1937–46; appeared in documentary film *Say Amen, Somebody,* 1983. **Teaching Career:** Gospel Choral Union of Chicago, Dean of Evangelistic Musical Research and Ministry of Church Music, 1940–70s; frequently toured nationally and internationally as speaker and lecturer, 1960s and 1970s. **Honors/Awards:** Simmons Institute, S.C., honorary Doctor of Gospel Music, 1946; American Music Conference National Music Award, 1976; first African American named to Nashville Song Writers Association, 1979; elected to Georgia Music Hall of Fame, 1981; named to Gospel Music Association's Living Hall of Fame, 1982; Chicago, Ill., Governor's Award for the Arts, 1985; Grammy National Trustee Award, 1992.

MUSIC LIST

[The following list of titles includes only works that were composed by the subject of the entry; it is not a list of recordings that were made by the subject. Although the composer may have made recordings of his own works, the list is not restricted to those recordings but in many cases includes performances by other artists of the composer's work. The list is made up of publication and discographical data, in cases where such information is available. Although no effort has been made to include documentation of the earliest recording of the works listed, the date of the earliest recording that is readily available has been given. —Ed.]

COLLECTIONS

Dorsey's Songs of the Kingdom, edited by Thomas A. Dorsey, Kathryn Dorsey, and Julia Mae Smith. Chicago: Thomas A. Dorsey, 1951.

Dorsey's Songs with a Message, no. 1, edited by Thomas A. Dorsey, Julia Mae Smith, and Mary Belle White. Chicago: Thomas A. Dorsey, 1951.

Great Gospel Songs. New York: Hill and Range Songs, 1965.

Great Gospel Songs of Thomas A. Dorsey. Winona, Minn.: Chappell/Intersong, 1988.

SONGS

"All Is Well." Chicago: Thomas A. Dorsey, 1940. Co-composer or arranger, Mattie Wilson.

"An Angel Spoke to Me Last Night." Chicago: Thomas A. Dorsey, 1953.

"Army Rock." Los Angeles: Unichappell, 1959.

"Be Thou Near Me All the Way (Prayer of the Righteous)." Chicago: Thomas A. Dorsey, 1943. In *Dorsey's Songs with a Message, no. 1.*

"Be Thou with Me All the Way." Chicago: Thomas A. Dorsey, 1943.

"Beautiful Me." Chicago: Thomas A. Dorsey, 1953.

"Beautiful Tomorrow." Chicago: Thomas A. Dorsey, 1953.

"Behold the Man of Galilee." Chicago: Thomas A. Dorsey and Louise Shropshire, 1957. Co-composer, Louise Shropshire.

"Blue Melody." Los Angeles: Unichappell, 1959.

"Boots, Boots." Los Angeles: Unichappell, 1959.

"Changes." Copyright, 1932. Los Angeles: Unichappell, 1951.

"Come unto Me." Chicago: Thomas A. Dorsey, 1946. In *Dorsey's Songs of the Kingdom.*

"Consider Me." Los Angeles: Unichappell, 1965.

"Consideration." Chicago: Thomas A. Dorsey, 1953. In *Great Gospel Songs of Thomas A. Dorsey.* Recorded: Vocalion VL 73745.

"Count Your Blessings from the Lord Each Day." Chicago: Thomas A. Dorsey, 1952.

"A Crown for Me." Copyright, 1934. Chicago: Thomas A. Dorsey, 1935.

"The Day Is Past and Gone." Beverly Hills, Calif.: Hill and Range Songs, 1952.

"Diamonds from the Crown of the Lord." Chicago: Thomas A. Dorsey, 1953. In *Great Gospel Songs of Thomas A. Dorsey.*

"Did It Happen to You Like It Happened to Me?" Copyright, 1934.

"Did You Ever Say to Your-self that I Love Jesus?" Chicago: Thomas A. Dorsey, 1962.

"Do You Know Anything about Jesus?" Chicago: Thomas A. Dorsey, 1933.

"Does Anybody Here Know My Jesus?" Chicago: Thomas A. Dorsey, 1937.

"Does It Mean Anything to You?" Copyright, 1940.

"Don't Forget the Name of the Lord." Chicago: Thomas A. Dorsey, 1950. In *Dorsey's Songs of the Kingdom.*

"Don't You Need My Savior Too?" Chicago: Thomas A. Dorsey, 1931. In *Dorsey's Songs with a Message, no. 1.*

"Down by the Side of the River." Chicago: Thomas A. Dorsey, 1940. In *Great Gospel Songs of Thomas A. Dorsey.*

"Ev'ry Day Will Be Sunday By and By." Chicago: Thomas A. Dorsey, 1947. In *Dorsey's Songs of the Kingdom* and *Great Gospel Songs of Thomas A. Dorsey.*

"Forgive Me Lord and Try Me One More Time." Chicago: Thomas A. Dorsey, 1950. In *Dorsey's Songs of the Kingdom.*

"Forgive My Sins, Forget, and Make Me Whole." Chicago: Thomas A. Dorsey, 1938.

"Get Ready and Serve the Lord." Chicago: Thomas A. Dorsey, 1938.

"Give Me a Voice to Sing Thy Praise." Chicago: Thomas A. Dorsey, 1950.

"Glory for Me." Copyright, ca. 1937. Los Angeles: Unichappell, 1951.

"Go with Me." Chicago: Thomas A. Dorsey, 1937.

"God Be with You." Chicago: Thomas A. Dorsey, 1940. Co-composer, Artelia W. Hutchins.

"God Is Good to Me." Chicago: Thomas A. Dorsey, 1943. In *Dorsey's Songs of the Kingdom.*

"The Gospel Train Is Coming." In *Great Gospel Songs of Thomas A. Dorsey.*

"He Has Gone to Prepare a Place for Me." Chicago: Thomas A. Dorsey, 1934. Co-composer, Sallie Martin.

"He Is Risen for He's Living in My Soul." Copyright, 1941. Chicago: Thomas A. Dorsey, 1941.

"He Is the Same Today." Chicago: Thomas A. Dorsey, [1933] 1949.

"He Never Will Leave Me." Chicago: Thomas A. Dorsey, 1949. In *Dorsey's Songs of the Kingdom.*

"He That Believeth." Los Angeles: Unichappell, 1951.

"He'll Know Me over Yonder." Chicago: Thomas A. Dorsey, 1930.

"He's All I Need." Chicago: Thomas A. Dorsey, 1944.

"Hide Me in Thy Bosom." Chicago: Thomas A. Dorsey, 1939. In *Great Gospel Songs of Thomas A. Dorsey.* Recorded: Columbia KG 32151; Columbia/Legacy CK-57164.

"Hide Me Jesus in the Solid Rock." Chicago: Thomas A. Dorsey, 1939. Co-composer, Effie Mason.

"Highway to Heaven (Walking up the King's Highway)." Chicago: Gardner-Dorsey Publishing, 1940. Co-composer and arranger, Mary Gardner. Recorded: Columbia KG 32151; Columbia/Legacy CK-57164; Justin Time Just 10-2.

"Hold Me (Please Don't Let Me Go)." Chicago: Thomas A. Dorsey, 1958.

"Hold On a Little While Longer." Chicago: Thomas A. Dorsey, 1945.

"Holy Ghost Gett'n Us Ready for That." Los Angeles: Unichappell, 1951.

"How about You?" 1932. Chicago: Thomas A. Dorsey, 1941. Recorded, 1932: Sound of Gospel SOG-3D110; Topaz Jazz TPZ-1011; Vocalion 1710, 04646.

"How Many Times?" Chicago: Thomas A. Dorsey, 1940. Recorded: Columbia KG 32151; Columbia/Legacy CK-57164.

"How Much More of Life's Burden Can We Bear?" Chicago: Thomas A. Dorsey, 1947. In *Dorsey's Songs with a Message, no. 1.*

"I Can't Forget It, Can You?" Chicago: Thomas A. Dorsey, 1933.

"I Claim Jesus First and That's Enough for Me." Copyright, 1941.

"I Don't Know What You Think of Jesus." Chicago: Thomas A. Dorsey, 1941.

"I Don't Know Why I Have to Cry Sometime." Chicago: Thomas A. Dorsey, 1942. Recorded: Columbia KG 32151; Columbia/Legacy CK-57164; Spirit Feel SF 1005.

"I Got Jesus in My Soul." Chicago: Thomas A. Dorsey, 1945. Co-composer, Thomas M. Dorsey.

"I Just Can't Keep from Crying." Recorded, 1934: Vocalion (unissued).

"I Know It Was Blood." Recorded: Sound of Gospel SOG-3D110.

"I Know Jesus." Chicago: Thomas A. Dorsey, 1935.

"I Know My Redeemer Lives." Chicago: Thomas A. Dorsey, 1940. In *Dorsey's Songs with a Message, no. 1.*

"I May Never Pass This Way Again." Chicago: Thomas A. Dorsey, 1947. In *Dorsey's Songs with a Message, no. 1.*

"I Thank God for My Song." Chicago: Thomas A. Dorsey, 1941. In *Dorsey's Songs of the Kingdom.*

"I Thought of God." Chicago: Thomas A. Dorsey, 1956. In *Great Gospel Songs of Thomas A. Dorsey.*

"I Thought on My Way." Chicago: Thomas A. Dorsey, 1952.

"I Want Jesus on the Road I Travel." Chicago: Thomas A. Dorsey, 1942. In *Dorsey's Songs with a Message, no. 1.*

"I Want to Go There." Chicago: Thomas A. Dorsey, 1942.

"I Will Trust in the Lord." Chicago: Thomas A. Dorsey, 1951. In *Dorsey's Songs with a Message, no. 1.*

"If I Could Hear My Mother Pray Again." Recorded: Document DLP 563; Vocalion 01719.

"If I Don't Get There." Copyright, 1922. In *Gospel Pearls* (Nashville, Tenn.: Secondary School Publishing Board, 1921). Recorded: Sound of Gospel SOG-3D110.

"If Jesus Bore His Cross So Can I." Chicago: Thomas A. Dorsey, 1938. In *Dorsey's Songs with a Message, no. 1.* Co-composer, Lucelia Sebastion.

"If We Never Needed the Lord Before (We Sure Do Need Him Now)." Chicago: Thomas A. Dorsey, 1943. In *Dorsey's Songs of the Kingdom.* Recorded: Columbia KG 32151; Columbia/Legacy CK-57164.

"If You Can't Speak Kindly of Me." Los Angeles: Unichappell, 1951.

"If You Meet God in the Morning." Chicago: Thomas A. Dorsey, 1940.

"If You Ring the Bell." Chicago: Thomas A. Dorsey, 1940.

"If You See My Savior (Tell Him that You Saw Me)" or "I Was Standing by the Bedside of a Neighbor." ca. 1926. Chicago: Thomas A. Dorsey, 1929. Recorded: Columbia/Legacy CK-57164; Topaz Jazz TPZ-1011; Vocalion 1710, 04646.

"If You Sing a Gospel Song." Miami, Fla.: Warner-Tamerlane Publishing, 1951.

"I'll Be Waiting for You at the Beautiful Gate." Chicago: Thomas A. Dorsey, 1955. Co-composer, Verlie Ramey.

"I'll Never Turn Back." Chicago: Thomas A. Dorsey, 1944. In *Dorsey's Songs with a Message, no. 1.* Recorded: DRB CDSBL 12584.

"I'll Take Jesus for Mine." Co-composer or arranger, Mary Gardner. Miami, Fla.: Warner-Tamerlane Publishing, 1951.

"I'll Tell It Wherever I Go." Chicago: Thomas A. Dorsey, 1938. In *Dorsey's Songs of the Kingdom.* and *Great Gospel Songs of Thomas A. Dorsey.* Recorded: Columbia KG 32151; Columbia/Legacy CK-57164; Sound of Gospel SOG-3D110.

"I'm a Pilgrim, I'm a Stranger." In *Great Gospel Songs of Thomas A. Dorsey.*

"I'm a Stranger Don't Drive Me Away." In *Dorsey's Songs of the Kingdom.*

"I'm Climbing up the Rough Side of the Mountain." Chicago: Thomas A. Dorsey, 1952.

"I'm Coming Back to Live with Jesus." In *Great Gospel Songs of Thomas A. Dorsey.* Recorded: Monitor MFS 335.

"I'm Goin' to Hold On 'til Jesus Comes for Me." Copyright, 1938. Pekin, Ill.: Despen Music Publishers, 1967.

"I'm Going to Follow Jesus All the Way" Copyright, 1935. Los Angeles: Unichappell, 1951.

Thomas Andrew Dorsey; courtesy of Hogan Jazz Archive, Howard-Tilton Memorial Library, Tulane University

"I'm Going to Live the Life I Sing About in My Song." Chicago: Thomas A. Dorsey, 1941. Recorded: Columbia KG 32151; Columbia/Legacy CK-57164.

"I'm Going to Wait until My Change Shall Come." Chicago: Thomas A. Dorsey, 1944.

"I'm Going to Walk Right In and Make Myself at Home." Chicago: Thomas A. Dorsey, 1938.

"I'm Going to Work until the Day Is Done." Chicago: Thomas A. Dorsey, 1951.

"I'm in Your Care." Los Angeles: Unichappell, n.d.

"I'm Just a Sinner Saved by Grace." Copyright, 1936. Chicago: Thomas A. Dorsey, 1937.

"I'm Looking for the Stone." Los Angeles: Unichappell, 1951.

"I'm Singing Every Day." Chicago: Thomas A. Dorsey, 1934.

"I'm Talking about Jesus." Chicago: Thomas A. Dorsey, 1936.

"I'm Waiting for Jesus, He's Waiting for Me." Chicago: Thomas A. Dorsey, 1945. In *Dorsey's Songs with a Message, no. 1*. Recorded: Columbia KG 32151; Columbia/Legacy CK-57164.

"In My Savior's Care." Chicago: Thomas A. Dorsey, 1953.

"In the Scheme of Things (The Wedding Song)." Chicago: Thomas A. Dorsey, 1958.

"Inside the Beautiful Gate." Chicago: Thomas A. Dorsey, 1950. In *Dorsey's Songs with a Message, no. 1*. Co-composer, Sallie Martin.

"It Don't Cost Very Much." Chicago: Thomas A. Dorsey, 1954.

"It Is Real with Me." Chicago: Thomas A. Dorsey, 1934.

"It Is Thy Servant's Prayer, Amen." Copyright, 1938. In *Dorsey's Songs with a Message, no. 1* and *Great Gospel Songs of Thomas A. Dorsey*.

"It Just Suits Me." Los Angeles: Unichappell, 1951.

"It's a Blessing Just to Call My Savior's Name." Chicago: Thomas A. Dorsey, 1950. In *Dorsey's Songs of the Kingdom*.

"It's All in the Plan of Salvation." Chicago: Thomas A. Dorsey, 1934.

"It's Not a Shame to Cry Holy to the Lord." Chicago: Thomas A. Dorsey, 1946. In *Dorsey's Songs with a Message, no. 1*.

"Jesus He Brought Me All the Way." Chicago: Thomas A. Dorsey, n.d. Recorded: Sound of Gospel SOG-3D110.

"Jesus Is the Light." Copyright, 1938. Recorded: Sound of Gospel SOG-3D110.

"Jesus Is the Light of the World." Miami, Fla.: Warner-Tamerlane Publishing, 1951.

"Jesus Lives in Me." Chicago: Thomas A. Dorsey, 1937.

"Jesus' Love Bubbles Over." Bronx, N.Y.: Soul Music, 1971.

"Jesus My Comforter." Copyright, 1931. Co-composer, Daisy M. White.

"Jesus Never Does a Thing That's Wrong." Chicago: Thomas A. Dorsey, 1936. In *Dorsey's Songs of the Kingdom*.

"Jesus Only." Chicago: Thomas A. Dorsey, 1950. In *Dorsey's Songs of the Kingdom*.

"Jesus Remembers When Others Forget." Chicago: Thomas A. Dorsey, 1941. In *Dorsey's Songs with a Message, no. 1* and *Great Gospel Songs of Thomas A. Dorsey*. Recorded: Spirit Feel SF 1005.

"Jesus Rose Again." Chicago: Thomas A. Dorsey, 1950. In *Dorsey's Songs with a Message, no. 1* and *Great Gospel Songs of Thomas A. Dorsey*.

"Just Look Around." Beverly Hills, Calif.: Hill and Range Songs, 1952. Co-composer, Dorcas Cochran.

"Just One Step." Chicago: Thomas A. Dorsey, 1950. In *Dorsey's Songs with a Message, no. 1*.

"Just Tell Jesus." Bronx, N.Y.: Soul Music, 1968.

"Just Wait a Little While." Copyright, 1941. In *Great Gospel Songs of Thomas A. Dorsey*.

"Keep Praying All the Time." Chicago: Thomas A. Dorsey, 1939. In *Dorsey's Songs of the Kingdom*.

"Lead Me Home." Miami, Fla.: Warner-Tamerlane Publishing, 1968.

"Lead Me On." Co-composer, B. Hooten.

"Lead Me to the Rock That's Higher Than I." Chicago: Thomas A. Dorsey, 1951. In *Great Gospel Songs of Thomas A. Dorsey*.

"Let Every Day Be Christmas." Beverly Hills, Calif.: Hill and Range Songs, 1956.

"Let Me Understand." Copyright, 1943. Chicago: Thomas A. Dorsey, 1949. In *Dorsey's Songs with a Message, no. 1*.

"Let the Savior Bless Your Soul Right Now." Chicago: Thomas A. Dorsey, 1955. In *Great Gospel Songs of Thomas A. Dorsey*.

"Let Us Go Back to God." Chicago: Thomas A. Dorsey, 1942. In *Dorsey's Songs with a Message, no. 1* and *Great Gospel Songs of Thomas A. Dorsey*. Recorded: Columbia KG 32151.

"Let Us Pray Together." Los Angeles: Unichappell, 1956.

"Let's Go Down to Jordan." Los Angeles: Unichappell, 1951.

"Life Can Be Beautiful." Chicago: Thomas A. Dorsey, 1940. In *Dorsey's Songs of the Kingdom*.

"A Little Talk with Jesus." Chicago: Thomas A. Dorsey, 1951. In *Dorsey's Songs of the Kingdom*.

"The Little Wooden Church on the Hill." Chicago: Thomas A. Dorsey, 1949. Recorded: Monitor MFS 335; Savoy SL 14604; Sound of Gospel SOG-3D110.

"Look, Look, Look Lord Down upon Me." Chicago: Thomas A. Dorsey, 1944.

"Look on the Brighter Side." Chicago: Thomas A. Dorsey, 1941. In *Dorsey's Songs of the Kingdom*.

"The Lord Has Laid His Hands on Me." Chicago: Thomas A. Dorsey, 1946. In *Dorsey's Songs with a Message, no. 1* and *Great Gospel Songs of Thomas A. Dorsey*.

"Lord Is My Shepherd." Copyright, 1951. Los Angeles: Unichappell, 1951.

"The Lord Knows Just What I Need." Copyright, 1942. Miami, Fla.: Warner-Tamerlane Publishing, 1951.

"Lord, Look Down upon Me (Mercy Lord)." Chicago: Thomas A. Dorsey, 1944.

"The Lord Will Make a Way Some How." Chicago: Thomas A. Dorsey, 1943. In *Dorsey's Songs with a Message, no. 1*. Recorded: Columbia/Legacy CK-57164; Savoy SL-14739; Sound of Gospel SOG-3D110.

"Make Me the Servant I Would Like to Be." Chicago: Thomas A. Dorsey, 1938.

"Makes Me Pray." Los Angeles: Unichappell, 1951.

"A Man Who Loves Music Should Be One Who Loves Devotedly Whether It Be His Country, His Family, His Home, or His God." Chicago: Thomas A. Dorsey, 1946.

"Maybe It's You and Then Maybe It's Me." Copyright, 1938. Chicago: Thomas A. Dorsey, 1951. In *Dorsey's Songs of the Kingdom*.

"Meet Me at the Pearly Gates." Copyright, 1941.

"My Desire." New York: Hill and Range Songs, 1937. In *Great Gospel Songs of Thomas A. Dorsey*. Recorded: Columbia KG 32151; Columbia/Legacy CK-57164.

"My Faith I Place in Thee." Chicago: Thomas A. Dorsey, 1954.

"My Mind on Jesus." Los Angeles: Unichappell, 1951.

"My Soul Feels Better Right Now." Chicago: Thomas A. Dorsey, 1951. In *Dorsey's Songs with a Message, no. 1* and *Great Gospel Songs of Thomas A. Dorsey.*

"My Time's Not as Long as It Has Been." Chicago: Thomas A. Dorsey, 1940. In *Dorsey's Songs with a Message, no. 1.*

"Never Leave Me Alone." Chicago: Thomas A. Dorsey, 1951. In *Dorsey's Songs of the Kingdom* and *Great Gospel Songs of Thomas A. Dorsey.*

"Never Turn Back." Recorded: Columbia KG 32151; Columbia/Legacy CK-57164; Justin Time Just 10-2.

"Oh Lord, Show Me the Way." Chicago: Thomas A. Dorsey, 1934.

"Old Ship of Zion." Chicago: Thomas A. Dorsey, 1950. Recorded: Columbia KG 32151; Columbia/Legacy CK-57164; Sound of Gospel SOG-3D110.

"Only Believe All Things Are Possible." Co-composer John Sellers. Los Angeles: Unichappell, 1960.

"Peace, It's Wonderful." Copyright, 1939. Chicago: Thomas A. Dorsey, 1951. In *Dorsey's Songs of the Kingdom.*

"Race Against Time." Co-composer or arranger, Mahalia Jackson. Miami, Fla.: Warner-Tamerlane Publishing, 1996.

"Remember Me (We Shall Be Remembered by Our Works)." Chicago: Thomas A. Dorsey, 1939.

"Right Now." Copyright, 1931. Chicago: Thomas A. Dorsey, 1951. In *Dorsey's Songs of the Kingdom.*

"Save Me as I Am." Chicago: Thomas A. Dorsey, 1936. In *Dorsey's Songs with a Message, no. 1.*

"The Savior Is Born." Chicago: Thomas A. Dorsey, 1950. In *Dorsey's Songs of the Kingdom.*

"The Savior's Here." Chicago: Thomas A. Dorsey, 1941. In *Dorsey's Songs with a Message, no. 1.*

"Say a Little Prayer for Me." Chicago: Thomas A. Dorsey, 1957. In *Great Gospel Songs of Thomas A. Dorsey.*

"Search Me, Lord." Chicago: Thomas A. Dorsey, 1948. Note: dedicated to the Brooklyn Westchester Choral Union and Associated Unions. Recorded: Columbia KG 32151; Columbia/Legacy CK-57164.

"Shake My Mother's Hand for Me." Chicago: Thomas A. Dorsey, 1932. In *Dorsey's Songs with a Message, no. 1.* Recorded, 1934: Vocalion (unissued).

"She Is Mine." Los Angeles: Unichappell, 1959.

"Singing Every-where." Chicago: Thomas A. Dorsey, 1960.

"Singing in My Soul." Chicago: Thomas A. Dorsey, 1932. Recorded: Document DLP 563; DRG CDSBL 12584; Vocalion 01719.

"Singing My Way to Rest." Chicago: Thomas A. Dorsey, 1940.

"Some Day I'm Goin' to See My Jesus." Chicago: Thomas A. Dorsey, 1941.

"Somebody Here Is a Witness." Los Angeles: Unichappell, 1951.

"Somebody's Knocking at Your Door." Chicago: Thomas A. Dorsey, 1945. In *Dorsey's Songs of the Kingdom.*

"Someday I'll Be at Rest." Chicago: Thomas A. Dorsey, 1956. Co-composer, Susie Cochran.

"Someday I'm Going Home." Chicago: Thomas A. Dorsey, 1946. In *Dorsey's Songs with a Message, no. 1.*

"Someday Somewhere." ca. 1926. Chicago: Thomas A. Dorsey, 1941. In *Dorsey's Songs of the Kingdom.* Recorded: Vocalion VL 73745.

"Something Has Happened to Me." Copyright, 1949. Chicago: Thomas A. Dorsey, 1954.

"Something New Burning in My Soul." Chicago: Thomas A. Dorsey, 1938.

"Someway, Somehow, Sometime, Somewhere." Copyright, 1951. Chicago: Thomas A. Dorsey, n.d. In *Dorsey's Songs of the Kingdom* and *Great Gospel Songs of Thomas A. Dorsey.*

"Somewhere." Copyright, 1941. Chicago: Thomas A. Dorsey, 1941.

"Standing Here Wondering Which Way to Go." Chicago: Thomas A. Dorsey, 1955. Recorded: Sound of Gospel SOG-3D110; Spirit Feel SF 1007.

"Take Me Through, Lord." Chicago: Thomas A. Dorsey, 1944. In *Dorsey's Songs of the Kingdom.*

"Take My Hand, Precious Lord." 1932. Chicago: Thomas A. Dorsey, 1938. In *Dorsey's Songs of the Kingdom, Dorsey's Songs with a Message, no. 1,* and *Great Gospel Songs of Thomas A. Dorsey.* Recorded: Antilles 91236-1; Columbia/Legacy CK-57164; DRG CDSBL 12584; Lection/Polygram 838 114-2; Savoy SL 14742; Warner Bros. 9 45990-2.

"Tell Jesus Everything." Chicago: Thomas A. Dorsey, 1949. In *Dorsey's Songs of the Kingdom.*

"Thank You All the Days of My Life." Chicago: Thomas A. Dorsey, 1946. In *Dorsey's Songs with a Message, no. 1.*

"That's All That I Can Do." Chicago: Thomas A. Dorsey, 1945. In *Dorsey's Songs of the Kingdom.*

"That's Good News." Chicago: Thomas A. Dorsey, 1949. In *Dorsey's Songs of the Kingdom* and *Great Gospel Songs of Thomas A. Dorsey.*

"There Is No Friend like Jesus." In *Great Gospel Songs of Thomas A. Dorsey.*

"There Isn't but One Way to Make It In." Chicago: Thomas A. Dorsey, 1946.

"There'll Be Peace in the Valley for Me." Chicago: Thomas A. Dorsey, 1939. In *Great Gospel Songs of Thomas A. Dorsey.* Recorded: Columbia CL 2053 (63); Columbia/Legacy CK 57164; Sound of Gospel SOG-3D110.

"There's a Better Day Coming Right Now." Chicago: Thomas A. Dorsey, 1936.

"There's a God Somewhere." Chicago: Thomas A. Dorsey, 1942. In *Dorsey's Songs of the Kingdom.*

"There's an Empty Chair at the Table." Copyright, 1941. Miami, Fla.: Warner-Tamerlane Publishing, 1951.

"This Man, Jesus." Copyright, 1949. Chicago: Thomas A. Dorsey, 1949. In *Dorsey's Songs with a Message, no. 1.*

"Thy Kingdom Come." Chicago: Thomas A. Dorsey, 1943. In *Dorsey's Songs with a Message, no. 1.*

"Thy Servant's Prayer Amen." Recorded: Columbia KG 32151; Columbia/Legacy CK-57164.

"Today (Evening Song)." Chicago: Thomas A. Dorsey, 1939. In *Great Gospel Songs of Thomas A. Dorsey.*

"Too Long." Recorded: Document DLP 563.

"Traveling On." Chicago: Thomas A. Dorsey, 1950. In *Dorsey's Songs of the Kingdom.* Co-composer, Paul Rosie Brooks.

"Treasure in Heaven." Copyright, 1931. Los Angeles: Unichappell, 1951.

"Trusting in Jesus." Los Angeles: Unichappell, 1951.

"Use My Heart, Use My Mind, Use My Hands." Copyright, 1938. Miami, Fla.: Warner-Tamerlane Publishing, 1951.

"Walk Close to Me, O Lord." Copyright, 1941. In *Dorsey's Songs with a Message, no. 1* and *Great Gospel Songs of Thomas A. Dorsey.*

"Walk over God's Heaven." Chicago: Thomas A. Dorsey, 1954. In *Great Gospel Songs of Thomas A. Dorsey.*

"Want to Go to Heaven When I Die." Chicago: Thomas A. Dorsey, 1951. In *Great Gospel Songs of Thomas A. Dorsey.*

"Wasn't That an Awful Time." Copyright, 1940. Miami, Fla.: Warner-Tamerlane Publishing, 1951.

"Watching and Waiting." Copyright, 1935. Chicago: Thomas A. Dorsey, 1951. In *Dorsey's Songs of the Kingdom.*

"We Must Work Together." Chicago: Thomas A. Dorsey, 1960.

"What Could I Do If It Wasn't for the Lord?" Chicago: Thomas A. Dorsey, 1944. In *Great Gospel Songs of Thomas A. Dorsey.* Recorded: Columbia KG 32151; Columbia/Legacy CK-57164.

"What Some Say about Jesus." Los Angeles: Unichappell, 1951.

"What the Good Lord's Done for Me." Chicago: Thomas A. Dorsey, n.d.

"What the World Needs Is Jesus Most of All." Copyright, 1942. Los Angeles: Unichappell, 1951.

"What Then?" Copyright, 1935. In *Dorsey's Songs with a Message, no. 1.*

"When Day Is Done." Chicago: Thomas A. Dorsey, 1947. In *Dorsey's Songs with a Message, no. 1.*

"When I Get to Heaven (I Got a Home)." Recorded: Savoy SL 14667.

"When I've Done My Best." Beverly Hills, Calif.: Hill and Range Songs, 1939. In *Dorsey's Songs of the Kingdom* and *Great Gospel Songs of Thomas A. Dorsey.* Recorded: DRG CDSBL 12584; Sound of Gospel SOG-3D110.

"When I've Done the Best I Can." Chicago: Thomas A. Dorsey, 1939.

"When I've Sung My Last Song." Chicago: Thomas A. Dorsey, 1943. In *Dorsey's Songs with a Message, no. 1* and *Great Gospel Songs of Thomas A. Dorsey.*

"When the Gates Swing Open, Let Me In." Chicago: Thomas A. Dorsey, 1941. In *Dorsey's Songs of the Kingdom.* Recorded: Columbia KG 32151; Columbia/Legacy CK-57164; Sound of Gospel SOG-3D110.

"When the Last Mile Is Finished." Chicago: Thomas A. Dorsey, 1939. In *Dorsey's Songs of the Kingdom.*

"When They Crown Him Lord of All." Chicago: Thomas A. Dorsey, 1951. In *Dorsey's Songs of the Kingdom.*

"When You Bow in the Evening at the Altar." Chicago: Thomas A. Dorsey, 1949. In *Dorsey's Songs with a Message, no. 1.*

"While He's Passing By." Chicago: Thomas A. Dorsey, 1964.

"While the Evening Shadows Fall, There's Morning in My Heart." In *Great Gospel Songs of Thomas A. Dorsey.*

"Who Is Willing to Take a Stand for the World?" Copyright, 1938. Los Angeles: Unichappell, 1951.

"Windows of Heaven." Chicago: Thomas A. Dorsey, 1955. In *Great Gospel Songs of Thomas A. Dorsey.*

"Won't You Come and Go Along?" Chicago: Thomas A. Dorsey, 1941.

"Your Sins Will Find You Out." Chicago: Thomas A. Dorsey, 1946. In *Dorsey's Songs of the Kingdom.*

"You've Got to Right Each Wrong Day." Chicago: Thomas A. Dorsey, 1934.

AS BARRELHOUSE TOM, GEORGIA TOM, MEMPHIS MOSE, RAILROAD BILL, OR THE HOKUM BOYS (WITH HUDSON "TAMPA RED" WHITAKER)

"All Alone Blues." Recorded, 1929: Best of Blues BOB 18; Champion 15903; Gennett 7041; RST BDCD-6021.

"Beedle Um Bum" or "My Beedle Um Bum." Copyright, 1928. Recorded, 1928: Disques Pierre Cardin 93520; EPM Musique JA157432; RST BDCD-6021.

"Been Mistreated Blues." Recorded, 1930: Champion 16237; Disques Pierre Cardin 93520; Document BDCD-6022; RST BDCD-6022.

"Billie the Grinder." Recorded, 1929: Brunswick 7143; Document DLP 563; RST BDCD-6021.

"Black Cat Hoot Owl Blues." Copyright, 1928. Recorded, 1928: Paramount 12687; Riverside RLP 12-108.

"Blame It on the Blues." Copyright, 1928.

"Blue Moanin' Blues." Recorded, 1929: Brunswick 7134; Document DLP 563; RST BDCD-6021.

"Broke Man's Blues." Recorded, 1929: Champion 15834; Disques Pierre Cardin 93520; RST BDCD-6021; Supertone 9508.

"Come on In (Ain't Nobody Here but Me)." Recorded: Disques Pierre Cardin 93520.

"Dark Hour Blues." Recorded, 1930: Best of Blues BOB 18; Champion 15950; RST BDCD-6021.

"Dead Cats on the Line." Recorded: Columbia/Legacy CT 52725.

"Don't Leave Me Blues." Recorded, 1930: Champion 16360; Document DLP 563; RST BDCD-6022; Superior 2560.

"Don't Mean to Mistreat You." Recorded, 1930: Best of Blues BOB 18; Oriole 8086; Perfect 187; Romeo 5086; RST BDCD-6022.

"Don't Shake It No More." Los Angeles: Unichappell, 1972. Recorded, 1924: Classics 756; Paramount 12211.

"Double Trouble Blues." Recorded: Disques Pierre Cardin 93520.

"The Duck's Yas Yas Yas." Recorded, 1929: Best of Blues BOB 18; Homestead 16100; Jewel 20014; Oriole 8014; Romeo 5014; RST BDCD-6022.

"Eagle Ridin' Papa." Recorded, 1929: Best of Blues BOB 18; Champion 15834; RST BDCD-6021; Supertone 9508.

"Fish House Blues." Recorded: Document DLP 563.

"Fix It." Recorded: Disques Pierre Cardin 93520.

"The Flag for You and Me." Copyright, 1942. Los Angeles: Unichappell, 1951.

"Gee, but It's Hard." Recorded, 1930: Champion 16682; Champion 50014; Decca 7362; Disques Pierre Cardin 93520; RST BDCD-6022.

"Gonna Catch You with Your Breeches Down." Copyright, 1928.

"Grievin' Me Blues." Recorded, 1928: Document DLP 563; RST BDCD-6021; Vocalion 1216.

"Gym's Too Much for Me" or "I Had to Give Up Gym." Recorded, 1930: RST BDCD-6021; Yazoo L-1041.

"Hear Me Beefin' at You." Recorded, 1929: Best of Blues BOB 18; Brunswick 7102; Origin Jazz Library OJL-25; RST BDCD-6021.

"Hip Shakin' Strut." Recorded: Disques Pierre Cardin 93520.

"Hustlin' Blues." Copyright, 1928.

"I Just Want a Daddy (I Can Call My Own)." New York: Jack Mills, 1923.

"If You Want Me to Love You." Recorded, 1932: RST BDCD-6022; Vocalion 1682.

"I'm a Married Man." Los Angeles: Unichappell, 1957.

"I'm the Lonesome One." Recorded: Best of Blues BOB 18.

"It's a Pretty Thing." Recorded: Document BDCD-6045.

"It's Been So Long." Recorded: Best of Blues BOB 18.

"It's Tight like That" or "Honey, It's Tight Like That." 1928. Co-composer, Hudson "Tampa Red" Whitaker. Recorded: Stomp Off SOS 1226; Vocalion 1216.

"Kunjine Baby." Recorded: Story of the Blues SB-3501; Vocalion 1450.

"Leave My Man Alone." Recorded: Disques Pierre Cardin 93520.

"Levee Bound Blues." Recorded, 1930: Champion 16682; Champion 50014; Decca 7362; Disques Pierre Cardin 93520; RST BDCD-6022.

"Lonesome Man Blues." Recorded, 1928: Document DLP 563; RST BDCD-6021; Vocalion 1246.

"Long Ago Blues." Recorded, 1928: Document DLP 563; RST BDCD-6021; Vocalion 1246.

"M and O Blues, Part I." Recorded, 1932: Document DLP 563; Melotone M12373; RST BDCD-6022.

"M and O Blues, Part II." Recorded, 1932: Document DLP 563; Melotone M12373; RST BDCD-6022.

"Mama's Leaving Town." Recorded, 1930: Best of Blues BOB 18; Jewel 20025; Oriole 8025; Romeo 5025; RST BDCD-6022.

"Maybe It's the Blues." Recorded, 1930: Champion 15994; Champion 50054; Gennett 7190; Disques Pierre Cardin 93520; RST BDCD-6022.

"McClellan Theme." Los Angeles: Unichappell, 1959.

"Mississippi Bottom Blues." Recorded, 1930: RST BDCD-6022; Yazoo L-1041.

"My Texas Blues." Recorded, 1929: Best of Blues BOB 18; Champion 15794; Document DLP 563; RST BDCD-6021; RST BDCD-6022.

"No Matter How She Done It." Co-composer, Hudson "Tampa Red" Whitaker. Recorded: Columbia/Legacy CT 52725.

"Parkway Stomp." Co-composer, A. Wynn. Recorded: Stomp Off Records SOS 1059 (83).

"Pat That Bread." Recorded: Document DLP 563; Supertone S2216; Vocalion 1286.

"Pig Meat Blues." Recorded, 1929: Best of Blues BOB 18; Champion 15815; Disques Pierre Cardin 93520; RST BDCD-6021; RST BDCD-6022.

"Pig Meat Papa." Recorded, 1929: Best of Blues BOB 18; Brunwick 7102; RST BDCD-6021.

"Poor Old Bachelor Blues." Recorded: Document BDCD-6045.

"Rent Man Blues." Recorded: Best of Blues BOB 18.

"Riverside Blues." ca. 1923. Recorded: Paramount 20292; World Records SH 358.

"Rollin' Mill Stomp." Recorded, 1929: Champion 15903; Gennett 7041; RST BDCD-6021; Supertone 9512.

"The Sailor Song (The Boy in the Boat)." Recorded, 1929: Brunswick (unissued).

"Second Hand Love." Recorded, 1930: Champion 15994; Champion 50054; Document DLP 563; RST BDCD-6022.

"Second-Hand Woman Blues." Recorded, 1930: Disques Pierre Cardin 93520; Gennett 7130; RST BDCD-6022; Supertone 9647.

"Selling That Stuff." Recorded: Disques Pierre Cardin 93520; Document DOCD-5050; EPM Musique JA157432.

"Sittin' on Top of the World." Recorded: Best of Blues BOB 18.

"Six Shooter Blues." Recorded, 1930: Best of Blues BOB 18; Champion 15950; Document DLP 563; RST BDCD-6022; Supertone 9647.

"Slave to the Blues." Recorded: Paramount 12332.

"Some Cold Rainy Day." Co-composer, Hudson "Tampa Red" Whitaker. Recorded, 1928: Yazoo L-1041.

"Somebody's Been Usin' That Thing, no. 2." Recorded, 1929: Champion 15794; Document DLP 563; Gennett 6933; RST BDCD-6021.

"Southern Melody." Los Angeles: Unichappell, 1959.

"Stormy Sea Blues." Recorded: Document 5582; Indigo 2004.

"Suicide Blues." Recorded, 1929: Best of Blues BOB 18; Champion 15815; Gennett 6933; RST BDCD-6021; Supertone 9506.

"Sworn to Stick Together." Los Angeles: Unichappell, 1959.

"Ta, Ta, Ta." Los Angeles: Unichappell, 1959.

"Terrible Operation Blues." 1928. Co-composer, Hudson "Tampa Red" Whitaker. Recorded: Champion 16171; Disques Pierre Cardin 93520.

"Then My Gal's in Town." Recorded, 1930: Best of Blues BOB 18; Jewel 20014; Homestead 16100; Oriole 8014; RST BDCD-6022.

"They Got It Fixed Right On." Co-composer, Hudson "Tampa Red" Whitaker. Recorded, 1930: Yazoo L-1041.

"Tomorrow Blues." Recorded, 1929: Brunswick 7134; Document DLP 563; RST BDCD-6021.

"What Can I Do? (I Love Her So)." Recorded, 1930: American Record Company (unissued).

"What Is It that Tastes Like Gravy?" Co-composer, Hudson "Tampa Red" Whitaker. Recorded, 1929: Document DOCD-5074; Indigo 2004.

"What's That Smell?" Recorded: Best of Blues BOB 18.

"You Got Me in the Mess (I Ain't Gonna Do It No More)." Recorded, 1930: Best of Blues BOB 18; Homestead 16101; RST BDCD-6022.

"You Got That Stuff." Recorded: Best of Blues BOB 18.

PUBLICATIONS

ABOUT DORSEY
Books and Monographs

Classic Gospel Song: A Tribute to Thomas A. Dorsey. Washington, D.C.: Smithsonian Institution, National Museum of American History, 1985.

Harris, Michael W. *The Rise of Gospel Blues: The Music of Thomas Andrew Dorsey in the Urban Church.* New York: Oxford University Press, 1992.

Smith, Ruth A. *The Life and Works of Thomas Andrew Dorsey: The Celebrated Pianist and Songwriter Poetical and Pictorial.* Chicago: Thomas A. Dorsey, 1935.

Williams, Joe. *Reflections on Mr. Thomas A. Dorsey.* Washington, D.C.: Smithsonian Institution, National Museum of American History, Program in African American Culture, 1985.

Dissertations

Harris, Michael Wesley. "The Advent of Gospel Blues in Black Old-Line Churches in Chicago, 1932–33 as Seen through the Life and Mind of Thomas Andrew Dorsey." Ph.D. diss., Harvard University, 1982.

Jackson, Jerma A. "Testifying at the Cross: Thomas Andrew Dorsey, Sister Rosetta Tharpe, and the Politics of African-American Sacred and Secular Music." Ph.D. diss., Rutgers, the State University of New Jersey, 1995.

Kalil, Timothy M. "The Role of the Great Migration of African-Americans to Chicago in the Development of Traditional Black Gospel Piano by Thomas A. Dorsey, circa 1930." Ph.D. diss., Kent State University, 1993.

Articles

Black World (July 1974). Special Dorsey issue.

Boyer, Horace Clarence. "'Take My Hand, Precious Lord, Lead Me On.'" In *We'll Understand It Better By and By: Pioneering African American Gospel Composers,* edited by Bernice Johnson Reagon, 141–163. Washington: Smithsonian Institution Press, 1992.

———. "Thomas A. Dorsey, 'Father of Gospel Music': An Analysis of His Contributions." *Black World* 23, no. 9 (1974): 20–28.

Broughton, Viv. "Working on the Building: Professor Dorsey and the Gospel Mothers." In *Black Gospel: An Illustrated History of the Gospel Sound,* 45–59. New York: Blanford Press, 1985.

Duckett, Alfred. "An Interview with Thomas A. Dorsey." *Black World* (July 1974): 4–18.

Harris, Michael. "Conflict and Resolution in the Life of Thomas Andrew Dorsey." In *We'll Understand It Better By and By: Pioneering African American Gospel Composers,* edited by Bernice Johnson Reagon, 165–182. Washington, D.C.: Smithsonian Institution Press, 1992.

Heilbut, Anthony. "'I Get These Special Vibrations': Thomas A. Dorsey." In *The Gospel Sound: Good News and Bad Times,* 21–35. 3rd ed. New York: Limelight Editions, 1989.

Helander, Olle. "Thomas A. Dorsey a.k.a. Georgia Tom." *Jefferson* 67 (Winter 1984): 4–9.

"King of the Gospel Song Writers (Thomas A. Dorsey)." *Ebony* (November 1962): 122–127.

O'Neal, Jim, and Amy O'Neal. "Living Blues Interview: Georgia Tom Dorsey." *Living Blues* 20 (March/April 1975): 16–34.

Oliver, Paul. "Georgia Tom: A Biographical Note." *Jazz Monthly* 7, no. 9 (1961): 6–8.

Phillips, Romeo Eldridge. "A Selected, Annotated Discography: Dorsey Songs on Record." *Black World* (July 1974): 29–32.

Rusch, Bob. "Georgia Tom Dorsey Interview." *Cadence* 4 (December 1978): 9–13.

BY DORSEY

"Gospel Music." In *Reflections on Afro-American Music,* edited by Dominique-René de Lerma, 189–195. Ohio: Kent State University Press, 1973.

"Gospel Songwriter Attacks All Hot Bands' Swinging Spirituals." Reprinted in *Black Sacred Music: A Journal of Theomusicology* 7, no. 1 (1993): 29.

Inspirational Thoughts. Chicago: Thomas A. Dorsey, 1935.

"Ministry of Music in the Church." In *Improving the Music in the Church,* Kenneth Morris, 42–45. Chicago: Martin and Morris, 1949.

"The Precious Lord Story and Gospel Songs." ca. 1969. Typescript, held by the Music Library, Indiana University, Bloomington, Indiana.

Songs with a Message: With My Ups and Downs. Chicago: Thomas A. Dorsey, 1941.

Treasure Chest of Favorite Hymns. New York: Treasure Chest Publications, 1940.

* * * * *

Thomas A. Dorsey did more than any other composer to define gospel music as it would come to be known in the second half of the 20th century. Popularly known as the "Father of Gospel Music," he was one of the unsung heroes and influential composer/ musicians of this century. Born in rural Carroll County, Georgia, in the town of Villa Rica, he was the oldest of four children. His father, Thomas Madison Dorsey, graduated from Atlanta Baptist College in the 1890s and married Etta Plant Spencer, a widowed landowner, whom he had met on an evangelizing mission. The early years of their marriage were spent moving around the region to Tennessee and Florida in search of a permanent pastorate. Etta gave birth to her first son, Thomas Andrew, in 1899. The Dorsey children were raised in a religious household, and Thomas sang in church choirs. He learned to play the keyboard from his mother, who was an organist, and he also imitated other church musicians. One of his uncles was a church choir director; another uncle was a guitarist for country dances. Although he studied with a local pianist, Edward Heywood, he did not learn to read music well until he was in his teens. He occasionally accompanied his father on the harmonium during evangelizing trips. Dorsey's religious upbringing later came into conflict with his career as a blues musician.

Because of dire economic circumstances, the family found it necessary to move from Villa Rica to Atlanta, and young Dorsey had to help support the family. He was educated in the Atlanta public school system but only went as far as the fourth grade in his formal schooling. Although Dorsey continued to play church music, he dropped out of school about age thirteen and began playing in a local saloon where he had also worked selling soft drinks. He adopted the stage name "Barrelhouse Tommy," which was one of many that he used. By the time he was fifteen, he had taught himself to read and notate music and had acquired a minor reputation as a blues pianist.

In 1916, Dorsey went to Chicago (en route to Philadelphia), and it became his home base for the rest of his life. He intermittently played with bands in the area but was regarded as "country" by the more seasoned Chicago musicians. Between 1919 and 1921, he studied at the Chicago School of Composition and Arranging. Dorsey also began to be sought after for his arranging skills and worked as an agent for the race record label Paramount. In that capacity, he sought out musicians for the label to record, coached singers for their recording dates, and did musical arranging. He worked with Will Walker's Whispering Syncopators in local Chicago clubs and scored a triumph when his "Riverside Blues" was recorded by the great cornetist Joseph "King" Oliver in December 1923.

Dorsey's fortunes gradually improved with the arrival of the southern blues singer Gertrude "Ma" Rainey as an exclusive Paramount artist. The music promoter J. Mayo "Ink" Williams, who had brought Ma Rainey to the attention of Paramount, asked Dorsey to become her accompanist, arranger, and coach. After a successful debut at Chicago's Grand Theater in spring 1924, Dorsey toured with Rainey and a five-piece band called the Wild Cats Jazz Band on the Theater Owner's Booking Association (TOBA) circuit. By his account in the documentary *Say Amen, Somebody,* Dorsey's association with Ma Rainey was the turning point in his career as a blues musician. Although he had seen her perform in Atlanta when he was a boy, his coaching her, directing her band, and accompanying the great singer was his break.

Dorsey's personal life at this time was blissful. He married Nettie Harper in 1925, and Rainey hired her to tour with the group as a wardrobe mistress. When Dorsey was not with Rainey, he played with various bands in the Chicago area. Dorsey was featured on many of Rainey's recordings, including "Titanic Man Blues" and "Booze and Blues," among others. His departure from Rainey was the result of his nearly having had a nervous breakdown, which, he said, was only remedied after a religious conversion.

In addition to his activities with Rainey, Dorsey also toured with blues singers Bertha "Chippie" Hill, Big Bill Broonzy, and Charlie Jackson. He was featured in several recordings of the 1920s on well-known race labels such as Paramount and Okeh.

Although Thomas A. Dorsey was well-known as a blues musician as a result of his arrangements, compositions, performances, and recordings, throughout much of the 1920s and beyond, he was only one of many such practitioners. His lasting contribution to the history of American music, if not the world, lay in his talent as a sacred music composer. He had frequent inner conflicts between his religious upbringing and his career as a blues musician; within African-American religious circles, the blues was seen as worldly, and as such, inappropriate for religious people. He experienced a religious rebirth as early as 1920 at the National Baptist Convention, and one of his religious songs, "If I Don't Get There," appeared in a later edition of the convention's landmark collection, *Gospel Pearls*, which was first produced in 1921. Dorsey credits his conversion to Reverend A. W. Nix, one of the many singing preachers who recorded brief sermons from the middle to late 1920s. Other "shout preachers" (as they were also called) with whom he had associations were J. M. Gates from Atlanta, J. C. Burnett from Kansas City, E. H. Hall from Chicago, and Theodore Frye from Mississippi, all of whom played a substantial role in the promotion of Dorsey's gospel music.

Dorsey had not altogether given up composing and playing the blues. In 1928, he collaborated with his friend Hudson Whitaker (whose stage name was Tampa Red) to compose "It's Tight Like That" and "Terrible Operation Blues." He also worked as an arranger for Brunswick Records. As early as 1927, however, he had begun "peddling" (i.e., accompanying a singer at the keyboard) his religious songs in area churches, but they were rejected by many ministers because of their stylistic affinity to the blues. In 1930, Dorsey's song "If You See My Savior" was performed at the National Baptist Convention to a tumultuous response. From this point on, he seems to have been more committed to composing, arranging, promoting, and recording gospel songs. He was clearly the genre's principal advocate.

In 1931, he organized with Theodore Frye what is generally recognized as the world's first gospel chorus at Chicago's Ebenezer Baptist Church. He formed choruses at other area churches as well. During this period, Dorsey opened his own publishing company dedicated to selling gospel music and co-founded the National Convention of Gospel Choirs and Choruses, Inc., with his colleague Sallie Martin. This organization became a vehicle for training gospel choirs and coaching soloists. This booming period in Dorsey's career was not without its personal tragedy, however. In 1932, his first wife, Nettie, died in childbirth, and the child died subsequently. This tragedy was the occasion during which Dorsey composed his most celebrated work, "Take My Hand, Precious Lord."

Through forming choruses, musical tours, workshops, and discovering and promoting other singers, Dorsey moved around the country promoting his brand of blues-based gospel music. He also had several prominent protégés. In addition to Sallie Martin, who also acted as his business manager, he discovered a talented singer, Willie Mae Ford Smith, whom Dorsey appointed in 1936 as the director of the Soloists Bureau of the National Convention of Gospel Choirs and Choruses. In this role, she demonstrated the proper style and delivery of gospel songs to a new generation of younger singers. Among Dorsey's other celebrated discoveries was Mahalia Jackson, who became gospel music's first international star. He first met her in 1929 and was her official accompanist between the years 1937 and 1946. He also discovered and promoted Clara Ward along with many other singers and groups.

Dorsey toured extensively in the 1930s and 1940s in the United States, Europe, Mexico, and North Africa, and he served as director of the National Convention of Gospel Choirs into the 1970s. By the late 1970s, failing health forced him into semi-retirement. Dorsey re-emerged in a 1983 documentary, *Say Amen, Somebody*, in which he appeared with Mother Willie Mae Ford Smith. The film featured their performances as well as those of many of their protégés, including the late Mahalia Jackson, the O'Neal twins, and Delois Barrett Campbell and the Barrett sisters. By the late 1980s, he was suffering from the effects of Alzheimer's disease. He died in Chicago in January 1993.

CHRISTOPHER A. BROOKS

TAKE MY HAND, PRECIOUS LORD (1932)

Dorsey's most celebrated work, "Take My Hand, Precious Lord," came from a period of great personal despair. As Dorsey recalled the scenario in an interview, he was testing out his new melody on his collaborator and friend, Theodore Frye, who suggested that instead of using "blessed Lord," he use "precious Lord" in the opening line. The melody is one that lends itself (as do many of Dorsey's gospel songs) to vocal embellishments such as *coloratura, glissandi,* grace notes, trills, and similar ornamental devices. Such was the tradition with the slow rhythmic songs or those songs without a noticeable rhythmic pulse. The harmony is relatively simple; in the key of C major, the chordal progression moves from the tonic to the subdominant to the dominant and back to the tonic.

The first verse of the song suggests a statement of faith from an individual who is either nearing the end of life or in great despair. Subsequent verses are similar in sentiment. The appeal of this work is found in its harmonic simplicity; however, the performance can become very complex in the hands of a skilled singer who may use the harmony as a mere springboard and alter the melody dramatically. The fact that the song has been translated into over fifty languages is an indication of its universal popularity and appeal.

Because of its poignant simplicity and profound message, "Take My Hand, Precious Lord" is probably one of the most frequently heard and performed songs in today's religious repertory. It has been sung at funerals, weddings, and a variety of other sacred and secular events.

CHRISTOPHER A. BROOKS

OLD SHIP OF ZION (1950)

This song is an excellent example of the power that Dorsey conveys through his music, a power that stems, in large part, from the highly personal narratives that he weaves through his texts. In "Old Ship of Zion," he uses the imagery of the sea—waves, swimming, ships—to describe a conversion experience. The singer, struggling to survive in "life's dark sea," sees a ship "far away." The captain, calling to her, asks her to come aboard; he has come to "save her." The song ends with an expression of joy because the singer is "on board"—"saved." The multiple layers of significance embedded in the text add to the emotional power of the song.

"Old Ship of Zion" borrows much of its imagery as well as the text of the chorus from the traditional spiritual of the same name, but Dorsey adds the narrative text of the verses and writes new music for the entire song, thus composing an entirely new work in the process. Its harmonic structure resembles that of many of Dorsey's other songs; he restricts himself to blues progressions, and the formal dimensions of the song are dictated by the text, suggesting that it is the element of primary importance, not the music. However, the text alone is not the only element that creates a powerful response in the audience. The music allows for a broad range of improvisation during the performance. With slowly unfolding phrases, a comfortable tessitura, a slow harmonic rhythm with textual repeats, and embellishments, the singer can take many interpretive liberties to communicate the emotive power of the text.

TIMOTHY ROMMEN

DURÁN, ALEJO

Born Gilberto Alejandro Durán Díaz, in El Paso, Cesar, Colombia, February 9, 1919; died in Montería, Córdoba, Colombia, November 15, 1989. **Education:** Mainly self-taught; learned the button accordion while working as a laborer; influenced by local maestros Octavio Mendoza and Víctor Silva. **Composing and Performing Career:** Began as composer, singer, accordion player, ca. 1943; Teatro Atenas, Mompós, Colombia, debut performance, 1949; made recordings and regional tours with his *conjunto vallenato*; moved to Magangué and Sahagún, ca. 1951; recorded first hit songs, "Cero treinta y nueve" and "Altos del Rosario," 1954; Tropical Records, signed as exclusive artist; moved to Planeta Rica, Córdoba, ca. 1965; recorded numerous LPs with various labels. **Honors/Awards:** Annual Festival Vallenato, Valledupar, Rey Vallenato Award, 1968; Gold Medal, Best Colombian Folk Music Artist; Cesar University, Silver Azafate.

MUSIC LIST
[The following list of titles includes only works that were composed by the subject of the entry; it is not a list of recordings that were made by the subject. Although the composer may have made recordings of his own works, the list is not restricted to those recordings but in many cases includes performances by other artists of the composer's work. The list is made up of publication and discographical data, in cases where such information is available. Although no effort has been made to include documentation of the earliest recording of the works listed, the date of the earliest recording that is readily available has been given. —Ed.]

"Altos del Rosario" or "La despedida del Alto." 1952. Recorded, 1954: Discos Fuentes 10070.
"Amor comprado." Recorded: Discos Fuentes 10070.
"Ayapel." Recorded: Victoria CDV 1244.
"Besito cortao." Recorded: Discos Fuentes 16031.
"El borracho." Recorded, 1974: Kubaney K-482.
"Bren."
"La cachucha bacana" (paseo). Recorded, 1982: CBS D2CS-7; Discos Fuentes 10070; Procultura 6.
"Caminito triste." Recorded: Discos Fuentes 16031.
"Caminito verde." Recorded: Discos Fuentes 10070.
"Los campanales." Recorded: Discos Fuentes 10070.
"Cata." Recorded, 1984: Discos CBS International DBL-15311.
"Cejas encontradas."
"Cero treinta y nueve" or "039." Recorded, 1954: Cariño DBL1-5212; Discos Fuentes 10070.
"Chave."
"El chinchorrito." Recorded, 1985: CBS D2CS-7.
"Clavo y martillo" (son). Recorded, 1982: Procultura 6.
"Las cocas."
"Comae consuelo."
"Compae Chemo." Recorded: Discos Fuentes 10070.
"Contestación a 'Pedazo de acordeón.'" Recorded: Discos Fuentes 16031.
"Los cuatro amigos." Recorded: Discos Fuentes 16031.

"De Juanito a Vifalero."
"El entusiasmo de las mujeres."
"Evangelina." Recorded: Discos Fuentes 16031.
"Fidelina." Recorded: Discos Fuentes 10070.
"La fortuna" (merengue).
"Güepaje (La trampa)" (paseo). Recorded: Discos Fuentes 10070.
"La hija de Amaranto."
"Hombre de malas."
"Hombre que se jugo la vida." Recorded, 1985: CBS D2CS-7.
"Honda herida." Recorded: Discos Fuentes 10070.
"Joselina." Recorded: Discos Fuentes 16031.
"La lengua" (paseo).
"Magangué."
"Mal de amor." Recorded: Discos Fuentes 10070.
"María Espejo." Recorded: Discos Fuentes 16031.
"El martillo." Recorded: Discos Fuentes 16031.
"Las mellas" (merengue). Recorded: Victoria CDV 1244.
"Mi dolor."
"Mi pedazo de acordeon."
"Mírame fijamente." Recorded: Discos Fuentes 16031.
"La niña Minga" (merengue). Recorded: Discos Fuentes 10070.
"Noche clara" (merengue).
"La ola vallenato." Recorded: Discos Fuentes 10070.
"Palmito." Recorded: Discos Fuentes 10070.
"El parrandero."
"Pasando penas."
"Pedazo de acordeón" (puya). Recorded: Discos Fuentes 10070.
"La pega pega." (son-paseo). Recorded: Discos Fuentes 10070.
"El pelionara." Recorded, 1985: CBS D2CS-7.
"Pena y dolor."
"La perra." Recorded, 1985: CBS D2CS-7; Discos Fuentes 1193-2.
"Pobre corazón."
"Pobrecito corazón." Recorded: Discos Fuentes 10070.
"La primavera." Recorded: Discos Fuentes 10070.
"Los primeros días." Recorded: Discos Fuentes 10070.
"La puya vallenata." Recorded: Discos Fuentes 10070.
"Quédate tranquila." Recorded: Discos Fuentes 16031.
"El querendón."
"La recorrida."
"Recuerdos de Alicia." Recorded: Discos Fuentes 16031.
"Sabina."
"El secreto." Recorded, 1974: Kubaney K-482.
"Sielva María." Recorded: Discos Fuentes 10070.
"Solito" (paseo).
"El tigre de Punta Brava." Recorded, 1974: Kubaney K-482.
"Toño el guapo."
"El trago garriao." Recorded, 1985: CBS D2CS-7.
"La trampa."
"Tristezas."
"La vieja necia" (paseo).
"La vieja Gabriela" (merengue).

Alejo Durán; courtesy of Egberto Bermudez

PUBLICATIONS

ABOUT DURÁN

Book

Vergara Contreras, José Manuel. *Alejo Durán*. Montería, Colombia: Grafisinú, 1989.

Video

Alejandro Durán, el inmortal. Barranquilla, Colombia: Guajira Producciones, 1995.

* * * * *

During his career, Gilberto Alejandro Durán Díaz (Alejo Durán) recorded more than 100 LPs with the Tropical, Discos Fuentes, Victoria, and Philips labels. Recognized as one of the founders of the *vallenato* tradition, he is the composer of numerous standards of this repertoire. His most popular songs include "Cero treinta y nueve," "El entusiasmo de las mujeres," "La perra," "La cachucha bacana," "Fidelina," and many others, covering a range of Colombian *son, paseo, puya,* and *merengue*. With some of his compositions, notably "Güepaje" (*paseo*) and "La pega pega" (*son-paseo*), Durán experimented in the late 1960s with the commercially successful blend of accordion and brass instruments found in the style of the "Corraleros del Majagual," an early example of the "fusions" of today.

Durán was born in 1919 in El Paso, Colombia, a small village in the southeastern savannahs of the northern coast. El Paso is located in a swampy lowland region irrigated by the Ariguaní and Cesar rivers and traditionally has been a cattle-raising area. Since the 18th century, several haciendas have flourished there, all belonging to absent proprietors who provide employment to a local black and mulatto population that maintain a traditional way of life based on agriculture.

El Paso and the entire Colombian northern coastal region share cultural traits based on Afro-Hispanic roots, including poetry improvisation, simultaneous singing and dancing, and funerary customs in which music plays an important role. These traditions were an integral part of the education and early life of Alejo Durán. His father owned and played an accordion and his mother is said to have been one of the renowned *cantadoras* of the local *tambora,* a music group that features responsorial singing accompanied by dancing and clapping to the music of two conical drums. The smaller drum, called *llamador,* keeps the main rhythmic pattern, and the other, *tambor alegre,* plays the alternating rhythmic variations characteristic of the style. His older and younger brothers, Luis Felipe and Nafer Durán, are also musicians, the latter, one of the foremost representatives of the so-called traditional, classical, or old-fashioned *vallenato*.

Around 1939, while still in his youth, Durán left his studies at the local elementary school to work as a cowboy in the Hacienda Las Cabezas, near his native village. There he learned the traditional musical forms such as the *tambora* and began to play instruments like the *caja* (conical drum) and the accordion with local fellow workers. He began composing shortly afterward and at age 24 began playing the accordion under the guidance of masters such as Víctor Julio Silva, Eusebio Ayala, and Octavio Mendoza. In 1949, he made his debut at the Teatro Atenas in Mompós, one of the most important commercial centers of the region. It possessed a flourishing cultural life as early as the second half of the 19th century and was one of the Colombian centers for the dissemination of European music and musical instruments in that period.

Spurred by the enthusiasm generated by the establishment in Cartagena of Discos Fuentes (Fuentes Recording Company) in the early 1940s, Durán participated in the company's recording sessions and toured the region with his own *conjunto vallenato,* which was comprised of the button accordion, the *guacharaca* (scraper), and the *caja*.

Durán soon settled in Magangué and Sahagún, which were both commercial and trading posts, and in 1954 recorded his first hit songs, joining the first generation of *vallenato* composers and accordion players, such as Abel Antonio Villa, Luis Enrique Martínez, Juancho Polo Valencia, and Manuel Francisco (Pacho) Rada; non-performing composers like Rafael Escalona; and interpreters such as Guillermo Buitrago and Julio César Bovea and their groups. Among his earliest recordings are "Noche clara" (*merengue*), "Solito" (*paseo*), "La vieja necia" (*paseo*), and "La vieja Gabriela" (*merengue*). He then signed as an exclusive artist with Tropical Records and settled in Planeta Rica, Córdoba.

In April 1968, Durán was acclaimed Vallenato King in the first Festival de la Leyenda Vallenata, which has since taken place yearly in Valledupar, one of the main urban centers of the area. His records from the 1970s show a close adherence to common schemes and a strong rural tinge, which he retained during the transformation of his style from a rural style to one modeled on *rancheras* and the Latin American pop *baladas* that reflected the change of social and economic patterns in the area.

On the occasion of the 20th anniversary of the Valledupar Festival Vallenato in 1987, a "Rey de Reyes" (King of Kings) contest was held, and Alejo Durán and all the winners of the previous festivals participated. Because the participants believed the jury to be partial and inadequate, Durán and most of the contenders withdrew days before the final event, demanding the election of another panel. After being refused, they returned to play, and the election of Nicolás "Colacho" Mendoza—instead of Durán, the audience's favorite—resulted in riots that, ironically, confirmed Alejo Durán as the people's "King of Kings." To his death, he lived as a peasant, cultivating his land and raising a small number of cattle, the owner of very little property, and the father of more than 20 children.

In general, all *vallenato* genres are strophic, with short instrumental introductions and interludes. One of the salient characteristics of Durán's style is the presence of sung melodies as introductions and interludes, all very rhythmic and within the compass of one octave. At the end of his pieces, Durán always includes a stereotypical closing *pase* ("pass," or short melodic run) common to the accordion players of his generation and universally present in their compositions.

Although the accordion's sound is the most distinctive feature of *vallenato* musicians, the general sound of the ensemble is created by the contribution of the *caja,* which adds free patterns to the steady *guacharaca* rhythm. Since the recording sessions of the 1970s, public performances have included, more and more frequently, the electric bass, which contributes to the rhythmic complexity of the texture. Also notable in *vallenato* is its duality. While more and more recordings rely on the electric bass and the addition of other instruments (*tumbadora, cencerro, timbaletas,* etc.), in the Festival Vallenato, with its almost antiquarian approach, only the three so-called traditional instruments are accepted. Textually and thematically, *vallenatos* are autobiographical, all of them linked to personal anecdotes, including themes of daily life, social critique, personal satire, and romance. In the 1980s, *vallenato* turned to foreign influences, especially those of Mexican *ranchera* and traditional *balada,* leaving aside its rhythmic and dance-like orientations and accepting a tamer and softer shape, concentrating on the lyrics, emphasizing a more dramatic and intense delivery of the texts, and displacing the attention from accordionists to singers.

One of the main characteristics of Durán's music is its harmonic simplicity and instability, possibly the result of the adaptation of *tambora* and *coplas* melodies to the disposition of the keys, related to Western harmonic practice, on the button accordion. The *tambora* schemes, the *coplas,* and *décimas* melodies—skeletons used by singers of the area—show different scalar formations, and their accommodation to a harmonically limited resource like the accordion could probably explain this harmonic ambiguity.

Rhythmically, Durán's music shows, as do most early *vallenato,* the prototypical structures used in other styles of the area. It is based on a steady *guacharaca* scheme (see Ex. 1) upon which the *caja* plays the freer role, following the techniques of *tambor alegre* playing in *cumbia* and *bullerengue* and producing variations based on divisions and amplifications of certain rhythmic schemes. In Durán's music, the voice and the accordion are highly dependent on each other and, paradoxically, this lack of independence of the accordion line converted him into the champion of "purity" in *vallenato.*

Example 1. *Guacharaca* rhythm

From the beginning of his public career, Durán was called the "Black King" of Vallenato and later on the "Grand Black" (Negro Grande) of Colombia, a male counterpart to the black singer Leonor González Mina, who was dubbed "La Negra Grande de Colombia."

SELECTED WORKS

In the *vallenato* repertoire, *sones* were common some decades ago but more recently have been losing terrain to the *paseo.* The *son* shows basically the same musical characteristics of the *paseo,* although the former uses shorter melodic motives and has a less-defined transition between the tonic and the dominant. The song "Altos del Rosario" (Rosario's Heights), sometimes called "La despedida del Alto" (Alto's Farewell), pays tribute to a village of that name. It was composed by Durán in 1952 in homage to the people of that village, who always welcomed Durán and celebrated his presence as a musician during his frequent stays there, which sometimes lasted for months. In this song, the names of important local personalities are mentioned, a practice that later became a very important feature of *vallenato.*

The *paseo* is the most prevalent genre in Alejo Durán's musical output, with "Cero treinta y nueve" (Zero Thirty-nine) being one of the most popular. Recorded in 1954, its theme is a poetic account of the unhappy ending of a love adventure. At the time of its composition, the piece aroused special interest because of its reference to the number (039) of the local transport system coach that is said to have taken away Durán's beloved. The song's musical and poetic structure is based on the alteration of sung strophes and contains a refrain and brief instrumental accordion interludes that use the same thematic material as the song. The lyrics use the vernacular idioms of the Colombian Spanish common to the Atlantic coastal region, articulated in the tradition of the popular Hispanic *copla,* which consists of a strophe of four verses of eight syllables each. In the refrain, the same poetic meter is used, with two verses repeated.

The *paseo* rhythm sticks to the common 2/4 meter of most *vallenato* genres, which frequently employ the dislocated accents that characterize Afro-Colombian peasant music. This *vallenato* tradition was most popular in Durán's home village and consists of a call-and-response pattern sung mainly by women who also clap their hands or play wooden clappers; the women are accompanied by three drums, two conical (*llamador* and *tambor alegre*) and one cylindrical (*tambora*). In the traditional *vallenato* ensemble, the melodic material is assigned to the voice, and the accordion and the *caja* (conical single-skin drum) take up the role of the *tambor alegre,* the larger of the two conical drums of the *tambora* ensemble, which usually make free variations of the rhythmic patterns. The third element of this ensemble, the *guacharaca* (tubular wooden scraper) keeps a steady single pattern, taking the role of the *llamador* (small conical drum) in the traditional peasant musical ensembles.

"Pedazo de acordeón" (Battered Accordion) is Durán's most well known *puya.* It refers to an old and battered accordion as a token and symbol of naturality and authenticity, especially in the context of the musical transformations that occurred in Colombian *costeño* music in the early 1960s. The structure of the *puya* is based on the musicalization of a *copla,* this time with even less harmonic flexibility, with quick changes from tonic to dominant, and a fast tempo. The music of *puya* is also used for the *piquerías,* or musical contests of improvised poetry, which are frequently performed as live events but are seldom recorded.

The *merengue* genre is one of the less performed of the *vallenato* repertoire. Its fast tempo recalls that of the *puya,* but it has a distinct rhythmic structure based on a structure similar to that of the *cinquillo* rhythm (see Ex. 2), which has changed in the last decades, becoming assimilated to triple groupings because of the high speed of its interpretation. The quick tempo is the most salient characteristic of *vallenato* and Durán's *merengues,* which, following the lines of his compositional techniques, are based on two musical motives that oscillate between tonic and dominant chords, although some of them present the same ambiguity found in the other genres of his repertoire. These motives are applied to the instrumental and sung sections of the songs. In his *merengues,* Durán frequently introduces a section in which improvisations are played on the bass buttons of the accordion. The improvisations usually stay within the simple harmonic framework already described, but in other pieces (e.g., "Las mellas"), it ventures into quasi-modulatory terrain. In "La niña Minga," the attempt of modulation in the improvisatory section on the basses is also matched by some rhythmic complexity; these pieces are probably the source of Durán's reputation as an accordion player.

Example 2. *Cinquillo* rhythm

One of the basic features of Durán's work is its simplicity. The musical structure of the majority of his pieces shows an apparent lack of consistency between their original style and the musical means used in their performances and recordings. Durán's work belongs musically to the traditional local style, especially to that of the *bullerengue* and *tambora*. This genre is based on the vocal performance of a refrain, usually a short musical motive, alternated with verses of the *copla* tradition. The same is found in the texts of most of Durán's works, especially in the *sones* and *puyas* and to a lesser degree in the *merengues* and *paseos,* these being more elaborate, with the full use of stanzas instead of the short musical phrases that derive from the peasant traditions that lie at the heart of Alejo Durán's musical style.

EGBERTO BERMUDEZ

EL-DABH, HALIM

Born in Cairo, Egypt, March 4, 1921; U.S. citizen, 1961. **Education:** Cairo, Egypt, received elementary education at Egyptian Public School and the Jesuit School; Heliopolis, Egypt, Kubeh Palace High School; Sculz Conservatory of Music, Cairo, studied piano and Western music, 1941–44; Cairo University, degree in agricultural engineering, 1945; University of New Mexico, Albuquerque, N. Mex., studied composition, 1950–51; Berkshire Music Center at Tanglewood, Lenox, Mass., studied composition with Aaron Copland and Irving Fine, 1951–52; New England Conservatory of Music, Boston, Mass., M.Mus., 1953; Brandeis University, M.F.A., 1954. **Composing and Performing Career:** All Saints Cathedral, Cairo, performed his own "It Is Dark and Damp on the Front" to great critical acclaim, launching his career in music, 1949; Metropolitan Museum, New York City, debuted as solo drummer at premiere of his "Tahmeela," Leopold Stokowski conducting, 1959. **Teaching Career:** Haile Selassie University, Addis Ababa, Ethiopia, Associate Professor of Music, 1962–64; Howard University, Washington, D.C., Associate Professor of Music and African Studies, 1966–69; Kent State University, Kent, Ohio, Professor of Ethnomusicology and Adjunct Professor of Pan-African Studies, 1969–1991; co-director, Kent State Center for the Study of World Music, since 1979; appointed University Professor, 1989, Professor Emeritus, 1991. **Commissions:** Martha Graham, 1958, 1961, 1962, 1975; Jerome Robbins, 1959; Ralou Manou, 1965; Howard University, 1967, 1968; Hawthorne School, 1971; Memphis Symphony Orchestra, 1987; Youngstown State University, 1988; Middletown, Ohio, 1991; Cleveland Museum of Art, Cleveland, Ohio, 1992; Delta Omicron, 1993. **Honors/Awards:** First prize, Egyptian Opera House composers competition, 1942; Fulbright Fellowship, 1950, 1967; Guggenheim Fellowship, 1959–60, 1961–62; Rockefeller Fellowship, 1961. **Mailing Address:** c/o Hugh A. Glauser School of Music, Kent State University, Kent, OH 44240.

MUSIC LIST

INSTRUMENTAL SOLOS
Harp
"Kalabsha on River Nile." 1991. Unpublished manuscript. Premiere, 1991.

Percussion
"Diversions." 1965. Unpublished manuscript. Premiere, 1965.

"Drum-Takseem." 1951. Unpublished manuscript. Premiere, 1952.

"Secrets of the Sky and Earth" (marimba). 1996. Unpublished manuscript. Premiere, 1996.

Sonics. 1955. Unpublished manuscript. ("Sonic no. 7" and "Sonic no. 10" published, New York: C. F. Peters, 1965.) Premiere, 1959.

Piano
"Arabiyaats." 1954. Unpublished manuscript. Premiere, 1954.

"Berceuse Amira." 1959. Unpublished manuscript. Also in a version for voice and piano. Premiere, 1959.

"Berceuse Shadia." 1955. Unpublished manuscript. Also in a version for voice and piano. Premiere, 1955.

"Egyptian Suite Ballet." 1947. Unpublished manuscript. Premiere, 1947.

Eulogy to Cairo's Earthquake Victims and Their Families. 1992. Unpublished manuscript. Contents: The City of Cairo; The Planet and the Earthquake; Lament, Love and Hope. Premiere, 1992.

"Evolution and Decadence." 1949. Unpublished manuscript. Premiere, 1949.

"Fantasia-Amira." 1946. Unpublished manuscript. Premiere, 1946.

"Felucca, the Celestial Journey." 1953. Unpublished manuscript. Premiere, 1953.

"Ifrikiyaats." 1954. Unpublished manuscript. Premiere, 1954.

"It Is Dark and Damp on the Front." 1948. Unpublished manuscript. Premiere, 1949.

March. 1947. Unpublished manuscript. Premiere, 1947.

"Mekta in the Art of Kita." 1955. New York: C. F. Peters, 1961. Premiere, 1955.

"Misriyaats." 1954. Unpublished manuscript. Premiere, 1954.

"Prelude Sheroude." 1946. Unpublished manuscript. Premiere, 1946.

"Soufiane." 1961. Unpublished manuscript. Premiere, 1991.

Chinese Zither
"Dragons and Water Lilies." 1991. Unpublished manuscript. Premiere, 1991.

Two Pianos
"Osmo-Symbiosis" or "Duo-Tahmeel No. 1." 1952. Unpublished manuscript. Premiere, 1952.

Electronic Music
Electronic Fanfare. 1963. Unpublished manuscript. Co-composer, Otto Luening. Premiere, 1963.

Elements, Beings and Primevals (tape). 1959. Unpublished manuscript. Premiere, 1959.

Leiyla and the Poet (tape). 1959. Unpublished manuscript. Premiere, 1959. Recorded: Columbia ML-5966.

Meditation on White Noise (tape). 1959. Unpublished manuscript. Premiere, 1959.

Ush Ka Masriya (harpsichord, tape). Unpublished manuscript. Premiere, 1959.

The Word (tape). 1959. Unpublished manuscript. Premiere, 1959.

SMALL INSTRUMENTAL ENSEMBLE
Strings
String Quartet no. 1. 1951. Unpublished manuscript. Premiere, 1951.

Woodwinds
"Ceremonial Fattening for Death and Resurrection" (bassoon ensemble). 1991. Unpublished manuscript. Premiere, 1991.

"Conversations with Shu." 1990. Unpublished manuscript. Premiere, 1990.

"Habeeb's Lullaby and Rebuttal" (saxophone, bassoon ensemble). 1991. Unpublished manuscript. Premiere, 1991.

Halim El-Dabh; shown holding an Egyptian-Sudanese seven-string harp (masks from Mali, wall rug from Ethiopia); photo courtesy of Kent State University

Brass

"Multicolored Sonata" (two trumpets). 1996. Unpublished manuscript. Premiere, 1996.

Percussion

"Hindi-Yaat no. 1" (cymbal-bells, medium-high drums, jingles, metallic discs, woodblocks/clappers). 1965. New York: C. F. Peters, 1965. Premiere, 1966.

"Juxtaposition no. 1" (two timpani, xylophone, marimba). 1959. New York: C. F. Peters, 1965. Premiere, 1959. Recorded: Indiana University School of Music, Program 1984–85 no. 832.

"Juxtaposition no. 2" (harp, timpani, tom-tom-xylophone, marimba). 1959. Unpublished manuscript. Premiere, 1959.

"Mosaic no. 1" (piano, double traps). 1965. New York: C. F. Peters, 1965. Premiere, 1965.

"Tabla Dance" (piano, percussion ensemble). 1952. New York: C. F. Peters, 1965. Premiere, 1952.

"Tabla-Tahmeel no. 1" (percussion ensemble). 1965. Unpublished manuscript. Premiere, 1966.

Combinations

"Big Tooth Aspen" (flute, *derabucca*). 1995. Unpublished manuscript. Premiere, 1995.

"Born from the World" (bass, sacred drums, cymbals, jingles). 1967. Unpublished manuscript. Commissioned by Howard University. Premiere, 1967.

"Dialogue for Double Bass and Ceramic Egyptian Drum" (*derabucca, bass*). 1991. Unpublished manuscript. Premiere, 1991.

"Egueypto-Yaat" (two trumpets, percussion). 1963. Unpublished manuscript. Premiere, 1985.

Fantasia-Tahmeel: Concerto for Darabukka and Strings. 1959. New York: C. F. Peters, n.d. Premiere, 1959.

"Frieze in Body Movement" (violin, piano, timpani, harp). 1954. Unpublished manuscript. Originally titled "Impressions from Gauguin, Léger and Dali." Premiere, 1954.

"Homage to Mohammed Ali-El-Kabir" (violin, cello, piano). 1946. Unpublished manuscript. Premiere, 1946.

"Monotone, Bitone, and Polytone" (wind sextet, percussion). 1952; revised 1985. Unpublished manuscript. Premiere, 1952.

"New Pharaohs Suite" (winds and percussion). 1996. Commissioned by Cleveland Museum of Art. Premiere, 1996.

"Spectrum no. 1: Symphonies and Sonic Vibration." (strings of the piano and drums of wood and pottery). 1955. Unpublished manuscript. Premiere, 1955. Also arranged for four harps and violins. Recorded: Folkways FX-6160.

"Tahmeela" (flute, oboe, clarinet, strings, bassoon, horn, violin). 1958. New York: C. F. Peters, n.d. Also arranged for *derabucca* and strings. Premiere, 1958.

"Theme Song: The New Renaissance" (flute, cello, piano). 1991. Unpublished manuscript. Premiere, 1991.

"Thulathiya" (violin, oboe, piano). 1955. New York: C. F. Peters, n.d. Premiere, 1955.

"Thumaniya" (two trumpets, percussion). 1984. Unpublished manuscript. Premiere, 1984.

"Tonography" (clarinet, bassoon, marimba, percussion). 1980; revised as "Tonography III," 1984. Unpublished manuscript. Premiere, 1980.

The World Order for Two Tubas and Egyptian Drum. 1994. Unpublished manuscript. Commissioned by the Delta Omicron chapter at Kent State University. Contents: The Pendulum; The Shiver; The Balance. Premiere, 1994.

STRING ORCHESTRA

Atshan Ya Sabaye. 1947. Unpublished manuscript. Premiere, 1947.

CHAMBER ORCHESTRA

Harmonies of the Spheres: Ten Nations Rejoice (wind symphony orchestra). 1991. Unpublished manuscript. Contents: Jangada—Brazil; Balladia—Egypt; Adriatica—Italy; Mexico; Japan; Switzerland; Ireland; India; Luxembourg; Canada. Commissioned by Middletown, Ohio, for the Middfest International Celebration. Premiere, 1991.

Nomadic Waves (double wind orchestra). 1965; revised 1981. Unpublished manuscript. Also in a version for double wind orchestra and percussion. Premiere, 1965.

FULL ORCHESTRA

Ballet Suite no. 2. 1958. Unpublished manuscript. Premiere, 1958.

Gahmela. 1960. Unpublished manuscript. Premiere, 1960.

Meditation on the Nile. 1952. Unpublished manuscript. Premiere, 1952.

National Anthem for Egypt for President Naguib. 1952. Unpublished manuscript. Premiere, 1952.

Ramesses the Great: Symphony no. 9. 1987. Unpublished manuscript. Commissioned by the Memphis Symphony Orchestra. Premiere, 1987.

Rhapsodia Egyptia-Brasileira. 1985. Unpublished manuscript. Premiere, 1985.

Symphony no. 1. 1950. Unpublished manuscript. Premiere, 1950.

Symphony no. 2. 1952. Unpublished manuscript. Premiere, 1952.

Symphony no. 3 of 37 Years. 1953. New York: C. F. Peters, n.d. (rental). Note: master's thesis, Brandeis University, 1954. Premiere, 1953.

Unity at the Crossroad. 1979. Unpublished manuscript. Premiere, 1979.

Ya Gamul Ya Nasser. 1947. Unpublished manuscript. Premiere, 1947.

ORCHESTRA (CHAMBER OR FULL) WITH SOLOISTS

Bahía (trombone, orchestra). 1986. Unpublished manuscript. Premiere, 1986.

Concerto (*derabucca*, clarinet, string orchestra). 1981. Unpublished manuscript. Premiere, 1981.

Concerto for Trombone. Unpublished manuscript. Premiere, 1987.

Pierre jusqu'au ciel (male voice, orchestra). 1960. Unpublished manuscript. Note: part of Egyptian Series also known as Music of the Pharaohs; sound and light music of the pyramids of Giza. Premiere, 1960.

Tahmeela, Concerto Grosso (timpani, orchestra). 1986. Unpublished manuscript. Premiere, 1986.

Urameshiya (voice or electronic tape, and small orchestra). 1959. Unpublished manuscript. Commissioned by Jerome Robbins. Premiere, 1959.

ORCHESTRA (CHAMBER OR FULL) WITH CHORUS

Lamentation de Pharaon (SA, soprano, baritone, orchestra). 1960. Unpublished manuscript. Note: part of Egyptian Series. Premiere, 1960.

Prayer to the Sphinx (SATB, solo voices, orchestra). 1960. Unpublished manuscript. Premiere, 1960.

Theodora in Byzantium (TB, soprano, orchestra). 1965. Unpublished manuscript. Commissioned by Ralou Manou. Premiere, 1965.

CONCERT BAND

Five Etudes. 1989. Unpublished manuscript. Premiere, 1989.

SOLO VOICE

"Hajer" (soprano). 1979. Unpublished manuscript. Premiere, 1979.

"The Jade Flute" (soprano, trumpet). 1989. Unpublished manuscript. Premiere, 1989.

VOICE WITH INSTRUMENTAL ENSEMBLE

"Isis and the Seven Scorpions" (soprano, flute, harpsichord, *derabucca*). 1975. Unpublished manuscript. Premiere, 1975.

"Juxtaposition no. 3" (mezzo-soprano, two harps, timpani, cymbals, bells, triangle, xylophone, marimba). 1959. Unpublished manuscript. Premiere, 1959.

CHORAL MUSIC

"Abongila's Love" (boys and men's chorus, three drums, shakers). 1974. Unpublished manuscript. Premiere, 1975.

Gloria Aton (SATB, percussion, strings). 1960. Unpublished manuscript. Note: part of Egyptian Series. Premiere, 1960.

"Kyrie for the Bishop of Ghana" (SATB, percussion). 1968. Unpublished manuscript. Premiere, 1968.

"Leiyla" (TB, mezzo-soprano, piano, timpani, cello, xylophone). 1965. Unpublished manuscript. Premiere, 1965.

Music of the Pyramids. 1960; revised 1983. Unpublished manuscript. Premiere, 1960.

"The Nile." 1960. Unpublished manuscript. Premiere, 1960.

Pyramide (TB, percussion, harps, strings). 1960. Unpublished manuscript. Note: part of Egyptian Series. Premiere, 1960.

"Salma Ya Salama." 1979. Unpublished manuscript. Premiere, 1979.

"Shades and Shadows" (TB, drums, jingles). 1965. Unpublished manuscript. Premiere, 1965.

"Shadows in Gallinia." 1947. Unpublished manuscript. Premiere, 1947.

DRAMATIC MUSIC

Aton, the Ankh, and the World (opera). 1972. Unpublished manuscript. Note: this work is part of the opera trilogy *Ptahmose and the Magic Spell.* Premiere, 1972.

The Birds (piano, synthesizer, flute, percussion, choruses, singers, actors, dancers). 1988. Unpublished manuscript. Commissioned by Youngstown State University. Premiere, 1988.

Black Epic. 1968. Unpublished manuscript. Commissioned by Howard University.

Black Genesis (opera). 1975. Unpublished manuscript. Premiere, 1975.

Clytemnestra (ballet). 1958; revised 1983. New York: C. F. Peters, n.d. (rental). Commissioned by Martha Graham. Premiere, 1958.

Drink of Eternity (flutes, ceramic pots, shakers, bells, narrator, dancers). 1981. Unpublished manuscript. Premiere, 1981.

The Eye of Horus (bass, percussion). 1967. Unpublished manuscript. Premiere, 1967.

A Look at Lightning (ballet). 1962. Unpublished manuscript. Commissioned by Martha Graham. Premiere, 1962.

Lucifer (ballet). 1975. Unpublished manuscript. Commissioned by Martha Graham. Premiere, 1975.

"Of Gods and Men" (chamber group, dancers, singers, drums, piano). 1973. Unpublished manuscript. Premiere, 1973.

One More Gaudy Night (ballet). 1961. New York: C. F. Peters, n.d. (rental). Commissioned by Martha Graham. Premiere, 1961.

Opera Flies. 1971; revised 1995. Unpublished manuscript. Commissioned by the Hawthorne School. Premiere, 1971 (first version); 1995 (second version).

The Osiris Ritual (opera). 1972. Unpublished manuscript. Note: this work is part of the opera trilogy *Ptahmose and the Magic Spell.* Premiere, 1972.

Prometheus Bound. 1969. Unpublished manuscript. Premiere, 1969.

Saladin and the Citadel (ballet). 1960. Unpublished manuscript. Also known as the Islamic Series. Premiere, 1960.

Sobek the Crocodile (children's opera). 1992. Unpublished manuscript. Commissioned by the city of Cleveland for the museum's Egyptian exhibit. Premiere, 1992.

The Twelve Hours Trip (opera). 1972. Unpublished manuscript. Note: this work is part of the opera trilogy *Ptahmose and the Magic Spell.*

Unnatural Acts. 1986. Unpublished manuscript. Premiere, 1986.

Yulei, the Ghost (soprano, oboe, clarinet, horn, trumpet, strings). 1962. Unpublished manuscript. Premiere, 1962.

MULTIMEDIA

"Lucy, Come Back" (singers, dancers, drummers, multimedia). 1993. Unpublished manuscript. Premiere, 1993.

PUBLICATIONS

ABOUT EL-DABH

Jarrett, Alfred Roosevelt. "New Music in the USA, 1960–1966." M.M. thesis, Howard University, 1967.

BY EL-DABH

The Derabucca: Hand Techniques in the Art of Drumming. New York: Peters, 1965.

"Egypt: The Religious Continuum." In *The Egyptian Continuum in Religion and Art,* edited by Edith Kohler. Middletown, Ohio: Middfest International Celebration, 1983.

"The Egyptian Aragouz Tradition." In *Puppetry at the Smithsonian,* edited by Jeffrey LaRiche. Washington, D.C.: Smithsonian Institution, 1980.

"Music Enriched by Traditions from the Depths of Time." *New York Times* (September 20, 1964): sect. 2, p. 15.

"Music from the Past." In *The Discovery Experience IV, Ancient Egypt: Arts and Artifacts,* edited by Marthalie Furber. Washington, D.C.: John F. Kennedy Center for the Performing Arts, 1979.

"The State of the Arts in Egypt Today." *The Middle East Journal* 35 (1981).

"Zebola and the Crocodile's Vengeance." In *Black People and Their Culture: Selected Writings for the African Diaspora*, edited by Rosi Lee Hooks. Washington, D.C.: Smithsonian Institution, 1976.

*   *   *   *   *

The son of Abdul Messieh El-Dabh, theologian and businessman, and Balsam Benyiamin Fam El-Dabh, Halim El-Dabh became fascinated by the folk music of his native country while working on a degree in agricultural engineering at Cairo University. For a class project, he conducted agricultural experiments in a remote Egyptian village, where he also became acquainted with traditional music. In the university his interests broadened to include Western music, and so he enrolled as a student in Cairo's Sculz Conservatory of Music. In 1942, El-Dabh won first prize in a composers' competition sponsored by the Egyptian Opera House, an important musical institution where Giuseppe Verdi's *Aida* received its premiere in 1871.

The turning point in Halim El-Dabh's artistic career occurred in 1948. Having witnessed the Jewish emigration from Germany to Palestine, El-Dabh concluded that "war truly begins in the heart of every human being." As a result of these events, he wrote "It Is Dark and Damp on the Front," for piano solo, which he played at the Music Center of the Cairo All Saints Cathedral the following year. A Swiss critic, who had previously objected to the unknown pianist's appearance in such a prestigious hall, wrote a front-page story in Cairo's French newspaper hailing the composer for his innovative use of sound and pedal technique.

An overnight sensation, El-Dabh was immediately invited by the American cultural attaché to perform in the United States; he arrived there in 1950. When Irving Fine heard "It Is Dark and Damp on the Front," he cabled Aaron Copland to offer El-Dabh an invitation to study at the Berkshire Music Center. The work had its American debut at Tanglewood in August 1951.

Those who influenced El-Dabh's early musical development include Francis Judd Cooke, Allen Barker, Hussein Helmy, Kamal Iskander, Pierre Nouri, Henry Shalala, Igor Stravinsky, Béla Bartók, Nicolas Slonimsky, Leopold Stokowski, and Arnold Schoenberg. Those who had great influence on his commitment to the African continent include El-Dabh's former chancellor, Haile Selassie; Sekou Tourré; and Leopold Sengor. The youngest of nine children, El-Dabh also credits two of his brothers, Bushra and Adeeb, for his early exposure to both music and philosophy. Their introduction to the writings of Sigmund Freud and Georg Wilhelm Friedrich Hegel, along with hearing his brothers perform, influenced and shaped El-Dabh's basic approach to life.

Blending elements of Egyptian music with the contrapuntal and harmonic devices of the West, El-Dabh's compositional style is noted for a special emphasis on rhythmic complexity and the incorporation of unusual percussive devices. His *Drink of Eternity* for flutes, ceramic pots, shakers, bells, narrator, and dancers (1981) and his three piano pieces "Arabiyaats," "Misriyaats," and "Ifrikiyaats" (all 1954) are known for their strong rhythmic qualities. His assertion that every instrument is a sound box with its own particular vibration potential is realized in "Spectrum no. 1" (1955), written

for the strings of the piano with drums of wood and pottery. It is conveyed also in his experimentation with sounds produced on a series of enamel musical instruments created during an enameling workshop held in 1991 on the campus of Kent State University. El-Dabh experiences rhythm and melody as a weave of physical and spiritual entities, and he has often invented new notational systems to be used along with standard notation, as in his *Sonics* (1955).

It is impossible, however, to address El-Dabh's compositional style without considering his approach to teaching and performing. For El-Dabh, the composer/performer/teacher cannot be separated from El-Dabh the man. All is integral to the whole. As a composer/performer he converses in a musical language that is essentially Egyptian, recalling ancient sounds by using contemporary instruments. This was perhaps best demonstrated when he was asked by the Cultural Ministry of the Egyptian government to compose *Lamentation de Pharaon* (1960), which is performed daily at the pyramids of Giza. Returning to Egypt in 1959, he lived literally in the tombs and temples of Abu Simbel. Every night the composer gathered the workers and the villagers into the temple chambers to sing and play instruments. Viewing the temple's bas-reliefs of musical processions, he experienced the sense that all the ancient sounds still remained.

As a teacher, he stresses that each cultural and geographical area deals with the organization of sound differently, and he emphasizes that one must work with sounds, not just ideas about sounds. In many of his introductory courses, students build their own African musical instruments and perform the music they are learning. By personally experiencing and sharing the music of Africa, the students receive a genuine feeling not only of the music but also of its relationship to the people who make it.

El-Dabh has enabled others to reach a heightened sense of awareness, teaching that insight into a culture may be achieved through understanding that culture's music. He has emerged as a musical ambassador of renown and has gained the respect and recognition of many. His drum manual, *The Derabucca: Hand Techniques in the Art of Drumming*, was published by Peters in 1965.

Noted for a preoccupation with large dramatic works intermediate between opera and pageant, El-Dabh often fashions his own texts, as in, for example, *Yulei, the Ghost* (1962), *The Eye of Horus* (1967), *Black Epic* (1968), *Prometheus Bound* (1969), *Ptahmose and the Magic Spell* (1972), and *The Birds* (1988). He is equally at ease composing works for full orchestra such as Symphonies nos. 1–3 (1950, 1952, 1953), *Unity at the Crossroad* (1979), and *Ramesses the Great: Symphony no. 9* (1987); chamber works such as String Quartet no. 1 (1951), and "Tonography" (1980); ballets, including *One More Gaudy Night* (1961), *A Look at Lightning* (1962), and *Lucifer* (1975); pieces for solo instruments like "Drum-Takes" (1951), "Meat in the Art of Kit" (1955), and "Dragons and Water Lilies" for Chinese zither (1991); and electronic music constructions such as *Meditation on White Noise* (1959), *Elements, Beings and Primeval* (1959), and *The Word* (1959).

With an energy level that belies his advanced years, Halim El-Dabh vigorously lives his life as a work-in-progress. An active man with many interests, he has a great propensity for transforming and reworking his scores. In fact, several of his works—*Music of the Pyramids* (1960, 1983), *Cleopatra* (1961, 1983), "Tonography" (1980, 1984), "Monotone, Bitone, and Polytone" (1952, 1985), *Opera Flies* (1971, 1995)—have subsequently been revised, which is a symbolic reflection of El-Dabh's belief that music is a living, organic entity that evolves and exists within its surroundings as a celebration of one's existence.

CLYTEMNESTRA (1958; REVISED 1983)

A pivotal moment in Halim El-Dabh's career occurred when, after hearing a performance of his "Monotone, Bitone and Polytone" for wind sextet and percussion (1952), Martha Graham, the famed American choreographer and pioneer in modern dance, commissioned him to compose the music for her epic dance-drama *Clytemnestra,* which was premiered on April 1, 1958, at the Adelphi Theatre in New York.

A relatively unknown composer at that time, El-Dabh's score elicited considerable interest among critics, who praised his ability to evoke an archaic atmosphere and to match, by means of rhythms and timbres, the choreographer's distinctive style of movement. Graham was so pleased with their collaborative effort that she solicited El-Dabh to compose another score—*One More Gaudy Night* (1961), based on scattered verses from William Shakespeare's *Anthony and Cleopatra.* The following year, she commissioned the score for *A Look at Lightning* (1962), which deals with three people and what happens to them when they are touched by a moment of inspiration.

Clytemnestra, based on the tragedy *Oresteia* by the Greek poet Aeschylus, is a large dramatic work for dancers, two narrators (dramatic soprano and baritone with falsetto range), and orchestra. In actuality, *Clytemnestra* is a cross between opera and pageant, involving spectacle and wonder. Appearing in concert attire, the narrators primarily intone vowels, which make up most of El-Dabh's text.

Clytemnestra consists of a prologue, two acts, and an epilogue. Masterfully, El-Dabh captured Aeschylus's mythological plot in which Orestes, the son of Agamemnon and Clytemnestra, avenges his father's honor. With the aid of his sister Electra, Orestes slays his mother and her lover, Aegisthus.

Halim El-Dabh's music for *Clytemnestra* cannot be discussed separately from Martha Graham's choreography. The energy of the music, inclusive of speech and song, generates the choreographic action, and the work is truly a collaborative effort undertaken equally between the composer and the choreographer. The young composer was inspired to write the first section of the music in Graham's dance studio, and she immediately created the choreography. This in turn inspired the composer, and he continued writing. For six months, this creative exchange of ideas, along with the give and take between sound and action, continued until the two-hour *Clytemnestra* was completed. Together, Halim El-Dabh and Martha Graham formed a modern dance-drama in which music and dance are not mere background to acting.

The score is unmistakably by El-Dabh, generating the choreographic action through its vivid timbres, rhythmic subtlety, and imaginative boldness. By uniting contemporary Western techniques with materials and instruments derived from Arabic, African, and Egyptian traditions, El-Dabh gives *Clytemnestra* the flavor of ritual and/or public ceremony. The work has been performed at the Metropolitan Opera House and on many stages around the world, including those in Paris, Edinburgh, London, Belgium, and Bangkok.

OPERA FLIES (1970; REVISED 1995)

During the aftermath of an anti-Vietnam War protest on the campus of Kent State University on May 4, 1970, Halim El-Dabh witnessed the shooting deaths of four students and the wounding of nine others. El-Dabh, who held a simultaneous creative residency at the Hawthorne School, an innovative private secondary institution in Washington, D.C., was commissioned by the school to write an opera about this tragic incident. At first reluctant to undertake this project, he was persuaded by students to compose the work. The result was a 90-minute score entitled *Opera Flies.* The premiere occurred on May 5, 1971, one year after the campus shootings, in Washington, D.C., and was given by a cast of students from the Hawthorne School. Demanding only modest vocal, instrumental, and stage resources, *Opera Flies* features seven soloists, three choruses, and an orchestra consisting chiefly of woodwinds and percussion. Combining austerity and grandeur, the music is reminiscent of such works as Erik Satie's 35-minute *Socrates,* Igor Stravinsky's 27-minute *Mavra,* and Benjamin Britten's 108-minute *Rape of Lucretia.*

Opera Flies deals with the eternal struggle of humankind, a common theme for the composer. A surreal commentary, it is not a conventional opera. The circumstances of the drama are not presented chronologically, but rather the work presents various reflections, through mythical and symbolic images, that address the May 4 shootings. Instead of a rifle, the murder weapon is a giant flyswatter, symbolic of the opera's title, and microtonal glissandi simulate the buzzing sound of the flies' wings.

In 1995, as the 25th anniversary of the shooting was approaching, El-Dabh revived the work in three transformations (one of which was a total, shorter metamorphosis that eliminated the original choruses) and added elaborate montages of light and video projections, tapes of the actual newscasters' reports remixed to produce a collage of sound, and narrative about current topics

In the opening scene, Vekeero, a young, runaway daughter, struggles to overcome a series of life tragedies and the domination of her overbearing mother, Kounia. Vekeero personifies the real-life Mary Anne Vecchio, the fifteen-year-old runaway from Florida who is depicted in John Filo's Pulitzer Prize–winning news photograph, kneeling over the dead body of Jeffery Miller. Kounia, the mother character, an obsessive-compulsive housewife, zealously exterminates truculent students as if they were bothersome flies. With her obsession for cleanliness, fear of filth, and passion for swatting flies, Kounia was modeled after the myriad letters to newspaper editors that appeared throughout the country. Several of the letter writers asserted that the National Guardsmen should have killed more students. The scene concludes with Vekeero witnessing the killing of four flies. Millijet, an archetype of the student protesters and Vekeero's love, is one of the four flies/students killed. (The character's name, Millijet, is derived from the name Jeffery Miller.)

African ritual dances conveying the rites of life and death comprise the climactic ritual scene in which Vekeero witnesses the union of the two disparate groups. As the two factions reemerge as one in this scene, all must reevaluate their individual belief systems and deal with the tragedy on various levels. The character Fobio, an administrative prototype, has the greatest difficulty in this struggle, which is so immense that his conscience actually comes to life as a separate entity known by the name Judumo. In order to come to terms with the situation, Fobio is forced to wrestle with Judumo.

Opera Flies concludes with the characters in a rather vague state. As they attempt a reconciliation, their earlier conflicts have become cryptic and ambiguous. They experience the eternal struggle between the rights of the individual and the social order. El-Dabh uses Jello, an undulating, diaphanous substance, to symbolize this dubious condition. The conclusion of *Opera Flies,* however, offers hope for the future. The message conveyed to the audience is one of survival, recovery, and progress.

The first of the three transformations of *Opera Flies* was performed March 1995, for narrator, soprano, and piano surrounded with light projections. The second transformation was performed in April 1995. This was an open improvisation for public participation. In addition to improvising on elements or themes from *Opera Flies,* the group included drumming, art, poetry, and reflections on the event of May 4, 1970. The third and final transformation is discussed at length and is really the culmination of the other ideas.

SONICS (1955)

In *Sonics,* special emphasis is placed on rhythmic complexity and structure. It is played on various drums from around the world. Sonic no. 1 is for *derabucca,* the Arabic name of a single-headed African drum in the shape of a vase. Known in the Nile and Niger regions, chiefly in Egypt, Mali, Guinea, and Senegal, its drumhead is usually made from the skin of fish or goats. The body of the *derabucca* is typically made from baked clay, although it is sometimes made from wood or gourds or, more lately, metal.

The score of Sonic no. 1 indicates that if the *derabucca* is not available, tabla, timbales, or tom-tom may be substituted. Sonics nos. 2–6 and 8–9 substitute African drums, Asian drums, or some types of Mexican manual drums. Sonics nos. 7 and 10, also for *derabucca* or multiple drums, premiered at the Living Theatre in New York on January 15, 1959, and have been the most widely performed of the set.

For one player, Sonics nos. 7 and 10 consist of alternating passages labeled as such by the terms "constant" and "variable," the former to be played strictly as written and the latter improvised. The score is designed in parallel lines—the upper for the right hand and the lower for the left, with the positions of the notes on the staff representing higher and lower relative pitches. Two relative pitches may be combined simultaneously or successively, as determined by the quality of the attack and the resulting resonance.

Although the rhythm is indicated in customary Western musical notation, El-Dabh's "drum-sign-symbol-notation," indicates "placement," "curvature and touch," "position," and "resonance." "Placement" refers to the location of the player's fingers in relation to the drum head—center, rim, rim over the edge, etc. "Touch" treats the various methods and techniques involved as the hand and fingers attack the drum head. Thus, every part of the hands and the ten fingers may be used upon the sounding surface, not only in producing the sound itself, but also in emphasizing or suppressing partial harmonics. "Position" is concerned with on which side of the drum the performer's hands are placed. "Resonance" addresses the quality of the sounds produced, which are labeled by the following terms: *dum, dhôuumm, tik, mma,* and *tak.* "Fingering" considers the training of the hand, the wrist, and the fingers.

RAMESSES THE GREAT: SYMPHONY NO. 9 (1987)

In 1987, a festival was held in Memphis, Tennessee, to commemorate the naming of the city after the Egyptian city of Memphis, once the capital of the Old Kingdom of ancient Egypt. As part of the festivities, the Memphis Symphony Orchestra commissioned a large work to mark the event. Searching for someone to bring knowledge and depth to the project, the orchestra selected Halim El-Dabh as the composer for this monumental undertaking. The resulting work was entitled *Ramesses the Great: Symphony no. 9* and was premiered on May 1, 1987, in the Vincent de Frank Music Hall in the city's Exhibition Center.

Ramesses the Great: Symphony no. 9 is a salute to the musical heritage of Egypt and is meant to portray the greatness of the king. Although El-Dabh had composed only three symphonies prior to *Ramesses the Great,* he named this work Symphony no. 9 in recognition of the influence of the nine religious energies, or gods, that dominated the daily lives of the Egyptians during the reign of the pharaoh. The symphony's three movements symbolize the life of Ramesses as a great builder and architect, as a king who was granted an extended life by the gods, and as a man who loved his wife.

The Symphony no. 9 portrays the classical, folk, traditional, and ritualistic music of the reign of Ramesses by juxtaposing and combining sounds reminiscent of ancient Egyptian musical instruments with those of the contemporary orchestral instrumentation. Says El-Dabh, "I am a contemporary composer using the orchestra in a contemporary manner yet conversing with a musical language that is basically Egyptian."

The symphony recalls the sounds of such ancient Egyptian instruments as the *bug* (trumpet), the *rebaba* (fiddle), the *derabucca* (drum), and the ancient cymbals known as the *systrum.* An ancient musical procession for Ramesses would have included each of these instruments along with perhaps 300 harps. El-Dabh depicts the powerful and prosperous reign of Ramesses in the shaping of the work's rhythmic phrases, in its timbres, and its dynamics. At times the orchestra players groan and shriek, and the work's pounding rhythms, often in ostinato (repeated) patterns, suggest the hammering and striking sounds of construction. The themes and harmonies capturing the movement representative of Ramesses's longevity and opulence are very contemporary yet they suggest the pageantry that might have taken place in the ancient amphitheaters. The melismatic melodies in the violins are drawn out in a type of *fortspinnung* that evolve much as the king's reign. The same repetition-variation principles are applied to the rhythms as well as to the melodies.

REFERENCES

El-Dabh, Halim. *The Derabucca: Hand Techniques in the Art of Drumming.* New York: Peters, 1965.

———. Personal conversation with the author, June 28, 1995.

———. Telephone conversation with the author, July 25, 1995.

DENISE A. SEACHRIST

ELIE, JUSTIN

Born in Cap-Haitien, Haiti, September 1, 1883; died in New York, N.Y., December 3, 1931. **Education:** Showed musical talent as a child; childhood teacher, Hermine Faubert; was sent to Paris, France, by his parents for further study; Conservatoire de Paris, studied piano with Charles Wilfred Bériot and Antoine François Marmontel, composition with Paul Vidal, harmony with Émile Pessard. **Composing and Performing Career:** Returned to Haiti and concertized in the Caribbean and Haiti, 1905–09; concertized widely in the Caribbean, and in North and South America; moved to New York City, found work as a composer, arranger, and conductor, 1921; Carnegie Hall concert, 1922; Washington, D.C., Pan American Union concert, 1928; WEAF, New York, hired by NBC to provide, conduct, and arrange music for weekly radio program "The Lure of the Tropics," ca. 1931. **Teaching Career:** Port-au-Prince, founded and directed first school of classical music in Haiti, ca. 1909–21.

MUSIC LIST

INSTRUMENTAL SOLOS
Violin
"Légende créole" (violin and piano). New York: Carl Fischer, 1928.

Piano
Les Chants de la montagne, nos. 1–3. Contents: The Echo (Ismao-o!); Homesickness (Nostalgie); Nocturne.
"Fantasies de la luciole (Caprice)." Unpublished manuscript.
"Doll's Parade." n.p.: Emil Ascher, 1928.
"Indian Dance and Ritual." New York: Belwin, 1929.
Polonaise and Invocation. Unpublished manuscript.
"Reine de la nuit." Unpublished manuscript.
"Rumba." New York: Belwin, 1929.
"Rustic Scherzo." New York: T. B. Harms, n.d.
"Six méringues populaires haïtiennes." New York: R. de la Roziere, 1920.
"Tropical Dance No. 1." Unpublished manuscript.
"Tropical Dance No. 2." New York: Carl Fischer, 1921.
Two Valses. Unpublished manuscript.

Two Pianos
"Labchanale." 1919. Unpublished manuscript.

CHAMBER ORCHESTRA
Prayer at Eventide (Prière du soir). New York: Carl Fischer, 1922.

FULL ORCHESTRA
Aphrodite, 1914. Unpublished manuscript.
Au Pied des Pyramides. Unpublished manuscript.
Babylon: A Suite of Four Oriental Sketches. New York: Carl Fischer, 1925.
Cléopâtre. 1917. Unpublished manuscript.
Firefly Fancies. New York: Carl Fischer, 1929.
Grande valse de concert. Unpublished manuscript.

Kiskaya: Suite aborigène. New York: Carl Fischer, 1928. Contents: In the Temple of the Sun God; Dance to the Sun God; Procession of the Shadows; Dance of the Cave Man.
Melida, A Creole Tropical Dance. New York: Carl Fischer, 1927.
Night in the Andes. New York: Carl Fischer, 1930.
Scènes vadouesques (Suite symphonique). Unpublished manuscript.
Le Sphinx. Unpublished manuscript.

ORCHESTRA (CHAMBER OR FULL) WITH SOLOISTS OR CHORUS
Fantaisie tropicale (piano and orchestra). Unpublished manuscript.
Hymne à Legba. Unpublished manuscript.
Hymne à Damballah. Unpublished manuscript.
Piano Concerto no. 1. Unpublished manuscript.
Piano Concerto no. 2. Unpublished manuscript.

SOLO VOICE
"Deux poèms vaudouesques" (low voice). Unpublished manuscript.
"Le Chant du barde indien" (medium voice). Unpublished manuscript.
"Lamentations" (medium voice). Unpublished manuscript.
"La Mort de l'Indien" (medium voice). Unpublished manuscript.
"Paysages indiens." Unpublished manuscript.
"Quand je serai vieux (From a Poem of Georges Sylvain)." Unpublished manuscript.
"Quiétude" (medium voice). Unpublished manuscript.

OPERA AND BALLET
Vaudou (ballet). Unpublished manuscript.

PUBLICATIONS

ABOUT ELIE
Dalencour, Micheline. "Justin Elie, ce musicien-compositeur d'avant-garde méconnu." *Revue de la Société Haïtienne d'Histoire et de Géographie* 52, no.191 (March 1977): 45–52.
Herrisé, Félix. "Justin Elie et la musique savante." In *Étoiles haïtiennes.* Unpublished typescript held in l'École Sainte Trinité Collection, Port-au-Prince.
Lassègue, Franck. "La Musique à travers Haïti." In *Ciselures.* Albert, France: Librairie Grossel, 1929.
———. "La Technique de M. Justin Elie." In *Études critiques sur la musique haïtienne.* Port-au-Prince: Imprimerie du Sacré-Coeur, 1919.

* * * * *

Born in Cap-Haitien, Haiti, Elie spent his formative years in Paris, where he began to study the piano. Like many young elite Haitians of his generation, he completed his education in Europe, enrolling in the Conservatoire de Paris, where he studied composition and piano.

Upon his return to Haiti, Elie gave several recitals, to great acclaim, in Port-au-Prince. Between 1905 and 1909, he made

Justin Elie; courtesy of Hildegard Gardere

recital tours in the Caribbean, with stops in the Dominican Republic, Puerto Rico, Jamaica, St. Thomas, Curaçao, Venezuela, and Cuba. During these travels, Elie transcribed the folksongs of some of the ethnic groups he encountered. He also made several trips to the Haitian countryside to gather musical material for his compositions. According to Simone Elie Strecher, the composer's daughter, his folksong transcriptions were lost when his family members, unaware of the nature of Elie's notes, burned the originals in a cleaning spree.

Like many elite Haitians of his day, Elie preferred to look to the Native American heritage of the Americas for musical inspiration rather than the music of the former African slaves. While there is little evidence to indicate that Elie adapted actual folk melodies into his compositions, his movement titles and evocative tempo markings are meant to connect the listener with the music of ancient America.

Elie left Haiti for the United States in 1921. The U.S. occupation of Haiti (1915–1934) was having a disastrous effect on the production and performance of *la musique savante haïtienne* (Haitian classical or "learned" music), and the task of organizing concerts larger than the popular "salon recitals" was difficult and financially unrewarding. In addition, Elie was unable to get performances of his orchestral works, since only one large musical ensemble was then active in Haiti—the Musique du Palais, a military wind band which had declined in quality following the ouster of its popular director, Occide Jeanty. So Elie moved to New York, where he became active as a composer, arranger, and conductor and had several of his works published by the music publishing firm Carl Fischer. These works included *Kiskaya: An Aboriginal Suite for Orchestra* (1928); *Prayer at Eventide (Prière du soir)* (1922); *Melinda, A Creole Tropical Dance for Orchestra* (1927); *Firefly Fancies (Fantaisie de vers luisant)* (1929); and *Night in the Andes (Noche en los Andes—La Nuit dans les Andes)* (1930). He arranged the music for a radio program on WEAF called "The Lure of the Tropics" and also arranged music for silent films. He collaborated on a theatrical production, "Voo-doo Moon," with Gilda Gray, owner and principal dancer for the dinner club Rendez-vous, located on West 45th Street in Manhattan. The show was a dance production set to music inspired by the Haitian vodou ceremony.

Elie's works for orchestra received several performances from the United Service Orchestra, a military band composed of 100 members drawn from the United States Army, Navy, and Marines. Ray Hart, the director of the Rialto Theater Orchestra, conducted a performance of Elie's "The Dance of the Cave Man" as a prelude to a screening of the film *Phantom of the Opera*.

On December 3, 1931, Elie died suddenly of either a heart attack or cerebral hemorrhage. He was buried in Haiti.

Among Haitian concert-goers, Elie is still considered to be one of Haiti's best composers; the centenary of his birth was celebrated in 1986 with a conference and concert in Port-au-Prince. The Orchèstre Philharmonique de la Sainte Trinité of Port-au-Prince, an ensemble affiliated with the music school of École Sainte Trinité, has performed several of Elie's concert works including the *Fantaisie tropicale,* a single-movement piece for piano and orchestra. His relative success as a composer living abroad still serves as an inspirational example to Haitian musicians.

SELECTED WORKS

The *Fantaisie tropicale* (n.d.) is a single-movement work for piano and orchestra. Built in short, two-measure phrases that return with a great degree of regularity, this work (in C minor) is episodic, with four major themes being explored through a variety of pianistic techniques. It opens with a ponderous four-measure statement of the first theme in the orchestra, which roots the work in minor mode and a relatively low tessitura. The piano responds with a series of chords that descend from the uppermost register and culminate in a rhythmic descent reminiscent of Grieg's Piano Concerto in A Minor. The piano and orchestra trade the opening theme, contrasting each appearance with either stark octaves or expansive harmonies. The second theme appears first in the orchestra, invoking the syncopated feel of the Haitian *méringue.* A third theme also exploits the five-note pulse of the *méringue quintolet.* A fourth, more lyric theme provides a restful harmonic backdrop for an acrobatic piano part. It is developed through a series of variations, each successively more demanding for the performer. Later, this lyric theme is blended with the opening motive in an imitative (*fugato*) style in the orchestra. With two cadenzas at the end, the *Fantaisie tropicale* closes with an exciting and technically demanding flourish.

Kiskaya: An Aboriginal Suite for Orchestra (1928) is a four-movement work for orchestra. As its subtitle implies, the piece is meant to invoke the music of so-called aboriginal peoples in the Americas, especially the native peoples of Central and South America. Cultural inspiration in the *Kiskaya Suite* comes, however, at the expense of historical accuracy. The suite is supposedly based on ideas from ancient Inca and Brazilian cultures, yet its name is the Arawak term for present-day Hispaniola: Quisqueya. Presumably, Elie was trying to connect the achievements and sophistication of the Inca empire with his own Native American forbears on Quisqueya. The result is an interesting mixture of stereotypical "primitive" musical motives.

While the music is not strictly programmatic, the descriptive notes that accompany the piece indicate that a llama was to be sacrificed to the deity. The first movement, "In the Temple of the Sun God," is a calm ceremonial invocation for the Inca sun god, Intip Rayme. Marked *Andante tranquillo,* the movement's introduction opens with horns and strings playing open fifths while the oboe contributes a descending triplet figure. The clarinet answers the oboe one octave lower with a dotted-eighth-sixteenth-note figure. The introduction's principal theme, a diatonic outline of G major by the English horn and flute, is stated in eighth and quarter notes and is supported by bassoons, horns, and strings.

At the *Poco più mosso* that begins the body of the movement, muted trumpets and horns restate the principal theme with a twist: an augmented fourth (*c*-sharp) is added to the melody and the rhythm is slightly syncopated with a sixteenth-eighth-sixteenth-note figure. The opening oboe and clarinet motives appear as the last four measures of the principal theme.

The lyrical quality of the principal theme is abruptly altered at *L'istesso tempo,* where the upper strings play offbeat *pizzicati* (plucked pitches) over a dotted-eighth-sixteenth-note in the celli and bassoons. An "Indian drum" provides additional rhythmic interest while the oboe and trumpet play a variation on the principal theme.

The first two measures of the augmented principal theme returns in the horns and bassoons and is answered by ascending triplet figures in the clarinets. The violins then combine the augmented theme with the triplet figures. The "Indian drum" maintains its syncopated sixteenth-rest-sixteenth-eighth-note figure throughout. The movement reaches its climax when the trombones enter to support the full orchestra on the principal theme. As the movement comes to a close, the orchestral texture thins very quickly, leaving only the celli and bassoons on the syncopated bass line and the "Indian drum" to fade quietly into the final *pianissimo* chord.

Movement two, a fast and vigorous "Dance to the Sun God," the ceremonial dance that follows the llama sacrifice in the previous movement, begins with a steady rhythm on an "Indian drum" and a bass drum. Heavily accented afterbeats in the brasses and winds and a steady, rhythmic drive in the bass lines give this movement strong forward momentum and a brash, exciting character. The third movement, "Procession of the Shadows," is slow, containing in its opening measures cadenza-like solos for the flute. It contrasts with the fourth movement, "Dance of the Cave Man," which purports to depict "sorcerers and medicine men" in the tropical rain forest of Brazil, in its reliance on an insistent rhythmic pulse and heavily accented chords, especially in the brass parts.

Before he emigrated to the United States, Elie wrote several piano works, one of which was published in Paris in 1920. Entitled "Méringues populaires" the work featured an alternating 2/4 and 5/8 rhythm, presumably to capture the syncopated feeling of the Haitian *méringue.* Elie also composed several pieces for solo piano including *Les Chants de la Montagne, nos. 1–3* (n.d.). The first piece, "The Echo (Ismao-o!)," is a short work that features a simple, descending melodic line in 6/8 meter. The second piece, "Homesickness (Nostalgie)," is somewhat static with arpeggiated figures in the right hand over two-measure phrases. The third movement, "Nocturne," like the first, is a contemplative piece with a conservatively harmonized melodic line.

Elie's works, whether for solo piano or for full orchestra, tend to feature single melodic themes. Rather than use his melodies as the basis of more extended rhythmic or harmonic variations, Elie keeps his melodies intact, occasionally substituting an augmented interval (as in "In the Temple of the Sun God") but preferring to allow contrasting orchestrations of the melody to provide musical interest.

REFERENCES

Baer, Frank. "A New Orchestra for Washington." Typescript held in the private collection of Simone Elie Stecher, Pétionville, Haiti.

Elie Stecher, Simone. Interview with the author, Pétionville, Haiti, 1988.

Herrisé, Félix. "Justin Elie et la musique savante." In *Étoiles haïtiennes.* Unpublished typescript held in l'École Sainte Trinité Collection, Port-au-Prince.

Lassègue, Franck. "La Musique à travers Haïti." In *Ciselures.* Albert, France: Librairie Grossel, 1929.

———. "La Technique de M. Justin Elie." In *Études critiques sur la musique haïtienne.* Port-au-Prince: Imprimerie du Sacré-Coeur, 1919.

Somers, Lee. "Prologues and Epilogues: Novelty!" Typescript held in the private collection of Simone Elie Stecher, Pétionville, Haiti.

"Voodoux at the Rendezvous." [New York] *Evening Telegram* (July 28, 1922).

MICHAEL LARGEY

ELLINGTON, EDWARD KENNEDY ("DUKE")

Born in Washington D.C., April 29, 1899; died in New York City, May 24, 1974. **Education:** Musical family, both his mother and father played piano; Washington, D.C., studied piano with a local teacher, Marietta Clinkscales; attended Armstrong High School; studied harmony with Henry Grant, 1918–19. **Composing and Performing Career:** Washington, D.C., formed his first band, Duke's Serenaders, 1918; Kentucky Club, New York City, performed regularly with his group, The Washingtonians, 1923–27; Cotton Club, hired as house band to provide music for revues, performers, and dancing, 1927–31; toured the United States regularly, including stops in Chicago, Cleveland, San Francisco, Denver, Pittsburgh, Philadelphia, Cincinnati, and Minneapolis, 1931–42; Chicago, regularly booked at the Oriental Theater, 1931; European tours, 1933, 1939; Carnegie Hall, New York City, premiered *Black, Brown and Beige,* 1943, Carnegie Hall, presented seven annual concerts, 1943–48; regularly toured with the band, 1950–74, including tours to Western Europe, 1958, 1962, 1963, 1964, 1965, India, the Middle East, and Near East, 1963, South American and Mexico, 1968, the Far East and Australasia, 1970, the Soviet Union, 1971; Newport Jazz Festival, 1956; San Francisco, Grace Cathedral, first Sacred Concert, 1965; Monterey Jazz Festival, 1958, 1960, 1970; wrote music for and appeared in several films including *Symphony in Black, Anatomy of a Murder,* and *Paris Blues;* New York, Cathedral Church of St. John the Divine, Second Sacred Concert, 1966. **Memberships:** ASCAP; National Council of Arts, appointed 1968; American Institute of Arts and Letters, elected 1970; Royal Academy of Music in Stockholm, Sweden, elected 1971; American Academy of Arts and Sciences, elected 1971. **Honors/Awards:** George Washington Carver Memorial Institute, Supreme Award of Merit, 1943; Art Director's Club, President's Medal, 1958; National Association for the Advancement of Colored People, Spingarn Medal, 1959; received Oscar nomination for *Paris Blues,* 1961; received several Grammy Awards, including Best Jazz Performance (Large Group) Instrumental for *First Time! The Count Meets the Duke,* 1962, Best Original Jazz Composition for *Night Creature,* 1964, Best Original Jazz Composition for *The Virgin Islands Suite,* 1965, Best Original Jazz Composition for "In the Beginning God," 1966, Bing Crosby Award, 1966, Grammy's for *Far East Suite,* 1968, *And His Mother Called Him Bill,* 1969, *Togo Brava Suite,* 1973; City of New York, Musician of Every Year, Gold Medal, 1965; Paris, France, Medal, 1965; City of Chicago, Gold Medal, 1965; City Club of New York Medal, Distinguished New Yorker Award, 1966; President's Gold Medal, 1966; Emmy Award for "Duke Ellington: Love You Madly," 1967; Ordem dos Músicos do Brasil, 1968; Presidential Medal of Freedom, 1969; special papal blessing from Pope Paul VI, 1969; Yale University, New Haven, Conn., Duke Ellington Fellowship Program established, 1972; National Association of Negro Musicians, Highest Award for Distinguished Service in Music, 1972; Eleanor Roosevelt International Workshop in Human Relations, International Humanist Award, 1972; commemorative stamp issued by the U.S. postal service, 1986; honorary doctorates from numerous schools, including: Wilberforce College, Wilberforce, Ohio, 1949; Milton College, Milton, Wisc., 1964; California College of Arts and Crafts, Oakland, 1966; Columbia College Chicago, Chicago, Ill., 1967; Morgan State College, Baltimore, Md., 1967; Yale University, 1967; Washington University, St. Louis, Mo., 1967; Brown University, Providence, R.I., 1969; Assumption College, Worcester, Mass., 1970; Christian Theological Seminary, Indianapolis, Ind., 1970; Berklee College of Music, Boston, Mass., 1971; Howard University, Washington, D.C., 1971; St. John's University, Jamaica, N.Y., 1971; University of Wisconsin, Madison, 1971; Rider College, Trenton, N.J., 1972.

SELECTED MUSIC LIST

[The following list of titles includes only works that were composed by the subject of the entry; it is not a list of recordings that were made by the subject. Although the composer may have made recordings of his own works, the list is not restricted to those recordings but in many cases includes performances by other artists of the composer's work. The list is made up of publication and discographical data, in cases where such information available. Although no effort has been made to include documentation of the earliest recording of the works listed, the date of the earliest recording that is readily available has been given. —Ed.]

Afro-Bossa or *Bula* or *Nova Exotique.* Recorded, 1963: Discovery 71002; Reprise R9-6069.

Afro-Eurasian Eclipse. Contents: Dash; Buss; Acac; Yoyo; True; Tenz; Tego; Soso; Nbdy; Gong; Dijb; Sche. Recorded, 1970: Fantasy OJCCD-645-2.

"All Too Soon" or "Slow Tune." Recorded, 1940: Mercury PPS 2028; Pablo OJCCD-450-2.

"Are You Sticking?" Recorded, 1941: RCA LPV517.

"Awful Sad." Recorded, 1928: Brunswick B-1011.

"Azure." Recorded, 1937: Master MA 131.

"Baby, When You Ain't There." Recorded, 1932: Jazz Information RBD 3001.

"Barzallai Lew." Recorded, 1942: Natasha n.n.

"Battle of Swing" or "Le Jazz Hot." Recorded, 1938: Brunswick M8239.

"The Beautiful Indians." Recorded, 1946: Everest Records FS-249; Unique Jazz VJ 001.

"Bensonality" or "Alavantin" or "The Band." Recorded, 1951: Columbia 39712; Skata 502.

"Best Wishes." Recorded, 1932: Jazz Information RBD 3001.

"Bird of Paradise." Recorded, 1964: Finnadar 9019-2.

"Birmingham Breakdown." Recorded, 1926: Brunswick BL 54007; Sounds Great SGS-5001.

Black, Brown and Beige. Contents: Emancipation Celebration; West Indian Dance; Sugar Hill Penthouse; Worksong; The Blues; Come Sunday. Recorded, 1943: Columbia CK64674; Milan 35656-2; RCA 07863-66679-2.

"Black and Tan Fantasy." Co-composer, Bubber Miley. Recorded, 1927: Family Records SFR-DP656; Fantasy Records F.9481; MCA Records MCA-349.

Edward Kennedy "Duke" Ellington; courtesy of Hogan Jazz Archive, Howard-Tilton Memorial Library, Tulane University

"Black Beauty" or "A Portrait of Florence Mills." Recorded, 1928: Brunswick 4009; EPM Musique 151122; Victor 21580.

"Black Butterfly." Recorded, 1936: Pablo 2310-815; Solid State SS 19000.

"Blind Man's Buff." 1923. Unpublished manuscript. Co-composer, Jo Trent.

"Blue Belles of Harlem." Recorded, 1943: Fairmont FA-1009.

"Blue Goose." Recorded, 1940: Merritt Records 049657-1; RCA Victor LPV517.

"Blue Light." Recorded, 1938: Aircheck Records 29; Columbia Cl633.

"Blue Tune." Recorded, 1932: Columbia C3L 27; Jazz Information RBD3001.

"Blues I Love to Sing." Co-composer, Bubber Miley. Recorded, 1927: Columbia KG33341; Victor 21490 or LPV-568.

"Blues in Blueprint" or "T.A." Recorded, 1959: Columbia CL1445.

"Blues in Orbit." 1958. Co-composer, Billy Strayhorn. Originally titled "Tender." Recorded: Atlantic SD-1643; Riverside RLP-9412.

"Blutopia." Recorded, 1944: Unique Jazz UJ001.

"Bojangles" or "A Portrait of Bert Williams." Recorded, 1940: Merritt 04954-1; RCA Victor LPT 3017.

"Bouncing Buoyancy" or "Exposition Swing." Recorded, 1939: Blue Ace 35240 or Columbia 257.

"Boy Meets Horn" or "Twits and Twerps." Recorded, 1938: Columbia 36123; FDC-1002.

"Braggin' in Brass." Recorded, 1938: Portrait Masters R2J 44395; TAX m8010; Telarc CD-80249.

"The Breakfast Dance" or "Ev'ry Day." Recorded, 1927: Victor 57542-1.

"The Brownskin Gal in the Calico Gown." Recorded, 1941: Verve V8635; Victor 27517.

"Bumpty Bump." 1930. New York: Mills Music. Co-composer, Irving Mills. Note: from *Blackberries Crop of 1930*.

"C-Jam Blues" or "C'Blues" or "Jam Session" or "Duke's Place." Recorded, 1942: EmArcy MG-36128; Riverside RLP 3510.

"Caravan." Co-composer, Juan Tizol. Recorded, 1936: Calligraph CLGLP002; RCA 09026-68173-2; Verve 833-291-2.

"Carnival in Caroline." Recorded, 1938: Brunswick m8099.

Check and Double Check. Co-composer, Irving Mills. Contents: Old Man Blues; Ring Dem Bells. Recorded, 1930: Columbia C3L 27; Impulse ASH 925812; Victor 23022.

"Chromatic Love Affair" or "Apollo Love Affair." Recorded, 1967: Eastman School of Music, 1988–89.

"Clarinet Lament" or "Barney's Concerto." Co-composer, Barney Bigard. Recorded, 1936: Columbia C3L-27.

"The Clothed Woman." Recorded, 1947: CBS 63563; Merritt 2003.

"Concerto for Cootie." Recorded, 1940: Atlantic SD 2-304; Prestige MUST 27; Victor 26598.

"Conga Brava." Co-composer, Juan Tizol. Recorded, 1940: Victor 26577.

The Controversial Suite. Contents: Before My Time; Later. Recorded, 1951: Columbia CL830; Encore P 14359.

"Cotton Tail" or "Hot Chocolate" or "Shuckin' and Stiflin'." Recorded, 1940: Allegro Elite 3105; Crown Records CST 183; Roulette R-52074.

"The Creeper." Recorded, 1926: Biltmore 1004; Decca DL 79224; Swaggie 57.

"Creole Love Call" or "Creole Love Songs" or "Creole Blues." Recorded, 1927: Jazz Information RBD 3001; Merritt 2003.

Creole Rhapsody. Recorded, 1931: Hot 'n' Sweet 152322; Brunswick B-1011.

"Dallas Doin's" or "Blue Eagle Stomp." Recorded, 1933: RCA LPV 506.

"Day Dream." 1940. Co-composer, Billy Strayhorn. Recorded: Concord Jazz CJ-326; RCA/Bluebird 6287-2-RB.

"Daybreak Express." Recorded, 1933: Victor 24501.

Deep South Suite. 1946. Co-composer, Billy Strayhorn. Contents: Happy Go Lucky Local; Sultry Sunset; Hear Say; There Was Nobody Lookin' (or Nobody Was Looking); Magnolias Dripping with Honey. Recorded: Nonesuch 79395-2; Red Baron 52760; Rhino R2 72033. Premiere, 1946.

"Delta Serenade" "Oh! Babe." Recorded, 1934: RCA P138.

"The Dicty Glide." Recorded, 1929: Victor 49767-1.

Diminuendo and Crescendo in Blue. Recorded, 1937: Brunswick m8004; Musidisc JA 5165; Unique Jazz UJ001.

"Dinah's in a Jam." Recorded, 1938: Blue Ace 248.

"Do Nothin' 'Til You Hear from Me." Recorded, 1943: Calligraph CLGLP 002; Impulse ASH 9285/2.

"Doin' the Crazy Walk." 1930. New York: Mills Music. Co-composer, Irwin Mills. Note: from *Blackberries Crop of 1930*.

"Doin' the Voom Voom." Co-composer, Bubber Miley. Recorded, 1929: Banner 6548; Columbia 35208.

"Don't Get Around Much Anymore" or "Never No Lament." Recorded, 1942: JA Records 1270; Verve 833-291-2.

"Dooji Wooji." Recorded, 1936: AJAX 116; Epic EE22002; Vocalion M977-1.

"Downtown Uproar." Co-composer, Cootie Williams. Recorded, 1937: Merritt 2002.

"Drop Me Off in Harlem." Recorded, 1933: Jazz Information RBD3002; Merritt 78827-1; Tall Poppy Tq151.

"Ducky Wucky" or "Dance." Co-composer, Irving Mills. Recorded, 1932: Brunswick 6432; Columbia C3L 27; Jazz Information RBD 3002.

"Dusk." Recorded, 1940: Victor 26677.

"Dusk on the Desert." Co-composer, Juan Tizol. Recorded, 1937: Sony AK57766.

"East St. Louis Toodle-O" or "Harlem Twist." Co-composer, Bubber Miley. Recorded, 1926: Brunswick 3480; Capitol T-1243; Velvet Tone 7072-V.

"Ebony Rhapsody." Recorded, 1934: RCA 20-2760; Victor 24674.

"Echoes of Harlem" or "Cootie's Concerto" or "Sweetest Gal Goin'." Recorded, 1936: Decca DL 5369; Intersound CDJ679.

"Esquire Swank." Recorded, 1945: Swing SW 230; RCA Victor LPV 553.

"Everything But You." Co-composers, Don George, Harry James. Recorded, 1944: Design DCF-1021; Victor 20-1697.

The Far East Suite. 1964. Co-composer, Billy Strayhorn. Contents: Tourist Point of View; Bluebird of Dekhi (Mynah Bird); Isfahan (originally titled "Elf"); Depk; Mount Harissa; Blue Pepper (Far East of the Blues); Agra; Amad. Recorded: Bluebird 7640-2-RB ; Jazz Heritage 514128F; RCA LSP 3782.

First Sacred Concert. 1965. Contents: Come Sunday; I Cried Then I Cried; Swing Low, Sweet Chariot; Tell Me, It's the Truth; Praise Ye the Lord; In the Beginning God; Christmas Surprise; New World A-Comin'; Will You Be There?; 99% Won't Do; Ain't But the One; The Lord's Prayer; David Danced Before the Lord; The Preacher's Song. Premiere, 1965.

"Flaming Sword." Recorded, 1940: RCA Victor LPM 1364.

"Flaming Youth." Recorded, 1929: Columbia C3L 39; RCA Victor LPV-568.

"Fleurette africaine." Also titled "Little African Flower." Recorded, 1962: Solid State Records, n.n.

"The Gal from Joe's." Recorded, 1938: Brunswick m8101; Columbia 37959; Phoenix PHX-303.

The Girls Suite. 1961. Contents: The Girls; Mahalia; Peg O' My Heart; Sweet Adeline; Juanita; Sylvia; Lena; Dinah; Clementine; Diane. Recorded: Columbia FC 38028.

The Golden Broom and the Golden Apple. 1965. Contents: The Golden Broom; The Green Apple; The Handsome Policeman. Recorded: Decca DL 710176.

"Golden Cress." Recorded, 1946: Columbia G 32564; Hindsight HSR-128; Merritt 2002.

The Goutelas Suite. 1971. Contents: Goof; Gogo II; Gogo I; Gigi. Recorded: Musical Heritage Society M419260M; Pablo J33J-20008.

Harlem or *Harlem Suite* or *A Tone Parallel to Harlem.* 1950. Recorded: Atlantic SD 2-304; Encore P14359. Premiere, 1951.

"Harlem Speaks." Recorded, 1933: EPM Musique FDC 5006; Jazz Information RBD 3003; Phoenix 10 Records PHX-303.

"Haunted Nights." Recorded, 1929: RCA Camden CAL 459; Time Life Records STL-J12.

"Hop Head." Recorded, 1927: Columbia C3L 27.

"Hot and Bothered." Recorded, 1928: Columbia C3L 27; EPM Musique FDC 5006.

"I Ain't Got Nothin' But the Blues." Recorded, 1944: Calligraph CLGLP 002; EmArcy MG-36128; RCA Victor LPV-566.

"I Didn't Know About You" or "Home." Recorded, 1943: Decca DL 4774; JA Records JA1270; Telestrar TRS 11100.

"I Don't Know What Kind of Blues I've Got." Recorded, 1941: RCA Victor LPM 1364; Smithsonian Institution RC 035; Victor 37804.

"I Got It Bad and That Ain't Good." Recorded, 1941: Calligraph CLGLP 002; Sony A22731; Verve 833 291-2.

"I Let a Song Go out of My Heart." Recorded, 1938: Calligraph CLGLP 002; Sony A22731; Verve 833 291-2.

"I Never Felt This Way Before." Recorded, 1939: Columbia 35353; Victor 27247.

"I'm Beginning to See the Light." Co-composers, Don George, Johnny Hodges, Harry James. Recorded, 1944: RCA Victor LM 2857; Smithsonian RD 031; Tetco 86801.

"I'm Just a Lucky So-and-So." Recorded, 1945: Riverside RLP 3510; Smithsonian Institution RC 035.

"I'm Slappin' Seventh Avenue (with the Sole of My Shoe)." Recorded, 1938: Brunswick M810-1; Jazz Panorama LP 14.

"I'm So in Love with You." Co-composer, Irving Mills. Recorded, 1930: Perfect 15649.

"Idiom." Recorded, 1959: Columbia CL 1400; Columbia C25 831.

"Immigration Blues." Recorded, 1926: Decca DL 79224; Swaggie S7.

"In a Mellow Tone" or "Baby, You and Me." Recorded, 1940: EPM Musique FDC 5006; JA Records JA 1270; Verve V6-8386.

"In a Sentimental Mood." Recorded, 1935: Columbia CL558; Decca 27603; Jon Mat Records CK 46059.

"It Don't Mean a Thing If It Ain't Got That Swing." Recorded, 1932: Sony A22731.

"Jack the Bear." Recorded, 1940: Bethlehem BCP 60; Crown Records 183; RCA Victor LPM 1715.

"Jam with Sam." Recorded, 1951: Atlantic SD 2-304; Columbia 39670.

"Jig Walk." Recorded, 1925: BYG Records 529 071; Paramount 14024; Sunbeam HB-310.

"Jubilee Stomp." Recorded, 1928: Bluebird 07863-66038-4.

"Just a Sittin' and a Rockin'." Co-composer, Billy Strayhorn. Recorded, 1941: RCA Bluebird 5659; Red Baron 52760; Rhino R2 72033.

"Just Squeeze Me" or "Subtle Slough." Recorded, 1946: Calligraph CLGLP 002; JA Records JA 1270; Mercury PPS-6028.

"Kinda Dukish." Recorded, 1953: Atlantic SD2-304; Capitol M11058.

"Ko-Ko" or "Kaline." Recorded, 1940: Bethlehem BCP-60; Fantasy Records F-9481; RCA Victor LPM 1715.

"Lady of the Lavendar Mist." Recorded, 1947: Columbia CL 6024.

Latin American Suite. 1968. Contents: Chico Cuadradino; Latin American Sunshine; The Sleeping Lady and the Giant Who Watches Over Her; Oclupaca. Recorded: Fantasy OJCCD-469-2.

"Lazy Duke." Recorded, 1929: Columbia C3L 27.

Liberian Suite. 1947. Contents: I Like the Sunrise; Dance no. 1; Dance no. 2; Dance no. 3.; Dance no. 4; Dance no. 5. Recorded: CBS 62686; Prestige 2PCD-24075-2.

"Lightning." Recorded, 1932: Columbia C3L 27.

"Lost in Meditation" or "Have a Heart." Co-composer, Juan Tizol. Recorded, 1938: Verve MGV-4008-2.

"Main Stem" or "Altitude" or "On Becoming a Square." Recorded, 1942: Crown 5153; Victor 20-1556.

"Me and You." Recorded, 1940: Victor 049017-1.

"Melancholia." Recorded, 1953: Capitol M11058.

"Merry Go Round" or "Ace of Spades" or "Cotton Club Shim Sham" or "142nd Street and Lenox Avenue." Recorded, 1933: Time Life Records STL J-02.

"Misty Mornin'." Co-composer, Arthur Whetsol. Recorded, 1928: Bluebird B-6565; Vocalion 3229.

"The Mooche." Co-composer, Irving Mills. Recorded, 1928: Columbia C3L 27; EPM Musique FDC 5006; RCA Victor LSP 3576.

"Mood Indigo" or "Dreamy Blues." Co-composers, Irving Mills, Albany Bigard. Recorded, 1930: Capitol 28106; Pro-Arte CDD 482; Sony A 22731.

"Moon Mist" or "Atmosphere." Recorded, 1941: Columbia C32564; Hindsight HSR-127; Victor 27856.

"Morning Glory." Recorded, 1940: Allegro Elite 3105; Victor 26536.

My People. 1963. Contents: Ain't But the One; Will You Be There; Blues at Sundown; Come Sunday; The Blues; King Fit the Battle of Alabam'; David Danced Before the Lord; Montage; My Mother, My Father; A Jungle Triangle; Strange Feeling; My People; Workin' Blues; Jail Blues; After Bird Jungle; What Color is Virtue; Walkin' and Singin' the Blues; My Man Sends Me; I Love My Lovin' Lover. Recorded: Reprise RS6154; Sony AK 52759.

"The Mystery Song." Co-composer, Irving Mills. Recorded, 1930: Privateer 403.

New Orleans Suite. 1970. Contents: Bourbon Street Jingling Jollies; Aristocray à la Jean Lafitte; Thanks for the Beautiful Land on the Delta; Blues for New Orleans; Second Line; Portrait of Wellman Braud; Portrait of Louis Armstrong; Portrait of Mahalia Jackson; Portrait of Sidney Bechet. Recorded: Atlantic Jazz 1580-2.

New World A-Coming. 1943. Recorded: RCA LSP 3582.

"New York City Blues." Recorded, 1947: Columbia CL 6024; Monologue 63563; Up-to-date 2003.

Newport Jazz Festival Suite. 1956. Co-composer, Billy Strayhorn. Contents: Festival Junction; Blues to Be There; Newport Up. Recorded: Columbia CS 8648.

Night Creature. 1955. Recorded: Discovery 71003.

"Old King Dooji." Recorded, 1938.: Columbia 36213; Vocalion v4849.

"Orson." Co-composer, Billy Strayhorn. Recorded, 1953: Capitol PRO 232.

Perfume Suite. 1944. Co-composer, Billy Strayhorn. Contents: Sonata (or Balcony Serenade; or Love; or Under the Balcony); Strange Feeling (or Violence); Dancers in Love (or Naiveté; or Stomp for Beginners); Coloratura (or Sophistication). Recorded: Columbia FC 38028; Prestige Records 2PCD-240732; RCA Victor LPM 6009. Premiere, 1944.

"Pitter Panther Patter" or "The Panther Patter." Recorded, 1940: New World Records NW 274.

"La Plus belle africaine." Recorded, 1966: Souvenir Record n.n.

"Portrait of the Lion." Recorded, 1939: Blue Ace 237.

"Prelude to a Kiss." Recorded, 1938: Philips 446 717-2; Sony A 22731; Time Life Records A-26243.

"Pretty Soft for You." 1924. Unpublished manuscript. Co-composer, Jo Trent.

"Pyramid." Co-composer, Juan Tizol. Recorded, 1938: Discovery 71002.

The Queen's Suite. 1959. Co-composer, Billy Strayhorn. Contents: Sunset and the Mockingbird; Lightning Bugs and Frogs; Le sucrier velours; Northern Lights; The Single Petal of a Rose; Apes and Peacocks. Recorded: Musical Heritage Society M419260M; Pablo Records PACD-2405-401-2; Pablo J33J-20008.

"Reflections in D." Recorded, 1953: Capitol Jazz CDP 7 92863 2.

Reminiscing in Tempo. 1935. Recorded: Columbia CK 48654.

"Retrospection." Recorded, 1953: Capitol Jazz CDP 7 92863 2; Mosaic S25 18515-1.

"Rhapsody Jr." 1926. Unpublished manuscript. Recorded, 1935: Decca 639.

"Riding on a Blue Note." Recorded, 1938: Brunswick m8083.

"Rockin' in Rhythm." Co-composers, Irving Mills, Harry Carney. Recorded, 1931: MCA-1360; Spa JHR 73504.

"Rude Interlude." Recorded, 1933: RCA LPV506.

"Rumpus in Richmond." Recorded, 1940: RCA LPM 1364.

"Satin Doll." Co-composer, Billy Strayhorn. Recorded, 1953: SPA JHR 73504.

"Saturday Night Function." Co-composer, Albany Bigard. Recorded, 1929: Vocalion 3012.

"Scrounch." Also titled "Skrontch." Recorded, 1938: Raretone/Brunswick 7771.

Second Sacred Concert. Contents: New World A-Comin'; Come Sunday; Montage; Come Easter; Tell Me, It's the Truth; In the Beginning God; West Indian Pancake; La plus belle africaine. Recorded: Prestige PCD-24045-2. Premiere, 1966.

"Sepia Panorama" or "Night House." Recorded, 1940: Indiana University School of Music Program 1995–96, no. 281; Victor LPM 1364.

"Serenade to Sweden" or "Moody" or "Kind of Moody." Recorded, 1939: Bethlehem BCP-76.

"The Sergeant Was Shy." Recorded, 1939: Columbia 35214; Epic EE 22027.

"Slap Happy." Recorded, 1938: Golden Era LP-15067.

"Soda Fountain Rag" or "Swing Session." ca. 1915. Recorded: Chiaroscuro CR 2001; Stomp Off Records SOS 1159.

"Solitude." Recorded, 1934: Calligraph Records CLGLP 002; RCA 09026-68124-2.

"Someone" or "You've Got My Heart" or "Alone Again" or "The Sky Fell Down." Recorded, 1942: Hindsight HSR-127; Victor 20-1584.

"Sophisticated Lady." Recorded, 1932: Retro SLD 13512; Spa JHR 73504; Victor Jazz 09026-68516-2.

"Steppin' into Swing Society." Recorded, 1938: Affinity AFF 194.

"Stompy Jones." Recorded, 1934: Verve 833-291-2; Victor P 128.

"Subtle Lament." Recorded, 1939: Indiana University School of Music, Program 1991-92, no. 759.

Such Sweet Thunder. 1957. Co-composer, Billy Strayhorn. Contents: Such Sweet Thunder; Sonnet for Caesar; Sonnet to Hank Cinq; Lady Mac; Sonnet in Search of a Moor; The Telecasters; Up and Down, Up and Down; Sonnet for Sister Kate; The Star Crossed Lovers; Madness in Great Ones; Half the Fun; Circle of Fourths. Recorded: Columbia CL 1033; Columbia 469140 2; Jazz Life CD 2673722. Premiere, 1957.

Suite Thursday. 1960. Co-composer, Billy Strayhorn. Contents: Misfit Blues; Schwiphthey; Zweet Sursday; Lay-By. Recorded: Columbia CL 1597; Columbia CT 46825.

"Swampy River." Recorded, 1928: Brunswick 6355; Jazz Information RBD 3001.

The Tattooed Bride. 1948. Recorded: Alpha Audio 203042; Sunburst 501.

Third Sacred Concert. 1973. Contents: The Lord's Prayer; My Love; Hallelujah; Is God a Three Letter Word for Love?; The Brotherhood; Every Man Prays in his Own Language; Tell Me, It's the Truth; Somebody Cares; The Majesty of God; Ain't Nobody Nowhere Nothi' Without God; Praise God and Dance; The Preacher's Song; In the Beginning God. Recorded: RCA APL1-0785. Premiere, 1973.

"Three Cent Stomp." Recorded, 1943: Columbia CL 6024.

Togo Brava Suite. 1971. Contents: Right on Togo; Soul Soothing Beach; Naturelement; Amour, Amour. Recorded: Capitol CDP 7243 8 30082 23.

Tonal Group or *Suite Ditty*. 1946. Contents: Rhapsoditti; Fugueaditti; Jam-a-ditty. Recorded: Merritt Record Society 2001.

Toot Suite or *Great South Bay Suite* or *Jazz Festival Suite*. 1959. Co-composer, Billy Strayhorn. Contents: Red Garter; Red Shoes; Red Carpet; Ready Go.

"Tootin' through the Roof." Recorded, 1939: Onyx OR 1209; Up Front UPF-144.

"Track 360" or "Trains That Pass through the Night." Recorded, 1958: Eastman School of Music, 1993–94.

"Transbluency." Recorded, 1946: Unique Jazz UJ001.

Les trois rois noirs. Co-composer, Mercer Ellington. Recorded: Musicmasters MMD 61076.

"Trumpet in Spades" or "Rex's Concerto." Recorded, 1936: Brunswick 7752.

The Virgin Islands Suite. 1965. Co-composer, Billy Strayhorn. Contents: Island Virgin; Virgin Jungle; Fiddler on the Diddle; Jungle Kitty. Note: received a Grammy Award for Best Original Jazz Composition, 1965. Recorded: Reprise n.n.

"Warm Valley." Recorded, 1940: Concord Jazz CJ-212-C; JA Records 1270.

"Washington Wobble." Recorded, 1927: Saville CDSVL 206; Victor
40156-4.

"What Am I Here For?" or "Ethiopian Notion." Recorded, 1942: Black
Lion 3702-4; Victor 071890-1.

"Who Knows." Recorded, 1953: Capitol M11058; Eastman School of
Music, 1993–94.

"Yam Brown." 1926. New York: Frazer-Kent. Co-composer, Jo Trent.

"Yearning for Love" or "Lawrence's Concerto." Recorded, 1936:
Brunswick 7752; Columbia CL 2029.

INCIDENTAL MUSIC

Anatomy of a Murder. 1959. Film soundtrack. Co-composer, Billy
Strayhorn. Contents: I'm Gonna Go Fishin'; Flirtibird; Way Early
Subtone; Hero to Zero; Low Key Lightly; Happy Anatomy;
Midnight Indigo; Almost Cried; Sunswept Sunday; Grace Valse;
Haupe; Upper and Outest; I Want to Love You.

"Asphault Jungle." 1960. Television theme.

Assault on a Queen. Film soundtrack.

Paris Blues. 1961. Film soundtrack. Contents: Battle Royal; Birdie Jungle;
Autumnal Suite; Nite: Wild Man Moore; Paris Stairs; Guitar
Amour; Paris Blues. Note: received an Academy Award nomination
for Best Score.

Symphony in Black. 1934. Film soundtrack.

DRAMATIC MUSIC

Beggar's Holiday. 1946. Unpublished manuscript. Note: music for the
stage. Recorded: Blue Pear Records BP-1013.

Jump for Joy. 1941; revised, 1959. Unpublished manuscript. Contents:
(1941) I Got It Bad and That Ain't Good; Brown-Skin Gal in the
Calico Gown; Chocolate Shake; Bessie, Whoa Babe; Nostalgia;
Flame Indigo; Jump for Joy; Give Me an Old-Fashioned Waltz; Sh,
He's on the Beat; Sharp Easter; Bli-Blip; The Giddy-Bug Galop.
(1959) The Natives are Restless Tonight; Nerves, Nerves, Nerves;
Resigned to Living; Strictly for Tourists; Within Me I Know; Three
Shows Nightly; Concerto for Clinkers; Don't Believe Everything You
Hear; So the Good Book Says (co-composer, Billy Strayhorn); Walk
It Off (co-composer, Billy Strayhorn). Note: music for the stage.
Premiere, 1941. Recorded, 1959: Smithsonian Institution RC 037.

Murder in the Cathedral. 1967. Unpublished manuscript. Contents:
Becket; Gold; Land; Martyr; Women's; Exotique Bongos. Note:
music for the stage.

Pousse-Café (Sugar City). 1962. Unpublished manuscript. Contents: Sugar
City; Spacious and Gracious; Spider and Fly; Settle for Less; Swivel;
Forever; Someone to Care For; Je n'ai rien; Here You Are; Follow
Me Up the Stairs; Do Me a Favor; These are the Good Old Days;
Let's; Amazing; The Colonel's Lady; Natchez Trace; Goodbye,
Charlie; Thank You, Sam; C'est comme ça. Note: music for the
stage.

Queenie Pie. Unpublished manuscript. Note: music for the stage;
incomplete.

The River (ballet). 1970. Unpublished manuscript. Contents: Well; The
Run; The Giggling Rapids; Meander; The Lake; The Falls; The
Whirlpool; The River; The Village of the Virgins; The Mother, Her
Majesty the Sea.

Timon of Athens. 1964. Unpublished manuscript. Contents: Impulsive
Giving; Ocean; Angry; Gold; Regal Formal; Regal; Skilipop;

Smoldering; Gossippippi; Counter Theme; Alcibiades; Gossip;
Banquet; Revolutionary. Note: music for the stage. Recorded:
Varèse Sarabande Records VSD 5466.

Turcaret. 1960. Unpublished manuscript. Contents: Overture; Annonce
de spectacle; Frontin; Lisette; La Baronne; Turcaret; Colère de
Monsieur Turcaret; Le Chevalier; Mathilde; Madame Turcaret;
Motif du Flamand. Note: music for the stage.

PUBLICATIONS

ABOUT ELLINGTON
Books and Monographs

Berini, Antonio. *Duke Ellington: Un genio, un mito.* Florence: Ponte alle
Grazie, 1994.

Bigard, Barney. *With Louis and the Duke: The Autobiography of a Jazz
Clarinetist.* New York: Oxford University Press, 1986.

Billard, Francois. *Duke Ellington.* Paris: Seuil, 1994.

Brown, Gene. *Duke Ellington.* Englewood Cliffs, N.J.: Silver Burdett Press,
1990.

Collier, James Lincoln. *Duke Ellington.* New York: Oxford University
Press, 1987.

Dance, Stanley. *The World of Duke Ellington.* New York: Scribner's Sons,
1970. Reprint, New York: Da Capo, 1981.

Dietrich, Kurt. *Duke's Bones: Ellington's Great Trombonists.* Rottenburg,
Germany: Advance Music, 1995.

Ellington, Mercer. *Duke Ellington in Person: An Intimate Memoir.* Boston:
Houghton Mifflin, 1978.

Franchini, Vittorio. *Duke Ellington.* Milan: Targa Italiana, 1989.

Frankl, Ron. *Duke Ellington.* Danbury, Conn.: Grolier, 1988.

Gammond, Peter. *Duke Ellington.* Tunbridge Wells, England: Spellmount,
1985. Reprint, London: Apollo, 1987.

George, Don. *Sweet Man, the Real Duke Ellington.* New York: Putnam,
1981.

Georgiady, Nicholas P. *Duke Ellington, American Negro Musician.*
Milwaukee, Wisc.: Franklin Publishers, 1969.

Hasse, John Edward. *Beyond Category: The Life and Genius of Duke
Ellington.* London: Simon and Schuster, 1993.

Jewell, Derek. *Duke: A Portrait of Duke Ellington.* London: Elm Tree
Books, 1977.

———. *Duke: Biografía novelada de Duke Ellington.* Mexico: Editores
Asociados Mexicanos, 1979.

Lambert, George Edmund. *Duke Ellington.* London: Cassell, 1959.

Montgomery, Elizabeth Rider. *Duke Ellington: King of Jazz.* New York:
Dell, 1972.

Moule, François-Xavier. *A Guide to the Duke Ellington Recorded Legacy on
LPs and CDs.* LeMans, France: Madly Productions, 1992.

Old, Wendie C. *Duke Ellington, Giant of Jazz.* Springfield, N.J.: Enslow
Publications, 1996.

Rattenbury, Ken. *Duke Ellington, Jazz Composer.* New Haven, Conn.: Yale
University Press, 1990.

Ruland, Hans. *Duke Ellington: Sein Leben, seine Musik, seine Schallplatten.*
Gauting-Buchendorf: Oreos, 1983.

Timner, W. E. *Ellingtonia: The Recorded Music of Duke Ellington and His
Sidemen.* Lanham, England: Scarecrow Press, 1996.

Travis, Dempsey J. *The Duke Ellington Primer.* Chicago: Urban Research
Press, 1996.

Trazegnies, Jean de. *Duke Ellington, Harlem Aristocrat of Jazz.* Brussells: Editions du hot club, 1946.

Tucker, Mark. *Ellington: The Early Years.* Urbana: University of Illinois Press, 1991.

———, ed. *The Duke Ellington Reader.* New York: Oxford University Press, 1993.

Ulanov, Barry. *Duke Ellington.* New York: Creative Age Press, 1945.

Valburn, Jerry. *The Directory of Duke Ellington's Recordings.* Hicksville, N.Y.: Marlor Productions, 1986.

———. *Duke Ellington on Compact Disc: An Index and Text of the Recorded Work of Duke Ellington on Compact Disc: An In-depth Study.* Hicksville, N.Y.: Marlor Productions, 1993.

Dissertations

Cooper, Matthew James. "Duke Ellington the Pianist." Ph.D. diss., University of Cincinnati, 1994.

Dietrich, Kurt Robert. "Joe 'Tricky Sam' Nanton, Juan Tizol and Lawrence Brown: Duke Ellington's Great Trombonists, 1926–1951." D.M.A. diss., University of Wisconsin-Madison, 1989.

Dodson, Leon. "Adapting Selected Compositions and Arrangements of Duke Ellington for High School Jazz Orchestra." Ed.D. thesis, New York University, 1979.

Hill, Wilbert Weldon. "The Sacred Concertos of Edward Kennedy 'Duke' Ellington." Ph.D. diss., Catholic University of America, 1995.

McLaren, Joseph. "Edward Kennedy (Duke) Ellington and Langston Hughes: Perspectives on Their Contributions to American Culture, 1920–1966." Ph.D. diss., Brown University, 1980.

Milnes, Harriett Elizabeth. "The Formation of Duke Ellington's Mature Style." M.A. thesis, Mills College, 1978.

Myers, Claudette. "Duke Ellington and His Expression of Creativity." M.Ed. diss., Texas Southern University, 1968.

Poole, Stephen R. "Every Man Prays in His Own Language: Reception and Critical Textual Analysis of Edward Kennedy 'Duke' Ellington's Sacred Concerts." M.M. thesis, Southwestern Baptist Thelogical Seminary, 1993.

Reid, Joseph Shuler. "An Analysis of Selected Songs by Edward Kennedy ('Duke') Ellington." M.M. thesis, University of Mississippi, 1976.

Rowell, Jules Edmund. "An Analysis of the Extended Orchestral Works of Duke Ellington, circa 1931 to 1972." M.A. thesis, San Francisco State University, 1983.

Steed, Janna T. "Duke Ellington's Jazz Testament: The Sacred Concerts." S.T.M. thesis, Yale Divinity School, 1993.

Taylor, Curtis Benjamin. "The Transcription and Stylistic Comparative Analysis of Two Recordings of Duke Ellington's Black and Tan Fantasy." M.A. thesis, Cornell University, 1974.

Articles

DeVeaux, Scott. "*Black, Brown and Beige* and the Critics." *Black Music Research Journal* 13, no. 2 (Fall 1993): 125–146.

Dietrich, Kurt. "Lawrence Brown—Duke Ellington's Versatile Trombone Virtuoso." *Proceedings of NAJE Research* 8 (1988): 29–40.

———. "The Role of Trombones in *Black, Brown and Beige.*" *Black Music Research Journal* 13, no. 2 (Fall 1993): 111–124.

Harvey, Mark Sumner. "New World A-Comin': Religious Perspectives on the Legacy of Duke Ellington." In *Sacred Music of the Secular City from Blues to Rap.* A special issue of *Black Sacred Music* 6, no. 1 (1992): 146–154.

Hoefsmit, Sjef, edited by Andrew Homzy. "Chronology of Ellington's Recordings and Performances of *Black, Brown and Beige,* 1943–1973." *Black Music Research Journal* 13, no. 2 (Fall 1993): 161–174.

Homzy, Andrew. "*Black, Brown and Beige* in Duke Ellington's Repertoire." *Black Music Research Journal* 13, no. 2 (Fall 1993): 87–110.

Hudson, Theodore R. "Duke Ellington's Literary Sources." *American Music* 9, no. 1 (1991): 20–42.

Knauer, Wolfram. "Simulated Improvisation in Duke Ellington's *Black, Brown and Beige.*" *Black Perspective in Music* 18, no. 1–2 (1990): 20–38.

Little, Patrick L. "The Poet and the Duke (Comparison of Machaut and Duke Ellington Songs)." *Early Music* 11 (February 1983): 217–220.

McKinney-Johnson, Eloise. "Some Memories of Duke Ellington's Premier Sacred Jazz Concert." In *Sacred Music of the Secular City from Blue to Rap.* A special issue of *Black Sacred Music* 6, no. 1 (1992): 155–161.

"Mingus et l'ombre de Duke." *Jazz Magazine* 120 (July 1965): 28–34.

Parker, B. "Edward Kennedy 'Duke' Ellington: A Unique Approach to Music." *Proceedings of NAJE Research* 9 (1989): 185–195.

Pilon, G. "Edward Kennedy 'Duke' Ellington." *St. Cecilia* 10 (1961): 38–46.

Peress, Maurice. "My Life with *Black, Brown and Beige.*" *Black Music Research Journal* 13, no. 2 (Fall 1993): 147–160.

Tucker, Mark. "The Genesis of *Black, Brown and Beige.*" *Black Music Research Journal* 13, no. 2 (Fall 1993): 67–86.

Welburn, Ronald G. "Duke Ellington's Music: The Catalyst for a True Jazz Criticism." *International Review of the Aesthetics and Sociology of Music* 17 (January 1986): 111–122.

Wiedemann, E. "Duke Ellington: The Composer." *Annual Review of Jazz Studies* 5 (1991): 37–64.

BY ELLINGTON

"The Duke Steps Out." *Rhythm* (March 1931): 20–22.

"From Where I Lie." *The Negro Actor* 11, no. 1 (July 1938): 4.

"Interpretations in Jazz: A Conference with Duke Ellington." *Etude* 65 (March 1947): 134, 172.

"Jazz As I Have Seen It." *Swing* (February 1940): 10–11, 33; (March 1940): 9, 32; (May 1940): 10, 23; (June 1940): 11, 22; (July 1940): 10, 23; (August 1940): 10; (September 1940): 8–9, 24.

"The Most Essential Instrument." *Jazz Journal* 18 (December 1965): 14–15.

Music Is My Mistress. New York: Doubleday, 1973. Reprint, New York: Da Capo, 1976.

"Reminiscing in Tempo." *Down Beat* 31 (July 2, 1964): 8–9.

"Thoughts on Composing." *Jazz Journal* 16 (January 1963): 3.

"Where Is Jazz Going?" *Music Journal* 20 (March 1962): 31.

PRINCIPAL ARCHIVES

Duke Ellington Collection, National Museum of American History, Smithsonian Institution, Washington, D.C.

* * * * *

Duke Ellington enjoyed a spectacular career marked by puzzles and paradoxes. Although he spent his entire professional life working with jazz musicians and mining the jazz tradition in his compositions, he repeatedly distanced himself from the term "jazz" itself, concerned that it might misrepresent his art and cloud the public's perception of his achievements. Setting enormously ambitious goals for himself as a composer, he nevertheless maintained a punishing schedule as a performer, accepting engagements of all kinds for his orchestra, often supplying dance music for audiences who viewed him mainly as a charming entertainer and celebrity bandleader—not as "our greatest composer," as Ralph Ellison once called him. Ellington wrote music incessantly but only for his own ensemble, taking no interest in making it available in written or published form (beyond simplified sheet-music arrangements of his popular songs and instrumentals). For nearly 30 years, he collaborated with fellow composer, arranger, and pianist Billy Strayhorn, the two developing a musical relationship so telepathic that one could literally continue writing a piece where the other had left off, with the listener unable to tell the difference. All these features—together with the far-ranging imagination, emotional depth, and enduring appeal of his music—make Ellington one of the 20th century's most intriguing creative figures.

Ellington launched his career in Washington, D.C., where he was born and reared in the midst of a close, nurturing, middle-class family, and where he lived until 1923, when he moved to New York at the age of 24. In Washington, Ellington's earliest musical ambition was to become an accomplished ragtime pianist. As a teenager, he listened intently to local black players, observed star performers like Luckey Roberts and James P. Johnson when they came through town, and gradually developed—mostly on his own—pianistic devices and flashy "tricks" for his own repertory. After acquiring basic keyboard proficiency, Ellington began leading pick-up groups around Washington in 1917–18 and by the early 1920s was operating a successful business furnishing ensembles for dances, parties, and society functions. During this time, Ellington showed virtually no interest in composing. His entire output before the age of 24 consisted of two loosely sketched ragtime pieces (including his earliest known composition, "Soda Fountain Rag," ca. 1914–15) and a risqué ditty, "What You Gonna Do When the Bed Breaks Down?"

During his first few years in New York, Ellington sought to establish himself as a bandleader and songwriter. He was more successful in the former goal, securing a long-term engagement for his group at the Kentucky Club in Times Square and gradually emerging as one of the city's leading black bandleaders. His songs, though, mostly written with lyricist Jo Trent, failed to stir much interest. It was not until 1926–27, on a series of recordings issued by Vocalion, Brunswick, Columbia, and Victor, that Ellington showed promise as a composer—not with songs but with brooding, atmospheric instrumentals like "East St. Louis Toodle-O" (1926), "Immigration Blues" (1926), and "Black and Tan Fantasy" (1927). These pieces derived much of their character from the singular performing styles of his players, most notably the expressive muted brass techniques of trumpeter James "Bubber" Miley and trombonist Joseph "Tricky Sam" Nanton. From this time on, specific performers in Ellington's ensemble would always play key roles in defining his voice as a composer.

Ellington's composing and recording activity accelerated in the late 1920s after he landed a job as house bandleader at Harlem's famous Cotton Club. Many pieces written then were probably fea-

tured at the nightspot, either used to accompany black performers in revues or played during intermission for the dancing of white patrons. "The Mooche" (1928) is an example of the former, titled after an African-American shuffle dance that had been around for years. This piece also had hallmarks of what came to be known as Ellington's "jungle style," in which snarling, plunger-muted brass, pulsating accompaniment in the bass and tom toms, minor-mode melodies, and weirdly dissonant chords gave a theatrical depiction of musical "primitivism." But the "jungle style" formed only a portion of Ellington's repertory. He also turned out sweet pop songs like "I'm So in Love with You" (1930), blistering dance pieces like "Jubilee Stomp" (1928), gentle laments like "Awful Sad" (1928), and earthy blues like "Saturday Night Function" (1929).

While employed at the Cotton Club, providing music for theatrical skits, song and dance acts, and social dancing, Ellington began to dream of writing extended compositions—pieces that would be longer than the roughly three minutes permitted by 78 rpm recordings. In 1930, a New York journalist interviewed Ellington and reported that he was "at work on a tremendous task," a piece that would depict "The History of the Negro." This work obsessed Ellington throughout the 1930s and finally emerged in January 1943 as *Black, Brown and Beige,* the three-movement "tone parallel to the history of the Negro in America" that his orchestra premiered on its first Carnegie Hall concert. After *Black, Brown and Beige,* a multi-movement model became one of Ellington's two main solutions to the problem of large-scale form in jazz, as seen in the series of suites he composed for subsequent Carnegie Hall concerts, among them the *Perfume Suite* (1944), *Deep South Suite* (1946), *Tonal Group* (1946), and *Liberian Suite* (1947). The other approach to large-scale form explored by Ellington in the 1930s and 1940s was that of a continuous, single-movement work integrated by theme, motive, tempo, program, or some combination of these elements. Ellington's first effort in this direction came with *Creole Rhapsody* (1931, in two different versions), loosely unified by a recurring rhythmic motive (see Ex. 1). This was followed by *Reminiscing in Tempo* (1935), a set of orchestral variations on a single theme, unfolding at a leisurely pace over four sides of two 78 rpm records; *Diminuendo and Crescendo in Blue* (1937), an essay in extended blues form and strict dynamic control; *New World A-Coming* (1943), a rambling, multi-section concerto for piano and orchestra; and *The Tattooed Bride* (1948), a through-composed programmatic work. This series of extended works culminated in *Harlem* (also known as *A Tone Parallel to Harlem* and *Harlem Suite,* 1950), one of Ellington's richest and most powerfully expressive compositions.

Example 1.

Making music for dancers was one of Ellington's main activities throughout his career. He viewed this as a worthy calling for a black composer, a way to address aesthetic concerns underlying African-American culture in general. As he wrote in 1931, "When we dance it is not a mere diversion or social accomplishment. It expresses our personality, and, right down in us, our souls react to the elemental but eternal rhythm, and the dance is timeless and unhampered by any lineal form." During the swing era of the 1930s and 1940s, many of the pieces written by Ellington were designed to move dancers across the floor, as some of their titles suggested: "Steppin' into Swing Society" (1938), "I'm Slappin' Seventh Avenue (with the Sole of My Shoe)" (1938), and "Bouncing Buoyancy" (1939). At the same time, Ellington finally began to realize his earlier songwriting ambitions when instrumentals were set with lyrics and became popular hits, among them "Sophisticated Lady" (1932), "Solitude" (1934), "Don't Get Around Much Any More" (1942), and "Do Nothin' 'Til You Hear from Me" (1943). Ellington's abundant gifts as a composer, together with his ensemble's virtuosity and outstanding soloists (especially saxophonists Johnny Hodges and Ben Webster, clarinetists Barney Bigard and Jimmy Hamilton, trumpeters Cootie Williams and Ray Nance, and trombonists Joe Nanton, Lawrence Brown, and Juan Tizol) made the Ellington orchestra one of the most popular big bands playing before the American public. It also won a prominent reputation abroad through its recordings and concertizing, beginning with tours to Europe in 1933 and 1939.

Success in the field of popular music brought Ellington other kinds of opportunities to compose and perform. The 1935 film short *Symphony in Black* depicted him as an established composer writing a programmatic "Rhapsody of Negro Life" for the concert hall, then conducting its premiere with a huge orchestra (his own, though expanded for the occasion). This cinematic vision of Ellington came to life in the 1940s with a series of high-profile concerts at Carnegie Hall, each featuring new pieces written for the occasion. The largest and most adventurous was *Black, Brown and Beige* (1943), a panoramic survey of African-American history that grew out of *Symphony in Black* and Ellington's earlier plans to fashion a large-scale piece based on this subject. Ellington also tried his luck in musical theater with the revue *Jump for Joy* (1941), but the show closed after a three-month run in Los Angeles and was never successfully revived afterwards. This experience typified Ellington's inability to break through with a hit show, although he kept trying in later years with such projects as *Beggar's Holiday* (1946) and *Pousse-Café* (1966).

In his later years, Ellington continued to compose steadily while maintaining a constant performing schedule. He wrote works for record dates, new members in his orchestra, jazz festivals, and concert appearances. He produced "A Drum Is a Woman" (1957) for television and *The River* (1970) for Alvin Ailey's ballet company. He supplied film scores for *Anatomy of a Murder* (1959) and *Paris Blues* (1961). Most significant—at least to Ellington—were the sacred concerts he staged from 1965 to 1973. In these performances, many of them held in cathedrals and churches, his orchestra joined forces with solo singers (including the ethereal Swedish soprano, Alice Babs), choral groups, and dancers. Ellington's texts preached the gospel of love, compassion, tolerance, freedom, peace, and universal brotherhood. Despite their mixed critical reception, the sacred concerts count among Ellington's last major musical statements, together with *The Latin American Suite* (1968), *The New Orleans Suite* (1970), *The Afro-Eurasian Eclipse* (1970), and the opera *Queenie Pie* (unfinished at the time of his death in 1974).

Ellington reaped many honors and awards for his achievements. But in a lifetime devoted to composing and performing, he gave far more than he received. His impressive musical legacy, constructed over a period of 50 years, stands as a towering monument of 20th-century art and a tribute to the miraculous powers of human creativity.

MOOD INDIGO (1930)

A relatively early piece that became one of Ellington's best-known works, "Mood Indigo" exhibits several key traits found throughout his career as composer and bandleader. One is the transformative approach he brought to compositions that stayed in his repertory. Issued first under the title "Dreamy Blues," "Mood Indigo" was performed and recorded by Ellington and his orchestra many times over the next 40 years. During this period, Ellington kept changing details in the scoring and arrangement to keep "Mood Indigo" fresh, while still preserving its basic identity. Differences can already be noted between the first recordings for Brunswick and OKeh in October 1930 and the version for Victor in December of that year; by 1932, newly orchestrated sections appeared when the piece was recorded as part of a medley. An extended "concert version" of "Mood Indigo," lasting 15 minutes instead of the original three, was released in 1950 on the album *Masterpieces by Ellington.* Together with Ellington's changes in length and structure, though, the work also consistently underwent transformation in the solos of members of the band. Over time, then, "Mood Indigo" became for Ellington not so much a single piece—frozen in details and sounding the same each time it was played—but a performance tradition with its own unfolding history. Certain fundamental features of the piece (melody, chord progression, themes) were always there, while others (tempo, key, harmonization, structure, solos) were varied. Like other pieces in Ellington's repertory, "Mood Indigo" existed in a constant state of self-renewal—born again during each performance, reincarnated at every record date.

Another aspect of Ellington's transforming touch is apparent in the genesis of "Mood Indigo." Ellington usually said he wrote the piece quickly for a record date, sketching it out in 15 minutes while waiting for his mother to cook dinner. But in doing so, Ellington patched in a section—the clarinet's secondary theme, a harmonic variation on the opening chorus—borrowed from his clarinetist Barney Bigard, who in turn had learned it from Lorenzo Tio, his teacher in New Orleans. Bigard's name thus appears as one of the co-composers of "Mood Indigo" (together with that of Ellington's manager Irving Mills, who routinely took credit for pieces even though he may have done little or none of the creative work). This collaborative process, while overly emphasized in accounts by journalists and by Ellington band members, did form an important part of Ellington's composing method. In addition, Ellington profited from the substantial contributions of his writing and arranging partner Billy Strayhorn and occasionally from composer-arrangers within his band (e.g., Juan Tizol and Jimmy Hamilton).

The title of "Mood Indigo" points to another salient trait in the world of Ellington's music: its haunting emotional landscape, often derived from the blues but usually drawing upon other elements to achieve a special blend. The critic R. D. Darrell noted this in 1931 when he called the first recorded "Mood Indigo" a "poignantly restrained and nostalgic piece." Ellington himself referred to the "plaintive sort of style" he began to develop in the late 1920s while performing at the Cotton Club, one that contrasted greatly with the grandiose symphonic jazz of Paul Whiteman and his imitators. One key player responsible for Ellington's "plaintive" style was trumpeter Bubber Miley, whose expressive blues lines and artful muting techniques helped forge an identity for the Ellington orchestra. Another was Joseph "Tricky Sam" Nanton, whose doleful lines on plunger-muted trombone distinguish the original recordings of "Mood Indigo." Nanton's melancholia, though, is counter-balanced by the sweeter and more hopeful tone of trumpeter Arthur Whetsol, especially on the Victor recording from December 1930, where on the second chorus he soars high above low-register clarinets in a wistful variation of the main tune.

The intense emotional expression in Ellington's music derives from the eloquent voices of players like Whetsol, Nanton, Bigard, Hodges, and Miley, and also from the subtle ways in which the composer blended their timbres together. The opening chorus (December 1930 version), for example, displays two features commonly found throughout Ellington's music: muted brass (Whetsol and Nanton), and three-voiced or "trio" textures.

Ellington's affinity for muted brass techniques resulted in part from environmental factors; these distorted sounds—whether sensual, bluesy, bestial, or uncanny—added "primitivist" touches to the theatrical revues and floorshows his orchestra accompanied in the 1920s. Such tonal effects became hallmarks of Ellington's musical identity, and he would continue to employ them long after leaving the Cotton Club (e.g., "Ko-Ko," 1940, and *Afro-Bossa*, 1963). The "trio" texture, on the other hand, reflected Ellington's interest in concocting new timbral combinations from disparate ingredients. For the first chorus of "Mood Indigo," he scored muted trumpet and trombone closely together more than an octave above the clarinet line. Later he claimed he did this to offset a certain microphone tone that resulted from technology of the time. Regardless, he returned to the trio texture of "Mood Indigo" in many later works, often employing it for similarly plangent effects, as in, for example "Dusk" (1940) and "Transbluency" (1946).

Timbre often serves a structural function in Ellington's music, with individual sections of a piece defined not just by theme, key, or harmonies but by tone colors. The December 1930 "Mood Indigo" provides an example, with the trio of muted trumpet, muted trombone, and clarinet in the first chorus; high muted trumpet over low clarinet trio in the second chorus; clarinet backed by open brass in the third; and the return of the opening trio in the last chorus to bring closure.

"Mood Indigo" provides a primer for studying Ellington's compositional manner and method. It illustrates the characteristic yet elusive quality once defined by Billy Strayhorn: "Each member of [Ellington's] band is to him a distinctive tone color and set of emotions, which he mixes with others equally distinctive to produce a third thing, which I like to call the 'Ellington Effect'."

"Mood Indigo" became a signature piece for Ellington, one of his most popular compositions and a staple of his orchestra's repertory. While others performed the piece—either as an instrumental or song with lyrics by Mitchell Parish—it always retained the stamp of the composer-bandleader's identity. In 1932, R. D. Dar-

rell hailed "Mood Indigo" as one of Ellington's best pieces, comparing its muted brass effects to orchestration in Stravinsky's *Rite of Spring*. And in his 1968 study *Early Jazz*, Gunther Schuller praised the piece's "originality of conception" and formal perfection.

JACK THE BEAR (1940)

Ellington was quick to exploit the talents of new orchestra members and adept at bending received forms into original designs. "Jack the Bear" illustrates both tendencies. It was first recorded in March of 1940, during a year hailed by many as one of the most fertile and artistically rewarding periods of Ellington's career. By this time, Ellington's orchestra had grown to 15 pieces, with five reeds, three trumpets, three trombones, and four players in the rhythm section. This instrumentation was conventional for dance bands during the swing era. But "Jack the Bear" is anything but a conventional composition for such an ensemble.

One unusual feature is the prominent role assigned to bassist Jimmy Blanton. The young virtuoso had joined Ellington in September of 1939, when he was 20 years old. Realizing Blanton's exceptional ability, Ellington went into the studio in November and recorded several duets for bass and piano. In "Jack the Bear"—named after a Harlem bass player who ran a tailor shop—Ellington displayed Blanton's skills within an orchestral framework. The introduction features a series of call-and-response exchanges, with Blanton answering brief phrases in the brass and reeds. The last chorus lets Blanton take the lead with two-measure calls followed by answers in the orchestra, and the tag is a four-bar *cadenza* for solo bass (in tempo) that culminates in a rising scale and a final chord shouted by the orchestra. In between these opening and closing sections of "Jack the Bear," Blanton's bass is also featured three times in a unison figure played with brass and reeds; it is thus liberated from its otherwise strict timekeeping function. Such treatment of the bass was uncommon for 1940 but characteristic of the imaginative assignments Ellington devised for individual members of his orchestra.

A second striking feature of "Jack the Bear" is its form, which follows no preset formulas or patterns commonly found in popular dance music of the time. Ellington fuses sections of different lengths, varies orchestral colors, and uses the African-American call-and-response principle as a unifying textural device (see Ex. 2). As the diagram shows, the core sections of the arrangement are three choruses of 12-bar blues—nearly four, but the last (D) is interrupted by a recurring unison interlude figure. In addition, the opening and closing A sections, also 12 bars long, imply a blues progression but leave out the move to subdominant in bars 5–6. Ellington inserts section B, which draws upon standard 32-bar popular song form, into these blues and blues-like choruses; but even this is handled unconventionally, since Cootie Williams's plunger-muted trumpet in a^1 (over a march-like rhythm in the ensemble) disguises the internal repetition of the AABA form. Add to this the thrice-repeated unison figure, the metrically ambiguous introduction (which begins with a pick-up, but the delayed entrance of the rhythm section creates doubt for the listener), and the short solo *cadenza* for Blanton in the tag, and the result is a degree of formal variety and complexity rarely found in big-band compositions of the period. Even more remarkable, however, is the musical narrative of "Jack the Bear," which is smoothly flowing despite such irregular structural components. Lawrence Gushee, in his liner notes for the album *Duke Ellington 1940,* has singled out this piece's "formal play and sleight-of-hand," identifying, among other features responsible for this, Ellington's "across the seams" scoring that stitches sections together.

"Jack the Bear" shows how in a single piece Ellington could meet different aesthetic challenges. When performed live by the Ellington orchestra, the piece served as inspiration for social dancers, driving them along with its steady beat and strong sense of swing. It was also a way of showcasing the talents of bassist Jimmy Blanton, one of the ensemble's outstanding musicians at the time. Finally it represented an ingenious reworking of formal types (blues, popular song) and conventions (call-and-response, riffs, fills, solo breaks) into an original composition in the jazz idiom.

"Jack the Bear" was performed by Ellington and his orchestra mainly in the 1940s, although a new version was recorded in 1956 for the Bethlehem LP *Historically Speaking.* Although few other bands played the piece, it was recorded by bassist Oscar Pettiford in 1954, and jazz repertory orchestras began progamming it in the 1980s and 1990s. Critics have praised Ellington's original 1940 recording both for compositional aspects and for Blanton's memorable performance.

HARLEM (1950)

In his memoirs, Ellington recalled writing *Harlem* in 1950 aboard the *Île de France* as he returned from a European tour. The piece had been commissioned by Arturo Toscanini and the NBC Symphony. For some reason the Toscanini performance never materialized, and Ellington premiered *Harlem* with his own orchestra at the Metropolitan Opera House in 1951. Eventually *Harlem* came to exist in three distinct versions: for jazz orchestra alone, as premiered on disc by Ellington in January 1951; for jazz and symphony orchestras together, as performed by Ellington with the Symphony of the Air in 1955; and as an arrangement for symphony orchestra, which was made by Maurice Peress in 1988. Ellington and his orchestra often featured *Harlem* in concerts into the 1960s and 1970s.

The inspiration for Ellington's *Harlem* was the great African-American community in upper Manhattan that had been his home since 1923, when he moved there from Washington, D.C. Ellington and his orchestra had performed often in Harlem in the 1920s and 1930s, not only at the Cotton Club but in such leading theaters as the Lincoln, Lafayette, and Apollo. He was on intimate terms with Harlem, its celebrities and common folk, its glittering nightlife and daytime realities, its sobering problems and shining possibilities, its religious fervor and resilient spirit. *Harlem* conveyed Ellington's impressions of the place, his attempt to capture in music the flavor of its street life and the essence of its soul. He had already made preliminary sketches of Harlem in a number of shorter pieces, including "Drop Me Off in Harlem" (1933), "Echoes of Harlem" (1936), "Blue Belles of Harlem" (1943), and the last movement of *Black, Brown and Beige,* especially the section "Sugar Hill Penthouse." But *Harlem* would become his most fully realized portrait of the place.

Example 2. "Jack the Bear," overview

	Number of measures	Main musical events
Introduction	8	Brass and reeds call, Blanton responds
A	12 (modified blues)	Piano calls, brass and reeds respond
Interlude	4	Unison figure for brass, reeds, bass
B	32 (aa^{1}ba)	Solos for clarinet (a) and muted trumpet (a^1) against background riff figures
Interlude	4	
C	12 (blues)	Baritone saxophone solo
C^1	12 (blues)	Plunger-muted trombone solo with background figures in reeds
C^2	12 (blues)	Ensemble: brass call, reeds respond
D	8 (abridged blues)	Ensemble: reeds call, brass respond
Interlude	4	
A^1	12	Bass calls, brass and reeds respond
Tag	4	Bass *cadenza* and final chord

The overall plan for *Harlem* follows a programmatic scheme in which the listener is taken on a musical tour of the community's sights and sounds. The resulting form is a series of different "scenes," like panels of a tableau, or like the individual pictures that make up the larger narrative in painter Jacob Lawrence's *Migration* series. The loose, random-seeming sequence of musical events reflects the casual movement of the interested observer from one site to the next as he strolls through Harlem, like the museum visitor in Musorgsky's *Pictures at an Exhibition.* Ellington renders this process, as Stanley Dance has noted in his liner notes to the CD issue of *Ellington Uptown,* with a technique similar to film montage, in which scenes follow "one another with bewildering rapidity, overlapping and dissolving [to] illustrate the different facets of the city within a city."

The creative risk in this sequential approach to structure is that the piece will seem to be fragmentary rather than unified. To integrate the varied panels in his tableau, Ellington fell back on a method he had employed in *Reminiscing in Tempo* (1935) and would repeat later in *Suite Thursday* (1960), embedding a recurring melodic motive in various sections of the piece. For *Harlem* it is a descending minor third, first heard in Ray Nance's solo trumpet introduction to the piece and conceived as an onomatopoeic rendering of the word "Harlem" (see Ex. 3). This minor-third interval permeates both the main and secondary thematic material in *Harlem.* During an up-tempo episode in the opening section, for example, it can be heard high in the reeds' light accompanying patterns and inverted (i.e., major sixth) in the baritone saxophone line below. In the middle of the piece, following the rumba evocation in the "Spanish Harlem" scene, the minor third appears in both calls and responses given out by the orchestra during choruses of 12-bar blues. And in the major-mode "spiritual" theme section depicting a storefront church worship service, the minor third appears at the end of phrases to provide closure. For the brilliant, triumphant coda, the full orchestra reiterates the minor third motive, which is sounded for the last time—as in the beginning—by the trumpet.

Example 3.

However, the power and beauty of Ellington's *Harlem* lies not in the motivic saturation of the minor-third interval but in other, more localized realms—especially its richly dissonant harmonies, sumptuously blended tone colors, and poignantly expressive "spiritual" theme. The latter section constitutes the emotional core of *Harlem,* in keeping with Ellington's oft-repeated remark that "there are more churches than cabarets in Harlem." Especially striking is the illusion of spontaneous, polyphonic harmonizing created by a small group of instruments after the trumpet and clarinet first state the theme, followed later by an eerily-voiced passage for reeds that resembles the keening voices of ancestors (or painful memories of the past crowding out faith in the future). To argue for

Harlem's merits on the grounds of unifying techniques or structural niceties is to miss the point of the piece and misconstrue Ellington's aesthetic. *Harlem* is not about large-scale structural control and intricate craft but rather about the visceral impact of a particular urban landscape translated into the language of tones. It reveals Ellington at his most sensational, bombarding the listener with musical images, vividly evoking the rhythms of the community and the complex, richly textured lives of its inhabitants.

Critical reactions to *Harlem* have been largely positive. The British jazz writer Raymond Horricks delivered a balanced appraisal of the work in 1956, hailing it as a compelling example of musical "pictorialism." Subsequent biographers of Ellington (James Lincoln Collier, John Edward Hasse) have identified it as one of Ellington's most successful extended works. *Harlem* has also been programmed repeatedly by both jazz repertory orchestras and symphony orchestras (using Maurice Peress's orchestration). It is one of the few longer compositions by Ellington to have earned both a high critical reception and popularity in the concert hall.

THE FAR EAST SUITE (1966)

The Far East Suite represents a series of musical impressions from Ellington's travels with his orchestra in the Middle East and Asia. The Ellington orchestra embarked on the first of these tours, organized by the State Department, in 1963. A visit to Japan in 1964 yielded the piece "Ad Lib on Nippon," which became the final movement of the suite. Although the Ellington orchestra began performing portions of *The Far East Suite* as early as 1964, the entire work was not recorded until late in 1966. Since the advent of the long-playing record era around 1950, Ellington had begun tailoring his writing to the temporal limits of this technology. *The Far East Suite*—like *Such Sweet Thunder* (1957) and *Afro-Bossa* (1963) before it—took up both sides of a 12-inch LP, its nine sections totaling roughly 45 minutes of music.

The importance of collaboration to Ellington is reflected in both the composition and performance of *The Far East Suite.* Of the work's nine movements, only two—"Blue Pepper" and "Ad Lib on Nippon"—are credited to Ellington alone; the rest are identified as co-composed by Ellington and his writing partner Billy Strayhorn. Moreover, as had been typical of Ellington's music since the 1920s, individual pieces were tailored for specific voices in the ensemble: "Isfahan" for alto saxophonist Johnny Hodges, "Agra" for baritone saxophonist Harry Carney (displaying his circular breathing technique at the end), "Amad" for trombonist Lawrence Brown, and "Ad Lib on Nippon" highlighting the skills of both Ellington on piano and Jimmy Hamilton on clarinet.

The Far East Suite's geographical theme provides the main unifying element for the work. Latin or *habanera*-derived rhythms abound in *The Far East Suite* as they had in *Afro-Bossa.* While hardly non-Western in origin, they served for Ellington as a signifier for musical exoticism, taking the listener away from the everyday family of American and African-American rhythms to a remote locale. Another way to suggest Middle Eastern and Asian musical practices was to introduce static harmonic fields over which extended melodic improvisation could unfold, replacing conventional chord movement that produced harmony-driven soloing. One-chord vamps in jazz were not new, of course, dating back to the 1920s (i.e., Louis Armstrong and the Hot 5's "Yes! I'm in the Barrel," 1925), and Ellington himself used the technique in one of his imitation train pieces, "Happy-Go-Lucky Local" (1946). But the unchanging harmonies (or oscillating two-chord backgrounds) in sections of *The Far East Suite*'s "Tourist Point of View" and "Agra" attempt to induce a repetitive, hypnotic response in the listener that Ellington and Strayhorn may have experienced on their travels. The point, as Ellington stressed, was not to recreate non-Western musical traditions in an authentic, ethnomusicologically informed way but rather to offer unapologetically the Westerners' reaction to the fresh sounds they heard—in other words, their "tourist point of view."

Not all of *The Far East Suite*, though, is "exotic" in character or self-consciously non-Western in effect. "Isfahan," the Johnny Hodges feature that takes its title from the ancient city in Persia, is a sensuous romantic ballad (in 32-bar, ABAC form). The "place" described by Hodges in "Isfahan" is not Iran but Eros; the fantasy he conjures up could have originated in Harlem, Berlin, or Rio. "Blue Pepper," by contrast, has a strong flavor of American rock from the 1960s, despite the modal cast of its melodic lines. Rufus Jones's funky back-beat would have fit right into a Stax or Motown session. And the switch to 12-bar blues form for Hodges's solo in the middle of "Blue Pepper" reveals the Western core of Ellington's inspiration beneath the trappings of orientalism.

Although occasionally relying on standard formal types—blues in "Blue Pepper" and "Ad Lib on Nippon," AABA popular song form in "Isfahan" and the middle of "Mount Harissa"—Ellington displays a willingness to break from these conventions and explore more unusual structures. The suite's opening "Tourist Point of View," for example, evokes the traveler's amazement and disorientation upon being thrust into the midst of a new culture. While the basic unit of structure is the four-bar phrase (often doubled), Ellington avoids ordering it in predictable groups, instead blurring the outlines of units to produce a sense of dazed dislocation. The familiar "West" is embedded in the basic musical syntax, but it is challenged and disrupted by powerful forces operating according to different rules. Paul Gonsalves's discursive, meandering tenor saxophone solo enhances the effect of being a stranger in a strange land. In the fourth movement, "Depk," which Ellington linked to a vigorous dance he saw performed in Jordan, ten-bar phrases alternate with sections based on three-bar groups, leading to a middle section that changes suddenly to triple meter. These atypical formal features, together with the hypnotic vamps and modal melodies, help Ellington and Strayhorn create the work's "exotic" soundscape.

Ultimately, though, the success of *The Far East Suite* as a large-scale composition results not so much from novel melodic, formal, and rhythmic features but from its arresting timbral effects and impressive sounds. The musical canvas painted by Ellington and Strayhorn blazes with bold colors and fresh tonal blendings. Only a few examples need be cited by way of illustration: in "Bluebird of Delhi," the chirping clarinet set off against low, parallel organum-like trombones; in "Depk," Ellington's brittle single-note piano interjections stabbing through the bright reed and brass textures; in "Agra," the mighty foghorn blasts of Harry Carney in the introduction, followed by his insinuating reading of the melody backed by distant-sounding muted trumpets; in "Amad," the expectation and excitement created in the long opening vamp, preparing the entrance of Lawrence Brown's eloquent trombone, cast in the role of the "muezzin" giving the call to prayer.

In *The Far East Suite,* as in so much of Ellington and Strayhorn's music, inspired composition and authoritative performance unite to create compelling art. The recording received favorable notices, and in subsequent years *The Far East Suite* was often cited by critics as one of Ellington's most successful extended works. Jazz musicians have been especially drawn to the section of the piece titled "Isfahan," performing and recording it many times.

REFERENCES

Bigard, Barney. *With Louis and the Duke: The Autobiography of a Jazz Clarinetist.* New York: Oxford University Press, 1986.

Collier, James Lincoln. *Duke Ellington.* New York: Oxford University Press, 1987.

Dance, Stanley. Liner notes, *Ellington Uptown.* Columbia Jazz Masterpieces, CK 40836.

Darrell, R. D. "Black Beauty" (1932). Reprinted in *The Duke Ellington Reader,* edited by Mark Tucker, 57–65. New York: Oxford University Press, 1993.

———. Review. *Phonograph Monthly Review* (January 1931). Reprinted in *The Duke Ellington Reader,* edited by Mark Tucker, 38–39. New York: Oxford University Press, 1993.

Ellington, Duke. "Career Highlights" *Down Beat* (November 5, 1952): 1+.

———. "The Duke Steps Out" *Rhythm* (March 1931): 20–22.

———. Interview with Jack Cullen, CKNW radio, Vancouver, Canada, October 30, 1962. Issued on Varèse International VS81007. Reprinted in *The Duke Ellington Reader,* edited by Mark Tucker, 338–341. New York: Oxford University Press, 1993.

———. *Music Is My Mistress.* New York: Doubleday, 1973. Reprint, New York: Da Capo Press, 1976.

Ellison, Ralph. "Homage to Duke Ellington on His Birthday." In *Going to the Territory,* 217–226. New York: Vintage Books, 1987.

Gushee, Lawrence. Liner notes, *Duke Ellington 1940.* Smithsonian Collection R 013, 1978.

Hasse, John Edward. *Beyond Category: The Life and Genius of Duke Ellington.* London: Simon and Schuster, 1993.

Horricks, Raymond. "Duke Ellington and the Harlem Suite." *Jazz Monthly* 2, no. 3 (July 1956): 8–10, 31.

Schuller, Gunther. *Early Jazz: Its Roots and Musical Development.* New York: Oxford University Press, 1968.

Tucker, Mark. *Ellington: The Early Years.* Urbana: University of Illinois Press, 1991.

———, ed. *The Duke Ellington Reader.* New York: Oxford University Press, 1993.

MARK TUCKER

EUBA, AKIN

Born in Lagos, Nigeria, April 28, 1935. **Education:** Studied piano with his father, 1943–48, with Major J.G.C. Allen and Tessier Rémi du Cros, 1948–1952; C.M.S. Grammar School, Lagos, Nigeria, 1944–51; Trinity College of Music, London, studied harmony and counterpoint with Eric Taylor, composition with Arnold Cooke, 1952–57; University of California, Los Angeles, B.A., 1964, M.A., 1966; University of Ghana at Legon, studied with J. H. Kwabena Nketia, Ph.D., 1974. **Composing and Performing Career:** Nigerian Broadcasting Corporation, senior program assistant, 1957–60, head of music and music research, 1960–65 (with some leaves for study abroad); Munich, *Dirges* performed at the Munich Cultural Olympics, 1972; has performed his own works for piano in recitals in Europe, the United States, and Africa; organizer of numerous concerts of African music at home and abroad. **Teaching Career:** University of Lagos, 1966–68; University of Ife, 1968–77; Centre for Cultural Studies, University of Lagos, director, 1978–81; Elekoto Music Centre, Lagos, director, 1981–86; Iwalewa-Haus, University of Bayreuth, Germany, research scholar, 1986–91; Centre for Intercultural Music Arts, London, director, 1988–present; has lectured widely in Africa and abroad, 1966–present; Department of Music, City University, London, Honorary Visiting Professor, 1993–96; University of Pittsburgh, Pa., Andrew Mellon Professor of Music, 1997–present. **Commissions:** United States Information Service, 1967. **Honors/Awards:** Nigerian Festival of the Arts, Lagos, first prize, piano performance, 1950–52, silver medal, best performance, 1952; Federal Government of Nigeria Scholarship, 1952–57; Rockefeller Foundation Fellowship for study at University of California, Los Angeles, 1962. **Mailing Address:** Department of Music, University of Pittsburgh, Pittsburgh, PA 15260.

MUSIC LIST

INSTRUMENTAL SOLOS
Cello
"The Wanderer." 1960. Unpublished manuscript. Recorded for radio broadcast.

Horn
Five Pieces for English Horn and Piano. 1963. Unpublished manuscript. Premiere, 1964.

Piano
Four Pictures from Oyo Calabashes. 1964. Unpublished manuscript.
"Impressions from an Akwete Cloth." 1964. Unpublished manuscript.
"Saturday Night at the Caban Bamboo." 1964. Unpublished manuscript.
Scenes from Traditional Life. 1970. Ile-Ife, Nigeria: Ife University Press, 1975. Premiere, 1974. Recorded: EMC LP 001.
"Themes from *Chaka* no. 1." 1996. Unpublished manuscript. Note: original reworking of themes from his opera *Chaka*. Premiere, 1996.
Wakar Duru: Studies in African Pianism, nos. 1–3. 1987. Unpublished manuscript. Premiere, 1989. Recorded: EMC LP 1001.

SMALL INSTRUMENTAL ENSEMBLE
Strings
String Quartet. 1957. Unpublished manuscript.

Woodwinds
Wind Quintet (flute, oboe, clarinet, bassoon, horn). 1967. Unpublished manuscript. Premiere, 1967.

Combinations
Four Pieces (flute, bassoon, piano, percussion). 1964. Unpublished manuscript.
"Igi nla so" (piano, gudugudu, kanago, iya-ilu, kerikeri). Ibadan: Oriki Publications, 1963.
"Legend" (violin, horn, piano, percussion). 1966. Unpublished manuscript.
"Music for Violin, Horn, Piano and Percussion." 1970. Unpublished manuscript. Premiere, 1970.

STRING ORCHESTRA
Ice Cubes. 1970. Unpublished manuscript. Premiere, 1970.

CHAMBER ORCHESTRA
Dance to the Rising Sun. 1963. Unpublished manuscript. Premiere, 1963.

FULL ORCHESTRA
Four Pieces for African Orchestra. 1966. Unpublished manuscript. Note: Master's thesis, University of California, Los Angeles.
Introduction and Allegro. 1956. Unpublished manuscript.
Olurounbi: A Symphonic Study on a Yoruba Legend. 1967. Unpublished manuscript. Commissioned by the United States Information Service. Premiere, 1967.

ORCHESTRA (CHAMBER OR FULL) WITH CHORUS
Two Songs (soloist, SATB, rock orchestra). 1983. Unpublished manuscript. Contents: Children Come and Hear and Be Told About Nigeria; 1900 Was the Beginning of Nigeria.

SOLO VOICE
Six Yoruba Folk Songs. 1975. Ile-Ife, Nigeria: Ife University Press, 1975. Contents: Mo le j'iyan yo; Ore meta; Mo ja'we gbegbe; Omo jowo; Agbe; O se gbe na.
"Time Passes By" (soprano). 1985. Unpublished manuscript. Premiere, 1985.
Two Tortoise Folk Tales in Yoruba. 1975. Unpublished manuscript. Contents: Ijapa ati agaramoku; Ijapa ati erin.

VOICE WITH INSTRUMENTAL ENSEMBLE
"Emi l'a nse l'oko d'oru" (female voice, piano, iya-ilu dundun, iya-ilu bata). Unpublished manuscript.
"The Fall of the Scales" (solo voice, prerecorded Nigerian instruments). 1970. Unpublished manuscript.
Seven Modern African Poems. 1987. Unpublished manuscript. Premiere, 1987.

Akin Euba; courtesy of the composer

Three Songs for Voice, Piano, and Iyalu Drum. Ibadan: Oriki Publications, 1963.

Two Modern African Poems (speaker, neo-African ensemble). 1987. Unpublished manuscript. Premiere, 1987.

CHORAL MUSIC

"Abiku II." 1968. Unpublished manuscript.

Dirges (speakers, singers, dancers, Yoruba drums, tape). 1970. Unpublished manuscript. Premiere, 1970.

"FESTAC 77" (SATB, jazz combo). 1977. Unpublished manuscript. Premiere, 1977.

The Laughing Tree (narrator, chorus, African instruments). 1970. Unpublished manuscript.

Two Yoruba Folk Songs (SATB). 1959. Unpublished manuscript. Contents: O se gbe na; Kori.

"West African Universities Games Anthem" (singers, rock ensemble, athletes). 1981. Unpublished manuscript. Premiere, 1981.

DRAMATIC MUSIC

Alantangana (ballet). Unpublished manuscript.

Bethlehem (opera). 1984. Unpublished manuscript. Premiere, 1984.

Black Bethlehem (opera). 1979. Unpublished manuscript. Premiere, 1979.

Chaka (opera). 1970; revised 1995. Unpublished manuscript. Premiere, 1970.

"Tortoise and the Speaking Cloth" (narrator, piano). 1964. Unpublished manuscript.

INCIDENTAL MUSIC

Abiku I. 1965. Unpublished manuscript. Note: this suite was composed for a dance-drama titled *Iya-Abiku*. Premiere, 1965.

PUBLICATIONS

ABOUT EUBA
Books and Monographs

Uzoigwe, Joshua. *Akin Euba: An Introduction to the Life and Music of a Nigerian Composer.* Bayreuth: E. Breitinger, University of Bayreuth, 1992.

Theses

Ogunnaike, Anna. "Contemporary Nigerian Art Music: The Works of Bankole, Euba and Ekwueme." Master's thesis, University of Lagos, 1986.

Uzoigwe, Joshua. "Akin Euba: An Introduction to the Life and Music of a Nigerian Composer." Master's thesis, Queen's University of Belfast, 1978.

Articles

Uzoigwe, Joshua. "A Cultural Analysis of Akin Euba's Musical Works." *Odu* [Ibadan] 24, no. 1 (1983): 44–60.

BY EUBA

"The African Composer in Europe: The Challenge of Interculturalism." In *Festschrift for Gamal Abdel-Rahim.* Cairo: Binational Fulbright Commission in Egypt, 1993.

"The African Guitar." *African Guardian* [Lagos] (April 1987): 30–31.

"African Traditional Music as a C
   and Research in African M
   Orpheus 3, no. 1 (1974):

Akin Euba in Interview with Dap
   of Theatre Arts, Universit

"Aspects of the Preservation and
   of Music 18, no. 4 (1976)

"Creative Potential and Propaga
   African Music: Meeting in
   edited by J. H. Kwabena

"Criteria for the Evaluation of N
   49 (1975): 46–50.

"The Dichotomy of African Mu
   (1975): 55–59; also in Co

"Drumming for the Egungun: T
   Theater." In *The Yoruba A*
   African Arts, edited by Ro
   John Pemberton, 161–16
   Institution Press, 1994.

"Dundun Music of the Yoruba."

Essays on Music in Africa. Vol. 1.
   Bayreuth, 1988.

Essays on Music in Africa. Vol. 2: I
   Music Centre, 1989.

"European Influences in Nigerian
   (July/September 1969): 4

"Evaluation and Propagation of A
   Music 15, no. 3 (1973): 3

"Évolution et diffusion de la mus
   Musicale 288/289 (1974):

"Ilu Esu (Drumming for Esu): A
   Essays for a Humanist: An
   Spring Valley, N.Y.: Town

"In Search of a Common Musica
   Nigerian Quarterly (1969):

Intercultural Music. Vol. 1, edited
   Euba. African Studies Seri

"Introduction to Music in Africa.
   by Richard Olaniyan, 224

"An Introduction to Music in Nige
   1–38.

"Islamic Musical Culture among t
   Essays on Music and History
   171–181. Evanston: North

"The Language of African Music.

Modern African Music: A Catalog
   Iwalewa-Haus, University o
   Haus, University of Bayreu

"Modern Popular Music in Zimb
   Antilopenfrauen: Kunst und
   Ronald Ruprecht, 8–15. B
   der University of Bayreuth

"Multiple Pitch Lines in Yoruba C
   International Folk Music Cc

"Music." In *The Living Culture of*
   20–24. Lagos: Thomas Ne

"Music in Traditional Society." *Nigeria Magazine* no. 101 (July/September 1969): 475–480.

"The Music of Nigeria." In *Development of Materials for a One-Year Course in African Music,* edited by Vada E. Butcher, 91–98. Washington, D.C.: Department of Health, Education, and Welfare, 1970.

"Musicology in the Context of African Culture." *Odu* [Ibadan] 2 (October 1969): 3–18.

"New Idioms of Music-Drama among the Yoruba: An Introductory Study." *Yearbook of the International Folk Music Council* 2 (1970): 92–107.

"Nigerian Music: An Appreciation." *Nigeria Magazine* no. 66 (October 1960): 199–208; also in *Negro History Bulletin* 24 (March 1961): 130–133.

"The Potential of Traditional Music as a Contemporary Art." *Black Orpheus* 3, no. 1 (1974): 54–60.

"Preface to a Study of Nigerian Music: In the Light of References Which Made It What It Is." *Ibadan* 21 (October 1965): 53–62.

"A Preliminary Survey of Musicological Aspects of Islamic Culture among the Yoruba." In *Les religions africaines comme source de valeurs de civilisation: Collogue de Cotonou 16–22 aout 1970,* 373–381. Paris: Présence Africaine, 1972.

"Traditional Elements as the Basis of New African Art Music." *African Urban Studies* 5, no. 4 (1970): 52–62.

Yoruba Drumming: The Dundun Tradition. Bayreuth: E. Breitinger, University of Bayreuth, 1990.

"Yoruba Music in the Church: The Development of a Neo-African Art among the Yoruba of Nigeria." In *African Musicology—Current Trends, Vol. 2: A Festschrift Presented to J. H. Kwabena Nketia,* edited by Jacqueline DjeDje, 45–63. Atlanta, Ga.: Crossroads Press, 1991.

* * * * *

In nearly 50 musical works, five scholarly books, and 80 articles, Akin Euba has pioneered, promoted, and theorized a genre that he terms "neo-African art music." To treat his music as simply another manifestation of the nationalist movement in the European "classical" tradition, however, is to discount a fundamental aspect of Euba's work: its role in the living tradition of African music. European classical music occupies a controversial space in African culture as it echoes the class distinctions, economic imperialism, and racial inequities of an only recently disabled colonial past. Compositions by Euba co-opt European cultural resources in service of a neo-African identity, just as Arabic and Islamic resources were transformed and incorporated into African culture in centuries past.

Born in Lagos, the capital city of Nigeria, on April 28, 1935, Euba was given a classical education in European art music. He began piano studies with his father in 1943. Euba's father encouraged his son's musical ambitions, sending him in 1948 to study with Major J.G.C. Allen, a senior civil servant in the Colonial Administration and later Director of Administration at what was then called the Nigerian Broadcasting Corporation. Winning the first prize in piano three consecutive times at the annual Nigerian Festival of the Arts (1950–52) and a silver cup for best all-around performance in 1952 helped create further educational opportunities. With the aid of Major Allen's connections in the colonial government, Euba received a Federal Government of Nigeria Scholarship for study at Trinity College in London (1952–57). As a youth, Euba was also exposed to traditional African musics that had broken into the sphere of popular entertainment musics, including the *Egungun* festival, *Eyo* masquerade processions, and *Apala* and *Waka*—two genres influenced by Islam and accompanied by the *dundun* drumming that would be the focus of his doctoral dissertation. Exposure to African children's songs served to further enculturate the future composer; according to Nketia, "Participation in children's games and stories incorporating songs enables [the child] to learn and sing in the style of his culture, just as he learns to speak its language."

Over the course of his career, Euba has become increasingly dedicated to the development of African musics in general. A proponent of creative ethnomusicology and musical interculturalism, he has responded to the implications of a global postmodern culture by writing music that functions on two social levels: (1) as a protective gesture that asserts a sense of African identity against a barrage of external influence and (2) as an agent of cultural vindication that argues against the outdated, European-based images of colonial and "third-world" Africa. Euba's scholarly efforts have further legitimized neo-African art music by giving it a history as well as a theorized aesthetic based on specifically African cultural values. He has also worked to bring traditional musics into Africa's primary and secondary school curricula.

In his analysis of neo-African art music, Euba has divided it into four main categories: (1) music based entirely on Western models in which the composer has not consciously introduced any African elements; (2) music in which thematic material is borrowed from African sources but is otherwise Western in idiom and instrumentation; (3) music in which African elements form an integral part of the idiom through the use of African instruments, texts, or stylistic concepts; and (4) music whose idiom is derived from African traditional culture, which employs African instruments, and in which the composer has not consciously introduced non-African ideas. This succession of categories also describes the course of his own musical growth.

Euba's European-based pieces (category 1), such as Introduction and Allegro for orchestra (1956) and the String Quartet (1957), are among his earliest student compositions. Written a few years later, his cello sonata, "The Wanderer" (1960), is based upon a Yoruba legend and quotes an African folk tune (category 2). First influenced by his research into African traditional music for the Nigerian Broadcasting Corporation (1957–65) and later by his academic studies in ethnomusicology (1962–74), which include a dissertation on Dundun drumming, Euba began to view his compositions as extensions of traditional African music. Works such as "Igi nla so" for piano and four African drums (1963) and *Chaka* (1970) create an African musical voice from a combination of European and African elements (category 3). *Abiku I,* composed for the dance-drama *Iya-Abiku* (1965), his University of California, Los Angeles master's thesis *Four Pieces for African Orchestra* (1966), and *The Laughing Tree* (1970) make exclusive use of African musical traditions (category 4). Although there are exceptions to this progression, Euba's artistic development from colonial to national parallels his homeland's political fortunes as his career bridged the shift in 1960 from Nigeria's subjugation to England to its current status as independent nation.

Euba's compositional approach involves two layers of signification and mediation that result in intercultural dialogue: the incorporation of African elements and the simultaneous use of and resistance to European classical models. His integration of African elements has become increasingly rich. Beginning with a preservationist approach, he set African folk songs to European-style piano accompaniments. He also sought intercultural synthesis by using African myths as a source of inspiration. Soon, however, the African drumming he learned as an ethnomusicologist began to dominate his musical thinking. He incorporated African instruments, especially drums, into his work and wrote "contemplative" music (as opposed to ritual or dance music) for traditional African ensembles. He also set neo-African poetry to music in hopes of following the successful path of modern African writers to the creation of an explicitly African idiom based upon the tonal characteristics of African language.

As his music's African voice grew stronger, Euba actively began to resist the dominating sound of European musical tradition, often by reinterpreting modernist techniques, such as *Sprechstimme* (speech song), indeterminacy, and improvisation, as a means of defamiliarization. Euba's use of 12-tone serialism reverses Schoenberg's intent to further the tradition of Brahms, Wagner, and Mahler, and radically reinterprets modernism as a strategy to resist the pull of European harmony. Finding precedent for an African atonality in the "shadow chord" behind a drumming ensemble, Euba adapts serialism's resistance to tonality for his own purposes. Even when he uses a 12-tone row to generate pitch materials, the European method does not control its use. Euba's serial compositions are sonic mosaics in which individual chips of tonally resistant melody form the larger patterns of the complete work. His tone rows are fragmented into smaller segments, overlaid with African rhythmic patterns, and then juxtaposed, layered, transposed, bent, and distorted, making the identification of the source row difficult.

The use of African traditional instruments in an intercultural context creates practical obstacles to performance. Euba borrows instruments from a wide variety of African nations, making groups of skilled performers difficult to assemble. Detailing varied oral traditions in written notation requires continual invention: many of Euba's Africanist pieces are essentially annotated scripts that use extensive improvisation, making the skilled performer even more essential to the work's realization. Euba has addressed these challenges by founding neo-African music ensembles, by using tape-recorded sounds when live performers are unavailable, and by adapting Western instruments, such as the piano, to uniquely African use. Euba coined the term "African pianism" in a 1970 essay entitled "Traditional Elements as the Basis of New African Art Music," reinterpreting the piano as an African percussive keyboard. Introduced by Western missionaries, the piano has been in use among Africans for two centuries. Expunging such Western concepts as authenticity and cultural pollution as essentially imperialist, Euba's African pianism validates the heterogeneity of contemporary African culture, fusing the traditional and the historically imposed into a rich cultural present.

Euba's aesthetic philosophy places the composer at the service of society, and many of his works carry political subtexts concerning freedom from Western domination. After Nigeria became independent, Euba focused on pan-African concerns, including anti-apartheid protest, through works such as the opera *Chaka*. Although he initially embraced the music of the European avant-garde, Euba's turn to African myths, pictorialism, theatrical works, traditional instruments, and songs with African texts signals an attempt to reach a broader African audience. Euba's *Wakar Duru* for piano solo (1987) translates pop accessibility to the keyboard through the use of a nondissonant idiom that embraces the melodies, harmonies, and rhythms of African popular musics, especially highlife. He has even composed pop tunes. Today, Euba's music effectively combines his modernist and populist impulses.

After a long hiatus, during which his academic career took precedence over composition, Euba has recently begun to revise and extend his musical approach. In 1988, he founded the Centre for Intercultural Music Arts in London and began to see his own aesthetic hurdles as part of a wider set of challenges to all composers in postmodern culture—African as well as Asian, South American, and European. Throughout his career, Euba has emphasized human themes that cross ethnic boundaries, such as birth, death, and children, revealing that interculturalism is fundamental to his aesthetic. Nevertheless, to overemphasize these "universal" aspects of his cultural project would obscure the achievements of a composer coming to terms with a very particular and extraordinary musical heritage.

THE WANDERER (1960)

As Euba's first original composition exploring elements of African culture, "The Wanderer," for cello and piano, marks a turning point in his career. Prior to 1960, Euba's role was primarily that of a Nigerian piano prodigy, and his compositions demonstrate mastery of European form and technique. Having lived his entire life under British colonial rule, Euba contributed his accomplishments to the argument supporting Nigeria's capacity for political self-determination. In 1960, the year "The Wanderer" was composed, Britain withdrew and Nigeria became independent, thus creating an opportunity for Euba to serve a new role as a composer forging a specifically Nigerian musical identity.

The work's premiere recording was commissioned by Radio Nigeria and executed in England. "The Wanderer" was to be broadcast as part of Nigeria's independence celebrations. While the commission sought to use Britain's waning influence to depict an image of Nigeria consonant with European cultural models, Euba found self-expression through the use of a traditional Yoruba song, "Okuta meta ona Ijofin/Three Stones on the Road to Ijofin." The text of this song reads: *Okuta meta ona Ijofin,/Okan gbun n lese/Okan ni imi a rora/Okan ni jigiragbada/lemi lo lese oru/Opopo omo, opopo omo/Emi le mise gbo o* (Three stones on the road to Ijofin,/One pierced my foot,/Another said, "Be Careful,"/The third demanded,/"What brings you out at peak of night?"/"Rituals for a child," I answered).

Not merely a source of melody, "Okuta meta ona Ijofin" provides the instrumental work's structural and emotional substance: "I was moved by the words of this song," Euba writes in the manuscript's preface, "and, though indicating no distinct story, they raised in my mind all kinds of ideas with regard to their meaning." On the surface, the song appears to depict an individual wandering along a road, performing a pilgrimage ritual for a child. It is not clear from the text whether this figure is a barren woman hoping to become pregnant (Euba's initial interpretation), if the child is sick and in need of a ritual cure, or if the child has died and is in need of a burial rite. Departing from this multivalent context, Euba views the stones as three manifestations of the same stone and makes this threefoldness a structural component of the work. On a symbolic level, this triplicity represents, according to Euba, "a trait which in human beings might be considered undesirable." This conflicted struggle with the question of triplicity could be autobiographical, as Euba's musical expression is torn by three forces: the self, the African, and the European. Biographical interpretation might view Euba as "the wanderer"—an artist moving across cultural boundaries in search of a compositional voice. Euba's professional career also attempts a difficult balance between three identities: composer, pianist, and scholar. A different interpretation privileging political context might consider the child to be the newborn independent nation of Nigeria. In political terms, the interference of a colonial government could introduce a third undesirable force between the government and people of Nigeria. Certainly, the introduction and first thematic area of the work's modified sonata form express struggle and conflict through striking dissonance and rapidly shifting asymmetrical meters. Euba's selection of sonata form reinforces the theme of triplicity, as this conventional European structure features three sections (exposition, development, and recapitulation) that present recurrent melodic material in different harmonic and transformational guises.

In many aspects, "The Wanderer" is a programmatic tone poem. The sonata encapsulates the folk song's narrative as the three appearances of the stone are reflected in the three-part recurrence of the sonata's melodic material. The introduction responds to the poem's dramatic shape, as piano and cello exchange unaccompanied solo statements, forming a conversational dialogue. The introduction's final, lyric cello solo, marked *Adagio assai, molto espressivo*, seems to evoke the protagonist's emotional response to the third stone's interrogation. With a return to the quick opening tempo, the piano extends the cello's melodic motive into a dramatic closing gesture punctuated by the cello's quintuplet exclamations. The next section, *Più allegro; con fuoco*, introduces the drumming, highly rhythmic first subject. Here, cello and piano begin in a tight rhythmic unison that soon explores the staggered, polyrhythmic attacks characteristic of African rhythm. The final result, however, owes more of a debt to Stravinsky than to the traditional African drumming of the composer's childhood memories, as Euba did not begin his ethnomusicological study of African drumming until 1962.

A radical shift in mood from anxiety to repose is created by the appearance in measure 97 of the Yoruba folk-song melody as the second subject. In sonata form, the harmonic tension associated to accompany the second subject usually creates a sense of departure. But Euba has undercut this harmonic convention to create a feeling of stability and arrival by using a slow tempo (*Largo*) and the consonant harmonies of the cello's triple-stop chords that decorate the folk melody. Generally, the work's harmonic idiom skirts European tonality through a linear conception of dissonant counterpoint in which nondiatonic melodies are punctuated by strident tone clusters that frustrate any sense of tonal center. However, when the form demands harmonic tension to accompany the second subject, Euba offers only harmonic tranquillity, ingeniously undercutting European tradition while highlighting the African melody.

Reflecting the conversational structure of the introduction, the cello and piano next alternate short solo gestures, the cello intoning phrases of the folk song and the piano echoing and commenting in a stubbornly dissonant voice. By marking the melody *rubato*, Euba gives the cellist some of the improvisational freedom of a ritual or folk performance in oral tradition. Euba soon cancels this marking and reintroduces the strict rhythmic interplay of his first subject against the lyricism of the second. The piano's quintuplets recall the anxious character of the opening and mark the beginning of the development section. After only 28 measures, the piano's opening fanfare chords return. Yet Euba's recapitulation is deceptive as the composer continues to rework and hybridize previous material. He even introduces new music: the piano's hesitant cadenza leads to a new percussive march theme. When the folk song finally returns, the piano and cello switch roles; the piano sounds the melody and the cello responds. In the coda, the piano recalls both the first subject and the march theme to accompany the cello's plaintive high-register solo. The work closes ambiguously, both harmonically and motivically, as the rhythmic pulse dissolves, the cello staggers between the two notes of a dissonant tritone interval, and the piano collapses with a cascade of descending fourths.

While pleased at its premiere, Euba became disenchanted with the work as it became clear that its European elements dominated the African in the ears of most listeners. Its unfamiliar timbres made the folk-song melody undetectable to African listeners, even to those familiar with the tune. One London critic wondered what the members of the African National Congress would think of Euba's European-based sonata. This lukewarm reception prompted Euba to search for additional strategies to make his music more accessible to his African audience.

THE PIANO COMPOSITIONS (1964–96)

Despite the piano's European heritage, Euba has treated the instrument as both a fundamental African voice and the ideal vehicle for intercultural exploration. Introduced to Nigeria in the mid-19th century by European missionaries, the keyboard was central to the establishment of a distinctly Nigerian tradition of performance and composition that began with church organists and composers such as Rev. Robert A. Coker, Thomas King Ekundayo Phillips, and especially Fela Sowande. As an intercultural instrument, the piano offers a composer such as Euba numerous pragmatic advantages: instruments and training are readily available in Nigeria (Euba grew up with a piano at home from the age of five and began lessons at eight); excellent performers for his music are found throughout the world; and Euba himself can perform at lectures about his piano compositions without the need to transport African instruments, find specialized performers, or rehearse musicians unfamiliar with African music.

Central to Euba's compositional thinking is his concept of "African pianism." (Although he coined the term in 1970, Euba was not the first to write African keyboard music.) His own earliest experiments with this genre date from 1964 and were inspired by his participation in the University of California, Los Angeles, African drumming ensemble. As defined by Euba, the elements of African pianism include "(i) thematic repetition, (ii) direct borrowing of thematic material (rhythmic and/or tonal) from African traditional sources, (iii) use of rhythmic and/or tonal motifs which, although not borrowed from specific traditional sources, are based on traditional idioms, (iv) percussive treatment of the piano, and (v) making the piano 'behave' like African instruments." According to Euba, as a percussion instrument, the piano adapts easily to an African aesthetic in which not only drums but also melodic instruments are frequently approached percussively. Euba has observed that polyrhythmic performance techniques of traditional African instruments such as the xylophone (e.g., the *ngedegwu* of the Igbo of Nigeria), thumb piano (e.g., the *mbira*), or the plucked lute (e.g., the *goge* of the Hausa of Nigeria) establish a firm basis for an African pianistic style.

Euba's six piano compositions cover the entire scope of his output and illustrate the development of his compositional approach. Euba's earliest studies in African pianism—*Four Pictures from Oyo Calabashes*, "Impressions from an Akwete Cloth," and "Saturday Night at the Caban Bamboo"—all date from 1964. In these works, Euba approached the keyboard "as if it were a set of drums," making use of repeated motivic cells that, as noted by Joshua Uzoigwe, present the illusion of communal drum ensemble performance through successive placement in contrasting registers. It is as if a rhythm is performed by one drummer and then passed among the other members of the ensemble. To create the illusion of a drum ensemble, in which each player has a different size drum that sounds a distinct pitch, Euba places these ostinato figures at various places on the keyboard, jumping from one pitch to another. The musical result is often that of a two-part invention for drum piano, featuring complex polyphonic interplay between the voices of each hand. Typically, each rhythmic motive retains its identity throughout the work as successive ideas create an ever-changing musical surface held together by repeated bass ostinatos.

Euba's acknowledged masterpiece, *Scenes from Traditional Life* (1970), has, in fact, no narrative or pictorial association, despite its association with Robert Schumann's *Scenes from Childhood*. Rather, the work extends African pianism into a modernist vein. The work's three untitled movements are based on a single 12-tone row. As detailed in Joshua Uzoigwe's analysis, Euba created 46 distinct rhythmic patterns either based on or borrowed from African drumming patterns. The first rhythmic motive of the work, for example, is borrowed from the first half of a Yoruba time-line pattern. Euba has assigned pitches from the 48 possible versions of the row to each of the rhythmic motives. Since the motives are short, each containing fewer than 12 pitches, the original row is fragmented beyond recognition. While rare examples of transposition and elaboration appear, the work is, on the whole, a collage of these rhythm and pitch amalgamations. Euba's use of serial technique frustrates the pull of European harmonic practice and brings his rhythmic ideas to the fore.

While the use of serialism might imply, for some, an entirely academic approach, many of Euba's piano works cross the boundary between classical and popular music by incorporating the rhythms of African popular music, especially highlife—the popular music of Euba's youth. "Saturday Night at the Caban Bamboo," for example, depicts a nightclub. Beginning on beat two, its third measure quotes a Ghanaian highlife bell pattern. Despite the serial idiom, the third movement of *Scenes from Traditional Life* also establishes a swinging rhythmic bass line. Composed in the style of a highlife bass, Euba's alternation between two bass motives, one beginning with a repeated pitch *e* and the second leaping up from

g-sharp, establishes two contrasting harmonic realms, yet without regard to functional harmony. This juxtaposition technique is adopted from highlife and juju harmonic practice.

Scenes from Traditional Life has been well received by European audiences and has entered the touring repertoire of such recitalists as the German concert pianist Peter Schmalfuss. Yet the piece has failed to reach African audiences, frustrating Euba's attempt to create a neo-African art music. Composed in 1987, *Wakar Duru: Studies in African Pianism, nos. 1–3* addresses the problem of audience by using a nondissonant idiom that Euba hoped would "make my work more approachable to audiences (particularly in Africa) who are unaccustomed to atonality." What is immediately striking about *Wakar Duru*, however, is not tonal harmony, but rather melody. Indeed, the title *Wakar Duru* could be translated as "Songs for Keyboard." Euba's earlier piano works highlight drumming patterns, whose interplay of brief rhythmic motives resists any semblance of song-like melody. The first movement of *Wakar Duru*, however, features an almost strophic conception, using a lengthy, 24-measure theme that recurs five times. The third study uses a melody that is already familiar to Euba's African audience—a quotation of "Omo laso," a hit song by the Nigerian highlife artist Ambrose Campbell. The three phrases of Campbell's melody appear in measures 5–12, 25–32, and 51–58 respectively.

Euba's most recent piano piece, "Themes from *Chaka* no. 1" (1996), bridges the gap between modernist and popular idioms. An original reworking of the themes from his opera *Chaka*, its single movement includes drumming patterns, 12-tone serialism, and lyric melody. The work's symbolic leitmotifs, such as the warlike "Chaka" or "conscience" theme that opens the piece and the graceful "Noliwe" theme of measures 413 and following, give the work an accessible melodic coherence. Euba's intercultural approach is evident from the extensive quotation and transformation of the *Dies irae* theme, a plainchant melody borrowed from the Roman Catholic mass for the dead. The use of this theme symbolizes, particularly in the Africanized rhythm of its first 6/8 appearance, both Britain's colonial presence and the martyrdom of the opera's main characters, the lovers Chaka and Noliwe.

OLUROUNBI: A SYMPHONIC STUDY ON A YORUBA LEGEND (1967)

Although written for an orchestra of exclusively European instruments, Euba's symphonic poem *Olurounbi: A Symphonic Study on a Yoruba Legend* exhibits a rich fusion of African and European musics. While Euba's String Quartet is essentially a European composition and "The Wanderer" adapts the European sonata as a vehicle for African expression, *Olurounbi* uses the European orchestra as if it were a traditional African ensemble. During the 1960s, Euba was concerned with writing exclusively for African instruments, but a commission from the United States Information Service requesting a symphonic work for a Voice of America radio broadcast entitled "Salute to Nigeria" prompted this work for European orchestra. The year 1967 marks not only the completion of *Olurounbi* but also the commencement of Euba's doctoral studies in ethnomusicology with J. H. Kwabena Nketia at the University of Legon, Ghana. *Olurounbi* reveals the artistic effects of the composer's research into traditional African musics, as well as his participation in the African drumming ensemble at the University of California, Los Angeles, in 1962–64 and 1965–66.

Based upon a Yoruba legend, the work "portray[s] the tragedy of *Olurounbi* and the anguish which faces her," according to the composer. Euba's program reads as follows:

> *Olurounbi* is a childless woman who goes to the powerful *Iroko* tree to pray for a child. Usually, women in her condition offer sacrifices of goats and sheep to the *Iroko* in order to have their wishes granted. However, *Olurounbi* is so anxious that she is prepared to offer anything; thus she promised to give her child to the *Iroko* after it is born. But when the child is born, she turns out to be so beautiful that *Olurounbi* is reluctant to give her up. Nevertheless, nobody makes vain promises to the *Iroko*: *Olurounbi* is forced to give up the child and she becomes childless once more.

By turning to a narrative, program music format, Euba accomplishes three goals: he begins the process of synthesizing African and European culture; he makes his music more accessible to an intercultural audience by depicting a story in sound rather than composing an abstract instrumental work; and he escapes the dictates of traditional European symphonic forms. Rather than a conventional European structure, such as sonata-allegro form, the shape of *Olurounbi* is dictated only by the dramatic requirements of the story. A single-movement work, *Olurounbi* moves in a three-part trajectory, Fast-Slow-Faster. The first and final sections are dances featuring the percussion section and are subtitled "Dances of Supplication" and "Sacrificial Dance." After the woman's wish is granted, a strident brass outburst punctuated by the full orchestra playing *fortississimo* (as loud as possible) reminds the listener of the Iroko's claim and a mother's agony. The slower central section represents the anguish of Olurounbi, forced to give up her child. Her lamentations are depicted by the woodwind choir and a series of lyric wind solos.

Euba features the percussion section in *Olurounbi*, treating it as an African drum ensemble. In such an ensemble, the master drummer often plays the largest and, hence, deepest-sounding instrument. Smaller, higher-pitched drums and bells perform less complicated, repeating ostinato patterns. Euba casts the timpanist of the orchestra as the master drummer, who begins the work with a timpani solo. The range of pitches available to the master drummer through damping and varied striking techniques are imitated on timpani by tuning three separate instruments: low (*g*), middle (*d*), and high (*f*). In traditional African performance, only the master drummer is allowed to freely improvise rhythmic gestures. With *Olurounbi*, however, Euba expands this improvisational role by writing variations into several parts. Unusually large, the percussion section includes tam tam, three timpani, snare drum (with snare disengaged), suspended cymbal, bass drum, triangle, wood block, xylophone, bongos, and maracas. Euba's complex polyrhythmic writing requires almost one percussionist per instrument.

For contrast, Euba leaves the percussion out of the work's central section. Yet, the role of the drum ensemble is picked up by the strings, who execute a percussive, although delicate and muted, ostinato pattern for much of the lament section. Euba sets the upper strings against the double bass in a polyrhythmic dialogue characteristic of African drumming. Points of attack alternate between the voices: when the upper strings sustain a pitch, the basses shift, and vice versa.

Throughout *Olurounbi*, Euba makes use of 12-tone serialism in order to avoid the sounds of European common practice harmony. The pitches performed by the wind and string sections are derived from a single row. Their rhythms, however, are not serialized but freely composed in polyrhythmic style. As Euba limits the timpani/master drum part to only three pitches, he must use other strategies to avoid the implication of major/minor harmony. In the typical European symphonic composition, the timpani reinforces tonal definition by sounding the structural pitches of the prevailing key, usually the tonic and dominant. Euba's timpani are tuned to a set of pitches that do not outline the guideposts of any functional European harmonic space. The dissonant interval of a seventh from *g* to *f* could function as a dominant of C major, yet the remaining pitch in Euba's set is not *c*, but *d*. Even if listeners hear *d* as the tonic, the atonal string writing following the opening timpani solo frustrates any latent harmonic implications.

While writing *Olurounbi*, Euba was also composing contemplative music for traditional African instruments and ensembles. For him, the European orchestra offered "an alternative language for African composers and not a substitute for traditional musical idioms." In contrast with his student days, Euba was now convinced that "African traditional music has such a wealth of untapped potential that there is no reason why it should not grow, as it has done before now, with little reference to foreign cultures." Although written for a European ensemble and performance context, *Olurounbi* does not represent a turning away from African traditional music. On the contrary, the tone poem makes use of traditional African musics on a deep, structural level. In *Olurounbi*, the timbre may be European, but the expression is in Euba's own intercultural voice.

CHAKA (1970; REVISED 1995)

When the White Voice spits out the first word of the libretto to *Chaka*, the principal questions of Euba's opera are set into motion: Who was Chaka? What does his life mean for contemporary society? Who has the authority to write history and decide? Based upon a poem of the same name by Leopold Sedar Senghor (b. 1906), president of Senegal at the time of Euba's first version and a prime mover of the pan-Africa movement, the opera recasts the history of Chaka as that of hero and martyr. Dedicated to the Bantu Martyrs of South Africa, the poem retells the story of a 19th-century king of the Zulu people, considered a blood-thirsty tyrant by European colonists. A brilliant military strategist, Chaka was among the first African leaders to resist the incursion of Europeans and the racist policies that became known as apartheid.

Euba adopts Senghor's narrative of Chaka's death as his libretto. The poem's first section, "Chant I," depicts the confrontation between the dying Chaka and a White Voice, which represents the colonial leaders who have engineered the warrior's assassination. "Chant II" is a love poem sung by Chaka to his now dead betrothed, Noliwe. As the curtain falls, Chaka dies of his wounds. Euba has interpolated another Senghor poem, "Man and the Beast" from *Ethiopiques*, as a bridge between Chants I and II. To Chant II, Euba has also added a eulogistic praise poem sung by a Yoruba chanter and the chorus, which represents Chaka's people. The praise poem was assembled from three sources: a poem composed by a traditional Yoruba chanter for the original 1970 production and two traditional praise poems collected during Euba's doctoral research, one for Oba Adetoyese Laoye, king of Ede, and another for Oba Adesoji Aderemi, king of Ile-Ife. The opera includes four primary characters and five main performers: Chaka (bass), the White Voice (a part split between two tenors), the Leader of the Chorus (bass or mezzo-soprano), and a Yoruba chanter. These characters are supported by dancers and a mixed chorus of adults and children.

The opera confronts apartheid and the misinformation that supports it by giving Chaka a voice, making him more human than myth. Chaka pleads his own case to an audience increasingly aware of the contradictions between the colonial and African versions of history. In the opera's 1995 version, the staging elucidates these historical contradictions by splitting the White Voice of Senghor's poem between two tenors, one dressed as a white British colonial officer and another as a black African chief. This African manifestation of the Voice represents Chaka's "conscience," his fears, and his understanding of the human and personal sacrifice necessary to confront the European invasion. Central to the White Voice's accusations of Chaka's inhumanity is the death of Noliwe. Chaka kills her after the sage Isanussi divines that Africa will be freed only if the warrior sacrifices "the blood of the dearest of all." While the White Voice concludes that Chaka must be incapable of love—a beast lusting only after power—Chaka replies that when confronted by colonial rule, "I became a mind, an untrembling arm. Neither a warrior nor a butcher. As you said, a politician, the poet I killed, a man of action alone. A man alone, dead already before the others, those you pity. Who will understand my passion?" Chaka's muse, his feeling, has died along with his love. Noliwe's death becomes, in a sense, his own suicide. Now, Chaka is pure will—a mind dedicated to the liberation of his people. Chaka's "passion" co-opts the Christian imagery of Christ's Passion, making Chaka's death an act of martyrdom and redemption for his people. His mocking references to the "politician" and the false pity of the White Voice redirect the accusations of inhumanity toward his executioners.

To avoid the clichés of European grand opera and heighten the emotional intensity of the text, Euba mixes three modes of vocal delivery: speech, chant, and song. By shifting quickly between modes, Euba highlights individual words and phrases critical to his interpretation. In Chaka's soliloquy quoted above, for example, Euba begins with speech mode, but shifts to song mode to emphasize Chaka's claim of being "neither a warrior nor a butcher." The use of song mode creates a sense of climax by a leap to the highest note of the passage on the words "dead already." The passion of Chaka's vocalism makes his humanity certain.

Euba's musical rhetoric also contributes to an understanding of Chaka's passion. To begin the prelude, a brass trio of trumpet, horn, and trombone sounds the Chaka "conscience" motive. This fanfare returns three times during the prelude in ever-increasing emotional turmoil. Euba shifts the motive off the beat, extends the cadence, and adds rhythmic complexity. In its fourth appearance, the horn sustains and produces a new melody. Here, the Chaka motive melts into the Noliwe theme, thus revealing the source of Chaka's anxiety.

For the accompanying orchestra, Euba combines European and traditional African instruments. Generally, the woodwind and brass trios play serial motives that help to dilute the tonal heritage of their European instrumental timbres. Euba frequently transforms the European winds into African percussion instruments through the use of staggered polyrhythmic attacks. Most prominent among the voices in the African ensemble are the nine drums and the ten *atentebens,* modernized versions of a traditional Ghanaian bamboo flute. More than coloristic timbres, these instruments become a source of traditional performance techniques, structures, and musical materials. For example, Euba borrows the first three *agogo* bell ostinatos from a traditional African time-line, the *Adowa* dance of the Ashanti (Ghana), and the *Atsiagbekor* dance of the Ewe (Ghana). In "Chant II," Euba's simultaneous layering of Chaka's love poem with the chanter's praise poem imitates the Yoruba festival practice of juxtaposing groups of performers playing in uncoordinated meters and tempos.

With *Chaka,* Euba turned away from the distancing effect of absolute music in favor of a narrative drama that could capture the attention of his African audience. First performed in a converted nightclub in Ile-Ife, Nigeria, *Chaka* has enjoyed broad popular appeal both in Africa and abroad due to its effective portrayal of powerful social themes. *Chaka* has been revised five times to fit changing performing resources and contexts, most recently in collaboration with Olusola Oyeleye for the City of Birmingham Touring Opera as part of the Africa '95 Festival.

REFERENCES

Agawu, Kofi. "Review of *Akin Euba: An Introduction to the Life and Music of a Nigerian Composer.*" *Research in African Literatures* 27, no 1 (1996): 232–236.

Alaja-Browne, Afolabi. "A History of Intercultural Art Music in Nigeria." In *Intercultural Music,* edited by Cynthia Tse Kimberlin and Akin Euba, 1: 79–86. Bayreuth African Studies Series. Beyreuth: E. Breitinger, 1995.

Baldacchino, John. "From 'African Pianism' to a New Commonwealth of Interculturalism." *Commonweath Music* 2 (1994): 2–5.

Euba, Akin. "Intercultural Expressions in Neo-African Art Music: Methods, Models and Means." In *Essays on Music in Africa: Intercultural Perspectives,* 2: 115–178. Lagos: Elekoto Music Centre, 1989.

———. Interview with the author, April 3, 1997.

———. "My Approach to Neo-African Music Theater." *In Essays on Music in Africa: Intercultural Perspectives,* 2: 74–114. Lagos: Elekoto Music Centre, 1989.

———. "Traditional Elements as the Basis of New African Art Music." *African Urban Studies* 5, no. 4 (1970): 52–62.

Irele, Abiola. "Is African Music Possible?" *Transition* 61 (1986–87): 56–71.

Nketia, Kwabena. *The Music of Africa.* New York: W. W. Norton, 1974.

Omojola, Bode. *Nigerian Art Music with an Introduction Study of Ghanaian Art Music.* Ibadan, Nigeria: Institut Français de Recherche en Afrique, 1995.

Uzoigwe, Joshua. *Akin Euba: An Introduction to the Life and Music of a Nigerian Composer.* Bayreuth: E. Breitinger, University of Beyreuth, 1992.

MARK CLAGUE

EUBANKS, RACHEL AMELIA

Born in San Jose, Calif. **Education:** Oakland, Calif., attended Roosevelt Junior High School and Oakland High School; University of California–Berkley, studied harmony with Edward G. Stricklen, counterpoint with David Boyden, orchestration and composition with Charles Cushing; B.A. (music theory and composition), 1945; Columbia University, New York City, studied composition with Douglas Moore, Otto Luening, and Normand Lockwood, orchestration with Randolph Thomas, music history with Paul Lang, also organ and ethnomusicology; M.A. (composition), 1947; Eastman School of Music, Rochester, N.Y., 1947; University of California–Berkeley, composition with Roger Sessions, 1948; Columbus, Ohio, studied organ at Capital University, 1949–50; Ohio State University, philosophy, religion, and economics, 1950–51; University of Southern California, film scoring with Miklós Rózsa, also studied organ, composition, completed all requirements except final draft of thesis for M.Mus. (church music), 1953–80; California State University–Los Angeles, education, language, 1954; University of California–Los Angeles, educational psychology, voice, electronic music, composition, ethnomusicology, and history of music theory, 1958–84; California State University–Long Beach, ethno-musicology, 1975; Westminster Choir College, music administration, 1976; American Conservatory, Fontainebleau, France, composition and analysis with Nadia Boulanger, summer 1977; Pacific Western University, Calif., D.M.A. (composition), 1979–80. **Composing and Performing Career:** Began composing, 1936; worked as a church organist. **Teaching Career:** Private piano instructor, 1940–45; Carmen Shepherd School of Music, New York City, taught piano, 1946–47; Albany State College, Albany, Ga., head of the department and associate professor of piano, theory, and choral music, 1947; New School of Music, Columbus, Ohio, founder, director, and associate professor of piano and theory, 1948; Wilberforce University, Wilberforce, Ohio, chairman and professor of theory, 1949–50; Los Angeles, Calif., founder, president, and professor of theory, composition, piano, and organ, Eubanks Conservatory of Music and Arts, since 1951. **Memberships:** Alpha Mu Honor Society; American Musicological Society; International Alliance for Women in Music; National Association of Music Teachers; Society of Ethnomusicology. **Honors/Awards:** Columbia University, Mosenthal Fellowship, 1946; National Association of Negro Musicians, Composition Award, 1948; Phelan Award (Honorable Mention). **Mailing Address:** 4928 Crenshaw Blvd., Los Angeles, CA 90043.

MUSIC LIST

INSTRUMENTAL SOLOS
Violin
Four Vietnamese Traditional Songs. 1992. Unpublished manuscript. Contents: Ruoc dèn tháng tám; Tháng cuôi; Dêm dông; Em bé quê.
"Kiep Nào Có Yeu Nhau." 1994. Unpublished manuscript. Note: melody by Pham Trong.
"Truöng Làng Tôi." 1994. Unpublished manuscript. Note: melody by Pham Trong.

Cello
Two Vietnamese Traditional Songs. 1992. Unpublished manuscript. Contents: La do muon chieu; Han do ban.

Oboe
"Kebili" (Intermezzo). 1995. Unpublished manuscript.

Piano
Five Interludes for Piano. 1984. Pullman, Wa.: Vivace Press, 1995. Recorded: (nos. 1 and 5) Leonarda CD-LE339.
Intermezzo. 1956. Unpublished manuscript.
Prelude. Oakland, Ca.: Music Mart, 1940.
"Postludium." 1995. Unpublished manuscript.
Sonata. 1992. Unpublished manuscript. Premiere, 1993.
"Waters of the Ganges." 1936. Unpublished manuscript.

Organ
Easter Suite. 1995. Unpublished manuscript. Contents: Palm Sunday; Last Supper; Crucifixion; Resurrection.

SMALL INSTRUMENTAL ENSEMBLE
Combinations
Trio for Clarinet, Violin, and Piano. 1977. Unpublished manuscript. Contents: Adagio con expressione; Allegro; Lento. Premiere, 1977.
"Xuân Ca" (two violins, cello, piano). 1992. Unpublished manuscript. Note: melody by Pham Duy.

ORCHESTRA (CHAMBER OR FULL) WITH SOLOISTS
Symphonic Requiem (four solo voices, orchestra). 1980. Unpublished manuscript. Note: Ph.D. diss., Pacific Western University, 1980. Premiere, 1980.

SOLO VOICE
"Autumn" (medium voice). Unpublished manuscript.
"By the Riverside" (bass/baritone). 1984. Unpublished manuscript. Also in a version for voice, pipa, and piano.
"A Curious Cloud" (high voice). 1948. Unpublished manuscript.
"Deus" (high voice). 1952. Unpublished manuscript.
"God" (medium voice). 1953. Unpublished manuscript.
"Heavy Snow" (bass/baritone). 1984. Unpublished manuscript.
"I Don't Feel Noways Tired" (medium voice). 1956. Unpublished manuscript.
"I've Been in the Storm So Long" (medium voice). 1955. Unpublished manuscript.
"Interlude no. 1" (medium voice). 1948. Unpublished manuscript.
"Interlude no. 2" (high voice). 1956. Unpublished manuscript.
"Like Rain It Sounded" (medium voice). 1952. Unpublished manuscript.
"The Sea Gull" (medium voice). 1954. Unpublished manuscript.

VOICE WITH INSTRUMENTAL ENSEMBLE
"Our God" (baritone, flute, gongs, gamelan, vibraphone, piano). 1984. Unpublished manuscript.

CHORAL MUSIC

"Attitude, Respect, Confidence." Unpublished manuscript.

"Be Still." 1956. Unpublished manuscript.

"Bless the Lord." 1958. Unpublished manuscript.

"Blessed Art Thou." Unpublished manuscript.

"A Christmas Folksong." 1956. Unpublished manuscript. Also in a version
    for medium voice.

"Commit Thy Way unto the Lord." 1957. Unpublished manuscript.

"Delight Thyself Also on the Lord." 1958. Unpublished manuscript.

"Inside the Eagle's Nest." 1984. Unpublished manuscript.

"Let the Children Come to Me" (SA). 1954. Unpublished
    manuscript.

"Peace I Leave with You." 1953. Unpublished manuscript.

"Psalm Eighty-four." 1955. Unpublished manuscript.

"Purple Straight-grown Bamboo Shoot" (SAT, flute). 1986. Unpublished
    manuscript.

"Saeya saeya" (Old bird) (SA). 1986. Unpublished manuscript.

"Sanctus." 1958. Unpublished manuscript.

"Shepherd of Eager Youth." 1955. Unpublished manuscript.

"We're Stepping Out." 1985. Unpublished manuscript.

"Zun nurgas visulin garlvdn" (Nine of us have left). 1986. Unpublished
    manuscript.

DRAMATIC MUSIC

Ode to Joy (cantata for chorus, orchestra). 1947. Unpublished manuscript.

PUBLICATIONS

BY EUBANKS

Musicianship. 1956. 2 vols.

PRINCIPAL ARCHIVES

Rachel Eubanks, Los Angeles, California

* * * * *

The compositions of Rachel Eubanks include sacred and secular works in many genres: songs, choral music, solo instrumental works, music for instrumental ensemble, cantatas, and orchestral works. Encompassing a variety of compositional techniques, they are intellectually challenging and emotionally engaging and exhibit a wide variety of ethnic influences. In many ways they are a reflection of her activities as a musician, ethnomusicologist, educator, and administrator.

The remarkable breadth of her interests and experiences began to be developed in her youth in Oakland, California. Born in San Jose, she moved with her family first to San Francisco when she was three or four, then to Oakland, where she attended Manzanita, Lockwood, and Allendale elementary schools, Roosevelt Junior High School, and Oakland High School. She began to play the alto horn and the clarinet while still in elementary school, and her parents regularly took her and her two brothers to operas at the Scottish Rite Auditorium in Oakland and to concerts at the Oakland Auditorium and the Greek Theater in Berkeley. Rachel began piano lessons at age eight; in college she began extensive organ studies while continuing to study the piano.

Her mother, a native of San Francisco, nurtured the international and artistic side of her children's education, taking them to museums, subscribing to the *National Geographic* magazine, and introducing them to family friends from many different backgrounds. Rachel had close friends who lived in Chinatown and recalls the appeal of the Chinese music she heard there. The travel accounts of a family missionary friend who had been to India inspired Rachel's first serious composition, "Waters of the Ganges" for solo piano (ca. 1936), composed when she was in her early teens. Later, while a graduate student at Columbia University in New York City, she often visited Chinatown and saw Chinese opera. At Columbia she studied ethnomusicology and subsequently traveled to many parts of the world, collecting musical instruments and recording the music that she heard. These experiences gave her the expertise that enables her to compose in traditional ethnic styles.

At the University of California–Berkeley, Eubanks studied undergraduate composition and orchestration with Charles Cushing, continuing in her master's degree work at Columbia University with Otto Luening, Douglas Moore, Seth Bingham, Randolph Thomas, and Normand Lockwood. While at Columbia, she taught at the Carmen Shepherd School of Music in New York City. After graduation, she attended the Eastman School of Music and moved to Georgia, where she served briefly as head of the music department at Albany State College. She returned to the University of California for a year to study composition with Roger Sessions and then moved on to Wilberforce University, Wilberforce, Ohio, to chair its music department. While in Ohio, she attended classes in philosophy, religion, and economics at Ohio State University and took organ lessons at Capitol University in Columbus. With this background, Eubanks determined to start her own independent school in California.

The Eubanks Conservatory of Music and Arts, which she founded in 1951, has grown from its humble beginnings as an independent studio in her living room into a substantial institution offering state-approved bachelor's and master's degrees in music and boasting a faculty drawn from the Los Angeles Philharmonic Orchestra and outstanding jazz musicians of the area. Its curriculum emphasizes an integrated perspective that includes the development of critical and analytical approaches to knowledge and the understanding of the essential nature and history of society. The conservatory is affiliated with the Korean Philharmonic Orchestra and the Korean Opera Company, and its museum collection of musical instruments contains items gathered in the course of Eubanks' travels to many countries.

At each stage of her professional career, Rachel Eubanks has continued to pursue knowledge of all kinds, taking courses at one time or another at California State University–Los Angeles; California State University–Long Beach; Westminster Choir College, Princeton, New Jersey; the American Conservatory, Fontainebleau, France; the University of California–Los Angeles; and the University of Southern California.

Eubanks' output begins with her "Prelude" for solo piano, published by Music Mart in 1942, and extends through the 1990s. She lists among her early influences the compositional styles of William Walton and Igor Stravinsky, particularly their harmonic

Rachel Amelia Eubanks; courtesy of Helen Walker-Hill

progressions and orchestration. These influences can be seen in the orchestral nature of her writing for chamber ensemble and in the extraordinary demands made on the performers to exploit the full range and textural possibilities of their instruments. From 1958 to 1976, she was involved in composing commercial and pedagogical piano music. Her educational and musicological compositions include her two-volume textbook, *Musicianship* (1956), and her choral works in Chinese and Korean traditional style composed for the courses in ethnomusicology. Some of the latter are "Saeva, Saeva" (Old bird), a traditional Korean lullaby arranged for sopranos, altos, flute, and piano; "Zun Nutgas Yisulin Garldvdn" (Nine of us are left), a traditional Oirat melody arranged for mixed chorus and piano; and "Purple Straight-Grown Bamboo Shoot," a traditional Chinese lullaby from Peking arranged for sopranos, altos, flute, and piano. Her involvement in church music began in her childhood, when she played piano for Sunday School and church services and at Sunday afternoon concerts. It has continued through her work as a church organist and her graduate studies in all aspects of church music at the University of Southern California; it has also found expression in her many sacred compositions. These have formed a great part of her compositional output, dating from her cantata, *Ode to Joy* of 1947, through her many arrangements during the 1950s of spirituals for both solo voice and chorus, her doctoral dissertation (the *Symphonic Requiem* of 1980), and numerous sacred choral works, to the *Easter Suite* for organ (1995). A number of these works combine Christian forms and texts with those of other religious traditions. *Our God,* on a text by Kahlil Gibran, is scored for baritone and Western and Indonesian instruments: flute, gongs, gamelan, vibraphone, and piano. Indonesian traditions are tapped further in Eubanks' use of gamelan stratification, pentatonic scales, and chanting vocal style. Her willingness to explore uncharted musical territory and her responsiveness to specific needs are illustrated by her settings of Vietnamese folksongs for violin and cello with piano accompaniment, composed for three of her Vietnamese students. Secular art works for voice, chorus, piano, and chamber ensemble complete her oeuvre. Characterized by intellectual rigor, spiritual and emotional depth, and reflective of the international experiences of their composer, her compositions are satisfying and worthy additions to the repertories of their respective media.

FIVE INTERLUDES FOR PIANO (1984)

Intellectual rigor and intense expressivity are combined in these five short pieces. The moods range from quiet and introverted to forceful and dramatic. While they vary in technical difficulty from moderate to considerable, they all require interpretive maturity and sensitivity from the performer. The pitch and dynamic range of the work is wide. Although there are few themes as such, similar intervallic cells are employed in all five movements. Changing meters prevail throughout.

The first interlude (*Moderato*), the shortest at one page long, is expressively tranquil. Gently dissonant, its quartal harmonies are presented in a soft dynamic level and *legato* articulation and suggest pensiveness rather than confrontation. The intervallic cells are mostly melodic rather than harmonic and are widely spread by octave displacements. This piece has a more open and relaxed feeling than the subsequent movements, while presaging what is to come in the intervals of its melody (combinations of fourths and fifths with half-steps).

The second interlude (*Moderato*) is more mysterious and concentrated, its mood intensified by doublings and smaller intervals (whole and half-steps) winding in closely convoluted melodic contours. Unlike the others, this second interlude has a strong sense of tonality, created by the reiterated *f* in the bass.

The closeness of the intervals (minor seconds and major or minor thirds) becomes even tighter in the agitated third interlude (*Moderato*). It opens and closes with tentative, fragmentary, repeated three-note phrases, building to *fortissimo* before subsiding and closing tentatively, as it began.

The tension that builds through the second and third pieces climaxes in the fourth (*Larghetto*), released in forceful, short phrases in octaves punctuated by exclamatory chords in which the intervallic cells of the first three pieces coalesce in hard-driving repeated patterns.

The fifth and final piece (*Larghetto*) is a contrast in texture and mood to all the others, particularly the fourth, climactic interlude. The intervallic cells, in the preceding work tight and intense, are now spread out in an expansive song-like melody in the right hand over a wide-ranging 16th-note accompaniment that meanders dreamily and mysteriously over most of the keyboard. Near the end, the melody shifts to expressively undulating triplet eighths before a quiet, mysterious close.

SONATA FOR PIANO (1992)

The Sonata for Piano is a two-movement work of approximately 20 minutes duration. The first movement, predominantly lyrical, is in sonata-allegro form and the second, more angular and percussive, is sectional (ABCDA). The two movements are tied together by the use of close (half-step and whole-step) motives that appear in their melodic material. The first movement adheres to the traditional format of exposition, development, recapitulation, and coda, but with some interesting variations upon the expected classical formula. Instead of the usual contrast between a "masculine" (assertive) Theme I and "feminine" (lyrical) Theme II, both main themes are lyrical. The development, instead of a concentrated motivic reworking such as one might expect in Beethoven or Haydn, provides contrast through a more transparent texture—a freer, more rhapsodic treatment of the themes.

The sparse intervallic and motivic structure of the themes promotes both homogeneity and variety, since the simplicity of the material allows for many permutations. The opening 21-bar theme consists of three phrases. It begins with four descending notes (the top four of the F-sharp Dorian scale), which are immediately repeated with the addition of chromatic half steps between them and which complete the descending scale. This expressively mournful melody is accompanied by six-note chords of a thick and richly chromatic texture. The theme continues in a second phrase with the same overall contour but with a greater variety of intervals that lend it more intensity. The third phrase repeats the first, this time in octaves, and ends with an extension in widely-spaced chords that build to a climax. Theme II opens with an upward leap (a fifth) that provides motivic material for both the melody and the accompaniment. The texture is more contrapuntal, and the phrases are interrupted by soft, mysterious arpeggiation that, becoming more elaborate, turns into undulating double fourth figurations.

The development reduces the themes to their initial motives, which are this time accompanied by figuration that becomes more and more elaborate and rhapsodic. The accompaniment gradually becomes the main material, spun out in a transparent, wide-ranging filigree. Theme II is the first to be developed, leading climactically to the return of Theme I's descending four-note motive repeated in rising sequence and culminating in rapid virtuoso scales.

In the recapitulation, Theme I starts in A minor (the "wrong" key) for two measures before reestablishing the original key of F-sharp major as the tonal center. With the second phrase, the accompaniment changes to a broken chord figuration that takes on the character of a counterpoint, and the recapitulation of Theme I becomes another development. Theme II is also varied and developed—doubled in octaves, its elaborations more intense—building to a coda in which the first four notes of Theme I return, doubled powerfully in treble chords that alternate antiphonally with a bass-chord pedal point. These continue to build in reiteration and dynamic level to the end.

The second movement of the sonata was composed in response to the Los Angeles riots of 1992 and expresses utter chaos, hopelessness, and despair. Its musical language is atonal and polytonal. (In the score, there are no sharps or flats in the treble/right-hand staff, and there are five sharps in the bass/left-hand staff.) The overall texture is dominated by vertical sound masses—sequences of chords containing massed, close intervals (dissonant seconds, and blocks of hand and arm clusters). Section A, marked *Lento*, begins after a five-measure introduction of ominous atonal cluster sonorities. Its theme, recalling the falling chromaticism of Theme I of the first movement, gathers clusters as it progresses. The succeeding B section accelerates to *Allegro*, with sharply accented dissonant chords in dotted rhythms. Section C is *Presto* with rapidly alternating clusters in both hands, which expand in widening leaps to arm clusters at the extremes of the keyboard. After a final, long-held treble arm cluster, Section D returns to *Lento* with a mournful ostinato falling figure that recalls the opening of the first movement. This leads into the last A (*Lento*) section, which recapitulates the opening material.

TRIO FOR CLARINET, VIOLIN, AND PIANO (1977)

This trio, 25 minutes long and in three movements (*Adagio con espressione, Allegro,* and *Lento*), begins quietly, as two principal motives are introduced in flowing three- and four-part counterpoint. The first motive outlines a gently rising and falling phrase spanning an octave, while the other, shorter motive answers with a terse repeated 16th-note figure. The instruments "converse," sometimes in alternating dialogue, more often all together. The motives are repeated more insistently and build in intensity. The melodic lines become more continuous and the texture thicker as all the instruments play simultaneously and the piano doubles its melody with chords, piling up blocks of sonorities. After a climax in which the repeated 16th-note motive is extended into continu-

ous figurations by all the instruments, then further intensified in double stop clarinet and violin tremolos, the movement subsides to end quietly.

The second movement, *Allegro,* is in 6/8 meter in the bright, open sound of the Dorian mode, evoking a medieval folk dance. It begins with a continuous, repetitive, triplet eighth-note accompaniment pattern, which moves in contrary motion in the piano and is accompanied by *pizzicato* double stops in the violin. The clarinet introduces a cheerful dance melody of narrow span and repeated motives. The rondo form is in five parts (ABACA) with the alternating episodes in simple meters, slower tempos, and plaintive, longer-flowing melodies in exotic gapped modes. On return, the A section is varied in figuration and texture.

The third movement, *Lento,* is in theme and variations form. The introductory motive is evocative of spirituals in its rising and falling thirds and in its call-and-response between the piano and the other two instruments. The melodic material uses fragments from Roman Catholic hymns that the composer heard during her travels in France. The theme itself dominates the entire movement and is identifiable in each of the variations. As the variations build, massive layers of shimmering sounds are piled up in octave doublings and figuration in the piano, and in the violin's double, triple, and quadruple stops. The texture of the movement finally thins and subsides to a quiet close.

SYMPHONIC REQUIEM (1980)

The *Symphonic Requiem* for orchestra and four solo voices is a 45-minute work in four movements. Two of the movements are based on the proper of the Mass (Introit, Offertorium), and two are based on the ordinary of the Mass (Sanctus, Agnus Dei). The work differs from other requiems in several respects: (1) the omission of portions of the liturgy; (2) the sources of the musical material; (3) the relationship of the voices to the orchestra; (4) the treatment of the text; and (5) the special effects employed.

Only portions of the Requiem Mass are used, and the Dies Irae has been omitted. The organization of the remaining sections into four movements suggests the four-movement structure of the symphony in the standard 19th-century sense; however, the tempi of the movements (primarily *largo*) do not reflect symphonic form.

The sources of Eubanks' musical material include not only Gregorian plainsong but also the Ethiopian Orthodox Mass, African-American spirituals, and Tibetan Buddhist chant. The composer uses the slow, sustained, and almost monotone Tibetan chant not only to create a calm, solemn mood but also to express the eternal sound of "aum," the eternal, divine essence of man. She cites the universality of this philosophy as the reason for combining musical themes and instruments of the East and West in this work.

The relationship of the voices is subordinate to the orchestra. Because this work is primarily a symphonic interpretation of the Requiem, the voices are treated as the vocal color of the instrumentation. They are not used at all in the second movement, the instrumental Offertorium. In the treatment of the text, English and Latin versions of the text are used alternately.

Special effects include the use of small Tibetan and Indian bells and the Ethiopian sistrum. Western instruments are played in unusual ways: the piano strings are struck with the open palms of both hands moving apart, and descending *glissandos* in the extreme low registers of the woodwinds, brass, strings, piano, and harp evoke an Eastern vocal style. In the first movement, pitch changes by microtonal increments are used in the trombones, cellos, and basses; this device was derived from a practice in the Ethiopian Orthodox Mass (originating in the ancient Byzantine chant), which was observed by the composer when she visited Ethiopia in 1972.

The first movement, Introit-Kyrie, opens with the Tibetan Buddhist chant "The Eternal Voice." Like Benjamin Britten's *War Requiem* (1961), it begins on *d*. But whereas the *War Requiem* begins with a seven-measure pedal tone on *d,* the *Symphonic Requiem* opens with 18 measures on *d* in the low register of the brass and woodwinds before ascending one-half step to *e*-flat, joined by tenor and bass. After 26 more measures, the piece ascends to *e,* at which point the alto joins the tenor and bass and then returns to *e*-flat and *d* just as slowly. A melodic response from the Ethiopian Mass is also heard in the first movement. This two-note response of an ascending minor third corresponds to the same interval in the more rhythmic African-American spirituals in the second movement. The Introit and Kyrie are combined in an ABA form. Passages alternating instrumental and vocal treatment flow smoothly from one to another.

The second movement, the instrumental Offertorium, is also in ABA form, and opens with the "Eternal Voice" chant for 18 measures in a high register of the violins. It is combined, at the end of the movement, with a Gregorian plainsong melody. There are also references to two spirituals in the second movement: "I've Been in the Storm So Long," and "I Want to Make Heaven My Home."

The third movement, Sanctus, gradually abandons the slow, sustained mood with a rhythmic climax created by an Indian *tala* (an abstract pattern of beats that serves as a time frame) superimposed upon a Western metrical rhythm. This movement also features an appearance of the Roman Catholic Sanctus Dominus Deus Sabaoth.

The fourth movement, the Agnus Dei, is in theme-and-variation form. "The Eternal Voice" reappears in the violins, then in the flutes, and then in the horns before, at the very end, it is transposed simultaneously up a major third (and down a minor sixth) in high and low registers. The variations flow smoothly from one to the next, each developing a particular melodic, harmonic, or rhythmic characteristic of the previous variation.

The *Symphonic Requiem* is highly innovative, both in overall concept and in its details. The ecumenical inclusiveness of its musical and philosophical approaches to the ancient Roman Catholic Requiem Mass may well be unprecedented in contemporary music. This work admirably sums up the global scope of Rachel Eubanks' life and work.

REFERENCES

Eubanks Conservatory of Music and Art Catalog. Los Angeles, Calif.: Eubanks Conservatory of Music, 1974.

Eubanks, Rachel. Correspondence with the author, April 24, 1991.

———. Telephone interview with the author, October 14, 1995.

———. Correspondence with the author, October 20, 1995.

HELEN WALKER-HILL

EUROPE, JAMES REESE

Born in Mobile, Ala., February 22, 1880; died in Boston, Mass., May 9, 1919. **Education:** Born into a musical family; educated in Washington, D.C. public schools; studied composition, piano, and violin with Enrico Hurlei and Joseph Douglass, ca. 1895; New York City, studied with Melville Charlton and Harry T. Burleigh, ca. 1903. **Military service:** Bandmaster for the 369th Infantry Regiment ("Hellfighters") in World War I. **Composing and Performing Career:** New York, established himself as a composer of popular songs and instrumentals and as musical director of major black theater productions including John Larkins's *A Trip to Africa* (1904), S. H. Dudley's *The Black Politician* (1904–08), Cole and Johnson's *Shoo-Fly Regiment* (1906–07), and *Red Moon* (1908–09), and Bert Williams's *Mr. Lode of Koal* (1909); joined Ernest Hogan's Memphis Students, 1905; founded the Clef Club, a union and booking agency for black musicians, 1910; organized and conducted annual concerts of African-American music at Carnegie Hall by the large Clef Club Symphony Orchestra, 1912–13, and the National Negro Symphony Orchestra, 1914; musical director with Ford Dabney of the team of Vernon and Irene Castle, 1913–14; Victor offered the first major recording contract for a black orchestra, 1913; principal composer and orchestra conductor for dancers Irene and Vernon Castle, 1913–16; continued to compose marches, dances, and songs and to collaborate with artists such as Ford Dabney, Eubie Blake, Noble Sissle, Henry Creamer, and Bob Cole; New York, recorded for Pathé, 1919.

MUSIC LIST

SONGS

"Ada, My Sweet Potater." 1908. New York: Joseph W. Stern, 1908. Note: from *The Red Moon.* Premiere, 1908.

"All of No Man's Land Is Ours." New York: M. Witmark, 1919. Co-composer, Eubie Blake. Recorded: Pathé Frere 22104-A.

"Arizona." New York: Sol Bloom, 1904.

"At that San Francisco Fair." n.p.: T. B. Harms and Francis, Day and Hunter, 1915. Note: from *Nobody Home.*

"Ballin' the Jack." 1913. New York: Jos. W. Stern, 1913. Co-composer, Chris Smith. Note: from *The Darktown Follies; The Girl from Utah.*

"Benefactors, A March." Unpublished manuscript. Premiere, 1913.

"Blue Eyed Sue." New York: Sol Bloom, 1904.

"Boy of Mine." 1915. n.p.: T. B. Harms, Francis, Day and Hunter. Co-composer, Ford Dabney.

"Breezy Rag." Unpublished manuscript. Premiere, 1913.

"Castle Combination Waltz." New York: Joseph W. Stern, 1914. Co-composer, Ford Dabney. Published version arranged for solo piano.

"The Castle Doggy Fox Trot." New York: Ricordi, 1915. Published version arranged for solo piano. Recorded: Herwin Records H-407.

"Castle House Rag: Trot and One-Step." 1913. New York: Joseph W. Stern, 1914. Co-composer, Ford Dabney. Published version arranged for solo piano. Recorded: New World NW269; RCA ARL1-0364.

"Castle Innovation Tango." New York: Joseph W. Stern, 1914. Co-composer, Ford Dabney. Published version arranged for solo piano.

"Castle Lame Duck Waltz" or "Congratulations." New York: Joseph W. Stern, 1914. Co-composer, Ford Dabney. Published version arranged for solo piano. Recorded: Victor 35372-A.

"Castle Maxixe." New York: Joseph W. Stern, 1914. Co-composer, Ford Dabney. Published version arranged for solo piano.

"Castle Perfect Trot: One Step." New York: Joseph W. Stern, 1914. Co-composer, Ford Dabney. Published version arranged for solo piano.

"Castle Walk." New York: Joseph W. Stern, 1914. Co-composer, Ford Dabney. Published version arranged for solo piano.

"Castle Walk: Trot and One-Step." 1914. New York: Joseph W. Stern, 1914. Co-composer, Ford Dabney. Note: for orchestra. Recorded: New World NW269.

"Castles' Half and Half." New York: Joseph W. Stern, 1914. Co-composer, Ford Dabney. Published version arranged for solo piano. Recorded: Vanguard VSD 79429.

"Castles in Europe." New York: Joseph W. Stern, 1914. Co-composer, Ford Dabney. Published version arranged for solo piano.

"Clef Club: Grand March and Two-step." 1910. New York: F. B. Haviland, 1910. Published version arranged for solo piano.

"Come, Cinda Be My Bride." New York: Sol Bloom, 1904.

"The Coon Band Parade." New York: Sol Bloom, 1905.

"The Darktown Band." Note: from *The Black Politician.*

"The Darktown Strutters' Ball." Recorded: Saydisc SDL 221.

"Don't Take Him Away." Note: from *The Black Politician.*

"Down Manila Bay." Note: from *The Black Politician.*

"Droop Dem Eyes." 1912. New York: Waterson, Berlin and Snyder, 1912.

"Election Time." Note: from *The Black Politician.*

"Father's Gone to the War." New York: Ricordi, 1915.

"Fiora: Valse." 1914. New York: G. Ricordi, 1914. Published version arranged for solo piano. Recorded: Victor 35372-A.

"Follow On: March Song." New York: Ricordi, 1915.

"Fox Trot." 1914. Unpublished manuscript.

"Good Night Angeline." New York: M. Witmark, 1919. Co-composer, Eubie Blake. Note: from *Shuffle Along.*

"Good-bye My Honey, I'm Gone." New York: Joseph W. Stern, 1918. Co-composer, Eubie Blake.

"Help Yourself." Note: from *The Black Politician.*

"Hey, There!" New York: Ricordi, 1915.

"Hezekiah" or "Hezekiah Doo." Note: from *The Black Politician.*

"Hi, There!" New York: Ricordi, 1915.

"Hilo: Hawaiian Waltz." New York: Ricordi, 1916.

"A Hot Step." Unpublished manuscript. Premiere, 1913.

"Hula, Hawaiian Dance." Unpublished manuscript. Premiere, 1912.

"I Ain't Had No Lovin' in a Long Time." 1908. New York: Joseph W. Stern, ca. 1908. Note: from *The Red Moon.* Premiere, 1908.

"I Must Have Somone Who Loves Me." 1915. New York: Ricordi, 1915.

"I'll Hit the Homeward Trail." New York: Ricordi, 1915.

"I've Got the Finest Man." New York: Waterson, Berlin and Snyder, 1912.

"I've Got the Lovin'es' Love for You." New York: Joseph W. Stern, 1918. Co-composer, Eubie Blake.

"Likin' Ain't Like Lovin'." Note: from *The Black Politician.*

"Lolita." Note: from *The Black Politician.*

"Lorraine Waltzes." Unpublished manuscript. Premiere, 1911.

"Mirandy, That Gal o' Mine." New York: Joseph W. Stern, 1918. Co-composer, Eubie Blake. Recorded: New World 260; Pathé Frere 22089-A.

"Monkey Doodle." New York: Ricordi, 1915.

"My Heart Goes Thumping and Bumping for You." New York: Sol Bloom, 1904.

"Myosotis Waltz." New York: Ricordi, 1915.

"The Nell Rose Waltz." Unpublished manuscript. Premiere, 1914.

"Nubiana." New York: Sol Bloom, 1904. Published version arranged for solo piano.

"Obadiah (You Took Advantage of Me)." New York: Gotham Music, 1905.

"Oh, Silvery Star." 1912. New York: Joseph W. Stern, 1912.

"Old Black Crow" or "Crow." Note: from *The Black Politician.*

"On Patrol in No Man's Land." ca. 1918. New York: M. Witmark, 1919. Co-composer, Eubie Blake. Note: from *Shuffle Along.* Recorded: New World 260; Pathé Frere 22089-B.

"On the Gay Luneta." 1906. New York: Joseph W. Stern, ca. 1906. Note: from *The Shoo-Fly Regiment.*

"Picanninny Days" or "Pickaninny Days." 1908. New York: Jerome H. Remick, 1909. Note: from *The Red Moon.* Premiere, 1908.

"Pliney, Come Out in the Moonlight." Note: from *The Red Moon.*

"Queen Louise." New York: Ricordi, 1915.

"Queen of the Nile." Unpublished manuscript. Premiere, 1910.

"Races, Races." Note: from *The Black Politician.*

"Rat-a-Tat Drummer Boy." New York: Ricordi, 1915.

"Red Moon." Note: from *The Red Moon.*

"Rouge et noir." New York: Ricordi, 1915.

"A Royal Coon." Chicago: Will Rossiter, 1907.

"Sambo." 1908. New York: Joseph W. Stern, ca. 1908. Note: from *The Red Moon.* Premiere, 1908.

"School Days" or "I Don't Like School." Note: from *The Black Politician.*

"The Separate Battalion." Unpublished manuscript. Premiere, 1911.

"The Smart Set Carbineers." Note: from *The Black Politician.*

"Society." Note: from *The Black Politician.*

"Someday You'll Want a Home of Your Own." New York: Ricordi, 1915.

"Someone Is Waiting Down in Tennessee." 1913. New York: Waterson, Berlin and Snyder, 1913.

"Spooney Sam." Note: from *The Black Politician.*

"Strength of the Nation." Unpublished manuscript. Premiere, 1911.

"Suwanee River." Note: from *The Black Politician.*

"Sweet Suzanne." New York: F. B. Haviland, 1910.

"Syncopated Minuet." New York: Ricordi, 1915.

"Take Him Away, the Law Commands It." Note: from *The Black Politician.*

"Tinkle a Little Tune." New York: Ricordi, 1915.

"Valse Marguerite." New York: Joseph W. Stern, 1914.

"The Victor." Unpublished manuscript.

"Wait for Me." 1915. New York: Ricordi, 1915.

"What It Takes to Make Me Love You, You've Got It." New York: Joseph W. Stern, ca. 1914.

"When I Rule the Town." Note: from *The Black Politician.*

"When the Moon Plays Peek a Boo." Note: from *The Black Politician.*

"Zola: Jungle Song." New York: Sol Bloom, 1904.

MUSICAL THEATER

The Black Politician (musical comedy). 1904–08. Premiere, 1904.

Darkydom or Darkeydom (musical revue). Co-composer, Will Marion Cook. Premiere, 1915.

PUBLICATIONS

ABOUT EUROPE
Books and Monographs

Badger, Reid. *A Life in Ragtime: A Biography of James Reese Europe.* New York: Oxford University Press, 1995.

Sissle, Noble Lee. "Memoirs of Lieutenant 'Jim' Europe." Unpublished manuscript held at Library of Congress.

Articles

Badger, Reid R. "James Reese Europe and the Prehistory of Jazz." In *Jazz in Mind: Essays on the History and Meanings of Jazz,* edited by Reginald T. Buckner and Steven Weiland, 19–37. Detroit: Wayne State University, 1991.

Goines, Leonard, and Mikki Shepard. "James Reese Europe and His Impact on the New York Scene." *Black Music Research Bulletin* 10, no. 2 (1988): 6–8.

Shirley, Wayne D. "The House of Melody: A List of Publications of the Gotham-Attucks Music Company at the Library of Congress." *Black Perspective in Music* 15, no. 1 (1987): 79–112.

Tirro, Frank. "Music of the American Dream: Brass Traditions and Golden Visions." *New Perspectives on Music: Essays in Honor of Eileen Southern,* edited by Josephine Wright, with Samuel A. Floyd Jr., 213–227. Warren, Mich.: Harmonie Press, 1992.

Welburn, Ron. "James Reese Europe and the Infancy of Jazz Criticism." *Black Music Research Journal* 7 (1987): 35–44.

BY EUROPE

"A Negro Explains Jazz." *Literary Digest* (April 26, 1919). Reprinted in *Readings in Black American Music,* edited by Eileen Southern, 240. New York: W. W. Norton, 1983.

"Negro Composer on Race's Music." *New York Tribune* (November 22, 1914). Reprinted in. *Reminiscing with Sissle and Blake,* 64. New York: Viking, 1973.

"Negro's Place in Music." *New York Evening Post* (March 13, 1914). Reprinted in *Reminiscing with Sissle and Blake,* edited by Robert Kimball and William Bolcom, 60–61. New York: Viking, 1973.

* * * * *

In his short lifetime, James Reese Europe was both a famous bandleader and a successful composer of popular songs, dance pieces, and marches; and some of his music continues to be performed by ragtime pianists, historic repertory ensembles, and military bands. Europe's greatest contributions to American musical culture, however, derive primarily from his championing of African-American musical expression in all of its forms—folk, popular, and symphonic—and from his remarkable success in engaging both others of his own race and those of the majority culture in his vision. Europe's pioneering efforts during the first and second decades of the 20th century led "New Negro" spokesman Alain Locke to include him among his four "arrangers of genius," who "organized Negro music out of a broken, musically illiterate dialect and made

James Reese Europe; courtesy of the Reid Badger Collection, Moorland-Spingarn Research Center, Howard University

it a national music with its own peculiar idioms of harmony, instrumentation, and technical style of playing." A major figure in the transformation of orchestral ragtime into jazz, Europe helped to open so many doors for the music of black Americans to be heard that pianist-composer Eubie Blake would later claim, with reason, that he was the Martin Luther King of black American musicians.

A member of the first generation born in the South after Reconstruction, Europe's early childhood was spent in Mobile, Alabama. His parents were both religious and musical, and his mother provided regular piano instruction for all of her five children. As a youngster, Europe was also drawn to fiddle and banjo music and to that of the brass bands that accompanied the popular cadet drill contests in the port city. In 1890, when his family moved to Washington, D.C., Europe continued his musical instruction as a student of concert violinist Joseph Douglass, grandson of Frederick Douglass, and Enrico Hurlei, assistant director of the U.S. Marine Corps Band. Reports suggest that he also studied briefly with Hans Hanke, a former member of the faculty of the Leipzig Conservatory. In 1894, at the age of 14, Europe gave his first public recital, performing a violin duet with his younger sister, and that same year won a prize for composition.

Upon the unexpected death of his father and following in the path of his older brother, a ragtime pianist, Europe left Washington in 1903 for the brighter prospects of New York City, which had emerged as the center for black professional musicians and entertainers. It did not take long for Europe to establish himself. In 1904, he was asked by John Larkins to direct the orchestra and chorus for a musical farce called *A Trip to Africa,* and the following year he joined Will Marion Cook, Abbie Mitchell, and Will Dixon in Ernest Hogan's famous Memphis Students troupe. Although he studied occasionally with Harry T. Burleigh, a former student of Dvořák during the Czech composer's tenure as director of the National Conservatory, and with Melville Charlton, the noted organist at St. Phillips Episcopal Church, for the next six years Europe's musical education came primarily from the challenges of being musical director for a series of important black musical theater productions; conducting, arranging, and writing for large touring companies led by such talented entertainers as Bob Cole, J. Rosamond Johnson, George Walker, Bert Williams, and S. H. Dudley served as his music conservatory.

Despite its popularity in the first decade of the century, black musical comedy entered a difficult period beginning in the spring of 1910. But the demand for black instrumentalists and singers for high society functions and for the expanding public nightlife of the city had never been greater. In order to capitalize on the situation, Europe organized and became president of the Clef Club, a combination of social club and booking agency and the first organization in New York's history to effectively improve working conditions for black musicians. (During its thirty-year life, the Clef Club included many of the most important performer-composers in the city, among them Will Marion Cook, Joe Jordan, William Tyers, James "Tim" Brymn, Ford Dabney, Clarence Williams, Henry Creamer, and Fletcher Henderson.) As leader of the Clef Club, Europe created something entirely new—a large, symphony-sized concert orchestra dedicated to the performance of the music of black Americans. Consisting of 125 singers and instrumentalists, the Clef Club

Orchestra played its historic first "Symphony of Negro Music" at Carnegie Hall on May 2, 1912, featuring compositions by Will Marion Cook, Harry T. Burleigh, J. Rosamond Johnson, William Tyers, Samuel Coleridge-Taylor, and himself. Between 1910 and 1915, Europe led several large, string-dominated ensembles that appeared in popular concerts before black and white audiences in New York and on tour of major cities in the eastern United States. Europe intended these orchestras to showcase the recent compositions of black composers and to demonstrate the orchestral skills of black performers. The list of such composers whose works were performed by his orchestras (many for the first time, often conducted by the composer) includes Harry T. Burleigh, Will Marion Cook, Will Vodery, Samuel Coleridge-Taylor, Paul C. Bohlen, Hugh Woolford, Luckey Roberts, Will Dixon, Al Johns, Ford Dabney, Joe Jordan, William Bryan, J. Rosamond Johnson, and William Tyers. Several of the works that were given exposure by Europe's orchestras (those by Jordan, Cook, and Burleigh, in particular) continued to be performed in later years.

In the fall of 1913, during the height of the prewar ragtime dance craze, Europe and fellow Clef Club member Ford Dabney became musical directors for the leading demonstration dancers of the time—Vernon and Irene Castle, with whom Europe's Society Orchestra toured the country. The most famous of the original Castle dances, the fox-trot, was the result of a collaboration between Europe, Vernon Castle, and blues composer W. C. Handy. Europe and his Society Orchestra recorded ten sides of dance music for Victor Records between December 1913 and October 1914; it was the first contract given by a major company to a black orchestra.

During World War I, Europe enlisted in the 15th Infantry Regiment of the New York National Guard, the first black unit organized in the state. Later, when the regiment was sent to the battlefields of France, he distinguished himself as a soldier (the first African-American officer to lead troops into conflict in the war) and as leader of the American Expeditionary Force's most celebrated Army band, which among others is credited with introducing French and British audiences to the live sounds of orchestrated ragtime, blues, and the new music called "jazz."

Dubbed by the newspapers in the United States as "America's first 'Jazz King,'" Jim Europe was tragically killed while on tour with his band in the spring of 1919; he was 39 years of age. One of his ambitions—that of seeing the establishment of a permanently funded symphony orchestra committed to performing the music of African-American composers—has yet to be fulfilled, but another— that of seeing African-American musical comedy restored to Broadway—was realized when his closest musical associates Eubie Blake and Noble Sissle brought *Shuffle Along,* with William Grant Still and Hall Johnson in the orchestra, to the Sixty-third Street Theatre on May 23, 1921. A generous man, when some of the pieces he wrote during World War I were later published, Europe also insisted that his friends and musical associates, Blake and Sissle, be listed as joint composers, regardless of their actual contributions.

ON THE GAY LUNETA (1906)

During his 16-year musical career in New York City, James Reese Europe played a major role in the development of American popular musical taste and expression. Though relatively few of his nearly 100 published popular songs, marches, concert waltzes, rags, and other dance pieces enjoyed major commercial success, they do demonstrate his ability to write charming melodies in the popular style of the day and to effectively interpolate new rhythmic elements derived from traditional African-American dance practice. Most of the several dozen song and dance numbers that he composed and arranged for black musical theater productions between 1905 and 1910 were never published, but one of those—"On the Gay Luneta" from Cole and Johnson's *The Shoo-Fly Regiment* of 1906—does provide evidence of Europe's skill in writing for the musical stage.

"On the Gay Luneta," with exceedingly sentimental lyrics by Bob Cole, is a lament for lost love, in this case a charming "Manila Belle." This song, comprised of a fairly standard 16-measure verse and 16-measure chorus, was sung in the second act of the musical, which, set in the Philippines, chronicles the poignancy of a brief moonlight encounter. The *habanera* rhythm in the bass line of the verse lends a Spanish feeling to the piece, and Europe's contrasting and musically interesting rhythms (the seductive *habanera,* especially) help save the lyrics by giving the song a degree of emotional sophistication. Musically, the most successful song of *The Shoo-Fly Regiment* was J. Rosamond Johnson's art song "Lit'l Girl" (lyrics by Paul Laurence Dunbar), but "On the Gay Luneta" was also a popular hit.

HI! THERE! (1915)

James Reese Europe was noted throughout his career for writing melodic, inspiring concert marches in the manner of John Philip Sousa, to whom he was occasionally compared. The brass band and march music reached their peak of popularity between 1890 and World War I and were embraced equally by white and black Americans. Europe's earliest march compositions were often written to celebrate a particular event or dedicated to a particularly worthy group of individuals. "The Separate Battalion" (1911) was dedicated to the High School Cadets of Washington, D.C., "Strength of the Nation" (1911) to the proposed black National Guard regiment for New York state, and "Benefactors, A March" (1913) to the philanthropists who supported the establishment of the Music School Settlement for Colored People in Harlem.

"Hi! There!," written for Europe's 100-piece Tempo Club Orchestra, was composed during the period of Europe's heaviest involvement with dance music, and in its looser, more swinging rhythmic conception, general playfulness, and absence of pretension (witness the title) reflects something of an influence of the popular dances. Described in the sheet music as a "One Step—March," the piece is a standard. It follows a four-part, three-theme (AABBAA'CC) pattern characteristic of both the march and of ragtime; like a rag, it is written in 2/4 time and employs a good deal of off-beat accenting. Europe was clearly manipulating in new and clever ways musical materials that were familiar to his audiences. The piece begins with quote from "The Star Spangled Banner," concludes with a quote from the last strain of Sousa's "Stars and Stripes Forever," and in between makes references to "Yankee Doodle" and "Dixie." Europe quotes with affection rather than ridicule, all the while, however, undermining the reverential pomp and stiff-

ness often associated with the performance of such nationalistic pieces. Such treatment strengthens the loosely swinging, playful feeling of his own composition.

For the July 14, 1989, recreation of Europe's historic first Clef Club Concert at Carnegie Hall (1912), conductor-arranger Maurice Peress selected Europe's "Hi! There!" for the closing number of the program because the music for the original finale—Europe's "Strength of the Nation"—is lost and because he felt that "Hi! There!" had the feel of a "good closer." It also reveals, Peress later commented on the National Public Radio rebroadcast of the concert, Europe "showing off a bit" by demonstrating his ability to "manipulate musical materials in a very conscious way." By making new music out of old and familiar material, Europe points toward a direction that would eventually include such highly developed artists as Louis Armstrong, Jelly Roll Morton, and Duke Ellington. "Hi! There!," which Europe copyrighted and published in 1915, is not a major work, but it does show the value he placed upon musical novelty and play.

CASTLE HOUSE RAG (1913)

"Castle House Rag," an instrumental one-step or turkey trot, was Europe's best-known composition during his lifetime and remains his most enduring to this day. It was written in late 1913 (copyright 1914) on the occasion of the opening of the Castle House, a school for social dance that the wildly popular Vernon and Irene Castle had established on East 46th Street in New York. Europe, along with Ford Dabney, wrote many syncopated dance pieces for the Castles, including "Castle Walk," "Castles' in Europe," "Castle Lame Duck Waltz," "Castle Innovation Tango," and "Castles' Half and Half," the latter piece carrying an unusual 5/4 time signature. "Castle House Rag," however, soon became the couple's signature piece. Written in 4/4 meter, it is nonetheless a classic rag which, in the published sheet music, consists of three contrasting themes (AABBACC') and concludes with an eight-measure chromatic break and a repeat of the C' strain. In "Castle House Rag," the A and B themes are in the key of C, but the A strain shifts back and forth between major and minor chords employing lowered third and seventh scale steps, interestingly suggesting spirituals and the blues. The third strain, a stop-time trio, is written in the contrasting key of F. As a piano piece, it is fresh and enjoyable to play and is often included in classic ragtime collections.

"Castle House Rag" was one of the four tunes that Europe and his Society Orchestra recorded for Victor in February of 1914, and a comparison of the written and the recorded versions of the piece is revealing. One obvious difference is that the tempo of the Society Orchestra's recording is very fast, much faster than the *Allegro moderato* instructions on the sheet music would seem to require. In his program notes for the Black Music Repertory Ensemble's 1989 slower recording of "Castle House Rag," Samuel A. Floyd Jr. suggests that the faster tempo of the original Europe recording may have been due to the constraints of the 78 recording process at the time. But speed is not the only difference in the written and recorded versions. In the recording, the first three strains are performed much as written, in the same AABBACC' sequence, and Europe alters the instrumentation giving some contrast to the different strains. The drums, for example, are absent in the trio (or C strain). From this point on, however, the recorded version goes its own separate way, and the orchestra, following the cornet's lead, plays an increasingly wild fourth strain that does not appear in the sheet music but which sounds very much like a variation of Wilbur Sweatman's "Down Home Rag," a piece the orchestra had recorded earlier. Drum breaks dominate a "ferociously wild climax," which may be the first of its kind on record. Moreover, as Lawrence Gushee suggests in his liner notes to the New World Record reissue, "with half a minute of recording time left, Europe may have let his band loose for three choruses of ad-hoc basic rag, accidentally transmitting to us the only example from its time of orchestral ragtime extemporization." If Gushee is correct, then, "Castle House Rag" is a very important composition because it constitutes the first recorded example of a piece of music that was, in part at least, composed during performance and thus initiated the recorded road toward jazz.

ON PATROL IN NO MAN'S LAND (1919)

"On Patrol in No Man's Land," which Europe began composing while recovering from the effects of a gas attack he suffered in France during the war, is as close to a vaudeville novelty number as he ever wrote. Its strictly musical interest is certainly limited as compared to its social and cultural importance; but it does reflect something of Europe's ability to translate personal experience into musical expression, and it is representative of the type of song that he wrote while serving in World War I ("Good-bye My Honey, I'm Gone" and "All of No Man's Land Is Ours" are other examples).

"On Patrol in No Man's Land" is a verse/chorus song in which the lyrics clearly determine the character of the musical accompaniment. The verse is basically spoken rather than sung, and the main melody of the chorus is reminiscent of the first strain of Europe and Ford Dabney's "Castle Walk" of 1914.

Europe may have arranged "On Patrol in No Man's Land" for his 369th Infantry Regiment "Hellfighters" Band during the time they were causing a sensation in Paris during the late summer of 1918. But it is likely, given its character, that he did not begin performing it until after returning to the United States in February of 1919. "On Patrol in No Man's Land" was performed by Europe (piano) and Sissle (vocal)—with flashing lights, sirens, and cymbal crashes—toward the end of each concert during the spring 1919 "Hellfighters" tour of the East and Midwest. Europe also included the piece, with Sissle as lead vocalist, among the two dozen recordings he and the band made for Pathé Records during the same

period. The recorded performance is lively, the sound effects (bombs, machine guns, etc.) well done, and at the climax, Sissle leads the cheering bandmembers "over the top" against an unfortunate enemy. "On Patrol in No Man's Land" remained popular for several years after Europe's death. Sissle and Blake performed it as the finale in their vaudeville act for a year and a half and even interpolated it into their path-breaking 1921 musical *Shuffle Along*.

Undoubtedly, the most interesting and important aspects of the music Europe wrote, arranged, and performed with the Hellfighters Band overseas, in the United States, and on record, are those that reflect the kind of instrumental interpretation that he was then consciously developing and which was being referred to by the term "jazz." Though the "On Patrol in No Man's Land" recording that Europe and the Hellfighters made in March of 1919 exhibits few jazz elements, the band's instrumental recordings made at the same time (especially of blues like "St. Louis Blues," "Memphis Blues," or "Hesitating Blues," all written by Europe's friend W. C. Handy) provide strong evidence of jazz interpretation, including paraphrased and sometimes improvised solo breaks by his instrumentalists. Thus, they are in part new compositions, new works created in the process of being performed, and the line between composition and performance, therefore, becomes very narrow indeed.

REFERENCES

Badger, Reid. *A Life in Ragtime: A Biography of James Reese Europe.* New York: Oxford University Press, 1995.

Floyd, Samuel A., Jr. Liner notes, *Black Music: The Written Tradition.* Black Music Repertory Ensemble. Center for Black Music Research CBMR001, 1990.

Grayck, Tim, and Brad Kay. Liner notes, *Lieut. Jim Europe's 369th U.S. Infantry "Hellfighters" Band.* Memphis Archives MA 7020, 1996.

Gushee, Lawrence. Liner notes, *Steppin' on the Gas: Rags to Jazz.* New World Records NW 269, 1976.

Locke, Alain. *The Negro and His Music.* Washington, D.C.: Associates in Negro Folk Education, 1936. Reprint, New York: Arno Press and the *New York Times,* 1969.

Peress, Maurice. Radio broadcast, *Performance Today,* National Public Radio, May 2, 1992.

Riis, Thomas. *Just Before Jazz: Black Musical Theater in New York, 1890–1915.* Washington, D.C.: Smithsonian Institution Press, 1989.

REID BADGER

FAÍLDE PÉREZ, MIGUEL

Born in Matanzas, Cuba, December 23, 1852; died in Matanzas, December 26, 1921. **Education:** Received his first musical education from his father, Cándido Faílde; studied harmony and composition with Federico Peclier, 1864. **Composing and Performing Career:** Matanzas Firemen's Municipal Band, played cornet, 1864; played variously the cornet, double bass, viola, violin, and piano in bands and orchestras; founded Los Faílde, served as conductor and cornetist, 1871–1920; composed first Cuban *danzón*, "Las Alturas de Simpson," ca. 1879. **Teaching Career:** Gave music classes in his home as a youth; Academia de Música del Cuerpo de Bomberos (Music Academy of the Firemen's Corps).

MUSIC LIST

DANCE ORCHESTRA

"A galleta vieja no hay que mirarle el gorgojo" (danzón). Premiere, 1892.

"A La Habana me voy" (danzón). Premiere, 1903.

"A la Sambambé" (danzón). Premiere, 1898.

"¿A mí qué me dices?" (danzón). Premiere, 1889.

"Abrete, penca de guano" (danzón). Premiere, 1891.

"Adelante, Directiva" (danzón). Premiere, 1894.

"Aflójate un cancharrazo" (danzón). Premiere, 1893.

"Ahora veremos" (danzón). Premiere, 1889.

"Ahueca, mujer, ahueca" (danzón).

"Las Alturas de Simpson" (danzón). ca. 1879. Premiere, 1879.

"El amolador" (danzón). Premiere, 1904.

"Angeles neopoblanos" (danzón). Premiere, 1889.

"Antón Pirulero" (danzón). Premiere, 1879.

"¡Aprieta Miguelito!" (danzón). Premiere, 1891.

"Aurora" (danzón). Premiere, 1892.

"Ausencia" (song). 1910.

"Ayayay, cómo baila Carmita" (danzón). Premiere, 1889.

"Los Bacocó" (danzón).

"El bandullo de José María" (danzón). 1879.

"La Belén" (march). Premiere, 1881.

"El Bill de Kinley" (danzón). Premiere, 1891.

"Los bohemios" (danzón).

"La bollera" (danzón).

"La brujería de la mulata" (danzón). Premiere, 1902.

"Los bueyes no mascan andullo" (danzón). Premiere, 1902.

"¡Cá, hombre, cá!" (danzón). Premiere, 1888.

"Calentico, maní tostao" (danzón). Premiere, 1895.

"Camaleón, deja las moscas" (danzón). Premiere, 1889.

"Carlos Morales" (danzón).

"Caterwich" (danzón). Premiere, 1890.

"Chacho" (danzón).

"El Champion" (danzón). Premiere, 1890.

"Los chinos" (danzón). Note: performed on April 3, 1886.

"Chocolate de Ametller" (danzón). Premiere, 1895.

"Círculo de artesanos" (danzón). Premiere, 1905.

"El Club Artesanos" (danzón).

"El Club Mercado" (danzón).

"El Comercio" (danzón). 1887.

"Con palo no, salao, si me das te entrego al celador" (danzón). Premiere, 1898.

"Con quién se casa Miguelito, con Petronila Pinto" (danzón).

"Con un perro chico se come galleta" (danzón). Premiere, 1891.

"Concertante" (danzón). Note: performed on October 8, 1899.

"El conuco de Fabián" (danzón).

"Cuadrilla." Premiere, 1874.

"Cuando escupas para arriba, zafa el cuerpo" (danzón). Premiere, 1891.

"Cuando vengan los perros grandes comerás de mi ajiaquito" (danzón). Premiere, 1891.

"Cuba libre" (danzón). Premiere, 1902.

"De la azucena el perfume y de la playa la brisa" (danzón). Premiere, 1891.

"De la Tribuna a la Romería" (danzón). Premiere, 1903.

"Delicias de la armonía" (danzón). Premiere, 1891.

"El dengue se pega" (danzón). Premiere, 1890.

"El desengaño" (waltz). Premiere, 1873.

"Día y noche" (danzón).

"El diablo me lleve" (danzón).

"La diosa japonesa" (danzón).

"Las dos mascotas" (danzón). Premiere, 1901.

"El de los cinco tríos" (danzón). Premiere, 1901.

"El envidioso" (danzón). Premiere, 1901.

"Los espejuelos de palacio" (danzón). Premiere, 1890.

"El espíritu del hombre no muere" (danzón).

"El que le debe a los muertos no pisa el suelo" (danzón).

"El que mira con ojos de caimán no sabe comer arroz con leche" (danzón). Premiere, 1892.

"Figurín, se acabó el merengue" (danzón). Premiere, 1887.

"Florita" (polka-song).

"4,000 guaguarnacos" (danza). Premiere, 1893.

"Los frijoles" (danzón). Premiere, 1892.

"Fuego tanillo" (danzón).

"El Ganyá" (danzón).

"El gato prieto come guabina" (danzón). Premiere, 1893.

"La Gran potpourri." Note: performed on October 10, 1908.

"La Gran Vía" (danzón). Premiere, 1888.

"La Guabina" (danzón). 1880.

"La habanera." Premiere, 1885.

"Helado, helado" (danzón). Premiere, 1891.

"El hombre es débil" (danzón). Premiere, 1879.

"El Jai Alai" (danzón). Premiere, 1902.

"José Ramón" (danzón).

"La jota aragonesa" (danzón). Premiere, 1892.

"Juanita" (danzón).

"Julio Ceijas" (danzón). Premiere, 1912.

"Liceo de Versalles" (danzón). Premiere, 1903.

"Linda cubana" (danzón).

"Lirita" (danzón).

"Llegué, vi y . . . me reventaron allí" (danzón). Premiere, 1889.

"La luz eléctrica" (danzón). Premiere, 1890.

"La malagueña" (danzón). Premiere, 1903.

"El Malakoff" (danzón).

"El malombe" (danzón). Premiere, 1902.

"El manisero" (danzón).

"Manuel García" (danzón).

"Los Mary Bruni" (danzón).

"Los mascavidrios" (danzón). Premiere, 1879.

"Mi chamalaco" (danzón).

"El mondonguito" (danzón). Premiere, 1880.

"El mudo dice lo que mira el ciego" (danzón). Premiere, 1891.

"Mulero" (danzón). Premiere, 1898.

"El naranjero" (danzón).

"El negro bueno" (danzón).

"Niña Pancha" (danzón). Premiere, 1888.

"No aguanto" (danzón).

"No hay contras" (danzón). Premiere, 1888.

"No juegues con los cheques" (danza). Premiere, 1873.

"No me botes, botoncito" (danzón). Premiere, 1887.

"No me mires con ojos de mamey colorado" (danzón). Premiere, 1891.

"No se puede pedir más" (danzón). Premiere, 1893.

"La ocarina" (danzón). Premiere, 1890.

"Los panaderos" (danzón). Premiere, 1898.

"Papá yo quiero galones" (danzón). Premiere, 1883.

"El papalote" (danzón).

"Paracaídas" (danza). Premiere, 1893.

"Piña, mamey y zapote" (danzón). Premiere, 1901.

"El Pirulero" (danzón). Premiere, 1911.

"¿Un plátano por medio? ¡Te embromaste, tasajo brujo!" (danzón). Premiere, 1892.

"Por nuestra parte sin novedad" (danzón). Premiere, 1895.

"Puerto Rico" (danzón). Premiere, 1889.

"¿Quién dijo miedo?" (danzón). Premiere, 1892.

"Quirina en la rumba" (danzón).

"Quítate el antifaz" (danzón). Premiere, 1890.

"Los rasca tripas" (danzón).

"La Recholata" (danzón).

"Reglita" (danzón). Note: performed on April 14, 1887.

"Respuesta a Yaka-Hula" (danzón).

"Resuélvete, Pepito" (danzón). Premiere, 1895.

"Resumen de un baile" (danzón). Premiere, 1899.

"La Revolución del 93" (danzón). Premiere, 1890.

"La roncha" (danzón). Premiere, 1890.

"Rusia y Japón" (danzón). Premiere, 1904.

"La sardina" (danzón). Premiere, 1879.

"Sr. Biscochuiti, arrempújeme un cigarro" (danzón). Premiere, 1891.

"Si la cebolla no pica, ¿por qué se te aguan los ojos?" (danzón). Premiere, 1891.

"El silencio" (danzón).

"Sin carboneras" (danzón). Premiere, 1901.

"La Sociedad Liceo de Matanzas" (danzón).

"Suprímeme todo, menos la comida" (danzón). Premiere, 1892.

"Terina" (danzón).

"Los tirabuzones" (danzón). 1880.

"Toros de punta" (danzón). Premiere, 1888.

"Trabajar, compañeros, trabajar" (danzón). Premiere, 1890.

"Los Tres Manolos" (danzón). Premiere, 1909.

"Tú estabas así, y yo estaba 'asao', vino el tomate y arrancó la verdolaga. ¡Reviéntate, cigüeña!" (danzón). Premiere, 1893.

Miguel Faílde Pérez; courtesy of Instituto Cubano Libro

"Los turcos" (danzón).

"Vals, sin nombre (waltz)." 1874.

"Vals tropical (waltz)."

"¡Venga el dúo!" (danzón). Premiere, 1891.

"Ventura" (danzón).

"La Virgen de Regla" (danzón).

"Yaka-Hula" (danzón).

"El Yambú" (danzón). Premiere, 1880.

"Yo me voy para el otro mundo" (danzón).

"Yo no me pongo chapa" (danzón). Premiere, 1901.

"Yo no puedo comer sin aguacate" (danzón). Premiere, 1888.

"Yo salgo y entro en todos lados porque a mí no me gobiernan las mujeres" (danzón). Premiere, 1901.

"Záfate" (danzón). Premiere, 1892.

"El zuncho de goma" (danzón).

PUBLICATIONS

ABOUT FAÍLDE PÉREZ
Books and Monographs

Castillo Faílde, Osvaldo. *Miguel Faílde, creador musical del danzón.* Havana: Editora del Consejo Nacional de Cultura, 1964.

PRINCIPAL ARCHIVES

Cándido Faílde, private collection

Centro de Investigación e Información de la Música Miguel Faílde,
    Matanzas, Cuba
Museo Nacional de la Música, Havana, Cuba

* * * * *

As the creator of the *danzón,* the musical and dance genre recognized as the national dance of Cuba, Miguel Faílde Pérez is considered to be one of the most outstanding Cuban musicians of the 19th century. His orchestra was very popular, and he was recognized in various regions of the country as a composer.

Faílde took his first music lessons from his father, the Galician trombonist Cándido Faílde. In 1864, he attended classes in harmony given by the French professor Federico Peclier. From a very early age, he was distinguished by his interpretive gifts, mastering the cornet, double bass, viola, violin, and piano. Faílde played the cornet in the Banda Municipal de Bomberos de Matanzas (Matanzas' Firemen's Municipal Band) and in other bands and dance orchestras. He also played the violin in chamber ensembles. While still very young, he began to give music classes in his home and in the Academia de Música del Cuerpo de Bomberos (Music Academy of the Firemen's Corps). Faílde was a tailor by trade.

During the period of Spanish domination in Cuba (16th-19th centuries), many of the dance orchestras were made up largely of free Negroes and mulattos, who were also dedicated to artisanal activities such as shoemaking, tailoring, or carpentry. The profession of musician was little rewarded, lacked social prestige, and was considered to be an artisan trade. The Negro and Creole mulattos brought a peculiar rhythm and timbre to original European forms and organized the musical content in a fresh way, and their participation in ensembles determined the stylistic features of much popular Cuban music.

In 1871, Miguel Faílde founded an *orquesta típica* (typical dance orchestra) that was initially known as Los Faílde, for which he acted as director and in which he played the cornet. His brothers Cándido (trombone) and Eduardo (second clarinet) were also members of the group, along with Pancho Morales (first violin), Juan Cantero (second violin), Anselmo Casalin (first clarinet), Pascual Carreras (ophicleide), Eulogio Garrido (double bass), Andrés Segovia (kettledrums), and Isidro Acosta (*güiro,* a notched gourd that is rasped with a stick). Other musicians who later achieved fame as instrumentalists and composers of *danzones,* such as Raimundo Velanzuela (1848–1905) and Aniceto Díaz (1881–1964), also played in this orchestra.

Faílde worked uninterruptedly for almost 50 years, playing at school and society dances and festivities of various kinds. He was an extremely prolific composer of *contradanzas, danzas,* waltzes, *pasodobles,* marches, and numerous other instrumental pieces for band. The titles of many of these scores are known, but documentary evidence of the majority of them has not survived. Among the most popular are "Florita," a polka-song; "Vals tropical" and "Vals, sin nombre" (1874), waltzes; "No juegues con los cheques," a *danza* (1873); "El desengaño," a waltz (1873); "La Belén," a march (1881); "Cuadrilla" (1874); "La habanera" (1885); and "La Gran potpourri" (ca. 1908). But his most outstanding work is to be found in the musical genre of *danzón,* a genre that emerged from the assimilation and modification of the famed Creole *danzas* and *contradanzas* that were so enjoyed in the Cuban dance halls of the 19th century.

Prior to 1877, the Cuban press had noted the musical pieces called *danzones,* as well as *danzones* that were composed by Faílde, such as "El delirio," "La ingratitud," "Las quejas," and "Las Alturas de Simpson." But the structure of these works was the same as that of the *contradanzas* and *danzas* with *habanera* rhythm (see Ex. 1a), for which reason they cannot be identified with what was later called *danzón.*

Faílde modified the binary form of the *danzas* and *contradanzas* (AB) and introduced the rondo form to the *danzón,* creating a more extensive form in which the introduction becomes a *ritornello* (recurrent section), alternating with other different sections (ABAC). Following the introduction, a contrasting, more rhythmic B section appears, led thematically by the flute and clarinets of the *orquesta típica*; the section was called the *trio de clarinetes* (clarinet trio). After a repetition of the introductory segment comes the C section, the *trio de metales* (brass trio, also with contrasting sound) in which the *habanera* rhythm of the *danzas* and *contradanzas* is now abandoned and the five-note *cinquillo* rhythm is characteristic (see Ex. 1b). The work that marked the new style was "Las Alturas de Simpson," first performed in the Matanzas Club on January 1, 1879, and considered to be the first Cuban *danzón* composition.

Example 1
a. Habanera Rhythm

b. Cinquillo Rhythm

In Osvaldo Castillo Faílde's book entitled *Miguel Faílde, creador musical del danzón,* there is reference to 144 *danzones* written by Miguel Faílde, including, for example, "El Malakoff," "Cuba libre," "El amolador," "El negro bueno," "Los turcos," "Rusia y Japón," "A La Habana me voy," and others that reflect both in their titles and musical content much Creole *costumbrismo* (culture) from the 19th century. The *danzones* include in their trios fragments of opera and *zarzuela* melodies and a large number of popular and folkloric themes. Miguel Faílde played his last dance as musical director and instrumentalist in 1920. His work is now dispersed, many of his scores lost, and only a few of the librettos have been preserved.

REFERENCES

Carpentier, Alejo. *La música en Cuba.* Mexico: Fondo de Cultura
    Económica de México, 1947.
Castillo Faílde, Osvaldo. *Miguel Faílde, creador musical del danzón.*
    Havana: Editora del Consejo Nacional de Cultura,
    1964.

Eli Rodríguez, Victoria, and Zoila Gómez. *Haciendo música cubana.* Havana: Editorial Pueblo y Educación, 1989.

León, Argeliers. *Del canto y el tiempo.* Havana: Editorial Pueblo y Educación, 1974.

Rodríguez, Ezequiel. *Iconografía del danzón.* Havana: Dirección Provincial de Música de La Habana, Consejo Nacional de Cultura, 1967.

VICTORIA ELI RODRÍGUEZ

FAX, MARK OAKLAND

Born in Baltimore, Md., June 15, 1911; died in Washington, D.C., January 2, 1974. **Education:** Studied piano with Carrie Mae Smith Cargill, beginning age 9; Baltimore, Md., Public School Number 112; Douglass High School, studied music with W. Llewellyn Wilson, graduated 1926; Syracuse University, Syracuse, N.Y., 1929–33, B.M. with honors, 1933; Morgan State College, Baltimore, Md., helped with stage productions and gave piano recitals, summer of 1934; Bennington, Vt., studied piano with Gregory Tucker, summer of 1942; Eastman School of Music, Rochester, N.Y., studied composition with Howard Hanson and Bernard Rogers, studied piano with Cecile Genhart, 1942–45, M.M., 1945; New York University, doctoral studies, 1945–46. **Composing and Performing Career:** Baltimore, Md., organist at Metropolitan Methodist Episcopal Church and Regent Theater, age 14; Mount Olivet Baptist Church, Rochester, N.Y., choir director, 1943–44; First Baptist Church of West Washington, Georgetown, Washington, D.C., choir director, ca. 1947–51; Asbury United Methodist Church, Washington, D.C., organist and director of music, 1951–74. **Teaching Career:** Paine College, Augusta, Ga., music department, chairman, 1934–42; Black Mountain College, Black Mountain, N.C., 1946; Howard University, Washington, D.C., 1947–73, director of the School of Music, 1972. **Commission:** Howard University, 1966. **Honors/Awards:** Rosenwald Fellowship, 1930, 1944; Syracuse University, All-University Honor Society, 1933; American Guild of Organists, Fellow, 1955.

MUSIC LIST

INSTRUMENTAL SOLOS
Violin
"Cantilenare for Violin and Piano." Unpublished manuscript.
"Twelve Tone Piece for Violin and Piano." Unpublished manuscript.

Clarinet
"Gospel Sonata." 1969. Unpublished manuscript. Premiere, 1975.
Sonata for Clarinet and Piano. 1946. Unpublished manuscript. Premiere, 1950.

Vibraphone
"Trees." Unpublished manuscript.

Piano
A Day in Retrospect. Unpublished manuscript. Contents: The Beginning; Humoresque; Gavotte; The End.
"All Peace Come to All Men." 1957. Unpublished manuscript.
"Dinah." 1947. Unpublished manuscript.
Prelude no. 1. 1968. Unpublished manuscript. Recorded: Opus One 35.
Theme and Variations. Unpublished manuscript.
"Thirty Measures for Your Birthday." Unpublished manuscript.
Three Cries. Unpublished manuscript. Contents: Strong Men Overture; Lullaby; To Be Free. Note: "Lullaby" is from *A Christmas Miracle.* Premiere, 1973.

Three Night Pieces. Unpublished manuscript. Note: only the second piece, "Shadows" is extant.
Three Piano Pieces. ca. 1946. Unpublished manuscript. Contents: Key of C; Key of C; Spring Dance.
Three Piano Pieces. 1968. Unpublished manuscript. Contents: Prelude; Fugue; Toccata.
Three Pieces for Piano. ca. 1945. Unpublished manuscript. Contents: Prelude; Untitled; Con fuoco.
Three Pieces for Piano. 1964. Unpublished manuscript. Contents: Simple, Flowingly; Vigorously Accented; Simple, Calmly. Note: "Vigorously, Accented" was revised in 1971 and titled "Rapidly, Noisily."
Toccatina. Unpublished manuscript.
Two Piano Pieces. Unpublished manuscript. Contents: Moderato; Vivo.
"Vegetable Man." Unpublished manuscript.
"Waltz for Piano." Unpublished manuscript.

Organ
"Bridal Processional." 1968. Unpublished manuscript.
Fantasy on "We Gather Together." 1968. Unpublished manuscript.
Offertory in F (Postlude on "I'll Never Turn Back"). 1972. Unpublished manuscript.
Prelude and Chorale. 1952. Unpublished manuscript.
"The Quiet Church." Unpublished manuscript.
Six Organ Pieces. 1945. Unpublished manuscript. Note: only one piece, "Offertory," survives.
"Study on Morecambe." Unpublished manuscript.
Three Organ Preludes. 1964. Unpublished manuscript. Contents: St. Martins; Crusader's Hymn; St. Anne's.
Toccata. Unpublished manuscript.
Three Pieces for Organ. 1963–65. Unpublished manuscript. Contents: Chant; Allegretto; Toccata. Recorded: Titanic Records TI-205.
Two Choral Preludes. 1968. Unpublished manuscript. Contents: Crusader Hymn; Kremser. Note: "Crusader Hymn" was formerly in *Three Organ Preludes.*
Variations on Maryton. 1960. Unpublished manuscript.

Two Pianos
Peace, War, Peace. 1947. Unpublished manuscript. Contents: Peace: Nazi Entrance, Democracy Entrance; Peace: Before War; War; Peace.

SMALL INSTRUMENTAL ENSEMBLE
Strings
String Quartet. Unpublished manuscript. Contents: Allegro-Moderato; Tranquillo; Allegro-Vivace.

Combinations
Piano Quartet. Unpublished manuscript.
"Sultry Sundown" (trumpets, piano). 1947. Unpublished manuscript. Premiere, 1948.
Trio for Piano, Violin, and Violincello. Unpublished manuscript.

FULL ORCHESTRA

Elegy to the Memory of R. Nathaniel Dett. Unpublished manuscript. Premiere, 1948.

The Lost Zoo: Symphonic Suite. 1945. Unpublished manuscript. Note: M.M. thesis, Eastman School of Music, 1945.

Motet. 1947. Unpublished manuscript. Premiere, 1948.

Music on a Happy Theme. Unpublished manuscript. Premiere, 1947.

Short Piece for Orchestra. ca. 1946. Unpublished manuscript.

ORCHESTRA (CHAMBER OR FULL) WITH SOLOISTS

Music (piano, orchestra). 1947. Unpublished manuscript.

You Can Tell the World (high voice, orchestra). Unpublished manuscript.

ORCHESTRA (CHAMBER OR FULL) WITH CHORUS

The Gettysburg Address (tenor and soprano soloists, SATB, orchestra). 1965. Unpublished manuscript. Premiere, 1965.

Incidental Music for Easter Resurrection Day (mixed voices, orchestra). 1964. Unpublished manuscript. Premiere, 1964.

Poem of America (SATB, orchestra). Unpublished manuscript.

Rhapsody on Psalm 137 (SATB, orchestra). 1954. Unpublished manuscript. Premiere, 1954.

BAND

Heritage March. 1971. Unpublished manuscript. Also arranged for piano.

VOICE AND INSTRUMENTAL ENSEMBLE

Po' Mo' Ner Got a Home at Las' (high voice, flute, oboe, clarinet, bassoon). Unpublished manuscript.

SOLO VOICE

"Entreat Me Not to Leave Thee." 1968. Unpublished manuscript.

First Book of Songs (high voice). 1946–55. Unpublished manuscript. Contents: Night Truths; Dreams; Impulse; Inspiration; Sunset; Tondell; Rain Song; Deep River; Great Day; If He Only Walked in Gardens.

Five Black Songs (high voice). Unpublished manuscript. Contents: Love; The Refused; Only Dreams; Selfishness; Advice to a Child. Note: "Love" published in *Anthology of Art Songs by Black American Composers,* edited by Willis Patterson (New York: Edward B. Marks, 1977).

"Longing." In *Negro Art Songs* (New York: Edward B. Marks, 1946).

"May Day Song." In *Negro Art Songs* (New York: Edward B. Marks, 1946).

"To an Unknown Soldier" (high voice). New York: G. Schirmer, n.d.

Two Lyrics (high voice). Unpublished manuscript. Contents: Autumn Leaves; Break, Break, Break.

"Use All Your Hidden Forces" (baritone). 1946. Unpublished manuscript.

"Who Shall Separate Us?" (baritone). 1946; revised 1957. Unpublished manuscript. Also arranged for SATB.

CHORAL MUSIC

"Allelujah" (SATB, organ). Unpublished manuscript.

"As the Heart Panteth" (SAB, organ). 1951. Unpublished manuscript. Also arranged for SATB and organ.

"Asbury Hymn" (SATB, piano). 1966. Unpublished manuscript.

"By the Waters of Babylon" (SAB, piano). 1950. Unpublished manuscript.

"Choric Song" (SATB, piano). Unpublished manuscript.

"Christ Is Risen" (SATB, piano). Unpublished manuscript.

"Except the Lord Built the House" (SATB, organ). 1957. Unpublished manuscript.

"For Mother's Day" (SATB, piano). 1937. Unpublished manuscript.

"Give Ear O Shepherd" (SA, small choir, organ). 1950. Unpublished manuscript.

"God Be Merciful unto Us" (SSAB, organ). Unpublished manuscript.

"Hallelujah" (SATB, organ). Unpublished manuscript.

"The Harp of the Wind" (TTBB, piano). 1948. Unpublished manuscript.

"He Hath Shewed Thee, O Man" (SATB unaccompanied). Unpublished manuscript.

"He That Dwelleth in the Secret Place" (SATB, organ). 1968. Unpublished manuscript.

"Home in That Rock" (SA, piano). Unpublished manuscript.

"Hope Thou in God" (SATB, piano). 1961. Unpublished manuscript.

"I Have a Dream" (SATB unaccompanied). 1970. Unpublished manuscript. Premiere, 1971.

"I Will Lift Up Mine Eyes" (SATB, organ). Unpublished manuscript.

"In My Father's House Are Many Mansions" (SATB, organ). 1968. Unpublished manuscript.

"Let Not Your Heart Be Troubled" (SATB, organ). 1947. Unpublished manuscript.

"The Lord Is My Light" (SATB, piano or organ). Unpublished manuscript.

Lost Chord (TTBB, piano). Unpublished manuscript. Contents: Deep River; Toll the Bell; I Got a Home.

"Out of the Depths" (SATB unaccompanied). Unpublished manuscript.

"Poem of America" (SATB, baritone solo). Unpublished manuscript. Premiere, 1951.

"Remember Now Thy Creator" (SATB, piano). 1949. Unpublished manuscript.

"Serenade" (TTBB, piano). 1952. Unpublished manuscript.

"Song of Praise" (SAB, piano). 1948. Unpublished manuscript.

"Sonnet" (TTBB, piano). 1952. Unpublished manuscript.

"Whatsoever a Man Soweth" (SATB, organ). Minneapolis, Minn.: Augsburg Publishing House, 1958.

"When the Heart Is Hard" (SAB, piano). Unpublished manuscript.

"Where Shall My Wondering Soul Begin" (SATB, piano). Unpublished manuscript. Note: written for Paine College and used as the Paine College Hymn.

"Who Can Find a Virtuous Woman" (SATB, piano). Unpublished manuscript.

DRAMATIC MUSIC

A Christmas Miracle (opera). 1956; revised 1970. Unpublished manuscript. Premiere, 1958.

Merry-Go-Round (liturgical opera). 1969. Unpublished manuscript.

Till Victory Is Won (opera). 1966. Unpublished manuscript. Commissioned by the Centennial Committee of Howard University. Premiere, 1974.

Mark Oakland Fax; courtesy of the Reid Badger Collection, Moorland-Spingarn Research Center, Howard University

PUBLICATIONS

ABOUT FAX
Dissertations

Caldwell, Hansonia LaVerne. "Black Idioms in Opera as Reflected in the Works of Six Afro-American Composers." Ph.D. diss., University of Southern California, 1974.

Davidson, Celia Elizabeth. "Operas by Afro-American Composers: A Critical Survey and Analysis of Selected Works." Ph.D. diss., Catholic University of America, 1980.

Jones, Velma. "The Life and Works of Mark Oakland Fax." M.A. thesis, Morgan State University, 1978.

* * * * *

Mark Oakland Fax was an organist, pianist, conductor, composer, and teacher. The second of two sons, Fax was born at his parents' home on Calhoun Street in West Baltimore, Maryland, on June 15, 1911. The Fax family was close-knit, stoic, and Methodist. His father, the elder Mark, was often described as a man of innate dignity and worked several menial jobs. His mother, Willie Estelle (Cargille), was a homemaker.

Fax was born near the time that the National Association for the Advancement of Colored People (NAACP) was founded (1910), segregated housing ordinances were passed in several large cities, including Baltimore, and violence was epidemic nationwide. But Baltimore, just north of the Mason-Dixon line, also became a haven for African Americans, with large numbers of jobs available to them, many of which were not domestic positions. Work on the docks paid good wages, for example, and most of the dock workers were black. The minority community strongly supported and encouraged the talents, abilities, ambitions, and successes of its young people. The *Baltimore Afro-American* newspaper and the earlier *Baltimore Crusader* championed these successes.

Shortly after the end of World War I, the elder Fax completed his training in chiropody, a lucrative profession in a port city with many dock workers and other haulers. But his untimely death in 1924 at age 45 forced the family to move into the home of Estelle's three sisters.

Although his father had been an amateur singer, the aunts' large classical phonograph record collection was a major influence on young Mark. The jazz and blues collection, treasured by one of the aunts, did not interest him at the time. Mark was an introvert, overprotected by a mother who often described him as frail. The upbringing of Fax and his elder brother was strict and loving in a climate in which the family took advantage of every cultural activity available to them. Young Mark's brother Elton, an extrovert, became a nationally respected artist, critic, and cultural essayist.

In addition to doing the usual errand-running and casual summer jobs, Fax, at age 14, became the organist at the Metropolitan Methodist Episcopal Church and at Baltimore's famous Regent Theater. His playing at a church of the size and prominence of the Metropolitan afforded him another large audience and the "pious respectability" that balanced his "worldly contacts" from the Regent, which was a popular center for silent movies and stage shows. In addition to the pay, other important benefits were avail-

able to the shy teenager. Fax recounted that playing for the shows made him a celebrity among his peers and that he saw all of the films and shows free of charge. Professionally, the job provided opportunities for him to develop his improvisational skills.

W. Llewellyn Wilson, an early mentor and Fax's music teacher at Douglass High School, was also a columnist for the *Baltimore Afro-American.* In this capacity, Wilson reported the numerous cultural activities of the community and chronicled the achievements of promising young people, including two of his favorite students, Ann Wiggins Brown and Mark Fax. (Years later, in 1935, Brown created the role of Bess in Gershwin's *Porgy and Bess.*)

Fax chose Syracuse University for his undergraduate studies and arrived on campus for his freshman year just a month before the stock market crash of 1929. In April 1930, he won a prestigious Rosenwald Fellowship. His mentor, Wilson, wrote on July 12, "Mr. Fax, during his freshman year at Syracuse University, has succeeded in winning a scholarship for superior attainment in piano, harmony, and counterpoint, which will assure his music study for the period of three years. Mr. Fax is the first freshman of our group to win a place on a major recital program at Syracuse." He was elected to the All-University Honor Society, graduated with honors in 1933, and won a graduate scholarship to the University of Michigan-Ann Arbor. However, he was forced by the Depression to abandon his studies at Ann Arbor.

Back home in Baltimore, Fax gave several recitals and worked with drama and music productions at Morgan State College. In September 1934, he joined the faculty at Paine College in Augusta, Georgia, where he developed the school's first music curriculum and chaired the department. He married Dorothy Stuckey, a Paine graduate, in 1938. Regrettably, the atmosphere at Paine was severely paternalistic and limiting. Permission to attend and participate in out-of-state seminars and workshops was denied, and attempts to improve and enlarge the school's music curriculum were also rejected. However, characteristically, Fax made his years at Paine positive ones. He composed operettas, a substantial number of vocal and piano compositions, and the music for the college hymn. (The verses were written by the successful novelist Frank Yerby.) Dismayed and financially troubled, the Faxes left Augusta in 1942 to study at Bennington College in exchange for domestic services performed by the couple. During this period, he wrote music for the Martha Graham dance troupe.

In September 1942, the Faxes moved to Rochester, New York, and Fax enrolled in the graduate program in composition at the Eastman School of Music. He found work at a local church, Mount Olivet, as choir director and janitor. A year later, a son, Jesse, was born. In 1944, the financial stress lessened when he was awarded a graduate assistantship and was named a Rosenwald Fellow in composition. He felt so indebted to the Mount Olivet Baptist Church for sustaining the family during the first year that he asked permission to continue serving the church as janitor during the summer without pay.

In 1945, with a master of music degree in composition in hand, the family moved to New York City, and Fax began doctoral studies at New York University. Again, a lack of funds forced him to abandon his plans, and, in 1946, he accepted a position as visiting lecturer at a uniquely progressive (for that era) North Carolina institution, Black Mountain College, for the spring semester.

In 1947, an invitation from Warner Lawson, dean of the music department at Howard University, brought the family to Washington, D.C. At Howard, Fax distinguished himself as a professor of piano, counterpoint, and composition, developing a solid curriculum in counterpoint, orchestration, and composition at the undergraduate and graduate levels. His studio on the first floor of the Conservatory building quickly became a favorite classroom for his students. In addition to remembrances about his early mentor, Llewellyn Wilson, Fax shared stories and insights gained during his studies at Eastman with pianist Cecile Genhart and composers Howard Hanson and Bernard Rogers. He also often entertained his students with stories about the occasions as a theater organist when, due to inattention and boredom, his background music did not fit the action on the celluloid scene. Fax became an indispensable member of several university committees and gradually accepted increasing responsibilities as administrative assistant to the Dean of the College of Fine Arts and later as dean of the same unit. He proved himself to be an able administrator—a skilled negotiator and mediator—and also served a term as the secretary of the National Association of Schools of Music, Region IV, and became a Fellow of the American Guild of Organists. Wise, unassuming, and sympathetic, he was content to be part of the background; however, for those who were privileged to be his friends and students, he was the foreground.

During his early years in Washington, Fax served as choir director at the First Baptist Church of West Washington in historic Georgetown. While there, he composed many anthems that minimized the small group's limitations. In 1951, Fax was appointed Minister of Music at the historic Asbury United Methodist Church in the heart of downtown Washington. A notable achievement during his tenure there was the planning and construction of a new Casavant organ in 1959, which has served through the years as a prototype for similar instruments in the area. His anthems, organ solos, and thoughtful arrangements of hymns and spirituals, both familiar and less well known, were highlights of the Asbury services. He gave frequent organ recitals at several historic churches in the metropolitan area and was invited to lecture and perform at colleges and schools of music.

A lawn mower accident during the summer of 1972 and the ensuing spiraling decline in his health shocked all who knew him. Though the prognosis was grave, he continued to make plans for the future. Even during his last hospital confinement in November 1973 until his death on January 2, 1974, he was generally optimistic. This writer spent most of a day in early December 1973 at his bedside in the Pavilion, Howard University Hospital. He talked with obvious pleasure about the impending performance of *Till Victory Is Won* at the John F. Kennedy Center for the Performing Arts and changes he still wanted to make in the work. He talked about the many things he still wanted to accomplish at the university and about an opera and several choral and organ works that he had mentally written as he lay in bed.

As a teacher, he was unsurpassed. His classes and lessons were exciting and motivating. His students became his friends, and each one knew that Mark Fax could always be called on for help. These friendships grew and the learning opportunities continued after graduation. Notes that he wrote in the margins of his students' scores continued to inspire and provoke even deeper consideration of the music. He counseled young teachers in selecting repertoire and guided them in developing creative ways of solving the unique technical problems presented by their students. Through the years, many returned for study and advice; his door was always open.

Fax was a *gebrauchsmusik* (functional music) composer. In fact, many of his compositions were written with specific persons in mind. Some were written quickly, when an imminent date loomed on the calendar, although the work itself may have been completed in his mind for some time. Others were sketched, worked and reworked, put aside, and revisited again and again. Fax was a perfectionist, and his ability to write counterpoint is evident in each of his works. Clarity, sincerity, and moderation, often to the point of understatement, are distinctive characteristics of his style.

SELECTED WORKS

The majority of Fax's choral works, sacred and secular, were written for specific choirs, including the Paine College Choir, the First Baptist Church of West Washington Choir, the famed Howard University Choir, several of the choral organizations at the Asbury United Methodist Church, and for special events. He wrote two compositions, "Serenade" and "Sonnet," for the Leonard de Paur group in 1952. *Rhapsody on Psalm 137*, for choir and orchestra, was premiered by the Wesleyan Choir of Asbury United Methodist Church with the National Gallery Orchestra during a Festival of American Music in 1954. *The Gettysburg Address*, for tenor and soprano soloists, chorus, and orchestra, was frequently programmed, including three performances at the 1965 New York World's Fair. It was composed for the District of Columbia Youth Chorale and Symphony Orchestra, a forerunner of the D.C. Youth Orchestra. Another favorite of several congregations was "Whatsoever a Man Soweth," an anthem for mixed voices and organ. The majority of the choral works remain in manuscript.

Fax's chamber works include several compositions for various instrumental combinations. Paul Hume, music critic for the *Washington Post* during the Truman era, described the Sonata for Clarinet and Piano as a striking work, difficult, and of surprising texture contrapuntally: "All of the music is of rare power." *Short Piece for Orchestra* was also very favorably received by the critics. Other orchestral compositions included *Music on a Happy Theme*, premiered at City College of New York in 1947; Motet for orchestra; and *Elegy to the Memory of R. Nathaniel Dett*, premiered in 1948 by the Eastman-Rochester Symphony Orchestra with Howard Hanson conducting.

Several of the keyboard compositions were loosely grouped in twos and threes. There are at least two collections of three organ pieces and several piano collections of three compositions. The Prelude for piano, written in 1968, has been recorded on the Opus One label. One collection, *Three Pieces for Organ*, written between 1963 and 1965, was recorded by Herndon Spillman. This group, like most of his keyboard compositions, is neoclassic in style. The arresting "Chant" uses a florid theme with an accompaniment of parallel fifth figures and an ostinato pedal. As Spillman notes, "These ideas are developed and then brought together in stretto." The "Allegretto" borrows from the waltz and the blues. Fax described the third piece (first simply entitled "Allegro" and later changed to "Toccata") as "big city" organ music.

Fax loved the voice and wrote sympathetically for it throughout his career. The list of his vocal works includes art songs, the lovely and demanding solos and ensembles in the operas, spiritual arrangements, thoughtful settings of religious texts, and nuptial dedications. A favorite spiritual arrangement is "Ride On, King Jesus" for high voice and orchestra. Two solos, "Longing" and "May Day Song," gained early popularity after their publication in 1946. Willis Patterson included two compositions, "Cassandra's Lullaby" (from the opera *A Christmas Miracle*) and "Love," in his *Anthology of Art Songs by Black American Composers*. "Cassandra's Lullaby" is increasingly programmed on recitals.

Especially beautiful is the wedding song "Entreat Me Not to Leave Thee," composed for the nuptials of Alece Howard, a Howard University School of Music graduate, and Charles Morgan in April 1968. After a dramatic eight-tone descending scale pattern of two octaves from high *a* to *a*-sharp below middle *c*, a poignant melody introduces the phrase "Entreat me not to leave thee." The glorious vocal lines implore, soar, and twice confirm "Thy people will be my people, and thy God shall be my God."

Fax completed three operas, *A Christmas Miracle* (1956; revised 1970), *Till Victory Is Won* (1966, with several revisions), and *Merry-Go-Round* (1969). A fourth opera, based on John O. Killens' satirical novel *Cotillion* was being planned when Fax's health failed. All three operas have been performed. *A Christmas Miracle* was premiered in 1958 at Howard University. *Merry-Go-Round*, a short liturgical opera, was first performed at Asbury United Methodist Church. His last opera, *Till Victory Is Won*, was premiered in 1974 at the Kennedy Center Opera House.

A Christmas Miracle, a one-act chamber opera with a libretto by Owen Dodson, is not the usual happy, frothy story that today's audiences have come to expect in the holiday season. The ten characters, performed by seven singers—one adult female, two pre-adolescent children, and four adult males—tell a brief story of the resistance to oppression and the miraculous workings of the forces of nature. Fax stated, "It reminds us that beautiful things may come through pain and suffering. The story is told from the black perspective, but its universality may be communicated from any point of view."

A family tries to find shelter and a safe hiding place from a group of marauders who burned to the ground their home and the homes of several neighbors. The story implies that the father is now being hunted by the lawless group because he had the courage to rally together a small fearful and exploited group. The young daughter, Cassandra, who is blind, has faith in the miracle of the Christmas star, and her protective brother bolsters this belief. The mother gives birth to another son, and later the father and older son go off in search of firewood. Three joyous strangers appear, and each leaves a cherished possession for the family: a religious medal for protection; a colorful blanket for warmth; and food packages, including fruit, for nourishment. In response, Cassandra sings a lullaby to the new baby. The older son is caught and tortured into revealing the family's hiding place. Moments after the father escapes, the mob arrives and, in a depraved frenzy, kills the infant before continuing the chase. At this moment, the "magic" star

appears and Cassandra sees it. The family's unswerving faith and the core of the story are revealed in the mother's closing aria, "Thank you, my Jesus, for all your miracles even though they come through pain and darkness, and sometimes evil doings. The sun has never gone out; the stars shine even in the day."

Till Victory Is Won is a moving work of epic proportions. The first complete stage production was at Washington's Kennedy Center Opera House on March 4, 1974, two months after the composer's death. The opera, commissioned by Howard University for its centennial celebration, was a major undertaking for Fax and Owen Dodson, who was at that time chair of the drama department. Their goal was to present a work of appropriate magnitude that would include highlights of the myriad events in the life of the black man from Africa to present-day America.

By selecting an event in the life of specific individuals, Fax and Dodson structured a manageable design to chronicle deeds and emotions paramount to the black diaspora in the United States. They organized the story in four episodes (purposefully avoiding the term "acts"), a prologue, and interludes. The unifying element is a recurring classroom scene with "Miss Truth" guiding her young charges through the different passages and events: episode 1, Africa; episode 2, Harriet Tubman; episode 3, Bessie Smith; and episode 4, Medgar Evers.

The staged work includes 21 soloists, a children's chorus, a mixed adult chorus, dancers, a large orchestra including five percussionists, the expected props, and a cyclorama that dramatically increases the impact of the events. The music is continuous throughout, and quick and precise scene changes are required. The large orchestra is skillfully used to reinforce, but never to overtake, the voice. The solo voice is at times unaccompanied, heightening the dramatic impact. The Medgar Evers character summarizes the theme of this epic work: "Remember, and always know/Our children must live without this foe/And if I'm killed—/My soul will not be stilled/Till victory is won."

Numerous compositional devices are employed in this panoramic work. They include strict and free contrapuntal imitation, sophisticated and earthy call-and-response techniques, layered and motivic development of rhythms, fragmented and plaintive settings of familiar ethnic melodies, and unexpected juxtapositions of harmonies.

This is an operatic message for our time. Had Fax been able to complete his planned revisions, several parts of the opera might have been fashioned for concert performances, as he had done earlier with the Bessie Smith episode. This material begs for greater exposure.

REFERENCES

Caldwell, Hansonia LaVerne. "Black Idioms in Opera as Reflected in the Works of Six Afro-American Composers." Ph.D. diss., University of Southern California, 1974.

Davidson, Celia Elizabeth. "Operas by Afro-American Composers: A Critical Survey and Analysis of Selected Works." Ph.D. diss., Catholic University of America, 1980.

Fax, Mark. Conversations with the author, 1951, 1954, 1971–73.

Jones, Velma. "The Life and Works of Mark Oakland Fax." M.A. thesis, Morgan State University, 1978.

McLellan, Joseph. "A Panorama of Black History." *Washington Post* (March 6, 1974): B9.

Patterson, Willis C., comp. *Anthology of Art Songs by Black American Composers.* New York: Edward B. Marks Music, 1977.

Spillman, Herndon. Liner notes, *A Diversity of Riches.* Titanic Records TI-205.

CELIA E. DAVIDSON

FLORES, PEDRO

Born in Naguabo, Puerto Rico, March 9, 1894; died in Río Piedras, San Juan, Puerto Rico, July 13, 1979. **Education:** probably finished eighth grade; University of Puerto Rico, teacher's certificate. **Military Service:** U.S. Army, sergeant, ca. 1919. **Composing and Performing Career:** First composition, "El jilguero," 1919; moved to New York City, 1926; formed Cuarteto Flores with Ramón Quirós, Pedro Marcano, Davilita, Fallito, and Pellín (the group also included other performers during its lifetime), 1930–ca. 1941; first recording, "Toma jabón pa' que laves," 1930; lived in Cuba for seven years, Mexico for ten; returned to Puerto Rico, 1956. **Teaching Career:** Humacao, Yabucoa, and Gurabo, Puerto Rico, worked as a rural schoolteacher, specializing in English, among other non-musical jobs, until 1926.

MUSIC LIST

[The following list of titles includes only works that were composed by the subject of the entry; it is not a list of recordings that were made by the subject. Although the composer may have made recordings of his own works, the list is not restricted to those recordings but in many cases includes performances by other artists of the composer's work. The list is made up of publication and discographical data, in cases where such information is available. Although no effort has been made to include documentation of the earliest recording of the works listed, the date of the earliest recording that is readily available has been given. —Ed.]

COLLECTIONS

100 éxitos de Puerto Rico, Barcelona: Southern Music Española/Peer International, n.d.

Este es Pedro Flores (solo voice). New York: Peer-Southern, 1975.

POPULAR SONG

"Adoración." Recorded, 1940: Harlequin HQ CD 49.

"Advertencia" (solo voice). Recorded: Caliente CLT 7258; Discos CBS DML-20632.

"Allí" (voice and jazz ensemble). Recorded: Qbadisc QB9011.

"Amor" (solo voice). In *Este es Pedro Flores.* Recorded, 1941: Discos CBS DML-20638; Harlequin HQ CD 49.

"Amor perdido" (solo voice). In *Este es Pedro Flores.* Recorded: Caliente CLT 7258; Fania SLP CD00489; Harmony CDDE-463854.

"Añoranza" (solo voice). In *Este es Pedro Flores.* Recorded: DYL 1.

"Arrímate." Recorded: Caliente CLT 7048.

"Así es mi amor." Recorded: Caliente CLT 7048.

"Aunque pasen años." Unpublished manuscript.

"¡Ay, qué bueno!" Unpublished manuscript.

"Azucenas" (solo voice). In *Este es Pedro Flores.* Recorded: Discos CBS DML-20565.

"Bailando una noche." Recorded: Caliente CLT 7048.

"Bajo un palmar." Recorded: Caliente CLT 7258; Discos CBS DML-20638.

"La batatita: Pregón cha cha" (solo voice). Recorded: Ansonia MCD-13034.

"Blanca" (solo voice). In *Este es Pedro Flores.*

"Blancas azucenas." Recorded: Egrem CD0222.

"Borracho no vale" (solo voice). In *Este es Pedro Flores.* Recorded: Caliente CLT 7258; Discos CBS DML-20632.

"Búsqueda." Recorded: Discos CBS DML-20565.

"El cafetero." Recorded: RCA Victor LPR-1002/RSRM-6515.

"El carbón." Recorded: Caliente CLT 7048.

"Celos" (solo voice). In *Este es Pedro Flores.* Recorded: Discos CBS DML-20638.

"Ciego de amor." Recorded: Caliente CLT 7048.

"Compay, póngase duro" (solo voice). In *Este es Pedro Flores.* Recorded: Ansonia SALP 1527.

"Congojas." Recorded: Caliente CLT 7048.

"Contestación." Recorded: Caliente CLT 7048.

"Contigo" (solo voice). In *Este es Pedro Flores.* Recorded: RCA Victor LPR-1002/RSRM-6515.

"Corazón." Recorded, 1939: Harlequin HQ CD 49.

"Déjame gozar." Recorded, 1942: Harlequin HQ CD 49.

"Desde que tú me quieres." Recorded: Discos CBS DML-20565.

"Desilusión." Co-composer, P. Robles. Recorded: RCA Victor LPR-1002/RSRM-6515.

"Despedida" (solo voice). Recorded, 1941: Caliente CLT 7258; Discos CBS DML-20638; Harlequin HQ CD 49.

"Despierta pueblo." Recorded: NYL 1.

"Echando chispas." Recorded: Ansonia SALP 1527.

"Esperanza inútil." Recorded: Discos CBS DML-20638.

"Esto no es un mambo" (solo voice). Recorded: Ansonia SALP 1527.

"Háblame amigo mío." Recorded: Ansonia SALP-1320.

"La historia de siempre" (solo voice). Recorded: Ansonia SALP 1527.

"Irresistible" (solo voice). Recorded, 1940: Caliente CLT 7258; Discos CBS DML-20638; Harlequin HQ CD 49.

"El jilguero." 1919.

"Juanita." Recorded, 1942: Harlequin HQ CD 49.

"Juramento." Recorded, 1940: Harlequin HQ CD 49.

"Lamento de amor." Recorded, 1940: Harlequin HQ CD 49.

"Lamentos del alma." Recorded, 1938: Caliente CLT 7048; Harlequin HQ CD 49.

"Linda" (solo voice). Recorded: Discos CBS DML-20638.

"Mañana es domingo" (solo voice). Recorded: Ansonia SALP 1527.

"Margie" (solo voice). Recorded, 1941: Caliente CLT 7258; Fania JM623; Harlequin HQ CD 49.

"Mentiritas de amor" (solo voice). Recorded: Ansonia SALP 1527.

"La mujer de Juan." Recorded, 1941: Harlequin HQ CD 49.

"Obsesión" (solo voice). In *Este es Pedro Flores.* Recorded: Caliente CLT 7258; Discos CBS DML-20638; Orfeón C4D11901; Peerless PCD-112-8.

"Olga." Recorded: RCA Victor LPR-1002/RSRM-6515.

"Oye mi ruego." Recorded, 1940: Harlequin HQ CD 49.

"Perdón." (solo voice). In *Este es Pedro Flores.* Recorded, 1940: Caliente CLT 7258; Discos CBS DML-20638; Harlequin HQ CD 49; Orfeón 25CDT-354.

"¿Por qué?" Recorded: Caliente CLT 7048.

"Preciosa añoranza." Co-composer, Rafael Hernández. Recorded: Ansonia ALP-1320.

"¿Qué culpa tengo yo?" Recorded: Odessa OLP-888.

"Qué extraña es la vida." Recorded: Discos CBS DML-20565.

"Qué te pasa" (solo voice). Recorded: Caliente CLT 7258; Discos CBS DML-20638.

"Querube." Originally titled "Luisa." Recorded: Odessa OLP-888.

"Quinto patio" (solo voice). Recorded: RCA 3407-4-RL.

"Rosita." Recorded, 1939: Harlequin HQ CD 49.

"Se fue." Recorded: Harlequin HQ CD 49.

"Se vende una casita" (solo voice). Recorded: Fania JM569.

"Será como tú quieras." Recorded: Discos CBS DML-20565.

"Si no eres tú" (solo voice). In *Este es Pedro Flores.*

"Si no fuera por ti." Recorded, 1940: Harlequin HQ CD 49.

"Si tú me quisieras." Recorded: Odessa OLP-888.

"Sin bandera." Recorded, 1935.

"Sólo fue un sueño." Recorded: NYL 1.

"Tesoro de amor." Recorded: Caliente CLT 7048.

"Toma jabón pa' que laves." 1927. Recorded, 1930.

"Tú séras mía." Co-composer, P. Robles. Recorded: RCA Victor LPR-1002/RSRM-6515.

"El último ruego" (solo voice). Recorded: Ansonia SALP 1527; Caliente CLT 7258.

"24 horas." Recorded: Discos CBS DML-20565.

"Veleidosa" (solo voice). Recorded: Ansonia SALP 1527.

"Ven." Recorded, 1940: Harlequin HQ CD 49.

"Venganza" (solo voice). Recorded: Caliente CLT 7258; Discos CBS DML-20632; RCA Victor LPR-1002/RSRM06515.

"Virgen de medianoche." Recorded: RCA MLK-1338.

"Virgen del Cobre" (voice and instrumental ensemble). Recorded: Fania JM569.

"Vuelve otra noche." Recorded: Discos CBS DML-20565.

"Y que tú sabes." Recorded: Caliente CLT 7048.

"Yo contigo." Recorded: Discos CBS DML-20565.

"Yo no sé nada." Recorded, 1938: Caliente CLT 7048; Harlequin HQ CD 49.

"Yo quisiera saber." Unpublished manuscript.

"Yo sé que es mucho." Recorded, 1940: Harlequin HQ CD 49.

PUBLICATIONS

ABOUT FLORES
Books and Monographs

Campagne, Jean-Marc. *Pedro Flores.* Paris: Les éditions françaises, 1958.

* * * * *

Pedro Flores; Courtesy of Naguabo Cultural Center, Naguabo, Puerto Rico

One of Latin America's most renowned composers, Pedro Flores is the author of over 1,000 compositions, many of which remain unpublished. Some of the most popular Puerto Rican hits of the 1930s, 1940s, and 1950s have come from his pen.

Born in Naguabo, in northeastern Puerto Rico, on March 9, 1894, to Julián Flores Hernández and Eulalia Córdoba Martínez, Pedro Flores was one of 12 sons raised in a very humble household. Flores probably finished eighth grade, despite economic limitations and thanks to his skill as a baseball player, in exchange for which the School Board paid for his schooling. He received a teacher's certificate from the University of Puerto Rico.

Flores taught English on the island until 1926, when he decided to move to New York. There, in 1930, he organized the Cuarteto Flores (Flores Quartet), which sometimes contained more than four musicians. His intention was to play mostly dance music with lyrics that spoke about the everyday life of the common Puerto Rican. In the same year as its founding, the Cuarteto Flores made its first recording, "Toma jabón pa' que laves," written by Flores.

Many of Flores's songs contain lyrics that depict comical situations, although he also wrote patriotic and romantic music. An example of the comical song is "Borracho no vale," which was made a hit by singer Daniel Santos; in this song, a mouse falls into a barrel of wine and asks his "compadre" the cat to take him out. Flores's patriotic songs were popular among Puerto Ricans living in New York during the Depression and later among the Puerto Rican soldiers fighting in World War II and Korea. Even though Flores never stated that he was an *independentista,* his patriotic songs reflect a strong influence of the pro-independence movement of the 1930s, 1940s, and 1950s in Puerto Rico. Songs such as "Sin bandera" (recorded in 1935) and "Despierta pueblo" (included in the album *Corazón musical de Puerto Rico-Añoranza,* by Moncho Usera and His Orchestra) contain lyrics that speak about the wish of having a nation free from the political influence of another country. In the song "Despedida," a man who has been drafted says goodbye to his friends. The soldier asks his buddies to take care of his mother, who is his most valued treasure, during his absence or if he is killed in battle. This song was a great success when it was sung during the 1950s by Daniel Santos.

Flores had a romantic view of life that is reflected in many of his compositions. Some of the most famous *boleros* in Latin America came from his pen, including "Obsesión," which became an international success. To this day, "Obsesión" and other of Flores's successes remain in the repertoires of major musical groups around the world. Although his romantic songs speak of love lost and found, some of them are written to the rhythm of *guaracha,* a rhythmic, festive, and lively genre with comical or satirical lyrics.

Although Pedro Flores was born in Puerto Rico, he lived for seven years in Cuba, 10 years in Mexico, and 30 years in New York, traveling often between New York and Puerto Rico. In the latter years of the 1920s, while living in New York, he reorganized his ensemble, Cuarteto Flores, under the direction of pianist-arranger Moncho Usera. Among its members during this period were Panchito Riset and Mirta Silva, two vocalists who later became renowned. Riset was later replaced by Daniel Santos, a fortunate change, since the combination of Flores and Santos created a dual success. Santos became one of Flores's most constant and better-known interpreters (together with Pedro Ortiz Dávila). During the 1950s, Flores returned to Puerto Rico, where he resided until his death on July 13, 1979.

Pedro Flores was a close friend of Rafael Hernández, the Puerto Rican composer of concert music, popular songs, and film scores. But unlike Hernández, Flores did not receive a musical education beyond the exposure to the music of his time. Some authors write of their mutual admiration, while others emphasize their rivalry; Ruth Glasser describes this situation as a love/hate relationship. A general observation may be expressed about the difference of their compositional styles: Flores's music is "folksy" in character, while Hernández' compositions are more academic, or "cultivated."

Flores had been a baseball player, a railroad worker (train inspector), a foreman in the sugar industry, an English teacher, a soldier, and a worker in different government agencies. All these occupations must have been necessary for subsistence but obviously took valuable time away from his musical career. Despite all these distractions, Pedro Flores was a popular and successful composer whose works are well known in Mexico, Cuba, his native Puerto Rico, and other Latin American countries as well. Some of his best known works are "Adelita," "Irresistible," "Yo no sé nada," "Vivir separados," "Contigo," "Aunque pasen años," "Obsesión," "Sin bandera," "Venganza," "Esperanza inútil," "Linda," "Perdón," "Amor perdido," "Celos," "Bajo un palmar," "Se vende una casita," "Margie," "Ciego de amor," "(¡Ay, qué bueno!," "Yo quisiera saber," and "Borracho no vale."

SELECTED WORKS

"Obsesión," one of Flores's most popular works, is set in an AABA form, each section being eight bars long, with an introduction and coda, each of four bars. It is a *bolero* in D minor and has a rich harmonic structure. The tempo of a *bolero* is relatively slow, with rhythms based on the *clave* patterns shown in Example 1. As is typical of the *bolero,* this composition is one of Flores's romantic songs. The lyrics speak of a man's obsession with a woman, demonstrated

by the last stanza (in translation): "I am obsessed with you/and the World is witness/of my frenzy, /and no matter how strong is Destiny's opposition/You shall be for me, for me."

Example 1. *Clave* pattern

"Perdón," another *bolero,* in F minor, has as its most notable characteristic a melody plus countermelody, which both have the same text. It suggests the Puerto Rican *danza* because of its contrapuntal aspects. The composition's harmonic structure is simple, and the topic is romantic. In the song's text, a man implores forgiveness for some unstated fault. A great emotional intensity is expressed by the two parts. One voice pleads for forgiveness while the other voice states security in one true love. Set in a binary ABAB form, with a solo-group format emphasized, the song features strong rhythmic contrast throughout. This contrast increases as the rhythmic activity itself increases in the B section, where interaction between solo and group intensifies and the solo and group lines become independent. The voice also appears alone, without group accompaniment of any kind, as the group becomes more independent, its part doubles in counterpoint the note values of the solo voice.

"Borracho no vale" (Drunk people don't count) is a *guaracha* in major mode, with much activity on the dominant and supertonic chords. It is reminiscent of the *seis mariandá,* a very rhythmic and syncopated variant of the *seis* genre that is usually sung with the *décima* poetic form (abbaaccdde). In fact, stanzas 2, 3, and 4 are octosyllabic *décimas* or *espinelas.* The topic is a fable with a moral: a mouse is drowning in a barrel of wine. He asks a cat to save him because otherwise the cat would not be able to eat him. The mouse promises to let the cat eat him if the cat lets him out. The cat accepts the deal. As soon as the mouse is taken out of the barrel, it runs and hides in a hole in the earth. Days later, the cat happens to see the mouse and reproaches him for the unkept promise. The mouse in turn simply states, "When somebody drinks liquor, who pays any attention to him?" The refrain says *Borracho no vale* or "Drunk people don't count." Set in verse/chorus form, the piece begins with a four-bar introduction to a through-composed verse. The chorus consists of three repetitions of an abcb phrase structure of 28 bars (8+8+4+8), in which the first two phrases are exactly the same and the last two are tailored to variations in the text. The song concludes with a ten-bar coda consisting of a repetition of the first half of the chorus plus a two-bar tag from the beginning of the second phrase.

REFERENCES

Brignoni, Bartolomé. "Sepelio de Pedro Flores hoy en Cementerio SJ." *El Mundo* (July 14, 1979): 1A, 12A.

Centro de Investigaciones y Ediciones Musicales de Puerto Rico. *Compositores de música popular.* San Juan: Instituto de Cultura Puertorriqueña, 1981.

Cesáreo, Rosa-Nieves, and Esther M. Melón. "Biografias." In *Colección Puertorriqueña,* 167–168. Sharon, Conn.: Troutman Press, 1970.

Flores, María. Interview with the author, 1998.

Glasser, Ruth. *My Music Is My Flag: Puerto Rican Musicians and Their New York Communities 1917–1940.* Berkeley: University of California, 1995.

Ramos, Josean. "Un conjunto de voces para Don Pedro." *El Nuevo Día* (March 13, 1994): Domingo section, 4–8.

Rico Salazar, Jaime. *Cien años de boleros: Su historia, sus compositores, sus mejores intérpretes y 600 boleros inolvidables.* 3rd ed. Bogotá, Colombia: Centro Editorial de Estudios Musicales, 1993.

Sánchez, Luis Rafael. *La importancia de llamarse Daniel Santos.* Hanover, N.H.: Ediciones del Norte, 1988.

Santiago, José G. "Identidad cultural latinoamericana en la importancia de llamarse Daniel Santos." *Revista Universidad de América* 3, no. 1 (May 1991): 94–101.

Suárez Alicea, Rafael [Pilo]. *Método para el cuatro puertorriqueño: 35 canciones con acompañamiento.* Vol. 1. San Juan: Rafael Suárez Alicea, 1975.

Martínez, Jan. "Un clásico de la música popular." *El Nuevo Día* (March 13, 1994): Domingo section, 9–11.

J. EMANUEL DUFRASNE-GONZÁLEZ

FOX, DONAL LEONELLIS

Born in Boston, Mass., July 17, 1952. **Education:** Piano study with Edna Ida Itkin, 1960–62; New England Conservatory of Music Preparatory Department, Boston, Mass., studied piano with Jeanette Giguère, 1962–64; continued private study with Giguère, 1964–68, 1971–72; Berklee College of Music, Boston, Mass., summer 1968; Berkshire Music Center, Tanglewood, Mass., summer 1969; studied theory and composition with Avram David, 1972–74, T. J. Anderson, 1975–76, and Gunther Schuller, 1977–81. **Composing and Performing Career:** Elma Lewis School, Roxbury, Mass., composer-in-residence, 1972–74; Fox/Hubbard Concert Series, co-founder, conductor, composer-in-residence, 1974–1976; Tanglewood Contemporary Music Festival, composer-in-residence, summer 1983; Tobin Middle School, Boston, artist-in-residence, 1985–86; St. Louis Symphony Orchestra, composer-in-residence, 1991–93; Videmus, conductor, composer-in-residence, 1992–94; Harvard University, visiting artist and lecturer, 1993; Spencer/Colton Dance Company, composer-in-residence, 1993–94; Summer Stages at Concord Academy, music faculty, composer-in-residence, 1996–present. **Commissions:** Fromm Foundation at Harvard University and Berkshire Music Center, 1983; Massachusetts Council on the Arts and Humanities, Heritage Program, and Vivian Taylor, 1988; Faina Bryanskaya, 1989; Videmus, 1989, 1991; Project Step, Inc., 1990, 1992; Dinosaur Annex, 1992; St. Louis Symphony Orchestra, 1992, 1995; Bermuda Triangle, 1993; Boston Ballet, 1993; Boston Musica Viva, 1993; Little Orchestra of Cambridge [Mass.], 1993; Tufts University New Music Festival, 1993; WGBH Educational Foundation, 1993; WGBH Educational Foundation/WGBH Radio/Videmus, 1993; Tufts University Department of Music, 1995; Paris New Music Review, 1996; Thomas Piercy, 1997. **Honors and Awards:** Scholarship to Berkshire Music Center, 1969; St. Boltoph Club Foundation, Boston, Mass., 1984; Institute for the Arts Grant, Boston, 1985; Ludwig Vogelstein Foundation, Inc., 1987; Massachusetts Artists Fellowship Program, 1988; National Endowment for the Arts/Meet the Composer/Rockefeller Foundation Grant, 1991; Massachusetts Cultural Council Grant, 1995; Guggenheim Fellowship, 1997. **Mailing Address:** Leonellis Music, 14 Highland Park Avenue, Roxbury, MA 02119.

MUSIC LIST

INSTRUMENTAL SOLOS
Two Violins
Toccata for Two Violins. 1990. Roxbury, Mass.: Leonellis Music. Commissioned by Project Step, Inc. Premiere, 1992.

Clarinet
"Duetto for Clarinet and Piano." 1991. Roxbury, Mass.: Leonellis Music. Commissioned by Videmus. Premiere, 1991. Recorded: New World Records 80423-2.

Ballade for Clarinet and Piano. 1993. Roxbury, Mass.: Leonellis Music. Commissioned by the WGBH Educational Foundation. Premiere, 1993. Recorded: New World Records 80515-2.

Variations for Clarinet and Piano. 1997. Roxbury, Mass.: Leonellis Music. Commissioned by Thomas Piercy. Premiere, 1997.

Bass Clarinet
"Golden Ladders." 1993. Roxbury, Mass.: Leonellis Music. Commissioned by WGBH Educational Foundation. Premiere, 1993. Recorded: Evidence ECD-223131-2.

"Vamping with T. T." 1993. Roxbury, Mass.: Leonellis Music. Commissioned by WGBH Educational Foundation. Premiere, 1993. Recorded: Evidence ECD-22131-2.

Saxophone
"Becca's Ballad." 1993. Roxbury, Mass.: Leonellis Music. Commissioned by WGBH Educational Foundation. Premiere, 1993. Recorded: Evidence ECD-223131-2.

"Jazz Sets and Tone Rows" (alto saxophone, piano). 1991. Roxbury, Mass.: Leonellis Music. Commissioned by Videmus. Premiere, 1991. Recorded: New World Records 80423-2.

"Jazz Sets with T. T." (alto saxophone, piano). 1991. Roxbury, Mass.: Leonellis Music. Commissioned by Videmus. Premiere, 1991. Recorded: New World Records 80515-2.

Suite in Three Movements. 1990. Roxbury, Mass.: Leonellis Music. Premiere, 1990. Recorded: Music and Arts CD-732.

"Variants on a Theme by Monk." 1990. Roxbury, Mass.: Leonellis Music. Premiere, 1990. Recorded: Music and Arts CD-732.

Piano
Children's Songs for Solo Piano. 1989. Providence, R.I.: White Lilac Press, n.d. Commissioned by Faina Bryanskaya. Premiere, 1989.

Concert Etude no. 1. 1989. Unpublished manuscript. Commissioned by Videmus. Premiere, 1989.

Fantasy Variations on Schoenberg's op. 23. 1989. Unpublished manuscript. Contents: Prelude; Capriccio; Intermezzo; Finale. Premiere, 1989.

"Four Chords from T. J.'s *Intermezzi.*" 1991. Roxbury, Mass.: Leonellis Music. Premiere, 1991. Recorded: New World Records 80423-2.

"Four Chords Revisited." 1995. Roxbury, Mass.: Leonellis Music. Commissioned by Tufts University Department of Music. Premiere, 1995.

"Improvisations on Themes of T. J. Anderson." 1989. Unpublished manuscript. Premiere, 1989. Recorded: New World Records CD-732.

Intermezzo. 1990. Roxbury, Mass.: Leonellis Music. Premiere, 1991. Recorded: Music and Arts CD-732.

"Polytonal Thirds for Béla." In *Extraordinary Measures—The League-ISCM, Boston Piano Book: 33 Easy-to-Intermediate Pieces.* West Somerville, Mass.: League-ISCM, 1994.

"Refutation and Hypothesis I: A Treatise for Piano Solo." 1979–81. Newton Centre, Mass.: Margun Music, 1982. Premiere, 1985.

"The Scream." 1996. Roxbury, Mass.: Leonellis Music. Commissioned by the Paris New Music Review for the Sixty Seconds Project. Premiere, 1997.

Suite in Three Movements. Unpublished manuscript. Recorded: Music and Arts CD-732.

"Variants on a Theme by Monk." Unpublished manuscript. Recorded: Music and Arts CD-732.

Two Pianos

Dialectics for Two Grand Pianos. 1988. Newton Centre, Mass.: Margun Music, 1992. Commissioned by the Massachusetts Council on the Arts and Humanities, Heritage Program, and Vivian Taylor for Videmus. Premiere, 1991. Recorded: New World 80423-2.

CHAMBER ORCHESTRA

Refutation and Hypothesis II (horn, trumpet, two trombones, two violins, viola, cello, double bass, two pianos, drum set). 1983. Roxbury, Mass.: Leonellis Music. Commissioned by the Fromm Foundation at Harvard University and the Berkshire Music Center. Premiere, 1983.

ORCHESTRA (CHAMBER OR FULL) WITH SOLOISTS

Chamber Improvisation I (piccolo/flute, vibraphone, trumpet, trombone, violin, cello, piano). 1992. Roxbury, Mass.: Leonellis Music. Commissioned by the St. Louis Symphony Orchestra. Premiere, 1992.

Chamber Improvisation II (flute, clarinet, violin, viola, cello, piano, percussion). 1992. Roxbury, Mass.: Leonellis Music. Commissioned by Dinosaur Annex. Premiere, 1992.

Chamber Improvisation III (voice, clarinet/bass clarinet, violin, cello, piano, percussion). 1992. Roxbury, Mass.: Leonellis Music. Commissioned by the St. Louis Symphony Orchestra Discovery Series. Premiere, 1992.

Chamber Improvisation IIIa (voice, flute, clarinet, violins, guitar, bass, harp, piano). 1993. Unpublished manuscript. Commissioned by Tufts University New Music Festival. Premiere, 1993.

Chamber Improvisation IV (soprano, flute, clarinet, violin, viola, cello, piano, percussion). 1993. Roxbury, Mass.: Leonellis Music. Commissioned by Boston Musica Viva. Premiere, 1993.

Concerto for Piano and Orchestra. Unpublished manuscript. Commissioned by the St. Louis Symphony Orchestra. Premiere, 1995.

ORCHESTRA

Letting Go. 1993. Roxbury, Mass.: Leonellis Music. Commissioned by the Little Orchestra of Cambridge [Mass.]. Premiere, 1993.

VOICE WITH INSTRUMENTAL ENSEMBLE

"T-Cell Countdown" (tenor or soprano, piano, double bass). 1993. Roxbury, Mass.: Leonellis Music. Commissioned by the Bermuda Triangle for the Political Songbook Project. Premiere, 1993. Recorded: New World Records 80515-2.

DRAMATIC MUSIC

"Following the North Star Boogaloo" (narrator and piano). 1993. Roxbury, Mass.: Leonellis Music. Commissioned by WGBH Educational Foundation, WGBH Radio, and Videmus. Premiere, 1993. Recorded: New World Records 80515-2.

Gone City (ballet for clarinet, piano, and double bass). 1993–94. Roxbury, Mass.: Leonellis Music. Commissioned by the Boston Ballet. Premiere, 1994. Recorded: New World Records 80515-2.

"The Old People Speak of Death" (narrator and piano). 1993. Roxbury, Mass.: Leonellis Music. Commissioned by WGBH Educational Foundation, WGBH Radio, and Videmus. Premiere, 1993. Recorded: New World Records 80515-2.

"River Town Packin' House Blues" (narrator and piano). 1993. Roxbury, Mass.: Leonellis Music. Commissioned by WGBH Educational Foundation, WGBH Radio, and Videmus. Premiere, 1993. Recorded: New World Records 80515-2.

PRINCIPAL ARCHIVES

Boston Public Library, Boston, Mass.

Brookline Public Library, Brookline, Mass.

Indiana University, Archive of African American Music, Bloomington, Ind.

Tufts University Library, Medford, Mass.

* * * * *

Composer, pianist, and conductor Donal Fox works comfortably in many idioms and brings together in his works an eclectic range of influences from jazz, blues, Western art music, and popular forms. Over the last few years, Fox's performing and writing activities have earned him several awards and commissions, confirming his position as one of the country's rising and innovative compositional voices. His work challenges the divide that exists between Western art music and jazz because he strives to create music that exploits and blurs the ideals of "improvisation" and "composition." As Fox has said: "I am interested in reaching out to both sides of the fence. Improvisation and jazz are not limited to the club and the smoke-filled room, nor are people associated with classical composition or concert music restricted to an elitist concert hall." Fox has composed works for solo piano and for chamber orchestra; chamber works for violin, alto saxophone, clarinet, voice, and bass clarinet; and a ballet. His tendency to straddle the fence between "classical" music and jazz makes his music particularly difficult to categorize, a fact that delights this composer. In his compositions, Fox creates the impression of a seamless connection between notated and improvised aspects of his work. He believes that this stylistic feature positions his work not only in the traditions of great jazz musicians like Thelonious Monk, Duke Ellington, and Charlie Parker but also within the improvisatory traditions of Western art music reflected in the likes of Bach, Mozart, and Beethoven.

Fox was born in 1952 in Boston, Massachusetts, to an interracial couple—a Jewish father and a Panamanian mother. In the formative years of his home setting, Fox heard an eclectic mix of musical styles. Educated in the public schools of nearby Brookline, Massachusetts, Fox was encouraged to pursue music study by his father, Herbert Leon Fox, who had studied composition at Boston University, and often improvised with his son. Listening sessions in the home featured recordings of Western art music—including, for example, Stravinsky's *Rite of Spring*—and jazz—including Miles Davis's *Birth of the Cool,* for example.

Fox began to study the piano at age eight with Edna Ida Itkin and later studied formally with the French pianist Jeanette Giguère at the New England Conservatory of Music, continuing with her through his teen years. Fox then began to take a musical path that would mark his future artistic profile, composing works that combined jazz and classical idioms. In 1968, he studied at Boston's Berklee College of Music and, in the following year, won a scholarship to the Berkshire Music Center in Tanglewood, Massachusetts. His studies during this period included counterpoint and fugue with Avram David. Fox's eclectic musical interests led him to seek out other like-minded composers as his teachers, and he found suitable ones in T. J. Anderson and Gunther Schuller, both of whom draw on musical materials from varied traditions. Anderson wrote of Fox's dual musical heritage: "From classical music Mr. Fox derives structure and design, cadenzas, disjunct lines, ostinato trills, development, and rubato. From jazz spring improvisation, harmony, riffs, walking bass, accents, polyrhythm, and free time."

Although Fox believes his work is rather cerebral, individualistic, and abstract, he has established an international reputation through his collaborations with other artists such as Oliver Lake, David Murray, Billy Pierce, John Stubblefield, Quincy Troupe, and Miquel Algarin. Fortunately, many of Fox's collaborations can be heard on recordings. For example, his ballet in three movements, *Gone City* (1993–94), commissioned by the Boston Ballet, was written with the input of the project's choreographers, Richard Colton and Amy Spencer. Inspired by the *film noir* genre, some of the thematic ideas conveyed in the ballet include boxing, dance halls, city streets, chase scenes, train stations at rush hour, lyricism, sexy women, and strong men. Fox's belief was that he could musically convey these modalities through collaboration not only with *Gone City*'s choreographers but also with his fellow musicians. So that he could control his music in "real time," Fox left parts of his score (for piano, clarinet, and bass) open for improvisation. This technique allowed Fox to create the sense of excitement that the thematic content of the choreography demanded and also to provide the score with a self-sufficiency that works independently of the ballet.

Fox's highly original approach has earned him a number of awards and commissions.

DIALECTICS FOR TWO GRAND PIANOS (1988)

Dialectics was commissioned through a grant from the Heritage Program of the Massachusetts Council on the Arts and Humanities and Vivian Taylor, pianist and founder and former artistic director of Videmus, a chamber organization established in 1986 to perform the music of minority composers. According to pianist Billy Taylor, Fox "abandoned traditional academic procedures and post-Romantic composing techniques, in favor of an organization of sounds based on the interaction of instrumental media and their performing environments." Demonstrating clearly the composer's interest in bridging improvisation and written composition, *Dialectics* is fully scored, and the performers are required to create a broad range of sonic effects, including guttural sounds, shouts, laughter, foot stomping, fist booms, tapping, and plucking.

Dialectics divides into six almost seamless episodes of varying length and sonority. The score indicates that each pianist will make sounds vocally, on the piano's strings, and on its keys. The piece opens with a dramatic gesture that requires each pianist to sing a nonsense syllable in unison with piano. The first section is characterized by an agitated mood in which there are combined florid arpeggio passages, flutter-tongued vocal utterances, plucked

strings, and intermittent chords struck in a percussive, almost unpianistic, manner. These gestures are gradually converted into the second episode, a section without vocals that makes use of shimmering piano effects that slowly thin out into gentle raindrop-like thumps. The third episode is humorously marked "relaxed groove" but abstracts various elements that comprise a typical jazz groove, especially in its percussive dimensions. Fox's treatment—complete with interjections such as "yeah" and "baby"—sounds very modernistic, pushing the boundaries of jazz stylings. Episode four is dominated by a robust ostinato pattern that almost references minimalism. Yet because of the rapid tempo (quarter note = 138) that gradually gets faster throughout the episode, Fox cleverly frustrates any direct connection to either minimalism or to African-American popular dance forms in which ostinato patterns dominate.

The next episode, which functions as the climactic point in the piece, is marked "rejoice" and begins with a *fortissimo* shout. In another humorous gesture, Fox punctuates the section with sporadic fits of loud, "gleeful demonic laughter," yelps, and calls. These vocal sounds are underscored by loud, rhythmically disjunct passages played by both pianos. The fury of this section gradually subsides into the much calmer episode six, in which the pianists sing a monosyllabic dyad accompanied by impressionistic piano passages and plucked strings. In the final episode, the energy in *Dialectics* further dissipates into sparse chords played on piano strings and keys. Fox brings the piece to a halt by slowly thinning out the soundscape into a hushed pedal point and a single-note triplet figure played on the strings.

T-CELL COUNTDOWN (1993)

This brief but emotionally charged piece is scored for tenor (or soprano), piano, and double bass. Although the score requires that the performers achieve the effect of improvisation, "T-Cell Countdown" is thoroughly notated. T. J. Anderson writes that this piece— "a wordless monodrama"—captures "the struggle of one dealing with AIDS." Fox moves the listener on an emotional continuum from anger and agony to resolution; he achieves this stunning effect by using two contrasting sections that represent these states of mind. The first section comprises a bundle of musical gestures that create the "anger" motives. "T-Cell Countdown" opens with rapid descending and ascending single-note passages in the piano. Built on two tonal areas, F Lydian and G-flat major, this bitonal, aggressive, and unstable gesture seems to plunge the listener into the kind of disorientation that one might feel on learning of the presence in his or her body of the AIDS virus. This opening gesture also might be heard as representing the aggressive disease itself wreaking havoc on the patient's immune system and psyche. Fox allows disorientation to give way quickly to anger. Pounding chords on the piano coupled with bowed, heavily accented passages in the double bass make the *fortissimo* lines in the singer's part convey an overwhelmingly visceral response to AIDS. The section culminates in rhythmically disjunct, repeated low notes on the piano, which are joined briefly and belatedly by the double bass. These repeated notes bridge the two emotional worlds represented in this piece. Following this clipped transition, Fox provides a plaintive, ascending vocal passage, again with soft nonsense vowels and occasional falsetto notes. This

Donal Leonellis Fox; courtesy of the composer; photo by Eric H. Antoniou

peaceful melody is accompanied by sparse piano passages that gently caress the vocal line.

RIVER TOWN PACKIN' HOUSE BLUES (1993), THE OLD PEOPLE SPEAK OF DEATH (1993), FOLLOWING THE NORTH STAR BOOGALOO (1993)

This trilogy of works features Fox's pianistic imagination in collaboration with poet Quincy Troupe, co-author of the prize-winning autobiography of Miles Davis. These collaborations combine two distinct traditions. Fox uses techniques derived from the piano experimentation championed by the American composer Henry Cowell and from the politically salient legacy of the poetry of the Black Arts Movement of the late 1960s and early 1970s. Because of its potential for direct communication, poetry was perhaps the movement's preferred medium.

Throughout "River Town Packin' House Blues," the story of a John Henry-like figure, Fox explores the piano's sonic possibilities, manipulating its strings by hand to create effects that enhance and dramatize Troupe's spoken words. Troupe's part in the collaboration is itself also quite musical, featuring direct statements that draw some of their form and delivery style from the structure of blues poetry and from African-American musical techniques such as riffs, repetition, and "worrying" the line. For example, early in the work Troupe declares: "Big Tom was a black nigga man, cold and black/I say, Big Tom was a black nigga man, black steel flesh." These two lines are clearly related to the first two lines of classic blues poetry. But after this set-up, Troupe moves into an elongated third line: "Standing like a gladiator, soaked in animal blood, bits of flesh, ringing wet, standing at the center of death, buzzards hovering, swinging his hammer called death, 260 work days, I say, swinging his hammer named death." Fox draws attention to this narrative play by undergirding the entire passage with a plodding, single low tone in the piano in an irregular rhythm. The resulting musical effect gives the passage a gripping force, especially as juxtaposed with Troupe's more urgent style of delivery, which in other sections Fox underscores with more agitated accompaniment.

Fox animates the accompaniment with a full range of techniques, including sweeping atonal passages, segments played on the strings of the piano, repeated melodic fragments that cluster into hypnotic rhythmic patterns, and rich, full-bodied jazz chords, among other gestures. Many passages are underpinned by the pounding lower notes that seem to stand for the "hammer called death" imagery. Fox combines and recombines all of these gestures throughout the piece, building to climaxes with each poetic stanza and providing a sense of drama that makes the emotional thrust of the piece gripping.

"The Old People Speak of Death" explores one aspect of the human condition, namely, mortality. A sparsely adorned backdrop is employed here, one that again remains rooted in two traditions—the 19th-century romanticism of Western art music and the approach of jazz pianists such as Herbie Hancock or Bill Evans. Troupe's text is a meditation on death and aging, the contemplative mood of which Fox supplements with delicately clustered harmonies that occasionally unleash scalar, *legato* melodies that soar above the chords. The harmonies themselves shift gently among a series of tonal centers in each of which Fox creates interest through lyric melodies and rhythmic nuance. Through delicate touch and subdued dynamics, a feeling of weightlessness is created—an effect that musically conveys the people of whom Troupe speaks—those who have died and "gone to spirit."

"Following the North Star Boogaloo" returns to an expressly African-American theme. Troupe's urgent delivery is upstaged by the lyrics as they move quickly through a number of themes, much as does a rap performance. Troupe's narrative is packed with references to popular culture, basketball, hip-hop culture, the black church, the dozens, and much more. T. J. Anderson has written of these lyrics that "the poet's basketball imagery serves as a metaphor for African-American life." Troupe critiques the "new-age home-boy's" lack of knowledge of previous historical African-American heroes and makes strident observations about the postmodern condition of urban black communities that are situated "north of where we entered from Africa." Fox chose not to match the energy of these lyrics with an equally shrill and agitated accompaniment; instead, it is restrained, limited to percussive work on the strings and the body of the piano, with occasional high notes on the keys. The overall effect is that of an extremely melodic conga drummer whose part unobtrusively complements the textual aspects of the piece. It should be noted that many rap recordings use a similar approach, stripping the accompaniment to its bare essentials in order to draw more attention to the unusually dense narrative content of the lyrics. Fox once again demonstrates his ability to draw on various musical traditions to achieve a desired musical treatment.

REFERENCES

Anderson, T. J. Liner notes, *Gone City*. New World Records 80515-2.

Davis, Miles, with Quincy Troupe. *Miles: The Autobiography*. New York: Simon and Schuster, 1989.

Taylor, Billy. Liner notes, *Videmus: Works by T. J. Anderson, David Baker, Donal Fox, Olly Wilson*. New World Records 80423-2, 1992.

GUTHRIE P. RAMSEY JR.

FREEMAN, HARRY LAWRENCE

[Because of the amount of conflicting information encountered in the preparation of this entry, with several sources giving different dates for particular events and different titles for particular compositions, we have chosen to take a cautious approach to it. Therefore, when conflicting data cannot be satisfactorily resolved, even when family members have provided it, we have chosen to rely solely on information provided by Eileen Southern's Biographical Dictionary of African-American and African Musicians. —Ed.]

Born in Cleveland, Ohio, October 9, 1869; died in New York, N.Y., March 21, 1954. **Education:** Cleveland public schools; studied piano with Edwin Schonert and Carlos Sobrino; studied theory, composition, and orchestration with Johann Beck. **Composing and Performing Career:** Cleveland, Ohio, organized, directed, and accompanied, Boys Quartette, age ten; worked as church organist; Denver, Colo., operas *Epthelia* and *The Martyr* premiered, 1893; World's Columbian Exposition, Chicago, Ill., Freeman Grand Opera Company performed *The Martyr,* 1893; Chicago, Ill., musical director, Ernest Hogan's Rufus Rastus Company, 1905; Pekin [Theater] Stock Company, musical director and composer; New York, N.Y., musical director, Bob Cole/Johnson brothers' *The Red Moon* company, ca. 1905–10; Negro Choral Society, conductor; Negro Grand Opera Company, founder, composer, producer, beginning 1920; opera *Voodoo* broadcast over radio, 1928; *Voodoo* staged at the 52nd Street Theater, 1928; Steinway Hall, New York, N.Y., excerpts from nine operas performed in concert, 1930; World's Fair, Chicago, Ill., music director and conductor for the pageant *O Sing a New Song,* 1934; Carnegie Hall, New York, N.Y., *The Martyr* performed in concert, 1947. **Teaching Career:** Wilberforce University, Wilberforce, Ohio, 1902–04; Salem School of Music, New York, N.Y., founder and director, 1910s; Freeman School of Music, New York, N.Y., founder and director, 1910s; Freeman School of Grand Opera, founder and director, beginning 1923. **Honors/Awards:** William E. Harmon Award, 1930.

MUSIC LIST

ORCHESTRA (CHAMBER OR FULL) WITH CHOIR
The Slave. 1917–25. Unpublished manuscript.

SOLO VOICE
"Broken Dreams."
"Down Where the Yazoo River Flows." 1924. Unpublished manuscript.
"I'd Choose a Southern Girl." New York: Jerome H. Remick, 1910.
"If Thou Didst Love" (high voice). 1935. New York: Handy Brothers Music Co., 1935.
Lives of Pompey (song cycle). ca. 1915. Unpublished manuscript.
"Whither?" (high voice). 1935. New York: Handy Brothers Music Co., 1935.

DRAMATIC MUSIC
An African Kraal or *Kiffer Grand Opera* (opera). 1902–03; revised 1934. Unpublished manuscript.

Allah (opera). 1932–47. Unpublished manuscript. Notes: believed to be lost; may have been part of the opera tetralogy *Zululand.*
An American Romance (opera). 1927. Unpublished manuscript. Note: unproduced.
Athalia (opera). 1915–16. Unpublished manuscript.
Captain Rufus (revue). 1907. Unpublished manuscript. Co-composers, Joe Jordan, James ("Tim") Brymn. Premiere, 1907.
Chaka (opera). 1927 or 1941. Unpublished manuscript. Note: may have been part of the opera tetralogy *Zululand.*
The Confederate (opera). ca. 1916. Unpublished manuscript.
Dark Canyon (opera). Unpublished manuscript. Note: unproduced.
Epthelia (opera). 1893. Unpublished manuscript. Note: lost. Premiere, 1893.
The Flapper (opera). 1929. Unpublished manuscript.
Fugitive (race drama). 1921. Unpublished manuscript.
The Ghost-Wolves (opera). 1941. Unpublished manuscript. Note: may have been part of the opera tetralogy *Zululand.*
Leah Kleschna (opera). 1930–31. Unpublished manuscript. Note: unproduced.
The Martyr (opera). 1893. Unpublished manuscript. Note: original title, *Platonus.* Premiere, 1893.
My Son (cantata). 1898. Unpublished manuscript. Premiere, 1898.
Nada (opera). 1925–47. Unpublished manuscript. Notes: may have been part of the opera tetralogy *Zululand;* not performed.
The Octoroon (opera). 1902–04. Unpublished manuscript.
Panama (opera). ca. 1908. Unpublished manuscript. Co-composer, James ("Tim") Brymn.
The Plantation or *A Modern Plantation* (revue). 1906–15. Unpublished manuscript. Premiere, 1912.
The Prophecy (opera). 1911. Unpublished manuscript. Premiere, 1911.
Rufus Rastus (revue). 1905. Co-composers, Ernest Hogan, Tom Lemonier, Joe Jordan. Premiere, 1905.
Slave Ballet from Salome (SATB, orchestra). 1923. Unpublished manuscript. Premiere, 1932.
Slaying of the Lion (opera). Unpublished manuscript.
The Stone-Witch (opera). 1941. Unpublished manuscript. Note: may have been part of the opera tetralogy *Zululand.*
The Tryst (opera). ca. 1908–09. Unpublished manuscript. Premiere, 1911.
Umslopagaas and Nada (opera). 1941. Unpublished manuscript. Note: may have been part of the opera tetralogy *Zululand.*
Uzziah (opera). ca. 1934. Unpublished manuscript. Note: unproduced.
Valdo (opera). 1905. Unpublished manuscript. Note: planned as the first of a cycle titled *The Destiny;* the other operas, not completed, listed as *Dulcina, Xerifa,* and *Florina.* Premiere, 1906.
Vendetta (opera). 1923. Unpublished manuscript. Premiere, 1923.
Voodoo (opera). 1912–14. Unpublished manuscript. Premiere, 1928.
The Wolf (children's cantata). 1899. Unpublished manuscript. Premiere, 1899.
Zulu King: Witch Hunt (ballet). 1934. Unpublished manuscript.
Zuluki (opera). 1897–98. Unpublished manuscript. Note: original title, *Nada.* Premiere, 1900.

*Harry Lawrence Freeman; Theodore Charles Stone Collection,
Center for Black Music Research, Columbia College Chicago*

PUBLICATIONS

ABOUT FREEMAN
Dissertations

Davidson, Celia E. "Operas by Afro-American Composers: A Critical
    Survey and Analysis of Selected Works." Ph.D. diss., Catholic
    University of America, 1980.

Articles

Abdul, Raoul. "Operas by Black Composers." In *Blacks in Classical Music.*
    New York: Dodd, Mead and Co., 1977.

BY FREEMAN

"The Negro in the Higher Altitudes of Music in This Country and
    Throughout the World." *AME Review* (1915).
The Negro in Music and Drama. Unpublished manuscript.
Regular column in *The Afro-American* newspaper, 1935–37.
Regular column in the *New Amsterdam News,* 1935–37.

* * * * *

Harry Lawrence Freeman received favorable press attention
throughout his career. An article in the *Cleveland Press* in 1898,
acclaiming him as "the Colored Wagner," stated that he was given
the title by "the musicians of Cleveland" and asserted, "This young
man is considered the foremost musical genius in the city." In an
appraisal of Freeman for the local press, Johann Beck, founder and
conductor of the Cleveland Orchestra, declared, "His compositions are wonderful—big in conception, the music faithfully portraying the sentiment in the words. He is the most promising music
student with whom I have met." In 1900, the Cleveland Orchestra,
conducted by Beck, performed several instrumental interludes
from Freeman's opera *Zuluki.* These works were believed to have
been the first by an Afro-American composer to be presented by a
major symphony orchestra in the United States.

Freeman was born in Cleveland, Ohio, on October 9, 1869,
in the house at 686 Sterling Avenue that his grandfather—who had

literally "walked away from slavery"—had built about 15 years before the Civil War. By the standards of the day for a black family, the Freemans were "well-to-do." As a boy, Harry had his own horse and buggy, his clothes were tailor-made, and he collected a sizable library of classics, popular fiction, moral tracts, and biographies. He attended public school music classes and sang in a boys' quartet that he organized and directed at the age of ten. This quartet sang frequently at the Euclid Avenue Baptist Church, the home church of John D. Rockefeller Sr. As an adult, Freeman had a few lessons on various instruments and in composition from Johann Beck.

The mid-19th century was an auspicious time to grow up in Cleveland. The city, bursting with energy, offered numerous political, economic, and cultural opportunities to its enterprising citizens. Freeman was certainly influenced by the success of such Clevelanders as attorney John P. Green, the first Negro to be elected to public office in Cleveland, and author Charles Waddell Chestnutt. A schoolmate was Rachel Walker Turner, who became known as the "Creole Nightingale" and was under contract to Oscar Hammerstein. Cleveland was then on the brink of phenomenal prosperity: steel and manufacturing companies were flourishing as several mergers had created the Standard Oil Company of Ohio. Education and the arts were strongly supported and generously endowed by some of the city's wealthiest citizens. Freeman was introduced to Wagner's *Tannhäuser* in 1892 at a Denver performance of the Emma Juch Grand Opera Company. The infatuation was immediate: Wagner's music became his model.

In 1893, Freeman, the avid reader and armchair adventurer, went west. On February 9, 1893, the *Rocky Mountain News,* a major Denver newspaper of the time, noted the first performance of his opera *Epthelia.* This work, now lost, is believed to be the second opera in the English language written by an American composer of African descent. (The first was John Thomas Douglass's *Virginia's Ball* [1868].) Freeman's second opera, *The Martyr,* was premiered in the late summer of the same year at the German Theater in Denver and was then performed by a group formed by the composer in October at the World's Columbian Exposition in Chicago. These performances occurred less than 50 years after the opening of William Fry's *Leonora,* which was noted in Edward Hipsher's *American Opera and Its Composers* as the first publicly performed "real American opera" and "the first serious American opera."

Freeman had grown to manhood during an optimistic period, when rapid industrial changes, suggestions of economic independence for the resourceful, the passage of the 13th, 14th, and 15th amendments, newly enacted public school laws, and the suffrage acts spawned dreams of equality and assimilation. But disenfranchisement, legislated discrimination, downward turns in education and employment opportunities, and broken promises shattered the hopes of African Americans.

Freeman taught music at Wilberforce University in Ohio from 1902 to 1904, when it was an educational and cultural haven for young black students. The school took pride in its numerous musical ensembles, and the students' dance orchestras were famous far beyond the boundaries of Ohio. This environment, however, did not persuade Freeman to pursue an institutional teaching career. There is no evidence that he studied for, or even contemplated getting, the valued credentials from academia that would have ensured him a comfortable and highly respected teaching position.

Freeman toured the states with various popular entertainment groups, including Ernest Hogan's blackface comedy ensemble known as the Rufus Rastus Company. (Valdo Freeman pointed out that his father wrote serious music for the shows and left the ragtime and popular ballad writing to Joe Jordan and Timothy Brown.) Freeman was also the musical director for Cole and Johnson's *Red Moon,* for the Ragoon Company, and for the Pekin Stock Company. Yet he resisted numerous urgings to sustain himself and cushion his family materially by composing blackface comedy and coon songs.

Around 1908, he moved his family to Harlem, an area of New York City that was soon to become the primary mecca for African Americans. In this setting, Freeman cut a rather dashing figure. Physically, he was quite modest in size, but his manner and bearing made him seem tall. He appeared formidable with his Vandyke beard, expertly tailored cutaway coat, pearl-gray spats, and handsome walking cane. By 1920, the college youth were calling the corner of 135th Street and 7th Avenue "The Campus." One could stand there and see such neighborhood celebrities as James Weldon Johnson, "Fats" Waller, Lawrence Brown, Florence Mills, and the "Hair-Dressing Heiress," A'Lelia Walker. The Lafayette Theater was on 132nd Street; the "Y" and the Harlem branch of the New York Public Library were on 135th Street. In spite of its glamorous facade, Harlem was a strong middle-class community with conservative attitudes and outlook. James Weldon Johnson called it "second generation respectability."

Many problems, especially financial ones, prevented Freeman from realizing two of his dreams until 1920. That year he opened his own music school on 133rd Street near Lenox Avenue and inaugurated the Negro Grand Opera Company, Inc., perhaps the first such company on the East Coast founded for the purpose of performing a particular composer's works. The group performed in theaters and in churches.

Although finances were a constant and nagging problem for Freeman, his wife, Carlotta (a respected singer-actress and member of the Lafayette Players), and their only child, Valdo (born in 1900), were always supportive. During the opera productions, Carlotta and Valdo did administrative and publicity work and performed on stage. Freeman wanted only to write and produce his operas, and his private teaching advanced this desire. Most of his students—children and adults—were poor, but Freeman promoted their talents. His voice students augmented the choruses and crowd scenes of his operas, and his instrumental students formed the nucleus of his pit orchestras. Freeman frequently had to rearrange his orchestrations to accommodate the instrumentalists' limitations, and more often than not, the piano was the only accompaniment. Freeman's interest in folklore is first evidenced in his opera *The Tryst,* an American Indian story. *The Octoroon* followed. Sometime after 1910, he completed *The Plantation,* which he described as a "Negro Grand Opera." Originally in three acts, it was a collage of spirituals, "Ethiopian" tunes, and popular-styled melodies. These three works appear to have been a series of preliminary exercises in preparation for *Voodoo,* which premiered early in 1928.

The greatest moments for Freeman and his company involved his opera *Voodoo,* which was presented on radio station WGBS in 1928. September 1928 saw the work in a full stage production with soloists, costumes, scenery, and orchestra at the 52nd Street Theater.

Several important recognitions followed the success of *Voodoo.* Freeman won a William E. Harmon Award in 1930, and in 1934 he was named music director for the expansive and elaborate pageant *O Sing a New Song,* which was to be held at Soldier Field during the Chicago World's Fair.

At various times during his many years in New York, Freeman was engaged as an arbiter of cultural matters in Harlem through his writings. For more than a year (1935–37), he wrote a column for *The Afro-American* newspaper in which he reviewed concerts, gave advice, and documented historic events. Freeman taught, composed, and planned new works until blindness and the infirmities of age curtailed these activities. He died on March 21, 1954, of a heart attack.

For all American-born composers and performers of serious music, this was the time when the "studied and performed in Europe" label was the necessary imprimatur of acceptance for assuring substantial financial backing, generous patrons, and the support of ticket-buying audiences; it was especially needed for the tremendous undertaking of opera production. Beyond the need for a European reference, the black creative artist was circumscribed by the crushing conditions and prevailing stereotypes of race and color. In the face of all these odds, Harry Lawrence Freeman stubbornly pursued his dream, grandly and against almost overwhelming odds. He was determined, self-assured, initially optimistic, and later fatalistic. His operas are uneven in quality. Some, apparently, were merely exercises in preparation for the more adventuresome works that followed. But considered in the context of the times, Freeman and his musical efforts represent a triumph in the segregated cultural society of that era.

Among Freeman's compositions are operas, a drama, incidental ballet music for chorus and orchestra, a sacred cantata, a fairy tale cantata for children, two symphonic poems, a song cycle, and a number of individual songs. According to Valdo Freeman, the exact number of works, especially operas, is unknown because several compositions were lost during Freeman's various moves between cities and homes in New York, because the composer changed the names of some operas after they were performed, and because he frequently mentioned the names of planned and incomplete works to friends and interviewers, who then mentioned the names in articles. But we do know that twelve different operas, excerpted or in their entirety and spanning some 40 years, were performed during the composer's lifetime.

Freeman, an insatiable reader from childhood, collected a sizable personal library. His favorite reading materials were essays on the history and geography of Africa, travel adventures, and novels involving "noble Egyptians" and the "un-Christian savages" that were exceedingly popular in the late 19th century. These preferences are seen in his choices of opera plots, with subjects that range from African history and fiction, and from native folklore and miscegenation in the United States, to the adaptation of a rather successful English drama. Opera locales included Mexico, the Orient,

southern Michigan, a southern plantation, and a successful Manhattan broker's office. *Voodoo* was billed as a "Negro Opera"; the unproduced *An American Romance* and *The Flapper* were called "Jazz Grand Opera."

The plots, usually original, observed the dramatic rule of cause and effect and, in true operatic style, were enhanced with intense sentiment and exaggerated emotion. The generally straightforward storyline avoided intricate subplots and intrigues. *The Martyr* is the story of a young Egyptian nobleman who, despite the pleading of his loved ones, accepts the sentence of death for his belief in Jehovah. In *The Tryst,* the wounded Indian brave kills the white hunter who ambushed and fatally shot his sweetheart. The opera *Valdo* presents an ironic twist of fate: a young wealthy Mexican, whose origins had never been revealed, tries to win the affections of Dulcinea, the sweetheart of a dangerous rogue. The men fight a duel, and as the young protagonist lies dying, the specific circumstances of his birth are revealed: Dulcinea is his sister. The universally favorite storyline, the romantic triangle, is used in *Vendetta,* and the opera *Voodoo* somewhat superficially explores the consequences of several pagan beliefs that cloud the path of two young lovers.

For all of the operas except one, Freeman was unfortunately his own librettist. The action usually is excruciatingly static; the language is often excessively flowery, stilted, and pompous. This problem is most glaring in *Voodoo,* in which heavy-handed Negro dialect is juxtaposed with such statements as, "Should there be one here who gainsays my right, Let him stand forth."

In contrast, Freeman's musical creativity showed promise. He loved the Wagner operas; he studied them carefully and, especially in his early works, consciously tried to imitate Wagner's techniques. The harmonic study of Freeman's later operas reveals his abundant use of random and sequential seventh chords (especially dominant, diminished, and half-diminished in quality, traditionally altered and enharmonically spelled), the use of quartal harmonies, and elusive tonalities created by rhythmic manipulations. The scores illustrate Freeman's fondness for writing the predominant melodies in the accompaniment rather than in the vocal line. He wrote some beautiful melodies but seldom developed them. He wrote a few interesting theme and variations sections but usually extended an idea simply by restating the original melody. Some of the more promising rhythmic motives, continuously repeated without alteration, become monotonous. Vocally, the works show Freeman's preference for high tessituras.

Only a few of Freeman's compositions were published. These include 32 pieces from *Voodoo,* including the "Voodoo Dance," a piano reduction of a symphonic poem, "Zulu King," and two songs for solo voice, published by Handy Brothers Music Company. The operas remain in manuscript.

THE MARTYR (1893)

The Martyr, originally entitled *Platonus,* is based on an original story and was written between February and July 1893. The complete work and excerpted portions were performed frequently during the next 45 years. In addition, the quintet from the opera was used in several Rufus Rastus productions, and an interesting and entertaining duet of various melodies was arranged for saxophones by Freeman for the talented entertainers, who worked under the name of the Housley Brothers.

The plot centers on Platonus, a noble Egyptian who becomes a follower of Jehovah. This denunciation of tradition and of the deity of the Pharaoh is heresy. Although friends beg him to repent and the Pharaoh threatens him with death, Platonus fails to recant and is burned at the stake.

Musically, *The Martyr* is the most naïve of Freeman's several performed operas. Much of the vocal writing is syllabic, and there is a preference for melodic lines that outline chord tones and sometimes move in wide skips and octave leaps. The da capo aria form is prevalent and several of the melodies are used like *leitmotifs* to represent a particular person or event. They do not appear as true motives or even melodic fragments but are usually heard as complete phrases. *The Martyr* contains no 19th-century *bel canto* arias and little contrast between the recitatives and solo sections that are labeled "aria."

The libretto, written by Freeman himself, was in the stilted style that was fashionable during the period. *The Martyr* shows a brashness of the young and the very naïve.

VOODOO (1928)

Voodoo was a "work in progress" for more than a decade. After its radio premiere on May 20, 1928, a stage production was given at the Palm Garden at the 52nd Street Theater on two successive nights in September of the same year. According to Edward Hipsher, this opera was credited as "the first opera on a Negro theme, by a Negro composer, presented by a Negro impresario and an all-Negro troupe, to invade the Broadway district."

Of *Voodoo*, the *Brooklyn Daily Times* quoted a WGBS spokesman as saying, "The story is tense and gripping and the songs, which include jazz, blues, spirituals and voodoo chants, are both novel and tuneful." The same article noted, "That unique piece deals with a love affair on a New Orleans plantation, immediately after the Civil War, and it is to be presented with a cast of 30 people and a 20-piece symphony orchestra." The *Telegraph* announced the number of performers and gave the names of soloists Carlotta Freeman, Doris Trotman, Ray Yates, and Otto Bohanan. There was no orchestra; Freeman played the accompaniment on the piano.

Voodoo is a work of numerous contrasts. The dialogue juxtaposes the pompous and flowery speech with the overexaggerations of minstrel-inspired Negro dialect. The opening of the prelude to act 1 strongly suggests the melodies of the spirituals "Nobody Knows the Trouble I've Seen" and "Steal Away." Later in the act, "Steal Away" and "Swing Low, Sweet Chariot" are used literally. In act 2, "Go Down Moses" and "There's a Meeting Here Tonight" are presented and interspersed between operatic arias and recitatives. A toe-tapping ragtime theme appears first in the prelude to act 1, and the infectious rhythm of the tango appears in act 2, followed by a cakewalk theme. The crowd-pleasing "Voodoo Dance" in the third act elicited prolonged applause.

In his compositions, Freeman constantly ignored the limitations of his amateur performers and was also fond of varying the rhythms of an individual part within the span of a few measures. These traits, together with a smorgasbord of ideas, thoughts, themes, and styles, not only contributed to a simulated complexity, but also created aural, and perhaps, visual confusion. There is

much interesting material in *Voodoo*—too much, in fact. The result is an experimental collage of undigested ideas.

The best known of Freeman's operas, *Voodoo* received a generous amount of attention in the press. More than a dozen New York newspapers, other metropolitan papers, and periodicals reviewed the radio broadcast and the stage premiere of the work. The reviews were mixed, and some reviewers admitted their bewilderment. The WGBS broadcast obviously suffered for lack of an orchestra. A *Musical America* columnist wrote, "The radio performance was incomplete and the singers engaged in its exposition did very little to set the opera in a favorable light. Replete with the spiritual atmosphere and containing reminiscences of the old 'cake walk' melodies the opus ran the gamut between the two extremes."

A *New York Times* article of September 11, 1928, commented on the staged version: "The composer utilizes themes from spirituals, Southern melodies and jazz rhythms which, combined with traditional Italian operatic forms, produce a curiously naïve mélange of varied style." Another reviewer stated, "When Mr. Freeman isn't relying on his memory, he falls quite amazingly into forms which are fresh, [and] rhythms which are new." From the *Billboard* (Cincinnati, Ohio), the critic patronizingly observed, "*Voodoo* is a most encouraging sign that the Negro is capable of entering the operatic field and of contributing valuable material and talent to it. This work, however, serves more as a shadow cast before future developments rather than the realization of a perfect production." Like several reviewers, the *Billboard* concluded that "The last act is unquestionably the finest, and here and there are touches of inspired creative powers."

Another reviewer, Robert Garland, wrote that "the libretto . . . is terrible. It sounds as if it had been translated from the Italian. . . . You may not admire *Voodoo*, but it'll seldom bore you." In the *Evening Telegram,* Garland also took notice of the other critics' reactions: "Listening in while music critics oh-ed and ah-ed, I gathered that *Voodoo* is important. It stands for something in the history of American music. Just what, I'm not prepared to say. But it stands for something, something big. As one music critic said to his mate, 'When you write your autobiography, you'll be proud that you were here.'" Charles D. Isaacson in the *Morning Telegraph* (New York City) wrote, "Because it is a beginning, I rise to commend H. Lawrence Freeman. . . . It has some mighty fine moments. The orchestration (scarcely articulate because of the orchestra [which is] below the standards of musicianship required for Freeman's intricate writing) is the best part of the opera." Isaacson further suggested that "If *Voodoo* could be brought to eliminate the first act almost completely, increase the tempo of the second and clarify the third, it would be a score which might prove useful to the major opera companies," and he gave special attention to the voodoo ceremonies and the holiday scene of the clog-dancing cotton-pickers. He concluded, "He can write. . . . Somebody called Freeman the Negro Wagner; maybe he is the Negro Monteverdi."

TWO SONGS

In 1935, Handy Brothers Music Company published two songs by Freeman: "If Thou Didst Love" and "Whither?" According to Valdo Freeman, the songs were well received by the general public, but the monetary rewards were few. At the height of Tin Pan Alley's dominance, music publishers usually titillated their patrons by including a "teaser," or first page of music from another composition they had published and were promoting. They invited the musicians to "try this over on your piano" and quoted the price of the sheet music. Freeman received more deferential treatment. Although Handy did include a "first page" of an alternate song in Freeman's publications, no such invitational "come-on" was included, and the Freeman songs were 40 cents, not the usual 30 cents.

"If Thou Didst Love" and "Whither?" like so many songs of the period, belong neither to the popular format of the day nor to the traditional classic art form of the concert stage. They do, however, have a kinship with the operetta genre. The words and music remind one of the local and regional contest repertory of the twenties, thirties, and forties. Temperate dissonances, *appassionata* melodic lines, and flowery verses characterize both songs.

REFERENCES

Benton, Elbert Jay. *Cultural Story of an American City, Cleveland. Ohio.* Cleveland: Western Reserve Historical Society, 1943.

Brown, Sterling A. *The Negro Caravan.* New York: Arno Press and the New York Times, 1970.

Chestnutt, Charles W. "The Wife of His Youth." In *Cavalcade,* edited by Arthur P. Davis and Saunders Redding, 179–188. Cleveland, Ohio: Cleveland Ohio Press, 1971.

Condon, George E. *Yesterday's Cleveland.* Seemann's Historic Cities Series no. 30. Miami, Fla.: E. A. Seemann Publishing, 1976.

Davidson, Celia E. "Operas by Afro-American Composers: A Critical Survey and Analysis of Selected Works." Ph.D. diss., Catholic University of America, 1980.

Davis, Arthur P. "Growing Up in the Negro Renaissance." In *Cavalcade,* edited by Arthur P. Davis and Saunders Redding, 428–437. Cleveland, Ohio: Cleveland Ohio Press, 1971.

Davis, Russell H. *Memorable Negros in Cleveland's Past.* Cleveland, Ohio: Western Reserve Historical Society, 1969.

Freeman, Harry Lawrence, and Valdo Freeman, compilers. "Scrapbooks." Private collection.

Freeman, Valdo. Interviews with the author, 1971–72.

Hipsher, Edward. *American Opera and Its Composers.* New York: Da Capo Press, 1972.

Johnson, James Weldon. *Black Manhattan.* New York: Atheneum, 1969.

Southern, Eileen. *Biographical Dictionary of Afro-American and African Musicians.* Westport, Conn.: Greenwood Press, 1982.

———. *The Music of Black Americans: A History.* 2nd edition. New York: W. W. Norton, 1983.

Spear, Allan H. Preface, *Black Manhattan,* by James Weldon Johnson, v-xv. New York: Atheneum, 1969.

CELIA E. DAVIDSON

FURMAN, JAMES

Born in Louisville, Ky., January 23, 1937; died in Danbury, Conn., September 9, 1989. **Education:** Early piano training with his aunt, Permelia Hansbrough; Louisville public schools, Coleridge-Taylor Elementary School, 1943–48, Madison Junior High School, 1948–51, Central High School, 1951–54; University of Louisville, studied composition with George Pearle, 1954–58, B.A., 1958, M.Mus.Ed., 1965; Brandeis University, Waltham, Mass., studied theory and composition with Irving Fine, Arthur Berger, and Harold Shapiro, completed Ph.D. coursework, 1962–64; Harvard University, Cambridge, Mass., post-graduate work in early music and choral literature, summer 1966. **Military Service:** U.S. Army, Fort Devens, Mass., 1960–62. **Composing and Performing Career:** Church of Our Merciful Savior, Louisville, organist and choir director, 1953–60; Congregation Church, Weston, Mass., 1953–65; Chapel no. 6, Fort Devens, organist, 1960–61; Jewish Scientist Church, New York, N.Y., 1964–65; Brandeis University, assistant choral director, 1962–64; Fort Devens, musical director, arranger, and pianist for world-touring army show, *Rolling Along of 1961,* 1961–62; BBC documentary film on Charles Ives, choral director, 1966; Town Hall, New York, N.Y., conducting debut, 1967; Ives Centennial Concert, Danbury, prepared American Symphony Orchestra Chorus, for Leonard Bernstein, 1974. **Teaching Career:** Louisville public schools, music instructor, 1958–59; Mamaroneck, N.Y., public schools, 1964–65; Western Connecticut State College, Danbury, assistant professor of music, choral director, and orchestra director, 1965–76, associate professor, 1976–89. **Commissions:** Joseph Muise, 1962; Greenwich Choral Society, 1970; Carl Smith, 1971; Kentucky State University, 1971, 1973; Philip DeLibero, 1979; Philip and Mary DeLibero, 1980; Eric Lewis and the Manhattan String Quartet, 1980; Manhattan String Quartet, 1986. **Memberships:** ASCAP, American Association of University Professors, American Federation of Teachers, Phi Mu Alpha, Phi Delta Kappa, Society of Black Composers. **Honors/Awards:** Louisville Philharmonic Society's Young Artist's Contest, first place, 1953; University of Louisville, Omicron Delta Kappa Award, 1958; Brandeis University fellowship, 1962–64; Brookline Library Music Committee, first place, 1964; National Federation of Music Clubs, Award of Merit, 1965–66, 1967; Connecticut Commission on the Arts, Individual Artists Grant, 1982–83; Danbury Cultural Commission, 1982; Paul Dunbar Foundation, 1982; Western Connecticut State University, Faculty Scholars Award, 1984–85.

MUSIC LIST

INSTRUMENTAL SOLOS
Violin
Sonata for Solo Violin. 1977. Unpublished manuscript. Contents: Allegro; Moderato; Allegro Vivace. Premiere, 1982.

Flute
Deux Movements pour flûte seule. 1982. Unpublished manuscript. Contents: Roulade; Le Cornemuse solitaire. Premiere, 1982.

Clarinet
Suite for Solo Clarinet. 1976. Medfield, Mass.: Dorn, 1981. Contents: Introitus; Moresca; Incantation; Motore Music. "Incantation" also arranged for clarinet and strings. Premiere, 1976.

Saxophone
Hichijin (Seven Buddhist Gods of Luck) (alto saxophone, piano). 1980. Unpublished manuscript. Contents: Benten, Goddess of Love; Ebisu, God of Abnegation; Daikoku, God of Wealth; Fukurokujin, God of Longevity; Jurojin, God of Longevity; Hotei, God of Generosity; Bishamon, God of War. Commissioned by Philip and Mary DeLibero. Premiere, 1982.
"Music for Saxophone and Piano." 1979. Unpublished manuscript. Commissioned by Philip DeLibero.

Trumpet
"Une Chanson pour trompette et piano." 1979. Unpublished manuscript. Also arranged for trumpet and strings.

Guitar
"Canti" (guitar, optional string orchestra). Unpublished manuscript. Contents: Cante hondo; Cante flamenco. Premiere, 1980.

Piano
Sonata. 1982. Unpublished manuscript. Contents: Fantasy; A Touch of Blue; Concert Piece. Premiere, 1982.

SMALL INSTRUMENTAL ENSEMBLE
Strings
String Quartet. 1986. Unpublished manuscript. Commissioned by the Manhattan String Quartet. Premiere, 1987.

Combinations
"Chanson" (trumpet or cornet, string quintet). Unpublished manuscript. Premiere, 1980.
"Fanfare and Finale" (brass, percussion). Unpublished manuscript.
"Recitative and Aria for Solo Horn and Woodwinds." 1976. Unpublished manuscript. Also arranged for horn and piano. Premiere, 1977.
"Triumphal Fanfare" (horn, trumpet, trombones, tuba, percussion). Unpublished manuscript. Premiere, 1980.
"Variants" (violin, cello, prepared piano, piano technician). 1963. Waltham, Mass.: n.p., 1963. Note: this work won the Brookline Library Music Composition Competition, 1964. Premiere, 1963.

STRING ORCHESTRA
Cantilena. Unpublished manuscript.
Fantasia and Chorale. Unpublished manuscript.

CHAMBER ORCHESTRA
Concerto for Chamber Orchestra. 1964. Unpublished manuscript. Note: piano score, probably not orchestrated.

FULL ORCHESTRA

The Declaration of Independence (orchestra, narrator, optional organ and bagpipes). 1976. Unpublished manuscript. Premiere, 1977.

Moments in Gospel. 1985. Unpublished manuscript. Contents: Walk to the Altar; Invitation and Prayer; Holy Dance. Premiere, 1985.

ORCHESTRA (CHAMBER OR FULL) WITH CHORUS

Mass (SATB, boys choir, soprano, alto, tenor, bass, orchestra). 1974. Unpublished manuscript. Note: possibly unfinished.

SOLO VOICE

"I Have a Friend in Jesus" (medium voice, piano or organ). 1978. Unpublished manuscript.

"In the Woods (Dans le bois fleuri)" (high or medium voice, piano). 1983. Unpublished manuscript. Premiere, 1984.

"Just Jesus" (high voice). Unpublished manuscript.

Songs of Juvenilia (Nursery Rhyme Cycle) (high voice, piano). 1956; revised 1984. Unpublished manuscript. Contents: Tom, Tom, the Piper's Son; Little Boy Blue; Contrary Mary; Humpty Dumpty. Also arranged for SATB and piano, or SATB and wind octet. Premiere, 1956.

"Valse romantique" (high voice, piano). 1976. Unpublished manuscript. Also arranged for trumpet, two violins, viola, cello, double bass.

VOICE WITH INSTRUMENTAL ENSEMBLE

"Gospel Anthem" (SATB, soprano, alto soloists, brass ensemble, percussion, piano, organ, electric bass). 1971. New York: Sam Fox, 1972. Commissioned by Carl Smith. Also arranged for SATB, soprano, alto soloists, piano. Premiere, 1971.

CHORAL MUSIC

"Ave Maria" (SSAATTBB). 1971. Unpublished manuscript. Premiere, 1971. Commissioned by Kentucky State University. Recorded: Gregg Smith Singers GSS111.

"A Babe Is Born in Bethlehem (Puer Natus)" (SSATB). 1978. Unpublished manuscript.

"Born in a Manger" (SATB unaccompanied). 1978. Unpublished manuscript. Premiere, 1979.

"Bye, Bye, Lully, Lullay" (medium solo voice, SATB unaccompanied). 1978. Unpublished manuscript. Premiere, 1979.

"Come Thou Long Expected Jesus" (SATB). 1971. New York: Lawson-Gould, 1979. Commissioned by Kentucky State University. Premiere, 1971. Recorded: Classics Record Library 10-5573.

"For Thanksgiving (Rejoice, Give Thanks, and Sing)" (SATB, optional organ or piano). 1978. Unpublished manuscript.

Four Little Foxes (SATB, soprano, alto soloists). 1962–63. New York: Oxford University Press, 1971. Contents: Speak Gently; Walk Softly; Go Lightly; Step Softly. Premiere, 1965.

"Glory to God in the Highest" (SATB). 1978. New York: Lawson-Gould, 1979. Premiere, 1982.

"The Grosse Fuge Revisited" (SSATTB, brass quintet, string quartet). 1980. Unpublished manuscript. Commissioned by Eric Lewis and the Manhattan String Quartet. Premiere, 1980.

"Hehlehlooyuh: A Joyful Expression" (SATB). 1976. Chapel Hill, N.C.: Hinshaw Music, 1978. Premiere, 1976. Recorded: Mark ACDA89MC-1.

"Hold On" (SSATB, solo voice, piano, electric organ). New York: Lawson-Gould, 1979. Commissioned by Kentucky State University. Premiere, 1973.

"Hymn" (SATB). Unpublished manuscript.

"I Keep Journeyin' On" (SATB, solo voice, piano). 1972. Unpublished manuscript. Commissioned by Kentucky State University. Premiere, 1972.

Jupiter Shall Emerge (SSAATTBB). 1978. Fort Lauderdale, Fla.: Music 70 Music Publishers, 1988. Contents: On the Beach at Night; Jupiter Shall Emerge. Premiere, 1984. Recorded: Gregg Smith Singers GSS111.

The Quiet Life (SATB, soprano, alto, tenor, bass soloists). 1968. Fort Lauderdale, Fla.: Music 70 Music Publishers, 1980. Contents: Fanfare and Pastorale; Quiet by Day; Sound Sleep by Night; Thus Let Me Live. Premiere, 1969.

Responses for Church Service (SATB). 1978. Unpublished manuscript. Contents: Bless Thou the Gifts; The Lord Bless Thee and Keep Thee; Amen.

Salve Regina (SSATB). 1966. Unpublished manuscript. Premiere, 1968. Recorded: Gregg Smith Singers GSS111.

"Some Glorious Day" (SATB, alto solo, piano). 1971. New York: Sam Fox, 1972. Commissioned by Kentucky State University. Premiere, 1973.

"There Is a Balm in Gilead" (SATB, alto, baritone soloists). 1984. Fort Lauderdale, Fla.: Music 70 Music Publishers, 1984. Premiere, 1984.

"The Threefold Birth" (boy's chorus, SATB, organ). 1962. Unpublished manuscript. Commissioned by Joseph Muise. Premiere, 1962.

"Trampin'" (SATB, mezzo-soprano solo). 1959. Unpublished manuscript.

DRAMATIC MUSIC

I Have a Dream (oratorio for SATB, gospel chorus, baritone solo, orchestra, gospel piano, organ, guitar, banjo, combo organ, electric bass, electric guitar, drum set). 1970. Unpublished manuscript. Contents: In the River of Life; I Have a Dream; Let Freedom Ring. Commissioned by the Greenwich Choral Society. Premiere, 1970.

It's 11:59 (opera). Unpublished manuscript. Note: withdrawn by the composer.

PUBLICATIONS

ABOUT FURMAN
Dissertations

Gardner, Effie Tyler. "An Analysis of the Technique and Style of Selected Black-American Composers of Contemporary Choral Music." Ph.D. diss., Michigan State University, 1979.

Articles

Tischler, Alice. "James Furman." In *Fifteen Black American Composers: A Bibliography of Their Works*, 135–147. Detroit Studies in Musical Bibliography, no. 45. Detroit: Information Coordinators, 1981.

BY FURMAN

"Black Gospel Music: A History and Performance." Unpublished manuscript.

James Furman; courtesy of Ruth S. Lanham

PRINCIPAL ARCHIVES

James Furman Collection. Center for Black Music Research, Columbia College Chicago, Chicago, Ill.

* * * * *

James Furman was a well-rounded individual: he was not only a composer but also a teacher, choral director, and church musician. He taught in a public school in his native Louisville, Kentucky, during 1958–59, and in Mamaroneck, New York, from 1964 to 1965; he was on the faculty at Western Connecticut State College in Danbury from 1965 until his death in 1989. Furman also served as choral conductor and organist at several churches in Kentucky, Massachusetts, New York, and Maine. A student of theory and composition at the University of Louisville (1954–58) and Brandeis University (1962–64), he also studied voice, piano, early music, and choral music. He received a number of grants, fellowships, awards, and honors throughout his career, many of which led to performances and recordings of his compositions; among these were grants from the Danbury (Conn.) Cultural Commission (1982) and the Paul Dunbar Foundation (1982) for performances of original compositions. A recording of "Ave Maria," *Jupiter Shall Emerge,* and the Salve Regina by the Gregg Smith Singers was made possible by another grant, in 1982–83, from the Connecticut Commission on the Arts. He was also an organ recital artist and a conductor and was often called on to conduct his premieres. Furman lectured on subjects of African-American music and music by black composers at Kentucky State University, which also commissioned and premiered a few of his choral works (1971 and 1973), Morgan State University (1976), Howard University (1977), and Fisk University (1980).

Furman's compositions number more than 50 works: several for chorus, an oratorio (*I Have a Dream*), orchestral works, chamber works, arrangements, and an off-Broadway musical. At the time of his death, he was completing a book on gospel music and had written journal articles as well.

In the compositions of James Furman can be found elements of the spiritual, blues song, gospel song, and jazz, including especially the manner in which he breaks up the syllables of his words by placing one short note per syllable and separating each with a rest—a feature that may be found extensively in African-American musical culture.

One of his notebooks dated in 1976 included notes on a speech titled "My Development as a Composer," in which he discussed painting, the blues, and theoretical issues such as counterpoint and 12-tone technique. An example of his own use of 12-tone writing appears in his choral cycle titled *Four Little Foxes.* In other works, he used music to encourage images and feelings of what the text conveyed. Furman's orchestral writing in *The Declaration of Independence,* for example, is presented in movie score fashion.

Furman is known primarily as a choral composer, because his choral works have been most often published and recorded and because he specialized in choral conducting. However, he seems to have been conversant with many musical styles and could compose effectively for a variety of different instruments and ensembles. His unpublished book on gospel music also attempts to place that subject within the full historical continuum of American religious music, attesting again to the breadth of his outlook. Both humor and a strong spirituality also characterize his music. He was able to call on his African-American heritage effectively when he wished, but he was equally at home in a variety of other American idioms.

ROBERT T. TOWNSEND

THE DECLARATION OF INDEPENDENCE (1976)

This work is for orchestra with narrator and optional organ and bagpipes, and the text is taken from sections of the Declaration of Independence. Approximately 18 minutes in duration, the work was composed between July 4 and December 24, 1976, and was premiered on April 28, 1977, with then-Connecticut Governor Ella Grasso as narrator and the composer conducting the Western Connecticut State College Orchestra in Danbury.

The Declaration of Independence contains eight sections, some for narrator or orchestra alone, and others for both orchestra and narrator. The opening "Fanfare," in 3/8 meter, begins with percussion rolls that introduce typical fanfare patterns in the brass. Wind instruments, double bass, and, finally, the narrator join in. The second section is for strings and narrator, with the text "We hold these truths to be self-evident . . ." in a slow tempo and at a soft dynamic level. The ending of the section is a D-seventh chord, a device that is often used in jazz at conclusions to give a sense of incompleteness.

The narrator alone continues with the text beginning "He has refused," and then, with the text "He has obstructed," percussion instruments—tambourine, cymbal, field drum—are added, followed gradually by others, all of which are instructed to improvise in accompanying the narrator. The section concludes with cellos, basses, and timpani playing repeated patterns with the percussion instruments, still accompanying the narrator. An instrumental section entitled "Infernalis," in 6/8 meter, follows immediately with percussion continuing in patterns from the preceding section and using motives from the opening "Fanfare."

Piccolo and field drum next suggest fife and drum music of the period of the American Revolutionary War, with two trumpet soloists and, later, bassoon and oboe solos added. The text begins with "He has abdicated." The next section, "In every stage," is again for narrator alone. It leads into the final section, "We, therefore . . .", which begins with string accompaniment. The woodwinds join with the strings in a slow, chordal accompaniment.

At the conclusion of the text, the brass play alone, with other instruments added, now including the organ and bagpipe, as the music builds to a majestic conclusion.

ROBERT T. TOWNSEND

FOUR LITTLE FOXES (1962–63)

This song cycle for unaccompanied mixed chorus, composed from 1962 to 1963, sets text by Lew Sarett. The four short songs were first performed on December 14, 1965, in Danbury, Connecticut, and Furman dedicated the cycle in memory of his aunt, Permelia Hansbrough.

A unifying device in this cycle is the use of the first words of the text of the songs—"Speak Gently," "Walk Softly," "Go Lightly," and "Step Softly"—in both the opening and closing of each; the closing statements are homophonic and in generally longer note values than the opening statements. The four songs are contrasted in tempo, changing meters, syncopation, and dynamics. This cycle features a favorite choral device of the composer—fragmenting the syllables of words between the several voices—and dissonant harmonic language.

"Speak Gently," the first piece, uses vocal word-painting to convey the meaning of the words, as in, for example, the setting of "squirming." The meter is predominantly 3/8 with a few measures of 2/8 and 4/8 interspersed. The piece opens and closes with a short motive on the text "Speak gently" and is otherwise through-composed. The dynamic range does not go above moderately loud, and Furman has instructed that the piece be performed "freely moving." The second piece, "Walk Softly," is to be sung *Andante legato* and features a soprano solo that is marked "off stage" and "misterioso." Furman has written fragmented syllables among the voices so that one section finishes a word that another section begins. The third song, "Go Lightly," has the most flowing lines of the four pieces in which melismas (more than one note per syllable) and contrapuntal writing occur.

"Step Softly," the last piece, has the fastest tempo of the four songs, being marked *Allegro leggiero* (lightly and moderately fast). Although through-composed, the piece consists of three sections. Section A begins with the bass and tenor parts in a staccato ostinato pattern. After the first statement of this pattern, a soprano and alto duet enters in which the parts are in unison or imitate each other. At measure 15, the ostinato pattern in the men's parts changes to a new pattern, over which an alto and then a soprano solo state the text. The third section is marked by the bass and tenor continuing their staccato style on each beat, but this time on a single pitch. The tempo gradually gets faster and the dynamic level louder. The women's parts feature a melisma on the phrase "shiv'ring in the rain"—another example of word-painting. The song stops abruptly with a full measure rest three measures before the end, and concludes with a return to the original tempo and a last statement of the "step softly" text.

The songs in *Four Little Foxes* display Furman's ability to write contemporary classical choral literature. But although his use of dissonances is vast, the parts are voiced in a manner so as not to be impossible to sing. *Four Little Foxes* exemplifies Furman's personal style of using syncopation, dissonant chords, and separated syllables.

ROBERT T. TOWNSEND

I HAVE A DREAM (1970)

Furman's *I Have a Dream* is an oratorio in three movements scored for mixed chorus, gospel chorus, baritone solo, folk singer, two gospel soloists, and orchestra. The work was commissioned by the Greenwich, Connecticut, Choral Society in commemoration of its 45th anniversary. Furman dedicated it to the memory of Dr. Martin Luther King Jr., whom he called his "beloved friend," and also based the text on King's words. Completed on March 12,

1970, it was premiered by the society on April 19, 1970, under Furman's direction.

The work has the basic characteristics of an oratorio, being a work for chorus and soloists with orchestral accompaniment and including recitatives and arias.

The first movement, "In the River of Life," opens with conga and timbale drums playing polyrhythmic patterns. A *crescendo* followed by a *diminuendo* lead to the entrance of the alto, tenor, and bass sections of the chorus with the text "I refuse to accept the idea that man is mere flotsam and jetsam in the river of life." Words of the text are broken between the voices and are sung staccato; for example, in the word "accept," the tenors sing "ac-" and the basses, "cept." The text is treated similarly throughout the work. Furman also employs such 20th-century vocal and instrumental techniques as frequent and lengthy glissandos, voiced (rather than sung) text, whispers, improvisation by the voices singing simultaneously any individually selected pitches, and the use of mallets to play the piano strings.

The second and third movements are more sectional in structure than the first, which is largely through-composed. The second movement, "I Have a Dream," opens with a recitative and aria for baritone soloist, whose part is heavily ornamented and includes glissandos within a wide vocal range. The text set at the end of the movement is in an African tongue. An off-stage trumpet solo ends this section. Immediately following is the "Fantasia and Chorale for Strings with Horn and Trumpet (*ad libitum*)," with blues violin solo, strings with no vibrato, and quarter-tone flutter tonguing by the trumpet soloist. The third and concluding section of the movement is labeled a hymn by the composer, and its vocal setting is homophonic with accompaniment only by double bass and organ.

The third movement, "Let Freedom Ring," is written in a gospel style and employs gospel choir, soloists, and other gospel instruments such as the electric bass. The driving and syncopated accompaniment makes "a joyful noise." The next section is "Poor People's March," which is sung by the folk singer using a microphone with reverberation and accompanied by the full orchestra. Added instruments include prepared piano, combs, guitar and banjo, and numerous percussion instruments. For the concluding section of the work, "Free at Last," the gospel choir returns. The text is based on the spiritual of the same title, but the musical setting is the composer's. The piece ends with full orchestration and all voices singing "we're free at last."

This work is a worthy tribute to the life and work of Dr. King and to his dream of freedom for all people. It is a creative work with much depth that should be more widely heard.

ROBERT T. TOWNSEND

JUPITER SHALL EMERGE (1978)

Jupiter Shall Emerge is a choral setting of Walt Whitman's poem "On the Beach at Night" from *Leaves of Grass*. Furman sets the first two sections of the poem in two related parts, which he entitled "On the Beach at Night" and "Jupiter Shall Emerge." Whitman's vignette of a child weeping at the sight of the stars devoured by clouds is a comment on death and immortality, as her father reassures her that their disappearance is not permanent. Furman's setting is for eight-part mixed chorus, although he seldom employs the full texture. His treatment is straightforward, mostly through-composed, and always expressive of Whitman's text. Rhythmically, Furman switches time signatures and employs triplets and dotted notes to match Whitman's metrically free speech patterns. He uses simple melodies or melodic motives. Harmonically, he juxtaposes triadic chords with fairly mild dissonances. Much of the piece is homophonic, emphasizing Whitman's speechlike meters, although Furman occasionally uses contrapuntal passages.

The entire piece is centered tonally in A minor/A major. Furman also often employs parallel fourths and open chords with no third. Dissonances are not extreme. A favorite device is the use of an inverted seventh or ninth chord with the seventh or ninth degree in the bass. Diminished fifths or major or minor sevenths embedded in chords are also used.

Each of the two parts is sectional. Furman sets one logical section of text, then moves on. The two parts share very little thematic material except for Furman's percussive repetition of the word "Jupiter," which appears in both. This one device serves to unify the two parts.

Part 1, "On the Beach at Night," begins low and soft, with men's voices only. There is a simple melody in the first tenor, a countermelody in the baritone, and a repeated octave on *a* in the second tenor and bass. The piece begins in A minor on parallel major seconds an octave apart, and for the first two lines of the poem, the droning *a* continues against the tenor melody. When the altos enter on the line "watching the east, the autumn sky," the equivocal modality of the piece begins, as their melody line employs both an *f*-sharp and a *g*-sharp, which, in an E-major triad, emphasizes the words "autumn sky." Furman introduces a device he uses repeatedly: emphasizing a word with a sudden consonant (and often unprepared) major triad.

The next section of text is expressive with its references to "burial clouds" and to "ravening clouds in black masses spreading," and Furman sets it with increasing dissonance and triplets and changing time signatures that reflect the rhythm of the words. The texture, with the addition of the sopranos, becomes more dense and complex but remains homophonic, as the emphasis is on conveying Whitman's words and rhythms. The following section is equally descriptive: a floating soprano line depicts a "transparent clear belt of ether" in which the stars and planets still shine. Furman's chord progression is startling but etherlike: from a somewhat equivocal chord with a diminished fifth (*c*-sharp-*g*) in the bass line, he jumps to a full measure of B major, to a full measure of G major, to A major with a *g* lingering in the bass. Against this background, he introduces his percussive "Jupiter" pattern, 32nd-note triplets in fourths, in the tenor. The percussive "Jupiter" pattern subsequently reappears, repeated in every part over a static E-minor harmony. The sopranos depict "the delicate sisters, the Pleiades" in a similar succession of 16th notes and intervals of fourths.

Having described the happenings in the sky musically, as the clouds engulf the stars, Furman reverts to his opening theme in the tenors and basses to describe the child's reactions, closing Part 1

with a final quiet A-major chord and a repetition of the word "weeps." This first part is narrative and descriptive, and Furman has maintained a homophonic texture, relying on chord changes and speech rhythms to move the narrative, stressing major points with simple triadic chords.

Part 2, "Jupiter Shall Emerge," is more complex. It begins with the words "Weep not child," which Furman sets contrapuntally, incorporating sweeping ascending and descending motives containing leaps of fifths, fourths, and sevenths. This extended treatment of the first three words is followed by a chordal section that recalls the second section of Part 1 in its rhythmic use of triplets, eighth notes, and changing time signatures, with references again to the "ravening clouds," this time to reassure the child that "they devour the stars only in apparition." Furman's next section, to the words "Jupiter shall emerge," departs again from homophony. Each voice has a quick, interlocking pattern over a droning *a* in the low bass producing a swinging effect; against it a soprano soloist continues the poem in an upward-sweeping vocal line reminiscent of the earlier setting of "weep not child." Furman then returns to a homophonic texture with the words "They are immortal," in a section that is dense harmonically, as he employs a series of seventh and ninth chords in six-part texture. The sopranos soar to high *a* on the words "the great stars" while the basses and tenors answer *pianissimo* "and the little ones." The entire chorus concludes "shall shine out again" on the first inversion of a D-major-ninth chord, so that the basses sing an *f*-sharp against the sopranos' *e*. This extended bit of word painting serves again to emphasize the meaning of Whitman's lines.

Furman then abandons through-composition, returning to the words "Jupiter shall emerge," now combining his quick and percussive treatment of the word "Jupiter" with a sweeping line reminiscent again of the "weep not child" motive. Those words do eventually reappear in the bass line. He then repeats almost exactly the following section, "with these kisses let me remove your tears. . . . The ravening clouds . . . devour the stars only in apparition," skipping then to the grand chordal sweep of "they are immortal." Through repetition, Furman stresses concepts of both reassurance and immortality.

Furman concludes with the final words of the second section of Whitman's poem, "The vast immortal suns and the long enduring pensive moons shall again shine," and brings together all his standard devices: for example, the time signature changes from 4/4 to 3/8 to 2/4 to 4/4, in the space of five measures, to reflect Whitman's speech-like meter exactly. The composer employs a series of fairly simple triadic chords (D minor to B-flat major to A-major seventh with the seventh in the bass) in various inversions for "the vast immortal suns." The phrase "the long enduring pensive moons" is a series of very dense, chromatic chords resolving to a G-minor seventh with the seventh in the bass. "Shall again shine" is a D-minor-seventh chord in first inversion repeated three times followed by a six-part *fortissimo* A-major chord. Furman's chord juxtapositions are startling, and his use of chromaticism is clearly intended to build to the climactic phrase.

Throughout *Jupiter Shall Emerge* Furman has shown great sensitivity to Whitman's text. Therefore, one may wonder why he did not set the entire poem. One explanation may be that in the final section of the poem, which moves from the immortality of the stars to hint at the immortality of the soul, Whitman's language becomes extremely allusive, almost coy. There is little opportunity for a strong musical statement, and the effect of setting it might almost be anticlimactic. As it stands, Furman's final extended A-major chord is an effective conclusion.

Jupiter Shall Emerge was composed in 1978 and published by Music 70 Music Publishers in 1988. It was recorded on a limited edition cassette by the Gregg Smith Singers (New American Choral Music Vol. III, GSS111).

SUZANNE FLANDREAU

REFERENCES

Tischler, Alice. "James Furman." In *Fifteen Black American Composers: A Bibliography of Their Works,* 135–147. Detroit Studies in Musical Bibliography, no. 45. Detroit: Information Coordinators, 1981.

GARCIA, JOSÉ MAURÍCIO NUNES

Born in Rio de Janeiro, Brazil, September 20 or 22, 1767; died in Rio de Janeiro, April 18, 1830. **Education:** Rio de Janeiro, received musical training from João Lopes Ferreira, his predecessor at the Rio de Janeiro Cathedral, ca. 1777–84; attended the seminary to become a priest, ordained, 1792; studied rhetoric with Manoel Ignacio da Silva Lavarenga, 1802–04. **Composing and Performing Career:** Choirboy and composer from early age; earliest known work, *Tota pulchra es Maria,* 1783; Irmandade de Sao Pedro dos Clérigos, may have served either as chapelmaster or music teacher, beginning in 1791; began collaborating with Rio de Janeiro Cathedral, 1795; composed *Vésperas de Nossa Senhora* (Our Lady Vespers), 1797; Rio de Janeiro Cathedral, Igreja da Irmande de Nossa Senhora do Rosário e São Benedicto dos Homens de Côr (Church of Our Lady of the Rosary's Brotherhood and of St. Benedict of Men of Color), designated chapelmaster, acting as organist, composer, and teacher, and providing music for feasts supported by the secular *Senado de Câmara,* July 2, 1798; master of the chapel of the emigrated Prince Regent, João VI, 1808–20; *Missa de Réquiem* composed, 1816; Rio de Janeiro, Igreja do Parto, conducted first South American performance of Mozart's *Requiem,* 1819; music and piano primer compiled, 1821; wrote and conducted his last work, *Missa de Santa Cecília,* 1826. **Teaching Career:** Gave free public music lessons at home, ca.1795–1822. **Memberships:** Helped found Brotherhood of St. Cecilia, 1784. **Honors/Awards:** Rio de Janeiro, Royal Chapel, won title of "Royal Preacher" for Innocents Day sermon; honorary habit of the Order of Christ from the king, 1809; awarded a yearly stipend by the Prince Regent, 1814.

MUSIC LIST

"A solis ortus cardine" (SATB, organ).

Ad Dominum cum tribularer (SATB, orchestra). 1800.

"Aeterna Christi munera" (SATB, organ).

Aleluia (para a Missa de Sábado de Aleluia) (SATB, orchestra).

Alleluia, alleluia (SATB, rebecs, violins, basso continuo). 1795. Recorded: Academia Santa Cecília de Discos ASC 58.

Alleluia, angelus Domini (SATB, rebecs, flute, horns). 1799.

Alleluia, ascendit Deos (SATB, rebecs, flute, horn, basso continuo). 1799.

Alleluia Confitemini Domino or *Vésperas para sábado de Aleluia* (SATB, two horns, double bass). 1799.

"Alleluia, emitte spiritum tuum" (SATB, organ). ca. 1800. Recorded: Philips 6598.308.

Alleluia specie tua or *Gradual dos Apóstolos* (SATB, rebecs, violins, basso continuo). 1795. Recorded: Academia Santa Cecilia de Discos ASC 58.

"Ascendens Christus" (soprano, alto, organ). 1809.

"Ave Maris Stella" (SATB, organ).

Ave Maris Stella (SATB, two flutes, two trumpets, two violins, cello, double bass, organ).

"Ave Regina caelorum" (SATB, organ).

"Bajulans" (SATB, organ).

"Beata nobis gaudia" (SATB, organ).

"Beate pastor Petre" (SATB, organ).

"Beijo a mão que me condena" (soprano, piano). Rio de Janeiro: Pierre Laforge, 1837. Recorded: Angel 3 CBX 411; Estudio Eldorado 187900596: RGE Fermata 303.1015; MEC-FUNARTE.

Bendito e louvado seja (SATB, two flutes, two clarinets, two bassoons, two horns, two trumpets, two violins, viola, cello, double bass). 1814.

Bendito e louvado seja (SATB, two flutes, two clarinets, two bassoons, two horns, trumpet, two violins, viola, cello, double bass). 1815.

"Benedicte Dominum omnes" (SATB, organ). 1798. Also arranged for orchestra.

Benedictus es, Domine (SATB, flute, horn, violins, viola, basso continuo). 1799.

Cântico Benedictus (SATB, organ). ca. 1798. Contents: Antífona para Benedictus.

Cântico de Zacarias (SATB).

Christus factus est (SATB, orchestra).

"Christus factus est em ré maior" (SATB, organ). ca. 1798.

Christus factus est em sol menor (SATB, two flutes, two horns, two violins, viola, cello, organ).

"Compêndio de música e método de pianoforte." 1821. Recorded: FUNARTE LP3-56-404-011.

"Confirma hoc Deus" (SATB, organ). 1809.

Constitues eos principes (SATB, rebecs, violins, basso continuo). 1795. Recorded: Academia Santa Cecília de Discos ASC 58.

Côro para o entremês (SSATB, orchestra). 1808

"Creator alme siderum" (soprano, flute, trumpets, violin, viola, cello, double bass).

"Credo em dó maior." 1820. Note: 1897 arrangement by Miguel Pereira.

"Credo em dó maior." (two voices, organ).

"Credo em dó maior." Note: arrangement.

"Credo em dó menor."

"Credo em fá maior." Note: arrangement.

"Credo em ré maior."

"Credo em si bemol." 1808.

"Credo em si bemol."

"Crudelis Herodes" (SATB, organ).

"Crux fidelis" (SATB). Recorded: Angel ST 3 CBX 410.

"Decora lux aeternitatis" (SATB, organ).

"Deus tuorum militum" (SATB).

Dextera Domini. (SATB, instruments).

Dies sanctificatus (SATB, orchestra, organ). 1793. Rio de Janeiro: FUNARTE, 1981.

Dilexisti justitiam (SATB, flutes, trumpets, strings). 1794.

Diliexisti justitiam (SATB, oboes, horns, violins, double bass).

Discite filliae Sion (SATB, flute, trumpet, violins, double bass). 1798.

Dolorosa et lacrimabilis (SATB, orchestra).

"Domare cordis" (SATB unaccompanied).

"Domine Jesu para a Procissão dos Passos" (SATB, double bass).

"Domine Jesu para o Pregador" (SATB, instruments).

"Domine tu mihi lavas pedes" (SATB). ca. 1799. Recorded: Abril Cultural G.C. 46; Seminários de Música Pro-Arte PRO 001.

Doze divertimentos (clarinets, horns, trumpets, bassoon, percussion). 1817. Note: lost.

Le due gemelle (opera). ca. 1809.

Ecce sacerdos (SATB, flutes, reeds, horns, strings, double bass, timpani, organ). 1798.

Ecce sacerdos (SSAATTBB, bassoons, cellos, basso continuo, organ). 1810.

Ecce sacerdos. Note: only tenor voice and bass instrument parts remain.

Ego sum panis vitae (SATB, orchestra).

Ego sum panis vitae (SATB, orchestra).

Emitte spiritum tuum (SATB, two flutes, oboes, trumpets, two violins, double bass).

"Exultet orbis gaudiis" (SATB, organ).

"Felix namque" (TTB, organ). 1809.

Flos carmeli (SATB).

Flos carmeli da Novena de Nossa Senhora do Carmo (SATB, orchestra). 1818.

Gradual para o Espírito Santo. 1800. Note: Only orchestra parts remain.

Grande missa em fá maior.

Haec dies quam fecit Dominus em dó maior (SATB, oboes, trumpets, violins, viola, cello, timpani).

Haec dies quam fecit Dominus em mi bemol menor (SATB, two oboes, two horns, two violins, viola, organ).

Heu Domine (SAT). ca. 1789.

Hinos e Credo para Domingos de Ramos (SATB).

Hodie nobis caelorum Rex. Note: only alto, tenor, bass, and some instrumental parts remain.

"Immutemur habitu" (SATB, organ).

"Inter vestibulum" (SATB, organ). ca. 1818.

"Invicto martyr" (SATB).

"Iste confessor" (SATB, organ). *In honorem beatissimae* (SATB, flutes, horns, violins, double bass). 1807.

Isti sunt qui viventes (SATB, two flutes, two clarinets, two bassoons, two horns, two trumpets, two violins, double bass). 1818.

Jacta cogitatum tuum (SATB, flute, horn, violins, basso continuo). 1800.

"Jam Christus astra ascenderat" (SATB, organ).

"Jam sol recedit" (SATB, organ).

Jesu, Jesu clamans (SATB, flute, clarinet, two violins, cello, double bass).

"Jesu Redemptor omnium" (SATB, organ).

"Judas mercator pessimus" (SSATBB). 1809. Recorded: Angel 3-CBX 410; Claves CD-50-9521; Seminários de Música Pro-Arte PRO 001.

Justus cum ceciderit (SATB, soprano soloist, two rebecs, flute, two trumpets, double bass, organ). 1799. Rio de Janeiro: FUNARTE, 1981.

Ladainha da Novena da Conceição de Nossa Senhora (SATB, two rebecs, flute, two obbligato horns, double bass). 1798.

Ladainha da Novena de Nossa Senhora do Carmo (SATB, orchestra). 1818.

"Ladainha da Novena de Santa Teresa." Note: only instrumental parts remain.

"Ladainha da Novena de São Joaquim" (SATB).

Ladainha da Novena do Santíssimo Sacramento (SATB, orchestra). 1822.

Ladainha de Nossa Senhora do Carmo (SATB, bassoons, cellos, double bass, organ). 1811.

"Ladainha do coração de Jesus" (SATB, organ). 1824.

Lauda Sion (SATB, orchestra). 1809. In *Latin American Colonial Music Anthology.* Washington, D.C.: General Secretariat, Organization of American States, 1975. Recorded: Eldorado USR-7746.

"Laudamus te" (soprano, contralto, two rebecs, two clarinets, two horns, violin, cello, double bass). 1821.

"Laudamus te" (soprano, flute, clarinets, trumpets, violins, viola, cello, double bass).

"Laudamus te" (two sopranos, orchestra).

"Laudate Dominum." Note: only violin part remains.

Laudate Dominum (SATB, two rebecs, two clarinets, two horns, double bass). 1821.

Laudate Dominum omnes gentes (SATB, soloists, flutes, horns, violins, cello). 1813. Rio de Janeiro: FUNARTE, 1981.

Laudate pueri (SATB, orchestra, basso continuo). 1813. Rio de Janeiro: FUNARTE, 1981. Recorded: PSP LP 1749.

Laudate pueri (SATB, two rebecs, two clarinets, two horns, bass). 1821.

Libera me (SATB, orchestra). 1799.

Libera me (SATB, orchestra).

Magnificat (SATB, instruments). 1797.

Magnificat (SATB, instruments). 1810.

"Marília, se me não amas, não me digas a verdade" (voice, piano). Rio de Janeiro: Pierre Laforge, 1840.

"Matinas" (bass).

Matinas da Assunção de Nossa Senhora (SATB, orchestra). 1813.

Matinas da Conceição (SATB, orchestra). ca. 1815.

Matinas da quarta-feira de Trevas (SATB, orchestra).

Matinas da Ressurreição (SATB, organ). 1809. Also arranged for orchestra.

Matinas de Nossa Senhora do Carmo. (SATB, orchestra). ca. 1815.

Matinas de Nossa Senhora do Carmo (SATB, organ).

Matinas de São Pedro (SATB, organ). 1809.

Matinas do Apóstolo São Pedro (SSAATB, organ, bassoon). 1815.

Matinas do Natal (chorus, cello, organ). 1799. Rio de Janeiro: FUNARTE, 1978. Also arranged for orchestra. Recorded: Clio ACC 100-002; Jade JACD 022; Seminários de Música Pro-Arte PRO 001.

Media nocte (soprano, orchestra). 1818.

Memento mei Deus (SATB, flute, clarinet, two horns, two violins, cello, double bass).

"Miserere" (SATB, organ).

Miserere para quarta-feira de Trevas (SATB, instruments). 1798. Recorded: Seminários de Música Pro-Arte PRO 001.

Miserere para quinta-feira Santa (SATB, instruments). 1798.

Missa a quatro em mi bemol.

Missa abreviada (SATB, two rebecs, two clarinets, two horns, cello, double bass). 1823. Recorded: Frank Justo Acker FJA 099.

Missa breve em dó maior.

Missa de Nossa Senhora da Conceição or *Missa oito de dezembro* (SATB, orchestra). 1810. Recorded: Angel 3-CBX 410.

Missa de Nossa Senhora do Carmo (SATB, soprano, mezzo-soprano, tenor, bass soloists, orchestra). 1818. Recorded: Jade JACD 031; Clio Discos L P V O 004.

Missa de Réquiem (SATB, continuo). 1799.

Missa de Réquiem (SATB, organ). 1809. Recorded: Abril Cultural G.C. 46.

Missa de Réquiem (SATB, soloists, two flutes, two clarinets, two horns, trumpet, two violins, two violas, two cellos, two double basses, timpani). 1816. New York: Associated Music Publishers, 1977 (piano arrangement). Recorded: CBS ST 25001; Columbia M 33431; Festa LDR 5012.

Missa de Santa Cecília (SATB, soprano, mezzo-soprano, tenor, baritone soloists, orchestra, organ). 1826. Rio de Janeiro: FUNARTE, 1984. Recorded: FUNARTE FUN 001-2M/95; Promemus MMB 82.024.

José Maurício Nunes Garcia; Acervo Escola Nacional de Música da UFRJ, Rio de Janeiro

Missa de São Pedro de Alcântara. 1808.

Missa de São Pedro de Alcântara. 1809.

Missa em dó maior.

Missa em fá. 1808.

Missa em fá para Nossa Senhora. Contents: Missa; Credo.

Missa em mi bemol. 1811.

Missa em mi bemol.

Missa em mi bemol.

Missa em si bemol (soprano, alto, tenor voices, accompaniment). 1801. Note: incomplete. Recorded: Academia Santa Cecilia de Discos ASC-140.

Missa mimosa (SATB, flutes, clarinets, trumpets, violins, violas, cellos, double bass, bass drum). 1820.

Missa pastoril para a noite de Natal (SATB, soprano, alto, tenor, bass soloists, organ or orchestra without violas). 1808; revised 1811. Rio de Janeiro: FUNARTE, 1982. Also arranged for orchestra. Recorded: Angel 3-CBX 262; EMI Odeon SC 10.119.

Missa pequena e Credo abreviado. 1813.

Modinha (opera).

"Moteto de São João Batista." Note: only orchestra parts remain.

Motetos para a Procissão dos Passos (SATB, flute, clarinet, trumpets, violins, viola, double bass).

"No momento da partida, meu coração te entreguei" (voice, piano). Rio de Janeiro: Pierre Laforge, 1837.

Novena da Conceição (SATB, orchestra).

Novena da Conceição (SATB, orchestra).

Novena da Conceição de Nossa Senhora (SATB, two rebecs, flute, two obbligato horns, double bass). 1798.

Novena da Nossa Senhora Mãe dos Homens (SATB, orchestra).

Novena de Nossa Senhora do Carmo (SATB, orchestra). 1818. Contents: Ladainha; Tantum ergo; Flos carmeli.

Novena de Nossa Senhora do Monte do Carmo. Note: only double bass part remains.

Novena de Santa Bárbara (SATB, organ). 1810.

Novena de Santa Teresa. Note: only instrumental parts remain.

Novena de São Joaquim (SATB). Contents: Tantum ergo; Ladainha.

Novena do apóstolo São Pedro (SATB, two rebecs, clarinets, trumpets, cello, organ). 1814. Contents: Tantum ergo.

Novena do Santíssimo Sacramento (SATB, rebecs, clarinets, trumpets, cello, double bass). 1822.

"O gloriosa virginum" (SATB, organ).

O Sacrum Convivium (SATB, two flutes, two horns, two violins, cello, organ). ca. 1810.

"O sola magnarum urbium" (SATB, organ).

Oculi Omnium (SATB, flutes, trumpets, violins, viola, double bass). 1793.

Ofício de defuntos (SATB, two horns, organ, cello, double bass). 1799.

Ofício de defuntos (SATB, two clarinets, two horns, two violins, two violas, cello, double bass). 1816. Rio de Janeiro: FUNARTE, 1982.

Ofício de Domingo de Ramos (SATB, flute, two clarinets, two horns, two violins, viola, cello, ophicleide). Contents: Paixão.

Ofício de Domingo de Ramos (SATB, cello, double bass). Recorded: Abril Cultural G. C. 46.

Ofício fúnebre a oito vozes (two choruses, two organs). 1816.

Omnes de Saba venient (SATB, rebec, flute, horns, basso continuo). 1800.

Os Justi meditabitur (SATB, orchestra).

O triunfo da América (soprano, SATB, orchestra). 1809.

Ouverture em ré maior. Rio de Janeiro: FUNARTE, 1982. Recorded: Angel ST 3 CBX 412.

Paixão (SATB, orchestra).

"Paixão" (SATB).

"Paixão" (SATB, cello, double bass).

"Pange lingua" (SATB).

"Pange lingua" (SATB, organ).

"Peça para piano."

"Placare Christe" (SATB, organ).

Popule meus (SATB, instruments). Recorded: Abril Cultural G.C. 46; Seminários de Música Pro-Arte PRO 001.

"Posuerunt" or "Antífona para Benedictus" (SATB, organ). 1798.

Praecursor Domini (SATB, two clarinets, two trumpets, two violins, cello, double bass). 1810.

Probasti Domine cor meum (SATB, oboes, trumpets, violins, viola, cello, timpani, organ).

Quarteto. ca. 1801.

"Quem terra pontus sidera" (SATB, organ).

Qui sedes. 1808. Note: only orchestra parts remain.

Qui sedes e quoniam (two tenors, orchestra). 1818.

"Quid Lusitanos deserens" (SATB, organ).

Quoniam. Note: only parts for bass voice, two clarinets, and horn remain.

Regem cui omnia vivunt. Note: only SATB and cello parts remain.

"Regina coeli laetare" (SATB, organ).

"Regina coeli laetare" (SATB, organ).

Responsórios fúnebres or *Matinas de finados* (SATB, flute, two clarinets, two horns, two violins, viola, cello, double bass). 1816. Recorded: Promemus MMB 80.016.

"Salutis humanae sator" (SATB, organ).

"Sepulto Domino" (SATB). 1789.

Segundas matinas de Santa Cecília (SATB, orchestra).

Setenário para Nossa Senhora das Dores (SATB, instruments).

Sinfonia fúnebre. 1790. Recorded: Angel 3 CBX 410; EMI Odeon SC 10.118.

Sinfonia tempestade or *Sinfonia da tempestade.* Note: incomplete.

Stabat Mater (ATB, flutes, bassoon, organ). 1809.

Stabat Mater das Dores (SATB, orchestra).

Stabat Mater do Setenário das Dores (SATB, orchestra).

"Stetit angelus juxta aram" (SATB, organ). 1798.

Sub tuum praesidium (SATB, soloists, flutes, trumpets, two violins, double bass). 1795.

"Surrexit Dominus" (SATB).

Tamquam auram (SATB, two flutes, two clarinets, two bassoons, two horns, two trumpets, two violins, cello, double bass). 1812.

Tantum ergo da Novena da Conceição de Nossa Senhora (SATB, two rebecs, flute, two obbligato horns, double bass). 1798.

Tantum ergo da Novena de Nossa Senhora do Carmo (SATB, orchestra). 1818.

"Tantum ergo da Novena de Santa Teresa." Note: only instrumental parts remain.

"Tantum ergo da Novena de São Joaquim" (SATB).

Tantum ergo da Novena do Apóstolo São Pedro (SATB, two rebecs, clarinets, trumpets, cello, organ). 1814.

Tantum ergo da Novena do Santíssimo Sacramento (SATB, rebecs, clarinets, trumpets, cello, double bass). 1822.

Tantum ergo do Setenário (SATB, violins, violas, double bass).

Tantum ergo do Te Deum alternado (SATB, orchestra).

"Tantum ergo em mi menor."

"Tantum ergo em ré menor."

Tantum ergo para a Reposição (SATB, flutes, trumpets, violins, double bass).

"Te Christe solum novimus" (soprano, flute, horns, two violins, viola, double bass). 1800. Recorded: Frank Justo Acker FJA-099.

Te Deum (SATB, bassoon, cellos, double bass, organ). 1811. Also arranged for flute, two clarinets, two violas, horns, and additional strings. Recorded: Angel 3 CBX 411; PSP-LP 1749.

Te Deum alternado (SATB, flute, horns, violins, double bass).

"Te Deum das Matinas de São Pedro" (SATB, organ). 1809.

"Te Deum em lá menor."

"Te Deum em ré." Recorded: PSP-LP 1749.

"Te Deum para as Matinas da Assunção." 1801.

"Te Joseph celebrent" (SATB, organ).

Tecum principium (SATB, two rebecs, flute, trumpets, violin, double bass). 1793.

Tota pulchra es Maria (SATB, two violins, viola, bass). 1783. Rio de Janeiro: FUNARTE, 1983.

Trezena do Patriarca São Francisco de Paula (SATB, orchestra). 1817.

Ulisséia (heroic drama). 1809.

"Ut queant laxis" (SATB, organ).

"Veni Creator Spiritus" (SATB, organ).

Veni Creator Spiritus (SATB, instruments).

"Veni Sancte Spiritus" (SATB).

Veni Sancte Spiritus (SATB, two violins, double bass).

Vésperas das dores de Nossa Senhora (SATB, rebecs, flutes, horns, violins). 1794. Contents: Credidi; Ad Dominum cum tribularer; Eripe me. Recorded (Credidi): Academia Santa Cecilia de Discos ASC 58.

Vésperas de Nossa Senhora (SATB, bassoon, horn, contrabass, bass, organ). 1797. Contents: Laetatus sum; Nisi Dominus; Magnificat.

Vésperas do Espírito Santo (SATB, flute, clarinet, bassoon, horn, trumpet, timpani, violin, cello, double bass). 1820. Contents: Dixit Dominus; Confitebor; Beatus vir; Laudate Dominum; Magnificat; Laudate pueri.

Vésperas dos Apóstolos (SATB, instruments).

"Vexilla Regis" (SATB).

Virgo Dei genitrix or *Gradual para a festa de Santa Cruz* (SATB, rebecs, violins, basso continuo). 1795. Recorded: Academia Santa Cecilia de Discos ASC 58.

Zemira: Abertura em ré (opera). 1803. Note: only the instrumental overture remains. Recorded: Angel 3 CBX-411.

PUBLICATIONS

ABOUT GARCIA
Books and Monographs

Fagerlande, Marcelo. *O método de pianoforte de José Maurício Nunes Garcia.* Rio de Janeiro: Relume Dumara, 1995.

Gama, Mauro. *José Maurício, o padre-compositor.* Rio de Janeiro: FUNARTE, 1983.

Lima, Rossini Tavares de. *Vida e época de José Maurício.* São Paulo, Brazil: Edição da Livraria Elo, 1941.

Mattos, Cleofe Person de. *Catálogo temático das obras do Padre José Maurício Nunes Garcia: nota editorial, informação biográfica,*

catálogo temático, comentários. Rio de Janeiro: Ministério da Educação Cultura, Conselho Federal de Cultura, 1970.

Segundo centenário do nascimento de José Maurício Nunes Garcia (1767– 1830). [Rio de Janeiro]: Biblioteca Nacional, Divisão de Publicaçoes e Divulgação, 1967.

Taunay, Alfredo d'Escragnolle. *Dous artistas máximos: José Maurício e Carlos Gomes.* São Paulo: Comp. Melhoramentos de São Paulo, 1930.

———. *Uma grande glória brasileira, José Maurício Nunes Garcia.* São Paulo: Comp. Melhoramentos de São Paulo, 1930.

Articles

Lange, Francisco Curt. "A música no Brasil durante o século XIX: Regência-império-república." In *Die Musikkulturen Lateinamerikas im 19 Jahrhundert,* 121–166. Regensburg, Germany: Gustav Bosse, 1982.

———. "Sobre las dificiles huellas de la música antigua de Brasil. La Missa abreviada del Padre José Mauricio Nunes Garcia." *Yearbook, Inter-American Institute for Musical Research* 1 (1965): 15–40.

de Lerma, Dominique-René. "The Life and Works of Nunes-Garcia: A Status Report." *Black Perspective in Music* 14, no. 2 (Spring 1986): 93–102.

Mattos, Cleofe Person de. "José Maurício Nunes Garcia (1767–1820): Offices for the Dead; Requiem Masses." In *Musices aptatio,* edited by Antonio Alexandre Bispo, 29–42. Rome: Urbanania University, 1981.

———. "La tradition européenne et la musique de José Maurício Nunes Garcia." *Brussels Museum of Musical Instruments Bulletin* 16 (1986): 211–220.

PRINCIPAL ARCHIVES

Cabido Metropolitano de Rio de Janeiro (Metropolitan Capitulary), Rio de Janeiro, Brazil

Escola de Música da Universidade Federal do Rio de Janeiro (School of Music, Federal University), Rio de Janeiro, Brazil

* * * * *

The most recorded of all colonial Brazilians, Nunes Garcia has also been the most published and the best catalogued. There are 19 extant masses (12 composed between 1801 and 1826) and three requiem masses, dated 1799, 1809, and 1816, the latter published in 1897 with the orchestral parts reduced for organ by Alberto Nepomuceno (Rio de Janeiro: Isidoro Bevilacqua). Composed in memory of Portuguese Queen Maria I (d. March 20, 1816), who had lived in Rio de Janeiro beginning in 1808, this masterwork is scored for four-part chorus (with solos for alto, tenor, and bass) with orchestral accompaniment calling for paired clarinets and horns, strings, and flutes, with trumpets and timpani *ad libitum.* In the words of Gerard Béhague, "This requiem confirms Garcia's position as the most distinguished Brazilian composer up to his time." Following in the footsteps of Mozart's Requiem, which Garcia premiered in Brazil on December 19, 1819, it echoes some of Mozart's thematic material in the "Kyrie eleison" and "Dies irae," but always in an individual manner.

Garcia was the son of Apolinário Nunes Garcia, a lieutenant who died in 1783, and Vitória Maria da Cruz, who died on March 20, 1816. He entered the Brotherhood of St. Cecilia and was ordained a priest in 1792. He received musical training from the priest João Lopes Ferreira, his predecessor as chapelmaster of the Rio de Janeiro Cathedral from about 1777 until Ferreira's death in 1784. Garcia served as master of the chapel of João VI, the Prince Regent, from 1808 until 1820.

As with any substantially great composer, Garcia's style matured during the 44 years from his earliest preserved, lightly scored motet, *Tota pulchra es Maria* (1783), composed at age 18, to his final colossal masterpiece, *Missa de Santa Cecília* (1826). Cleofe Person de Mattos' massive *Catálogo temático das obras do Padre José Maurício Nunes Garcia* reaches 237 entries, organized by genre. In the introduction to this collection, the editor lists 17 graduals for masses dated between 1793 and 1800, and ten for undated masses. In addition, Garcia wrote graduals for his three requiem masses and a half-dozen undated graduals for Holy Week and Easter observances. The following annotated list of eight works in Mattos' editions reveals aspects of Garcia's stylistic growth between 1793 and 1826. Each musical score includes full instrumentation, and each contains notes about the work by the editor in both Portuguese and English.

Dies sanctificatus, gradual para o dia de Natal para coro, orquesta e orgão, the 1793 Christmas gradual, is 96 measures long, in D major and 3/4 meter. It is scored for four-part chorus, two horns, first and second violins, viola, cello, double bass, and figured organ. Notable among characteristics of this early work for the Rio de Janeiro Cathedral are the dynamic markings, which call for sharp contrasts between loud and soft.

Justus cum ceciderit, gradual de São Sebastião para coro, soprano solo, orquesta e orgão, was composed for the annual celebration of St. Sebastian's feast day (January 20, 1799). This charming D-major gradual in 3/4 meter is the only one that survives among many that Garcia wrote honoring Rio de Janeiro's patron saint.

Matinas do Natal, para coro, solistas, orquesta e orgão, was composed for performance on December 25, 1799, the year after Garcia became music director of the Rio de Janeiro Cathedral. These eight Christmas responsories for four-part chorus and soloists are of the highest value. They show how accomplished a composer Garcia had already become a decade before the court moved from Lisbon to Rio de Janeiro. They also prove how capable were both singers and instrumentalists in the Rio de Janeiro Cathedral in 1799, the date of the organ-accompanied version, and 1801, the date of the orchestral version. On their evidence, Rio de Janeiro did not lag notably behind contemporary Lisbon. In conformity with classical-era preferences, every responsory is in a major key (B-flat, F, G, D, G, C, E-flat, C [starting in C minor]). Where key shifts occur, they are always to the dominant (responsories 1, 2, 5–8). For variety, Garcia relies on meter, tempo, and texture changes. In her valuable introduction, Mattos—the leading authority on Garcia—ascribes the manuscripts used as sources for her edition to the chapter library of the Rio de Janeiro Cathedral. Of Garcia's seven *matinas* surviving in whole or part, this set is both the earliest and the only one for Christmas.

The original parts used by Leopoldo Miguez in the late 19th century to prepare the score of *Zemira: Abertura em ré* (Garcia's most substantial independent orchestral work) carried the legend (in Portuguese), "Overture or introduction expressing light and thunder [*relâmpagos e trovoadas*] for violins, viola, cello, horns, *trombe lunghe,* flutes, bassoon, and bass." The form displays Garcia's mastery of classic sonata-allegro key and modulation schemes. (Of Garcia's four single-movement orchestral works, only the 1790 *Sinfonia fúnebre* is extant in the composer's autograph. The so-called *Zemira* overture survives only in the late-19th-century arrangement by Miguez, who dated the now-lost original parts to 1803. The *Ouverture em ré maior* exists only in 12 orchestral parts at the Carlos Gomes Museum in Campinas, and *Sinfonia tempestade* is located at the Rio de Janeiro Escola de Música in a partial score arranged by Alberto Nepomuceno.)

Missa pastoril para noite de Natal, para solistas, coro e orquestra (1811), a Christmas mass originally composed in 1808 for SATB soloists and SATB chorus with organ accompaniment, was rewritten with orchestra minus violins three years later. The 1811 score includes paired clarinets, bassoons, horns, trumpets in B-flat, first and second violas, first and second cellos, organ, and timpani. The 6/8 meter, C-major music for the Kyrie, Gratias, Cum Sancto Spiritu, and Agnus Dei movements is substantially the same. The solo passages demand virtuoso operatic singers. The "Qui sedes" movement pits a soprano solo against three harmonizing basses.

The psalm settings *Laudate pueri* (Psalm 112) and *Laudate Dominum omnes gentes* (Psalm 116), para flautas, trompas, coro, solos, violinos, violoncelo, contrabaixo, are two of nearly 90 psalms composed by Garcia between 1797 and 1820. (Those antedating 1809 call for organ accompaniment; thereafter, orchestral accompaniment is the rule. Most heavily orchestrated is the *Laudate pueri* for Holy Ghost vespers [1820].) The Latin settings of both Psalms 112 and 116 are in D major, and both were composed in 1813 at the request of his friend João dos Reis. The *rondo* structure of both is the same: an opening choral ritornello repeated after each vocal solo in a related key. *Laudate pueri,* the longer of the two (291 measures), has the shorter ritornello (13 measures). Each solo is assigned a different voice (or pair, in Psalm 116). Joviality is the intended hallmark of these two psalms.

A sense of personal loss may have suffused both the 1816 *Missa de Réquiem* and the preliminary office of the dead, the *Ofício de defuntos,* para solistas, coro e orquestra, written for Queen Maria I of Portugal, as the composer's mother, Victoria Maria da Cruz (b. Cachoeira do Campo, Minas Gerais), died the same day as the queen, March 20, 1816. The latter work, consisting of nine responsories, preceded the first performance of Garcia's most famous composition, his requiem mass, sung "in the Chapel Royal with extraordinary pomp" during a ceremony sponsored by the Third Carmelite Order in memory of the queen. The musical quality of the responsories matches that of the requiem. Orchestral forces include paired clarinets and horns, plus strings (first and second violins, first and second violas, cello, and double bass).

In the introduction to her edition of *Missa de Santa Cecília,* para solistas, coro e grande orquestra (1826), Mattos explains why this work should be considered the apex of Garcia's creative achievement. Among the characteristics of this St. Cecilia Mass common to his other masses are the following: (1) the Kyrie and Gloria are much longer than the Credo, Sanctus, and Agnus Dei together; and (2) the Kyrie starts in his favorite key, E-flat major (ten of his 19 masses start in E-flat). The solo movements in this mass ("Laudamus," "Qui tollis," "Quoniam") call for operatic voices. Evidently, the tenor singer, Cândido Inácio da Silva, who was responsible for commissioning the St. Cecilia Mass and who was Garcia's former pupil and himself a celebrated composer of *modinhas,* wanted a number of virtuosic display numbers. After quickly composing the first version of the mass (in 30 days), Garcia spent his last four years revising the orchestration. Because of its monumental proportions, this mass has not been frequently performed, but, becoming better known through adequate interpretations, it confirms his renown as a great master.

Garcia's requiem mass of 1809 had strayed into keys alien to the opening D minor (Sanctus and Agnus Dei in C minor, Benedictus and Communio ending in C minor), but in the 1816 requiem, he returned to the initial D minor in both the concluding Agnus Dei and the Communio. Dominique-René de Lerma's edition of the 1816 requiem, although indebted to the Nepomuceno 1897 edition, fleshed out the orchestration with additional paired oboes and bassoons, "with some textural changes in the orchestration." This edition served for the recording issued by Columbia in 1975. De Lerma stated: "I also took the liberty of rearranging some of the solo parts so that the *Liber scriptus* is now for contralto rather than the bass, and the *Ingemisco,* originally for soprano, is given to the tenor. A *da capo* in the *Kyrie* has been inserted and the *Ingemisco, Sanctus,* and *Benedictus* in particular have been provided with additional music so the ideas may prove somewhat more complete for concert use." These adumbrations enter his 1977 edition, which "is an amplification, and at times, recomposition of that issued by Alberto Nepomuceno in 1897." Moreover, Nepomuceno himself had made changes in his 1897 edition from the original manuscript in the Rio de Janeiro Escola de Música library catalogued as 3110-3166. Just as Haydn's masses sound tame in Novello's organ arrangements, so also does anything by Garcia reduced from full orchestra to organ. Among Nepomuceno's changes from Garcia's autograph: the Kyrie is marked *Fugato* in the autograph but *Allegro moderato* in the 1897 imprint; the Gradual is headed *Andantino* in the autograph but *Larghetto* in the 1897 imprint; in the autograph Offertory, the bass soloist does not sing in unison with the instrumental bass, as prescribed by Nepomuceno. In the autograph, the requiem mass itself is, moreover, preceded by the office of the dead, the last responsory of which ("Libera me") begins with material anticipatory of the "Requiem aeternam"—evidence of the intended continuity of the office and mass. Since Nepomuceno printed only the mass, Garcia's architectural unity escapes the listeners.

In the office, Garcia prescribed different keys and different solo voices or duets for each successive verse of the nine responsories. Garcia's skillful alternation of first and second bass in the verse of the eighth responsory, "Amplius lava me" in E-flat and 3/8 meter, marked *Andantino,* and with string accompaniment, typifies his sensitive reaction to text. The full import of Garcia's "acknowledged masterpiece" therefore awaits the availability of both the office and mass in a conjoint recording (Mattos edited the 1816 *Oficio* in 1982).

The first large work by Garcia published outside Brazil, *Lauda Sion Saluatorem, Sequencia da 5.ª fr.ª do Corpo de Deis em*

1809 (Thursday Sequence, Corpus Christi, 1809 [text by St. Thomas Aquinas]), for mixed chorus, soloists, paired flutes, *trompas* and *clarines,* violins I and II, *violeta* (=viola), cellos, and *basso geral* appears in the *Latin American Colonial Music Anthology.* Transcribed from Garcia's manuscript in the library of the Escola de Música of the Universidade Federal do Rio de Janeiro by Robert Stevenson, this sequence, catalogued by him in *Renaissance and Baroque Musical Sources in the Americas,* also takes pride of place as Garcia's first masterpiece recorded in the United States (*Festival of Early Latin American Music,* recorded at the University of California–Los Angeles under the supervision of Roger Wagner in 1975). Tenor, contralto, and soprano soloists singing virtuosic solos alternate with the chorus in a long, joyous outburst (596 measures) circling around B-flat and its related keys. Garcia rhythmically punctuates lines of text such as "Laudis thema specialis" and "Panis vivus et vitalis" with *forte* accents on the first beats of every other measure, followed immediately by a *piano* dynamic. This brilliant work demands concert singers of the most accomplished level and reminds the listener of the expenses for music incurred by Dom João VI when he moved his royal court from Lisbon to Rio de Janeiro in 1808. A classically perfect work such as this not only demonstrates Garcia's consummate mastery of the idiom spoken by Haydn and Mozart, but it also rebukes the narrow-mindedness of critics who deny any composers of African descent the right to dominate European musical modes.

Apart from the already mentioned orchestral overture entitled *Zemira* (1803), Garcia's secular works include incidental music for a drama staged at the Teatro Régio on May 13, 1809, entitled *O triunfo da America,* a "heroic drama" called *Ulisséia* performed June 24, 1809, 12 *divertimenti* for wind orchestra (1817), and a didactic *Compendio de música e methodo de pianoforte* (1821) used in his own teaching. The enormous quantity of his sacred works, nearly all of which require orchestral accompaniment, has thus far inhibited any attempt at a complete edition. Instead, his one extant *modinha* published at Rio de Janeiro by Pierre Laforge in 1837, "Beijo a mão que me condena" (I kiss the hand that rejects me), has too frequently been allowed to do him the same kind of service that "Für Elise" provides for Beethoven. Meanwhile, not even his name is spelled correctly in more than one representative reference work.

REFERENCES

Béhague, Gerard. "Garcia, José Maurício Nunes." In *New Grove Dictionary of Music and Musicians,* edited by Stanley Sadie, 7: 153–155.

Mattos, Cleofe Person de. *Catálogo temático das obras do Padre José Maurício Nunes Garcia: nota editorial, informação biográfica, catálogo temático, comentários.* Rio de Janeiro: Ministério da Educação Cultura, Conselho Federal de Cultura, 1970.

Stevenson, Robert, ed. *Latin American Colonial Music Anthology.* Washington, D.C.: General Secretariat, Organization of American States, 1975.

———. *Renaissance and Baroque Musical Sources in the Americas.* Washington, D.C.: General Secretariat, Organization of American States, 1970.

ROBERT STEVENSON

GHONEIM, MAUNA

Born in Cairo, Egypt, August 21, 1955. **Education:** Cairo Conservatoire, preparatory and secondary education, studied piano with Maria Nos and Marcella Matta, 1963–70; Cairo Conservatoire, studied piano with Ettore Puglisi, composition with Gamal Abdel-Rahim, 1970–78, B.Mus. in composition, 1977, B.Mus. in piano performance, 1978; Hochschule für Musik und darstellende Kunst, Vienna, studied composition with Thomas Christian David and Francis Burt, 1981–88, Graduate Diploma, 1987, Magister Artium, 1988. **Composition and Performing Career:** First acknowledged composition, 1977; two to three new works each year, 1983–88. **Teaching Career:** Cairo Conservatoire, teaching/research assistant to Gamal Abdel-Rahim, 1978–81; Cairo Conservatoire, Associate Professor of Composition, 1988–present. **Honors/Awards:** Syndicate of the Arts prize, 1991; Academy of Arts, 1991; Ismaelia Festival prize for film music, 1990. **Mailing Address:** Cairo Conservatoire, Avenue of the Pyramids, Giza, Egypt.

MUSIC LIST

INSTRUMENTAL SOLOS
Flute
"Nacht Bäume Suite for Flute Solo." 1991. Unpublished manuscript.
Suite for Flute and Piano. 1991. Unpublished manuscript.

Piano
"Piano Pieces for Two Voices." 1986. Unpublished manuscript.
Sonata for Piano. 1977. Unpublished manuscript.

Two Pianos
"Three Pieces for Two Pianos." 1993. Unpublished manuscript.

SMALL INSTRUMENTAL ENSEMBLE
Strings
String Quartet. 1985. Unpublished manuscript.
String Trio. 1985. Unpublished manuscript.

Woodwinds
Quartet for Woodwinds. 1986. Unpublished manuscript.

Percussion
"Small Pieces for Percussion Instruments." 1984. Unpublished manuscript.

Combinations
Suite for Flute and Harp. 1993. Unpublished manuscript.
"Tanz für Klavier und zwei Schlagzeuger" (Dance for Piano and Two Percussionists). 1988. Unpublished manuscript. Premiere, 1988.

STRING ORCHESTRA
"El Mashrabia" for String Orchestra. 1988. Unpublished manuscript.
Two Portraits for String Orchestra. 1988. Unpublished manuscript.

FULL ORCHESTRA
Elegy for Orchestra. 1990. Unpublished manuscript.

ORCHESTRA (CHAMBER OR FULL) WITH SOLOISTS
Concerto for Piano and Orchestra. 1984. Unpublished manuscript.
Fantasy for Piano and Strings. 1978. Unpublished manuscript. Premiere, 1978.
Suite for Flute, Oboe and String Orchestra. 1986. Unpublished manuscript.
Two Pieces for Woodwinds and String Orchestra. 1984. Unpublished manuscript.

SOLO VOICE
"Aria for Voice and Piano." 1977. Unpublished manuscript.
"Lied for Soprano and Piano." 1985. Unpublished manuscript.

VOICE WITH INSTRUMENTAL ENSEMBLE
"Die Däume der Nacht" (soprano, alto flute, percussion instruments). 1988. Unpublished manuscript.

INCIDENTAL AND COMMERCIAL MUSIC
El Adkar El Dameya (Blood Density). 1980. Film soundtrack.
Hadith El Hajar (Talking Stones). 1979. Film soundtrack.
Hadith El Karya (The Village). 1979. Film soundtrack.
Little Songs for Children. 1991. Incidental music for children's television programs.
Sahara Safari. 1978. Film soundtrack.
Sunlight Fishing. 1990. Film soundtrack.

* * * * *

Mauna Ghoneim is one of modern Egypt's leading composers. Working within a culture where the composer has traditionally played a less significant role than the performer and improviser, Ghoneim has become one of Egypt's most active composers of art music and one of her country's best writers of film music. Through the assimilation of Arabic and Western ideas into her compositions, she has become an important composer of intercultural music and has encouraged many of her students in this direction. Although she grew up in a society that has traditionally regarded women as second-class citizens, Ghoneim is now recognized as one of the most significant female composers in the Arabic world and one of Egypt's most sought-after composition teachers.

Following the tradition of many others on the African continent who have been interested in acquiring some knowledge of Western European music, Ghoneim began her musical education by studying the piano. Between the ages of eight and 15 (1963–70), she took piano lessons through the Cairo Conservatoire; then, between the ages of 15 and 22 (1970–77), she studied at the Conservatoire proper, where she studied piano at a higher level while taking composition classes from Gamal Abdel-Rahim. In addition to receiving an undergraduate degree in piano performance in 1978, Ghoneim was one of the first students to graduate from the Cairo Conservatoire with a degree in musical composition (1977). Between 1978 and 1981, she developed her skills as a teacher of harmony and analysis as an assistant to Abdel-Rahim.

Mauna Ghoneim; courtesy of the Commission for Educational and Cultural Exchange between the U.S.A. and the A.R.E. (The Binational Fulbright Commission)

In 1981, Ghoneim won a scholarship from the Austrian Ministry of Education, which enabled her to pursue graduate studies in composition at the Hochschule für Musik und darstellende Kunst, Vienna (hereafter referred to as the Hochschule). Along with her husband, Rageh Daoud, she became one of the first two graduates of the Cairo Conservatoire to be admitted to a foreign graduate school without being required to do any remedial work at the undergraduate level. The Hochschule awarded her the master's and doctoral degrees in composition in 1987 and 1988, respectively. Her career as a composition and theory professor at the Cairo Conservatoire began with her return to her native country late in 1988.

Ghoneim's initial development as a composer took place from 1970 to 1977, during which time she was particularly influenced by the music of Abdel-Rahim, Bartók, and Stravinsky. From Abdel-Rahim, she acquired a thorough knowledge of the traditional Arabic modes, at a time when this knowledge was beginning to die out among Egyptian musicians. She also developed a basic understanding of contrapuntal writing and motivic development. This knowledge is reflected in Ghoneim's earliest works, mostly small-scale pieces for solo piano and for voice and piano written between 1977 and 1981.

Ghoneim's Vienna period lasted from 1981 to 1988. As a modern composer working within a Third-World nation, Ghoneim has been frustrated by the unavailability of recently published books, scores, and recordings. Thus, her years in Vienna were extremely important, since they enabled her to develop her knowledge of modern music written by Viennese and other Western European composers. During this prolific period, Ghoneim experimented with chamber music for strings, music involving woodwinds, and pieces featuring a variety of percussion instruments. Her works from this Viennese period contain a large amount of motivic development and reflect her tendency to manipulate and reorder motivic ideas in a manner analogous to that of a serial composer.

Ghoneim's third period began with her return to Egypt in 1988. Since that time, she has continued to compose music that relies heavily on the Egyptian modes, which she uses to construct her melodies and harmonies. Her contrapuntal textures are usually of the non-imitative variety. In addition to asymmetrical rhythmic patterns (which reflect her knowledge of the Arabic rhythmic modes), another distinctive stylistic trait of her music is the wide presence of melodic and rhythmic ostinatos, which suggests the influence of Bartók and Stravinsky. Ghoneim's consistent use of ternary form appears to be a concession to Egyptian concertgoers, who, she says, have a greater appreciation for music written in ABA form than for compositions utilizing other formal structures.

Recently, Ghoneim has devoted much of her attention to the composition of film music and music for children's television shows. Through this endeavor, she has helped the children and younger adults of her country to stay in touch with their musical heritage despite the influx of Western ideas, and the experience has given her the opportunity to play a significant role in the musical education of the Egyptian people.

FANTASY FOR PIANO AND STRINGS (1978)

Ghoneim's Fantasy for Piano and Strings is a relatively short work, approximately six minutes in duration. As the title implies, the piece reflects the spirit of improvisation that has been such an essential element in traditional Arabic music. The piece is in ternary form, with the three sections being approximately equal in length.

The A section begins with a five-measure thematic idea stated by the piano, which is immediately reiterated by the orchestra. Both the theme and its chordal accompaniment illustrate the duality that sometimes exists in intercultural music. To Western ears, the material can be heard as emerging from a minor scale (natural, with a raised fourth degree: *b*-flat-*c*-*d*-flat-*e*-*f*-*g*-flat-*a*-flat-*b*-flat). Arabic musicians, however, might hear this melody as outlining a pair of four-note scales, each having its own distinct intervallic structure. In whichever manner it is perceived, one of the distinctive features of this opening material is the use of the augmented second (*d*-flat to *e*), which receives emphasis particularly because the intervals immediately on either side of it are half-steps (*c*-*d*-flat and *e*-*f*) that create additional tension. Dissonant conflicts frequently enter the texture as well.

The spirit of improvisation is reflected in both the rhythm and the melodic contour of the opening theme. Slower note values are placed on the first half of each measure, with most of the rhythmic motion taking place in the latter half of each measure, suggesting the concept of "filling in" between the points of main rhythmic emphasis. At the same time, the melody in measures 1 and 2 gradually rises and falls, emphasizing the pitches *b*-flat-*f*-*b*-flat. After surprising the listener by touching upon unexpected pitches, the melody returns to the tonic (*b*-flat) before reaching a climax (high *d*-flat) at the end of its fifth measure. During the remaining portion of the A section, both the melodic material in the piano and the

accompaniment in the orchestra become more animated, just as an Egyptian improvisation might become more intense as the musicians' original ideas are developed.

The B section contrasts with A in that its texture is more contrapuntal, its emphasis is on descending melodic lines, and it contains a constantly shifting array of accidentals that partially obscures the tonal center. Throughout the B section, descending melodic lines are found in the viola and cello parts, while material that moves primarily in contrary motion to these parts is found in the right-hand piano part and the violin lines. During the 11-measure piano cadenza that follows, melodic ideas from the A section are reintroduced along with other melodic material outlining perfect or augmented fourths. The entrance of the orchestra after measure 44 signals the end of the B material and the return of the A section. With the exception of the five-measure piano solo that introduces the fantasy, the material is restated, and the piece ends with a clear-cut cadence on the tonal center (B-flat). This work, somewhat reminiscent of the highly chromatic, written-out improvisations of Chopin, is one of Ghoneim's most lyrical, expressive, and neo-romantic compositions.

The Fantasy for Piano and Strings was given its premiere performance in 1978 by the Cairo Conservatoire Symphony Orchestra, conducted by Alfred Mishorin, with the composer as the piano soloist.

STRING QUARTET (1985)

Written in the middle of her Viennese period, this composition is one of the finest string quartets written by an Egyptian composer to date. With the entire three-movement quartet based on the motivic material presented in the opening three measures, the first movement begins with a four-note motive in the cello that exhibits both Egyptian and Western traits: it features characteristic Arabic intervals (augmented fourth, minor second, and augmented second) but also places some emphasis on common Western intervals (major and minor thirds). Simultaneously, the violins play a four-note, syncopated idea that appears to be a variant of the cello motive. Both of the four-note motives, each one measure in duration, are reiterated simultaneously in ostinato fashion for the next seven measures. Other intervals and rhythms figure prominently in two other variants, one in the viola (mm. 3–4) and one in the first violin (mm. 9–10). The result is a complex, contrapuntal texture that lasts for 10 measures, when the lower three instruments play a five-note chord derived from this material (*f*-*a*-flat-*b*-*c*-*e*-flat). Similar motivic development continues throughout the movement, which ends with a dissonant chord (*f*-sharp-*g*-*c*-sharp-*d*), a suitable conclusion to an *Allegro vivace* movement that is agitated in style.

In the lyrical second movement of the quartet, this basic motivic transformation continues to take place. The main melodic idea continues for two measures (beginning with an augmented fourth, and concluding with a pair of descending fourths). From this material, Ghoneim derives several other ideas that utilize her characteristic structural intervals (minor seconds, augmented seconds, perfect fourths, and augmented fourths) in various guises. A third idea, first presented in measure 13, is based on the latter portion of the movement's melody and is rhythmically altered as the piece progresses. A new transformation with four half steps in a row appears in measure 31, with interest added through changes in rhythm and meter (constant eighth notes in 9/8 meter with syncopation—hemiola, specifically). Another transformation begins with ascending leaps and continues in descending, stepwise motion. Both transformations are reworkings of the movement's main thematic idea.

The quartet is brought to a quick conclusion by a rapid and highly articulated third movement, which opens with a series of half-steps in 6/8 meter. Close intervals shift to wider ones, which are transposed and restated beginning on different portions of the measure. The entire quartet is one of the best examples of Ghoneim's ability to develop short motivic ideas that utilize the intervals common to many Egyptian modes.

TANZ FÜR KLAVIER UND ZWEI SCHLAGZEUGER (1988)

The "Tanz für Klavier und zwei Schlagzeuger" (Dance for Piano and Two Percussionists) was written when the composer was completing her doctoral studies in Vienna and preparing to return to Egypt. Like Bartók in his Sonata for Two Pianos and Percussion, Ghoneim in this composition exploits the combined sonorities of the piano and various percussion instruments.

In Ghoneim's one-movement work in ternary form, colorful effects are created by five percussion instruments: tam-tam, marimba, tambourine, large drum, and tom-tom. The entire piece is based on three of her favorite intervals, the minor second, the major second, and the augmented fourth. In the A section (mm. 1–40), the piano dominates for the first eleven measures, using these intervals; the intensity increases as the marimba enters with a variant of the same melodic material in measures 12–15. Half-steps govern the top, middle, and bottom lines of the piano part in measures 1–9. Beginning with the marimba's entrance in measures 12–15, this idea is expanded to outline a fourth from *e*-flat to *b*-flat and a third from *g* to *e*-flat; simultaneously, the bass line of the piano outlines another interval, the tritone. In the latter half of the A section, this material is inverted with an ascending variant of it moving toward the climax of the section. Additional expansion then takes place, along with the appearance of constantly changing asymmetrical rhythms (3+3+2+2, 2+3+3+2, and 2+3+2+3 in 10/8 meter). The section concludes with dissonant, very loud (*fortissimo*) chords that outline close intervals (*d*-flat-*e*-flat-*g*-flat-*g*).

The percussion instruments play a dominant role in the animated B section (mm. 41–101). Although characterized by asymmetrical rhythmic patterns, this middle section combines units of two and three eighth notes in various ways without using any of the Egyptian rhythmic modes. It begins with the tambourine setting an asymmetrical (3+3+2+2) rhythm in an asymmetrical meter 6+4/10, with the marimba adding melodic material that features close and dissonant intervals. Occasionally, the piano supplies dissonant harmonies in chains of minor, major, and augmented thirds (such as *e*-flat-*g*-*b*-flat-*d*-flat-*f*-sharp). Throughout much of the section, the bass line of the piano sounds a 3+3+2+2 rhythm that outlines consonant and dissonant intervals (perfect and augmented fourths).

The most unusual writing in the piece comes just after its central point, where a solo part for tuned tom-toms introduces material derived from the beginning of the work. Here the composer outlines and emphasizes wide and open intervals (minor sevenths, diminished and perfect fourths) in an exciting passage characterized rhythmically by both syncopation and asymmetrical rhythms.

The last 40 measures of the piece are an almost exact repetition of the A section, the only exception being the addition of an extra measure that makes a *crescendo* into the final dissonant chord. Because of its colorful use of percussion instruments, this composition is one of the most unique pieces in the entire repertory of modern Egyptian chamber music.

First performed at the Vienna Hochschule für Musik in 1988, this work was enthusiastically received by the audience.

SUNLIGHT FISHING (1990)

One of Ghoneim's prize-winning film scores, *Sunlight Fishing* consists of six movements, each approximately two to three minutes in length, written for different combinations of instruments, and intended for a particular place in the film. The ensemble includes two flutes, an oboe, cello, French horn, xylophone, drum, and a group of soprano voices. The first movement, scored for two flutes and cello, is based on a melody derived from the Egyptian *busahlik* mode (comprised of two four-note scales consisting of a major second, a minor second, and a major second). The movement opens with a solo flute stating a two-measure melodic line that rises and falls. The cello enters solo at measure three. The opening melodic material is then repeated at various pitch levels by both flutes in the remaining portion of the movement (mm. 3–14). The descending portion of the melodic material is first presented by the flute and when expanded thereafter, is stated by both flutes in open intervals (parallel fourths and later in parallel fifths). The gentle ascending and descending lines, played in the low register of the flutes, suggests the image of a peaceful sunrise.

The second movement, scored for flute, oboe, and cello, consists essentially of a one-measure *pizzicato* (plucked) cello ostinato, a cello drone underneath it, and a lyrical melody played on the oboe and later on the flute. The cello ostinato is stated five times before being varied and transposed to other pitch levels. Poignancy is added to the melody that continues over it through chromatic alteration. Although the oboe and cello are quite independent of one another, their simultaneity creates open intervals that are more consonant than those that are found in Ghoneim's concert music.

A more unusual combination of instruments is called for in the third movement. To the flute, oboe, and cello, a French horn is added; it plays sustained notes in the manner of cantus-firmus-based medieval polyphony. The A section (mm. 1–24) begins with a solo flute playing a melody consisting of two balanced four-measure phrases. The movement is primarily in the *hijazi* mode (characterized by a half step followed by an augmented second). The initial appearance of the melody is stated by the solo flute, which repeats it, then it moves to the oboe, while underneath the cello has an arpeggiated, *pizzicato* part and the horn has sustained notes that complement the cello. In the B section (mm. 25–40), the horn and cello continue with variants of their previous material, while the woodwinds present material that alternates between chains of open intervals (fourths) and step-wise chromatic motives. The movement concludes with a full return of the A section, but with alterations that negate the augmented seconds that appeared earlier in the piece.

Except for the melody that is vocalized by a group of sopranos, the fourth movement is similar in melodic material to the second movement. The mysterious sound of the soprano vocalise conjures images of ancient Greek epic poems in which the enchanting female sirens lured sailors to their deaths with their singing. In the background, the flutes restate this textless vocal melody at the distance of a quarter note, creating another unusual effect. The form of this short movement could be described as ABA', since the melodic idea is stated, then there is a brief departure from it, and a varied return of the first idea follows.

The fifth movement contrasts strongly with the slow-moving, lyrical movements discussed above. This is a light-textured duet for flute and cello, one in which the composer creates a more frivolous mood by using a faster tempo, *staccato* articulations, and a xylophone that doubles the flute part. The melody unfolds in a series of four-measure phrases and, in the second section of the movement, is fragmented into one- or two-note events, each of which is imitated by flute and cello in an echo effect similar to that found in Western European medieval music.

The sixth movement also has a light, two-voiced texture, with the melody doubled in the flute and oboe, a cello ostinato, and an Egyptian *mazhar* drum (a large, fairly loud frame drum with a single membrane) complementing the cello part by playing strong and weak patterns typical of Arabic music. The plaintive melody and the ostinato from the second movement are transformed to create a lively, articulated dance in a quick 10/8 meter featuring an asymmetrical rhythmic pattern (3+3+2+2). Over a *pizzicato* cello ostinato derived from the first four notes of the second movement's ostinato, a fragmented, cleanly tongued version of the oboe melody of the second movement appears, is restated, and then motivically developed for eight measures. After repeating the first 20 measures of the movement, the piece ends as it began, with only the cello ostinato part.

Any evaluation of *Sunlight Fishing* must take into account the fact that it is film music rather than music for the concert hall. Just as one would not judge a Mozart divertimento on the same terms as a Mozart symphony, so one should not criticize Ghoneim for writing a film score that lacks the intricacies of the compositions discussed earlier; rather, she deserves praise for her ability to write music in disparate styles—music that, regardless of the occasion, reflects the spirit of the Egyptian people. Her success as a composer of film music is indicated by the fact that *Sunlight Fishing* has been praised at both the Ismaelia Film Festival in Cairo (1991) and the Oberhausen Film Festival in Berlin (1992).

REFERENCES

El-Kholy, Samha. *Nationalism in Twentieth-Century Music.* Kuwait: Alam Al Maarifa, 1992. (In Arabic)

Robison, John O. "Intercultural Music in Modern Egypt: The Third Generation." In *Intercultural Music,* vol. 3, edited by Akin Euba and Cynthia Tse Kimberlin. Bayreuth, Germany: E. Breitinger, forthcoming.

JOHN O. ROBISON

GILLESPIE, JOHN BIRKS ("DIZZY")

Born in Cheraw, S.C., October 21, 1917; died in Englewood, N.J., January 6, 1993. **Education:** Taught himself trumpet and trombone in early teens; Laurinburg Institute, Laurinburg, N.C., 1932–35. **Composing and Performing Career:** Philadelphia, Pa., Frank Fairfax's band, which included Charlie Shavers, 1935; New York, N.Y., joined Teddy Hill's band at the Savoy Ballroom and for a European tour, 1937; worked in several groups, including Al Cooper's Savoy Sultans and the Afro-Cuban band of Alberto Socarras; joined Cab Calloway's big band, 1939–41; Minton's Playhouse, New York, participated in jam sessions with Charlie Parker, Thelonious Monk, Kenny Clarke, and others, early 1940s; worked briefly in various big bands, including those led by Claude Hopkins, Les Hite, Lucky Millinder, Charlie Barnet, Fletcher Henderson, Coleman Hawkins, and Benny Carter, ca. 1941; Down Beat Club, Philadelphia, led own band, 1942; joined the Earl Hines band, ca. 1942; New York, N.Y., played briefly with Duke Ellington, 1943; co-led small band with bassist Oscar Pettiford, 1943–44; joined Billy Eckstine's Big Band, 1944; participated on some of the first small-group bebop recordings, Manor, Guild, and Dial, 1944; several performances and recordings with Charlie Parker, 1945–46; led big band, 1945–50; formed unsuccessful record company, Dee Gee, 1951; led various small and big bands, 1950s and 1960s; toured as soloist with the "Jazz at the Philharmonic" presentations, 1953–67; formed big band for U.S. State Department-sponsored international tour, 1956; guest star in the all-star touring line-up "the Giants of Jazz," 1971–72; continued to tour widely during late 1970s; performed mainly with quintet, 1980s. **Honors/Awards:** Laurinburg Institute scholarship, 1932–35; *Metronome* awards, Best Trumpet, 1947–50; Grammy Awards for performance, 1975, 1980; Chicago, Ill., Columbia College Chicago, honorary doctorate, 1988; Grammy Lifetime Achievement Award.

MUSIC LIST

[The following list of titles includes only works that were composed by the subject of the entry; it is not a list of recordings that were made by the subject. Although the composer may have made recordings of his own works, the list is not restricted to those recordings but in many cases includes performances by other artists of the composer's work. The list is made up of publication and discographical data, in cases where such information is available. Although no effort has been made to include documentation of the earliest recording of the works listed, the date of the earliest recording that is readily available has been given. —Ed.]

"Alternate One." New York: Pablito, 1982. Recorded: Pablo OJCCD-744-2.

"And the Melody Still Lingers On." Los Angeles: MCA, 1981. Co-composers, Frank Paparelli, Arif Mardin. MCA. Recorded: Reprise 45865.

"And Then She Stops" or "And Then She Stopped." Copyright, 1964. Co-composer, Lorraine Gillespie. Recorded: Enja 6044-2; Limelight 86007; Original Jazz Classics OJCCD-733-2; PolyGram 832 574-2; Verve 314-513875-2.

"Anthropology." Copyright, 1946. New York: Music Sales. Co-composer, Charlie Parker. Recorded, 1946: BMG Classics 09026-68499-2; Indigo 2068; Philips 830 224-2; RCA Victor 09026-68517-2.

"Antilles." Englewood, N.J.: Dizlo, [1990?]. Recorded, 1989: A&M 75021-6404-2.

"Anythin'." Recorded, 1957: Verve 835253-2.

"Are You There?" Englewood, N.J.: Dizlo.

"Back to the Land." New York: Pablito. Co-composer, Count Basie. Recorded: Original Jazz Classics 886.

"Ballad." Copyright, 1987. Recorded, 1985: GRP GRD-9512.

"Barbados Carnival." Recorded, 1964: Limelight 86007.

"Bebop" or "Be-bop." New York: Music Sales, 1949. Also arranged and published as "Be Bop (Dizzy's Fingers)," "The Things Are Here," and "Things to Come." Recorded, 1945: Heads Up International HUCD 3032; Indigo 2068; Pablo OJCCD-443-2; Smithsonian LP 2004.

"Birks." New York, Pablito, 1976. Co-composers, Roy Eldridge, Flip Phillips, Bill Harris, Oscar Peterson, Ray Brown, Herb Ellis, Louie Bellson. Recorded, 1955: Pablo PACD-2310-713-2.

"Birk's Blues." Englewood, N.J.: Dizlo.

"Birk's Works." Englewood, N.J.: Dizlo, 1957. Recorded, 1953: Blue Note 80507; Delta 55605; Heads Up International HUCD 3032; RCA Victor 09026-68360-2; Moon Records MCD-009-2.

"Blue for You." Los Angeles, Calif.: MCA. Co-composer, Verges.

"Blue 'n' Boogie." Copyright, 1944. Los Angeles, Calif.: MCA. Co-composer, Frank Paparelli. Recorded, 1945: Bulldog BCD-2006; Indigo 2068; Philips 830 224-2; Steeple Chase SCCD 31290.

"The Blues." Englewood, N.J.: Dizlo. Recorded: Habacan HABCD-2435.

"Blues for Bird." Copyright, 1957. Englewood, N.J.: Dizlo, 1985. Co-composer, Sonny Stitt. Recorded, 1956: Pablo PACD-2310-740-2; Verve VE 12533.

"Blues for Max." Englewood, N.J.: Dizlo. Recorded, 1967: Blue Note 80507; Delta 55605; LRC CDC 9011.

"Blues for Norman." New York: Pablito, 1976. Co-composers, Louis Bellson, Niels Pederson, Clark Tevey, Oscar Peterson, Roy Eldridge. Recorded: Clef MG vol. 2; Verve 11368.

"Blues People." Recorded, 1991: Mainstream 721.

"Bopsie's Blues." Recorded, 1951: Savoy Jazz SV-1057.

"Bop 'n' Boogie." Los Angeles, Calif.: Co-composer, Frank Paparelli.

"'Bout to Wail." Recorded: American Recording Society G 405; Verve 314-513875-2.

"Brother K" or "Brother King." Englewood, N.J.: Dizlo. Recorded: Accord 556 572; LRC MC-9016; Pablo 2120116.

"Bye." Recorded: GRP/Impulse MCAD-33121.

"Caprice." Copyright, 1944. Co-composer, Frank Paparelli.

"Carambola." Copyright, 1950. New York: Music Sales. Co-composer, Chico O'Farrill. Recorded: Capitol 892.

"Carnival." Englewood, N.J.: Dizlo, 1964. Co-composer, Lorraine Gillespie. Recorded: Pablo 52625-708.

"The Champ." Copyright, 1957. Recorded, 1953: Original Jazz Classics OJCCD-603-2; Pablo OJCCD-381-2; Philips 830 224-2; RCA Victor 09026-68360-2.

"Changes." Copyright, 1944.

John Birks "Dizzy" Gillespie; courtesy of the Frank Driggs Collection

"Chicken Wings." New York: Pablito. Co-composers, Ray Brown, Freddie Hubbard, Joe Pass, Oscar Peterson. Recorded, 1980: Original Jazz Classics OJCCD-603-2.

"Clappin' Rhythm." Recorded, 1952-53: Vogue 68361.

"Coast to Coast." New York: Music Sales, 1964. Co-composer, Buster Harding. Recorded: Capitol M-11059; Capitol H-326.

"Come Sunday." Englewood, N.J.: Dizlo. Recorded: Verve V-8386.

"Con Alma." Copyright, 1956. Englewood, N.J.: Dizlo. Recorded, 1957: Heads Up International HUCD 3032; Mainstream 721; PolyGram 832 574-2; Telarc 83421; Verve 835253-2.

"Confusion." Copyright, 1956. Englewood, N.J.: Dizlo, 1956. Co-composer, Buster Harding. Recorded: Norgran MGN-1090.

"Constantinople." Copyright, 1961. Englewood, N.J.: Dizlo, 1989. Recorded, 1977: Original Jazz Classics 886.

"Contraste." Copyright, 1954. Englewood, N.J.: Dizlo, 1982. Co-composer, Chico O'Farrill. Recorded, 1959: Norgran MGN-1003.

"Cool Breeze." Copyright, 1948. Co-composers, Tadd Dameron, Billy Eckstine. Recorded: Bandstand BDCD 1534; Capitol 57061; Jazz Hour JH-1029; RCA Victor 09026-68517-2; Verve 314 511 393-2.

"Cripple Crab Crutch." Recorded: Storyville 8208; Vogue n.n.

"Cubana Be/Cubana Bop." Copyright, 1949. New York: Music Sales. Co-composer, George Russell. Recorded, 1947: Artistry 110; Bluebird 5785-1; RCA PM 42 408.

"Daisy Chain." New York: Music Sales. Co-composers, Ray Brown, Gil Fuller.

"Dartmouth Duet." Co-composers, Mitchell, Willie Ruff. Recorded: Mainstream 721.

"Devil and the Fish." Copyright, 1956. Englewood, N.J.: Dizlo, 1984. Co-composer, Buster Harding. Recorded: American Recording Society G 405; Verve MGV-8173.

"Diamond Jubilee Blues." Recorded: Telarc CD-83316; Telarc 83421.

"Diddy Wa Diddy (Mozambique)." Englewood, N.J.: Dizlo, 1971. Co-composer, Oscar Peterson. Recorded, 1970: Pablo PACD-2310-740-2; Perception 13; Rhino R2 79170.

"Dizzy Atmosphere" or "Dynamo A (Dizzy Atmosphere)." Copyright, 1944. Los Angeles: MCA. Recorded, 1946: Allegro Elite 3083; Classics 935; Moon MCD045-2; Indigo 2068; Savoy Jazz SJ-0152; Smithsonian R004.

"Dizzy Meets Sonny." Copyright, 1957. Englewood, N.J.: Dizlo, 1985. Recorded, 1956: Verve VE 12533.

"Dizzy the Duck." Englewood, N.J.: Dizlo, n.d. Recorded, 1982: Original Jazz Classics OJCCD-733-2.

"Do What You Want." Copyright, 1975.

"Down Under." New York: Edwin H. Morris, 1943. Recorded: GRP GRD-606.

"Drebirks." New York: Pablito. Co-composers, Roy Eldridge, Oscar Peterson. Recorded, 1975: Original Jazz Classics 807; Pablo PACD-2310-816-2.

"Droppin' a Square." Recorded, 1946: Moon MCD045-2.

"Du Carnival." Copyright, 1974.

"DW." Englewood, N.J.: Dizlo.

"Dynamo B." Recorded: Classics 935; EPM Musique 158812; Jazz Archive 158812.

"Easy Swing." Englewood, N.J.: Dizlo.

"Emanon." New York: Music Sales. Co-composer, Milt Shaw. Recorded, 1946: Bandstand BDCD 1534; Bulldog BCD-2006; Musicraft 1046-70053-2; Savoy Jazz SJ-0152.

"Evening Sound." Verve 314-513875-2.

"Exotica." Englewood, N.J.: Dizlo, 1971. Recorded: Blue Note 93901.

"Fais Gaffe (Watch Out)." Englewood, N.J.: Dizlo. Recorded, 1952–53: BMG Classics 09026-68361-2; Vogue 68361.

"Fast Freight." Copyright, 1944.

"Fiesta." Copyright, 1954. Englewood, N.J.: Dizlo, 1982. Co-composer, Chico O'Farrill.

"Fiesta Mo-Jo." Englewood, N.J.: Dizlo. Co-composers, Lorraine Gillespie, Martin Mel. Recorded: GRP GRD-9512; Mercury 832 574-2.

"First Chance." Recorded, 1982: Pablo OJCCD-733-2.

"Follow the Leader." New York: Pablito. Co-composer, Count Basie. Recorded, 1977: Original Jazz Classics 886.

"Fountain Blues." Copyright, 1990. Englewood, N.J.: Dizlo. Recorded: A&M 75021-6404-2.

"Get the Booty." Recorded, 1980: Original Jazz Classics 882.

"Good Dues Blues." New York: Music Sales. Co-composers, Ray Brown, Gil Fuller. Recorded, 1946: Allegro Elite 3083; Bulldog BCD-2006; Musicraft 1046-70053-2.

"Grand Central Getaway." Copyright, 1944. New York: Music Sales. Co-composer, Jimmy Dorsey. Recorded: Laserlight 15759.

"Groovin' High." Copyright, 1961. Los Angeles: MCA. Recorded, 1945: Bulldog BCD-2006; Indigo 2068; Moon MCD-009-2; Savoy Jazz SV-0152.

"Guachi Guaro (Soul Sauce)" or "Wachi Wara." New York: Music Sales, 1965. Co-composer, Chano Pozo. Note: originally titled "Guarachi Guaro." Recorded: Concord Picante CCD-247; Original Jazz Classics 274; Rhino 72238; Verve 314-521007-2.

"Hand Fulla Gimmie." Copyright, 1946. New York: Music Sales. Co-composers, Gil Fuller, Ray Brown.

"Harlem Samba." Englewood, N.J.: Dizlo, 1977. Recorded, 1976: Original Jazz Classics 823.

"Haute Mon'." Copyright, 1958. Englewood, N.J.: Dizlo, 1986. Recorded, 1946: Verve 835253-2.

"He Beeped When He Shoulda Bopped." Englewood, N.J.: Dizlo, 1974. Co-composers, Ray Brown, Gil Fuller. Recorded: Allegro Elite 3083; Moon MCD045-2; Musicraft 1046-70053-2; Tradition 1027.

"Here 'Tis" or "Here It Is" or "Oh Yeah!" or "Shake Your Booty." Englewood, N.J.: Dizlo, 1962. Recorded: Verve 822 897.

"Hey Pete Le's Eat Mo' Meat." New York: Music Sales, 1977. Co-composers, Buster Harding, Oscar Peterson. Recorded, ca. 1948: Bluebird 66528-2; Columbia/Legacy 52454; RCA PM 42 408; Verve 314 511 393-2.

"Hob Nail Special." Copyright, 1956. Englewood, N.J.: Dizlo, 1984. Co-composer, Buster Harding. Recorded: Norgran MGN-1090.

"Hollywood and Vine." Copyright, 1945. Co-composer, Frank Paparelli. Recorded, 1991: Indiana University School of Music, 1991-92, no. 136.

"Hot Potato." Englewood, N.J.: Dizlo, n.d. Co-composers, Davis, Glen, Hayes, Larsen.

"How Can We Part." Copyright, 1940. Co-composers, Barnhill, Carter.

"I Waited for You." Copyright, 1953. Co-composer, George Russell. Recorded, 1946: Bandstand BDCD 1534; Heads Up International HUCD 3032; Moon MCD045-2; Musicraft 1046-70053-2; Rhino R2 79170.

"Impromptu." Copyright, 1954. Englewood, N.J.: Dizlo, 1982. Recorded, 1953: Verve 833 559-2; Verve VE-2-2521.

"Improvisations." Copyright, 1954. Englewood, N.J.: Dizlo, 1982. Co-composer, Chico O'Farrill.

"(I've Got) The Bluest Blues." Recorded, 1953: RCA Victor 09026-68360-2; Roulette RE-105; Vogue DP18.

"Jambo." Englewood, N.J.: Dizlo. Co-composer, Lorraine Gillespie. Recorded: Polygram 533846; Verve 314-513875-2.

Jazz Suite in Three Movements. Copyright, 1984.

"Jew's Harp." Recorded, 1970: Black Hawk BKH 51801.

"Joogie Boogie." Copyright, 1957. Englewood, N.J.: Dizlo. Recorded: Verve 527900.

"Juice." Copyright, 1945. Los Angeles: MCA. Co-composer, Frank Paparelli.

"Jump Did Le Ba." Recorded: BMG Classics 09026-68499-2; Rhino/Atlantic 71551.

"Jungla." Copyright, 1954. Englewood, N.J.: Dizlo, 1982. Co-composer, Chico O'Farrill. Recorded: Verve 8191.

"Just a Thought." Englewood, N.J.: Dizlo, 1997.

"Kerouac." 1941. Englewood, N.J.: Dizlo, 1985. Recorded, 1941: Smithsonian LP 2004.

"Kisses." Recorded, 1980: Original Jazz Classics 882.

"Kush." Englewood, N.J.: Dizlo. Recorded, 1960: Delta 17126; Heads Up International HUCD 3032; Impulse IMPD-178; LRC MC-9016; Verve 314 519809-2.

"Land of Milk and Honey." Englewood, N.J.: Dizlo. Recorded, 1976: Original Jazz Classics 823.

"Latin Stuff." Englewood, N.J.: Dizlo.

"Lights and Shadows." Copyright, 1947. Co-composer, Frank Paparelli.

"Little David." Copyright, 1976. Co-composers, Roy Eldridge, Flip Phillips, Bill Harris, Oscar Peterson, Ray Brown, Herb Ellis, Louie Bellson.

"The Lonely One." Englewood, N.J.: Dizlo.

"Lorraine." Englewood, N.J.: Dizlo. Recorded, ca. 1955: GRP GRD-9512; Mercury 832 574-2; Omega OCD 3025; Pro Arte 698; Riverside RLP 3508.

"Love Me Pretty Baby." Beverly Hills, Calif.: Planetary Music. Recorded, 1951: Savoy Jazz SV-1057.

"Manhattan Mood." Copyright, 1944. Co-composer, Frank Paparelli.

"Manteca" or "I'll Never Go Back." New York: Music Sales. Co-composers, Chano Pozo, Gil Fuller. Recorded, 1946–49: BMG Classics 09026-68499-2; Heads Up International HUCD 3032; Rhino R2 79170; Verve 314-513875-2.

"M'bani" or "N'bani." Englewood, N.J.: Dizlo, 1970. Recorded: Delta 17107.

"Me 'n Them." Englewood, N.J.: Dizlo, 1971. Recorded: Perception 13.

"Mic's Jump." Copyright, 1962. Englewood, N.J.: Dizlo. Recorded, ca. 1958: Polygram 512674; Polygram 834752.

"Minor Walk." Co-composer, Linton Garner. Recorded, 1947: BMG Classics 09026-68499-2; LRC MC-9016; RCA PM 42 408.

"Ms. Five by Four." Copyright, 1974.

"Nearness." Copyright, 1945. Co-composer, Tadd Dameron. Recorded: Capitol 57061; Jazz Showcase 5002.

"Night in Tunisia." 1942. Los Angeles: MCA. Co-composer, Frank Paparelli. Note: also known as "Interlude" when lyrics are included. Recorded: BMG Classics 09026-68499-2; Heads Up International HUCD 3032; Indigo 2068; Jazz Hour JH-1029.

"Norm's Norm." Recorded: Omega OCD 3025.

"Olé (For the Gypsies)." Englewood, N.J.: Dizlo, 1962. Recorded, 1991: Laserlight 15751.

"Olinga." Englewood, N.J.: Dizlo. Recorded: Collectables 5616; Columbia 2K-44174; Pablo 2620116; Smithsonian Folkways SF40811.

"One Alone." Copyright, 1956. Recorded, 1953–56: Verve 833 559-2.

"One Bass Hit." New York: Music Sales. Co-composers, Ray Brown, Gil Fuller. Recorded, 1946: Bandstand BDCD 1534; Capitol 57061; Indigo 2068; Philips 830 224-2; Savoy Jazz SV-0152.

"Oo Pa Pa Da." Copyright, 1990. Co-composers, Gil Fuller, Babs Brown. Recorded, 1947: Delta 17126; Disques Vogue 68213; Telarc CD-83316.

"Ooh-Shoo-Be-Doo-Be." Recorded, 1953: RCA Victor 09026-68360-2.

"Ool Ya Koo" or "Ool Ya Coo." Copyright, 1948. New York: Music Sales. Co-composer, Gil Fuller. Recorded, 1948: BMG Classics 09026-68499-2; Musica Jazz 2 MJP-1053; Verve 314-513875-2; Vogue 68213.

"Oop Bop Sh' Bam." Copyright, 1946. New York: Music Sales. Co-composer, Ray Brown, Gil Fuller. Recorded, 1946: Allegro Elite 3083; Bandstand BDCD 1534; Indigo 2068; Moon MCD045-2; Musicraft 1046-70053-2; Savoy Jazz SJ-0152.

"Ow." Copyright, 1958. Los Angeles: Advanced Music. Recorded, 1949: Bandstand BDCD 1534; Original Jazz Classics 886; Philips 830 224-2; RCA PM 42 408; Verve 314 519803-2.

"Paradiddle" or "Paradiddles." Copyright, 1940. Englewood, N.J.: Dizlo, 1967. Co-composer, Cozy Cole.

"Pickin' the Cabbage" or "Pickin' Cabbage." Copyright, 1940. Recorded, 1940: Classics 595; EPM Musique 158812; Smithsonian LP 2004.

"Pile Driver." Copyright, 1956. Englewood, N.J.: Dizlo, 1984. Co-composer, Buster Harding. Recorded, 1954: Norgran MGN-1090.

"Purple Sounds." Copyright, 1958. Englewood, N.J.: Dizlo, 1988. Recorded: Verve 840 039.

"Quasi-Boogaloo." New York: Pablito. Co-composers, Roy Eldridge, Oscar Peterson. Recorded, 1975: Pablo PACD-2310-816-2.

"Rails." Copyright, 1956. Englewood, N.J.: Dizlo, 1984. Co-composer, Buster Harding. Recorded, 1954: Polygram 513630; Verve MGV-8173.

"Rehearsal Blues." Englewood, N.J.: Dizlo.

"Reverend 'G'." Englewood, N.J.: Dizlo, 1974.

"Rhumba Finale." Copyright, 1956. Englewood, N.J.: Dizlo. Co-composer, Chico O'Farrill. Recorded: Verve 8191.

"Rhythm Man (Do Not Disturb)." Copyright, 1992. Recorded: Blue Moon 79170.

"Rimsky." Recorded, 1982: Original Jazz Classics OJCCD-733-2.

"Rio Pakistan." Copyright, 1957. Englewood, N.J.: Dizlo. Recorded: Verve 314-513875-2.

"Romany Joe." Copyright, 1938.

"Rumbola." Copyright, 1956. Englewood, N.J.: Dizlo, 1984. Co-composer, Buster Harding. Recorded, 1954: Verve 8143.

"Runison Fantasy." Englewood, N.J.: Dizlo.

"Salt Peanuts." Copyright, 1941. Los Angeles: MCA. Co-composer, Kenny Clarke. Recorded, 1945: Artistry 110; Capitol 57061; Indigo 2068; Musicraft 1046-70053-2; Smithsonian Collection P 13454/5.

"Saturday Night." Englewood, N.J.: Dizlo.

"Say Eh" or "Say A." Recorded, 1952: BMG Classics 09026-68361-2; Intermedia 5033; RCA Victor 09026-68361-2; Vogue 68361.

"Say When." Englewood, N.J.: Dizlo. Co-composer, Tadd Dameron. Recorded: Capitol 797; Capitol M-11059.

"Shaw Nuff." Copyright, 1946. New York: Music Sales. Co-composer, Charlie Parker. Recorded, 1945: Indigo 2068; Moon MCD045-2; Musicraft 1046-70053-2.

"6/8." Copyright, 1956. Englewood, N.J.: Dizlo. Co-composer, Chico O'Farrill.

"Slam Blues." Englewood, N.J.: Dizlo.

"Soulphony in Three Hearts." Los Angeles: Bregman, Vocco and Conn, 1948. Co-composer, Tadd Dameron.

"Stay on It." Los Angeles: Bregman, Vocco and Conn, 1948. Co-composer, Tadd Dameron. Recorded: BMG Classics 09026-68499-2; RCA PM 42 408.

"Steeplechase." Copyright, 1948. Englewood, N.J.: Dizlo, 1986. Co-composers, Oscar Peterson, David Eldridge, Harry Edison. Recorded, 1955: Verve 8212.

"Study in Soulphony." Recorded, 1993: Intermedia 5033.

"Sugar Hips." Copyright, 1957. Englewood, N.J.: Dizlo, 1986. Co-composer, Wade Legge. Recorded: Polygram 40031.

Suite in Five Movements. 1986. Englewood, N.J.: Dizlo. Contents: Birk's Works; Lorraine; Tenor Song; Ballad; Fiesta Mo-Jo; Tin Tin Deo.

"Sumphin'." Copyright, 1958. Englewood, N.J.: Dizlo, 1986. Recorded, 1957: Verve 835253-2.

"Swing Shift." Copyright, 1942. Englewood, N.J.: Dizlo, 1942.

"Swingin' Easy." Copyright, 1944. Co-composer, Frank Paparelli.

"Tally Ho." New York: Music Sales. Recorded, 1984: Tall Tree TTC-6002.

"Tanga" or "Frelimo." Copyright, 1974. Englewood, N.J.: Dizlo. Recorded, 1974: Enja 6044-2; Jazz Heritage 513 280A; Pablo 020116; Pablo OJCCD 443-2.

"Tangorine." Los Angeles: Silhouette Music, 1957. Recorded: Verve 314 511 393-2.

"That's Earl, Brother." Copyright, 1946. New York: Music Sales. Co-composers, Ray Brown, Gil Fuller. Recorded, 1946: Allegro Elite 3083; Indigo 2068; Rhino R2 79170; Savoy Jazz SJ 0152.

"There Is Something Wrong." Copyright, 1975.

"This Is the Way." Copyright, 1946. New York: Music Sales. Co-composer, Gil Fuller. Recorded, 1951–52: BMG Classics 09026-68361-2; Heads Up International HUCD 3032; Verve 314 519809-2; Vogue 68621.

"Timet." Englewood, N.J.: Dizlo, 1971. Recorded: Perception 13.

"Tour de Force." Copyright, 1957. Englewood, N.J.: Dizlo, 1985. Recorded, 1955: Blue Note 80507; Delta 55605; Verve 314 516 319-2; Verve VE1-2533.

"Trumpet Blues." Copyright, 1956. Englewood, N.J.: Dizlo, 1984. Co-composer, David Eldridge. Recorded, 1954: Verve 8110.

"Two Bass Hit" or "Bright Lights" or "Rococo" or "Second Base Hit." New York: Music Sales. Co-composer, John Lewis. Recorded, 1947: BMG Classics 09026-68499-2; Delta 17126; Jazz Guild 1010; LRC MC-9016; Philips 830 224-2.

"Um Hmmm." Englewood, N.J.: Dizlo. Recorded: RTE 1008.

"Ungawa" or "Oon-ga-wa." Copyright, 1961. Englewood, N.J.: Dizlo, 1989. Co-composer, Oscar Nunes. Recorded, 1959: Timeless CDSJP 250; Verve 314-513875-2.

"Walk Me to the Mountain." Copyright, 1988.

"We Love to Boogie." Recorded, 1946: Rhino R271255; Savoy Jazz SV-1057.

"Wetu." Copyright, 1974.

"Whasidishena." Recorded: Timeless CDSJP 250.

"Wheatleigh Hall." Copyright, 1958. Englewood, N.J.: Dizlo, 1986. Recorded, 1957: Accord 56572; Original Jazz Classics OJCCD-733-2; Rhino R2 79170; Verve 835253-2.

"Winter Samba" or "Tenor Song." Copyright, 1987. Englewood, N.J.: Dizlo. Recorded, 1966: Limelight LM-82042; GRP GRD-9512.

"Woody 'n' You" or "Algo Bueno (Woody 'n' You)." New York: Music Sales. Note: also known as "Wouldn't You" when lyrics are included. Recorded, 1944: BMG Classics 09026-68213-2; Mainstream 721; Smithsonian LP 2004.

"Yale Blue Blues." Co-composers, Dwike Marshall, Willie Ruff. Recorded, 1977: Black Hawk BKH 51801.

"You Got It." New York: Pablito. Co-composer, Count Basie. Recorded, 1977: Original Jazz Classics 886.

INCIDENTAL AND COMMERCIAL MUSIC

The Cosmic Eye. 1986. Co-composers, Benny Carter, Conrad Cummings, William Russo, Elizabeth Swados. Film score.

"Fanfare." 1965. Theme for the *Al Hirt Show* (television).

"Theme from Formula 409." Copyright, 1960. Commercial theme.

The Winter in Lisbon or *El Invierno en Lisboa.* 1990. Film soundtrack. Contents: Opening Theme; San Sebastian; Lucretia's Theme; Magic Summer; Isthmus; Lisbon; Burma; Bill's Song; Final Theme. Recorded: Milan 73138-35600-2.

PUBLICATIONS

ABOUT GILLESPIE
Books and Monographs

Evensmo, Jan. *The Trumpets of Dizzy Gillespie, Irving Randolph, Joe Thomas, 1937–1943.* Hosle, Norway: Jan Evensmo, 1982.

Gleason, Ralph J. *Celebrating the Duke, Louis, Bessie, Billie, Bird, Carmen, Miles, Dizzy, and Other Heroes.* Boston: Little, Brown, 1975.

Götze, Werner. *Dizzy Gillespie: Ein Porträt.* Wetzlar, Germany: Pegasus, 1960.

Horricks, Raymond. *Dizzy Gillespie and the Be-bop Revolution.* Tunbridge Wells, England: Spellmount, 1984.

James, Michael. *Dizzy Gillespie.* New York: A. S. Barnes, 1961.

Jepsen, Jorgen Grunnet. *A Discography of Dizzy Gillespie, 1953–1968.* Copenhagen: K. E. Knudsen, 1969.

Koster, Piet. *Dizzy Gillespie.* Amsterdam: Micrography, 1985.

———. *Dizzy Gillespie: A Discography, Volume 2.* Amsterdam: Micrography, 1988.

Lyons, Jimmy, and Ira Kamin. *Dizzy, Duke, the Count and Me: The Story of the Monterey Jazz Festival.* San Francisco: Hearst, 1978.

McRae, Barry. *Dizzy Gillespie: His Life and Times.* New York: Universe Books, 1988.

Morgenstern, Dan, Ira Gitler, and Jack Bradley. *Bird and Diz: A Bibliography.* New York: New York Jazz Museum, 1973.

Tanner, Lee, ed. *Dizzy: John Birks Gillespie in His 75th Year.* San Francisco: Pomegranate Artbooks, 1994.

Wölfer, Jürgen. *Dizzy Gillespie: Sein Leben, seine Musik, seine Schallplatten.* Waakirchen, Germany: Oreos, 1987.

Dissertations

Carlson, William Ralph. "A Procedure for Teaching Jazz Improvisation Based on an Analysis of the Performance Practice of Three Major Jazz Trumpet Players: Louis Armstrong, Dizzy Gillespie, and Miles Davis." D.Mus.Ed. diss., Indiana University, 1980.

Levy, James Daniel. "A Model of Phrase Improvisation in the Music of John Birks 'Dizzy' Gillespie (1940–1955)." M.M. thesis, University of Maryland at College Park, 1993.

Parkinson, William M. "Innovations in the Jazz Trumpet Styles of Louis Armstrong, Dizzy Gillespie, and Miles Davis." M.M. thesis, Kent State University, 1975.

Articles

Coss, B., and D. Solomon. "A Visit to the King in Queens: An Interview with Dizzy Gillespie." *Metro* 78 (February 1961): 15–18.

Dance, Stanley. "Dizzy Gillespie: Past, Present and Future." *Jazz* 2 (July 1963): 8–10.

Gardner, M. "Dizzy's (Back in) Business." *Jazz Journal* 21 (October 19, 1968): 2–4.

Knauss, Zane. "Dizzy Gillespie." In *Conversations with Jazz Musicians,* edited by Louis Bellson, 63–76. Detroit, Mich.: Gale Research, 1977.

Koenig, Wolfgang. "Dizzy Gillespie und sein Cuban Connection." *Jazz Podium* 37 (June 1988): 12–14.

Laber, Bob. "Dizzy Gillespie: An American Original." *Instrumentalist* 45 (December 1990): 24–31.

Laplace, Michel. "Un hommage á Dizzy Gillespie." *Brass Bulletin* 62 (1988): 10–15.

Lees, Gene. "Bird et Diz." *Jazz Magazine* 7 (August, 1961): 29–31.

———. "The Years with 'Yard': Interview with Dizzy Gillespie." *Down Beat* 28 (May 25, 1961): 21–23.

Meckna, Michael. "'It's Like the Spokes of a Wheel': Dizzy Gillespie at 75." *International Trumpet Guild Journal* 17 (September 1992): 7–10.

Priestley, Brian. "Dizzy Gillespie and Jimmy Smith at Bristol." *Jazz Monthly* 11 (February 1966): 2–5.

Terry, Clark, and Lee Underwood. "Dizzy Gillespie: Blowin' with Diz, via Mumbles." *Down Beat* 45, no. 8 (April 20, 1978): 12–14+.

Woodfin, H. "The Dizzy Gillespie Band: 1946–1950." *Jazz Monthly* 10 (October 1964): 12–14.

Wright, Josephine R. B. "Conversation with John Birks "Dizzy" Gillespie: Pioneer of Jazz." *Black Perspective in Music* 4, no. 1 (1976): 82–89.

BY GILLESPIE

"Dizzy and Monk at Minton's," with Al Fraser. *Jazz Times* (April 1982): 11.

"James Moody's My Man Now." *Melody Maker* 38 (June 15, 1963): 8.

"Ne tirez pas sur le bebop." *Jazz Magazine* 298 (June 1981): 61–63.

To Be or Not . . . to Bop: Memoirs, with Al Fraser. Garden City, N.Y.: Doubleday, 1979.

* * * * *

With his trumpet bell upturned, his spinnaker cheeks, easy virtuosity, pathbreaking compositions, and puckish bonhomie, Dizzy Gillespie epitomized the very spirit of jazz. He was one of the principal developers of bop style in the early 1940s and one of the most widely imitated trumpeters in the 1940s and 1950s. During the Cold War, he was the first musician commissioned by the U.S. State Department to take a jazz orchestra on an international goodwill tour. With a Grammy Lifetime Achievement Award, Kennedy Center Honors, National Medal of Arts from President Bush, Commandeur d'Ordre des Arts et Letters from French President Mitterand, a scholarship fund endowed in his name at Stanford University, and over a dozen honorary doctorates, he was one of the most famous persons of the 20th century. The noun "musician" truly fits this man who wrote as well as performed music and whose life was dedicated to his art. He composed nearly 200 works, many of which have become jazz standards.

Gillespie's was a far from easy career. Born in 1917 in Cheraw, South Carolina, he was the ninth and last child of Lottie Powe Gillespie and James Gillespie, a bricklayer and part-time musician who led a local band and died a few months before his youngest child's tenth birthday. By then, however, Dizzy, an inquisitive and often unruly child, had developed the ability to play several instruments. At age 12, he focused on trombone, but the following year he switched to trumpet. By the time he left the Robert Smalls Public School in 1933, he was accomplished enough to win a music scholarship to the Laurinburg Institute in Laurinburg, North Carolina, where his teacher was Shorty Hall. Gillespie flourished in Laurinburg's atmosphere of strong discipline, good teaching, and high ideals. However, a few months before graduation in 1935, he moved to Philadelphia with his family. (In a special ceremony at Laurinburg 12 years later, he received both his diploma and a football letter.)

With his trumpet in a paper bag, Gillespie joined the musicians' union in Philadelphia and soon thereafter began playing in Frank Fairfax's band, where fellow trumpet player Charlie Shavers taught him Roy Eldridge solos. Gillespie's ribald behavior with Fairfax won him the nickname by which all the world, even his wife, eventually called him. In 1937, he moved to New York to seek fame and fortune. Largely on the strength of his ability to imitate Eldridge, Gillespie was hired by Teddy Hill, with whom Eldridge had until recently been a soloist. Gillespie made his first recordings with the Teddy Hill band, including "King Porter Stomp" and "Blue Rhythm Fantasy," and spent a happy summer touring France and Great Britain. Back in New York, Gillespie played with such groups as Al Cooper's Savoy Sultans and Alberto Socarras's Afro-

Cuban band in addition to Hill's ensemble. In September 1939, he recorded in a group led by Lionel Hampton, with whom he began to find his own voice on such pieces as "Hot Mallets." Two months later he joined Cab Calloway's big band.

While in Calloway's group, Gillespie made some 50 recordings, most of which are dominated by the bandleader's singing. However, Gillespie's occasional solos reveal an emerging artist who could improvise with skill. He also became interested in Afro-Cuban music under the influence of fellow trumpeter Mario Bauzá, and he began to explore new musical territory with bassist Milt Hinton. In extracurricular jam sessions, he and Charlie Parker, Thelonious Monk, Kenny Clarke, and others experimented with the style that was to develop into bop.

From 1941 until he formed his own big band in 1945, Gillespie worked with Charlie Barnet, Benny Carter, Billy Eckstine, Duke Ellington, Ella Fitzgerald, Coleman Hawkins, Earl Hines, Les Hite, Lucky Millinder, and Oscar Pettiford. "Dizzy's the greatest," fellow Barnet trumpeter Joe Guy later told Leonard Feather. "He never gets tired of playing. He'll do sixteen sets and then go across the street and jam with someone else." During this period, Gillespie also further developed his talent as a composer-arranger. "Salt Peanuts," "Woody 'n' You," and the now classic "Night in Tunisia" all date from this time. So does the term "bebop," an onomatopoetic word that was frequently used to convey the rhythm and articulation of one of the new style's characteristic phrase endings.

Gillespie's own big band won *Metronome* magazine awards, and from 1947 to 1950, he outdistanced Roy Eldridge for Best Trumpet. However, there was more than a little resistance to the new bop style. For the next few years, he made recordings such as "Cubana Be/Cubana Bop," "Manteca," and "Things to Come," which eventually changed the course of jazz. Dissatisfied with his treatment by record company executives, he created his own label, Dee Gee, in 1951, but it lasted barely two financially unrewarding years. In the meantime, the jazz spotlight had turned its focus on the new cool style as represented by performers such as Miles Davis. On the whole, these were relatively lean years for Gillespie, although in 1953, he began a professional association with Norman Granz and toured as a headliner with Jazz at the Philharmonic.

In 1956, the U.S. State Department was looking for a musician to undertake a cultural mission, and invited Gillespie to participate. He reorganized his big band and took it to Africa, the Near East, Asia, and Eastern Europe. The tour was so successful that a few months later he was asked to take the group to South America. "Gillespie was an ideal ambassador," Leonard Feather has observed. "He made no speeches but mingled with crowds, pointed to his interracial personnel when the subject of American racism was raised, brought gifts for fans, and made countless new friends in every city." Gillespie's band lasted another two years, but without government support he had to return to leading smaller combos.

Gillespie continued to be a major presence on the jazz scene. Although he basically let the Free Jazz movement pass him by, he did participate in Third Stream experiments, notably with Lalo Schifrin in the jazz suite *Gillespiana* (1960). However, he was most at home playing with his own small groups, serving in all-star ensembles such as the Giants of Jazz, and appearing as a featured artist aboard Caribbean cruise ships. Highlights of his career include a mock-serious bid for the U.S. presidency in 1964; a 1977 visit to Cuba; singing "Salt Peanuts" with President Carter during a 1978 performance at the White House; publication to wide critical acclaim of his memoirs, *To Be or Not . . . to Bop*; playing trumpet for Oscar the Grouch on a 1982 *Sesame Street* episode; trips to Havana in 1985 and 1986; numerous festivals on the occasion of his 70th birthday in 1987; the release in 1989 of his documentary *A Night in Havana*; dozens of appearances on NBC's *Tonight Show*; and of course the various honorary doctorates and Grammys. Gillespie became an elder statesman of jazz, as reissues of his old recordings alternated with new recordings.

As is usually the case with composers who are primarily performers, the development of Gillespie's compositional output is inextricably linked with his trumpet playing of both his own compositions and those of others. In 1937, his style on "King Porter Stomp" and other recordings purposely resembled that of Roy Eldridge, but by 1939, he had begun to find his own voice. A brief, muted solo of high-speed eighth notes on "Hot Mallets" foreshadows the future bop style, and on "Pickin' the Cabbage" from the following year he plays in both swing- and even-note values. He began to use less vibrato, perhaps because he did not spend all that much time on any one note. By 1942, the year of "Jersey Bounce," his style was in place. This piece, probably the first recorded example of bop, exhibits Gillespie's characteristic trait of abruptly alternating mid-register passages with startling high notes.

Gillespie moved around the horn with the speed and agility of a saxophone player, and so, naturally, do his compositions. "Night in Tunisia," which he wrote in 1942 and recorded several times, has amazing long runs of notes. On this piece and others such as "Shaw 'Nuff," he exhibited another of his stylistic characteristics, an infectious good humor. "Our Delight" and especially the manic "Things to Come," which was the first translation of the bop style into the big band language, are more excellent examples of his boisterous, extroverted style.

Gillespie's improvisations invariably exhibit certain signature effects such as the glissando, half-valve smear, and shake, even in his ballad style. If his sound is not particularly broad and warm, and if he sometimes seems little concerned with intonation, he still constructs memorable solos on such standards as "Stardust," "Lover Man," and "All the Things You Are." In 1945, he bravely attempted "I Can't Get Started," which had belonged to Bunny Berigan since 1937. Gillespie's silver tone, restless filigree, and hint of desperation made the piece his. A subsequent recording of the Quincy Jones arrangement of "I Can't Get Started," which Gillespie took on the 1956 State Department tour, shows a more restrained, thoughtful soloist.

"Dizzy Gillespie has been at the forefront of American music spiritually, intellectually, and humorously for 50 years," observed Wynton Marsalis to Bob Laber. "He's the father of the modern trumpet style, an innovator . . . whose true accomplishments still have yet to be properly assessed let alone digested." He was also one of those rare men who, according to close friends, was as great a man in his life as he was in his art. It is little wonder that his death in 1993 was mourned throughout the world and made headlines in many prominent newspapers.

SELECTED WORKS

While Gillespie is most commonly associated with trumpet playing, he also wrote many outstanding jazz works. Many of these were spontaneous tunes created with Charlie Parker, and several have become standards. From 1941, when he left the Calloway band, until 1945, when he formed his own big band, Gillespie developed his talent as a composer. "Night in Tunisia," "Salt Peanuts," and "Woody 'n' You" all date from this time. "Things to Come," recorded by Gillespie's second big band on July 9, 1946, is an early translation of the bop style into the big band language. Energetic, adventuresome, and witty, all four works are characterized by a firm structural framework that, in the hands of an able performer, supports endlessly elaborate improvisation.

Gillespie wrote "Night in Tunisia" while he was in the Earl Hines band, and he brought it along when he played briefly with Boyd Raeburn. Like so many musical compositions, jazz or otherwise, it had its origins in the exploration of two closely related chords, a B-flat-minor ninth and a D-minor ninth (see Ex. 1a). From these, Gillespie derives an insouciant melody (see Ex. 1b) that is elaborated upon as it makes its way around an ensemble. In a typical performance of "Tunisia," a Latin-tinged rhythm undergirds the melody (although it has been recorded in blues and funk among other styles by a wide variety of ensembles). Subtle but insistent, this rhythm, together with unusual harmony and intonations (ninth chords and lowered fifths) provided a fresh approach to big band jazz writing. An alternate title, "Interlude," is frequently used when "Night in Tunisia" is performed with lyrics.

Example 1. "Night in Tunisia"
a. Basic chords

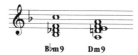

b. Melody

Like "Night in Tunisia," "Salt Peanuts" is more preoccupied with rhythmic, harmonic, and melodic complexities than with form. A familiar riff is its salient melodic aspect, (see Ex. 2) and the harmony is based on "I Got Rhythm." The form of "Salt Peanuts" is the familiar bop scheme of a brief introduction, a theme played in unison, a number of improvised solo choruses, a return to the theme, and a coda. It moves along at a rapid pace, and the riff serves as both a punctuation and a breathing point. Like "Night in Tunisia," "Salt Peanuts" has become a standard. Thirty years after its

composition, Gillespie coaxed President Jimmy Carter onto a bandstand set up on the South Lawn of the White House and, with the help of Max Roach, cajoled him into singing along.

Example 2. "Salt Peanuts" theme

"Woody 'n' You" is more dance-like than Gillespie's fast-paced music; in fact, he wrote it for the Woody Herman band as an accompaniment for tap dancers. Herman never recorded it, but Gillespie did, initially with Coleman Hawkins in 1944 and later in 1947 with his big band. Also known as "Algo Bueno," "Woody's" melody is derived from chords: a B-flat minor sixth followed by an A-flat minor sixth and then a simple D-flat major chord. Gillespie saw in this progression both a melody, which he punctuated with a few notes from "Night in Tunisia," and a countermelody. "I didn't try to express anything particular, just music, just what the chords inspired," Gillespie later recalled to Ira Gitler. The sophisticated "Woody 'n' You" is nonetheless evocative of Gillespie the hipster, who at the time wore a beret, horn-rimmed glasses, and a goatee, and served as the interpreter of bebop to white beatniks.

While "Woody 'n' You" fit comfortably into the jazz groove, nothing like "Things to Come" had ever been heard before. After several years of experimentation in small groups, Gillespie tried out bop's frantic speed, emotional tension, and new harmonic ideas (such as half-diminished seventh chords) in a big band format. The result was a qualified success. Listeners were startled by the manic tempos, and many musicians found the phrases nearly impossible at Gillespie's suggested metronome marking (quarter-note = 180). (By way of comparison, "Night in Tunisia" typically goes at the unusually rapid clip of 144, and Glenn Miller's version of "In the Mood," considered *Presto* in its day, moves along at 152.) "Things to Come" found its share of admirers, though, and it served as a harbinger of the end of the swing era. Gillespie himself subsequently moved laterally and wrote the Latin-inspired "Manteca," the more harmonically oriented "Con Alma," and the blues-style "Birk's Works."

REFERENCES

Balliett, Whitney. "Profiles: Dizzy." *New Yorker* 66 (September 17, 1990): 48–56.

Feather, Leonard. *From Satchmo to Miles.* New York: Stein and Day, 1972.

Gillespie, Dizzy, with Al Fraser. *To Be or Not . . . to Bop.* Garden City, N.Y.: Doubleday, 1979.

Gitler, Ira. *Swing to Bop.* New York: Oxford University Press, 1985.

Gourse, Leslie. *Dizzy Gillespie and the Birth of Bebop.* New York: Atheneum, 1994.

Laber, Bob. "Dizzy Gillespie: An American Original." *Instrumentalist* 45 (December 1990): 24–31.

Lees, Gene. *Waiting for Dizzy.* New York: Oxford University Press, 1991.

McDonough, John. "Gillespiana." *Jazz Educators Journal* 28, no. 4 (January 1996): 30.

McRae, Barry. *Dizzy Gillespie: His Life and Times.* New York: Universe Books, 1988.

Meckna, Michael. *Twentieth-Century Brass Soloists.* Westport, Conn.: Greenwood Press, 1994.

Tanner, Lee, ed. *Dizzy: John Birks Gillespie in His 75th Year.* San Francisco: Pomegranate Artbooks, 1994.

Terry, Clark, and Lee Underwood. "Dizzy Gillespie: Blowin' with Diz, via Mumbles." *Down Beat* 45, no. 8 (April 20, 1978): 12–14+.

MICHAEL MECKNA

GOLSON, BENNY

Born in Philadelphia, Pa., January 25, 1929. **Education:** Began piano study, wage nine; Philadelphia, Pa., public schools, studied saxophone from age 14; Howard University, studied saxophone with Sterling Thomas and theory with Bernard Mason, 1947–50; studied composition with Henry Brant, 1960. **Composing and Performing Career:** Mainly New York, N.Y., arranged for and played saxophone with bands led by "Bull Moose" Jackson, 1951, Tadd Dameron, 1953, Lionel Hampton, 1953, Johnny Hodges, 1954, Earl Bostic, 1954–56, Dizzy Gillespie, 1956–58, Art Blakey, 1958–59; co-leader of Jazztet with Art Farmer, 1959–62; writer and producer of music for radio and television commercials, 1963–present; producer, arranger, and composer for various artists including Miles Davis, Sammy Davis Jr., Ella Fitzgerald, Connie Francis, Dizzy Gillespie, Eartha Kitt, Lou Rawls, Max Roach, and Diana Ross; Hollywood, Ca., retired from performing to write music for television and feature films including scores for *M*A*S*H, Ironside, Mission Impossible, Mod Squad, Room 222, The Partridge Family, Mannix, Run for Your Life,* pilots for ABC, CBS, and others, 1967–74; resumed performing career, appearing regularly in concerts and festivals around the world and recording and producing his own albums and those of others, 1974–present; composed television commercial theme music for Coca-Cola, Chrysler Motors, Chevrolet, Canada Dry Ginger Ale, and others. **Teaching Career:** William Paterson College, artist-in-residence, ca. 1991–92; as a lecturer, has spoken at the Conservatoire National des Arts et Métiers, Paris, Eastman School of Music, Howard University, Jazz at Lincoln Center, Juillard School of Music, Loyola University, New Orleans, La., Manhattan School of Music, New York University, Stanford University, and others. **Honors/Awards:** *Down Beat* International Jazz Poll, New Star Composer award, 1952; *Down Beat* International Jazz Poll, New Star Saxophonist award, 1952, 1953; William Paterson College, honorary doctorate, 1993; Guggenheim fellowship, 1994; National Endowment for the Arts, American Jazz Masters Award, 1996. **Mailing Address:** 101 West 90th Street, #22J, New York, N.Y. 10024.

MUSIC LIST

COLLECTION

The Genius of Benny Golson. Miami: Columbia Pictures Prod., 1985. Reprint, Milwaukee, Wis.: Hal Leonard, 1989. Contents: Along Came Betty; Are You Real; Blues March; Briellesamba; Caribbean Runabout; Fair Weather; Five Spot after Dark; From Dream to Dream; I Remember Clifford; Just by Myself; Killer Joe; Out of the Past; Stablemates; Time Speaks; Whisper Not. Note: piano versions arranged by the composer.

JAZZ ENSEMBLE

[The following list of titles includes only works that were composed by the subject of the entry; it is not a list of recordings that were made by the subject. Although the composer may have made recordings of his own works, the list is not restricted to those recordings but in many cases includes performances by other artists of the composer's work. The list is made up of publication and discographical data, in cases where such information is available. Although no effort has been made to include documentation of the earliest recording of the works listed, the date of the earliest recording that is readily available has been given. —Ed.]

"Along Came Betty" or "Along Came Manon." 1958. Los Angeles: Time Step Music. Recorded: Blue Note 4003; Dreyfus FBM 36552-2; JA Records 1223; Soul Note SN 1066CD.

"Are You Real?" Los Angeles: Time Step Music. Recorded, 1958: Blue Note 4003; Prestige PRT 7361; Riverside OJCCD-1750-2.

"Back to the City." Recorded, 1986: Contemporary C-14020; Original Jazz Classics 842.

"Bean Bag." Los Angeles: Time Step Music. Recorded, 1960: Chess 802.

"B. G.'s Holiday." Recorded, 1957: Contemporary OJCCD-164-2.

"Blue Streak." Recorded, 1959: New Jazz NJLP-8248; Prestige OJCCD-1873-2.

"Blue Thoughts." Los Angeles: Time Step Music. Recorded, 1958: Original Jazz Classics OJCCD-207-2.

"Blue Walk." Los Angeles: Time Step Music. Recorded, 1954: Original Jazz Classics OJCCD-1837-2; Prestige PRST-7663.

"Blues After Dark." Los Angeles: Time Step Music. Recorded, 1959: New Jazz NJLP-8235; Prestige OJCCD-1850-2.

"Blues It." Los Angeles: Time Step Music. Recorded, 1957: Contemporary OJCCD-164-2.

"The Blues March (March On)." Los Angeles: Time Step Music. Recorded, 1958: Blue Note 4003; Columbia JC35359; Riverside 53505; Timeless Records CDSJP 177.

"Blues on Down." Los Angeles: Time Step Music. Recorded, 1957: Jazzland JLP 85; Riverside 93505; Riverside OJCCD-1797-2.

"Blues on My Mind." Los Angeles: Time Step Music. Recorded, 1959: DRG Disques Swing CDSW 8418; Riverside OJCCD-6009-2.

"Bob Hurd's Blues." Recorded, 1959: New Jazz NJLP 8248; Prestige OJCCD-1873-2.

"Briellesamba." In *The Genius of Benny Golson.*

"Caribbean Runabout." In *The Genius of Benny Golson.* Recorded: Eastman Jazz Ensemble recording.

"Change of Heart." Recorded, 1983: Timeless Records SJP235.

"City Bound." Recorded, 1989: Hep CD2047.

"City Lights." 1958. Recorded: Mosaic MD4-162.

"Cool One." Los Angeles: Time Step Music. Recorded, 1985: Red House RHR-07.

"Cry a Blue Tear." Recorded, 1958: Milestone M-47048; Riverside OJCCD-1750-2.

"Dear Kathy." Recorded, 1963: Mercury SR-60801; Verve 840-951-4.

"Domingo." 1956–58. Recorded: Dreyfus FDM 36557-2; Mosaic MD4-162.

"The Drum Thunder Suite." Los Angeles: Time Step Music. Recorded, 1958: Blue Note 4003.

"Ease Away Walk." Recorded, 1983: Soul Note SN 1066CD.

"Easy All Day." Recorded, 1977: Columbia 34678.

"Fair Weather." Los Angeles: Time Step Music. Recorded, 1983: Riverside 93505; Soul Note SN 1066 CD.

"Five Spot after Dark." Los Angeles: Time Step Music. Recorded, 1960: Chess 802.

Benny Golson; courtesy of Dreyfus Records, Inc.

"From Dream to Dream." In *The Genius of Benny Golson.* Recorded, 1986: Contemporary C-14020; Original Jazz Classics 842.

"Gypsy Jingle-Jangle." Recorded, 1987: Delta 17076; Denon 71838.

"Happy I'm Happy." Recorded, 1979: Columbia JC 35359.

"Hasaan's Dream." Los Angeles: Time Step Music. Recorded, 1957: Blue Note CDP 7 46817 2; Mosaic MD4-162.

"Heartstrings." Recorded, 1992: Evidence 22141-2.

"I Remember Clifford." Los Angeles: Time Step Music. Recorded, 1957: Argo 664; Mosaic MD4-162; Prestige PRT 7361; Timeless Records CDSJP 177.

"I'll Do It All with You." Recorded, 1977: Columbia 34678.

"I'm Always Dancin' to the Music." Recorded, 1978: Columbia JC 35359.

"Impromptune." Los Angeles: Time Step Music. Recorded, 1961: Cadet CA 681.

"Jam for Bobbie." Recorded, 1959: New Jazz NJLP-8235.

"Jam the Avenue." Recorded, 1983: Dreyfus FDM 36552-2; Timeless Records CDSPJ 235.

"Junction." 1961. Los Angeles: Time Step Music. Recorded: Cadet LP 688; Chess 802.

"Just by Myself." Los Angeles: Time Step Music. Recorded, 1957: Argo LP-716; Contemporary OJCCD-164-2; Mosaic MD4-162.

"Killer Joe" or "That's Killer Joe." 1959. Los Angeles: Time Step Music. Recorded: Blue Rock' It BRCD 124.

"Little Karin." 1958. Los Angeles: Time Step Music. Recorded: Cadet CA 681.

"Mesabi Chant." 1956–58. Recorded: Mosaic MD4-162.

"Minor Vamp." Recorded, 1959: Riverside RLP 93505; Savoy Jazz 127.

"Moment to Moment." Recorded, 1983: Soul Note SN 1066 CD.

"My Blues House." Los Angeles: Time Step Music. Recorded, 1959: Dreyfus FDM 36557-2; Prestige OJCCD-226-2.

"New Killer Joe (Rap)." Co-composer, Quincy Jones. Note: based on "Killer Joe." Recorded, 1977: Columbia 34678.

"No Dancin'." Recorded, 1985: Timeless Records CDSJP 187.

"One Day Forever (I Remember Miles)." Recorded, 1992: Arabesque AJ 0118; Evidence 22141-2.

"Out of the Past." Los Angeles: Time Step Music. Recorded, 1957: Jazzland JLP 85; Riverside OJCCD-1797-2; Riverside OJCCD-226-2.

"Outta Sight." North Hollywood, Calif.: Maggio Music Press, 1970.

"Park Avenue Petite." Los Angeles: Time Step Music. Recorded, 1960: Cadet CA664; Prestige/Fantasy OJC-5248.

"Portrait." Los Angeles: Time Step Music.

"Reggie of Chester." 1956–58. Los Angeles: Time Step Music. Recorded: Mosaic MD4-162.

"Roland Speaks." Los Angeles: Time Step Music. Co-composer, Rahsaan Roland Kirk. Recorded: Mercury MG 20844; Polygram 846-630-2.

"Sad to Say." Recorded, 1987: Denon CY-1838; Enja ENJ-7047-2.

"Slightly Hep." 1956–58. Recorded: Mosaic MD4-162.

"Soul Me." Recorded, 1959: New Jazz NJLP-8235.

"Stablemates." Los Angeles: Time Step Music. Recorded, 1955: Delta 17176; LRC MC-9018; United Artists 4020.

"Stand By." 1956–58. Recorded: Delta 17075; Mosaic MD4-162.

"Starfire." Los Angeles: Time Step Music.

"Step Lightly" or "Junior's Arrival." Los Angeles: Time Step Music. Recorded, 1956: Contemporary OJCCD164-2.

"Stockholm Sojourn." Recorded, 1965: Prestige 7361.

"Strut." Los Angeles: Time Step Music. Recorded, 1954: Prestige PRLP-192.

"A Swedish Villa." Recorded, 1965: Prestige PRT 7361.

"Swing It." Los Angeles: Time Step Music. Recorded, 1961: Cadet CA 681.

"Thinking Mode." Recorded, 1991: Dreyfus FDM 36557-2.

"Thursday's Theme." Recorded, 1958: DRG Disques Swing CDSW 8418.

"Timbale Rock." Recorded, 1977: Columbia 34678.

"Time Speaks." In *The Genius of Benny Golson.* Recorded, 1986: Dreyfus FDM 36557-2; Timeless Records CDSJP 187.

"Time's Past (This Is for You, John)." Recorded, 1983: Timeless Records CDSJP 235.

"Tippin' on Thru." Los Angeles: Time Step Music. Recorded, 1959: New Jazz NJLP-8248; Original Jazz Classics 1873.

"Tip-Toeing." Recorded, 1957: Blue Note CDP 7 46817 2; Mosaic MD4-162.

"Tomorrow, Paradise." Recorded, 1977: Columbia 34678.

"Touch." Los Angeles: Time Step Music. Recorded, 1961: Cadet CA 681.

"Tryst." 1968. Recorded: Prestige PRT 7361.

"Two Part Inventions for the Trumpet." North Hollywood, Calif.: Maggio Music, 1970.

"Up, Jump, Spring." Recorded, 1987: Delta 17076.

"Uptown Afterburn." Recorded, 1992: Evidence 22141-2.

"Vas Simeon." Recorded, 1986: Original Jazz Classics 842.

"Venetian Breeze." Recorded, 1957: Jazzland JLP 85; Milestone M-47048; Riverside OJCCD-1797-2.

"Walkin' and Stalkin'." Recorded, 1977: Columbia 34678.

"Where Am I?" 1956–58. Los Angeles: Time Step Music. Recorded: Mosaic MD4-162.

"Whisper Not." Los Angeles, Calif.: Model Music and Los Angeles: Time Step Music. Co-composer, Leonard Feather. Recorded, 1956: Contemporary OJCCD-164-2; Epic 16009; Mosaic MD4-162; Timeless Records CDSJP 177.

"Without Delay." Recorded, 1986: Original Jazz Classics 842.

"Yesterday's Thoughts." Los Angeles: Time Step Music. Recorded, 1983: Soul Note SN 1066 CD.

"You're Not the Kind." Recorded, 1958: DRG Disques Swing CDSW 8418.

ORCHESTRA (CHAMBER OR FULL) WITH SOLOISTS

Two Faces (double bass, orchestra, jazz piano, drums). 1991. Unpublished manuscript. Premiere, 1992.

INCIDENTAL AND COMMERCIAL MUSIC

"Another Turn in the Road." From the motion picture soundtrack *Ed's Next Move.* Recorded, 1996: Milan 35776-2.

"City Walking." From the motion picture soundtrack *Ed's Next Move.* Recorded, 1996: Milan 35776-2.

The Creative Spirit. 1994. Music for the television miniseries.

Ironside. 1968. Los Angeles: On Back Street Music. Television series soundtrack.

It Takes a Thief. 1967–68. Los Angeles, Calif: On Back Street Music. Television series soundtrack.

"Looking for a Home." From the motion picture soundtrack *Ed's Next Move*. Recorded, 1996: Milan 35776-2.

"Manhattan Bound." From the motion picture soundtrack *Ed's Next Move*. Recorded, 1996: Milan 35776-2.

Mannix. 1968. Television series soundtrack.

M*A*S*H*. 1968–71. Television series soundtrack.

Mission Impossible. 1968–69. Television series soundtrack.

Mod Squad. 1969. N.p.: Haven Music. Television series soundtrack.

"Morning Groove." From the motion picture soundtrack *Ed's Next Move*. Recorded, 1996: Milan 35776-2.

The Partridge Family. 1971. Television series soundtrack.

Room 222. 1967–70. Los Angeles: Fox Music Corp. Television series soundtrack.

"Rough at First." From the motion picture soundtrack *Ed's Next Move*. Recorded, 1996: Milan 35776-2.

Run for Your Life. 1967. Television series soundtrack.

Silent Force. Los Angeles: Warner Brothers Music Corp. Television series soundtrack.

Skifascination. Film soundtrack. 1966.

"Something There." From the motion picture soundtrack *Ed's Next Move*. Recorded, 1996: Milan 35776-2.

Where It's At. 1968. New York, N.Y.: EMI Unart Catalog. Television series soundtrack.

PUBLICATIONS

ABOUT GOLSON
Articles

"Benny Golson." *Swing Journal* 36, no. 5 (1982): 248.

Blum, J. "The Jazztet." *Jazz Times* (November 1986): 18–19.

Carles, P., and D. Michel. "Benny Golson: I Remember Blue March." *Jazz Magazine* 399 (December 1990): 40–42.

"Forward Motion: An Interview with Benny Golson." *Boundary* 22, no. 2 (1995): 53.

Frost, H. "Benny Golson." *Down Beat* 25, no. 10 (1958): 19.

Keepnews, P. "Blue Notes' Two New Theatrical Efforts in Search of Support." *Billboard* 99 (March 7, 1989): 54.

Lees, Gene. "The Philadelphia Connection: Benny Golson." In *Cats of Any Color: Jazz Black and White*, 123–142. New York: Oxford University Press, 1995.

———. "Benny Golson." In *Jazz Lives: One Hundred Portraits in Jazz*, 96. New York: Firefly, 1994.

Tomkins, Les. "Balancing Creativity and Commercialism." *Crescendo International* 25 (January 1988): 8–9.

———. "Benny Golson: Getting into a Different Bag." *Crescendo International* 21 (December 1982): 6–7.

———. "Benny Golson: How to Succeed in Music—By Really Trying." *Crescendo International* 21 (September 1983): 12–13.

———. "Benny Golson: Variety and Its Virtues." *Crescendo International* 21 (May 1983): 16–17.

———. "The Dilemma of the Playing Writer." *Crescendo International* 21 (November 1982): 20–22.

Voce, S. "Benny Golson." *Jazz Journal* 35 (1982): 8; 36 (January 1983): 6–7.

———. "The Tenorist and Composer Benny Golson." *Jazz Journal* 35 (December 1982): 8–9.

BY GOLSON
Television

The Sophisticated Gents. 1987. Television miniseries.

*   *   *   *   *

Benny Golson emerged in the late 1950s, at a time when bebop-derived music was undergoing consolidation. His overnight success had been preceded by a lengthy and fruitful apprenticeship during which he had progressed from keyboard studies to the saxophone and from European classical music to the full range of vernacular styles. Within the jazz field, he rapidly established himself as a leading composer with an individual and highly recognizable approach.

Golson's interest was initially sparked by the piano performances of two uncles. At about the age of eight, he began to take lessons, at 75 cents an hour, from J. Walker Freeman. About 1943, Golson turned from his ambition to be a concert pianist when he heard the Lionel Hampton band, featuring saxophonist Arnett Cobb, which led to his taking up the tenor saxophone and eventually becoming part of the Philadelphia jazz scene. In 1947, Golson entered the music department of Howard University and studied saxophone with Sterling Thomas and theory with Bernard Mason. Acquiring the nickname "Professor" among colleagues, Golson was a self-described "musical rebel" while at Howard. More valuable, however, for his chosen path were his early years as a professional saxophonist when, in the band of singer Ben "Bull Moose" Jackson, he was befriended by the pianist-composer Tadd Dameron, who unselfishly passed on to Golson his accumulated knowledge. This strong influence marks many of Golson's best-known compositions, as does his admiration for the work of Quincy Jones, Gigi Gryce (Basheer Quism), and Ernie Wilkins, whom he replaced in the Dizzy Gillespie band. Although Golson denies any influence from composer John Lewis, his frequent use of simple triads and unadorned seventh and half-diminished chords, in an era when more extended chords were becoming common, is a point of similarity.

During his development as a jazz composer, Golson's reputation became established as he released pieces such as "Stablemates" (recorded by Miles Davis with John Coltrane in 1955), "Step Lightly" (1956, also known as "Junior's Arrival" and first recorded by Clifford Brown), "Whisper Not" (1956, recorded by Lee Morgan and later, Dizzy Gillespie) and "I Remember Clifford" (1957, recorded variously by Donald Byrd, Morgan, and Gillespie). In the same period, he wrote original arrangements for the bands of James Moody (1956) and Oscar Pettiford (1957) and produced attractive items for the band of his next employer, Art Blakey (e.g., "Blues March" and "Along Came Betty," 1958), and for record sessions led by friends such as Art Farmer. In 1959, he founded The Jazztet with Farmer, which achieved a hit record with "Killer Joe" (1959). In every case, memorable melodies, notably simple and direct compared to much jazz of the period, are underpinned by harmonies that, while also apparently simple, move in logical but surprising directions.

In 1960, Golson studied privately with film composer Henry Brant, who taught him valuable structural techniques. His career moved into another phase when, in 1967, with the encouragement of Quincy Jones and Oliver Nelson, Golson followed their example and settled in Hollywood, where he began to compose for film and television dramas and for advertising agencies. None of this work is easily available for study, unlike some of his recorded scores for popular singers, which hew more closely to his 1950s style.

Also unavailable is a double bass concerto titled *Two Faces,* which was written for Rufus Reid and premiered on October 21, 1992, at Lincoln Center. Golson is not solely a jazz composer, and more study is needed of the totality of his output. It is, however, true to say that his works of the 1955–59 period, and some pieces of the 1980s in a similar vein, were of such individuality that they had an immediate impact on the world of jazz and laid the foundation for Golson's reputation.

SELECTED WORKS

The four Golson works discussed here all belong to the period of his greatest impact on the jazz scene, and all have stood the test of time. "Whisper Not" (1956), his first widely popular piece, was completed in a single short burst of inspiration, and its directly appealing melody is contained in a simple AA'BA'' framework (a separate introduction, used on its premiere recording by Lee Morgan, was dropped on subsequent recordings). Recalling the work of Tadd Dameron, the melody proceeds mainly in long notes that last three beats, one for each main harmonic movement. "Whisper Not" has several points in common with the slower and somewhat more complex "I Remember Clifford" (1957) which, by comparison, required considerable time for Golson to complete, including a melodic introduction of six bars, which is repeated in the work's eight-bar coda. Memorable also are the long notes of its opening, which are contrasted with faster-moving phrases. Much of the harmonic movement of the piece is cut from the same cloth as "Whisper Not," bars 1–4 of the latter being similar to bars 4–7, 17–18, and 22–24 of "I Remember Clifford."

"Blues March" (1958) is ostensibly different than "Whisper Not" and "I Remember Clifford" in several respects, not the least of which is the fact that it is an example of jazz with a martial beat. Although the alternative theme at the end of "Whisper Not" and that in the closing chorus of "Along Came Betty" were already quite martial, the latter even being described as "march-like" in the piano score, Glenn Miller's arrangement of "St. Louis Blues" was the best-known of this genre. In bars 5–9 of the blues chord sequence of "Blues March," the composer introduces greater harmonic movement than is usual (via the key cycle and then chromatically) and ends each two-bar division of this section with a prominent (half-diminished) chord at the start of bars seven and nine. This represents an excellent combination of a programmatic idea with the typical harmonic language of the composer (especially as punctuated by its first performer, Art Blakey, and decked out with his solo drum interludes).

Something comparable may be said of the famous "Killer Joe" (1959), which, on its initial recording by the Jazztet, was preceded by an unaccompanied "rap" by Golson that has acquired different verbal contexts on later versions, including those by Quincy Jones (1969 and 1995). In "Killer Joe," Golson is clearly moving in the direction of "modal jazz," but the piece is also inspired by the danceable qualities of contemporary "soul jazz." Thus, the introduction and the first two A sections are built on a two-note figure from the piano (with juicy eight-note voicings of C and B-flat 13th chords in alternate bars) that is answered, on the fourth beat of each bar, by a third note from the drummer (see Ex. 1). The actual melody is cryptic and is intriguingly placed against this rhythmic piano-and-drums figure, but the mood changes completely for the B section. Here, Golson drops the insistent rhythm, replacing it with long chords, the first of which is half-diminished, the top notes of which gradually ascend (through the diminished scale from G to E in the space of eight bars) before resuming the melody and rhythmic figure of the A section.

Example 1. "Killer Joe," basic chord pattern

In addition to their inherent qualities, these four pieces enjoyed immediate acceptance from Golson's contemporaries, his contemporaneous seniors, and his listeners. After a period of comparative neglect, they have been revived by various performers and may accurately be described as examples of this composer's craftsmanship.

REFERENCES

Golson, Benny. Interview with the author.

BRIAN PRIESTLEY

GONZAGA, CHIQUINHA

Born Francisca Edviges Gonzaga do Amaral, in Rio de Janeiro, October 17, 1847; died in Rio de Janeiro, February 28, 1935. **Education:** Early education unknown; studied piano as a child; mentored by Joaquim António da Silva Callado Jr. **Composing and Performing Career:** Began composing earliest pieces as a child; played the piano in Callado's *choro* group; "Atraente," first published work, 1877; composed *Festa de São João* for the musical theater, 1884; composed "Ó abre alas!," the first Carnival song of Brazil, 1899; traveled to Europe, 1902, 1904; moved to Lisbon, 1906; theatrical works regularly performed, 1906–09; returned to Brazil, 1909. **Memberships:** Sociedade Brasileira de Artistas Teatrais (SBAT), organizer and founding member, 1917. **Honors/ Awards:** Festival given in her honor by SBAT, 1925.

MUSIC LIST

INSTRUMENTAL SOLOS
Piano

"Ada" (*polca inglesa*). Unpublished manuscript.

"Água do vintém" (*tango brasileiro*). Rio de Janeiro: Buschmann e Guimarães, ca. 1897.

"Aguará" (*valsa*). Unpublished manuscript.

"Alegre-se viúva" (*tango*). Rio de Janeiro: Casa Artur Napoleão, n.d. Also arranged for small orchestra. Recorded: FENAB 114-115.

"Alerta!" (*polca militar*). Rio de Janeiro: Artur Napoleão, n.d.

"Angá" (*mazurca*). Unpublished manuscript. Originally titled "Antoinette." Also arranged for instrumental ensemble.

"Animatógrafo" (*valsa*). Rio de Janeiro: Manoel Antônio Guimarães, n.d.

"Anita" (*polca*). Rio de Janeiro: Buschmann e Guimarães, ca. 1894.

"Araribóia" or "Não morreu" (*polca*). Unpublished manuscript. Also arranged for instrumental ensemble.

"Arcádia" (*quadrilha*). Rio de Janeiro: Buschmann e Guimarães, 1885.

"Ari: Filha do céu" (*valsa de salão*). Unpublished manuscript. Also arranged for various instrumental ensembles.

"Atraente" (*polca*). 1877. Rio de Janeiro: Narciso, A. Napoleão e Miguéz, 1881. Also arranged for various instrumental ensembles. Recorded: Eldorado 13.79.0333; Philips-Phonogram 6349 156.

"O bandolim" (*serenata espanhola*). ca. 1899. Rio de Janeiro: Manoel Antônio Guimarães, n.d.

"Bandolineira." 1898. Unpublished manuscript. Note: lost.

"A bela jardineira" (*valsa*). Rio de Janeiro: Buschmann e Guimarães, n.d.

"Bella fanciulla io t'amo" (*walzer d'amore*). Rio de Janeiro: Viera Machado e Cia., n.d. Recorded: EMI-Angel 064 422884.

"Bijou" (*tango*). Rio de Janeiro: Nascimento Silva e Cia., 1909. Also arranged for band.

"Biónne" (*tango*). 1883. Rio de Janeiro: Buschmann e Guimarães, ca. 1895. Also arranged for small orchestra. Recorded: Eldorado 13.79.0333; EMI-Angel 064 422884.

"Borboleta" (*valsa*). Unpublished manuscript. Also arranged for instrumental ensemble.

"O Boulevard da Imprensa: El amor es la vida" (*habanera do Café da Cascata*). Rio de Janeiro: Manoel Antônio Guimarães, ca. 1888.

"Café de São Paulo" (*tango*). Unpublished manuscript. Note: from *Cá e lá*.

"Camila" (*polca*). Rio de Janeiro: Artur Napoleão e Miguéz, 1879. Also arranged for chamber orchestra.

"Cananéa" (*valsa*). ca. 1900. Rio de Janeiro: Manoel Antônio Gomes Guimarães. Also arranged for band; string orchestra.

"Candomblé" (*dança africana*). 1888. Rio de Janeiro: Buschmann e Guimarães, ca. 1893. Also arranged for voice and piano; chorus and piano; small orchestra.

"Cariri" (*valsa*). Unpublished manuscript. Also arranged for instrumental ensemble.

"Carlos Gomes" (*valsa brilhante*). ca. 1880. Rio de Janeiro: Artur Napoleão e Miguez, ca. 1880. Also arranged for orchestra.

"Catita" (*polca*). Rio de Janeiro: Buschmann e Guimarães, n.d.

"Ceci" (*valsa*). Unpublished manuscript. Also arranged for instrumental ensemble.

"Conspiradores" (*tango*). Rio de Janeiro: Manoel Antônio Guimarães, n.d.

"Cubanita" (*habanera*). Rio de Janeiro: Manoel Antônio Guimarães, n.d.

"Dama de ouros" (*habanera*). ca. 1890. Rio de Janeiro: Buschmann e Guimarães, n.d. Also arranged for *mezurca*.

"Dança brasileira" (*polca*). ca. 1892. Rio de Janeiro: Buschmann e Guimarães, ca. 1898. Also arranged for chamber orchestra. Recorded: EMI-Angel 064 422884.

"Dança das fadas" (*valsa de salão*). Rio de Janeiro: Buschmann e Guimarães, ca. 1887.

"Day-break: Ainda não morreu" (*tango*). Rio de Janeiro: Buschmann e Guimarães, ca. 1888. Recorded: EMI-Angel 063 422908.

"Desalento" (*valsa de concerto*). 1877. Rio de Janeiro: Artur Napoleão, n.d.

"Desejos" (*fado português*). 1901. Rio de Janeiro: Vieira Machado e Cia., n.d.

"O diabinho" (*tango carnavalesco*). Rio de Janeiro: Artur Napoleão e Cia., n.d.

"Diário de notícias" (*polca*). Rio de Janeiro: Buschmann e Guimarães, ca. 1886.

"Djanira" (*polca*). 1881. Rio de Janeiro: Buschmann e Guimarães, ca. 1881.

"É enorme!" (*polca*). Rio de Janeiro: Buschmann e Guimarães, ca. 1888.

"Em guarda!" (*dobrado*). Rio de Janeiro: Manoel Antônio Guimarães, n.d. Recorded: EMI-Angel 064 422884.

"Eu já volto" (*polca*). Rio de Janeiro: Buschmann e Guimarães, n.d.

"Evoé" (*tango carnavalesco*). Rio de Janeiro: Buschmann e Guimarães, ca. 1897.

"Faceiro" (*tango*). Rio de Janeiro: Buschmann e Guimarães, ca. 1889.

"Fado de Coimbra." Unpublished manuscript.

"Falena" (*valsa*). ca. 1899. Rio de Janeiro: Manoel Antônio Guimarães, n.d. Recorded: Abril Cultural MPBCHIG A.

"Fantasia: Introdução no. 1." Unpublished manuscript.

"Fênix" (*habanera*). Rio de Janeiro: Buschmann e Guimarães, n.d.

"Filha da Noite" (*polca*). Rio de Janeiro: Buschmann e Guimarães, 1885.

"Gaúcho" (*tango brasiliero*). ca. 1895. Rio de Janeiro: Vieira Machado e Cia., 1895. Recorded: Abril Cultural MPBCHIG A; Orpheus 01.

"Genéia" (*valsa*). Rio de Janeiro: Buschmann e Guimarães, ca. 1894. Also arranged for voice and piano. Recorded: EMI-Angel 063 422908.

"Gondolineira" (*barcarola*). Unpublished manuscript.

"Grata esperança" (*valsa*). Rio de Janeiro: Buschmann e Guimarães, ca. 1886.

"Gruta das flores" (*polca*). 1887. Rio de Janeiro: Buschmann e Guimarães, n.d.

"Guaianazes" (*polca brasileira*). Unpublished manuscript. Also arranged for instrumental ensemble.

"Guasca" (*polca*). Unpublished manuscript.

"Harmonia das esferas" (*valsa brilhante*). Rio de Janeiro: Cia. de Música e Pianos Sucessora de Artur Napoleão, 1881.

"Harmonias do coração" (*valsa de concerto*). 1877. Rio de Janeiro: Artur Napoleão e Cia., n.d.

"Heloísa" (*valsa de salão*). Rio de Janeiro: Buschmann e Guimarães, ca. 1897.

"Hip!!!" (*polca-galope*). Rio de Janeiro: Manoel Antônio Guimarães, 1881. Recorded: EMI-Angel 063 422908.

"Iara: Coração de fogo" (*valsa de concerto*). 1885. Rio de Janeiro: Buschmann e Guimarães, n.d. Recorded: EMI-Angel 063 422908.

"Invocação" (*capricho elegíaco*). Unpublished manuscript. Also arranged for voice and orchestra.

"Io t'amo" (*gavota*). Rio de Janeiro: Manoel Antônio Guimarães, n.d.

"Ismênia" (*valsa*). Rio de Janeiro: Cia. de Música e Pianos Sucessora de Artur Napoleão, 1881.

"Itararé" (*polca*). Rio de Janeiro: Buschmann e Guimarães, ca. 1897.

"O jagunço" (*tango característico brasileiro*). Rio de Janeiro: Artur Napoleão e Cia., ca. 1897.

"Jandira" (*quadrilla*). Rio de Janeiro: Manoel Antônio Guimarães, ca. 1903.

"Janiquinha" (*schottisch*). Rio de Janeiro: Buschmann e Guimarães, ca. 1897. Recorded: EMI-Angel 064 422884.

"Júlia" (*tango*). Rio de Janeiro: Artur Napoleão, n.d.

"Jurací" (*valsa de salão*). Rio de Janeiro: Buschmann e Guimarães, ca. 1897. Recorded: EMI-Angel 064 422884.

"Laurita" (*mazurca*). Rio de Janeiro: Buschmann e Guimarães, ca. 1889. Recorded: EMI-Angel 064 422884.

"Leontina" (*habanera*). Rio de Janeiro: Buschmann e Guimarães, ca. 1889.

"Linda morena" (*choro*). 1919. Unpublished manuscript. Also arranged for instrumental ensemble.

"Marcha fúnebre" or "Á memória do general Osório." 1879. Rio de Janeiro: Narciso e Artur Napoleão, 1879. Recorded: EMI-Angel 064 422884.

"Marcha palaciana." Unpublished manuscript.

"Maria" (*valsa*). Rio de Janeiro: Manoel Antônio Gomes Guimarães, ca. 1899.

"Meditação" (*noturno*). 1893. Rio de Janeiro: Buschmann, Guimarães e Irmão, n.d. Also arranged for chamber orchestra. Note: from *O crime do Padre Amaro*. Recorded: EMI-Angel 064 422884.

"A meia noite!" (*polca*). Rio de Janeiro: Buschmann e Guimarães, ca. 1890.

"Minha pátria" (*marcha palaciana*). Rio de Janeiro: Manoel Antônio Gomes Guimarães, ca. 1904.

"Mordaguinha" (*polca*). N.p.: Newparth e Carneiro, n.d.

"Musiciana" (*polca*). Rio de Janeiro: Buschmann e Guimarães, 1882. Also arranged for various instrumental ensembles.

"Não insistas, rapariga!" (*polca*). ca. 1877. Rio de Janeiro: Narciso e Artur Napoleão, 1881. Also arranged for chamber orchestra.

"A noite" (*gavota*). Unpublished manuscript.

"Oh! Não me iludas" (*habanera*). Rio de Janeiro: I. Bevilacqua e Cia., n.d. Recorded: EMI-Angel 063 422908.

"Os olhos dela" (*polca*). ca. 1881. Rio de Janeiro: Cia. de Música e Pianos Sucessora de Artur Napoleão, 1881. Recorded: Orpheus 01.

"Olhos irresistíveis" (*polca*). Porto: Costa Mesquita, n.d.

"Ortruda" (*valsa*). Rio de Janeiro: Artur Napoleão e Cia., n.d.

"O Padre Amaro" (*valsa*). Rio de Janeiro: Buschmann e Guimarães, ca. 1890.

"Paraguaçu" (*choro*). Unpublished manuscript. Also arranged for instrumental ensemble.

"Passos no choro" (*polca brasileira*). 1911. Unpublished manuscript.

"Pehô-Pekim" (*dança característica chinesa*). Rio de Janeiro: Buschmann e Guimarães, ca. 1889. Recorded: EMI-Angel 064 422884.

"Perfume: Feno de Atkinsons" (*valsa de salão*). 1892. Unpublished manuscript.

"Piu-dudo: Beija Flor" (*batuque brasileiro*). 1889. Rio de Janeiro: Buschmann e Guimarães, ca. 1896. Also arranged for chamber orchestra.

"Plangente" (*valsa sentimental*). ca. 1877. Rio de Janeiro: Cia. de Música e Pianos Sucessora de Artur Napoleão, n.d. Recorded: EMI-Angel 063 422908.

"Polca militar." 1900. Rio de Janeiro: Manoel Antônio Guimarães, n.d.

"Prelúdios." Unpublished manuscript.

"Primeira gavota." Rio de Janeiro: Buschmann e Guimarães, n.d.

"Promessa!" (*valsa americana*). Rio de Janeiro: Artur Napoleão e Cia., n.d. Also arranged for voice and piano.

"Psique" (*habanera*). Rio de Janeiro: Buschmann e Guimarães, ca. 1885. Also arranged for instrumental ensemble.

"Radiante" (*polca de salão*). ca. 1885. Rio de Janeiro: Buschmann e Guimarães, 1885. Also arranged for instrumental ensemble.

"Robertinha" (*valsa*). Rio de Janeiro: Buschmann e Guimarães, ca. 1897.

"Rosa" (*valsa característica*). Rio de Janeiro: Buschmann e Guimarães, n.d.

"Saci-pererê" (*cateretê brasileiro*). Unpublished manuscript. Also arranged for chamber orchestra as *batuque*.

"São Paulo" (*tango brasileiro*). 1885. Rio de Janeiro: Manoel Antônio Guimarães, 1902. Also arranged for chamber orchestra. Recorded: EMI-Angel 064 422884.

"Satã" (*lundu brasileiro*). 1891. Rio de Janeiro: Manoel Antônio Guimarães, n.d. Also arranged for chamber orchestra; orchestra.

"Saudade" (*valsa de salão*). Unpublished manuscript. Also arranged for instrumental ensemble.

"SBAT" (*tango*). 1917. Unpublished manuscript. Also arranged for orchestra.

"Se o ferreta está de veneta" (*polca*). ca. 1885. Rio de Janeiro: Buschmann e Guimarães, ca. 1885.

"Sedutor" (*tango*). 1877. Rio de Janeiro: Artur Napoleão e Cia., 1881.

"Serenata" (*balada*). Unpublished manuscript.

"Si fuera verdad!" (*habanera*). 1885. Rio de Janeiro: Manoel Antônio Guimarães, 1885. Also arranged for voice and piano.

"Só na flauta" (*polca*). 1911. Unpublished manuscript. Note: lost.

"Só no choro" (*tango característico*). 1889. Rio de Janeiro: I. Bevilacqua e Cia., n.d.

"Soberano" (*tango*). Rio de Janeiro: Buschmann e Guimarães, n.d.

"Sonhando" (*habanera*). 1879. Rio de Janeiro: Artur Napoleão e Cia., 1881. Also arranged for instrumental ensemble; chamber orchestra. Recorded: EMI-Angel 063 422908.

"Sultana" (*polca*). 1878. Rio de Janeiro: Viúva Banongia, 1878. Also arranged for instrumental ensemble; guitar; chamber orchestra. Recorded: FENAB 114-115.

Chiquinha Gonzaga; courtesy of Codecria Publishers, Rio de Janeiro

"Suspiro" (*tango*). Rio de Janeiro: Artur Napoleão e Cia., ca. 1881. Recorded: EMI-Angel 063 422908.

"Tambiquererê" (*tango*). ca. 1894. Rio de Janeiro: Manoel Antônio Guimarães, n.d.

"Tamoio" (*pas-de-quatre*). Unpublished manuscript. Also arranged for instrumental ensemble.

"Tango" or "Carlino." Rio de Janeiro: Buschmann e Guimarães, ca. 1887. Note: from *Carlino desempregado.*

"Tango brasileiro." ca. 1880. Rio de Janeiro: Manoel Antônio Guimarães, ca. 1898. Also arranged for chamber orchestra.

"Tango característico." ca. 1887. Rio de Janeiro: Buschmann e Guimarães, ca. 1889. Also arranged for chamber orchestra.

"Tapuia" (*mazurca*). Unpublished manuscript. Also arranged for instrumental ensemble.

"Teu sorriso" (*polca*). 1879. Rio de Janeiro: Cia. de Música e Pianos Sucessora de Artur Napoleão, 1881.

"Tim-tim" (*tango*). ca. 1885. Rio de Janeiro: Buschmann e Guimarães, n.d. Recorded: Eldorado 13.79.0333.

"Timbira" (*valsa*). Unpublished manuscript. Also arranged for instrumental ensemble.

"Toujours et encore" (*polca*). Rio de Janeiro: Buschmann e Guimarães, ca. 1897.

"Tupã" (*tango brasileiro*). ca. 1890. Rio de Janeiro: Buschmann e Guimarães, n.d. Also arranged instrumental ensemble; chamber orchestra.

"Tupí" (*valsa*). Unpublished manuscript. Also arranged for instrumental ensemble.

"Tupiniquins" (*valsa*). Unpublished manuscript. Also arranged for instrumental ensemble.

"Vida ou morte" (*dobrado*). Unpublished manuscript. Note: lost.

"La Violette" (*pas-de-quatre*). Unpublished manuscript.

"Viva la gracia" (*valsa espanhola*). Rio de Janeiro: Vieira Machado e Cia. Ed., n.d. Recorded: EMI-Angel 064 422884.

"Viva o Carnaval!" (*polca*). 1884. Rio de Janeiro: Buschmann e Guimarães, ca. 1886. Also arranged for chamber orchestra.

"Viver é folgar" (*valsa*). 1885. Rio de Janeiro: Buschmann e Guimarães, n.d.

"Vou dar um banho em minha sogra" (*polca*). Rio de Janeiro: Artur Napoleão e Cia., n.d.

"Xi!" (*tango*). Rio de Janeiro: Buschmann e Guimarães, ca. 1883.

"Yo te adoro" (*tango*). 1881. Rio de Janeiro: Buschmann e Guimarães, 1881. Also arranged for orchestra as *Eu te adoro*.

INSTRUMENTAL ENSEMBLE

"Aguará: Garca vermelha" (*valsa*). Rio de Janeiro: [Author's edition], 1932. Also arranged for piano.

"Ai que amor!" 1889. Unpublished manuscript. Note: lost.

"Angá-catu-rama: Alma bondosa" (*rancheira*). ca. 1890. Rio de Janeiro: [Author's edition], 1932. Also arranged for piano.

"Aracê: O Dia sai" (*polca*). Rio de Janeiro: [Author's edition], 1932. Also arranged for piano.

"Caobimpará: Mar azul" (*polca*). Rio de Janeiro: [Author's edition], 1932. Also arranged for piano.

"Carijó" (*choro*). Rio de Janeiro: [Author's edition], 1932. Also arranged for piano.

"Carioca" (*polca*). Rio de Janeiro: [Author's edition], 1932. Also arranged for piano.

"Rancheira-platina" (*choro*). Rio de Janeiro: [Author's edition], 1932. Also arranged for piano.

"Sabiá da mata" (*polca*). Rio de Janeiro: [Author's edition], 1932. Also arranged for piano.

STRING ORCHESTRA

Juriti (*prelúdio*). 1919. Unpublished manuscript.

Dança no. 1 or *Uma página triste* (*minueto*). 1915. Unpublished manuscript.

CHAMBER ORCHESTRA

Coco velho (*dança*). 1902. Unpublished manuscript.

Dança no. 2. 1915. Unpublished manuscript.

Os mineiros (*chula*). Rio de Janeiro: [Author's edition], n.d.

A noite. 1901. Unpublished manuscript.

Os oito batutas (*tango*). 1919. Unpublished manuscript.

FULL ORCHESTRA

Habanera. Rio de Janeiro: [Author's edition], n.d.

Menina faceira (*tango*). 1885. Unpublished manuscript. Also arranged for voice and piano as a *canção*; chorus and piano as a *canção*.

Sada (tango). 1886. Rio de Janeiro: [Author's edition], n.d.

Valquíria (*valsa*). 1884. Unpublished manuscript. Also arranged for piano.

ORCHESTRA (CHAMBER OR FULL) WITH SOLOISTS

Meu Deus por fim já creio (*romance de Luiz*). Unpublished manuscript.

BAND

Chautemoc (*marcha*). Unpublished manuscript. Also arranged for voice and piano.

Duquesne (*marcha militar*). 1894. Unpublished manuscript.

SOLO VOICE

"À Nossa Senhora das Dores" (*prece*). 1908. Unpublished manuscript.

Agnus Dei. ca. 1899. Unpublished manuscript.

"Ai morena" (*canção*). Rio de Janeiro: Buschmann e Guimarães, n.d.

"Ai que broma!" (*bolero*). Rio de Janeiro: Manoel Antônio Guimarães, 1885.

"Amarguras" (*balada*). In *Futuro das moças* 18 (August 1917).

"Amendoim" (*cançoneta*). Unpublished manuscript.

"Amor" (*canção*). Unpublished manuscript.

"L'Ange du Seigneur" (*invocação*). ca. 1894. Unpublished manuscript.

"Angelitude." ca. 1900. Unpublished manuscript.

"Aurora" (*fado*). 1909. Unpublished manuscript.

Ave Maria. 1909. Unpublished manuscript.

"A Baiana dos pastéis" (*canção*). N.p.: Almanaque Editora, n.d. Note: lost.

"Balada." Rio de Janeiro: Buschmann e Guimarães, n.d. Also arranged for violin and piano.

"Barcarola." Unpublished manuscript.

"O beijo" (*romance*). ca. 1914. Unpublished manuscript. Also arranged for chamber orchestra.

"Beijos." Rio de Janeiro: Manoel Antônio Guimarães, ca. 1899.

"Beijos do céu: Um sonho" (*romance*). ca. 1900. Unpublished manuscript.

"A brasileira" (*canção*). Rio de Janeiro: Manoel Antônio Guimarães, n.d.

"Cá por coisas!" (*canção brasileira*). Rio de Janeiro: Manoel Antônio Gomes Guimarães, 1904.

"Canção brasileira." Unpublished manuscript. Also arranged for orchestra.

"Canção dos pastores" (*noite de Natal*). 1858. In *Chiquinha Gonzaga: Grande compositora popular brasileira* (Rio de Janeiro: FUNARTE, 1978).

"Carmencita" (*tango*). 1901. Rio de Janeiro: Manoel Antônio Guimarães, n.d.

"Carta à Zitinha" (*canção brasileira*). Rio de Janeiro: Artur Napoleão e Cia., n.d.

"O coió" (*cançoneta*). Rio de Janeiro: Manoel Antônio Gomes Guimarães, n.d.

"Compensação" (*cançoneta*). Unpublished manuscript.

"Coro de virgem." Unpublished manuscript.

"O cozinheiro" (*canção brasileira*). Unpublished manuscript.

"Democrático" (*tango*). Unpublished manuscript.

"Desejos" (*fado português*). Rio de Janeiro: Vieira Machado e Cia. Ed., n.d. Recorded: Odeon 40.491.

"Diálogo" (*valsa*). Unpublished manuscript.

"Doce fado." 1909. Unpublished manuscript.

"Dona Adelaide" (*cançoneta*). Rio de Janeiro: Manoel Antônio Guimarães, n.d. Recorded: Odeon 108185; Victor 98.953.

"Dueto de amor." Unpublished manuscript.

"Eis a sedutora." Rio de Janeiro: Buschmann e Guimarães, 1896. Note: from *O burro de carga*.

"Elvira" (*fado português*). 1901. Rio de Janeiro: Buschmann e Guimarães, n.d.

"O esfolado" (*tango da quitandeira*). 1902. Rio de Janeiro: Manoel Antônio Gomes Guimarães, 1904. Note: from *O esfolado*. Recorded: Odeon 10.091.

"Espanha e Brasil" (*canção*). Rio de Janeiro: Manoel Antônio Guimarães, ca. 1903.

"Faceira" or "Faceira, escuta" (*raconto*). In *Boletim SBAT* 240 (October 1947).

"Fado da sabina." Rio de Janeiro: Buschmann e Guimarães, n.d. Notes: lost; included in *A República,* by Artur Azevedo.

"Fani" (*valsa de salão*). Rio de Janeiro: Buschmann e Guimarães, n.d.

"Feijoada do Brasil" (*canção*). Rio de Janeiro: Vieira Machado e Cia., 1909.

"A fiandeira" (*raconto*). 1913. Unpublished manuscript.

"Foi um sonho!" (*barcarola*). Rio de Janeiro: Manoel Antônio Gomes Guimarães, ca. 1890. Note: from *O crime do Padre Amaro*.

"A guitarra" (*fado*). Unpublished manuscript. Also arranged for chamber orchestra.

"Iaiá fazenda etc. e . . . tal!" (*canção brasileira*). Rio de Janeiro: Manoel Antônio Gomes Guimarães, 1911.

"Lua branca" (*canção*). 1911. Rio de Janeiro: Irmãos Vitale, 1939. Also arranged for chamber orchestra; accordion. Recorded: Abril Cultural MPB CHIG A; Atlantic/WEA BR 20054; Contintental 16.425; Odeon 10.420.

"Machuca" (*cançoneta*). Rio de Janeiro: Manoel Antônio Gomes Guimarães, n.d. Recorded: Columbia 12.193; Eldorado 12.79.0333.

"Manhã de amor" (*balada*). Rio de Janeiro: Artur Napoleão e Cia., 1881. Recorded: Eldorado 13.79.0333.

"O mar" (*balada*). 1926. Unpublished manuscript.

"A morena" (*canção*). Rio de Janeiro: Manoel Antônio Gomes Guimarães, ca. 1901.

"Morena" (*canção luso-brasileira*). Rio de Janeiro: Manoel Antônio Gomes Guimarães, ca. 1901. Recorded: Columbia B 211; Eldorado 12.79.0333.

"A mulatinha" (*canção brasileira*). Rio de Janeiro: Manoel Antônio Gomes Guimarães, n.d. Recorded: Odeon 120378.

"Os namorados da lua" (*serenata*). ca. 1900. Rio de Janeiro: Manoel Antônio Gomes Guimarães, n.d. Recorded: Eldorado 13.79.0333; Victor 98.950; Zon-o-phone 1516.

"O namoro" (*canção brasileira*). Rio de Janeiro: Manoel Antônio Gomes Guimarães, n.d. Recorded: Odeon 10008.

"A noiva." Unpublished manuscript.

"Noivado" (*valsa de amor*). Rio de Janeiro: Artur Napoleão e Cia., n.d.

"Ó abre alas!" (*maxixe*). 1899. Unpublished manuscript. Also arranged for chamber orchestra as a *marcha carnavalesca*. Recorded: Abril Cultural MPBCHIG A; Favorite 1-452023; Odeon 120174; SECC-1000.

"Oh! Mon étoile" or "Duas horas" (*tango brasileiro*). ca. 1881. Rio de Janeiro: Artur Napoleão e Cia., 1881.

"Para a cera do Santíssimo" (*cançoneta cômica*). Rio de Janeiro: Manoel Antônio Gomes Guimarães, ca. 1886.

"A Peroba." Rio de Janeiro: Buschmann e Guimarães, n.d.

"Poesia e amôr" (*romance*). 1888. Unpublished manuscript.

"As pombas." 1890. Rio de Janeiro: Casa Bevilacqua, ca. 1929. Also arranged for piano; string orchestra.

"Por que choraste?" (*romance*). Unpublished manuscript.

"Prece à Virgem." ca. 1894. Unpublished manuscript.

"Roda ioiô" (*cançoneta*). Rio de Janeiro: Manoel Antônio Gomes Guimarães, n.d.

"Rondolini-Rondolão" (*cançoneta cômica*). Rio de Janeiro: Manoel Antônio Gomes Guimarães, ca. 1886.

"Santa" (*canção brasileira*). Rio de Janeiro: Manoel Antônio Gomes Guimarães, n.d.

"A sereia" (*balada*). 1887. In *A semana* 127 (June 9, 1887): 180.

"Simpatia" or "Que é simpatia?" (*modinha*). Rio de Janeiro: Buschmann e Guimarães, n.d.

"A sorte grande" (*cançoneta*). 1909. Unpublished manuscript.

"Tachi!" (*romance*). ca. 1900. Unpublished manuscript.

"Teus olhares" (*canção brasileira*). Unpublished manuscript. Also arranged for orchestra.

"Trigueira" or "Desgarrada minhota." Rio de Janeiro: Manoel Antônio Gomes Guimarães, n.d.

As tricanas de Coimbra: Pus-me a cantar . . . e chorei (*fado*). Unpublished manuscript. Recorded: Columbia B 290.

"Vamos à Missa." ca. 1901. Rio de Janeiro: Manoel Antônio Gomes Guimarães, n.d.

"Villancete" (*balada*). Unpublished manuscript.

VOICE WITH INSTRUMENTAL ENSEMBLE

"Não sonhes" (*romance* for voice, harp, piano). 1909. Unpublished manuscript.

CHORAL MUSIC

"Heróica" (*marcha*). Unpublished manuscript.

"Hino à redentora." 1888. Unpublished manuscript.

"Vinde! Vinde!" (*sacro*). Unpublished manuscript. Note: lost.

DRAMATIC MUSIC

Abacaxi! 1893. Unpublished manuscript. Note: lost. Premiere, 1893.

Abolindemrepcochindego. 1889. Unpublished manuscript. Premiere, 1889.

Abre alas! 1913. Unpublished manuscript. Co-composer, Luz Junior. Note: lost. Premiere, 1913.

Alba (operetta in three acts). 1921. Unpublished manuscript. Note: incomplete.

Amapá. 1896. Unpublished manuscript. Co-composers, Cavallier, Costa Junior, L. Moreira, Manoel Passos, Elia Pompilio, A. Gama, Luiza Leonardo. Premiere, 1896.

Os amores de um taberneiro. ca. 1903. Unpublished manuscript.

A avozinha (operetta in two acts). 1917. Unpublished manuscript. Premiere, 1917.

A batota. 1908. Unpublished manuscript. Premiere, 1908.

A bicha de sete cabeças. 1892. Unpublished manuscript. Co-composers, Henrique Alves de Mesquita, R. Domenech, Luiz Moreira, and others. Note: lost. Premiere, 1892.

A bota do diabo (fantastic play in three acts). 1908. Unpublished manuscript. Premiere, 1908.

Casei com titia (operetta in one act). 1911. Unpublished manuscript. Premiere, 1911.

Os ciganos (drama in three acts). ca. 1893. Unpublished manuscript. Note: lost.

Colégio de senhoritas (operetta in three acts). 1912. Unpublished manuscript. Premiere, 1912.

Conspiração do amor (burlesque in three acts). 1920. Unpublished manuscript. Premiere, 1920.

O conto do vigário (burlesque in three acts). 1900. Unpublished manuscript.

Cora (comic opera in three acts). ca. 1891. Unpublished manuscript.

A corte na roça (operetta in one act). 1885. Unpublished manuscript. Premiere, 1885.

O crime do Padre Amaro. 1890. Unpublished manuscript. Note: incomplete manuscript. Premiere, 1890.

A dama de ouros (*zarzuela* in three acts). 1890. Unpublished manuscript. Co-composers, Chueca, Valverde. Note: lost. Premiere, 1890.

De 13 de maio a 15 de novembro. 1890. Unpublished manuscript. Note: lost. Premiere, 1890.

Depois do forrobodó (burlesque in three acts). 1913. Unpublished manuscript. Premiere, 1913.

A desfilada dos mortos (fantastic tragedy in three acts). 1915. Unpublished manuscript.

O destino (O que é o destino!). 1886. Unpublished manuscript. Note: lost.

É êle! 1915. Unpublished manuscript. Note: incomplete manuscript. Premiere, 1915.

O esfolado. 1903. Unpublished manuscript. Co-composers, Assis Pacheco, Luis Moreira, Hallier, Paulino Sacramento, Luis Amabile, Nicolino Milano, and others. Note: lost. Premiere, 1903.

Estrela d'alva (pastoral operetta in two acts). 1920. Unpublished manuscript. Premiere, 1920.

Festa de São João (operetta in one act). 1884. Unpublished manuscript.

FFF e RRR (comedy in one act). 1903. Unpublished manuscript. Note: lost.

A filha do Guedes. 1885. Unpublished manuscript. Premiere, 1885.

Forrobodó (burlesque in three acts). 1912. Unpublished manuscript. Premiere, 1912.

Há alguma novidade? 1886. Unpublished manuscript. Note: lost.

Idalio. 1917. Unpublished manuscript. Note: incomplete manuscript.

Jandira (operetta in three acts). 1921. Unpublished manuscript. Premiere, 1921.

Jurití (operetta in three acts). 1919. Unpublished manuscript. Premiere, 1919.

Manobras do amor (operetta in three acts). 1911. Unpublished manuscript. Premiere, 1911.

Manto de arlequim. 1925. Unpublished manuscript. Co-composers, Assis Pacheco, Eduardo Souto, Sá Pereira, Freire Júnior, Paulino Sacramento. Premiere, 1925.

Maria! 1933. Unpublished manuscript. Premiere, 1933.

O Minho em festa or *De volta á pátria* (operetta in three acts). 1919. Unpublished manuscript.

Os mistérios do convento (drama in three acts). 1890. Unpublished manuscript. Note: lost. Premiere, 1890.

A mulher homem. 1886. Unpublished manuscript. Co-composers, Henrique Alves de Mesquita, Carlos Cavalier, Miguel Cardoso, Henrique Magalhães. Premiere, 1886.

Não venhas! (dramatic parody of *Quo Vadis?*). 1904. Unpublished manuscript. Premiere, 1904.

Nú e crú. 1906. Unpublished manuscript. Co-composers, Costa Júnior, Luiz Amabile. Premiere, 1906.

Ordem e progresso. 1917. Unpublished manuscript. Premiere, 1917.

O perdão (lyric drama in three acts). 1901. Unpublished manuscript. Note: only one piece for voice and piano extant.

Quebra primas (comedy in one act). ca. 1905. Unpublished manuscript. Note: lost.

Pomadas e farofas. 1912. Unpublished manuscript. Premiere, 1912.

Pudesse esta paixão (burlesque in three acts). 1912. Unpublished manuscript. Premiere, 1912.

Redes ao mar (operetta in two acts). 1921. Unpublished manuscript. Premiere, 1921.

Romeu e Julieta or *Mário e Beatriz*. 1921. Unpublished manuscript.

O sargento de milícias (operetta in three acts). 1926. Unpublished manuscript. Note: incomplete.

A sertaneja (burlesque in three acts). 1915. Unpublished manuscript. Premiere, 1915.

As três graças (comic opera). 1908. Unpublished manuscript. Premiere, 1908.

A trombeta mágica. ca. 1904. Unpublished manuscript.

Viagem ao Parnaso. 1883. Unpublished manuscript. Premiere, 1891.

Você me conhece? ca. 1913. Unpublished manuscript.

Zé Caipora. 1887. Unpublished manuscript. Premiere, 1887.

Zizinha maxixe (burlesque operetta). 1895. Unpublished manuscript. Premiere, 1895.

PUBLICATIONS

ABOUT GONZAGA
Books and Monographs

Boscoli, Geysa. *A pioneira Chiquinha Gonzaga*. [Natal]: Departamento Estadual de Imprensa, 1968.

Diniz, Edinha. *Chiquinha Gonzaga: Uma história de vida*. Rio de Janeiro Coderi, 1984. Reprint, [Rio de Janeiro]: Editora Rosa dos Tempos, 1991.

Lira, Mariza. *Chiquinha Gonzaga: Grande compositora popular brasileira*. Rio de Janeiro: [Impressão da Pap. e typ. Coelho], 1939. Reprint, Rio de Janeiro: FUNARTE, 1978.

Dissertations

Fernandes, Adriana. "O balanço de Chiquinha Gonzaga: Do carnaval à opereta." M.A. thesis, Universidade de Campinas, Instituto de Artes, n.d.

Articles

Andrade, Mário de. "Chiquinha Gonzaga." In *Música, doce música,* 329–333. São Paulo: Martins, 1963.

Azevedo, Luiz Heitor Corrêa de. In *150 anos de música no Brasil: 1800–1950,* 148–151. Rio de Janeiro: José Olympio, 1956.

Mariz, Vasco. "O início de uma nova era: Chiquinha Gonzaga." In *A canção brasileira,* 64–68. Rio de Janeiro: Serviço de Documentação do Ministério da Educação e Cultura, 1959.

Vasconcelos, Ary. "Chiquinha Gonzaga (1847–1935)." In *Panorama da música popular brasileira,* 33–35. São Paulo: Martins, 1964.

———. "Chiquinha Gonzaga." In *Raízes da música popular brasileira (1500–1889),* 263–289. 2nd ed. Rio de Janeiro: Rio Fundo, 1991.

Vidal, Barros. "A primeira maestrina." In *Precursoras brasileiras,* 191–199, 252, 260. Rio de Janeiro: A Noite, n.d.

PRINCIPAL ARCHIVES

Divisão de Música e Arquivo Sonoro, Fundação Biblioteca Nacional, Rio de Janeiro

Sociedade Brasileira de Autores Teatrais, Av. Almirante Barroso, Rio de Janeiro

* * * * *

Francisca "Chiquinha" Hedviges (or Edviges) Gonzaga do Amaral (1847–1935) was Brazil's first woman composer and one of the principal originators of the music that evolved into the *samba*. A talented *mulatta*, she defied tradition in order to fulfill her musical abilities and ambitions. Struggling with family ostracism and with prejudice against women who participated in public life, Gonzaga finally won respect and acceptance.

Gonzaga was born on the margins of upper-class life as the illegitimate child of a *mulatta* woman and an upper-class military man. Because Gonzaga's father recognized her and eventually married her mother, his unhappy family was insistent that Gonzaga overcome her *mulatta* appearance and lower-class origins by playing the rigid, limiting upper-class female roles of society hostess and pampered wife and mother.

Gonzaga's education included piano lessons and a musical environment of recitals by relatives. From an early age, she excelled at the piano and composed music. The family's attempts to mold the strong-willed, rebellious teenager into a society matron resulted in her marriage into a moderately high-class family. Her dowry piano was her constant companion and consolation in her stifling home environment. When forced by her jealous husband to choose between her music and the society life he offered, Gonzaga chose music. This decision caused her to be expelled from the family, who denied her access to her daughter and second son and considered her dead. Alone and ostracized, she pursued a career as a music teacher, composer, and musician in the Bohemian fringes of Rio de Janeiro society.

Because of this life, Gonzaga came to value Africa-inspired popular music and became one of the first to bridge the gap between the African and European musical cultures. Her compositions were some of the earliest to combine elements from these two cultures. She found the polka to be the European form that best lent itself to fusion with the African *lundu* because of the similarities of their tempos and sensual implications.

After a brief interlude in the countryside, where she and a lover were forced to reside because of social criticism, Gonzaga returned to Rio, ending the liaison. Although already an accomplished composer of polkas and a skilled pianist, Gonzaga had to restart her career. For this purpose, Gonzaga chose as her mentor the *mestiço* flutist Joaquim António da Silva Callado Jr. (1848–80). He had created a special type of musical group that fused popular African rhythms with socially acceptable European melodies and popularized the African innovations that were still scorned by the elite. The hybrid form that resulted evolved into the *choro,* the first nationalized form of popular music.

The Callado/Gonzaga relationship was mutually beneficial. Callado's support of the young, struggling musician helped launch Gonzaga's professional career, while she, in turn, through her piano accompaniments supported his innovations on the flute and made arrangements of his music. Through her collaboration with Callado, Gonzaga became the first professional piano player to be associated with the *choro,* which stimulated the popular success of her own compositions. Callado even introduced her into Rio's elitist musical society when he dedicated his song "Querida por todos" (Loved by All) to the aspiring composer.

After Callado's premature death in 1880, Gonzaga pursued even more actively her mentor's work in Afro-Brazilianizing popular music and became one of the principal promulgators of the innovative genre of the *choro*. Gonzaga's work and Afro-Brazilianized music in general gained widespread acceptance during the tumultuous period between Callado's death and the end of the century, and she emerged as a composer of the majority of the most successful pieces of the period.

Always the rebel, Gonzaga gave her first pieces (written in 1877) such provocative titles as "Atraente" (Captivating), "Não insistas, rapariga!" (Don't Insist, Wench!), and "Sedutor," thereby increasing the hostility she experienced in this period of already intense societal rejection (the years 1877–85). Even in her style of dress, she was iconoclastic and flouted convention, such as when she replaced the customary hat with silk scarves entwined in her hair.

Not only was Gonzaga one of the first composers to move traditional Brazilian music toward the composition of national forms through her fusion of European and African styles, but she was also the first to use lower-class speech and customs in songs, in the theater, and in light opera. After Callado's death, Gonzaga began to compose for an early Brazilian, popular (lower-class) musical theater called the magazine theater (*o teatro de revista*). In this style of musical theater, several events and personalities of the past year were presented; happy, charming, and spirited music sustained the action and added sensuality and decorative exuberance.

In 1884, Gonzaga wrote the libretto and music for one such show, *Festa de São João* (The Feast of St. John). Although this love story filled with rural customs was neither published nor performed, it revealed Gonzaga's audacity and determination to excel and was a prelude to better works to come. Five years later when she wrote the music for a work titled *A corte na roça* (Court in the Hinterlands), she broke with convention by ending the work with a *maxixe* dance that was subsequently censored by the police. Still, this theatrical piece was praised for its happy, spirited instrumentation, its national character, its use of rhythms from popular songs and dances, and its touch of lasciviousness. These works were followed by various light operas such as *Corta-Jaca Gaúcho,* which was composed in 1895 and played in the presidential palace.

In 1899, Gonzaga wrote the first song for a Carnival march of a particular Carnival group, the Rosa de Ouro. This popular *marcha-rancha,* "Ó abre alas!/Que eu quero passar" (Oh, Open the Wings [of Dancers]/I Want to Go Through) is noteworthy because it was composed specifically for Carnival and definitively established the relationship between the *marcha-rancha* and Carnival songs. This song also brought social recognition to the previously scorned street manifestations of Carnival and established a new genre that persists to this day. Another of her famous Carnival songs, "Forrobodó," was part of a theater piece by the same title that caricatured the customs and speech of the lower classes. The malicious, sexual, common language of this piece reveals the revolutionary nature of its themes.

As Gonzaga approached middle age, she was finally accepted in elite musical circles. Despite this acceptance and her enhanced popularity, Gonzaga was never accepted by her family, and although she helped her now penniless and aged father, she continued to suffer from his insistence that she had died many years before. Only her adult sons were part of her life, her daughter having long since been lost to her.

Because she was marginalized for her nonconformist behavior, Gonzaga identified with other marginalized people and extended herself to help them. She was especially active in the abolitionist movement, even selling her music door to door in order to buy a slave's freedom. In reaction to her own exploitation by others who gained financially by using her music without her permission, she organized a group to protect artists' rights, the Sociedade Brasileira de Artistas Teatrais (Brazilian Society for Theater Artists). Her contribution to this movement was recognized by the festival given in her honor by the Sociedade in 1925 when she was 78 years old.

At the end of her life, Gonzaga was recognized as a composer who radically changed Brazilian music to reflect the various components of Brazilian life. This music, which evolved into the *samba,* finally became accepted by the upper classes. She was recognized as a woman who had made her way alone in a man's world, a woman who had held true to her artistic and humanistic convictions in spite of prejudice and condemnation.

JOYCE CARLSON-LEAVITT

SELECTED WORKS

Chiquinha Gonzaga achieved great success with the polka "Atraente" (Captivating), composed in 1877, her first published work. This short piano piece appeared in February 1877, and by November of the same year it was already in its 15th edition. "Atraente" is a rondo in five sections (ABACA) with an introduction. Each of the three main parts has an individual character, demonstrating the influence of her mentor, Joaquim António da Silva Callado. According to Gerard Béhague, this piece reconstructs the musical dialogue between different instruments of the *choro,* such as the flute and clarinet in section A and the *cavaquinho*—a ukulele-like instrument—in section B, but overall it presents few national characteristics. Nevertheless, "Atraente" marks the beginning of Gonzaga's career as a composer in a male-dominated field.

"Gaúcho" (1895), a tango for piano, is arguably Gonzaga's most famous composition. It first appeared in the operetta *Zizinha maxixe,* which premiered in 1895, and left the stage that same year, after only three performances. "Gaúcho" began to circulate widely only after the piano score was published by Casa Vieira Machado. It was later recycled as the last number of the musical revue *Cá e lá* (Here and There) from 1904, in which it achieved a remarkable success. In this revue, "Gaúcho" was danced as a *maxixe,* widely regarded as an extremely indecent and lascivious dance. In 1910, a performance of "Gaúcho" during a presidential festivity caused a great scandal due to the risqué connotations of the piece. Nevertheless, the work continued to be very popular, and in 1920, Darius Milhaud, who was then living in Rio, borrowed the whole of section A for his ballet *Le boeuf sur le toit.* The first part of "Gaúcho" is in D minor and alternates the original sung parts with a *batuque,* imitating the beating of Afro-Brazilian percussion instruments. Section B is explicitly labeled "Chorus and Dance," and its melody in double thirds and sixths is in the key of F, the relative major. Overall, "Gaúcho" clearly exemplifies a typical characteristic of Gonzaga's works, which is the constant repetition of syncopated rhythmic patterns of one or two measures over entire sections.

Forrobodó (1912) was Gonzaga's most successful theatrical work. It was frequently revived and performed during the first quarter of the 20th century, more than 1,500 times throughout Brazil. Its outstanding feature, however, is the libretto written by Carlos Bettencourt and Luíz Peixoto, which depicts the way of life of the lower classes of Rio de Janeiro, including their spicy use of slang and bawdy language; and it portrays in vivid terms the musicians known as *chorões.* Two of its individual numbers acquired a

life of their own—the Brazilian tango "Não se impressione" (Don't Be Impressed) and the *modinha* "Lua branca" (White Moon), both of which received new lyrics and, in the case of the latter piece, a new title as well.

The first act concludes with the exuberant "Não se impressione," also known as the "Tango of the Night Guard." A lively syncopated rhythm, typical of the *choros,* provides unity to this ternary piece (ABA), and the middle section, with its modulation to the subdominant, has deliciously chromatic melodic lines. "Lua branca," originally set as a duet between Escaldanhas and the *mulatta* Zeferina, consistently employs the chromatically descending bass so typical of the *modinha.* Its brief introduction sets the key of D minor and is followed by two eight-measure phrases ending with the same melodic refrain (abcb). In its simplicity and lyrical pathos, "Lua branca" successfully captures the sentimentality and nostalgia of the Brazilian *modinha.*

Juriti (1919) can appropriately be described as an operetta, and its action takes place in one of the rural and less developed villages of the northeastern states of Brazil. According to Mário de Andrade, it is a work of lasting significance and perhaps the most important of Gonzaga's compositions. She was at the height of her career, and the combination of her music and the libretto by Viriato Correia, a member of the Academia Brasileira de Letras, was a winning one. The premiere of *Juriti* on July 16, 1919, at the Teatro São Pedro de Alcântara in Rio was highly acclaimed by both the public and the press. This operetta was the most successful work of its kind and was revived many times and widely performed throughout the country during the first half of the century. The main heroine is Juriti, whose name is that of a dove from Brazil. She is genuinely loved by two locals, Graúna, her fiancé, and Corcundinha (the hunchback), who is hopelessly in love with her. Juriti is also desired by the son of the powerful Major Fulgêncio, Dr. Juca, who comes back to his native village after completing his studies in Rio. Temporary havoc ensues when Sofia, a woman of dubious reputation, is seen with Dr. Juca and is mistakenly identified as Juriti by the gossipy Bonifácia. As a result, Juriti is rejected by Graúna but is rewarded with the sincere love of Corcundinha, who remains by her side through adversity. Local color is provided by an onstage marching band in the first act and the celebration of the Feast of St. John in the third act, including scattered bonfires, colorful banners, and a performance of the *bumba-meu-boi,* a dramatic folk dance that mixes native Indian and African elements.

Gonzaga composed a total of 27 individual pieces for this work, including numbers for soloists and chorus, solo songs, duos, trios, and ensembles. The opening instrumental prelude is a slow *samba,* an Afro-Brazilian dance and musical form. Lively syncopated rhythms, bright major keys, and simple harmonies predominate throughout, such as in Juriti's opening number with chorus. All this provides a deep contrast with the melancholic song of Corcundinha, marked by gloomy diminished chords and pedal tones, which reappears many times in different minor keys. The trio for Juriti, Raposo (Juca's friend from Rio de Janeiro), and Juca finds its counterpart in the trio for Sofia, Raposo, and Juca, both pieces being typical Brazilian waltzes set in F major. In these two trios, Gonzaga treats the wholesome Juriti and the dubious Sofia with equal sympathy through similar musical means, perhaps reflecting the two sides of

Gonzaga's own personality, as a woman of strong morals rejected by a society who frowned on female composers. Comic relief is provided in numbers such as the automobile song of Major Fulgêncio, which like the *revistas* (musical revues) of the day, often provided an ironic framework for contemporary events. The operetta ends with the reprise of "Number Eight," a *samba* for Juriti and chorus, now entitled "Fogo, foguinho" (Fire, fire) and accompanied by handclaps.

Chiquinha Gonzaga belongs to a period of transition in Brazilian music, in which imported and native elements still coexisted. *Juriti,* however, is a late work in which the example of Offenbach's operettas is left far behind while the powerful influence of the European polka is subtly but unequivocally transformed, and the whole can be considered as a legitimate contribution to musical nationalism in Brazil.

LUIZ FERNANDO VALLIM LOPES

REFERENCES

Andrade, Mário de. "Chiquinha Gonzaga." In *Música, doce música*, 329–333. São Paulo: Martins, 1963.

Appleby, David. *The Music of Brazil.* Austin: University of Texas Press, 1983.

Béhague, Gerard. "Popular Musical Currents in the Art Music of the Early Nationalist Period in Brazil, circa 1870–1920." Ph.D. diss., Tulane University, 1966.

Diniz, Edinha. *Chiquinha Gonzaga: Uma história de vida.* Rio de Janeiro: Codecri, 1984.

Guillermoprieto, Alma. *Samba.* London: Jonathan Cape, 1990.

McGowan, Chris, and Ricardo Pessanha. *The Brazilian Sound: Samba, Bossa Nova, and the Popular Music of Brazil.* New York: Billboard, 1991.

Vasconcelos, Ary. *Raízes da Música Popular Brasileira.* 2nd ed. Rio de Janeiro: Rio Fundo, 1991.

GUTIÉRREZ (Y) ESPINOSA, FELIPE

Born in San Juan, Puerto Rico, May 26, 1825; died in San Juan, Puerto Rico, November 27, 1899. **Education:** Mostly self-taught; first studies with father, Julián Gutiérrez, then with José Alvarez, both musicians in the Regimiento Granada; studied organ with Fr. Domingo Delgado; studied in Europe (mainly Vienna and Paris), 1873–74. **Military Service:** Músico Mayor (Chief Musician), Regimiento de Iberia, beginning 1845. **Teaching Career:** San Juan, founder, head, and teacher of free Academia de Música, 1871–74. **Composing and Performing Career:** First opera by a Puerto Rican composer, *La palma del cacique,* 1856; won open competition for the position of *maestro de capilla* of the Cathedral of San Juan, 1858–98; conductor, orchestra of the Teatro Municipal; lost cathedral post as a result of American occupation, 1898. **Honors/Awards:** Received awards in various competitions in San Juan throughout his career; received gold medal for opera *Macías,* 1872; subsidy from San Juan town council to establish the Academia de Música, 1871–74, and for travel abroad 1873–74.

MUSIC LIST

INSTRUMENTAL SOLOS
Clarinet
"Petición de clarinete número 2." Unpublished manuscript.

Horn
"Allegro en la menor." Unpublished manuscript.
"Setimino." Unpublished manuscript.

Piano
Cuaderno con estudios para piano. Unpublished manuscript.

INSTRUMENTAL ENSEMBLE
"Petición A de clarinete." Unpublished manuscript.
"Petición a dúo, número 3" (flute and clarinet). Unpublished manuscript.
"Petición de violín, número 1" (violin and organ). Unpublished manuscript.
"Peticiones de las siete palabras" (three flutes and horns in E-flat). 1870. Unpublished manuscript. Note: incomplete.
"Tota pulchra" (horns in E-flat, double bass, and *bombardino*). Unpublished manuscript.

FULL ORCHESTRA
Aire de fandango. Unpublished manuscript.
La familia. 1875. Unpublished manuscript.
La manganilla. Unpublished manuscript.
"Marcha fúnebre." 1883. Unpublished manuscript.
El parto de los montes. Unpublished manuscript. Note: fragment.
La peseta. 1883. Unpublished manuscript.
Peticiones. Unpublished manuscript.
Salve de gallo. Unpublished manuscript.
Tonidán. Unpublished manuscript.
La yuca. Unpublished manuscript.

ORCHESTRA (CHAMBER OR FULL) WITH SOLOISTS
Agnus Dei (high voice, orchestra). Unpublished manuscript.
"Elisa" (soprano solo, violins, viola, clarinet in A, horns in D). Unpublished manuscript.
Magnificat a tres voces (three voices, chorus, and instrumental ensemble). 1860. Unpublished manuscript. Note: incomplete.
Réquiem a dos voces y orquesta. Unpublished manuscript.
"Salve número 3 para dos voces y orquesta." Unpublished manuscript.
Sonatina de violín (violin, orchestra). Unpublished manuscript.

SOLO VOICE
"La despedida." In *Canciones populares.* Boston: Silver Burdett, 1921.
"Salve a solo." 1865. Unpublished manuscript.

VOCAL ENSEMBLE
Misa a dos voces (two voices and organ). Unpublished manuscript.
Réquiem a tres voces. Unpublished manuscript.
Salve a dúo in B-flat major (two voices and organ). Unpublished manuscript.
"Salve a dúo" in E-flat major. Unpublished manuscript.
"Salve a dúo" in F major. Unpublished manuscript.
"Salve a dúo de contralto." Unpublished manuscript.
"Salve a dúo número 1." Unpublished manuscript.
Salve a dúo número 1 (obligada a tenor). Unpublished manuscript.
"Salve a dúo número 2." Unpublished manuscript.
"Salve a dúo número 3." Unpublished manuscript.
"Salve número 5 a dos voces." Unpublished manuscript.
Te Deum a dos voces. Unpublished manuscript.
"Tota pulchra" (piano and two voices). Unpublished manuscript.

CHORAL MUSIC WITH KEYBOARD OR INSTRUMENTAL ACCOMPANIMENT
Adiós a la Virgen. Unpublished manuscript.
"Adorate devote." Unpublished manuscript.
Así-así (four voices, choir, and orchestra). Unpublished manuscript.
Conclusión de novenas, número 1 y número 2. Unpublished manuscript.
Conclusión número 5. Unpublished manuscript.
"Dios te salve." Unpublished manuscript.
Easter Mass. 1876. Unpublished manuscript.
Finales para triduns, novenas y misas. Unpublished manuscript.
Gozos a la Purísima Concepción. Unpublished manuscript.
Gozos de la Inmaculada Concepción (tenors, basses, organ, flute, clarinets, violins, double bass). 1878. Unpublished manuscript.
Gozos de la Purísima. Unpublished manuscript.
Gran salve a Nuestra Señora de la Providencia (SATB, orchestra). Unpublished manuscript.
Gran salve número 1. Unpublished manuscript.
"Grandes letanías." Unpublished manuscript.
"Lamentación número 1." Unpublished manuscript.
"Lamentación segunda." Unpublished manuscript.
Lamentación tercera del Jueves Santo. 1867. Unpublished manuscript.
"Letanía de la Providencia." Unpublished manuscript.
Letanía número 3. Unpublished manuscript.

Letanías a cuatro voces, coros y orquesta (soprano, alto, tenor, bass, SATB, orchestra). Unpublished manuscript.

Letanías de Nuestra Señora de Belén. Unpublished manuscript.

Letanías jesuitas (SATB, orchestra). Unpublished manuscript.

Letanías número 1 y número 2. Unpublished manuscript.

Letanías pastoriles. Unpublished manuscript.

Misa a dos contraltos de niños o dos bajos. 1859. Unpublished manuscript.

Misa a dúo para coro y orquesta. 1872. Unpublished manuscript.

Misa de Jueves Santo. Unpublished manuscript.

Misa de la Anunciación (three voices). Unpublished manuscript.

Misa de la Anunciata (tenor and orchestra). Unpublished manuscript.

Misa de la Ascensión (three voices). Unpublished manuscript.

Misa de la Circuncisión (three voices). Unpublished manuscript.

Misa de la Purificación (three voices). Unpublished manuscript.

Misa de Nochebuena. Unpublished manuscript.

Misa de Réquiem. Unpublished manuscript.

Misa de Réquiem número 2. 1867. Unpublished manuscript.

Misa de San José. Unpublished manuscript.

Misa de San Juan. 1861. Unpublished manuscript.

Misa de Santa Cecilia (four soloists, SATB, and orchestra). Unpublished manuscript. Premiere, 1865.

Misa del Corpus Christi (three voices). Unpublished manuscript.

Misa en sol menor. Unpublished manuscript.

Misa para voces de niños. Unpublished manuscript.

Misa pastorela. Unpublished manuscript.

Misa pequeña en do mayor (two voices and orchestra). Unpublished manuscript.

Misa pequeña en la menor (two voices). Unpublished manuscript.

Miserere (three-part chorus, orchestra). Unpublished manuscript.

No recorderis. Unpublished manuscript.

Novenario de la Concepción. Unpublished manuscript.

Novenario de San Francisco. Unpublished manuscript.

Novenario de San Juan Bautista. Unpublished manuscript.

Novenario de San Miguel. Unpublished manuscript.

Novenario de Santa Rosa de Lima. Unpublished manuscript.

"Ofertorio." Unpublished manuscript.

"Parce mihi." 1871. Unpublished manuscript.

Pasión del Domingo de Ramos y Viernes Santo y Credo a dos voces solas. 1870. Unpublished manuscript.

Pasión del Viernes Santo. Unpublished manuscript.

Reservas. Unpublished manuscript.

Responso de entierros. Unpublished manuscript.

Responso número 1. Unpublished manuscript.

Responso número 2. Unpublished manuscript.

Responso para entierros, Parce mihi. Unpublished manuscript.

"Salve." Unpublished manuscript.

"Salve a coro" (voices and organ). Unpublished manuscript.

Salve a cuatro voces, coro y orquesta. 1891. Unpublished manuscript.

Salve grande a dos voces y coro. 1878. Unpublished manuscript.

Salve Mediana número 7 del Patrón San Juan. Unpublished manuscript.

Salve número 8. Unpublished manuscript.

Salve obligada de barítono. 1864. Unpublished manuscript.

Salve solemne. 1892. Unpublished manuscript.

"San Juan en do mayor" (two-part children's chorus). 1859. Unpublished manuscript. Note: written for the inauguration of the San Juan Cathedral.

Secuencia de Resurrección y Corpus. Unpublished manuscript.

"Segunda lamentación." Unpublished manuscript.

"Septenario de Dolores." Unpublished manuscript.

"Tercera lamentación." Unpublished manuscript.

"Tota pulchra a tres voces." Unpublished manuscript.

Tota pulchra es (SATB, orchestra). Unpublished manuscript.

Untitled notebook with religious music. Unpublished manuscript. Note: includes 24 compositions.

"Vigilia de difuntos." Unpublished manuscript.

DRAMATIC MUSIC

El amor de un pescador (zarzuela). 1857. Unpublished manuscript. Premiere, 1857.

El bearnés (opera). Unpublished manuscript.

Guarionex (opera). 1856. Unpublished manuscript.

Las siete palabras (oratorio). 1892. Unpublished manuscript.

Macías (opera). 1871. Unpublished manuscript. Premiere, 1872. Note: reorchestrated, revised, and reconstructed by Raphael Aponte, Ledíc, 1971.

PERFORMING FORCES UNKNOWN

"Contradanza." Unpublished manuscript.

"El recuerdo." 1856. Unpublished manuscript.

"Tota pulchra." Unpublished manuscript. Note: in C major.

"Tota pulchra." Unpublished manuscript. Note: in D minor.

"Tota pulchra." Unpublished manuscript. Note: in C minor.

PUBLICATIONS

ABOUT GUTIÉRREZ
Books and Monographs

Menéndez Maysonet, Guillermo. *Catálogo Temático de la Música de Felipe Gutiérrez y Espinosa (1825–1899).* Río Piedras: Universidad de Puerto Rico, 1993.

Dissertation

Muñoz de Frontera, Nélida. "A Study of Selected Nineteenth Century Puerto Rican Composers and Their Musical Output." Ph.D. diss., New York University, 1988.

Article

De Lerma, Dominique-René "Black Composers in Europe: A Works List." *Black Music Research Journal* 10, no. 2 (1990): 275–334.

BY GUTIÉRREZ

Teoría de la música. San Juan: Imprenta de Sancerrit, 1875.

* * * * *

Felipe Gutiérrez (y) Espinosa is considered one of the most distinguished of Puerto Rican musicians, and he has been acknowledged as his country's leading composer from the 19th century. During the latter half of that century, he was an active participant in the

Felipe Gutiérrez y Espinosa; from La Gran Enciclopedia de Puerto Rico *(C. Corredera, Madrid, 1976)*

musical life of San Juan as chapelmaster of the cathedral, head of his own free music academy, and conductor of an opera orchestra at the Teatro Municipal. His accomplishments and significance have been widely recognized during the last 20 years or so.

Gutiérrez was the second child of Julián Gutiérrez, a military band musician who emigrated from Spain in 1815, and Lucía Espinosa, a native of Puerto Rico. Early musical instruction was provided by his father and two others: José Alvarez, a band musician, and Father Domingo Delgado, organist of the cathedral. He learned to play a full range of instruments, of which his favorite was the piano. In 1845 he was appointed Músico Mayor (chief musician) within the Regimiento de Iberia, one of the two local military regiments in which his father had served earlier.

On September 9, 1858, at the age of 33, Gutiérrez was appointed chapelmaster of the newly formed musical ensemble of the Cathedral of San Juan by Bishop Pablo Benigno Carrión de Málaga (1798–1871). He held this position until 1898, when events associated with the Spanish-American War forced the dissolution of the ensemble. Most of his extant works were written for the church. In 1865 he was involved in the organization of a society that supported musicians while promoting performances of operas and *zarzuelas* (short plays with music and dancing). He frequently conducted the orchestra at the Teatro Municipal de San Juan (now the Teatro Tapia). In 1871, with the approval and subsidy of the

Ayuntamiento de San Juan (town council), he founded a free Academia de Música and continued as its director until 1874. Within three months of the opening of the academy, 360 students had matriculated. Subjects and performance instruction covered theory, solfège, harmony, composition, flute, clarinet, cornet, *bombardino* (saxhorn or baritone horn), trumpet, violin, and string bass. From April 1873 until mid-1874, Gutiérrez was on leave for study in Europe, which included extended visits to Vienna and Paris. He was disappointed that Parisian musicians showed little recognition of Puerto Rico or its music. (In contrast, the renowned piano virtuoso and composer Louis Moreau Gottschalk, a native of New Orleans, visited Puerto Rico during 1857–58 and produced a piquant remembrance: *Souvenir de Porto Rico,* op. 31, for piano.) Gutiérrez's music theory text, *Teoría de la música,* is known to have been issued in at least three editions, the last in 1875 (San Juan: Imprenta de Sancerrit).

The work for which he is perhaps most well known, the opera *Macías,* was entered into a competition at San Juan and won a gold medal in 1872. Five years later, on October 4, 1877, the work was dedicated to King Alfonso XII of Spain; a copy was deposited at the Biblioteca de Palacio in Madrid. Almost a century after the dedication, on August 19, 1977, this three-act opera was finally mounted for a premiere performance at the Teatro Tapia in San Juan; a microfilm copy of the Biblioteca de Palacio score made the performance possible. Other stage works have all been lost, including the operas *Guarionex* (1856), which was based on Alejandro Tapia y Rivera's *La palma del cacique* (Madrid, 1852) and lauded as the first opera by a Puerto Rican composer; *El bearnés* (libretto by Antonio Biaggi); and the *zarzuela El amor de un pescador* (*The Love of a Fisherman;* libretto by Carlos Navarro y Almansa).

In 1882 Gutiérrez married Juana Bautista Medina, a widow with two children, who died in 1887. His last years were clouded by social disruption and the deaths of family members and friends (especially Alejandro Tapia y Rivera). Toward the end of 1897, the salaries of the cathedral musicians were suspended. Gutiérrez subsequently worked at a much reduced monthly salary (40 pesos) as a concierge at the Instituto de Segunda Enseñanza and received for seven months a miniscule monthly pension (20 pesos) from the San Juan municipal government. He died in the city of his birth on November 27, 1899, as a result of chronic nephritis. His residence during much of his life was Calle del Sol No. 108 in Old San Juan, not far from the cathedral.

Gutiérrez has been described in a recent dissertation as "a tall man, dark-complexioned, and with an aloof glance. A mixture of Catholic and free-thinker, he was kind-hearted and loved children."

Since the modern premiere of *Macías* and the publication of several recent books and articles on Puerto Rican music, interest in Gutiérrez and his music has risen markedly. Héctor Campos Parsi calls him "our first great musician" ("nuestro primer gran músico"). Unfortunately, almost all of his works remain in relatively inaccessible manuscript copies, and some have been lost. The only known publication is the song for voice and piano "La despedida" (The Farewell) in the out-of-print anthology *Canciones populares.* Robert Stevenson in 1978 convincingly argued that the sacred works alone "may yet place Gutiérrez on a pedestal shared with only two or three other great Latin Americans of his century."

SELECTED WORKS

In a recent publication, Guillermo Menéndez Maysonet, Professor of Music History, University of Puerto Rico, has provided a detailed thematic catalog of the musical works. One hundred eighteen compositions (designated GE 1 to GE 118) are listed in groupings by genre, with those in the sacred category (GE 1–110) far outnumbering those in the secular (GE 111–118). There are 13 Masses, including four requiem masses, three passions, 16 Salve Regina settings, eight litanies, and a host of other liturgical pieces, as well as 23 sacred pieces with Spanish text and 19 instrumental works for church services. The secular listings include *Macías,* three songs with instrumental accompaniment (including "La despedida"), two overtures, a "sinfonía," and a fragmetary instrumental work entitled "El parto de los montes" ("The Creation of the Mountains").

Macías (GE 111) was not the first of Gutiérrez's operas–it follows *Guarionex* (1856) and *El bearnés* (n.d.)–but it may have been his most ambitious. Winner of a gold medal in 1872, it was dedicated in 1877 to Alfonso XII of Spain. The libretto for *Macías,* possibly by Martín Travieso y Rivero or by the composer himself, was adapted from a play of the same name by Mariano José de Larra (1809–1837). The legend of Macías, "the enamored" ("el enamorado"), can be traced back to the mid-15th century. The tragic story of love and death revolves around the troubador Macías (tenor) and his beloved, Elvira (soprano), and the action takes place at the castle of Don Enrique de Villena in Andújar, Spain (near Córdoba), in 1406. After a forced marriage between Elvira and Fernán Pérez (baritone), Macías returns from a contrived mission to challenge Pérez. Macías is subsequently imprisoned. Elvira seeks out Macías in prison with the aid of Beatriz (mezzo-soprano), finds him mortally wounded, and curses Pérez as she kills herself. Nineteen musical numbers are distributed among the three acts and four scenes; the overture has been lost. Musical forces include nine soloists, four-voice choir, and full orchestra.

Critical reaction to the first performance on August 19, 1977, in San Juan was positive. Tomás Marco, in the Madrid newspaper *Arriba,* enthusiastically applauded the opera's originality, maturity, and brilliant orchestration. In the *San Juan Star,* music critic and historian Donald Thompson characterized the opera as "the tip of an iceberg," i.e., the recently made visible part of a rich and largely unknown mid-19th-century musical culture in San Juan, and "an original work . . . which deserves to become much better known."

Among the sacred works, *Tota pulchra es* for voices and orchestra (GE 63) has been singled out as the first composition from Puerto Rico to utilize the saxophone. Other works found especially praiseworthy are the *Lamentación tercera del Jueves Santo* in G minor (GE 62, dated 1867), certain of the *Letanías* (Litanies) and Salve Regina settings, and the *Magnificat a tres voces* in D major (GE 65), for three voices, chorus, and orchestra.

The music historian Braulio Dueño Colón discerns two styles of religious music. The first is more melodious and free, more Italianate, with voices more prominent than instruments and yielding to the flow of the melody, as in the early *Misa a dos contraltos de niños o dos bajos* (GE 1, 1859). It is worth noting here that the operas of Gutiérrez have been considered Italianate by Braulio Dueño Colón, with the influence of Bellini and Donizetti being noticeable. The second style is more like plainchant, with its generally narrower compass and modal scales; this style anticipates to some extent the style of certain 20th-century composers, such as Vaughan Williams and Bloch. Dueño Colón cites the Gloria and Credo movements of Gutiérrez's last Masses as examples. This second style, or "new school" (*nueva escuela*), came under severe criticism. It has been described in terms of a sonata for orchestra with vocal accompaniment because of the suppression of the more florid vocal melodies. Some faulted Gutiérrez for his orchestrations, which, due partly to the instrumental resources assigned to the cathedral ensemble, were somewhat unbalanced. The ensemble lacked violas, oboes, and bassoons but did include trumpets, clarinets, and a *bombardino.* The winds typically overpowered the strings. Gutiérrez may have preferred that kind of sound, but it apparently went against the grain of the clergy and parishioners.

A more detailed picture of Gutiérrez and his significance will be possible with the publication of his works and more widespread performance. We have seen, as Donald Thompson suggested, only the tip of the iceberg and eagerly await the distribution of the many works tantalizingly described in the thematic catalog by Menéndez Maysonet.

REFERENCES

Batista, Gustavo. "Felipe Gutiérrez y su Academia de Música de Puerto Rico." *Revista/Review Interamericana* 8, no. 4 (1978–79): 640–645.

Dower, Catherine. *Puerto Rican Music Following the Spanish American War; 1898: The Aftermath of the Spanish American War and Its Influence on the Musical Culture of Puerto Rico.* Lanham, Md.: University Press of America, 1983.

Dueño Colón, Braulio. Quoted in "Felipe Gutiérrez Espinosa (1825–1899)," by Héctor Campos Parsi. In *La Gran Enciclopedia de Puerto Rico.* Vol. 7, *La Música en Puerto Rico,* 185–188. Madrid: C. Corredera, 1976.

Fowlie-Flores, Fay, comp. *Index to Puerto Rican Collective Biography.* Bibliographies and Indexes in American History, no. 5. Westport, Conn.: Greenwood Press, 1987.

Kuss, Malena. Felipe Gutiérrez y Espinosa. In *Pipers Enzyklopädie des Musik Theaters,* vol. 2, 623–624. Munich: Piper, 1987.

Marco, Tomás. "'Macías' de Gutiérrez Espinosa: Estreno actual de una ópera romántica." *Inter-American Music Review* 1, no. 1 (1978): 96–97. (Originally published: *Arriba* [Madrid], September 1, 1977.)

Menéndez Maysonet, Guillermo. *Catálogo Temático de la Música de Felipe Gutiérrez y Espinosa (1825–1899).* Río Piedras: Universidad de Puerto Rico, 1993.

Muñoz de Frontera, Nélida. "A Study of Selected Nineteenth Century Puerto Rican Composers and Their Musical Output." Ph.D. diss., New York University, 1988.

Stevenson, Robert M. "Caribbean Music History: A Selected Annotated Bibliography with Musical Supplement." *Inter-American Music Review,* 4, no. 1 (1981): 1–112.

———. "Music in the San Juan, Puerto Rico, Cathedral to 1900." *Inter-American Music Review* 1, no. 1 (1978): 73–95.

Thompson, Donald. "Gutiérrez (y) Espinosa." In *The New Grove Dictionary of Opera,* edited by Stanley Sadie, 2: 585. London: Macmillan, 1992.

———. "Macías." In *The New Grove Dictionary of Opera,* edited by Stanley Sadie, 3: 133. London: Macmillan, 1992.

———. "Music Research in Puerto Rico." *College Music Symposium* 23, no. 1 (1983): 81–96.

———. "Musical Archaeology, Fine Talent Bring 'Macías' to Life." *Inter-American Music Review* 1, no. 1 (1978): 98–99. (Originally published in the *San Juan Star* June 7, 1978.)

Thompson, Donald, and Annie F. Thompson. *Music and Dance in Puerto Rico from the Age of Columbus to Modern Times: An Annotated Bibliography.* Metuchen, N.J.: Scarecrow Press, 1991.

JOHN E. DRUESEDOW

HAILSTORK, ADOLPHUS CUNNINGHAM

Born in Rochester, N.Y., April 17, 1941. **Education:** Early musical training included violin, piano, and organ; Albany High School, Albany, N.Y., 1956–59; Howard University, Washington, D.C., studied with Mark Fax (composition); B.Mus., music theory, *magna cum laude,* 1963; American Institute at Fontainebleau, France, studied with Nadia Boulanger, summer 1963; Manhattan School of Music, New York, N.Y., studied with Ludmila Ulehla, Nicholas Flagello, Vittorio Giannini, and David Diamond, B.Mus., composition, 1965, M.Mus., composition, 1966; Michigan State University, East Lansing, studied conducting with Warner Lawson and Hugh Ross, composition with Nicholas Flagello, Ph.D., 1971; Electronic Music Institution, Dartmouth College, Hanover, N.H., studied with John Appleton and Herbert Howe, summer 1972; Seminar on Contemporary Music, State University of New York at Buffalo, summer 1978. **Military Service:** Captain in U.S. Armed Forces, active in western Germany, 1966–68. **Composing and Performing Career:** Early compositions performed under his baton while in high school; Howard University, musical comedy, *The Race for Space,* performed during senior year in college, 1963; National Symphony Orchestra, read works written while a student at Howard University; Howard University Chorus, appointed assistant conductor, 1963; *Statement, Variations, and Fugue,* written while a student, performed by Baltimore Symphony Orchestra, 1966, and Atlanta Symphony Orchestra, 1968; Michigan State University Male Chorus, served as conductor, while completing doctoral work. **Teaching Career:** Michigan State University, teacher and graduate assistant, 1969–71; Youngstown State University, Youngstown, Ohio, assistant professor, 1971–76, associate professor, 1976–77; Norfolk State University, Norfolk, Va., composer-in-residence, 1977, associate professor of music, 1977–85, professor of music, 1985–present; University of Michigan, Ann Arbor, visiting professor, 1977. **Commissions:** J. C. Penney Bicentennial Celebration Committee, 1974; Virginia Symphony, 1984; Nova Trio, 1985; Boys Choir of Harlem, 1987; Baltimore Symphony, 1990; Meet the Composer/Reader's Digest/National Endowment for the Arts, 1990; American Guild of Organists, 1993; Barlow Endowment for Music Commission, 1993; Dayton Opera Company, 1995. **Memberships:** ASCAP, NANM, American Music Center. **Honors/Awards:** Lucy E. Moten Travel Fellowship, 1963; one of 25 participants selected nationally to attend Electronic Music Institute at Dartmouth College, 1972; Ernest Bloch Award for choral composition, co-winner, 1970–71; Belwin-Mills/Max Winkler Award, 1977; Virginia CBDNA College Band Symposium, winner, 1983: Virginia Band Directors award 1987; Fulbright Fellowship for study and travel in Guyana, 1987; University of Delaware Festival of New Music, winner, 1995. **Mailing Address:** 521 Berrypick Lane, Virginia Beach, VA 23462-1927.

MUSIC LIST

INSTRUMENTAL SOLOS
Violin

"American Landscape no. 2." Unpublished manuscript.

"Sanctum." Unpublished manuscript. Also arranged for clarinet, piano.

Sonata for Violin and Piano. 1972. Unpublished manuscript.

Suite. Unpublished manuscript. Contents: Prelude; Tango; Meditation; Demonic Dance. Premiere, 1979.

Variations on a Guyanese Folksong. Unpublished manuscript. Also arranged for viola, piano.

Flute

Sonatina. Naperville, Ill.: Fema Music Publications, 1977. Premiere, 1975.

Clarinet

"A Simple Caprice." Unpublished manuscript. Recorded: Capstone Records CPS-8604.

"Three Smiles for Tracy" (clarinet unaccompanied). Unpublished manuscript.

Trumpet

Sonata. Unpublished manuscript. Also arranged for trumpet, string quartet.

Variations (unaccompanied trumpet). Unpublished manuscript.

Tuba

"Duo, for Tuba and Piano." 1973. Naperville, Ill.: Fema Music Publications, 1981. Premiere, 1975.

Guitar

Fanfares and Waltzes. Unpublished manuscript.

Three Preludes. Unpublished manuscript.

Harp

Two Impromptus (harp unaccompanied). Unpublished manuscript.

Piano

"Ignis Fatuus." 1976. Unpublished manuscript. Premiere, 1976.

Piano Sonata no. 1. 1978–80. St. Louis, Mo.: MMB Music, 1980. Recorded: Albany TROY 266.

Piano Sonata no. 2. Unpublished manuscript.

Trio Sonata. 1991. Unpublished manuscript.

Two Scherzos. Unpublished manuscript.

Two Pianos

Sonata for Two Pianos. Unpublished manuscript.

Organ

First Organ Book. Unpublished manuscript.

Suite for Organ. Chapel Hill, N.C.: Hinshaw Music, 1976. Contents: Prelude; Andantino; Scherzetto; Fugue. Premiere, 1975.

"Who Gazes at the Stars." 1978. Unpublished manuscript.

SMALL INSTRUMENTAL ENSEMBLE
Brass

Bagatelles (two trumpets, two trombones). 1973. Naperville, Ill.: Fema Publications, 1977. Contents: Sousalute; Tranquility Base; Untitled. Premiere, 1973.

Combinations

Arabesques (flute, percussion). Unpublished manuscript.

Lachrymosa: 1919 (two clarinets, two bassoons, strings). Unpublished manuscript.

Piano Trio (violin, cello, piano). 1985. St. Louis, Mo.: MMB Music, 1985. Commissioned by the Nova Trio.

STRING ORCHESTRA

Sonata da chiesa. San Antonio, Tex.: Southern Music, 1992 (rental).

CHAMBER ORCHESTRA

Consort Piece (flute, clarinet, trumpet, violin, cello, piano, percussion). 1995. Unpublished manuscript. Winner of the University of Delaware Festival of New Music.

Music for Ten Players (flute, oboe, clarinet, trumpet, two violins, viola, cello, percussion). Unpublished manuscript.

My Lord What a Mourning. St. Louis, Mo.: MMB Music.

Two Romances (harp, strings). Unpublished manuscript.

FULL ORCHESTRA

An American Port of Call. 1984. Unpublished manuscript. Commissioned by the Virginia Symphony. Recorded: Fanfare 3534; First Edition LCD 009; Intersound International 3534.

Epitaph (In Memoriam to Dr. Martin Luther King). 1979. Century City, Calif.: Wimbledon Music (rental). Recorded: Connell Communications CDR0497; Fanfare 3534; Intersound International 3534.

Festival Music. 1993. Unpublished manuscript. Commissioned by the Barlow Endowment for the Baltimore Symphony. Premiere, 1993.

Intrada. 1990. Unpublished manuscript. Commissioned by the Baltimore Symphony for its 75th anniversary.

Symphony no. 1. 1988. Unpublished manuscript. Premiere, 1988. Recorded: Albany TROY 104.

ORCHESTRA (CHAMBER OR FULL) WITH SOLOISTS

Four Spirituals (two sopranos, orchestra or piano). Unpublished manuscript.

Piano Concerto. 1990. Century City, Calif.: Wimbledon Music. Commissioned by a consortium of the Virginia, Richmond, Roanoke, Louisville, and Phoenix Symphony Orchestras. Premiere, 1992. Recorded: Columbia Masterworks M34556; Connell Communications CDR0497.

Sonata for Trumpet and Strings. Unpublished manuscript.

Three Romances for Viola and Chamber Orchestra. 1988. Unpublished manuscript.

ORCHESTRA (CHAMBER OR FULL) WITH CHORUS

Songs of Isaiah (SATB, orchestra or piano). ca. 1987. St. Louis, Mo.: MMB Music (rental). Commissioned by the Boys Choir of Harlem.

CONCERT BAND

An American Fanfare (brass, percussion). 1985. New York: Theodore Presser (rental).

American Guernica. 1982. Unpublished manuscript. Awarded first prize in a national contest sponsored by the Virginia College Band Directors, 1983.

. . . And Deliver Us from Evil (band, percussion). St. Louis, Mo.: MMB Music.

Celebration. 1974. New York: J. C. Penney, 1975 (rental). Commissioned by J. C. Penney for their bicentennial. Premiere, 1975. Recorded: Columbia M34556; Connell Communications CDR0497.

Norfolk Pride. Unpublished manuscript.

Out of the Depths. 1974. Unpublished manuscript. Winner of the Belwin/ Max Winkler award for best band composition, 1977.

SOLO VOICE

A Charm at Parting (mezzo-soprano, piano). 1969. New York: Edward B. Marks, 1977. Contents: Call this Whatever Name; I Loved You; Finis: A Charm at Parting. Premiere, 1970. Recorded: University of Michigan Records SM0015.

"Create in Me" (soprano, piano). Unpublished manuscript.

Four Love Songs (tenor, piano). Unpublished manuscript.

"If We Must Die" (baritone, piano). 1978. Unpublished manuscript.

"I've Seen the Day" (soprano, double bass). Unpublished manuscript.

"Slave Song" (bass, four cellos, double bass, timpani). Unpublished manuscript.

"Sunset and Night" (soprano, piano). Unpublished manuscript.

Songs of Love and Justice (soprano, piano). Unpublished manuscript.

Three Simple Songs (soprano, piano). Unpublished manuscript.

Two Sonnets (soprano, piano). Unpublished manuscript.

"A Woman's Song" (soprano, piano). Unpublished manuscript.

CHORAL MUSIC

"Arise My Beloved" (SATB unaccompanied). Unpublished manuscript. Recorded: Albany TROY 156.

"Break Forth" (SATB, brass, timpani, organ). Bryn Mawr, Penn.: Theodore Presser.

"A Carol for All Children" (SATB unaccompanied). Houston, Tex.: Alliance Music. Recorded: Albany TROY 156.

"Entreat Me Not to Leave Thee" (women's chorus, harp). Unpublished manuscript.

Five Short Choral Works (SATB unaccompanied). Bryn Mawr, Penn.: Theodore Presser, 1994. Contents: I Will Sing of Life; Nocturne; Crucifixion: He Never Said a Mumblin' Word; The Cloths of Heaven; The Lamb. Recorded: Albany TROY 156.

"God" (SATB). Unpublished manuscript.

"Hodie (Christus natus est)" (SATB unaccompanied). Unpublished manuscript.

"A Kwanzaa Litany" (male chorus, bass soloist, five percussionists). Unpublished manuscript.

"Let the Heavens Be Glad" (SATB unaccompanied). Unpublished manuscript.

"Look to This Day" (SATB, organ). N.p.: Marvel, n.d. Also arranged for chorus, band.

"Mourn Not the Dead" (SATB unaccompanied). 1966. Unpublished manuscript. Co-winner of the Ernest Bloch Award, 1970–71. Premiere, 1971.

"Now I Recall My Childhood" (SATB). Unpublished manuscript.

"O Praise the Lord" (SATB unaccompanied). St. Louis: MMB Music. Recorded: Albany TROY 156.

"Of Tenderness and Grace" (SATB). Unpublished manuscript.

Adolphus Cunningham Hailstork; courtesy of the composer; photo by Phil Schexnyder

"Psalm 72" (SATB, brass, organ). 1981. Unpublished manuscript. Premiere, 1981.

"The Richness of Life" (women's chorus unaccompanied). Unpublished manuscript.

"Set Me as a Seal upon Thy Heart" (SATB unaccompanied). 1979. New York: Boosey and Hawkes. Recorded: Albany TROY 156.

Seven Songs of the Rubaiyat (SATB unaccompanied). 1981. Unpublished manuscript. Recorded: Albany TROY 156.

"Shout for Joy" (SATB, brass, timpani, organ). Bryn Mawr, Penn.: Theodore Presser.

"The Song of Deborah" (SATB unaccompanied). ca. 1983. N.p.: Alliance Music. Commissioned by the American Guild of Organists.

"Stages" (SATB). Unpublished manuscript.

"The Stars" (SATB). Unpublished manuscript.

Two Madrigals. 1968. Contents: Cease Sorrows Now (SSATB); The Silver Swan (SATB). Note: "Cease Sorrows Now" published by Marks Music. Premiere, 1971.

"Ye Shall Have a Song" (SATB). N.p.: Marvel Music.

DRAMATIC MUSIC

Done Made My Vow: A Ceremony (oratorio). 1985. Unpublished manuscript.

I Will Lift Up Mine Eyes (cantata). 1989. New York: Theodore Presser (rental).

Paul Laurence Dunbar: Common Ground (opera). Unpublished manuscript. Commissioned by the Dayton Opera Company. Premiere, 1995.

PUBLICATIONS

ABOUT HAILSTORK
Articles

Tischler, Alice. "Adolphus Cunningham Hailstork." In *Fifteen Black American Composers: A Bibliography of Their Works,* 149–164. Detroit Studies in Music Bibliography, no. 45. Detroit, Mich.: Detroit Information Coordinators, 1981.

* * * * *

Adolphus Hailstork has established himself as an important voice in contemporary concert music, having numerous performances and recordings of his symphonic, choral, and chamber works. Known as a composer of both instrumental and vocal works, he credits his vocal experiences as a teenager as "most influential" in the development of his style. In an interview with the author, he said that "My stuff is always lyrical, always tonal, it sings. I can't help it. Singing is as natural to me as anything." He has also stated, "I've always been interested in trying to create an amalgam between European structural principles and African-American melodic and rhythmic materials."

Born in 1941 in Rochester, New York, Hailstork began studying violin when he was eight years old. He attended public school there, but in 1949 his family moved to Albany, New York, where he became a member of the choirs of the Cathedral of All Saints, Episcopal. His first instrument was the violin, and by the age of 15 he had also studied piano, singing, and conducting. He then decided to learn to compose: "This revelation to be a composer occurred in 1956 at the age of 15." Upon graduating from high school in 1959, Hailstork entered Howard University, where he majored in music theory and studied with composer Mark Fax. Having earned a bachelor of music degree at Howard in 1963, he studied that summer with Nadia Boulanger at the American Institute at Fontainebleau, France. He continued work at the Manhattan School of Music, where he studied with David Diamond; he received a bachelor of music degree in composition in 1965 and a master of music degree in 1966. After a two-year tour of duty with the United States Army (1966–68), Hailstork took a teaching position at Youngstown (Ohio) State University and worked toward a doctorate, which he earned in 1971 from Michigan State University in East Lansing.

It was during this period that Hailstork's awareness of a "black consciousness" or black arts tradition and of the death of Dr. Martin Luther King Jr. brought a deeper understanding of his calling as a composer and his responsibility as a black American. It was, in fact, the continuous reporting of news of Dr. King's death that inspired him to pursue the doctorate. From then on, his goal has been "to create a part of the Black repertoire."

His training with composer David Diamond at the Manhattan School of Music and the compositional influences of Aaron Copland, Samuel Barber, and Igor Stravinsky were the factors that shaped much of Hailstork's career. Said Hailstork: "I liked their music more than the stuff I heard by Schoenberg. Serialism had become dominant. But I liked the American school." His music, like that of the composers he particularly admires, is appealing and familiar, and thus he is one of the most performed black composers of his generation.

In the 1970s, many academically trained African-American composers wrote music that was decidedly "noncultural," having been influenced by then-current serialistic and atonal practices. Hailstork, however, always contained within his orchestral and instrumental/vocal frameworks some features of traditional African-American music. In many of his works, even if well hidden, there are blues riffs or pulsating "black rhythms." While many of his orchestral landscapes do contain such references to African-American vernacular music, many of his vocal and choral works do not reflect this cultural identity.

Since the late 1970s, Hailstork's works have been performed throughout the United States by organizations such as the Boys Choir of Harlem, the McCullough Chorale, the Brazeal Dennard Choral, and the symphony orchestras of Baltimore, Chicago, Detroit, and Savannah, to name a few. His piano concerto, commissioned in 1990 by Meet the Composer, Readers Digest, and the National Endowment for the Arts, was performed by pianist Leon Bates with the Norfolk, Virginia, Louisville, Phoenix, Roanoke, and Rochester symphony orchestras. An award-winning composer, he has been honored with the Ernest Bloch choral composition award for "Mourn Not the Dead" and the Belwin-Mills/Max Winkler award for the band composition *Out of the Depths.* Among the composer's best-known works are *Celebration,* an overture for orchestra (1974), the oratorio *Done Made My Vow* (1985), the cantata *I Will Lift Up Mine Eyes* (1989), and his Piano Trio (1985). In

1995, Hailstork's opera *Paul Laurence Dunbar: Common Ground* was premiered by the Dayton (Ohio) Opera Company.

Hailstork characterizes his work as "evolving postmodern pluralism," which can be heard in his *An American Port of Call, Festival Music,* Sonata for Trumpet, Symphony no. 1, *Epitaph,* the Piano Trio, and Piano Sonata no. 1.

Hailstork's approach to composition is organic. That is, he "grows" whole works from precreated melodic/sonority cells that he has stockpiled from hundreds of themes and motives from works he began but never finished. This rich repository is kept near his piano, always available. He frequently retrieves themes from this rich trove of discarded motives and breathes new life into them as they become materials of new works. A capable craftsman, sensitive musician, and inspired creator, Hailstork in this way builds his contributions to the concert repertoire.

Adolphus Hailstork is an American composer who uses European structural principles fused with African-American conventions and sensibilities to consciously create a "black" concert music. To dismiss the cultural spirit of his works would be to miss a critical and essential element in them. Hailstork, a practical composer, believes in writing music that will be performed. He desires to communicate with people through the music: "I just enjoy music. I prefer to write music. I'm a pragmatist. I write music to get performed. I don't write esoteric, Ivory Tower works to be played by a few people in a loft for an audience of a few people. That's just not me. I'm a populist, but so was Verdi!" He believes profoundly in the notion of cultural nationalism but also believes his music is universal, transcending categorical cultural and aesthetic differences.

SYMPHONY NO. 1 (1988)

Hailstork's Symphony no. 1 may be described as spirited, brightly orchestrated, and melodic, driven by a continuous underlying rhythmic pulsation. The first movement (*Allegro*) of the four-movement, 20-minute work is a simple and colorful sonata form. It opens with eight attacks of the strings and brass, which alert the listener that the work will be rhythmically engaging. Constant shifting of instrumental families pushes the work through the ongoing themes, secondary motives, a development section, and an anticipated and welcome recapitulation of the opening chords and materials.

After the work's opening chords, a theme appears first in the clarinet; it is then quickly passed to the strings and accompanying orchestration. The orchestra completes this principal theme, which is then repeated. A transition leads to a less busy secondary theme area in which the second theme is presented, again first by the clarinet, then by the strings. The development section follows, in which the rhythmic focus is transferred to the cellos and basses, which introduce an engaging rhythmic cell, as the clarinet, violins, and violas handle the thematic material. A series of modulations occurs in which melodic material is heard in the solo trumpet and the horns, and the rhythmic cell is picked up by the timpani. Soon the strings slow the pace, modulate, and prepare for the return of the opening material.

Within the composer's colorful harmonic and theme-driven palette, there exists a subtle but nonetheless constant foundational pulse, first heard in the timpani and used in the accompanying strings throughout the work. The recapitulation of the first theme area is signaled by the return of the opening, eight chordal attacks of the strings and brass. The principal and secondary theme areas are heard only once in the recapitulation, and the work ends energetically with the opening chords, to which is appended a surprising coda and a final cadence.

The second movement (*Lento ma non troppo*) is a simple three-part design, ABA, characteristically slow and tuneful. While reminiscent of slow movements such as Samuel Barber's *Adagio for Strings* or Copland's *Appalachian Spring,* with its large expanding and pyramiding gestures, the movement is more mood-oriented and solemn than tune-driven. The movement ends quietly on a sustained major chord played by the strings and high woodwinds.

The third movement (*Allegretto*) returns to a busier texture that makes use of the orchestra's characteristic voices: the oboe, bassoon, clarinet, and solo flute. Unlike the smooth melodic curves of the first two movements, this movement's contour is less predictable and angular in shape, propelling the music toward the fourth and final movement.

The fourth movement (*Vivace*) begins with the opening chords of the first movement but quickly moves into new material—a highly rhythmic, pulsating texture with hints of the opening themes in the cellos. Themes used earlier are present, although manipulated and submerged, and they hearken back to the opening movement. Some of the same modulations and transferring of musical activity throughout the orchestra from strings to woodwinds to brass found in the first movement are used in the last, further connecting the work as a whole. There is then a triumphant final attack on the ending chord.

The work was composed in 1988 for a summer festival, the premiere conducted by the composer in Ocean Grove, New Jersey. It has also been recorded on the Albany label by the Bohuslav Martinu Philharmonic of Gottwaldov, Czechoslovakia, conducted by Julius Williams.

AN AMERICAN PORT OF CALL (1984)

An American Port of Call, written for orchestra, launches immediately into a pulsating drive that carries a myriad of colorful themes, the most prevalent being the characteristically American blues riff heard in the lead clarinet, a favorite Americanism. In almost standard sonata form, the work contains strands again reminiscent of Bernstein, Copland, and Gershwin as well as a Stravinskian allure after a fast flurry of runs, a playful and catchy foundational motive heard in the brass (see Ex. 1). The high bells and cascading mallet instruments combined with piccolo trills, high register piano, brass calls, and riffing violins give the work an agitated and energetic texture similar to that of the opening of George Gershwin's *American in Paris.* The work slows, moving into a more solemn but lyric section carried by the strings and horn. The entire orchestral fabric then returns, presenting the busy and energetic theme-filled opening, moving into a development section, on to a literal repeat of the opening motives, and finally to the coda, which is a variant of the main theme. According to the composer, "All the events of the piece are variations of this core theme heard in the trumpets and horns early in the work."

Example 1. *An American Port of Call,* brass motive

An American Port of Call was commissioned and first performed by the Virginia Symphony and recorded by the Rundfunk-Sinfonia Orchestra.

PIANO TRIO (1985)

The Piano Trio, which explores the individual voices of the piano, violin, and cello, is an excellent example of carefully balanced ensemble writing. Monothematic, with the violin theme presented in various permutations in every movement, the work opens with a piano and violin lament commemorating the Jewish holocaust. The lyric melody and static harmony played softly in the opening are interrupted by an intruding *forte,* dissonant and stark, played by the piano and cello. Soon, the violin and cello emerge from the musical mix to restate the themes, which are accompanied by the piano's low pedal note. There is then a return to the opening lyricism, the piano leading, with a soaring violin recapitulation of the theme in the upper register underlying the intense emotion evoked by the subject matter.

The second movement, a scherzo in 11/8 meter, opens with a lively string figure, clearly a festive "dance," almost Bartókian in nature. After this opening, there is a return to the more solemn themes presented in the first movement, this time led by the cello and accompanied by a dance-like piano part. The violin joins the cello theme in unison at the octave. A lively imitative section with *pizzicato* strings follows; then comes a sudden return to the opening dance that lasts to end the movement.

The third movement, clearly a rendition of an ethnic Eastern European folk dance, is comprised of imitation heard in unison lines between and among the three instruments. The middle of the work bridges into a blues-tinged segment, which is followed by a lyric section that acts as a transition to and a recall of the opening movement's principal thematic material. A festive close, featuring the livelier dances of the earlier movements, brings the movement, and the work, to a close.

The Piano Trio was commissioned by the Nova Trio of Norfolk, Virginia.

SEVEN SONGS OF THE RUBAIYAT (1981)

This work, according to the composer, was written "to explore the possibilities of choral works based on a series of different scales." Based on a text written by Omar Khayyam, its lyricism and sonorities immediately capture the listener's attention. Sounding neither contrived nor plotted out, the music flows very naturally in praise of the invincibility of the "Life of Spirit."

Seven Songs of the Rubaiyat is liturgical concert music for unaccompanied chorus. Clearly inspired by the vocal training, traditions, and repertoire the composer heard as a youth in the Episcopal church, the spirit of these seven songs varies from one to the other, alternately buoyant, celebratory, and reflective. The first song celebrates the wonders of life ("Come fill the cup"), beginning with a plaintive chant of male voices (in parallel fifths) on the words "The worldly hope men set their hearts upon turns ashes . . . Like snow upon the desert's dusty face lighting a little hour or two is gone." Another example of this more reflective quality of the work is song six, which opens with a solo baritone voice, again almost chant-like, accompanied by a low (alto) vocal drone on the words "The Revelation of the Devout and Learn'd who rose before us, . . . I sent my Soul to the Invisible, some letter of that after-life to spell; and by and by my soul returned to me, and answered, 'I myself am Heaven and Hell.'" In addition to texts with spiritual and reflective moods, existentialist and celebratory nature (as in the opening and closing segments, "Come fill the cup, and in the fire of Spring your Winter-garment of Repentance fling"), there is also the realism of life's fleeting duration. The penultimate song is set to the text "O threats of Hell and hopes of Paradise! One thing at least is certain, This Life Flies; One things is certain and the rest is Lies; The Flower that once has blown forever dies." The work ends with a return of the opening text, "Come fill the cup."

As a composer born in the mid-20th century, Adolphus Hailstork has internalized, processed, and recreated compositional trends of the past century, including the Americanist, post-romantic tendencies of an earlier generation, as seen in his Symphony no. 1, and his use of the Negro spirituals, blues, and Eastern European ethnic dances, as in the Piano Trio. The four works discussed here justify the claim that Hailstork is a noteworthy American voice in contemporary concert music. Further proof of this can be seen in his rich and varied collection of published works, which are part of the contemporary concert experience.

REFERENCES

Banfield, William C. "Conversations with Adolphus Hailstork, April 9, 1996." In *Landscapes in Color: Conversations with Black American Composers.* Metuchen, N.J.: Scarecrow Press, forthcoming.

Hailstork, Adolphus. Liner notes, *Symphonic Brotherhood.* Albany TROY 104.

———. Liner notes, *The McCullough Chorale in Concert Singing the Music of Adolphus Hailstork.* Albany TROY 156.

———. Personal interview with the author, April 9, 1996.

WILLIAM C. BANFIELD

HAIRSTON, JESTER JOSEPH

Born in Belews Creek, N.C., July 9, 1901. **Education:**
Massachusetts Agricultural College (now the University of
Massachusetts-Amherst), studied landscape architecture, 1920–21,
1926–27; Tufts University, Medford, Mass., studied music, 1927–
29, B.A. *cum laude,* 1929; Juilliard School of Music, New York,
N.Y., studied harmony and composition, 1931–33. **Composing
and Performing Career:** Homestead, Pa., performed with church
choirs as a young boy; New York, N.Y., performed with the Eva
Jessye Choir, 1929; performed in the Broadway musical *Hello Paris,*
1930; Hall Johnson Choir, assistant conductor, 1931–ca. 1940;
Los Angeles, with the Hall Johnson choir, provided music for the
films *The Green Pastures* and *Lost Horizon,* 1936; arranged choral
music and organized his own choir for film soundtracks, 1936–49;
San Francisco, directed Federal Theatre Project productions of *Run
Little Chillun,* 1938, *The Swing Mikado,* 1939; Europe, toured
with Noble Sissle in USO show, 1945–46; frequent U.S. State
Department goodwill ambassador to various countries in Europe,
Africa, and the Americas, conducting choirs, lecturing, and hosting
clinics, 1961–75; acted in numerous films and television programs
throughout his career, including *To Kill a Mockingbird, Lady Sings
the Blues, That's My Mama,* and *Amen.* **Teaching Career:** University
of the Pacific Summer Camps, instructor, 1949–ca. 1969; U.S. and
abroad, led numerous workshops and music clinics, beginning
1949. **Honors/Awards:** Honorary doctorates from University of
the Pacific, Stockton, Calif., 1964, University of Massachusetts-
Amherst, 1972, Tufts University, 1972; African Sisters Committee,
Los Angeles mayor's office, citation for achievement and
outstanding contributions to music, 1982.

MUSIC LIST

CHORAL MUSIC

"Amen" (SATB unaccompanied). New York: Bourne, 1957. Recorded:
Epic BN26094; MCA 1500.

"Christmas Gift" (SATB, piano). New York: Schumann Music, 1965.

"Christmas in de Tropics" (tenor soloist, SATB unaccompanied). 1970.
New York: Bourne, n.d.

"Go Down in de Lonesome Valley" (SATB unaccompanied). New York:
Bourne, 1965.

"Goodbye Song" (SATB, piano). New York: Bourne, 1967.

"He's Gone Away" (SSA unaccompanied). New York: Schumann Music,
1957.

"Hold My Mule While I Dance Josey." (SATB unaccompanied). New
York: Bourne, 1960.

"Home in Dat Rock" (SATB, piano). New York: Bourne, 1957.

"I'll Take Sugar in My Coffee-o" (SATB soprano soloist, piano). New
York: J. C. Penney, 1975. Co-composer, Scott.

"Mary, Mary, Where Is Your Baby" (SATB unaccompanied). North
Hollywood, Calif.: Schumann Music, 1950. Recorded: Silver Crest
MOR-111977.

"Mary's Little Boy Child: Calypso Christmas." New York: Bourne, 1956.
Recorded: Sony SK48235.

"No ne li domi" (TTBB unaccompanied). New York: Bourne, 1971.

"Our Troubles Was Hard" (SATB unaccompanied). New York: Bourne,
1961.

"Ring de Christmas Bells" (SATB, soprano soloist, piano). 1972. New
York: Schumann Music, 1972. Recorded: Audio House AHS-
30F75.

"Swing a Lady Gum-Pum" (SATB unaccompanied). New York:
Schumann Music, 1956.

"That Old House Is Ha'nted" (SATB, soprano or tenor soloist, piano).
1970. New York: Bourne, n.d.

"You Better Mind" (SATB unaccompanied). New York: Bourne, 1965.

INCIDENTAL AND COMMERCIAL MUSIC

Tanganyika. 1954. Film soundtrack. Co-composers, Henry Mancini,
Hans Salter, Herman Stein.

PUBLICATIONS

ABOUT HAIRSTON
Books and Monographs

Fullen, M. K. *Pathblazers: Eight People Who Made a Difference.* Seattle,
Wash.: Open Hand Publishers, 1992.

Dissertations

Manzo, Maria Paulette. "A Compositional and Interpretive Analysis of the
Arranged Negro Spiritual, as Represented by the Choral Music of
Jester Hairston." Ph.D. diss., University of Northern Colorado,
1990.

Wyatt, Gwendolyn. "Jester Hairston: His Approach to Spirituals." D.M.A.
diss., Claremont Graduate School, 1996.

Articles

Ramsey, William. "Jester Hairston: Afro-American Ambassador." *Music
Journal* 28 (October 1970): 33, 49.

Sharer, Tim. "Jester Hairston: Background and Interpretation of 'Elijah
Rock.'" *Choral Journal* 20, no. 1 (1979): 34.

BY HAIRSTON

Just Jester. New York: Bourne, 1979.

* * * * *

Jester Hairston made his musical mark in his home base of Los
Angeles. He developed a multifaceted career as an arranger, composer, touring choir leader, singer, actor, and storyteller, and he is
the last African-American musician who works almost exclusively
in the genre of the Negro spiritual. His influence may be felt more
for his talent as an arranger than as a composer; as an arranger,
Hairston is second to none. Hairston also formed and trained his
own racially mixed choir (working particularly as the choral
arranger for Dmitri Tiomkin), which was to perform in such films
as *She Wore a Yellow Ribbon, Carmen Jones, Land of the Pharaohs,
Portrait of Jenny, Foxes of Harrow, Friendly Persuasion, Duel in the
Sun, Red River, Tales of Manhattan, The Long Night, It's a Wonderful*

Life, Tap Roots, and *Three Godfathers.* Tiomkin, who had written the score for the movie *Lost Horizon* in 1937, in which the Hall Johnson choir performed, remembered Hairston and used his choir for his later pictures.

Born in Belews Creek, North Carolina, July 9, 1901, Jester Joseph Hairston was raised in the steel-mill town of Homestead, Pennsylvania, and remained there through his high school years. He had an impoverished home life. His father, Louis Austin Hairston, died when he was barely 14 months old, and his mother worked as a domestic to support the family.

His academic interests centered upon athletics (football) and music, subjects not open for study to blacks at the University of Pittsburgh near his home. He therefore traveled further north in 1920 to attend the Massachusetts Agricultural College (now the University of Massachusetts-Amherst) and studied agriculture for two years before having to drop out to replenish his funds. He also took voice lessons from a private teacher. During the next four years, he worked in the steel mills and later as a waiter on passenger boats that traveled between New York and Boston. Fate intervened in the person of Anna Laura Kidder, a wealthy New England aristocrat who had become aware of his singing abilities and provided the funds to enable him to transfer to Tufts University in Boston. He continued his study of voice and completed his education, graduating *cum laude* in the class of 1929.

Upon graduation, he sought to establish a career in music in New York City. He worked at first with Eva Jessye's choir and other black choirs in Harlem. Then, he went to stand on Seventh Avenue, beside the "Tree of Hope," and was immediately hired for his first real job. Hairston explained in 1985 that "black actors without a job would stand there and rub up against that tree hoping for a job in a show. It's part of our theatrical history—the Tree of Hope." He was hired for a part in the 15-man black chorus in the play *Hello Paris,* which starred the comedian Chic Sales. However, the person in charge of the music stated that he did not feel Hairston could sing well enough and suggested to him that with his background, particularly his ability to read music, Hairston might train the chorus instead. This bit of advice directed his future endeavors, which have been centered ever since in the field of choral directing and arranging. His abilities in this area were strengthened by his study of theory at the Juilliard School of Music.

Hairston joined the Hall Johnson Choir in New York in 1931, where he received his early training in the performance of African-American folk music. He soon became Johnson's assistant conductor, working with him over a period of 13 years. With that group, he appeared in several black Broadway shows in the 1930s, most notably *Run Little Chillun* (1938). He then traveled with the choir to Los Angeles in 1936 to provide the music for the movie version of *The Green Pastures.* Shortly thereafter, the choir worked with Dmitri Tiomkin as he produced the score for the film *Lost Horizon.* Because Hall Johnson was ill during most of the filming, Hairston undertook the responsibility for making most of the choral arrangements and for training the choir. Hairston also performed with Hall Johnson in the Hollywood Bowl George Gershwin Memorial Concert on September 8, 1937, a nationally broadcast performance on CBS memorializing George Gershwin, who had recently died. In 1938 and 1939, Hairston directed WPA

productions of *Run Little Chillun* and *The Swing Mikado* in San Francisco. He performed the role of Koko in *The Swing Mikado,* which was also performed at the San Francisco World's Fair of 1939. When Hall Johnson and the choir returned to New York in 1943, Hairston remained in Los Angeles, which became his permanent residence.

Hairston met Walter Schumann and worked with him both as an arranger and as a soloist with the singing ensemble The Voices of Walter Schumann. Schumann served as Hairston's publisher until his death. Thus arose the series *The Jester Hairston Spirituals,* two books of arrangements that are performed throughout the world.

These works were often introduced to choirs at workshops and choir festivals with Hairston serving as guest clinician. He began this special teaching effort in 1949 at the summer music camps of the College of the Pacific (now the University of the Pacific—UOP). The connections he made at these camps helped create the market for his arrangements. As he explained in 1985, "When the kids went off to their various schools, they told the teachers about the Negro spirituals that they had learned at camp. The teachers began to write to me for copies of them."

Hairston taught at the UOP summer camps for the next 20 years and went on from there to build a special career training hundreds of choirs all over the United States and in foreign countries. He has appeared numerous times with the Mormon Tabernacle Choir and has been a featured artist with the choirs of the Orange County Crystal Cathedral.

Hairston often supported himself in the lean times by working as an actor in film and television shows. He began as an extra in *The Green Pastures* and in Tarzan pictures (including *Tarzan's Hidden Jungle* in 1955) and subsequently played many character roles in film and on television. Among the film roles were parts in *Band of Angels, St. Louis Blues, Samson and Delilah, Stormy Weather, The Alamo, Summer and Smoke, To Kill a Mockingbird, Finian's Rainbow, In the Heat of the Night, Lady Sings the Blues, The Bingo Long Traveling All Stars and Motor Kings,* and *The Last Tycoon.* For 16 years, he played first in bit roles and then in the comedy role of LeRoy, the Kingfish's brother-in-law, and Henry Van Porter on the *Amos 'n' Andy* radio and television shows, and he has had roles in segments of *Gunsmoke* and *The Outcasts.* Hairston arranged the choral music for the film *Lilies of the Field* (1963), and his performance of his colorful arrangement of the song "Amen" was dubbed over Sidney Poitier's voice in the film. He was a regular character on the television shows *That's My Mama* and *Nichols,* and he played Deacon Rolly on *Amen.* He brought his career as a television actor to a close in 1996 with appearances in television commercials for Milk! and Heineken beer, the latter broadcast only in the U.K. and Europe.

Hairston's musical talents have taken him around the world, his frequent travels beginning with a USO tour of Europe with Noble Sissle in 1945–46. In 1961, the State Department sent Hairston to Germany, Austria, and Norway to teach American folk songs, and in 1963, to Germany, Vienna, Yugoslavia, Denmark, Norway, Sweden, and Finland. Hairston describes one of the experiences as follows:

In Bad Godesberg, 1,600 men all together sang in that chorus. I taught them "Amen." You should have heard them.

Jester Joseph Hairston; courtesy of the Eva Jessye Collection, Leonard H. Axe Library, Special Collections, Pittsburgh State University

There were about 1,500 in the audience. I made a little speech in German, telling them that I was especially happy and honored to be sent by my country to honor their 100th anniversary [the choir had been formed in 1863] because, I said, my grandmother was a slave in Virginia. She was set free by Abraham Lincoln with the Emancipation Proclamation in 1863—the same year. She was 18 years old. They set her free along with all the other slaves, and here my country sent me to celebrate their 100th anniversary. Well, when I told them that, they just about brought the house down!

In 1965 and 1966, he served as a State Department goodwill ambassador to Mali, the Ivory Coast, Nigeria, the Cameroons, and Ghana, and in 1968, to Ghana, Senegal, Tanzania, Kenya, Uganda, Madagascar, Zambia, and the Ivory Coast. In 1971 and 1973, he conducted festivals and performed on television specials about spirituals in Denmark. He also recorded an album with a Danish choir of students and teachers entitled *Jester Hairston and His Chorus: A Profile of Negro Life in Song*. In 1975, the State Department sent him to Mexico to teach spirituals to music teachers. Since then, he has traveled abroad with various professional and church-affiliated choirs: to a choir festival in Canada in 1980 and 1984; to China in 1983 and 1984 with the William Hall Chorale; to China in 1985 with the Jester Hairston Chorale; to Tallinn, Estonia, in 1991 with Reverend Schuller and the Crystal Cathedral choirs; and to Spain and Italy in 1993 and 1994 with Gwendolyn Wyatt and the West Los Angeles Spiritual Choir.

In this, the ninth decade of his life, Hairston energetically continues to serve as an ambassador of goodwill and as a clinician. In a recent tribute program, he explained that "I never thought about retiring. I have to work right on up until He calls me. . . . I don't think I could be happy sitting in an old folks home, playing checkers and talking about what we did years ago." John Lovell suggests, "It is very likely that Jester Hairston has been the cause of more people singing spirituals in more places than any other single individual." In appreciation for his accomplishments, Hairston was presented with an honorary doctorate degree from the University of the Pacific in 1964 and from both the University of Massachusetts-Amherst and Tufts University in 1972. He is saluted across the world as one of America's living legends.

Hairston's spirituals are imbued with the authoritative air of his ex-slave grandmother, who lived with the family until her death, and with that of other ex-slaves he interviewed to obtain the correct words and music. His goal has been to unearth the unknown spirituals and bring them to the public in well-thought-out, unsophisticated arrangements that retain their African-American flavor. In a body of music that should be of exceptional interest to high-school, college, and church choral directors, Hairston's spirituals maintain a respectful use of dialect and are harmonically vital, formally cohesive, and rhythmically stimulating.

HANSONIA L. CALDWELL

RING DE CHRISTMAS BELLS (1972)

Although Jester Hairston is best-known for his arrangements of African-American spirituals, his contributions to the choral reper-

tory in the "style" of spirituals are highly original and demonstrate his deep commitment to the genre. "Ring de Christmas Bells," a work for chorus, soprano soloist, and piano, captures the power and expressive nature of the spiritual while infusing it with the energy of calypso.

This work is a strophic formal structure in which the soloist is responsible for the verses while the chorus provides a strong response in the refrain. The Caribbean aspects of the work are revealed immediately, in the piano introduction and its generic calypso rhythmic pattern (3 + 3 + 2). Allusions to the Caribbean, continuing throughout the song, extend to speech patterns as well. These allusions are made explicit in the pronunciation of "the" as "de" in the text. However, Hairston was not necessarily interested in constructing a type of rhythmic or linguistic authenticity within this piece. Rather, he seems to have been interested in borrowing more general aspects of Caribbean rhythmic and speech patterns.

Hairston creates an energetic interaction between the soloist and the chorus throughout the work by calling for syncopated, non-texted lines (la, la, la) that are sung by the chorus while the soloist sings the verses. These non-texted lines create an effect that emulates that of the bell-patterns so characteristic of African and Caribbean musics. The chorus, then, serves as an additional accompanimental instrument during the verses, adding rhythmic complexity to the piano part and providing additional harmonic support to the vocalist. Hairston provides textural contrast in the refrains, which are constructed so that the chorus is divided into two independent groups. The text of the refrain contains three main ideas. Hairston calls for the first group to sing sustained lines to the first idea, "Ring de bells." The second group repeats the first fragment of text and adds the second textual idea, "Ring de bells, shout Christ i' born," singing more rapidly over the sustained notes of the first group. The third idea, "And he shall be King of kings," is sung by both groups, ending the refrain.

The harmonic progression that Hairston uses in the verses (I–IV–V) is altered only slightly in the refrains, where it consists of I–V–I–IV–V–I. The straightforward nature of the progressions contributes to the calypso-like nature of the work. A modulation, which occurs after three verse/refrain pairs and raises the material by a half-step, heightens the intensity of the final verse/refrain pair. This is followed by a final repetition of the refrain, which brings the piece to a close.

"Ring de Christmas Bells" is an excellent example of Hairston's ability to incorporate various other influences (such as calypso) into his style while maintaining the essentially jubilee spiritual-like quality for which he is known, accomplished in part by maintaining a call-and-response pattern between the soloist and the chorus throughout the piece. In addition to its normal scoring, the work has been recorded with Jester Hairston singing the solo part (instead of a soprano) along with additional percussion instruments.

TIMOTHY ROMMEN

MARY'S LITTLE BOY CHILE (1956)

Hairston refers to this choral work as an original Christmas spiritual on West-Indian rhythms. Scored for SATB chorus, soprano soloist, and piano accompaniment, the work is subtitled "Calypso

Christmas," with reference to the syncopated character of the rhythmic structures. In similar fashion to "Ring de Christmas Bells," Hairston utilizes approximate spellings of Caribbean dialects (which, in most cases, amounts to a rather stereotypical replacement of "th" with "d").

This piece once again demonstrates Hairston's ability to emulate traditional elements in his original works. A short piano introduction is followed by a brief passage of untexted choral accompaniment ("la, la, la" [for the sopranos, altos, and tenors] and "tum" [for the basses]). Throughout most of this strophic piece, the basses sing lines identical to the left-hand piano part, adding emphasis to the lower register and helping to punctuate the harmonic processes (which consist primarily of I–IV–V progressions). Conversely, the sopranos, altos, and tenors are responsible for providing harmonic support to the soloist as they continue to sing the untexted material of the introduction. While the harmonic function of the soprano, alto, and tenor lines matches that of the left-hand piano part, Hairston utilizes these voices to introduce added syncopation into the piece. The right-hand piano part can be considered the equivalent of a bell-pattern, while the chorus adds rhythmic intensity to the texture.

The chorus also joins the soloist in singing parts of the text, and Hairston uses a consistent pattern in accomplishing this. At the end of each strophe, there is a short choral response to the soloist during which the chorus sings, "My, my, my Mary boy chile; Jesus Christ, he born on Chris-a-mas day." A total of four strophes of this drawn-out call-and-response pattern are sung, bringing the piece to a close.

The straightforward quality of this piece makes it memorable and singable. It also defines the compositional style of Hairston, who was, above all, interested in conveying the character and sentiment of the traditional African-American spiritual.

TIMOTHY ROMMEN

REFERENCES

Hairston, Jester. Personal interviews with Hansonia L. Caldwell, 1969, 1985, 1995.

———. Personal journals, held by the composer.

Lovell, John. *Black Song: The Forge and the Flame.* New York: Macmillan, 1972. Reprint, New York: Paragon House Publishers, 1986.

Maxwell, Jessica. "Make a Joyful Noise." *PSA Magazine* (July 1979).

Ramsey, William. "Jester Hairston: Afro-American Ambassador." *Music Journal* 28 (October 1970): 33, 49.

Sharer, Tim. "Jester Hairston: Background and Interpretation of 'Elijah Rock.'" *Choral Journal* 20, no. 1 (1979): 34.

Wyatt, Gwendolyn. "Jester Hairston: His Approach to Spirituals." D.M.A. diss., Claremont Graduate School, 1996.

HAKIM, TALIB RASUL

Born Stephen Alexander Chambers, in Asheville, N.C., February 8, 1940; died in New Haven, Conn., April 2, 1988. **Education:** Studied clarinet as a child; sang in church choir; Chester, Pa., public schools, until 1958; Manhattan School of Music, New York, N.Y., studied clarinet and piano, 1958–59; New York College of Music, studied clarinet, composition, and piano, 1959–63; the New School for Social Research, 1963–65; pursued private composition study with teachers, including Robert Starer, William Sydeman, Hall Overton, Morton Feldman, Chou Wen-Chung, Ornette Coleman, David Reck, Hale Smith, Charles Whittenberg, Eric Dolphy, and Margaret Bonds, 1964–67; Adelphi University, Garden City, N.Y., B.A., 1978. **Composing and Performing Career:** Chester High School, Chester, Pa., played in marching band, symphony orchestra, various other instrumental groups; performed with the All-State Orchestra of Pennsylvania; began writing music, 1963; New York, N.Y., pieces performed in the Music in Our Time concert series directed by Max Pollikoff, 1965–69; first publication of his work, "Sound-Gone," 1967; published first book of poems, *Forms on #3,* 1968; numerous performances of his works, 1970s; University of Wisconsin–River Falls, guest artist-in-residence, 1973; Nassau Community College, Garden City, N.Y., produced his own radio program; Brooklyn Philharmonic Community Concert Series, New York, N.Y., co-founder and director, 1976–79. **Commissions:** Brooklyn Chamber Orchestra, 1972; University of Wisconsin–River Falls, 1973; New Haven Symphony Orchestra, 1985. **Teaching Career:** Pace College, New York, N.Y., 1970–72; Nassau Community College, Garden City, N.Y., assistant professor, 1971–81; Adelphi University, Garden City, N.Y., 1972–79; Morgan State University, Baltimore, Md., visiting professor in composition, 1978–79; lecturer and panelist at various schools, including Hofstra University, Hempstead, N.Y., 1968; Barnard College, New York, N.Y., 1969; Bowdoin College, Brunswick, Maine, 1969; University of Connecticut, 1974. **Memberships:** Society of Black Composers, co-founder and president, ca. 1970–72; ASCAP; Black Music Research Associate, Fisk University; Connecticut Composers, Inc.; Creative Musicians Improvisers Forum. **Honors/Awards:** Bennington, Vt., Bennington Composers Conference Fellowship, four times between 1964 and 1969; ASCAP Composers Award, three times between 1967 and 1973; Cultural Council Foundation grant, 1972; National Endowment for the Arts grants, 1973, 1978; Connecticut Commission on the Arts grant, 1981.

MUSIC LIST

INSTRUMENTAL SOLOS
Cello
"Images." 1964. Unpublished manuscript.

Clarinet
"Fragments and Things." Unpublished manuscript.
"Holiday Sketches." Unpublished manuscript.

Prelude for Clarinet and Piano. Unpublished manuscript.
"Segments—Four" (unaccompanied B-flat clarinet). 1981. Unpublished manuscript.

Trombone
Prelude. Unpublished manuscript.

Piano
"Contemplation." 1964. Unpublished manuscript.
"Episodes." 1965. Unpublished manuscript.
"A Piano Piece in Six Sections." 1965. Unpublished manuscript.
"Sectional." 1964. Unpublished manuscript.
"Sound-Gone." 1967. Berlin: Bote and Bock, 1976. Recorded: Composers Recording Inc. CD629; Orion ORS 84357.

SMALL INSTRUMENTAL ENSEMBLE
Strings
"Currents" (string quartet). 1967. Unpublished manuscript.

Woodwinds
"Duo" (flute, clarinet). 1963. New York: Galaxy Music, 1965. Premiere, 1964.
Impressions (woodwind quintet). Unpublished manuscript.
"Moments" (E-flat alto saxophone, bassoon, horn). 1966. Unpublished manuscript.
Peace-Mobile or *Piece-Mobile* (woodwind quintet). 1964. Unpublished manuscript.
"Quartet in Four Sections" (flute/piccolo, oboe/English horn, clarinet/bass clarinet, bassoon). 1965. Unpublished manuscript.
"Titles" (flute, oboe, clarinet, bassoon). 1965. Unpublished manuscript.

Percussion
"Fragments from Other Places—Other Times" (five percussion instruments). 1982. Unpublished manuscript.
"Placements" (piano, five percussion instruments). 1970. Berlin: Bote and Bock, 1975. Recorded: Folkways Records FTS 33901.

Combinations
"Abstractions for Three" (flute, oboe, cello). Unpublished manuscript.
"Contours" (oboe, bassoon, horn, trumpet, cello, double bass). 1966. Unpublished manuscript.
"Elements" (flute/alto flute, clarinet/bass clarinet, violin/viola, cello, piano, glass and bamboo wind and hand chimes). 1967. Unpublished manuscript. Premiere, 1969.
"Encounter" (flute, oboe, clarinet, bassoon, horn, trumpet, trombone). 1965. Unpublished manuscript.
"Evening Impressions" (clarinet, cello, double bass). Unpublished manuscript.
"Excursion" (flute, cello, piano). Unpublished manuscript.
"Excursions: Now and Then" (oboe, viola, trombone, piano). Unpublished manuscript.
"Four" (clarinet, trumpet, trombone, piano). 1965. Unpublished manuscript.

Talib Rasul Hakim; courtesy of C. Zakiah Barksdale-Hakim

"Inner-Sections" (flute, clarinet, trombone, piano, percussion). 1967. Unpublished manuscript.

"Lailatu'l-qadr" (bass clarinet, double bass, percussion). 1984. Unpublished manuscript.

"Mutations" (bass clarinet, horn, trumpet, viola, cello). 1964. Unpublished manuscript.

"Ode to Self" (flute, clarinet in C, cello, double bass). Unpublished manuscript.

"On Being Still—on the 8th" (alto flute, English horn, bass clarinet, bassoon, cello, double bass, piano, percussion). 1978. Unpublished manuscript.

"Parables" (flute, clarinet/bass clarinet, cello, double bass, piano, percussion). 1979. Unpublished manuscript.

"Passages" (flute, clarinet, cello). 1964. Unpublished manuscript.

"Portraits" (alto flute, bass clarinet, piano, three percussion instruments). 1965. Unpublished manuscript.

"Profiles" (clarinet, trumpet, trombone, cello). 1964. Unpublished manuscript.

"Ramadhan Meditations" (flute, oboe, clarinet, bassoon, horn, piano). 1986. Unpublished manuscript.

"Three Play Short Five" (bass clarinet, percussion, double bass). 1965. Unpublished manuscript.

"Timelessness" (flugelhorn, horn, trombone, tuba, percussion, double bass, piano). 1970. Unpublished manuscript.

"Transitions" (trumpet, bass clarinet, horn, viola, cello). Unpublished manuscript.

CHAMBER ORCHESTRA

A-B-C-L-S; 10-27-81 (three trumpets, two trombones, alto, tenor and baritone saxophones, three double basses, three timpani, two vibraphones, drum set, miscellaneous percussion). 1981. Unpublished manuscript.

A Beginning. Unpublished manuscript.

Reflections on the Fifth Ray (narrator, chamber orchestra). 1972. Unpublished manuscript. Note: commissioned by the Brooklyn Chamber Orchestra. Premiere, 1972.

Roots and Other Things (flute/alto flute, oboe/English horn, clarinet/bass clarinet, trumpet, horn, trombone, viola, cello, double bass). 1967. Unpublished manuscript. Premiere, 1968.

Shapes. 1965. Unpublished manuscript. Premiere, 1970. Recorded: Desto DC-7107.

FULL ORCHESTRA

As-Zahir . . . al Batin. 1985–86. Unpublished manuscript.

Bir-ming-ham Reflections (narrator, orchestra). 1985. Unpublished manuscript. Note: commissioned by the New Haven Symphony Orchestra. Premiere, 1986.

Concepts. 1974. Unpublished manuscript.

Connotations. Unpublished manuscript. Note: only the trombone parts for this work are extant.

Re/Currences. 1974. Unpublished manuscript. Premiere, 1975.

Visions of Ishwara. 1970. Berlin: Bote and Bock, 1970. Premiere, 1971. Recorded: CBS P9 19424; Columbia M33434.

ORCHESTRA (CHAMBER OR FULL) WITH CHORUS

Sound-Images (brass ensemble, three percussion, strings, female chorus). 1969. Unpublished manuscript. Premiere, 1969.

Spiritual and Other Fragments from Another Time and Other Places (three alto saxophones, two tenor saxophones, baritone saxophone, three trumpets, two trombones, tuba, percussion, piano, strings, SAT). 1983. Unpublished manuscript.

JAZZ ENSEMBLE

"Rhu-barb." 1976. Unpublished manuscript.

"Sketchy Bluebop." 1973. Unpublished manuscript. Note: commissioned by the University of Wisconsin–River Falls. Premiere, 1973.

SOLO VOICE

"Ode to Silence" (unaccompanied soprano). 1964. Unpublished manuscript.

"The Seeker" (soprano). 1981. Unpublished manuscript.

VOICE WITH INSTRUMENTAL ENSEMBLE

"Chorus—From a Love Poem" (soprano, alto flute, English horn, bass clarinet, horn, trombone, cello, double bass, piano, percussion). 1986. Unpublished manuscript.

"Music for Nine Players and Soprano Voice" (soprano, alto flute, English horn, bass clarinet, horn, trombone, cello, double bass, piano, percussion). 1977. Unpublished manuscript. Premiere, 1977.

"Psalm of Akhnaton: ca. 1365–1348 B.C." (mezzo-soprano, piccolo/flute/ alto flute, piano). 1978. Unpublished manuscript.

"Quote-Unquote" (tenor, oboe, trumpet, percussion). 1983. Unpublished manuscript.

"Set Three" (soprano, cello, piano). Unpublished manuscript.

"Six Players and a Voice" (soprano, clarinet, trumpet, cello, piano, percussion). 1964. Unpublished manuscript. Premiere, 1969.

"Song-Short" (soprano, alto flute, English horn, bass clarinet, horn, trombone). 1967. Unpublished manuscript.

"Tone-Poem" (soprano, piano, double bass, percussion). 1969. Unpublished manuscript. Premiere, 1969.

"Uranian-Projections" (soprano, piano, percussion). 1970. Unpublished manuscript.

"Words and Music" (soprano, oboe, bassoon, xylophone). Unpublished manuscript.

CHORAL MUSIC

"And They Called Him Paul" (SATB). 1976. Unpublished manuscript.

"Tone-Prayers" (SATB, percussion). 1973. Unpublished manuscript. Note: commissioned by the University of Wisconsin–River Falls. Premiere, 1973.

MULTIMEDIA

Arkan-5 (tape, orchestra). 1980. Unpublished manuscript. Premiere, 1980.

PUBLICATIONS

ABOUT HAKIM
Dissertation

Oliver, Christine Evangeline. "Selected Orchestral Works of Thomas J. Anderson, Arthur Cunningham, Talib Rasul Hakim, and Olly Wilson." Ph.D. diss., Florida State University, 1978.

Article

Baker, David N., Lida M. Belt, and Herman C. Hudson, eds. "Talib Rasul Hakim." In *The Black Composer Speaks*, 93–107. Metuchen, N.J.: Scarecrow Press, 1978.

PRINCIPAL ARCHIVES

Talib Rasul Hakim Collection, Center for Black Music Research, Columbia College Chicago, Chicago, Ill.

* * * * *

Talib Rasul Hakim was one of the most individual voices among the American composers who came into prominence in the late 1960s and 1970s. He is remembered for enigmatic titles, avant-garde performance techniques, directed improvisation, atonality, and similar devices that he used to develop his unique compositional sound.

Born Stephen Alexander Chambers, Hakim had ample opportunity to study traditional Western music. His earliest musical experiences came through his family and the church. His first instrument was the clarinet, which he played in his high school band, although he later studied piano and developed a fascination for exotic percussion. He discovered European classical music in high school and admired Beethoven, Mozart, Brahms, and Debussy. After attending high school in Chester, Pennsylvania, graduating in 1958, Hakim moved to New York, studying clarinet and piano at the Manhattan School of Music (1958–59) and taking up composition as well as clarinet and piano at the New York College of Music (1959–63). He also studied composition privately; his composition teachers—among them William Sydeman, Robert Starer, Chou Wen-Chung, Hall Overton, and Hale Smith—were academically trained modernists who also made use of non-Western music and jazz. Although Hakim took an interest in jazz, there is no evidence that he performed it seriously. He named Miles Davis and Ornette Coleman as major influences on his music, but there is little or no overt jazz presence in his compositions.

The strongest influences on Hakim's music appear to have been internal and spiritual: in the 1960s, he became interested in Eastern religions and in Islam, especially in its more personal and mystical forms. An affinity for Sufism, an ecstatic and mystical branch of Islam, led him to adopt his Arabic name in the early 1970s. His spiritual interests are reflected in the titles he employed (*Visions of Ishwara,* "Psalm of Akhnaton," "Ramadhan Meditations," and others) and in the concepts behind his music.

Hakim was a versatile composer. He wrote symphonic pieces, vocal and choral works, and chamber works for various combinations of instruments. In his vocal pieces, he usually employed his own texts, although an exception is his "Tone-Poem" (1969), an adaptation of Langston Hughes' "The Negro Speaks of Rivers." He also used proverbs, biblical texts, sayings of the Buddha, and other Eastern writings, usually in his own adaptations. He tended to treat voices equally with any accompanying instruments; for example, *Spiritual and Other Fragments from Another Time and Other Places* (1983) is scored for various wind instruments, piano, percussion, and wordless SAT choir.

Hakim's earlier chamber works are written for traditional ensembles such as string quartet ("Currents," 1967) and woodwind quintet (*Piece-Mobile,* 1964), but his later pieces are more adventurous in their juxtaposition of instrumental timbres. *A-B-C-L-S; 10-27-81* (1981) uses three trumpets, two trombones, alto, tenor, and baritone saxophones, three double basses, three timpani, two vibraphones, drum set, and miscellaneous percussion. "On Being Still—on the 8th" (1978), for alto flute, English horn, bass clarinet, bassoon, cello, double bass, piano, and percussion, led Tom Johnson, an appreciative critic, to write in the February 20, 1978, issue of the *Village Voice,* "The piece is scored with great care. Without ever resorting to bizarre instrumental techniques, the composer manages to come up with numerous fresh sounds and combinations of sounds." Hakim made extensive use of percussion in his chamber works, a development, perhaps, from his successful "Placements" (1970) for five percussionists and piano, which reflects his habit of going beyond standard drums and timpani to incorporate bells, gongs, and tuned percussion instruments.

His chamber works were well-received, but it was probably as a composer for orchestra that Hakim achieved his greatest success. *Shapes* (1965), *Visions of Ishwara* (1970), *Re/Currences* (1974), and *Bir-ming-ham Reflections* (1985) all received performances, and *Shapes* and *Visions of Ishwara* were commercially recorded. *Bir-ming-ham Reflections,* a setting of Martin Luther King's "Letter from a Birmingham Jail," written for orchestra and narrator and commissioned by the New Haven Symphony, has remained in that orchestra's repertoire. His writing for orchestra gave Hakim the greatest range and opportunity to develop his unique compositional style.

Although some of his earliest extant works (perhaps student compositions) show the influence of serialism and he regularly made use of variations of the chromatic scale, Hakim early abandoned strict academic compositional techniques in order to explore and develop his own style. When asked about his music in the 1970s, as reported by David Baker, he described his style as "percussive," not in the European sense, as loud, or accented, but in its employment of an underlying pulse and rhythmic intricacy characteristic of non-Western music. He implied that the rhythmic density of his music, a texture he described as "heavy," derived from "the African concept of rhythmic nuances." He also described his music as "functional," again in a non-Western (and perhaps African) sense in that it forms part of a "social-political" awareness of his cultural origins. Most of all, however, his music is frankly spiritual, intended to make "both performer and listener . . . experience some degree of inner stirring."

The specific ways in which Hakim achieved these goals are fairly consistent: he used drones or ostinatos of brief, repeated melodic/rhythmic motives; he emphasized scales and intervals rather than harmony, with "chords" made of widely-spaced tone clusters and interlocking intervals (tritones, or fourths and fifths); and his interlocking rhythmic patterns and intervallic juxtapositions make the most of the various instrumental or vocal timbres he employed. Each instrumental part is fairly repetitive, designed to achieve a total effect he described to Baker as "sound continuums—blocks of sound moving."

Hakim employed experimental performance techniques in which the performer is required to play an instrument in nonstandard ways. He also used a process he called "directed improvisation," in which he provided a scale or melodic pattern rather than a completely written part, expecting the performer to improvise rhythmically and melodically within the context of the piece. His scores, therefore, often contain fairly detailed instructions to performers. In these instructions, he seldom used words such as "melody" or "harmony," referring instead to "sound material." Another of his favorite terms was "sound atmosphere," or "sound sphere," referring again to his goal of involving performer and listener in music as a mode of enlightenment.

It is difficult to judge the long-term importance of a man whose career was interrupted by death at the comparatively early age of 48. Certainly he had his share of success during his lifetime: fellowships, performances, a few published scores, and recordings. He made his mark as a teacher and lecturer. While he was academically trained and made his living as an academic, his music is remarkably nonacademic and approachable, and critical response to it seems to have been favorable. His most memorable pieces— "Sound-Gone" for solo piano, for example, or *Visions of Ishwara* for orchestra—undoubtedly succeed at sustaining the musical/spiritual atmosphere he intended. Among 20th-century black composers, his is a unique voice.

For several years after his death in 1988, Talib Rasul Hakim's unpublished music was virtually inaccessible. In 1994, family members placed his scores in the Library and Archives of the Center for Black Music Research, making it possible for his music to be studied and performed.

SOUND-GONE (1967)

In "Sound-Gone," the composer makes use of nontraditional performance techniques and contrasting passages to create his desired "sound-atmosphere" while exploring both the percussive and the expressive possibilities of the piano. The performance notes in the score specifically state that the performance should be "introspective" and "loose-lingering," admonishing that "only where indicated is a precision-like execution desired."

"Sound-Gone" is sectional, with four contrasting sections and a final fifth section that refers to material and devices from earlier sections. The piece begins with a single low *b*-flat, pedaled and allowed to fade. Then comes a slow, upward progression of chords, some of which overlap, ending on a dissonant, open interval (an augmented octave: high *b*-flat and the *b*-natural above) over a lingering chord in the bass. A brief rhythmic passage involving successive open chords (major sevenths and augmented octaves) then introduces the piece's first nontraditional element: the performer is instructed to play one loud "chord" along the keyboard with arms and elbows. A slower passage follows, a series of chromatically moving augmented octaves in the piano's middle range, rising again, and again allowed to fade. Although this section is reminiscent of academic serialism, it is by no means strict, exploring instead the sonorities of dissonant intervals and widely spaced tone clusters and employing changing dynamics to achieve a floating sound.

A dramatic change occurs with the second section: the performer is instructed to play the inside of the piano—to strike the low strings with the hand, to pluck the very top strings, and to "rub, strike, glide, etc. [a] drinking glass at various locations." The performer is in control of "dynamics—duration—sequence—pulse" with only the composer's admonition to "be sensitive and purposeful." This section also closes with widely spaced tone clusters that fade to inaudibility.

The third section of "Sound-Gone" gently introduces other percussive possibilities. Quickly repeated rhythmic and chromatic patterns centered on the note *c*-sharp play over a sustained inner part, producing dissonant intervals (tritones and sevenths) while the bass plays slowly moving octaves. The effect here is one of layering with hints of melodic chromaticism. This percussive and slightly dissonant section sets up the most radical change in the piece: the fourth section is both harmonic and melodic. A rocking ostinato based on an open fifth in the bass uses repeated impressionistic chords (sevenths and ninths) to support a high, wandering melody. Open intervals (fifths, fourths, and octaves) are also explored with quotations of both the percussive patterns and half-step chromaticism of earlier sections. The performer is allowed to "play with" the "descant-like" melody, with the instruction to "be sensitive and tasteful."

The piece ends with a fifth section that reintroduces earlier motives. The wandering descant becomes increasingly abstract until the dissonant sevenths and tritones again predominate over a bass line of parallel fifths. A series of fades and pauses separates the final elements: the bass strings are struck from inside the piano, and a last, widely spread combination of wide intervals (major sevenths: *c*-natural to *b* and *c*-sharp to *d*) fades away. The ultimate sound is a slow rhythm tapped on the sideboard of the piano: a final "sound-gone."

"Sound-Gone," despite its idiomatic exploration of the sounds of the piano, right down to the wood of the sideboard, incorporates elements that are standard in Hakim's compositional vocabulary. These include atonality; the use of percussive patterns, melodic fragments, and ostinatos, usually layered; a fondness for sevenths, tritones, fourths, and fifths, and for tone clusters, usually widely spaced to mitigate their dissonance; and a willingness to give a performer scope for controlled improvisation and experimental techniques. In the process, the listener recognizes the piano as a percussion instrument and perceives the effective melodic contrast in the fourth section and the closing reiteration of earlier elements, fading away, leaving one waiting for the final sound, the sound that will not be heard.

"Sound-Gone" was often programmed by the late Natalie Hinderas, who recorded it in 1970. Reviewers of the Hinderas recording of "Sound-Gone" dwell on the piece's avant-garde qualities, particularly the use of experimental performance techniques. Howard Klein describes the effect of the piece as "eerie. . . . It mixes melodic and rhythmic keyboard passages with sounds produced by scraping the strings while the sustaining pedal is depressed, producing a beautifully lyrical and haunting effect." Albert Frankenstein describes the piece as "a pianistic sonority study making much use of the plucked strings, strings made to sound by friction of the hand, cavernous tone clusters and all such; in addition there is an episode . . . which is simply tuneful and quiet and sparsely harmonized." He singles out "Sound-Gone" as the finest piece on the entire recording, calling it "a masterpiece."

VISIONS OF ISHWARA (1970)

The theme of this work is taken from Hindu mythology, in which, according to the liner notes of the recording, Ishwara is a manifestation of Brahma, the ultimate godhead, made accessible to his "ultimate creation: Man." The piece is quite programmatic, depicting a spiritual journey with three orchestral "visions"—flashes of enlightenment or encounters with the god—along the way.

The three central orchestral sections of *Visions of Ishwara* build to a climax and are bracketed by a wandering melody in the alto flute set against a muted bass drum. The drum beat, written first in 4/4 time, then in 3/4, then again in 4/4, always followed by a quarter rest, sets the basic pulse of the entire work. The time-changes from 4/4 to 3/4 and back, over which the flute melody is stated, underscore the importance of pulse over time signature, because it is only a written change, imperceptible to the hearer. The flute melody consists largely of dissonant tritone leaps (written as diminished fifths or augmented fourths) that resolve to open consonant intervals (perfect fourths or fifths).

After the brief flute introduction come the contrasting timbres of the instruments of the orchestra, which create the first sound block—the first "vision." The winds begin with interlocking ostinato patterns, more rhythmic than melodic, subdividing the drum pulses with heavily accented (*sforzando*) entrances on off-beats or with triplet patterns. The most melodic wind parts, the English horn and bass clarinets, stress open, slightly different intervals (sev-

enths and ninths). The low brasses then enter with their own ostinato of widely spaced tone clusters. When the horns and trumpets enter, they play overlapping tritones and overlapping minor seconds while the cellos enter with parallel fifths in tremolo. When the brasses enter, the bass drum pulse is replaced with quick seven- and five-note patterns on the timpani, a suggestion of increasing suspense and change. The bassoon and marimba double on an agitated 16th-note pattern, alternating very close intervals with more open and dissonant ones (chromaticism with tritone jumps) accompanied by a five-note pattern on the timpani, which is then taken up by the cellos. Finally, the high strings begin fifths and fourths in tremolo while the clarinets and flutes play chromatic 16th notes. A climax is signaled by snare drum rolls: the entire orchestra is engaged, and the sound block for the first "vision" is in place.

The first section ends with an almost instantaneous *diminuendo,* as most of the instruments drop out. The high winds continue their short patterns while the snare drum and timpani play a roll and the tuba holds a low drone. The tuba becomes the basis for a new ostinato as the bassoons and bass clarinets add widely spaced additions to the tone cluster in alternating rhythmic patterns. This time, the sound block builds more quickly, beginning with the alto flute and the English horn playing quick, angular tritone passages. The percussion is more pronounced: temple blocks play a jumpy pattern of alternating 16th notes in groups of six and five. Flute, oboe, and clarinet add a sustained chordal pattern, and immediately the trumpets play a quick dotted fanfare motive in closely packed intervals (minor seconds). *Pizzicato* (plucked) cellos and upper strings playing in tremolo enter, executing a pattern of chromatic 16th notes while the horns play sustained parallel fourths. The percussion again indicates a climax: temple bells play major sevenths against a continuously ringing triangle. Once again, all parts of the musical structure are in place, and a second "vision" has been achieved.

This time, a change is signaled more slowly, by triplet figures in the bass clarinet and bassoon. The high winds drop out, leaving *agitato* strings, chimes playing an open fifth on the second beat of every measure, and droning chords in the trombones and horns. The third "vision" is, however, more intense; this section builds rapidly. The strings continue, and with the snare drum, the horns and brasses enter together, playing interlocking fanfare patterns that are punctuated by a repeated single loudly accented 16th-note pattern played by the trumpets in interlocking fifths. Just as suddenly, everything stops, leaving only the single-note drone in the tuba. A gong announces quick *pizzicato* triplet figures in the cellos and basses against open fifths and fourths played with tremolo in the strings. The timpani commences an alternating pattern of 16th notes in groups of six and five. This rhythmic agitation once more signals a climax: the rest of the orchestra immediately enters playing a single chord on the first and third beats against an off-beat drone in the tuba. This massive chord is built of the intervals that have been featured throughout the piece: ninths in the trombones, minor seconds in the trumpets, tritones in the horns, a perfect fourth in the bassoons, and widely spaced tone clusters in the upper winds. Timpani and sleigh bells provide rhythmic agitation against this unchanging orchestral chord, which is sounded squarely on beats one and three until three final one-beat blasts signal an ultimate sustained sound. Even as this climax occurs, the bass drum once more sounds the pulse that began the opening section. Then the orchestra fades, and a reprise of the wandering flute melody closes the piece.

Visions of Ishwara substantiates Hakim's claim that his music is percussive rather than melodic or harmonic. Certainly, percussion figures prominently in the piece, but standard instruments are also utilized to achieve its rhythmic complexity. The instrumental patterns cannot usually be described as melodic, and they depend for their interest on the ways in which they interlock, interact, or contrast rhythmically with other parts. Even drone patterns are interlocking. Harmonically, the piece is atonal, depending as it does on short, repeated units combined with drones. Hakim piles up his favorite intervals (seconds, ninths, and tritones), often resolving them or combining them with fourths and fifths. He uses the full pitch range of the orchestra, preferring bass instruments at their lowest ranges and high winds and strings at their highest. The combination of rhythmic patterns, atonal harmonies, and a spectrum of instrumental timbres creates the sound blocks from which he builds, quite literally, this particular "sound-atmosphere."

Visions of Ishwara for orchestra was premiered by the Symphony of the New World in 1970 and recorded in 1975 by Paul Freeman and the Baltimore Symphony as part of CBS Records' Black Composers Series. Volume 8 of the series, on which it appears, was issued in 1975. Alfred Frankenstein once again singles out a piece by Hakim for his highest praise. He describes *Visions of Ishwara* as "a great, shaggy, harsh piece, infinitely larger in its implications than its relatively modest (nine minute) time span would indicate." He calls it "serious, heroic and inspired . . . great music on a great theme."

RAMADHAN MEDITATIONS (1986)

Ramadhan is the month in the Islamic calendar devoted to prayer and fasting, and the composer's performance instructions state that "for the overall success of this work, it is essential that the performers make a serious effort to transport themselves into a quiet-meditative state of consciousness." The goal is to achieve "a quiet-meditative sound-sphere." Like Hakim's earlier pieces, "Ramadhan Meditations" is sectional, with five distinct sections labeled A through E, although "movement from one sound-material to the next should be smooth/easy/flowing," and not give a sectional feeling. The piano is the pivotal instrument, "the center around which the other materials evolve."

Like "Sound-Gone," "Ramadhan Meditations" makes use of experimental techniques. To begin the piece, the pianist is instructed to play the inside of the piano in the lower/middle range with a timpani mallet, swelling the sound and then fading it away. The piano then begins an ostinato quarter-note pattern in 6/4, on the note *f,* against a chromatic pattern alternating between *a*-flat and *g* but accented on the first and third beats, over a bass line of dotted half notes that alternate between low *g*-flat and *e*-flat below. The tone cluster is widely spaced, and the rhythm equivocal: six equally accented quarter notes over a chromatic two-note pattern accented on alternating *a*-flats and *g* naturals over a bass line in two. This rhythmic interplay stresses the importance of the quarter-note pulse.

The horn enters on the half beat with a syncopated one-note ostinato on *a,* followed by the bassoon on the second beat with a deliberate two-note ostinato on *d* and *e.* When the upper parts enter, they do so on the three beats of a quarter-note triplet, with a sustained two-octave chord stretching from middle *c* to *b*-natural above to high *b*-flat. After a few repetitions, the piano ostinato slows to conclude the section. Extreme dissonance has been avoided by the spread of the tone clusters over a wide pitch range—in spite of the presence of a series of notes within a half tone or whole tone of each other. The atmosphere established is one of sustained, meditative sound, despite its rhythmic complexity.

The piano continues its repetition of the note *f,* this time in a triplet-based pattern, to begin section B, although it adds sustained wide intervals (sevenths) in the treble and a line that descends slowly from *e*-flat to *d*-flat to the *b*-flat under the *f* ostinato. The upper instruments play another widely spread tone cluster (*a*-flat–*b*-*a*), and the bassoon adds another slow bass pattern that moves in fourths and fifths. Once this ostinato is established, the horn does the unexpected, quoting against it the first two lines of the well-known "Pilgrim's Chorus" from Wagner's opera *Tannhäuser.* Section C, which follows after a brief pause, is equally unexpected: it consists of a hymn-like passage in parallel harmony, quartal if not tonal, to be played "in the manner of the traditional Negro Spiritual," with the markings "Mournful—Soulful—Rubato." The composer clearly intends to emphasize this section, so different in sound from the preceding (and following) material. Both sections B and C, introducing music from his varied musical heritage, are striking and thought-provoking.

Section D begins with another slow piano ostinato, this time on low *c*-sharp, with a syncopated beat. The right hand plays an *a*-flat, accented but held. The clarinet (alternating *e* and *e*-flat) and bassoon (on *b* to *g* to *a*) play short patterns on the beat, while the horn enters on the half beat with a single-note drone on *d.* This "chord" is, again, a widely spaced tone cluster, although high notes are lacking: the piano's *a*-flat above middle *c* is the highest sounding note. Once the ostinato is established, the flute and oboe, entering separately, are given overlapping four-note "scales" (the oboe on *a, b, c*-sharp, and *d*-sharp, the flute on *c, d*-flat, *e*-flat, and *e*-natural), and instructed to "create several short-long melodic sound materials that relate to the overall sound atmosphere of the ostinato material." (A variant score has parts for the flute and oboe written out against more meticulous timings in the ostinato parts, perhaps so that musicians uncomfortable with directed improvisation have an alternative available.)

The final section, section E, repeats the ostinato material in section A, with a few sustained chords at the end. Again, the composer begins and ends his piece with the same contemplative strain. Other compositional devices in "Ramadhan Meditations" are similar to the composer's *Visions of Ishwara*: short, rhythmic/melodic motives; interlocking rhythms with a pulse either implied or played; widely spaced tone clusters; and layered ostinatos created by incremental entrances until the desired "sound atmosphere" has been achieved. In this case, it is sustained, slow, and meditative.

Against these devices, however, Hakim has juxtaposed music from his various cultures: the European Judeo-Christian (and classical music) past of Wagner's *Tannhäuser* and his own African-American heritage of spirituals. He has provided (for the month of Ramadhan) a commentary on the concept of pilgrimage, so important in Islam, concluding with an improvisatory section that perhaps represents his own response to this heritage and his own journey beyond into mysticism. Within its meditative aura, the music, simpler in its way than *Visions of Ishwara* or even "Sound-Gone," invites a spectrum of intellectual and emotional responses from the listener.

"Ramadhan Meditations" is a late chamber work for woodwind quintet and piano that exemplifies a refinement of both the spirituality and the musical techniques of Hakim's earlier works. It was performed at least once, although it has not been published or commercially recorded. The score and a tape cassette recording of an unidentified performance are held in the Talib Rasul Hakim Collection at the Center for Black Music Research.

REFERENCES

Baker, David, Lida M. Belt, and Herman C. Hudson, eds. "Talib Rasul Hakim." In *The Black Composer Speaks,* 93–107. Metuchen, N.J.: Scarecrow Press, 1978.

Frankenstein, Albert. Review of "Sound-Gone." *High Fidelity* (February 1971).

———. Review of *Visions of Ishwara. High Fidelity* (October 1975).

Johnson, Tom. "Talib Rasul Hakim Has Found His Music." *Village Voice* (February 20, 1978): 80.

Klein, Howard. "Overdoing Benign Neglect." *New York Times* (March 7, 1971).

SUZANNE FLANDREAU

HALL, FREDERICK DOUGLASS

Born in Atlanta, Ga., December 14, 1898; died in Atlanta, December 28, 1982. **Education:** Began keyboard study with his mother, age five; Atlanta, studied piano with Hattie Kelly, voice and piano with Sidney Woodward, voice with Emma Azalia Hackley; early education in Atlanta's public schools; Morehouse College, Atlanta, studied music theory, history, piano, and strings with Kemper Harreld, B.A., 1921; Pittsburgh Musical Institute, Pittsburgh, Pa., studied theory and composition with Charles M. Boyd, summer 1921; Chicago Musical College, B.Mus., 1924; Columbia University Teachers College, New York, N.Y., M.A., 1929, Ph.D., 1952; additional study, Royal College of Music, London, England, and London Academy of Music, 1933–35; West Africa, studied folk music, 1935. **Composing and Performing Career:** As a boy, sang in church choirs, played various instruments with school groups and the Atlanta Theatre Orchestra; began writing music at an early age; Mt. Olive Baptist Church, Atlanta, music director, 1915–21; composed the alma-mater hymns for Jackson College and Dillard University. **Teaching Career:** Jackson College, Jackson, Miss., 1921–26; Jackson, Miss., part-time supervisor of music for the public schools, 1921–26; Clark College, Atlanta, 1926–33; Morris Brown College, Atlanta, director of music, 1926–33; Gammon Theological Seminary, Atlanta, lecturer on hymn interpretation and hymnology, 1926–33; School of Social Work, Atlanta University, lecturer on socialized music, 1926–33; Dillard University, New Orleans, La., 1935–41, 1960–74; Alabama State College, Montgomery, music department chairman, 1941–55; Southern University, Baton Rouge, La., 1955–60; Morehouse College, Distinguished Visiting Professor, 1975. **Memberships:** National Association of Music Teachers in Negro Schools, founder, ca. early 1940s; Phi Mu Alpha Sinfonia, New York chapter vice president, ca. 1951–52; Phi Delta Kappa. **Honors/Awards:** Julius Rosenwald Fellowship, 1929; General Education Board Fellowship, 1934–35; Phelps-Stokes Fund Research Grant, 1935; fellow of the Royal Anthropological Institute, 1935; citation made by Representative Augustus Hawkins in the Congressional Record of the United States, April 30, 1964; Distinguished Service Citation, National Fellowship of Methodist Musicians, 1969.

MUSIC LIST

INSTRUMENTAL SOLOS
Piano
Suite for Piano, op. 5, no. 1, or *Suite Romantique* or *Romantic Suite*. ca. 1936. Unpublished manuscript. Contents: At Twilight; The Canebreak; The Brooklet.

SOLO VOICE
A Cycle of Afro-American Religious Songs. ca. 1948. Winona Lake, Ind.: Rodeheaver, 1949. Contents: Lord, How Come Me Here?; Po' Me; How Long Befo' the Sun Go Down?; Day Is Done; Get Up Chillun.
Four Songs, op. 4. 1926. Winona Lake, Ind.: Rodeheaver, 1926. Contents: Dawn; Morning; Mandy Lou; Good Night.

CHORAL MUSIC
"Fair Dillard." ca. 1936. New Orleans, La.: Dillard University, 1966.
"Violets" (SSAA and soloist). Unpublished manuscript.

DRAMATIC MUSIC
Adi Dako and His Songs (pageant/play). ca. 1936–37. Unpublished manuscript.
The Birth of a Song (pageant). ca. 1937. Unpublished manuscript. Premiere, 1937.
Deliverance (oratorio). 1938. Winona Lake, Ind.: Rodeheaver, 1963.
Heritage (pageant). ca. 1938–39. Unpublished manuscript.
Pearly Gates (pageant). Unpublished manuscript. Premiere, 1936.
Youth for God and Country (pageant). 1970. Unpublished manuscript. Contents: Scene I: Voices from Africa; Scene II: In a Strange Land; Scene III: A Call to Worship; Scene IV: In the Midst of Oppression/A Proclamation; Scene V: Christian Education; Scene VI: The Living Cross/Calvaree; Scene VII: The Living Flag; Finale: For God and Country (Convention Youth Hymn). "Youth Hymn," Nashville, Tenn.: Townsend Press. Premiere, 1970.

NOT VERIFIED
"Angels Done Changed My Name" (two pianos); "Sinner, Please Don't Let This Harvest Pass" (two pianos).

PUBLICATIONS

ABOUT HALL
Dissertation
Prescott, Camille J. "A Selected Work by Frederick Douglass Hall, Sr., Transcribed for Strings and Piano with Historical Documentation." M.M. thesis, Bowling Green State University, 1986.

Articles
Bowers, Violet G. "In Retrospect: Frederick Douglass Hall—He Was My Teacher." *Black Perspective in Music* 8, no. 2 (1980): 215–242.
Phillips, Romeo Eldridge. "Some Perceptions of Gospel Music." *Black Perspective in Music* 10, no. 2 (1982): 167–178.

BY HALL
"A New Program in Music Education for the Teacher Training College." Ph.D. diss., Columbia University, 1952.

PRINCIPAL ARCHIVE
Frederick Hall Archives, Atlanta, Georgia.

* * * * *

Frederick Douglass Hall is often described as an "educator-composer," indicating that he placed service to his students as his primary goal even though he possessed a keen and uncommon quality as a composer. As a musical arranger, Hall's contributions are enviable. He stands in the top echelon of arrangers of African-American

Frederick Douglass Hall; courtesy of Dr. Frederick D. Hall Jr. (former chairman of the Division of Fine Arts, Spelman College)

spirituals and folk music. Although not very prolific as a composer, his contributions are serious and genuine works.

In the era of the Negro Renaissance, many artists and scholars were intimately involved in the major activities at the heart of the movement in Harlem; many responded and moved to the city. Others, however, remained on the periphery and responded to the call in their own way. Such a person was Frederick Douglass Hall, who was named for the abolitionist, orator, and journalist Frederick Douglass. During her pregnancy with Hall, his mother, Laura, was so impressed by a speech given by the elder statesman that she promised, if her child was a boy, to name him after Douglass.

Hall's mother and father, Samuel, were both teachers in Atlanta. Widowed at an early age, his mother was responsible for his and his four sisters' upbringing. She recognized early his musical talent and taught him to play the reed organ. When he was nine, the family acquired a piano, and he began to write short pieces. His first piano teacher was Hattie Kelly. Also aware of Hall's talent, the school music supervisor introduced him to the music director of the First Presbyterian Church, where he attended weekly rehearsals of the chorus and continued to develop his musical skills. In 1915, while still a teenager, Hall became director of music at the Mt. Olive Baptist Church and remained there until he graduated from Morehouse in 1921 with a bachelor of arts degree.

The range of Hall's music experiences was expanded when he entered the private high school at Morehouse College, where he studied music theory and history, piano, and string instruments with violinist Kemper Harreld, performed in both the glee club and orchestra, sang in the Morehouse Quartet, and served as accompanist for college events and for local and visiting artists. In the summer after graduation in 1921, he studied theory and composition with Charles Boyd, editor of the American Supplement for the *Grove Dictionary of Music,* in Pittsburgh, Pennsylvania. He then went to Jackson College in Mississippi where he had been hired to develop a music program. He also received permission to become a part-time supervisor of music for the Negro public schools. He held these positions until 1926. Among his many activities, he also formed a community chorus to create more local support for the college, especially its music program. In later academic appointments, he would form similar organizations for similar purposes. All the while, he continued to refine his skills as an arranger, especially in the areas of folk music and the spiritual.

Meanwhile, in 1923, Homer Rodeheaver, the song leader with the Billy Sunday Crusade, had visited Jackson. While there, he met Hall, and the result was the publication and recording of many of Hall's works by the Rodeheaver Music Publishing Company and its Rainbow Record label. The next year, John Finley Williamson of the Westminster Choir (then in Ohio) asked Hall for eight-part arrangements and programmed them for performances in the United States and in Europe. In 1925, Dudley Buck Jr. of the Dudley Buck Singers heard the Westminster Choir in a Carnegie Hall performance, and this led to a request by Buck for more eight-part arrangements ("Carry Me Back to Ole Virginny" and "My Old Kentucky Home").

From 1921 to 1974, Hall was associated with several black colleges, including Jackson College in Mississippi, Clark College and Morris Brown College in Atlanta, Dillard University in New Orleans, and Southern University in Baton Rouge. He took time off during 1933–35, when he lived and studied first in England and later in Africa. On the day he left for New York to sail to Europe in September 1933, he married pianist Mildred Greenwood, a fellow musician and associate, who accompanied him on his foreign travels.

While pursuing the master of arts and doctorate degrees in music education at Columbia University Teachers College (New York City), he studied with Peter Dykema and Howard Murphy; he did additional work at the Institute of Musical Arts (now the Juilliard School) with Percy Goetschius, a highly influential theorist of the day. Through Dykema, Hall was introduced to Herbert Weissman, a prominent conductor in Edinburgh, Scotland, who recommended that Hall study vocal music and singing in Cardiff, Wales. Before Hall did so, he studied at the Royal College of Music in London, with Arthur Benjamin in composition and R. O. Morris in counterpoint. He was encouraged in his studies by Sir Adrian Boult. While in England, Hall was fortunate to meet Dr. Albert Schweitzer, who not only gave the American tips on travel to Africa but also discussed with him his interest in Negro spirituals and improvised on a spiritual melody for him.

After his stay in London, Hall and his wife went to Cardiff and stayed for several months. Wales, its music, and its people made a deep, positive impression on them. Then came six months in West Africa, where Hall studied the music of parts of that region and began to consider its relationship with African-American practices. On his return to London, he lectured about his travels and study for the Royal Anthropological Institute and was made a Fellow of the Institute.

Hall's American destination was Dillard University in New Orleans, where he arrived in 1935 and became responsible for planning a well-balanced liberal arts program in music and a strong music education curriculum. During his six-year stay, he expanded his compositional range by writing larger works, including the oratorio *Deliverance* and the pageant *Pearly Gates.*

From 1941 to 1955, Hall taught at Alabama State College in Montgomery, where he planned statewide programs in music, both graduate and undergraduate. In 1955, he heeded a call from Southern University in Baton Rouge, Louisiana, to assist the university in receiving accreditation by the National Association of Schools of Music. In 1960, Hall returned to New Orleans and Dillard University, where he spent the remainder of his long and successful career, which he brought to a close with retirement in 1974.

As a composer and arranger, Hall's contributions are impressive. He wrote primarily for voices, solo or in chorus, and the majority of his works are arrangements, especially of spirituals. Characteristic of his direct and dignified style of composition is his *A Cycle of Afro-American Religious Songs,* on texts by Hall and "composed after the manner of the spiritual," which was frequently performed by the tenor Roland Hayes.

Hall's legacy includes not only his musical works but also his varied and influential contributions as a music educator, especially as a choral music conductor. He was a teacher's teacher and, as many of his students claim, "I am happy to say, he was my teacher." Hall has said that his reward came from having been able to develop successful and serviceable leaders for our society, especially for African-American leadership in music.

FOUR SONGS, OP. 4 (1926)

The four short but sensitive settings that make up this cycle, all on texts of Paul Laurence Dunbar, one of America's leading African-American poets, are early examples of Hall's compositional style. The four songs that comprise the collection are "Dawn," "Morning," "Mandy Lou," and "Good Night." Clothed in the traditional art-song style of the romantic period, they display a complete fusion of words and music, with the accompaniment supporting the painting of the text as well as the melodic line.

The accompaniment in "Dawn" begins and ends with running 16th-notes in the treble with supporting chords in the bass. The short middle section employs a descending chromatic passage that mirrors the vocal melody, with syncopated chords in the left hand descending chromatically. A tertian relationship from G to B-flat and back to G—by way of secondary dominants and other altered chords—determines the tonal scheme, and the short movement ends with a beautiful and lyrical *ppp* on the final words, "Man called it Dawn."

In contrast to the other three songs, the text of "Mandy Lou," from Dunbar's poem "Dreamin' Town," uses dialect. Choosing a musical style that complements the text, Hall has set this song in a "minstrel style," with a wavering, syncopated melodic line that is mirrored in the piano accompaniment. "Mandy Lou" follows a *da capo*-like plan, using a structural scheme of AABAA, with a harmonic scheme of A-flat-F minor (B section)-A-flat. In the A section (*Allegro moderato*), with its syncopated melodic line, the protagonist paints a happy-go-lucky picture for Mandy Lou: "Come away to dreamin' town, whaih de skies don' nevah frown . . . Whaih de street is paved with gol', Whaih de days is nevah col'."

In the B section (*Andante cantabile*), plaintive and melancholy, the piano accompaniment becomes a series of rolling, arpeggiated chords that descend chromatically to the dominant by the end of the first eight measures. The second eight measures proceed in the same manner, at first hesitating, then moving chromatically to the dominant, fulfilling the plea of the protagonist—the lover—to come "to the place [with me where] my love will be its crown . . . whaih dreams is king . . . An' my soul kin always sing Mandy Lou."

In the serene and peaceful setting of the final song, "Good Night," Hall sets off the text "Good night my love, Good night, good night" at the end of each of the three sections of this short work. With different elaborations in the melodic texture, these short closing sections each vary in mood and quality.

The form of "Good Night" is rounded binary with an extension (ABA'). It begins with an eight-measure instrumental introduction followed immediately by the voice in another eight-measure phrase. The piano accompaniment displays arpeggiated chords and harmony that are similar to those in the introduction. The next group of phrases articulates the same words: "Sleep love and peaceful be thy rest." This section ends as it began in the key of C, abruptly modulating to the subdominant, the key of F, for the B section. The key change is accompanied by a meter change to 6/8 for the B section. The slowly rollicking, dream-like movement—marked *con moto*—portrays "Dreams [to] attend thee . . . To soothe thy rest . . . and angels [to] keep vigil [over] thee." *Tempo primo* brings a return to the melodic and harmonic texture

of the opening section. The uneven phrases of the final A' section mirror the similar phrasing in the first A section. Several key areas are related to the C major tonality of the work by way of secondary dominants (V of V, V of vi, and V of IV). The final melodic line, which sets "Good night, my love," is characteristically chromatic—*g, f*-sharp, *f, e*, which is mirrored in the piano.

DELIVERANCE (1938)

Deliverance, the largest of Hall's works, is an oratorio for full chorus; soprano, tenor, and baritone solos; and piano accompaniment. In the 1930s, *Deliverance* was written and performed from manuscript at Dillard University during Hall's first tenure at that institution, but the vocal score was not published until 1963. The dedication gives an idea of his vision for the work: "To Dr. Homer A. Rodeheaver [Hall's close friend and publisher], whose interest in better religious music, whose efforts toward making life more abundant for the thousands who had the privilege of contact with him, and whose concern in the DESPAIR of any people, with delight in their HOPE and satisfaction in their DELIVERANCE, and To my mother, whose musical genius and Christian fortitude inspired and guided me through the years, this work is humbly dedicated." In the introduction to the work, Hall writes that "In several sections of the Old Testament writers tell the story of the despair, hope, and deliverance of the Hebrew Children. The lot of the Children of Israel has been shared by people of all races and creeds through the ages. In bondage and under oppression they despair, but if they hope and pray in earnest the God of the ages will deliver them!"

The oratorio is divided into three parts—"Despair," "Hope," and "Deliverance"—each part having five movements, resulting in a 15-movement sequence of arias (airs) and recitatives, choruses, and other ensemble combinations (e.g., duos and trios). "Despair" begins with the biblical lament "My God, My God, why hast thou forsaken me?" set for soprano and chorus. "Hope," the second section, contains a soprano air, "I will lift up mine eyes unto the hills from whence cometh my help," and a duet for soprano and tenor entitled "The Lord is my portion . . . Therefore will I hope in Him." "Deliverance," the final section, sums up the relief with joy and happiness in two choruses, "Come let us sing unto the Lord a new song" (no. 13) and "The Lord is my light and my salvation, whom then shall I fear" (no. 15).

Unlike R. Nathaniel Dett, who used African-American musical sources as the basis of his two early oratorios, *The Chariot Jubilee* (1921) and *The Ordering of Moses* (1937), Hall wrote in the more romantic style favored by many of his colleagues of the time. The choral and chorale-like passages, sometimes unaccompanied, are highly tinged with chromaticism and contain imitative sections. The chorale melody and the basic harmonization used in the chorus, "Hear the Voice of My Supplication" (no. 4), are used again in the final chorus (no. 15), "The Lord Is My Light," which serves to unify the work.

The trio "As the Hart Panteth" (no. 5), for female chorus—sopranos 1 and 2 and alto—hints of Mendelssohn's "Lift Thine Eyes" from the oratorio *Elijah*. As Mendelssohn had written his great oratorios under the influence of Bach, Hall probably received inspiration from Mendelssohn and Haydn. One of the first oratorios Hall had learned at the First Presbyterian Church of Atlanta, the large church in Atlanta where he sat at the foot of "his Mr. Smith," was Haydn's oratorio *The Creation*. In fact, as a young male soprano, he had sung from this work the aria "In Verdure Clad."

Movements 4, 8, and 15 illustrate the compositional style of *Deliverance*. Movement no. 8, "The Lord Is My Portion," a duet for soprano and tenor from the first section, is possibly the most popular piece in the entire work. After a short introduction in the key of F major, the soprano sings the first two phrases, which give melodic shape to the thematic material that will dominate the movement. After modulating to the dominant, the soprano soars through the first part, written in a Schubertian manner, with its floating chords and harmonies. It moves to remote keys through chromatic alteration, finally returning to the key of F by way of an augmented sixth chord. The tenor then enters with the melodic idea from the opening four measures, which had been sung by the soprano. The soprano and tenor, alternating back and forth with this original melodic idea, bring the opening section to a close.

The B section, moving to the key of B-flat minor, capitulates the back-and-forth motion of the two voices—the tenor initially responding in short contrapuntal spurts, later joining the soprano as they prepare to reenter the key of F through a sequence of augmented sixth chords. The piece closes with a recapitulation of the original melodic idea. A four-measure instrumental *ritornello* ends the movement as it began. The schematic design for the movement is ABA'—rounded binary.

Choruses no. 4, "Hear the Voice of My Supplication," and no. 15, "The Lord Is My Light," are unified by a common chorale melody. The words are different, but the harmonization of the chorale melody is basically the same. In each movement, the chorale is preceded and followed by a short fugal section. The meter changes from a rollicking 6/8 to a more subtle and moderate 4/4 that prepares for the chorale. The chorales in both movements follow a traditional ABA' form. In no. 4, after the chorale, there is a change of key and then a move to a brief *fugato* section. This movement closes in chorale style.

No. 15, "The Lord Is My Light," is the most powerful and dramatic choral section of *Deliverance*. The movement begins with a short fugal section in C major, moving chromatically with unresolved secondary dominants and cadencing on the dominant of the key; then it moves directly into the chorale from no. 4, which, as in no. 4, is followed by another fugue-like section. This leads to a repeat of the first eight measures of the movement. On the words "Amen" and "Alleluia," another *fugato* section follows. The coda is a powerful choral section in which a string of secondary dominants and chromatically altered chords digress from, then return to, the home key of C, effecting a dramatic close to a project that moves from despair, through hope and deliverance by faith.

Deliverance is an ambitious work, especially for a composer most comfortable with small forms and relatively short musical essays. The work has been performed in whole or in part throughout the United States, including a performance with the New Orleans Black Chorale. Because of the dense chromaticism found in *Deliverance*, and a number of unaccompanied chorales, a strong choral group is needed for a successful performance.

A CYCLE OF AFRO-AMERICAN RELIGIOUS SONGS (CA. 1948)

In these five wonderful settings from *A Cycle of Afro-American Religious Songs*, Hall has composed sincere but simple and dignified portraits of authentic spirituals. The cycle goes from despair in the plight of enslaved blacks in the first three settings, to hope in "Day Is Done" ("I thank God day is done"), to deliverance from a workaday syndrome (working in the hot southern sun from morning to night), to dance/pantomime as catharsis from the weary burdens of the long day.

Hall created these songs from the imagined plight and feelings of the slaves, conceiving them from this thesis: "After an unpleasant trip across the ocean aboard the slave ship, the worker finds himself in a strange land." The five songs and summaries of their theme, as expressed by their composer, are: "Lord, How Come Me Here?" (When the African laments, he usually exclaims "I wish I'd never been born"); "How Long Befo' the Sun Go Down?" (He toils from sunrise to sunset, and always welcomes the end of the day); "Po' Me, Po' Me" (He pities himself and calls upon the Lord to take him away); "Day Is Done" (As shadows gather, he shoulders his implements and moves wearily toward the cabin in the distance); and "Git Up Chillun" (Tired from the work of the day, but never too burdened to spend a little while in singing and acting songs of jollification). In these poignant songs of pathos and, finally, cathartic relief, Hall follows in a dramatic manner his reflections of what a spiritual of the African American should be—simple, dignified, emotional, religiously based, reflective of a common condition, music of the heart, and sincere in purpose.

The first setting, following a blues-like formal pattern with a refrain, stresses through repetition the question "Lord, How Come Me Here?" The schematic design is AABA (where the A represents the refrain). The mood is "pathos," the mode is E minor.

"Po' Me" moves between the key of A-flat major and its relative minor (F minor). Both the A and B sections contain four four-measure phrases (or a 16-measure double period)—a binary plan, with a two-measure instrumental *ritornello* (instrumental music that functions as a refrain) at the beginning and the end of this song. The first eight measures of the vocal line are based on a descending major third—*c* to *a*-flat. The piano part is representative of Hall's rich accompaniments—full of chromatic meandering, but clever writing.

The third setting, "How Long Befo' the Sun Go Down?" like the first, uses the scheme AABA. A refrain on the words "befo' de sun go down" is repeated throughout the entire movement, in exactly the same form each time, although the first statement uses a full cadence, while the second statement creates an incomplete or half cadence. The syncopation in the melodic line gives rise to the basic technique used in African-American song and dance music.

The unifying factor of the fourth song, "Day Is Done," as in the preceding song, is a refrain, this time on the words "I thank God day is done." Again the scheme is AABA. The key is F major, the mood is hopeful, and the musical setting is dignified and stately. With each of the three statements of "day is done," the mood proceeds with controlled feelings of hope and fulfillment. Finally, the refrain exults, "I thank God day is done."

Hall remembered that "the slave made songs for work and play; dance and pantomime were warp and woof of his daily existence." In the final song, "Get Up Chillun," a dance song with an oom-pah ragtime-style piano accompaniment and a syncopated rhythm, Hall produces a foot-tapping ode to music and dance. A call-and-response technique is also used in this movement, with the leader as instigator and the dancers and the instrumentalists responding. The weary workers sing and dance through the evening.

Roland Hayes, the great interpreter of this cycle of songs, portrayed superbly the personal and fulfilling qualities embodied in Hall's opus. In a letter to Hall, Hayes wrote that, since November 1949, "I have sung your [*Cycle of Afro-American Religious Songs*] from Boston to Seattle, Chicago to St. Louis and Lincoln, Nebraska. I have sung it from New York to Washington, Washington to Atlanta, Atlanta to Austin, Texas, from Texas to Denver, Colorado, and from Denver to Philadelphia. . . . I am glad to tell you that in each of the cities . . . only enthusiastic acclaim . . . has greeted their rendition. . . . I must tell you that the unusual setting . . . so suited to the mode and mood of the songs captivated me upon first acquaintance with the songs which means that from here on out . . . [you] will find them on my programs. . . . I was so delighted that you could be present at my New York Carnegie Hall concert . . . to, yourself, witness the whole hearted enthusiasm that the great audience gave your songs."

REFERENCES

Bowers, Violet G. "In Retrospect: Frederick Douglass Hall—He Was My Teacher." *Black Perspective in Music* 8, no. 2 (1980): 215–242.

Butcher, Margaret Just. *The Negro in American Culture*. New York: New American Library of World Literature, 1956.

Cureau, Rebecca. Telephone conversation with the author, September 1995.

Dunbar, Paul Laurence. *The Complete Poems of Paul Laurence Dunbar*. New York: Dodd, Mead, 1934.

Eskew, Harry. Taped interviews with Frederick Douglass Hall, July-August 1976.

Floyd, Samuel A., Jr. *Black Music in the Harlem Renaissance: A Collection of Essays*. New York: Greenwood Press, 1990.

Hall, Frederick. Program notes, *A Cycle of Afro-American Religious Songs*. Unpublished manuscript, 1948. Held by the author.

———. Liner notes, *Yonder Come Day: A Program of Afro-American Spirituals*. Dillard University Choir, Frederick Hall, director, 1974. Recording released by the General Education Board, United Methodist Church.

Hayes, Roland. Letter to Frederick Hall, from Roland Hayes, March 29, 1950. Held by Frederick Hall Archives, Atlanta, Georgia.

Locke, Alain. *The Negro and His Music*. New York: Arno Press and The New York Times, 1969.

Southern, Eileen. *The Music of Black Americans: A History*. 2nd ed. New York: W. W. Norton, 1983.

Whalum, Wendell. "Frederick Douglass Hall, Sr., 1898–1982." *Signature* [A publication of the Metropolitan Atlanta Musicians Association] 1, no. 1 (April 1983): 6–10.

MALCOLM J. BREDA

HANCOCK, HERBIE

Born Herbert Jeffrey Hancock in Chicago, Ill., April 12, 1940. **Education:** Chicago, Ill., public schools including Hyde Park High School; studied piano from the age of seven; Grinnell College, Grinnell, Iowa, studied electrical engineering and music composition, 1956–60; Chicago, attended Roosevelt University, 1960; New York, N.Y., Manhattan School of Music, 1962; New School for Social Research, 1967. **Composing and Performing Career:** At the age of 11, performed the first movement of Mozart's D Major Piano Concerto (K. 537) with the Chicago Symphony Orchestra, 1951; formed his own jazz ensemble while still in high school; formed, composed, and arranged for 17-piece big band while at Grinnell College; returned to Chicago and performed with touring jazz artists such as Coleman Hawkins and Donald Byrd, 1960; New York, N.Y., worked with Phil Woods and Oliver Nelson, 1961; first professional recording date with Donald Byrd, ca. 1961; signed with Blue Note Records and recorded first album as leader, *Takin' Off,* 1962; joined Miles Davis quintet, including Wayne Shorter, Tony Williams, and Ron Carter, 1963–68; organized first permanent group, the Herbie Hancock Sextet, and signed with Warner Brothers Records, 1968; moved to Los Angeles and signed with Columbia Records, 1972; released *Headhunters,* the best-selling jazz album of its time (certified platinum), 1973; formed V.S.O.P. Quintet and performed at the Newport Jazz Festival, 1976; broke new ground in electronic musical technology with group, Material, 1983; recorded "Rockit," the largest-selling 12-inch single in Columbia Records' history, 1983; has continued to compose, record, and perform in concert and on television throughout the 1980s and 1990s. **Honors/Awards:** *Down Beat* Readers' Poll winner for Jazz Piano, 1968–71, and for Jazz Composer, 1967, 1971; *Time Magazine,* "One of the Ten Best Recordings of 1971" award for *Mwandishi,* 1971; Grinnell College, Grinnell, Iowa, honorary doctorate, 1972; Grammy for Best Soul/R&B Single, "Doin' It," 1976; Grammy for Best R&B Instrumental Performance, "Rockit," 1983; Grammy for Best R&B Instrumental Performance, *Sound System,* 1984; Academy Award for Best Original Score, *Round Midnight,* 1986; Grammy for Best Instrumental Performance, "Call Sheet Blues," 1987; California State University–Fresno, honorary doctorate, 1997.

MUSIC LIST

JAZZ ENSEMBLE

[The following list of titles includes only works that were composed by the subject of the entry; it is not a list of recordings that were made by the subject. Although the composer may have made recordings of his own works, the list is not restricted to those recordings but in many cases includes performances by other artists of the composer's work. The list is made up of publication and discographical data, in cases where such information is available. Although no effort has been made to include documentation of the earliest recording of the works listed, the date of the earliest recording that is readily available has been given. —Ed.]

"Actual Proof." Recorded, 1974: Columbia PC-32965.

"Alone and I." Recorded, 1962: Blue Note BST-84109 or Blue Note CDP 746506 2.

"And What If I Don't?" Recorded, 1963: Blue Note CDP 7 84126 2 or Blue Note BN-LA399-H2.

"Aung San Suu Kyi." Recorded, 1997: Polygram 314 537 564-2.

"Autodrive." Recorded, 1984: Columbia CK 38814; Westwood One SE 85-03.

"Birdhouse." Recorded: Warwick W-2041.

"Blind Man, Blind Man." Recorded, 1963: Blue Note CDP 7 84126 2 or Blue Note BST-89907; Verve V6-8609.

"Bluesville." Co-composers, A. Davis, Joe Josea.

"Bo Ba Be Da." Recorded, 1994: Verve 314 522 681-2.

"The Bomb." New York: BMI. Co-composer, Rodney Temperton. Recorded, 1982: Columbia 32474.

"Bubbles." Co-composer, Melvin Ragin. Recorded: Columbia CK 33812.

"Butterfly." Co-composer, Bennie Maupin. Recorded, 1974: Columbia PC-32965; RCA Victor APDI-1025.

"Button Up." Recorded: Columbia COL 477296 2; Tri-Star Music 35467.

"Call It '95." Recorded, 1994: Verve 314 522 681-2.

"Call Sheet Blues." 1987. Note: received a Grammy Award in 1987.

"Can't Hide Your Love." Co-composers, Jeffrey Cohen, Narada Michael Walden. Recorded, 1982: Columbia 32474.

"Cantaloupe Island." Recorded, 1964: Blue Note CDP 784175 2 or Blue Note 512740X; Columbia CK34280.

"Chameleon." Co-composers, Harvey Mason, Bennie Maupin, Paul Jackson. Recorded, 1973: Columbia CK 36309; Columbia CK-47478; Pablo 2310755; Pickwick 3301.

"Come and See Me." Recorded, 1994: Verve 314 522 681-2.

"Crossings." 1974. Recorded: Warner Brothers WB-2807.

"D.C.H." New York: BMI. Co-composers, Stanley Marvin Clarke, George Duke.

"Dis Is da Drum." Recorded, 1994: Verve 314 522 681-2.

"Doin' It." Co-composers, Melvin Ragin, Ray Parker Jr. Note: received a Grammy Award in 1976. Recorded: Columbia CK 34280.

"Dolphin Dance." Recorded, 1965: Avion Records AVCD 511; Blue Note B2-46339; Milestone OJCCD-754-2.

"Doom." Recorded, 1976: Atlantic CS 1696.

"Driftin'." Recorded, 1962: Blue Note CDP 746506 2.

"The Egg." Recorded, 1964: Blue Note CDP 784175 2 or Blue Note BCT-84175.

"Einbahnstrasse." Recorded, 1976: Atlantic CS 1696.

"Empty Pockets." Recorded, 1962: Blue Note CDP 746506 2 or Blue Note BST-84109 or Blue Note BN-LA399-H2.

"Everybody's Broke." New York: BMI. Co-composers, Alphonse Mouzon, Jeffrey Cohen, Gavin Wright.

"The Eye of the Hurricane." Recorded, 1965: Blue Note B2-46339; Columbia CGK 38275; Pausa PR 7115.

"Fair Thee Well." Encino, Calif.: Masong Music. Co-composer, Harvey W. Mason Jr. Recorded, 1976: Arista 4054.

"Fat Albert Rotunda." Recorded, 1969: Warner Brothers 9 45732-2.

"Fat Mama." Recorded, 1969: Fantasy 9416; Warner Brothers 9 45732-2.

"Firewater." Recorded: Blue Note BST-84321.

"Free Form." Co-composer, D. Zeitlin. Recorded: Columbia C2 38430.

Herbie Hancock; courtesy of Verve/Polygram Records; photo by James Minchin

"Future Shock." Recorded, 1984: Columbia CK 38814.

"Gentle Thoughts." Co-composer, Melvin Ragin. Recorded: Columbia CK 34280.

"Getting to the Good Part." Co-composer, Rodney Temperton. Recorded, 1982: Columbia 32474; Westwood One SE 85-03.

"Give It All Your Heart." New York: BMI. Co-composer, Rodney Temperton. Recorded, 1982: Columbia 32474.

"Go for It." Northridge, Calif.: Mouzon Music. Co-composers, Jeffrey Cohen, David Rubinson, Alphonse Mouzon. Recorded: Columbia 36415.

"Goodbye to Childhood." Recorded, 1968: Blue Note CDP 7 46136 2 or Blue Note BST-89907.

"Groove Is in the Heart." Co-composers, Dmitry Brill, Kierin Kirby, Dong-Hwa Chung. Recorded: Elektra Entertainment 60957.

"Hale-Bopp, Hip-Hop." Recorded, 1997: Polygram 314 537 564-2.

"Hang Up Your Hang Ups." Co-composers, Melvin Ragin, Paul Jackson. Recorded: Columbia CK 36309 or Columbia CK 33812 or Columbia AS 360.

"Hard Rock." Recorded: Columbia CK 39478; Westwood One SE 85-03.

"He Who Lives in Fear." Recorded, 1969: Blue Note CDP 7 46845 2 or Blue Note BST 89907.

"Heartbeat." Co-composers, Melvin Ragin, Paul Jackson. Recorded: Columbia CK 33812.

"Help Yourself." New York: BMI. Co-composers, Gavin Wright, Jeffrey Cohen, David Rubinson.

"Herbie's Blues." Recorded, 1980: Manhattan 5021; Retro Music SLD21122.

"Hey Ho." Recorded: Atlantic 1483.

"Hidden Shadows." 1974. Recorded: Columbia KC-32212.

"Honey from the Jar." Co-composer, Jeffrey Cohen. Recorded: Columbia CK 35764.

"The Hook." Co-composer, Chick Corea. Recorded: Polygram 835680.

"Hornets." Recorded: CBS 2K 45218; Columbia KC-32212; CTI 6049.

"Hump." Recorded, 1994: Verve 314 522 681-2.

"I Have a Dream." Recorded, 1969: Blue Note CDP 7 46845 2 or Blue Note BST 89907.

"I Love New York." Recorded: Co-composer, Claire Lynn Francis.

"I Thought It Was You." New York: BMI. Co-composers, Jeffrey Cohen, Melvin Ragin. Recorded: Columbia CK 36309.

"Jack Rabbit." Recorded: Blue Note CDP 7 46845 2.

"Jammin' with Herbie." Recorded, 1980: Manhattan 5021; Retro Music SLD21122.

"Jessica." Recorded: Columbia CGK 34976; Warner Brothers 9 45732-2.

"Juju." Recorded, 1994: Verve 314 522 681-2.

"A Jump Ahead." Recorded: Blue Note CDP 7 46845 2 or Blue Note BN-LA152-F.

"Junku." Co-composer, Ayzb Dieng. Note: field theme for the 1984 Los Angeles Summer Olympics. Recorded: Columbia CK 39478 or Columbia BJS 39322; Westwood One SE 85-03.

"Just around the Corner." Co-composer, Melvin Ragin. Recorded: Columbia COL 471240 2; Hollywood 162102.

"Karabali." Co-composer, Daniel Ponce. Recorded: Columbia CK 39478.

"King Cobra." Recorded, 1963: Blue Note CDP 7 84126 2 or Blue Note BST-89907.

"Knee Deep." Co-composer, Melvin Ragin. Recorded: Columbia CK 35764.

"Li'l Brother." Recorded, 1969: Warner Brothers 9 45732-2.

"Little One." Recorded, 1965: Blue Note B2-46339; Columbia PC-9150.

"Madness." Recorded, 1977: Columbia CS-9594.

"Magic Number." New York: BMI. Co-composers, Jeffrey Cohen, David Rubinson. Recorded, 1981: Columbia 37387.

"Maiden Voyage." Recorded, 1965: Blue Note CDP 7 46530 2; Columbia COL 477296 2; Polydor 835 680-2.

"Manhattan (Island of Lights and Love)." Co-composer, Jean Hancock. Recorded: Verve 314 529 584-2.

"Manhattan Lorelie." Recorded, 1997: Polygram 314 537 564-2.

"Maxxed Out." New York: BMI. Co-composer, Gregory Phillinganes. Recorded, 1981: Planet 52299.

"The Maze." Co-composer, John Scott. Recorded, 1962: Blue Note CDP 7 46506 2 or Blue Note BST-84109.

"The Melody (On the Deuce by 44)." Recorded, 1994: Verve 314 522 681-2.

"Memory of Enchantment." Recorded, 1997: Polygram 314 537 564-2.

"Meridianne: A Wood Sylph." Recorded, 1997: Polygram 314 537 564-2.

"Metal Beat." Recorded, 1985: Columbia CK 39478; Westwood One SE 85-03.

"Mimosa." Recorded: Blue Note CDP 7 46845 2.

"Mojuba." Recorded, 1994: Verve 314 522 681-2.

"New Concerto." New York: Duchess Music, n.d.

"Oliloqui Valley." Recorded, 1964: Blue Note CDP 7 84175 2 or Blue Note BCT-84175 or Blue Note BST-89907.

"One Finger Snap." Recorded, 1964: Blue Note CDP 7 84175 2 or Blue Note BCT-84175; Pausa PR 7115.

"Ostinato (Suite for Angela)." Recorded, 1971: Warner Brothers 9 45732-2.

"Palm Grease." Recorded, 1974: Columbia PC-32965.

"Paradise." Co-composers, Jay Graydon, David Foster, William Champlin. Recorded, 1982: Columbia 32474.

"People Music." Co-composers, Melvin Ragin, Paul Jackson. Recorded: Columbia CK 34280.

"The Pleasure Is Mine." Recorded, 1963: Blue Note CDP 7 84126 2.

"The Prisoner." Recorded, 1969: Blue Note CDP 7 46845 2.

"Promise of the Sun." Recorded, 1969: Blue Note CDP 7 46845 2.

"Rain Dance." Recorded: Columbia KC-32212.

"Ready or Not." Recorded: Columbia CK 35764.

"Riot." Recorded, 1968: Blue Note CDP 7 46136 2 or Blue Note BST 89907; Columbia CS-9594.

"Rockit." Recorded, 1983: Columbia CK 38814; Rhino Records R4 71834; Westwood One SE 85-03.

"Rubber Soul." Recorded, 1994: Verve 314 522 681-2.

"Sanctuary." New York: BMI. Co-composers, Madonna, Dallas Austin, Anne Preven, Scott Cutler. Recorded: Maverick 45767.

"Shooz." Recorded, 1994: Verve 314 522 681-2.

"Sister Cheryl." Co-composers, Wynton Marsalis, Wayne Shorter, Charlie Haden, Tony Williams. Recorded: Blue Note 46289; Columbia 37574.

"Sleeping Giant." Recorded, 1971: Warner Brothers 9 45732-2.

"Sly." Recorded, 1973: Columbia CK-32731 or Columbia CK-47478.

"Sonrisa." Recorded, 1997: Polygram 314 537 564-2.

"The Sorcerer." Recorded, 1967: Blue Note CDP 7 46136 2; Columbia CGK 38275.

"Sound System." Note: received a Grammy Award in 1984. Recorded: Columbia CK 39478.

"Spank-a-Lee." Recorded, 1974: Columbia PC-31965.

"Speak Like a Child." Recorded, 1968: Blue Note CDP 7 46136 2; Pausa PR 7115.

"Spider." Co-composers, Melvin Ragin, Paul Jackson. Recorded: Columbia PC-34280 or Columbia AS 360.

"Stars in Your Eyes." New York: BMI. Co-composers, Ray Parker Jr., Gavin Wright. Recorded, 1985: Westwood One SE 85-03.

"Steppin' in It." Recorded: Columbia CK 33812.

"Succotash." Recorded: Blue Note CDP 7 46845 2 or Blue Note BST 89907.

"Sun Touch." Recorded: Columbia CK 33812.

"Survival of the Fittest." Recorded, 1965: Blue Note B2-46339.

"Swamp Rat." Co-composers, Melvin Ragin, Paul Jackson. Recorded: Columbia CK 34280.

"TCB with Herbie." Recorded, 1995: Retro Music SLD21122.

"Tell Everybody." New York: BMI. Co-composers, David Rubinson, Jeffrey Cohen, B. Good. Recorded, 1979: Columbia CK 35764 or Columbia CK 36309.

"Tell Me a Bedtime Story." Recorded, 1969: A&M Records SP-4685; Warner Brothers 9 45732-2.

"Terry." Co-composers, Jerry Heyward, Robert Leak, James MacCawthall, David Cox.

"There's a Better Way." Co-composers, Marlon Williams, Simone Johnson. Recorded, 1993: Warner Brothers 45054-2.

"Three Bags Full." Recorded, 1962: Blue Note CDP 7 46506 2 or Blue Note BST-84109.

"Three Wishes." Recorded: Blue Note CDP 7 84118-2.

"Tonight's the Night." Calabasas, Calif.: Raydiola Music. Co-composer, Ray Parker Jr.

"Toys." Recorded, 1968: Blue Note CDP 7 46136 2.

"The Traitor." Co-composers, Melvin Ragin, Louis Johnson, Wayne Shorter. Recorded: Columbia CK 33812.

"Triangle." Recorded: Blue Note CDP 7 46845 2.

"A Tribute to Someone." New York: BMI. Recorded, 1963: Blue Note CDP 7 84126 2.

"Trust Me." Co-composers, David Rubinson, A. Willis. Recorded: Columbia CK 35764.

"The Twilight Clone." Co-composer, Adrian Belew. Recorded, 1981: Columbia 37387.

"Vein Melter." Recorded, 1973: Columbia CK-32731 or Columbia CK-47478.

"Visitor from Nowhere." Recorded, 1997: Polygram 314 537 564-2.

"Visitor from Somewhere." Recorded, 1997: Polygram 314 537 564-2.

"Watch It." Recorded, 1977: Columbia 650.

"Watcha Waiting For." Recorded, 1977: Columbia 650.

"Watermelon Man." Recorded, 1962: Blue Note CDP 7 46506 2 or Blue Note CDP 0777 7 97960-2; Columbia CK-32731.

"Wiggle-Waggle." Recorded, 1969: Pausa PR 7115; Warner Brothers 9 45732-2.

"Yams." Recorded: Capitol 54904B.

"You'll Know When You Get There." Recorded, 1971: Warner Brothers WS-1898.

"You Bet Your Love." New York: BMI. Co-composers, Jeffrey Cohen, A. Willis. Recorded: Columbia CK 35764.

"You Know What to Do." Co-composer, Billy Towne. Recorded, 1966: United Artists Ual-3496.

INCIDENTAL MUSIC

Action Jackson. 1988. Film soundtrack.

Blow Up. 1966. Film soundtrack. Contents: The Bed; Blow Up; Verushka Part I; Verushka Part II; The Naked Camera; Bring Down the Birds; Jane's Theme; Stroll On; The Thief; The Kiss; Curiosity; Thomas Studies Photos; End Title: Blow Up. Recorded: Atlantic CDCBS 702.

Colors. 1988. Film soundtrack. Co-composers, Robert Musso, Tony Meilandt, Charles Drayton, Jeffrey Bova.

Death Wish. 1974. Film soundtrack. Contents: Death Wish; Joanna's Theme; Do a Thing; Paint Her Mouth; Rich Country; Suite Revenge; Ochoa Knose; Party People; Fill Your Hands. Recorded: Columbia PCT 33199.

The George McKenna Story. 1986. Television film soundtrack.

Harlem Nights. 1989. Film soundtrack.

"Hey, Hey, Hey, It's Fat Albert." 1969. Television special score.

Jo Jo Dancer, Your Life Is Calling. 1986. Film soundtrack. Contents: Michelle; Off the Cliff; Theme for Mother.

"Livin' Large." 1991. Film theme song. Recorded, 1991: Def Jam CT 48501.

Round Midnight. 1986. Film soundtrack. Note: received an Oscar Award in 1986. Contents: Berangere's Nightmare; Chan's Song (Never Said); Still Time. Recorded: Columbia 40464.

"Sesame Street." Incidental music for the television show of the same name.

A Soldier's Story. 1984. Film soundtrack.

The Spook Who Sat by the Door. 1973. Film soundtrack. Contents: Main Theme; CIA; Are in Bee; Am I Doing the Right Thing?; Cobra Theme; Blues for an I.O.U.; Cobra Training; Freeman and Joy; Pretty Willie; Old Friends; Pipes. Recorded: Columbia KC-32944.

PUBLICATIONS

ABOUT HANCOCK
Books and Monographs

Suzuki, Naoki. *Herbie Hancock, A Discography, 1961–69.* Fujieda-shi, Sizuoka, Japan: N. Suzuki, 1988.

Thesis

Lapey, Sarah Elisabeth. "Inventions and Dimensions: An Analysis of Herbie Hancock's Compositional and Improvisational Techniques between 1962 and 1968." B.A. thesis, Williams College, 1993.

Articles

Baker, David N., Lida M. Belt, and Herman C. Hudson, eds. "Herbert Jeffrey Hancock." In *The Black Composer Speaks,* 108–138. Metuchen, N.J.: Scarecrow Press, 1978.

Balleras, J. "Herbie Hancock's Current Choice." *Down Beat* 49, no. 9 (September 1982): 15–17.

Heckman, Don. "Discovery Channeling: Wayne Shorter and Herbie Hancock." *Down Beat* 64, no. 12 (December 1997): 20–22+.

———. "Watermelon Man: Herbie Hancock." *Down Beat* 32, no. 22 (October 1965): 12–13+.

Johnson, Brooks. "Herbie Hancock: *Into His Own Thing.*" *Down Beat* 38, no. 2 (January 1971): 14–15+.

Korall, B. "Herbie Hancock." *Orkester Journalen* 36 (March 1968): 8–9.

Lyons, Len. "Herbie Hancock: Keyboard Wizard." *Contemporary Keyboard* 1, no. 2 (February 1975): 18–20+. Reprinted in *The Great Jazz Pianists: Speaking of Their Lives and Music,* by Len Lyons, 269–283. New York: Quill, 1983.

Mandel, Howard. "Herbie Hancock: Of Films, Fairlights, Funk . . . And All That Other Jazz." *Down Beat* (July 1986): 17–19.

Mehegan, John. "Herbie Hancock Talks to John Mehegan." *Jazz* 3, no. 5 (May 1964): 23–25+.

Muro, Don. "Herbie Hancock: On the Cutting Edge." *Jazz Educators Journal* 20, no. 3 (March 1988): 17–20.

Townley, Ray. "Hancock Plugs In." *Down Beat* 41, no. 17 (October 1974): 13–15+.

Stewart, Zan. "Herbie's Search for New Standards." *Down Beat* 63 (April 1996): 22–25.

Waters, Keith. "Blurring the Barline: Metric Displacement in the Piano Solos of Herbie Hancock." *Annual Review of Jazz Studies* 8 (1996): 19–37.

Woodard, Josef. "Herbie and Quincy." *Down Beat* 57 (January 1990): 16–21.

———. "The Herbie Hancock Interview." *Down Beat* 55 (June 1988) 16–19.

* * * * *

Herbie Hancock has achieved a perhaps unprecedented combination of critical acclaim and popular favor in his domain. Few jazz composers of any era have produced a larger repertory of standards, including "Blind Man, Blind Man" (1963), "Speak Like a Child" (1968), "Riot" (1968), "One Finger Snap" (1964), "Cantaloupe Island" (1964), "Palm Grease" (1974), "Butterfly" (1974), and "Chameleon" (1973).

Hancock's earliest influence, only apparent during his years as a professional jazz and rock composer and pianist, came from the European classical tradition. Beginning piano lessons at the age of seven, he performed, four years later, the first movement of Mozart's Piano Concerto in D major (K. 537) in his native city with the Chicago Symphony Orchestra. By his early twenties, Hancock's taste in classical music had expanded to include that of Igor Stravinsky and other modernists, such as Karlheinz Stockhausen, Edgard Varèse, Olivier Messiaen, and John Cage.

Although he would continue to perform classical music until the advent of his professional jazz work with saxophonist Coleman Hawkins and trumpeter Donald Byrd, Hancock had, by his early teen years, shifted his interest to rhythm and blues. Despite a somewhat belated introduction to jazz in high school (courtesy of a knowledgeable classmate), Hancock quickly learned to transcribe solos of George Shearing and Oscar Peterson as well as the sophisticated harmonizations of Clare Fisher, the arranger for the vocal group the Hi-Lo's, and Robert Farnon, a British arranger of "mood music." While in high school, he also led a student jazz band.

Hancock's interest in electrical engineering led to his first declared major at Grinnell College in Iowa, which he attended from 1956 to 1960. Although he left Grinnell one sociology unit short of a bachelor of arts degree in music, he later was awarded an honorary doctorate (1972) from his alma mater. Beginning in the late 1960s, Hancock's college training and his aptitude for electronic technology proved useful in his exploration of electronic keyboards and synthesizers.

Hancock's career as a performer and a composer is characterized by an oscillation among contrasting styles and ideologies: rhythm and blues ("Watermelon Man," 1962), modal jazz ("Maiden Voyage," 1965), traditional jazz ("Dolphin Dance," 1965, and "The Sorcerer," 1967), free jazz (*Sextant,* 1972), and jazz-rock fusion (*Headhunters,* 1973). After performing with swing legend Hawkins while still in college, Hancock joined Byrd in 1960 to produce such funky rhythm-and-blues-style recordings as "Pentecostal Feeling" (*Free Form,* Blue Note B2-84118). Hancock would popularize this funky blues-style more broadly in his early compositions "Driftin'" and "Watermelon Man," both of which appeared on the first album under his own name, *Takin' Off.* Before gaining universal recognition in the jazz world as a performer when he joined Miles Davis in May 1963, Hancock had also worked briefly with avant-garde woodwind virtuoso Eric Dolphy several months earlier. Thus, by the age of 23, Hancock had mastered several distinctive jazz styles and had already composed a song, "Watermelon Man," that would eventually become perhaps the best-known funky blues song of all time.

During his five years of touring and recording with Davis, Hancock also created his most widely circulated jazz standards and recorded them with his own groups (including "Maiden Voyage" and "Dolphin Dance") and occasionally with Davis's ("The Sorcerer"). Near the end of his tenure with Davis, Hancock was introduced to the electric piano and played this instrument on one cut each on *Miles Davis Quintet + Joe Beck* ("Water on the Pond," 1967) and *Miles in the Sky* ("Stuff," 1967) and exclusively on *Filles de Kilimanjaro* (1968), *In a Silent Way* (1969), and other albums.

For the next four years (1969–73), Hancock developed in new directions as a leader of his own group, Mwandishi (Swahili for composer), also known as the Herbie Hancock Sextet, which performed music ranging from traditional jazz to free jazz to fusion. While still leading this group, Hancock gained a practical knowledge of synthesizers from Patrick Gleeson. Two years later, he made his recorded debut on the synthesizer on *Headhunters,* the top-selling jazz album of its time.

Hancock continued to focus mainly on fusion but also returned to acoustic jazz with the group V.S.O.P. in 1976–77. As part of his search to "find that part of my musical being that relates to the most people," Hancock would continue to focus on rock styles. In 1983, Hancock produced the mega-hit, "Rockit" (from the album *Future Shock*), which he considered stylistically removed from jazz, and he also continued to record with such non-jazz artists as Stevie Wonder and the Pointer Sisters. Although he had scored the music for several films, including *Blow Up* (1966) and *Death Wish* (1974), it was not until 1986 that he gained major recognition for his film work when *Round Midnight,* which also featured Hancock as actor and performer, received an Oscar for best movie scoring.

WATERMELON MAN (1962)

"Watermelon Man," which appeared on Hancock's first album as a leader, *Takin' Off* (1962), remains arguably the most popular funky blues tune ever composed. According to Len Lyons, of all his compositions, Hancock would come to regard "Watermelon Man" and the perennially popular "Maiden Voyage" as his two "strongest pieces." Townley reports that "Watermelon Man" also represents Hancock's conscious attempt at "projecting something from the black experience." In a 1980 interview with Leonard Feather, Hancock explained further the origins and purposes of the tune: "I wanted to make something that would be an authentic reflection of my background. When I was a child, the watermelon man would go through the alley a couple of times a day. So I wrote a phrase that sounded like 'Hey! Watermelon Man!'" According to Hancock, the phrase came first, the only time a title preceded the music.

On the 1962 recording, a funky rhythmic vamp (eight measures, all on the tonic) played by Hancock, Butch Warren (bass), and Billy Higgins (drums) sets the stage for the blues tune to follow. In addition to its memorability and its widely imitated rock-like accompaniment figure, the form of the tune eventually departs from the standard 12-bar blues (I–I–I–I IV–IV–I–I V–V–I–I), although the opening eight measures conform to the expected formula. But the tune soon evades this norm by delaying the return to the tonic and twice repeating the V–IV progression (mm. 9–14). Also distinctive in the 1962 recording are rhythmic breaks that separate expected climactic returns to the tonic in each of the 13 choruses (mm. 15–16). The overall form of the 1962 recording consists of the main tune in harmony between Dexter Gordon (tenor saxophone) and Freddie Hubbard (trumpet): three choruses of trumpet, four choruses of tenor saxophone, and two choruses of piano, each chorus delineated by two measures of the opening vamp. The recording concludes with a two-chorus return of the original tune, again featuring tenor saxophone and trumpet in harmony, followed by a longer statement of the vamp, which fades into near nothingness after 16 measures.

In 1973, Hancock reworked "Watermelon Man" for the album *Headhunters* and, in the liner notes, credits drummer Harvey Mason for the conception and percussionist Bill Summers with the new opening: "The intro was actually from Pygmy music with Bill blowing in a beer bottle and making a melodic, rhythmic thing." The use of other African instruments along with the West-African practice of combining independent rhythmic layers heterophonically in "Chameleon" surpassed the other, more amorphous "return to Africa" efforts of the period. For the first time, a large jazz public was exposed to a jazz-rock style that also attempted to incorporate authentic African elements. While Davis's more jazz-oriented rock album *Bitches Brew* (1969) managed to sell an impressive 500,000 recordings after four years, *Headhunters* accomplished the same commercial feat within a matter of months. After more than 20 years, the album continues to sell well.

In light of Hancock's attributions to Mason for the basic new conception and Summers for the introduction, the extent to which Hancock can be credited for the formal alterations to his original tune is unclear. In any event, the most notable departure in the latter version is the abandonment of the traditional blues progression for the first eight measures and its replacement by a static tonic seventh chord. The most distinctive formal-harmonic feature of 1962, however, is preserved: the repeated V–IV progression alterations in

measures 9–14. Although Hancock retained the break between measures 15 and 16, the harmony on these measures is now an A-flat seventh instead of the expected tonic on F. Other changes include new repetitions, returns, extensions, and harmonies.

The performance concludes with a modified return of the original introduction, this time with the sound of the synthesizer compatibly accompanying the simulated Pygmy tribal music. Just as the introduction presented first the bass and then the drums, these instruments are quickly removed (drums first) before the synthesizer, whistles, and yelps gradually fade out into near silence.

Hancock openly acknowledged that he composed "Watermelon Man" "with a commercial goal in mind." Nevertheless, in a view now shared by most jazz historians as well as the general jazz public, Hancock steadfastly defended the artistic integrity of both versions of his popular song and denied the critical charges that he was abandoning traditional jazz in the 1973 recording and "selling out."

MAIDEN VOYAGE (1965), DOLPHIN DANCE (1965), AND THE SORCERER (1967)

Although considerably slower-moving harmonically than standard bop or even swing tunes, the harmonies in "Maiden Voyage" move at double the rate of change in tunes like "So What," an extremely constrained approach to modality. Instead of a single modal chord stretching over 16 consecutive measures, Hancock's modal tune changes harmony after each four-measure unit. The piano introduction presents a recurring rhythmic vamp that can be interpreted as a subtle transformation of what Kernfeld has called "the stereotypical bossa nova" pattern. The work has no cadences, according to the composer; it "just keeps moving around in a circle," with its repetitive rhythmic ostinato, recurrent melodic figures, and constrained harmonic language.

Like the vast majority of jazz, the architecture of the recorded performance consists of a single statement of the tune followed by a series of solo choruses with rhythm accompaniment and a return to the tune. In the original recording, the tune precedes and follows choruses by tenor saxophonist George Coleman (one chorus), trumpeter Freddie Hubbard (two choruses), and Hancock (two choruses).

Although "Maiden Voyage" was literally conceived for the commercial marketplace (a television commercial for Fabergé perfume), the work was highly regarded by scholars as well as jazz aficionados for its imaginative harmonies, voicings, and rhythms. After more than 30 years, it has maintained its stature as one of the two or three most famous, widely discussed, and anthologized modal tunes.

"Dolphin Dance" exhibits a dazzling display of harmonic variety and virtuosity underlying a melody of great interest. Its form might be most accurately described as a 32-bar song form, ABA'C, with a two-measure extension before the repeat of the chorus. The A and B sections share the rhythm of the principal melodic figure (mm. 1–2 and 10–11), which is varied through syncopation; the principal rhythmic contour (mm. 9 and 13) is also varied. What is most striking about the piece, however, is the constantly fluctuating harmonizations of these identical or related figures. The variety takes several forms, including reharmonizations and altered starting chords. After the B section, the return to A with different pitches (mm. 35–36) and different harmonies (mm. 37–38), while idiosyncratic, conveys a sense of circularity and continuity to the tune not unlike that of "Maiden Voyage." In sharp contrast to the purposefully static modal tune, however, the chords in "Dolphin Dance" rarely repeat from one measure to another. The chords themselves range from major, minor, and dominant sevenths to half-diminished sevenths.

Among Hancock's compositions, beyond the principal melodic phrase inspired by the words "Hey, Watermelon Man," programmatic correspondences between his tunes and titles are more generic than specific. Thus, as Heckman reports, although he intended "to try to make some kind of rhythmic sound like a soulful [watermelon] wagon going over the cobblestones, with the horse's hooves and everything," Hancock's attempt to reflect the black experience is manifest mainly by the funky blues style itself. Similarly, the relationship between the melody of "Maiden Voyage" and its title is more suggestive than literal, and specific musical properties suggestive of dolphins are not immediately apparent in "Dolphin Dance."

Unlike these amorphous programmatic references, "The Sorcerer" bears a considerable metaphoric musical resemblance to its dedicatee, Miles Davis. In the liner notes for his 1968 recording of the tune on his own album *Speak Like a Child,* Hancock explains: "Miles *is* a sorcerer. His whole attitude, the way he is, is kind of mysterious. I know him well but there's still a kind of musical mystique about him. His music sounds like witchcraft. There are times I don't know where his music comes from." The connections between the melody and rhythm of "The Sorcerer" and the character it attempts to portray are especially apposite in that the 16-measure tune perfectly captures the mysteriousness and unpredictability of Davis's mercurial personality.

"The Sorcerer" appeared as the title tune on Davis's album *Sorcerer* in 1967. Hancock's trio performance with Ron Carter (bass) and Mickey Roker (drums), which was recorded one year later on *Speak Like a Child,* was selected for the prestigious anthology *Jazz Piano* (Smithsonian Collection of Recordings RD 039, vol. 4, 1989). Despite its apparent inscrutable nature, an unusual but logical harmonic plan gives the tune a distinctive stamp, Dick Katz tells us, since it "doesn't depend on the usual circle-of-fifths or II-to-V chord progressions." The asymmetrical phrasing within the four-bar frames, the strikingly varied syncopated rhythms, and the silence at the opening of the final phrase combine to create an element of constant surprise that is analogous to the ever-surprising Davis.

REFERENCES

Baker, David N., Lida M. Belt, and Herman C. Hudson, eds. *The Black Composer Speaks.* Metuchen, N.J.: Scarecrow Press, 1978.

Brown, Charles T. *The Jazz Experience.* Dubuque, Iowa: Wm. C. Brown, 1989.

Carr, Ian. *Miles Davis: A Biography.* New York: William Morrow, 1982.

Chambers, Jack. *Milestones 2: The Music and Times of Miles Davis Since 1960.* New York: William Morrow, 1985.

Dobbins, Bill. "Hancock, Herbie." In *New Grove Dictionary of Jazz,* edited by Barry Kernfeld, 1: 477–479. London: Macmillan, 1988.

Feather, Leonard. "Piano Giants of Jazz: Herbie Hancock." *Contemporary Keyboard* 6, no. 3 (March 1980): 62–63.

———. *The Pleasures of Jazz.* New York: Horizon Press, 1976.

Hancock, Herbie. Liner notes, *Speak Like a Child.* Blue Note BST 84279, 1968.

Heckman, Don. "Watermelon Man: Herbie Hancock." *Down Beat* 32, no. 22 (October 1965): 12–13+.

Jagajivan. "Musing with Mwandishi." *Down Beat* 40, no. 10 (May 24, 1973): 14–15+.

Johnson, Brooks. "Herbie Hancock: *Into His Own Thing.*" *Down Beat* 38, no. 2 (January 1971): 14–15+.

Katz, Dick. Liner notes, *Jazz Piano.* Smithsonian Collection of Recordings RD 039, 1989.

Kernfeld, Barry. *What to Listen for in Jazz.* New Haven, Conn.: Yale University Press, 1995.

Lyons, Len. "Herbie Hancock: Keyboard Wizard." *Contemporary Keyboard* 1, no. 2 (February 1975): 18–20+. Reprinted in *The Great Jazz Pianists: Speaking of Their Lives and Music,* by Len Lyons, 269–283. New York: Quill, 1983.

———. *The 101 Best Jazz Albums: A History of Jazz on Records.* New York: William Morrow, 1980.

Martin, Henry. *Enjoying Jazz.* New York: Schirmer Books, 1986.

Mehegan, John. "Herbie Hancock Talks to John Mehegan." *Jazz* 3, no. 5 (May 1964): 23–25+.

Porter, Lewis, and Michael Ullman. *Jazz: From Its Origins to the Present.* Englewood Cliffs, N.J.: Prentice Hall, 1993.

Townley, Ray. "Hancock Plugs In." *Down Beat* 41, no. 17 (October 1974): 13–15+.

GEOFFREY BLOCK

HANDY, W(ILLIAM) C(HRISTOPHER)

Born in Florence, Ala., November 16, 1873; died in New York, N.Y., March 28, 1958. **Education:** Florence District School for Negroes, studied solfège there with Y. A. Wallace, a Fisk graduate, ca. 1881–ca. 1891; Henderson, Ky., studied music informally with a Professor Bach, ca. 1895; Birmingham, Ala., passed exam for teacher's certificate, 1892. **Composing and Performing Career:** Toured briefly in a minstrel company at age 15; Hampton Cornet Band, Evansville, Ind., 1892; toured with W. A. Mahara's Minstrels as cornetist, 1896; first recording (no known extant copies), 1897; W. A. Mahara's Minstrels, bandmaster, 1900; toured with Frank Mahara's Minstrels, 1902–03; Clarksdale, Miss., organized and played in local bands, 1903–05; Memphis, Tenn., organized and played in local bands, 1905–13; Memphis, established the Pace and Handy Music Co. with Harry Pace, 1913; composed and published "The Memphis Blues," 1912, "St. Louis Blues," 1914, and "Beale Street Blues," 1916–17; formed and recorded with Handy's Memphis Blues Band, 1919; New York, N.Y., relocated Pace and Handy Music Co., 1918; became sole proprietor of Handy Brothers Music Company, 1922; Carnegie Hall, organized and produced concert of "the variety of black music," 1928; toured with the Clarence Davis band, 1932, and Joe Laurie's *Memory Lane* show, 1933; Apollo Theater, performed with Billy Butler's orchestra, 1936; "The Memphis Blues" copyright restored to him, 1940; performed in "Violins over Broadway" revue at Billy Rose's Diamond Horseshoe, 1948; guest appearances on Edward R. Murrow's *Person to Person*, the *Ed Sullivan Show*, and the "Stars of Tomorrow" radio show, 1950s. **Teaching Career:** Crittenden Cross Road School, ca. 1891; Bethel School, ca. 1892; Alabama A&M College, Normal, Ala., music teacher and bandmaster, 1900–02. **Memberships:** American Federation of Musicians; ASCAP; Detroit Musicians Association; National Association of Negro Musicians; National Music Publishers Association; Negro Actors Guild; Prince Hall Lodge, Harlem; 33rd degree Mason (Grand Master); Songwriters Guild of America; W. C. Handy Foundation for the Blind. **Honors/Awards:** Handy Park on Beale Street, Memphis, Tenn., named in his honor, 1931; National Association of Negro Musicians Award, 1937; 65th birthday concert in his honor, 1938; Wilberforce University, Wilberforce, Ohio, honorary doctorate, 1953; Lewisohn Stadium Concert in his honor, featuring Louis Armstrong and Leonard Bernstein, 1954.

MUSIC LIST

[The following list of titles includes only works that were composed by the subject of the entry; it is not a list of recordings that were made by the subject. Although the composer may have made recordings of his own works, the list is not restricted to those recordings but in many cases includes performances by other artists of the composer's work. The list is made up of publication and discographical data, in cases where such information is available. Although no effort has been made to include documentation of the earliest recording of the works listed, the date of the earliest recording that is readily available has been given. —Ed.]

COLLECTIONS

Blues: An Anthology. Introduction by Abbe Niles. New York: Albert and Charles Boni, 1926. Revised and published with additional songs as *A Treasury of the Blues: Complete Words and Music of Sixty-Seven Great Songs from "Memphis Blues" to the Present Day.* Introduction by Abbe Niles. New York: Charles Boni, 1949. Revised by Jerry Silverman and published with additional songs as *Blues: An Anthology.* New York: Macmillan, 1972.

Blues Folio: Words and Music Complete with Guitar Chords. New York: Robbins Music, 1914.

Unsung Americans Sung. New York: Handy Brothers Music, 1944.

W. C. Handy's Collection of Blues: Words and Music Complete. New York: Robbins Music, 1924.

INSTRUMENTAL SOLOS
Piano
"Evolution of the Blues." 1924.

"No Name Waltz." 1918. Co-composer, Charles Hillman.

POPULAR SONGS

"Aframerican Hymn." 1916. New York: Handy Brothers Music. Also arranged for military band; mixed chorus; male chorus. Recorded, 1928: Audio Archives A-1200.

"Ape Mister Eddie." 1922.

"Atlanta Blues." Copyright, 1923. New York: Handy Brothers Music.

"Aunt Hagar's Children." 1920; text added 1922. New York: Pace and Handy Music, 1920. Also titled "Aunt Hagar's Children Blues" or "Aunt Hagar's Blues." In *Collection of Blues, Blues Folio,* and *Blues: An Anthology.* Recorded: Columbia CK-40242; Musica Jazz 2 MJP-1060; Odeon 03193; Okeh 4789 or Okeh 8046; Parlophone E5115.

"The Basement Blues." 1924. In *Collection of Blues* and *Blues: An Anthology.* Recorded: Columbia 14039-D.

"Beale Street Blues." 1916. Memphis: Pace and Handy Music, 1917. Originally titled "Beale Street: Another Memphis Blues." In *Collection of Blues, Blues Folio,* and *Blues: An Anthology.* Recorded: Capitol CDP 7243-8-32612-2-2; Columbia CK-40242; Lyratone 4211.

"Beale Street Serenade." 1938. Co-composers, Gene Van Ormer, Porter Grainger.

"The Big Stick Blues March." New York: Handy Brothers Music, 1951. Co-composer, Charles L. Cooke. Recorded: Audio Archives A-1200; DRG SL-5192.

"The Birth of Jazz." 1927. Co-composer, Chris Smith.

"Black Patti (Sissieretta Jones)." Copyright, 1940. In *Unsung Americans Sung.* Also arranged for chorus.

"Blue Gummed Blues." 1926. In *Blues: An Anthology.*

"Bright Star of Hope." 1925. New York: Handy Brothers Music. Co-composer, Martha E. Koenig.

"Chantez les bas (Sing 'em Low)." 1931. In *Blues: An Anthology.* Recorded: Capitol CDP 7243-8-32612-2-2; Columbia CK-40242; Smithsonian Folkways FG-03540.

"The Chicago Gouge." 1924. In *Blues: An Anthology.*

"Darktown Reveille." Copyright, 1923. New York: Robbins Music. In *Collection of Blues* and *Blues Folio.* Co-composer, Chris Smith. Note: adaptation of "Bugle Blues." Recorded: Okeh 8110.

"Ever After On (I'll Love My Baby 'till the Sea Runs Dry)." 1946.

"Feelin' Blues." 1923. Co-composer, William Farrell.

"Finis (In Memory of Richard B. Harrison)." Copyright, 1940. In *Unsung Americans Sung.* Also arranged for chorus.

"Friendless Blues." 1926. In *Blues: An Anthology.* Recorded: Capitol CDP 7243-8-32612-2-2; Forum SF-9058.

"The Girl You Never Have Met." 1913.

"Go and Get the Enemy Blues." New York: Handy Brothers Music, 1942. Co-composer, Clarence M. Jones.

"Golden Brown Blues." 1927. New York: Handy Brothers Music, 1927. In *Blues: An Anthology.*

"The Good Lord Sent Me You." 1936.

"The Gouge of Armour Avenue." 1924. New York: Handy Brothers Music, 1924. In *Blues: An Anthology.* Recorded: Vocalion 14859.

"Hail to the Spirit of Freedom (March)." 1915. Memphis: Pace and Handy Music, 1915. Recorded: DRG SL-5192.

"Harlem Blues." 1923. New York: Handy Brothers Music. In *Blues: An Anthology.* Note: adapted for clarinet and string quartet as "Harlem." Recorded: Capitol CDP 7243-8-32612-2-2; Cub CUB-8002; Verve MG VS-6061.

"The Hesitating Blues." 1915. Memphis: Pace and Handy Music, 1915. In *Blues: An Anthology.* Recorded: Columbia CK-40242; Lyratone 4212; Musica Jazz 2 MJP-1060.

"The Hooking Cow Blues." 1917. New York: Pace and Handy Music, 1917. Co-composer, Douglass Williams. Recorded: Columbia A2420 or Columbia A2913; Memphis Archives MA-7006.

"I See though My Eyes Are Closed." New York: Handy Brothers Music. Recorded: Audio Archives A-1200; DRG SL-5192.

"I'm Tellin' You in Front." 1937. Co-composer, Russell Wooding.

"In the Cotton Fields of Dixie." 1907. Cincinnati: George Jaberg, 1907.

"In the Land Where Cotton Is King." 1916. Memphis: Pace and Handy Music.

"Joe Turner Blues." 1915. Memphis: Pace and Handy Music, 1915. In *Collection of Blues, Blues Folio,* and *Blues: An Anthology.* Recorded: Capitol CDP 7243-8-32612-2-2 ; DRG SL-5192; Lyratone 4211.

"The Jogo Blues." 1913. Memphis: Pace and Handy Music, 1913. In *Blues: An Anthology.* Note: originally titled "The Memphis Itch." Recorded: Columbia A2327.

"John Henry Blues." 1922. New York: Handy Brothers Music. In *Blues: An Anthology.* Recorded: Grey Gull 7023; Paramount 12003.

"The Kaiser's Got the Blues." 1918. Co-composer, Domer C. Browne.

"Keep the Love Ties Binding." 1918. Co-composer, J. P. Schofield.

"Lincoln's Gettysburg Address." Copyright, 1943. New York: Handy Brothers Music. In *Unsung Americans Sung.* Co-composer, Jean Stor.

"Long Gone (from Bowling Green)." 1920. New York: Pace and Handy Music, 1920. In *Blues: An Anthology.* Recorded: Columbia CK-40242; Emerson 10365, 41700-2.

"Loveless Love." 1921. New York: Pace and Handy Music, 1921. In *Blues: An Anthology.* Recorded: Columbia CK-40242; Davis DA22; Smithsonian Folkways FG-03540; Varsity 8162.

"The Memphis Blues." 1912; republished with text, 1913; new arrangement, 1940. Memphis: W. C. Handy, 1912. Originally known as "Mr. Crump." Recorded: Capitol CDP 7243-8-32612-

2-2; Columbia CK-40242; Lindström American Record A4169; Okeh 4896.

"Mozambique." 1934. New York: Handy Brothers Music.

"Mr. Crump." 1909; revised as "The Memphis Blues," 1912. Recorded: Audio Archives A-1200; DRG SL-5192.

"Natives Singin'." New York: Handy Brothers Music.

"Negrita." 1935. New York: Handy Brothers Music. Co-composer, Alfonso D'Artega.

"Newspaperman's Blues." 1953. New York: Handy Brothers Music. Co-composer, Charles L. Cooke.

"Ole Miss Blues." 1916. New York: Handy Brothers Music, 1916. In *Collection of Blues, Blues Folio,* and *Blues: An Anthology.* Also titled "Ole Miss" or "Ole Miss Rag." Recorded: Columbia A2420; Columbia CK-40242; Memphis Archives MA-7006.

"Opportunity." New York: Handy Brothers Music, 1932.

"Pasadena." 1927. New York: W. C. Handy Music, 1927.

"Remembered (Impressions of Florence Mills)." 1940. New York: Handy Brothers Music. In *Unsung Americans Sung.* Co-composer, Joe Jordan.

"Roosevelt Triumphal March" or "President Roosevelt's Triumphal March." Note: lost, ca. 1906.

"(Shine like a) Morning Star." New York: Handy Brothers Music. Recorded: Capitol CDP 7243-8-32612-2-2.

"Shoeboot's Serenade." 1915. Memphis: Pace and Handy Music, 1915. In *Blues: An Anthology.* Notes: originally subtitled "Rag Song with Trombone Obligato"; based on Schubert's "Ständchen."

"Somebody's Wrong about Dis Bible." 1930. New York: Handy Brothers Music.

"Sounding Brass and Tinkling Cymbals." 1922. New York: Handy Brothers Music.

"Southside." 1922.

"The St. Louis Blues." 1914. Memphis: Pace and Handy Music, 1914. In *Collection of Blues, Blues Folio,* and *Blues: An Anthology.* Recorded: Black Swan 2053; Capitol CDP 7243-8-32612-2-2; Famous 3092; Memphis Archives MA-7006.

"Sundown Blues." 1923. New York: Handy Brothers Music, 1923. In *Collection of Blues* and *Blues: An Anthology.* Recorded: Lindström American Record A4167; Okeh 4886.

"The Temple of Music (A Tribute to Robert T. [Bob] Motts)." 1940. New York: Handy Brothers Music. In *Unsung Americans Sung.* Co-composer, Joe Jordan.

"Thinking of Thee." 1917.

"Though We're Miles Apart." 1919. Co-composer, Charles Hillman.

"Vesuvius (There's a Red Glow in the Sky above Vesuvius)." 1935. New York: Handy Brothers Music.

"Wall Street Blues." 1929. New York: Handy Brothers Music. In *Blues: An Anthology.*

"Way Down South Where the Blues Began." Copyright, 1932. New York: Handy Brothers Music. In *Blues: An Anthology.* Recorded: Audio Archives A-1200; DRG SL5192; Varsity 8162.

"When the Black Man Has a Nation of His Own." Copyright, 1925. New York: Handy Brothers Music. In *Unsung Americans Sung.*

"The White Man Said 'Twas So, So It Must Be So." 1927.

"Who Was the Husband of Aunt Jemima (The Mammy of the Gold Dust Twins)." New York: Handy Brothers Music, 1921.

"Who's That Man?" 1928. Co-composer, Spencer Williams.

W. C. Handy; courtesy of Handy Brothers Music Company, Incorporated, New York

"Wool-Loo-Moo-Loo Blues." New York: Handy Brothers Music, 1942. Co-composer, Clarence M. Jones.

"Yellow Dog Blues" or "Pattona Rag." 1914. Memphis: Pace and Handy Music, 1914. In *Collection of Blues, Blues Folio,* and *Blues: An Anthology.* Originally titled "The Yellow Dog Rag." Recorded: Capitol CDP 7243-8-32612-2-2; Lyratone 4212; Memphis Archives MA-7006.

PUBLICATIONS

ABOUT HANDY
Books and Monographs

Adams, Paul R. *Bibliography of W. C. Handy-Related Holdings.* Memphis: Memphis State University, 1982.

Currotto, William F. *A Newspaper Scrapbook of William Christopher Handy: Father of the Blues.* Memphis: W. F. Currotto, 1995.

Lee, George W. *Beale Street: Where the Blues Began.* New York: Robert O. Ballou, 1934.

————. *The Legend of W. C. Handy, "Father of the Blues."* Memphis: W. C. Handy Memorial Fund Committee, 1960.

Moore, Craig. *W. C. Handy, 1873–1958: A Collection of the Memphis/ Shelby County Room, Memphis/Shelby County Public Library and Information Center.* Memphis: The Library, 1985.

W. C. Handy 85th Birthday Year Celebration Committee. *W. C. Handy 85th Birthday Celebration Year: November 17, 1957–November 17, 1958.* New York: R. W. Kelly, 1957.

Dissertations

Packard, Donald Wheeler. "The Blues, 1912–27." Master's thesis, Eastman School of Music, 1947.

Reichenbach, Allan Metz. "Four American Musician Autobiographies." Master's thesis, Emory University, 1973.

Articles

Blau, George. "W. C. Handy." *Music Memories* 3, no. 2 (1963): 16–18.

Cerulli, Dom. "W. C. Handy's Story of the Blues." *Down Beat* 25, no. 7 (1958): 15–16, 42.

Fox, Mrs. Jesse W. "Beale Street and the Blues." [Memphis] *West Tennessee Historical Society Papers: Papers* 13 (1959): 128–147.

Harkin, G. E. "Mr. Handy's Beale Street." *Sepia* 8 (July 1960): 24–28.

Levine, Henry. "Gershwin, Handy and the BLUES." *Clavier* (October 1970): 10–20.

Kay, George W. "William Christopher Handy, Father of the Blues: A History of Published Blues." *Jazz Journal* 24, no. 3 (1971): 10–12.

Morrison, Allan. "Broadway's Grand Old Man of Music." *Ebony* (November 1953): 59–70.

Morton, Jelly Roll. "I Created Jazz in 1902, Not W. C. Handy." *Down Beat* (August and September 1938). Reprinted in *Down Beat: 60 Years of Jazz,* edited by Hal Leonard, 35–36. Milwaukee, Wis.: Hal Leonard, 1995.

Niles, Abbe. "Blue Notes." *New Republic* 45 (February 3, 1926): 292–293.

————. "Sad Horns." Introduction to *Blues: An Anthology* (New York: Albert and Charles Boni, 1926). Reprinted as "The Blues." In *Frontiers of Jazz,* edited by Ralph De Toledano, 32–57. New York: Durrell, 1947. Reprinted as "The Story of the Blues," in W. C. Handy, *A Treasury of the Blues,* 9–32. New York: Charles Boni, 1949.

Rossi, Nick. "Father of the Blues." *Music Journal* 29, no. 5 (1971): 24–26, 58–59.

Scarborough, Dorothy. "Blues." In *On the Trail of Negro Folk-Songs,* 264–280. Cambridge, Mass.: Harvard University Press, 1925. Originally published as "The 'Blues' as Folk-Songs." *Texas Folklore Society Publications* no. 2 (1923).

Smith, Charles E. "Introduction." *W. C. Handy Blues Sung by His Daughter, Katharine Handy Lewis.* Cassette recording. Washington, D.C.: Smithsonian Institution, 1991.

Souchon, Edmond. "W. C. Handy: An Enigma." *Record Changer* 4, no. 5 (May 1952): 3–4, 16.

Southern, Eileen. "Letters from W. C. Handy to William Grant Still." *Black Perspective in Music* 7, no. 2 (1979): 199–234; 8, no. 1 (1980): 65–119.

Van Vechten, Carl. "The Black Blues." *Vanity Fair* 24 (August 1925): 57, 86, 92.

Wilson, Edmund. "American Ballads and Their Collectors." *New Republic* 47 (June 30, 1926): 168–170.

————. "Shanty Boy Ballads and Blues." *New Republic* 47 (July 14, 1926): 227–229.

BY HANDY

"The Birth of the Blues." *Victor Record Review* 4, no. 5 (1941): 12–13, 23.

"The Blues." *Chicago Defender* (August 30, 1919): 9.

"An Explanation of the 'Blues.'" *Musical Journal* 15 (November/December 1957): 8–9.

Father of the Blues: An Autobiography, edited by Arna Bontemps. New York: Macmillan, 1941.

"From Minstrel Songs to St. Louis Blues." *Variety* 196, no. 7 (1954): 51.

"The Heart of the Blues." *Etude* 58, no. 3 (1940): 152, 193–94. Reprinted in *Readings in Black American Music,* edited by Eileen Southern, 212–217. 2nd ed. New York: W. W. Norton, 1983.

"How I Came to Write the 'Memphis Blues.'" *New York Age* (December 7, 1916): 6.

"I Would Not Play Jazz if I Could." *Down Beat* (September, 1938). Reprinted in *Down Beat: 60 Years of Jazz,* edited by Hal Leonard, 36–37. Milwaukee, Wis.: Hal Leonard, 1995.

Negro Authors and Composers of the United States. New York: Handy Brothers Music, 1938.

PRINCIPAL ARCHIVES

Handy Brothers Music Co., Inc., New York, New York

W. C. Handy Collection, Schomburg Center for Research in Black Culture, New York Public Library, New York, New York

W. C. Handy Home and Museum, Beale and Fourth Streets, Memphis, Tennessee

W. C. Handy Home and Museum, Florence, Alabama

W. C. Handy (1873–1958) Collection, Library, Fisk University, Nashville, Tennessee

* * * * *

W. C. Handy, composer, publisher, and bandleader, was widely regarded in his time as one of the greatest American songwriters. In retrospect, he stands as an equally important codifier and disseminator of black American folklore, and he assimilated folk blues materials into the wider commercial and urban culture, adding a blue note to American music as it existed in 1910 by creating an aggregate of Anglo-Celtic folksong and hymnody, minstrelsy, spirituals, Victorian parlor ballads, band music, and the newer strains of ragtime and blues. Handy's role in the synthesis of these materials was crucial, and his achievement places him alongside Stephen Foster and James Bland as a seminal figure in the history of American song.

Born in 1873, in Florence, Alabama, Handy grew up in relatively comfortable circumstances and was well educated. His father was a minister who prized respectability, hard work, and achievement. Despite the discouragement of this formidable patriarch, who sanctioned only organ and sacred music study, Handy managed to learn the cornet and guitar in his youth. He also learned solfège and the rudiments of music in grade school. Well into adulthood, he continued to augment his musical knowledge through the study of printed texts, by self instruction, and through study with others; for example, he is said to have studied orchestration with a teacher in Memphis.

Handy served an unusually long musical apprenticeship before making his reputation. He began arranging music when in grade school and set to music a popular ballad for a quartet of female friends; he sang with various male quartets as a teenager. In 1892, he earned a teacher's certificate, intending to teach, but instead he found better-paid work as a laborer. In 1900–02, however, he put his certificate to good use, teaching music at A&M College in Normal, Alabama, near Huntsville.

Handy was far more deeply involved with the entertainment field than with education. He traveled with Mahara's Minstrels in the United States, Cuba, and Mexico (1896, 1900, 1902–03); he led the Knights of Pythias band in Clarksdale, Mississippi, from 1903 to 1905, then moved to Memphis, where he led Thornton's Knights of Pythias Band while continuing to lead and play with other ensembles in the Mississippi Delta. At the peak of his band-leading career in Memphis, Handy was managing three bands that were providing much of the music for an extensive entertainment circuit. He was a disciplinarian and perfectionist who nevertheless enjoyed a warm relationship with his musicians.

Before he ever released a publication, Handy spent ten years as a bandleader, honing his arranging skills and hearing his work played. Not surprisingly, he left behind no juvenilia. Some of his earliest surviving works date from his mid-thirties and already show a mature sense of form; these works give no hint, however, that he was destined to go down in history as the "Father of the Blues." Handy's first songs generally reflect older musical styles that were common in the early decades of the 20th century. With his first lyricist and publishing business partner, Harry Herbert Pace, Handy wrote four songs, all firmly based in two of the most common older genres. Thematically and lyrically, "In the Cotton Fields of Dixie" (1907) and "In the Land Where Cotton Is King" (1916) rely on plantation melody conventions. "The Girl You Never Have Met" (1913) and "Thinking of Thee" (1917) are sentimental, polite post-Victorian songs, the latter a "mother" song. These genres, like band music and spirituals, were important components in Handy's background as a musician.

Later in life, he maintained a high regard and even nostalgia for the older traditions. He staged a minstrel entertainment in

1925 and wrote fondly of minstrelsy in his autobiography, *Father of the Blues*. Beginning in the 1920s, he turned increasingly to the Negro spirituals for inspiration, an activity that culminated in 1938 with the publication of *W. C. Handy's Collection of Negro Spirituals*. Handy's spirituals, like those of his protégé William Grant Still or those of his friend J. Rosamond Johnson (Handy published some by each man), are set in a straightforward, even conservative style that was prevalent in the 1930s. All of Handy's spirituals are settings of traditional melodies, as he was happy to acknowledge. Characteristic examples of his work in the area include "I'm Drinking from a Fountain That Never Runs Dry" (1924), "Let Us Cheer the Weary Traveler" (1927), and "I've Heard of a City Called Heaven" (1928). The last-named of these derives much of its power from the dramatic use of stark, repeated unison passages.

In 1913, Handy joined forces with Atlanta businessman Harry Pace in a publishing venture, Pace and Handy Music Company. For the next 45 years, Handy was a leading publisher of compositions by other musicians, black and white. He was as important in this respect as in his creative endeavors. Many of the pieces he published, including some he wrote, seem old-fashioned even for the time in which they appeared, but this reflects the fact that Handy, born in 1873, was no longer young by the time he became a composer-publisher. He arrived in the first rank of songwriters simultaneously with a number of major talents a decade younger than he, among them Eubie Blake, Jerome Kern, Shelton Brooks, and Irving Berlin.

Alongside his more conservative musical activities, Handy was simultaneously forging a stylistic revolution. In the years 1914–24, his creative output peaked in two separate bursts of songwriting activity. In the first of these phases, roughly from 1914 to 1917, he was and was still active primarily as a bandleader. Although the firm name, Pace and Handy Music Company, appeared on their published sheet music, Harry Pace was generally preoccupied with the Standard Life Insurance Company of Atlanta between 1913 and 1920. During these years, Handy was writing songs on his own, with his own lyrics, and was copyrighting them solely in his own name. During this surge of productivity, he wrote and published his greatest blues, "The St. Louis Blues" and "Yellow Dog Blues" (originally titled "The Yellow Dog Rag", both 1914), "Joe Turner Blues" and "The Hesitating Blues" (both 1915), and "Ole Miss" and "Beale Street" (both 1916, the latter renamed "Beale Street Blues" and not published until 1917).

Handy spent much of 1916–18 managing the growing company and guiding its transition from a Memphis business into one rooted in the North. Handy joined the Great Migration, first in an abortive move to Chicago and then in a successful resettlement in the summer of 1918 in New York, where the business remains to this day.

A second important creative period for Handy was that roughly between 1921 and 1924, years marked also by adversity. In 1921, Harry Pace left Pace and Handy to found Black Swan Records, causing a disruption by taking with him the best talent in the office, including William Grant Still and Fletcher Henderson. This disruption exacerbated business difficulties that Handy was already experiencing and nearly caused the business to fail. In 1922, in debt and facing ruin from a steep decline in record royalties, Handy took measures to keep his business from collapsing. In addition to selling his house on Harlem's Striver's Row and staffing the office with immediate family members to cut expenses, he sold or licensed a number of valuable copyrights to less vulnerable white publishers. The reorganized business, Handy Brothers Music Company, would not be truly profitable again for almost 20 years.

In the 1920s, Handy relied more than ever on the folk sources that had fed so many of his earlier blues, especially "Joe Turner Blues." "Loveless Love" (1921) is easily recognizable as the old folksong "Careless Love," and the chorus of "Atlanta Blues" (1924) had a long folk pedigree as "Make Me a Pallet on the Floor." But his best music of this period is found in newly composed pieces that use folklore only for inspiration. "Aunt Hagar's (Children) Blues" (1920; revised 1922 with words by J. Tim Brymn), is an exceptionally witty character portrait whose protagonist is a sassy matriarch who battles churchly prohibitions against blues music. "The Basement Blues" (1924) includes a riotous catalog of puns, corny jokes, and period slang, much of it commenting on race and caste distinctions within black society in Handy's era. These two last-mentioned numbers are among his most original works. They express his growing personal authority and reflect an increasing willingness to comment on his own experiences and attitudes. Other mature products of this second period mirror Handy's personal and business experiences, including "Harlem Blues" (1923) and "The Chicago Gouge" (1924). In the latter, Handy paints a vivid picture of black Chicago, familiar to him from many visits and several short residencies.

Handy, like Irving Berlin and Cole Porter and unlike most other major songwriters, was his own best lyricist. His attorney, adviser, and editor, Abbe Niles, in the foreword to *Father of the Blues,* referred to him as a lyric poet, someone who wrote distinctively in short forms. Handy's best blues lyrics and melodies seem to combine effortlessly and organically. This is remarkable considering his frequent use of a composite compositional method that combined collected and new material. In *Father of the Blues,* Handy wrote about his encounters with itinerant Mississippi Delta singers who sold their ballads on small pieces of paper similar to broadsides. These ballads provided the basis for some of his blues and spirituals.

Handy's blues are often, but by no means always, classic blues, which are generally understood to have certain musical features that do not vary much from song to song: a stanza of three lines, the first of which is literally repeated as the second, and the third entirely new. This scheme is sometimes varied with a nearly new second line or a third line that repeats the first, this time elongated and with additional material at the end. The subject matter of the genre includes romantic intimacy, epics and tall tales, lost love, bad luck, and other kinds of trouble conveyed through tales and legends, evocations of place, and much else. Most blues, including Handy's, are measured in multiples of four bars, with 12 being the most common since it works so naturally with three-line stanzas and four-bar melodic phrases. The chords that occur most frequently are those built on the first, fourth, and fifth degrees of the scale (tonic, subdominant, dominant). Blue notes, lowered tones (usually the third and seventh degrees of the scale) foreign to the key signature of the pieces in which they appear, are frequently used and are the most commonly recognized melodic feature of blues.

Handy's books—especially his autobiography, *Father of the Blues,* but also *Blues: An Anthology* (1926) and his other collections—and his song lyrics comprise an impressive contribution to American culture. Due to the ubiquity of his best songs in the 1920s, (such as "St. Louis Blues") and particularly in the wake of the release of *Blues: An Anthology,* Handy became culturally influential, and his blues influenced the writers of the Harlem Renaissance. Langston Hughes, the greatest poet among them, produced a seminal volume entitled *Weary Blues* in 1926. The following year, Handy published his own song setting of a Hughes text, "Golden Brown Blues," and Hughes's second collection of poems, *Fine Clothes to the Jew* (1927) contained a section titled "Beale Street Love," reflecting his familiarity with Handy's "Beale Street Blues." In addition, Handy provided a venue in Times Square where black entertainers could gather and mingle with white ones. The Handy Brothers office in Manhattan was an informal meeting place as well as a business. Major artistic figures, such as Eubie Blake, Bessie Smith, and George Gershwin, were among a steady stream of visitors to the premises.

Handy's reputation is problematic. His fame as "Father of the Blues" was enormous and international in his lifetime. Yet 20 years before his death, the first doubts about his accomplishments were raised in the press. Jelly Roll Morton (first in the Baltimore *Afro-American,* then in *Down Beat*) accused Handy of stealing "St. Louis Blues" from his former guitarist, Guy Williams, and "The Memphis Blues" from a triumvirate of musicians, including Morton himself. These 1938 attacks were provoked by Morton's jealousy over Handy's considerable press attention. Morton's claims cannot be substantiated but have come to be widely believed. There are also other disputed songs in the Handy catalog, such as his "The Hesitating Blues" (1915). Handy was always forthcoming about his borrowings from folk sources, if not from his contemporaries in commercial music. The worlds of black vaudeville and Tin Pan Alley in which he circulated were somewhat lawless and chaotic, and Handy tried to look after his interests as best he could. He functioned in a world in which plagiarism was common, not exceptional.

After his death, W. C. Handy was honored in a variety of ways. In 1960, a bronze statue of him was erected in Handy Park in Memphis, and another bronze statue was installed in the business district of Florence, Alabama, in 1995. The U.S. Post Office issued a commemorative Handy stamp in 1969. His childhood home in Florence, Alabama, was preserved as a museum in 1971. Two years later, his portrait was hung in the Tennessee state capitol building in Nashville, making him the first African American so honored. Another "first" was the designation by Columbia Records of the first week in February as "W. C. Handy Week." New York City joined the roster of locations honoring Handy in 1979, when West 52nd Street between Seventh Avenue and the Avenue of the Americas was renamed "W. C. Handy Place." And last, but not least, the Memphis Blues Awards have been named in his honor.

THE MEMPHIS BLUES (1912)

"The Memphis Blues" combines blues structure with characteristics of a ragtime song. The first of its three sections is a classic 12–bar blues form and has a blues chord pattern, a feature that made the piece unusual in 1912. Thereafter, the song has a variable structure, with a chord progression in the second strain that is too sophisticated to be mistaken for a genuine blues. The second 16-bar strain is harmonically and, especially, rhythmically in ragtime style; the third section, structurally again closer to a blues, also retains ragtime harmonic features.

There are many altered pitches in "The Memphis Blues," but it would not be entirely accurate to call them blue notes. Equally notable is a more decorative feature of the piece, a repeated figure alternating leaps and semitones, played *legato* and with a persistent syncopation. Handy referred to this as "the first jazz break."

Handy was always especially fond of "The Memphis Blues," his first hit and the song he felt entitled him to the appellation "Father of the Blues." Actually, there were a number of other blues of the same vintage and a few that were earlier. "The Memphis Blues," like many early blues, is not a pure blues throughout, but it was the piece through which the blues concept entered world culture.

"The Memphis Blues" was the first composition by Handy to become a major success, and it gave him a bitter lesson in copyright protection that he was never to forget. The piece originated in 1909 as a campaign song for Memphis mayoral candidate Edward Crump. The popularity of this song and the Handy band's performance of it were credited with helping elect Crump. (In fact, the lyrics lampooned the politician, a professed reformer.) Three years later, Handy published the piece in its second incarnation as "The Memphis Blues" (a piano solo). Several publishers turned the work down before Handy decided to issue it himself. He then took the word of unscrupulous business acquaintances that the piece was a failure and sold the rights for $50, retaining only authorship credit. With slightly modified music and words by George A. Norton, it went on to become an enormous hit, and Handy had to wait 28 years to regain control of the copyright.

"The Memphis Blues" enjoyed enormous popularity in the first years after its appearance. It played a seminal role in the history of popular dance music. Both Irene Castle and James Reese Europe claimed that the fox-trot was born in 1914 when Europe played "The Memphis Blues" slowly at the piano for Vernon and Irene Castle. Handy himself described the electrifying effect the piece had on dancers. The number soon gained wide acceptance in more genteel settings. According to *Father of the Blues,* Handy's band had to encore the piece nine times in a famous 1916 concert in Atlanta. It became an international hit in 1918–19, when James Reese Europe's 369th Infantry Band played it in France. Europe's unit, dubbed the "Harlem Hellfighters Band," was tremendously popular with the French people, and although there were racial tensions with the white American troops in France, there was nothing but acclaim for the band. "The Memphis Blues" in particular won the hearts of American troops of both races and, if anything, was even more of a sensation with the French.

"The Memphis Blues" was first recorded in 1914 by the Victor Military Band (instrumental) and by the vaudeville-style singer Morton Harvey (in the George Norton version). (The instrumental recording, which stylistically resembles a Sousa march more than a blues, uses the first and second sections almost exclusively, all but ignoring the third strain. By contrast, Harvey particularly emphasizes the third section.) The piece retained much of its popularity for decades. Ironically, Handy came to particularly enjoy Norton's lyr-

ics, which, while they glorify Handy personally, were written for the 1913 edition of the song used to rob Handy of considerable potential income. Both Fletcher Henderson and Duke Ellington recorded "The Memphis Blues" in the 1930s. The piece continued to reappear in updated band versions in the 1940s. By this time, Handy had reclaimed his copyright, and he was finally able to profit from the piece in the last years of its commercial viability.

ST. LOUIS BLUES (1914)

"St. Louis Blues," one of the most widely acclaimed compositions of all time, is striking for its sheer abundance of ideas; it is packed with enough memorable phrases to have carried two or three memorable songs to success. It appeared when America was in the grip of a dance craze in 1913–14, personified by the celebrity of Vernon and Irene Castle. There was a mania for new dance sensations, and this need fueled or coincided with an eruption of great popular music.

"St. Louis Blues" consists of two rhythmically distinct blues strains bridged by a dramatic tango that also serves as a brief introduction. The first section or strain consists of a standard 12-bar blues pattern repeated. The three lines of poetry are each spread over 12 bars of music in a natural, organic way so that the repetition of this pattern is doubly effective rather than redundant, reflecting the origins of the theme in a folk melody Handy overheard in his travels. The dominant chord is used sparingly, the prevailing tonic and subdominant harmonies giving the tune a mournful and repetitious quality. This lugubrious strain, with its unmistakable blues inflections, is one of the most celebrated and characteristic melodies of the twentieth century (see Ex. 1).

Example 1. "St. Louis Blues," mm. 9–12

The second section of "St. Louis Blues" is a tango, or *habanera,* a style that Handy first heard during his sojourn in Cuba with Mahara's Minstrels in 1900. He would later come to see the tango as an African-derived dance rhythm—originally the "tangana," as he calls it in *Father of the Blues*—and to view his appropriation of this Latin strain as a unifying, even pan-Africanist, cultural gesture. Without question, the tango measures of "St. Louis Blues" provided a jolt of surprise when the song was new and allowed Handy to benefit from the huge commercial vogue of the tango during the years around World War I.

The repeated three-note figure that comprises the final chorus of "St. Louis Blues," a rising semitone followed by a descending major third, derives from a chant Handy heard in his native Florence, Alabama, in the early 1890s. According to Abbe Niles's commentary in *Blues: An Anthology,* Brother Lazarus Gardner, an elder of the African Methodist Episcopal Church, repeatedly sang the words "Come along, come along" to this three-note pattern as he summoned the faithful to the collection plate. This passage is the barest and most elemental part of the song—and probably the oldest trope in it. (Handy had used it before, as the opening strain of a 1913 instrumental, "The Jogo Blues," and he would use it again in "Golden Brown Blues" in 1927.) The text of this final section is a lament, but the music has an irrepressible jauntiness, an eerie aural paradox that is common to blues and other folk music. Musicians instinctively tend to swing hard on the closing bars.

Like so many of his greatest songs, "St. Louis Blues" is rich in textual and melodic folk quotations that were charged with personal overtones for Handy. The doleful line "Ma man's got a heart like a rock cast in de sea" was uttered by a dejected woman in St. Louis, where Handy wandered the streets after finding himself stranded and destitute during his youthful travels in 1893. The line, fused with the experience, created a memory of suffering that Handy claimed he never forgot. Significantly, it was this line from the middle of the song that was used to open a 1929 film short entitled "St. Louis Blues," which featured Bessie Smith and in the production of which Handy took part.

The song immediately found favor with dancers, and by the 1920s had established itself as the greatest of all international pop standards. Members of the English royal family were sufficiently taken with "St. Louis Blues" that the pipers at Balmoral Castle in Scotland were required to add it to their repertoire. Emperor Haile Selassie of Ethiopia had the piece played at his palace in Addis Ababa. Handy received amused letters from correspondents from Moscow, Tokyo, and Seoul, informing him of futile efforts to render idiomatic translations of the lyrics.

According to the evidence of Richard Crawford and Jeffrey Magee's *Jazz Standards on Record,* "St. Louis Blues" was recorded at least 165 times by jazz bands alone between 1915 and 1942, far more often than any other piece by an African American. It was first recorded in 1915 by Prince's Band, and several other recordings followed within the first few years. As with his other songs, white performers (such as blackface singer Al Bernard) played a crucial role in the early reception history of "St. Louis Blues"; Handy was particularly grateful to singer Marion Harris for the part she played in popularizing the piece.

Handy himself recorded "St. Louis Blues" in 1922; his interpretation proceeds at a fast clip but sounds more like martial music than dance music. All of the early Handy recordings betray his background in marches and other turn-of-the-century styles. Bessie Smith's famous 1925 recording is diametrically opposed to Handy's: doleful in the extreme, rich in blues inflection, but too slow to retain an adequate pulse for dancers. This would remain true of her later interpretations, as the 1929 film attests. Her recordings reflect a general change in blues performance during the 1920s. The blues as dance music waned in popularity after 1920 and, in the next two decades, became entirely associated with slow tempos, mourning, and complaint.

"St. Louis Blues" lends itself to creative reinvention, and in the 1920s, new versions of the piece began to proliferate. Fats Waller, who was on very friendly terms with Handy, arranged "St. Louis Blues" for organ. Handy Brothers Music Company published this setting, and Waller's 1926 recording (substantially different from the printed version) is one of the best recorded performances. Toward the end of the recording, Waller digs deep into the primal roots of the melody, producing a foreshadowing of much later rhythm and blues music. This tendency is also audible

at the end of Louis Armstrong's great 1930 recording and in the very similar closing passages of a version Cab Calloway recorded later in the same year. There have also been symphonic treatments of "St. Louis Blues," including one published by Handy Brothers, although these, predictably, have been less successful.

YELLOW DOG BLUES (1914)

"Yellow Dog Blues" is a response song, drawing on the competitive but friendly interrelationships among black songwriter/entertainers of the day. "Yellow Dog Blues" answered Shelton Brooks's 1913 hit, "I Wonder Where My Easy Rider's Gone," the tale of a girl who loses her money betting on a favorite jockey. Brooks's song fits firmly into the vaudeville blues style, and Handy's response, while more of a blues than its antecedent, mirrors "Easy Rider" in its use of sexual double entendre.

In Handy's response to Brooks, he used a snatch of folk poetry he had overheard at the railroad station in Tutwiler, Mississippi, about 1903. A man seated beside him sang repeatedly, to the accompaniment of his own bottleneck guitar, the line "Goin' where the Southern 'cross' the Dog," a reference to the crossing point of two railroad lines in nearby Moorhead. This was one of Handy's first exposures to genuine Mississippi Delta blues, and he was struck by the "weird" (we might say "eerie") quality of this music.

With "Yellow Dog Blues," Handy combined homage to a fellow black songwriter with a lesson in one-upmanship and song styling. Brooks had carefully prepared the chorus of his song, its most memorable passage. Handy used the chorus of "Easy Rider" as the introduction to his song. He had much stronger material, both original and culled from the folk tradition, to use for his own chorus. Brooks was one of the greatest black songwriters of the era, with hits like "Some of These Days" and "The Darktown Strutters' Ball" to his credit; however, in this instance, Handy's reuse of Brooks's "Easy Rider" chorus bested his competitor at his own game, and Handy emerged from this contest with the bigger hit.

In keeping with its lighthearted character, "Yellow Dog Blues" is fundamentally rooted in D major, with minor harmonies and lowered tones being added primarily as decoration and for variety. Compared with "St. Louis Blues," this work is structurally simple with only two melodic strains. It opens with an eight-bar anticipation of the second strain, an introductory gesture familiar from parlor song and other older genres. Following a two-bar transition in the dominant key (a vamp, to be played until the singer is ready to begin), the blues song proper begins, again in the tonic key.

In reusing the chorus of Brooks's "Easy Rider" as his verse, Handy stretched and deformed the original melody, subdividing and adding strings of eighth notes to accommodate his text. Brooks's melody was already something of a monotone; in Handy's treatment, Brooks's melody is recast as two three-note figures (*a-b/ b*-flat-*c* and *d-e-f*). In the former figure, the tonic chord supports the melody throughout; in the latter, the subdominant underpins the use of the lowered third in the melody, just as tonic chords offset the lowered sixth and seventh in the earlier phrase. These phrases are set in a classic blues pattern with three 12-bar phrases in the lengthy verse and two in the shorter chorus. This chorus, with its pervasive use of stepwise motion, is one of Handy's best-known melodies. Throughout, Handy relies heavily on the tonic and subdominant, the dominant appearing only at a few structurally significant points, such as the lead-in to the chorus.

"Yellow Dog Blues" enjoyed considerable popularity through the 1920s, once Handy changed the title from "The Yellow Dog Rag." An early recording by white bandleader Joe Smith made a good deal of money for Handy. Bessie Smith's 1925 recording with a reduced Fletcher Henderson unit was typified by her slow, bluesy approach to the music and her stunningly powerful voice. At the opposite end of the spectrum, Ben Bernie's nearly contemporary recording emphasized the comic, vaudeville aspects of the song—an approach taken by most performers through the 1920s. Louis Armstrong's 1954 recording of "Yellow Dog Blues" was particularly assured, demonstrating his unerring ability to use dramatic emphasis and phrasing to tell a story.

BEALE STREET BLUES (1916)

"Beale Street Blues" was inspired by Handy's deep feeling for Beale Avenue (later renamed Beale Street in Handy's honor), the center of the black neighborhood in Memphis where he had come to maturity as a songwriter and founded a publishing business. The song may also reflect a certain nostalgia on Handy's part, since he wrote it at a time when he was beginning to broaden his horizons and consider a move to the North. The chorus of "Beale Street Blues" contains the line, "It's goin' to take the Sargent [sic] for to make me go." Despite this declaration of faithfulness to Beale Street, in a few short years Handy would leave for New York, where for four decades he would reign as the dominant black figure in Tin Pan Alley.

"Beale Street Blues," like most of Handy's songs, contains phrases taken from the folk tradition. The "Beale Street" quotations are woven into the lyric in a particularly seamless way and on two levels. Of these, Handy's happiest discovery was the statement of a Beale Avenue barber, which was made in response to Handy's question of why the shop was open so late: "I never close till somebody gets killed."

Later, the text includes the line, "I'd rather be here than any place I know," a phrase obviously taken from an itinerant street singer, "the blind man on the corner, who sings the Beale Street Blues." At this point, Handy adds a bluesy element to what to that point had retained vestiges of commercial song style. Again, the stylistic progress is gradual. Handy's technique here is masterful, culminating in a passage that transcends the commercial blues genre. Here, as he had done in "St. Louis Blues," Handy made the division between "genuine" and "commercial" blues virtually disappear.

"Beale Street Blues," like "Joe Turner Blues" and other mature Handy compositions, displays classic blues features within a popular song framework that ultimately derives its structure from parlor song. By the time it was written, Handy had learned to write songs that adhered closely to the textbook definition of a blues, a definition that he himself helped to create, and he was freely mixing blues and Tin Pan Alley elements. These pieces mimic folk-derived musical traits, such as the chantlike, "monotonous" quality that so impressed Handy (as he says in *Father of the Blues*) when he was first exposed to genuine folk blues.

"Beale Street Blues" has one of the longest introductions of any of Handy's songs. Following a four-bar opening phrase derived from the chorus and a two-bar vamp, the introduction/verse begins. This 24-bar passage is predominantly centered in B-flat major, the dominant key of the song, an unusual feature in the context of Handy's usual practice.

The chorus is in two parts, both based on folk sources and both among the most memorable phrases Handy ever wrote. The first eight-bar phrase maintains the tension of the verse through frequent use of dominant chords. Here, too, we find some of Handy's most skilled and evocative lyrics, particularly in the third of the three sets of lyrics for this passage: "If Beale Street could talk/ Married men would have to take their beds and walk,/Except one or two, who never drink booze,/And the blind man on the corner who sings the Beale Street Blues."

This leads, naturally and seemingly effortlessly, into the second part of the chorus, introducing the blind street singer with his declaration of fealty to Beale Street. Here the music finally resolves to the tonic, a long-delayed release of the tension engendered by the previously prevailing dominant. At the same time, the final 24-bar passage opens with a rhythmic figure consisting of four eighth notes followed by a long held note, echoing the tango rhythm in "St. Louis Blues." Indeed, "Beale Street Blues," in its brilliant yet unostentatious blending of disparate musical elements and multiple folk quotations, stands alongside "St. Louis Blues" as one of Handy's two masterpieces.

"Beale Street Blues" was recorded often in the first few decades after its publication. The earliest version, by white bandleader Earl Fuller (1917), was enormously lucrative for Handy at a time when he was deeply in debt. Another white bandleader, trombonist Jack Teagarden, adopted "Beale Street" with particular fervor, performing and recording it many times over a period of 30 years. Teagarden had a particular genius for the blues, and his trombone improvisations and vocals on "Beale Street" are deeply felt. Fats Waller prepared an organ arrangement of "Beale Street," as he had done with "St. Louis Blues" and "Loveless Love." Two versions were recorded in 1927, of which one, with Alberta Hunter adding a vocal chorus at the end, is extraordinary. F. Scott Fitzgerald made evocative reference to "Beale Street" in *The Great Gatsby* (1925), a further measure of the extent to which Handy's music pervaded the Jazz Age. It is largely due to Handy that, by the middle of the 1920s, the blues had indelibly colored American culture. In this respect, at least, as in his work as a folklorist, Handy's importance for American music can hardly be overstated.

REFERENCES

Abbott, Lynn, and Doug Seroff. "'They Cert'ly Sound Good to Me': Sheet Music, Southern Vaudeville, and the Commercial Ascendancy of the Blues." *American Music* 14, no. 4 (1996): 402–454.

Badger, Reid. *A Life in Ragtime: A Biography of James Reese Europe.* New York: Oxford University Press, 1995.

Berlin, Edward A. *Ragtime: A Musical and Cultural History.* Berkeley: University of California Press, 1980.

"'Blues Daddy' Gives an Unique Concert." *Baltimore Afro-American* (May 30, 1925): 5.

Crawford, Richard, and Jeffrey Magee. *Jazz Standards on Record, 1900–1942: A Core Repertory.* CBMR Monographs, no. 4. Chicago: Center for Black Music Research, Columbia College, 1992.

Handy, William Christopher. *Blues: An Anthology.* Introduction and notes by Abbe Niles. New York: A. and C. Boni, 1926.

————. *Father of the Blues: An Autobiography,* edited by Arna Bontemps. New York: Macmillan, 1941.

Kay, George W. "William Christopher Handy, Father of the Blues: A History of Published Blues." *Jazz Journal* 24, no. 3 (1971): 10–12.

Southern, Eileen. *Biographical Dictionary of Afro-American and African Musicians.* Westport, Conn.: Greenwood, 1982.

————. "Handy, William Christopher." In *New Grove Dictionary of American Music,* edited by H. Wiley Hitchcock and Stanley Sadie, 2: 318–319. New York: Macmillan, 1986.

Van der Merwe, Peter. *Origins of the Popular Style: The Antecedents of Twentieth-Century Popular Music.* New York: Oxford University Press, 1989.

ELLIOTT S. HURWITT

HAYES, ISAAC

Born in Covington, Tenn., August 20, 1942. **Education:** Memphis, Tenn., musical education in public schools. **Composing and Performing Career:** Covington, Tenn., sang as member of church choir, beginning age four; Memphis, Tenn., played saxophone in high school band, 1950s; began to work in local clubs, including Curry's Tropicana, the Tiki Club, and Plantation Inn, early 1960s; first solo recording, 1962; played in bands led by Jeb Stuart and Floyd Newman and in various local groups including the Teen Tones, the Morning Stars, the Ambassadors, the Missiles, and Calvin Valentine and the Swing Cats, 1962–65; formed Sir Isaac and the Doo-dads, playing the R&B club circuit, mid-1960s; Stax-Volt Records, Memphis, worked as studio musician, playing piano and organ and recording with and arranging for various R&B artists, including Otis Redding, Sam and Dave, and the Mar-Keys, 1964–69; songwriting collaboration with David Porter produced many hits for Stax artists, including "Soul Man," "Hold On! (I'm Comin')," and "B-A-B-Y," 1965–69; recorded first solo album, *Presenting Isaac Hayes*, 1968; follow-up album, *Hot Buttered Soul*, garnered national attention and reached Top Ten on pop album charts, eventually going platinum, 1969; composed soundtrack for the film *Shaft* and released *Black Moses*, 1971; turned to acting, appeared in films including *Truck Turner*, *Three Tough Guys*, and *Escape from New York*, and on television in *The Rockford Files*, 1970s; formed own recording label, Hot Buttered Soul, 1975–77; hosted syndicated radio program, *Black Music Countdown Featuring Isaac Hayes*; made several recordings for Columbia, mid-1980s; signed with Virgin Records, 1995. **Honors/Awards:** Oscar award, Song of the Year, Grammy award, Best Instrumental Arrangement and Best Original Score Written for a Motion Picture, "Theme from *Shaft*," 1972; Grammy awards, Best Pop Instrumental Performance by an Arranger, Composer, Orchestra and/or Choral Leader, *Black Moses*, 1972; Grammy nominations, Composer and Best Male R&B Vocal Performance, "Deja-Vu," 1978.

MUSIC LIST

POPULAR SONG

[The following list of titles includes only works that were composed by the subject of the entry; it is not a list of recordings that were made by the subject. Although the composer may have made recordings of his own works, the list is not restricted to those recordings but in many cases includes performances by other artists of the composer's work. The list is made up of publication and discographical data, in cases where such information is available. Although no effort has been made to include documentation of the earliest recording of the works listed, the date of the earliest recording that is readily available has been given. —Ed.]

"Accused Rap." Recorded, 1988: Columbia CK-40941.

"After Five." Recorded, 1976: ABC/Hot Buttered Soul ABC5022-923.

"Ain't That Lovin' You (for More Reasons Than One)." Recorded, 1970: Stax 4133; Stax 5S1-88003; Stax FCD-60-001.

"Aruba." Recorded, 1976: ABC/Hot Buttered Soul ABC5022-923.

"As Long As I've Got You." Co-composer, David Porter. Recorded: Atlantic 82218.

"B-A-B-Y." 1966. Co-composer, David Porter. Recorded: Atlantic 82218.

"Believe in Me." Recorded, 1978: Polydor CT-1-6164.

"Birth of Shaft." Recorded, 1995: Virgin 7243 8 40336 2 0.

"Body Language." Recorded, 1975: ABC 5022-874.

"Boot-Leg." Co-composers, Duck Dunn, Packy Axton, Al Jackson Jr. Recorded: Atlantic 82218.

"Branded." Recorded, 1995: Charisma 7243 8 40335 4 05; Pointblank 24 or Pointblank 40335.

"Candy." Co-composer, Steve Cropper. Recorded: Atlantic 82218.

"Chocolate Chip." Recorded, 1975: ABC 5022-874.

"Choppers." Recorded, 1976: ABC/Hot Buttered Soul ABC5022-923.

"Come Live with Me." Recorded, 1975: ABC 5022-874.

"Come On." Recorded, 1973: Stax 2SCD-88004-2.

"Deja-vu." 1978. Recorded: Arista n.n.

"Dime a Dozen." Co-composer, David Porter. Recorded: Atlantic 82218.

"Didn't Know Love Was So Good." Recorded, 1995: Virgin 7243 8 40336 2 0.

"Disco Connection." Recorded, 1976: ABC/Hot Buttered Soul ABC5022-923.

"Doesn't Rain in London." Recorded, 1970: Stax 4133.

"Don't Take Your Love Away." Co-composer, Lee Hatim. Recorded, 1977: Polydor CT-1-6120.

"Eye of the Storm." Recorded, 1988: Columbia CK-40941.

"The Feeling Keeps On Coming." Recorded, 1973: Stax SCD-8530-2; Stax/Fantasy 5MP S8530.

"A Few More Kisses to Go." Recorded, 1979: Polydor PD-1-6224; Polygram 529487.

"The First Day of Forever." Recorded, 1976: ABC/Hot Buttered Soul ABC5022-923.

"Foreplay Rap." Recorded, 1988: Columbia CK-40941.

"The 405." Recorded, 1995: Virgin 7243 8 40336 2 0.

"Funkalicious." Recorded, 1995: Virgin 7243 8 40336 2 0.

"Funky Junky." Recorded, 1995: Virgin 7243 8 40336 2 0.

"Groove-a-thon." Recorded, 1975: Hot Buttered Soul ABCD-925.

"Hold On! (I'm Comin')." 1966. Co-composer, David Porter. Note: reached no. 1 on the R&B charts, 1966. Recorded: Atlantic 81279-2; Flashback R4 72664.

"How Can You Mistreat the One You Love." Co-composer, David Porter. Recorded: Atlantic 82218.

"Hyperbolicsyllabicsesquedalymistic." Recorded, 1969: Pointblank 24 or Pointblank 40335; Stax 4114.

"I Ain't Never." Recorded, 1980: Polydor PD-1-6269.

"I Ain't Particular." Co-composer, David Porter. Recorded: Atlantic 82218.

"I Can't Turn Around." Recorded, 1975: ABC 5022-874.

"I Got to Love Somebody's Baby." Co-composer, David Porter. Recorded: Atlantic 82218.

"I Had a Dream." Co-composer, David Porter. Recorded: Atlantic 82218.

"I Love You That's All." Recorded, 1973: Stax SCD-8530-2; Stax/Fantasy 5MP S8530.

"I Take What I Want." 1965. Co-composer, David Porter. Recorded: Atlantic 81279-2; Bell 6010.

Isaac Hayes; courtesy of BMI Photo Archives

"I Thank You." 1968. Co-composer, David Porter. Recorded: Atlantic 81279-2; Flashback R2 71664; Warner Brothers HS 3369.

"I Want to Make Love to You So Bad." Recorded, 1975: ABC 5022-874.

"If I Never Needed Love (I Sure Do Need It Now)." Co-composer, David Porter. Recorded: Atlantic 82218.

"If We Ever Needed Peace." Recorded, 1978: Polydor CT-1-6164.

"Ike's Mood I." Recorded, 1970: Stax SCD-4133-2.

"Ike's Plea." Recorded, 1995: Charisma 7243 8 40335 4 05; Pointblank 24 or Pointblank 40335.

"Ike's Rap I." Recorded, 1970: Stax SCD-4133-2.

"Ike's Rap V." Recorded, 1973: Stax 2SCD-88004-2.

"Ike's Rap VI." Recorded, 1973: Stax 2SCD-88004-2.

"Ike's Rap VII." Recorded, 1980: Polydor PD-1-6269.

"Ike's Rap VIII." Recorded, 1970: Stax 4133.

"I'll Always Have Faith in You." Co-composer, Alvertis Isbell. Recorded: Atlantic 82218.

"I'll Do Anything (to Turn You On)." Recorded, 1995: Charisma 7243 8 40335 4 05; Pointblank 24 or Pointblank 40335.

"I'll Gladly Take You Back." Co-composer, David Porter. Recorded: Atlantic 82218.

"I'll Run Your Heart Away." Co-composer, David Porter. Recorded: Atlantic 82218.

"I'm a Big Girl Now." Co-composer, David Porter. Recorded: Atlantic 82218.

"I'm Gonna Make It (without You)." Recorded, 1973: Stax SCD-8530-2; Stax/Fantasy 5MP S8530.

"It's Heaven to Me." 1977. Recorded, 1977: Polydor CT-1-6120; Polygram 529487.

"Joy." Recorded, 1973: Stax SCD-8530-2; Stax 5S1-88003; Stax FCD-60-002.

"Juicy Fruit (Disco Freak)." Recorded, 1976: ABC/Hot Buttered Soul ABCD-953.

"Lady of the Night." Recorded, 1976: ABC/Hot Buttered Soul ABCD-953.

"Let Me Be Good to You." 1966. Irving Music. Co-composers, David Porter, Carla Wells. Recorded: Atlantic 82340-2; Rhino 71633.

"Let Me Be Your Everything." Recorded, 1988: Columbia CK-40941.

"Let Me Love You." Recorded, 1995: Charisma 7243 8 40335 4 05; Pointblank 24 or Pointblank 40335.

"Let's Don't Ever Blow Our Thing." Recorded, 1976: ABC/Hot Buttered Soul ABCD-953.

"Let's Stay Together." Recorded, 1980: Fantasy 53304; Stax 5S1-88003; Stax FCD-60-002.

"Life's Mood." Recorded, 1995: Charisma 7243 8 40335 4 05; Pointblank 24 or Pointblank 40335.

"Life's Mood II." Recorded, 1995: Charisma 7243 8 40335 4 05; Pointblank 24 or Pointblank 40335.

"Lifetime Thing." Recorded, 1981: Polydor PD-1-6329; Polygram 529487.

"Little Bluebird." Co-composers, David Porter, Booker T. Jones. Recorded: Atlantic 82218.

"Love Attack." Recorded, 1988: Columbia CK-40941.

"Love Has Been Good to Us." Recorded, 1980: Polydor PD-1-6269.

"Love Me or Lose Me." Recorded, 1976: ABC/Hot Buttered Soul ABCD-953.

"Make a Little Love to Me." Recorded, 1975: Hot Buttered Soul ABCD-925.

"Make It Me." Co-composer, David Porter. Recorded: Atlantic 82218.

"Making Love at the Ocean." Recorded, 1995: Virgin 7243 8 40336 2 0.

"Man Will Be a Man." Recorded, 1973: Stax SCD-8530-2; Stax/Fantasy 5MP S8530.

"May I Baby?" Co-composer, David Porter. Recorded: Atlantic 81279-2.

"Memphis Trax." Recorded, 1995: Virgin 7243 8 40336 2 0.

"Mistletoe and Me." Recorded, 1970: Stax 4133.

"Monologue." Recorded, 1970: Stax 4133; Stax SCD-4133-2.

"Moonlight Lovin' (Ménage à trois)." Recorded, 1977: Polydor CT-1-6120; Polygram 529487.

"Music to Make Love By." Recorded, 1976: ABC/Hot Buttered Soul ABCD-953.

"Never Like This Before." Co-composers, David Porter, Booker T. Jones. Recorded: Atlantic 82218.

"The Night Before." Recorded, 1995: Virgin 7243 8 40336 2 0.

"Out of the Ghetto." Recorded, 1977: Polydor CT-1-6120; Polygram 529487.

"Patch My Heart." Co-composer, Steve Cropper. Recorded: Atlantic 82218.

"Please Uncle Sam (Send Back My Man)." Co-composer, David Porter. Recorded: Atlantic 82218.

"Precious, Precious." Recorded, 1968: Stax 8596; Stax SD-1599.

"Rock Me Easy Baby." Recorded, 1975: Hot Buttered Soul ABCD-925.

"Said I Wasn't Gonna Tell Nobody." Co-composer, David Porter. Recorded: Atlantic 81279-2.

"Same Time, Same Place." Co-composer, David Porter. Recorded: Atlantic 82218.

"Shaft II." Recorded, 1978: Polydor CT-1-6164.

"Showdown." Recorded, 1988: Columbia CK-40941.

"Sister's Got a Boyfriend." Co-composers, David Porter, Jones. Recorded: Atlantic 82218.

"Small Portion of Your Love." Co-composer, David Porter. Atlantic 81279-2.

"Someone Who Will Take the Place of You." Recorded, 1979: Polydor PD-1-6224.

"Something Good (Is Going to Happen to You)." Co-composer, David Porter. Recorded: Atlantic 82218.

"Sophisticated Sissy." Co-composers, David Porter, Mack Rice, Joe Shamwell. Recorded: Atlantic 82218.

"Soul Fiddle." Recorded, 1995: Virgin 7243 8 40336 2 0.

"Soul Girl." Co-composer, David Porter. Recorded: Atlantic 82218.

"Soul Man." 1967. Co-composer, David Porter. Note: reached no. 1 on the R&B charts, 1967. Recorded: Atlantic 81279-2; Flashback R2 72664.

"Soul Sister (Brown Sugar)." 1968. Co-composer, David Porter. Recorded: Atlantic 81279-2; Flashback R2 72644.

"Soulsville." 1971. Recorded, 1971: Pointblank 24 or Pointblank 40335.

"Southern Breeze." Recorded, 1995: Virgin 7243 8 40336 2 0.

"St. Thomas Square." Recorded, 1976: ABC/Hot Buttered Soul ABC5022-923.

"The Storm Is Over." Recorded, 1976: ABC/Hot Buttered Soul ABCD-953.

"Sugar Singer." Co-composer, Alvertis Isbell. Recorded: Atlantic 82218.

"Summer." Recorded, 1981: Polydor PD-1-6329.

"The Sweeter He Is." 1968. Co-composer, David Porter. Recorded, 1969: Stax STA-0050.

"Tahoe Spring." Recorded, 1995: Virgin 7243 8 40336 2 0.

"Thank You Love." Recorded, 1976: ABC/Hot Buttered Soul ABCD-953.

"Toe Hold." Co-composer, David Porter. Recorded: Atlantic 82218.

"Type Thang." Recorded, 1973: Stax 2SCD-88004-2.

"Urban Nights." Recorded, 1995: Virgin 7243 8 40336 2 0.

"Vykkii." Recorded, 1976: ABC/Hot Buttered Soul ABC5022-923.

"We've Got a Whole Lot of Love." Recorded, 1975: Hot Buttered Soul ABCD-925.

"What Does It Take." Recorded, 1979: Polydor PD-1-6224; Polygram 529487.

"When My Love Comes Down." Co-composer, David Porter. Recorded: Atlantic 82218.

"When Something Is Wrong with My Baby." 1966. Co-composer, David Porter. Recorded: Atlantic 81279-2; Flashback R2 72664.

"When Tomorrow Comes." Co-composer, David Porter. Recorded: Atlantic 82218.

"When You Move You Lose." Co-composer, David Porter. Recorded: Atlantic 82218.

"Wherever You Are." Recorded, 1980: Polydor PD-1-6269; Polygram 529487.

"Willy Nilly." Co-composer, David Porter. Recorded: Atlantic 82218.

"Winter Snow." Recorded, 1970: Atlantic 82218; Stax 4133.

"Wish You Were Here (You Ought to Be Here)." Recorded, 1975: Hot Buttered Soul ABCD-925.

"Wonderful." Recorded, 1970: Fantasy 53304; Stax 4133.

"Wrap It Up." 1970. Co-composer, David Porter. Recorded: Atlantic 8205; Atlantic 81279-2; Sony A24202.

"You Can't Run Away from Your Heart." Co-composer, David Porter. Recorded: Atlantic 82218.

"You Don't Know Like I Know." Co-composer, David Porter. Recorded: Atlantic 81279-2; Stax SD-1599.

"You Got Me Hummin'." Co-composer, David Porter. Recorded: Atlantic 81279-2.

"You Make Me Live." Recorded, 1995: Virgin 7243 8 40336 2 0.

"Your Good Thing (Is About to End)." 1966. Co-composer, David Porter. Recorded: EMI 7243-8-57181-2-0; Warner Brothers HS3369.

"Your Loving Is Much Too Strong." Recorded, 1975: Hot Buttered Soul ABCD-925.

"You're Taking Up Another Man's Place." Co-composer, David Porter. Recorded: Atlantic 82218.

"Zeke the Freak." Recorded, 1978: Polydor CT-1-6164; Polygram 529487.

INCIDENTAL MUSIC

Maidstone. 1970. Film soundtrack.

Shaft. 1971. Film soundtrack. "Theme from Shaft" received a Grammy Award, 1972. Contents: Theme from Shaft; Bumpy's Lament; Walk from Regio's; Ellie's Love Theme; Shaft's Cab Ride; Cafe Regio's; Early Sunday Morning; Be Yourself; Friend's Place; Soulsville; No Name Bar; Bumpy's Blues; Shaft Strike's Again; Do Your Thing; End Theme. Recorded: Stax CD 88002.

Three Tough Guys. 1974. Film soundtrack. Contents: Title Theme; Randolph and Dearborn; Red Rooster; Joe Bell; Hung Up on My Baby; Kidnapped; Run Fay Run; Buns O'Plenty; End Theme. Recorded: Stax 25CD 88014-2.

Truck Turner. 1974. Film soundtrack. Contents: Main Title; House of Beauty; Blue's Crib; Driving in the Sun; Breakthrough; Now We're One; Duke; Dorinda's Party; Pursuit of the Pimpmobile; We Need Each Other Girl; A House Full of Girls; Hospital Shootout; You're in My Arms Again; Give It to Me; Drinking; Insurance Company; End Theme. Recorded: Stax 25CD 88014-2.

"Two Cool Guys (Theme from *Beavis and Butt-head Do America*)." Motion picture theme. Recorded, 1996: Geffen GEFC-25002.

PUBLICATIONS

ABOUT HAYES
Articles

Corcoran, M. "We Like Ike: Isaac Hayes Has Come Back to Save Our Soul." *Spin* 11 (July 1995): 25.

Crouse, T. "Presenting Isaac Hayes Superstar." *Rolling Stone* 102 (1972): 14.

DiMartino, Dave. "Shaftmeister Returns." *Musician* 189 (July 1994): 13.

Gest, D. "Isaac Brings Soul to the Bowl." *Soul* 7 (September 1972): 8.

Goddet, L. "1973 année R 'n' B?" *Jazz Hot* 292 (March 1973): 20–21.

Henderson, W. T. "Isaac Hayes—Black Moses Wins Seal of Approval." *Soul* 7 (April 2/3, 1973): 16.

Ivy, A. "Black Moses Spreads a Lot of Joy." *Soul* 8 (June 11, 1973): 8.

Morgenstern, Dan. "Isaac Hayes: His Own Story." *Down Beat* 38 (April 29, 1971): 14–15.

Palmer, R. "Isaac Hayes: Black Moses Moves On." *Rolling Stone* 197 (1975): 18.

Pitts Jr., Leonard. "The First King of Rap." *Musician* 101 (March 1987): 29.

Rubine, N. "Isaac Hayes, the Black Moses." *Soul* 8 (February 1974): 2–3.

"The Sandpaper Soul of Isaac Hayes." *Rolling Stone* 58 (1970): 24.

Shaun, J. "Isaac Hayes: The Three Dimensional Man." *Soul Illustrated* 3, no. 1 (1971): 42–46.

Spiegelman, J. "Jazz Artist of 1971." *Soul* 7 (May 1, 1972): 16.

* * * * *

More than any other single musician, Isaac Hayes defined the compositional possibilities for African-American popular music between 1966 and the late 1970s. Between 1965 and 1969, Hayes and partner David Porter wrote many of the finest southern soul compositions that came out of Stax/Volt Records in Memphis, Tennessee. In the 1970s, on his own, Hayes pioneered the scoring of soundtracks for black films, helped to redefine the use of the voice in the soul idiom, developed several of the signature gestures of disco music, expanded the sonic palette available to black popular composers, and made the LP a meaningful mode of dissemination for black vernacular compositions. The latter, of course, had two immediate ramifications: (1) it made it possible for black vernacular composers to write extended works, and (2) as a medium, the LP record generated substantially more profits than the 45 r.p.m. single, making possible larger recording budgets for black composers of popular music. Larger recording budgets allowed these composers to spend longer amounts of time in studios experimenting with sounds, structures, techniques, orchestration, and overdubbing, and a greater number of musicians could be hired to help realize the final work.

Hayes was largely a self-taught musician. What little "formal" training he did receive was a result of the music program offered in the black sector of the Memphis school system. Upon graduation from high school, he was offered several scholarships in vocal music, but after having lived in abject poverty for the previous several years, Hayes elected not to continue his schooling, opting instead to enter the work force. While working at a variety of jobs unrelated to music, such as work in a meat packing plant, Hayes continued to develop his performing, arranging, and, ultimately, his compositional skills. During his high school years and immediately following, the budding musician worked in a number of ensembles that variously performed on the school, amateur hour, and nightclub circuits. Hayes sang doo-wop with the Teen Tones and the Ambassadors and gospel with the Morning Stars, and he played blues saxophone with Calvin Valentine and the Swing Cats, rhythm and blues piano with Jeb Stuart, and jazz sax and piano with the Missiles and Floyd Newman's band. Hayes was also well acquainted with country music, fondly recalling Saturday evenings listening to the Grand Ole Opry as a child, first in Covington, Tennessee, and later in Memphis.

Unable to read and write music fluently and possessing only an *ad hoc* sense of music theory, Hayes created head arrangements (memorized composition structures), a not-uncommon technique for small rhythm and blues or jazz ensembles. Hayes, though, would eventually take this idea much further, creating complex full orchestral scores by humming into a tape recorder the various parts that would later be transcribed by arrangers. Hayes would then supervise every detail to make sure the final orchestration was exactly what he had heard in his head. Hayes' lack of formal training often freed him to create original parts that trained composers may have been unable to conceive. This is especially evident in the keyboard parts he wrote at Stax in the 1960s.

Hayes worked his way into composition gradually. In 1964, he began playing sessions at Stax, replacing keyboard player Booker T. Jones while Jones was away at college. Slowly Hayes began volunteering ideas for arrangements, and by the summer of 1965, lyricist David Porter had approached him about a songwriting partnership. Hayes and Porter's first significant work was crafted for the fiery, gospel-tinged duo of Sam and Dave. Such Hayes-Porter compositions as "You Don't Know Like I Know," "Hold On! (I'm Comin')," "Said I Wasn't Gonna Tell Nobody," "You Got Me Hummin'," "When Something Is Wrong with My Baby," "Soul Man," "I Thank You," and "Wrap It Up" rank among the finest compositions in the history of southern soul. All of the above, save "Wrap It Up," were Top Ten R&B hits. Most of these compositions have been covered innumerable times in the intervening years, with several of the subsequent recordings turning into chart hits. Examples of covers that charted include Cold Blood's 1970 version of "You Got Me Hummin'," the Blues Brothers' 1978 reworking of "Soul Man," ZZ Top's 1980 reading of "I Thank You," the Fabulous Thunderbirds' 1986 take on "Wrap It Up," and Linda Ronstadt's and Aaron Neville's 1990 duet on "When Something Is Wrong with My Baby." With both the originals and covers being reissued several times, it is safe to say that all of these compositions have now become standards.

By his early twenties, Hayes was a virtual cornucopia of musical knowledge. His jazz experiences helped cultivate an aesthetic that preferred extended harmonies (dominant seventh chords with added ninths and elevenths, etc.), while his gospel background informed much of his piano style and sense of phrasing. This eclectic background encouraged continual growth and experimentation throughout his career. Beginning in 1969, rock and classical influences began to emerge. Taken together, these disparate influences helped propel five LPs in a row—*Hot Buttered Soul, Isaac Hayes Movement, To Be Continued, Shaft,* and *Black Moses*—to simultaneously chart in the categories of pop, rhythm and blues, jazz, and easy listening. Such crossover success was and remains virtually unprecedented.

When Hayes began his solo career in earnest with *Hot Buttered Soul* (1969), his second album, he surprised many listeners by recording the works of other writers. Even more surprising was the fact that the material he featured was that of white pop writers, specifically Burt Bacharach and Hal David's "Walk on By" and Jim Webb's "By the Time I Get to Phoenix." In both cases, Hayes totally reconstructed these three-minute pop songs as extended mélanges of pop, R&B, gospel, rock, and classical traits. "Walk on By" was stretched to 12 minutes, and "By the Time I Get to Phoenix" became an 18-minute tour de force. Hayes himself views these reworkings as, in effect, new compositions. In each case, he created a new composition by "sampling" the chords, lyrics, and melodies of preexistent works within the context of newly written material.

Hayes has continued this deconstruction/reconstruction approach right through the late-1990s. He has also continued to write original material in the more traditional sense. Much of his most successful work in this vein has been in the context of soundtrack scoring, beginning with the soundtrack to *Shaft* in 1971 and continuing with *Truck Turner* and *Three Tough Guys* in 1974. Hayes has also written extensively in the extended funk-vamp and the jazz-inflected romantic ballad styles. "Hyperbolicsyllabicsesquedalymistic" and "Joy" are the finest examples of the former, while "Wonderful" and "It's Heaven to Me" are superb examples of the latter. In the 1980s and 1990s, much of Hayes' funkier writing has been extensively sampled by rap artists, making Hayes into a musical hero with extensive influence on artists who were not born when he originally created his most important work.

SOUL MAN (1967)

The most successful songwriting partnership at Stax Records in the second half of the 1960s was that of Isaac Hayes and David Porter. As a team, they created some of the most enduring classics of the soul genre. "Soul Man," written, recorded, and released in 1967, was their most successful effort and was inspired by the heightened black pride that characterized the second half of the 1960s. In 1994, Hayes told this author:

That was during the days of the Civil Rights struggle. We had a lot of riots. I remember in Detroit, I saw a newsflash where they were burning [the city], and the only buildings that weren't burned, people would write "soul" on the building. At the time the big thing was "soul brother." So I said why not do something called "Soul Man" and tell a story about one's struggle to rise above one's present conditions. It was almost boasting—"I'm a soul man"—a pride thing. "Soul Man" came out of the black identification.

Sung by Sam Moore and David Prater, better known as Sam and Dave, and produced as well as written by Hayes and Porter, "Soul Man" was a number one hit for seven straight weeks on the rhythm and blues charts while also managing to reach number two on the pop charts.

By the time "Soul Man" was recorded, Hayes and Porter were tailoring their songs specifically to the vocal ranges and phrasing proclivities of individual artists. By late 1966, they had worked out an unofficial arrangement formula for their brightest stars, Sam and Dave. Sam's higher and stronger voice would be given the first verse, Dave's thinner, lower, and rougher timbre took the second, and the third verse would either be split between the two voices or assigned to Sam's alone. If there was a bridge, it was most often given to Dave, and the first verse was often reprised at the end, with Sam singing lead. Behind each singer's solo vocals, the other partner would inject cries and shouts of urging and affirmation (Sam was especially effective at this). Connections between sections would be seamless, and the choruses would be sung in unison. The ending would most often be in a call-and-response, *ad lib.* format. Solos were rare, although four-bar instrumental interludes and/or reprises of the introduction would often be included about two-thirds of the way through the piece.

"Soul Man" follows this formula to the letter, with the exception that the bridge is split between the two vocalists, with Dave singing the first two lines and Sam giving voice to the final couplet. When Hayes and Porter have Sam and Dave sing in unison or in harmony, they opt for a fluid conception of time in which Sam is generally slightly ahead of the beat, while Dave lags slightly behind it. The tension created by these different approaches to the beat is one of the central aesthetic components of Hayes and Porter's composition and production style.

Another such trademark of their style, which appears in "Soul Man," is the slight strain in the soloists' voices as they sing at the tops of their ranges. While Sam Moore intensely disliked doing this, the timbral results infuse "Soul Man" and other Hayes and Porter's compositions with an urgency and tension that is palpable. To this end, Hayes and Porter would commonly rehearse a song in a lower key and then, for the recording, suddenly force the vocalist higher up in his or her range.

The introduction to "Soul Man" is eight bars long and embraces the characteristic sound of an open-sixth voicing in the guitar. The chorus and verse are each also eight bars in length; the instrumental reprise of the introduction is four bars long, and the bridge has a one-bar extension that makes it an asymmetrical five bars in length. Sam and Dave engage in call-and-response throughout the verses, the bridge, and the *ad lib.* fade. In the chorus, where they sing in unison, Hayes has written for the horns and lead guitar response lines typically supplied by background vocals in the works of other soul songwriters. For the lead-guitar response, Hayes asked guitarist Steve Cropper to supply "some Elmore James, man," referring to one of the great blues slide guitarists. Cropper, not having a proper slide with him, used a cigarette lighter to achieve the desired sliding effect. Sam's famous response, the clarion call "Play it, Steve" on the second chorus, apparently came about spontaneously. The slide-guitar passage in the chorus is one of the most recognizable moments in soul music.

In keeping with his usual practice, Hayes uses the horn section as a substitute for background vocalists and employs lines in which short, syncopated off-beat "shots" are interjected by the trumpet. These "shots" are not used during the first verse of the piece but later in the song, as his additive compositional technique continually intensifies the texture over the course of the work's unfolding. On the verses, in the rhythm section, the bass, guitar, and piano all repeat one-bar, syncopated rhythmic vamps that lay out the harmony and articulate an infectious rhythmic groove.

The chorus and verse of "Soul Man" are in one key (G major), but the bridge contains an unusual modulation to a different key (E-flat major). The verse is written on one chord, the tonic, for all of its eight bars, but the harmonic rhythm intensifies on the chorus with five chord changes over the course of its eight bars. The bridge is written with a chord change at the beginning of each bar. The dominant chord is used only once in the whole composition, which is typical of Hayes' writing style. (Hayes tended to downplay the dominant in favor of the subdominant, reflecting the gospel roots of so much soul music.)

The song, a huge hit when it was originally released by Sam and Dave, also charted in 1967 in a version by Ramsey Lewis. In 1980, the composition once again was heard regularly as it charted for a third time in a version by the Blues Brothers, a version that attempted to replicate as closely as possible the Sam and Dave model. As a composition, "Soul Man" epitomizes the very essence of the soul era in both its music and lyrics.

THEME FROM SHAFT (1971)

After his illustrious career as one of the most significant writers of southern soul music in the 1960s, Isaac Hayes wrote very little for his first four solo albums. It was not until the soundtrack for the film *Shaft*, in 1971, that he began in earnest the second phase of his career as a composer. The commission to score *Shaft* was a bit of a surprise. While Hayes had always been interested in pursuing an acting career, he had never actually thought about writing soundtracks for films, since at that time no black composers other than Quincy Jones were writing music for films.

The opportunity to score *Shaft* emerged when MGM decided to create a film that would target black consumers. The project was discussed initially by Stax vice president Al Bell, Joel Freeman (the film's producer), and Gordon Parks (the director), who quickly agreed that Hayes was the most likely candidate to write the score. With no experience in composing for the screen, Hayes leapt at the opportunity, and the commission to score *Shaft* turned out to be one of the artistic and commercial high points of his career. *Shaft* became a box-office success, jump-starting the "blaxploitation" era. The soundtrack album went platinum, earned Hayes an Oscar (only the second African American so honored) and two Grammy Awards, and opened the door for Hayes, Curtis Mayfield, Bobby Womack, and others to embark on careers as bona fide film composers.

The "Theme from *Shaft*" was pulled from the soundtrack album and released as a single, topping the pop charts and peaking at number two on the rhythm and blues charts. It remains one of the most instantly recognizable compositions of the early seventies. The 16th-note hi-hat ride figure, dramatic string flourishes, and high speed wah-wah break that Hayes wrote for the composition would become bedrocks and eventually clichés of the disco era. They were first introduced to the general public in the "Theme from *Shaft*."

In light of the ultimate influence of these gestures, it is interesting to note that the 16th-note hi-hat pattern first appeared in a two-bar break at the climax to Otis Redding's 1966 recording of the Tin Pan Alley standard "Try a Little Tenderness." Hayes had played organ on that session and had helped work out the arrangement. On the Redding record, the figure is buried beneath a succession of Redding vocables and dramatic bass drum work. On "Theme from *Shaft*," the ride pattern (continuous pattern) is mixed front and center for the duration of the piece. The similarly continuous wah-wah pattern that is so inextricably identified with *Shaft* had actually been worked out by Hayes and guitarist Charles "Skip" Pitts for an earlier composition that was never finished. When Hayes began working on the title theme for the film, he was told that the film's hero, John Shaft, was a relentless character, on the move all the time, never stopping. Hayes recalled both the wah-wah figure from the earlier abandoned piece and the hi-hat pattern from "Try a Little Tenderness," concluding that both would convey the appropriate energy to make manifest aurally John Shaft's personality. Both were ingenious decisions that did much to set the pace of the film and soundtrack.

On being commissioned to score the film, Hayes had to learn the techniques involved in writing for the cinema. A number of people offered advice, including Quincy Jones. Most prescient was Tony McIntosh's suggestion that Hayes was writing what was in effect too much. McIntosh suggested that Hayes could conserve his energies and create some continuity within the film score by recycling themes in different contexts. One of the results of this advice was Hayes' use in the title theme of the major melodic line from a composition entitled "Bumpy's Lament." In "Theme from *Shaft*," the "Bumpy's Lament" theme is scored for flutes and heard prominently at about the one-minute mark. Similarly, the main melodic gesture from another tune called "Ellie's Love Theme" is recycled in the title theme, where it is scored for strings and horn and juxtaposed with the material derived from "Bumpy's Lament."

Much of the writing in "Theme from *Shaft*" is ingenious. In addition to the already mentioned motives, Hayes' ability to layer string and wind parts is superb. Particularly notable is the repeated four-bar motive that immediately precedes the vocal section; with each repetition of the section, Hayes adds more and more parts, gradually building the tension, which is finally released with the verse. The vocal is set between two keys (E minor and F major), with the harmony simply going back and forth between them. The final chord of the composition is a surprise (D minor, with a flat seventh and major ninth). The effect of this juxtaposition and progression immediately transports the listener from the opening credits and scenes to the beginning of the film proper.

On his very first project, Hayes had quickly developed into a mature film composer. It was an impressive achievement. "Theme from *Shaft*" was unlike anything he had previously written or recorded. This type of action-filled, dramatic writing for the screen would continue to be an important part of his career well into the 1990s.

SOULSVILLE (1971)

"Soulsville" is one of Hayes' most poetic lyrics.

> Black man, born free; at least that's the way it's supposed to be.
> Chains that binds him are hard to see, unless you take this walk with me.
> Place where he lives has got plenty of names; slums, ghetto and black belt, they are one
> and the same,
> But I call it Soulsville.
>
> Any kind of job is hard to find, that means an increase in the welfare line.
> Crime rate is rising too, if you were hungry what would you do?
> Rent is two months past due in a building that's falling apart.
> Little boy needs a pair of shoes, and this is only a part
> Of Soulsville.

"Soulsville" was written for the soundtrack of the film *Shaft*. Set in a lilting 3/4 meter, all instruments play a shuffle rhythm. The groove centers around a syncopated bass drum part in which beat one is strongly accented, followed by off-beats after beats two or three. On the first half of the verse, the drummer plays on the rim of the snare drum on beat three, coupling this with a straight quarter-note ride pattern on a closed hi-hat. The second half of the verse is much more active, with a ride pattern consisting of nine triplet eighths per bar while the snare is playing the head of the drum on beats two and three.

Hayes has set the evocative lyrics in B-flat major. The verse is 16 bars in length. In the first half of each of the first eight bars, the piano plays a progression that gives the composition a Mixolydian feel (B-flat major, A-flat major, C minor, with the B-flat major chord in second inversion and the C minor chord in first inversion). Such prominent articulation of the tonic chord in second inversion is a very common device in gospel music. In the second eight bars of the verse (mm. 9–16), Hayes alternates the G minor and C minor (second inversion) chords until the final bar, where the dominant chord (F major) is finally introduced. This chord sets up a perfect cadence at the beginning of the four-bar turnaround, which returns to the ostinato harmonic pattern in the first half of the verse. As was noted with "Soul Man," Hayes tends to use the dominant chord sparingly, an aesthetic strongly rooted in gospel music.

During the introduction and the first half of the verse, the guitar and bass play ostinato patterns, the bass part repeating every bar, the guitar part every two bars. In the guitar line's second beat, there occurs a wide interval (open-fourth dyad), played staccato; this interval serves as a response to the piano and bass lines, which cycle back to an emphasis on the first beat of each bar. In the second half of the verse, both the guitar and the bass are quite a bit more active in playing variants of triplet eighth-note arpeggios.

The melody of "Soulsville" is absolutely gorgeous, with much of the melodic movement consisting of thirds within an overall range of an octave and a half. Female voices, written at a significantly higher level than most of the other pitches in the piece (as is typical for Hayes), double the piano's chords on the second half of the verse; the background vocals also sing the final "soulsville" of each verse. The net effect is ethereal.

"Soulsville" was re-recorded for Hayes' 1995 comeback album, *Branded*. (Although he had never announced his retirement, it had been seven years since his last recording.) The new recording was similar to the *Shaft* version, with textual changes referring to contemporaneous conditions in inner-city black America. Most reviews of *Branded* mentioned the re-recording of "Soulsville" as one of the album's highlights.

IT'S HEAVEN TO ME (1977)

Lush, romantic love ballads have from the beginning of Hayes' solo writing career comprised a prominent part of his *oeuvre*. It was in this type of composition that he most often fully expressed his love of jazz-inflected harmony and delicate melodies and textures.

The treatment of lyrics in "It's Heaven to Me" is straightforward, with an abaab rhyme scheme used for each of the first three verses (the final verse uses a slightly varied aabba). Musically, the song is structured as follows: an eight-bar introduction, two 16-bar verses, a 16-bar interlude, and two more 16-bar verses with a 16-bar concluding tag that is modeled on the material from the interlude. While the verses are written in G major (with a melody that ranges from *b'* to *b''*), the interlude is set in contrast, suggesting G minor (with a melody that ranges from *b''*-flat to *d'''*). Hayes has crafted a melody that alternates disjunct (leaps of a third and occasionally a fourth or fifth) with conjunct motion. The melody's phrases tend to begin midway through a bar and end on a sustained final note at the end of the following or subsequent bar.

The harmonic rhythm in this piece is slow (one chord per bar), although the fourth bar of the interlude contains chord changes on every beat. The harmonies are rich and the orchestration superb. The first four bars of the introduction are scored for flutes accompanied by the harp, with glockenspiel and electric piano entering for the second half of the introduction. The net effect of these instruments' metallic, high-pitched timbral qualities is a lushness wholly appropriate to the lyric imagery that immediately follows. Subtle and restrained drum and bass parts underscore the electric piano during the first two verses, with the bass drum being played on beat one and occasionally on beat four, and the hi-hat pedal on beat three. The third and fourth verses are marked by increases in the density of the vocal accompaniment, most notably with a countermelody in the violas and violins. In the tag, acoustic guitar and glockenspiel are prominent as Hayes' vocal ascends into a wordless falsetto as if his feelings for his loved one have simply gone beyond what language can convey. Adding to the suggestion of romance is the use throughout the composition of audible breath inhalations and voiceless exhalations.

Written and recorded in 1977 for the *New Horizon* album, "It's Heaven to Me" was never released as a single. It remains one of the many lesser-known jewels within the Isaac Hayes canon.

REFERENCES

Bowman, Rob. *Soulsville U.S.A.: The Story of Stax Records.* New York: Schirmer Books, 1997.

Hayes, Isaac. Interviews by the author, August 6, 1986, and March 8, 1994.

ROB BOWMAN

HEMPHILL, JULIUS

Born in Fort Worth, Tex., 1938; died in New York, N.Y., April 2, 1995. **Education:** Fort Worth, studied clarinet with John Carter; North Texas State College, Fort Worth, Tex.; Lincoln University, Jefferson City, Mo. **Military service:** U.S. Army band, 1964. **Composing and Performing Career:** Early performances in local blues bands and jazz groups, including a band led by Ike Turner; St. Louis, Mo., founding member of the Black Artist Group (BAG) with Oliver Lake and Hamiet Bluiett, 1968; toured with pianist John Hicks, 1971; formed recording company, Mbari Records, 1972; first recording as leader, *Dogon A.D.,* 1972; moved to New York, N.Y., 1973; founding member and principal composer/arranger for the World Saxophone Quartet, with Hamiet Bluiett, Oliver Lake, and David Murray, 1976–89; founded Julius Hemphill Sextet, 1989; *The Last Supper at Uncle Tom's Cabin: The Promised Land,* toured Europe and the United States, 1990–91. **Commissions:** Arditti String Quartet and pianist Ursula Oppens, 1991; Richmond Symphony, 1993. **Honors/Awards:** Two Bessie Awards, 1991.

MUSIC LIST

INSTRUMENTAL SOLOS
Piano
"Parchment." Long Island City, N.Y.: Subito Music, n.d. Recorded: Music and Arts CD-604.

ELECTRONIC MUSIC
"Antecedent" (alto saxophone, tape). Long Island City, N.Y.: Subito Music, n.d.

"CME" (saxophone, tape). Long Island City, N.Y.: Subito Music, n.d.

"Dirty Row" (saxophone, tape). Long Island City, N.Y.: Subito Music, n.d.

"Homeboy Tootin' at the Dog Star" (saxophone, tape). Long Island City, N.Y.: Subito Music, n.d.

"Hot-End" (alto saxophone, tape). Long Island City, N.Y.: Subito Music, n.d.

"OK Rubberband" (alto saxophone, tape). Long Island City, N.Y.: Subito Music, n.d.

SMALL INSTRUMENTAL ENSEMBLE
Strings
"Mingus Gold" (string quartet). Long Island City, N.Y.: Subito Music, 1988.

Combinations
"One Atmosphere" (piano, string quartet). Long Island City, N.Y.: Subito Music, 1991. Commissioned by the Arditti String Quartet and Ursula Oppens. Premiere, 1992.

ORCHESTRA (CHAMBER OR FULL) WITH SOLOISTS
Plan B (alto saxophone, orchestra). Long Island City, N.Y.: Subito Music, 1993. Contents: Bordertown; What I Know Now; Dogon II. Commissioned by the Richmond Symphony. Premiere, 1993.

Sweet Lucy (for Impork) (soprano voice, orchestra). Unpublished manuscript.

JAZZ ENSEMBLE
[The following list of titles includes only works that were composed by the subject of the entry; it is not a list of recordings that were made by the subject. Although the composer may have made recordings of his own works, the list is not restricted to those recordings but in many cases includes performances by other artists of the composer's work. The list is made up of publication and discographical data, in cases where such information is available. Although no effort has been made to include documentation of the earliest recording of the works listed, the date of the earliest recording that is readily available has been given. —Ed.]

"About Itself" (alto saxophone, trumpet, cello, drums). Long Island City, N.Y.: Subito Music, n.d.

"Affairs of the Heart" (saxophone quartet). Long Island City, N.Y.: Subito Music, n.d. Recorded: Black Saint 120056-2.

"Air Rings" (soprano saxophone, trumpet, cello/bass, drums). Long Island City, N.Y.: Subito Music, n.d.

"Anchorman" (bass clarinet, soprano saxophone, tenor saxophone, trumpet). Long Island City, N.Y.: Subito Music, n.d. Also arranged for saxophone sextet.

"Another Feeling" (saxophone quartet). Long Island City, N.Y.: Subito Music, n.d. Recorded: New World 80524.

"The Answer" (saxophone sextet). Long Island City, N.Y.: Subito Music, n.d. Recorded: Black Saint 120115.

"At Harmony (for Baikida)" (alto saxophone, trumpet, cello, drums). Long Island City, N.Y.: Subito Music, n.d. Also arranged for big band. Recorded: Elektra/Nonesuch 9 60831-4.

"Basso Pro/Bird" (big band). Long Island City, N.Y.: Subito Music, n.d.

"Bayou Sketch" (saxophone quartet). Long Island City, N.Y.: Subito Music, n.d. Recorded: Moers Music 01034 CD.

"Big Foot" (saxophone quartet). Long Island City, N.Y.: Subito Music, n.d.

"Blued" (saxophone sextet). Long Island City, N.Y.: Subito Music, n.d.

"Bordertown" (alto saxophone, trumpet, cello, drums). Long Island City, N.Y.: Subito Music, n.d. Also arranged for big band; saxophone quartet; alto saxophone, cello, percussion; alto saxophone, orchestra as a movement of *Plan B.* Recorded: Black Saint 120077-2; Elektra/Nonesuch 9 60831-4; Music and Arts CD-731.

"Bumpkin" (saxophone quartet). Long Island City, N.Y.: Subito Music, n.d.

"Buster Bee" (two alto saxophones). Long Island City, N.Y.: Subito Music, n.d. Recorded: Sackville 3018.

"C (Those Blues)" (alto saxophone, trumpet, cello, drums). Long Island City, N.Y.: Subito Music, n.d. Also arranged for alto saxophone, cello, percussion; alto saxophone, cello; big band. Recorded: Black Saint 120015-2; Music and Arts CD-791.

"C/Saw" (big band). Long Island City, N.Y.: Subito Music, n.d. Recorded: Elektra 60831-1.

"Children's Song" (saxophone quartet). Also arranged for saxophone sextet as a movement in *The Last Supper at Uncle Tom's Cabin: The Promised Land.* Long Island City, N.Y.: Subito Music, n.d. Recorded: New World Records 80524-2.

Julius Hemphill; courtesy of American International Artists; photo by Guzman

"Choo-Choo" (saxophone quartet). Long Island City, N.Y.: Subito Music, n.d.

"Connections" (saxophone quartet). Long Island City, N.Y.: Subito Music, n.d. Recorded: Black Saint 120046-2.

"Cool Red" (saxophone quartet). Long Island City, N.Y.: Subito Music, n.d. Recorded: Elektra 79164-4.

"Country Side" (alto saxophone, trumpet, cello, drums). Long Island City, N.Y.: Subito Music, n.d. Recorded: Mbari Music n.n.

"Dar el Sudan" (saxophone quartet). Long Island City, N.Y.: Subito Music, n.d. Recorded: Moers Music 01034 CD.

"Dear Friend" (alto saxophone, cello, bass, drums). Long Island City, N.Y.: Subito Music, n.d.

"Dogon A.D." (alto saxophone, trumpet, cello, drums). Long Island City, N.Y.: Subito Music, n.d. Also arranged for alto saxophone, cello, percussion; big band. Recorded: Arista AL 1028; Minor Music 003; Music and Arts CD-731.

"Dream" (alto saxophone, cello). Long Island City, N.Y.: Subito Music, n.d. Recorded: Music and Arts CD-791.

"Dream Scheme" (saxophone quartet). Long Island City, N.Y.: Subito Music, n.d. Recorded: Black Saint 120027-2.

Drunk on God (big band, speaker). Long Island City, N.Y.: Subito Music, n.d. Contents: Big Drum Speaks; Cosmic Country Boy; Float; Gates of Kansas City (also arranged for saxophone sextet, big band); High on a Mountain; Leora; Maliaka: Drum/Woman; Motion as the Terrible Language of the Future; Nago: Testament; Radiant Number. Recorded: Elektra/Nonesuch 9 60831-4.

"Dung" (alto saxophone, trumpet, cello/bass, drums). Long Island City, N.Y.: Subito Music, n.d.

"Ebony?" (big band). Long Island City, N.Y.: Subito Music, n.d.

"Echo 1 (Morning)" (alto saxophone, cello). 1976. Long Island City, N.Y.: Subito Music, n.d. Recorded: Red RR 123138.2.

"Echo 2 (Evening)" (alto saxophone, cello). Unpublished manuscript. Recorded: Red RR 123138.2.

"Fat Man" (saxophone sextet). Long Island City, N.Y.: Subito Music, n.d. Recorded: Black Saint 120115.

"Fertility" (saxophone quartet). Long Island City, N.Y.: Subito Music, n.d. Also arranged for alto saxophone, soprano saxophone/flute. Recorded: Sackville 3018.

"Fifteen" (alto saxophone, cello, drums). Long Island City, N.Y.: Subito Music, n.d. Recorded: Music and Arts CD-731.

"Five Chord Stud" (saxophone sextet). Long Island City, N.Y.: Subito Music, n.d. Recorded: Black Saint 120140-2.

"Fixation" (saxophone quartet). Long Island City, N.Y.: Subito Music, n.d.

"Flair" or "Flare" (saxophone quartet). Long Island City, N.Y.: Subito Music, n.d.

Flat-Out Jump Suite (tenor saxophone, cello, trumpet, drums). Long Island City, N.Y.: Subito Music, n.d. Contents: Body; Ear; Mind; Heart. Recorded: Black Saint 120040-1.

"Float" (alto saxophone, trumpet, cello, drums). Long Island City, N.Y.: Subito Music, n.d. Also arranged for big band as a movement of *Drunk on God.*

"Floating" (big band). Long Island City, N.Y.: Subito Music, n.d. Recorded: Elektra/Nonesuch 9 60831-4.

"Floppy" (saxophone sextet). Long Island City, N.Y.: Subito Music, n.d. Recorded: Black Saint 120115.

"Flush" (saxophone sextet). Long Island City, N.Y.: Subito Music, n.d. Recorded: Black Saint 120140-2.

"For Billie" (alto saxophone, cello). Long Island City, N.Y.: Subito Music, n.d. Also arranged for band; alto saxophone, trumpet, cello, drums. Recorded: Elektra/Nonesuch 9 60831-4; Music and Arts CD-791.

"Functions" (saxophone quartet). Long Island City, N.Y.: Subito Music, n.d.

"Funny Paper" (saxophone quartet). Long Island City, N.Y.: Subito Music, n.d. Recorded: Black Saint 120077-2.

"G Song" (soprano saxophone, cello, drums). Long Island City, N.Y.: Subito Music, n.d. Recorded: Black Saint 120015-2.

"Georgia Blue" (alto saxophone, two guitars, bass, percussion, drums). Long Island City, N.Y.: Subito Music, n.d. Also arranged for saxophone quartet; saxophone sextet, orchestra as a movement in *Long Tongues: A Saxophone Opera;* alto saxophone, cello, percussion; saxophone sextet. Recorded: Black Saint 120096-2, 120140-2; Minor Music 003; Music and Arts CD-731.

"Glide" (big band). Long Island City, N.Y.: Subito Music, n.d. Also arranged for saxophone sextet. Recorded: Black Saint 120115.

"The Hard Blues" (alto saxophone, trumpet, cello, drums). Long Island City, N.Y.: Subito Music, n.d. Also arranged for alto saxophone, baritone saxophone, trumpet, cello, drums; big band; saxophone sextet. Recorded: Arista AL 1012; Black Saint 120115.

"Headlines" (saxophone sextet). Long Island City, N.Y.: Subito Music, n.d. Recorded: Black Saint 120115.

"Hearts" (saxophone sextet). Long Island City, N.Y.: Subito Music, n.d. Recorded: Black Saint 120027-2.

"Impulse" (saxophone quartet). Long Island City, N.Y.: Subito Music, n.d.

"In Space" (alto saxophone, cello). Unpublished manuscript. Recorded: Red RR 123138.2.

"Ink" (saxophone quartet). Long Island City, N.Y.: Subito Music, n.d.

"Ishaac the Terrible" (alto saxophone, trumpet, cello, drums). Long Island City, N.Y.: Subito Music, n.d.

"It's a Mystery to Me" (big band). Long Island City, N.Y.: Subito Music, n.d. Also arranged for two alto saxophones, guitar, cello, drums. Recorded: JMT 514003-2.

"Ji, Ji Tune" (saxophone quartet). Long Island City, N.Y.: Subito Music, n.d.

"Lady S" (alto saxophone, trumpet, cello, drums). Long Island City, N.Y.: Subito Music, n.d. Also arranged for big band.

"Leora" (saxophone quartet). Long Island City, N.Y.: Subito Music, n.d. Also arranged for big band as a movement of *Drunk on God;* alto saxophone, orchestra as a movement of *Plan B.*

"Little Samba" (saxophone quartet). Long Island City, N.Y.: Subito Music, n.d. Recorded: Black Saint 120056-2.

"Long Rhythm" (alto saxophone, cello, percussion). Long Island City, N.Y.: Subito Music, n.d. Recorded: Black Saint 120015-2.

"Loopology" (alto saxophone, trumpet, cello, drums). Long Island City, N.Y.: Subito Music, n.d. Recorded: Elektra/Musicians 60864-2.

"Lyric" (alto saxophone, trumpet, cello, drums). Long Island City, N.Y.: Subito Music, n.d. Also arranged for two alto saxophones, baritone saxophone, cello, drums. Recorded: Arista AL 1012.

"Me and Wadud, Part 1" (alto saxophone, cello). Long Island City, N.Y.: Subito Music, n.d. Recorded: Music and Arts CD-791.

"Me and Wadud, Part 2" (alto saxophone, cello). Long Island City, N.Y.: Subito Music, n.d. Recorded: Music and Arts CD-791.

"Mirrors" (alto saxophone, trumpet, cello, drums). Long Island City, N.Y.: Subito Music, n.d. Also arranged for alto saxophone, cello, percussion; saxophone sextet. Recorded: Black Saint 120015-2; Black Saint 120140-2.

"Moat and the Bridge" (saxophone sextet). Long Island City, N.Y.: Subito Music, n.d. Recorded: Black Saint 120140-2.

"Mr. Critical (for Ornette)" (saxophone sextet). Long Island City, N.Y.: Subito Music, n.d. Recorded: Black Saint 120140-2.

"My First Winter" (saxophone quartet). Long Island City, N.Y.: Subito Music, n.d. Recorded: Black Saint 120077-2.

"New Prayers" (saxophone quartet). Long Island City, N.Y.: Subito Music, n.d.

"Number Four" (alto saxophone, trumpet, cello, drums). Long Island City, N.Y.: Subito Music, n.d.

"One for Eric" (big band). Long Island City, N.Y.: Subito Music, n.d.

"One for Stub" (flute, alto saxophone, tenor saxophone, piano, bass, drums). Long Island City, N.Y.: Subito Music, n.d.

"One Waltz Time" (saxophone quartet). Long Island City, N.Y.: Subito Music, n.d. Recorded: Black Saint BSR 120096-2.

"Open Air" (alto saxophone, trumpet, cello, drums). Long Island City, N.Y.: Subito Music, n.d. Also arranged for alto saxophone, trumpet, drums; big band. Recorded: Black Saint BSR 120096-2.

"Out of Regular" (two alto saxophones, guitar, cello, drums). Long Island City, N.Y.: Subito Music, n.d. Recorded: JMT 514003-2.

"The Painter" (alto saxophone, trumpet, cello, drums). Long Island City, N.Y.: Subito Music, n.d. Recorded: Arista AL 1028.

"Pensive" (alto saxophone, trumpet, cello, drums). Long Island City, N.Y.: Subito Music, n.d. Also arranged for alto saxophone, cello. Recorded: Douglas NBLP 7045-7049; Red RR 123138.2.

"Pillars Latino" (saxophone quartet). Long Island City, N.Y.: Subito Music, n.d. Recorded: Black Saint 120046-2.

"Plain Song" (alto saxophone, trumpet, cello, drums). Long Island City, N.Y.: Subito Music, n.d. Also arranged for saxophone quartet. Recorded: Black Saint 120046-2.

"Plateau" (alto saxophone, cello, percussion). Long Island City, N.Y.: Subito Music, n.d. Also arranged for alto saxophone, trumpet, guitar, drums. Recorded: Black Saint 120015-2.

"Point of No Return" (saxophone quartet). Long Island City, N.Y.: Subito Music, n.d. Recorded: Moers Music 01034 CD.

"R & B" (saxophone quartet). Long Island City, N.Y.: Subito Music, n.d. Recorded: Black Saint 120027-2.

"Reflections" (alto saxophone, trumpet, cello, drums). Long Island City, N.Y.: Subito Music, n.d. Also arranged for two alto saxophones, baritone saxophone, cello, drums. Recorded: Arista AL 1012.

"Revue" (saxophone quartet). Long Island City, N.Y.: Subito Music, n.d. Also arranged for saxophone sextet as a movement of *Long Tongues: A Saxophone Opera*. Recorded: Black Saint 120056-2.

"Rites" (alto saxophone, trumpet, cello, drums). Long Island City, N.Y.: Subito Music, n.d. Recorded: Arista AL 1028; JMT 514003-2.

"Romance in Time" (saxophone quartet). Long Island City, N.Y.: Subito Music, n.d.

"Scatter Brain" (alto saxophone, trumpet, cello, drums). Long Island City, N.Y.: Subito Music, n.d.

"Serial Abstractions" (two alto saxophones, guitar, cello, drums). Long Island City, N.Y.: Subito Music, n.d. Recorded: JMT 514003-2.

"Shorty" (saxophone sextet). Long Island City, N.Y.: Subito Music, n.d. Recorded: Black Saint 120140-2.

"Sigure" (saxophone, cello). Unpublished manuscript. Recorded: Music and Arts CD-791.

"Sixteen" (alto saxophone, cello, percussion). Long Island City, N.Y.: Subito Music, n.d. Recorded: Music and Arts CD-731.

"Skin 1" (two alto saxophones, baritone saxophone, cello, drums). Long Island City, N.Y.: Subito Music, n.d. Recorded: Arista AL 1012.

"Skin 2" (two alto saxophones, baritone saxophone, cello, drums). Long Island City, N.Y.: Subito Music, n.d. Recorded: Arista AL 1012.

"Slide" (saxophone quartet). Long Island City, N.Y.: Subito Music, n.d. Recorded: Black Saint 120056-2.

"Sounds in the Fog" (two alto saxophones, guitar, cello, drums). Long Island City, N.Y.: Subito Music, n.d. Recorded: JMT 514003-2.

"Steppin'" (saxophone quartet). Long Island City, N.Y.: Subito Music, n.d. Recorded: Black Saint 120027-2; Black Saint 120077-2; Black Saint BSR 0027C; CBS RD-033.

"Stick" (saxophone quartet). Long Island City, N.Y.: Subito Music, n.d. Recorded: Black Saint 120077-2.

"Sweet D" (alto saxophone, trumpet, cello, drums). Long Island City, N.Y.: Subito Music, n.d. Also arranged for saxophone quartet; saxophone sextet. Recorded: Elektra 79164-4.

"Tendrils" (saxophone sextet). Long Island City, N.Y.: Subito Music, n.d. Recorded: Black Saint 120115.

"Testament no. 5" (alto saxophone, cello, percussion). Long Island City, N.Y.: Subito Music, n.d. Also arranged for alto saxophone, trumpet, cello, drums; three parts, drums. Recorded: Minor Music 003; Music and Arts CD-731.

"Three-Step" (saxophone sextet). Long Island City, N.Y.: Subito Music, n.d. Recorded: Black Saint 120115.

"Touchie" (saxophone quartet). Long Island City, N.Y.: Subito Music, n.d. Recorded: Black Saint 120077-2.

"The Unknown" (two alto saxophones, guitar, cello, drums). Long Island City, N.Y.: Subito Music, n.d. Recorded: JMT 514003-2.

"Untitled" (saxophone sextet). Long Island City, N.Y.: Subito Music, n.d. Recorded: Black Saint 120115.

"What I Know Now" (alto saxophone, trumpet, guitar, drums). Long Island City, N.Y.: Subito Music, n.d. Also arranged for big band; saxophone, orchestra as a movement of *Plan B*.

"Wind Rhythms" (saxophone quartet). Long Island City, N.Y.: Subito Music, n.d.

"Would Boogie" (alto saxophone, trumpet, cello, drums). Long Island City, N.Y.: Subito Music, n.d.

"Writhing Love Lines" (two alto saxophones, guitar, cello, drums). Long Island City, N.Y.: Subito Music, n.d. Recorded: JMT 514003-2.

DRAMATIC MUSIC

Last Supper at Uncle Tom's Cabin: The Promised Land (saxophone sextet). Long Island City, N.Y.: Subito Music, n.d. Contents: Ascension (two saxophones); Children's Song (saxophone sextet); Crossformation (saxophone sextet); Four Saints (saxophone sextet); Lenny (saxophone sextet); Opening (saxophone sextet); Spiritual Chairs (saxophone sextet). Note: winner of a Bessie Award, 1991. Premiere, 1990.

Long Tongues: A Saxophone Opera (tenor, two rap singers, saxophone sextet, piano, bass, drums, strings). 1989. Long Island City, N.Y.:

Subito Music, n.d. Also arranged for saxophone, orchestra. Contents: Ballad no. 1 (saxophone sextet); Band Theme (saxophone sextet); Beating Time (saxophone sextet); Bop Scene (or KC Line) (alto saxophone, trumpet, cello, drums); Contra Rhythm (saxophone sextet); Crackhead Dance (improvised); Degravitational Muse (saxophone sextet); Dogan II (saxophone sextet; also arranged for two guitars, alto saxophone, bass, drum); For Andrew (saxophone sextet, orchestra); Georgia Blue; Juke Joint (saxophone sextet, orchestra); Mask Dance (music off-stage); Otis' Groove (saxophone sextet); Revue (saxophone sextet); Sketch no. 4 (saxophone sextet, orchestra); Swing Things (saxophone sextet, orchestra); This Jazz Don't Jive with Me (saxophone sextet, orchestra); Tribute (saxophone sextet). Note: winner of a Bessie Award, 1991. Premiere, 1989.

Roi Boye and the Gotham Minstrels (audio-drama). 1976–77. Unpublished manuscript. Recorded: Sackville 3014-3015.

INCIDENTAL AND COMMERCIAL MUSIC.

"Soft Lines." From the film soundtrack for *Suite Willie's Rollbar Orientation.*

PUBLICATIONS

ABOUT HEMPHILL
Articles

Ardonceau, P. H. "Julius Hemphill." *Jazz Magazine* 289 (1980): 18.

Giacomo, P. "Spirit of Saint Louis." *Jazz Magazine* 309 (1982): 50.

Giardullo, Joe. "Julius Hemphill: Five Chord Stud." *Coda* 259 (1995): 19.

Jackson, D. "Profile: Julius Hemphill, Oliver Lake." *Down Beat* 42, no. 12 (1975): 32.

Ratliff, B. "Under the Weather." *Option* (May/June 1994): 40–43.

Shoemaker, Bill. "Julius Hemphill." *Jazz Times* 25, no. 5 (1995): 58.

———. "Julius Hemphill and the Theater of Sound." *Down Beat* 53, no. 2 (1986): 20–22.

Smith, B., and D. Lee. "Julius Hemphill Interviews." *Coda* 161 (1978): 4.

Smith, Will. "Julius Hemphill." *Coda* (April/May 1989): 21–23.

Stern, Chip. "Backside." *Musician* 202 (1995): 98.

Ware, C. "Julius Hemphill Times Two." *Jazz Spotlite News* 2, no. 2 (1980–81): 54.

* * * * *

Although probably best known for his affiliation with the World Saxophone Quartet, Julius Hemphill's compositional output includes an opera, an audio-drama, and numerous other collaborative efforts featuring a wide variety of artists and ensembles. Not only do his compositions illustrate his knowledge of and love for a wide chronological cross section of jazz, blues, and rhythm and blues, but they also explore the dense, ever-shifting harmonic voicings often associated with modern classical music. Throughout his career, Hemphill made a conscious effort to be responsive to new currents in jazz, and he continually provided audiences of the 1970s and 1980s with unique ensembles (most of which did not include rhythm sections) and innovative musical ideas. Although increasingly beset by illness during the last years of his life, Hemphill's prolific compositional output continued throughout the early

1990s. His brilliant career as both performer and composer demonstrates the creativity and innovation that drove him to the forefront of the jazz scene during the 1970s and 1980s.

Born in Fort Worth, Texas, in 1938, Julius Hemphill received his early musical training from John Carter (of Clarinet Summit fame). After studying clarinet with Carter, Hemphill pursued further study at North Texas State College in Fort Worth, followed by stints in U.S. Army ensembles. During these years, he fell in love with the alto saxophone and became a virtuosic performer on the instrument. By 1966, he was working with guitarist-pianist-composer Ike Turner, and in 1968, he moved to St. Louis, Missouri, where, in addition to undertaking further study at Lincoln University in Jefferson City, Missouri, he became a founding member of the Black Artists Group (BAG), an interdisciplinary arts collective that also included Hamiet Bluiett and Oliver Lake. During his time in St. Louis, Hemphill founded his own record label, called Mbari Records, and recorded two albums: *Dogon A.D.* (1972) and *'Coon Bid'ness* (1975). These albums illustrate his place at the crossroads of the saxophone tradition, reaping the benefits of the Parker and Coleman generation of altoists, drawing upon rich Texas roots, and being in the thick of the Midwestern revolution in jazz during the late 1960s and early 1970s. In the early 1970s, Hemphill toured with pianist John Hicks. In addition to these projects, Hemphill collaborated with poet K. Curtis Lyle, creating a tribute to blues great Blind Lemon Jefferson: "The Collected Poem for Blind Lemon Jefferson."

In 1973, forced away from St. Louis by lack of work, Hemphill moved to New York with his wife and two young sons. They took up residence in Brooklyn, and he began working with alto saxophonist Anthony Braxton and trumpeter Lester Bowie. Hemphill also became heavily involved in the "loft sessions" that were taking place around the city at that time. Will Smith once wrote of New York, "In the new jazz it has too often been a matter of where you play, not how you blow, that is the criterion—a politics of location, it seems." This "political" move to New York proved to be a successful one for Hemphill. The most visible outgrowth of this success was the formation in 1976 of the World Saxophone Quartet. Hemphill formed this quartet along with Oliver Lake, Hamiet Bluiett, and David Murray, and became the principal writer/arranger for the group.

The period from 1976 to 1989 was the most prolific in Hemphill's career. Among the notable compositions he contributed to the World Saxophone Quartet songbook are stirring ballads like "My First Winter" and "Open Air," as well as whimsical and lyrical titles such as "One Waltz Time." In addition to his commitment to the World Saxophone Quartet, Hemphill completed an audiodrama titled *Roi Boye and the Gotham Minstrels* (1976–77), worked on outside projects with cellist Abdul Wadud, and completed a three-act opera titled *Long Tongues: A Saxophone Opera* (1989), which documents the history of Washington, D.C.'s historic Bohemian Caverns nightclub.

Hemphill's interest in the expressive possibilities of theater is clearly demonstrated in his opera and audio-drama works, but he strove to incorporate the theatrical into his instrumental work as well. Compositionally, Hemphill does not simply tell a story, he stages it, milking it for all the humor, melodrama, and pathos he can.

Hemphill's work in the early 1990s includes an album with the Julius Hemphill Sextet titled *Fat Man and the Hard Blues* (1991), "One Atmosphere," commissioned and performed by the Arditti String Quartet and pianist Ursula Oppens (1992), and a work commissioned by the Richmond Symphony Orchestra called *Plan B* (1993). His death on April 2, 1995, marked the passing of one of the great jazz composer/performers of the 1970s and 1980s.

REUBEN JACKSON

SELECTED WORKS

It is difficult to put the aesthetic that governs Julius Hemphill's music into words. At times lyrical, at others verging on the atonal, but always forward-looking and daring, his compositions challenge the conventions of jazz and raise interesting questions concerning the relationship between composition and improvisation. This essay examines two works from the outer poles of Hemphill's career. While this is an admittedly evolutionary perspective, it proves useful in determining the various aspects that have come to define his style. While Hemphill has worked in theatrical, multimedia, and orchestral genres, the works included in this essay are scored for smaller ensembles. More specifically, they focus on his work with cellist Abdul Wadud and the Julius Hemphill Sextet, an ensemble that can be considered an extension of the sound and ideals that Hemphill pursued in the works written for the World Saxophone Quartet.

The first piece, "Echo 1 (Morning)," illustrates the unique approach that Hemphill takes to jazz. Recorded on May 28, 1976, the same year that he helped found the World Saxophone Quartet, "Echo 1 (Morning)" is a live performance given by Hemphill and cellist Abdul Wadud at the La Mama Jazz Workshop in New York. The cello introduces the harmonic progression in the plucked style usually reserved for double bass. It is a disjunct, chromatically inflected bass line that suggests numerous harmonic interpretations—harmonic possibilities that Hemphill is quick to exploit in his solo part. Without a bow in hand, Wadud employs strummed chords, which not only increases the percussive element within the song but also adds textural diversity to his part and creates an aural means of demarcating sections. Throughout this seven-and-a-half minute performance, Wadud explores the dynamic and expressive aspects of the cello part, creating a sense of almost continuous discovery and renewal and demonstrating the relative freedom of expression that came to characterize the sound of the World Saxophone Quartet.

For his part, Hemphill introduces the melodic material in an unornamented and straightforward manner before moving on to ever more nuanced and ornamented elaborations of the material. The melodic material consists of a descending fifth followed by an ascending fifth that originates on the lower octave of the original note (for example: *b*-flat to *e*-flat, followed by *b*-flat to *f*). The piece unfolds in cyclic fashion, spiraling ever farther from the initial statement and gaining in intensity as it does so. Hemphill employs a very wide pitch-range in this piece and adds emphasis to certain passages by growling, squeaking, and generally exploring the catalog of extended techniques, sounds, and noises that his instrument is capable of producing. The conclusion of the piece finds both Hemphill and Wadud exploring the highest registers of

their respective instruments. As they work through the upper registers, they gradually reduce the volume and intensity of their playing. The piece is brought to a close while the musicians are still playing in high registers, which generates an effect similar to that of a fade-out on a recording. In other words, the conclusion implies continuation rather than closure.

The traditional rhythm section is not missed here. In fact, its presence would most certainly wash out the subtleties of the cello part. Particularly striking in the performance of this piece is the artful, classical/recitalesque manner with which it is executed. Thus, an unusual ensemble, modern techniques, and an especially artful performance style mark the recording of "Echo 1 (Morning)."

"Floppy," recorded by the Julius Hemphill Sextet in 1991, near the end of Hemphill's *oeuvre,* is scored for three alto saxophones, two tenor saxophones, and a baritone saxophone. Even though the music is scored and requires a great deal of precision from the performers, Hemphill manages to create the illusion of spontaneity. Speaking of his compositional style, he once stated that he attempted to attain something akin to a conversational flow between instruments: "This is the quality I try to get into my charts. It's a situation where nothing should sound forced. Even though it's scored and there's a great need for precision, the parts should have the feeling of a head arrangement where everything comes together because it's something the musicians have been playing forever."

The concepts of conversationality and freedom are quite evident in "Floppy." A straightforward reading of the theme (or head) establishes the harmonic progression as well as the melodic material for the piece. Hemphill then repeats the head in a more ornamented and sonically dense fashion. This is accomplished by adding off-beat accents and weaving additional layers of syncopation into the parts. The harmonic progression remains the same in the following section, but the instruments themselves begin to leave the thematic and rhythmic elements of the head motive behind. Thus, while the first portion of the piece is communicated as a joint statement by the entire sextet, the following section focuses on the independence of each individual part within the sextet, a technique that gives the impression of free conversation. The rhythmic pulse of the piece remains steady, but there is little shared rhythmic activity, making the performance sound quite spontaneous. The harmonic progression, however, remains constant throughout and is the connecting link between the opening section, the improvisatory section, and Hemphill's alto saxophone solo. His solo, which not only showcases his virtuosity but also demonstrates his tasteful phrasing, is accompanied by sustained chords that provide welcome relief from the previously active and somewhat unstable rhythmic field.

After the solo, Hemphill revisits the opening theme, coming full circle in much the same way that bebop and swing charts do. This return to the head is executed with a more complex harmonization and with greater intensity, owing to the thorough exploration of the possibilities afforded by the harmonic progression and to the momentum generated by Hemphill's solo. Although this piece is far from being Hemphill's most experimental or difficult music, "Floppy" illustrates the combination and blurring of improvised and composed sections, the conversational quality of his music, and the artful virtuosity of his playing. As with "Echo 1 (Morning)," a traditional rhythm section would only detract from the timbres and nuances that are generated by the ensemble. Of his ensemble choices, Hemphill remarked, "An audience responds to music, not instrumentation." It would seem, though, that an audience also responds to excellent use of instrumentation, which is another quality always present in Hemphill's music.

TIMOTHY ROMMEN

REFERENCES

Jackson, D. "Profile: Julius Hemphill, Oliver Lake." *Down Beat* 42, no. 12 (1975): 32.

Ratliff, B. "Under the Weather." *Option* (May/June 1994): 40–43.

Shoemaker, Bill. "Julius Hemphill and the Theater of Sound." *Down Beat* 53, no. 2 (1986): 20–22.

Smith, Will. "Julius Hemphill." *Coda* (April/May 1989): 21–23.

HENDERSON, FLETCHER HAMILTON, JR. ("SMACK")

Born in Cuthbert, Ga., December 18, 1897; died in New York, N.Y., December 29, 1952. **Education:** Studied piano with his mother; Cuthbert, Ga., attended Howard Normal School, where his father was a prominent teacher; attended high school in the Atlanta University college preparatory program, graduated 1916; Atlanta University, Ga., B.A. in chemistry, 1920. **Composing and Performing Career:** New York, N.Y., Pace and Handy Music Company, song demonstrator, 1920; Black Swan Records, house pianist, 1921; Pace Phonograph Corp., musical director, 1921–23; recording debut, 1921; New Orleans, La., toured with blues singer Ethel Waters, 1921–22; performed on first known jazz radio broadcast, 1922; New York, N.Y., regularly backed singers, including Bessie Smith, Ma Rainey, 1923–27; regularly led bands at several clubs, including Club Alabam, 1924, Roseland Ballroom, 1924–30; first hit, "Sugar Foot Stomp," 1925; Chicago, Ill., Grand Terrace Ballroom, performed regularly, 1936–39; joined Benny Goodman's band, staff arranger and pianist, 1939; returned to bandleading and arranging, 1941–47; toured again with Ethel Waters, 1948–49; New York, N.Y., performed occasionally, 1950.

MUSIC LIST

[The following list of titles includes only works that were composed by the subject of the entry; it is not a list of recordings that were made by the subject. Although the composer may have made recordings of his own works, the list is not restricted to those recordings but in many cases includes performances by other artists of the composer's work. The list is made up of publication and discographical data, in cases where such information is available. Although no effort has been made to include documentation of the earliest recording of the works listed, the date of the earliest recording that is readily available has been given. —Ed.]

"Ain't That Funny Good Time Busse." Copyright, 1927. New York: Robbins Music, n.d. Co-composer, Jo Trent.

"Blue Moments." Copyright, 1932. Recorded: CBS 66423; Classics 546.

"Bumble Bee Stomp." Copyright, 1939. New York: Robbins Music, n.d. Co-composer, Henri Wood. Recorded: HEP Records CD 1038.

"Can You Take It?" Recorded: CBS 66423; Classics 535.

"Chris and His Gang." Copyright, 1937. New York: Robbins Music, n.d. Co-composer, Horace Henderson. Recorded: CBS 66423; Classics 519.

"Come outa the Swamp." Copyright, 1963. New York: Mills Music, n.d.

"'D' Natural Blues" or "Grand Terrace Rhythm." Copyright, 1928. New York: Fletcher Henderson, n.d. Recorded: ABC Records 842-735-2; CBS 66423; Classics 572.

"Dicty Blues." Copyright, 1923. New York: Down South Music, n.d. Recorded: CBS 66423; Classics 697; MCA 1346.

"Do Right Blues" or "If Somebody Wants Somebody (Take a Chance with Me)." 1923–24. New York: Mills Music, 1961. Co-composer, Spencer Williams.

"Do Doodle Oom." Copyright, 1923. New York: Irving Berlin, n.d. Co-composer, Porter Grainger. Recorded: Classics 697; MCA 1346.

"Down South Blues." Copyright, 1923. New York: Down South Music, n.d. Recorded: Classics 697; MCA 1346.

"Down South Camp Meeting." Copyright, 1934. New York: Milsons Music, n.d. Co-composer, Irving Mills. Recorded: Classics 535; Decca 213.

"Drowning in the River of Love." Copyright, 1937. Chicago: Will Rossiter, n.d.

"Dying with the Blues." Copyright, 1920. New York: Arrow Music, n.d. Recorded: Black Swan 2038.

"Dynamite." Copyright, 1926. New York: Triangle Music, n.d. Co-composer, Jack Palmer. Recorded: Classics 610; Disques Swing 8445-8446.

"Feelin' Kinda Good." Copyright, 1927. New York: Robbins Music, n.d. Co-composer, Jo Trent.

"Fletcher's Blues." Copyright, 1941. New York: Robbins Music, n.d.

"The Gidgy Gidgy." Copyright, 1939. New York: Bregman, Vocco, and Conn, n.d.

"The Gin House Blues." Copyright, 1926. New York: Tune-House, n.d. Co-composer, Henry Troy.

"Gonna Shoot My Nelson Now." Copyright, 1961. New York: Mills Music, n.d. Co-composer, Spencer Williams.

"Goose Pimples." Copyright, 1927. New York: Gotham Music, n.d. Co-composer, Jo Trent. Recorded: Disques Swing 8445-8446.

"Got the World in a Jug, Got the Stopper in My Hand" or "I've Got the World in a Jug" or "Got the World in a Jug (The Stopper's in My Hand)." Copyright, 1924. New York: Down South Music, n.d.

"Harlem Madness." Copyright, 1934. New York: Exclusive, n.d. Co-composers, Irving Mills, Ned Williams. Recorded: Classics 535; RCA 6676-2 B.

"Have It Ready." Copyright, 1927. Chicago: Forster Music, n.d. Recorded: Classics 597; Disques Swing 8445-8446.

"A Heart, Who Wants to Buy?" Copyright, 1933. Unpublished manuscript.

"The Henderson Stomp." Copyright, 1926. New York: Robbins-Engel, n.d. Recorded: Best of Jazz 4019; CBS 66423; Classics 597.

"High Yellow Blues." Copyright, 1963. New York: Mills Music, n.d.

"Hot Mustard." Copyright, 1927. New York: Gotham Music, n.d. Note: for solo piano. Recorded: Classics 597.

"I Ain't Goin' to Marry, I Ain't Goin' to Settle Down" or "I Ain't Gonna Marry, Ain't Gonna to Settle Down." Copyright, 1924. New York: Fletcher Henderson, n.d. Co-composer, Ethel Waters. Recorded: Historical Records ASC 18.

"I Did Not Think I Cared for You." Copyright, 1926. New York: Matthew Solomon, n.d.

"I Like My Sugar Sweet." Copyright, 1941. New York: Freddie Van Scoyk and Fletcher Henderson, n.d. Co-composer, Freddie Van Scoyk. Recorded: Classics 648.

"I Miss You Most of All." Copyright, 1920. New York: Arrow Music, n.d.

"I Need You to Drive the Blues Away." Copyright, 1923. New York: Melody Music, 1923.

"I Often Think about You." Copyright, 1933. Co-composer, Frank Pepe.

"If Your Good Man Quits You, Wear No Black." Copyright, 1924. New York: Down South Music, n.d. Co-composer, J. Wesley Holmes. Recorded: Historical Recordings 5829-18.

"I'm Allergic to You" or "Baby, I'm Allergic to You." Copyright, 1941. New York: Murray B. Tannenholz, n.d. Co-composer, Bert Tannen.

"I'm in a Crying Mood." 1948. New York: Regent Music, n.d. Co-composer, Wilmette Ward.

"It's Wearin' Me Down." Copyright, 1932. New York: Harms Music, n.d. Recorded: Classics 519.

"Jangled Nerves." Copyright, 1936. New York: Robbins Music, n.d. Recorded: ABC Records 836-093-2; Classics 527.

"Just Blues." 1931. Recorded: ABC Records 836-093-2; GRP/Decca 643; Melotone 12239.

"Kind Lovin' Blues." Copyright, 1922. New York: Fletcher Henderson, n.d.

"Kitty on Toast." Copyright, 1940. Recorded: Classics 648.

"Love Houn' Blues." Copyright, 1926. New York: E. Dacey and Fletcher Henderson, n.d.

"Mason Dixie Blues." Copyright, 1923. New York: Down South Music, n.d. Co-composer, Gus Smith.

"My Honey, My Dear." Copyright, 1932. Co-composer, Todd Marx.

"No, Baby, No." Copyright, 1947. New York: Regent Music, n.d. Co-composers, Eddie Gardner, Frank Lewis, Bobby Troup.

"Oh Baby, How Long." Copyright, 1923. New York: Irving Berlin, n.d. Co-composers, Roland C. Irving, J. H. Trent. Recorded: CBS 66423; Disques Swing 8445-8446; Sarabandas MCJT 39.

"Old Black Joe Blues." Copyright, 1924. New York: Jack Mills, n.d. Recorded: CBS 66423; Classics 697; Classics 683.

"A Pixie from Dixie." Copyright, 1941.

"Pretty Ways." ca. 1923. Unpublished manuscript. Co-composer, William Grant Still. Recorded: Best of Jazz 4019; Classics 794.

"Red Dust." Copyright, 1942. New York: American Academy, n.d.

"Rhythm Crazy" or "I'm Rhythm Crazy Now." Unpublished manuscript.

"Rocky Mountain Blues." Copyright, 1927. New York: Forrest B. Chilton, n.d. Co-composers, Patty Carroll, Ken Macomber. Recorded: CBS 66423; Classics 597.

"Screaming the Blues." Copyright, 1925. New York: Fletcher Henderson, n.d.

"Sock-a-Bye, Rock-a-Bye Baby." Copyright, 1936. Chicago: Isadore J. Wagner, n.d.

"Something in Your Eyes." Copyright, 1942. New York: American Academy, n.d.

"Stampede." Copyright, 1926. New York: Robbins-Engel, n.d. Recorded: CBS 66423; Classic 597; Columbia 654D.

"Superstitions Never Worry Me." Copyright, 1950. New York: Record Music, n.d.

"Sweetheart, This Is Our Night of Love." Copyright, 1938. Chicago: Will Rossiter, n.d. Co-composers, Herman Peters, Milton Kay.

"Tozo." Copyright, 1926. Cleveland: M. A. Cowdery, n.d. Co-composer, M. A. Cowdery. Recorded: CBS 66423; Classics 597.

"A Twilight Mood." Copyright, 1945. In *Down Beat* (March 1, 1945): 12.

"The Unknown Blues." Recorded: Best of Jazz 4019; Classics 794.

"Variety Stomp." Copyright, 1927. New York: Robbins-Engel, n.d. Co-composers, Jo Trent, Abel Green. Recorded: Classics 580; Disques Swing 8445-8446; RCA 6676-2 B.

"Wait'll It's Moonlight, Wait for a Moonlight Night." Copyright, 1925. New York: Broadway Music, n.d.

"Want Me." 1952. New York: Miller Music, n.d. Co-composer, Andy Razaf.

"Water Boy Serenade." Copyright, 1929. New York: Vincent Youmans, n.d.

"What Kind of Man Is You." Copyright, 1963. New York: Mills Music, n.d.

"What's Your Story, What's Your Jive?" Copyright, 1937. New York: Robbins Music, n.d. Recorded: Classics 519; Jazz Document va-7995.

"When I'm All Set with Daddy." Copyright, 1961. New York: Mills Music, n.d. Co-composer, Spencer Williams.

"Whoop-ee!" Copyright, 1927. New York: Mimic Music, n.d. Co-composers, George Bennett, William Morice.

"Why Put the Blame on You, Little Girl" or "Why Put the Blame on You." Copyright, 1924. New York: Down South Music, n.d. Recorded: Classics 673.

"Wrappin' It Up, the Lindy Glide." Copyright, 1934. New York: Milsons Music, n.d. Recorded: ABC Records 836-093-2; Classics 535; Decca 157.

"You're Everything to Me." Copyright, 1963. New York: Mills Music, n.d.

"Zanzibar Stomp." Copyright, 1927. New York: Robbins Music, n.d. Co-composer, Jo Trent.

AS GEORGE BROOKS

"Back Woods Blues." Copyright, 1924. New York: George Brooks, n.d. Recorded: Historical Recordings 5829-13.

"Dyin' by the Hour." Copyright, 1927. New York: George Brooks, n.d.

"Far Away Blues." Copyright, 1924. New York: George Brooks, n.d. Recorded: Columbia 13007-D.

"Hard Drivin' Papa." Copyright, 1926. New York: George Brooks, n.d. Recorded: Columbia 14137-D.

"Honey Man Blues." Copyright, 1924. New York: George Brooks, n.d.

"I Don't Know and I Don't Care" or "Don't Know and Don't Care" or "I Don't Know and I Don't Care Blues." Copyright, 1924. New York: George Brooks, n.d. Recorded: Classics 657; Historical Recordings 5829-13.

"If Mamma Quits Papa What Will Poor Papa Do?" Copyright, 1924. New York: George Brooks, n.d. Recorded: Columbia 13006-D.

"Jazzbo Brown" or "Jazzbo Brown from Memphis Town." Copyright, 1926. New York: George Brooks, n.d.

"No Second Hand Lovin' for Mine" or "No Second Handed Lovin' for Mine." Copyright, 1924. New York: George Brooks, n.d.

"One and Two Blues." Copyright, 1926. New York: George Brooks, n.d. Recorded: Columbia GL 505.

"Pork Chop Blues." Copyright, 1924. New York: Fletcher Henderson, n.d. Recorded: Columbia 14036-D.

"Rainy Weather Blues." Copyright, 1924. New York: Fletcher Henderson, n.d. Recorded: Columbia 14037-D.

"Salt Water Blues." Copyright, 1924. New York: Fletcher Henderson, n.d. Recorded: Columbia 14037-D.

"Send Me to the 'lectric Chair." Copyright, 1927. New York: George Brooks, n.d. Recorded: Columbia G 30818.

"Them's Graveyard Words." Copyright, 1927. New York: George Brooks, n.d. Recorded: Columbia G 30818.

"Trombone Cholly." Copyright, 1927. New York: George Brooks, n.d. Recorded: Columbia G 30818.

"When You Go Huntin' I'm Goin' Fishin'." Copyright, 1924.

Fletcher Hamilton "Smack" Henderson Jr.; courtesy of the Frank Driggs Collection

NOT VERIFIED
"My Right Man." Recorded, 1923: Vocalion 14831.

PUBLICATIONS

ABOUT HENDERSON
Books and Monographs
Allen, Walter C. *Hendersonia: The Music of Fletcher Henderson and His Musicians: A Bio-Discography.* Highland Park, N.J.: Walter C. Allen, 1973.

Audibert, Michel. *Fletcher Henderson et son orchestre 1924–1951: Sa place dans l'histoire du jazz.* Bayonne, France: M. Audibert, 1983.

Dews, Margery P. *Remembering: The Remarkable Henderson Family.* Chicago: Adams Press, 1978.

Dissertations
Aloiso, Gerard Salvatore. "A Historical Summary of Major Musical Developments in American Jazz from the End of World War I to the Beginning of World War II." D.M.A. thesis, University of Cincinnati, 1995.

Garner, Charles. "Fletcher Henderson, King of Swing: A Summary of His Career, His Music, and His Influence." Ed.D. diss., Columbia University Teachers College, 1991.

Magee, Jeffrey Stanford. "The Music of Fletcher Henderson and His Orchestra in the 1920s." Ph.D. diss., University of Michigan, 1992.

Spring, Howard Allan. "Changes in Jazz Performance and Arranging in New York, 1929–1932." Ph.D. diss., University of Illinois at Urbana-Champaign, 1993.

Articles
Fayenz, F. "La Storia di Fletcher Henderson." *Musica Jazz* 19 (March 1963): 24–28; (April 1963): 28–32; (May 1963): 12–18.

Havens, Daniel F. "Oh, Play That Thing! (Dippermouth Blues and the Transition from New Orleans Jazz to Swing)." *Proceedings of NAJE Research* 8 (1988): 67–79.

Konow, A. von. "Fletcher Henderson—han grundade storbandsjazzen." *Orkester Journalen* 51 (April 1983): 14–16.

Magee, Jeffrey. "Revisiting Fletcher Henderson's 'Copenhagen'." *Journal of the American Musicological Society* 48, no. 1 (Spring 1995): 42–66.

Panassié, Hugues. "Fletcher Henderson et son orchestre." *Bulletin du Hot Club de France* no. 25 (1953): 3; no. 26 (1953): 6; no. 27 (1953): 6.

Smith, Norman. "Fletcher Henderson." In *Jazz Orchestras,* edited by Bill Kinnell. Chilwell, England: B. Kinnell, 1946.

Stewart, Rex. "Smack! Memories of Fletcher Henderson." *Down Beat* 32 (June 3, 1965): 15–17.

PRINCIPAL ARCHIVES
Fletcher Henderson Collection, Amistad Research Center, Tulane University, New Orleans, La.

* * * * *

Fletcher Henderson was a major figure in jazz in the 1920s and 1930s, and his enduring impact has been acknowledged by such disparate figures as Duke Ellington, Benny Goodman, Miles Davis, and Sun Ra, among many others. Henderson exerted influences as a bandleader who consistently hired the premiere jazz musicians of his day and as a composer whose polished, swinging arrangements of popular songs and original jazz works brought fame to Benny Goodman in the mid-1930s.

Arriving in New York City from his native Georgia in 1920, Henderson would have seemed an unlikely figure to shape the history of jazz. Born James Fletcher Henderson, he grew up in a well-educated, middle-class family in the small but progressive community of Cuthbert, Georgia. His parents encouraged their three children in music but allowed only classical and church music in the home. Above all, as teachers, they stressed education as the path to a respectable career. To that end, Henderson attended Atlanta University and earned a degree in chemistry. He was a well-rounded student, participating in athletic, theatrical, and musical activities, the last under the mentorship of Kemper Harreld, one of Atlanta's leading black classical musicians. Upon graduation, Henderson moved to New York City, ostensibly for graduate training in chemistry at Columbia University. He never enrolled at Columbia, and it is unclear how serious his intentions were to do so, for soon after his arrival in New York, he began working as a musician.

Henderson came to New York at an auspicious moment, at the dawn of the Harlem Renaissance. By the time America entered World War I, Harlem had become a predominantly black community, and Henderson found a home there. With his middle-class background, college education, and cultivated mien, Henderson embodied all the traits of the New Negro as that term came to be understood after 1925, when Alain Locke published his seminal anthology by that title. Henderson's musical career began modestly in the fall of 1920, when he landed a job as a song demonstrator for the Harlem-based music publishing firm of Pace and Handy. In January 1921, Pace left the publishing concern in Handy's care and established the Pace Phonograph Corporation, with Fletcher Henderson as musical director. While Pace's enterprise struggled, Henderson gained valuable experience working on its behalf. As musical director, he developed a wide range of musical contacts in the black community. By 1923, when the company went out of business, he was in high demand as the piano accompanist for dozens of female vocalists—most notably Bessie Smith—on "race records," which had become the industry's term for recordings by black musicians. Henderson also began to lead a group of musicians in recordings of instrumental dance music. In 1924, he got his band a job at the Club Alabam, near Times Square, and then moved a few blocks north to the Roseland Ballroom. There, as Fletcher Henderson and His Orchestra, the band established a home base and, thanks to a radio wire, a far-reaching reputation for the following decade.

The band's repertory included several compositions by its leader. Henderson wrote pieces in small forms current in the twenties and thirties, such as the 12-bar blues, multi-strain ragtime and march forms, and popular-song forms, reflecting the syncretic nature of the jazz tradition. Within the strict conventions of such forms, however, Henderson explored a wealth of possibilities. In the early and mid-1920s, Henderson became intimately familiar with the blues as a piano accompanist on dozens of recordings with blues singers. During that period, he wrote several blues-based tunes under the pseudonym "George Brooks," but his best work included instrumental pieces written for his band and under his real name, demonstrating the flexibility and imagination with which he approached the 12-bar blues form, as in "Dicty Blues" (1923), "Hot Mustard" (1927), "'D' Natural Blues" (1928), and "Jangled Nerves" (1936).

Henderson also wrote music in the prevailing forms of Tin Pan Alley song and the earlier march and ragtime forms that jazz had adopted. "Do Doodle Oom" (1923) marks an early attempt to capture the syncopated excitement of jazz. In the later 1920s, Henderson hit his stride as a composer for his band with such works as "Stampede" and "The Henderson Stomp" in 1926 and "Rocky Mountain Blues" and "Variety Stomp" in 1927. All are multisectional works with strains comprising 16 to 32 bars in which solo and ensemble passages are combined. All are masterpieces of early big-band jazz, exhibiting Henderson's ability to integrate seamlessly the improvised solos by his sidemen and composed passages for sections of the band. In 1934, with "Down South Camp Meeting" and "Wrappin' It Up," Henderson reached his compositional peak. These two works demonstrate how Henderson could translate the language of jazz improvisation into the big-band idiom and write intricate background figures supporting the solo choruses and further integrating the compositions. Benny Goodman added both works to his repertory, and his band continued to play them until the end of his life.

For Fletcher Henderson, composing music was a by-product of bandleading. To maintain an edge on the competition, band-leaders had to play new material as well as arrangements of popular hits. Duke Ellington's repertory, for example, included an unusually high proportion of original compositions. Most bands did not play their leader's compositions as exclusively as Ellington's. Yet through the 1920s and 1930s—especially after 1926—Henderson's orchestra played many works by its leader.

Many of Henderson's earliest pieces are 12-bar blues tunes, reflecting his extensive work as piano accompanist for blues singers during the "blue craze" of the early 1920s. Writing for his dance band, Henderson sought to cast the earthy music of the blues into a context more familiar to New York record buyers—the foxtrot. In fact, Henderson's band consistently performed the blues at faster tempos than the singers did, and his band's blues records usually carried labels identifying them as dance music, such as "Blues Tempo, for Dancing" or "Blues Fox Trot."

With Goodman in the 1930s, Henderson perfected his ability to "recompose" existing tunes, and in fact, his best-known works included such recompositions. In "King Porter Stomp," for example, Henderson took a short figure in Jelly Roll Morton's original piano piece and transformed it into a call-and-response chorus for brass and reeds that became, in Schuller's words, "the single most influential ensemble idea in the Swing Era." Recorded by numerous bands in the 1930s and 1940s, Henderson's "King Porter Stomp" became a staple of the big-band repertory, and many big-band arrangers included a call-and-response passage as the final, climactic chorus of their arrangements. Henderson also wrote original syncopated, swinging melodies, riffs, and background figures for band scores of "Sometimes I'm Happy," "Blue Skies," "Between the Devil and the Deep Blue Sea," and "Honeysuckle

Rose," and these scores reached a wide audience, as they remained in Goodman's repertory for decades.

Fletcher Henderson perfected a style of writing for large ensembles that became paradigmatic for generations of jazz arrangers and composers. Although he continued his career as a bandleader, arranger, and composer until his death in 1952, his most innovative music had been completed more than a decade earlier, but its impact still resonated strongly in the jazz tradition, and his work continued to reach a mass audience in polished performances and recordings by Benny Goodman's Orchestra until Goodman's death in 1986. Since then, Henderson's compositions and arrangements have remained vital through the many vintage jazz records reissued on compact disc and in the performances of repertory orchestras such as the Smithsonian Jazz Repertory Ensemble and Loren Schoenberg and his Orchestra, which includes several members of Goodman's last band.

SELECTED WORKS

One of the Henderson band's blues records for dancing featured his earliest distinctive piece. Originally conceived as a piano piece called "Chimes Blues," "Dicty Blues" (1923) serves up the blues with a wry twist. Its 12-bar theme presents a chimes break followed by several bars of quasi-New Orleans style polyphony. By introducing the "dicty," or high-class, sound of chimes into a piece based on a traditional African-American idiom from the South, Henderson lightheartedly captures the unique tensions in Harlem life in the early 1920s, where aspiring New Negroes sought to refashion traditional cultural forms.

"Hot Mustard" (1927) elaborates on ideas that "Dicty Blues" introduced. The descending chord sequence that opens the first section recalls the earlier piece, although its harmony, changing on every beat, is richer. In fact, "Hot Mustard" is more elaborate than "Dicty Blues" in every way. With four different strains of different lengths, three modulations, and instrumentation that changes not only in four- and two-bar units, but often in *every* bar, it reveals the self-conscious formal and orchestrational devices that typified so-called symphonic jazz of the later 1920s.

"'D' Natural Blues" (1928) represents another effort to "elevate" the blues into the realm of symphonic jazz. Here, blues conventions serve as points of reference. The slow tempo and the gritty, grunting tuba lend the recorded performance a lowdown character. The middle section—for clarinets and trombone—simulates the familiar interaction of a blues singer and instrumentalist. Along with these blues effects, the piece also reveals a composer striving for symphonic sophistication. Harmonically, Henderson once again demonstrates his penchant for enriched blues progressions. The piece contains three different versions of the 12-bar blues, including chromatic substitutions and secondary dominants, all in the context of D major, a key unusual enough in early jazz to merit recognition in the title. The piece also reveals careful planning in its overall design, with an orchestrated *crescendo* calculated to peak in the final chorus. With no room for improvisation, the whole recording radiates the poised quality of a performance read from a fully written score. Henderson later transformed "'D' Natural Blues" into an up-tempo swing tune and dubbed it "Grand Terrace Rhythm," after the Chicago cabaret where his band—reorganized after more than a year's hiatus—took up an extended residence in 1936.

That same year, Henderson conceived and recorded another up-tempo blues called "Jangled Nerves," a *tour de force* of big-band orchestration and solo improvisation performed at an undanceably fast tempo. The opening section displays muted trumpets and saxophones in a quietly urgent call-and-response dialogue of riffs. From this texture emerges a masterful tenor saxophone solo by Chu Berry, followed by several other inventive solos and ensemble passages.

Throughout his career, Henderson also composed pieces in popular song forms and in multi-strain structures. He conceived these works as jazz instrumentals, pieces to be played by his band, and many of them remain his most enduring compositions. Together, these works demonstrate Henderson's mastery of the unique demands of big-band writing: setting the sections of the band in dialogue with one another and inciting an entire ensemble to swing—with chains of syncopated figures, call-and-response patterns, riffs, and a variety of other underscoring devices—while providing ample solo space for improvisers who can meet the challenge.

Two pieces from 1926 illustrate Henderson's varied approach to such forms early in his career. The first, "Stampede," is notable for the way the composer provides a platform on which the band's soloists can shine. The other, "The Henderson Stomp," has been called "a virtuoso band piece," displaying the band's ability to play as a unit.

With its antiphonal phrases played by discrete sections of the band, its composed variation, and its improvised solos, "Stampede" stands out as "almost an archetype of the big band score." In its 1926 recording, Henderson's ten-piece band rises to the occasion with a performance brimming with the reckless abandon of a smaller combo. Played at just under 240 beats per minute, the recorded performance surges with power and energy befitting the title. More than most of Henderson's previous recordings, "Stampede" presents its ensemble and sectional passages as frameworks for the featured soloists, all of whom were well-known stars of 1920s jazz: Rex Stewart, Coleman Hawkins, and Joe Smith. Henderson prepares each solo with an ensemble passage. For example, in the beginning, Henderson introduces a one-bar rhythmic figure that accumulates energy as the piano, saxophones, trumpets, and full band play it in succession. The result—a terraced, orchestrated *crescendo* building from a single instrument to sections to the entire ensemble—dramatically sets up Rex Stewart's clamorous trumpet phrases. The piece enjoyed wide circulation, and within six months of the arrangement's publication, several leading bands had made their own recordings of "Stampede."

"The Henderson Stomp" explores some of the same territory that "Stampede" trod. Henderson's band recorded it in late 1926, taking virtually the same tempo (just under 240 beats per minute) that it had for the earlier piece. Moreover, "Henderson Stomp" begins with another "terraced" introduction based on a one-bar rhythmic idea. Whereas in "Stampede," the terracing effect was chiefly created by shifts in instrumentation, in "Henderson Stomp," the introduction is dominated by one color—the clarinet trio—and marked by shifts in register, from high to middle to low then up again. Unlike "Stampede," moreover, "Henderson Stomp" mainly exhibits the band as a unit, not the solo stars within it, and makes more palpable the composer-arranger's presence.

"Rocky Mountain Blues" and "Variety Stomp," two Henderson compositions from the late 1920s, rank with "Stampede" and "Henderson Stomp" among those most successfully realized on record by his band. "Rocky Mountain Blues," despite its title, is a complex and multi-strain piece with no links to the blues in form or style. As recorded by Henderson's band in an arrangement credited to Don Redman, the piece reveals a deft and darting style of jazz orchestration, made up of a tightly woven collage of one-, two-, four-, and six-bar units—including 17 two-bar breaks. From the off-tonic, whole-tone introduction to the final, rather inconclusively chattering woodblock break, every section of the piece brims with well-played ideas. The third strain features a six-voice reed/brass harmonization that Schuller calls a "prophetic ensemble background" because it anticipates big-band writing of a decade later. Throughout, the work displays break-like textures in mid-strain; that is, the arrangement suspends the rhythm section for four-bar phrases not only for solo flourishes but also as a technique of structural contrast. A rapid-fire call-and-response dialogue between the brass and tenor saxophone soloist (Coleman Hawkins) shows how the musicians could deftly deliver a vital, polished performance through a thicket of tricky scoring.

"Variety Stomp," named after the entertainment weekly whose music columnist, Abel Green, receives co-composer credit for the tune, is a fiercely driving piece that begins in a minor key. Typical for its time, it features a frequent alternation of composed ensemble passages and improvised solos. In the first of two versions recorded in 1927, the piece comes alive as a searing, aggressive "stomp." Indeed, the piece could not be more aptly named, for variety is another of its hallmarks. It features four different strains, including a 32-bar chorus, and at least four modulations. Moreover, Henderson subdivides each strain into four-bar units, shifting among passages for full band, sections within the band, and six different solos (for two trombones, trumpet, alto saxophone, piano, and tenor saxophone). Whole-tone effects and a strange final cadence that avoids the home pitch add a touch of urbane wit typical of late-1920s New York jazz.

Two pieces that Henderson wrote in the mid-1930s—"Down South Camp Meeting" and "Wrappin' It Up"—represent his masterworks for the big band. Henderson scored many works for big band, but the majority of his works in the 1930s are *arranged* popular songs; that is, vocal pieces transformed for the swing band. "Down South Camp Meeting" and "Wrappin' It Up" stand out because they are swing *compositions*—works conceived for the big band, with melodies and rhythms better suited to instruments than voices and with ample space for improvised solos. While they share many traits with Henderson's jazz works of the 1920s, these swing pieces are qualitatively different. Gone are the tuba and banjo that marked the beat in the bands of the 1920s; in the 1930s, a guitar and string bass articulate a gentler, lighter, yet still vibrant pulse. Moreover, these pieces move at more moderate tempos, making the earlier pieces sound urgent and manic by comparison. Such tempos allow for a more swinging performance—that is, a highly nuanced rendering of rhythm and articulation that incites dancing. (Benny Goodman considered Henderson a composer-arranger of dance music *par excellence,* probably the highest compliment a swing bandleader could give after several thousand nights on the bandstand.) Performed and recorded by Henderson's own band as well as by Goodman's, "Down South Camp Meeting" and "Wrappin' It Up" reached a wide audience and helped to plant the sound of big-band swing in the national consciousness. Along with just a few other scores in Goodman's huge book, both pieces remained in the repertory of the "King of Swing" for half a century.

The version of "Down South Camp Meeting" that Henderson's band recorded in 1934 presents the piece as it would be played by Goodman for years. All the traits for which Henderson's style would become well known are here: passages that set the band's sections in dialogue with one another, carefully worked out background figures designed to interact with the soloist or section in the foreground, chains of syncopation in which the off-beat notes tug and push against the solid regular pulse, and a quality of understated, relaxed swing—powerfully present but hard to describe—that suffuses the whole.

While "Down South Camp Meeting" represents Henderson's use of the multi-strain form derived from marches and ragtime, "Wrappin' It Up" embodies the 32-bar ABAC popular-song form. The forms produce contrasting effects. "Down South Camp Meeting" is progressive, in the sense that it proceeds from one section to the next, modulates to a new key for each new section, and never recapitulates one section after introducing another. "Wrappin' It Up" is cyclical, presenting a single 32-bar theme with three variations. The saxophones state the theme, punctuated by pointed brass interjections. The first two "variations" are solo choruses featuring (on Henderson's classic 1934 recording) Hilton Jefferson on alto saxophone and Henry "Red" Allen on trumpet. The final chorus presents Henderson's own orchestrated variation of the theme. This format represents a common approach to swing-era scoring: a first chorus stating the melody, a series of solo improvisations on the melody, and a composer-arranger's chorus. The tune contains more rhythmic than melodic interest, and its darting, syncopated line is conceived for instruments, not voices. In fact, many phrases of the melody bear a striking resemblance to figures that Louis Armstrong played in his solos with Henderson a decade earlier. These figures, along with the blues inflections laced throughout the melody, are almost entirely composed, and even during the solos, the underscoring interacts with the soloists and often rises up to take over the discourse, only to recede into the background and allow the soloist to continue. For their part, the soloists obviously thrive on the foundation Henderson provides.

Adopting such scores as "Down South Camp Meeting" and "Wrappin' It Up," Benny Goodman's orchestra became the medium by which big-band jazz reached a mass audience. For the first time, jazz had become America's most popular music, and its style bore Henderson's stamp. With their call-and-response figures, their distinctive interaction of solo and group, and their rhythmic verve, Henderson's compositions brought music with deep African-American roots into national popularity.

REFERENCES

Connor, D. Russell. *Benny Goodman: Listen to His Legacy.* Studies in Jazz, no. 6. Metuchen, N.J.: Scarecrow Press, 1988.

Goodman, Benny, and Irving Kolodin. *The Kingdom of Swing.* New York: Stackpole Sons, 1939.

Hammond, John. Liner notes, *A Study of Frustration: The Fletcher Henderson Story.* Columbia Legacy 57596.

Schuller, Gunther. *Early Jazz: Its Roots and Musical Development.* New York: Oxford University Press, 1968.

———. *The Swing Era: The Development of Jazz, 1930–1945.* New York: Oxford University Press, 1989.

Schuller, Gunther, and Martin Williams. Booklet accompanying *The Smithsonian Collection of Big Band Jazz.* Smithsonian Collection of Recordings R 030.

Williams, Martin. Booklet accompanying *The Smithsonian Collection of Big Band Jazz.* Smithsonian Collection of Recordings R 033 (revised edition).

JEFFREY MAGEE

HENDRIX, JIMI

Born in Seattle, Wash., November 27, 1942; died in London, England, September 18, 1970. **Education:** Taught himself guitar while growing up in Seattle; Garfield High School, Seattle, 1959–60. **Military Service:** United States Army paratroopers, 101st Airborn Division, 1961; formed band with another paratrooper, bass guitarist Billy Cox; discharged due to injury, 1962. **Composing and Performing Career:** Seattle, Wash., played in high school band, the Rocking Kings (renamed the Tomcats), 1958–61; played with numerous touring rhythm-and-blues revues, 1962–64; lead guitarist with Little Richard's band, 1963; New York, N.Y., hired by Isley Brothers and joined Curtis Knight's band, 1964; England, brought over by manager Brian "Chas" Chandler, 1966; formed the Jimi Hendrix Experience with bass guitarist Noel Redding and drummer Mitch Mitchell; the Olympia Theater, Paris, The Experience debut, late 1966; released first single, "Hey Joe," December 1966; recorded first album, *Are You Experienced?*, 1967; Monterey Pop Festival, Monterey, California, U.S. debut, summer 1967; recorded second album, *Axis: Bold as Love*, 1967; extensive U.S. and European tours, 1967–69; released third album, *Electric Ladyland*, 1968; New York, N.Y., supervised construction of own recording studio, Electric Ladyland, 1968–69; Woodstock festival, appeared with Billy Cox and Mitch Mitchell, 1969; formed Band of Gypsys with Billy Cox and drummer Buddy Miles, 1969; released live album, *Band of Gypsys*, 1970; made numerous studio recordings, released posthumously, 1969–70. **Honors/Awards:** *Billboard* magazine, artist of the year, 1968; *Playboy* magazine, artist of the year, 1969.

MUSIC LIST

[The following list of titles includes only works that were composed by the subject of the entry; it is not a list of recordings that were made by the subject. Although the composer may have made recordings of his own works, the list is not restricted to those recordings but in many cases includes performances by other artists of the composer's work. The list is made up of publication and discographical data, in cases where such information is available. Although no effort has been made to include documentation of the earliest recording of the works listed, the date of the earliest recording that is readily available has been given. —Ed.]

"Ain't No Telling." Seattle: Experience Hendrix. Recorded, 1967: MCA MCA-11601; MCA MCAD-10894.

". . . And the Gods Made Love." Seattle: Experience Hendrix. Recorded, 1968: MCA MCA-11600; MCA MCAD-10895.

"Angel." Seattle: Experience Hendrix. Recorded, 1971: MCA MCA-11599; Reprise 2034-2.

"Are You Experienced?" Seattle: Experience Hendrix. Recorded, 1967: MCA MCA-11602; MCA MCAD-10893; Reprise/CBS 1-22306.

"Astro Man." Seattle: Experience Hendrix. Recorded, 1971: MCA MCA-11599; Reprise 2034-2.

"Belly Button Window." Seattle: Experience Hendrix. Recorded, 1971: MCA MCA-11599; Reprise 2034-2.

"Bleeding Heart." Seattle: Experience Hendrix. Recorded, 1972: MCA MCA-11684; MCA 11060; Reprise/CBS 1-22306; Reprise MS2103.

"Bold as Love." Seattle: Experience Hendrix. Recorded, 1967: MCA MCA-11601; MCA MCAD-10894.

"Burning of the Midnight Lamp." Seattle: Experience Hendrix. Recorded, 1967: MCA MCA-11600; MCA MCAD-10895; Reprise MS 2025; Ryko RCD 20078.

"Can You See Me?" Seattle: Experience Hendrix. Recorded, 1967: MCA MCA-11602; Reprise 25358-1; Reprise MS 2025; Reprise MS 2029.

"Castles Made of Sand." Seattle: Experience Hendrix. Recorded, 1967: MCA MCA-11601; MCA MCAD-10894.

"Crosstown Traffic." Seattle: Experience Hendrix. Recorded, 1968: MCA MCA-11600; MCA MCAD-10895.

"Dolly Dagger." Seattle: Experience Hendrix. Recorded, 1971: MCA MCA-11599; Reprise MS2040.

"Drifting." Seattle: Experience Hendrix. Recorded, 1971: MCA MCA-11599; Reprise 2034-2.

"Earth Blues." Seattle: Experience Hendrix. Recorded, 1971: MCA MCA-11599; Reprise MS2040.

"EXP." Seattle: Experience Hendrix. Recorded, 1967: MCA MCA-11601; MCA MCAD-10894.

"Ezy Rider." Seattle: Experience Hendrix. Recorded, 1971: Capitol/EMI 12416; MCA MCA-11599; Reprise 2034-2.

"51st Anniversary." Seattle: Experience Hendrix. Recorded, 1967: MCA MCA-11602; Reprise MS 2025.

"Fire." Seattle: Experience Hendrix. Recorded, 1967: MCA MCA-11602; MCA MCAD-10893; MCA MCAD-11063; Reprise/CBS 1-22306; Ryko RCD 20038; Ryko RCD 20078.

"Foxy Lady." Seattle: Experience Hendrix. Recorded, 1967: Capitol/EMI 12416; MCA MCA-11602; MCA MCAD-10893; Polydor 2302016; Reprise 25358-1; Ryko RCD 20038; Ryko RCD 20078.

"Freedom." Seattle: Experience Hendrix. Recorded, 1971: MCA MCA-11599; Polydor 2302016; Reprise 2034-2.

"Gypsy Eyes." Seattle: Experience Hendrix. Recorded, 1968: MCA MCA-11600; MCA MCAD-10895.

"Have You Ever Been (to Electric Ladyland)." Seattle: Experience Hendrix. Recorded, 1968: MCA MCA-11600; MCA MCAD-10895.

"Hear My Train a' Comin'." Seattle: Experience Hendrix. Recorded, 1971: Capitol/EMI 12416; MCA MCA-11060; MCA MCAD-11063; Reprise/CBS 1-22306; Reprise MS2040; Ryko RCD 20078.

"Here He Comes (Lover Man)." Seattle: Experience Hendrix. Recorded, 1997: MCA MCA-11684.

"Hey Baby (Land of the New Rising Sun)." Seattle: Experience Hendrix. Recorded, 1971: MCA MCA-11599; Reprise MS2040.

"Highway Chile." Seattle: Experience Hendrix. Recorded, 1967: MCA MCA-11602; Reprise MS 2025; Reprise MS2103.

"House Burning Down." Seattle: Experience Hendrix. Recorded, 1968: MCA MCA-11600; MCA MCAD-10895.

"I Don't Live Today." Seattle: Experience Hendrix. Recorded, 1967: MCA MCA-11602; MCA MCAD-10893; Reprise/CBS 1-22306.

"If 6 Was 9." Seattle: Experience Hendrix. Recorded, 1967: MCA MCA-11601; MCA MCAD-10894.

"In from the Storm." Seattle: Experience Hendrix. Recorded, 1971: MCA MCA-11599; Polydor 2302016; Reprise 2034-2; Reprise 2RS 6481.

Jimi Hendrix; printed by permission of Authentic Hendrix, L.L.C.; all rights reserved

"Izabella." Seattle: Experience Hendrix. Recorded, 1970: Cotillion SD 2400; MCA MCA-11599; MCA MCAD-11063; Reprise MS2103.

"Little Miss Lover." Seattle: Experience Hendrix. Recorded, 1967: MCA MCA-11601; MCA MCAD-10894.

"Little Wing." Seattle: Experience Hendrix. Recorded, 1967: MCA MCA-11601; MCA MCAD-10894; Reprise 2049; Reprise/CBS 1-22306.

"Long Hot Summer Night." Seattle: Experience Hendrix. Recorded, 1968: MCA MCA-11600; MCA MCAD-10895.

"Look Over Yonder." Seattle: Experience Hendrix. Recorded, 1971: MCA MCA-11684; Reprise MS2040.

"Love or Confusion." Seattle: Experience Hendrix. Recorded, 1967: MCA MCA-11602; MCA MCAD-10893; Ryko RCD 20078.

"Machine Gun." Seattle: Experience Hendrix. Recorded, 1970: Capitol CDP 7 96414 2; MCA MCA-11607.

"Manic Depression." Seattle: Experience Hendrix. Recorded, 1967: MCA MCA-11602; MCA MCAD-10893; Reprise MS 2025; Ryko RCD 20038.

"May This Be Love." Seattle: Experience Hendrix. Recorded, 1967: MCA MCA-11602; MCA MCAD-10893.

"Message to Love." Seattle: Experience Hendrix. Recorded, 1970: Capitol CDP 7 96414 2; MCA MCA-11607; Reprise MS 2204.

"Midnight." Seattle: Experience Hendrix. Recorded, 1972: MCA MCA-11684; Reprise MS2103.

"Midnight Lightning." Seattle: Experience Hendrix. Recorded, 1975: MCA MCA-11684; Polydor 2302016; Reprise MS 2229.

"Moon, Turn the Tides . . . Gently Gently Away." Seattle: Experience Hendrix. Recorded, 1968: MCA MCA-11600; MCA MCAD-10895.

"My Friend." Seattle: Experience Hendrix. Recorded, 1971: MCA MCA-11599; Reprise 2034-2.

"Night Bird Flying." Seattle: Experience Hendrix. Recorded, 1971: MCA MCA-11599; Reprise 2034-2.

"1983 . . . (A Merman I Should Turn to Be)." Seattle: Experience Hendrix. Recorded, 1968: MCA MCA-11600; MCA MCAD-10895.

"One Rainy Wish." Seattle: Experience Hendrix. Recorded, 1967: MCA MCA-11601; MCA MCAD-10894.

"Pali Gap." Seattle: Experience Hendrix. Recorded, 1971: MCA MCA-11684; Reprise MS2040.

"Power of Soul." Seattle: Experience Hendrix. Recorded, 1970: Capitol CDP 7 96414 2; MCA MCA-11607.

"Purple Haze." Seattle: Experience Hendrix. Recorded, 1967: MCA MCA-11602; MCA MCAD-10893; MCA MCAD-11063; Reprise 25358-1; Ryko RCD 20038; Ryko RCD 20078.

"Rainy Day, Dream Away." Seattle: Experience Hendrix. Recorded, 1968: MCA MCA-11600; MCA MCAD-10895.

"Red House." Seattle: Experience Hendrix. Recorded, 1967: MCA MCA-11602; MCA MCA-11060; MCA MCAD-11063; Reprise 2049; Reprise/CBS 1-22306; Ryko RCD 20038.

"Remember." Seattle: Experience Hendrix. Recorded, 1967: MCA MCA-11602.

"Room Full of Mirrors." Seattle: Experience Hendrix. Recorded, 1971: MCA MCA-11599; Reprise MS2040.

"South Saturn Delta." Seattle: Experience Hendrix. Recorded, 1989: MCA MCA-11684.

"Spanish Castle Magic." Seattle: Experience Hendrix. Recorded, 1967: MCA MCA-11601; MCA MCAD-10894; Ryko RCD 20038; Ryko RCD 20078.

"The Stars That Play with Laughing Sam's Dice." Seattle: Experience Hendrix. Recorded, 1967: MCA MCA-11684; Reprise MS 2025.

"Stepping Stone." Seattle: Experience Hendrix. Recorded, 1970: MCA MCA-11599; MCA MCAD-11063; Reprise MS2103.

"Still Raining, Still Dreaming." Seattle: Experience Hendrix. Recorded, 1968: MCA MCA-11600; MCA MCAD-10895.

"Stone Free." Seattle: Experience Hendrix. Recorded, 1966: Capitol/EMI 12416; MCA MCA-11602; Reprise/CBS 1-22306; Reprise MS 2025; Ryko RCD 20078.

"Straight Ahead." Seattle: Experience Hendrix. Recorded, 1971: MCA MCA-11599; Reprise 2034-2.

"Third Stone from the Sun." Seattle: Experience Hendrix. Recorded, 1967: MCA MCA-11602; MCA MCAD-10893.

"3 Little Bears." Seattle: Experience Hendrix. Recorded, 1972: Reprise MS2103.

"Up from the Skies." Seattle: Experience Hendrix. Recorded, 1967: MCA MCA-11601; MCA MCAD-10894.

"Voodoo Chile." Seattle: Experience Hendrix. Recorded, 1968: Capitol/EMI 12416; MCA MCA-11600; MCA MCAD-10895.

"Voodoo Child (Slight Return)." Seattle: Experience Hendrix. Recorded, 1968: MCA MCA-11600; MCA MCAD-10895; MCA MCAD-11063; Reprise 2049; Reprise/CBS 1-22306.

"Wait Until Tomorrow." Seattle: Experience Hendrix. Recorded, 1967: MCA MCA-11601; MCA MCAD-10894; Ryko RCD 20078.

"Who Knows." Seattle: Experience Hendrix. Recorded, 1970: Capitol CDP 7 96414 2; MCA MCA-11607.

"The Wind Cries Mary." Seattle: Experience Hendrix. Recorded, 1967: MCA MCA-11602; MCA MCAD-10893; Reprise 25358-1; Reprise MS 2025.

"You Got Me Floatin'." Seattle: Experience Hendrix. Recorded, 1967: MCA MCA-11601; MCA MCAD-10894.

PUBLICATIONS

ABOUT HENDRIX
Books and Monographs

Ala, Nemesio. *Morire di musica: Jimi Hendrix, Janis Joplin, Jim Morrison: Il rock, l'eroina, la morte la fine di una cultura nei testi di tre grandi musicisti scomparsi.* Roma: Savelli, 1979.

Benson, Joe. *Uncle Joe's Record Guide: Eric Clapton, Jimi Hendrix, The Who.* Glendale, Calif.: J. Benson Unlimited, 1987.

Boot, Adrian, and Chris Salewicz, comps. *Jimi Hendrix: The Ultimate Experience.* New York: Macmillan, 1995.

Brown, Tony. *Jimi Hendrix: A Visual Documentary—His Life, Loves and Music.* London: Omnibus Press, 1992.

Carey, Gary. *Lenny, Janis, and Jimi.* New York: Pocket Books, 1975.

Danneman, Monika. *The Inner World of Jimi Hendrix.* New York: St. Martin's Press, 1995.

Dister, Alain. *Jimi Hendrix.* Collection: Histoire du rock, no. 1. Paris: Nouvelles Editions Polaires, 1973.

Feller, Benoit. *Jimi Hendrix.* Paris: Editions Albin Michel, 1976.

Goldman, Albert. *Sound Bites.* New York: Turtle Bay Books, 1992.

Green, Martin. *The Illustrated Legend of Jimi Hendrix.* New York: Penguin Studio, 1995.

Giuliano, Geoffrey, Brenda Giuliano, and Deborah Lynn Black. *The Illustrated Jimi Hendrix.* Edison, N.J.: Chartwell Books, 1994.

Hatay, Nona. *Jimi Hendrix: Reflections and Visions.* San Francisco: Pomegranate Artbooks, 1995.

———. *Jimi Hendrix—The Spirit Lives On: Experimental Photo/Art, Concert Photographs, Concept and Interviews.* San Francisco: Last Gasp, 1983.

Henderson, David. *'Scuse Me While I Kiss the Sky: The Life of Jimi Hendrix.* New York: Bantam Books, 1981. Note: condensed and revised edition of *Jimi Hendrix: Voodoo Child of the Aquarian Age* (Garden City, N.J.: Doubleday, 1978).

Hopkins, Jerry. *Hit and Run: The Jimi Hendrix Story.* New York: Perigee Books, 1983.

Knight, Curtis. *Jimi: An Intimate Biography of Jimi Hendrix.* New York: Praeger, 1974.

———. *Jimi Hendrix: Starchild.* Wilmington, Del.: Abelard Productions, 1992.

Kramer, Eddie, and John McDermott. *Hendrix: Setting the Record Straight.* New York: Warner Books, 1992.

McDermott, John, Billy Cox, and Eddie Kramer. *Jimi Hendrix Sessions: The Complete Studio Recording Sessions, 1963–70.* Boston: Little, Brown, 1995.

Mitchell, Mitch, with John Platt. *The Hendrix Experience.* London: Pyramid, 1990.

———. *Jimi Hendrix: Inside the Experience.* New York: Harmony, 1990.

Murray, Charles Shaar. *Crosstown Traffic: Jimi Hendrix and the Post-War Rock 'n' Roll Revolution.* New York: St. Martin's Press, 1989.

Nolan, Tom. *Jimi Hendrix: A Biography in Words and Pictures,* edited by Greg Shaw. New York: Sire Books, 1977.

Ordovas, Jesus. *Jimi Hendrix/Jesus Ordovas.* Madrid: Ediciones Jucar, 1974.

Potash, Chris, ed. *The Jimi Hendrix Companion: Three Decades of Commentary.* New York: Schirmer Books, 1996.

Purple Haze Archives and Dave Armstrong, comps. *Jimi Hendrix: A Discography.* Tucson, Ariz.: Purple Haze Archives, 1981. Rev. ed., Tucson, Ariz.: Purple Haze Archives, 1982.

Redding, Noel, and Carol Appleby. *Are You Experienced? The Inside Story of Jimi Hendrix.* London: Fourth Estate, 1990.

Robertson, John. *Complete Guide to the Music of Jimi Hendrix.* London: Omnibus, 1995.

Salvatori, Dario. *Jimi Hendrix.* Rome: Lato Side, 1980.

Sampson, Victor. *Hendrix.* London: Proteus, 1984.

Shapiro, Harry, and Caeser Glebbeek. *Jimi Hendrix: Electric Gypsy.* New York: St. Martin's Press, 1991.

Sonderhoff, Achim. *Jimi Hendrix—Voodoo Chile: Die Biographie einer Rocklegende.* Bastei-Lübbe-Taschenbuch, bd. 60040. Bergisch Gladbach, Germany: Lübbe, 1981.

St. Pierre, Roger. *Jimi Hendrix Recorded Poems.* Milwaukee, Wisc.: Hal Leonard Books, 1986.

Welch, Chris. *Hendrix: A Biography.* New York: Delilah/Putnam, 1982.

Dissertation

Valdez, Stephen Kenneth. "The Development of the Electric Guitar Solo in Rock Music, 1954–1971." D.M.A. thesis, University of Oregon, 1992.

Articles

Chenoweth, Lawrence. "The Rhetoric of Hope and Despair: A Study of the Jimi Hendrix Experience and the Jefferson Airplane." *American Quarterly* 23 (1971): 25–45.

Goertzel, Ben. "The Rock Guitar Solo: From Expression to Simulation." *Popular Music and Society* 15, no. 1 (1991): 91–101.

Keena-Levin, Richard. "Call and Response: Jimi Hendrix." *Popular Music* 10, no. 1 (1991): 89–91.

Schwartz, Jeff. "Writing Jimi: Rock Guitar Pedagogy as Postmodern Folkloric Practice." *Popular Music* 12, no. 3 (1993): 281–288.

Whiteley, Sheila. "Progressive Rock and Psychedelic Coding in the Work of Jimi Hendrix." *Popular Music* 9, no. 1 (1990): 37–60.

BY HENDRIX

Cherokee Mist: The Lost Writings, compiled by Bill Nitopi. New York: HarperCollins, 1993.

Crosstown Conversation. Recorded interview with Jimi Hendrix. Bak Tabak 4082.

In His Own Words, edited by Tony Brown. London: Omnibus, 1994.

PRINCIPAL ARCHIVES

Experience Music Project, 110 110th Avenue NE, Suite 550, Bellevue, WA 98004.

Purple Haze Archives, P.O. Box 41133, Tucson, AZ 85717.

* * * * *

Images of Jimi Hendrix playing his guitar—or burning it, or using it in any of the other burlesque antics that made his stage shows famous—are central both to his reputation and to the iconology of the late 1960s. They are also a very inadequate guide to his achievements. He was a master guitarist and showman, to be sure. But he was also a remarkable vocalist, an extraordinarily inventive studio musician, and a gifted and original composer.

His years playing in bands with high school and army acquaintances exposed Hendrix to the gamut of early 1960s popular music: blues, rhythm and blues, soul, rock 'n' roll, chart-topping pop. His subsequent touring as a backup player for Little Richard and other rhythm-and-blues artists allowed him to hone his guitar technique and to take part in some of the era's most theatrical pop-music performances, the spirit of which he maintained in his own concert appearances, especially those of the years 1966–68. Moving to London in 1966 offered the first real opportunity to write and record original material and to sing, activities he pursued in tandem with his guitar playing from 1966 until his death.

Hendrix's musical roles should not be too sharply distinguished from one another, particularly those of the composer, guitarist, and studio artist. To the extent that he provided his songs with words, melodies, and chord progressions, Hendrix can be seen as a composer or songwriter in the traditional sense. But his music is distinguished as much by its sound and manner of performance as by its verbal or musical structures, and thus it should be seen in part as the product of his performing experience and of his continuing experiments with the electric guitar and with modern studio technique. Just how important these were to his creative process can be judged from his recordings of other people's music, such as Bob Dylan's "All Along the Watchtower" (on *Electric Ladyland*) or the "Star-Spangled Banner" (on the film and recording of the Woodstock festival); so thoroughly are these transformed by his treatment that they become, in effect, Hendrix songs.

His style lies at the confluence of several different traditions. As Charles Shaar Murray has emphasized, he frequently drew on black American genres, most importantly blues, rhythm and blues, and soul. These are sometimes cultivated as themselves: his "Red House" (on *Are You Experienced?*) is a traditional blues in structure, subject matter, and performance. More often, however, elements of the genres are incorporated into some new context, as when his guitar solos use blues idioms in songs that are not, strictly speaking, blues, or when his accompanying guitar parts use the rhythms and voicings of rhythm and blues in contexts otherwise far removed from the genre. Hendrix also drew on, and helped to develop, aspects of contemporary white rock music. Like many other songwriters of the period, he was influenced by the song lyrics of Bob Dylan, whose literary sophistication and use of mythical and allegorical imagery found frequent echo in Hendrix's own texts. In addition, he was one of several rock artists to experiment with advanced recording techniques. The first two albums by Hendrix's band, The Experience, were released in the same year as the Beatles' *Sgt. Pepper's Lonely Hearts Club Band* and, like that album, contained music that could be produced only in the recording studio. With this, both bands helped to draw a line between the recording and the performing artist, which was relatively new to rock music and which contributed to the notion that rock was not merely a popular entertainment but an art form, requiring as much careful preparation and commitment as any other art.

The recordings made with The Experience, which include several singles as well as the three albums discussed below, remain Hendrix's most influential work. In them may be heard the breadth of his musical and topical interests in songs ranging from down-to-earth blues to science fiction fantasy and from lyrical ballad to hard rock. Also evident is his elaborate studio technique, which frequently makes use of overdubbed instrumental and vocal tracks to create dense and variegated textures. The guitar playing is remarkable, not only for the virtuosity and emotional range of the solos but also for the complexity of the frequently changing accompaniments and, perhaps most of all, for the variety of tone colors produced by many different electronic manipulations of the guitar's sound. The recordings also display Hendrix's often underestimated skills as a vocalist, in which role he moves freely between song and speech with the same flexible sense of timing that characterizes his guitar playing. Remarkably, the singles and all three albums—of which the third, *Electric Ladyland,* is a "double" album—were completed in only two years. This is productive by any standard and especially impressive given that nearly all of the songs were written by Hendrix himself and required extensive studio production.

The two years between *Electric Ladyland* and Hendrix's death in 1970 were less productive. The reason, presumably, is that much of his energy was taken up by an extensive touring schedule as well as by the construction of a new recording studio, a legal battle over the rights to his music, an arrest and eventual acquittal on charges of drug possession, and a search for new musical collaborators. Nevertheless, he still managed to release the live album *Band of Gypsys,* played by his short-lived group Band of Gypsys, and to finish or nearly finish enough studio recordings to fill several additional albums. Undoubtedly, his most famous work from this period is the "Star-Spangled Banner," as performed and recorded at the Woodstock festival. The anthem is played by the guitar alone (with muted drums) and is provided with what amounts to a critical commentary, accomplished through an interpolation of "Taps" and a series of electronic screams and explosions. Its unmistakably anti-war message signals a new political consciousness in his music, one also reflected in his own song "Machine Gun" (on *Band of Gypsys*).

Band of Gypsys shows Hendrix interacting with a rhythm section whose sound is far closer to rhythm and blues or soul than was that of The Experience. Moreover, this album, the Woodstock performance, and the many live recordings released after his death give some idea of his style in concert, in which premiere place was given to his guitar playing. For the most part, the late studio recordings show him continuing to explore his earlier interests, writing blues, hard rock songs, and lyrical ballads, and performing them in characteristically complex and imaginative arrangements.

Hendrix's popular success has never really waned, thanks in part to the ongoing release of live recordings and videos and to the re-release of his original albums on compact disc. For the most part, critics and musicians have likewise responded favorably, although attitudes about what aspects of Hendrix's music are most valuable have changed over the years (for an excellent sampling see Chris Potash's book). Writers and players alike immediately recognized Hendrix as a phenomenally gifted and innovative guitarist, and since his death, he has come to be seen as a crucial figure in the history of electric guitar-playing generally. In particular, he is credited with having exploited the instrument's unique ability to produce a wide variety of timbres and sonic effects; Hendrix pioneered the use of the wah-wah pedal and similar sound-altering devices and also learned to manipulate feedback (the electronic noise that results when an electric guitar picks up its own sound signal from an audio speaker and feeds it back into an amplifier). Equally important, he is thought to have made these unusual effects an integral part of his musical conceptions rather than to have displayed them as a repertoire of gimmicks. *Guitar Player* and related publications have devoted considerable space to explaining his technique, and guitarists working in rock, funk, blues, heavy metal, and jazz have all attested to his influence.

As Hendrix's career has receded further into the past, however, critics and musicians have tended to place more emphasis on what he achieved outside the realm of guitar technique. A number of specific innovations have been praised, among them his introduction of electronically derived pure sound into the compositional vocabulary of rock music, his exploitation of the creative possibilities offered by the recording studio, and his transformation of the blues and other black American genres on which he drew. An increasing number of artists have recorded Hendrix's songs, indicating a growing interest in his abilities as a composer: the catalogue of Hendrix covers includes entries by jazz bandleader Gil Evans, the Kronos Quartet, and numerous rock, soul, and blues artists. More than any given song or stylistic innovation, however, Hendrix is probably most valued for what *New York Times* critic Jon Pareles called "his experimental spirit—his determination to smash through limits of timbre, harmony and structure." Hendrix devoted his career to exploring new possibilities, setting an example that artists could follow even if they did not wish to explore the same territory he had. His music served and continues to serve as a goad to invention, a reminder that stylistic and generic boundaries are never immutable.

ARE YOU EXPERIENCED? (1967)

Three singles preceded the recording of *Are You Experienced?*, and while they were not included in the original, British version of the album (they were inserted into the later, American release), they belong to the same phase of Hendrix's development. One song in particular, "Purple Haze," exemplifies the style for which The Experience was best known. Its most distinctive feature is a somewhat unorthodox division of duties between the bass, drums, and rhythm guitar. The bass is the real keeper of the beat. The drums occasionally provide the "backbeat" emphasis (1 *2* 3 *4*) so typical of rock music, but at least as often, both they and the rhythm guitar play offbeat patterns against the bass. The drums also add frequent rolls and other rhythmic ornaments, a practice that becomes more pronounced in "Fire," "Foxy Lady," and other songs. The effect is to propel the rhythms forward, giving each song a sense of urgency.

Other aspects of "Purple Haze" are likewise heard elsewhere. It begins with a striking introduction, in which the guitar plays a repeated, dissonant tritone and then a brief, sharply etched melody over a drone in the bass. Only when this is concluded does the music launch into the chord progression of the song proper. Several other examples begin similarly, and in some, the introduction also returns at a later point; for example, in "Purple Haze" the opening melody is reprised between the end of the guitar solo and the beginning of the final verse. The solo is likewise typical insofar as it centers around an abrupt shift in color: after a variation on the opening melody is delivered in the same angry "fuzztone" heard at the beginning of the song, a new, higher tone enters that is largely free of fuzz. It is as if another guitarist has begun to play, an effect Hendrix produces elsewhere either by a similar juxtaposition or by the superimposition of one guitar sound over another. The solo resembles others still further in that it is filled with various vocalisms, including half-spoken, half-sung interjections as well as an underlying growl created by playing recorded vocal sounds at speeds slower than normal. Comments, laughs, throat-clearings, and similar sounds are also found throughout many other songs, giving the performances an air of informality.

The vocal style itself is forceful and passionate, almost shouted. This is one of Hendrix's more characteristic voices, one that, taken together with the typically first-person construction of his lyrics, encourages his being personally identified with his protagonists. Here, a tale of confusion is rendered in brilliant, fantastic images, including those of the "purple haze" itself and of the singer "kissing the sky" at the end of the first verse. Elsewhere, his topics include love, desire, and depression, and he also casts himself in the typical blues persona of the "rolling stone."

Short of describing each of the songs included on *Are You Experienced?* in detail, it would be difficult to summarize the many different ways in which they treat the ingredients found in "Purple Haze." Even songs with very similar sounds and structures, such as "Fire" or "Manic Depression," have characteristics all their own. In the former, for instance, the opening instrumental melody is transformed on its return after the guitar solo, and the solo itself is actually played by two guitars that remain in unison except for one searing moment when they diverge. "Manic Depression," for its part, begins with fragments of an instrumental melody that really coalesce only in a postlude; moreover, it is in a rolling triple meter, which makes the rhythm sound even more propulsive than usual. Similar variations throughout the album keep the music from ever lapsing into formula.

There are also songs that depart entirely from the style of "Purple Haze." Most important, insofar as they represent interests pursued further on Hendrix's later albums, are "The Wind Cries Mary" and "Third Stone from the Sun." The first is a slow, evocative ballad. Its accompaniment is subdued, although not simple; what begins as a simple offbeat pattern in the guitar soon turns into an active part that accents different beats, fills in the spaces between the vocal phrases, and provides a counterpoint during the guitar solo. There is also a brief, three-note riff that serves as an introduction and then provides a coda to each verse. All the same, the principal emphasis is on Hendrix's now soulful voice and on his graceful lyrics. The first three verses all call on different images to suggest a sense of loss or ending, beginning in the real world with the end of a carnival and moving to a fantasy land where "the traffic lights . . . turn blue." Each concludes with some version of the song's title, and its significance is then clarified by a fourth verse, which characterizes the wind as the carrier of soon-to-be-lost memories.

There could hardly be a greater contrast than "Third Stone from the Sun," a tongue-in-cheek science fiction fantasy that lasts nearly seven minutes and has virtually no lyrics. Instead, the emphasis is on a series of wide-ranging explorations by the guitar, most of which unfold over a light pulse reminiscent of jazz. A context is provided by two spoken voice-overs in which an alien first expresses a desire to see Earth (the "third stone"), then resolves to destroy its incomprehensible inhabitants, so that, as he sarcastically puts it, they may "never hear surf music again." The guitar solos are accompanied by the groaning sounds of voices played at half speed, and as time goes on, the guitar sound makes increasing use of feedback and other electronic effects. The work is articulated, finally, by a threefold repetition of one of Hendrix's most memorable instrumental melodies, each rendering of which becomes increasingly distorted in a reflection of the story's ominous outcome.

AXIS: BOLD AS LOVE (1967)

This is Hendrix's gentlest album. A few songs, such as "Spanish Castle Magic" and "Little Miss Lover," retain the hard beat and biting timbres that characterize much of *Are You Experienced?* The majority, however, switch to less aggressive rhythms and to smoother sounds in both the instruments and the voice. This may reflect the influence of rhythm and blues or soul; many of the songs have comparatively slow tempos that sound more characteristic of those genres than of rock, and several feature choral answers to the vocal soloist, a trademark of soul. Whatever its source, however, the album's relative tranquility allows aspects of Hendrix's style to emerge that were less evident amid the excited energy of the earlier recordings.

One is his penchant for striking, fantastical imagery. The most brilliant example comes in the final song, "Bold as Love," where feelings are equated with colors and then used as characters in a ballad that ultimately serves to express the singer's own feelings. This is matched at the beginning of the album by "Up from the Skies," whose protagonist is an alien with similar but less malevolent interests in the Earth than the alien of "Third Stone from the Sun." In between are found "Little Wing," a romantic ballad that places the lover in a fairy-tale world of "butterflies and zebras and moonbeams"; "Spanish Castle Magic," which describes a utopia best reached "by dragonfly"; and "One Rainy Wish," a dream tale told, like "Bold as Love," mostly in term of colors. The fantastical images are often presented in quick succession and sometimes with alliteration or other devices to emphasize their rhythmic accumulation. This renders Hendrix's visions all the more vivid.

The album also displays his interest in a wide array of sounds and tone colors. This is evident directly in "EXP," an instrumental prelude to the album that is created entirely from feedback and other electronic noises. Subsequent songs explore many other sounds: "Up from the Skies" features Hendrix's first extended use of the "wah-wah" pedal; "Castles Made of Sand" includes a guitar solo that has been taped and played back in reverse; "Bold as Love" uses "phasing," in which the sound is given a luminous sheen by being simultaneously recorded on tape players running at different speeds. In addition, both the instruments and the voices are frequently subject to spatial shifts, either from one stereo channel to the other or between points located closer or farther away from the listener. Remarkably, it is rare that any of these seems like a mere special effect. On the one hand, the fact that the sounds result from electronic manipulation and seem so distant from "normal," acoustic music is curiously suited to the surrealism of Hendrix's lyrics. On the other, their treatment is typically such that they seem integrated into the very substance of each song. The reverse-tape effect in "Castles Made of Sand," for instance, is most prominent in the guitar solo that follows the second verse. However, it maintains a muted but clearly audible presence throughout the verses as well, so that its emergence in the solo seems wholly natural.

With the greater variety in color comes something of a de-emphasis on the guitar solos, which had formed the rhetorical high point of nearly every song on the early singles and on *Are You Experienced?* Here, one song, "Wait Until Tomorrow," has no solo, and several others leave only enough time for the guitar to make a brief statement. In addition, the solos that remain do not always exhibit the traditional focus on the solo instrument. In "You Got Me Floatin'," for instance, the solo passage is devoted to an instrumental mélange composed of the sounds of several guitars and the bass.

In some instances, Hendrix also departs from the typical forms of his earlier songs, in which a guitar solo would usually follow two verses and then be followed by one or two more. This was already dispensed with, of course, in "Third Stone from the Sun." In "If 6 Was 9," it seems to be progressively dismantled. The song

is in many ways similar to "Third Stone" insofar as it lasts nearly six minutes and combines spoken text with extensive instrumental passages. The topic, however, is self-determination rather than alien impressions of Earth, and the structure resembles a broken rather than a free form. First are heard two blues-like verses, sung by Hendrix and accompanied by a characteristic two-note rhythmic pattern. There follows, as expected, a guitar solo, but it is preceded by a spoken passage and accompanied by a jazz-like texture that has little in common with the music of the previous verses. The guitar solo ends, moreover, not in more verses but in a second spoken passage, in which the only holdover from the earlier music is the two-note rhythmic pattern. Even this then disappears in the ensuing section, another guitar solo over still another new accompanimental texture. It is as if Hendrix first distorts and then finally abandons the form implied by his opening verses.

Equally unusual is "One Rainy Wish," which is constructed so as to allow two widely different styles to be juxtaposed. Following a meditative introduction, the song begins with two verses in a slow waltz time, during which the singing is lyrical and the accompaniment dominated by descending scales in the guitar. The words describe a dream of an idyllic retreat, luminously colored, and with a lover waiting under a "tree of song." The music pauses for a moment, then shifts to duple meter and a hard rock sound reminiscent of "Purple Haze." The words address the loved one directly and are delivered in Hendrix's passionate shout, and they are followed by a brief but intense guitar solo. The words, meter, and tone color of the opening section then return, and the song concludes with a spoken passage in which the singer continues to describe the dream. In this case, the effect is to combine into one song two quite different texts and their settings.

ELECTRIC LADYLAND (1968)

The Experience's final album is a much darker affair than *Axis: Bold as Love*, as harsh as the other is gentle. It gives no hint of this at first, beginning with an electronic instrumental not unlike the previous album's "EXP" and continuing with "Have You Ever Been (to Electric Ladyland)," an invitation to utopia for which Hendrix employs a light, crooning voice. This gives way, however, first to "Crosstown Traffic," a tale of difficult love delivered in the Experience's hardest rock sound, and then to "Voodoo Chile," a brooding, autobiographical blues. Later in the album, even moments of potential lightness are usually tempered: in "1983 . . . (A Merman I Should Turn to Be)," for instance, the singer's dreamy descent into the sea is undertaken only to escape a torn and violent world above, and in a cover of Earl King's "Come On (Let the Good Times Roll)," any optimism in the lyrics is contradicted by an aggressive performance and by some of Hendrix's most savage guitar playing.

In this context, it is unsurprising that there should be no lyrical ballad in the tradition of "The Wind Cries Mary" or "Little Wing." The nearest thing is "Gypsy Eyes," in which a desperate search for a loved one is described in Hendrix's characteristically vivid and fantastical language. But the words are belied by the music. The rhythm is never allowed to settle; after a lengthy introduction based on a simple, steady pulse, a transition to the verses is effected by a more complex rhythmic pattern, and then the words themselves are sung over a quick-moving, "walking" bass line. In addition, many of the vocals are doubled by an angry-sounding guitar, and the instrument also provides percussive interjections in the style of the later, onomatopoeic gunfire in "Machine Gun." Most telling, when the singer at last collapses in the final verse—the point at which he also, finally, hears the "sweet call" of Gypsy Eyes—the music is washed over by distortion, as if to suggest that even so bittersweet an ending could not be real.

Hendrix transforms others of his favorite themes as well. Most importantly, the expanded, double-album format allows for lengthier explorations of certain interests than had previously been possible. The most space is given to the blues and especially to "Voodoo Chile," which lasts some 15 minutes and includes guitar, organ, and drum solos as well as four verses of text. The words combine traditional blues imagery with Hendrix's surrealism. They begin with the claim that "the night I was born/ . . . my poor mother cried out loud the gypsy was right," a reference to Willie Dixon's "Hoochie Coochie Man" and other blues songs that deal directly or indirectly with voodoo magic. The story then turns to fantasy, as the singer is taken "past . . . infinity" and his "arrows . . . of desire" come "from far away as Jupiter." The music, too, moves between harmonies and soloistic figurations characteristic of the blues and electronic sounds typical of Hendrix's own music. The result is a blues as seen through the lens of his own personal style.

Nearly the same amount of time is devoted to "1983," the last and most complicated of his science fiction fantasies. Unlike "If 6 Was 9," where a longer form resulted from the progressive abandoning of regular song structure, here the expansion is within. Four verses are spaced out across the song's length. Between the second and third comes a traditional pop song "break," with words sung to a different melody than that of the verses and then an instrumental interlude. Between the third and fourth verses comes a much longer and decidedly untraditional instrumental section, in which the song's meter breaks down and the music ranges from electronic sounds, to sitar-like improvisations in the guitar, to drum and bass solos. The whole structure is bracketed by an introduction, which features a majestic instrumental melody that is also heard several times later, and by a long postlude in which a guitar solo slowly dissolves into electronic noise. The song is remarkably effective despite its length, largely because of its well-calculated contrasts. Frequent shifts between instruments, including a flute at one point, prevent the long instrumental section from losing focus. And the song as a whole hinges on the affective distance between the majestic opening melody and the dreamy, introspective verses, in which a chromatically descending bass line traces the singer's descent into the sea and away from the real world.

The remainder of the album pays tribute to others of Hendrix's interests and to some of his contemporaries. "Rainy Day, Dream Away" is a long rhythm-and-blues jam recorded not with The Experience but with a band that includes drummer Buddy Miles; it is split into two parts to provide a down-to-earth frame around "1983." "All Along the Watchtower" transforms Dylan's unpretentious folk ballad into a rock epic, while the electric harpsichord and dense textures of "Burning of the Midnight Lamp" recall the Beatles' "Lucy in the Sky with Diamonds." The last word, however, is given to the blues. In "Voodoo Child (Slight Return)," Hendrix plays the same role he had in "Voodoo Chile," only this time his performance is shorter, faster, and angrier. The text consists of only two verses, and in both of them the singer asserts power, destroying a mountain in the first and summoning the listener to the afterworld in the second. These are surrounded by guitar solos in Hendrix's most aggressive style, the last of which never really ends but simply fades as he reiterates, over and over, the melodic riff on which the song is based. It is a fitting capstone to the album's somber moods.

REFERENCES

Murray, Charles Shaar. *Crosstown Traffic: Jimi Hendrix and the Rock 'n' Roll Revolution*. New York: St. Martin's Press, 1989.

Pareles, Jon. "The Jazz Generation Pays Tribute to Jimi Hendrix." *New York Times* December 4, 1989. Reprinted in *The Jimi Hendrix Companion: Three Decades of Commentary*, edited by Chris Potash, 164–166. New York: Schirmer Books, 1996.

Potash, Chris, ed. *The Jimi Hendrix Companion: Three Decades of Commentary*. New York: Schirmer Books, 1996.

Shapiro, Harry, and Ceasar Glebbeek. *Jimi Hendrix: Electric Gypsy*. New York: St. Martin's Press, 1991.

RICHARD WILL

HERNÁNDEZ, RAFAEL

Born in Aguadilla, Puerto Rico, October 24, 1891; died in San Juan, Puerto Rico, December 11, 1965. **Education:** Received formal instruction in music first from José Ruellán Lequerica and later with Jesús Figueroa, 1903–14; learned to play violin, trombone, baritone horn, guitar, and piano; National Music Conservatory, Mexico City, Mexico, studied with Juan León Marsical and Julián Carrillo, ca. 1932–47. **Military Service:** U.S. Army, 369th Regiment, trombonist in James Reese Europe's "369th Hellfighters" regimental band, served in France, later sergeant and assistant director to the 15th Infantry band, 1917–18. **Composing and Performing Career:** First composition, "María Victoria," a danza, 1912; toured Puerto Rico with a band that accompanied the Japanese circus, 1914; by 1915, was an accomplished trombonist; San Juan, played with the Municipal Band under the direction of Manuel Tizol; recorded several works for Victor Talking Machine Company, played with diverse ensembles, including one that accompanied silent films, 1916–17; sold first composition, "Mi provisa," a waltz, 1917; New York, N.Y., toured with Luckey Roberts Band, organized and directed Orquesta Hispanoamericana, 1920; Fausto Teatro, Havana, Cuba, played in cinema orchestra, 1920–24; New York, N.Y., formed Trío Borinquen, 1926; continued composing and recording, 1926–30; founded Conjunto Victoria, later called Cuarteto Victoria, 1930–31; lived and worked in Mexico, conducted orchestra for radio program on XEW, 1932–47; composer of film scores, 1936–early 1950s; returned to Puerto Rico, 1947; conducted Sinfonietta Puertorriqueña, 1949–52; music consultant to station WIPR, 1952–60.

MUSIC LIST

INSTRUMENTAL SOLO
Piano
"Adoración." Recorded: Instituto de Cultura Puertorriqueña ICP-37.
"Aristocracia negra."
"Bagatelles." Recorded: Instituto de Cultura Puertorriqueña ICP-37.
"Canto y danza Quembe." Recorded: Instituto de Cultura Puertorriqueña ICP-37.
"Ebano temas oscuros."
"Rapsodia negra." Recorded: Instituto de Cultura Puertorriqueña ICP-37.
"Romanza." Recorded: Instituto de Cultura Puertorriqueña ICP-37.
Tríptico. Contents: Preludio; Elegía canicular; Jolgorio. Recorded: Instituto de Cultura Puertorriqueña ICP-37.
"Variaciones sobre 'Mataron a Elena.'" Recorded: Instituto de Cultura Puertorriqueña ICP-37.

FULL ORCHESTRA
Japonesita. Recorded: Decca 21022A.

ORCHESTRA (CHAMBER OR FULL) WITH SOLOISTS OR CHORUS
El abuelito enojado (chorus, orchestra). Recorded: Instituto de Cultura Puertorriqueña ICP-MP1.

Caminá (chorus, orchestra). Recorded: Instituto de Cultura Puertorriqueña ICP-MP1.
Campanitas de cristal (chorus, orchestra). Recorded: Ansonia ALP 1221; Kubaney MT-260; Orfeón CD350; Polygram 314 523 712-2; Royal CDR-7019.
Le-lo-lai (chorus, orchestra). Recorded: Instituto de Cultura Puertorriqueña ICP-MP1.
Qué lindo besas tú (chorus, orchestra). Recorded: Instituto de Cultura Puertorriqueña ICP-MP1.
Rabelida negra (chorus, orchestra). Recorded: Instituto de Cultura Puertorriqueña ICP-MP1.
Todo para ti (solo voice, orchestra). Recorded: Gema LPGS-1145.

CHORAL MUSIC
"Aleluya" (*villancico*). ca. 1956.
"Los carreteros" (SATB unaccompanied). Recorded: Orfeón CD350; Tico SLP-1131.
"Me la pagarás" (SATB unaccompanied). Recorded: Disco Hit DHCD-1126.
"El negrito que vivió un mes" (SATB unaccompanied). In *Arreglos corales* (San Juan, Puerto Rico: Sociedad Puertorriqueña de Directores do Coros, 1981).
"Noche de navidad." ca. 1955.
"Para ti" (SATB unaccompanied). Recorded: Disco Hit DHCD-1126.
"La trulla" (SATB unaccompanied). ca. 1953. In *Villancicos corales de Navidad* ([Puerto Rico]: Ediciones Coral Interdenominacional, 1983).

DRAMATIC MUSIC
Alma criolla (operetta).
Amarga Navidad (one-act operetta). ca. 1947.
Colegiales: Zarzuela en tres actos.
El príncipe negro (zarzuela for solo voice, orchestra). 1935. Recorded: FAME P8301.

INCIDENTAL MUSIC
Aguila o sol. 1937. Music for the motion picture.
El gendarme desconocido. 1941. Music for the motion picture.

POPULAR SONGS
[The following list of titles includes only works that were composed by the subject of the entry; it is not a list of recordings that were made by the subject. Although the composer may have made recordings of his own works, the list is not restricted to those recordings but in many cases includes performances by other artists of the composer's work. The list is made up of publication and discographical data, in cases where such information is available. Although no effort has been made to include documentation of the earliest recording of the works listed, the date of the earliest recording that is readily available has been given. —Ed.]

"A mis amigos." Recorded, 1958: Ansonia ANSCD-1241.
"Adiós, muñequita." Recorded, 1958: Ansonia ANSCD-1241.

"Ahora seremos felices" (*bolero*). 1939. Recorded: Kubaney MT-260; Multinational DG-1124; Orfeón CD350; Polygram 314 523 712-2; Seeco SCLP 9146.

"Amigo." Recorded: Kubaney MT-260; Polygram 314 523 712-2.

"Amor ciego." Recorded: Disco Hit DHCD-1126; Kubaney MT-260; Multinational DG-1124; Orfeón CD350.

"Amor de mi bohío." Recorded: Caytronics CYS 1377.

"Ausencia." Recorded: Columbia EX 5181; Fonovisa FPCD-9231.

"Bajo un palmar." Recorded: Discos CBS International DML-20413.

"Buche y pluma na ma." Recorded: Tico SLP-1131.

"Cachita" (*guaracha*). 1936. Also arranged for band. Recorded, 1945: Decca 23462; Polygram 314 523 712-2; Rodven TH-2792.

"Canción del alma." Recorded: Multinational DG-1124; Orfeón CD551; Peerless PCD-006-7; Polygram 314 523 712-2.

"Canta, canta." Recorded: Tico SLP-1131.

"Capullito de Alelí" (*bolero*). 1929. New York: Peer International, 1948. Recorded: International de Cultura Puertorriqueña ICP-MP1; Orfeón CD350; Qbadisc QB-9011; Royal CDR-7019.

"Casita de la montaña."

"Con mi corazón te espero." Recorded: Ji Records Ji-003.

"Congoja." Recorded: Multinational DG-1124; Orfeón CD350; Polygram 314 523 712-2; Velvet 1344.

"Corazón adentro." Recorded: Disco Hit DHCD-1126.

"Cuando te volveré a ver." Recorded, 1958: Ansonia ANSCD-1241.

"Cuatro personas." Recorded: Kubaney MT-260; Orfeón CD350.

"Cuchifritos." Recorded: Tico SLP-1131.

"El cumbanchero" (piano, bass, percussion ensemble). Miami, Fla.: Peer International, 1943. Also arranged for solo voice. Recorded, 1949: Kubaney MT-260; Mercury 5288; Orfeón CD350.

"Desdichadamente." Recorded: Orfeón CD551.

"Desmayo." Recorded: Disco Hit DHCD-1126.

"Despedida." Recorded: Discos CBS International DML-20413.

"Desvelo de amor." Recorded: Orfeón CD551; Polygram 314 523 712-2; Seeco SCLP 9146; Sony DIC 80647.

"Diez años." Recorded: Orfeón CD551; Polygram 314 523 712-2; RCA 3405-4-RL.

"Dulces besos." Recorded, 1958: Ansonia ANSCD-1241.

"Enamorado de ti." Recorded: Orfeón CD551; RCA Victor MKS-1763; Velvet 1344.

"Ese soy yo." Recorded: Instituto de Cultura Puertorriqueña ICP-MP1.

"Los hijos de Buda." Recorded: Rodven THC-3079.

"Inconsolable." Recorded: Fuentes 200219; Multinational DG-1124; Polygram 314 523 712-2.

"Jugando, mamá, jugando." Recorded: RCA 3405-4-RL; Tico SLP-1131.

"Lamento borincano" (voice, guitar, percussion). 1929. Also arranged for orchestra. Recorded, 1958: Ansonia ALP 1221; Decca 21022A; Kubaney MT-260; Orfeón CD350; Polygram 314 523 712-2.

"Lejos de ti." Recorded: Seeco SCLP 9146; Tropical TRLP 5106.

"El limonar." Recorded: Daro International DIS-91.1139.

"Lo siento por ti." Recorded: Falcon Records FLP-3001; RCA 3405-4-RL.

"Madrigal." Recorded, 1958: Ansonia ANSCD-1241.

"Malditos celos." Recorded: Disco Hit DHCD-1126; RCA 3405-4-RL; Velvet 1344.

"Mi delito." Recorded: Orfeón CD551.

"Mi querer." Recorded: Disco Hit DHCD-1126; Orfeón CD350.

"Mosaico jíbaro." Recorded: Orfeón CD350.

"Muchos besos." Recorded: Tico SLP-1131.

"Muñoz." ca. 1926. Recorded, 1958: Ansonia ANSCD-1241.

"Murió la reina." Recorded: RCA Victor FPM-1159.

"No me quieras tanto." Recorded: Musart CMP-1233; Orfeón CD350; Seeco SCLP 9146.

"Noche y día." Recorded: Seeco SCLP 9146; Tropical TRLP 5106.

"Las palomitas." Recorded: Tico SLP-1131.

"El pastorcillo." Recorded: Orfeón CD551.

"Perfume de gardenia" (*bolero*). Recorded, 1958: Ansonia ALP 1221; Kubaney MT-260; Orfeón CD551; Seeco SCLP 9146.

"Pobre jibarito." New York: Peer International, 1956. Recorded, 1958: Ansonia ANSCD-1241.

"Potpourri Hernández." Recorded: Orfeón CD350.

"Preciosa." 1937. Recorded: Kubaney MT-260; Multinational DG-1124; Orfeón CD551; Polygram 314 523 712-2; Seeco SCLP 9146.

"La puerta de tu casa." Recorded: Ji Records Ji-003.

"Purísima." Recorded: Velvet 1344.

"Puro engaño." Recorded: Disco Hit DHCD-1126.

"Purrupita." Recorded, 1958: Ansonia ANSCD-1241.

"¡Qué chula es Puebla!"

"Que te importa." Recorded: Multinational DG-1124; Musart CEM-717; Orfeón CD551; Sony CDS-80662.

"Quimbamba." Recorded: Manhattan School of Music n.n.

"Quisqueya." Recorded: Montilla CD3022.

"Reminiscencia." Recorded, 1958: Ansonia ANSCD-1241.

"Romance." Recorded: Kubaney MT-260; Seeco SCLP 9146; Tropical TRLP 5106.

"Las seis de la mañana." Recorded: Disco Hit DHCD-1126.

"Si me muero, madre mia." Recorded, 1958: Ansonia ANSCD-1241.

"Si pudiera." Recorded, 1958: Ansonia ANSCD-1241.

"Siciliana." Recorded: Disco Hit DHCD-1126.

"Silencio" (*bolero*). Recorded, 1958: Ansonia ALP 1221; Kubaney MT-260; Orfeón CD551; RCA 3405-4-RL; Seeco SCLP 9146.

"Las seis de la mañana." Recorded: Discos CBS International DML-20440; Orfeón CD551.

"Tabú." Recorded: Disco Hit DHCD-1126; Instituto de Cultura Puertorriqueña ICP-MP1.

"Traición" or "Dos letras." Recorded: Discos CBS International DML-20440; Velvet 1344.

"Tú no comprendes." Recorded: Disco Hit DHCD-1124; Polygram 314 523 712-2; Seeco SCLP 9146.

"Tristes recuerdos." Recorded, 1958: Ansonia ANSCD-1241.

"El último suspiro." Recorded: Disco Hit DHCD-1126.

"Una mañana de domingo." Recorded: Qbadisc QB-9011.

"Vaya con Dios." Recorded: Ji Records Ji-003.

"Ven a verme." Recorded: Disco Hit DHCD-1126.

"Venus." Recorded: Disco Hit DHCD-1126.

"Villancico de Navidad-Hosanna." 1958. Recorded: Custom Fidelity CFS-3077.

"Víspera de Reyes." Recorded: Velvet LPVS-1516.

"Ya los verás." Recorded: Kubaney K-10021; Orfeón CD551.

"Ya no te quiero." Recorded: Columbia EX 5181; Orfeón CD350; Sony CDS-80662.

PUBLICATIONS

ABOUT HERNÁNDEZ
Books and Monographs
Javariz, Jorge, and Alejandro "Chalí" Hernández. *Apuntes biográficos del compositor Rafael Hernández (1891–1965).* San Juan: Universidad Interamericana de Puerto Rico, n.d.

Rafael Hernández vive . . . y siempre está en nosotros. Aguadilla, Puerto Rico: WNOZ Radio Nosotros, 1991.

Dissertations
Glasser, Ruth. "Que vivío tiene la gente aquí en Nueva York: Music and Community in Puerto Rican New York, 1915–1940." Ph.D. diss., Yale University, 1991.

Laracuente, Nahir. "Rafael Hernández: Critical Study." M.M. thesis, University of Mississippi, 1969.

Articles
Ayala, Cristóbal Díaz. "Rafael Hernández: Varias dudas y una gran verdad." *El Nuevo Día* (October 13, 1991): 8–9.

Ayoroa-Santaliz, José Enrique. "Rafael Hernández es Rafael Rosa." *El Nuevo Día* (July 24, 1991): 88.

Bloch, Peter. "Rafael Hernández and the Black Heritage." *Kalinda!* (Summer 1994): 8–10.

Bentez, Jaime. "Recuerdo de Rafael Hernández." *El Nuevo Día* (March 22, 1992): 19.

Betancourt, Ma Dhyan Elsa. *Hasta siempre, Rafael.* Río Piedras: Yaraví, 1981.

Campos-Parsi, Héctor. "La música." In *Enciclopedia clásicos de Puerto Rico*, vol. 7, 202–204. Barcelona: Ediciones Latinoamericanas, 1976.

Delgado, Ileana. "Doña María y Rafael." *El Nuevo Día* (October 13, 1991): 9.

González, Elmer. "Rafael Hernández en al pentagrama: Treinta años después." *Latin Beat* 5, no. 9 (November 1995): 28–29.

Malavet Vega, Pedro. "El Rafael Hernández que conocieron los mexicanos durante años." *El Nuevo Día* (October 25, 1991): 94–95.

Quintero Rivera, A. G. "Rafael Hernández, lo íntimo y lo social." *El Nuevo Día* (October 27, 1991): 4–9.

Reichard de Cancio, Haydée E. "Rafael: Del niño al soldado." *El Nuevo Día* (October 24, 1991): 92.

Schooler, Sara. "La vida artística de Rafael Hernández en Méjico." *Puerto Rico Ilustrado* 36, no. 1888 (May 12, 1945): 20.

Vélez Jiménez, Augustine. "Rafael, el mejor de los mejores." *El Nuevo Día* (October 24, 1991): 86–87.

Zervigón, Pedro. "De las últimas entrevistas a Rafael Hernández." *El Nuevo Día* (December 9, 1991): 65.

* * * * *

Rafael Hernández; from La Gran Enciclopedia de Puerto Rico (C. Corredera, Madrid, 1976)

In Puerto Rico, Rafael Hernández is considered a national hero. His music is well known in Latin America and in Spain. Two of his pieces, "Cachita" and "El cumbanchero," are renowned the world over.

Rafael Rosa-Hernández was born in Aguadilla (northwestern Puerto Rico) on October 24, 1891. His father was José Miguel Rosa-Espinosa, who played the guitar and sang. His paternal grandfather, Guillermo Rosa, played the button accordion, most probably of the diatonic type. His sister, Victoria, reports that all the family members were musicians: "In our house, music was breathed in the morning, it was eaten for breakfast." Hernández learned to play trombone, flute, cornet, guitar, bombardino, and violin. He received his first formal music instruction in Aguadilla from José Ruellán Lequerica, a famed teacher, and from Jesús Figueroa, who was the founder of the town's Fireman's band. By 1915, Hernández was an accomplished trombonist. He joined the U.S. Army during World War I and played trombone in a unit band. In 1917, he joined James Reese Europe's 369th Infantry Regimental band. During 1920, he performed in the U.S. as the director of the Luckey Roberts Band and of the Orquesta Hispanoamericana, which he founded. Hernández was invited to conduct the Fausto Theatre Orchestra at Havana, Cuba, and stayed in that capital city from 1920 to 1924. He moved to New York in 1925. He organized the Trío Borinquen in 1926 with Manuel "Canario" Jiménez (lead vocalist, later replaced by Antonio Mesa) and Salvador Ithier (second voice and second guitar). In 1928, Trío Borinquen recorded for Columbia Records.

In 1929, Hernández and his Trío Borinquen traveled to Puerto Rico to perform, returning to New York at the conclusion of the tour. During this time, he composed "Capullito de Alelí" and "Lamento borincano." A series of compositions and recordings from this period were the beginning of Hernández's fame.

In 1930–31, he founded his Conjuncto Victoria (previously Grupo Hernández), whose members were Hernández (second guitar and director), Francisco López Cruz (first guitar), Pedro "Dávila" Ortiz (first voice), and Rafael Rodríguez (second voice). The group later became known as Cuarteto Victoria.

In 1932, Hernández went to Mexico to perform, initially for three months, but he stayed 16 years. He continued his studies at the National Music Conservatory with Juan León Mariscal and Julián Carrillo. Living in Mexico was quite advantageous for Hernández because his works were immediately performed and broadcast by the orchestra of 35 musicians that he conducted for radio station XEW, which was owned by the Spaniard Bernardo Sancristóbal.

During his years in Mexico, Hernández wrote music for or contributed individual pieces to films such as *Honrarás a tus padres* (1936, directed by Juan Orol), *La gran cruz* (1937), *Aguila o sol* (1937, directed by Arcady Boytler), and *El crimen del expreso* (1938). In 1939, William Rowland produced for RKO the film originally titled *La mujer que amó en vano*, later retitled *Perfidia*, with music by Alberto Domínguez and Rafael Hernández. Hernández's songs were also included in *La liga de las canciones* (1941), *El gendarme desconocido* (1941), *Carnaval en el trópico o fiesta en Veracruz* (1941), *Las cinco noches de Adán* (1942), *Cruel destino: Allá en la frontera* (1943, directed by Juan Orol), *Pasiones tormentosas* (1945), *Humo en los ojos* (1946), *El amor no es ciego* (1950), and *El beisbolista fenómeno* (1951).

In 1947, Hernández returned triumphantly to Puerto Rico, where he was received as a national hero. He directed the Sinfonietta Puertorriqueña, a symphonic ensemble that performed under the auspices of the Puerto Rican government. About this same time, Hernández composed his one act operetta *Amarga Navidad*. In 1952, when the Sinfonietta disbanded, Hernández became a musical consultant to WIPR Radio, the government radio station. He also resumed his formal study of piano under Alfredo Romero, a private teacher. Around this time, he also composed *villancicos* (Christmas carols) such as "La trulla," "Casita de la montaña" and "Aleluya." Many of these songs were later arranged for choirs and other vocal ensembles. Hernández also composed piano works inspired by his Afro-Caribbean heritage, including "Ebano temas oscuros" and "Aristocracia negra."

Two of Rafael Hernández's most famous songs are "Preciosa" (1937) and "Lamento borincano" (1929). The first, which is about the beauties of Puerto Rico and its people, is considered by Puerto Ricans to be their second, unofficial national anthem. The lyrics of "Preciosa" also include a strong comment against colonialism. On the other hand, many scholars criticize the song because, although it mentions the Spanish and Taíno role in the formation of the Puerto Rican nation, it does not mention the strong African influence in the development of the country. Despite these contrasting views of the song, "Preciosa" remains one of the great patriotic songs in the musical history of Puerto Rico. It is included in the repertoire of several Puerto Rican musical groups, and, when they travel abroad, it is one of the songs they are obliged to perform wherever Puerto Ricans are found.

"Lamento borincano," the "Puerto Rican Lament," speaks about the situation of a poor *jíbaro*, or country dweller, who comes to town to sell his goods and tries to buy a dress for his mother. But,

due to the economic situation of the times (the turn-of-the-century Puerto Rican Depression), he is unable to sell his goods. The story begins with the countryman's dreams of happiness and well-being while he is on his way to town. As the morning goes on, however, he fails to sell his merchandise and must return home empty-handed and very unhappy. His *lamento* rhetorically asks what will become of his home, his family, and his country, and finishes by saying, "Borinquen, the land of Eden, the one whom Gautier [José Gautier Benítez, Puerto Rican poet] called the Pearl of the Seas, now that you die because of your sorrows, let me also sing to you." To this day, this last stanza is used as a metaphor for Puerto Rico's political situation by many pro-independence movements on the Island.

But not all of Rafael Hernández's songs speak of tragedy or loss. Some of the most beautiful are his *villancicos* and love songs. Hernández's "Aleluya" is an obligatory carol in the repertoire of most Puerto Rican choirs. In this 6/8 song, the composer praises the birth of Jesus and tells the story of the Nativity with a sweet melody about an important part of the religious culture of Latin America. Thus, the "Aleluya" is not only Puerto Rican in character but also Latin American.

In his "La trulla," Hernández speaks again about Christmas, this time writing of Puerto Rican Christmas traditions. He mentions not only this most popular celebration but also the foods that are prepared and consumed during the Christmas season. "Casita de la montaña," a standard of the Christmas repertoire in Puerto Rico, is sung in church and at secular events as well. Here, Hernández speaks about Christmas in the countryside, the preparations for the festivities, the excitement that precedes the holidays, and the religious meaning of the Christmas celebration in the family. This composition is written in 3/4 time, thus giving it a more international appeal than Christmas songs from other Puerto Rican authors.

It is his songs about romance, however, for which Hernández is most renowned. A whole generation of Puerto Ricans and Latin Americans fell in love while listening to his music. His songs that speak of lost love, mad love, and platonic love are the backbone of the repertoire of professional musicians in Puerto Rico. The *serenata* tradition that was popular during the 1940s, 1950s, and well into the 1960s was nurtured to a large extent by Hernández's songs. His compositions are popular, yet very cosmopolitan.

Because his music contains praise not only of his birthplace but also of other Latin American countries, countries such as Cuba and Mexico have claimed to be the homeland of this great composer. Examples of this are his songs "(Qué chula es Puebla!" and "Quisqueya," which speak respectively of the beauty of the city of Puebla, Mexico, and of the island of the Dominican Republic. Just as "Preciosa" is considered the second national anthem in Puerto Rico, so too, are these songs in their respective countries.

By far, the most famous song by Hernández is "El cumbanchero." This song became the trademark of Hernández's work and helped to place Puerto Rico on the international music scene.

SELECTED WORKS

"Cachita" (1936) is a *guaracha* (a festive, rhythmic song usually in a quick tempo and often on comical topics and with funny lyrics), with lyrics by Bernardo Sancristóbal. It is a rhythmic and exciting work. The constant use of the first inversion tonic and dominant seventh chords contribute to the work's enchantment. It is written in the key of C and speaks of a character who tells a lady called Cachita that he has an irresistible little *rhumba,* and that a hot *rhumba* is better than a fox trot. This character also states that the maracas are about to burst because of pleasure and that the *timbales* musician is eager to play. He adds that his music would be fun for a Frenchman, a German, an Irishman, or even a Muslim. He continues, saying that an Englishman or a Japanese would be possessed by the song's delight and that this music has no boundaries because it is heard even in the polar area, where Eskimos dance to it.

"El cumbanchero" is a stirring work composed in *rhumba-guaracha* style (a festive song with strong Afro-Cuban drumming). This piece is included in Cuba's repertoire as a standard, and its energy, rich harmony, and simple melody offer the arranger many possiblities for diverse orchestrations and arrangements. Its fascinating conception is rich in chromaticism and rhythmic variations, and its exoticism makes it reminiscent of "Sabre Dance" from the 1942 ballet *Gayane* by Aram Khachaturian. The lyrics are onomatopoeic, imitating the sounds of bongo and conga drums. Singers such as Cuba's Miguelito Valdés and Puerto Rico's Ismael Rivera have been renowned for their interpretations, variations, and improvisations on the themes of this composition.

"Ahora seremos felices" (Now We Shall be Happy) (1939) is a *bolero* (a slow dance, usually with romantic lyrics, elaborate harmonic structure, and rhythmic affinity to the *guaracha*) written in E-flat major. Its harmonic structure, shown in Example 1, is quite logical and conventional. This love song speaks of the new house acquired by a man in love. He speaks to his fiancée with great joy about their future love nest, which will be complete with the birth of their offspring. The song ends with a petition to God for a long and happy life. This *bolero* is usually enriched by arrangers with a section in *chachachá* rhythm to create contrasts, which accent the sense of great joy or happiness of the characters.

Example 1. "Ahora seremos felices," harmonic progression

| I | IV | V | v7 | V | V | V7 | | IV | IV | I | | | |

"Quimbamba" is an unusual type of song for Hernández. It celebrates African ancestry and heritage and has a mythic quality because of the poetic and epic use of language, vocabulary, and imagery from a distant, fascinating, and magical continent. The composer uses words of African origin, which are also exploited for their onomatopoeic qualities. Changes of key from major to minor are artistically employed by the composer, adding great emotion to the work.

REFERENCES

Campos Parsi, Héctor. "La música." In *Enciclopedia clásicos de Puerto Rico,* vol. 7, 202–204. Barcelona: Ediciones Latinoamericanas, 1976.

———. "La música en Puerto Rico." In *La Gran Enciclopedia de Puerto Rico,* vol. 7, 127–130. San Juan: Puerto Rico en la Mano/La Gran Enciclopedia de Puerto Rico, 1977.

Figueroa, Frank M. *Encyclopedia of Latin American Music in New York.* St. Petersburg, Fla.: Pillar, 1994.

Glasser, Ruth. *My Music Is My Flag: Puerto Rican Musicians and Their New York Communities, 1917–1940.* Berkeley: University of California Press, 1995.

Glasser, Ruth, and Jaime Jaramillo. Liner notes, *Rafael Hernández 1932–1939.* Harlequin HQ CD68, 1996.

Hernández, Alejandro "Chalí." Interview with the author, San Juan, Puerto Rico, January 13, 1998.

Hernández, Rafael. *Colegiales: Zarzuela en tres actos.* Unpublished manuscript, 1928.

———. "Pobre jibarito," arranged for piano by Horace Díaz, with vocal part. New York: Peer International, 1956.

Javariz, Jorge, and Alejandro "Chalí" Hernández. *Apuntes biográficos del compositor Rafael Hernández (1891–1965).* San Juan: Universidad Interamericana de Puerto Rico, n.d.

Malavet Vega, Pedro. *Del bolero a la Nueva Canción (La música popular en Puerto Rico: De los años '50 al presente),* 19, 101. Ponce: Pedro Malavet Vega, 1988.

Marianna, Sister, O.P., ed. *Cantares de Navidad: Aguinaldos puertorriqueños,* 126. San Juan: Oficina del Supervisor de Colegios Católicos, 1969.

Melón, Esther M., and Cesáreo Rosa Nieves. "Biografías puertorriqueñas: Perfil histórico de un pueblo." In *Colección Puertorriqueña,* 200–202. Sharon, Conn.: Troutman Press, 1970.

Música del Sur: Cien éxitos de Puerto Rico. Barcelona: Southern Music Española, n.d.

Orovio, Helio. *Diccionario de la música cubana, biográfico y técnico.* Havana: Letras Cubanas, 1992.

Rafael Hernández Song Folio. 3 vols. New York: Peer International, ca. 1966.

Torregrosa, José Luis. *Historia de la radio en Puerto Rico.* San Juan: Comisión del Quinto Centenario and Asociación de Radiodifusores, ca. 1992–93.

Torres Torres, Jaime. "De perenne vigencia la huella del jíbarito." *El Nuevo Día* (October 24, 1991): 89.

J. EMANUEL DUFRASNE-GONZÁLEZ

JAMES, WILLIS LAURENCE

Born in Montgomery, Ala., September 18, 1900; died in Atlanta, Ga., December 27, 1966. **Education:** Florida Baptist Academy, Jacksonville, Fla., studied violin and music with Sidney Woodward, age eight; Morehouse College, Atlanta, Ga., high school division, studied violin with Kemper Harreld, 1916–19; Morehouse College, additional study with Kemper Harreld, 1919–23, B.A., 1931; Chicago Musical College, summers, 1926–28; studied musicology, composition, and violin with Oswald Blake, 1926–28; studied composition privately with Edwin Gershefski, 1928. **Composing and Performing Career:** Morehouse College, violin soloist, assistant to conductor, member of several ensembles including orchestra and glee club, 1916–23; Leland College, Baker, La., composed school's alma mater, gave violin and tenor solo recitals, 1923–50s; Paramount Record Company, performed and recorded several Louisiana folk songs, 1927; Alabama State Teachers College, Montgomery, Ala., composed fight song, "Hail Alabama," 1929; music performed on NBC and CBS network programs, including *Voice of Firestone, Bell Telephone Hour,* and *Contented Hour,* ca. 1948–50. **Teaching Career:** Leland College, Baker, La., choral director, 1923–28; Alabama State Teachers College, Montgomery, conducted choir, orchestra, marching band, and coached the school's jazz ensemble, 1928–33; Spelman College, Atlanta, Ga., directed the glee club, orchestra, Atlanta-Morehouse-Spelman Chorus, and Morehouse College band, 1933–66; Fort Valley State College, Fort Valley, Ga., summer faculty, 1941–44; Fort Valley College Folk Music Festival, co-founder, 1941–55; Library of Congress Archive of Folk Song, field recorder, 1942, 1943; lecture-performances on folk songs and dialect, Jazz Round Table, 1952–53, Newport Jazz Festivals, 1954–66, Tanglewood Music Festival, 1954–66, Newport Folk Festivals, 1959–66; National Education (NET), *Lyrics and Legends,* lectured on African-American music, ca. 1962; Center for Negro Arts, Lagos, Nigeria, lectured at opening, 1961. **Memberships:** Institute for Jazz Studies, Rutgers University, Newark, N.J., Board of Directors, 1952–ca. 1966. **Honors/ Awards:** General Education Board fellowship, 1939; Rosenwald fellowship, 1942; Carnegie Foundation grant, early 1940s; U.S. Department of Health, Education, and Welfare, Honorary Superior Degree for Service in Music, 1953; Wilberforce University, honorary doctorate, 1955.

MUSIC LIST

INSTRUMENTAL SOLOS
Violin
"Bells and Shadows." ca. 1943. Unpublished manuscript.
"Hermit Dove." ca. 1943. Unpublished manuscript.
"Melodesque." Unpublished manuscript.
"Minstrel Serenade." 1927. Unpublished manuscript.
"Negro Dance." Unpublished manuscript.

Piano
"Edgewater Saturday Night." Unpublished manuscript.
"Impromptu Serenade." Unpublished manuscript.
"Southland Caprice." Unpublished manuscript.

INSTRUMENTAL ENSEMBLE
Strings
String Quartet. ca. 1940s. Unpublished manuscript.

SOLO VOICE
"Cabin Boy Call (A Negro Steamboat Song)" (tenor). New York: Carl Fischer, 1942. Premiere, 1927.
Four Songs Based on the Poetry of Wilbert Snow. 1952. Unpublished manuscript. Contents: Child Wonder; Conflict; Immortality; Nature Worships.
"I Stan' an' Fol' My Arms." Unpublished manuscript.
"I Want to Climb Up Jacob's Ladder." Unpublished manuscript.
"My Good Lord's Done Been Here" (medium voice). Unpublished manuscript.
"My Song to You." 1928. Unpublished manuscript.
"Negro Folk Lullaby ('Dis Chile)." Unpublished manuscript.
"Pity a Poor Boy." Unpublished manuscript. Recorded: Narthex N 64085.
"Roberta Lee." Unpublished manuscript.
Work Songs of the Negro Boatmen. Unpublished manuscript. Contents: Shallo' Water; Cabin Boy Call. Premiere, 1934.

BAND
"Hail, Alabama." 1929. Unpublished manuscript.

CHORAL MUSIC
"Captin Look-a Yonder" (TTBB unaccompanied, tenor solo). ca. 1920. Unpublished manuscript.
"Here's a Pretty Little Baby" (SATB). Unpublished manuscript.
"Lord Thou Hast Been Our Dwelling Place: Anthem for Women's Voices." ca. 1960. Unpublished manuscript.
"Negro Bell Carol" (SATB unaccompanied, soprano solo, tenor solo). New York: Carl Fischer, 1942. Recorded: RPC ZB 89591.
"O, Po' Little Jesus" (SATB). New York: G. Schirmer, 1937.
"Roberta Lee" (TTBB). ca. 1938–39. New York: Lawson Gould, 1972. Also arranged for solo and male chorus.
"Roun' de Glory Manger" (mixed voices unaccompanied, soprano solo). 1935. New York: G. Schirmer, 1937. Originally titled "De Glory Manger." Premiere, 1935.

DRAMATIC MUSIC
The Ballad of Candy Man Beechum (folk opera). 1964. Unpublished manuscript.

INCIDENTAL MUSIC
"Boy with a Cart" (drama). Note: three-part music in "madrigal style" for violin, cello, and recorder.

Willis Laurence James; courtesy of Rebecca T. Cureau

PUBLICATIONS

ABOUT JAMES
Dissertations
Cureau, Rebecca T. "Willis Laurence James (1900–1966): Musician, Music Educator, Folklorist." Ph.D. diss., Atlanta University, 1987.

Articles
Cureau, Rebecca T. "Black Folklore, Musicology, and Willis Laurence James." *Negro History Bulletin* 43, no. 1 (1980): 16–20.
———. "Willis Laurence James and the Preservation of Black Religious Folk Song." *Black Sacred Music: A Journal of Theomusicology* 4 no. 2 (Fall 1990): 1–13.

BY JAMES
Afro-American Music: A Demonstration Recording. New York: Moses Asch, 1970. Recorded: Smithsonian Folkways 2692.
"The Romance of the Negro Folk Cry in America." *Phylon* 16 (1955): 15–30.
Stars in de Elements. Special issue of *Black Sacred Music* 9, nos. 1 and 2. Durham: Duke University Press, 1995.

PRINCIPAL ARCHIVES
Willis Laurence James Papers, Archives, Spelman College, Atlanta, Georgia

* * * * *

Willis Laurence James achieved widespread recognition as a composer during his lifetime, though his original compositions have been largely overshadowed by his vocal solo and choral arrangements based on his collected Negro spirituals and folk songs. He used folk sources as inspiration or incorporated folk idioms such as jazz or blues rhythms into some of his compositions. Examples include "Negro Folk Lullaby (Dis Chile)" for solo voice, "Minstrel Serenade" for violin, "and "Edgewater Saturday Night" for piano. However, his largest body of works are choral settings in which he used the folk songs he collected as melodic or thematic material. He expanded or developed this material with rich harmonies, repeated phrases with subtle changes in melody or harmony, frequent changes of mode, contrasting textures (solo voice, unison chorus, treble or male chorus), and expressive devices (dynamics, tempo, mood). James generally retained the original dialect of the song texts, which he regarded as "having its own unique rhythm and tonal qualities." Examples of these "transformed" or "recomposed" spirituals include "Roun' de Glory Manger," "Negro Bell Carol," and "O, Po' Little Jesus." Though a number of his published and unpublished songs carry attributions of having been "arranged" or "adapted," some are closer to being original compositions—the result of the creative transformation that he gave to his collected folk songs. It is also evident that James used the word "arranged" in the sense of "setting," since many of the songs that he described as "arranged" bear little resemblance to the original folk song or

source of inspiration. Most of his songs exist only in unpublished versions, but his choral music became well known through performance by his own and other collegiate, high school, and community choral ensembles, making an important contribution to the African-American folk song repertory.

James's compositional output spans a period of more than 40 years and includes original compositions for men's and women's voices, mixed chorus, and solo voice; instrumental chamber works; a string quartet; incidental music for dance and drama; and a folk opera based on a short story by Erskine Caldwell. An accomplished singer and violinist, James often performed and premiered his original solo works on recitals; many of his songs were written for and performed by his students and other well-known artists.

Throughout his career, James also composed vocal and instrumental music that was not inspired by folk sources. However, as a folklorist he was naturally drawn to the folk music that was the focus of his study and collection throughout his life. He believed that the music of the slavery and post-slavery periods could best be preserved through performance in artful arrangements or as inspiration for original composition. This philosophy was also promoted by leaders of the Harlem Renaissance movement, which coincided with James's early career and work as a folklorist, composer, and arranger, though there is no evidence to suggest that he was involved in that activity.

Although the performance of James's music waned somewhat in the decade after his death, a period of reassessment of his life and contributions that began in the late 1970s has resulted in renewed interest in the performance of his music and newer and wider audiences for his works, some of which were published after his death. Many of his published and unpublished compositions and arrangements for solo voice, including art songs, are frequently programmed on recitals and have been included on recordings by a number of concert artists, including Roland Hayes, Mattiwilda Dobbs, John Patton, William Brown, and others.

James spent his entire life as a student and music educator in historically black institutions. Born in Montgomery, Alabama, he spent his early childhood in Jacksonville, Florida. He credited his mother with inspiring his love for his folk heritage and remembered many folk songs that she sang to him as a child and others from his boyhood in Florida. It is not surprising that music so deeply rooted in a culture he respected and with which he so closely identified would serve as the inspiration for his creativity. In drawing on folk sources for inspiration, he worked in the tradition of composers such as Béla Bartók, Antonín Dvořák, and others who celebrated the gift of simple folk in "cultivated" European-style compositions and arrangements.

James demonstrated unusual musical talent from an early age. He began studying violin at age eight at the Florida Baptist Academy in Jacksonville with Sidney Woodward, a concert singer who also trained the academy's vocal ensembles, in which James was a frequent tenor soloist. Recognizing that this student needed more advanced musical training than the academy could provide, Woodward took James to Atlanta, where from the age of 16 he was the protégé of Kemper Harreld, a concert violinist who headed the music department at Morehouse College. James completed his high school studies in the college's academy and excelled as an accomplished violinist and singer throughout his collegiate years. His studies included the traditional core of music courses, study of the violin and several other musical instruments, and membership in the college's glee club, quartet, and orchestra, for which he served as a student conductor. James showed great promise as a concert violinist; he performed as a member of a string quartet for a number of years and as recitalist and soloist for much of his career.

James began his teaching career at Leland College in Baker, Louisiana, in 1923, when the former Leland University relocated from New Orleans to a site near Baton Rouge, the state capital. As founder of the college's music department, he developed a music program that included a small orchestra and a choir that was reputed to be "first rate," and he composed the school's alma mater, "Leland, Dear Leland." His folk song collecting and early work as a serious folklorist date from this period.

In 1928, James joined the faculty of Alabama State Normal College (now Alabama State University) in Montgomery, Alabama. There he organized and conducted the choral ensemble and developed an instrumental music program and a small orchestra. He directed the college's marching band, observing the students' styles of "yells" and "calls" at football games, which would later figure in his theory on the Negro folk "cry." He composed the college's fight song, "Hail, Alabama." In 1933, James joined the faculty of Spelman College in Atlanta, Georgia, where he spent the remainder of his long and multifaceted career as music educator and choral director and gained national recognition as composer, arranger, and authority on Negro folk song. During the summers from 1926 to 1928, James studied composition and musicology at the Chicago Musical College and studied the violin privately with Oswald Blake. In 1928, he also studied with Edwin Gershefski, a pianist and composer who introduced him to the mathematics-based Schillinger System of Musical Composition.

From the beginning of his career, James's choral arrangements and compositions were well received by audiences in the college communities where he served; for example, the performance in 1935 of his unpublished "Roun' de Glory Manger," for mixed voices, was widely publicized throughout the Atlanta community, was well received by Atlanta audiences, and was later published. The performances and publication of other Christmas spirituals—notably "O, Po' Little Jesus," "Here's a Pretty Little Baby," and the "Negro Bell Carol"—were also widely publicized, as was his extensive fieldwork in the Deep South on grants from the General Education Board and the Rosenwald Foundation in the late 1930s and early 1940s. One goal of his fieldwork was to collect seldom-heard Christmas spirituals and other "rare and beautiful" religious folk songs, as he described them; another was to write a treatise or study of the development of Negro music in America "from the point of view of a Negro . . . based on first-hand observation." He completed this treatise, entitled *Stars in de Elements: A Study of Negro Folk Music*, in 1945, but was unable to find a publisher for it. It was published posthumously in 1995.

Religious folk songs constitute the largest body of James's compositional output. However, he also composed a considerable body of secular works, many of them inspired by work songs. He began to take special notice of the songs and cries of longshoremen along the Mississippi River while in Louisiana in the early 1920s. Already a committed folklorist, he frequented the levees, where he initiated friendships with workers who were themselves, he noted, "fascinated by his interest in their songs." The seeds for this theory of the folk-cry, in which he suggests that calls, cries, and hollers are easily identifiable in all types of Negro music, doubtless took root during this time. His published theory received much attention and critical reaction from folklorists and ethnomusicologists. James later collected work songs in the mining areas of Alabama and along the docks of the Savannah River in Georgia. The texts of several of his collected work songs were published in 1941 in a landmark publication by his friend and fellow folklorist, Sterling Brown. One of them, "Roberta Lee," described as a love ballad, was widely performed in solo, quartet, and male chorus versions and still enjoys popularity.

James composed a large number of songs for solo voice inspired by his collected folk songs, including "Negro Folk Lullaby ('Dis Chile)," which he wrote for his student, the concert artist Mattiwilda Dobbs, "Pity a Poor Boy," "I Stan' and Fol' My Arms," and "I Want to Climb Up Jacob's Ladder." Though still unpublished, these and other songs by James are widely performed, and many are included on recordings of concert artists. Of his songs not inspired by folk sources, "Immortality," one of four songs for solo voice based on poems by Wilbert Snow and written for his student, singer Alpha Brawner Floyd, enjoys wide performance by concert artists.

ROUN' DE GLORY MANGER (1935)

"Roun' de Glory Manger," set for six-part chorus of mixed voices, *a cappella,* with incidental soprano solo, is a striking example of James's skill in maintaining the folk character of songs he heard during his fieldwork while enhancing their effect in his settings and recompositions. As do many African-derived religious songs, "Roun' de Glory Manger" begins in a call-and-response pattern. In each verse, the first line is repeated twice and the fourth line is contrasting. A joyful refrain follows each verse.

The key of this song is G major, though James does not restrict himself to chords based on the scale; he uses dissonant nonchord tones that move in and out of the harmonies, as is true of most of his writing. He permitted students who had a natural inclination to use these "twists and turns," as he described them, in their singing, giving the effect of spontaneous folk singing to music sung by trained choral ensembles. This effect was a hallmark of James's writing for chorus, as was his ability to retain the rhythmic flow of his sources by adapting meters to the word rhythms of the originals.

With few exceptions, James retained the dialect in songs that he set, since he considered its unique rhythmic and tonal qualities to be an indispensable part of Negro folk song. He stated that, "In the symphony of languages, Negro dialect has the role of the cello!" In "Roun' de Glory Manger," the text of the refrain is set in alternating meters of 5/4 and 4/4 with subtle syncopations not unexpected in the lilting tempo of the beginning. The telling of the Christmas story is embellished through the imagination of slaves who fancy themselves witnesses to the event ("An' all His pretty little fingers played in de straw"). The song ends with the full chorus singing the music of the first phrase but moving into an extended cadence with lush, slow-moving dissonant chords on the final text ("In de Glory Manger, Laid Him in de Glory, Glory Manger") resolving in the last, long-held chord.

Despite its seeming simplicity, part of the beauty of "Roun' de Glory Manger" is found in the rich, full harmonies interspersed with unexpected dissonances, altered chords, and a bass line set in the lowest register—a typical example of James's skill in reconstructing the folk harmonies of which he often spoke and which were in his ears from years of listening to folk singing in churches, camp meetings, and other gatherings. Audiences that heard him conduct his choruses in performances of this piece and other Christmas spirituals and jubilees experienced his skill in "translating" this sound from his ears through his singers to his listeners. (James identified "jubilees" as spirituals that expressed "great exultation of the spirit, a feeling of joy, and in which the tempo is vigorous.")

One columnist from the *Atlanta Constitution,* who regularly attended and reported on performances by Spelman and Morehouse College ensembles and James's activities as a folklorist, wrote enthusiastically about the song's first performance. Entitled "De Glory Manger" in the original collected version, this work has become a perennial favorite of Spelman audiences and is still often performed by the Morehouse-Spelman Chorus in the Annual Christmas Candlelight Concerts, at which it was first performed in 1935.

NEGRO BELL CAROL (1942)

Published in 1942, "Negro Bell Carol" is a striking example of James's use of folk songs as inspiration for original composition. It is written for *a cappella* chorus of mixed voices with soprano or tenor solo. A Christmas jubilee collected in north Georgia is clearly recognizable as the inspiration for the carol, with "words adapted by W.L.J. from folk sources" and "music by Willis Laurence James." The text adaptation recasts the words in a somewhat fanciful, playful verse, with angels taking a leading role in the lyrics. There is virtually no use of dialect, but the words suggest the Christmas story as told by untutored preachers, and illustrate James's imaginative interpretation of the folk character.

In G major, the song is in ABA form, with introduction and codetta. In the introduction, James mimics the sound of bells swinging back and forth using moving chords, some on the beat—"Ding!"—and some off—"Dong!" The dynamic level fades from loud to silence. The first refrain commences with the basses, who are then joined by treble voices ("Ring, golden bells, in Glory Christmas morning"). A soprano solo over sustained chords in the lower voices makes up the first verse ("O holy Jesus, So meek and so mild"), followed by the refrain repeated. The second verse, which is strophic, reflects James's understanding of folk religious beliefs. The final refrain ("Mercy for all, Mercy for all") is followed by an ending slightly reminiscent of the introduction, with the melody in the soprano voices and the simulated bell sounds. While the harmonic texture of this work is mainly triadic and consonant, it is colored by James's judicious use of dissonance and altered tones.

More than 50 years after its publication, "The Negro Bell Carol" continues to enjoy great popularity and wide performance. On Christmas Eve 1994, the Morgan State University Choir performed the carol on a nationwide public radio network broadcast.

CABIN BOY CALL (A NEGRO STEAMBOAT SONG) (CA. 1920) AND CAPTIN LOOK-A YONDER (CA. 1920)

Included among James's secular vocal compositions are unique examples of folk song genres that engaged his interest and attention throughout his life, namely, work songs, folk cries, calls, and hollers. Two that date from his earliest work as folklorist and composer are "Cabin Boy Call," a composition for tenor solo and piano; and "Captin Look-a Yonder," a composition for *a cappella* mixed men's chorus and tenor solo. The songs are both work songs that also use calls or call motives.

First performed in Louisiana and recorded by a Chicago record company in 1927, a news report in the *Baton Rouge State Times* concerning the release of the recording described "Cabin Boy Call" as a "new type of Negro song." What is true of that "new song," however, is that James had used as the basis of the composition very *old* vocal sounds transported by slaves from Africa to America; these "strange and peculiar sounds," as one traveler in the early 1800s described them, could be heard in rural areas of the Deep South far into the post-slavery era and, indeed, may still be heard in various transformations in some rural areas. In using these calls in a work that would be performed in concert halls and other similar settings more frequently associated with "high art," James removed them from the places of their origin and preserved them as musical artifacts of a time now in the distant past for audiences to whom they may, indeed, be new.

In an author's note in the score, James describes "Cabin Boy Call" as "a series of musical cries, sung for me by an old cabin boy in the Louisiana lowlands." He notes that, contrary to common practice, in which the calls are single expressions heard in various forms and in various settings, he has "put them together in one continuous song." The introduction consists of only two chords in the piano accompaniment. The song begins with the text "yaa hoo," which James indicates "should be sung each time with hands cupped around the mouth." While "yaa hoo" is used only twice—at the beginning and end of the song—most of the words of the relatively brief song use "call" motives such as that shown in Example 1.

Example 1. "Cabin Boy Call," "call" motive

Boy,   Cab-in   Boy!_____   Cab-in   Boy,   Cab - in

In explaining the text, James says, "'Cabin Boy Call' is an expression of resentment felt by one cabin boy who has been forced to do the work of another, who is hiding away somewhere on the boat." He calls out for the missing cabin boy 16 times, which gives a sense of his anger at being overworked:

> Yaa hoo, yaa hoo, Cabin Boy, Cabin Boy,
> Cabin Boy, You hear me calling you Cabin Boy!
> Capti'n calling, Boat highballin' down to NEZ [Natchez]
> All while you hidin' 'bout yo' bizness,
> Working hell out me!
> Yaa-hoo, yaa-hoo, Cabin Boy!

The song is in ABA form. The calls, which are altered with each repetition, represent the three types of calls or cries (plain, florid, and coloratura) that are described in James's later treatise on "The Negro Folk-Cry in America." Though the song is written in a major tonality (A major), the singer is expected to use the slightly altered "off-key" pitches peculiar to this style of folk expression. The mainly chordal piano accompaniment contains many altered and dissonant chords, suggesting James's intention of helping the singer to achieve this effect. A recording of James's own performance of the song is illustrative of the style of interjecting "off-key" pitches. Published in 1942, "Cabin Boy Call" has been widely performed by James's former voice students and by concert artists such as Roland Hayes, William Brown, John Patton, and many others.

"Captin Look-a Yonder," the second example of James's composed work songs, is an outstanding example of James's skill in writing for male voices. The use of the chorus as background for the soloist in his composed work songs allowed James to interpret in music his observations of the settings in which the songs were born: whether in the fields, on riverboats, on railroad crews, or even chain gangs, a leader served as spokesperson for the group to express their anger, bitterness at their lot, dissatisfactions, and frustration—the range of emotions that singly none could express. Few songs demonstrate this group feeling more forcefully than "Captin, Look-a Yonder."

James gives the song's background and story in the foreword to the musical score:

> In the early days of this century, [N]egro labor gangs in Louisiana uttered this sung protest against being worked from "can't to can't"—from when it is so early that one *can't* see to when it is so *late* that one can't see. The laborers were not allowed to dispute with "captin" over quitting time. . . . Therefore, they pointed to the sun and cried out, "Captin, look-a yonder where de sun done gone!"
>
> In this dramatically expressed plea for liberation from the oppressively long work day, there is a reflection of hope, radiant as the sun itself, provided by the love of *the* woman and the home. This anticipated joy of eventual reunion serves as a strong antidote against the abuses of the "captin."

The chorus begins the song, dramatically descending with the words that describe the sun's sinking direction: "Sun done gone so low down, low, low, low, low." The upper voices hum, accenting each hum, almost like sung grunts, with the bass voices calling to get the Captin's attention: "Oh captin, oh captin, hm, hm."

The solo voice picks up the words in plaintive calls, each more impatient than the last, and ends in an ascending vocal glissando that becomes an impassioned cry (see Ex. 2). Over the chorus's continued calls to the "captin," the soloist tells of his sadness in leaving his beloved, pleading all the time: "Why don't you tell me for to go on home, go on home—/Ain't but one watch in this shanty town, 'blong to the captin, but I wish it was mine." Hoping for the sun to hurry down so that he can return to his gal who is waiting, he petitions the sun to aid his cause.

Example 2. "Captin Look-a Yonder," tenor solo motive

Typical of his compositions for male chorus, the song is placed in the deep, low registers of the bass voice and uses the close harmony that is effective in the upper voices. Four-part writing is used throughout, providing primarily an uncluttered harmonic background for the solo voice. The song is through-composed. The tempo is indicated as "Slow, forcefully, steady," which allows for the soloist and chorus to draw out the melodic lines of the brief text. Written in the key of G minor, the harmony is almost totally consonant. James used dynamics and other expressive markings to suggest the mood of the song and gives precise directions to the soloist ("faster, impatiently"). On the ascending call, he commands the soloist to "yell it!"

Considering James's youth—he was in his early twenties when he collected the songs, and 27 when he composed, performed, and recorded "Cabin Boy Call"—one wonders whether he could foresee the value of his efforts, for his settings of these two work songs gave a voice to otherwise anonymous laborers whose place in African-American history would be forgotten except for their songs, which he has preserved as veritable works of art.

REFERENCES

"Annual Carol Concert Is Thrilling to Music Critic." *Atlanta World* (December 17, 1939).

Brown, Sterling A., Arthur P. Davis, and Ulysses Lee, eds. *The Negro Caravan.* New York: Dryden Press, 1941.

Carte, A. E. Interview with the author, Baton Rouge, La., November 6–8, 1979.

Cureau, Rebecca T. "Willis Laurence James (1900–1966): Musician, Music Educator, Folklorist." Ph.D. diss., Atlanta University, 1987.

"Hunt for Negro Songs Is Planned: Spelman Teacher Will Seek Unknown Songs." *Atlanta Constitution* (September 25, 1939).

James, Willis L. *Stars in de Elements.* Special issue of *Black Sacred Music* 9, nos. 1 and 2. Durham: Duke University Press, 1995

Levine, Lawrence W. *Black Culture and Black Consciousness: Afro-American Folk-Thought from Slavery to Freedom.* London: Oxford University Press, 1977.

Perkins Huggins, Naomi. Interview with the author, Atlanta, Ga., October 8, 1979.

Powell, I. S. Interview with the author, Baton Rouge, La., November 6–8, 1979.

"Saving a Faded Page." *New York Buffalo Courier* (October 15, 1939).

Sevien, John. "Leland Alumni Gather Here." *Baton Rouge Morning Advocate* (June 29, 1980).

Sibley, Celestine. "Negro Jubilee to Be Presented for the First Time." *Atlanta Constitution* (December 19, 1935).

REBECCA T. CUREAU

JEANTY, OCCILIUS

Born in Port-au-Prince, Haiti, March 18, ca. 1860; died in Port-au-Prince, January 28, 1936. **Education:** Came from a musical family; his father, Occilius Jeanty, was a military bandsman, flutist, and founded the École Centrale de Musique in Port-au-Prince; Port-au-Prince, studied at the École Polymathique de Coupeaud and the Lycée Pétion; Conservatoire de Paris, studied harmony, composition, and the *cornet à pistons* with Arban, Marmontel, and Douillon, with support of a Haitian government scholarship, 1881–85. **Composing and Performing Career:** Director of the Musique du Palais national military band, 1892–1916, 1922–1934; "1804" commemorated Haitian independence and came to symbolize anti-United States resistance.

MUSIC LIST

INSTRUMENTAL SOLOS
Piano
"Les Pleures d'Estelle." 1872. Unpublished manuscript.

CONCERT BAND
"Chéry Hyppolite" (military band). 1896. Unpublished manuscript.
"1804." 1904. Unpublished manuscript.
"Imprécations de Dessalines: Jacques 1er" (miltary band). 1892.
       Unpublished manuscript.
"Maria." Unpublished manuscript.
"L'Obsédante." Unpublished manuscript.
"Oratorio" (military band). Unpublished manuscript.
"La Rentrée à Jérusalem." Unpublished manuscript.
"Le Retour du vieux lion." Unpublished manuscript.
"Sur la tombe" (military band). 1908. Unpublished manuscript.
"Ti Sam" (military band). 1902. Unpublished manuscript.
"Les Trompettes des anges." Unpublished manuscript.
"Les Vautours du 6 décembre." 1887. Unpublished manuscript.
"Les Zéphyrs: Grande Valse de Concert." Unpublished manuscript.

PUBLICATIONS

ABOUT JEANTY
Books and Monographs

Dissertations
Largey, Michael. "Musical Ethnography in Haiti: A Study of Elite Hegemony and Musical Composition." Ph.D. diss., Indiana University, 1991.

Articles
Herissé, Félix. "Étoiles haïtiennes." Unpublished typescript, held in l'École Sainte-Trinité Collection, Port-au-Prince.
Jeanty, Lydia. "Biographie d'Occide Jeanty." Unpublished typescript, held in the private collection of Lydia Jeanty, Port-au-Prince.
Largey, Michael. "Composing a Haitian Cultural Identity: Haitian Elites, African Ancestry, and Musical Discourse." *Black Music Research Journal* 14, no. 2 (1994): 99–117.

BY JEANTY
Jeanty, Occide. *Père et fils. Petite grammaire musicale.* Paris: Librairie Évangélique, 1882.

* * * * *

Perhaps the most beloved composer of Haitian audiences is Occilius Jeanty, *fils,* known to Haitian audiences as Occide Jeanty. Trained to be a military musician, Jeanty was best known as the leader of the Haitian presidential band and as a *konpositè nasyonalis ayisyen* (Haitian nationalist composer). His renown among Haitian audiences today is an indication of his former popularity and current importance to debates about Haitian national identity. His compositions are staples of the Haitian military band repertoire.

A native of Port-au-Prince, Jeanty received his elementary schooling at L'École Polymathique de Coupeaud and his secondary school training at the Lycée Pétion. Although these two schools were among the most prestigious in Haiti at the time, Jeanty is reported by Étienne Dumervé, in his *Histoire de la musique en Haiti,* to be an indifferent student, preferring to sing children's songs to himself while beating time with his ruler or pencil. His father, the director of the École Centrale de Musique, a professor of mathematics at Lycée Pétion, and the director of the Musique du Palais, the president's military band stationed at the Palais National, encouraged his son to study music from a young age. And the young Occide produced his first musical composition at the age of 12, a piece for piano entitled "Les Pleurs d'Estelle." Very little is known of Jeanty's early years, but based on his accomplishments in early adulthood, Jeanty must have pursued his musical education with his father and performed informally as a cornet player with his high school *fanfa* or wind band.

In 1881, he dazzled a Haitian jury with his technique and was awarded a scholarship from the government of Haitian president Lysius Felicité Salomon to study with Jean-Baptiste Arban in France at the Conservatoire de Paris. Before Occide traveled to France, he and his father authored *Petite grammaire musicale* (1882), an introductory music theory textbook with lessons for forming musical scales, performing ornamentation, and using clefs and dynamic markings.

When his father died on November 2, 1892, Occide was appointed to replace him as the director of the Musique du Palais. During his tenure as band director, the younger Jeanty wrote much of the repertoire that is still performed by the band, including many polkas, waltzes, marches, and *méringues.* Jeanty's duties as director of the Musique du Palais included composing music for the band's weekly concerts. Popular genres of the day included valses, gavottes, and *méringues.* Among Jeanty's valses were "L'Obsédante" and "Les Zéphyrs," and among the marches "La Rentrée à Jérusalem," "Les Trompettes des anges," and "Le Retour du vieux lion," the last-named a tribute to Cuban diplomat Ben Como. In addition, there were several *méringues,* a favorite dance in Haiti among elite audiences. Jeanty's "Maria" featured the syncopated *quintolet* rhythm, first in the saxophones and horns, then answered by the flutes and clarinets. This alternation of the *quintolet* rhythm between upper and lower voices was a common characteristic of the Haitian concert *méringue.*

Since the directorship of the band was both a military and a political appointment, Jeanty was called upon to write music that not only served the daily needs of the armed forces but also promoted Haitian political figures. He wrote a series of funeral marches for Haitian heads of state including "Chéry Hyppolite" (Dear Hyppolite) for President Florville Hyppolite (1896), "Ti Sam" (Little Sam) for President T. Augustin Simon Sam (1902), and "Sur la tombe" (On the Tomb) for President Nord Alexis (1908).

Not all of his politically motivated works were flattering to the Haitian state. In 1887, under the T. Simon Sam administration, German warships sailed into Port-au-Prince harbor demanding the release of a German citizen imprisoned for assaulting the police. Without resistance, the Haitian government capitulated to German demands and, within a week of the incident, as a condemnation of the ineffectiveness of the Simon Sam government during the conflict, Jeanty wrote "Vautours du 6 décembre" (Vultures of 6 December). Despite brutal repression of political criticism during the Simon Sam adminstration, Jeanty was not punished for his musical outburst, perhaps escaping censure because the work lacked a specific musical program.

On July 28, 1915, U.S. Marines landed in Port-au-Prince, ostensibly to restore order to Haiti after an angry mob lynched President Vilbrun Guillaume Sam. The invasion was also intended to limit German financial interests in the Caribbean and to make Haiti more economically dependent on the United States. Haitian intellectuals interpreted the invasion as a reminder of the early days of Saint-Domingue (colonial Haiti) when the majority of the population was held in slavery. As the only country founded on a successful slave revolt, Haiti had prided itself on keeping foreign invaders from its shores. The occupation of the country was made all the more distasteful since the contingent of U.S. Marines sent to Port-au-Prince were almost entirely white and were insensitive to class differences in Haiti. Haitian intellectuals, some of whom initially welcomed the U.S. invasion force, eventually became disenchanted with the Marines, whom they considered boorish and uncultured.

During the initial phase of the U.S. invasion, Jeanty remained at his post as head of the Musique du Palais. He directed the band until 1916 when, under the U.S. occupation government, he was demoted to the rank of first lieutenant. Rather then serve the needs of an occupation government at a subordinate rank, Jeanty resigned his commission and took up the directorship of a small band in the town of Petit-Goâve.

In 1922, Jeanty was reappointed director of the Musique du Palais by President Louis Borno, after which he continued his outspoken criticism of the U.S. occupation. In 1929, Jeanty was conducting a performance of "1804" in front of the Palais National; riots broke out and were later attributed by Haitian poet Jean Brierre to the evocative power of Jeanty's music. Jeanty remained in the post until he retired from the military in 1934. He died on January 28, 1936, in Port-au-Prince.

Occilius Jeanty (right) and his father, also named Occilius Jeanty; illustration from Petit grammaire musical *(Librairie Évangélique, Paris, 1882), courtesy of Lydia Jeanty*

SELECTED WORKS

With the exception of a few songs and piano solos, Occide Jeanty's work was written almost entirely for *fanfa,* the Haitian Kreyòl word for wind band. His *fanfa* consisted of flutes; piccolos; three clarinet parts; soprano, alto, tenor, and baritone saxophones; trombones; and solo cornet. While many of his pieces carried titles suggesting a variety of genres, Jeanty's *oeuvre* was dominated by short pieces for band. For example, his "Oratorio" was not a piece for chorus and instrumentalists but a slow march for military band.

Jeanty's work is important not so much for its stylistic variety, but for its symbolic importance to Haitian audiences, especially during the U.S. occupation of Haiti in the early 20th century. His most famous work is "1804," a *marche guerrier,* or warrior's march, written in commemoration of the 100th anniversary in 1904 of Haitian independence. After the U.S. Marines invaded Haiti in July 1915, "1804" became a symbol of Haitian resistance to the U.S. occupation. Jeanty, who led the Musique du Palais in weekly concerts on the Champs de Mars, or public park, in front of the Palais National, was eventually banned from giving public performances of "1804" because it reminded the Haitian crowds of the similarities between the U.S. occupation of Haiti and the imposition of slavery 100 years earlier. Jeanty was removed from his post as director of the Musique du Palais in 1916 by President Sudre Dartiguenave under pressure from the U.S. military. Eventually, Jeanty was reinstated by President Louis Borno in 1922.

Jeanty's "1804" continues to have political overtones for Haitian audiences. During the tempestuous years immediately after the fall of the Jean-Claude Duvalier regime, Haitian musicians cited it as a piece of music that could help unite disparate political factions, and one, Micheline Delancour, claims that its melody was an amalgamation of the regimental calls of many of the units in the Haitian army, the *Garde d'Haïti*.

This musical material of "1804" alone is hardly incendiary. It is a march with a first and second theme and a trio section with a *da capo* repetition to the first section. "1804" begins in 6/8 meter with an arpeggiated fanfare figure in the upper voices. The martial character of the first strain is tempered by the relatively lyric second theme in G major. The break strain is in 2/4 time, providing contrast to the lilting 6/8 meter of the opening of the piece. The saxophones and low brass carry the heavily accented melody.

While "1804" does not depart from the style and structure of a typical march for wind band of the period, its importance as a symbol of Haitian identity makes it a significant work in Haitian music history.

Another of Jeanty's important works was "Les Zéphyrs: Grande Valse de Concert," a concert waltz for three B-flat clarinets; soprano, alto, tenor, and baritone saxophones; three cornets; three alto horns; trombones; baritone horns; contrabasses; and drum battery. The entire ensemble begins the piece with the low brasses and baritone saxophones on the melody and the upper winds providing eighth-note passage work that follows the outline of the melody.

The "valse" proper, after the introduction, features a playful exchange of the notes of the melody between the upper saxophones and the clarinets. Each note of the melody is preceded by a grace note, giving the line a twittering quality reminiscent of bird calls. After eight measures, the brasses take the melody while the upper winds play eighth-note runs in a countermelody.

The second theme of "Les Zéphyrs" features a figure of six eighth notes in one measure followed by a half note and quarter note in the following measure. This figure is used in a call-and-response fashion; while the cornets play the second measure of the theme, the clarinets and saxophones answer the cornets with the eighth-note theme. The third theme features an expansive cornet solo on quarter and half notes while the upper winds play descending and ascending chromatic runs in eighth notes.

While most of Occide Jeanty's *oeuvre* has survived in the form of march music for the Haitian Musique du Palais, he was considered an eclectic composer during his lifetime. The *méringues,* valses, polkas, and other dance forms that Jeanty employed were expected by his loyal Sunday-in-the-park concert public. His musical works explored the limits of the wind band, using programmatic touches such as the birdcalls in "Les Zéphyrs" or the cannon fire in "1804." However, it is the memory of Jeanty as a defender of the Haitian republic that is cherished by Haitian audience members; his musical contributions were part of a much larger personal service to his country.

REFERENCES

Brierre, Jean. Interview with the author, Port-au-Prince, July 28, 1988.

Dalencour, Micheline. Interview with the author, Port-au-Prince, 1988.

Dumervé, Étienne Constantin Eugène Moise. *Histoire de la musique en Haïti.* Port-au-Prince: Imprimerie des Antilles, 1968.

Herissé, Félix. "Étoiles haïtiennes." Unpublished typescript, held in l'École Sainte-Trinité Collection, Port-au-Prince.

Jeanty, Lydia. "Biographie d'Occide Jeanty." Unpublished typescript, held in the private collection of Lydia Jeanty, Port-au-Prince.

Jeanty, Occide. *Père et fils. Petite grammaire musicale.* Paris: Librairie Évangélique, 1882.

Nicholls, David. *From Dessalines to Duvalier: Race, Colour and National Independence in Haiti.* Cambridge: Cambridge University Press, 1979.

MICHAEL LARGEY

JEFFERSON, BLIND LEMON

Born near Wortham, Tex., September 1893; died in Chicago, Ill., December 1929. **Education:** Self-taught guitar player from childhood. **Composing and Performing Career:** Played for local country dances and picnics at early age; Wortham, Tex., area, worked as singer at farm parties, picnics, and on streets, ca. 1912; Texas, performed in brothels and at parties in East Dallas, Silver City, and Galveston, ca. 1914; Waco, Tex., worked at Taborian Park, 1914; Dallas, Tex., performed in streets, barrelhouses, brothels, and saloons of Upper Elm Street area, begining 1915; teamed up with Huddie (Leadbelly) Ledbetter, ca. 1917; Gill, Ariz., performed at Alf Bonner's Place, ca. 1917; itinerant singer on streets throughout Louisiana, Mississippi, Alabama, Virginia, and elsewhere, 1920s; made his first recording with Paramount, 1925; made numerous recordings, chiefly for Paramount, while continuing to travel and perform, 1925–29. **Honors/Awards:** Numerous organizations named in his honor, including clubs in San Pablo, Calif., and New York City, the rock bands Jefferson Airplane and Blind Melon, and the Swedish blues magazine, *Jefferson*; gravesite historical marker erected by State of Texas in Wortham.

MUSIC LIST

[The following list of titles includes only works that were composed by the subject of the entry; it is not a list of recordings that were made by the subject. Although the composer may have made recordings of his own works, the list is not restricted to those recordings but in many cases includes performances by other artists of the composer's work. The list is made up of publication and discographical data, in cases where such information is available. Although no effort has been made to include documentation of the earliest recording of the works listed, the date of the earliest recording that is readily available has been given. —Ed.]

"Bad Luck Blues." Recorded, 1926: Milestone MCD-47022-2; Paramount 12443; Yazoo CD-1069.

"Bakershop Blues." Recorded, 1929: Collectables COLCD-5194; Milestone MCD-47022-2; Paramount 1285.

"Balky Mule Blues." Recorded, 1928: Collectables COLCD-5194; Document Records DOCD-5019; Paramount 12631.

"Bed Springs Blues." Recorded, 1929: Matchbox MSE-1001; Melodeon MLP-7324; Paramount 12872 or Broadway 5056.

"Beggin' Back." Recorded, 1926: Document Records DOCD-5017; Paramount 12394; Yazoo CD-1069.

"Big Night Blues." Recorded, 1929: Collectables COLCD-5194; Paramount 12801; Yazoo CD-1069.

"Black Horse Blues." Recorded, 1926: Milestone MLP-2004; Paramount 12367; Yazoo CD-1069.

"Black Snake Dream Blues." Recorded, 1927: Biograph BLP-12015; Document Records DOCD-5018; Paramount 12510.

"Black Snake Moan." Recorded, 1926: Columbia/Legacy CK-47060; Okeh 8455; Smithsonian Folkways Records 02802.

"Blind Lemon's Penitentiary Blues." Recorded, 1928: Collectables COLCD-5194; Milestone MCD-47022-2; Paramount 12666.

"Booger Rooger Blues." Recorded, 1926: Document Records DOCD-5017; Paramount 12425; Yazoo CD-1069.

"Booster Blues." Recorded, 1926: Biograph BLP-12000; Document Records DOCD-5017; Paramount 12347.

"Bootin' Me 'bout." Recorded, 1929: Document Records DOCD-5020; Milestone MLP-2004; Paramount 12946.

"Broke and Hungry Blues." Recorded, 1926: Milestone MCD-47022-2; Paramount 12443; Yazoo CD-1069.

"Cat Man Blues." Recorded, 1929: Biograph BLP-12015; Document Records DOCD-5020; Paramount 12921.

"Change My Luck Blues." Recorded, 1928: Matchbox MSE-1001; Milestone MCD-47022-2; Paramount 12639.

"The Cheaters Spell." Recorded, 1929: Document Records DOCD-5020; Matchbox MSE-1001; Paramount 12933.

"Chinch Bug Blues." Recorded, 1927: Collectables COLCD-5194; Document Records DOCD-5018; Paramount 12551.

"Chock House Blues." Recorded, 1926: Collectables COLCD-5194; Milestone MCD-47022-2; Paramount 12394.

"Christmas Eve Blues." Recorded, 1928: Biograph BLP-12000; Document Records DOCD-5019; Paramount 12692.

"Competition Bed Blues." Recorded, 1928: Document Records DOCD-5019 or Document Records DOCD-5020; Paramount 12728; RST Records BD-2082.

"Corinna Blues." Recorded, 1926: Milestone MLP-2004; Paramount 12367; Yazoo CD-1069.

"D B Blues." Recorded, 1928: Document Records DOCD-5019; Musical Heritage Society MHS-9379; Paramount 12712.

"Deceitful Brownskin Blues." Recorded, 1927: Collectables COLCD-5194; Document Records DOCD-5018; Paramount 12551.

"Disgusted Blues." Recorded, 1929: Document Records DOCD-5020; Matchbox MSE-1001; Paramount 12933.

"Dry Southern Blues." Recorded, 1926: Biograph BLP-12000; Document Records DOCD-5017; Paramount 12347.

"Dynamite Blues." Recorded, 1929: Biograph BLP-12040; Document Records DOCD-5020; Paramount 12739.

"Eagle Eyed Mama." Recorded, 1929: Biograph BLP-12040; Document Records DOCD-5020; Paramount 12739.

"Easy Rider Blues." Recorded, 1927: Milestone MCD-47022-2; Paramount 12474; Yazoo CD-1069.

"Empty House Blues." Recorded, 1929: Document Records DOCD-5020; Matchbox MSE-1001; Paramount 12946.

"Fence Breakin' Yellin' Blues." Recorded, 1929: Biograph BLP-12015; Document Records DOCD-5020; Paramount 12921.

"Gone Dead on You Blues." Recorded, 1927: Matchbox MSE-1001; Paramount 12578; Yazoo CD-1069.

"Got the Blues." Recorded, 1926: Document Records DOCD-5017; Matchbox MSE-1001; Paramount 12354.

"Hangman's Blues." Recorded, 1928: Milestone MLP-2004; Milestone MCD-47022-2; Paramount 12679.

"Happy New Year Blues." Recorded, 1928: Biograph BLP-12000; Document Records DOCD-5019; Paramount 12692.

"Hot Dogs." Recorded, 1927: Paramount 12493; Yazoo CD-1004; Yazoo CD-1069.

"Jack o' Diamond Blues." Recorded, 1926: DejaVu 5-114-2; Document Records DOCD-5017; Paramount 12373.

"'Lectric Chair Blues." Recorded, 1928: Biograph BLP-12015; Document Records DOCD-5019; Paramount 12608 or Broadway 5059.

"Lemon's Cannon Ball Blues." Recorded, 1928: Document Records DOCD-5019; Matchbox MSE-1001; Paramount 12639.

"Lemon's Worried Blues." Recorded, 1928: Document Records DOCD-5019; Milestone MLP-2004; Paramount 12622.

"Lock Step Blues." Recorded, 1928: Milestone MLP-2004; Milestone MCD-47022-2; Paramount 12679.

"Lonesome House Blues." Recorded, 1927: Milestone MCD-47022-2; Paramount 12593; Yazoo CD-1069.

"Long Distance Moan." Recorded, 1929: Collectables COLCD-5194; Milestone MCD-47022-2; Paramount 12852.

"Long Lastin' Lovin'." Recorded, 1928: Document Records DOCD-5019; Milestone 47022; Paramount 12666.

"Long Lonesome Blues." Recorded, 1926: Document Records DOCD-5017; Matchbox MSE-1001; Paramount 12354.

"Low Down Mojo Blues." Recorded, 1928: Document Records DOCD-5019; Milestone MLP-2004; Paramount 12650.

"Maltese Cat Blues." Recorded, 1928: Biograph BLP-12015; Document Records DOCD-5019; Paramount 12712.

"Match Box Blues." Recorded, 1927: Milestone MCD-47022-2; Okeh 8455; Paramount 12474; Yazoo CD-1069.

"Mean Jumper Blues." Recorded, 1928: Document Records DOCD-5019; Milestone 47022; Paramount 12631.

"Mosquito Moan." Recorded, 1929: Document Records DOCD-5020; Milestone MCD-47022-2; Paramount 12899.

"Oil Well Blues." Recorded, 1929: Milestone MLP-2016; Paramount 12771; Yazoo CD-1069.

"Old Rounders Blues." Recorded, 1926: Document Records DOCD-5017; Paramount 12394; RST Records BD-2082.

"One Dime Blues." Recorded, 1927: Matchbox MSE-1001; Paramount 12578; Yazoo CD-1069.

"Peach Orchard Mama." Recorded, 1929: Collectables COLCD-5194; Milestone MLP-2016; Paramount 12801.

"Piney Woods Money Mama." Recorded, 1928: Document Records DOCD-5019; Milestone MLP-2004; Paramount 12650.

"Pneumonia Blues." Recorded, 1929: Document Records DOCD-5020; Milestone MCD-47022-2; Paramount 12880.

"Prison Cell Blues." Recorded, 1928: Milestone MCD-47022-2; Paramount 12622; Yazoo CD-1069.

"Rabbit Foot Blues." Recorded, 1926: Milestone MCD-47022-2; Paramount 12454; Yazoo CD-1069.

"Rambler Blues." Recorded, 1927: Document Records DOCD-5018; Paramount 12541; Yazoo CD-1069.

"Right of Way Blues." Recorded, 1927: Document Records DOCD-5018; Paramount 12510; Yazoo CD-1069.

"Rising High Water Blues." Recorded, 1927: Document Records DOCD-5018; Milestone MCD-47022-2; Paramount 12487.

"Sad News Blues." Recorded, 1928: Document Records DOCD-5019 or Document Records DOCD-5020; Paramount 12728; RST Records BD-2082.

"Saturday Night Spender Blues." Recorded, 1929: Document Records DOCD-5020; Matchbox MSE-1001; Paramount 12771.

"See that My Grave's Kept Clean" or "See that My Grave Is Kept Clean." Recorded, 1927: DA Music 3704; Paramount 12585; Yazoo CD-1069.

"Shuckin' Sugar Blues." Recorded, 1926: Milestone MCD-47022-2; Paramount 12454; Yazoo CD-1069.

"Southern Woman Blues." Recorded, 1929: Document Records DOCD-5020; Milestone MCD-47022-2; Paramount 12899.

"'Stillery Blues." Recorded, 1927: Okeh (unissued).

"Stocking Feet Blues." Recorded, 1926: Document Records DOCD-5017; Milestone MCD-47022-2; Paramount 12407.

"Struck Sorrow Blues." Recorded, 1927: Document Records DOCD-5018; Matchbox MSE-1001; Paramount 12541.

"Sunshine Special." Recorded, 1927: Collectables COLCD-5194; Milestone MCD-47022-2; Paramount 12593.

"Teddy Bear Blues." Recorded, 1927: Document Records DOCD-5018; Milestone MCD-47022-2; Paramount 12487.

"That Black Snake Moan." Recorded, 1926: Collectables COLCD-5194; Milestone MCD-47022-2; Paramount 12407.

"That Black Snake Moan No. 2." Recorded, 1929: Collectables COLCD-5194; Document Records DOCD-5020; Paramount 12756.

"That Crawlin' Baby Blues." Recorded, 1929: Document Records DOCD-5020; Paramount 12880; Yazoo CD-1069.

"Tin Cup Blues." Recorded, 1929: Document Records DOCD-5020; Milestone MLP-2013; Paramount 12756.

"Wartime Blues." Recorded, 1926: Document Records DOCD-5017; Paramount 12425; Yazoo CD-1069.

"Weary Dogs Blues." Recorded, 1927: Biograph BLP-12040; Document Records DOCD-5018; Paramount 12493.

"Yo Yo Blues." Recorded, 1929: Biograph BLP-12000; Document Records DOCD-5020; Paramount 12872 or Broadway 5056.

PUBLICATIONS

ABOUT JEFFERSON
Books and Monographs

Groom, Bob, ed. *Blind Lemon Jefferson*. Blues World Booklet, no. 3. Knutsford, England: Blues World, 1970.

Articles

Becket, Alan. "Two Country Blues Singers." *New Left Review* 29 (January/February 1965): 73–77.

Govenar, Alan. "Blind Lemon Jefferson. That Black Snake Moan: The Music and Mystery of Blind Lemon Jefferson." In *Bluesland: Portraits of Twelve Major American Blues Masters,* edited by Pete Welding and Toby Byron, 16–37. New York: Dutton Books, 1991.

Groom, Bob. "The Legacy of Blind Lemon." *Blues World* no. 18 (January 1968): 14–16; no. 20 (July 1968): 33–37; no. 21 (October 1968): 30–31; no. 23 (April 1969): 5–7; no. 24 (July 1969): 9–10; no. 25 (October 1969): 9–10; no. 27 (February 1970): 13–14; no. 28 (March 1970): 8–9; no. 29 (April 1970): 8–9; no. 30 (May 1970): 13–14; no. 35 (October 1970): 19–20; no. 36 (November 1970): 20; no. 40 (Autumn 1971): 4–6.

Nilsson, Charley. "Blind Lemon Jefferson (1897–1930)." *Jefferson* no. 45 (Fall 1979): 24–28.

Obrecht, J. "Big Boss Blues: Blind Lemon Jefferson—The First Star of Blues Guitar." *Guitar Player* 25 (July 1991): 46–49+.

Blind Lemon Jefferson; courtesy of the Frank Driggs Collection

Oliver, Paul. "Blind Lemon Jefferson." *Jazz Review* 2, no. 7 (1959): 9–12.

Roberts, Bruce. "It's a Long Old Lane Ain't Got No End." *Blues and Rhythm* 119 (June 1997): 4–5.

Rust, Brian, Andre Gillet, and Serge Tonneau. "Discography of Blind Lemon Jefferson." *Rhythm & Blues Panorama* 22, no. 1 (1963): 10–14.

Silverman, Jerry. "Three Immortal Bluesmen." *Frets* 4, no. 2 (1982): 18–22.

Spencer, J. M. "The Mythology of the Blues." *Sacred Music of the Secular City: From Blues to Rap.* A special issue of *Black Sacred Music* 6 (1992): 98–140.

Stewart-Baxter, Derrick. "Blind Lemon Jefferson" [Discography]. *Jazz Journal* 7 (February 1954): 21, 23.

———. "Blind Lemon Jefferson: A New Discography." *Jazz Journal* 7 (May 1954): 15, 14.

Swinton, Paul. "A Twist of Lemon." *Blues and Rhythm* 121 (August 1997): 4–9.

Trubswasser, Gunther W. "Blind Lemon Jefferson." *Blues Notes* 7 (1970): 5–12.

Uzzel, R. L. "Music Rooted in the Texas Soil: Blind Lemon Jefferson." *Living Blues* 83 (November–December 1988): 22–23.

Venturini, Fabrizio. "Blind Lemon Jefferson: Bluesman Vagabondo." *Musica Jazz* 35, no. 2 (1979): 7–9.

Virgo, E. S. "A Note on the Death Date of Blind Lemon Jefferson." *Black Music Research Bulletin* 10, no. 2 (1988): 14–15.

* * * * *

Blind Lemon Jefferson was the first community-based folk blues singer/guitarist to become a star on phonograph records. As such, he virtually defined the genre for a period of time and became a role model for countless other musicians, setting musical standards that few could even hope to approach. Several of his recorded songs have consistently been covered by other artists, and verses and musical ideas attributable to him show up everywhere. Other Texas artists, especially ones who had some direct contact with him, such as Leadbelly and Lightnin' Hopkins, show the greatest degree of influence, but elements of his music show up occasionally in the work of dozens of blues artists from Mississippi, Georgia, Virginia, and elsewhere.

The early and middle 1920s were an era in which the recording of blues was dominated by female singers drawn from the vaudeville stage circuit and accompanied by a pianist or small jazz combo. For the most part, they sang material provided by professional songwriters. Between 1923 and 1925, a few male blues guitarists, such as Sylvester Weaver, Papa Charlie Jackson (who actually played a six-string banjo), and Lonnie Johnson, began to launch successful recording careers, but they too were from the vaudeville stage. Blind Lemon Jefferson represented the pure folk tradition that these other artists had taken to the level of popular music. He was the real thing from the streets of Dallas, with a tin cup attached to his instrument. Although he was a handicapped musician, he was a full-time professional and was able to develop his artistry to a level of complexity every bit as awesome as that of his vaudeville counterparts.

Jefferson's recording career was brief (only four years), but prolific: not counting alternate takes and versions, he recorded 74 blues, five spirituals, and two ragtime songs. His compositional talents clearly lay mainly in the blues arena, yet it is often difficult to distinguish compositional intent from spontaneous improvisation, particularly in the first half of his recording career.

In 1926 and 1927, his blues are made up mostly of traditional verses without thematic consistency or development through a whole song. Rather, they present various contrasts of theme, attitude, and mood in the manner of many other folk blues. His melodies during this period display a great deal of variation, and his guitar work, frequently at dazzlingly fast tempos with sudden breaks and hesitations, exhibits a profusion of ideas. Jefferson sounds like the genie of traditional blues escaping from the lamp where he had been confined for years, bursting forth with one striking image after another, melodies that range up to two octaves, and non-stop guitar ideas that would cause other musicians to give up in despair.

In 1928 and 1929, Jefferson's blues were much less improvisational in character. His lyrics were almost entirely thematic throughout a song and clearly had been rehearsed. In his final year, he even recorded some pieces credited to another songwriter, although they may actually be his own compositions. His melodies and guitar parts contain many of the same phrases that he used earlier, but he gives the impression of having chosen a few such phrases in advance and used them throughout the piece. In other words, Jefferson had become a composer in a conventional sense. During this final year, he recorded 22 blues and probably could have gone on for years doing so if he had not tragically frozen to death in Chicago in a snowstorm at the end of the year.

GOT THE BLUES (1926)

This is the first blues song that Jefferson recorded, around March 1926. Approximately two months later, he recorded another version, evidently because the first version had been worn out from pressing so many copies. Both versions employ a similar melody featuring descending lines ranging between a high and low tonic note, and in both versions, the guitar plays some of the same figures in open G tuning (D–B–G–D–G–D, from high to low). There are many improvisations, however, and some musical elements occur in one version only. Each version contains seven lyric stanzas, but only the first two are found in both versions. Although the other stanzas are completely different, they do share some thematic material.

Version 1 is set at a breakneck tempo, as Jefferson "whips" the guitar strings, leaps up the neck to play complex patterns on the high strings, extends his lines with improvised passages, and introduces rhythmic shifts and bursts of speed. His opening verse contains the remarkable image of "The blues come to Texas loping like a mule." This is followed through the second stanza by an image of a "high brown woman" who is "hard to fool" and who fools men by quitting them when they think she loves them. Jefferson reintroduces the theme of the blues in a stanza that probably gave the song its title, stating that he woke up with the blues all around his bed and found them in his bread when he went to eat his breakfast. He returns to the idea of "quitting" and "fooling," claiming now to be able to tell "when a woman gonna put you down," and contrasting this with a statement that he has been trying to quit a woman for two years but doesn't know how.

The final two stanzas present two potential resolutions to the dilemmas of breaking off a relationship. In the first of these, Jefferson states that he is "going to the river," a common metaphor for suicide, so that he can have "those tadpoles and minnows arguing over me." But in the last stanza, he threatens his woman with death, stating, "The next time I try to quit you, I'll hang crepe on your door." This song, then, deals with the blues as some kind of a creature or spirit that can beset someone and with the issue of fooling a partner or breaking off a relationship. But the song does not deal with this subject from a single perspective; instead, we see it from the point of view of the man and the woman, the perpetrator and the victim, the knowing and the unknowing. Like an African dilemma tale, it raises the range of possibilities in a common human situation without explaining or proposing a single solution.

Version 2 of this song is set at a slightly slower tempo. Although Jefferson introduces some new mandolin-like trills, his guitar playing is on the whole more conservative, yet this gives him the opportunity to be somewhat more adventurous in his singing. He opens with the same images of the blues "loping like a mule" and the deceitful and inscrutable "high brown woman." In the third stanza, however, he introduces a contrasting image of a woman who "ain't so good looking" but has a "nice disposition." He returns to the theme of the blues, but now he is trying to escape them by going to the river carrying his "rocker chair" and asking the crew of the transfer boat, "Have the worried blues reached here?" He returns again to a description of his "good gal" calling his name. In the final two stanzas, however, he reverts to the theme of the woman trying to fool him. In this version of the song, then, we find rather different emphases in a set of contrasts between the arrival of the blues and escape from them and between the deceitful woman and the good woman.

The theme of death is absent in the second version, and the singer himself is not trying to quit his woman but is instead trying to run away from the blues. Such significant differences raise the question of whether these two recordings might better be regarded as two separate songs despite their many similarities. They also suggest that Jefferson's concept of this song consisted of a core of musical and lyric elements or ideas to which he added others, either in an ongoing compositional process involving some degree of deliberation or, more likely, in a spontaneous manner at the time of performance. These introduced elements, however, were evidently more or less fixed building blocks within his "repertoire," no matter what degree of forethought he may have employed in expressing them, as many of them turn up in his other blues recordings.

'LECTRIC CHAIR BLUES (1928)

This song was recorded in February 1928, a bit past the midpoint in Jefferson's abbreviated recording career. By this time, his blues had mostly taken on the appearance of being more deliberate compositions, particularly with respect to their lyrics.

In this piece, Jefferson sings a more or less set melody with some degree of improvisational variation, displaying his typically wide melodic range of an octave and a fifth. His guitar is played in the E position of standard tuning at a medium tempo. His playing ranges over 12 frets of the instrument but is only moderately difficult and inventive by his own admittedly high standards. He

extends most lines beyond the usual four measures in this otherwise typical AAB blues. One of the most noticeable features of his guitar work is the playing of a varied countermelody behind his singing, a device that he regularly used and one that distinguished him from the majority of folk blues guitarists. This countermelody displays every bit as much freedom as Jefferson's singing does. It also seems especially designed for this piece, as he frequently snaps out treble notes in a manner suggestive of bolts of electric current.

Jefferson's theme in this song is related to two significant topics of lyric preoccupation in his repertoire. One is the legal system and prison, as found in such blues as "Blind Lemon's Penitentiary Blues," "Prison Cell Blues," "Lock Step Blues," and "Hangman's Blues." The other is the topic of sudden attack, bodily harm, and death, as in "Chinch Bug Blues," "Mosquito Moan," "Bootin' Me 'bout," and "See that My Grave Is Kept Clean." The latter preoccupation is easy to understand in the case of a blind man who made himself vulnerable by performing on the streets. This same handicap, however, meant that he would have had few opportunities to engage in criminal behavior or test the legal system. His preoccupation with this subject, therefore, is more likely explained by his feeling like a prisoner because of his blindness. Whatever the case, there can be no doubt that he penetrates with the deepest insight into the situation of a man condemned to be electrocuted.

The electric chair was quite a new method of execution in 1928 and undoubtedly the topic of much conversation. Unlike hanging, the method that it largely replaced, its effects on the body could be tested and imagined by anyone who had ever experienced a mild electric shock, making it undoubtedly even more frightening. In his text, Jefferson foregoes the opportunity to state the obvious and familiar by describing the electric chair or its effects. In fact, he largely foregoes the opportunity to direct audience pity toward himself as the condemned criminal, even though it is quite clear that we are to view him in that role. In only one line out of five stanzas does he clearly place himself in that position, stating "I sat in the 'lectric room, my arms folded up and crying." Jefferson instead deflects attention from himself, representing a process of denial not uncommon among the condemned but also forcing the audience to examine the effects of capital punishment on those who are close to its victims as well as the complicity of society at large in taking a human life.

Jefferson begins his song as a prisoner on death row shaking hands with another prisoner, his "partner," and asking him "how come he's here." The man answers, "I had a wreck with my family; they gonna send me to the 'lectric chair." The reason for the execution, therefore, is not seen as a crime so much as an accident, a "wreck" that resulted from the buildup of domestic pressures and problems. His next stanza is one of his most poignant, in which he informs society just how directly they are involved in the process of execution: "I wonder why they 'lectrocute a man after the one o'clock hour at night. Because the current is much stronger; babe, the folks is turned out all their lights." After placing himself in "the 'lectric room," Jefferson turns his attention to the woman who will survive him. First she asks the pitiful question, "Was they gonna 'lectrocute that man of mine?" Then she decides to take a taxi, presumably from the prison where she has had her last visit, saying, "I don't have but one friend in this world; he's to be murdered in the 'lectric chair." In the final stanza, Jefferson reintroduces the image of the "wreck with my family," but now it is the woman who is wrecked by her man's execution: "I've seen wrecks on the ocean; I've seen wrecks on the deep blue sea. But none like that wreck in my heart when they brought my 'lectrocuted daddy to me." By shifting the persona of the singer and the perspective of the song on the issue of execution, Jefferson has created a much more effective blues than if he had merely described a situation from the standpoint of himself as the condemned prisoner.

PEACH ORCHARD MAMA (1929)

This blues typifies Jefferson's late compositional approach, if such a term can be used in a discussion of a recording career that was so brief. It was recorded in March 1929, the last year of Jefferson's life. It is performed with a duple beat at a rather slow pace with the guitar played in open G tuning but raised a half step.

Jefferson sings a melody that ranges over an octave and a minor third with rather little variation. The entire performance is rather perfunctory in comparison to most of Jefferson's earlier work, although it would undoubtedly be deemed spectacular in comparison to most country blues by other artists. The pace and regularity of the piece suggest that Jefferson wanted to make his singing and playing absolutely clear to listeners. Indeed, this would be a good choice for beginning a project of trying to learn Jefferson's complex performance style. He even provides an entire guitar chorus for the listener before the final stanza.

Jefferson's text is not only consistently thematic, as all of his blues had become by this time, but also is entirely a single extended metaphor. The use of fruit in imagery of women and particular parts of their sexual anatomy is virtually universal in poetic expression. One common traditional stanza in the blues is "If you don't like my peaches, don't shake my tree; get out of my orchard and let my peaches be." A stanza of this sort seems to have been the inspiration for Jefferson's original text. It is addressed throughout to a "peach orchard mama," with the singer claiming that he has worked in her orchard, keeping it clean. He was led to believe that he had the exclusive right to harvest her fruit, but instead he "found three kid men shaking down your peaches tree." Over the course of five stanzas, Jefferson elaborates this basic idea, describing the activities of his rivals, begging the woman to "kick out all those kid men," but also threatening to kill her. Following the guitar chorus, he simply tells her, "Don't turn your papa down; because when I gets mad, I acts just like a clown." It is a well-crafted piece of work that shows that Jefferson had learned the technique of composing popular commercial blues.

SEE THAT MY GRAVE'S KEPT CLEAN (1927)

Jefferson recorded this piece in October 1927 and again four months later as "See that My Grave Is Kept Clean." The first version was coupled for release with a spiritual song. This was withdrawn, and the new recording coupled the song with "'Lectric Chair Blues" and marketed it as a blues song. Apparently his first recording was perceived by some purchasers and listeners as a blues, and his record company, Paramount, wanted to exploit the song's sales potential in this direction. It became, in fact, one of Jefferson's best remembered pieces and ultimately the inspiration for erecting an official marker at his gravesite.

The melody and words of this song are essentially traditional, and Jefferson's compositional contribution consists mainly of his brilliant arrangement of this material. The second version contains only minor variations in the lyrics and basic musical features of the melody and guitar part from the first version. It sounds a bit more careful, controlled, and planned than the first version, but thereby a bit less exciting and less powerfully frightening. The words are drawn largely from 19th-century religious and popular sentimental songs common especially in southern white culture. Jefferson arranges the words in an AAAB fashion, using a structure of 16 bars that is often extended by a few notes on the guitar at the ends of lines. The melody is similar to others in the spiritual tradition, such as "Nobody's Fault but Mine." It ranges over an octave in a pentatonic scale, on rare occasions moving a step above or below the high or low tonic. Jefferson's singing, especially in the first version, is so extremely melismatic and ornamented that he could be said to sound many other notes and shadings of notes in passing. The lowered fifth is particularly evident in this respect. Jefferson's performance style here may well be influenced by long meter hymn singing.

Jefferson's guitar is played in the E position of standard tuning, mostly in the bass and middle register with his left hand not venturing beyond the fourth fret of the instrument. Although this represents a rather conservative approach for Jefferson, his guitar part once again constitutes an independent countermelody that perfectly complements the text and mood of the piece. The pace is quite rapid, which might at first seem odd in a song about death and burial, but it proves effective in conveying the rapid approach of death and suggesting that these were the singer's last words. (Many people have stated erroneously that this was the last song Jefferson recorded.) His playing is rumbling, incessantly busy, and ultimately most ominous. In the fifth stanza of the first version, he abruptly slows the pace during the words "Have you ever heard a coffin sound?" In the second version, he snaps his open bass string following the words "Have you ever heard a church bell tone?" in the final stanza.

The text as a whole is full of awesome imagery and mystery. It is set in the point of view of someone who is dying and imagining his own burial. Only one verse, the opening line of the fourth and middle stanza, actually describes the act of dying, and it quickly moves to the burial "by the cypress grove," which is the main topic of the song. The two opening stanzas provide a kind of overview of the situation. In the first, the singer asks "one kind favor": that the listeners keep his grave clean. The second stanza consists of a pair of proverbial expressions that evoke the idea of eternity: "It's a long lane that never ends; and it's a bad wind that never change." In the remaining four stanzas, Jefferson introduces images of the sights and sounds of the burial itself: the procession of two white horses, the "coffin sound," the digging of the grave with a silver spade, the lowering of the coffin with a golden chain, and the tolling of the church bell. It is altogether a most effective piece.

DAVID EVANS

JENKINS, EDMUND THORNTON

Born in Charleston, S.C., April 9, 1894; died in Paris, France, September 12, 1926. **Education:** Jenkins Orphanage, Charleston, S.C., studied music as a child with tutors who worked for his father, Rev. Daniel Joseph Jenkins, founder of the orphanage; performed in choirs and bands at Jenkins Orphanage; played all band instruments, by age 14; Avery Institute, Charleston, S.C., ca. 1908; Atlanta Baptist College (now Morehouse College), Atlanta, Ga., studied with Kemper Harreld, 1908–14; London, traveled with the Jenkins Orphanage band to play at the Anglo-American Exposition, 1914; Royal Academy of Music, London, studied composition with Frederick Corder, clarinet with Edward J. Augarde and Herbert Stuteley, also took piano, oboe, bassoon, singing, and organ lessons, 1914–21; received the Associate of the Royal Academy of Music diploma, 1921. **Composing and Performing Career:** London, worked as church organist and played clarinet in theater orchestras, 1914–21; made recordings with the Versatile Three, the Queen's Dance Orchestra, and Jack Hylton's Jazz Band, 1920–21; associated with Will Marion Cook's Southern Syncopated Orchestra, 1919–22; settled in Paris, using it as his home base from which to tour, 1922; England, associated with James P. Johnson, 1923; played with bands in France, Italy, and Belgium, 1922–26; Paris, established Anglo-Continental-American Music Press, 1925; Paris, took over directorship of Ermitage orchestra, a 13-man dance band, 1925; Ostende, Belgium, *American Folk Rhapsody: Charlestonia* performed at the Kursaal, 1925; *A Negro Symphony* accepted for performance in Paris, apparently canceled due to composer's death, 1926. **Teaching Career:** Royal Academy of Music, subprofessor of clarinet, 1918–21. **Honors/Awards:** Oliveira Prescott Gift, 1917; Charles Lucas Prize, 1918; Battison Haynes Prize, 1919; Ross Scholarship, 1919; Holstein Prize, 1926.

MUSIC LIST

INSTRUMENTAL SOLOS
Violin
"Commodo quasi allegro (Poco martial)." Unpublished manuscript. Note: incomplete.

"Rêverie: Fantasie pour violon et piano." Unpublished manuscript. Premiere, 1919.

"Romanesque." 1918. Unpublished manuscript. Note: unfinished.

"Sonate in A minor: Violin and Pianoforte." Unpublished manuscript.

Cello
"Dance for Cello and Piano" or "Esperanto Dance, no. 1." Unpublished manuscript. Premiere 1916.

"Rêverie." Unpublished manuscript. Premiere 1916.

Sonata in A minor. 1926. Unpublished manuscript. Note: winner of the Holstein Prize, 1926.

Saxophone
"The Saxophone Strut" (saxophone, piano). 1925. Unpublished manuscript. Arranged for saxophone and orchestra under the title *Milano Strut.*

Piano
"The Cabaret Brawl, or Double Crossing the Stool Pigeon." Unpublished manuscript.

"Characteristic American Indian Dances." Unpublished manuscript. Note: may be unfinished.

"Spring Fancies." 1920. Paris: Anglo-Continental-American Music Press, ca. 1925.

Organ
"Prélude religieux." 1917. Paris: Anglo-Continental-American Music Press, 1925. Also arranged for organ and orchestra. Premiere, 1917.

SMALL INSTRUMENTAL ENSEMBLE
Combinations
"Andante quasi lento" or "Allegro Energico" or "Quintet: Slow Movement and Rondo" (flute, two clarinets, horn, piano). 1919. Unpublished manuscript. Notes: incomplete; winner of Battison Haynes Prize, 1919. Premiere, 1919.

Overture to Much Ado About Nothing (piano and strings). 1916. Unpublished manuscript. Premiere, 1916.

CHAMBER ORCHESTRA
Ballet (strings, woodwinds). Unpublished manuscript. Contents: Processional; Pas Seul; Danse Général.

FULL ORCHESTRA
African War Dance. 1925. Unpublished manuscript. Note: winner of the Holstein Prize, 1926.

Allegro Strepitoso. Unpublished manuscript. Note: unfinished.

American Folk Rhapsody: Charlestonia or *Folk Rhapsody.* 1917. Unpublished manuscript. Premiere, 1925.

Folk Rhapsody (on American Folk Tunes). 1919. Unpublished manuscript. Premiere, 1919.

Negro Symphonie Dramatique. 1925. Unpublished manuscript. Note: probably never orchestrated.

Rhapsodic Overture. Unpublished manuscript. Note: incomplete.

ORCHESTRA (CHAMBER OR FULL) WITH SOLOISTS
Andante (clarinet, cello, orchestra). Unpublished manuscript. Note: unfinished.

Concerto (unidentified solo instrument [probably clarinet], orchestra). Unpublished manuscript. Note: unfinished.

How Sweet Is Life (medium voice, orchestra). 1917. Unpublished manuscript. Premiere, 1917.

"A Prayer" (medium voice, orchestra). 1917. Unpublished manuscript. Also arranged for low voice and organ: Premiere, 1917.

Romance (violin, orchestra). 1917. Unpublished manuscript.

SOLO VOICE
"Baby Darling, Baby Mine" (medium voice). 1919. Unpublished manuscript. Premiere, 1919.

"I Want You Near Me" (Je te désire près de mois). Unpublished manuscript.

"If I Were to Tell You I Love You" (Si je vous dis, je vous aime).
Unpublished manuscript.

"Jungle Blues." Unpublished manuscript. Note: unfinished.

"Kiss Baby Goodnight." Unpublished manuscript.

"The Lilac Tree." Unpublished manuscript. Note: unfinished.

"Love's Hour" (medium voice). 1916. Unpublished manuscript. Also
arranged for voice and orchestra. Premiere, 1916.

"Pampa Blues." Unpublished manuscript.

"That Place Called Italy." Paris: Anglo-Continental-American Music
Press, n.d. Also arranged for dance orchestra.

Three Songs (medium voice). Paris: Anglo-Continental-American Music
Press, 1925. Contents: Doubting; A Romance; The Fiddler's
Fiddle. Premiere, 1917.

"Through the Metidja to Abd-el-Kadr." Unpublished manuscript.

"Trying: Waltz Song." Unpublished manuscript. Note: i
ncomplete.

"Your Voice I Hear." Unpublished manuscript.

DRAMATIC MUSIC

Afram ou la belle Swita (operetta). 1924. Unpublished manuscript.

Charleston Revue. Unpublished manuscript. Contents: Charleston on
Broadway; Underneath the Palmettos and Pines; The Carolina
Strut; The Levee Lounge Lizard (Blues Comique); The Charleston
Crawl: Danse Eccentrique; Pretty Kids; Joy Time. Note: also
incorporated into Act III of *Afram.*

NOT VERIFIED

"Amber Eyes." (voice and piano); Folk Rhapsody no. 2: Rhapsodie
Spirituelle, Negro Folk Rhapsody (orchestra).

PUBLICATIONS

ABOUT JENKINS
Books and Monographs

Chilton, John. *A Jazz Nursery: The Story of the Jenkins' Orphanage Bands.*
London: Bloomsbury Bookshop, 1980.

Green, Jeffrey P. *Edmund Thornton Jenkins: The Life and Times of an
American Black Composer, 1894–1926.* Westport, Conn.:
Greenwood Press, 1982.

Articles

Brawley, Benjamin. "Edmund T. Jenkins, An Appreciation." *Opportunity*
(December 1926). Reprinted in *Black Perspective in Music* 14, no. 2
(1986): 152–153.

De Lerma, Dominique-René. "Black Composers in Europe: A Works
List." *Black Music Research Journal* 10 (1990): 275–334.

Hillmon, Betty. "In Retrospect: Edmund Thornton Jenkins, American
Composer: At Home Abroad." *Black Perspective in Music* 14, no. 2
(1986): 143–180.

PRINCIPAL ARCHIVES

Edmund Thornton Jenkins Collection, Center for Black Music Research,
Columbia College, Chicago.

Edmund Thornton Jenkins Collection, Manuscript, Archives, and Rare
Books Division, Schomburg Center for Research in Black Culture,
New York Public Library.

* * * * *

The musical career of Edmund Thornton Jenkins reflects both his
Deep South origins and an internationalism that provided the
arena in which he honed his skills. Recognized as a significant figure by Benjamin Brawley, R. Nathaniel Dett, Will Marion Cook,
Alain Locke, and W.E.B. Du Bois, among other significant figures
of the Harlem Renaissance, Jenkins had no impact on that movement because of his early death in 1926, in France. His manuscripts were largely lost and unplayed until the 1980s.

The jazz/dance band recordings he made during 1920–23,
the testimony of surviving contemporaries, and the prizes and
medals he was awarded by the Royal Academy of Music in London,
where he studied and taught between 1914 and 1921, are all indications of his musical worth and accomplishments. Yet his concert-
hall compositions are known largely only from contemporary
reviews and concert program notes, and most of his works have not
been traced. From 1908 to 1914, Jenkins participated in music
making in church and at Morehouse College, in Atlanta, Georgia,
where he studied with Kemper Harreld and other professors. Those
college years in Atlanta built on a remarkably solid base, for Jenkins
had attended the reputable Avery Institute in Charleston, South
Carolina, and had benefited from music lessons at the Jenkins
Orphanage, which had been founded three years before his birth by
his Baptist minister-father. Practical training at the school for
orphans gave pupils skills that broadened their opportunities as
adults. During the summertime, the child musicians of the
orphanage toured around the area and into other states. On these
occasions, Edmund Jenkins, although just a child himself, had
social and musical responsibility for the children, and the tours
exposed him to a variety of experiences and contacts. Able to play
every band instrument, he also gave violin recitals and performed
sacred music.

In May 1914, Jenkins arrived in England with the Jenkins
Orphanage band, whose success at a major London exhibition led
to extended contacts, and he entered the Royal Academy of Music,
where he studied composition, worked with musicians who had a
broad experience in European music, and took lessons on orchestral instruments.

As a student in London in 1919, Jenkins conducted at a reputable concert hall, directing a talented orchestra that included
four members of Will Marion Cook's show orchestra. The music
was largely that of Samuel Coleridge-Taylor, the London-born son
of an African and an Englishwoman. Jenkins contributed one
piece, a folk rhapsody. It was described in the program by Wendell
Bruce-James, a West Indies-born Oxford University graduate and
a skilled pianist, as containing the themes "Swing Low, Sweet
Chariot," "Nobody Knows the Trouble I See," and a wharf fisherman's song from Charleston, "Br'er Rabbit, What Do You Do
Dere." A fascinating aspect of Jenkins' composition is his use of a
secular theme alongside two hardly unexpected spirituals. Turning
to genuine Southern roots, and using skills acquired in Atlanta and
London, he produced an orchestral piece based in the music of his
personal experience.

Among the other blacks living in England during Jenkins'
time were a substantial number of American entertainers—many of

Edmund Thornton Jenkins; courtesy of Jeffrey Green

whom Jenkins knew—Africans, people from the Caribbean region, and students of music, law, and medicine from many parts of the world. He socialized with prize-winning instrumentalists, a pioneer Marxist music tutor, Africans unwilling to accept the role of imperial subjects in a British empire, and the family of a future foreign minister of China. These contacts broadened Jenkins' cultural perspective and focused his attention on aspects of black life in Charleston.

Around 1920, Will Marion Cook asked Jenkins to direct the Southern Syncopated Orchestra, with the hope that they might collaborate on orchestral presentations back in the United States. But when, late in 1923, Jenkins returned to America, no commercial audience existed for black orchestral music, and opportunities for financing were limited. Jenkins' ambition was to establish a

school of music and an all-black orchestra that would tour America. He was bitterly disappointed when his fundraising efforts in New York, Chicago, Baltimore, and Washington, D.C., were unsuccessful.

After ten months in America, the composer returned to Europe. In Paris he worked in dance bands playing jazz with other Americans and local enthusiasts. Although this pursuit could be well paid, it was also far from restful, with late nights, continual relocation, and uncertainty about the next employment. This schedule did, however, keep Jenkins in contact with popular music, and when he established a music publishing company in Paris, in 1925, he composed and published dance tunes. He also wrote an operetta that was set in South Carolina.

Jenkins was reported to have completed a symphony just prior to his death that, along with the operetta, had been accepted for performance in Paris. This activity indicates that Jenkins was beginning to concentrate on concert repertoire. One can only speculate how, had he not died so early, his writing would have shown his absorption of African-American and European musical traditions and how he would have forged his own distinct musical personality from them.

JEFFREY GREEN

AMERICAN FOLK RHAPSODY: CHARLESTONIA (1917)

After his death in Paris in 1926, Edmund Thornton Jenkins' belongings were sent to his family in the United States. His music manuscripts came into the possession of his sister, Mildred Jenkins Haughton. In 1990, after her death, the music was placed at the Center for Black Music Research by her son, Jomo Zimbabwe. Until then, Jenkins' music had been inaccessible and unperformed for more than 60 years.

The music that survives consists of manuscripts of Jenkins' student compositions, some pieces he published at his own press in Paris (Anglo-Continental-American Music Press), and a few works from his Paris days: his operetta *Afram* and his *Negro Symphonie Dramatique,* which he completed just before his final illness. These later works, barely completed and never performed, may reflect Jenkins' attempts to merge his career as the leader of a dance orchestra with his aspirations as a composer.

The published works consist of songs, a piano piece entitled "Spring Fancies," and the "Prélude Religieux" for organ, orchestrated and performed in 1917 while Jenkins was a student in London, but published in an arrangement for grand organ alone. These pieces demonstrate his competence in the idioms of his time, from parlor music to popular songs. The organ piece, for example, is typical of late-romantic organ style, chromatic but not particularly dissonant, exploiting the various colors of the instrument in an orchestral fashion. Most of the surviving works are not particularly forward-looking. *Charlestonia* is a possible exception.

American Folk Rhapsody: Charlestonia is a student composition, written in 1917 while Jenkins was still at the Royal Academy of Music. However, Jenkins subsequently orchestrated it, and it was performed by the orchestra of the Kursaal in Ostende, Belgium, in July 1925. The orchestral score and nearly all the parts from the 1925 performance have been lost, however, and for an American premiere by the Charleston Symphony in October 1996, *Charlestonia* was reorchestrated from surviving manuscript versions by the Australian composer Vincent Plush. Even in its somewhat fragmentary state, *Charlestonia* is significant since there were so few African-American composers writing for full orchestra at the time, much less receiving performances. (The Paris edition of the *New York Herald* announced *Charlestonia* as "the first symphonic work by an American Negro.") Also, in *Charlestonia,* Jenkins, an expatriate African-American writing for an audience of Europeans, pays affectionate homage to his own musical heritage.

There are two surviving manuscripts of *Charlestonia,* both piano scores dating from the summer of 1917. The earlier, dated July 30, is the most complete: the later revision of August 10 lacks the final pages. There is also a single harp part, possibly from the Ostende performance. Both manuscript scores have orchestral cues, and both have penciled additions, some by Jenkins and some probably by one of his teachers at the Royal Academy of Music. The title of the piece on the 1917 manuscript is *Folk Rhapsody.* Jeffrey Green speculates that the name *Charlestonia* was added for the Ostende performance because of the popularity of the Charleston at that time. It would have been a logical title for a native of Charleston to use.

Jenkins took as his main theme a folk song sung by Charleston fishermen, "Brer Rabbit, What Do You Do Dere," remembered from his childhood. He used the tune also in another *Folk Rhapsody (on American Folk Tunes),* in which he combined it with two spiritual tunes. That piece, which appears to share other musical material with *Charlestonia,* was performed in London at Wigmore Hall in 1919. Jenkins, who was politically aware and active in African causes in London, undoubtedly used folk themes from his own heritage with the encouragement of his teachers, prompted by the nationalistic use of English folk music by composers at that time. Jenkins also had the example of Samuel Coleridge-Taylor, whom he greatly admired and who had used African and American themes for his works. The "Brer Rabbit" tune is simple, rhythmic, and catchy, and Jenkins takes many opportunities to play with its sprightly dotted rhythms. It is clearly the main theme unifying *Charlestonia,* although Jenkins juxtaposes it with another slower and more stately theme derived from its second strain (slightly reminiscent of the first line of Stephen Foster's "Old Folks at Home") and transmutes it into a similarly dotted but jazzier third theme.

Charlestonia is a true rhapsody. It is episodic, with brief contrasting sections providing interest and propulsion rather than any extended harmonic development. Harmonically, it never moves very far from F major/D minor, with occasional forays into D major/A major and B-flat major/G minor. Jenkins employs the string-heavy orchestral sound so beloved of the English composers of the early 20th century, although some of his most interesting effects are achieved with the winds and brass. At the same time, he flirts with additive rhythm, syncopation, and a jazzy sound.

Jenkins begins *Charlestonia* by introducing two of his major themes. Opening the piece is a solo horn playing the first line of the "Brer Rabbit" theme, which is answered by the slower second theme, stated by a solo flute and then by the clarinet. Some chromatic wandering leads to a complete statement of the "Brer Rabbit" theme by the English horn. In this brief expository section, "Brer Rabbit" is first played by the horn in F minor, then stated completely in F major and repeated immediately in B-flat minor. Frequent shifts in the main theme from major to minor are characteristic of the entire piece: Jenkins is clearly exploring the modal ambiguities of African-American folk music, and this modal shifting adds constant interest throughout *Charlestonia.*

A rather flashy clarinet cadenza introduces the next segment, which is based on the "Brer Rabbit" theme. Marked *tranquillo,* it is a kind of barcarolle in 4/4 time, in which the strings and winds engage in a canonic treatment of the theme over an arpeggiated eighth-note accompaniment by the low strings and harp. In some ways, this is the least successful part of the piece: the dotted rhythms of the theme seem awkward against the very square arpeggios. Jenkins seems to be trying for a syncopated effect, but for a few measures, there is simply too much going on, until he smooths out the bass and melody lines, hinting at his second theme and adding progressions of thirds in the winds. He also replaces his groups of four eighth notes with sextuplets, giving the section the rocking feel of a true barcarolle and creating one of the most lyrical episodes in the rhapsody.

Jenkins then introduces a contrasting third theme, a jazzy melody in G minor that retains the dotted rhythms and melodic thirds and fourths of the "Brer Rabbit" theme. He alternates measures in 3/4 and 2/4 time to provide a swinging effect and adds trombone slides to punctuate the bass line. Eventually, at a modulation to G major, the entire orchestra is involved, and off-beat accents and *sforzando* upward slides appear in other instruments as well. The orchestra very briefly becomes a jazz orchestra until, as the texture thins to a transition, the "Brer Rabbit" theme reasserts itself.

A full statement of the slower second theme happens quickly, after a few measures of ascending parallel thirds. It appears first in the cellos, which do justice to its chromatic and sweeping line, accompanied by the other strings, in a section marked *Andante espressivo*. The theme appears to undergo constant modulation because it consists of a chromatic turn in sextuplet eighth notes followed by an upward leap of an octave, which allows for considerable chromatic meandering. This section succeeds at achieving the lush orchestral sound so admired at the time. However, strings shortly give way to winds and another transitional section, a dance-like chordal passage in 3/4 time with lingering octave sweeps in the violins.

Again, Jenkins changes mood radically, providing one of the most surprising and most dissonant sections in *Charlestonia.* Suddenly *fortissimo* and *allegro strepitoso*, the entire orchestra engages in repeated passages of downward 16th notes in 4/4 time, punctuated by upward slides and *sforzando* notes in the bass instruments. Out of this section emerges the "Brer Rabbit" theme again, played *con spirito* by the strings. The flutes begin the octave pattern of the slow theme while the jazz theme emerges in the trumpet as the orchestra builds to another full statement of the "Brer Rabbit" theme, this time in 3/4 time. Jenkins' attempts at syncopation are more successful here: in the bass line, he accents the second beats or ties third beats over to the next measure, enhancing the ambiguities created by his use of 3/4 rather than 4/4 time. Finally, with strings and winds repeating a phrase from the jazz theme, the low brasses boom out a slow but syncopated bass line, marked *pomposo*. The syncopation here is rudimentary but quite effective.

As the texture thins again, a muted trumpet plays the jazz theme with support from the horns, entering on the half beat. This time, the slow theme is restated by the full orchestra *allegro grandioso* with fugal interplay among the various instruments, an interesting progression of whole-tone thirds in the horns, and, finally,

sweeping scalar passages in the strings. Jenkins succeeds again at a full, lush orchestral sound, and he is clearly preparing for some sort of grand climax. Unfortunately, at this point the manuscript sources fail. It is unclear exactly how Jenkins intended the piece to conclude. The later of the two manuscripts (from August 10, 1917) lacks its final pages altogether, and although the earlier manuscript (July 30, 1917) has an ending, added pencil sketches introducing interpolations or changes indicate that Jenkins, or perhaps his teacher, was unhappy with his original version.

The harp part from the orchestrated version has rests for the final sections of the piece, which only indicates that Jenkins had added at least ten additional measures that are not found in the July 30 piano score. If this earliest manuscript with its sketches is any indication, Jenkins at first intended *Charlestonia* to end with a final replay of the "Brer Rabbit" theme in a fairly thin texture, accelerating to a flurry of converging sounds: high instruments descending and low instruments rising in syncopated patterns to end in two quick, full chords.

Frustrating as it may be to lack any reliable sources for the conclusion to *Charlestonia,* the piece still proves interesting for what it says about Jenkins' sense of his own music. There is no doubt that the Ostende performance presented *Charlestonia* in a version far more polished than the ones that survive. Jenkins even told an American reporter that the piece was written in 1921. However, even the early versions show his interest in folk material, syncopation and additive rhythms, ambiguous modality, and the possibilities of symphonic jazz.

Charlestonia was well received at Ostende. Newspaper accounts called it "a great triumph" and "an unprecedented success," and the performance was also reported by the African-American press in the United States. Ten years after Jenkins' death, Alain Locke, who may have attended the Ostende performance, praised Jenkins as an early composer of "classical jazz." It is plain that Jenkins was considered something of a pioneer, and not only because he was an African-American in the European world of classical music. His unfortunate early death cut short a career that, had he continued the explorations of black idioms begun in *Charlestonia,* might have been interesting indeed.

SUZANNE FLANDREAU

REFERENCES

Green, Jeffrey P. *Edmund Thornton Jenkins: The Life and Times of an American Black Composer, 1894–1926.* Westport, Conn.: Greenwood Press, 1982.

Locke, Alain. *The Negro and His Music.* Washington, D.C.: The Associates in Negro Folk Education, 1936. Reprint, New York: Arno Press and the *New York Times,* 1969.